W9-CAX-872

MODERN MICROECONOMICS

Analysis and Applications

MODERN MICROECONOMICS

Analysis and Applications

Third Edition

David N. Hyman

North Carolina State University

IRWIN

Homewood, IL 60430

Boston, MA 02116

Senior sponsoring editor: *Gary Nelson*
Developmental editor: *Joan Hopkins*
Marketing manager: *Ron Bloecher*
Project editor: *Susan Trentacosti*
Production manager: *Ann Cassady*
Interior designer: *Alan Wendt*
Cover designer: *Michael Warrell*
Art manager: *Mark Malloy*
Compositor: *BiComp, Inc.*
Typeface: *10/12 Times Roman*
Printer: *R. R. Donnelley & Sons Company*

Library of Congress Cataloging-in-Publication Data

Hyman, David N.
Modern microeconomics : analysis and applications / David N. Hyman.—3rd ed.
p. cm.
Includes index.
ISBN 0-256-08377-0 (alk. paper)
1. Microeconomics. I. Title.
HB172.H96 1993
338.5—dc20 92–27614

Printed in the United States of America
1 2 3 4 5 6 7 8 9 0 DOC 9 8 7 6 5 4 3 2

For Linda,
who knows how much textbooks cost,
and
To the Memory of My Parents,
who were my first economics teachers

The Irwin Series in Economics

Appleyard and Field
International Economics

Baily and Friedman
Macroeconomics, Financial Markets, and the International Sector

Barron and Lynch
Economics
Third Edition

Blair
Urban and Regional Economics

Bornstein
Comparative Economic Systems: Models and Cases
Sixth Edition

Brown and Moore
Readings, Issues, and Problems in Public Finance
Third Edition

Colander
Economics

Colander
Microeconomics

Colander
Macroeconomics

Denzau
Microeconomic Analysis: Markets and Dynamics

Hyman
Economics
Second Edition

Hyman
Microeconomics
Second Edition

Hyman
Macroeconomics
Second Edition

Hyman
Modern Microeconomics: Analysis and Applications
Third Edition

Katz and Rosen
Microeconomics

Lehmann
Real World Economic Applications: *The Wall Street Journal* Workbook
Third Edition

Lindert
International Economics
Ninth Edition

Maurice and Phillips
Economic Analysis: Theory and Application
Sixth Edition

Maurice, Thomas, and Smithson
Managerial Economics: Applied Microeconomics for Decision Making
Fourth Edition

Nadler and Hansen
Microcomputer Macroeconomics with IBM Disk

O'Sullivan
Urban Economics
Second Edition

O'Sullivan
Essentials of Urban Economics

Peterson
Principles of Economics: Micro
Eighth Edition

Peterson
Principles of Economics: Macro
Eighth Edition

Prager
Applied Microeconomics: An Intermediate Approach

Rima
Development of Economic Analysis
Fifth Edition

Roger and Daniel
Principles of Economics Software Simulation

Rosen
Public Finance
Third Edition

Schwarz and Van Dyken
Manager: Managerial Economics Software

Seo
Managerial Economics: Text, Problems, and Short Cases
Seventh Edition

Sharp, Register, and Leftwich
Economics of Social Issues
Tenth Edition

Shepherd
Public Policies Toward Business
Eighth Edition

Shugart
The Organization of Industry

Slavin
Introduction to Economics
Third Edition

Streifford
Economic Perspective

Walton and Wykoff
Understanding Economics Today
Third Edition

PREFACE

Learning microeconomic theory represents a challenge to students, and meeting that challenge provides many rewards and insights. This new edition of *Modern Microeconomics: Analysis and Applications* has been thoroughly revised to help students meet the challenge. I have drawn on 25 years of teaching experience to make *Modern Microeconomics* an effective tool to aid students in learning and using microeconomic theory. I believe the key to understanding the theory is to use it. Therefore, relevant examples are consistently integrated with theory and theories developed in the text are applied as soon as feasible.

Applications

Rather than having separate chapters devoted to applications, I prefer to have students exposed to applications immediately after theoretical ideas are developed. This emphasizes and reinforces the relevance of the theory. There are usually three to six fully developed applications per chapter. The motivation for these applications is carefully established so the reader knows the purpose to which the theory is being applied.

Numerical Examples

It is easier for many students to see functional relationships when numbers are used. In almost every chapter there is a hypothetical numerical example that is fully developed to aid the student in understanding the theory. Income and substitution effects are illustrated by a numerical example that shows how an airline club whose benefit is lower fares will allow observation of the substitution effect if the membership fee is high enough. In Chapter 7, a continuing numerical example is introduced that gives production data for a hypothetical producer of a standardized chair. These data are carried through to Chapter 8, where they are used to derive cost curves. These numbers are then coupled with additional data in Chapters 9 and 10 to illustrate the behavior of the competitive firm. In Chapter 11, data on the demand for an entertainer's performances are used to derive marginal revenue curves and explain the profit-maximizing number of performances, assuming that the entertainer has a monopoly. Similarly, numerical examples are used to discuss input markets and illustrate externalities and the Coase theorem in later chapters.

Graphs and Tables

I want students to understand the importance of graphic tools to the study of economics. I have therefore been careful in using proper units of measurement in examples and graphs. A special effort has also been made to coordinate the placement of all graphs and tables with the appropriate textual discussion so that they can be easily referred to and understood by students.

Terms and Definitions

I have been careful to define terms when they are first introduced. Key terms are presented in **boldfaced** type and in the text margins when they first appear. There is also a comprehensive glossary at the end of the book.

Concept Reviews

Each major section of the chapter is followed by concept review questions so students can check their understanding of the preceding discussion before going on to the next section.

Changes in This Edition

As we move toward the 21st century, students must have the tools to understand the workings of the price system in a modern global economy. The numerous improvements and additions to this third edition of *Modern Microeconomics: Analysis and Applications* have been made with this in mind. Because examples take on new meaning when actual data are used, more real-world data have been added throughout the book. More important, I have given greater emphasis to international trade and global economic problems.

A new feature entitled "Modern Microeconomics in Action" appears in all chapters. These self-contained short essays provide up-to-date insights, information, and analysis of microeconomic issues in three major areas—their subtitles reflect these various focuses:

- *International Report* focuses attention on microeconomic aspects of international trade, issues in foreign nations, and international aspects of business to provide students with a perspective on the global economy of the 1990s.
- *The Business World* highlights issues in business, management, and marketing, and applies microeconomic theory to business situations to show students the relevance of the theory.
- *Government and the Economy* shows students how microeconomic theory can be used to understand trade-offs in social policy and helps them understand the role of government in the economy.

I have also added three new chapters that cover modern topics:

- Chapter 6: Choices under Uncertainty
- Chapter 13: Business Strategies in Oligopolistic Markets and the Theory of Games
- Chapter 17: Asymmetric Information and Market Performance

These new topics are treated at an appropriate level for intermediate coverage and are loaded with many new applications integrated with the development of theory.

Chapter 6 provides an introduction to the analysis of choices under uncertainty for undergraduates who have not had a course in statistics. The chapter uses lots of examples and keeps the technical analysis at a reasonable level. Attitudes toward risk are discussed using both product attributes and expected utility approaches. Risk-yield indifference curves are drawn and students are shown how variation in the marginal utility of income underlies risk-taking attitudes. The analysis is applied to insurance markets and capital markets. There is a brief discussion of the capital-asset pricing model. Actual β values for selected stocks are displayed in a table. Special features in this new chapter discuss risks of foreign investment, actual yields and variance on stocks and bonds, and government-run lotteries.

Chapter 13 provides a "user-friendly" exposition of the theory of games with many applications to modern oligopoly theory. The goal is to provide students with a flavor of the insights that game theory can provide into understanding business behavior while at the same time making it clear that any analysis of oligopoly must be ad hoc because of the variety of competitive conditions that can prevail. There is discussion of prisoner's dilemma situations, first mover advantages, repeated and sequential games, strategic moves, and other basic game theory situations. There are applications to retailing, expansion of productive capacity, pricing strategies, advertising, price fixing, cartels, strategic trade policy, the development of new products, entry deterrence, and other business issues.

Chapter 17 brings recent advances in the theory of information into the text. The approach emphasizes the impact of asymmetry of information on market performance and efficiency. The chapter applies the theory to help students understand markets for used products, price dispersion, and the economics of insurance. Among the important issues covered are health care, bank failure, and deposit insurance.

In addition to these new chapters, I added more welfare economics analysis of the gains and losses from economic policy in several chapters. The third edition also contains coverage of many new "hot topics" including:

The move toward free markets in Eastern Europe and the CIS.
GATT and international trade policy.
Income growth and living standards.
Health care and health insurance.
The stock market.
Government finance and state lotteries.
Environmental protection policy.
Total quality management.
The globalization of business.
Advances in technology.
Monopoly pricing and regulation of monopoly.
New antitrust cases.
Business strategies.

Deposit insurance and bank failure.

Competiveness of U.S. business.

And finally, a few pedagogical changes have been made to make it even easier for students to master microeconomics. All chapter introductions have been rewritten to include real-world situations that better motivate the discussions that follow. Key terms, which appear boldfaced in text, now are accompanied by definitions in the margin. All graphs have been redrawn to improve clarity and many of the captions have been rewritten. In general, I have tried to provide a balanced exposition of microeconomics, covering all the basic topics and applying the analysis to business, government policy, and international issues.

Supplementary Resources

Instructor's Manual

I have taken considerable care to write a useful, comprehensive manual. Each chapter contains a detailed set of notes and list changes in the new edition.

Test Bank

Also included is a bank of test items that are carefully matched and correlated with topics discussed in the text. The questions include multiple choice, as well as problems requiring calculations and graphic exposition. All test items have been reviewed and thoroughly checked for accuracy, clarity, and range of difficulty by several instructors who also served as reviewers of the text.

Transparency Masters

To further facilitate use of the text, you will find another unique feature: every graph and table in the text is reproduced as a transparency master.

Study Guide

The accompanying Study Guide has also been carefully planned and developed. It contains numerous elements designed to assist the student in mastering the content of this course. Included for each chapter are concept overviews, additional exercises and problems—all graded according to complexity—and sample questions to aid students in learning and preparing for exams.

Acknowledgments

I have benefitted from the assistance and expertise of the editorial staff at Richard D. Irwin throughout the development of this book. In this edition I worked closely with Joan Hopkins, developmental editor at Irwin, and I have benefitted from her careful synthesis of reviews of the third edition. Gary Nelson, senior editor, provided me with encouragement throughout the project.

I must also commend my editors for their choice of prepublication reviewers. Writing a textbook is a learning experience for the author. Putting down ideas on paper requires complete understanding of the theories and ideas to be explained. My reviewers have aided in helping me sort out my thoughts. They have provided criticism, suggestions, and insights that I have absorbed, reacted to, and used extensively to produce the final version of this book. I have learned a great deal from them and wish to thank them for their conscientious efforts. I hope they are pleased with the results and with how many of their suggestions I have incorporated in the book. The following economists participated as reviewers of one or more drafts of the first edition:

Bryan Boulier
George Washington University

Alvin Cohen
Lehigh University

Randall Ellis
Boston University

Louis Esposito
University of Massachusetts—Boston

Roger Frantz
San Diego State University

David Gay
Brigham Young University

Timothy Gronberg
Texas A&M University

William Gunther
University of Alabama

Thomas Ireland
University of Missouri—St. Louis

Arthur Kartman
San Diego State University

Jeffrey Krautkraemer
Washington State University

Leonard Lardaro
University of Rhode Island

Michael Magura
University of Toledo

Lawrence Martin
Michigan State University

Swati Murkerjee
Boston University

Peter Murrell
University of Maryland

Jon Nelson
Pennsylvania State University

Richard Peck
University of Illinois—Chicago

Michael Ransom
University of Arizona

Charles Rockwood
Florida State University

Robert Schmitz
Indiana University

Gary Sellers
University of Akron

David Sisk
San Francisco State University

James Stephenson
Iowa State University

Helen Tauchen
University of North Carolina—Chapel Hill

Roy Van Til
University of Maine—Farmington

Additionally, another group of professors reviewed the prospectus of this project and offered valuable suggestions at this early but critical stage:

Lawrence Blume
University of Michigan

James L. Dietz
California State University—Fullerton

Otis Gilley
University of Texas

John Goddeeris
Michigan State University

Edward Kittrell
Northern Illinois University

Charles Knoeber
North Carolina State University

Bruce Seaman
Georgia State University

Richard Tontz
California State University—Northridge

I am grateful for the comments and recommendations made by the following for the second edition of the book:

Oscar Brookins
Northeastern University

Charles Capone
Baylor University

Arthur H. Chan
New Mexico State University

Charles C. Fischer
Pittsburg State University

Ralph Gray
DePauw University

William Gunther
University of Alabama

John Helmuth
Rochester Institute of Technology

Donald L. Hooks
University of Alabama

David Hula
Kansas State University

Jeffrey Krautkraemer
Washington State University

Richard Long
Georgia State University

Charles Meyer
Iowa State University

Anthony O'Brien
Lehigh University

Kenneth M. Parzych
Eastern Connecticut State University

Bee Yan Roberts
Pennsylvania State University

William V. Weber
Illinois State University

Robert Wichers
University of Pittsburgh

In preparation of the third edition, I have benefitted from the comments and suggestions of the following economists. Their careful reviews have greatly improved the book and I am indebted to them:

Louis P. Cain
Loyola University of Chicago

Maria Dacosta
University of Wisconsin

Raymond J. Farrow
University of Washington

Roger Frantz
San Diego State University

James Henderson
Baylor University

Charles G. Leathers
University of Alabama

Nolan Masih
St. Cloud University

Donald Schaefer
Washington State University

David Hula provided additional questions and problems that have been incorporated with those appearing at the end of each chapter. I also received useful suggestions from my colleagues at North Carolina State University and from many users of the first edition who took the time to write to me. I thank them all and hope they forgive me for not mentioning them all by name.

I must also thank Carolyn Smith for her expert secretarial assistance in getting chapters ready for review and publication.

David N. Hyman

Contents in Brief

CONTENTS

PART I

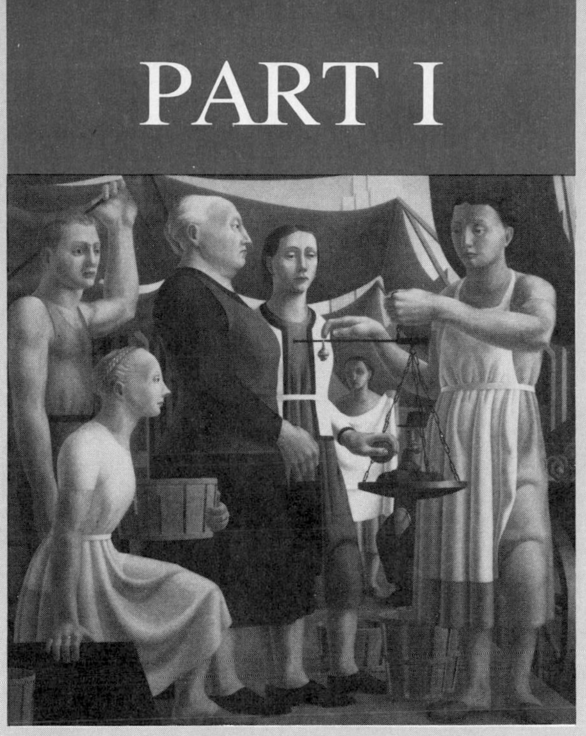

INTRODUCTION TO MICRO-ECONOMICS

1

Modern Microeconomics and Its Methodology

Economics is about the opportunities and obstacles all of us must confront as we seek to satisfy our needs and desires. Each day workers, business managers, consumers, investors, voters, and government officials make decisions that affect our opportunities to enjoy goods and services. Much of the information these people use in making their decisions is embodied in prices for the resources, products, and services they buy and sell. In the field of microeconomics we seek to understand how those prices are established and how they, in turn, affect decisions to buy, sell, and use resources.

You may not have thought about how prices affect you or of how chaotic the world would be if everything were unpriced. A simple example can help you visualize the chaos of a world without prices: Suppose you were given the privilege of obtaining anything you desired free. Anything that caught your fancy in any store would be yours at no charge. You could have the car, house, and wardrobe you always wanted but could not afford. Who would not come home with more and better goods after shopping without having to pay?

Now suppose that every consumer, business manager, and government official were given the same privilege. Every other consumer would have shopping lists as long as yours if the goods were free. Who can doubt that the shelves of stores would soon be bare and that the car lots of automobile dealers would soon be empty? Meanwhile, government officials and business managers would be scrambling around to get free labor, free equipment, free office space, and free fuel. There would not be enough goods and services to go around if everything were free. Who would get first choice? And who would want to produce and sell goods that were to be given away free? Would you work for an employer if you were not paid wages?

Scarcity The imbalance between desires for goods and services and the means of satisfying those desires.

The fantasy world described here illustrates two basic economic principles. First, although desires for goods and services are apparently limitless, the resources to satisfy them are not. **Scarcity** is the imbalance between desires for goods and services and the means of satisfying those desires. Scarcity is a universal problem faced by poor and rich nations alike. The starving children of sub-Saharan Africa demonstrate the problem of scarcity at its extreme. Yet even the vast wealth of the United States cannot satisfy all the desires of its citizens. Second, prices are both a natural consequence of scarcity and a means of rationing scarce resources, products, and services. Desires for goods and services must be backed up by purchasing power. We must live within our budgets and reconcile our desire to earn income with our conflicting desire to enjoy leisure. We must balance our desire for government spending on Social Security, roads, schooling, and national defense against what we must give up to finance these programs. If we devote more resources to government programs, fewer resources are available to satisfy our other desires.

Scarcity, Choice, and the Tasks of the Economy

Economics The study of how scarce resources are allocated among alternative uses.

The discipline of **economics** studies how scarce resources are allocated among alternative uses. Such resources as labor, structures, equipment, and raw materials are scarce. In any year a given quantity and quality of such resources are available in an economy to satisfy the seemingly unlimited desires for them. In any year technology, the knowledge of how to use resources to produce goods and services, is also given. Over time, growth in the quantity and quality of resources and improvements in technology help alleviate the problem of scarcity by increasing the productive capacity of an economy.

Microeconomics The study of public choices, business choices, and personal choices to understand how the economy functions.

Microeconomics is about decision making. It provides a framework for understanding public choices, business choices, and personal choices. As its name implies, microeconomics takes a close-up view of economic relationships. A microscopic perspective offers insights that would otherwise be unobtainable. Analysis of the countless decisions made each day by business managers, consumers, workers, investors, and government officials is the key to understanding how an economy functions.

Opportunity cost of a choice The next best alternative use of resources sacrificed by making a choice.

The problem of scarcity compels persons to make choices. The **opportunity cost of a choice** to use resources is the next best alternative use of those resources that is sacrificed by doing so. In allocating your own labor between study and recreation, for example, you must grapple with the fact that the more time you devote to one, the less time you have for the other. If your next best alternative to studying for an hour is an hour of tennis, then the opportunity cost of that hour of study is the loss of the hour of tennis. In making choices, persons must weigh the gain of using resources for a particular purpose against the opportunity cost of doing so. Daily decision making by workers, managers, investors, and households using the scarce resources available to them makes the economy function. In any society, scarcity requires choices to deal with the following basic problems:

1. *What to produce?* Each year choices must be made about how to allocate resources among alternative desired products. These choices must determine not only which products will be made available but also how much of each of these products will be produced. Because resources are scarce, however, when more of any good is made available over a given period, other goods must be sacrificed. When an automobile manufacturer uses more of the available workers, machinery, and plant area to produce minivans, less of those resources is available to produce sedans. This implies that the manufacturer forgoes the opportunity to produce the sedans that could have been made with the resources reallocated to minivan production. In this case the annual opportunity cost of choosing to produce more minivans is the annual quantity of sedans whose production is sacrificed by that choice.

The problem of what to produce is also faced in a society at large in that a society must make decisions to allocate resources among such broad uses as national defense and other government programs as opposed to consumer goods such as televisions, new homes, and automobiles. Increased expenditures for national defense involve the sacrifice of other goods as more resources are used to produce tanks, bombs, and aircraft and as more labor is allocated to the military. During a war, the availability of goods and services in consumer retail outlets typically shrinks. The familiar "guns versus butter" trade-off illustrates the concepts of both scarcity and opportunity cost. The opportunity cost of additional military goods (guns) is the consumer goods and services (butter) that are sacrificed when military spending is increased.

2. *How are chosen items to be produced?* Alternative means are available to produce goods and services. For example, furniture of a given quality can be made in highly mechanized factories with few workers or it can be made in factories with more workers and less machinery. Crops can be harvested by hand, using many workers, or they can be harvested by far fewer workers using mechanized devices. In utilizing available scarce resources, the methods of production chosen can affect the overall well-being of a nation's citizens. In nations where labor is relatively abundant and prices are low, as is the case in China and India, methods of production that use lots of labor are common. However, in nations such as the United States, where machinery is readily available, mechanized methods of production are preferred. Thus, agriculture in the U.S. Midwest uses lots of land and machinery and relatively little labor, while agriculture in Southeast Asia, where machinery is not readily available, uses lots of labor and little machinery.

Production methods that allow more output to be squeezed from available resources enable those resources to satisfy more human wants. When advances in technology result in new methods of production, decision makers must decide whether the benefits of adopting the new technology outweigh the costs of doing so. The goal of efficiency is to allow available resources to be used so as to permit maximum satisfaction to the members of a society.

3. *Who gets what is produced?* A person's well-being is influenced in part by the quantities of goods and services that he or she consumes each year. Persons with high annual incomes can purchase more and better goods than persons with low annual incomes. Both individual and political choices influence the way in which income is distributed in a nation. The income a person has available for spending depends on earnings from work, income from investments or rent, and any gifts received. It also depends on the taxes the person must pay and the payments the person receives from governments. For example, retired persons typically receive Social Security income from the U.S. government.

4. *How much production is for future as opposed to current consumption?* Resources can be used to gratify desires for immediate consumption. We could spend all of our current income on fine food, fine clothing, and travel to exotic

MODERN MICROECONOMICS IN ACTION: INTERNATIONAL REPORT

Coping with Scarcity: Firewood and Deforestation in the Third World

In the Third World nations of Africa, Asia, and Central and South America, there is a massive imbalance between the availability of firewood and the desire for this good. Because of the high price of gas, kerosene, and other fuels, the most common source of energy for cooking in these nations is firewood. Energy used for cooking accounts for one half to two thirds of the energy used in these nations, compared to 5 percent in more developed nations. In sub-Saharan Africa three fourths of the energy used comes from firewood. In Tanzania over 90 percent of the energy used comes from firewood.

Poor households in tropical nations typically spend from one fifth to one third of their budget on firewood. Some families spend more on firewood than on food! Families too poor to buy firewood spend considerable time searching for twigs and other pieces of wood. Women in poor villages typically walk 6 miles or more a day in search of wood. Spending time in this way is apparently harmful to the health of African women and their children. A UNICEF study found that infant mortality rates in Ethiopia increase as the time mothers spend in hauling wood goes up.

In some communities firewood is simply unavailable or is priced too high for impoverished inhabitants to afford. In some of these cases food cannot be cooked properly. As a result, food parasites are not killed and the risk of disease increases. In other cases, people turn to less expensive substitutes for firewood. For example, families in India too poor to afford firewood use cow dung to cook their food. But the burned dung cannot be returned to the soil as fertilizer. The ultimate result of this method is reduced crop yields.

To satisfy the desire for firewood, forests in developing nations have been and are being destroyed. This deforestation has unfortunate environmental consequences, including increased erosion, decreased fertility of agricultural lands, and reduced water supplies. The once magnificent forests of Haiti are gone, and the shrubs and saplings that currently grow there are sold for firewood before they can reach maturity. Major urban areas in Africa now have no woodlands within 10 miles of their boundaries. Ethiopia currently has less than 3 percent of its land in forest, while it had over 40 percent in forest at the turn of the century. Each year, for every tree planted in Africa, 10 are lost for use as firewood.

In Africa the traditional method of cooking uses an open fire with three stones to hold pots. To cope with the rising price of firewood, some African nations are distributing new types of cookstoves to peasants. The most promising of these devices is the mud stove, which is made by the Burayo Basic Technology Center, sponsored, in part, by UNICEF. The standard model uses 24 percent of the energy available in firewood, while open fires use only 5–10 percent. Widespread use of mud stoves would economize greatly on wood.

places. Alternatively, we could allocate a portion of our resources to the production of machinery, equipment, roads, bridges, structures, and skills that will allow us increased consumption in the future. Decisions must be made about how much of current income to *save*. By saving, we allow resources to be allocated to uses other than the production of goods and services for immediate consumption. *Investment goods* are goods that increase the capacity of an economy to satisfy future desires. By studying to acquire skills, you and others like you make an investment: You give up consumption today (because you sacrifice current income by not working when you devote your time to study) in the hope of consuming more in the future. Similarly, owners of businesses must decide how much to borrow or save for the purpose of acquiring new equipment and expanded facilities.

Investment is a key influence on our future living standards and on the rate at which our living standards improve over time. By investing, we can develop new technology and equip our work force with the skills needed to compete in the modern business world. *Economic growth* is the growth in a nation's productive potential that results from the increased availability and productivity of resources. Investment allows labor and other resources to become more productive and earn greater income. When a nation's income (after adjustment for inflation) grows faster than its population, living standards improve because individuals can then purchase growing amounts of goods and services.

Modern microeconomics studies the decisions that must be made to answer the above four questions. The focus of this book is on the ways in which such decisions are influenced by a variety of economic considerations, especially prices. You will see how markets, governments, and other economic and social institutions, such as the family, play a role in the functioning of the economy as we all seek to cope with the problem of scarcity.

Microeconomics helps us understand how businesses decide what products to develop and offer for sale. For example, as we use microeconomic analysis to study the interaction of buyers and sellers in the marketplace, you will see how such factors as the price of gasoline, the age distribution of the population, the price of labor, and competition from foreign producers influence the prices and types of cars produced.

The Role of Prices in Allocating Resources

Prices The sum of money that must be given up to obtain a unit of a good or service.

Prices represent what must be given up to obtain each unit of goods and services desired. The price of a good makes buyers reconcile their desire for the good with the opportunity cost of acquiring it. Consumers consider the prices of alternative goods and services when they make choices about how to spend their limited income. Prices are also what producers receive in compensation for their efforts and expenses for each unit of output they sell. Prices affect the profitability of producing alternative goods and services and thereby provide signals that induce producers to choose particular uses for their available resources.

Prices are usually measured in amounts of money. However, the money price of a good is not always the best indication of what must be given up to obtain a unit of the good. One reason for this is that the purchasing power of money can change over time. For example, when an average of the prices of all the goods available in our economy increases by 5 percent, the *quantity* of goods that each dollar will buy will fall on average. This means that the purchasing power of the dollar is less.

Change in the relative price of a good A change in the price of a good relative to the change in the average prices of all goods.

A **change in the relative price of a good** is a change in the price of that good relative to the change in the average price of all goods. The relative price of a good need not always change when its money price changes. For example, suppose that the average money price of all goods goes up 7 percent over a year. If the money price of a car also goes up 7 percent, its relative price has not changed. If the price of college tuition increases 10 percent over the same year, its relative price has risen because its money price has increased by a percentage that exceeds the average. Similarly, if the money price of television sets increases only 3 percent, the relative price of these sets has fallen even though their money price has gone up. This is because the money price of the sets has increased by less than the average increase in the prices of all goods. In the 1980s, the relative price of medical services and a college education increased in the United States because the prices of physician and hospital services and college tuition increased more rapidly than the average rate of price increases. In the same decade the relative price of personal computers and many electronic products decreased.

Changes in the relative price of a good measure the opportunity cost of purchasing it better than do changes in its money price when the purchasing power of money is not constant. Throughout this book, whenever the price of a good is said to change, it will be presumed that there is a change in its relative price.

A world in which goods and services are unpriced, such as that described at the beginning of this chapter, would be chaotic. The function of prices is to facilitate the orderly allocation of goods, services, and natural resources among alternative uses. Microeconomics is sometimes called *price theory* because a chief objective of its analysis is to explain how prices are determined and how they affect economic decisions.

Economic Transactions and Markets

Even in the most primitive societies, self-sufficiency is rare.[1] Persons depend on others to supply their most basic needs. They must enter into transactions with others to obtain food, energy for heat and light, clothing, medical assistance, transportation, and communication services.

A basic choice all persons make concerns what to provide for themselves by retaining the use of their labor, skills, and other resources rather than selling the use of those resources to others. It is clear that all persons rely on themselves, their friends, and their families for important services. Some of these services, such as food preparation, child care, transportation, and household repairs, can be purchased. Others, such as the sharing of experiences, memories, and love, cannot be purchased. The family provides a means for obtaining such unpurchasable services; in that sense the decision to marry and form a family can be viewed as partially influenced by the desire to obtain these services.

By and large, however, modern industrial societies rely heavily on economic transactions with others to satisfy desires. The services of productive resources are sold for cash to provide income. The sale of labor services provides wages. Saving and investing provide interest and dividend income. The sale of the services of land, structures, and equipment provides rental income. The amount of

[1] An interesting analysis of economic relations in primitive societies is Richard A. Posner, "A Theory of Primitive Societies with Special Reference to Primitive Law," *Journal of Law and Economics* 23, no. 2 (April 1980), pp. 1–50.

goods and services a person can purchase depends on the income that person earns through such transactions, which in turn depends on the productive resources that person owns, that person's willingness to sell the services of those resources to others, and the prices at which that person can sell them.

The Purpose and Functions of Markets

Market An arrangement through which buyers and sellers can meet for the purpose of trading goods or services.

A **market** is an arrangement through which buyers and sellers can meet for the purpose of trading goods or services. Markets constitute means through which buyers and sellers can trade at mutually agreeable terms. Competition and interaction in markets establish the prices on which many choices are based. Markets function to disseminate information as to what sellers want to sell and buyers want to buy. The local flea market is a place where sellers offering a wide array of items, such as antiques, handicrafts, and secondhand clothing, can conveniently display their wares and meet with prospective buyers.

A market need not be a specific geographic place. The classified advertisements section of the local newspaper constitutes a market. This section provides a means of communication between those wishing to sell and those wishing to buy various goods and services. It is used to market labor services of various kinds, as well as automobiles, housing, furniture, and many other items. It enables persons who wish to engage in transactions to contact trading partners by telephone.

Buyers and sellers use information available through markets to decide what and how much to buy and sell. Markets also communicate new information and thereby allow prices to change as buyers and sellers react accordingly. Prices act as signals to buyers and sellers by conveying information on the scarcity of goods and services and productive resources.[2] For example, if the price of crude oil rises, there is a complex and rapid communication of the increased scarcity of this resource as the prices of gasoline and heating oil rise. Substitute sources of energy, such as natural gas and firewood, also increase in price as consumers seek alternatives to petroleum products. The prices of automobiles may fall as increased fuel prices lead to less driving. The prices of wood stoves rise as persons in areas in which wood is relatively cheap purchase these devices to decrease their reliance on petroleum products as a source of heat. Over time the price of electricity rises, as do the prices of other commodities that use petroleum products as inputs. These include synthetic fabrics, roofing materials, and dry cleaning fluids. The process goes on and on as businesses and individuals respond to the chain reaction induced by the increase in the price of crude oil. Eventually, higher prices for such goods as wood stoves encourage more production of these goods. A decrease in the price of crude oil results in correspondingly opposite changes in the prices of other items.

[2] A classic analysis of the role of prices and markets in conveying information is found in F. A. Hayek, "The Use of Knowledge in Society," *American Economic Review* 35 (September 1945), pp. 519–30. Hayek points out that markets economize on the resources necessary to communicate information about scarcity.

Property Rights: The Prerequisites for Market Exchange

Suppose a law is passed tomorrow that abolishes all penalties for car theft and also makes it a crime to remove the key and lock the door of a private automobile. This patently ridiculous law would encourage people to use the first unattended vehicle they see to get to their destination. Consider the implications of the law for the automobile market.

Those who currently own cars will lose the right to the exclusive use of their cars. This will cause them only minor inconveniences at first because they will gain the right to use anyone else's unattended car, which might be rather convenient. To get from one point to another, a person merely uses the first available car and then leaves it at his or her destination. It is unlikely to be there when the person returns, but perhaps another car will be available.

There will, however, be little incentive for drivers to put in the car they use at the moment more gasoline than the amount necessary to get to their destination. There will be even less incentive to keep such a car in good operating condition. Who would replace a transmission in a car that is unlikely to be available for personal use after the next ride? Thus, because of lack of maintenance and lack of gasoline in the tank, after a while no automobiles in operable condition may be available for anyone's use.

And what of the market for automobiles? Who would buy a car if the right to its exclusive ownership and use does not exist?[3] Because no one would be willing to exchange money for cars, no cars are likely to be produced. In other words, the market for cars would collapse as the price of cars fell to zero.[4]

Property rights Privileges to own or use scarce resources.

Incentives to engage in market transactions are based on the property rights that can be acquired by exchanging cash for the items desired. **Property rights** are privileges to own or use scarce resources. The acquisition of those rights in market exchanges motivates consumer purchases. On the seller's side of the market, incentives to produce goods and services and offer them for sale are based on the presumption that sellers have the right to trade the product of their efforts for cash. This means that markets can exist only for items for which property rights can be easily established, enforced, and transferred.

When markets do not exist because of difficulty in assigning property rights, prices cannot be established. Moreover, the establishment of property rights allows orderly and civilized transactions. Without property rights the allocation of resources would be determined through force. In this "might makes right" world, the strong would gain title to resources by threats and violence.

Throughout most of this book it is assumed that government establishes property rights and uses its power to enforce those rights, and that government permits

---

[3] Governments could purchase and maintain the cars. With government motor pools, however, restrictions are usually placed on who can use government vehicles and many forms must be filled out before the right to use such a vehicle is obtained.

[4] This example is similar to one discussed by Demsetz in an article that investigates the relationship between property rights, incentives to trade, and prices. See Harold Demsetz, "The Exchange and Enforcement of Property Rights," *Journal of Law and Economics* 7 (October 1964), pp. 11–26.

people to trade established property rights to others for cash. Government can, and often does, use its power to change property rights and restrict their use. In the 1970s, the federal government began to alter the rights of business firms to dispose of wastes that damaged environmental resources.

Transaction Costs

Transaction costs The value of the resources used in locating trading partners, negotiating terms of trade, drawing up contracts, and enforcing the property rights acquired in a transaction.

Transaction costs are the value of the resources used in locating trading partners, negotiating terms of trade, drawing up contracts, and enforcing the property rights acquired in a transaction. When transaction costs are incurred by buyers rather than sellers, the price paid is not always a complete measure of what must be given up in trade for something desired. Transaction costs include such items as brokerage fees, advertising fees, and the value of the time and effort required to locate a trading partner. Other transaction costs are the cost of insuring oneself against fraud, the cost of transporting goods from the point of acquisition to the point of use, and the value placed on the time required to reach an agreement.

Transaction costs influence the incentive to engage in trade. For example, the transaction costs of going to a popular movie on a Saturday night include the time consumed in waiting in line to obtain tickets. A person may very well decide not to go to the movie on that night because of this transaction cost. The transaction costs involved in selling a used stereo system may include the cost of advertising the system in a newspaper and the time spent in answering the telephone and showing the system to prospective buyers. If these costs outweigh the price expected for the system, trying to sell it will not be worthwhile.

Transaction costs also affect the desirability of establishing property rights. Willingness to trade or purchase an item depends on the transaction costs involved in enforcing the rights exchanged through trade. Suppose, for example, you are very talented in landscaping and gardening and the garden in your front yard is a marvel to behold. Your neighbors enjoy looking at the garden, and people drive down your street to look at it. Can you sell the right or privilege of others to view the garden? To do so requires that you find a means of preventing nonpayers from viewing it. This might involve building a high fence and hiring someone to sell tickets to those who wish to tour the garden. These costs might not be worth the income you would gain from selling the right to see your garden. You may therefore allow others to view your garden at zero price. In this case the transaction costs of establishing property rights outweigh the gains obtained from doing so.

In discussing market interaction, economists usually ignore transaction costs or assume that they are zero. However, because transaction costs determine what is worth trading, their value is important in determining whether or not a market for a particular good or service will develop.

Market Systems

Most modern economies have vast systems of interconnected markets. To help visualize how these market systems operate, it is useful to define two specific types of decision-making units: households and business firms. Households possess the property rights to productive resources such as labor, capital (which includes the structures, equipment, and human skills acquired through both education and training), and land that are used as inputs in the production of goods and services by business firms. Households engage in transactions with business firms through two broad sets of markets. In *product markets,* households are buyers who seek to purchase food, clothing, housing, and the amenities of life from business firms. In *input markets,* business firms buy productive services offered for sale by households.

Circular flow diagram A diagram that demonstrates how households and business firms are linked through input and output markets and how expenditure on products generates revenue that business firms use to pay for productive services.

Figure 1–1 shows how productive services that flow from households to business firms through input markets result in the production of goods and services that are in turn offered for sale to households in product markets. As households sell input services, they obtain income that they then use to purchase the products of business firms. The **circular flow diagram** demonstrates that households and business firms are linked through input and output markets and that expenditure on the products of business firms generates revenue that these firms use to pay for productive services. The supply of resources by households shown in the lower linkage between households, input markets, and business firms generates income for the households while providing the resources necessary to produce goods and services. The purchase of goods and services in product markets shown in the upper linkage between households, product markets, and business firms results in expenditures that generate revenue for business firms. This revenue is used to finance the payments that business firms make to households for the productive services they provide. The circular flow of income, expenditure, products, and productive services is a continuous one that keeps the economy functioning. Prices determined through the interaction of buyers and sellers in both product and input markets play an important role in this process by influencing what is produced and how income is allocated among households.

The circular flow diagram simplifies the operation of modern economies in several ways. First, it does not consider the roles of government and international trade in the economy. As you know, governments supply education, roads, national defense, and many other services and finance these services through their power to tax. Modern economies also engage in international trade transactions. For example, about one third of U.S. income is used to pay taxes and about 15 percent of U.S. production is exported. In the 1980s and early 1990s, U.S. households spent about 16 percent of their income on products imported from foreign nations. Second, the circular flow diagram does not consider that many transactions take place between business firms. For example, General Motors purchases tires from such firms as Firestone when it manufactures cars. Third, the diagram does not consider that some production takes place in households, within which family members cook and clean for themselves and engage in many do-it-yourself activities as an alternative to purchasing goods and services in product markets. Nonetheless, the circular flow diagram provides important insights into the way a system of markets functions, and it is therefore used as a basis for organizing microeconomic analysis. In this book we will first analyze the way in which buyers and sellers interact in markets. We will then examine, in turn, how house-

FIGURE 1–1 The Circular Flow of Income and Expenditure in a Market System

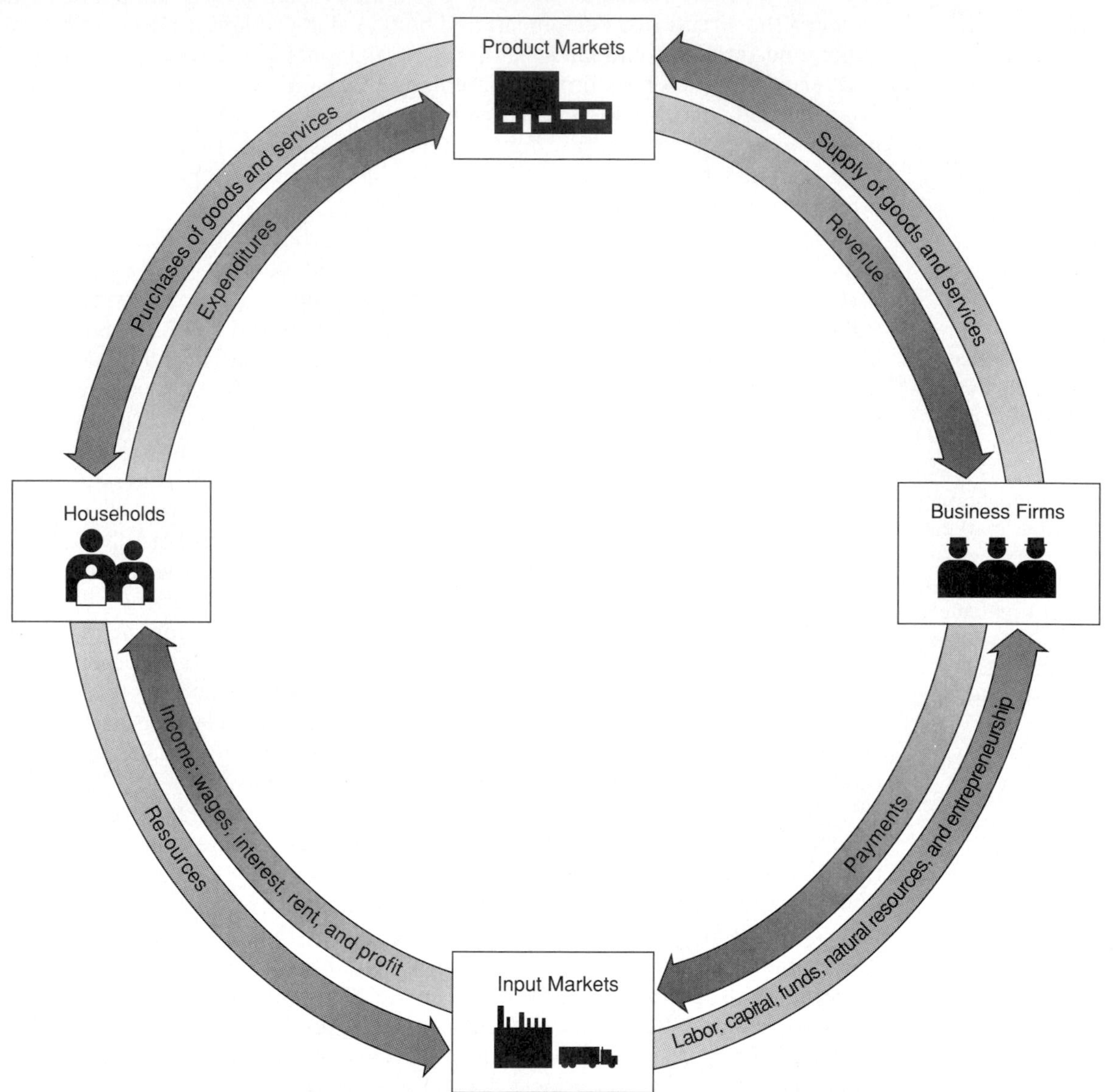

Business firms acquire resources from households in input markets. The income earned by households is then spent on goods and services that business firms offer for sale in product markets.

MODERN MICROECONOMICS IN ACTION: THE BUSINESS WORLD

Capitalism Comes to Russia: Property Rights, Markets, and the Economy of the Former Soviet Union

For most of the 20th century the economy of the former Soviet Union was dominated by a cumbersome system of central planning that excluded markets and business firms from playing a significant role in resource allocation. Under communism, the Soviet Union functioned as a centrally planned economy in which virtually all productive resources were owned or controlled by the state. Under that system there was little legal private enterprise and the economy was managed by politically appointed committees that set prices and production targets to achieve political goals. All business was conducted by the government, and markets as places for the free exchange of goods and services were a rarity.

The dramatic events of the early 1990s as well as a process of reform that began under Gorbachev's *perestroika* of the 1980s have been changing the economies of the republics that previously comprised the Soviet Union. As we approach the 21st century, business firms and markets will be playing a much greater role in Russia and the other former Soviet republics and in the former communist nations of Eastern Europe. However, the transition to a market system is going to be a very painful one for these economies. Let's look at how the economy of the former Soviet Union operated under communist-dominated central planning and at how it must change to become a market economy.

Despite the political upheavals, as of 1991 the republics of the former Soviet Union still had economies in which the government owned much of the means of production and *most* labor was allocated according to central plans. The system of central planning used throughout most of the 70-year history of the Soviet Union set the prices for all inputs and outputs and regulated economic activity by deciding what would be produced, how it would be produced, and to whom goods and services would be distributed. The economy was dominated by large government enterprises whose managers received state orders for production. The reforms of the 1980s encouraged these government enterprises, the Soviet equivalent of business firms, to earn profit. In the past, however, profit was not considered in evaluating the performance of these enterprises. Instead, grossly inefficient enterprises and enterprises whose products no one wanted to buy were allowed to operate. Enterprises whose products, such as bread and vodka, were in strong demand, due in part to very low prices set by the central planners, produced less than buyers wanted to buy, causing great shortages. Although prices for such basics as meat, bread, and housing were remarkably low, there were not enough of these items to satisfy the desires of all who wanted to buy them at their artificially low prices. The one safety valve for the economy was a vast underground economy in which illegal markets channeled products to consumers who could afford to pay very high prices for them.

Under central planning, the leaders of the Soviet Union favored the production of military goods and heavy industrial products over the production of consumer goods. The Soviet economy lacked the flexibility of market economies because it rarely used prices to signal the scarcity of products and to encourage the production of items in strong demand by allowing sellers to profit from making such items available. Although some private firms were operating in the Soviet Union in the early 1990s, most of these firms were very small because Soviet laws limited their ability to hire workers.

To move to free markets, the governments of the republics comprised by the former Soviet Union must transfer their property rights to productive resources. "Privatizing" former government enterprises means selling them to domestic or foreign buyers who will operate them as business firms. In this process the unprofitable enterprises that cannot find buyers will be shut down and their workers will have to find other jobs. As government enterprises become business firms, the economy will begin to have a functioning market sector. Prices for goods and services that have been in

(*Continued*) short supply will then increase. These price increases will serve as signals of scarcity and of potential profitability to the new firms that make the scarce goods and services available in markets.

The world of business will come to the former communist regimes as business firms are set up and as markets for the trading of inputs and products are established. But the process of transition to free markets will be a long and painful one!

holds make their choices as both buyers of products and sellers of resources, how business decisions affect the supply of goods and services in product markets, and how business and household decisions affect the demands for productive resources and the incomes of households. Finally, throughout the book we will analyze the role of government and international trade in the economy to understand how government policies and international trade affect the well-being of members of society and their incentives to engage in market transactions.

CONCEPT REVIEW

1. Why does scarcity imply that the opportunity cost of each choice to use resources will never be zero?
2. What is the function of a market?
3. How do property rights to resource use and transaction costs influence incentives to engage in market trading?

METHODOLOGY OF MICROECONOMICS: THEORIES AND MODELS

Microeconomics seeks to understand the forces influencing the choices individuals make as they cope with the problem of scarcity. Much of the analysis in this book is based on the assumption that human behavior is quite predictable. Economists generally presume that persons systematically pursue certain objectives, such as maximizing satisfaction from purchases or maximizing profit from the sale of products. In analyzing economic phenomena, economists make many simplifications to isolate the basic constraints under which persons must make decisions. The role of prices in influencing economic decisions is studied extensively in microeconomics.

Theory A framework for understanding relationships of cause and effect.

Theory establishes relationships between cause and effect that explain observed phenomena. Any theory, be it formulated by physicists or by economists, simplifies reality by making assumptions about the basic factors that influence these phenomena. Meteorology, for example, seeks to explain and predict the weather by studying how such factors as air currents and air pressure influence temperature and precipitation.

Economic theories make assumptions about how people behave. The implications of these assumptions for human actions are then traced out logically. For example, a theory of the way owners of business firms make decisions can be constructed by assuming that they seek to maximize the profit they obtain by selling a product over a certain period. The most important factors that influence the profitability of selling the product would be examined. These would logically include the quantity sold, the price of the product, and the factors influencing the cost per unit. The theory would also make assumptions about the way the price sellers receive and their costs per unit might change when they produce more or fewer units of the product in the given period. It would then trace out how changes in the influences on profit would change the choices made by sellers. For example, the imposition on manufacturers of a new tax on cigarettes would increase the cost of selling the cigarettes. The implications of this tax for cigarette production would be traced out using logic and assuming that the goal of the sellers remains profit maximization.

Knowing the causes and consequences of a process may even allow the control of outcomes; for example, it may be possible to treat or eradicate diseases once their causes are known. Before nuclear energy could be harnessed, a theory of atomic particles had to be developed. An atomic particle has never been observed. The theory of nuclear reactions is based on assumptions about protons, electrons, and other atomic particles and about the forces that are assumed to influence movements of these particles. Whether or not these assumptions are realistic, the theory is useful if it can be used to unleash or harness atomic energy. The group of scientists who developed the atom bomb during World War II had no idea whether their theory of nuclear reactions was valid until they actually tested the device they constructed.

In other words, a good theory predicts results that are borne out by facts. A theory based on the assumption that businesses act to maximize profits may be unrealistic because owners and managers of business firms might have other goals as well. They might be concerned not only with the profit of their firm but also with its public image, its sales revenue, or its dividend payments. Nonetheless, despite the simplification, a theory based on the assumption of profit maximizing will be useful if it predicts actions actually undertaken by business firms. Economic theories are no different from those developed by physicists, chemists, or any other scientists. Just as the physicist's model of the atom need not capture all of its complexity, the economist's model of the business firm need not include all aspects of such organizations. Scientists in the 1920s did not know that atoms had particles other than protons, neutrons, and electrons; however, their model of the atom was sufficient to predict the awesome explosive reaction that allowed development of the first atom bomb.

Model Building

Economic model
A simplified way of expressing how some sector of the economy functions; consists of assumptions that establish relationships among economic variables.

An **economic model** is a simplified way of expressing how some sector of the economy functions. Economic models consist of assumptions that establish relationships among economic variables. Such models work out the implications of a theory by using logic, graphs, or mathematics to deduce the consequences of the assumptions for the phenomena that the theory seeks to explain. In this way models can be used to make predictions about how changes in economic conditions result in changes in decisions and changes in such magnitudes as prices and quantities traded.

Economic variables Measurable quantities that can take on a number of possible values.

Economic variables are measurable quantities (such as price or the amount of a good produced annually) that can take on a number of possible values. An economic model usually seeks to explain how key economic variables are affected by economic conditions. Variables whose values are taken as given in a model are called *parameters*. An economic model usually considers only a few influences on the variables it seeks to explain and relates these variables by making certain assumptions about how people behave and about the constraints under which people must make their choices. A model is like a blueprint or schematic drawing of a complex mechanism that attempts to show what happens when various levers or buttons are pressed. The purpose of an economic model is to help understand how some sector of the economy functions.

For example, an economic model designed to explain the rate of marriage and divorce might hypothesize that the reduction in wage differentials between men and women would reduce the marriage rate. This model would make assumptions only about the economic motivation for marriage and would ignore all the other reasons that persons choose to marry. Economic models might also be used to explain how the purchase of automobiles is related to the interest rates charged on loans or how changes in mortgage interest rates, tax laws, and household incomes influence the price and availability of housing. Economic models concentrate on the relationship among a few economic variables.

Behavioral assumptions Assumptions about the motivations of people.

The **behavioral assumptions** of a model are assumptions about the motivations of persons. The assumption that managers of business firms seek to maximize profits is a behavioral assumption. Such assumptions are used to establish cause-and-effect relationships among the variables of the model. For example, the behavioral assumption that consumers seek to maximize the satisfaction they receive from purchasing goods might be used to establish the conditions that must prevail if the monthly consumption of a good is to achieve this objective. A model based on the assumption of profit maximization might be used to explain the influences on the quantities that sellers willingly offer for sale. For example, such a model might seek to show how an increase in the price of lumber affects the cost of new housing. Logic can then be used to show how the increased cost of lumber affects the incentive of profit-maximizing contractors to make housing available. If the model can show, given this increased cost, that reducing construction maximizes the profits of contractors, it will have established a relationship between the price of lumber and housing starts, assuming that nothing else changes.

The implications of an economic model for economic relationships are expressed as *hypotheses,* which are statements of cause and effect that can be confirmed or refuted by facts. The statement that an increase in the price of lumber reduces housing starts, assuming that nothing else changes, is an example of a hypothesis.

Unfortunately, a number of influences on an economic variable usually change at the same time. Housing starts are influenced not only by the price of lumber but also by interest rates on construction loans. Lower interest rates tend to encourage more housing construction by increasing its profitability. If the price of lumber increases while interest rates fall, the number of housing starts will reflect the influence of both these changes on the decisions of contractors. Thus, finding factual support for a hypothesis about the relationship between two economic variables often requires a method of accounting for the effect of other economic variables on the variables the model seeks to explain.

The behavioral assumptions of a model need not be realistic for the model to be useful. The goals of consumers and business managers are indeed multifaceted. However, the consideration of many, often conflicting, goals increases the complexity of a model and limits its applicability. The models used in microeconomic theory usually simplify reality by assuming that persons are motivated to achieve a single goal.

Ultimately, the usefulness of an economic model depends on the degree to which its predictions correspond with the facts, not on the realism of its assumptions. Models are, after all, simplifications and abstractions. They do not pretend to mirror reality in all of its complexity.[5]

The Pursuit and Maximization of Net Gain: A Key Behavioral Assumption in Microeconomic Models

A key behavioral assumption in models used in modern microeconomics is that persons are motivated by the desire to maximize the net gains they receive from engaging in transactions. Any market transaction results in both costs and benefits to a person. When you buy a car, for example, you receive the benefits of ownership and use of that good. On the other hand, the purchase of a car involves paying a price to the seller. The opportunity cost of your decision to buy the car is your next best use of the money you give up to buy it.

The net gain from all of the transactions a person undertakes over a certain period is the difference between the total benefits received and the total costs incurred. The net gain consumers earn in purchasing goods and services over a month is the difference between the benefits they receive from those purchases and the costs they incur in making the purchases. The net gain to a business owner from engaging in market transactions over a certain period can be measured by the profit earned over that period. Profit is the difference between the revenue earned by selling products over a period and the costs incurred to make those products available.

The presumption of maximization of net gains from transactions is a simplification. Economists do not mean to portray human beings as economic automatons that seek only gain. There is no doubt that persons are often motivated by noneconomic considerations and often do things for others without expecting cash payment in return. The presumption of maximization of net gains is merely a convenient starting point for explaining economic relations. It has proved to be a fruitful assumption; as will be shown repeatedly in this text, hypotheses based on it have been consistently supported by facts.

---

[5] See Milton Friedman, "The Methodology of Positive Economics," in *Essays in Positive Economics*, (Chicago: University of Chicago Press, 1953). For an elaboration of the role of assumptions in economics, see Lawrence A. Boland, "A Critique of Friedman's Critics," *Journal of Economic Literature* 17, no. 2 (June 1979), pp. 503–22; and Eugene Rotwein, "Friedman's Critics: A Critic's Reply to Boland," *Journal of Economic Literature* 18, no. 4 (December 1980), pp. 1553–55.

Marginal Analysis of Net Gains of Transactions

Marginal analysis A technique of analyzing the way persons who seek to maximize net gains make decisions.

Marginal benefit The extra benefit of one more unit of something.

Marginal cost The extra cost of one more unit of something.

Marginal analysis is a technique of analyzing the way persons who seek to maximize net gains make decisions. This technique examines the way each additional transaction of an individual over a period affects the goal that the individual is presumed to pursue. For example, marginal analysis of a profit-maximizing producer of automobiles would view each extra car produced and sold to dealers each month as a separate transaction. The cost of the transaction would include all of the production, shipping, and other costs involved in making that car available to dealers. The benefit to the producer would be the additional revenue that the producer receives from selling the car. The extra benefit associated with one more unit of an activity or transaction (such as selling one more car) is its **marginal benefit.** The extra cost associated with one more unit, in this case producing and selling one more car, is the **marginal cost** of the transaction. If the marginal benefit exceeds the marginal cost of the transaction, the net gain on the transaction is positive. When the net gain (profit) of an additional transaction during a month is positive, the transaction increases the total profit earned over the month.

Similarly, marginal analysis of buyers' decisions examines both the benefits obtained and the costs incurred by buyers when they engage in transactions. Buyers would purchase an additional unit of a good if the marginal benefit they obtain by doing so exceeds the marginal cost they incur. The marginal benefit of the purchase is the extra satisfaction obtained from acquiring another unit of the good. The marginal cost is the sacrifice of the opportunity to use the money spent to purchase something else.

Persons who maximize net gains will buy more, sell more, play more tennis, study more, and so on as long as the marginal benefit of doing so does not fall below the associated marginal cost. As you go through this book, you will see how marginal analysis is used over and over again to analyze the implications of models based on the behavioral assumption of maximization of net personal gain. Marginal analysis has proved to be both a powerful way of explaining decisions and a useful guide to decision making. Marginal analysis views persons as weighing the marginal costs against the marginal benefits of their actions in making decisions. The key to using marginal analysis is to carefully investigate all of the influences on the benefits and costs of decision makers while assuming that their goal is to maximize the net gains from transactions.

CONCEPT REVIEW

1. What is the purpose of an economic model?
2. What is the behavioral assumption used most often in microeconomic models?
3. The marginal cost of shipping another washing machine this month is $300. Assuming that the manager of the business making the machines seeks to maximize monthly profit, under what circumstances would you predict that he will choose *not* to ship this extra machine during the month?

Positive versus Normative Analysis

Positive economic analysis Analysis of the effects of changes in economic policies or economic conditions on economic variables.

Positive economic analysis of changes in economic policy or conditions seeks to predict the impact of these changes on observable phenomena such as production, purchases, prices, or personal income. Using positive economic theory, the economist can make statements of the "if . . . then" variety that may then be confirmed or refuted by comparison with available facts and figures. For example, a positive analysis of agricultural policy in the United States might seek to determine the impact of agricultural price supports on consumer prices and the incomes of farmers. The analysis might be used to make this prediction: "If price supports to U.S. farmers are reduced, agricultural surpluses and the prices of agricultural products to U.S. consumers will fall." The prediction could be verified if the price supports are actually reduced. Positive analysis might also be used to predict the impact of reduced price supports on the incomes of farmers and on the distribution of income among farmers. For example, the analysis might predict that farmers with large farms would be hurt more than farmers with small farms if price supports were reduced.

Normative economic analysis Analysis of the desirability of alternative outcomes on the basis of underlying value judgments.

Positive analysis makes no judgment as to whether an outcome is good or bad. The relative merits of alternative outcomes require value judgments to set criteria concerning what is good and bad. **Normative economic analysis** is used to evaluate the desirability of alternative outcomes on the basis of underlying value judgments. A normative analysis can be used to make recommendations regarding what ought to be. It can prescribe remedies in the form of government policy to correct results of market interaction that are not in accord with the underlying value judgments. Normative statements make recommendations; they say this or that *should* be done. "Policies that impede free international trade *should* be eliminated" is an example of a normative statement. Embodied in this statement is the judgment that it is good to have free trade.

A normative statement cannot be refuted by facts; it embodies a prescription rather than a prediction. Normative theory does, however, benefit from positive analysis. For example, if citizens agree that it is good to support policies that reduce poverty, there remains a factual problem concerning whether or not particular programs designed to reduce poverty can achieve this objective. Positive analysis can help citizens to intelligently choose among proposed policies whose predicted outcomes are in accord with their value judgments.

Techniques for positive analysis will be developed throughout much of this book. However, the book will also show how economists often prescribe changes in resource allocation and distribution to help achieve various normative goals.

MODERN MICROECONOMICS IN ACTION: GOVERNMENT AND THE ECONOMY

Can Beer Taxes and Raising the Legal Drinking Age Save Your Life?: Positive Economic Analysis in Action

Drinking and driving do not mix. For young people this is especially true in view of the fact that automobile accidents are the leading cause of death of persons between the ages of 16 and 24. But what do drinking and driving have to do with economics? The answer is that the decision to drink is in part an economic one, influenced by both the price of alcoholic beverages and the transaction costs of obtaining them.

A number of studies have utilized economic models to understand and predict what impact raising the legal drinking age and increasing the taxes levied on beer will have on fatal motor vehicle accidents. The models are based on the assumption that laws increasing the cost of obtaining alcoholic beverages change the decisions of persons who seek to maximize their net gains from consuming those beverages. Although laws that raise the legal drinking age do not directly affect the price of beer and other alcoholic beverages, they do increase the transaction costs that young people incur in trying to obtain these items. Raising the legal drinking age to 21 does not guarantee that no persons under that age will drink. However, by making it more difficult for these persons to obtain alcoholic beverages, such a law does increase the transaction costs of obtaining them.

The current trend toward increasing the drinking age in the United States was preceded by an earlier trend toward reducing it. Between 1970 and 1975 nearly half of the states reduced the minimum age required to buy beer to 18 in most cases. In 1976 a trend toward raising the drinking age back to 21 was inaugurated, and today all of the states have a minimum legal drinking age of 21. A number of studies have shown that the reduction in the drinking age in the early 1970s was associated with an increase in traffic fatalities for drivers under the age of 21.*

Based on data from 1975 to 1984, a period when many states were raising the drinking age, a recent study used statistical methods to test the hypothesis that raising the drinking age would reduce highway fatalities. The study concluded that raising the minimum drinking age would reduce nighttime driver fatal crash involvements by 13 percent.†

Two recent studies have suggested that another way to reduce highway deaths is to increase the tax on beer. Douglas Coate and Michael Grossman argue that a tax on beer is likely to be very effective in reducing drinking by young people.‡ They reason that young drinkers have not been drinking long enough to develop the habit and that young people typically have low incomes. The price increase resulting from a higher tax on beer will take a bigger chunk of income from the young beer drinkers than from the relatively more affluent older drinkers. And because people between the ages of 21 and 24 are unlikely to be habitual drinkers, they are more likely to respond to the higher price by cutting back consumption.

Analysis of beer consumption by youths based on data from a survey conducted between 1975 and 1982 supported the hypothesis that people between the ages of 18 and 24 would sharply reduce their consumption of beer in response to an increase in its price relative to the price of other goods. A study by Grossman and Henry Saffer supported the hypothesis that higher beer taxes can save lives. Grossman and Saffer estimated that over 1,000 lives of youths between the ages of 18 and 20 could have been saved per year over the period studied if the excise tax on beer had been increased annually by a percentage equal to the average rate of increase of all prices.§

Congress passed legislation in 1984 requiring that a portion of federal aid for highway construction be withheld from states with legal drinking ages below 21. As a result of this legislation, all of the states raised their legal drinking age to 21. Then in 1990, as part of a deficit reduction package of tax

(*Continued*) increases, Congress doubled the federal tax on beer to 32 cents per six-pack!

The research summaries provided above show how economists use positive economic analysis to help citizens and politicians evaluate economic policies. You may have your own views on what the legal drinking age should be or on whether the taxes on beer should be increased. Those views might be influenced by positive economic analysis showing that raising the drinking age and increasing beer prices are quite likely to reduce the number of the young people who die on the highways!

* For example, see Philip J. Cook and George Tauchen, "The Effect of Minimum Drinking Age Legislation on Youthful Auto Fatalities, 1970–1977," *Journal of Legal Studies* 13 (1984), p. 169.

† William Du Mouchel, Allan F. Williams, and Paul Zador, "Raising the Alcohol Purchase Age: Its Effects on Fatal Motor Vehicle Crashes in Twenty-six States," *Journal of Legal Studies* 16, no. 1 (January 1987), pp. 249–66.

‡ Douglas Coate and Michael Grossman, "Effects of Alcoholic Beverage Prices and Legal Drinking Ages on Youth Alcohol Use," Working Paper no. 1852, National Bureau of Economic Research, March 1986.

§ Michael Grossman and Henry Saffer, "Beer Taxes, the Legal Drinking Age, and Youth Motor Vehicle Fatalities," National Bureau of Economic Research, Working Paper no. 1914, May 1986.

Summary

1. Microeconomics studies the behavior of persons as they make choices and engage in transactions to provide themselves with goods and services.
2. Scarcity is the imbalance between desires for goods and services and the means of satisfying those desires.
3. The opportunity cost of choosing to use scarce resources for one purpose is the next best alternative use of those resources that is sacrificed by doing so. Scarcity compels persons to make daily choices regarding resource use in which they consider both the benefits and the opportunity costs of their choices. Basic economic decisions determine what gets produced, how it gets produced, and who gets the products.
4. Prices represent what must be given up to obtain each unit of goods and services desired. The relative price of a good increases when its money price increases more rapidly than the average rate of increase of the money prices of all goods.
5. Markets allow communication and trade between buyers and sellers. Interaction among buyers and sellers in markets establishes prices, and these market prices ration available supplies of goods and services.
6. A prerequisite to market exchange is the establishment of property rights. Trade involves an exchange of property rights. Persons are willing to trade only when the rights they acquire by doing so can be established, enforced, and transferred at low cost. Transaction costs are the value of the resources used to locate trading partners, to negotiate, and to protect property rights acquired through trading.
7. Economic models consist of assumptions that establish relationships between and among economic variables.
8. Hypotheses derived from economic theories must be tested against facts. A useful economic theory explains the economic phenomena for which it was developed and is the basis for predictions that can be supported with factual data.
9. A key behavioral assumption used to construct economic models is that persons maximize the net gains they obtain from engaging in transactions. This implies that over a given period persons will undertake additional transactions provided that the marginal benefit of such a transaction does not fall short of its marginal cost.
10. Positive analysis seeks to explain and understand economic relationships. Normative analysis seeks to change the use of resources in order to achieve goals based on underlying value judgments.

Important Concepts

scarcity
economics
microeconomics
opportunity cost of a choice
prices
change in the relative price of a good
market
property rights
transaction costs
circular flow diagram
theory
economic model
economic variables
behavioral assumptions
marginal analysis
marginal benefit
marginal cost
positive economic analysis
normative economic analysis

Questions for Review

1. Why would a zero price for an item indicate the item is not scarce? An example of an item with a zero price is pine needles freshly fallen from the tree. Yet garden supply stores commonly sell baled pine needles at a positive price. Is there a contradiction?
2. Suppose you have a $20 per week allowance that you use to buy only records and ice cream cones. The price of a record is $5, and the price of an ice cream cone is $1. This week you buy four records. What is your opportunity cost of choosing to buy these records?
3. Make a list of the markets you use. Which of these are located at particular places? Describe the communication that takes place in these markets.
4. When you purchase a good or service, you really purchase the right to use it in certain ways. Zoning ordinances limit the purposes for which land can be used. Suppose a parcel of land can be used only for residential purposes. How would this affect your willingness to purchase that parcel as an investment?
5. On occasion, a good that is truly scarce is not priced. An example is unpolluted air. Those who live in cities in which the air is foul would be willing to pay for the right to breathe pure air. Why is it difficult to price the air we breathe and use the revenue collected to improve its quality?
6. How can transaction costs influence the incentives to engage in trade? Think of the items you currently do not choose to buy or sell because of high transaction costs. How much would these costs have to decline to induce you to buy or sell the items?
7. Suppose household expenditure on goods and services produced by domestic firms declines because households allocate more of their incomes to the purchase of imports. Other things being equal, how will this affect household incomes?
8. What type of behavioral assumption underlies many microeconomic models? Give some examplés of economic variables that economic models seek to explain and predict.
9. When a prediction is based on an economic model, why does the qualification "other things being equal" have to be stipulated? What is the ultimate test of the usefulness of a theory?
10. Indicate whether each of the following statements is positive or normative, and explain why.
    - **a.** If the price of men's suits were to rise 20 percent, the quantity sold would fall by 30 percent.
    - **b.** Tariffs should be imposed on foreign automobiles.
    - **c.** Tariffs on foreign automobiles will increase wages in the domestic automobile industry.
    - **d.** Policies that increase gross domestic product are good for the nation and ought to be pursued.
    - **e.** Government budget deficits should be eliminated.
    - **f.** The elimination of government budget deficits will decrease interest rates.

PROBLEMS

1. The tuition at your college goes up 6 percent in 1994. During the same year the average price of all goods and services goes up only 4 percent. What has happened to the relative price of attending college as measured by tuition? How can the relative price of a product fall even if its money price goes up?

2. Suppose that your marginal benefit from going to another rock concert this month is $25. The price of a ticket to rock concerts is currently $45, which is the marginal cost you will incur if you go to another rock concert this month. What would your net gain be if you attended another rock concert this month. Assuming that you seek to maximize your net gain from going to rock concerts, will you attend another one this month?

3. The following table shows how Mary's marginal benefit from purchasing sweaters varies with the number she purchases per year. The current market price of sweaters is $49.99, and there is no sales tax on the purchase. The purchase price represents the marginal cost of sweaters for Mary.

Sweaters Purchased per Year	***Marginal Benefit***
1	$80
2	70
3	60
4	50
5	40
6	30

How many sweaters will Mary buy this year? How many will she buy if a 9 percent sales tax is imposed on sales of sweaters and the market price remains $49.99 after the tax has been imposed?

2

Market Interaction

Basic Supply and Demand Analysis and Its Uses

The political upheaval that resulted from the unsuccessful coup in the former Soviet Union in August 1991 brought down more than an empire that had endured for over 70 years. When the Soviet Union died, changes in government policies and the need for dollars and other hard currencies (such as marks and yen) in the republics of the new Commonwealth of Independent States released a flood of exports. The demise of central control of exports in the republics of the former Soviet Union released stockpiles of various commodities and also changed many of the former Soviet Union's commercial relationships with agents for exporting such products as beluga caviar. As a result, the prices for such commodities as platinum, uranium, aluminum, gold, fertilizer, and even caviar plummeted in world markets.

For example, platinum, which was selling for $500 an ounce in 1989, was priced at $340 an ounce in January 1992. Gold prices were also down as a result of increases in supplies from the Soviet Union. Aluminum was selling for 51 cents a pound in early 1992, down from 70 cents a pound a year earlier. Urea fertilizer from former Soviet enterprises was being dumped on world markets in January 1992, and its price was plummeting. A pound of yellowcake uranium (a lightly processed ore) from the former Soviet Union was selling for $7 a pound in early 1992, down from $12 a pound in 1990. American uranium producers were filing complaints against the Russians for unfair competition![1]

The increase in the supplies of products from former Soviet enterprises in world markets put inevitable downward pressure on the prices of these products. You can predict the effects of changes in supplies and demands for goods and services if you understand how the market mechanism works. Markets facilitate exchange between buyers and sellers. Supply and demand analysis explains how prices are established in markets through competition among many buyers and sellers and how those prices affect the quantities traded. Such analysis, which many of you have already studied in your principles of economics course, is an indispensable tool for showing how the market mechanism works and how prices influence incentives to use resources.

[1] See Matthew L. Wald, "Soviet Aftershocks Include a Global Commodities Glut," *The New York Times,* January 12, 1992, p. 4E.

The laws of supply and demand, which we review in this chapter, are fundamental observations about human behavior. These laws cannot be repealed. Supply and demand analysis shows that there are easily predictable consequences when governments seek to intervene in the market mechanism to achieve such social objectives as low rents for tenants, minimum wages for unskilled workers, and price supports for farmers. It also shows the consequences of central planning, such as was used by the nations of Eastern Europe and the former Soviet Union. Under central planning, the economies of these nations were highly regulated by government authorities who controlled the use of most resources and prevented markets from functioning to establish prices. Yet another use of supply and demand analysis is to show how taxes, subsidies, and import quotas affect market prices and the quantities of goods and services consumers can enjoy.

After you read this chapter, you will be able to apply supply and demand analysis to a variety of business and social issues. The chapters that follow will use marginal analysis to help you understand the forces of supply and demand more completely and to show you how government intervention in markets and the degree of competition affect market prices and freedom of choice.

Free and Competitive Markets

Free and competitive market A market in which many sellers compete for sales to many buyers who compete for available supplies and in which there are no restrictions on the participation of buyers or sellers.

In a **free and competitive market** many sellers compete for sales to many buyers who compete for available goods and services. In such a market all who wish to participate as either buyers or sellers can do so without any restrictions. No participant in a competitive market has the power to affect the market price. Each seller takes the market price as given and merely reacts to it.

In competitive markets buyers have no reason to prefer one seller over another because there is little difference between the products or services offered by the many sellers participating in the market. For example, in a typical farmers' market many sellers are likely to be selling a commodity of a certain standard quality, such as grade A eggs. Each unit of the commodity trades at the same price. In such a market, no single individual controls the forces that influence the price of the commodity. Instead, the process of competition among buyers and sellers creates impersonal forces that influence its price. The quantities willingly bought and sold are in turn influenced by the price. Supply and demand analysis concentrates on the relationship between prices and quantities willingly bought and sold, but it also considers other influences on prices and quantities.

Let's begin our analysis by looking at the buyers' side of the market. To do so, we must first introduce the concept of *demand*.

The Demand Curve

The quantity of an item buyers purchase in a market over a given period is influenced by such factors as

1. The price of the item.
2. The income of those who want to buy it.

3. The wealth of those who want to buy it (this is the value of the assets owned by potential buyers, such as stock, bonds, bank deposits, homes, and real estate).
4. Expectations of changes in future prices and future income or wealth.
5. The prices of alternative items.
6. Tastes or current fashions.
7. The population served by the market.

In supply and demand analysis we concentrate on each of these factors, one at a time, paying special attention to the relationship between the price of a good and the quantities buyers will purchase. **Demand** is a relationship between the price of a good and the quantity that buyers are willing and able to purchase. The **law of demand** states that, other things being equal, the lower the price of a good, the greater is the quantity demanded by buyers.[2] This law is really a hypothesis that the facts have consistently supported.

Demand The relationship between the price of an item and the quantity buyers are willing and able to purchase.

Law of demand The lower the price of an item, the greater is the quantity demanded, other things being equal.

A change in any of the demand influences listed above will affect the quantities that buyers are willing and able to purchase at various prices. The law of demand is therefore qualified by saying that the hypothesized inverse relationship between the price of a good and the quantities buyers willingly purchase presumes that *all other influences on demand are held fixed.*

The law of demand can be shown to be consistent with the behavioral assumption that individual consumers seek to maximize the net gains they receive from purchasing goods in markets. The following chapters investigate consumer choices more fully and show how the law of demand can be derived from a model that assumes maximizing behavior. At this point, a bit of introspection is likely to convince you that the law of demand is quite reasonable. How much rib eye steak do you purchase each week? For many Americans rib eye steak is a coveted delicacy. It is, however, more expensive than chicken, ground beef, pork, and various other meats. Surely you consider the price of steak when deciding how much of it to eat each week. Would you eat it more often if, given your income, tastes, and the prices of alternative foods, its price were $2 per pound instead of $7 per pound? Provided that you are not a vegetarian, you probably would. So would other consumers.

Table 2–1 presents hypothetical data on the way in which consumer purchases of rib eye steak would vary with its price (other things being equal). Such a table, called a **demand schedule,** shows how the quantity of a good that consumers willingly purchase during a period increases as the price of the good declines. The **quantity demanded** is the amount that would be purchased at a certain price given all the other influences on demand. For example, according to the data in Table 2–1 the quantity of rib eye steak demanded per month would be 5 million pounds if the price were $6 per pound. The monthly quantity demanded varies with the price. Each price is associated with a certain quantity demanded. The demand for the good is represented by the entire relationship expressed in the table between price and quantity demanded.

Demand schedule A table showing how the quantity demanded of an item varies with the price of the item.

Quantity demanded The amount of an item that would be purchased at a certain price given all of the other influences on demand.

[2] These other influences on demand are sometimes called *demand parameters*.

TABLE 2–1 Demand for Rib Eye Steak

Price per Pound (In Dollars)	*Quantity Demanded (Millions of Pounds per Month)*
9	3.5
8	4
7	4.5
6	5
5	5.5
4	6
3	6.5
2	7
1	7.5

Demand curve A graph of the relationship between price and quantity demanded.

The law of demand can be illustrated by plotting the data from the demand schedule on a set of axes. A **demand curve** depicts the inverse relationship between price (P) and the quantity of good buyers are willing and able to buy. Each point on the demand curve associates the quantity demanded (Q_D) with the corresponding price. The demand curve drawn in Figure 2–1 plots thc prices in Table 2–1 on the vertical axis and the corresponding quantities demanded on the horizontal axis. The negative (downward) slope of the demand curve illustrates the law of demand. As price declines, the quantity demanded increases.

A demand curve can be drawn only if all the other influences on the quantities of a good that consumers will purchase, other than the price of the good, are held constant. The demand curve in Figure 2–1 shows the relationship between the price of rib eye steak and the amount of rib eye steak that consumers would buy per month given all the other influences on demand.[3] If any of these influences were to change, there would be a corresponding change in the relationship between price and quantity demanded and a whole new demand schedule and demand curve would have to be drawn up.

The concept of demand isolates the relationship between price and quantities demanded during a period. Economists often qualify their statements about demand with the phrase *other things being equal* or the Latin equivalent, *ceteris*

[3] The demand curve illustrates an inverse functional relationship between price and quantity demanded. A *demand function* is a mathematical way of expressing the law of demand. Such a function could be written as follows:

$$Q_D = f(P, I, T, P_S, P_C, E)$$

This states that quantity demanded depends on price and such other influences as income, I; tastes, T; the prices of substitutes, P_S; the prices of complements, P_C; and E, expectations of changes in future prices. The law of demand implies that $\partial Q_D/\partial P < 0$.

FIGURE 2–1 The Demand Curve

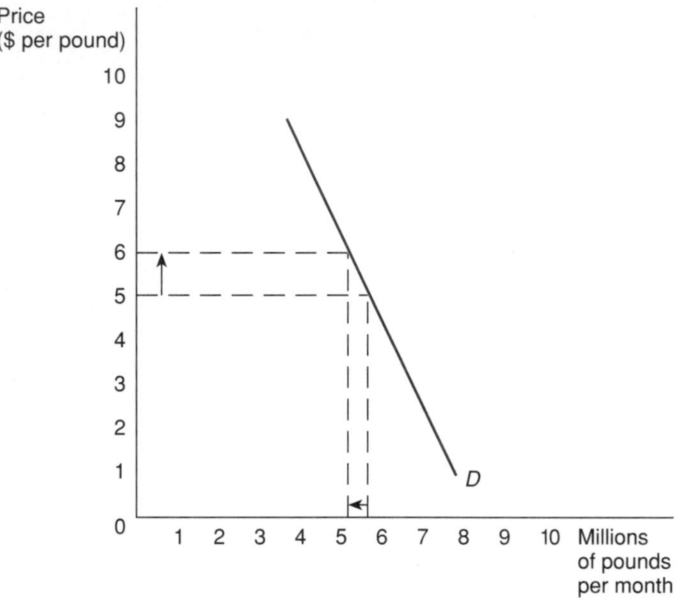

The demand curve depicts the relationship between price and quantity demanded. If price increases from $5 per pound to $6 per pound, quantity demanded decreases from 5.5 million to 5 million pounds per month. A price decrease causes an increase in quantity demanded.

paribus. For example, other things being equal, the law of demand hypothesizes that an increase in price decreases the quantity demanded. To support this hypothesis, the impact of price on quantity demanded must be isolated by adjusting for any other influence on the willingness or ability of consumers to buy the good that might simultaneously change.

Change in quantity demanded A change in the amount of an item buyers are willing and able to buy in response to a change in its price.

A movement along a demand curve is called a **change in quantity demanded**. It represents a change in the quantity of a good purchased that results from a change in the price of the good. Figure 2–1 shows that an increase in the price of rib eye steak from $5 to $6 per pound results in a decrease in quantity demanded from 5.5 to 5 million pounds per month.

A demand curve also provides information about the maximum price consumers will pay for various quantities of a good that are made available per period. This alternative view of the demand curve is useful in determining how price will vary with the availability of a good. The data in Table 2–1 can be interpreted as giving the maximum price that will be paid for various quantities of rib eye steak available in different months. When rib eye steak is less abundant during a month, the maximum price that would be paid for it increases accordingly.

Changes in Demand

Change in demand A change in the relationship between the price of an item and the quantity demanded caused by a change in something other than the price of the item.

A **change in demand** is a change in the relationship between the price of a good and the quantity demanded that is caused by a change in something other than the price of the good. A change in demand is represented by a movement of an entire demand curve. Such a change implies that consumers will buy more or less of a good at any given price. For example, an increase in consumer income tends to increase the demand for steak. This means that a greater quantity of rib eye steak would be bought by consumers at each of the prices listed in Table 2–1. Conversely, a decrease in consumer income tends to cause a decrease in the demand for steak.

For some goods an increase in income can decrease demand. In general, economists can only make hypotheses about the effects of changes in various influences on the variables the model seeks to explain. The hypothesis that an increase in consumer income increases the demand for steak at various possible prices would therefore have to be checked against the facts. A good for which an increase in income results in an increase in demand is called a *normal good*. For some goods, called *inferior goods*, an increase in income results in a decrease in demand. For example, hamburger and less expensive cuts of meat may be inferior goods since increases in income induce consumers to replace them with steak and other better-quality meats. An increase in income, other things being equal, might therefore *decrease* the demand for hamburger.

An increase in the price of pork or chicken is also likely to increase the demand for steak. As the prices of these meats go up, consumers will find steak a more attractive buy and the demand curve for steak will shift outward. Similarly, a decrease in the prices of goods that go well with steak dinners, such as potatoes or beer, could also increase the demand for steak.

Changes in demand are illustrated in Figure 2–2. An increase in demand shifts the demand curve from D_1 to D_2. After the increase in demand, the quantity demanded at a price of $6 is now 7 million pounds per month on demand curve D_2 instead of the 5 million pounds per month that prevailed on demand curve D_1. Similarly, after the increase in demand, the quantity demanded at each possible price is greater on the new demand curve than on the old demand curve.

The Supply Curve

The quantity of an item that sellers will offer for sale in market can be affected by such factors as

1. The price of the item.
2. The current prices of inputs required to produce and market the item.
3. The current technology available to produce the item.
4. The prices of other items that can be produced with inputs used or owned by the sellers.
5. Expectations about future prices.
6. The number of sellers.

FIGURE 2–2 Changes in Demand

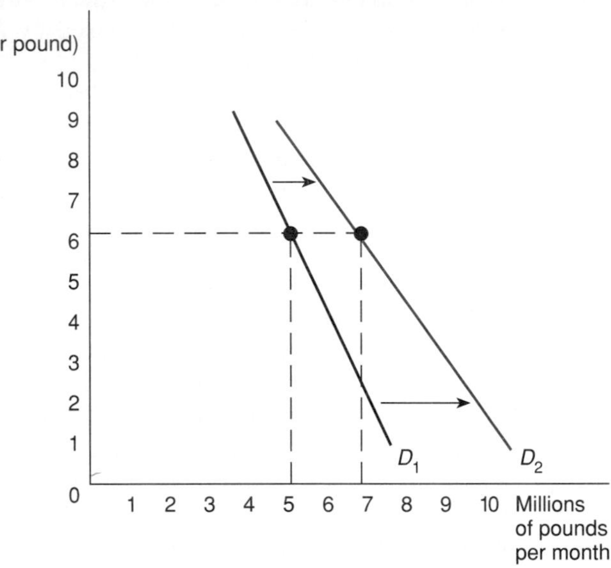

An increase in demand shifts the demand curve outward from D_1 to D_2. When demand increases, the quantities demanded at *all* prices increase. For example, at a price of $6 the quantity demanded is 5 million pounds per month when demand curve D_1 prevails but is 7 million pounds per month when demand curve D_2 prevails. A decrease in demand would be represented by a shift in the demand curve from D_2 to D_1. Changes in the demand for an item can be caused by

- An increase in income or in wealth if the item is a normal good (if the item is an inferior good, an increase in income would decrease demand).
- An increase in the price of a substitute.
- A decrease in the price of a complement.
- Expectations of a future increase in the relative price of the item.
- A change in tastes or fashion that makes the item more popular.
- An increase in the number of buyers served by the market.

In supply and demand analysis we seek to isolate the effects of each influence on the supply of an item while paying special attention to the influence of the item's price on the willingness of sellers to make it available for sale in markets. **Supply** is a relationship between price and the quantity sellers are willing and able to sell. The **law of supply** states that, other things being equal, the higher the price of a good, the greater is the willingness of sellers to make that good available. In general, higher prices increase the profitability of selling more of an item and thus induce sellers to increase the quantity supplied. Sellers require higher prices to gain from increasing the quantity supplied because the unit costs of production rise when the quantity supplied over a given period increases. Unit and marginal costs of production rise as the quantity supplied is increased because as existing facilities are worked more intensively and less experienced workers are hired, the efficiency of operations is impaired.

Supply A relationship between price and quantity supplied.

Law of supply The higher the price of an item, the greater is the quantity supplied.

The concept of supply isolates the relationship between the price of a product and the quantities of the product sellers willingly offer for sale in a market over a certain period, assuming that all other influences on incentives or ability to sell are held fixed. When one of the other influences changes, so does the relationship between the price of the product and the quantities supplied. For example, an increase in the price of fuel makes it more expensive to operate taxis. This decreases the willingness of taxi owners to offer their services at any given price. The technology available to produce a good can also affect the willingness of sellers to make it available. Improvements in technology can reduce the amount of labor and the other inputs required to produce a given amount of a good. When fewer inputs are required to produce a given amount of output, costs will also decline, thereby increasing the profitability of making a good available. An improvement in the technology of meat cutting decreases the cost of making each pound of steak available.

Changes in the prices of other goods that can be produced with the same inputs will affect the opportunity cost of a good whose supply is being analyzed. For example, an increase in the price of corn might decrease the willingness of farmers to make wheat available by inducing them to use more land for corn and less for wheat as corn production becomes more profitable. Expectations of changes in the future profitability of producing a good might also influence its current supply. The number of sellers in the market is an important determinant of supply over longer periods. For example, a reduction in international trade barriers that increases the number of automobile sellers in a nation will increase the supply of automobiles. Noneconomic conditions are also sometimes important influences on supply. For example, the weather is important in explaining the market supply of wheat because it can affect the quantity of wheat harvested no matter what the price of wheat. The weather is not, however, important in explaining the quantity of typewriters bought or sold.

Supply schedule
A table showing how the quantity supplied of an item varies with the price of that item.

A **supply schedule** is a tabular way of expressing the relationship between price and the amounts sellers are willing to sell over a certain period. The quantity associated with each price in a supply schedule is the **quantity supplied.** Table 2–2 gives hypothetical data for price and the quantity of rib eye steak supplied per month. The data in the table illustrate the law of supply because the quantity supplied increases as the price goes up.

Quantity supplied
The amount of an item that would be supplied at a certain price given all of the other influences on supply.

A **supply curve** is a graph that isolates the relationship between price and quantity supplied over a period. The supply curve in Figure 2–3 is obtained by plotting price (P) against the corresponding quantity supplied (Q_S) in Table 2–2. The upward slope of the supply curve reflects the law of supply.[4]

Supply curve
A graph of the relationship between price and quantity supplied.

[4] The law of supply can also be expressed by using a mathematical relationship. Supply is a functional relationship between price (P) and quantity supplied (Q_S) that also depends on other variables. The supply function can be written as

$$Q_S = f(P, P_I, T, E)$$

where P_I are input prices, T is technology, and E are expectations of future changes in price. The law of supply implies that $\partial Q_S/\partial P > 0$.

Change in quantity supplied A change in the amount of an item offered for sale in response to a change in its price, other things being equal.

A **change in quantity supplied** is a change in the amount of a good offered for sale in response to a change in its price, other things being equal. A change in the quantity supplied is represented by a movement along a given supply curve. For example, in Figure 2–3 an increase in price from $6 to $7 per pound results in an increase in the quantity supplied from 5 million to 6 million pounds per month. A supply curve illustrates the relationship between price and quantity supplied over a given period. The data in Table 2–2 refer to a certain month.

TABLE 2–2 Supply of Rib Eye Steak

Price per Pound (In Dollars)	*Quantity Supplied (Millions of Pounds per Month)*
9	8
8	7
7	6
6	5
5	4
4	3
3	2
2	1

FIGURE 2–3 The Supply Curve

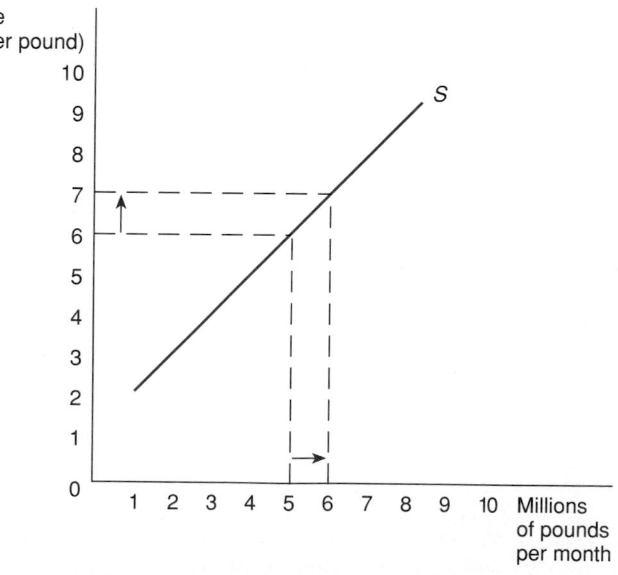

An upward-sloping supply curve implies that quantity supplied increases with price. As price increases, there are corresponding increases in quantity supplied. A decrease in price reduces quantity supplied.

A supply curve can also be interpreted as a relationship between quantity supplied and the minimum price required to make that amount available. For example, the supply curve in Figure 2–3 indicates that, other things being equal, the minimum price necessary to induce sellers to offer 5 million pounds of rib eye steak per month is $6 per pound.

Changes in Supply

Change in supply
A change in the relationship between the price of a good and the quantity supplied that results from a change in something other than the price of the good.

A supply curve is drawn under the presumption that influences other than the price of the good on the incentive to make it available are fixed. A **change in supply** is a change in the relationship between the price of a good and the quantity

FIGURE 2–4 Changes in Supply

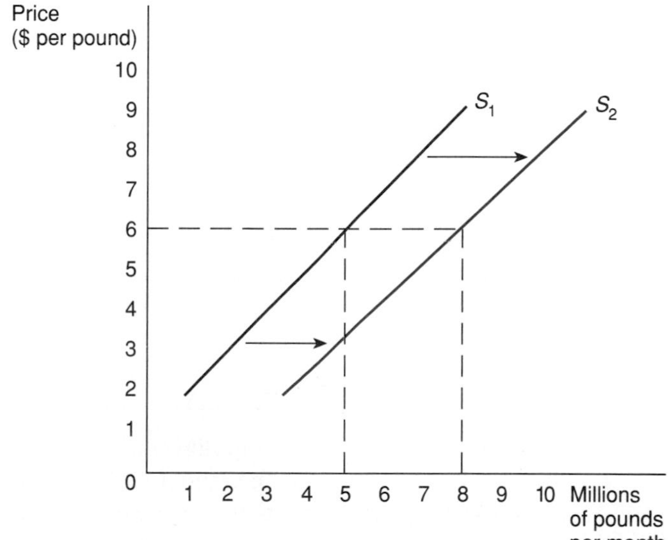

A change in supply is a movement of the entire supply curve. A movement from S_1 to S_2 signifies an increase in supply. After this increase has occurred, the quantity supplied at a price of $6 per pound is 8 million pounds per month instead of the 5 million pounds that were supplied with the initial supply curve. A movement from S_2 to S_1 signifies a decrease in supply.

A change in the supply of an item can be caused by

- A change in the prices of the inputs used to produce it: An increase in input prices decreases supply, while a decrease in input prices increases supply.
- A change in technology: An improvement in technology increases supply, while the unlikely event of a deterioration in technology (caused by some catastrophe) would decrease supply.
- A change in the prices of other items: An increase in the relative price of an alternative item that can be produced with the same resources decreases the supply of the first item, while a decrease in the relative price of the alternative item increases the supply of the first item.
- A change in the number of sellers serving the market: A decrease in the number of sellers decreases supply, while an increase in the number of sellers increases supply.

supplied that results from a change in something other than the price of the good. A change in supply is represented by a movement of an entire supply curve. For example, a decrease in the price of cattle feed could cause an increase in the supply of steak. Thus, the supply curve would shift outward. At each possible price the quantity supplied would be greater. When an input price falls in this way, the cost per unit falls and sellers are willing to accept a lower minimum price to make any given quantity available for sale. This accounts for the fact that the new supply curve lies below the old one at each quantity after supply increases. Conversely, an increase in the price of cattle feed increases the cost of producing steak and therefore decreases the supply. This means that the amounts sellers will sell at each price will decline. The supply curve would shift inward toward the vertical axis of the graph.

Changes in supply are shown in Figure 2–4. An increase in supply that shifts the supply curve from S_1 to S_2 increases the quantity supplied at all possible prices. For example, along the new supply curve, S_2, the quantity supplied at a price of $6 is 8 million pounds per month compared to the 5 million pounds per month that were supplied before the increase in supply.

CONCEPT REVIEW

1. What information is provided in a demand schedule?
2. What could cause a change in the demand for wheat?
3. Explain the distinction between a change in supply and a change in quantity supplied.

MARKET EQUILIBRIUM

Equilibrium
A balance of forces that keeps economic variables from increasing or decreasing.

Market equilibrium
A condition that exists in a market when price adjusts so that quantity demanded equals quantity supplied.

In an economic model an **equilibrium** is a balance of forces as a result of which the economic variables that the model seeks to explain neither increase nor decrease. A **market equilibrium** exists when the price of an item is such that the quantity demanded exactly equals the quantity supplied. *When a market is in equilibrium, the quantity buyers wish to buy is exactly balanced by the quantity sellers wish to sell and there is no tendency for the market price to increase or decrease.* When prices reach equilibrium values, all buyers who wish to buy at the market price will find goods readily available and all sellers who wish to sell at that price will readily find buyers for their goods.

Plotting demand and supply curves on the same set of axes, graphic analysis can be used to show how the equilibrium price and quantity are determined. In Figure 2–5 the equilibrium price is $6 per pound and the equilibrium quantity is 5 million pounds per month. Only at that price is the monthly quantity demanded equal to the monthly quantity supplied. Any movement away from the equilibrium price sets up forces that return the market to its previous equilibrium, other things unchanged. At a price of, say, $3 per pound, the quantity demanded would exceed the quantity supplied (based on the data in Tables 2–1 and 2–2). When, given the

FIGURE 2–5 **Market Equilibrium**

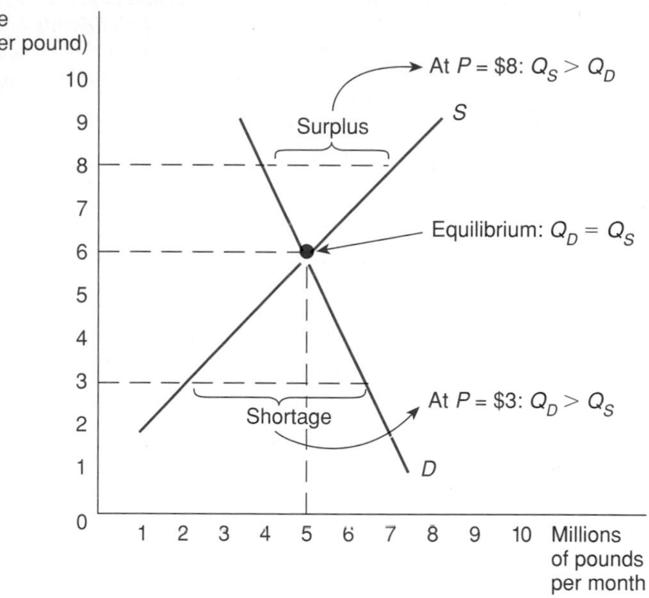

The equilibrium occurs where the demand curve, *D*, and the supply curve, *S*, intersect. The equilibrium price is $6 per pound. At that price quantity demanded equals quantity supplied. At any other price there would be a shortage or surplus of rib eye steak. If the market price were $3 per pound, there would be a shortage ($Q_D > Q_S$). A surplus would prevail if the market price were $8 per pound ($Q_S > Q_D$).

Shortage The difference between quantity demanded and quantity supplied in a market when quantity demanded is greater than quantity supplied.

Surplus The difference between quantity supplied and quantity demanded in a market when quantity supplied is greater than quantity demanded.

price, quantity demanded exceeds quantity supplied ($Q_D > Q_S$), a **shortage** exists. The shortage measures the difference between the quantities buyers want to buy and sellers are willing to sell at that price. A shortage is sometimes also called an *excess demand*. As shown in Figure 2–5, at a price of $3 per pound of rib eye steak, suppliers will supply only 2 million pounds per month and buyers want 6.5 million pounds per month. The shortage is therefore 4.5 million pounds per month. Competing buyers, unable to obtain as much rib eye steak as they demand at that price, begin to offer higher prices, and sellers, seeing that buyers are willing to pay more, begin to raise the price. As the price rises, the quantity demanded by buyers declines and the quantity supplied by sellers increases. This continues until the price reaches its equilibrium level of $6 per pound.

If price is above the equilibrium level, quantity demanded will fall short of quantity supplied ($Q_D < Q_S$). When this is the case, the difference between quantity supplied and quantity demanded is called a **surplus** (or an *excess supply*). At a price of $8 per pound, for example, buyers would be willing to purchase 4 million pounds of steak per month and sellers would be willing to supply 7 million pounds per month. The difference between what sellers would offer and buyers would buy at that price is a monthly surplus of 3 million pounds. Rib eye steak then piles up

TABLE 2–3 Market Equilibrium

Market Condition	*Relationship between Quantity Demanded and Quantity Supplied*	*Market Price*
Equilibrium	$Q_D = Q_S$	Equilibrium
Shortage	$Q_D > Q_S$	Rises
Surplus	$Q_D < Q_S$	Falls

in the supermarkets and starts to spoil. As the competing sellers see the unsold steak accumulating, they begin to cut their prices. As price begins to decline, quantity demanded increases and quantity supplied declines until the monthly surplus has been eliminated.

Table 2–3 summarizes the conditions for equilibrium and shows how market price changes when a shortage or surplus exists. The changes always adjust price to its equilibrium level.

Changes in Market Equilibrium: Comparative Static Analysis

Market Response to a Change in Demand

Comparative static analysis The use of logic to trace out the effects of a change in economic conditions on equilibrium values of the variables of an economic model.

Comparative static analysis uses logic to trace out the effects of a change in economic conditions on equilibrium values of the variables that an economic model seeks to explain. Comparative static analysis of supply and demand is used to develop hypotheses of how conditions that change either demand or supply affect market equilibrium prices and quantities traded. This type of analysis is a way of using an economic model to explain previous events or make predictions.

For example, suppose that the current market equilibrium price of rib eye steak is $6 per pound when the demand curve is D_1 in Figure 2–6. At that price, quantity demanded and quantity supplied balance and the market equilibrium quantity is 5 million pounds of rib eye steak per month. The current market equilibrium corresponds to point E_1 on the graph.

Now suppose that next month a sharp reduction in consumer income decreases the demand for rib eye steak. The demand curve for rib eye steak shifts inward from D_1 to D_2, and the equilibrium price of steak must therefore decline. To see why this is so, suppose that price were to remain at its previous equilibrium level of $6 per pound. At that price the quantity demanded of rib eye steak, based on the new demand curve (D_2), would be less than the quantity supplied. As a result there would be an excess supply of rib eye steak in the market, putting downward pressure on price.

The new equilibrium occurs where $Q_D = Q_S$ along D_2, namely at a price of $5 per pound. The equilibrium shifts from point E_1 to E_2, where the quantity sold decreases to 4 million pounds per month. The impact of the decrease in demand is

FIGURE 2–6 **Impact of a Decrease in Demand in the Market for Rib Eye Steak**

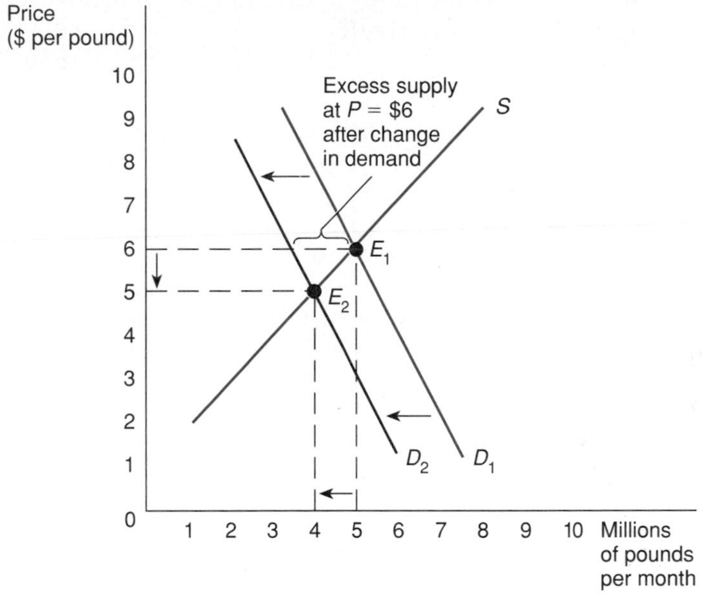

A decrease in demand changes the market equilibrium point from E_1 to E_2. Price declines from \$6 per pound to \$5 per pound. The new equilibrium quantity is 4 million pounds per month.

a decrease in the market equilibrium price, to which sellers respond by decreasing the quantity supplied, moving the supply curve down from point E_1 to point E_2.

Similarly, an increase in demand, other things being equal, will increase equilibrium price and quantity supplied. For example, an increase in the price of chicken, other things being equal, will increase the demand for steak. It will therefore result in an increase in the market equilibrium price and the quantity of steak supplied.

Market Response to a Change in Supply

Market equilibrium will also change in response to a change in supply. In Figure 2–7 the market equilibrium price and quantity initially correspond to point E_1, at which the price is \$6 per pound and the quantity bought and sold is 5 million pounds per month.

Now suppose that next month there is an increase in the price of cattle feed. This will decrease the supply of rib eye steak. The decrease in supply results in a new market equilibrium at point E_2. The equilibrium price of rib eye steak increases to \$7 per pound, and the quantity demanded declines to 4.5 million pounds per month. If price did not increase to this new level, there would be a shortage of rib eye steak on the market. At the new equilibrium price of \$7, quantity supplied based on the new supply curve is just equal to quantity demanded.

MODERN MICROECONOMICS IN ACTION: **THE BUSINESS WORLD**

Where's the Beef?

The price of beef in the United States soared in the late 1980s and early 1990s. In mid-July 1991, T-bone steak was selling for $5.65 a pound according to a survey of retail prices in 19 cities. The retail price of steak in 1991 was 38 percent higher than it had been five years earlier, and in 1990 the retail price of beef rose 8.9 percent, outpacing the rates of increases in the prices of other food products.*

The higher retail price of beef has been a boon to ranchers. As of early 1990 ranching was one of the strongest sectors of the U.S. farm economy, bringing prosperity to such states as Nebraska, where cattle is still a major industry. Ranchers throughout the Great Plains have been earning record profits and plowing those profits into new farm machinery.

A sustained high price of beef is somewhat unusual for the U.S. cattle industry and is particularly surprising in view of the fact that the U.S. demand for beef has been declining since 1976 because of health concerns about the impact of fat and cholesterol in food. U.S. per capita consumption of beef has fallen by nearly one third since 1976. Typically when the price of beef rises, ranchers rush to increase the size of their herds. The resulting increase in supply tends to put downward pressure on the price of beef.

The price of beef did not fall in the early 1990s in part because rising exports of beef, particularly to Japan, helped offset the declining U.S. demand for beef. Also, U.S. ranchers *did not* increase the size of their herds in response to the run-up in the price of beef. In fact, as of 1991 the size of those herds was at a 30-year low. The supply of beef has actually fallen more than the demand has decreased, resulting in an increase in the price of cattle and beef products.

The reluctance of ranchers to expand their herds has puzzled agricultural economists, who have grown to expect a boom-and-bust cycle of rising and then falling beef prices. One possible explanation for the decreased responsiveness of supply is the increase in the average age of ranchers. The older and more experienced present-day ranchers are more interested in reducing their debt burdens than in borrowing to expand productive capacity.

* See Scott Kilman, "Beef Prices Stay Lofty as Ranchers Avoid Usual Overexpansion," *The Wall Street Journal*, July 23, 1991. The information presented here is based on this article.

The decrease in the supply of steak causes its price to increase. Buyers respond to the price increase by decreasing the quantity demanded. The market adjustment to the new, higher equilibrium price serves to ration the decreased supply of steak according to the willingness of buyers to pay. At the higher price buyers are willing to purchase less steak than before.

An increase in the supply of steak would have opposite effects. If the equilibrium price of steak does not decline in response to the increase in supply, there will be a surplus of steak on the market. An increase in supply therefore communicates information on the increased availability of a commodity by putting downward pressure on its price. Consumers respond by increasing the quantity demanded of that commodity. Once again the link between a change in supply and a change in quantity demanded is through a change in price.

FIGURE 2–7 Impact of a Decrease in Supply on the Market for Rib Eye Steak

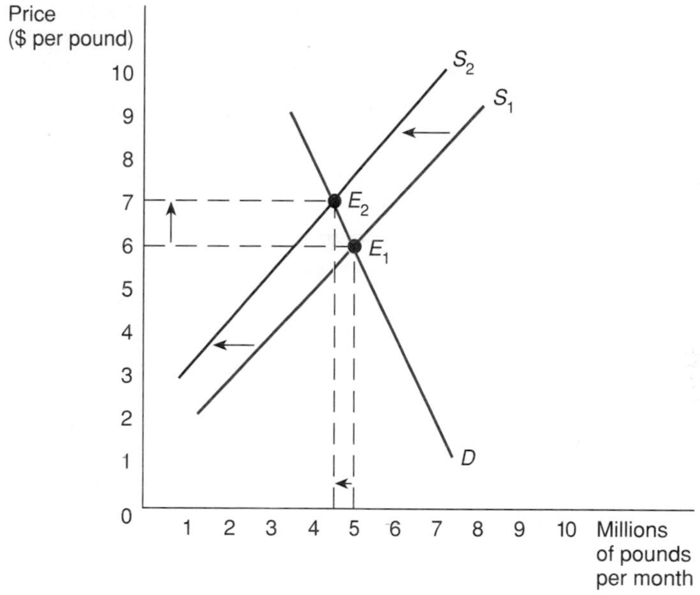

A decrease in supply changes the market equilibrium from point E_1 to E_2. The price of rib eye steak increases. Buyers respond to the higher price by decreasing the quantity demanded.

CONCEPT REVIEW

1. What forces must balance for a market equilibrium to be achieved?
2. Suppose that the current market equilibrium price of laser videodiscs is $35. Other things being equal, show the impact on market equilibrium of an increase in the demand for these discs.
3. A change in the tax law results in a decrease in the supply of rental housing. Other things being equal, predict the effect of the decrease in supply on monthly rents and on the quantity of rental housing demanded.

APPLICATIONS OF SUPPLY AND DEMAND ANALYSIS

Analysis of the Consequences of Taxation

Suppose that a tax, T, equal to 10 cents per gallon, is imposed on sellers of gasoline. Assume that 10 million gallons of gasoline are currently sold per month at a price of $1 per gallon. Will the tax collect a million dollars in revenue each month? A little reflection will indicate that this is unlikely. What effect will the tax have on the market price of gasoline? How will the tax affect the net price received by sellers?

Imposition of the 10-cent per gallon gasoline tax is likely to raise the price of gasoline and thereby reduce the quantity demanded. Figure 2–8 shows the impact of the tax on the market for gasoline. From the sellers' point of view the tax is an increase in the cost of making gasoline available to consumers. At the end of each month the seller will have to remit to the government an amount equal to 10 cents multiplied by the number of gallons sold. This is equivalent to an increase of 10 cents per gallon in their costs of production. It increases the minimum price per gallon that sellers will require to sell any given quantity of gasoline per month. By decreasing the profitability of selling the gasoline, the tax will affect its supply in exactly the same way as any increase in cost. As a result of the tax, the supply curve of gasoline shifts inward from S_1 to S_2, as shown in Figure 2–8.

Figure 2–8 also shows that the decrease in the supply results in a new market equilibrium price and quantity. The market price rises to P_G = \$1.04 per gallon. This is the gross price paid by consumers and received by sellers *before* payment of the 10-cent tax, which is the legal liability of the seller. The net price received by sellers after payment of the tax is

$$P_N = P_G - T = \$1.04 - \$0.10 = \$0.94$$

Consumers of gasoline make decisions about how much to purchase on the basis of the new market equilibrium price. Sellers decide how much gasoline to sell on the basis of the net price they receive after paying the tax.

Note that the new equilibrium price does *not* increase the market price of gasoline by the full amount of the 10-cent tax. If the sellers simply increased the price of gasoline to \$1.10 by adding the tax per gallon to the old equilibrium price,

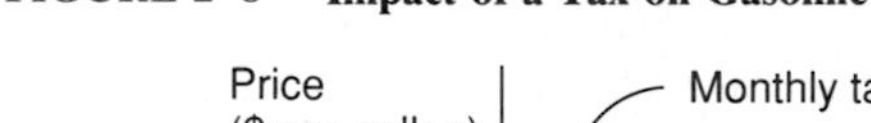

FIGURE 2–8 Impact of a Tax on Gasoline

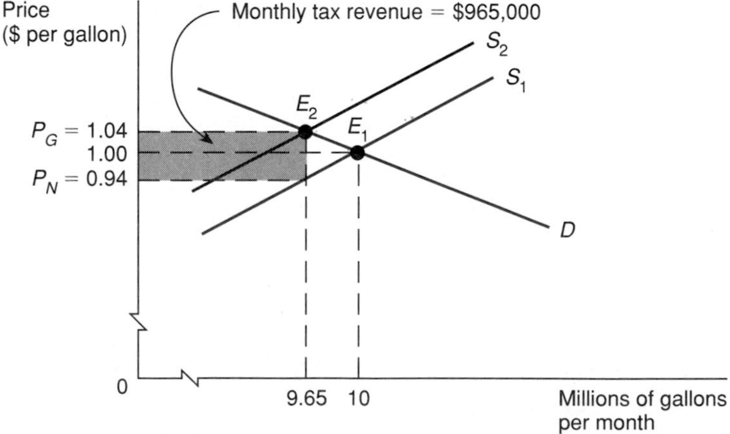

A 10-cent per gallon tax on gasoline collected from sellers decreases its supply from S_1 to S_2. The new market equilibrium is attained at point E_2. The tax increases market price to P_G = \$1.04 while reducing the net price received by sellers to P_N = 94 cents. The shaded area represents the tax revenue collected.

a surplus of gasoline on the market would cause the price to fall below $1.10. At the new equilibrium price of $1.04 buyers pay 4 cents more per gallon, whereas sellers receive a net price that is 6 cents less than the initial price of $1 per gallon. Before the tax there was no difference between the net and gross prices. Also note that even though the tax is collected from sellers, buyers in effect pay 4 cents of the 10-cent tax in the form of an increase in price. The increase in the market price of gasoline is the portion of the tax that sellers succeed in shifting to buyers as a result of their decrease in supply.[5]

As shown in Figure 2–8, the monthly consumption of gasoline declines by 350,000 gallons, from 10 million to 9.65 million gallons per month. Because of the decrease in the equilibrium quantity of gasoline traded each month, the tax will yield $965,000 in revenue per month instead of $1 million. To project government revenues from the tax therefore requires an assessment of the impact of the tax on market equilibrium. Figure 2–8 represents the monthly tax revenue collected as the area of the shaded rectangle. This area equals the new equilibrium quantity after the tax (9.65 million gallons) multiplied by the 10-cent per gallon tax.

In summary, a per unit tax levied on sellers of an item is likely to make them worse off by reducing the net price they receive for the item. Sellers are likely to shift part of the tax to others as the decrease in supply increases price and reduces the sellers' employment of inputs. Ultimately, the decline in sales adversely affects the tax revenue collected by governing authorities. The actual distribution of the per unit tax will depend on the responsiveness of both quantities demanded and quantities supplied to the changes in market price that the tax causes.

Import Quotas, Tariffs, and the Consequences of Protecting Domestic Industries from Foreign Competition: A More Complex Application

Import quotas Restrictions on the quantity of foreign goods that can be sold in a nation.

Tariffs Taxes levied on imported goods.

Domestic industries often use political means to obtain governmental protection from foreign competition. For example, the U.S. automobile industry in the early 1980s persuaded governing authorities to negotiate quotas on the number of Japanese cars that could be imported into the United States. **Import quotas** restrict the quantity of foreign goods that can be sold in a nation. An alternative means of achieving the same objective is a tariff. **Tariffs** are taxes levied on imported goods. A probable outcome of both tariffs and import quotas is an increase in the prices of the goods involved. This harms consumers of those goods but is likely to benefit their domestic producers. Supply and demand analysis can illuminate these and other gains and losses stemming from the two policies.

In 1981 President Reagan negotiated a "voluntary export restraint" agreement with Japan that placed limits on the annual exports of Japanese cars to the United States. This agreement established import quotas for Japanese cars that were in effect until 1985. The annual limit on imported Japanese cars, initially set

[5] For a more complete analysis of the impact of taxes on prices, see David N. Hyman, *Public Finance: A Contemporary Application of Theory to Policy*, 4th ed. (Fort Worth, Tex: HBJ The Dryden Press, 1993), chap. 11.

at 1.68 million, was increased to 1.85 million in 1983. These temporary quotas were designed to protect the ailing U.S. automobile industry, thereby improving its job opportunities, its profits, and its incentive to invest in new facilities.[6]

A quota on imports restricts supply to a certain quantity of sales. The supply curve is upward sloping until it reaches the quantity corresponding to the annual import quota. Thereafter the quota prevents quantity supplied from increasing in response to higher prices. Assuming that the initial import quota of $Q_L = 1.68$ million cars corresponded to the market equilibrium at E_1, the demand curve D_1 is drawn. Market price is initially P_1. In Figure 2–9 the supply curve after the quotas have been imposed is the kinked curve labeled SE_1S_L.

As the United States came out of a recession in 1983, an increase in demand for Japanese automobiles took place in response to increased consumer income. In the absence of the quotas, quantity supplied would have increased to Q'along the dashed portion of the actual market supply, E_1S'. Price would have risen to P'. But the quotas prevented quantity supplied from increasing beyond the limit of 1.68 million cars per year; price therefore increased to P_2 along the vertical portion of the supply curve as the new equilibrium was attained at point E_2. Because of the quotas, consumers paid a higher price for Japanese cars than they would have otherwise. This increment in price was

$$\Delta P = P_2 - P'$$

Japanese automobile producers and domestic dealers benefited from this positive price differential resulting from the quotas even though they sold fewer cars than they would have sold without the quotas. Without the quotas, the sales revenues of Japanese auto sellers would have been $P'Q'$, represented by the area $OP'E'Q'$. With the quotas, these revenues were P_2Q_L, represented by the area $OP_2E_2Q_L$. The difference in the revenues of Japanese automobile sellers that resulted from the use of quotas was

$$(P'Q' - P_2Q_L)$$

This difference could have been positive or negative. If ΔPQ_L (represented by shaded area A), exceeded $P'\Delta Q$ (represented by area B), the sales revenues from Japanese cars would have increased. Area A is the increase in seller revenues resulting from the quotas. Area B is the revenue decline caused by the lost sales. Note that this analysis does not discuss the profits of Japanese automobile sellers. This would require data on cost as well as revenue.

Empirical research indicates that the price of imported Japanese cars increased on average by nearly $1,000 per car as a result of the import quotas in 1981–82. This resulted in increases of close to $2 billion in the revenues of Japanese auto producers and their dealers.[7] Because Japanese cars are substitutes for

---

[6] For an analysis of the background and details of this agreement, see Robert W. Crandall, ''Import Quotas and the Automobile Industry: The Costs of Protectionism,'' *Brookings Review* 2, no. 4 (Summer 1984), pp. 8–16.

[7] Ibid., p. 13.

FIGURE 2–9 Import Quotas versus Tariffs

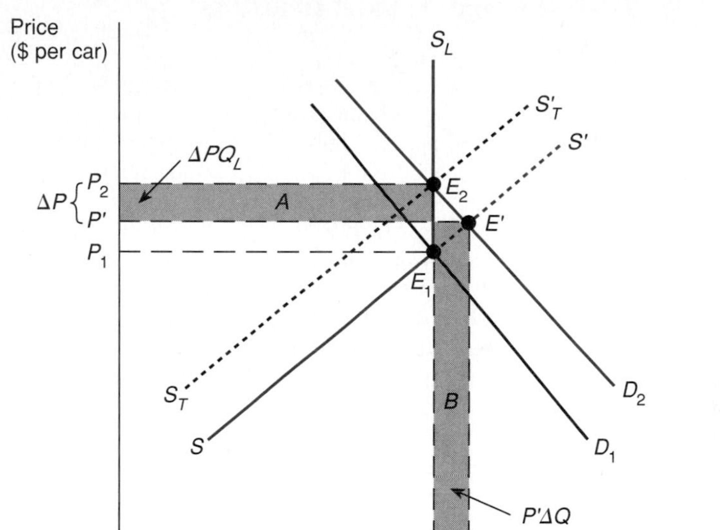

An import quota places a limit, Q_L, on the quantity of foreign goods that can be sold. The supply curve under the quota is SE_1S_L, which is a vertical line at Q_L. A tariff can be used to decrease the supply of imported goods to $S_TS'_T$, thereby reducing consumption to Q_L.

American-built cars, the increase in their price contributed to an increase in the demand for domestic cars. It has been estimated that the resulting price increase averaged about $370 per domestic car from 1981 to 1983.[8]

Figure 2–9 also shows that the same reduction in the quantity of Japanese cars sold could have been achieved by a tariff on these cars. A tariff represented by the vertical distance E_1E_2 dollars per car has the same effect as a tax. It decreases the supply from SS' to the dotted supply curve $S_TS'_T$. This would result in a new market equilibrium at point E_2. The price of Japanese cars would be the same as it was with the quotas when demand was D_2. The difference in this case is that a tariff would not only make consumers worse off but would also directly reduce the revenues of Japanese producers and their dealers. The Japanese sellers must pay an amount represented by the area $P_2E_2E_1P_1$ to the U.S. government, which equals Q_L multiplied by the tariff per car. This results in a substantial decline in the net revenue they receive from sales after paying the tariff. It is clear therefore

[8] Ibid., p. 15.

Modern Microeconomics in Action: **International Report**

The Effects of Tariffs and Import Quotas: The Case of the U.S. Textile and Apparel Industries

The U.S. textile and apparel industries have benefited from protectionist trade policies of the U.S. government since 1930. Both tariffs and import quotas have insulated these industries from import competition and have contributed to high U.S. prices for textile products and clothing. In 1930 the average tariff was 46 percent on cotton goods and 60 percent on wool products. As of 1988 the average tariff on textile imports was 10.1 percent and 18.4 percent on apparel imports—rates considerably higher than the average tariff of 3.4 percent for all U.S. merchandise imports.

Quotas on textile and apparel imports were first imposed in 1936, on imports from Japan. As of late 1991 various informal "voluntary export restraints" negotiated between the United States and other nations restricted imports from 41 countries that accounted for 69 percent of U.S. textile imports and 88 percent of U.S. apparel imports.* Most of these quotas affected developing nations in which labor costs were low.

In the 1980s and early 1990, Congress passed several bills to extend protection to the U.S. textile and apparel industries by tightening quotas. The president vetoed them, but each time Congress came close to overriding his veto. At the same time, international negotiations under the General Agreement on Tariffs and Trade (GATT) sought to reduce U.S. protection of its textile and apparel industries.

Let's take a look at the benefits that restraints on international trade have conferred on workers and owners of capital in these U.S. industries and at the costs of the restraints over time. Remember that quotas and tariffs raise the prices of both domestic and imported products. A study by the International Trade Commission in 1987 concluded that U.S. quotas on textile imports were equivalent to a 21.8 percent tariff and that U.S. quotas on apparel imports were equivalent to a 28.3 percent tariff. The combined effect of tariffs and quotas was equivalent to a 32 percent tax on textiles and a 46 percent tax on apparel. The study concluded that the elimination of all U.S. tariffs and quotas on textiles and apparel would reduce domestic employment in the U.S. textile and apparel industries by between 13 and 16 percent—a "loss" of nearly 60,000 jobs. The jobs wouldn't really be "lost," since the workers whose jobs were eliminated would eventually find other employment. Instead, trade restriction removal would change the distribution of employment within the United States. The beneficiaries of the restrictive trade policies are concentrated in several Southeastern states in industries that generally pay below-average wages. Despite the low wages these labor-intensive industries pay, they face competition from producers in developing nations whose wages are still lower.

Estimates from various studies indicate that the cost of each job saved in the apparel industry as a result of tariffs and quotas ranges from $39,000 to $46,000 per year. Estimates of the cost of protecting the jobs of workers in the textile industry range from $50,000 to $52,000 per year for each job saved. These estimates include the higher consumer costs for textiles and apparel that transfer well-being from consumers to workers and owners of capital in the textile and apparel industries. They also include the waste that results from allocating our resources to relatively inefficient industries.†

The protection of the textile and apparel industries will undoubtedly be a source of political strife throughout the 1990s. There is no doubt that the protectionist policies save jobs. However, the price per job saved is very high. That imported suit or dress you would pay $200 for in the absence of trade restraints costs $292 based on an effective tariff rate of 46 percent! The costs of protectionism in this case appear to far outweigh the losses to workers in textile and apparel industries who would be displaced if the trade restraints were removed. It costs the United States as much as $52,000 per year to save a job that on average pays less than $20,000 per year. Displaced workers in the textile and apparel industries could be compensated for loss of wages while searching for new jobs at a much lower cost per job than the current cost of tariffs and quotas in these industries.

* See Congress of the United States, Congressional Budget Office, *Trade Restraints and the Competitive Status of the Textile, Apparel, and Nonrubber-Footwear Industries* (Washington, D.C.: Congress of the United States, December 1991).

† Ibid., p. xvi.

why the Japanese prefer the quotas to tariffs. The result of both tariffs and quotas is the same for consumers in both cases, but sellers are better off with quotas. Finally, a tariff could be used to finance tax reductions because it would substitute for alternative sources of tax revenues for the government. This would benefit all U.S. citizens.

Import quotas can be a very expensive way of saving domestic jobs from the threat of foreign competition. One study of the effects of import quotas on Japanese cars in the early 1980s estimated that these quotas saved about 26,000 domestic jobs in the U.S. automobile industry. Because of the quotas, however, consumers paid more that $4 billion more per year for both domestic and foreign cars between 1981 and 1983. This means the cost per job saved amounted to $160,000 per worker per year! It therefore cost consumers much more *per worker* to save those jobs than the value of the jobs to the workers as measured by the wages received by workers. Put another way, if the average annual wage of the workers whose jobs were saved was $30,000, then the benefits of the import quotas to those workers was $780 million—their average annual wage multiplied by the 26,000 jobs saved. U.S. consumers paid $4 billion to provide $780 million in benefits to U.S. workers—a bad deal. The import quotas also contributed to the increase in profit of about $300 per car for the U.S. automobile industry. They therefore made U.S. car consumers worse off while making both U.S. workers and U.S. automobile manufacturers better off.

The United States makes extensive use of import quotas as a means of protecting domestic industries. For example, as of the early 1990s it imposed import quotas on sugar and many types of clothing. These quotas inevitably raised product prices and often weighed heavily on low-income households, which spend relatively high portions of their income on consumer goods. Other nations also use import quotas as a means of protecting domestic industries.

Rent Controls: Impact of a Price Ceiling

Government-imposed price controls can prevent markets from achieving equilibrium. The almost inevitable result of such market intervention is a sustained market disequilibrium that manifests itself in the form of either a chronic surplus or a chronic shortage of the good or service whose price is being controlled.

One type of price control regulates the rents of residential housing. The simple supply and demand model is useful in analyzing the impact of such price controls on the parties involved. Rent controls are laws limiting the rents that owners of rental housing may charge. They either limit increases in monthly rents or establish rules that are used to determine "fair" monthly rental rates for housing of various kinds and quality. The impetus of such controls is the desire to keep housing rents lower than those that would prevail if the market were allowed to establish its own equilibrium rent. Many supporters of rent controls believe that in the absence of such controls lower-income citizens would have to pay higher percentages of their income in rent.

The impact of rent controls is illustrated in Figure 2–10. Suppose that the equilibrium rent would be R_E in the absence of rent controls. The equilibrium quantity of housing rented at that price would be Q_E, measured in square feet of

MODERN MICROECONOMICS IN ACTION: GOVERNMENT AND THE ECONOMY

Rent Regulation in Practice: Tenants' Rights, Warehousing of Apartments, Condominium Conversions, and Flipping in the Big Apple during the 1980s Give Way to Rent Declines in the 1990s

During the 1980s a common method New York City landlords used to avoid the adverse effects of rent control on their incomes was to convert rental units into condominiums. Condominiums are owner-occupied units that can be sold instead of rented. Landlords could therefore escape the undesirable effects of rent controls on their income by converting rental units into condos!

When an apartment subject to rent control became vacant, landlords in many cases chose not to re-rent the unit. It has been estimated that in 1987 as many as 90,000 of the city's 1.2 million rent-regulated apartments were being held off the market. Landlords not renting rent-regulated apartments "warehouse" these units to avoid difficulties in converting them into condominiums. Under New York City law a building cannot be converted into a condominium unless 15 percent of the units in the building have been sold. However, landlords typically must sell considerably more than 15 percent of the units to make a profit on the conversion. But you can't sell units occupied by tenants whom rent regulation law protects against eviction!

Warehousing aggravates the shortage of rental units caused by rent controls. Landlords argue that it is their right not to rent apartments they own. Critics of warehousing argue that it should be outlawed.

You can easily understand the motivation for warehousing if you look at some of the costs that landlords incur in converting rental units into salable condominium units. When a building is converted into a condominium, New York City's current regulation laws not only protect the tenants in rent-regulated apartments against eviction but also grant them the right to renew their leases at modest increases in rent. Tenants have the option of retaining their right to rent, buying their apartment at a discounted "insider" price, or accepting a payment from the landlord in return for giving up their tenant rights. Insider prices in condominium conversions typically run 20–45 percent below the market equilibrium price of the condominium units. For example, one Manhattan tenant was given the option of purchasing his apartment at a price of $72,000, which represented a 28 percent discount from the outsider price. Alternatively, the landlord would have gladly paid him $36,000 to give up his tenant rights. This tenant chose to keep renting the apartment at the current regulated rent of about $400 per month. The tenant reasoned that holding on to his lease would minimize his housing costs over the long run.

Landlords offered discount condominium prices as an incentive to get tenants to give up their legal rights to their rent-regulated apartments. Without this incentive most tenants would never give up those rights! So landlords have no alternatives other than to offer what amounts to a bribe or to warehouse apartments vacated because of death or voluntary relocation.

Not all tenants choose to retain their rights. Some reason that buying their apartments at the insider price is a good investment.* Some tenants engage in a practice known as *flipping*. In flipping a tenant purchases his or her rent-controlled apartment at the insider price and then immediately resells it at a price closer to its market value. It has been estimated that if all of the tenants in a recent condominium conversion had purchased their apartments at the insider price and then flipped by selling the apartments at the market price, they would have earned a total profit of $170 million!† This $170 million represents the value of the income transfer from landlords to tenants as a result of rent control.

As profitable as it is, flipping has been the exception rather than the rule in New York City. About two thirds of the tenants in the city's condominium conversions find keeping their rent-controlled apartments a better deal than flipping.

(*Continued*) New York City's boom in condominium conversions came to a screeching halt in 1990 as an economic slowdown in the city caused a sharp decrease in the demand for housing. The collapse of the real estate market in the early 1990s all but put an end to flipping and even resulted in falling apartment rents. The market rents actually fell below the regulated levels in some cases, and some landlords found that they could not find tenants for their apartments at the legal rent ceilings. With some apartments renting for less than the legally allowed rents, the incentive to convert apartments into condominiums was sharply reduced.

* See Michael deCourcy Hinds, "For New Yorkers, Is There Life after Rent Regulation?" *The New York Times*, October 26, 1986, Sec. 8, p. 2.

† Michael deCourcy Hinds, "The Windfall Profits in Insider Flips," *The New York Times*, August 30, 1987, Section 8, p. 1.

housing rented per year. If, however, rents are controlled and thus are not allowed to rise to their equilibrium level, the market will fail to reach an equilibrium.

Price ceilings Maximum prices established by law.

Price ceilings establish a maximum price that can be legally charged for an item. Rent controls are price ceilings. Of course, if the legal rent ceilings were above the market equilibrium rents, there would be no disequilibrium in the market. When rents are controlled to a level below the market equilibrium rents, they

FIGURE 2–10 Rent Control: An Example of a Price Ceiling

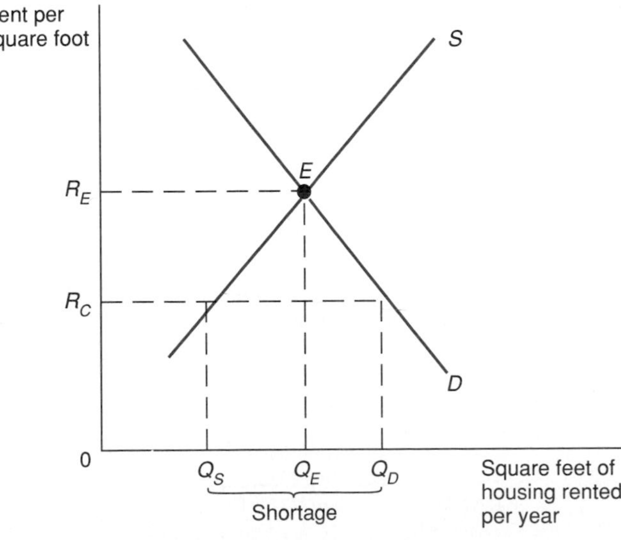

Establishment of a controlled rent, R_C, below the equilibrium rent, R_E, results in a shortage of rental housing space.

are said to be *effective* price ceilings. They are effective in the sense that they establish rents at levels below those that would prevail if the market were allowed to equilibrate.

At the controlled rent, R_C, the quantity of rental housing demanded is Q_D, whereas the quantity that landlords are willing to supply at that price is Q_S. Because quantity demanded exceeds quantity supplied, there is a shortage of rental housing units at the controlled rent. The shortage arises out of an increase in the quantity of housing demanded above that which would prevail at the equilibrium rent and a decrease in the quantity of housing space supplied below that which would prevail at the equilibrium rent. The rent controls make housing less expensive than it would otherwise be; unfortunately, however, not all of those who wish to rent housing at the controlled price will be successful in finding it.

Rent controls also reduce the income of landlords. Some of them respond to the reduction in rental income by reducing the amount of housing they rent. The loss in rental income can be substantial. One study concluded that the cost of rent controls to landlords greatly exceeded the benefits to the tenants who lived in rent-controlled housing.[9] Another study concluded that between 1965 and 1967 rent controls contributed to the withdrawal of 114,000 housing units from the market by landlords in New York City.[10]

Why are rent controls still popular in many communities and nations despite the fact that they benefit only some housing consumers? Perhaps it is because most consumers find the idea of lower rents appealing and are unaware of the shortages that inevitably develop as a result of rent controls. Or perhaps it is because most renters believe that they will be lucky enough to find housing at the controlled prices and support rent controls in the hope of winning the housing "lottery" that inevitably results from these controls. Moreover, some people do benefit from rent controls, and this explains at least part of their popularity.[11]

Nonprice Rationing of Shortages Caused by Price Controls

Price controls usually stimulate the development of means other than price for rationing the use or sale of commodities whose prices are below market equilibrium levels. These means often reflect a high degree of ingenuity. **Nonprice rationing** devices distribute goods and services in short supply on a basis other than willingness or ability to pay. For that reason, many people contend that these devices give lower-income groups the opportunity to consume goods and services that they would otherwise be unable to afford. Although there is some truth to this

Nonprice rationing The distribution of available amounts of goods and services on a basis other than willingness or ability to pay.

[9] E. Olsen, "An Econometric Analysis of Rent Control," *Journal of Political Economy* 80, no. 6 (November–December 1972), pp. 1081–1100.

[10] RAND Corporation, "The Effects of Rent Control on Housing in New York City: Confronting the Crisis," RM–6190–NYC, February 1970.

[11] For further analysis of rent controls and their impact, see Lee S. Friedman, *Microeconomic Policy Analysis* (New York: McGraw-Hill, 1984), chap. 12, pp. 436–61; and Walter Block and Edgar Olsen, eds., *Rent Control: Myths and Realities* (Vancouver, B.C.: Fraser Institute, 1981).

contention, it remains to be shown in each case that it is the poor who in fact obtain available supplies when there is a shortage. Many economists argue that interference with the natural rationing function of prices is an unfortunate side effect of this method of aiding the poor. These economists say that assisting the poor through direct cash grants from government allow the poor to purchase more in markets without impairing the rationing function of prices.

Price ceilings, as has been demonstrated, are likely to result in shortages of the commodities whose price is controlled. A shortage implies that some buyers who are willing to pay higher prices to obtain a commodity will be unable to purchase the commodity at the controlled price. Because price no longer serves to ration goods and services in short supply, an alternative means must be devised to allocate the available amounts of those goods and services to the people who wish to purchase them. The simplest form of nonprice rationing is the "first come, first served" principle. Under this principle available supplies are rationed by having people spend time waiting in a line (or, as it is sometimes called, a *queue*). Queuing is perhaps the most common form of nonprice rationing.

Another method of rationing goods and services in short supply is to allocate them on the basis of personal characteristics of buyers. This requires people to fill out forms on which they state such characteristics as marital status, age, and number of children. Government officials then decide who gets served first on the basis of predetermined criteria. For example, if there were a milk shortage, families with children might get first priority for the available supplies of milk; if there were a housing shortage, families might get priority over single persons.

During World War II this country used rationing stamps to ration the available supplies of goods whose prices were controlled. Rationing stamps establish a dual price system for allocating goods and services. In addition to the controlled price, citizens must surrender a certain number of stamps that the government has distributed according to predetermined criteria. The stamps serve the purpose of rationing available supplies. When gasoline price controls were imposed in the 1970s, the use of rationing stamps was suggested as a means of shortening the lines at gas stations.

Price ceilings always result in dissatisfied potential buyers who would be willing to pay more. Sales at prices higher than those legally set are a crime. Those who make such sales usually operate clandestinely. A market in which buyers pay sellers prices that exceed those legally set is referred to as a *black market*. In a black market prices are often far higher than those that would prevail if the controlled market were allowed to reach equilibrium. This is because illegal sellers incur risks and expenses that increase their costs of production, including the risk of apprehension, fine, prison sentences, and the payment of bribes. Ticket scalpers engage in black market sales of admissions to sports events and rock concerts when the official prices for these admissions are below the market equilibrium prices. The prices charged by these scalpers are usually way above the official prices.

Black market suppliers search out goods in short supply. They may acquire these goods from abroad or from persons who can legally buy amounts in excess of their requirements.

Minimum Wages: The Impact of a Price Floor

Price floor
A minimum price established by law.

A **price floor** is a minimum price established by law. A minimum wage established by law is an example of a price floor. A price floor is said to be effective if it is established at a level above the one that would prevail if the market were free to equilibrate.

Minimum wage laws stipulate a minimum price for labor services and enforce it with rules and regulations that impose penalties on those who pay below the stipulated minimum. Minimum wage laws typically are effective only for unskilled workers. In developed nations most skilled workers and most workers in factories typically earn more than the minimum wage. Thus the market for unskilled labor is the labor market most likely to be affected by minimum wage legislation.

An effective minimum wage reduces the quantity of labor demanded below that which would prevail if the market were free to equilibrate, while at the same time increasing the quantity of labor hours supplied. The inevitable result is a surplus of labor at the minimum wage. In other words, an effective minimum wage contributes to the unemployment of unskilled workers. This is illustrated in Figure 2–11. The equilibrium wage is W_E; the minimum wage established by law is W_M. At W_M a surplus of labor hours equal to the difference between Q_S and Q_D hours is offered for sale.

Minimum wage legislation enjoys broad political support despite its disequilibrating impact on the labor market for unskilled workers. Yet a growing body of evidence indicates that minimum wage laws contribute to teenage unemployment.

FIGURE 2–11 Minimum Wages: An Example of a Price Floor

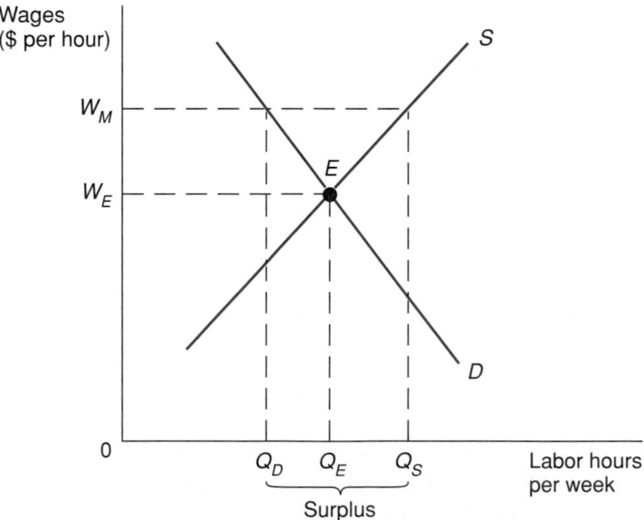

Establishment of a minimum wage, W_M, above the market equilibrium wage, W_E, results in a surplus of labor hours offered for sale in the labor market.

Evidence also indicates, however, that a substantial number of middle-income housewives engaged in part-time or full-time employment benefit from minimum wages.[12] This could explain the strong political support for minimum wage laws: They benefit the middle-income classes.

It is possible to have an illegal market for goods and services subject to price floors. In the case of minimum wages, for example, there will be unemployed sellers who would be willing to work for lower wages. Employers who illegally hire these workers at wages below the legal floor would be operating in an illegal market for labor. Wages paid in this market are often lower than those that would prevail if the market were allowed to reach an equilibrium. This is because of the risks involved in illegal hiring. To cover those risks, employers pass some of them on to the workers in the form of lower wages.

As of April 1991 the minimum wage for most workers in the United States was $4.25 per hour. The minimum wage does help some of the working poor. However, nearly 90 percent of the workers who earn the minimum wage live in households with income above the poverty level. In addition, approximately three quarters of the poor do not benefit from minimum wages, because they are dependent children in households in which the head is not in the labor force. The self-employed poor also do not benefit from minimum wages, and employees of small businesses are often not covered by minimum wages. These data indicate that many who are not poor benefit from the minimum wage law while many who are poor receive no benefit from the law because they are not in the labor force or because they work in jobs not covered by the law. Finally, minimum wages increase the production costs of products that are produced with unskilled labor and thus contribute to higher product prices. These higher prices can harm low-income consumers by decreasing the purchasing power of their income.

Government and the Business of Agriculture

U.S. agricultural policy has sought to benefit U.S. farmers by guaranteeing farmers minimum and reasonably stable prices for their crops. The price floors or supports established by the U.S. government have contributed to huge surpluses of agricultural commodities that governing authorities have purchased or stored to keep prices from plummeting. Agricultural price supports along with other policies that pay farmers to keep land out of production have also contributed to increased food prices paid by U.S. consumers while requiring substantial government outlays to subsidize farmers.

Supply and demand analysis can be applied to analyze the consequences of recent U.S. agricultural policies. In 1992 the federal outlays to support farm prices and incomes totaled nearly $12 billion. The U.S. government uses a complex of price support programs to benefit agricultural firms. The simplest of these pro-

[12] See Donald O. Parsons, *Poverty and the Minimum Wage* (Washington, D.C.: American Enterprise Institute for Public Policy Research, 1980). Parsons concludes that minimum wage laws seriously reduce job opportunities for teenagers while allowing modest increases in earnings for women, some of whom come from families with poverty-level incomes.

grams is a price floor similar to the one discussed above for wages. Such a program has been used for many years to bolster the incomes of dairy farmers. However, the impact of this type of price floor is somewhat different from that of a minimum wage program. In the case of an effective minimum wage, the surplus of workers seeking work is not employed. However, in the case of an effective price floor established for a dairy product such as milk, the government actually purchases the surplus and in that way uses taxpayers' money to increase the income of dairy farmers. When the price floor is above the equilibrium price of milk, consumers pay higher prices for milk and thus also increase the income of dairy farmers. Because milk is not storable for long periods, the surplus milk is usually converted into powder, cheese, or butter before being stored.

Figure 2–12 shows the impact of the dairy price supports. Each of these supports is a floor on prices set above the market equilibrium price by the U.S. Department of Agriculture. Farmers decide how much to supply on the basis of the support price. Suppose that the support price is $4 per gallon of milk while the market equilibrium price would be $3 per gallon. Farmers produce 22 million gallons per year, which corresponds to point *L* on the supply curve. At a price of $4 per gallon consumers will purchase only 20 million gallons per year. As a result there is a surplus of 2 million gallons per year. To prevent this surplus from putting

FIGURE 2–12 Impact of Agricultural Price Supports

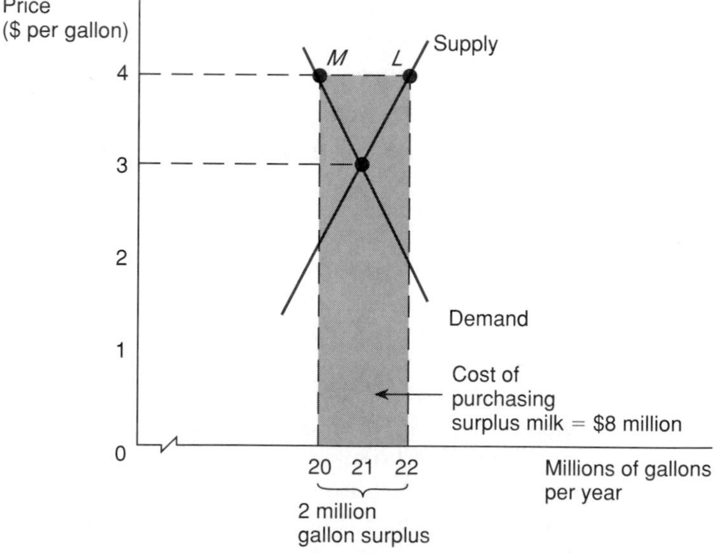

The support price for milk is above the market equilibrium price. As a result there is a surplus of milk on the market corresponding to the distance *ML*. To prevent the surplus from putting downward pressure on price, the government purchases it and stores it in the form of cheese and other milk products. The price support increases the prices consumers pay for milk and requires taxpayers to pay an amount equal to the shaded rectangle to finance the government's purchase of milk.

downward pressure on price, each year agents of the government purchase the 2 million gallons at the support price and store it. The total cost of the program to taxpayers, which in this case would be $8 million, is represented by the shaded rectangle in Figure 2–12. In addition, consumers pay $4 per gallon of milk rather than the $3 per gallon that would have emerged as the market equilibrium price in the absence of price supports. At the higher price the quantity demanded by consumers is 20 million gallons per year instead of the 21 million gallons per year they would have demanded if the market price had not been supported by the government.

In recent years government purchases of surplus milk have amounted to about 10 percent of total production! During the early 1980s the federal government spent over $2 billion annually to purchase surplus milk. To reduce the costs of the program, in 1986 it initiated a new program under which it purchased the dairy herds of farmers who agreed to stay out of the milk business five years. The dairy cows purchased under this program were slaughtered. The price support floors for milk were also reduced in 1986. High milk prices in the late 1980s sharply reduced the surplus. However, the surplus increased substantially in 1990, and that year the federal government spent about $400 million to purchase surplus milk products. Outlays for the purchase of surplus milk products have been projected to average between $600 million and $800 million from 1991 to 1996.[13]

The federal government also intervenes in the market in other ways to support the prices that farmers receive for agricultural commodities. The imposition of "target prices" for crops is the method that has been used most recently to support the incomes of grain producers. Target prices are price floors to sellers. However, unlike the price supports discussed above for milk, target prices do *not* directly increase the market price paid by buyers. Instead, the entire quantity farmers supplied at the target price is dumped on the market. The resulting price depends on the demand for the commodity. The government then subsidizes farmers through a payment for each bushel sold equal to the difference between the target price and the price paid by buyers.[14]

At the beginning of each crop year the U.S. Department of Agriculture announces the target prices for various crops and the requirements for participation in the target price program. In 1992, for example, the target price for wheat was $4 per bushel. Typically, farmers are required to hold a certain percentage of their acreage idle to be eligible for the target price. In 1992 farmers had to withhold 12.5 percent of base acreage owned from production to gain the right to the target price.

---

[13] See Congress of the United States, Congressional Budget Office, *The Outlook for Farm Commodity Program Spending, Fiscal Years 1991–1996* (Washington, D.C.: Congressional Budget Office, June 1991), p. 69.

[14] Actually, the program is a bit more complicated in that a support price is also established through government loan programs that place a limit on the extent to which the price paid by buyers can fall. Moreover, a limit based on historical production statistics is placed on the subsidy payments to individual farms.

FIGURE 2–13 Impact of Agricultural Target Prices

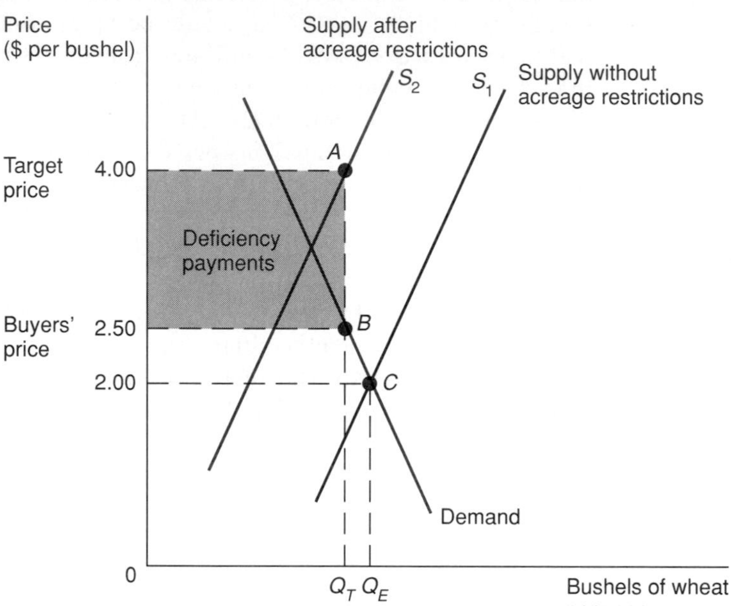

The target price results in quantity supplied of Q_T bushels of wheat per year, corresponding to point *A* on the supply curve after acreage restrictions. This amount is sold on the market at the price buyers will pay. The buyers' price corresponds to point *B* on the demand curve. Farmers receive deficiency payments, which are financed by tax revenues, corresponding to the shaded rectangle. Without acreage restrictions the price to buyers corresponding to point *C* could be lower than the price corresponding to point *B*.

Figure 2–13 uses supply and demand analysis to analyze the impact of a target price on farmers, consumers, and taxpayers. Two supply curves are illustrated. The supply curve labeled S_1 shows the relationship between price and the quantity of a crop, say wheat, that would be supplied per year in the absence of acreage controls. Given the demand curve for wheat, the market equilibrium price per bushel would be \$2 and without acreage restrictions the equilibrium quantity would be Q_E bushels per year corresponding to point *C* in Figure 2–13.

The acreage restriction decreases the supply of wheat, so that the actual supply curve is the one labeled S_2. The quantity supplied in any year depends on the target price guaranteed to farmers, assuming that the target price exceeds the anticipated market equilibrium price with the acreage restriction. In Figure 2–13 the quantity supplied at the target price is Q_T bushels, which corresponds to point *A* on the supply curve after acreage restrictions. Note that supply is not fixed despite the acreage restrictions because farmers can vary the quantity produced on the remaining acreage by working it with varying amounts of labor, machinery, and fertilizer.

With target prices, unlike the milk price floor discussed above, the government does not purchase the surplus that would prevail at the target price. Instead, the entire quantity supplied is offered for sale to buyers in the market. At the quantity Q_T the price that buyers are willing to pay corresponds to point B on the demand curve. As a result buyers are able to purchase wheat at a price of $2.50 per bushel instead of at the target price of $4 per bushel. However, farmers do receive the target price because the government pays them an amount equal to the difference between the price paid by buyers per bushel and the target price. In Figure 2–13 this payment, which is a government subsidy that varies with the quantity sold by farmers, corresponds to the distance AB. With a target price of $4 and a buyers' price of $2.50 per bushel, the government's deficiency payment is $1.50 per bushel. The government's total deficiency payments to all farmers are represented by the shaded rectangle in the graph, whose area equals the deficiency payment per bushel multiplied by the Q_T bushels that farmers supply over a year. The cost to taxpayers of the target price program is represented by that total.

Consumers are clearly better off under the target price program than they would be under a price floor of $4 per bushel. In fact, one of the justifications of the target price program in recent years has been that it contributes to lower prices for U.S. crops, thereby increasing the ability of U.S. producers to win out over foreign competitors in international commodity markets. Because of the program's acreage restrictions, however, prices can be higher than they would be in the absence of any subsidies. In Figure 2–13 the market equilibrium price in the absence of any government programs to subsidize farmers or support prices would be $2 per bushel, which is lower that the $2.50 per bushel that prevails under the target price program. Subsidizing farmers in this way therefore transfers income from taxpayers in general to farmers, but it does not necessarily result in commodity prices to consumers lower than those that would prevail in a free market.

The United States is not the only nation that subsidizes farmers in ways that increase quantities supplied. Other nations also have subsidy programs that tend to raise prices received by their farmers above the equilibrium level. In recent years these programs have resulted in a glut of grain on international markets that has sharply reduced prices. Farmers in nations without subsidy programs have suffered from this glut. For example, in Canada, where farm subsidies are lower than those of other nations, many farmers have been forced out of business.

SUMMARY

1. The law of demand states that there is an inverse relationship between the price of a good and the quantity of the good demanded, represented by a downward-sloping demand curve.
2. A change in quantity demanded is a movement along a given demand curve in response to a change in the price of a good, other things being equal. A change in demand is a movement of an entire demand curve in response to a change in some demand determinant other than the price of a good.
3. The law of supply states that quantity supplied increases with the price of a good. A change in quantity supplied is a movement along a given supply curve, while a change in supply is a shift of an entire supply curve in response to a

change in input prices, technology, or some other supply determinant other than the price of the good.

4. A market equilibrium is established when price has been adjusted to the level that equates quantity demanded with quantity supplied.
5. Market equilibrium price and quantity are likely to change in response to changes in demand or supply.
6. When price ceilings are set below the market equilibrium price, they result in shortages. When a shortage exists, quantity demanded exceeds quantity supplied.
7. When price floors are established above the market equilibrium price, quantity supplied exceeds quantity demanded and a surplus of goods results.

IMPORTANT CONCEPTS

free and competitive market
demand
law of demand
demand schedule
quantity demanded
demand curve
change in quantity demanded
change in demand
supply
law of supply
supply schedule
quantity supplied
supply curve
change in quantity supplied
change in supply
equilibrium
market equilibrium
shortage
surplus
comparative static analysis
import quotas
tariffs
price ceilings
nonprice rationing
price floor

QUESTIONS FOR REVIEW

1. Below is a demand schedule for milk in a certain city.

Price per Gallon	*Quantity Demanded per Month (Gallons)*
$1	10,000
2	9,000
3	8,000
4	7,000
5	6,000

Draw the demand curve for milk.

2. The supply schedule for milk in the same city is as follows:

Price per Gallon	*Quantity Supplied per Month (Gallons)*
$1	4,000
2	6,000
3	8,000
4	10,000
5	12,000

Draw the supply curve for milk and the demand curve for milk based on the demand schedule in Question 1. What is the equilibrium price of milk?

3. Show how the equilibrium price of milk will be affected by a decrease in the demand for milk.
4. "Import quotas act to make demand increases for imported goods more inflationary than they would otherwise be." True or false? Explain your answer using a diagram.
5. Suppose that a per unit tax is imposed on good X, whose before-tax supply curve is S_1 as illustrated. D_1 and D_2 are alternative demand curves for good X. After imposing the tax.
   a. Will equilibrium price be higher with demand curve D_1 or D_2?
   b. Will equilibrium quantity be higher with demand curve D_1 or D_2?
   c. Will the government's tax revenue be higher with demand curve D_1 or D_2?

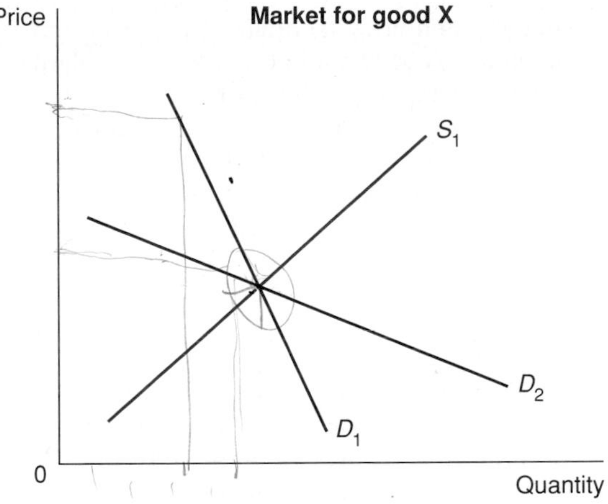

6. Suppose that the demand for good Y and the supply of good Y both increase.
   a. Is it possible to predict whether the equilibrium price of good Y will increase, decrease, or remain the same as a result of these changes?
   b. Will the equilibrium quantity of good Y increase, decrease, or remain the same as a result of these changes?
   c. Is it possible to predict whether the equilibrium total revenue of good Y producers (equilibrium price multiplied by equilibrium quantity) will increase, decrease, or remain the same as a result of these changes?
7. Using supply and demand analysis, show how a decrease in supply can result in a decrease in quantity demanded. Also show how an increase in demand will result in an increase in quantity supplied.
8. Briefly explain the equilibrium adjustment process for a competitive market. Also explain why the competitive market model may be a better short-term predictor of actual market prices and quantities when the equilibrium adjustment process occurs "quickly" rather than "slowly."
9. At $1 per dozen the monthly quantity of eggs demanded equals the monthly quantity supplied. Many consumers complain that this price is too high and persuade government authorities to require sellers to charge only 50 cents per dozen. Predict the effect of the government price controls on the market for eggs.
10. "Technological advance benefits producers but not consumers." Do you agree or disagree with this statement? Justify your position.

Problems

1. An electronics company is anxious to market a new amplifier that greatly enhances the quality of recorded sound. The minimum price at which the new device can be sold is $6,000. Assuming that the maximum price any buyer would pay for the device is $5,000, draw the market demand and supply curves. What is the equilibrium quantity? How can an improvement in technology better the market prospects of the new device?
2. Suppose that the supply curve of rental housing over a five-year period is a horizontal line. Interpret the shape of this supply curve, plotting the price per square foot of housing on the vertical axis and the number of square feet supplied per year on the horizontal axis. Show how an increase in the demand for housing will affect the market equilibrium price and quantity if the supply curve is flat.
3. The demand curve for backpacks in a small town is described by the following equation:

   $$Q_D = 600 - 2P$$

   where Q_D is the quantity demanded per month and P is the price.

   The supply curve of backpacks is described by the following equation:

   $$Q_S = 300 + 4P$$

   where Q_S is monthly quantity supplied.

   What is the market equilibrium price and quantity per month?
4. Suppose that a $10 ceiling is placed on the price of backpacks. Use the equations in Question 3 to calculate the shortage of backpacks that would result.

5. Suppose that all nations abandon policies supporting the prices of agricultural commodities. Use supply and demand analysis to forecast the effect that abandonment of agricultural price floors will have on commodity prices, government spending, and farmer incomes in various nations. Why will farmers in some nations actually benefit from the abandonment of these price floors?

6. Suppose that both oranges and grapefruits are sold by their producers in competitive national markets. The initial equilibrium price and quantity of oranges are $1.20 per pound and 500 million pounds, respectively, so that the initial equilibrium total revenue of orange growers (equilibrium price multiplied by equilibrium quantity) is $600 million. Answer the following questions regarding this case:
   a. If the supply of grapefruits decreases, will the equilibrium total revenue of orange growers increase or decrease?
   b. If the demand for oranges increases, will the equilibrium total revenue of orange growers increase or decrease?
   c. Suppose that grapefruit groves are infested by a grapefruit fruit fly that reduces the supply of grapefruits but does not affect the supply of oranges. How will the equilibrium price and quantity of grapefruits be affected? How will the equilibrium price and quantity of oranges be affected?

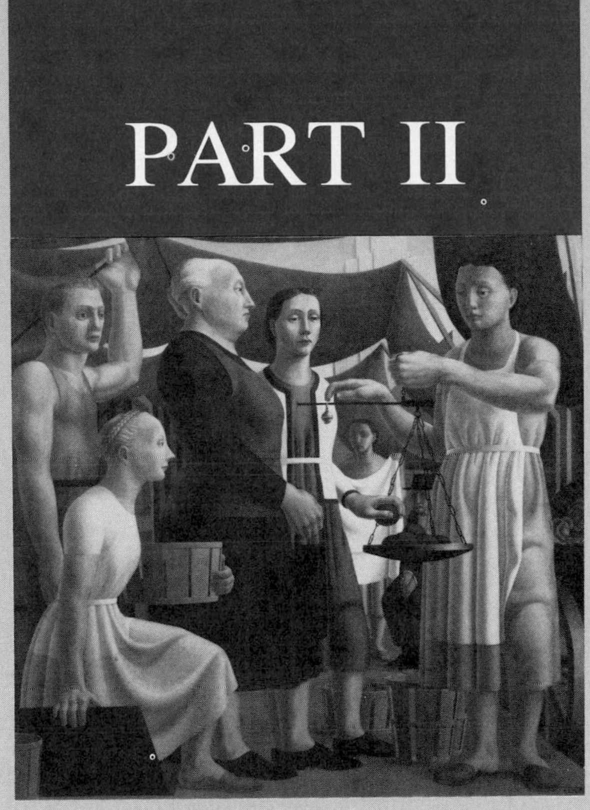

The Theory of Demand

3

The Theory of Consumer Behavior

The European clothing designer Karl Lagerfeld is wild about Lycra, an elastic fiber invented by the Du Pont company over 30 years ago as a rubber substitute for use in women's girdles. The fiber is now used in disposable diapers, swimsuits, hosiery, sportswear, T-shirts, ladies' dresses, and men's jackets. The designer Donna Karan likes to mix Lycra with wool in her men's jackets. Lycra fits in with the active lifestyles of the 1990s, and it is priced attractively enough to make it affordable to consumers.

With Lycra, Du Pont is making inroads into European consumer markets by catering to the tastes of Europeans who like the fabric and find clothes made with it reasonably priced and attractive. In the early 1990s the nations of the European Community were taking action to create a vast European market of over 300 million consumers and U.S. businesses were quick to see the opportunities for exporting products to the consumers of the European Community. Du Pont, the chemical giant based in Wilmington, Delaware, was relying on sales to Europe to account for much of its profit in the 1990s. Many other U.S. companies were also wooing European consumers. For example, the Timberland Company, headquartered in New Hampshire, was having great success selling its shoes and boots to French, Italian, and British schoolchildren who didn't think they were well dressed unless they were wearing Timberland boots! Europeans were also devoted consumers of U.S. tobacco products. Even ailing U.S. car dealers were having success in Europe. Chrysler's Jeep Cherokee was a hot item in Europe and the Middle East. In 1991 Chrysler exported 12.2 percent of the Jeep Cherokees it produced in the United States. General Motors hoped to be exporting a quarter of a million of its vehicles in the 1990s. Meanwhile, indications in the early 1990s were that income growth in the United States would be declining. This means that U.S. consumers will have less to spend. Concern about the declining income of U.S. consumers has led U.S. businesses to scramble for export markets.

Businesses need to know how individual consumers make choices about what to buy and how those choices affect consumer demand for products. They need to know how the market for their products is affected by consumer reactions to price changes and by changes in the income and tastes of consumers. The microeconomic theory of consumer behavior helps us understand how consumer choices are influenced by prices, preferences, and incomes. That theory, which we develop in this chapter, underlies individual and market demand for goods and services. However, as you will see, the theory of consumer choice has broad applicability. It can show how government subsidies to consumers for housing and food affect their well-being and how taxes influence taxpayers' choices. It can also illuminate the factors influencing decisions to marry, to have children, and to allocate time between leisure and work.

Preferences and Choices

Preferences The rankings consumers give to the alternative opportunities available to them.

Persons differ widely in their preferences; one person's pleasure is another person's pain. The way people rank the alternatives available to them provides information about their likes and dislikes. **Preferences** are represented by the rankings consumers give to the alternative opportunities available to them. Preferences are but one determinant of consumers' choices. Their choices of goods and services also depend on their incomes and on the prices of items they desire.

Do not confuse preferences with choices. Preferences are likes and dislikes. Persons must reconcile their desires with their actual budgets. Budgets depend on income and on the prices of desired goods and services. Consumers must choose how to best satisfy their preferences without spending more than their budget permits.

Also do not confuse preferences with demand. Economic circumstances often force the choice of alternatives other than those that would be preferred if they were available without charge. You may prefer prime rib to hamburger. Nonetheless, after viewing a restaurant menu you often choose the hamburger because prime rib is too expensive for your budget. The economic realities of price and ability to pay prevent most persons from getting everything they desire. The fact that you drive a 20-year-old wreck does not mean that you prefer it to a spanking new Corvette or other sports car. Most people would choose more or better clothes, cars, or housing *if* their incomes were greater or *if* prices were lower. In markets we must all confront the fact that our income may be insufficient to purchase products that rank high in our preferences. Despite your preference for the BMW 525i over the Ford Escort, you may demand the Ford because, given your current income, you can't afford the BMW at its current price.

Assumptions about Consumer Preferences

The economist's model of consumer choice is based on a few underlying assumptions about individual preferences for goods and services. These assumptions include the following:

1. *Persons are able to rank alternatives.* It is assumed that persons can rank alternative combinations of goods in an order that reflects their preferences. When a person is confronted with two baskets containing different amounts or kinds of goods, she is presumed to be capable of indicating that she prefers one basket to the other or that she is indifferent between the two. If she prefers basket *A* to basket *B*, it can be inferred that basket *A* gives her more satisfaction than basket *B*. If, however, she indicates that she is indifferent between basket *A* and basket *B*, it can be inferred that both baskets provide her with the same level of satisfaction.

At any point in time, the ranking of alternatives describes a consumer's preferences. For any two alternatives, a consumer either prefers one to the other or is indifferent between the two. All that the model of consumer choice assumes is the ability to rank. There is no need to presume that persons can measure the intensity of their preferences. It is sufficient that they know when they are better off.

Transitivity A property of preferences indicating that a person who prefers alternative *A* to alternative *B* and alternative *B* to alternative *C* must also prefer *A* to *C*.

2. *Preferences are transitive.* **Transitivity** means that if a person prefers basket of goods *A* to basket *B* and also prefers basket *B* to basket *C*, he must also prefer *A* to *C*. This is because it can be inferred from those rankings that *A* provides him with more satisfaction than *B* and that *B* provides him with more satisfaction than *C*. It must follow that *A* definitely provides him with more satisfaction than *C* because it was chosen over *B*. For example, if a person prefers a new car to a European vacation and also prefers a European vacation to a new stereo system, then her preferences are transitive if she also prefers the new car to the stereo. A person who indicates that he prefers the car to the vacation, the vacation to the stereo, and the stereo to the car would be regarded as having inconsistent preferences. Transitivity also implies that a person who is indifferent between *A* and *B* and between *B* and *C* must also be indifferent between *A* and *C*.

3. *More of a good is preferred to less.* It is usually assumed that people always prefer more of a good or service to less of it. This implies consumers have insatiable desires for economic goods. Thus, a consumer would always rank a basket containing 2 pounds of rib eye steak and two bottles of wine over a basket that contains only 1 pound of steak and one bottle of wine.

Items that persons prefer less of are sometimes called *economic bads* rather than *economic goods*. Examples of economic bads are garbage and polluted water. One person might regard as an economic bad an item that others regard as an economic good. Your roommate might love spinach and liver but if you view spinach and liver as economic bads, you would prefer that your college cafeteria serve less rather than more spinach and liver. Consumers will never voluntarily sacrifice goods to obtain bads.

THE UTILITY FUNCTION AND INDIFFERENCE CURVES

Utility The satisfaction obtained from consuming an item.

Utility is a term used by economists to indicate the satisfaction that consumers obtain from consuming goods and services or engaging in activities. It would be nice if the utility of goods and services could be precisely measured in, say, "utils" in the same way the length of objects can be precisely measured in feet and inches. If utility were measurable, it would be possible to add up the satisfaction participants in an economy obtain each year and thus determine the total annual "national utility" obtained from purchases and other activities. It would also be possible to find out how many utils one person enjoyed compared to another. If policymakers were able to measure and compare utility from resource use, they could develop precise methods of redistributing utility to attain social objectives regarded as fair.

Despite the hopes of early developers of the theory of consumer choice, it appears that utility can be neither observed nor measured; it can only be inferred by interpreting a consumer's actions. The assumptions made above about consumers imply that they can specify their first, second, third, and other rankings for alternatives available to them. It can be inferred that the first-ranked alternative has more utility than the second-ranked alternative, but there is no presumption that the consumer can measure how much more. Utility is **ordinally measurable** when alternatives can be ranked. Utility would be **cardinally measurable** if persons could attach a *specific number of utils* to each alternative. If utility were cardinally measurable, a consumer could say that one vacation to Florida each year is worth 500 utils, while two vacations to Florida each year are worth 800 utils. From this it would be inferred that the second vacation adds 300 utils to the consumer's total utility. Attaching a number to the difference in utility between two alternatives would be possible only if utility were cardinally measureable.

Ordinal measurement The ranking of alternatives as first, second, third, and so on.

Cardinal measurement Placing a number on alternatives so that their utility can be added.

Because it is assumed that a person is merely capable of ranking alternatives, the model of consumer choice developed below assumes that utility is only ordinally measureable. Once the theory based on ordinal measurements has been developed, it will be possible to show how the theory could be refined if utility were cardinally measureable.

What utility actually is and whether it can be measured are not of fundamental importance in analyzing human behavior. Because utility is a personal concept, the activities and items that provide it vary from person to person. Altruistic behavior is consistent with utility maximization if it provides a person with satisfaction.

The Utility Function

Utility function A relationship between the quantities of goods and services consumed and the utility level achieved by the consumer.

A **utility function** is a relationship between the quantities of goods and services consumed and the utility level achieved by the consumer. Utility functions are a way of representing a person's preferences. A utility function may be written as follows:

$$U = f(Q_X, Q_Y) \tag{3–1}$$

where f indicates that U, the utility level, depends on the variables within the parentheses. The utility function in Equation 3–1 presumes that a person's utility depends only on the quantity of good X, Q_X, and the quantity of good Y, Q_Y, the person consumes over a certain period, such as a week. Of course, you can include as many variables as you wish in the utility function. Naturally, a person's utility level depends on the quantities of many goods and services that the person purchases over a period and on the extent to which the person engages in various activities. The simplified utility function in Equation 3–1 can concentrate on the basic influences on a person's choice by explaining his choice of the quantities of only two economic goods.

Indifference Curves

It is possible to represent a person's preferences graphically by asking questions about how that person would rank alternatives. The assumptions made about preferences guarantee that persons can indicate preference or indifference among

Market basket A combination of goods and services for consumption over a period.

Indifference curve A curve connecting points on a graph that correspond to market baskets of equal utility to a consumer.

alternatives. Suppose that your teenage brother, who gets a weekly allowance from your parents, is interested in consuming only two products each week: cassette tapes for his collection of heavy metal music and gasoline for his 1965 Mustang so he can go cruising on the weekend. A **market basket** of goods is a combination of goods and services for weekly (or daily, or annual) consumption. For example, one market basket for your brother might be four cassette tapes and ten gallons of gasoline per week. The symbol Q_X represents the number of cassette tapes consumed per week, and the symbol Q_Y represents the number of gallons of gasoline consumed per week. This weekly market basket may therefore be represented by the coordinates $Q_X = 4$, $Q_Y = 10$.

In Figure 3–1, plot Q_Y on the vertical axis and Q_X on the horizontal axis. The point *M*1 on the graph represents the market basket composed of ten gallons of gasoline and four cassette tapes per week. An **indifference curve** connects points on a graph that correspond to a set of market baskets among which the consumer is indifferent. Suppose that the consumer is indifferent between the market basket of ten gallons of gasoline and four cassette tapes and another market basket, *M*2, consisting of five cassette tapes and six gallons of gasoline per week. This second market basket would lie on the same indifference curve as *M*1. If the consumer were also indifferent between market basket *M*3, consisting of six cassette tapes

FIGURE 3–1 An Indifference Curve

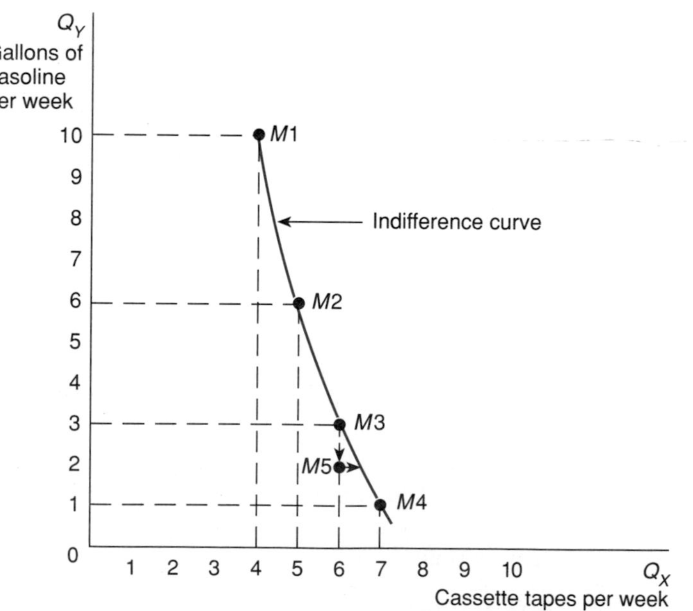

Each point on an indifference curve represents a market basket of goods. The consumer is indifferent among all of the market baskets on the curve.

and three gallons of gasoline per week, and market basket *M*1, point *M*3 would be on the same indifference curve. Market basket *M*4, consisting of seven cassette tapes and one gallon of gasoline is also on the curve.

An indifference curve for a person represents all the combinations of Q_X and Q_Y that provide the person with a certain level of satisfaction. The indifference curve drawn in Figure 3–1 shows market baskets among which the consumer is indifferent. Any market basket on the curve provides the same satisfaction as that provided by the initial market basket, *M*1. Table 3–1 summarizes the data on which this indifference curve is based. Because the consumer is indifferent among the market baskets on an indifference curve, it can be inferred that the level of utility of each market basket is the same. An indifference curve can therefore be thought of as showing alternative market baskets of goods that provide a person with equal utility.

The assumptions made about preferences imply that indifference curves for economic goods must be negatively sloped. If both cassette tapes and gasoline are economic goods for the consumer, more of each good will be preferred to less of it. If confronted with two different market baskets of the goods *X*, which in this example is cassette tapes, and *Y*, which in this example is gasoline, the consumer will always prefer the basket that has more *X*, provided that the two baskets have the same amount of *Y*. Similarly, when two baskets have the same amount of *X*, but one of the baskets has more *Y*, the consumer will prefer the one with more *Y*. This also implies that a basket containing more of both goods will be preferred to a basket with less of both.

To see why this implies negatively sloped indifference curves, imagine that the consumer is currently consuming the weekly market basket *M*3. This basket consists of three gallons of gasoline (the *Y* good) and six cassette tapes (the *X* good). If one gallon of gasoline per week were removed from the basket, the consumer would be worse off because more is preferred to less. Thus, a market basket *M*5, consisting of two gallons of gasoline and six cassette tapes per week, will provide less utility than that provided by *M*3. *M*5 cannot, therefore, be on the same indifference curve as *M*1. To return the consumer to the same indifference curve, the reduction in the weekly amount of gasoline consumed must be offset by the addition of some number of cassettes. In general, to remain on a given indiffer-

TABLE 3–1 Data for an Indifference Curve

Market Basket	Q_Y *(Gallons of Gasoline per Week)*	Q_X *(Cassette Tapes per Week)*
*M*1	10	4
*M*2	6	5
*M*3	3	6
*M*4	1	7

ence curve, any reduction in the amount of good Y, $-\Delta Q_Y$, must be replaced by an increase in the amount of good X, $+\Delta Q_X$. It follows that the slope of indifference curves for economic goods, $\Delta Q_Y/\Delta Q_X$, will always be negative because its numerator and denominator will always be of the opposite sign.

Indifference Maps

If both gasoline and cassette tapes are economic goods, then any market basket that contains more of at least one of these goods will be preferred to a market basket with less. For example, in Figure 3–2 basket *M*6, consisting of ten gallons of gasoline and five cassette tapes per week, is preferred to basket *M*1. This is because *M*6 has one more cassette tape than *M*1 and the same number of gallons of gasoline per week.

It is now possible to find the baskets among which the consumer would be indifferent as compared to basket *M*6. This allows the tracing of another indifference curve. By the same token, an indifference curve could be drawn through point *M*5, which consists of two gallons of gasoline and six cassette tapes per week. An indifference curve could be drawn through the point corresponding to any given market basket on the graph.

FIGURE 3–2 An Indifference Map

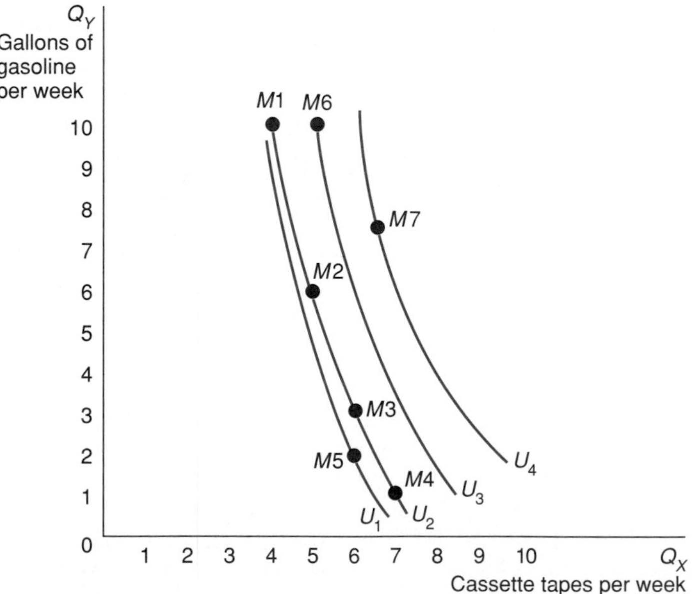

An indifference map is a way of describing a person's preferences. An indifference curve could be drawn for any market basket on the graph. Only four indifference curves have been drawn above. Indifference maps farther out from the origin correspond to higher levels of utility. In the graph $U_1 < U_2 < U_3 < U_4$.

Indifference map A set of indifference curves used to describe a person's preferences.

The indifference curves that can be drawn in this way constitute a person's **indifference map.** An indifference map is a way of describing a person's preferences. A consumer's indifference map for gasoline and cassette tapes is illustrated in Figure 3–2. The assumptions made about consumer preferences for economic goods imply that indifference maps have the following properties:

1. *Market baskets on indifference curves farther from the origin are preferred to market baskets on indifference curves closer to the origin.* If X and Y are economic goods, market baskets lying on indifference curves farther from the origin must be preferred to those lying on curves closer to the origin. This follows from the assumption that more is preferred to less. For example, removing cassette tapes from the market basket labeled $M2$ must make the consumer worse off if they are not replaced by some number of gallons of gasoline. This would move the consumer to a lower indifference curve providing less satisfaction. Market baskets corresponding to a given amount of X are preferred according to the amount of Y in the baskets. Similarly, market baskets with a given amount of Y are ranked according to the amount of X in them. The market basket $M7$ is preferred to any market basket on the indifference curve going through the point $M2$ because it has more of *both* X and Y than are contained in basket $M2$. All market baskets on the indifference curve going through the point $M7$ are therefore preferred to those on the indifference curve going through the point $M2$.

It can be inferred that market baskets on higher indifference curves provide the consumer with more utility than is provided by those on lower indifference curves. This is because the consumer would always choose a basket on the higher curve over one on a lower curve provided that nothing constrained the choice. The indifference map is really a way of *describing* a person's utility function for two goods. The level of utility provided by any combination of goods X and Y can be inferred from the indifference curve on which it lies. For example, in Figure 3–2 all market baskets on the indifference curve labeled U_1 provide a level of utility that is less than the level U_2 provided by baskets on the curve labeled U_2. Similarly, all market baskets lying on the indifference curve labeled U_4 provide more utility to the consumer than is provided by baskets lying on the curve labeled U_3. The farther away from the origin, the higher is the utility associated with a given indifference curve for economic goods.

2. *Indifference curves cannot intersect.* To see why this is so, consider the implications of having the two indifference curves in Figure 3–3 intersect. Market basket A is at the point of intersection common to both indifference curves. Since A and B are both on indifference curve U_1, the consumer is indifferent between them. Similarly, since C is on indifference curve U_2 along with A, the consumer is also indifferent between A and C. It must follow that the consumer will also be indifferent between B and C.

It is easy to see, however, that if both X and Y are economic goods, the consumer will prefer basket C to basket B. The reason is that basket C corresponds to more of both good X and good Y than does basket B. Reading off the coordinates in Figure 3–3 it can be seen that C contains three units of Y and six units of X, whereas B contains only five units of X and two units of Y. Be-

FIGURE 3–3 **Intersecting Indifference Curves Imply a Contradiction**

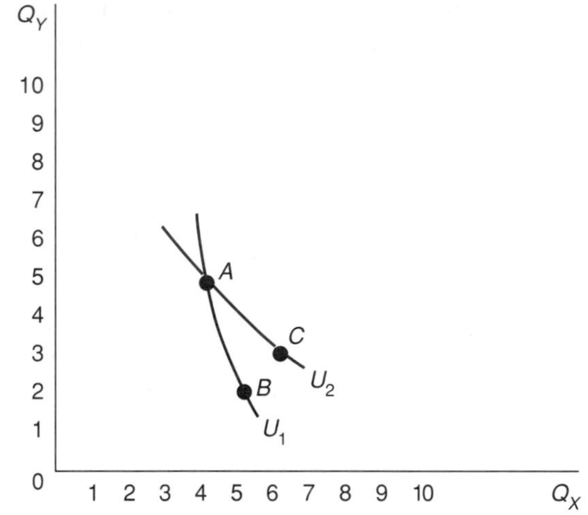

If the market basket represented by point A is on both indifference curves, U_1 and U_2, where $U_2 > U_1$, this implies that the consumer is indifferent between A and B and between A and C. It follows that he is indifferent between B and C. But basket B has less of both good X and good Y than C has. It must therefore follow that he prefers C to B. This is a contradiction because the consumer cannot simultaneously prefer one basket to another and be indifferent between the two.

cause the consumer cannot simultaneously prefer C to B and be indifferent between them, the intersection of the two indifference curves implies a contradiction.

Diminishing Marginal Rates of Substitution and the Curvature of Indifference Curves

Marginal rate of substitution of *X* for *Y* The amount of good Y that a consumer would give up to obtain one more unit of good X while holding utility constant.

The **marginal rate of substitution (MRS_{XY}) of *X* for *Y*** is the amount of good Y that the consumer would give up to obtain one more unit of good X while remaining on a given indifference curve. Giving up more than the amount of Y corresponding to MRS_{XY} for another unit of X would make the consumer worse off. Giving up less than the amount of Y corresponding to MRS_{XY} for another unit of X would make the consumer better off. The marginal rate of substitution therefore measures the willingness of a consumer to exchange one good for another while neither gaining nor losing utility in the process. The curvature of indifference curves that have been drawn thus far implies that the amount of Y that a consumer is willing to give up for another unit of X in this way diminishes as more X is substituted for Y in the consumer's market basket.

To see this, move along the indifference curve illustrated in Figure 3–4. If a consumer neither gains nor loses utility by giving up some weekly consumption of Y to get one more unit of X per week, it follows that he remains on the same indifference curve. Call "ΔQ_Y" the amount of weekly consumption of good Y the

FIGURE 3–4 Diminishing MRS_{XY} along an Indifference Curve

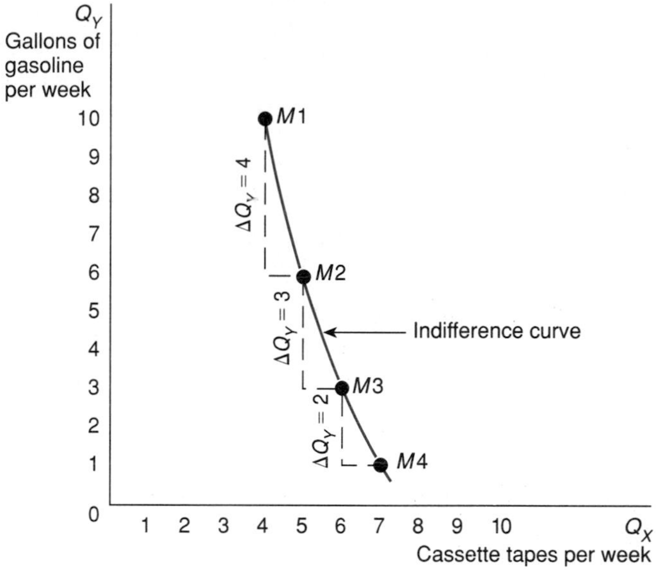

Along any indifference curve the amount of good Y the consumer will give up to get another unit of good X decreases as X is actually substituted for Y in the consumer's market basket.

consumer will give up to obtain another unit of good X. The gain in weekly consumption of one unit of X is $\Delta Q_X = 1$. The amount of Y that will be exchanged for a unit of X between any two points along the indifference curve can therefore be written as $\Delta Q_Y/Q_X$. This is the slope of the indifference curve along which the consumer moves when giving up units of Y for additional units of X. However, the slope of the indifference curve is negative. Thinking of the MRS_{XY} in this way results in a negative number. The marginal rate of substitution is defined as a *positive* amount of Y the consumer is willing to give up for an additional amount of X. It is therefore the slope of the indifference curve multiplied by -1:

$$MRS_{XY} = -\Delta Q_Y/\Delta Q_X \tag{3–2}$$

The curvature of the indifference curve illustrated in Figure 3–4 implies diminishing marginal rates of substitution of X for Y. Notice how the slope of the curve changes as the consumer substitutes X for Y. The marginal rate of substitution between points $M1$ and $M2$ on the indifference curve illustrated in Figure 3–4 is 4. This is the amount of Y the consumer would give up to get one more unit of X where Y is gasoline and X is cassette tapes. A marginal rate of substitution of 4 means that the consumer would be willing to give up four gallons of gasoline per week to receive one more cassette tape each week while remaining on the same indifference curve. However, $MRS_{XY} = 4$ only when the consumer's market basket contains ten gallons of gasoline and four cassette tapes each week (the amounts in market basket $M1$).

TABLE 3–2 Marginal Rate of Substitution of X for Y

Market Basket	Q_Y	Q_X	MRS_{XY}
*M*1	10	4	
			4 units of *Y* per unit of *X*
*M*2	6	5	
			3 units of *Y* per unit of *X*
*M*3	3	6	
			2 units of *Y* per unit of *X*
*M*4	1	7	

Suppose the consumer has the market basket of goods represented by point *M*2 (six gallons and five cassette tapes). The consumer would now be willing to give up only three cassette tapes in exchange for another gallon of gasoline each week while still remaining on the same indifference curve. The marginal rate of substitution has declined as the consumer has moved from market basket *M*1 to market basket *M*2. Notice how the indifference curve becomes flatter as *X* is actually substituted for *Y* along the curve. The convex shape of the indifference curve implies that as the consumer's market basket contains fewer gallons of gasoline and more cassette tapes, the number of gallons of gasoline he is willing to trade for more cassette tapes declines. When the consumer is at point *M*3 on the indifference curve illustrated in Figure 3–4, he is willing to give up only two gallons of gasoline per week to get another cassette tape. Table 3–2 summarizes the data used to calculate MRS_{XY} at various points on the indifference curve.

Diminishing marginal rates of substitution of *X* for *Y* The assumption that as good *X* is substituted for good *Y* along an indifference curve, while keeping utility constant, there is a decline in the amount of good *Y* that the consumer will give up for each additional unit of good *X*.

Diminishing marginal rates of substitution of *X* and *Y* is an important assumption made about the shapes of indifference curves. As good *X* is substituted for good *Y* along such a curve, the curve becomes less steep. Consumers differ in their preferences. Differences in preferences imply differences in the amounts of one good they would be willing to exchange for another good while neither gaining nor losing satisfaction. However, it is presumed that the marginal rate of substitution of *X* for *Y* tends to decline as more *X* is substituted for *Y* along any consumer's indifference curve. Exceptions to this tendency do exist.

Using your own experience, a little introspection might convince you that the assumption is quite reasonable. Suppose you were given a monthly market basket consisting only of food. You would exchange that food for other goods, such as entertainment and clothing, only if the exchange would not make you worse off. Is it not reasonable that at first you would be willing to exchange fairly large amounts of food to get small amounts of goods that you do not have? If you are naked but have a lot of food, you would give up a fair amount of food to get some clothes on your back. However, as your monthly food stock dwindles and you obtain more of other goods, you would become less willing to surrender food to get one more unit of any other good.

The Cardinal Approach: Marginal Utility and the Slope of Indifference Curves

As discussed earlier in this chapter, cardinal measurement of utility (were it possible) would allow calculation of the *difference* in total utility between two market baskets. Given cardinally measureable utility, it would be possible to calculate *how much* better off the consumer would be if one more unit of a good were added to a market basket.

Marginal utility The gain in utility obtained from consuming another unit of an item.

Marginal utility is the gain in utility attained from consuming an additional unit of a good or service. Economists often use the term *marginal utility* in discussing the extra benefit that consumers receive from additional goods and services even though they realize that it would be very difficult, if not impossible, to measure that benefit.[1]

The marginal rate of substitution along an indifference curve can be related to the marginal utilities on the goods on each axis. Removing ΔQ_Y units of Y from the consumer's market basket makes him worse off. The loss in utility is $\Delta Q_Y \text{MU}_Y$, where MU_Y is the marginal utility of Y to the consumer. If this lost Y is replaced with just enough X to make him just as well off as he was previously, the gain in utility would be $\Delta Q_X \text{MU}_X$, where MU_X is the marginal utility of X. If the consumer is to return to the same indifference curve, the gain in utility from the X added to the market basket must exactly equal the loss in utility from the Y removed from it. Thus,

$$\Delta Q_X \text{MU}_X = -\Delta Q_Y \text{MU}_Y \tag{3–3}$$

Therefore,

$$-(\Delta Q_Y / \Delta Q_X) = \text{MU}_X / \text{MU}_Y = \text{MRS}_{XY} \tag{3–4}$$

The marginal rate of substitution of X for Y can therefore be thought of as the ratio of the marginal utility of X to the marginal utility of Y[2].

The marginal utility of a good tends to decline as more of it is consumed over a given period. As persons have more of an item over a period, they tend to tire of it. For example, the marginal utility you receive from one steak dinner per week might be quite high. However, the second steak dinner that week is likely to add less to your total utility than the first one. This means that the marginal utility of steak dinners is lower when two instead of one are purchased per week. By the time you have your fifth steak dinner during a week, the marginal utility of a steak dinner is likely to be much lower than it was when you had your first.

Assume that a consumer currently has a market basket consisting of ten gallons of gasoline and four cassette tapes, corresponding to point *M*1 on the indifference curve in Figure 3–4. Also assume that this consumer is indifferent between that market basket and another consisting of six gallons of gasoline and five cassette tapes, corresponding to point *M*2 on the same indifference curve. It is now easy to see why MRS_{XY} must decline as the consumer exchanges gallons of

---

[1] Given the utility function $U = f(Q_1, Q_2, Q_3 \ldots Q_N)$, the marginal utility of each good i is its first derivative: $\text{MU}_{Q_i} = \partial U / \partial Q_i$

[2] The same result can be obtained more precisely using calculus. If the utility function is $U = f(Q_X, Q_Y)$ then the total differential is

$$dU = dQ_X(\partial U / \partial Q_X) + dQ_Y(\partial U / \partial Q_Y) = 0$$

To keep total utility constant, the total differential must be equal to zero.

Solving the above equation for dQ_Y / dQ_X, which is the slope of the indifference curve, gives

$$dQ_Y / dQ_X = -(\partial U / Q_X) / (\partial / Q_Y)$$

gasoline for cassette tapes along an indifference curve. Because the consumer now has *more cassette tapes*, the marginal utility of cassette tapes (MU_X) must be lower. However, because the consumer now has *less gasoline*, the marginal utility of gasoline (MU_Y) must be higher. Just as marginal utility tends to decline when you have more of a good, so does it tend to increase when you have less of a good. Because MU_X declines while MU_Y increases when the *X* good is substituted for the *Y* good along a given indifference curve, it follows that the ratio MU_X/MU_Y, which equals MRS_{XY}, declines. Thus, the marginal rate of substitution of *X* for *Y* must also decline when *X* is substituted for *Y* if the marginal utilities of both *X* and *Y* are inversely related to the amounts of each purchased over a period. The declining marginal utility of goods, which could be ascertained if that utility were cardinally measurable, explains the convex shape of indifference curves.

CONCEPT REVIEW

1. What assumptions must be made to draw a person's indifference curves? Does utility have to be cardinally measurable in order to draw an indifference map?
2. Explain why the indifference curves for market baskets of any two economic goods must be downward sloping.
3. Explain how the diminishing marginal rates of substitution of good *X* for good *Y* affect the shape of indifference curves.

BUDGETS AND PRICES

A consumer's choices regarding how much of each good to purchase over a given period depend on economic influences as well as preferences. The next step in understanding consumer choices is to examine the economic forces that influence those choices. To do this, it is necessary to examine how prices for goods and income available for spending over a period constrain the consumer's opportunities to purchase goods and services.

The Budget Constraint

Budget constraint The market baskets of goods and services that a consumer can afford, given the consumer's income and the prices of the goods and services in the baskets.

A budget tells how much money is available to spend in a given period, such as a week. The amount the consumer has available to spend in the given period is his income. How much that income will buy depends on the prices of the goods and services the consumer desires. The consumer's income defines the **budget constraint**. The budget constraint shows the market baskets of goods and services a consumer can afford, given the consumer's income and the prices of the goods and services in the baskets.

Suppose your brother, who is interested in buying only gasoline and cassette tapes, receives a \$15 per week allowance from mom and dad. That \$15 is your brother's weekly income. Suppose that the price of gasoline is \$1.50 per gallon

TABLE 3–3 Affordable Market Baskets*

Market Basket	*Gallons of Gasoline (Q_Y)*	*Cassette Tapes (Q_x)*	*Total Expenditure*
*B*1	0	5	$15
*B*2	2	4	15
*B*3	4	3	15
*B*4	6	2	15
*B*5	8	1	15
*B*6	10	0	15

* Income = $15 per week; P_Y = $1.50; P_X = $3.

and the price of a cassette tape is $3. Table 3–3 shows the various combinations of gasoline and cassette tapes your brother can buy with his weekly income assuming that he spends all of it.

If your brother spent all of the $15 on cassette tapes, he could buy five cassette tapes during a week. This is represented by market basket *B*1. If your brother bought five cassette tapes during a week, that week he would exhaust his income on cassette tapes and not be able to afford any gasoline. He would then be able to listen to a lot of new music at home but would have to give up cruising in his Mustang. At the other extreme is market basket *B*6, where your brother spends all of his income on gasoline and purchases no cassette tapes. At $1.50 per gallon, the maximum amount of gasoline that he can buy is 10 gallons per week. Market baskets *B*2, *B*3, *B*4, and *B*5 show other combinations of gallons of gasoline and cassette tapes that can be purchased with a $15 weekly income.

Budget line A line showing all combinations of two goods that a consumer can afford if all income is spent over a period.

These combinations are graphed in Figure 3–5. The resulting **budget line** shows all the combinations of two goods, *X* and *Y*, that the consumer can afford, given the consumer's income and the prices of the two goods. Market baskets represented by points above the line require more income per week than is currently available. For example, market basket *B*7, consisting of eight cassette tapes and four gallons of gasoline per week, would require a weekly income of $30, of which $24 would be needed for the cassette tapes and another $6 would be needed for the gasoline. This exceeds your brother's current $15 income, so he would not be able to get to point *B*7. Market baskets below the line could be purchased without using up all of his weekly income.

Points on the budget line imply that the sum of the expenditure on good *X* and good *Y* must equal the consumer's income. In general, if I is the consumer's income (say per week), P_X is the price of good X, and P_Y is the price of good Y, we can derive a simple equation for the budget line. As before, Q_X is the quantity of good X consumed and Q_Y is the quantity of good Y consumed. It follows that P_XQ_X is the amount the consumer spends on good X and P_YQ_Y is the amount the consumer spends on good Y. The budget constraint may therefore be written as

$$I = P_XQ_X + P_YQ_Y \tag{3–5}$$

FIGURE 3–5 The Budget Constraint Line

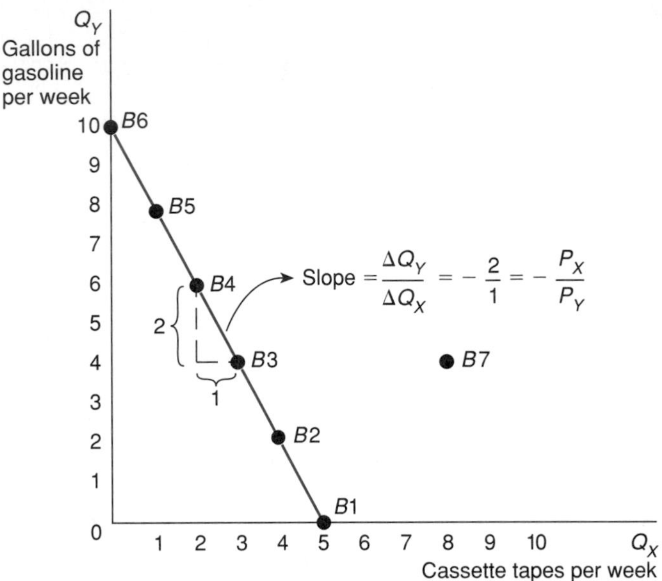

The budget constraint line shows all the market baskets of good *X* and good *Y* that the consumer's budget allows him to purchase. This line is based on the data in Table 3–3. The market basket represented by point *B*7 would require more income per week than the consumer has to spend.

or

$$\text{Income} = \text{Expenditure}$$

The Economic Significance of Intercepts of the Budget Line with the Axes

The intercept of the budget line with the *Y* axis occurs at market basket *B*6, where all of the \$15 weekly income is spent on gasoline and no cassette tapes are purchased. Similarly, the intercept of the budget line and the *X* axis occurs at market basket *B*1, where all of the \$15 weekly income is spent on cassette tapes and no gasoline is purchased.

Each of the budget line intercepts shows the *maximum* amount of the one good that the consumer can purchase with his available income at current prices when he purchases none of the other good. You can use Equation 3–5 to find out how the maximum amounts of each good that the consumer can purchase depend on the consumer's income and on the price of the good. If you set Q_Y equal to zero in Equation 3–5 and solve for Q_X, you will get an expression for the maximum amount of good *X* the consumer can purchase over a period. When $Q_Y = 0$, $Q_X = I/P_X$. The maximum amount of good *X* a consumer can purchase over a period depends on the consumer's income and on the price of good X. Similarly, the maximum amount of good Y a consumer can purchase over a period is I/P_Y. In this case $I/P_X = \$15/\$3 = 5$, which corresponds to the X intercept in Figure 3–5, and $I/P_Y = \$15/\$1.50 = 10$, which corresponds to the Y intercept.

In effect, the consumer's income can be expressed in terms of either cassette tapes or gallons of gasoline instead of dollars. If the consumer were to spend all of his weekly income on gasoline, the maximum amount of gasoline he could purchase would be ten gallons. Income expressed in terms of the maximum amount of gasoline that it could purchase is a way of measuring the consumer's real (as opposed to money) income. Similarly, the consumer's real income in terms of cassette tapes is five cassette tapes.

The Economic Significance of the Slope of the Budget Line

Notice that in Table 3–3 the possibility of consuming two gallons of gasoline is gained for each cassette tape given up. When the consumer gives up the opportunity to buy a cassette tape, \$3 of his budget is freed. He can then use this money to buy two gallons of gasoline at the current price of \$1.50 per gallon. The extra gasoline that can be bought each time one cassette tape is given up is the price of a cassette tape divided by the price of a gallon of gasoline: $\$3/\$1.50 = 2$.

In general, how many extra units of Y a consumer can purchase by sacrificing a unit of good X depends on the relationship between the price of X and the price of Y. By giving up one unit of X, the consumer frees a sum of money equal to the price of X. The amount of Y that the consumer will be able to purchase with that sum is P_X/P_Y units of Y. If the price of Y were exactly equal to the price of X, the consumer could buy exactly one unit of Y for each unit of X sacrificed. If the price of Y were less than the price of X, the consumer could buy more than one unit of Y for each unit of X sacrificed.

The amount of good Y obtained by giving up each unit of good X is represented by the slope of the budget line. To see this, look at Figure 3–5 and note how each time the consumer gives up one unit of good X measured by $\Delta Q_X = -1$, two units of good Y, represented by $\Delta Q_Y = 2$, are obtained. The slope of the budget line is $\Delta Q_Y/\Delta Q_X$, which in this case is equal to -2. This slope can also be interpreted as meaning that the consumer must sacrifice two units of good Y (gasoline) to obtain an additional unit of good X (cassette tapes) at the current prices for these two goods. Notice that $P_X/P_Y = \$3/\$1.50 = 2$. If you multiply the slope of the budget line by -1, you obtain the ratio of the price of X to the price of Y. In general,

$$-\text{Slope of budget line} = -\Delta Q_Y/\Delta Q_X = P_X/P_Y \qquad (3\text{–}6)$$

Because the budget line is linear, it will have the same slope at all points. The consumer must always give up the same amount of good Y to obtain each extra unit of good X, given the prices of these two goods.[3]

[3] Assuming that the consumer always spends all his weekly budget income along the budget line, it follows that $-dQ_YP_Y = dQ_XP_X$. Therefore, $-dQ_Y/dQ_x = P_X/P_Y$.

You can also see how the slope of the budget line depends entirely on the ratio of the price of good X to that of good Y by solving Equation 3–5 for Q_Y:

$$Q_Y = -(P_X/P_Y)Q_X + (I/P_Y) \tag{3–7}$$

The slope of the budget line is the coefficient of Q_X, which is $-(P_X/P_Y)$. Multiplying this coefficient by -1 gives the ratio of the price of X to the price of Y. The steeper the budget constraint, the higher is the price of X relative to the price of Y and the more of good Y that must be sacrificed to obtain each extra unit of good X. The term (I/P_Y) in Equation 3–7 represents the intercept of the budget line on the Y axis.

Changes in Income and Prices

Changes in income or prices shift the position of the consumer's budget constraint line. An increase in income makes it possible for the consumer to purchase market baskets of goods and services that were previously unaffordable. It therefore shifts the budget constraint outward. It does not, however, change the slope of the budget line. The slope of the budget line depends only on the prices of the goods consumed and is independent of the consumer's income. An increase in income shifts the budget constraint line out parallel to itself. A decrease in income results in an inward parallel shift of the budget line. The effect of changes in income on the budget constraint is shown graphically in Figure 3–6(a).

Referring to Table 3–3, suppose that your brother's income were to double, from \$15 per week to \$30 per week. The number of cassette tapes and gallons of gasoline that he could purchase in each market basket would then also double,

FIGURE 3–6 Changes in Income and Prices

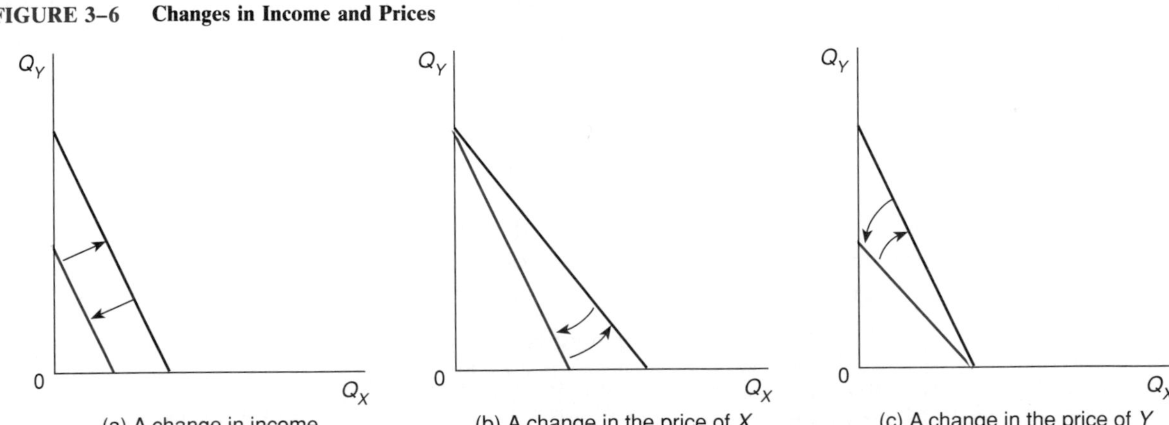

A change in income shifts the budget constraint outward or inward parallel to itself. A change in the price of X rotates the budget line to a new intercept on the X axis without changing the intercept on the Y axis. Similarly, a change in the price of Y rotates the budget line to a new intercept on the Y axis without changing the intercept on the X axis.

MODERN MICROECONOMICS IN ACTION: GOVERNMENT AND THE ECONOMY

Income Stagnation and the Budget Constraint of the Middle Class: A Political Issue for the 1990s

As the 1992 presidential campaign opened in an economy struggling to recover from a stubborn recession, politicians began to notice the plight of the middle class. The average American family seemed to be running on an almost level treadmill. Although average family income nearly tripled between 1970 and 1990, from $9,867 to $35,353, inflation substantially eroded the purchasing power of that income during the same period. Expressed in 1990 dollars, average family income in 1970 was $33,328. Thus the real income of the average American family increased by only about 6 percent over the 20-year period from 1970 to 1990.*

As the accompanying graph shows, nearly all of the gains from increased money income have been offset by higher prices. While increased money income has shifted the average family's budget constraint outward, inflation (the increase in the average level of prices) has shifted the budget line inward. The net result has been only a small increase in the consumption possibilities of families with average income.

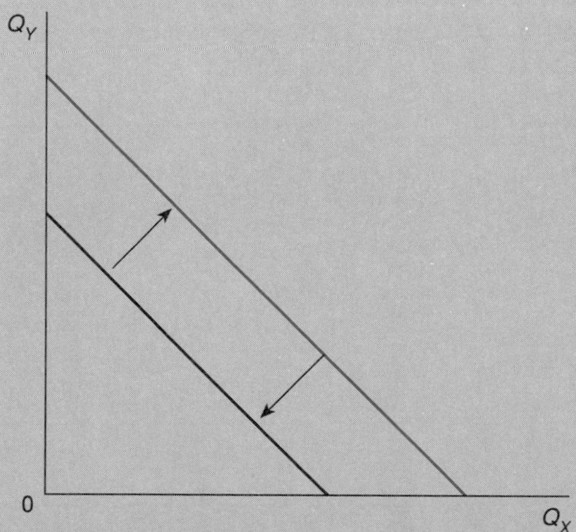

Increases in money income have shifted the budget line of the average family outward since 1970. However, inflation has shifted the budget line inward over the same period, just about wiping out the increased consumption possibilities that increased money income would have otherwise afforded.

The middle class has kept its standard of living from falling in the 1970s and 1980s mainly through the increased participation of wives in the labor force. That increased participation is the main reason why average family income managed to achieve a meager 6 percent increase from 1970 to 1990. Increased income has been achieved at the expense of less time spent at home by women and fewer children per household.

The average family is also spending its money differently today than it did 20 years ago. Today, families whose principal breadwinner is between 35 and 44 years of age spend considerably more of their after-tax income on housing than was the case in 1970. They also spend less on clothing and food, mainly because the size of these families is smaller, and less on out-of-pocket expenses for medical care, mainly because they are typically covered by employer-provided health insurance plans. Even though the average family of the 1990s is not much better off than the average family of the 1970s, the average 1990s family spends a higher proportion of its income on recreation and a smaller proportion on necessities than was the case in 1970.

The reasons for stagnating income are complex, so it is difficult to place the blame for the problem on any particular government policy. However, you can be sure that Democrats and Republicans will be blaming each other for it.

* See Peter T. Kilborn, "The Middle Class Feels Betrayed, but Maybe Not Enough to Rebel," *The New York Times*, January 12, 1992, sec. 4, p. 1.

provided there were no changes in their prices. As long as prices are constant, an increase in money income is equivalent to an increase in real income. Similarly, a cut in your brother's income would reduce the amounts of goods that he could purchase.

A change in the price of X will rotate the budget line along the X axis without changing its intercept on the Y axis. For example, suppose the price of X were to decrease. If the consumer were to spend all of his income on X, he would be able to buy more at the lower price. Thus the intercept on the X axis moves outward. Because the price of Y is unchanged, the intercept on the Y axis remains the same. Similarly, an increase in the price of X would swivel the budget line inward, as illustrated in Figure 3–6(b). A change in the price of Y affects the intercept on the Y axis and swivels the budget line upward or downward, as illustrated in Figure 3–6(c).

Suppose the prices of X and Y change by the same proportion. They could, for example, both change by 10 percent. This would be equivalent to a change in the purchasing power of the consumer's income. It therefore changes the consumer's real income. If both prices were to increase by 10 percent, the purchasing power of the consumer's income would decline by 10 percent. This would be equivalent to a decrease in consumer income. It would therefore be shown on the graph of the budget constraint as a parallel inward shift of the line. A change in both prices by the same percentage does not alter their ratio and therefore does not affect the slope of the budget constraint line. The intercepts on the X and Y axes will change when both prices change because a given amount of income would buy changed amounts of both X and Y were it to be spent on those goods alone.

Concept Review

1. If $P_X = \$5$ and $P_Y = \$2.50$, calculate the number of units of Y that the consumer can purchase for each unit of X sacrificed. What is the slope of the budget line?
2. What can cause the slope of a budget line to change?
3. A budget line intersects the X axis at 5. What is the economic significance of 5 units of X in this case?

Consumer Choices

The model of consumer behavior is based on the behavioral assumption that consumers seek to obtain the highest level of utility possible from spending their income on goods and services available in markets. Consumers are presumed to maximize utility *subject to* the constraint of a budget. This implies that they seek the greatest possible net gain from exchanging income for goods and services over each period. However, the market baskets that consumers can purchase are limited because they cannot spend more than the income available over each period.

The purpose of the model of consumer behavior is to *explain* how consumer choices are influenced by preferences, income, and the prices of goods. To accomplish this goal, the conditions under which the assumed consumer objective is attained are derived by means of the model. Given all of the assumptions made about indifference curves and the budget constraint, logic can then be used to show how consumers' decisions are related to preferences and the economic variables of the analysis.

Maximization of Utility Subject to the Budget Constraint

Figure 3–7 superimposes a typical consumer's indifference map on the axes of the same consumer's budget constraint line. The model of consumer behavior can now be used to determine the consumer's choice of weekly consumption of gasoline and cassette tapes. Remember that the assumed objective of the consumer is to make purchases maximizing the utility level, subject to the constraint that no more than the available income per period can be spent. The market basket that achieves this objective indicates the consumer's most preferred weekly purchases of goods *X* and *Y*, given his income and the prices of *X* and *Y*.

Look first at point *B*5, which corresponds to a market basket of one unit of good *X* and eight units of good *Y* per week. This basket of goods gives the consumer a utility level of U_1. Similarly, the market basket corresponding to point *B*2, where $Q_X = 4$ and $Q_Y = 2$, also gives the consumer a utility level of U_1. To find

FIGURE 3–7 Consumer Equilibrium

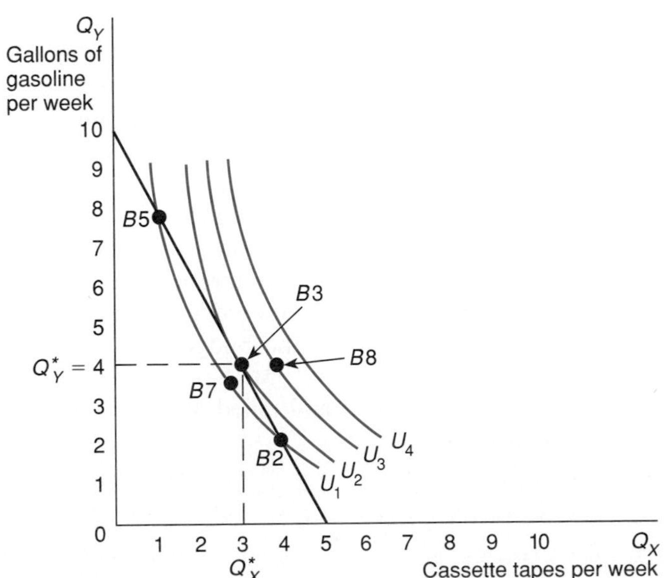

The consumer is in equilibrium when the highest possible level of utility has been attained, given available income and the prices of goods *X* and *Y*. This occurs when an indifference curve is just tangent to the budget constraint line. Market basket *B*3 is the combination of goods *X* and *Y* that the consumer chooses.

out whether either of these market baskets will achieve the consumer's objective, you must determine whether or not other market baskets can provide the consumer with a higher level of utility.

It is easy to see that other baskets provide more utility from spending available income on X and Y at their current prices. By moving along the budget constraint line from $B5$ to the market basket represented by $B3$ and thus moving to a higher indifference curve, the consumer can increase utility. This is done by substituting good X for good Y in the weekly market basket. Similarly, the consumer increases utility by moving toward $B3$ from $B2$. Keep in mind that even though they have not been drawn, indifference curves go through each and every point on the budget line.

A market basket corresponding to a point inside the space below the budget line and the axes, such as $B7$, also provides the consumer with lower levels of utility than basket $B3$. This is so because market baskets such as $B7$ must lie on lower indifference curves than the one going through $B3$. Market baskets corresponding to points above the budget line, such as $B8$, provide more utility than $B3$ but are unaffordable because they require more income than is available to the consumer. Because no affordable basket can provide the consumer with more utility than that represented by $B3$, the consumer has no incentive to further exchange one good for the other once that basket has been chosen.

In general, the maximum utility attainable from a budget is achieved when the combination of goods consumed corresponds to the point at which the budget line touches the highest possible indifference curve. The combination of goods X and Y corresponding to this market basket $Q_X^* = 3$, $Q_Y^* = 4$ is the consumer's chosen market basket of goods. No other combination will provide the consumer with more utility or satisfaction, given the available income. *The* ***consumer equilibrium*** *is the combination of goods purchased that maximizes utility, subject to the budget constraint.* It is an equilibrium in the sense that, given the behavioral assumption of the model, once the consumer has acquired that basket, there is no incentive to trade it for another.

Consumer equilibrium A condition that is achieved when the consumer purchases the market basket that maximizes utility, subject to the budget constraint; achieved when consumption is adjusted so that $MRS_{XY} = P_X/P_Y$ for any two goods.

Geometrically, the equilibrium can be described as the combination of goods that corresponds to the point at which the budget constraint line is just tangent to the highest attainable indifference curve on the consumer's indifference map. At that point the slope of the budget line is just equal to the slope of an indifference curve. The slope of the budget line is $-P_X/P_Y$. The slope of the indifference curves at any point is $-MRS_{XY}$ (recall that MRS_{XY} was defined as the slope of the indifference curve multiplied by -1). The equilibrium condition can therefore be written as

$$-(P_X/P_Y) = -MRS_{XY}$$

or **(3–8)**

$$(P_X/P_Y) = MRS_{XY}$$

This condition, when achieved, implies that the consumer is maximizing utility subject to the budget constraint.

The marginal rate of substitution gives the maximum amount of Y the consumer is willing to forgo for an additional unit of X. The ratio of prices in Equation 3–8 gives the amount of Y the consumer must forgo when an additional unit of X is purchased at current market prices for these goods. The equilibrium condition therefore implies that the consumer purchases good X up to the point at which the maximum amount of Y she is willing to give up for an additional unit of X equals the amount that must be given up for that last unit at current market prices. By varying the amounts purchased, the consumer can adjust marginal rates of substitution until the equilibrium condition has been achieved. Note that consumers must take the prices of X and Y as given. In equilibrium a consumer's valuation of the last unit of X purchased equals the cost of that last unit in terms of the amount of good Y actually given up to acquire it.[4]

A numerical example will make the above interpretation of the equilibrium conditions represented by Equation 3–8 clear. Suppose that at point $B5$ in Figure 3–7 the marginal rate of substitution of X for Y is equal to 3 on indifference curve U_1. In Figure 3–7 the ratio of the price of X to the price of Y is always 2. At point $B5$, therefore, the consumer is willing to give up three gallons of gasoline to get one more cassette tape during the week. However, it takes the sacrifice of only two gallons of gasoline to free the income required to purchase another cassette tape at the current market prices. The *marginal benefit of good* X *in terms of good* Y is measured by the amount of Y the consumer is willing to forgo for another unit of X. The *marginal cost of* X *in terms of* Y to the consumer is the amount of Y that must be given up to obtain an extra unit of X at current market prices for the two goods. If MRS_{XY} exceeds P_X/P_Y, this implies that the marginal benefit of X to the consumer exceeds the marginal cost that must be incurred to purchase it. Remember from the discussion of marginal analysis in the first chapter of this book that a

[4] The solution to the constrained maximization problem can be obtained mathematically using calculus. The utility function is

$$U = f(Q_i)$$

where $i = 1, \ldots, n$ and Q_i is the quantity of the ith good consumed over a period. The budget constraint is

$$\Sigma P_i Q_i = I$$

where $i = 1, \ldots, n$, P_i is the price of the ith good, and I is available income. Lagrange's technique is used to solve for the equilibrium conditions. Set up the expression

$$L = f(Q_i) - \mathcal{L}(\Sigma P_i Q_i - I)$$

where $\mathcal{L}$ is the Lagrangean multiplier. The first-order condition for a maximum is

$$\partial L/\partial Q_i = \partial U/\partial Q_i - \mathcal{L}P_i = 0 \text{ and } \partial L/\partial \mathcal{L} = \Sigma P_i Q_i - I = 0$$

This implies that the market basket satisfying the following conditions will maximize the consumer's utility subject to the budget constraint:

$$\partial U/\partial Q_i = \mathcal{L}P_i \text{ and } \Sigma P_i Q_i = I, \text{ for all } i$$

Each of the derivatives in the above equation represents the marginal utility of the good i. The marginal rate of substitution between any two goods can be thought of as a ratio of their marginal utilities. For any pair of goods i and j

$$\text{MRS}_{ij} = \frac{\partial U/\partial Q_i}{\partial U/\partial Q_j} = \frac{\mathcal{L}P_i}{\mathcal{L}P_j} = \frac{P_i}{P_j} \text{ in equilibrium}$$

net gain is achieved whenever the marginal benefit of a transaction does not fall short of its marginal cost. You can now see that whenever $\text{MRS}_{XY} > P_X/P_Y$, a net gain can be achieved by giving up more Y to obtain more X.

You can now also see why a consumer would never choose a point such as $B2$ in Figure 3–7. At that point the indifference curve is flatter than the budget line. This implies that $\text{MRS}_{XY} < P_X/P_Y$. The market basket represented by $B2$ is therefore one whose marginal benefit to the consumer falls short of its marginal cost. Moving to $B2$ would therefore involve trading Y for X beyond the point at which this is worth doing. Thus, a consumer at point $B2$ would achieve a net gain by trading X for more Y. By adjusting the goods in the purchased market basket to equate the marginal rate of substitution of X for Y with the ratio of the price of X to that of Y, the consumer makes sure that no additional net gains are possible from changing the mix of goods. When the consumer is in equilibrium, the marginal benefit obtained from consuming a good is just balanced by the marginal cost of doing so.

The Equimarginal Principle

Interpreting the marginal rate of substitution of one good for another as a ratio of marginal utilities allows the condition for consumer equilibrium to be expressed as follows:

$$\text{MU}_X/\text{MU}_Y = P_X$$

$$\text{MU}_X/P_X = \text{MU}_Y/P_Y \tag{3–9}$$

Equimarginal principle Equalization of the marginal utility per dollar spent on all goods so as to maximize utility given income.

Equation 3–9 says that a consumer who maximizes utility buys the two goods so that their *marginal utilities per dollar* are equal. The **equimarginal principle** generalizes the conditions required for consumer equilibrium by pointing out that a consumer allocates expenditure on *all goods* in equilibrium to equalize the marginal utility per dollar spent on each. For example, if the marginal utility per dollar of cassette tapes were 5 while that of gasoline were 2, the consumer could enjoy a net gain by reallocating expenditure. This is because each extra dollar spent on cassette tapes would result in a gain of 5 units of utility. The consumer would lose only 2 units of utility by spending $1 less on gasoline. Because the gain in utility from reallocating the dollar exceeds the loss, the consumer is made better off. The consumer can always gain in this way until the condition in Equation 3–9 has been met. If the marginal utility per dollar of any good exceeds that of another, the consumer can gain in the same way by reallocating expenditure.

The hypothesis of diminishing marginal utility of a good as more of the good is obtained implies that the marginal utility per dollar of a good available at a given price will also decline. This explains why consumers tend to diversify spending over a period. For example, suppose that your first use of a fixed weekly income is used to purchase cassette tapes. Eventually the marginal utility of cassette tapes will decline to the point at which you can get more marginal utility per dollar by spending your income on an alternative good. For this reason you can think of your budget allocation problem as one of balancing declining marginal utilities per dollar for all goods.

USING INDIFFERENCE CURVE ANALYSIS TO EXPLAIN CHOICES

Differences in Tastes among Consumers

The way indifference curves are shaped and the way a consumer's marginal rate of substitution of one good for another varies along indifference curves provide information on the consumer's tastes. Suppose that your brother's friend Alfred (consumer *A*) really likes to cruise and therefore has a strong preference for gasoline over cassette tapes, while another friend, Betsy (consumer *B*), strongly prefers cassette tapes to gasoline. Also suppose that both Alfred and Betsy pay the prices for these two goods that have been indicated above and have the same $15 weekly income. Indifference curve analysis shows that consumption of these goods, other things being equal, will depend on preferences. This is illustrated in Figure 3–8.

Consumer *A*'s indifference curves, shown in Figure 3–8(a), are relatively flat. In Figure 3–8(b), consumer *B*'s indifference curves are steeper than those shown in Figure 3–8(a) at *any given market basket*. This means that consumer *A* has a lower MRS_{XY} than consumer *B* for any given amount of *X* (cassette tapes) and *Y* (gallons of gasoline) consumed. This implies that, given identical market baskets, the marginal benefit of *X* to consumer *A* is lower than the marginal benefit of *X* to consumer *B*. At any given point Alfred would be willing to give up fewer gallons of gasoline to obtain an additional cassette tape than would Betsy. For example, take

FIGURE 3–8 Differences in Tastes

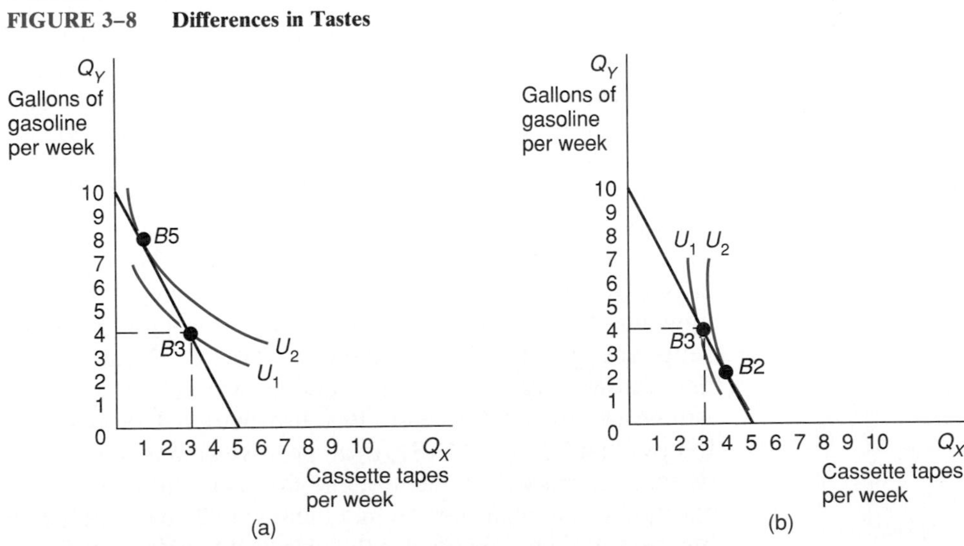

For any given market basket, the consumer whose indifference curves are shown in (a) has a lower MRS_{XY} than does the consumer whose indifference curves are shown in (b). If both consumers have the same budget and pay the same prices, the consumer in (a) is in equilibrium at a market basket containing relatively more of good *Y* (gasoline) and less of good *X* (cassette tapes) than the market basket of the consumer in (b).

market basket $B3$, which corresponds to four gallons of gasoline and three cassette tapes. At that market basket, Alfred has a lower marginal rate of substitution of cassette tapes for gasoline than does Betsy. This would hold true for the relationship between the MRS_{XY} of these two consumers at any other market basket.

It is clear that market basket $B3$ is not an equilibrium market basket for either Alfred or Betsy because the indifference curve corresponding to it intersects their budget lines. Equilibrium for Alfred occurs at basket $B5$, where weekly consumption is eight gallons of gasoline and one cassette tape. Equilibrium for Betsy occurs at basket $B2$, where two gallons of gasoline and four cassette tapes are consumed each week. Not surprisingly, the consumer with a stronger preference for cassette tapes consumes more cassette tapes in equilibrium than does the other consumer. Note, however, that in equilibrium MRS_{XY} is the *same for both consumers* because they both adjust consumption of the two goods until $MRS_{XY} = P_X/P_Y = 2$. This occurs at a market basket with relatively more gasoline for Alfred and relatively more cassette tapes for Betsy.

The Choice Not to Consume a Good: Corner Equilibrium

Persons do not always choose to purchase every good. If you examine your own buying patterns, you will observe that you do not make any purchases of some goods. You may want to take a European vacation this year but choose not to do so because what you must give up to take it exceeds what you expect to get in return. In some instances you choose not to purchase goods because you simply do not like them. Indifference curve analysis can be used to explain the conditions under which consumers choose to purchase none of a particular good. An equilibrium for the consumer in which one of the goods is not purchased is called a **corner equilibrium.** It occurs on one of the axes at the corner of the budget line. An equilibrium in which the consumer purchases both goods is called an *interior equilibrium*.

Corner equilibrium A consumer equilibrium in which one of the goods is not purchased.

Figure 3–9(a) shows the indifference curves between cassette tapes and gasoline for a consumer who strongly prefers gasoline to cassette tapes. The equilibrium is at market basket $B6$, which corresponds to ten gallons of gasoline and no cassette tapes purchased each week. At the current market prices this consumer is unwilling to give up the opportunity of consuming any gasoline for a single cassette tape. The number of gallons of gasoline he has to give up to purchase that first cassette tape at current market prices (P_X/P_Y) exceeds the number he is willing to give up (MRS_{XY}). Because marginal rates of substitution decline, it follows that $P_X/P_Y > MRS_{XY}$ at all positive amounts of X (cassette tapes). In other words, the marginal benefit of the first cassette tape purchased each week falls short of its marginal cost, so that there would be no net gain from purchasing even one cassette tape. Whenever the marginal benefit of a single unit of a good is less than its marginal cost at current prices, a corner equilibrium results.

Figure 3–9(b) shows the indifference curves for a consumer with a corner equilibrium at market basket $B1$. This consumer is in equilibrium when he is consuming five cassette tapes and no gasoline each week. At current market

FIGURE 3–9 **Corner Equilibrium**

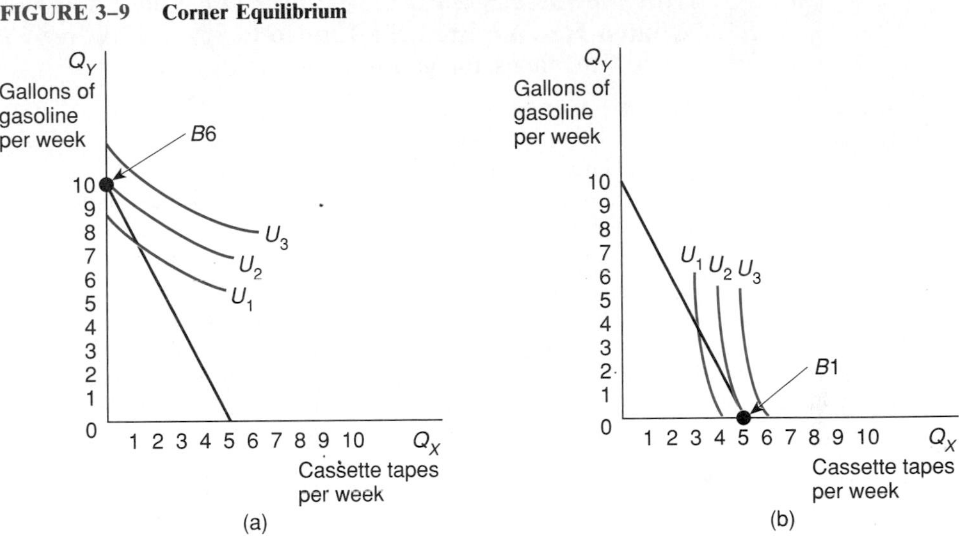

The consumer whose indifference curves are shown in (a) is in equilibrium at point *B*6. This is a corner equilibrium in which the consumer purchases no cassette tapes. In (b) a consumer with strong preferences for cassette tapes spends all of his weekly food budget on cassette tapes in a corner equilibrium at point *B*1.

prices he is unwilling to give up the opportunity of consuming even one cassette tape in exchange for gasoline. There is no net gain possible from giving up, in exchange for gasoline, any of the five cassette tapes purchased each week. If the consumer were to make such a trade of cassette tapes for gasoline, he would move to a lower indifference curve and become worse off.

Whether or not you are in equilibrium at a corner depends not only on your tastes, as represented by the shapes of your indifference curves, but also on your income and on the price of *X* relative to the price of *Y*. For example, you might be at a corner equilibrium for jewelry at your current income and at the current price of jewelry relative to the prices of other goods. However, either an increase in your income or a decrease in the relative price of jewelry could move you to an interior equilibrium for this good.

Perfect Substitutes and Perfect Complements

The shapes of indifference curves provide information on the willingness of consumers to substitute one good for another while neither gaining nor losing satisfaction. Figure 3–10(a) shows a case in which indifference curves are negatively sloped lines with a slope equal to -1. Here MRS_{XY} is equal to 1 at all market baskets. If this is the case, the consumer can be said to view the two goods, coffee and tea, as perfect substitutes. She would always be willing to exchange one cup of coffee for one cup of tea.

Modern Microeconomics in Action: The Business World

How the Increased Earning Power and Labor Force Participation of Women Has Affected the Choice to Have Children

The choice to have children is complex and involves many considerations. There is an economic dimension that can have an important effect on a couple's decision to have children. For couples engaging in family planning, choosing to have a child entails a "price" in terms of the material goods, services, and personal time per year that must be sacrificed to raise each child. Indifference curve analysis is used in the accompanying graphs to illustrate how economic considerations influence the choice to have children.

The quantity of material goods for a couple's annual use is plotted against the number of children. The intercept of the budget line on the *Y* axis measures income in terms of the maximum amount of goods that the couple could enjoy per year without children. The slope of the budget line is the annual amount of material goods the couple must give up per child. In (a) the couple is at a corner equilibrium. They choose not to have children. The couple in (b) has the same income and faces the same price of children as the couple in (a). However, they are in equilibrium at point *E*, where they choose to have one child. They give up the amount of material goods indicated on the graph per year for the child. Persons with stronger preferences for children would choose to have more of them, either by bearing more of their own or through adoption. The choice to have children clearly depends on economic variables, including family income and the value of time. The value of time is an important determinant of the "price" of children.

There has been a reduction in the size of the family in the United States and other nations since the end of World War II. Increased employment opportunities for women have affected the choice to have children. It is likely that the increased earning power of women has contributed to a significant portion of the decline in birthrates in recent years. Women must now give up more to bear and raise their children. The "price" of a child has increased.

In recent years higher family income has been negatively related to the number of children. Upper-income persons apparently have fewer children but devote more of their income to educating their offspring. They seem to have tried to improve the quality of their children while reducing the quantity.*

* See Gary S. Becker, *A Treatise on the Family* (Cambridge, Mass.: Harvard University Press, 1981).

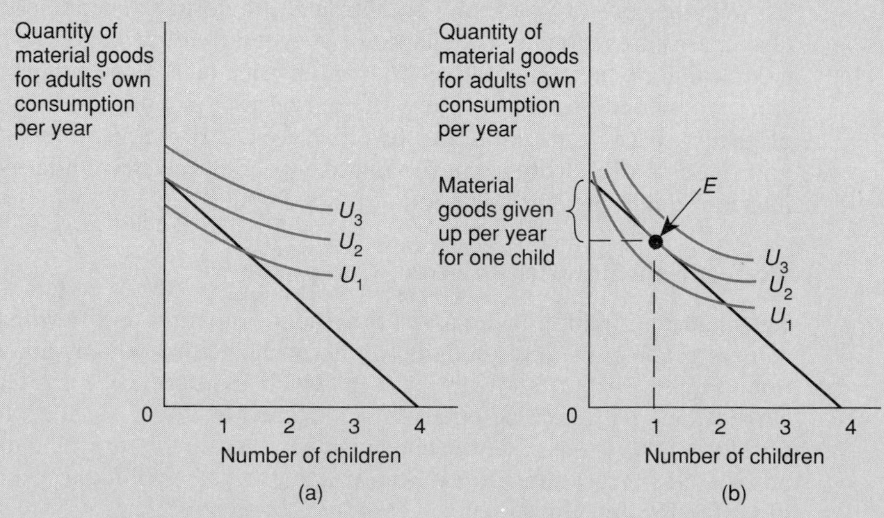

FIGURE 3–10 Perfect Substitutes and Perfect Complements

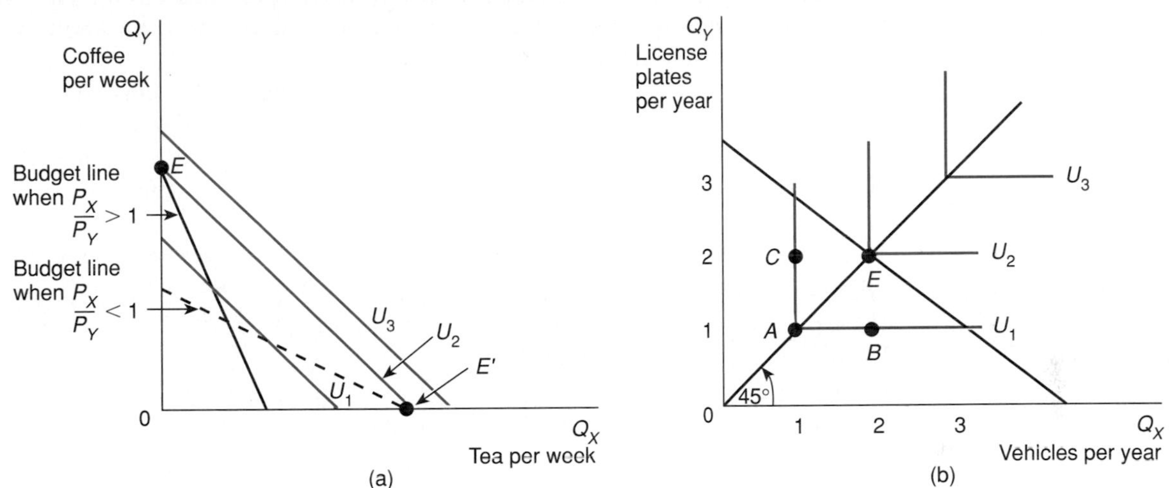

The graph in (a) shows the indifference curves for perfect substitutes. These indifference curves are straight lines of slope −1. The consumer is always at a corner equilibrium in which he buys either *X* or *Y*, depending on which is cheaper. The graph in (b) shows the indifference curves for perfect complements. In this case both goods must be increased in the same proportion before the consumer can experience a gain in utility. Equilibrium always occurs at a vertex point, such as *E*.

Drawing the budget line shows that the consumer would spend all of her budget on coffee if $P_X/P_Y > \text{MRS}_{XY}$. Equilibrium would be at point *E*. Similarly, the consumer would spend all of her budget on tea if $P_X/P_Y < \text{MRS}_{XY}$. Equilibrium would be at point *E'*. Because $\text{MRS}_{XY} = 1$ in this case, the consumer would buy coffee when $P_X/P_Y > 1$ and would buy tea when $P_X/P_Y < 1$.

Some goods are always bought in the same ratio. These goods can be considered perfect complements. The enjoyment of some goods requires the purchase of a certain amount of another item. Examples of perfect complements include automobiles and license plates. An additional license plate is useless without another vehicle to put it on. An additional car is useless unless you get an additional license plate for it so that it can be driven on public roads. Coffee and nondairy coffee creamer are examples of goods that are close to being perfect complements.

Figure 3–10(b) shows the indifference curves for perfect complements. These indifference curves are right angles. In the case of cars and license plates the two goods would have to be increased in a 1:1 ratio to provide increments in utility. The vertices of the right angles would lie along a 45-degree ray emanating from the origin. These indifference curves imply that neither an additional license plate nor an additional vehicle can make the consumer better off unless it is also accompanied by one of the other.

To see this, look at the market basket at point *A* in Figure 3–10(b). This market basket consists of one license and one vehicle. If the consumer acquires another vehicle and moves to market basket *B*, he remains on indifference curve

U_1, implying no gain or loss in utility. If he moves to market basket C by acquiring another license plate, he also remains on the same indifference curve. He can move to a higher indifference curve only when he acquires both an additional license plate and an additional vehicle.

The consumer will always be in equilibrium at a market basket corresponding to the vertex of the indifference curves. This holds true irrespective of the prices of the two goods and the consumer's income. In Figure 3–10(b) the consumer is in equilibrium at point E, where he uses two vehicles and two license plates per year.

CONCEPT REVIEW

1. The price of good X is \$5, and the price of good Y is \$2.50. Assuming no corner equilibrium, calculate the marginal rate of substitution of X for Y for a consumer in equilibrium.
2. Suppose that $MRS_{XY} < P_X/P_Y$ before a single unit of good X has been purchased. How much of good X will the consumer purchase?
3. The marginal utility of good X for a consumer is 5 utils, the marginal utility of good Y is 3 utils, and the price of each of these goods is \$1. Is the consumer in equilibrium?

EXPANDING THE MODEL: THE CHOICE BETWEEN SPENDING ON ONE GOOD AND SPENDING ON ALL OTHER GOODS

Graphic depiction of utility functions with indifference curves and maps permits analysis of the choice between only two goods. Such graphic analysis can be expanded by considering the choice the consumer makes between spending available income on *all* other goods and spending it on some particular good, X. The consumer is viewed as choosing between spending some income on good X per week (or any other period) and spending what is left over on *all* other available goods. This innovation can be used to analyze more than two goods on the axes. The budget constraint may now be written as

$$I = P_X Q_X + \Sigma P_i Q_{Yi} \qquad \textbf{(3–10)}$$

where I is the consumer's available income. The first term in the sum is the consumer's weekly expenditure on good X and the second term is the sum of the consumer's weekly expenditure on *all* other goods. The Greek letter Σ symbolizes the sum of the quantities of all the other goods consumed, Q_{Yi}, multiplied by their respective prices, P_i. The amount of any particular good other than good X that the consumer buys each week (or any other period), Q_{Yi}, cannot be determined from the model. The model can be used to observe and explain only the sum of the amounts spent on purchases of all other goods, $\Sigma P_i Q_{Yi}$.

The expanded budget constraint is plotted graphically in Figure 3–11. On the horizontal axis, the quantity of the good X consumed, Q_X, is plotted as before. However, the variable on the vertical axis is *expenditure* on all other goods, $\Sigma P_i Q_{Yi}$. The unit of measurement on the Y axis is therefore dollars.

FIGURE 3–11 **An Expanded Budget Constraint Line**

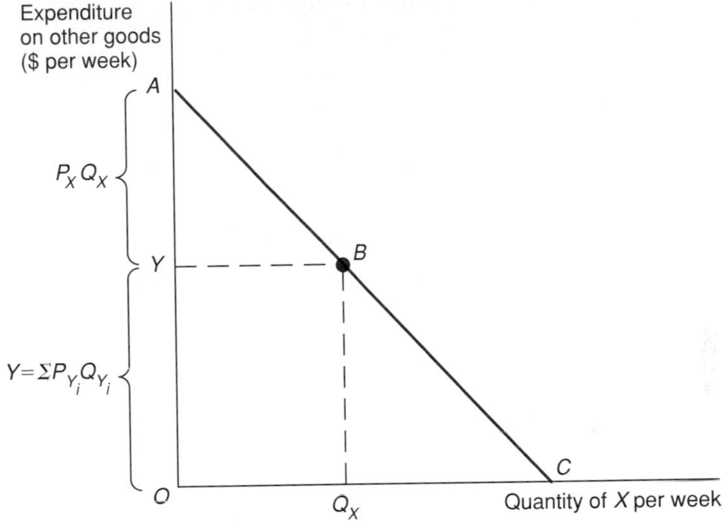

The expanded budget constraint line plots expenditure on all other goods against the quantity of good X consumed. At pont A the consumer spends all available income on other goods and consumes no X. At point C the consumer spends all available income on X and nothing on other goods. At point B the weekly amount represented by the distance OY is spent on all other goods and the weekly amount represented by the distance YA is spent on X. The sum of expenditure on X and all other goods equals weekly income: $\$OY + \$YA = \text{Income}$.

The budget constraint line looks similar to that used when only two goods are considered. Given the price of good X and the prices of all other goods, the line gives all the combinations of good X and all the other goods that the consumer can buy with his available income, OA. Suppose that the consumer has the weekly market basket represented by the point A on the budget constraint line. This means that the consumer buys no X and keeps his entire income to spend on all other goods. The choice of market basket C in Figure 3–11 means that the consumer is spending all of his income on good X and has none left over for expenditure on other goods. Finally, a market basket like that represented by point B in Figure 3–11 means that the consumer buys Q_X units of good X and spends $\$Y$ of his income on all other goods. The amount that the consumer spends on good X is equal to the difference between his total income and the amount that he spends on all other goods. This is shown as the distance YA. The sum of $\$OY$ and $\$YA$ is the consumer's income, which is represented by the distance OA.

Figure 3–12 shows the consumer's equilibrium market basket for good X and expenditure on all other goods. The consumer is in equilibrium at point E, where he buys Q_X^* units of good X each week and spends $\$Y^*$ on all other goods. If his income is I, it follows that he spends $(I - Y^*)$ dollars on good X, which is represented by the distance AY^* in Figure 3–12.

FIGURE 3–12 The Choice between Buying X and Spending Income on Other Goods

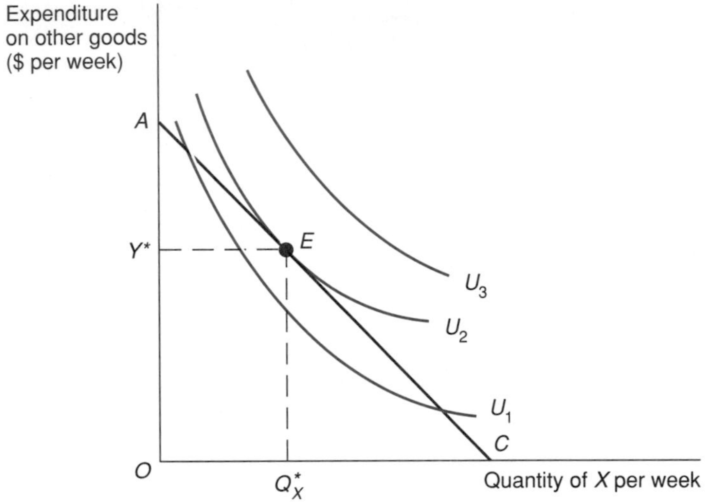

The consumer is in equilibrium at point E. In equilibrium he consumes X up to the point where its marginal benefit is just equal to its price. The weekly amount of X purchased is O_x^*. The consumer spends $\$Y^*$ on other goods.

Marginal benefit of a good A measure of the number of dollars of expenditure on all other goods a consumer will sacrifice to purchase a particular item.

The marginal rate of substitution of good X for the consumer's expenditure on all other goods (measured in dollars) is the marginal benefit of good X in terms of dollars. The **marginal benefit of a good** in dollars is a measure of the willingness to sacrifice the opportunity to spend income on other goods for one more unit of good X while remaining on a given indifference curve. It is therefore a measure of the *willingness to pay* for an extra unit of good X.

In Figure 3–12 the slope of indifference curves at any point equals the marginal benefit of X in terms of dollars multiplied by -1. The slope of the budget line represents the number of dollars of expenditure on other goods that must be sacrificed to purchase each extra unit of X. The number of dollars necessary to purchase a unit of X is nothing more than its market price! The slope of the budget line is therefore $-P_X$.

Thus the equilibrium condition may be written as follows:

$$\text{MRS}_{XY} = P_X$$

or

$$\text{MB}_X = P_X \tag{3–11}$$

where MB_X is the marginal benefit in dollars of good X. Equation 3–11 says that the consumer continues to buy good X until its marginal benefit measured in dollars is equal to its price. If X were to be consumed beyond that point, it would cost more than it is worth to the buyer and the buyer would be made worse off.

MODERN MICROECONOMICS IN ACTION: **INTERNATIONAL REPORT**

Caviar for the Masses: How Changes in the Former Soviet Union Could Add a Coveted Delicacy to the Diet of the Common Consumer

"This is a delicacy—we need to keep it elite." These are the words of Sergei Dolya, an employee of Sovrybflot, the enterprise that for years monopolized the export of fine caviar from the former Soviet Union.* Up until the demise of the Soviet Union, that's the way it was—caviar was just for the elite. As of late 1991 the very best Russian beluga caviar was selling for more than $1,000 per pound at the Petrossian Restaurant in New York City. At that price most of us were at a corner equilibrium for Russian caviar—we did not include it in our market baskets of commodities.

However, if you like fish eggs (Russian caviar is the eggs of the sturgeon, a long-snouted prehistoric fish that is caught in the Caspian Sea, whose salinity is just right for producing fish eggs with an exquisite flavor), you may soon move from a corner equilibrium to an interior one. The price of caviar is coming down as a result of institutional changes in what for 70 years was the Soviet Union.

Caviar has been deliberately kept scarce in the West to keep its price up. Its supply was controlled by the government, and the Paris-based Petrossian company had near-exclusive rights to distribute it commercially to the non-Soviet market. Of the total annual harvest of 2,000 tons or so of caviar, only 150 tons were exported. In 1991 a kilogram of caviar sold for $5 on the black market in Russia and for $500 in New York.

But now things are changing. Competition is eating away at the former state monopoly of the caviar supply. Individual Caspian fishermen, who are learning about markets and competition, are beginning to stake their own claims to caviar and to develop their own export channels. The effects are already being felt on the market. The export price of caviar fell a whopping 20 percent in 1991, and further price declines are likely. If the price of caviar falls far enough, the masses may soon be enjoying caviar sandwiches for lunch!

* See Jane Mayer, "Horrors! Fine Caviar Now Could Become as Cheap as Fish Eggs," *The Wall Street Journal*, November 18, 1991. The quote and the information in this report come from Mayer's article.

The indifference maps in the remainder of the text show as the variable on the Y axis expenditure on all goods other than good X. This approach is more descriptive of actual consumer choice. It concentrates on the consumer's conflict between purchasing a particular good and retaining income to spend on other things. When the term *marginal benefit* is used, the reference will be to the willingness to give up *dollars of income* in exchange for another unit of a good.

Diminishing Marginal Benefit of a Good

The marginal benefit of X tends to decline over a period as more X is purchased. The reason for this is the same as that given for diminishing marginal rates of substitution of any good X for any other good Y. When you give up more and more of your income to buy more X, each extra unit of X is worth less to you. Also, by buying more X, you have less income available to spend on other goods. Your remaining income is therefore more valuable to you in other uses, and you are less willing to give more of it up to purchase more of X. The convex shape of the indifference curves drawn in Figure 3–12 is therefore based on the assumption of declining marginal benefit of X.

The marginal benefit of a good is a measure of the maximum sum of money that a person is willing to give up to obtain another unit of the good. The assumption of declining marginal benefit means that, given available income, preferences, and the price of good X, the *willingness to pay* for X tends to decline as more of X is purchased. For example, your willingness to pay for a compact disc tends to decline as you purchase more compact discs with available income over a certain period. Equilibrium is attained when you have purchased enough discs so that the marginal benefit of discs falls to equal the marginal cost of a disc as measured by its market price.

Summary

1. The theory of consumer behavior assumes that persons maximize utility, given their preferences and incomes and the market prices of goods.
2. Consumer preferences are represented by the rankings given to alternatives. These rankings provide information on the consumer's likes and dislikes. Economic theory assumes that consumers can always indicate whether they prefer one market basket of goods to another or that they are indifferent between the two. At any point in time, for any two alternatives, consumers must be indifferent between the two or must prefer one to the other.
3. Consumer preferences are assumed to be transitive. Consumers are presumed to prefer more economic goods to less.
4. Indifference curves and maps are used to represent a person's preferences among available goods and services. All points along an indifference curve give the consumer the same level of utility or satisfaction. The indifference map is a way of graphing the person's utility function. The utility function is a more general mathematical expression of preferences when more than two variables are considered.
5. Indifference curves for economic goods slope downward. Indifference curves can never intersect and usually exhibit diminishing marginal rates of substitution of good X for good Y. Diminishing marginal rates of substitution means that as good Y is given up for good X, there is a decline in the amount of good Y a consumer would give up to get one more unit of good X while being made neither better nor worse off by the exchange. Diminishing marginal rates of substitution give indifference curves their convex shapes.
6. A consumer's budget constraint represents the amount of income he or she has available to spend per period. Expenditures must equal income. How far a consumer's income will go toward buying goods and services depends on prices.
7. A consumer's equilibrium market basket of goods X and Y is the basket that achieves maximum utility, given the consumer's income and given the prices of the goods and services consumed. This occurs where the marginal rate of substitution of X for Y is equal to the ratio of the price of X to the price of Y.
8. The theory of consumer behavior requires only that consumers be able to rank alternatives. This implies that utility is ordinally but not cardinally measurable. If cardinal measurement of utility were possible, a specific number could be applied to the utility of each market basket that the consumer acquires. This would allow measurement of the intensity of the consumer's preferences and calculation of the marginal utility of additional amounts of goods.
9. Indifference curve analysis is useful in explaining consumer choices between purchasing a

given good and retaining available income to spend on all other goods. A consumer is in equilibrium when consumption of a good is adjusted to a point at which its marginal benefit measured in dollars is equal to its price.

10. The marginal benefit of a good measured in dollars is its marginal rate of substitution for expenditure on other goods. It measures the amount of income a consumer is willing to sacrifice for an extra unit of a particular good.

Important Concepts

preferences
transitivity
utility
ordinally measurable
cardinally measurable
utility function
market basket
indifference curve
indifference map
marginal rate of substitution
diminishing marginal rates of substitution
marginal utility
budget constraint
budget line
consumer equilibrium
equimarginal principle
corner equilibrium
marginal benefit of a good

Questions for Review

1. Examine your own preferences between any two goods you consume. Construct your own indifference curves for various market baskets of these goods by asking yourself whether you prefer one basket to the other or are indifferent between the two.
2. What assumptions do economists make about consumer preferences? Is it necessary to assume that consumers know *how much* better off they are when they acquire additional economic goods?
3. What is meant by transitivity? Explain why indifference curves for economic goods could intersect if persons did not have transitive preferences.
4. Explain why indifference curves for economic goods must be negatively sloped. What is the implication of positively sloped indifference curves?
5. Suppose that a consumer has two goods to choose from, food and gasoline. Government rationing forces the consumer to purchase less gasoline then he or she otherwise would, reducing the consumer's maximum possible utility. Illustrate in an indifference curve diagram how a reduction in the price of food could increase the consumer's maximum possible utility to the level achievable without rationing.
6. "If positive marginal utility is derived from consuming a good, some of that good will always be purchased by a utility-maximizing consumer." True or false? Explain.
7. If a consumer's indifference curves are straight, downward-sloping lines with the same slope as the consumer's budget line, does a single, unique utility-maximizing combination of goods exist? Illustrate your answer with a diagram.
8. Your brother spends all of his $50 weekly allowance on renting videocassettes and buying hamburger dinners. The price of a cassette rental is $2, and the price of a hamburger dinner is $4. Draw your brother's budget line, and calculate the opportunity cost of a cassette rental.
9. Draw a budget constraint line showing opportunities to purchase a particular good, X, and to spend income on all other goods. Show the consumer equilibrium point, the amount of good X purchased, expenditure on good X, and expenditure on all other goods.
10. John is currently at a corner equilibrium in his choice to consume Remy Martin XO cognac, which is currently priced at $125 a bottle. Draw John's indifference curves between cognac and expenditure on all other goods with cognac consumed per year plotted on the X axis and expenditure per year on all other goods plotted

on the Y axis. Draw John's budget line, and show his current equilibrium. What can you say about the relationship between the marginal benefit of the cognac to John and its current market price? What can move John from a corner equilibrium to an interior equilibrium?

PROBLEMS

1. The price of chicken is \$1 per pound, and the price of beef is \$3 per pound. For any given market basket the marginal rate of substitution of chicken for beef of consumer A exceeds that of consumer B. Assuming that neither of the two consumers is in equilibrium at a corner, draw the indifference curves for both consumer A and consumer B. Assume that both consumers have a \$30 budget spent entirely on chicken and beef. Plot chicken purchased per week on the X axis and beef purchased per week on the Y axis.

   Prove that the marginal rate of substitution of chicken for beef will be identical for both consumers in equilibrium. Given the assumption that A's marginal rate of substitution of chicken for beef exceeds B's for any given market basket, does this imply a contradiction?

2. Suppose your weekly allowance is \$40 and that you spend all of it on ice cream and rock concerts. Assuming that the price of ice cream is \$4 per half gallon and the price of each rock concert ticket is \$10, draw your budget constraint line.

   How many rock concerts could you attend if you spent your money on nothing else? How much ice cream can you buy for each rock concert you forgo? Show how a cut in your allowance to \$20 per week will affect the amounts of these goods you can purchase. Show the effect of an increase to \$20 in the price of rock concerts.

   Suppose you received a quantity discount on ice cream in which its price would vary with the amount purchased. You would pay a price of \$4 per half gallon if you purchased one-half gallon per week. If you purchased more than one-half gallon per week, the price would be \$2 per half gallon. Draw your budget line given these circumstances. Show how such a budget line for economic goods could result in *more* than one most preferred outcome.

3. Suppose that the marginal rate of substitution of X for Y increased as the good X was substituted for the good Y. Show that in this case a tangency between the consumer's budget line and an indifference curve would indicate the equilibrium market basket that the consumer *least preferred*. Show that the most preferred market basket occurs at a corner equilibrium.

4. Suppose the marginal utility per dollar of a shirt for you is 5 and the marginal utility per dollar of a pair of shoes is 10. Have you attained a point of equilibrium in your consumption of these two goods? Explain your answer.

   Now draw the indifference curves for these two goods. Show why the data on marginal utility and price correspond to an intersection of your budget line and an indifference curve. How must you adjust your consumption of these two goods to attain equilibrium?

5. Suppose that a consumer may choose between two goods, X and Y, whose prices are \$5 and \$10, respectively. Diagram a case in which the consumer is indifferent between the following:
   a. Receiving 20 more units of good X.
   b. Receiving a \$50 cash grant that may be spent on good X, good Y, or a combination of the two.

   Explain why the consumer would not spend the entire grant on good X if he or she received it.

6. Answer the following questions regarding the accompanying indifference curve diagram:
   a. If the consumer's income is \$300, what is the price of good X? Of good Y?
   b. What is the marginal rate of substitution at point A?
   c. Could the marginal rate of substitution be 5 at point B?
   d. If the consumer's income is held constant, how do the prices of goods X and Y have to change to make point B the consumer's equilibrium?

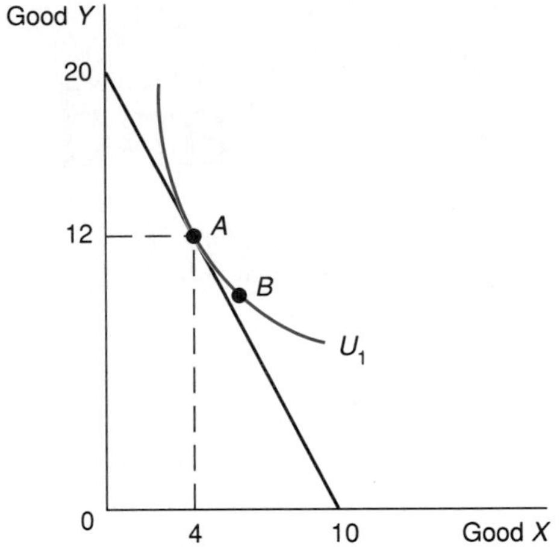

7. Draw a graph of a typical family's indifference curves between the quantity of housing (measured by number of rooms of standard size rented or owned during the year), plotted on the X axis, and expenditure on all other goods, plotted on the Y axis. Suppose that the current monthly rental rate of housing for the typical family is $100 per room per month and that the family is currently in equilibrium renting five rooms per month. If the family's current monthly income after taxes is $1,500 per month, show its current equilibrium on the graph along with the amount that it spends on housing. What is the marginal benefit of housing to this family? Suppose that this year housing prices rise by an amount equal to the general rate of inflation for all goods, which is 5 percent. If the family's money income also increases by 5 percent, how will its equilibrium allocation of income between housing and expenditure on all other goods be affected? The average American family of the 1990s is spending a higher percentage of its income on housing than did the family of the 1970s. What can explain the increase in the percentage of income allocated to housing?

4

Prices, Incomes, and Consumer Demand

In the United States in the late 1980s an increase in the supply of personal computers caused their prices to plummet. As a result, more and more students and people who had thought they would never own a computer chose to buy one.

The U.S. recession of 1991 caused declines in income for many families. As their incomes fell, these families cut back on their purchases of clothing and new automobiles. Lower incomes also decreased the demand for new homes, so housing construction fell.

When the price of a good changes, the effect is often felt not only in the market for that good but in the market for complements and substitutes as well. For example, in 1990, when the price of U.S. air travel increased substantially, the demand for intercity travel by train soared and Amtrak passengers had to book tickets well in advance to assure themselves of seats.

As these examples demonstrate, consumer choices are sensitive to changes in incomes and prices. When prices or our incomes change, so do the choices we make. When our incomes fall, we adjust our choices to the realities of tighter budget constraints. When our incomes rise, we consume more and better products.

We can now use the theory of consumer choice we developed in the previous chapter to examine consumer reactions to changes in prices and incomes. In doing this, we will derive an individual consumer's demand curve for an item and show how that demand curve is affected by preferences, income, and the prices of related items. We will also show how indifference curve analysis can be used to help us understand a variety of business and policy issues relating to changes in prices and incomes. Among these issues are the impact of taxes and subsidies on choices.

Income Changes and Consumer Choices

How often do you eat out at restaurants? How many videotapes do you rent per week? How many rock concerts do you attend each semester? Would you consume more or less of these items over any given period if your income were to increase? The incomes of many U.S. families fell in the early 1990s as a recession and a slowdown in economic growth decreased the demand for the services of many workers. Because of the fall in their incomes, many families cut back on dining out and postponed purchases of such items as vacations, new cars, appliances, and furniture. For example, auto production cutbacks in 1991 caused many Michigan families to suffer income reductions and in the New England states, a severe decline in employment and income tightened the budget constraints of thousands of families. When incomes fall, however, the demand for some items goes up. The demand for used cars and used furniture often increases in periods of declining incomes, as does the demand for meals at modestly priced fast-food restaurants such as McDonald's. Let's use our theory of consumer choice to analyze how changes in income affect what people buy and how they allocate their budgets.

Income-Consumption Curves

Income-consumption curve A graph connecting equilibrium points on a consumer's indifference map as income changes; shows how consumption of goods varies as income changes.

A consumer's choice to consume good *X* depends in part on the income available to him or her over a certain period. Changes in income are likely to result in changes in the quantities of good *X* purchased. An **income-consumption curve** is one that connects all of the equilibrium points on a consumer's indifference map as income changes. Such a curve shows how the market baskets consisting of good *X* and expenditure on other goods change as income changes.

FIGURE 4–1 An Income-Consumption Curve

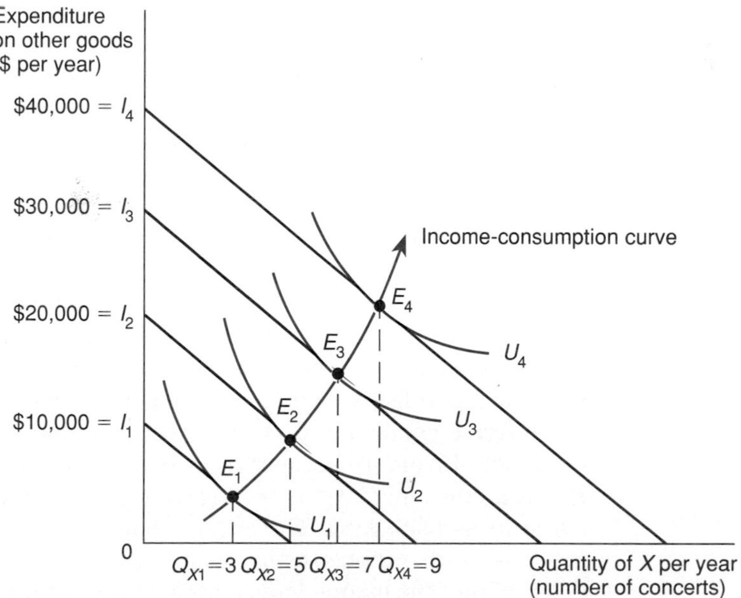

An income-consumption curve connects the equilibrium points and shows how the consumption of good *X* changes as the consumer's income increases. The curve shown is for a normal good. As income increases, the consumption of good *X* per year increases.

An income-consumption curve for good X is drawn in Figure 4–1. Initially, the consumer is in equilibrium at the market basket corresponding to point E_1, at which Q_{X1} units of good X are consumed per year. For example, suppose that good X is the number of rock concerts you attend per year. If your annual income were $\$I_1 = \$10,000$ per year, you would be in equilibrium at point E_1, where you choose to buy tickets for three rock concerts per year. Because we are measuring expenditure on other goods on the vertical axis, we can easily read off your income from the graph (see Chapter 3). The intersection of the budget line with the vertical axis shows your annual income as measured by the number of dollars you would be able to spend on all other goods if you did not buy any of good X.

Suppose you get a new job and your annual income doubles from $I_1 = \$10,000$ per year to $I_2 = \$20,000$ per year. An increase in income from I_1 to I_2 shifts the budget line out parallel to itself. An increase in income, other things being equal, allows the purchase of some market baskets of goods that were previously unaffordable. This results in a new equilibrium at point E_2. In Figure 4–1 in response to the increase in income from I_1 to I_2 the consumer increases the annual consumption of good X to Q_{X2}, or five rock concerts per year.

Figure 4–1 also shows other income levels and the equilibrium corresponding to each of these levels. The income-consumption curve is obtained by connecting all of the equilibrium points. It shows how the quantity of good X consumed per year changes as the consumer's annual income *and nothing else* changes.

Normal versus Inferior Goods

Normal goods Goods that a consumer purchases more of as income increases.

Normal goods are those that a person consumes more of when the person's income increases. The income-consumption curve drawn in Figure 4–1 indicates that X, rock concerts, is a normal good. As your income increases, you buy more tickets to rock concerts. If X is a normal good, its income-consumption curve will be positively sloped. Every time the consumer receives an increase in income, he will buy more of this normal good. You might want to reflect on which goods are normal goods for you. Most people tend to buy more or better automobiles and drive more for pleasure per year as their income increases. If you are like most people, you probably tend to buy more clothing and more home entertainment items such as televisions, stereo equipment, and electronic recording devices per year as your income increases. Photographic equipment, jewelry, and vacation travel are also likely to be normal goods for most people.

Inferior goods Goods that a consumer purchases less of as income increases.

Inferior goods are those whose consumption tends to decrease as income increases. Figure 4–2 draws an income-consumption curve for an inferior good. When a consumer begins to regard a good as inferior, its income-consumption curve turns backward. This means that after a certain level of income has been reached, further increases in income result in less rather than more consumption of the good. The income-consumption curve therefore becomes negatively sloped after income reaches this level. In Figure 4–2 increases in income above level I_2 result in decreases in the consumption of good X. For example, suppose that travel by bus is an inferior good for you. This means that after your income has risen above a certain level, you will travel less by bus. Your higher income would allow you to travel more often within a city by car instead of by bus and to afford

FIGURE 4–2 An Income-Consumption Curve for an Inferior Good

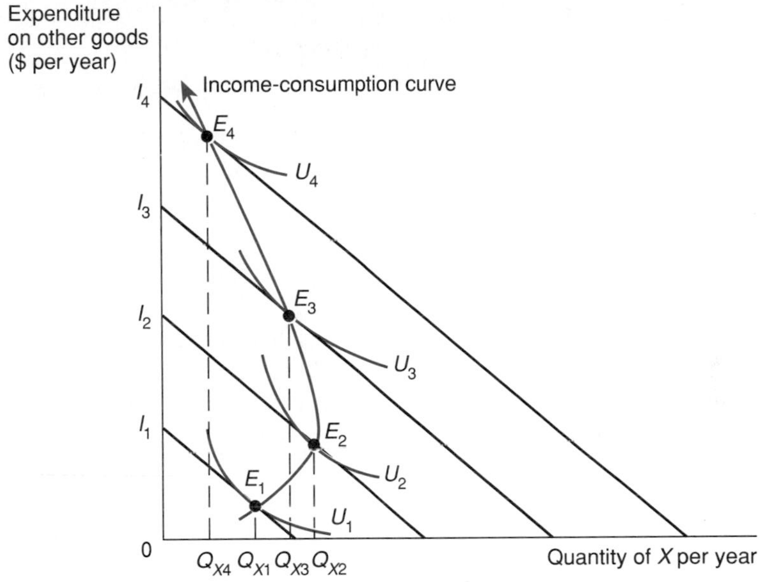

When a good is regarded as inferior, its income-consumption curve is negatively sloped. In the graph increases in income result in decreased consumption of X when income is greater than I_2.

gas, parking, and tolls. It would also allow you to travel between cities more often by air or in your own car instead of by bus. If a consumer's income increases enough, he will eventually drop an inferior good from his equilibrium market basket. Thus, if your income increases enough, you may not do any traveling by bus.

Examples of goods that consumers are likely to regard as inferior are poor-quality cuts of meat such as tripe and secondhand items such as used cars, clothing, or furniture. As income increases, many consumers substitute steak for hamburger in their equilibrium market baskets.

Keep in mind that whether a good is normal or inferior depends on consumer tastes. In the South many rich people still eat chitlins. Tripa alla Florentina (tripe, Florentine style) is a coveted dish in Florence, Italy, found only in the best restaurants. Some people choose to drive their own cars less and to take advantage of taxis for short trips and air travel for long trips when their income rises. For these people, travel in their own cars is an inferior good.

Finally, some goods are neither inferior nor normal for the consumer. These are goods whose quantity consumed remains constant at all levels of income. This is likely to be true for goods that constitute relatively small portions of the consumer's budget or are regarded as necessities, for example, such goods as salt, toilet paper, and toothpaste. The income-consumption curve for goods of this kind is a vertical line, as illustrated in Figure 4–3.

FIGURE 4–3 A Vertical Income-Consumption Curve

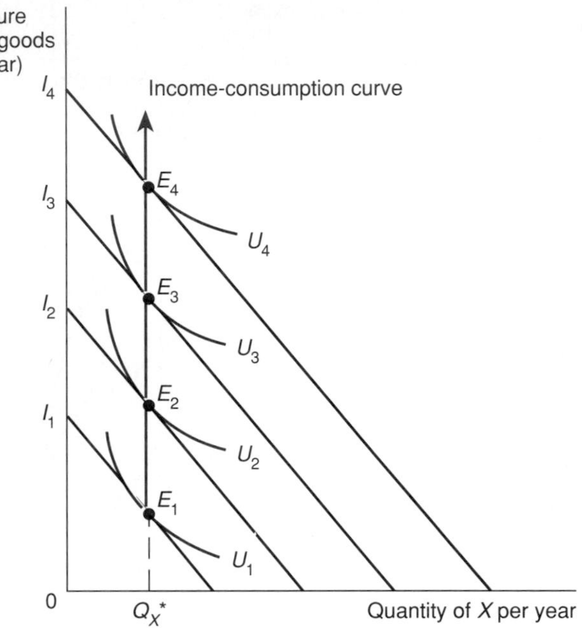

The consumption of the good X is independent of income. The consumer continues to consume Q_x^* units as income increases above its initial level, I_1.

Engel Curves

Engel curve A graph showing the relationship between money income and the quantity of a good purchased.

An **Engel curve** shows the relationship between a person's money income and the quantity of X purchased by plotting money income over a period on the vertical axis and the quantity of X purchased over that period on the horizontal axis. Engel curves can be drawn for a person with particular preferences, given the price of X and the prices of all other goods. These curves are similar to demand curves in that they show the relationship between an important determinant of demand and the quantity of a good purchased. A demand curve gives the relationship between price and quantity demanded, given income, preferences, and the prices of all other goods and any other demand determinants. An Engel curve shows the relationship between *income* and quantity purchased, *given all of the other influences on demand.* Engel curves are named after Ernst Engel (1821–96), who studied how the consumption of goods and services varied with family income in the 19th century.

To derive an Engel curve from an income-consumption curve for a good, simply plot income on the vertical axis and on the horizontal axis plot the equilibrium quantity of the good purchased that corresponds to that income. For example, the income-consumption curve in Figure 4–1 indicates that when the person

FIGURE 4–4 Engel Curves

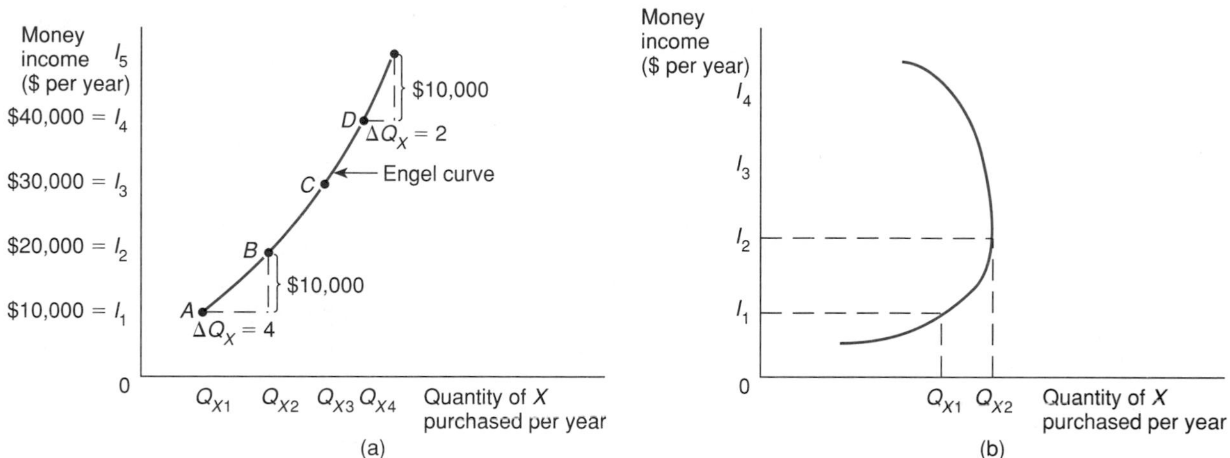

An Engel curve shows how the quantity of a good purchased is related to a consumer's money income. (a) shows the Engel curve for a normal good, (b) shows the Engel curve for an inferior good.

whose indifference curves are drawn has an annual income of $\$I_1$, the equilibrium quantity of X purchased, E_1, is Q_{X1} units per year. This is plotted as point A in Figure 4–4(a). Similarly, point B in Figure 4–4(a) corresponds to point E_2 in Figure 4–1, for which income is $\$I_2$ per year and the quantity of X consumed is Q_{X2}. Points C and D on the Engel curve correspond to points E_3 and E_4, respectively, on the income-consumption curve. The Engel curve is traced out by connecting all of the coordinates corresponding to income and the associated equilibrium quantity of yearly purchases of X. The Engel curve for a normal good is upward sloping because increases in income always increase the quantities of such goods purchased. The Engel curve for an inferior good bends backward after reaching some point. Figure 4–4(b) shows the Engel curve corresponding to the income-consumption curve drawn in Figure 4–2. The Engel curve is upward sloping up to the point at which income increases to I_2. After income rises above that level, the curve bends backwards and becomes negatively sloped, which implies that further increases in income will reduce the demand for the given item. The curve illustrated in Figure 4–4(b) could be the Engel curve for Hardy's hamburger dinners per year for someone who regards hamburger dinners as an inferior good.

The slope of an Engel curve is

$$\Delta I/\Delta Q_X = \text{Change in income/Change in } Q_X \text{ purchased} \qquad (4\text{–}1)$$

The slope of the Engel curve drawn in Figure 4–4(a) increases as income per year goes up. For example, suppose that good X is the number of clothing outfits purchased per year. The curve shows that for a person whose income is only

\$10,000 per year, an *extra* \$10,000 in annual income results in the purchase of four more outfits per year. However, if the person's income is \$40,000 per year, an extra \$10,000 in income results in the purchase of only two extra outfits per year. The shape of an Engel curve conveys important information about the responsiveness of a consumer's purchases of a good to changes in income. The Engel curve drawn in Figure 4–4(a) shows that purchases of clothing outfits become *less* responsive to changes in income as income increases.

For a good whose consumption is independent of the level of the buyer's income, the Engel curve is a vertical line. Figure 4–5(a) illustrates the Engel curve for such a good. For example, if you buy half a gallon of orange juice per week no matter how much your income increases, the Engel curve for your weekly purchases of orange juice will be a vertical line.

Figure 4–5(b) shows an Engel curve whose slope decreases as income increases. Such an Engel curve indicates that the consumer's purchases of good X become *more* responsive to changes in income as income increases. For example, if good X were compact discs purchased per year and the consumer's annual income were only \$10,000, an extra \$1,000 of income might result in the purchase of 10 extra compact discs per year. However, if the consumer's annual income were \$40,000, an extra \$1,000 of income might result in the purchase of 30 extra compact discs per year. The rate of increase in the purchase of this good increases as income increases.

The way consumers respond to increases in income is important in analyzing changes in the market conditions for a product. For example, a sharp decrease in income is likely to result in an even sharper decrease in furniture purchases if many consumers have Engel curves for furniture like the one in Figure 4–4(a). By

FIGURE 4–5 Engel Curves Showing the Responsiveness of Purchases to Changes in Income

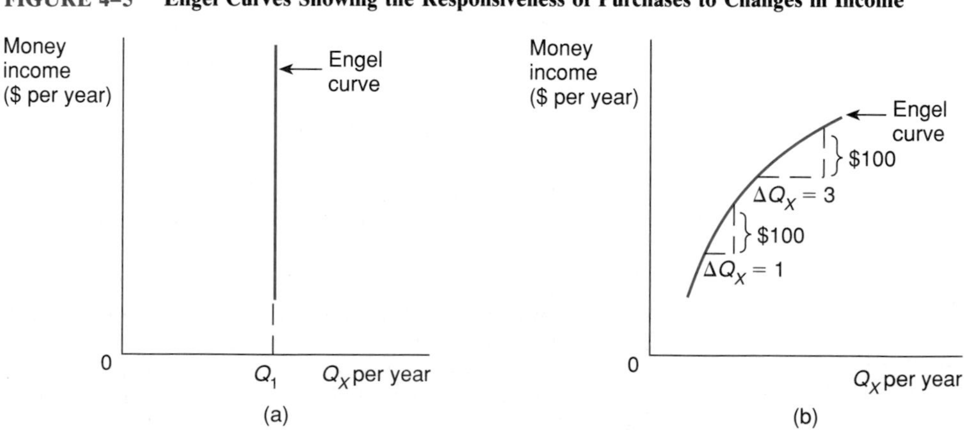

Changes in income in (a) do not result in changes in the quantity of X purchased. The Engel curve for the good in (b) shows that the extra quantity of X purchased increases for each \$100 increase in income.

the same token, a sharp increase in income is likely to result in only a modest increase in food purchases because most consumers regard their food purchases as necessary.

Engel's research on the relationship between income and purchases of goods in the 19th century suggested certain patterns that have become known as "Engel's Laws." Engel's research suggested that, given the prices of all goods, the proportion of a family's income spent on food tends to decline as family income rises. This suggested that household purchases of food are very unresponsive to changes in family income, implying a nearly vertical Engel curve for food. Engel's research also suggested that the consumption of education, legal, health, and leisure services tends to increase more rapidly than income as income increases. In recent years the growth of the services sector of the economy as personal income has grown suggests that many services have an Engel curve like the one shown in Figure 4–5(b).

Price-Consumption Curves and the Derivation of Individual Consumer Demand Curves

As was shown in Chapter 3, a reduction in the price of good X will result in a swiveling outward of the budget line to a higher intercept on the X axis. Assuming no change in money income or in the prices of other goods, there will be no change in the intercept of the budget line on the Y axis. Similarly, an increase in the price of X will result in a swiveling inward of the budget line to a lower intercept on the X axis.

Indifference curve analysis can now be used to illustrate how the law of demand is consistent with the model of consumer behavior. To accomplish this, vary the price of some good, X, while holding fixed the consumer's income and the prices of all other goods. Trace out this consumer's equilibrium positions, given his preferences, while observing the changes in the quantities of good X in his market basket as he reacts to the price changes.

Each reduction in the price of X swivels the budget line outward to a new intercept of the X axis. As the budget line becomes flatter, the consumer reacts by consuming more X so as to reduce its marginal benefit to equal the new lower price. The curve connecting all the points of consumer equilibrium as prices change is called a **price-consumption curve**. This is shown in Figure 4–6(a). The consumer's income is fixed at I as indicated by the intercept of the various budget lines and the vertical axis. As the price of X falls, the consumer moves to new equilibrium points on the graph. The consumer is initially in equilibrium at point E_1. Figure 4–6(a) shows that as the price of X falls, he moves to point E_2. Two other price declines are shown, and the consumer moves to point E_3 and then to E_4 in response to these price declines. Connecting these points gives the price-consumption curve.

Price-consumption curve A graph connecting points of consumer equilibrium as prices change; shows how the consumption of a good changes as its price changes.

On the graph the points on the X axis showing the amounts of X the consumer could buy if he were to spend all of his income on that good are indicated by $F1$, $F2$, $F3$, and $F4$. These points can be used to calculate the price of X. Plotting these prices against the corresponding amounts of X consumed allows derivation of the demand curve.

FIGURE 4–6 **Price-Consumption Curve and Derivation of the Law of Demand**

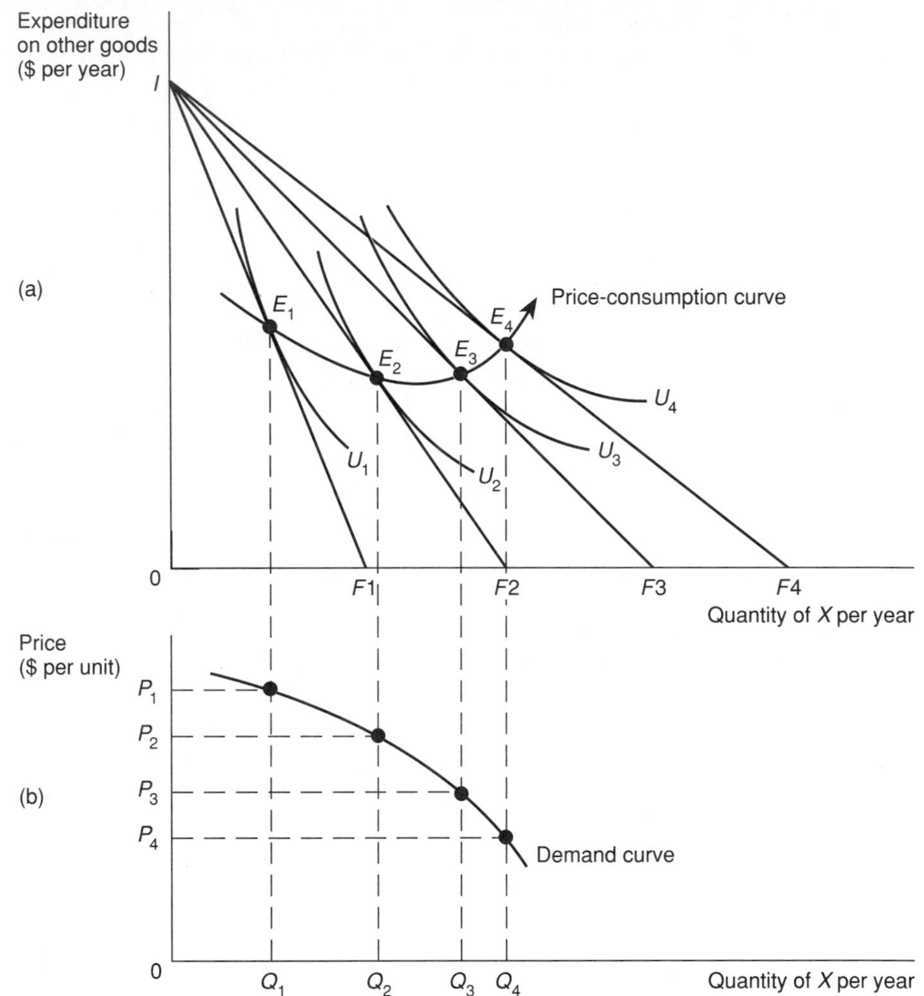

The price of good X at any point may be calculated as I/F, where F is the amount of X that could be bought if the consumer spent all of his income on it. Plotting this price on (b) against Q_X consumed per year gives the consumer's yearly demand curve for X.

Begin with the budget line $F1$ in Figure 4.6(a). The price of good X must be $I/F1$, the consumer's income divided by the amount of X he could buy if he were to spend all of his income on X. This follows because his expenditure on all other goods would then be zero. Therefore, the budget constraint would be

$$I = P_1F1 + 0 \tag{4–2}$$

Therefore,

$$P_1 = I/F1 \tag{4–3}$$

At the price $I/F1$ the consumer is in equilibrium at point E_1, at which he consumes Q_1 units of good X. In Figure 4–6(b), Q_1 has been brought down directly to the quantity axis, where price is plotted against quantity. When price equals P_1, the quantity demanded by the consumer is Q_1.

As the price of good X falls, the budget line moves outward along the X axis. The intercept of the X axis increases accordingly. When the intercept is $F2$, the price of X equals $I/F2$, or P_2. P_2 must be less than P_1 because $F2$ is greater than $F1$. In this case the new consumer equilibrium is at point E_2 and the amount of X consumed increases to Q_2. The coordinates P_2, Q_2 are plotted below the indifference curves as another point on the demand curve. Similarly, as the price of X falls to P_3 and to P_4, the quantity of X consumed per year increases further. By pairing the price with quantity demanded by the consumer at that price, Figure 4–6(b) traces out the demand curve. This curve gives the quantity that the consumer demands at various prices. This is the consumer's demanded curve for good X.

The demand curve and the price-consumption curve are merely two different ways of showing how, other things being equal, the quantity of a good demanded varies inversely with its price.

CONCEPT REVIEW

1. What does a vertical income-consumption line imply about the way the consumption of a good will vary with changes in consumer income?
2. What is the distinction between normal and inferior goods? Draw an Engel curve for a good that a consumer regards as inferior after his or her income has reached a certain level per week.
3. Explain the relationship between an individual consumer's price-consumption curve for a good and his or her demand curve for a good.

INCOME AND SUBSTITUTION EFFECTS OF PRICE CHANGES

Will demand curves always slope downward? The theory of consumer behavior can be used to answer this question. When the price of a good changes, consumers' opportunities to purchase market baskets of goods also change. Consumers find the good whose price has changed either more or less attractive, depending on whether its price has risen or fallen. However, a price change also alters consumers' opportunities to purchase all *other* goods by affecting their real income.

When the price of a good falls, a consumer's real income, expressed as the maximum amount of the good that could be purchased with his money income, goes up. Conversely, a consumer's real income goes down when the price of a good increases. The consumer's reaction to a change in the price of a good depends *both* on the change in real income caused by the change *and* on the change in the relative price of the good.

The change in real income depends on the extent of the price change and on the portion of the consumer's income spent on the good. For example, if the price of salt declines 20 percent and you spend only a tiny fraction of your money income on salt, the increase in real income caused by that price change will be negligible. If, however, housing rents decline 20 percent and you spend one third of your money income on housing rents, you will experience a generous increase in your real income. Conversely, an increase in housing rents would cause a substantial decrease in the purchasing power of your money income. The change in real income resulting from a price change affects the incentive to purchase all goods, not just the good whose price changes.

Income effect The change in the consumption of a good that results from the change in real income caused by a change in the price of the good.

Substitution effect The change in the consumption of a good that results from the change in its price relative to the prices of other goods.

Economists divide the change in the quantity of a good purchased into two parts that results from a change in its price. The **income effect** is the change in the consumption of the good that results only from the variation in real income caused by the price change. The **substitution effect** is the change in the consumption of the good that results only from the change in its price relative to the prices of other goods. The substitution effect is the change in the quantity of the good purchased (per period) that would be observed if the consumer's real income were adjusted so that he was *neither better nor worse off* because of the change in the price of the good.

Income and substitution effects can rarely be observed independently of each other. When prices change, the resulting consumer responses reflect the impact of *both* substitution and income effects. However, it is important to understand that the well-being of consumers depends on both types of effects. Thus, in evaluating economic policies, for example, estimates of consumer sensitivity to changes in income and changes in relative prices are used to predict changes in consumer choices.

Income and Substitution Effects of a Price Decrease

Indifference curve analysis can be used to isolate the separate income and substitution effects of price changes. Suppose, for example, that at the current price of a round-trip airline ticket a college student has been taking four plane trips each year to visit his parents, who live in Toledo. The student then receives some good news (assuming that he likes his parents enough to visit them more often). The price of airline tickets has been reduced significantly. This price change shifts the budget line outward from *IA* to *IB* in Figure 4–7. The student would now move to a new equilibrium, from point E_1 to E_2, where he increases his consumption of plane trips to Toledo to eight per year. This movement would be the result of the combined income and substitution effects of the price reduction. The increase in the quantity of trips demanded from four to eight is the movement along a demand curve that would actually be observed for this consumer after the price decline.

To see how the income effect and the substitution effect might actually be observed separately, suppose that along with the good news of the price reduction comes some bad news: The lower fare is available from only one airline, and to take advantage of the lower fare, the student must join a special club whose annual dues are $200. Assume that this extra fee is just high enough to make him indifferent between flying that airline at the reduced fare and continuing to use other airlines at the regular fare but without having to pay a membership fee. For the sake of argument, let us say he joins the club.

FIGURE 4–7 Income and Substitution Effects of a Price Decrease for a Normal Good

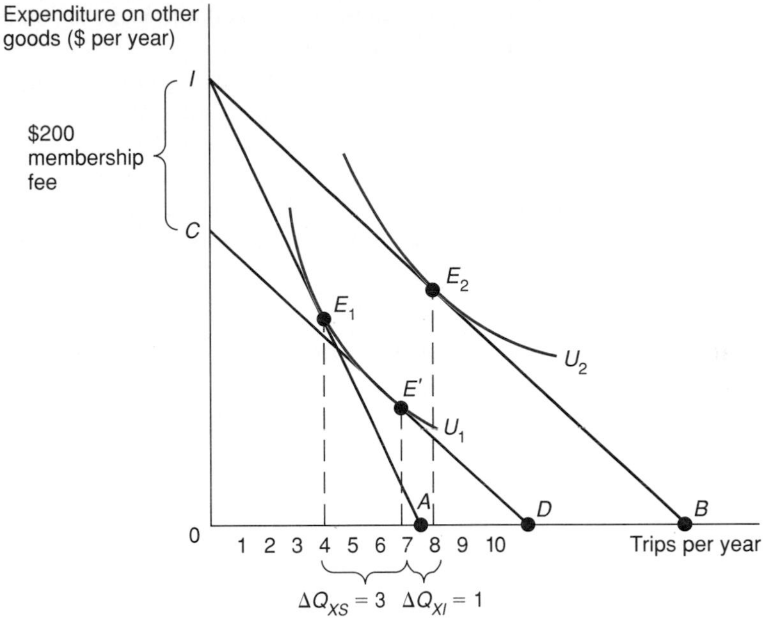

A price decrease shifts the budget line from *IA* to *IB*. Charging a fee of *IC* = \$200 for the privilege of consuming at the lower price shifts the budget line to *CD*. The substitution effect is three trips. If the fee were refunded, the income effect would be observed. In this case it is one additional trip per year.

It is easy to show that even though the student will be just as well off either by paying the regular fare or by joining the club and paying the reduced fare, he will consume more trips to Toledo per year if he joins the club. The increase in the number of trips to Toledo, after paying the fee to join the club, is the substitution effect of the decrease in the price of air travel. *The substitution effect represents the consumer's increased air travel in response to the lower relative price of air travel independent of the effect of the increase in the consumer's real income caused by the reduction in the price of air travel.* The \$200 fee removes the impact of the increased real income on the consumer's well-being.

The \$200 fee is represented by a reduction in income of the amount *IC* in Figure 4–7. Once this fee has been paid, the student is no better off than he was before the reduction in the airfare. Payment of the fee therefore moves him to the original indifference curve, U_1. However, because the slope of the budget line *CD* reflects the airfare discount, the student is now in equilibrium at point E', where seven instead of four round-trip tickets to Toledo are purchased each year. Joining the club induces the student to travel more because membership makes lower price of air travel possible. The increase in the number of his annual trips to Toledo, $\Delta Q_{XS} = 3$, is the substitution effect of the price cut. It is the increase that results only from the change in the relative price of good *X*. The \$200 fee has eliminated the impact on the student's well-being of the change in real income that would have otherwise resulted from the price decline. This confines the student to the original indifference curve and allows isolation of his reaction to the decline in the relative price of air travel.

Now suppose that the student's parents, eager to see him more often, reimburse him for the $200 membership fee after his first visit home. The income effect is the extra purchase of round trips to Toledo, $\Delta Q_{XI} = 1$, that the student chooses after receiving this increase in income from his parents. This change in his consumption of air travel results only from the impact of the increase in real income caused by the price decline. It is represented by the movement from E' to E_2 in Figure 4–7.

Income and Substitution Effects in General and the Demand Curve for Normal Goods

In general, when the price of any good changes, the change in the quantity of X, ΔQ_X, that the consumer demands can be thought of as the *sum* of the resulting income and substitution effects:

$$\Delta Q_X = \Delta Q_{XS} + \Delta Q_{XI} \tag{4–4}$$

Both the income effect and the substitution effect of a price change influence the choices made by a consumer. In reality, these two effects cannot be easily observed separately because price changes are rarely accompanied by fees that allow isolation of the substitution effect from the income effect. It is, however, useful to understand that separate and distinct forces influence the consumer's reaction to a price change.[1]

The substitution effect of a price decline always increases the consumption of the good whose price declines. This is easy to demonstrate in Figure 4–7. When the income effect is removed by payment of the fee, the consumer must, by definition, remain on U_1, the indifference curve on which he started out. However, the new budget constraint line (CD) is flatter than the initial budget constraint line (IA) because P_X is lower along that line. It *must* follow that tangency E' corresponds to a higher value of X than the initial tangency, E_1. This is because declining marginal rates of substitution of air travel for expenditure on other goods along a given indifference curve (the marginal benefit of air travel to the student) imply that indifference curves become flatter only as more air travel is purchased.

---

[1] The income and substitution effects of a price change can be separated using the following equation:

$$\partial Q_X/\partial P_X = \underset{\text{for constant } U}{(\partial Q_X/\partial P_X)} - \underset{\text{for constant prices}}{[Q_X(\partial Q_X/\partial I]}$$

This is called the *Slutsky equation*. The first term on the right side gives the change in the purchase of good X resulting from a price change when utility is held constant so the consumer is confined to a given indifference curve. This is the substitution effect. The second term gives the change in purchases resulting from a change in income with the prices of all goods constant. This is the income effect. For the derivation of this equation, see J. M. Henderson and R. E. Quandt, *Microeconomic Theory: A Mathematical Approach* (New York: McGraw-Hill, 1980), pp. 25–30.

The convex shape of the indifference curve therefore guarantees that the substitution effect of a price decline always increases the consumption of the good whose price falls. If this were the only effect of a price decline, decreases in the relative price of a good would always increase its consumption.

On the other hand, the income effect on the consumption of a good whose price falls can either increase or decrease purchases of the good. In Figure 4–7 the student chose to consume one more round trip to Toledo when his parents refunded his membership fee. The increase in the student's consumption of air travel resulting from the increase in income represented by the refund shows that air travel is a normal good for the student. If air travel had been an inferior good for the student, the increase in income represented by the refund would have *decreased* rather than increased the student's consumption of air travel. Thus, the impact of the income effect on the consumption of a good whose price changes depends on whether the consumer regards that good as normal or inferior.

Using the insights afforded by the theory of consumer behavior, it can now be concluded that the demand curves for normal goods will always be downward sloping. The law of demand is consistent with the implications of the model of consumer choice for normal goods because both the income and substitution effects of price decreases always act to increase purchases of those goods.

The Case of Inferior Goods

For goods that the consumer regards as inferior, the income and substitution effects work in opposite directions. For a price decrease, the substitution effect increases the amount purchased, whereas the income effect decreases the amount purchased. For a price increase, the substitution effect decreases the amount purchased, whereas the income effect increases the amount purchased.

The income and substitution effects of a price decrease for a good that is regarded as inferior are shown in Figure 4–8(a). As before, the price decrease swivels the budget line from *IA* to *IB*. If the consumer were charged a flat fee to take advantage of the price decrease, the substitution effect could be isolated. As before, the fee must be large enough to make the consumer indifferent between purchasing the good at the lower price and purchasing it at the regular price. As shown in Figure 4–8(a), the substitution effect is ΔQ_{XS}.

However, if the fee were refunded and the consumer were to move from E' to E_2, he would *decrease* his consumption of X. The income effect would work against the substitution effect. In this case, the two effects would also work against each other if the price were to increase.

Could the income effect of a change in the price of an inferior good ever be strong enough to outweigh the substitution effect? If so, the consumer would react to a price decrease by consuming *less* of the good and to a price increase by consuming *more* of the good. This would be in violation of the law of demand.

The answer to the question is that it is possible for the income effect to outweigh the substitution effect. However, this answer must be qualified by saying that it is extremely unlikely that such a state of affairs has ever existed or will ever exist. An inferior good for which the income effect exceeds the substitution

Modern Microeconomics in Action: International Report

Spending on Health Care in the United States and Abroad

As of 1992, spending for health care in the United States was approaching 14 percent of the gross domestic product and was increasing at a double-digit annual rate. The growth of health care spending has meant that more and more income is being allocated to health care at the cost of sacrificing enjoyment of other goods and services. In 1991 U.S. businesses spent more to provide their employees with health care and through taxes to help fund Medicare, the government's program of health insurance for the elderly, than they earned in profits after taxes! Federal and state tax revenues are also allocated to fund Medicaid, the government-financed program of health care for the poor.

The American system of health care is mainly a mix of private and government insurance programs. Spending per person on health care in the United States is double the amount spent in Japan, three times as much as in the United Kingdom, and one third higher than in Canada. How can we explain the spiraling health care costs in the United States, and why are such costs being contained more successfully in other countries?

First, let's examine the U.S. system. In the United States 80 percent of the health bills of Americans are paid by insurance firms and government insurance programs. *Third parties* other than buyers and sellers of health care services pay the bills. Most of the insurance plans have *deductibles*, which means that before the plan starts paying, the insuree must first pay for a certain amount of health care costs out of his or her own pocket each year. Once the insuree has met the deductible, he or she pays only *coinsurance*, a small fraction (between 10 and 20 percent) of the costs of health care services. Finally, in most private plans, after the consumer has paid a certain maximum of out-of-pocket health care costs for the year, the insurance company pays all of the consumer's remaining health care costs.

The accompanying graph shows how this insurance system affects the budget line for health

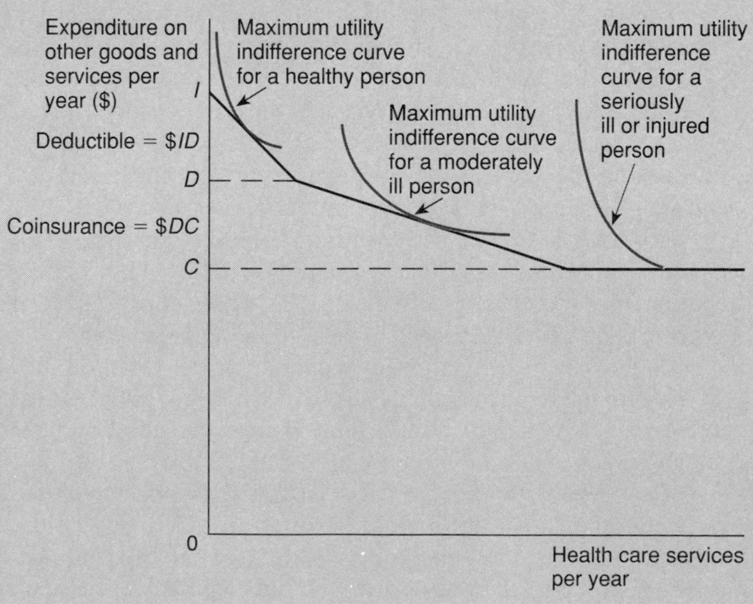

(*Continued*) care and the choices of typical insurees regarding the consumption of health care. Notice the strange shape of the budget line. Starting from zero expenditure on health care up until the point at which the deductible has been met, an individual with a typical employer-provided health insurance policy pays the full price of medical and other covered health care services. After the deductible has been met, the out-of-pocket price of health care services falls to the coinsurance. Finally, once the insuree has paid the maximum annual out-of-pocket amount, the insurance company pays all of the insuree's health care expenses (up to a maximum lifetime benefit, which is usually $1 million). When this point has been reached, the insuree's out-of-pocket health care cost falls to zero and the budget line is flat.

Naturally, the amount of health care services a person chooses depends on the person's state of health as well as prices and incomes. The graph shows the maximum utility indifference curves for three people—a healthy person, a moderately ill person, and a seriously ill or injured person. The healthy person who does not meet the deductible during the past year pays the full price of health care and consumes health care services up to the point at which the marginal benefit of such services falls to equal the market price. The moderately ill person behaves similarly, but because the out-of-pocket price is lower for this person, both income and substitution effects encourage the person to consume more health care services. Finally, the seriously ill or injured person pays zero out-of-pocket costs for health care and therefore consumes health care services until the marginal benefit falls to zero. Health care providers are also more likely to prescribe services and tests to a patient when they know that the insurance company and not the patient will pay the bill. By lowering the price of health care services to many patients, insurance itself has contributed to the spectacular growth in health care spending that we have seen in recent years.

To control health care spending, many insurers have been increasing both deductibles and copayments required under coinsurance. Many have also been trying to get insurees to enroll in health maintenance organizations because the physician in such organizations operate under strict budget rules and are paid a fixed amount per patient rather than according to the services they provide.

How is health care spending controlled in countries with national health insurance, such as the United Kingdom? In the United Kingdom the government owns and operates hospitals and pays physicians' salaries. Although patients pay no fees for most services, their ability to choose is severely limited. The National Health Service budgets for health care, deciding which hospitals get equipment and how much equipment they get. Doctors employed by the government decide priorities for such medical procedures as hernia operations, and there are often long waiting lists for surgery. In early 1991, for example, more than 700,000 people were waiting for surgery in the United Kingdom. In effect, in the United Kingdom and other nations with national health insurance the government rations health care according to its own criteria and individuals are not free to choose how much health care they will consume according to their preferences and incomes. Many wealthy Britons opt out of the system by going to the few private hospitals in the United Kingdom or by going abroad for health care when they are seriously ill.*

* For an excellent discussion of health insurance and health spending in the United States and abroad, see Congress of the United States, Congressional Budget Office, *Rising Health Care Costs: Causes, Implications, and Strategies* (Washington, D.C.: U.S. Government Printing Office, April 1991).

Giffen good An inferior good for which the income effect exceeds the substitution effect.

effect is sometimes called a **Giffen good.** Such goods are named after Sir Robert Giffen (1837–1910), a famous British statistician and economist. Giffen claimed to have observed very poor workers increase their consumption of cheap, starchy bread when its price increased. These workers spent large portions of their income on bread, which was apparently an inferior good for them. When the price of bread rose, the income effect could have been so strong as to force them to drop

FIGURE 4–8 Income and Substitution Effects of Price Declines for Inferior Goods

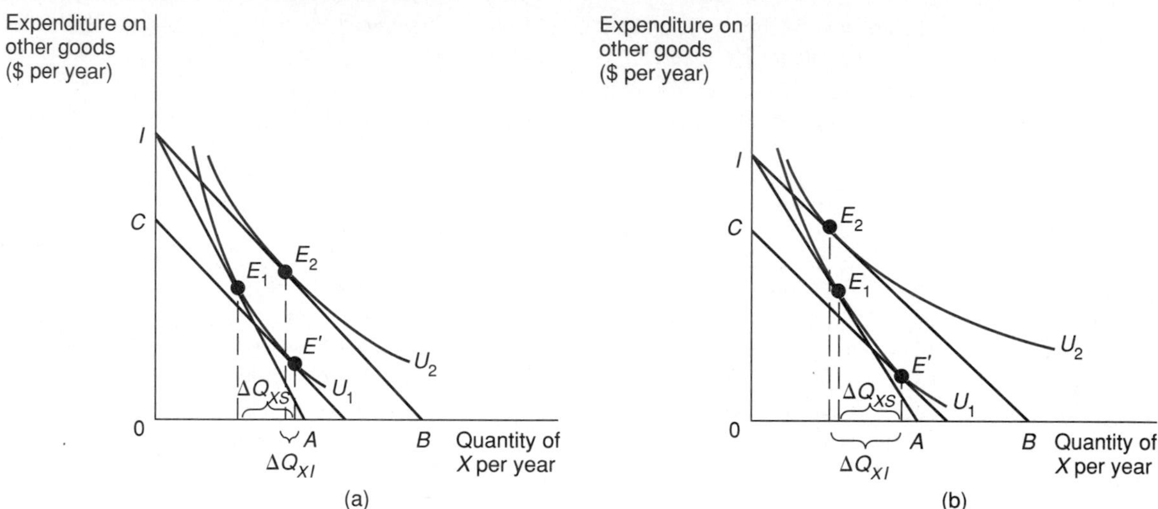

In (a) the consumer regards X as an inferior good. The income effect diminishes the substitution effect. In (b) the income effect for the inferior good is so strong that it overcomes the substitution effect. The price decrease actually decreases the consumption of the good. This illustrates the unlikely Giffen paradox.

meat and other more expensive foods from their diet. Because bread was still the cheapest food available, they purportedly consumed more even though its price had risen.[2]

A Giffen good must be both one that is strongly inferior and one on which the consumer spends large portions of income. Goods on which the consumer spends relatively high percentages of income, such as housing, transportation, and clothing, are unlikely to be regarded as inferior. Goods that consumers might consider inferior, such as poor cuts of meat, potatoes, and cheap bread, are unlikely to absorb large portions of income. Changes in real income resulting from changes in the price of such goods are therefore likely to have only negligible influence on consumer well-being. Goods that modern consumers regard as inferior also have ample substitutes; the substitution effects of changes in the price of such goods are likely to be substantial. Because the income effect of price changes for these goods is likely to be small and the substitution effect large, it is unlikely that their demand curves would ever slope upward. It is so difficult to find an example of Giffen goods in the modern world that it must be concluded that the so-called

[2] Many believe that Giffen had potatoes in mind and had observed the reaction of the Irish to the famous potato famine in the 1840s. Historical analysis indicates that the demand for potatoes was extremely unlikely to have been upward sloping at that time. See Gerald P. Dwyer, Jr., and Cotton M. Lindsay, "Robert Giffen and the Irish Potato," *American Economic Review* 74, no. 1 (March 1984), pp. 188–92.

Giffen paradox is very unlikely. The illustration of the paradox in Figure 4–8(b) can therefore be regarded as a geometric curiosity with little empirical relevance. There is no likely exception to the law of demand.

There are some notable bogus "exceptions" to the law of demand. One such exception occurs when consumers judge the quality of a good by its price. Such consumers may therefore buy more of a good whose price has risen. An antique dealer may be able to sell more when he raises his prices because uninformed consumers think that the higher prices indicate better quality. Another bogus exception occurs when consumers expect prices to rise in the future. Such expectations may be triggered by actual price increases. This may result in hoarding and therefore increased sales of the goods whose price goes up.

These are not really exceptions to the law of demand because other things are not being held equal when price changes. In the first case consumers are fooled into thinking that quality changes when price changes; in the second case they view price increases as indicative of further increases. In each case a change in some other demand determinant is associated with changes in price.

CONCEPT REVIEW

1. Explain the distinction between the income and substitution effects of price changes and why the two effects cannot be easily separated.
2. Why will the substitution effect of a price increase always act to decrease purchases of the good whose price goes up?
3. Under what circumstances will the substitution effect of a price change be exactly offset by the income effect of that change?

PRICES, INCOMES, AND UTILITY: USING THE THEORY OF INDIVIDUAL DEMAND

The theory of individual demand is applicable to a wide variety of business and social issues. In this section we apply the theory to understand how consumer choices are affected by business pricing policies. We also use the theory to examine some of the difficulties involved in measuring changes in the cost of living. Finally, we investigate the effects of taxes and subsidies on consumer choices by examining how they affect incentives to use resources.

Business Bonus Gifts to Consumers: Frequent Flier Plans

Businesses often offer bonuses to certain regular customers. For example, many airlines have "frequent flier plans" that reward passengers who fly more than a certain number of miles over a period with the "bonus" of a free ticket. The ticket can be used for a number of miles of additional travel. Recipients of the ticket cannot convert it into cash for expenditures on other goods. Although the bonus increases the consumer's real income (the increment being measured in additional air travel), it does not allow the consumer the option of spending it on other goods. Let's use indifference curve analysis to analyze the impact of the frequent flier plan on the consumer's demand for air travel on a specific airline.

A frequent flier plan creates a "notch" in a consumer's budget line. To see how a plan of this kind affects a consumer's spending possibilities, Figure 4–9 shows the budget line for air travel and expenditure on other goods for a consumer with annual income equal to $*I*. Assume that the price per mile of air travel is constant. In the absence of a frequent flier plan the budget line for the consumer would be *IR* and the price per mile of travel would be the slope of *AR* multiplied by −1. Now suppose an airline announces that after having flown Q_A miles per year, a passenger is entitled to *M* miles of free travel. This means that after having reached point *A*, corresponding to Q_A miles of air travel per year on the budget line, the passenger receives a bonus of *M* miles of travel. The line segment *AB* in Figure 4–9 represents the *M* travel miles the passenger receives after having consumed Q_A miles per year. Of course, a passenger who has used up the *M* miles of free travel can undertake additional travel on the airline at the initial market price per mile. The segment *BC* of the budget line shows that after the free travel has been used up, the passenger still has the option of purchasing more travel at the same price that he or she paid before.

The budget line available to passengers of an airline with a frequent flier plan is represented by the notched line *IABC*. The notch is the section *AB*, which represents the "gift" of free mileage to the frequent flier. Note that the cash value

FIGURE 4–9 Impact of a Notched Budget Line: Frequently Flier Plans

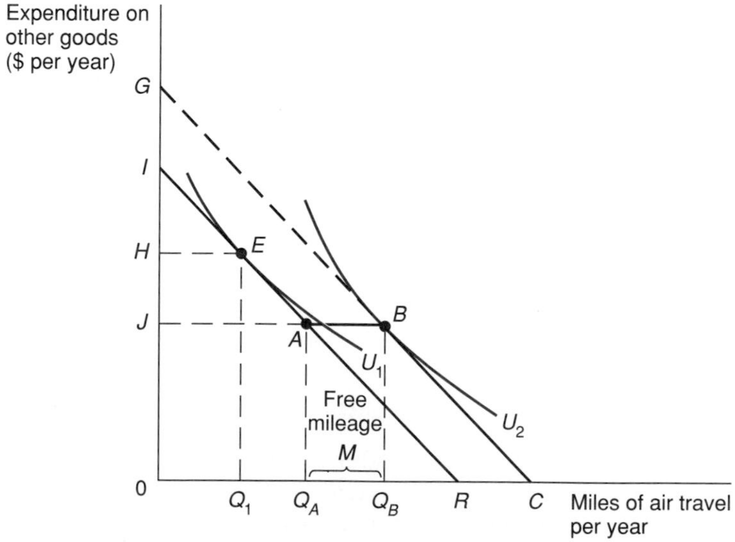

After purchasing Q_A miles of travel on an airline, the consumer gets *M* miles of free travel, represented by the notch *AB* in the budget line. The consumer whose indifference curves are illustrated increases purchases of air travel as a result of the bonus.

of the free mileage can be determined from the graph by following the dashed line from point B to point G on the vertical axis. The distance IG shows how much expenditure on other goods the passenger would have to give up to purchase the amount of air travel that the airline offers to give away free to frequent fliers. Because the passenger does not have the option of redeeming the free ticket for cash, he or she cannot move along the dashed line segment BG to obtain the opportunity to purchase market baskets along that segment. The availability of the in-kind bonus therefore shifts the budget line for the passenger from IR to $IABC$, with the notch at AB corresponding to the gift of free travel.

It is easy to show that the frequent flier plan gets some passengers to travel more on the airline. Prior to the announcement of the bonus plan, the consumer whose indifference curves are shown in Figure 4–9 is in equilibrium at point E at which Q_1 miles of travel on the airline are consumed and $\$H$ are spent on other goods, including travel on other airlines. At E utility level U_1 is achieved. After the frequent flier plan has been announced, the consumer finds it gainful to move to point B, at which Q_B miles are traveled on the airline and $\$J$ are spent on other goods. At point B utility level $U_2 > U_1$ is achieved. Of the total miles traveled, the consumer pays for Q_A miles and receives M miles as a free bonus. The frequent flier plan has therefore been effective in increasing *purchase* of air travel on the airline by this consumer from Q_1 miles per year to Q_A miles per year.

As you might expect, the frequent flier plan does not affect every consumer in the same way. Consumers with the same income and different indifference maps will react differently. Figure 4–10 shows the case of a consumer who chooses not

FIGURE 4–10 Nonresponse to a Bonus

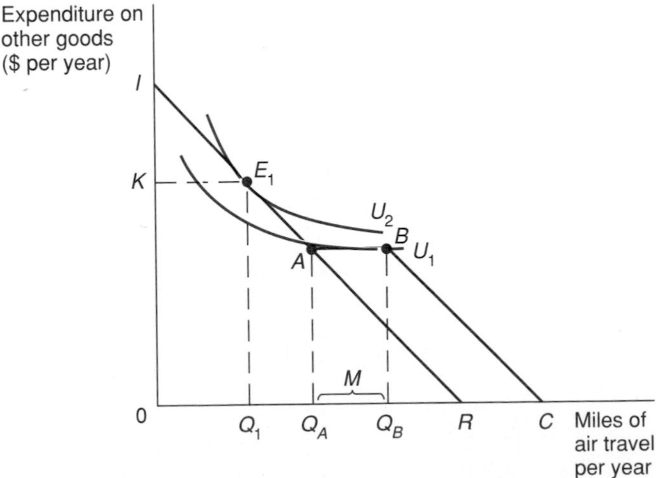

The frequent flier bonus has no effect on the choice to purchase air travel for the consumer whose indifference curves are shown. This consumer achieves a higher level of utility at point E_1, the initial equilibrium, than is possible at point B, where he or she would enjoy the bonus.

Modern Microeconomics in Action: The Business World

Transaction Costs and the Incentive to Sell

Many people have home gardens in the summer. Sometimes they are fortunate enough to have bumper crops. Yet these home gardeners rarely go into the business of selling tomatoes and cabbages. The required transaction costs usually prevent them from doing so. The transaction costs of selling a product often influence the incentive to enter the market as a seller. Let's look at a simple example to show the relationship between transaction costs and the willingness of people to start up a business.

The graph plots the indifference curves of a typical home gardener. The good on the X axis is the weekly crop of home-grown tomatoes. Expenditure on other goods per week is plotted on the Y axis. With the weekly tomato crop the person finds himself at point B on indifference curve U_2. At that point the person can enjoy T_1 pounds of tomatoes per week and spend $\$I_1$ on other goods. The dashed line PB has a slope that indicates the market price of tomatoes. If the person could sell tomatoes at this price, he would move to an equilibrium at point E, where he would retain T_2 pounds of tomatoes per week for his own consumption and sell T_1T_2 pounds of tomatoes to others. He would then be able to consume $\$I_2$ of other goods each week.

It is unlikely that the person could move to point E. To sell tomatoes he would have to build or rent a stand at the local farmers' market or incur other costs, such as the costs of advertising and transportation, to get his goods to buyers. These transaction costs of selling are likely to be a fixed amount per week independent of the number of tomatoes sold. They have the effect of reducing the incentive to sell tomatoes.

Suppose that transaction costs are $\$C$ per week. Independent of the amount of tomatoes sold, these costs would reduce the gardener's expenditure on other goods by $\$C$ if he tried to sell toma-

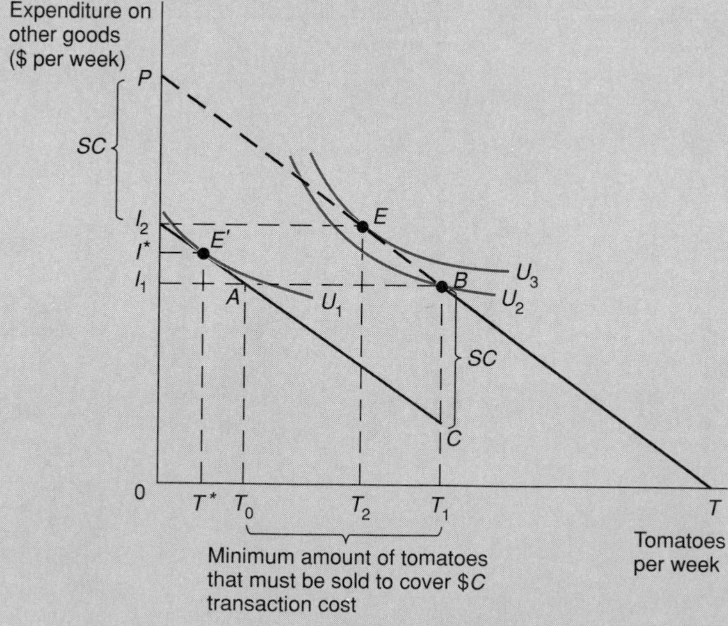

(*Continued*) toes. These fixed transaction costs put a notch in the actual budget line between tomatoes and expenditure on other goods per week. Before one tomato can be sold, the seller must sacrifice the opportunity to consume $\$C$ of other goods, represented by the distance BC. Once this has been done and the seller has set up his stand, he can begin to market his tomatoes along the line segment I_2C, whose slope is the same as the line segment PB. The budget line possible from selling tomatoes is therefore I_2CBT, with the notch BC representing the weekly transaction costs of marketing tomatoes. The gardener can remain at point B, set up a stand, and sell tomatoes along the segment I_2C, or he can buy more tomatoes than he grows by moving along the segment BT of his budget line.

The gardener would have to sell a minimum of T_0T_1 pounds of tomatoes per week just to recoup $\$C$, his transaction costs. To see this, move from point C on the notched budget line to point A. If the gardener were to give up T_0T_1 pounds of tomatoes per week at the price represented by the slope of the budget line, he would earn $\$C$ at the current market price. For example, suppose that tomatoes sell at 50 cents per pound. If the transaction costs were \$50 per week, the distance T_0T_1 would correspond to 100 pounds of tomatoes. If the gardener were to sell more than this amount, he would be able to increase his expenditure of other goods above I_1 by earning more than his transaction costs. If he were to sell all of his weekly tomato production, he would be at point I_2, where he would spend $\$I_2$ on other goods and consume no tomatoes.

The highest level of utility that the gardener can achieve by selling tomatoes occurs at point E', where he sells T^*T_1 pounds of tomatoes per week and spends $\$I^*$ on other goods per week. There he achieves utility level U_1. Because this is less than the utility level at point B, the gardener decides that going into the business of selling his produce is not worthwhile.

Note that the incentive to sell depends both on transaction costs and on preferences represented by the indifference map. It is possible that gardeners with different preferences might achieve higher utility by selling tomatoes. For example, a gardener whose very flat indifference curve implies low marginal benefit from consuming tomatoes might achieve higher utility at a point like E' than at a point like B. A decrease in the transaction costs of selling tomatoes, which would decrease the height of the notch in the budget line, might also induce more home gardeners to sell home-grown tomatoes. A cheap means of advertising intentions to sell (such as a freely distributed classified publication with low advertising rates) or cheap weekend rental of stalls at a local flea market might have this effect. At the extreme, if the transaction costs were zero, even the gardener whose indifference curves have been drawn might choose to sell some of his crop.

to increase air travel on the airline despite the availability of the frequent flier plan. This consumer has relatively flat indifference curves compared to those of the consumer whose indifference curves are illustrated in Figure 4–9. This means that for any given mileage the marginal benefit of air travel on the airline offering the plan is lower for the second consumer than for the first.

In the absence of a frequent flier plan the second consumer would be in equilibrium at point E_1, at which Q_1 miles are traveled per year on the airline and $\$K$ are spent on other goods. At that market basket the utility level U_2 is achieved. With the frequent flier plan this consumer's maximum utility market basket remains that represented by point E_1. For example, if the consumer were to increase air travel to Q_A so as to be eligible for the bonus and reach point B on the notched budget line, he or she would achieve utility level U_1, which is less than the level U_2 available at E_1. This consumer therefore chooses not to increase travel on the airline.

Are frequent flier plans effective in increasing airline profits? Although at this point not enough theory has been developed to answer this question precisely, a rough analysis of the impact of such plans on airline profits can be outlined. The cost of a frequent flier plan to an airline is that of free travel to passengers who find it in their interest to take advantage of the bonus. The gain is the revenue from the extra travel that these passengers pay for to gain the bonus. Of course, the airline could also gain extra travel revenue by simply lowering its price per mile of travel for *all* consumers instead of giving a bonus to its frequent fliers. Because the marginal benefit of air travel declines for all fliers, a general price reduction is likely to increase the miles traveled by all of the airline's clientele instead of a select few. The price reduction might even attract new passengers. The managers of the airline must therefore carefully weigh the net gains from each of these alternatives before deciding whether it is, in fact, in the airline's interest to initiate a frequent flier plan.

Measuring Changes in the Cost of Living

Measures of the cost of living, such as the consumer price index, are indexes of the cost of buying a given market basket of goods. For example, the consumer price index assumes that consumers allocate their income in a certain way to buy a market basket of housing, clothing, food, and so on. This measure suffers from a fundamental defect. Unless the prices of all the goods in the basket increase in the same proportion, consumers will change the mix of goods purchased in response to changes in relative prices. Indifference curve analysis can be used to show this problem.

Suppose you wish to construct a measure of the increased expenditure on clothing and food that is required to give a certain level of satisfaction when their prices rise. The current price of clothing is $\$P_{C1}$ per unit, and that of food is $\$P_{F1}$. Figure 4–11 shows a typical consumer's indifference curves for clothing and food. The budget line C_1F_1 has a slope of $-P_{F1}/P_{C1}$. In equilibrium the consumer chooses the market basket represented by point $B1$, which includes Q_{C1} units of clothing and Q_{F1} units of food per year. The consumer's total annual expenditure on food is

$$\$M1 = P_{C1}Q_{C1} + P_{F1}Q_{F1} \tag{4–5}$$

Laspeyres price index A measure of changes in the price level that calculates the cost of living in the current year relative to the cost of living in a base year.

Now suppose in year 2 the price of food increases relative to the price of clothing. The price of clothing is now P_{C2}, the price of food is P_{F2}, and $P_{F2}/P_{C2} > P_{F1}/P_{C1}$. If the consumer were to purchase the market basket B1, it would now cost

$$\$M2 = P_{C2}Q_{C1} + P_{F2}Q_{F1} \tag{4–6}$$

A **Laspeyres price index** calculates the cost of living in the current year relative to the first year as

$$L = (M2/M1)100 \tag{4–7}$$

FIGURE 4–11 Measuring Changes in the Cost of Living

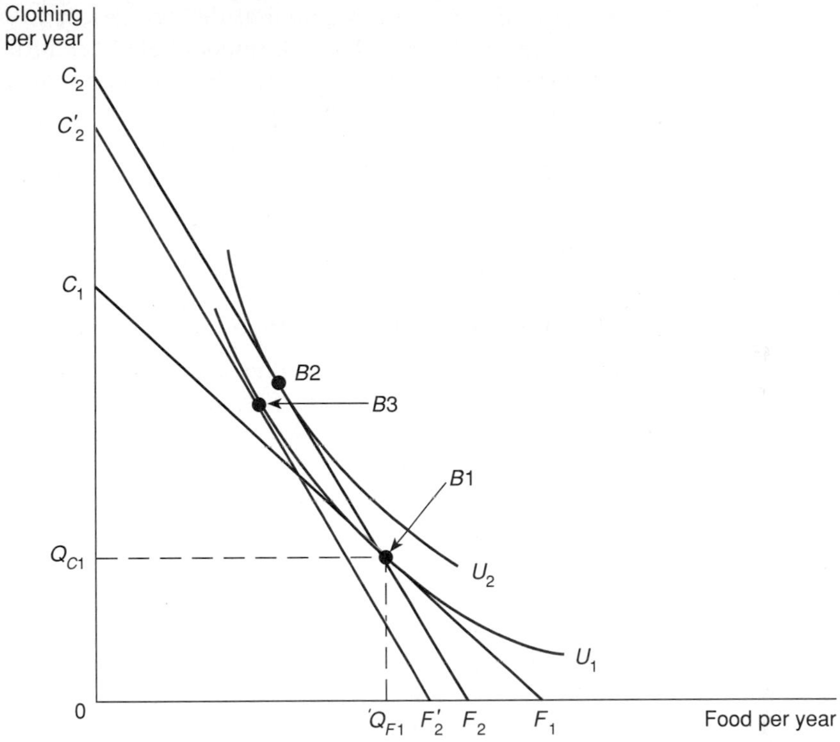

When prices are represented by the budget line C_1F_1, the consumer buys the market basket at $B1$. Expenditure on these goods is $M_1 = P_{C1}Q_{C1} + P_{F1}Q_{F1}$. When prices rise in unequal proportions, the budget line is C_2F_2. To buy the market basket at $B1$, the consumer must now spend $M_2 = P_{C2}Q_{C1} + P_{F2}Q_{F1}$. The consumer can spend the lesser amount represented by the budget line $C'_2F'_2$ and be just as well off as when the market basket $B1$ was purchased. The consumer does this by buying market basket $B3$.

This is the method used to calculate the *consumer price index* (CPI) in the United States. The first year (or period) is called the *base* or reference period. Current prices are compared to prices during this period. For example, if $L = 110$, this means that it costs \$110 to purchase a market basket that cost \$100 during the base period.

The problem with this index—and any alternative index of the cost of living—is that it neglects the fact that a change in relative prices will change the equilibrium market basket. If the consumer had \$$M2$ to spend in year 2, he or she would still be able to buy market basket $B1$. But the budget constraint represented by Equation 4–11 is steeper than the previous one, based on year 1 prices, and goes through point $B1$. Figure 4–11 shows that if the consumer had that budget in year 2, the chosen market basket would be $B2$ and he or she would achieve utility level $U_2 > U_1$. If enough income were taken away from the consumer to make him or her just as well off as in year 1, basket $B3$ would be chosen. This is the equilibrium corresponding to the budget line $C'_2F'_2$. That budget line corresponds to the amount of expenditure required at the new prices to make the consumer as well off as in the first year. This is the amount of expenditure necessary to compute the true increase in the cost of living. The market basket $B3$ has less food in it than it had in year 1, but more clothing.

Because the expenditure required for $B3$ is less than that required for $B1$, the price index overstates the actual increase in the cost of living. It does so by failing to take into account the consumer's adjustment to the increase in the relative price of food.

Taxes and Economic Welfare

No one enjoys paying taxes. Other things being equal, taxes make persons worse off. We can use the concepts of income and substitution effects to understand the impact of taxes on choices and resource allocation.

Lump-sum tax A tax that does not distort relative prices and therefore has only an income effect on incentives.

Most types of taxes have both income and substitution effects because taxes usually affect prices. A tax that has *only* income effects provides a benchmark for evaluating taxes that have *both* income and substitution effects. Such a tax is called a **lump-sum tax.** It is a once-and-for-all levy that cannot be influenced by any change in behavior. An example of a lump-sum tax is a head tax on adults. This fixed payment would come due when a person reaches age 18. At that age all persons with heads would receive a bill from the government as a sort of initiation fee into society. They could pay the tax at once or pay it out (with interest) over a number of years. They could do nothing to avoid the tax (except for removing their heads). No prices would be affected by the tax because it is not levied on any salable goods or services. It would, however, clearly reduce every person's income.

A tax on the sale of clothing has the effect of raising the price of clothing. The amount paid under such a tax varies with the amount of clothing that a person purchases. The increased price of clothing resulting from the tax swivels the consumer's budget line inward. In Figure 4–12 the impact of the tax is shown as a movement of the budget line from IG to ID. As a result of the tax-induced price increase the consumer moves from equilibrium at point E to equilibrium at point E'. Consumption of clothing is reduced from C_1 to C_2. Expenditure on all other goods rises from OB to OB'. The amount of tax paid is represented by the distance $B'T$. To purchase C_2 units of clothing per year, the consumer gives up a total of \$$IB'$ of income, of which \$$IT$ are retained by sellers of the good and the remainder $B'T$ goes to the government. In moving from equilibrium at point E to equilibrium at point E', the consumer suffers a reduction in utility from U_3 to U_1. Thus the tax makes the consumer worse off. The movement from E to E' is the combined result of the income and substitution effect.

Now suppose the person were to pay the same amount of taxes per year in the form of a lump-sum tax. Such a tax would have no direct effect on the price of clothing or of any other goods. Because the lump-sum tax would not change relative prices, it would not result in a substitution effect. It would cause only an income effect.

FIGURE 4–12 A Lump-Sum Tax versus a Price-Distorting Tax

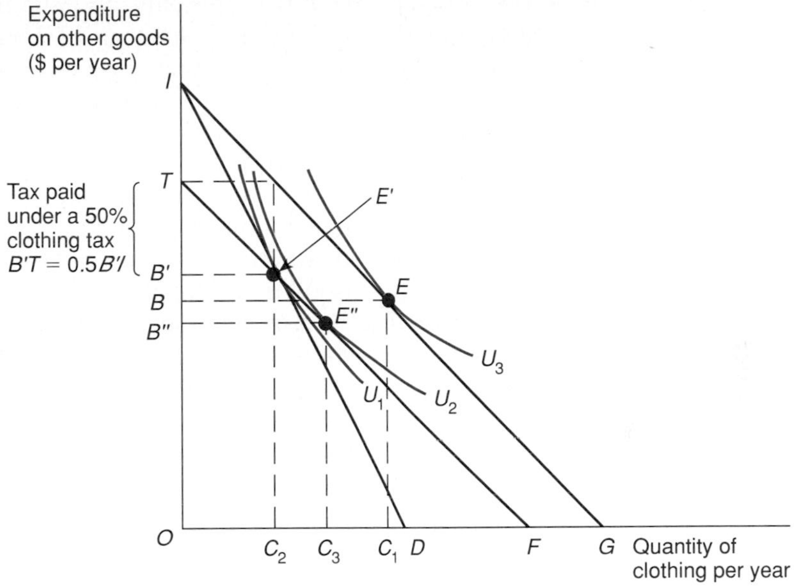

The person attains utility level U_2 under the lump-sum tax. If he were to pay the same amount as a tax on clothing, his attainable level of utility would be $U_1 < U_2$.

It is easy to show that the person would be better off under the lump-sum tax, provided that he pays the same amount of taxes annually that he would under the tax on clothing. A lump-sum tax equal to the tax on clothing would reduce the consumer's income by an amount $B'T$, shifting the budget line to TF. (Note that although the tax reduces income, it is *not* the same as an income tax because it does not distort the prices of labor services and other productive services supplied to employers.) The tax has an income effect that reduces the consumption of clothing, provided clothing is a normal good. There is no substitution effect; therefore the amount of clothing consumed under the lump-sum tax is greater than the amount consumed under the clothing tax. Under the lump-sum tax the consumer's equilibrium moves from E to E'' and his consumption of clothing becomes $C_3 > C_2$. The level of utility achieved by the consumer under the lump-sum tax (U_2) exceeds the level that he could achieve if he paid the same amount of tax under the clothing tax (U_1). This is so because although the consumer's real income is the same in both cases, in the case of the lump-sum tax he consumes more clothing.

The difference in a person's well-being under the lump-sum tax and under the price-distorting tax when the annual payment for the two taxes is the same is the excess burden of taxation borne by the person. The difference between utility levels U_2 and U_1 in Figure 4–12 represents the *deadweight loss* borne by the consumer whose indifference curves are illustrated. This deadweight loss of taxation can be thought of as a measure of the loss in utility caused by the substitution effect of a price-distorting tax.

Income and Substitution Effects of a Rebated Tax on Gasoline

The 1970s were a period of rising gasoline prices in the United States. As a result of an oil embargo imposed by Arab states in 1973 and of further decreases in the supply of oil in the late 1970s, the price of gasoline soared. The U.S. government sought ways to reduce reliance on imported oil and hit on the idea of taxing gasoline. Naturally, a tax on gasoline was likely to raise its price still further and to further reduce the well-being of U.S. households already smarting from the effect of increasing gas prices on their purchasing power. To reduce the sting of the tax, the Carter administration proposed that it be refunded to consumers as a "rebate" on household income tax returns. Although this scheme was never enacted into law, it is useful to use the theory of consumer choice to trace out its effects and show that even though the tax paid by consumers would have been rebated to them, their consumption of gasoline would have nonetheless declined.

Suppose the price of gasoline is $1 per gallon and that its price increases as a result of the tax designed to reduce energy use. This is illustrated in Figure 4–13. The budget line of a typical motorist is *IA* before the price increase. She is in equilibrium at point E_1, where she consumes 800 gallons of gasoline per year when

FIGURE 4–13 Income and Substitution Effects of a Price Increase for a Normal Good

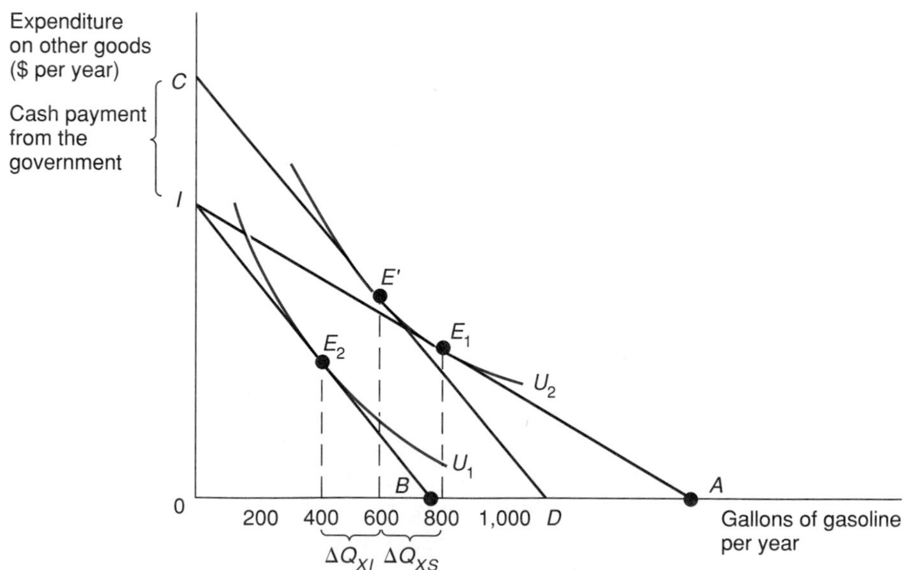

An increase in the price of gasoline shifts the budget constraint line from *IA* to *IB*. A government cash payment large enough to make the consumer just as well off as she was before the price increase allows observation of the substitution effect. The 200-gallon decrease from 800 to 600 gallons per year is the substitution effect of the price increase. The income effect in this case is a further 200-gallon reduction of consumption, to 400 gallons per year. This reduction would be observed if the consumer's income were allowed to decline by $*IC*.

the price of gasoline is $1 per gallon. The price increase swivels the budget line inward to *IB* and results in a new equilibrium at point E_2, where her consumption of gasoline declines to 400 gallons per year. This movement is the result of the combined income and substitution effects. It reduces the motorist's utility level from U_2 to U_1. However, suppose that the tax rebate mailed to this motorist is just enough to make her as well off as she was before the new gasoline tax was introduced. This would imply that her income increases enough to return her to indifference curve U_2. The rebate shifts the budget line from *IB* to *CD*.

Such a scheme results in only a substitution effect on the motorist's choice. In Figure 4–13 the amount she receives from the government is equal to the distance *IC*. This keeps her on indifference curve U_2. After receiving the payment, she is in equilibrium at point E'. Her consumption of gasoline declines from 800 to 600 gallons per year. This reduction in consumption is the substitution effect of the price increase. In this case ΔQ_{XS} is a decrease of 200 gallons in annual gasoline consumption. Even though the government's policy has made this motorist no worse off, she reduces her consumption of gasoline because of the substitution effect caused by the tax.

The substitution effect must decrease the consumption of gasoline in response to an increase in its price. This follows from the convex shape of the indifference curves. Because the budget line *CD* is steeper than the original budget line, *AC*, the tangency E' must lie to the left of E_1. Just as the substitution effect of a price decrease always acts to increase the consumption of the good whose price falls, so does the substitution effect of a price increase always act to decrease the consumption of the good whose price rises.

If the government were to merely tax gasoline while providing no refunds, the budget line would be *IB*. Equilibrium would be at point E_2, where consumption would decline by an additional 200 gallons per year. This additional decline would be the income effect of the price increase. It is shown as the distance ΔQ_{XI}. If gasoline is a normal good for the motorist, there would be a greater decline in her consumption when the tax is not accompanied by a rebate.

Note that it would be difficult to implement such a rebate scheme. Only the individual knows what determines his well-being. How would the government decide how much income to rebate to each person? Some are likely to get more than enough to return them to their initial level of utility; others might not get enough to make them as well off as they were before the tax on gasoline. Thus it would be difficult to eliminate income effects entirely from the incentive to purchase gasoline.

Also note how the substitution effect of the tax distorts the motorist's choices. Even if she is no worse off as a result of the tax, she still consumes less gasoline than she would have consumed otherwise.

Subsidies and Economic Welfare

Subsidies are the opposite of taxes. They are payments that persons receive, usually from governing authorities. Subsidies are not payments for services rendered; they do, however, influence prices and incomes. The impact of subsidies, like that of taxes, can be examined with the aid of indifference curve analysis. The analysis is analogous to that for taxes. If a lump-sum subsidy entails a payment to all persons when they reach a certain age, the amount of the subsidy will always be the same and cannot be influenced by anything the person does. A subsidy of this kind has only an income effect. A price-distorting subsidy has both an income effect and a substitution effect. For example, governments typically subsidize food, housing, and medical services purchased by certain eligible persons, including elderly and poor persons. A subsidy that pays a certain amount or percentage of the price of each unit of these goods purchased by eligible persons would be a price-distorting subsidy.

Suppose the government offers a subsidy for expenditure on rental housing to eligible persons. The government promises to pay a certain fraction of the actual rental payments made by these persons. Eligibility could be based on age. Typically, the elderly are eligible for such subsidies. The subsidy reduces rent per room to eligible consumers. As a result the budget line in Figure 4–14 swivels out from *ID* to *IG* and consumer equilibrium moves to *E′* from *E*. This induces the recipient to consume more housing (that is, it increases the number of square feet rented). As shown in Figure 4–14, the amount of housing consumed by an eligible person increases from H_1 to H_2. The subsidy is the distance *BB′*. The consumer pays *IB* dollars for H_2 units of housing per year. The net cost after receipt of the subsidy for this amount of housing is $IB' = IB - BB'$ dollars per year.

FIGURE 4–14 A Lump-Sum Subsidy versus a Price-Distorting Subsidy

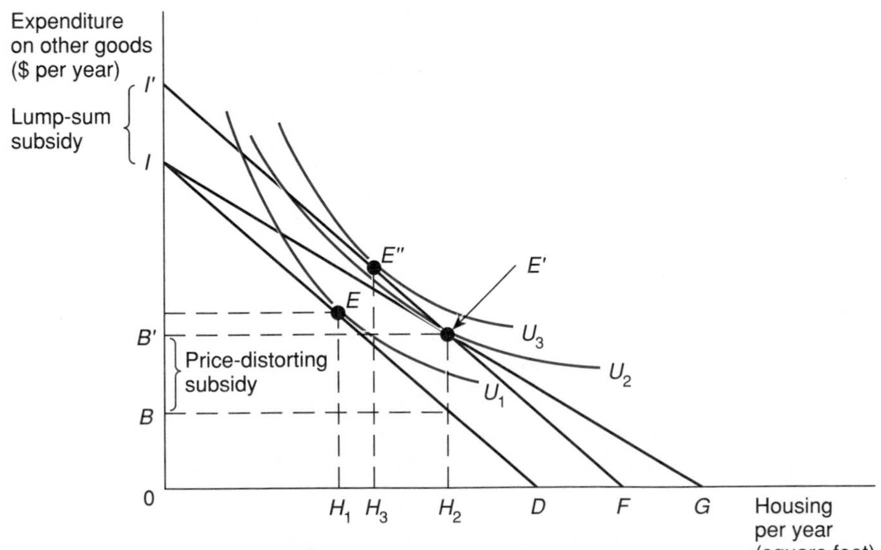

A lump-sum subsidy allows a person to obtain a higher level of utility than is obtainable from a price-distorting subsidy of equal dollar amount.

Modern Microeconomics in Action: **Government and the Economy**

Food Stamps and Consumer Choices

Food stamps are a major form of assistance to the needy in the United States. Eligible recipients receive a certain dollar amount of stamps that can be used *only* to purchase food and related items.

These stamps are equivalent to a cash transfer to the poor in most cases. Suppose a typical recipient receives $F in stamps each month. In the absence of the stamps this person's cash income would be $OM. Graph (a) shows that the cash value of the stamps could result in an increase in expenditure on goods other than food by as much as $MM'. However, the $F can be used only for food purchases. Persons eligible for the stamps have a notch placed in their budget line. The budget constraint line is *MB2N'* for recipients of food stamps. The market baskets represented by points on *M'B2* cannot be purchased by the consumer with income $OM and food stamps whose cash value is $F.

If, instead, the recipient got an unrestricted cash grant of $F, he could purchase *all* of the market baskets on the budget line *M'N'*. Unless the equilibrium market basket for food and expenditure on other goods when the budget constraint is *M'N'* lies to the left of basket *B*2, the recipient is just as well off with food stamps as with an equivalent unrestricted cash grant. This is because an equilibrium at a market basket such as *B*2 or *B*3 means that the consumer would choose to spend at least $F on food even if he were given that amount in cash instead of stamps. The consumer whose indifference curves are illustrated in graph (a) is in equilibrium at basket *B*3. This consumer would choose that basket if he were given food stamps or a cash grant equal to the market value of the food stamps.

A consumer such as the one whose indifference curves are shown in graph (b) would be in equilibrium with the cash grant at a point where *less* than $F were spent on food. This consumer is made worse off by having stamps instead of their cash equivalent. He is induced to buy Q_F units of food per month when he is eligible for food stamps. With a cash grant of $F he would spend $M'L on Q'_F units of food per month. For this consumer utility at *B*2 is less than that at *B*1.

It is commonly believed that the cash value of food stamps is so modest that most recipients would normally spend at least that much on food even in the absence of the subsidy. This means that recipients of food stamps are likely to be just as well off and spend the same amount of income on food per month if they receive the cash value of their stamps.

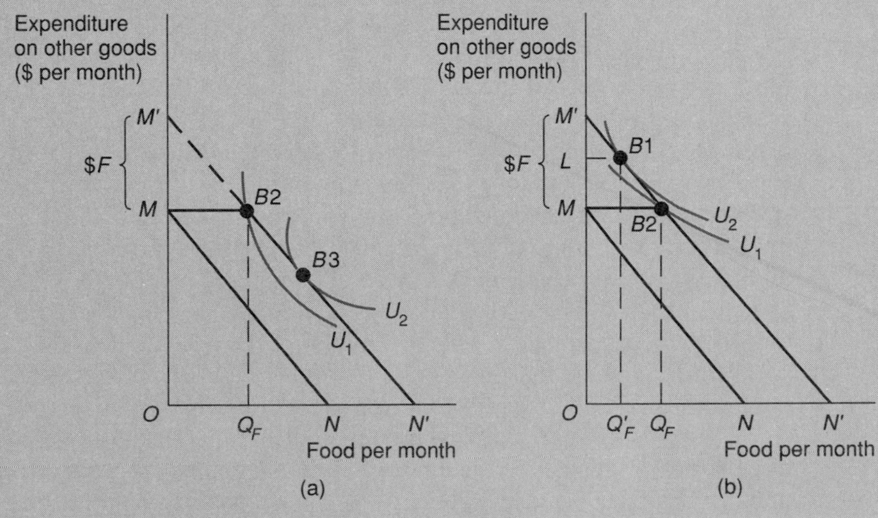

Now suppose the consumer were given a direct lump-sum subsidy equal to BB' dollars per year instead of the price-distorting subsidy. This will shift the budget line outward to $I'F$ as the consumer's income increases from I to I', where $II' = BB'$ is the lump-sum subsidy. The equilibrium is now at E'', where the consumer receives the level of utility $U_3 > U_2$. At E'' he would consume less housing than at E', but he would be better off.

Consumers are better off under the lump-sum subsidy because it gives them greater freedom of choice to spend the dollars they receive. The price-distorting subsidy provides benefits only to the extent to which housing is consumed; but the consumer can buy more of other goods under the lump-sum subsidy. The price-distorting subsidy has an excess burden resulting from its substitution effect. The consumer is worse off with a price distorting-subsidy than with an equal lump-sum subsidy. If consumers were given the equivalent value of such subsidies in cash (evaluated at the amount of the subsidized item they would choose under the price-distorting subsidy), they could always choose to purchase the same amount of the subsidized good anyway. Under the cash subsidy, however, they have the option of purchasing more of other goods as well and can therefore be better off.

In-Kind Subsidies: How Government Policies Can Result in Effects Opposite to Those Intended

Governments typically subsidize persons by supplying them with in-kind subsidies instead of cash income. These subsidies are in the form of goods or coupons to purchase goods. In the United States, for example, low-income persons are eligible for food stamps that can be redeemed only for food or related items. Elderly and low-income persons are often eligible for government-supplied public housing made available at rents below those prevailing on the market. The purpose of such in-kind subsidies is often stated to be the increased consumption of basic goods and services by eligible persons. The subsidy programs are designed to ensure that persons consume at least minimum amounts of the subsidized goods. However, these programs restrict the choices of those eligible to only a few market baskets of the subsidized goods and other goods. Some of the programs could actually *decrease* the consumption of the subsidized goods below the levels that would prevail in the absence of the subsidy!

For example, suppose local housing authorities provide a standardized 600-square-foot apartment to eligible low-income persons at a rental rate of 10 cents per square foot per month. The monthly rent on this apartment is therefore \$60 per month. Assume that the market price of equivalent housing is 30 cents per square foot per month. The 600-square-foot apartment would therefore cost \$180 per month without a subsidy. This means the cash equivalent of the subsidy is \$120 per month. Assume that there is no difference in quality between a square foot of public housing and a square foot of private housing purchased on the market.

Figure 4–15 shows how the availability of public housing could induce an eligible person to reduce the amount of housing space rented. All public housing units provide 600 square feet of space. Those wishing to rent the public housing have no choice in the size of the apartment; they must accept the standardized apartment offered or forgo the subsidy. The person whose indifference curves are

FIGURE 4–15 **How an In-Kind Subsidy Can Reduce Consumption**

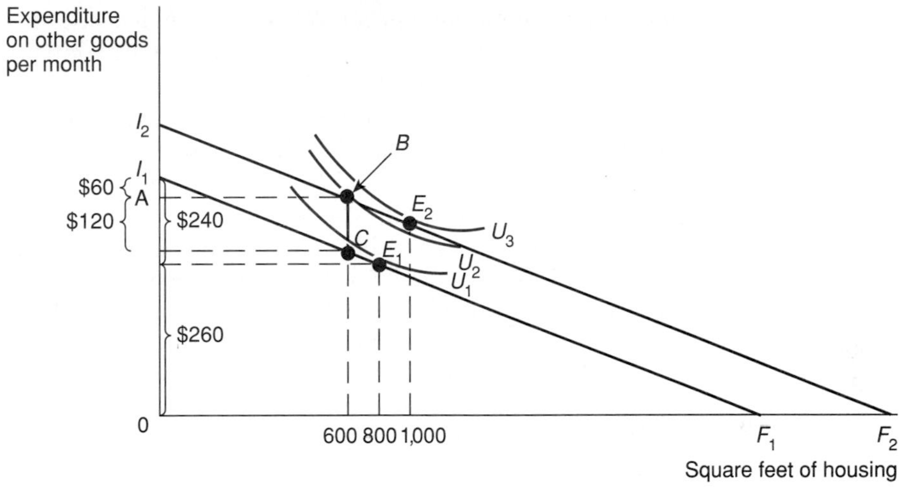

The person is in equilibrium initially at point E_1. Provision of a standardized 600-square-foot apartment induces a movement to point B, where $U_2 > U_1$, but the amount of housing consumed declines. If the person is given the cash value of the subsidy, her equilibrium would be at E_2, where her housing consumption would increase to 1,000 square feet per month.

shown in Figure 4–15 has income I_1 = \$500 per month and is in equilibrium at point E_1, where she currently occupies 800 square feet of housing without a subsidy at a monthly rent of \$240. Her budget line is I_1F_1, and in equilibrium she purchases housing at the market price and therefore spends \$240 on housing and \$260 on other goods.

If she is eligible for public housing, she can rent the standardized 600-square-foot apartment at \$60 per month. This would be a quarter of her current monthly expenditure on housing. The availability of the 600-square-foot public housing unit places a notch in her budget line. She can buy a housing unit of less than 600 square feet at the market price by moving along the segment *IC* of her original budget line. However, if she desires a 600-square-foot apartment, she can move directly from point *C* to point *B*, at which she can move from a 599-square-foot apartment to a 600-square-foot apartment and get the subsidy to boot! The cash value of the subsidy is represented by the distance *CB* on the budget line. If she wanted a 601-square-foot apartment, she could not get the subsidy and would have to pay the market rent. Her budget line when she is eligible for the subsidy is therefore I_1C up to point *C*, which corresponds to the 600-square-foot apartment. There is then a discontinuity in the budget line at point *C*, at which there is a sharp notch up to point *B*. For more housing than 600 square feet per month the budget line notches down again to point *C* and the segment CF_1 of the original budget line becomes relevant. This strange budget line reflects the fact that the public housing is an all-or-nothing offer by the government. To get the subsidy, the woman must agree to consume exactly 600 square feet per month. If she wishes to consume either more or less than this amount, the subsidy is not available. If she wants more than 600 square feet, she must buy it at the market price of 30 cents per square foot along the portion CF_1 of her budget line. If she wants less than 600 square feet, she must buy it at 30 cents per square foot along the portion I_1C of her budget line.

The person whose indifference curves are illustrated in Figure 4–15 is better off in public housing. This is because she achieves utility level U_2 at point B while only enjoying utility level $U_1 < U_2$ along the segment CF_1 of her budget constraint. She therefore chooses to move out of her 800-square-foot apartment into the 600-square-foot subsidized unit. At point B she spends \$60 a month on housing, leaving \$440 per month available for spending on other goods—an increase of \$180 over her previous level. The subsidy induces her, and others like her, to *decrease* the consumption of housing space!

The cash value of the subsidy is \$120 per month. If this were given to the woman each month as a cash subsidy, her monthly money income would increase to \$620. Her budget line would then be I_2F_2, and she would be in equilibrium at point E_2, where she would increase her consumption of housing to 1,000 square feet per month. Thus, an equivalent cash subsidy would be more effective in increasing the consumption of housing than the provision of in-kind standardized public housing. A study of public housing in New York City concluded that nearly half of the tenants enjoying its benefits would have consumed more housing had they been given an equivalent cash grant.[3]

CONCEPT REVIEW

1. Explain how a frequent flier plan affects the budget constraint line of a typical air traveler. Why do different air travelers react differently to such plans?
2. Why will \$1,000 collected in the form of a lump-sum tax cause less reduction in utility for a taxpayer than the same sum collected in the form of a price-distorting tax?
3. How do government subsidies influence the choices of recipients?

SUMMARY

1. Income-consumption curves are used to chart the way a consumer's purchases of goods vary with changes in his or her income. Normal goods are those whose consumption increases with increases in income. The income-consumption curves for such goods are positively sloped when the consumption of the goods is plotted on the horizontal axis. Inferior goods are those whose consumption decreases with increases in income. The income-consumption curves for inferior goods turn backward and become negatively sloped.

[3] John Kraft and Edgar Olsen, "The Distribution of Benefits from Public Housing," in *The Distribution of Economic Well-Being: Studies in Income and Wealth,* ed. F. Thomas Juster, vol. 1 (Cambridge, Mass.: Ballinger, 1977), pp. 51–64.

2. Engel curves show the relationship between money income and the quantity of a good purchased. Engel curves for normal goods slope upward. The slope of an Engel curve indicates the responsiveness of consumer purchases of a good to changes in income.
3. A demand curve can be derived from a price-consumption curve by allowing the price of a good to change while income, the prices of other goods, and preferences are held constant.
4. In analyzing the reaction of consumers to changes in prices, it is important to realize that two separate effects influence the purchasing incentives of consumers. The substitution effect of a change in the price of a good is the change in the quantity of the good purchased that would be observed if the consumer's real income were adjusted so that the price change would make him neither better nor worse off. This effect measures the change in the purchase of a good that results from the change in its relative price alone. The income effect is the change in the consumption of a good resulting from the change in the purchasing power of money that results from a price change. The income and substitution effects for normal goods work in the same direction. For inferior goods the income effect diminishes the substitution effect. However, it is unlikely that the income effect for an inferior good would ever be strong enough to offset the substitution effect.
5. Government subsidies and bonuses that businesses give to frequent users of their services can create notches in consumer budget lines that influence the choices of some but not all consumers.
6. Taxes on products and subsidies for purchases can distort the choices of consumers and make them worse off than they would be if the same dollar amount of taxes collected or subsidies given were in the form of a lump-sum tax or subsidy that does not distort market prices.

Important Concepts

income-consumption curve
normal goods
inferior goods
Engel curve
price-consumption curve
income effect
substitution effect
Giffen good
Laspeyres price index
lump-sum tax

Questions for Review

1. What is the distinction between normal goods and inferior goods? Draw the income-consumption curve for an inferior good. Can you think of any goods you consume that you would regard as inferior?
2. Can a good be an inferior good at *all* levels of income? Explain your answer.
3. Explain the difference between the income effect and the substitution effect of a price change. Why is the income effect of a 50 percent increase in housing rent likely to be much more substantial than that of a 50 percent increase in the price of tissue paper?
4. A book club membership would allow you to purchase books at a 50 percent discount. However, the club's annual membership fee makes you indifferent between buying books at the regular price and buying them through the club at the reduced price. Explain why, if you join the club, the change in your purchase of books observed would be the substitution effect of the 50 percent price reduction.
5. Explain why the substitution effect always acts to increase the consumption of a good whose price declines and to decrease the consumption of a good whose price increases as long as indifference curves are convex. Draw the change in the budget line for both increases and decreases in the price of a good after removal of the income effect to convince yourself that this is true.
6. Why does the income effect for an inferior good offset the substitution effect of a price change?

7. After you buy five books per year from a book club, you get two free books. Books purchased from the club always sell for $20. Show the impact of the bonus on your budget line, and explain why not all members of the club take advantage of the bonus.

8. In the diagram, PC_A and PC_B are price-consumption curves for good *X* for Mr. *A* and Mr. *B*, respectively, both of whom have the same money income. Demonstrate that Mr. *B* demands more of good *X* at any particular good *X* price than does Mr. *A*. (*Hint:* Draw a budget line.)

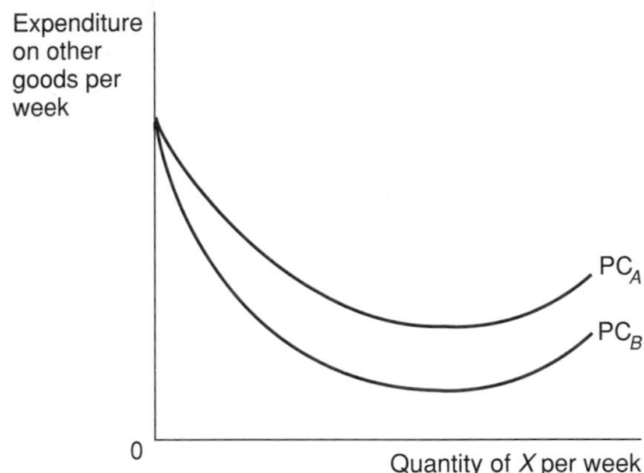

9. Explain why a lump-sum tax results in an income effect for a taxpayer but no substitution effect.

10. Suppose the government decides to subsidize the purchase of bread by rebating 20 percent of the price of bread to consumers. Use indifference curve analysis to show how this price-distorting subsidy will affect the choices of a typical consumer. Use your graph to show the amount of the payment that a recipient of the subsidy will get from the government and to show that if he received this amount as a lump sum, he would purchase less bread than the quantity purchased under the subsidy.

Problems

1. Suppose you join a country club. To be a member, you must pay $1,000 a year. As a member, you can enjoy the club's golf course for a price equal to one quarter of what you would have to pay to use a commercial course. Assume that the annual fee is just high enough to make you indifferent between joining the club and continuing to golf on commercial courses. Also assume that you choose to join the club. Use indifference curve analysis to show the impact of both the fee and the reduced price on your choice.

2. Show that the government's provision of 600 square feet of housing to eligible persons could result in a multiple equilibrium for a recipient. A person with a multiple equilibrium has more than one most preferred outcome in equilibrium. Draw an indifference curve for a person who will *turn down* the opportunity to move into a 600-square-foot housing unit if that opportunity is offered.

3. Suppose you spend all of your budget on two goods. Use indifference curve analysis to show that it is impossible for both goods to be inferior.

4. The diagram depicts a consumer's income-consumption curve for good *X*. Answer the following questions regarding this case:
   a. What is the price of good *X*?
   b. What is the consumer's spending on other goods at point *A*? At point *B*?

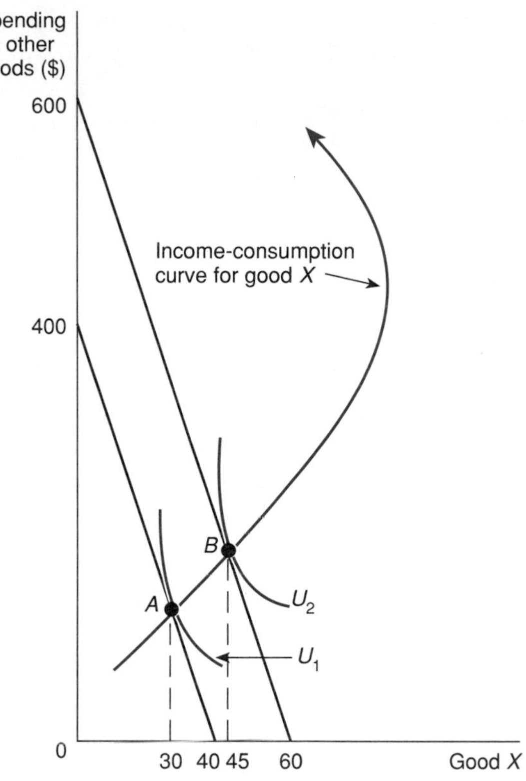

c. What are the coordinates of two points on the consumer's Engel curve for good X?

d. Could good X be an inferior good for the consumer at an income level of $600? At an income level of $2,000?

e. Is the consumer willing to give up the same amount of spending on other goods to obtain one more unit of good X at all points on her income-consumption curve? In other words, is the marginal benefit the same at all points on her income-consumption curve for good X?

5. The indifference curve diagram applies to Michael, whose utility-maximizing goods combinations for two different prices of good M are represented by points A and B. Answer the following questions regarding this case:

   a. What is Michael's income?

   b. What is the price of good M at point A? At point B?

   c. What are the coordinates of two points on Michael's demand curve for good M?

   d. If Michael's demand curve for good M is a straight, downward-sloping line, what is its slope?

   e. Does Michael's price-consumption curve for good M slope upward or downward?

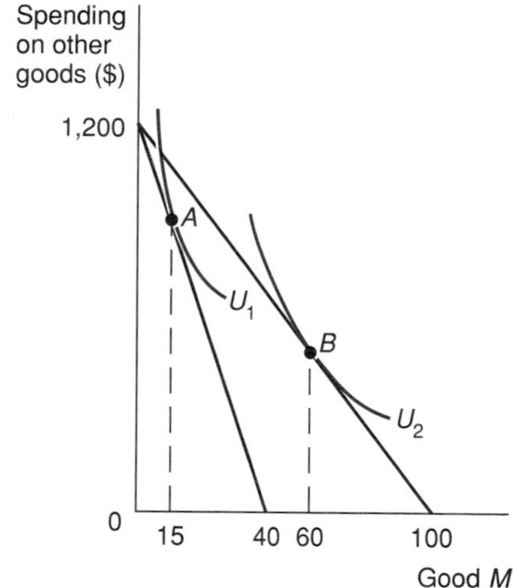

5 Market Demand and Its Elasticity

During 1991 the marketing strategy of Apple Computer, Inc. changed dramatically. Up to that point the prices of Apple's Macintosh computers had been higher than those of competing brands, many of which lacked the graphics capability and user-friendly operating systems of the Macs. In 1991, however, Apple's managers decided that it would be in the company's best interests to increase its market share of the personal computer market. Apple's long-term goal was to gain 20 percent of the market. To achieve this goal, Apple introduced a new line of computers and a new pricing strategy. It reduced the prices of its basic models substantially—by 50 percent and even more.

The market response to the new pricing strategy was phenomenal: by the end of the year Apple reported an 85 percent jump in unit sales of its Macs! The dramatic response to price cuts took even Apple's managers by surprise. Apparently the demand for their company's computers was much more sensitive to changes in price than they thought.

Like most businesses, Apple would have benefited from more precise information on the market demand for its products. Business firms competing for sales are more concerned with the market demand for their product than with the demand of any individual consumer for their product. Market demand for a product depends on total population and its age distribution as well as individual consumer incomes, preferences, tastes, and prices. Knowledge of market demand is the key to a successful marketing and sales program. Without such knowledge it is impossible to forecast the effect of price changes on unit sales and business revenues.

We can now show how market demand is related to individual demand. We can also show how various measures of the sensitivity of market demand to changes in prices and incomes can be useful to both businesses and government officials in formulating economic policies. You will see how measures of the sensitivity of quantities demanded to prices and other demand determinants can be used to help in forecasting changes in consumer expenditure on a good when the price of that good changes.

Market demand also indicates the maximum prices that would be paid for an economic good as its quantity is varied. Information about the willingness and ability of consumers to pay for goods as a function of the availability of those goods is embodied in a market demand curve. You will learn how market demand curves can be used to approximate the benefits consumers receive from purchasing goods and how policies influencing prices affect the net benefits enjoyed by consumers.

DERIVATION OF MARKET DEMAND CURVES

Market demand curve A demand curve derived from individual demand curves for a product in a market by adding the quantities demanded by all consumers at each possible price.

A **market demand curve** is derived from individual demand curves for a given product by adding the quantity demanded by all consumers at each possible price. Because, as the previous chapter demonstrated, individual demand curves are downward sloping, market demand curves are also downward sloping.

This can be illustrated with a simple example. Assume that there are only five consumers in the market for Rolls-Royces in your city. The demand curve for each of these consumers is drawn separately in Figure 5–1(a). These separate demand curves tell how many Rolls-Royces each consumer will purchase per year at various possible prices. In Figure 5–1(b), the market demand curve is derived by adding the quantities demanded by each consumer per year at each of the possible prices.

At any price above P_1, total sales of the good would be zero because no consumer will buy it when its price exceeds P_1. As the price of the good falls below P_1, consumers begin to purchase it. At any price above, say, \$300,000 the quantity demanded for Rolls-Royces would be zero. At a price below P_1 but above P_2, the market demand would be the same as the demand curve D_5. In other words, the market demand would be that of only one consumer. As price falls below P_2, a second consumer enters the market. For example, at a price between

FIGURE 5–1 Derivation of a Market Demand Curve

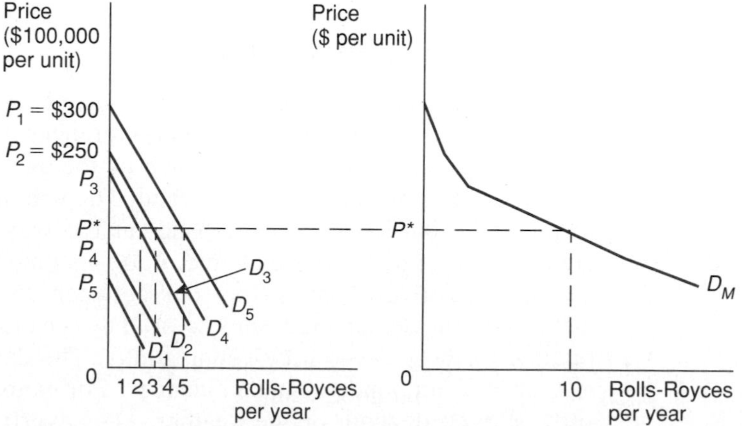

The market demand curve, D_M, is the sum of the quantities demanded by all consumers at each possible price. At price P^* the total quantity demanded in the market is $2 + 3 + 5 = 10$ units.

\$250,000 and \$300,000 for these splendid machines, only one (presumably very rich) buyer would buy any. As price falls below \$250,000, an additional buyer enters the market.

At any price between P_2 and P_3, market demand consists of the *sum* of the quantities demanded of two consumers. As price falls below P_3, a third consumer enters the market and the total quantity demanded is equal to the sum of the quantities demanded by each of the three consumers. For example, if price were $P^* = \$175{,}000$, which is below P_3 but greater than P_4, the consumer whose demand curve is D_5 would purchase five Rolls-Royces per year. This very rich consumer might use one car in his business and give the rest to other family members, or he might use a different one every day of the week. At that price the consumer whose demand curve is D_4 would buy three Rolls-Royces per year and the consumer whose demand curve is D_3 would buy two per year. The remaining two consumers would not buy any Rolls-Royces at price P^*. The total market demand at price P^* would therefore be $2 + 3 + 5 = 10$ Rolls-Royces per year. This is shown as a point on the market demand curve corresponding to the price P^*.

If price were to fall below P_5, the consumer with demand curve D_1 would begin purchasing Rolls-Royces and the total market demand would be the sum of the quantities demanded by all five consumers. This is shown in Figure 5–1(b).

In general, for any number of consumers, the total quantity demanded at any price is obtained by summing the quantities demanded at that price by each consumer. When this is done for each possible price, the result is the market demand curve. The market demand curve represents the horizontal summation of quantities demanded at each price because all of the addition takes place along the horizontal axis. In a typical market the amount demanded by any one buyer at any given price is likely to be a very small share of the total quantity demanded. An important determinant of market demand is therefore the *number* of consumers who are willing to purchase a good at each of its possible prices. Population is therefore a major influence on market demand.

Determinants of Market Demand

Market demand depends on all the determinants of individual demands, including income, prices of related goods, and preferences of consumers. In addition, various demographic characteristics, such as the age distribution of the population, are major influences on market demand. The willingness and ability of consumers to purchase particular items depend on the way income is distributed among demographic groups. For example, if the income of persons over the age of 65 increases relative to that of persons between 25 and 35, you would expect an increase in the demand for items favored by the elderly, such as medical services, relative to those favored by young adults. The demand for particular goods can also depend on noneconomic influences. For example, the demand for sleds and snow shovels depends on the weather. The advertising and promotional efforts of business firms can influence consumers' choices by providing information (be it true or slightly misleading) affecting their preferences. Finally, the market demand for a good is also influenced by the number of consumers in foreign nations who are willing and able to purchase it.

Income and preferences for certain goods are likely to be correlated with age. Clearly, the greater the birthrate and the greater the proportion of children in the population, the greater is the demand for youth-oriented goods and services such as diapers and baby clothes, toys, schooling, and the services of obstetricians and pediatricians. On the other hand, the demand for rest home services and pacemakers can be expected to increase if the proportion of elderly persons in the population increases. If more elderly persons retire early, the demand for such leisure-time activities as vacations in Florida is likely to increase and the demand for life insurance is likely to decline. Businesses carefully project changes in the age distribution of the population in an attempt to forecast changes in the pattern of demand.

Household size, like the age distribution of the population, is a major influence on the demand for various goods. Household size is measured by the number of related persons who live together. A trend toward smaller households will increase the demand for small condominium housing units and apartments but will decrease the demand for large homes. An increase in the number of persons living alone probably means an increase in the demand for convenience food services and for apartments and condominiums. It could even contribute to an increase in the demand for pets as substitutes for children.

The number of households headed by persons between the ages of 18 and 25 increased from 4.6 million in 1970 to 6.4 million in 1980. During the same period the increase in the number of households headed by 25–34-year-olds increased from 12 million to about 18 million. This increase was coupled with a sharp increase in the number of single-person households and households of nonrelated persons living together. There was an increase in the number of persons of all ages who lived alone.

Surveys indicate that younger households borrow more often and spend higher portions of their income than do households headed by older persons. The residential housing construction boom of the 1980s was undoubtedly influenced by increased household formation among the baby boomers. The rising rate of single-person households in all age groups also contributed to increased housing demand.

Younger households also tend to spend higher proportions of their incomes on durable goods. These goods include automobiles, furniture, and household appliances. As the proportion of national income earned by such households increases, there will be a tendency toward increased demand for durable goods.[1]

A population is said to "age" when the average age of the population rises. The children of the postwar baby boom that lasted until the late 1950s are now adults. The proportion of children in the U.S. population will decline steadily at least up to the beginning of the 21st century. In 1960 children below the age of 18 accounted for about 35.7 percent of the population; by 1995 they are expected to account for 27 percent of the population. The proportion of persons 65 years of

[1] For in-depth analysis, see Louise B. Russell, *The Baby Boom Generation and the Economy* (Washington, D.C.: Brookings Institution, 1982).

age and over, which was 9.2 percent in 1960, is expected to reach 12.4 percent in 1995. Population projections indicate that by the year 2080 nearly 25 percent of the U.S. population will be over the age of 65.

Analysis of the effect of changes in age distribution and household size on broad categories of consumer purchases suggests that a number of items are particularly sensitive to these changes. Purchases of furniture and vehicles tend to decline with increases in average age and decreases in the number of persons per household. Decreases in the number of children per household are associated with decreases in the consumption of education and in housing construction. Changes in age distribution have little effect on health care expenditures. Increased expenditure by elderly persons is apparently offset by decreased birth-related medical expenses.[2] The aging of the population is likely to decrease the enrollments of educational institutions and thus to decrease the demand for education-related goods and services. As the population ages, the demand for housing construction and related activities is also likely to decline.

Price Elasticity of Demand

Price elasticity of demand The percentage change in quantity demanded that would result from each 1 percent change in price along a demand curve.

Price elasticity of demand is a measure of the percentage change in quantity demanded that would result from each 1 percent change in price along a demand curve. Price elasticity of demand is a number used to measure the responsiveness of quantity demanded to a change in the price of a good, assuming no change in any other demand determinant.

Along a demand curve, price elasticity of demand, E_D, is defined as

$$E_D = \% \text{ change in } Q_D / \% \text{ change in } P \qquad \textbf{(5–1)}$$

where Q_D is the quantity demanded of a good measured along a demand curve and P is the price of the good. For example, suppose that a 1 percent increase in the price of new automobiles (other things being equal) over last year's price results in a 2 percent decrease in the annual quantity of automobiles sold. The price elasticity of demand for automobiles would be $-2\%/1\% = -2$.

Price elasticity of demand is a negative number because the law of demand implies that for any given change in price, the change in quantity demanded is in the opposite direction. In other words, when the denominator of Equation 5–1 is positive, the numerator is negative, and vice versa. The ratio of the two percentage changes is always negative because the numerator and denominator always have different signs.[3]

---

[2] Philip Musgrove, *U.S. Household Consumption, Income, and Demographic Changes, 1975–2025* (Baltimore: Resources for the Future, Johns Hopkins University Press, 1982), pp. 30–35.

[3] Sometimes economists report the absolute values of estimated price elasticities of demand. This ignores the minus sign and presumes that those using the estimates realize that the estimated elasticities are, in fact, negative.

Calculating Price Elasticity of Demand

The following formula can be used to calculate the price elasticity of demand from actual data corresponding to points along a demand curve.

$$E_D = (\Delta Q_D/Q_D)/(\Delta P/P) \qquad \textbf{(5–2)}$$

It is easy to see that the formula corresponds to the definition of elasticity. Suppose that at a price of \$100 monthly sales of bicycles in a city are 2,000. Next month the price of bicycles goes up to \$101 and nothing else affecting the demand for bicycles changes. As a result of the price increase the quantity of bicycles demanded per month falls to 1,990. The percentage change in the price of bicycles is the \$1 increase in price (ΔP) divided by the initial price (P) of \$100 and then multiplied by 100 percent to convert the resulting decimal into a percentage. The percentage change in price is therefore

$$[\Delta P/P](100\%) = [\$1/\$100](100\%) = 0.01(100\%) = 1\%$$

The percentage change in quantity demanded is

$$[\Delta Q_D/Q_D](100\%) = [-10/2{,}000](100\%) = -0.005(100\%) = -0.5\%$$

The price elasticity of demand is therefore

$$(\Delta Q_D/Q_D)(100\%)/(\Delta P/P)(100\%) = -0.5\%/1\% = -0.5$$

Because 100 percent appears in both the numerator and denominator of the above equation, it cancels out, giving the formula for elasticity shown in Equation 5–2. Equation 5–2 therefore corresponds to the ratio of the percentage change in quantity demanded to the percentage change in price that caused the change.

Elasticity versus Slope

Equation 5–2 can also be written in the following way to show how price elasticity of demand is related to the slope of a demand curve.

$$E_D = (\Delta Q_D/Q_D)/(\Delta P/P) = (P/Q_D)(\Delta Q_D/\Delta P) \qquad \textbf{(5–3)}$$

The slope of a demand curve is $\Delta P/\Delta Q_D$. The fraction $\Delta Q_D/\Delta P$ in Equation 5–3 is simply the inverse of the slope of the demand curve at a point. Price elasticity of demand, however, depends not only on the slope of the demand curve but also on the actual price and quantity demanded.

The slope of the demand curve has different units of measurement for different goods. For example, the unit of measurement for the slope of the demand curve for automobiles is dollars per vehicle. The unit of measurement for the slope of the demand curve for wheat is dollars per bushel. The difference in units makes it difficult to compare the relative responsiveness of the quantities purchased of different goods. No such problems exist for elasticity. Economists therefore regard elasticity as a more useful measure of sensitivity to price changes than slope.

It is easy to show the defects of slope as a measure of responsiveness. Suppose that for each \$1 increase in the price of a bottle of wine the quantity of bottles demanded in a city per month declines by 1,000. The slope of the demand curve for wine would therefore be $-\$1/1{,}000$ bottles $= -\$0.001$ per bottle. Suppose the quantity of wine is measured by the case instead of by the bottle. If there are 10 bottles to the case, the change in the number of cases sold when price increases by \$1 is 100. Measuring wine by the case therefore results in a measured slope of the demand curve of $-\$1/100$ cases $= -\$0.01$ per case. The two slopes differ by a factor of 10! Yet nothing has changed except the units of measurement.

There are no such problems when elasticity is used to measure the responsiveness of demand. Suppose the price of a bottle of wine rises by 10 cents, amounting to, say, a 1 percent increase, and as a result the number of bottles demanded per month falls by 100. The percentage change in bottles demanded, assuming that the initial quantity was 10,000 bottles per month, would be

$$[-100/10{,}000](100\%) = -1\%$$

The 100-bottle reduction in quantity demanded is equivalent to a 10-case reduction, assuming 10 bottles to the case. The percentage change in cases sold would be $[-10/1{,}000](100\%)$, which also equals -1 percent. The price elasticity of demand would therefore be -1 independent of the units of measurement of quantity demanded.

Slope is an unreliable indicator of the sensitivity of quantity demanded to changes in the price of a good because the value of slope depends on the units used. Moreover, elasticity is merely a *measure* of the responsiveness of demand and *not* a determinant of demand. Elasticity is used to characterize the sensitivity of buyers' willingness to buy to changes in price along a demand curve.

The Range of Variation of Price Elasticity of Demand

Price elasticity of demand can range from zero to minus infinity. The greater the absolute value of price elasticity of demand, $|E_D|$, the more price elastic is the demand. The absolute value of a number ignores the sign in front of it. For example, demand is more price elastic when $E_D = -5$ than when $E_D = -1$ because the number 5, which is the absolute value of -5, exceeds the number 1, which is the absolute value of -1.

It is common for economists to report estimates of E_D as negative numbers. Demand is said to be *elastic* if the absolute value of its price elasticity ranges between 1 and infinity. Demand is characterized as *inelastic* if the absolute value of its price elasticity is between zero and 1. If price elasticity of demand is exactly equal to -1, its absolute value is 1 and demand is characterized as *unit elastic*. When price elasticity of demand is zero, demand is said to be *perfectly inelastic*, while it is said to be *perfectly elastic* when the absolute value of its price elasticity is equal to infinity. Table 5–1 summarizes the range of variation for price elasticity of demand, showing both the numerical and absolute values in each range.

Perfectly Inelastic and Perfectly Elastic Demand Curves

What would the demand curve look like for a product whose price elasticity of demand is zero no matter what its price? A *perfectly inelastic demand curve*

TABLE 5–1 Price Elasticity of Demand: Range of Variation as an Index of Degree of Responsiveness

Numerical Value of E_D	*Absolute Value of E_D*	*Relative Responsiveness of Quantity Demanded to Price (Ignoring Direction of Change)*	*Demand Response Is*
$-1 < E_D < 0$	$0 < \|E_D\| < 1$	% change in Q_D < % change in P	Inelastic
$E_D = -1$	$\|E_D\| = 1$	% change in Q_D = % change in P	Unit elastic
$-\infty \leq E_D < -1$	$1 < \|E_D\| < \infty$	% change in Q_D > % change in P	Elastic

FIGURE 5–2 Perfectly Inelastic and Perfectly Elastic Demand Curves

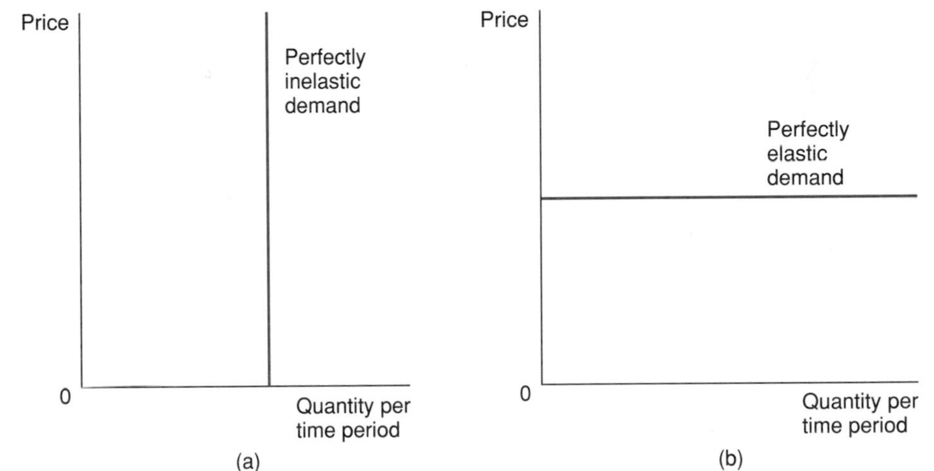

The demand curve in (a) is perfectly inelastic, while the one in (b) is perfectly elastic.

would be a vertical line, as illustrated in Figure 5–2(a). Along this demand curve the quantity demanded is always the same and is therefore insensitive to change in price. No matter how much the price changes, the change in quantity demanded is always zero.

It is unlikely that the demand curve for any product will be perfectly inelastic. In most cases we expect the demand curve for a product to have at least some downward slope in accordance with the law of demand. Products with virtually no substitutes might have a demand curve that is *nearly* vertical. For example, the demand curve for insulin by diabetics might be close to perfectly inelastic because insulin has no substitutes. However, higher prices for insulin are likely to induce at least some diabetics to watch their diet more carefully and to pursue other measures that can reduce the amount and frequency of their required insulin doses.

Figure 5–2(b) illustrates a *perfectly elastic demand curve*. Think of the curve as one that is approached in the limit when a downward-sloping demand curve becomes so flat that it can't be distinguished from a horizontal line. A nearly flat demand curve means that the tiniest change in the price of a product will result in a nearly infinite change in the quantity demanded. Along the perfectly elastic demand curve at any point, a price change that is as close as possible to zero will result in infinite changes in quantities demanded, giving a price elasticity of demand of minus infinity.

An infinitely elastic demand curve would prevail for a product that has abundant and perfect substitutes. For example, if you are one of a million sellers in a competitive market for a standardized product such as grade A eggs, buyers will view your eggs as a perfect substitute for any other seller's eggs. You could sell all the eggs you wished at the market price of, say, $1 per dozen, as illustrated in Figure 5–2(b), without causing the price to decline.

Determinants of Price Elasticity of Demand

Price elasticity of demand for a good depends on the following determinants:

1. *The availability of substitutes*. The more substitute goods (goods serving a similar purpose) there are for a good whose price rises, the more elastic is the demand for the good. It is rare for a good to have no substitutes. A particular automobile brand is likely to have a number of competing brands that are similar. The demand for Chevrolets is therefore likely to be quite elastic because there are many substitute cars available for consumers to choose among. The availability of substitutes varies from good to good. As a result there is considerable variability in price elasticity of demand for various goods.

2. *The period of adjustment to price changes*. Economists generally estimate both short-term and long-term price elasticities of demand. The demand for a good is generally more elastic in the long run than in the short run because persons generally find more substitutes for a good as time goes by. In the short run there might be little that drivers can do in response to a sharp increase in the price of gasoline. In the long run, however, they can replace gas guzzlers with fuel-efficient cars. Over longer periods buyers have more time to find substitutes for goods whose prices increase and sellers develop substitutes and make them available. For these reasons, demand is likely to be more elastic in the long run than in the short run.

3. *The portion of consumer budgets allocated to the product*. Large percentage increases in the price of goods that constitute small portions of your total budget might have little effect on your purchases of these goods if you regard them as necessities. For example, a 20 percent increase in the price of toilet paper might have little effect on the quantity demanded of this item because the increase is likely to cost the typical consumer only a small portion of his or her income. On the other hand, a 20 percent increase in housing rents might induce tenants to seek out smaller apartments when their leases expire because consumers typically spend between 25 percent and 35 percent of their income on housing. There are, however, numerous exceptions to the rule that price elasticity for a good varies inversely with the portion of the budget allocated to it. Consumers who allocate very small percentages of their budgets to olives might be quite responsive to increases in the price of olives.

TABLE 5–2 Estimated Price Elasticities of Demand

Item	*Short Run*	*Long Run*
Stationery	−0.47	−0.56
Jewelry and watches	−0.41	−0.67
Tires and tubes	−0.86	−1.19
Gasoline	−0.4*	−1.5†
Foreign travel by U.S. residents	−0.14	−1.77
Housing	−0.3	−1.88
Household electricity use	−0.13	−1.89
Tobacco products	−0.46	−1.89
Household natural gas use‡	−1.4	−2.1
Automobiles and parts	−1.87	−2.24
China, glassware, and tableware	−1.54	−2.55
Toilet articles and preparations	−0.20	−3.04
Intercity rail travel	−1.4	−3.19
Movies	−0.87	−3.67
Radio and TV repair	−0.47	−3.84

* Robert Archibald and Robert Gillingham, "The Review of the Short-Run Consumer Demand for Gasoline Using Household Survey Data," *Review of Economics and Statistics* 62 (November 1980), pp. 622–28.

† J. M. Griffin, *Energy Conservation in the OECD, 1980–2000* (Cambridge, Mass.: Ballinger, 1979).

‡ G. R. Lakshmanan and William Anderson, "Residential Energy Demand in the United States," *Regional Science and Urban Economics* 10 (August 1980), pp. 371–86.

Source: Except where otherwise indicated, data are from Hendrik S. Houthakker and Lester D. Taylor, *Consumer Demand in the United States: Analyses and Projections* (Cambridge, Mass.: Harvard University Press, 1970).

Empirical Estimates of Price Elasticities of Demand: How the Sensitivity to Price Changes Differs among Goods

Table 5–2 presents both short-run and long-run estimated price elasticities of demand for a number of items. For most of these items, as would be expected, demand is more price elastic in the long run than in the short run.

Table 5–2 indicates inelastic short-run demand for all of the items presented except china, glassware, and tableware; intercity rail travel; household natural gas use; and automobiles and parts. The short-run price elasticity of demand for household electricity use is nearly zero. All of the long-run price elasticities exceed the short-run values. Demand is quite elastic for most products in the long run.

Using Price Elasticities of Demand to Analyze Consumer Expenditures

Sellers are very interested in the amounts consumers will spend on a good because such expenditures are an important determinant of their profits. Total expenditures on a good over a period is the quantity purchased multiplied by the price of each unit. From the sellers' point of view, expenditures by consumers represent the total revenue they take in from selling their output, which is the quantity (Q) sold (and therefore purchased) multiplied by the price (P) per unit:

$$\text{Total expenditure} = \text{Total revenue} = PQ \qquad \textbf{(5–4)}$$

If, for example, the price of beef is \$1.50 per pound and 20 million pounds are sold at that price each month, the monthly total expenditure by buyers is \$30 million. From the sellers' point of view this represents \$30 million of sales revenue. Because total expenditure is the product of the price and the quantity sold, it can be represented by the area of the rectangle in Figure 5–3 whose height is the market price and whose width is the quantity sold per month. When the price is P_1, total revenue is represented by the area $OP_1E_1Q_1$.

Suppose an increase in the price of cattle feed increases the cost per pound of producing beef. As illustrated in Figure 5–3, this cost increase will cause a decrease in the supply of beef and will therefore increase its price per pound. The increase in price causes a decrease in quantity demanded.

When the supply decreases to S' and the price increases to P_2, total expenditure on beef by buyers is represented by the area $OP_2E_2Q_2$. This area also represents the monthly revenue that sellers of beef will take in at the new, higher price. Do not confuse the total revenue with the price of the product. Price is revenue per unit output (also called *average revenue*) because $P = PQ/Q$.

A price increase because of a decrease in supply would increase PQ were it not for the fact that the *increase* in price induces a *decrease* in quantity demanded. As quantity demanded declines, it exerts a downward influence on PQ. Whether

FIGURE 5–3 Changes in Total Expenditure by Consumers

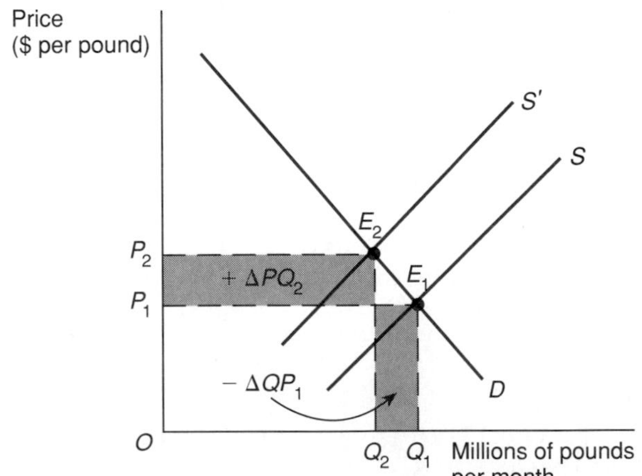

At a price of P_1 quantity sold is Q_1 and total expenditure is represented by the area $OP_1E_1Q_1$. This is also the total revenue from sales received by beef distributors. A decrease in supply from S to S' causes price increases to P_2 and quantity demanded falls to Q_2. Total expenditures by consumers are now the area $OP_2E_2Q_2$.

expenditure by buyers increases or decreases depends on the relative strength of the upward pressure of the price increase and the downward pressure of the decline in quantity demanded. Knowledge of a product's price elasticity of demand can be used to predict the relative magnitudes of the upward and downward forces influencing expenditure. Sellers can therefore use that knowledge to predict changes in their total revenue when prices change as a result of changes in supply.

The short-run price elasticity of demand for beef has been estimated to be about −0.5, implying an inelastic demand. An inelastic demand means that, ignoring the sign of the change, the percentage change in quantity demanded will be less than the percentage change in price that caused it.

Suppose that the price of beef is expected to go up to $1.88 per pound as a result of the decrease in supply. This is a 25 percent increase in price. Inelastic demand implies that the reduction in the quantity of beef demanded will be less than 25 percent. In fact, because the price elasticity of demand is −0.5, the percentage reduction in quantity demanded will be exactly one half of the increase in price. This means that the reduction in quantity demanded will be 12.5 percent. The quantity of beef demanded will therefore fall to 17.5 million pounds per month. Because the percentage increase in price is greater than the percentage decrease in quantity demanded, total revenue, PQ, increases. In this case, total expenditure on beef increases from $30 million to $32.9 million per month as a result of the decrease in supply. In Figure 5–3 the gain in revenue from the higher price is shown as the shaded rectangle ΔPQ_2 and the loss in revenue is shown as the shaded area ΔQP_1. Because demand is inelastic, $\Delta PQ_2 > -\Delta QP_1$ and the gain in revenue from the price rise exceeds the loss in revenue from the reduction in quantity demanded.

Price Elasticity of Demand and Changes in Total Revenue

Whenever the demand for a good is inelastic, an increase in its price raises total expenditure on that good and therefore also raises total revenue taken in by sellers. This is because when demand is inelastic, the upward pressure on revenue resulting from a price increase is greater than the corresponding downward pressure on revenue resulting from the consequent decrease in quantity demanded. At the extreme, suppose the price elasticity of demand for a good is zero. This implies that an increase in price would have no effect on quantity demanded. If this were the case, ΔQ would be zero and total revenue taken in by sellers would increase by the percentage increase in price.

When demand is elastic, any percentage change in price results in a larger percentage change in quantity demanded. The short-run price elasticity of demand for pork has been estimated to be −1.25. What would happen to the revenue of pork producers if an increase in feed costs resulted in a decrease in the supply of pork? The answer is that their revenue would decline because an elastic demand for pork means that the percentage change in quantity demanded caused by the price increase would exceed the percentage change in price. The positive effect of the increase in price on revenue would be offset by the negative effect of the decrease in quantity demanded, causing the product PQ to decline in value.

TABLE 5–3 Price Elasticity of Demand and Total Revenue or Expenditures

Price Elasticity	*Implication (Ignoring the Sign of the Change)*	*Change in PQ for Price Decrease*	*Change in PQ for Price Increase*
Elastic	% change in Q_D > % change in P	+	–
Unitary	% change in Q_D = % change in P	0	0
Inelastic	% change in Q_D < % change in P	–	+

Suppose the demand for a product is unit elastic. This implies that any given percentage change in price would result in an equal but opposite percentage change in quantity demanded. Any price increase therefore causes an equal but opposite percentage decrease in quantity demanded. The net effect is an unchanged total revenue because the upward force on revenue is exactly offset by the downward force.

The logic is the same for decreases in prices. When price decreases, it exerts downward pressure on total expenditures that can be offset by increases in quantity demanded. The net effect on revenue or expenditures of a price decrease depends on the relationship between the percentage decrease in price and the percentage increase in quantity demanded. Why would a decrease in price have a favorable effect on the revenue of pork producers? If the demand for pork is elastic, the downward pressure on revenue caused by a price decline is more than offset by the increase in quantity demanded. The opposite is true for a decrease in the price of beef caused by an increase in its supply. Because the demand for beef is inelastic, the decrease in price decreases the total revenue taken in by cattle producers.

Table 5–3 summarizes the relationship between price elasticity of demand and total revenue.

Unit-Elastic Demand

Figure 5–4 illustrates the demand curve for a good whose price elasticity of demand is unitary at all possible prices. This means that no matter what the price, the total expenditure on the good is constant.[4] Unitary elasticity of demand implies that any percentage change in price will be accompanied by a corresponding equal and opposite percentage change in quantity demanded. Along the curve, PQ_D must therefore be constant if demand is unit elastic at all points on the curve.

[4] The equation of the curve is $PQ = K$, where K is a constant.

FIGURE 5–4 A Unit-Elastic Demand Curve

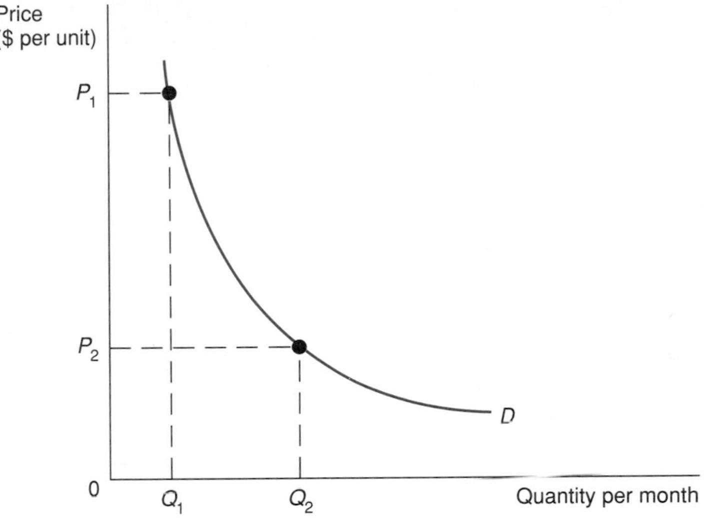

All points along the demand curve illustrated above, are unit elastic. This means that no matter what the price, total expenditure by consumers is always the same. For example, at price P_1, total expenditure is P_1Q_1; at price P_2, total expenditure is P_2Q_2. However, $P_1Q_1 = P_2Q_2$.

A good whose price elasticity of demand is always unitary is therefore one on which consumers always spend the same amount. Some estimates of the demand for housing indicate that its price elasticity of demand is close to -1. These estimates, if accurate, indicate that consumers tend to spend constant amounts on housing irrespective of its price. Note that this does not imply that they consume constant *amounts* of housing. It implies that they tend to adjust to any given percentage change in the price of housing by changing the quantity of housing consumed in an equal but opposite percentage amount.

CONCEPT REVIEW

1. How are market demand curves related to individual demand curves? What important determinants of market demand are not considered in deriving individual demand curves?
2. If the price elasticity of demand for cameras is -3, calculate the percentage change in the quantity of cameras demanded that would result from a 10 percent price increase for cameras.
3. The price elasticity of demand for wheat is estimated to be -0.5. What will happen to the revenue of wheat producers if supply increases and the market price of wheat falls?

MODERN MICROECONOMICS IN ACTION: **INTERNATIONAL REPORT**

The Price of the Dollar and the Price Elasticity of Demand for Imported Goods and U.S. Exports

The price of the dollar in terms of the currency of the key trading partners of the United States dropped sharply in international currency markets between 1985 and 1988. In early 1985 $1 could be exchanged for 260 Japanese yen in these markets. By early 1988 the conditions of supply and demand had changed significantly and $1 could be exchanged for only about 120 yen! Between 1988 and 1990 the price of the dollar increased to 145 yen, but by early 1992 it was again down to 120 yen. The ups and downs of the price of the dollar in terms of foreign currency have important implications for the prices of foreign goods in the United States and for sales of U.S. goods in foreign markets.

For example, suppose that the minimum price a Japanese seller of a quality 35-mm camera will accept is 100,000 Japanese yen. If the market price of the dollar is currently 250 yen, then the price of the camera *in dollars* will be

$$100{,}000 \text{ yen } (\$1/250 \text{ yen}) = \$400$$

It will take $400 to provide the Japanese seller with the 100,000 yen to cover costs and provide a profit from selling the camera in the United States when the exchange rate is 250 yen to the dollar.

If the price of the dollar falls to 120 yen, assuming no change in the minimum 100,000-yen supply price, the dollar price of the camera will be

$$(100{,}000 \text{ yen})(\$1/120 \text{ yen}) = \$833.33$$

A decrease in the price of the dollar in terms of foreign currency therefore puts upward pressure on the dollar price of foreign goods sold in the United States.

It is also easy to see that a decline in the price of the dollar in terms of foreign currency decreases the price of U.S. goods to foreigners. If the dollar price of U.S. wheat is $1 per bushel, the price of a bushel of U.S. wheat sold in Japan will be 250 yen when the exchange rate is 250 yen to the dollar. When the exchange rate is only 120 yen to the dollar, the Japanese can get the same $1 worth of wheat for only 120 yen!

You would expect the higher prices of foreign goods to decrease the quantity of these goods demanded in the United States, thereby contributing to lower U.S. expenditures for imports. Similarly, the decrease in the price of the U.S. dollar can be expected to increase the quantity of U.S. goods demanded abroad, thereby contributing to increased expenditure by foreigners for U.S. exports.

Despite the lower price of the dollar in 1987 and 1988, U.S. expenditures on Japanese goods did not decrease substantially in those years. In fact, in 1986 and 1987 U.S. buyers continued to spend record amounts on imported goods. In 1986, despite the sharp decline in the price of the dollar that year, Americans spent a record $170 billion more on imports than on exports.

One possible explanation for the increased expenditure on imported goods, despite rapid increases in the price of these goods in dollars, is that the demand for such goods is price inelastic over a period of one year. When demand for any good is price inelastic, an increase in the price of the good results in an *increase* in consumer expenditures on it. Apparently, U.S. consumers were reluctant to cut back significantly on their purchases of Japanese VCRs, televisions, cameras, and automobiles despite steep dollar increases in their prices. If foreign demand for U.S. exports is price inelastic, then expenditures on U.S. exports will also decline despite increased quantities exported. When the demand for imports and exports is price inelastic, the gap between expenditures on exports and on imports will increase despite the decline in the price of the dollar.

This does not necessarily imply that permanent price increases will not be effective in reducing expenditures on imports and increasing revenue from exports over a longer period. Remember that demand is always more price elastic in the long run than in the short run. As time goes by, U.S. consumers are likely to find more substitutes for Japanese and other imported goods. Also, the higher the prices of these goods, the more likely it is that U.S. producers can market goods of comparable quality to U.S. consumers at prices that these consumers find more competitive than the prices charged by foreign sellers. Foreign buyers are also likely to be more responsive to lower prices of U.S. exports over longer periods than over a one-year period.

Calculating Price Elasticity of Demand for Points on a Demand Curve

The price elasticity of demand can be measured for infinitesimally small changes in price at a given point on a demand curve.[5] A linear demand curve has a constant slope, but it does *not* have a constant price elasticity. In fact, a linear demand curve has a price elasticity that varies continuously from zero to minus infinity. This is illustrated in Figure 5–5. When price is zero, price elasticity of demand is also zero because the ratio P/Q_D in the formula for price elasticity of demand (Equation 5–4) is also zero. When price is so high that quantity demanded approaches zero, the value of price elasticity becomes minus infinity because the ratio P/Q_D approaches infinite value.

In other words, demand is more price elastic along a linear demand curve at higher prices than at lower prices. Each 1 percent increase in price can be expected to result in a greater percentage reduction in quantity demanded. If a seller

FIGURE 5–5 Price Elasticity at Points along a Demand Curve

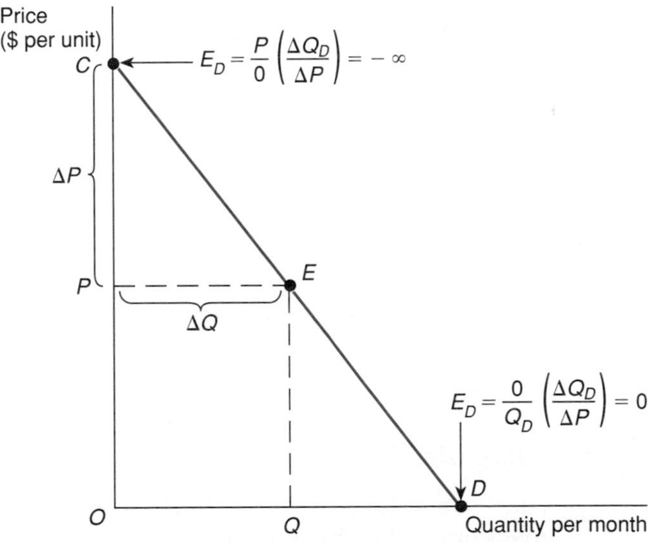

Although a linear demand curve has constant slope, price elasticity of demand varies along the curve. At point *E*, using the distance formula, price elasticity of demand is $-(OP/PC)$. At zero price, price elasticity of demand equals zero. As price approaches an amount represented by the distance *OC*, price elasticity of demand approaches minus infinity.

[5] The point elasticity of demand is therefore

$$(P/Q_D)(dQ_D/dP)$$

and it is measured for the given P and Q_D.

faces a linear demand curve for his product, this implies that his customers are more sensitive to price increases when price is already high than when price is low, that market demand becomes more inelastic with respect to price as supply increases. For example, as the supply of personal computers increased in the 1980s, sellers found it increasingly difficult to increase revenue despite continued price cuts. As a market becomes saturated with a product and price falls as a result of increased supply, demand for the product often tends to become more inelastic.

Price Elasticity of Demand as a Ratio of Distances at Points on a Demand Curve

For D, the linear demand curve illustrated in Figure 5–5, price elasticity of demand at price P may be calculated as a ratio of distances on the price axis. The fraction $\Delta Q_D/\Delta P$ is the same at all points along the demand curve because the demand curve has constant slope. At price P

$$\Delta Q_D/\Delta P = -PE/PC = -OQ/PC$$

because $\Delta P = PC$ and $\Delta Q = PE$ at that point. The ratio PE/PC can also be written as $-OQ/PC$ because $PE = OQ$ in Figure 5–5. At point E price is represented by the distance OP, while quantity demanded is represented by the distance OQ. Price elasticity of demand is therefore equal to

$$(P/Q_D)(\Delta Q_D/\Delta P) = (OP/OQ)(-OQ/PC) = -OP/PC$$

Price elasticity of demand is the ratio of the distance OP to PC multiplied by -1. As can be seen, at low prices OP is small relative to PC and elasticity is close to zero, or inelastic. At the midpoint of the linear demand curve, demand is of unitary elasticity because OP equals PC. Moving up along the demand curve to price C, demand becomes more elastic as OP becomes large relative to PC.[6] Conversely, moving down along the demand curve, demand becomes more inelastic as price declines.

Comparing Point Elasticity of Two Demand Curves

The distance formula can be used to compare the price elasticities of demand for a given price along two demand curves. Two linear demand curves are shown in Figure 5–6(a). For any given price, the relatively flatter curve (D_2) is more elastic. For example, at price P^*, where the two curves intersect, the price elasticity of D_1 is $-OR^*/R^*C_1$ and the price elasticity of D_2 is $-OP^*/P^*C_2$. Because P^*C_1 ex-

[6] The distance formula can also be used to compute the price elasticity of demand along nonlinear demand curves. To do so, select the point on the nonlinear curve at which price elasticity is to be computed and then draw a linear demand curve *tangent* to that point. The price elasticity of demand at that point on the nonlinear curve will be the same as that of the tangent linear curve. This is so because the slopes of the two curves are the same at the point of tangency, as are the respective prices and quantities.

FIGURE 5–6 Using the Distance Formula for Price Elasticity of Demand

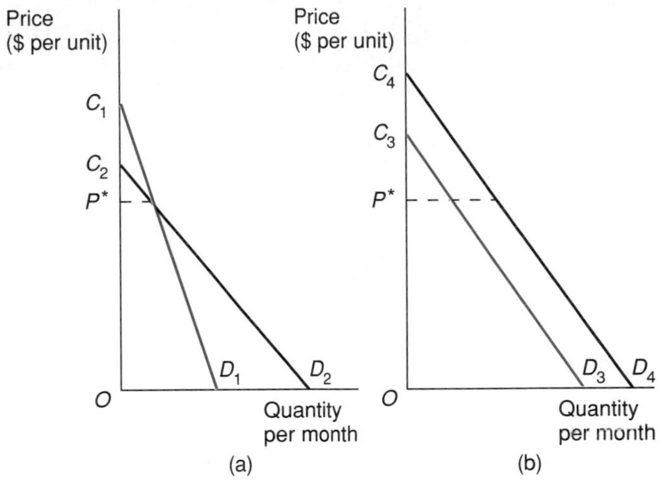

In general, at any given price a steeper demand curve is less price elastic than a flatter one. As illustrated in (a), at price P^* demand is more price elastic on demand curve D_1 then on demand curve D_2 because $P^*C_1 > P^*C_2$. For the two demand curves illustrated in (b), demand is more price elastic at price P^* on D_3 than on D_4 because $P^*C_3 < P^*C_4$.

ceeds P^*C_2, demand is less elastic at price P^* on curve D_1 than on curve D_2. Making the same calculation for any possible price would show that demand is more elastic on the relatively flatter curve, D_2, than on D_1.

The distance formula can also be used to compare the elasticity at given prices of two demand curves that do not intersect. This is illustrated in Figure 5–6(b). At price P^* the demand curve D_3 is more elastic than the demand curve D_4. The intercept on the price axis for D_4 is above that for D_3. Using the distance formula, we find that at price P^* demand is more elastic for the curve with the intercept C_3 than it is for the curve with the intercept C_4. This is because the distance P^*C_3 is less than the distance P^*C_4. These comparisons are valid only for given prices; because the demand curves in Figure 5–6(b) are linear, it is always possible to find a point on one curve that is more elastic than a point on the other curve at different prices.

Calculating Price Elasticity from Data Corresponding to Two Points on a Demand Curve

Because price elasticity of demand can differ at different points on the same demand curve, it is necessary to calculate elasticity for the average price and quantity between the two points for fairly large percentage changes in the price or quantity demanded. For example, suppose the price of wine increases from $5 to $7 per bottle. As a result of the price increase, quantity demanded of wine in a

Modern Microeconomics in Action: The Business World

Maximizing Revenue from the Sale of Tickets to Sports Events: Why Pricing to Fill the Stadium Is Not Always the Best Policy*

The cost of a sports event is usually independent of the number of fans attending such an event. Promoters of a sports event (and similar exhibitions, including rock concerts) often seek to maximize revenue from selling tickets to the event. By maximizing revenue from ticket sales, the promoters also maximize profits because the cost of the event is fixed.

Knowledge of the price elasticity of demand for tickets is very important to promoters of the event if they seek to maximize revenue from the sale of tickets. Surprisingly, it is not always the best policy to price the tickets so as to fill a stadium to capacity! In considering what price to charge to maximize revenue, promoters must take into account *both* the price elasticity of demand for tickets

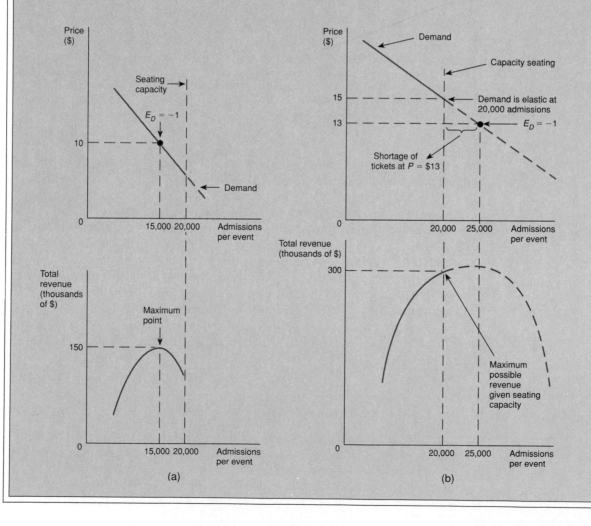

Price ($)
Seating capacity
$E_D = -1$
10
Demand
0
15,000 20,000
Admissions per event
Total revenue (thousands of $)
Maximum point
150
0
15,000 20,000
Admissions per event

(a)

Price ($)
Demand
Capacity seating
15
Demand is elastic at 20,000 admissions
13
$E_D = -1$
Shortage of tickets at $P = \$13$
0
20,000 25,000
Admissions per event
Total revenue (thousands of $)
300
Maximum possible revenue given seating capacity
0
20,000 25,000
Admissions per event

(b)

(Continued) and the capacity of the stadium. Suppose that the capacity of the stadium is 20,000 and the demand for tickets is linear, as shown in the upper graph of (a). Along a linear demand curve total revenue increases in response to price reductions as long as demand is elastic. When demand becomes inelastic, total revenue starts to fall when price is reduced. As shown in the lower graph of (a), total revenue increases at first in response to reductions in price and then starts to decrease. The point of maximum total revenue occurs at a price of $10 per ticket, at which price elasticity of demand is −1. At that price 15,000 tickets will be sold to the event. Because the capacity of the stadium is 20,000, this means that there will be 5,000 empty seats. To fill these empty seats, the promoters would have to lower the price below $10. However, lowering the price below $10 would decrease revenue, as you can see in the lower graph of (a). The promoters therefore do not want to fill the stadium because doing so would not maximize revenue!

When will the promoters choose to price tickets so as to fill the stadium? The answer to this question can be inferred from (b). If the demand for tickets is still elastic at the point at which the capacity sales of 20,000 are achieved, the promoters will price the tickets to fill the stadium. In (b) the demand for tickets is stronger than in (a). At a price of $15 per ticket, demand is still elastic and 20,000 tickets will be sold. Further reduction in price to the point at which demand is unit elastic would result in a shortage of tickets because quantity demanded would exceed the 20,000-seat capacity. For example, at a price of $13 per ticket, the quantity demanded of 25,000 would imply a 5,000-seat shortage.

The lower graph in (b) shows that in this case the maximum possible revenue occurs at the 20,000-seat capacity. Total revenue would increase further were it possible to squeeze more fans into the stadium when price is lowered to the point at which price elasticity of demand is −1. However, the capacity constraint prevents promoters from moving along the dashed portions of the demand and total revenue curves.

Whether to set a price to fill the stadium therefore depends both on the level of demand and on the capacity of the stadium.

* I am indebted to Professor David Hula of the Department of Economics of Kansas State University for suggesting this example to me.

certain city declines from 10,000 bottles per day to 5,000 bottles per day. In this case ΔP is \$2 and ΔQ_D is −5,000 bottles per day. If the *initial* price and quantity are used to calculate price elasticity of demand, its value would be

$$(P/QD)(\Delta Q_D/\Delta P) = (\$5/10{,}000 \text{ bottles})(-5{,}000 \text{ bottles}/\$2) = -1.25$$

If, however, the *new* price and quantity are used to calculate price elasticity of demand, its value would be

$$(\$7/5{,}000 \text{ bottles})(-5{,}000 \text{ bottles}/\$2) = 3.5$$

To correct the ambiguity resulting from a price change large enough to move from one point to another along an arc on a demand curve, the *average* of the initial and final prices and quantities is used in calculating price elasticity of demand:

$$\text{Price elasticity of demand along an arc on a demand curve} = \frac{\text{Average of initial and final } P}{\text{Average of initial and final } Q_D} \times \frac{\Delta Q_D}{\Delta P} \qquad \textbf{(5–5)}$$

In this case the average price is (\$5 + \$7)/2, which is \$6, while the average quantity demanded is (5,000 + 10,000)/2, which is 7,500. The price elasticity of demand along the arc between the two prices based on the average price and quantity is therefore

$$\$6/7{,}500 \text{ bottles } (-5{,}000 \text{ bottles}/\$2) = -2$$

The formula for price elasticity along an arc is used when percentage changes in prices or quantities are believed to be large enough to result in substantial movements along points on a demand curve.

Other Demand Elasticities

In addition to price elasticity of demand, income elasticity of demand and cross elasticity of demand provide useful information. Income elasticity of demand measures the sensitivity of consumer purchases to each 1 percent change in income. Cross elasticity of demand measures the sensitivity of consumer purchases of a good to changes in the prices of substitute or complementary goods.

Income Elasticity of Demand

Income elasticity of demand The percentage change in quantity purchased of a product in response to each 1 percent change in income.

The level of income and its fluctuations are important determinants of market demand. **Income elasticity of demand** (E_I) measures the percentage change in quantity purchased in response to each 1 percent change in income. It can be calculated from the following formula:

$$E_I = \Delta Q/Q/\Delta I/I \qquad \textbf{(5–6)}$$

where I is a measure of consumer income and Q is the quantity of a particular good purchased. For example, an income elasticity of 3 for foreign travel means that a 1 percent increase in income will result in a 3 percent increase in foreign travel.

E_I may be positive, negative, or zero. Income elasticity is zero for goods whose consumption is completely unresponsive to changes in income. A good that is a necessity might have a zero income elasticity. A positive income elasticity implies that increases in income (other things being equal) are associated with increases in the quantity of a good purchased. Normal goods always have positive income elasticity of demand. A good whose income elasticity is greater than 1 is a *luxury good*. The share of income a person spends on a luxury good increases as the person's income goes up. Foreign travel has, in fact, an estimated income elasticity of about 3, indicating that it can be considered a luxury good.

Given percentage increases in income result in *larger* percentage increases in purchases of goods whose income elasticity is greater than 1. By the same token, given percentage decreases in income result in larger percentage decreases in purchases of such goods. For example, when income in the economy is growing rapidly, the demand for such goods as furniture and household appliances, whose demand is quite income elastic in the short run, is likely to grow even more rapidly. However, when there is a recession and income declines, there are likely to be even sharper declines in the demand for such goods. Retail firms are very interested in the value of the income elasticities for the goods they sell. If they have good estimates of these elasticities, they can adjust their inventories and orders accordingly so as to be prepared for anticipated recessions and booms.

A negative income elasticity of demand implies an inverse relationship between income and the amount of a good purchased. An inferior good has a negative income elasticity. For example, you might expect income elasticity of demand for poor cuts of meat to be negative because many consumers regard such cuts as inferior goods. Estimates of income elasticity of demand from market data indicate whether goods are, on average, normal or inferior. Such estimates also provide indications of the sensitivity of consumer purchases of goods to fluctuations in consumer income.

Table 5–4 presents empirical estimates of income elasticities for various goods and services. Estimated income elasticities for such goods as automobiles, foreign travel by U.S. citizens, and household appliances are quite high (greater than 1) and positive. These are normal goods whose demand is quite responsive to changes in income.

TABLE 5–4 Estimated Income Elasticities of Demand

Item	*Short Run*	*Long Run*
Potatoes*	N.A.	−0.81
Pork†	0.27	0.18
Beef†	0.51	0.45
Furniture	2.6	0.53
China, glassware, and tableware	0.47	0.77
Dental services	0.38	1.00
Chicken†	0.49	1.06
Automobiles	5.5	1.07
Spectator sports	0.46	1.07
Physician services	0.28	1.15
Clothing	0.95	1.17
Gasoline and oil	0.55	1.36
Household appliances	2.72	1.40
Shoes	0.9	1.5
Jewelry and watches	1.0	1.6
Owner-occupied housing	0.07	2.45
Foreign travel by U.S. citizens	0.24	3.09
Toilet articles and preparations	0.25	3.74

* Dale M. Heien, "The Structure of Food Demand: Interrelatedness and Duality," *American Journal of Agricultural Economics* 64, no. 2 (May 1982), pp. 213–21.

† Michael K. Wohlgenant and William F. Hahn, "Dynamic Adjustment in Monthly Consumer Demand for Meats," *American Journal of Agricultural Economics* 64, no. 3 (August 1982), pp. 553–57.

Source: Unless otherwise indicated, data are from Hendrik S, Houthakker and Lester D. Taylor, *Consumer Demand in the United States* (Cambridge, Mass.: Harvard University Press, 1970).

Both short-run and long-run estimates of income elasticities are presented in Table 5–4. In most cases, as would be expected, long-run elasticity exceeds short-run elasticity. Notable exceptions are household appliances, furniture, and automobiles. These are durable goods that consumers do not always replace as their incomes increase. Note that the income elasticity of demand for potatoes is negative, indicating that consumers, on average, regard potatoes as an inferior good.

Cross Elasticity of Demand

Cross elasticity of demand The percentage change in the quantity of a good consumed in response to each 1 percent change in the price of some other good.

Another useful price elasticity concept is **cross elasticity of demand.** Cross elasticity of demand measures the percentage change in the quantity of good X consumed in response to each 1 percent change in the price of some other good, Y. The formula for cross elasticity of demand, E_C, between the demand for good X and the price of some other good, Y, is

$$E_C = \Delta Q_X/Q_X/\Delta P_Y/P_Y \quad \textbf{(5–7)}$$

Cross elasticity of demand may be positive, negative, or zero. *Substitutes* are items whose cross elasticity of demand is positive. Whenever the price of one good changes, other things being equal, demand for the other moves in the same direction. This means that a price increase for one of the goods leads to an increase in the amount purchased of the other. For example, one estimate of the cross elasticity of demand between chicken and the price of pork is 0.299. This positive cross elasticity indicates that consumers treat these two meats as substitutes for each other. If the estimate is correct, each 1 percent increase in the price of pork can be expected to increase the demand for chicken at any given price by one third of 1 percent. Thus a 10 percent increase in the price of pork, other things being equal, can be expected to result in a 3 percent increase in chicken purchased.

In general, the greater the substitutability between two goods, the higher is the value of their cross elasticity of demand. Cross elasticity of demand between two competing brands of a good, such as Coca-Cola and Pepsi-Cola, is likely to be quite high. A sharp increase in the price of one of these beverages can be expected to result in a sharp increase in sales of the other, assuming that the price of the other is fixed. Similarly, for any two brands of automobiles, cross elasticity of demand is likely to be high. Cross elasticity of demand for unrelated goods, such as ice cream and typewriters, is likely to be zero.

Complements have a negative cross elasticity of demand. Coffee and nondairy coffee creamers are complements. You would therefore expect an increase in the price of coffee to decrease the demand for nondairy creamers. Cross elasticity of demand of nondairy creamers with respect to coffee is therefore expected to be negative. The greater the complementarity of two goods, the greater is the absolute value of their negative cross elasticity of demand.

If two goods are viewed neither as substitutes nor as complements, their cross elasticity of demand is zero. A zero cross elasticity of demand indicates that the consumption of one good is independent of the price of the other.

TABLE 5–5 Estimated Cross Elasticities of Demand*

Item	*Estimate*
Natural gas with respect to price of electricity	0.8†
Margarine with respect to price of butter	1.53‡
Pork with respect to price of beef	0.40‡
Chicken with respect to price of pork	0.29‡

* These are long-run elasticities.
† G. R. Lakshmanan and William Anderson, "Residential Energy Demand in the United States," *Regional Science and Urban Economics* 10 (August 1980), pp. 371–86.
‡ Dale M. Heien, "The Structure of Food Demand: Interrelatedness and Duality," *American Journal of Agricultural Economics* 64, no. 2 (May 1982), pp. 213–21.

Knowledge of the cross elasticity of demand for a product is important for corporate planning. For example, suppose that a sharp increase in the price of natural gas is expected. This increase is likely to increase the demand for electricity because natural gas and electricity are regarded as substitutes for heating and cooking purposes. Gas companies could therefore plan to meet the increased demand for their product if they know the value of the cross-price elasticity of demand for natural gas with respect to the price of electricity. For example, if that cross-price elasticity is 0.8 over the long run, then a 20 percent increase in the price of electricity can be expected to increase the demand for natural gas by 16 percent.

Table 5–5 presents some estimated cross elasticities. The estimates indicate that pairs of goods such as margarine and butter, pork and beef, and natural gas and electricity are regarded as substitutes by consumers. The estimated cross elasticities for these goods are positive.

CONCEPT REVIEW

1. How does price elasticity of demand vary along a linear demand curve?
2. Of what use are measures of income elasticity of demand for a good?
3. Suppose that orange juice and apple juice are substitutes. What can you say about cross elasticity of demand for apple juice with respect to the price of orange juice?

DEMAND CURVES AND CONSUMER BENEFITS

How much value do consumers place on the goods and services they consume? We can use a market demand curve to answer questions regarding the marginal benefit of a product to consumers and to evaluate the costs or benefits of increasing or decreasing production of the product. Points on a demand curve provide us with information on the maximum price that consumers would pay for a good at each quantity. The relationship between this maximum price and the market price provides a useful approximation of the net social value of a good.

Consumer Surplus

Consumer surplus The difference between the market price of a good and the maximum price a consumer is willing to pay for an additional unit of the good.

The difference between the market price of a good and the maximum price a consumer is willing to pay for an additional unit of the good is the **consumer surplus** of that unit. Downward-sloping individual demand curves indicate that this maximum price declines as a consumer has more of this good in his monthly (or weekly) market basket.

For example, suppose you go shopping to purchase a shirt. You know exactly what kind of shirt you would like and you are prepared to pay $45 for it. That $45 represents the maximum price you would pay for an additional shirt in your wardrobe. It is your marginal rate of substitution of shirts for expenditure on other goods, which represents the marginal benefit in dollars of an additional shirt. If, on arriving at the store, you find that the market price of the shirt you want is $20, you would earn $25 consumer surplus if you bought just one. Consumer surplus on each unit can be thought of as the difference between the consumer's marginal benefit from that unit measured in dollars and the price paid to acquire the unit. This represents the **marginal net benefit,** MNB, of the unit. In general, the marginal net benefit of good X is

Marginal net benefit The difference between a consumer's marginal benefit from a good and the price of that good.

$$\text{MNB}_X = \text{MB}_X - \text{P}_X \quad \textbf{(5–8)}$$

where MB_X is the good's marginal benefit measured in dollars to a consumer and P_X is its price.

In equilibrium, consumers purchase goods up to the point at which the marginal benefit just equals the price. It follows that consumers continue to purchase until it is no longer possible to earn additional consumer surplus. In equilibrium the marginal net benefit of a good must be zero because $\text{P}_X = \text{MB}_X$ at that point.

Thus, if you are able to earn $25 consumer surplus on the purchase of a shirt, you could add to your satisfaction by purchasing more shirts. In this case you would continue to purchase shirts until their marginal benefit to you fell to $20, the market price. Purchase beyond that point would make you worse off because the shirts would cost more than the extra benefit they give you. Of course, this implies that your indifference curves between shirts and other goods are convex. The marginal benefit of additional shirts therefore falls.

Figure 5–7 shows how consumer surplus can be represented graphically. The maximum price a consumer would pay for each shirt purchased per month is plotted against the quantity available. The maximum price the consumer illustrated would pay for one shirt per month rather than do without it is $45. The area of the rectangle whose height is $45 and whose width is one shirt measures this dollar amount. This rectangle represents the marginal benefit of that shirt to the consumer. Note that if the market price of shirts exceeds $45, this consumer would do without that first shirt.

Figure 5–7 shows that the marginal benefit of a second shirt is $40. This is the maximum price the consumer would pay for a second shirt per month. If the market price exceeds $40, this consumer would buy only one shirt. The marginal

FIGURE 5–7 Total Consumer Surplus for an Individual Consumer

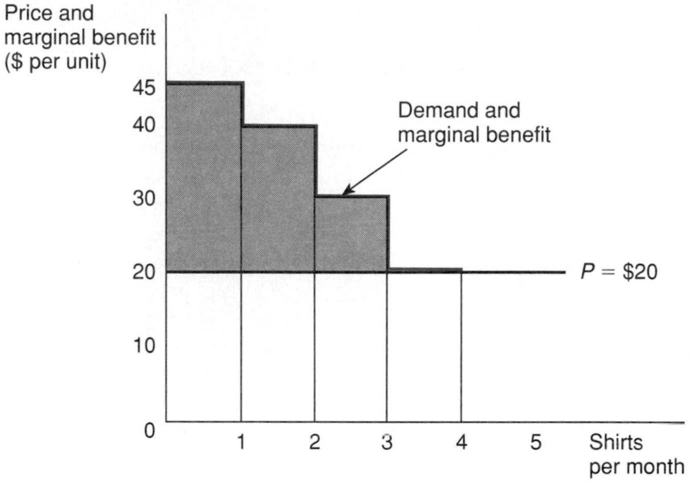

The person whose marginal benefit for good X is illustrated earns consumer surplus on three of the four units purchased. Total consumer surplus is the shaded areas of the first three rectangles. These areas represent the difference between the maximum price that would be paid for each of the units consumed and the $60 actually given up for the first three units.

benefits for additional shirts decline further. The marginal benefit of a third shirt is $30. The price of shirts would therefore have to fall to $30 for the consumer to purchase three. The marginal benefit of a fourth shirt is $20. If the market price of shirts is in fact $20, the consumer illustrated in the graph would purchase four shirts per month. This is the number of shirts that corresponds to equality between price and marginal benefit. The curve shown on the graph has a stepped shape because the consumer cannot buy a fraction of a shirt. The curve indicates how the marginal benefit that the consumer receives from shirts declines as more are purchased. Because the consumer buys the number corresponding to $P =$ MB, the marginal benefit curve can also be interpreted as the consumer's demand curve for shirts. At any price the corresponding quantity on the step curve is the number of shirts the consumer chooses to purchase per month.

In equilibrium the consumer buys four shirts and spends $80 on shirts in the given month. The total benefit received from those shirts is represented by the sum of the marginal benefit of each of the shirts. This is the maximum amount that the consumer would sacrifice to buy each of the four shirts separately, or $45 + $40 + $30 + $20 = $135. This amount represents the total benefit of the four shirts. *The difference between the number of dollars the consumer would give up rather than going without the four shirts purchased and the total expenditure on those shirts is the total consumer surplus.* In this case the total consumer surplus equals $55. It is represented by the shaded areas above the market price of $20 in Figure 5–7. Note that consumer surplus is not earned on the last unit consumed. This is sometimes called the *marginal unit.* The consumer surplus on the first three inframarginal units is the sum of the three shaded rectangles.

MODERN MICROECONOMICS IN ACTION: GOVERNMENT AND THE ECONOMY

Evaluating Willingness to Pay for Government Services

The values placed on government services not sold in a market are difficult to estimate, but information on such values is vital to deciding whether the benefits of new government projects outweigh their costs. Suppose, for example, your local government is considering the purchase of land for the development of a new park. It knows the cost of purchasing, developing, and maintaining the land. Is there any way it can find out how much citizens would be willing to pay for this new service?

Using indifference curves, the conceptual problems involved in obtaining a measure of willingness to pay can be explored. The graphs show a person's indifference curves between keeping income to spend on other goods and consuming the benefits of public parks. The income of the person whose indifference curves are depicted in (a) is $\$I$ per year. How much of that income would he be willing to give up each year to have one park made available by the government?

Assume that no parks are now available. The person is therefore in equilibrium at point I, where all of his income is spent on other goods and no park services are consumed. At that equilibrium he achieves a utility level of U_1. If the park were constructed, he would move to point C, where he would have the benefits of using the park. Point C corresponds to the market basket at which the person spends the same amount as before on other goods and has the benefits of using one new park. This clearly makes him better off, as the utility level enjoyed rises to U_2.

What is the maximum amount of income the person would be willing to give up per year for a new park? Put another way, what annual fee (or tax) imposed for the use of the new park would make the person indifferent between consuming the services of one park and forgoing them?

The answer to the question is ambiguous. It could be the sum of money represented by the vertical distance between the two indifference curves corresponding to zero parks on the X axis. This would be an annual fee of $\$IA$. Paying this fee would return the person to indifference curve U_1, and he would be indifferent between paying the fee and having the new park and holding on to all of his income to spend on other goods but not having the park. Notice, however, that as drawn in (a), the

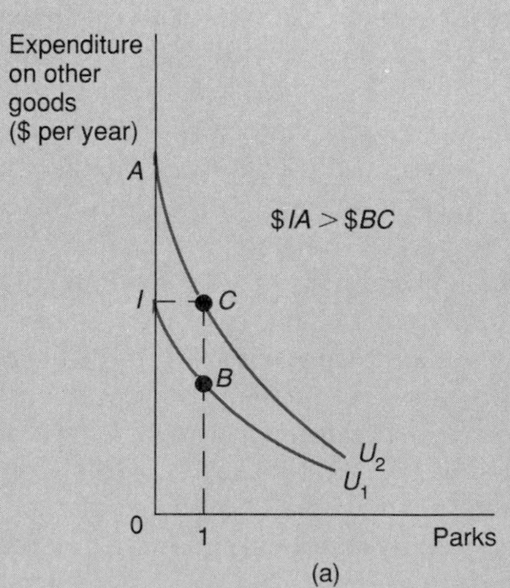

(a)

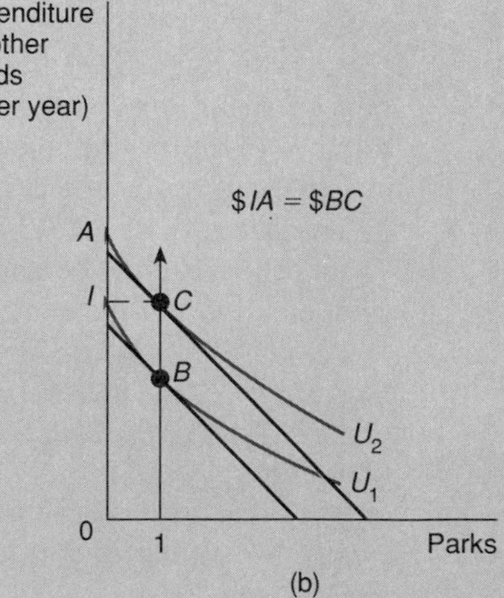

(b)

(*Continued*) vertical distance between the two indifference curves narrows as the good on the X axis increases. This means that if the consumer were charged a fee of $\$BC$, the difference between the two indifference curves when one park is available, he would also be indifferent between the two options. Because $\$BC$ is less than $\$IA$ in (a), the analysis gives two different answers to the question.

The cause of this measurement problem is that the amount of income the consumer will sacrifice per year to get the new park depends on the amount he has. This amount will decline after he has paid the fee. As the person gives up income to get the good, the value of his remaining dollars changes. The crux of the difficulty lies in the fact that a dollar measure is being sought for the change in utility the person receives from a park. This gets back to the controversy regarding the cardinal versus ordinal measurability of utility, a problem that has haunted economists for a long time.* Some economists have argued that it is impossible to obtain an unambiguous measure of willingness to pay. This means that the gain in well-being from the park is being measured with a stretchable yardstick! Note also that from the cardinal perspective the problem can be summarized by saying that unless the marginal utility of income is constant, dollars cannot be used to measure utility changes.

If a few simplifying assumptions are made, it is possible to resolve the ambiguity. Assume that the indifference curves are parallel throughout, as shown in graph (b). This means that the vertical distance between U_1 and U_2 is always the same. It also means that slopes of the indifference curves are equal along a vertical line drawn from a given point on the X axis. If income were to increase or decrease and the budget line were to move up or down, the tangency to the curves would always correspond to the same amount of X. This is shown on (b).

The economic implication of this is that the income effect of any price change would be zero and thus that the amount of good X chosen would be independent of income. The vertical line would represent the income-consumption line for X. It can be concluded that if income effects are negligible, an unambiguous measure of willingness to pay for a good rather than go without it is obtainable.

When will income effects be zero? They are likely to be so when the amount that must be given up per year for a good does not constitute a significant portion of total annual income. If this is so, the amount by which income changes after the fee has been paid is so small as to result in negligible income effects. Under these circumstances the willingness to pay of all consumers can be summed, thereby measuring the benefits they would receive from the park. These benefits can be compared with the cost of the park to see whether it is worth building.†

* For an excellent discussion of this controversy, see Edward R. Morey, "Confuser Surplus," *American Economic Review* 74, no. 1 (March 1984), pp. 163–73.

† This approach provides the basis for a technique of evaluating the benefits of public projects called *cost-benefit analysis*. See Edward M. Gramlich, *A Guide to Benefit-Cost Analysis*, 2nd ed. (Englewood Cliffs, N.J.: Prentice Hall, 1990), for a good survey of this technique.

Using Market Demand Curves to Approximate Consumer Surplus

The market demand curve for shirts is shown in Figure 5–8. At a market price of \$20, 10,000 shirts are sold in a given month. At that price *each and every consumer* of shirts buys shirts that month up to the amount at which the market price of shirts equals his or her personal marginal benefit. Thus at the market price, P_X, the following condition holds for any good:

$$MB_1 = MB_2 = MB_3 = \ldots = MB_N = P_X \tag{5–9}$$

where the subscript indicates each of the N consumers of shirts that month. If 10,000 shirts are sold, there will be fewer than 10,000 consumers because many consumers buy more than one shirt.

FIGURE 5–8 Measuring Total Consumer Surplus

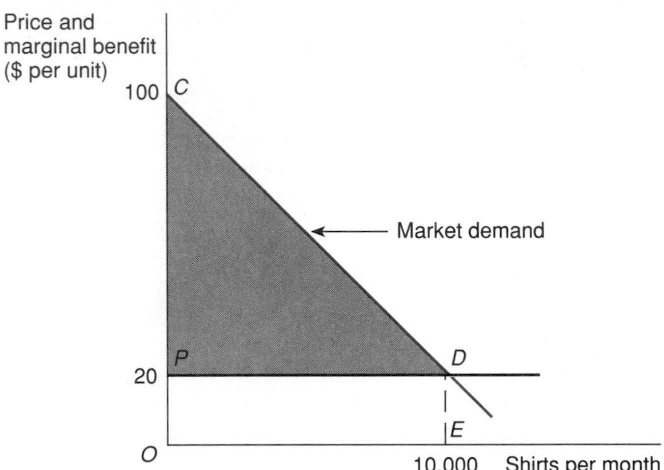

The total consumer surplus for all persons purchasing good *X* is approximated by the shaded triangle *PCD*. Actual expenditure on shirts is the area *OPDE*.

The total consumer surplus earned by the buyers of the 10,000 shirts in Figure 5–7 is the difference between the maximum amount that those buyers would pay for that number and their actual expenditure of $200,000. This maximum is the amount that sellers could collect if they sold each shirt at the maximum price consumers would pay for it. For example, if the maximum price some consumer would pay for the first shirt purchased is $100, then the first shirt sold would fetch that amount. This is the maximum price that the person who buys that shirt would pay if he thinks no other shirts will be sold that month. It is the marginal benefit of a shirt when only one shirt is sold per month. Similarly, the marginal benefit of two shirts represents the maximum price that some buyer would pay for the second shirt if only two shirts are to be sold in a month. The scale of measurement is very compact on the horizontal axis in Figure 5–8, where 10,000 shirts are sold in equilibrium. The market demand curve does not have the stepped appearance of the individual demand curve in Figure 5–7 because the distance on the horizontal axis between successive units sold is microscopic.

The market demand curve can now also be interpreted as a marginal benefit curve. Each point on the curve represents the maximum price that the consumer of each extra unit produced would be willing to pay for it. This maximum price is the marginal benefit of that unit to the consumer who purchases it. The demand curve therefore gives the marginal benefit as a function of the quantity made available. The total consumer surplus of the 10,000 shirts can be approximated by the difference between the area under the demand curve up to $Q = 10{,}000$ and the area representing the $200,000 expenditure on shirts (*OPDE*). The total consumer surplus is the shaded triangular area *PCD* in Figure 5–8.

Downward-sloping demand curves imply that some consumer surplus exists at the market equilibrium price and quantity. This assumes that consumers are free to purchase as much of a good as they choose at the market price, which is the usual case in markets.

However, there are exceptions. Take the case of a good only one unit of which can be purchased in a lifetime. Assume that this good is supplied by a single seller who has no competitors. For example, suppose only one surgeon in the world has the knowledge to perform a certain transplant operation. This surgeon could conceivably charge each patient the maximum price equal to the marginal benefit of that operation to the paticnt. Only one operation could be consumed by each patient in his or her lifetime. If the surgeon is skillful in estimating the maximum price each patient would pay for the operation, the entire consumer surplus would be extracted from buyers. Compare this with the situation that would prevail if there were a single market price, say $2,000, for the operation. Persons who valued the marginal benefit of their single operation above this amount then enjoy consumer surplus.

Willingness to Pay, Availability, and Price

Many goods that are required for survival, such as drinking water, are priced at very low levels. Presumably, persons would be willing to give up considerable amounts of money for water if they did not have any. By the same token, it would be possible to live without gold, diamonds, Rolls-Royces, and other luxuries. Yet these goods command very high market prices despite the fact that they are not essential for life. Is there a paradox?

Figure 5–9 shows that there is no paradox. The marginal benefit of one gallon of drinking water per day would be very high if only one gallon were available per day. The marginal benefit of one gallon of water (MB_{W1}) would exceed the marginal benefit of one ounce of gold (MB_{G1}). At the *actual* amounts available (Q_{GE} and Q_{WE}), however, the marginal benefit of a gallon of drinking water is only a fraction of a cent, whereas the marginal benefit of an ounce of gold is $400. Persons are willing to pay more per unit of gold than per unit of water because $MB_{GE} > MB_{WE}$ at current quantities supplied.

Using Consumer Surplus to Evaluate the Burden of Taxes

The concept of consumer surplus is also useful in evaluating economic gains and losses resulting from economic policies. Assume that the government levies a tax on sales of new cars equal to $1,000 per car. Also assume that this tax raises the price of cars by exactly that amount over a period. As a result of the tax the number of new cars sold declines from 5 million to 4 million per year. The loss in net benefits incurred by consumers of cars is illustrated in Figure 5–10.

The price of cars increases from $10,000 to $11,000. Before the price increase, consumer surplus was equal to the triangular area *ABC*. The price increase reduces consumer surplus to the area *FBE*. The loss in net benefits from car purchases is therefore represented by the area *AFEC*. This area can be broken up into

FIGURE 5–9 Marginal Benefit and Price

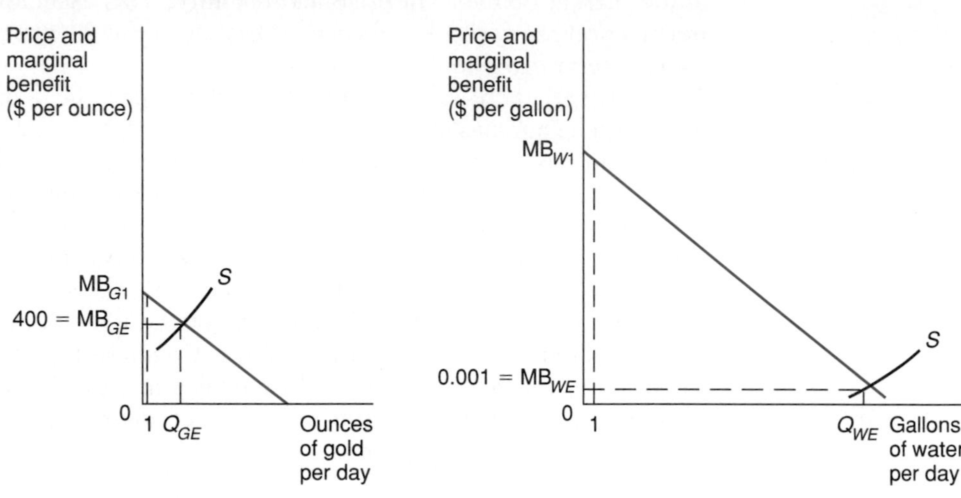

The marginal benefit of drinking water when only one gallon is available per day greatly exceeds the marginal benefit of gold when only one ounce is available per day. However, the price of gold greatly exceeds the price of water. This is because at the quantities *actually* available MB_G is much higher than MB_W.

FIGURE 5–10 The Loss in Consumer Surplus from a Tax

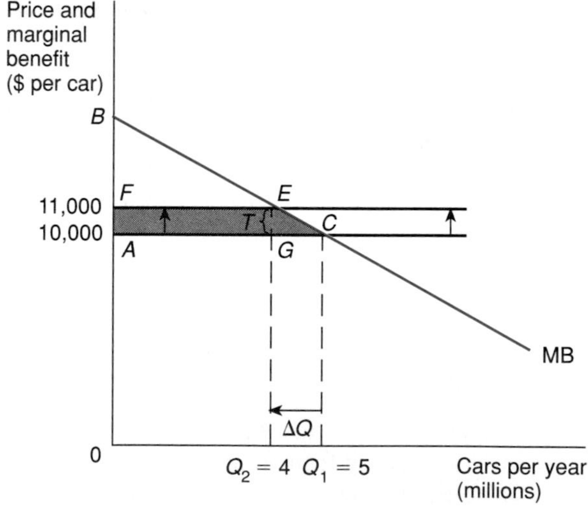

If a tax increases the price of cars by $1,000, total consumer surplus declines by the shaded area *AFEC*. The triangle *GEC* is the excess burden of the tax.

two components. The first component, the rectangular area *AFEG*, represents the reduction in consumer surplus as a result of increased expenditures on the 4 million cars that in the absence of the tax would be selling for only $10,000 each instead of $11,000 each. This area is also the tax revenue taken in by the government. It is equal to TQ_2, the tax per car multiplied by the number sold, which in this case amounts to $4 billion. The second component is the triangular area *GEC*, which represents the loss in consumer surplus on the 1 million extra cars that would have been sold had the tax not been levied. The area GCQ_1Q_2 is the amount that would have been spent on these cars. This amount is *not* part of the loss in consumer benefits, because consumers choose to spend it on other goods after the price of cars rises.

The area of the triangle *GEC* is equal to $\frac{1}{2}T\Delta Q$, where *T*, the height of the triangle, represents the tax per car and ΔQ, the base of the triangle, represents the tax-induced decline in car sales. The total loss in the net benefits of consumers, *L*, is therefore.

$$L = TQ_2 + \tfrac{1}{2}T\Delta Q \qquad \textbf{(5–10)}$$

Excess burden of a tax The difference between the dollar value of consumer surplus lost as a result of the tax and the tax revenue collected.

Notice that the total loss of consumer surplus exceeds the tax revenue collected by the area of the triangle *GEC*. The **excess burden of the tax** is the difference between the dollar value of consumer surplus lost as a result of the tax and the tax revenue collected. It costs *more than one dollar to raise each dollar of tax revenue*. Even if at the end of the year the total tax revenue were given back in a lump-sum payment to those from whom it was received, they would still be worse off by *GEC* because the tax-induced increase in car prices caused them to cut back car purchases.

Using Consumer Surplus to Evaluate the Gains from Subsidies

A similar analysis can be used to evaluate the impact of a subsidy. Assume that the government subsidizes the home construction industry. The marginal benefit of new housing construction is shown in Figure 5–11. Also assume that the subsidy reduces the price of new housing construction from $50 to $40 per square foot. As a result of the decrease in price, the quantity of new housing construction demanded increases from 10 million to 12 million square feet per year. What is the net social gain from the subsidy?

The decrease in the cost of new housing construction increases total square feet purchased per year from Q_1 to Q_2. In this case $\Delta Q = 2$ million square feet per year. The gain in total consumer surplus is the area *ABCE*. This gain to consumers, *G*, is

$$G = SQ_1 + \tfrac{1}{2}S\Delta Q \qquad \textbf{(5–11)}$$

where *S* is the subsidy per square foot. SQ_1 represents the decreased expenditure on the Q_1 square feet that would have cost $10 per square foot more without the subsidy. This amounts to $100 million. These are benefits to persons who would have purchased new homes anyway but can now do so at lower prices. The term $\frac{1}{2}S\Delta Q$ is the gain in consumer surplus on the extra housing construction induced by the subsidy, which amounts to $10 million. The total gain is $110 million.

FIGURE 5–11 The Gain in Total Consumer Surplus from a Subsidy

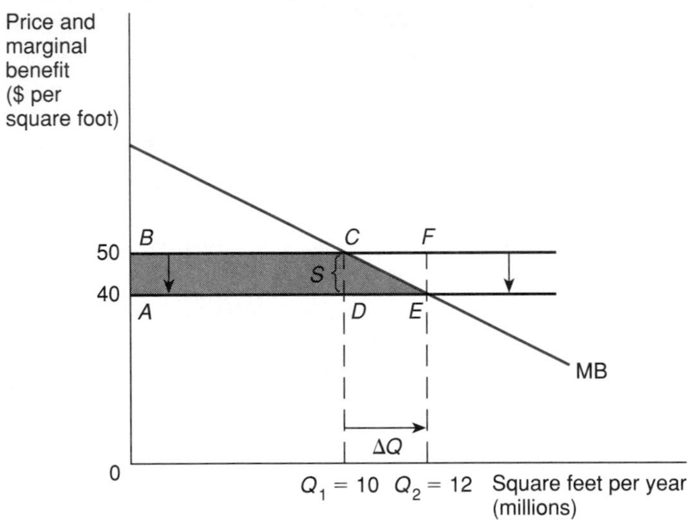

A subsidy reduces the price per square foot by $10. The gain in total consumer surplus is the area *ABCE*. The total cost of the subsidy to the government is the area *ABFE*. This cost exceeds the gain in total consumer surplus by the area *CFE*.

The total cost of the subsidy to the government is $120 million, represented by the area *ABFE*. This cost, presumably borne by taxpayers, falls short of the gain to home buyers. Buyers of new homes could have been given $110 million in lump-sum cash grants. Had this been done, they would have been just as well off and taxpayers would have saved $10 million. The excess burden of the subsidy is the difference between its total cost to taxpayers and the gain in consumer surplus to recipients. In this case the excess burden of the subsidy is represented by the triangle *CFE*, which amounts to $10 million.

Some Qualifications

The area under market demand curves can be interpreted as net benefits to consumers only under certain conditions. These conditions relate to the way a person's willingness to give up income for extra units of a particular good varies with the amount of income actually given up. Consumer surplus is a dollar measure of the net benefits that a person receives when purchasing goods. Using a dollar measure of these benefits in effect presumes that utility is cardinally measurable in dollar units and that it is possible to add these units to obtain measures of social benefits.

This is true only when the amount of the goods that persons would choose is independent of their income. The income effects of price changes for these goods must be negligible. Under such circumstances the maximum amount of income that any person would give up to get an additional unit of a good is independent of the amount actually surrendered. In certain cases the price changes being evaluated are small enough for their income effects on purchases to be ignored. In those cases the area under the demand curve accurately reflects consumer gains or losses. However, in cases in which price changes are believed to have substantial income effects on purchases, the area under the demand curve provides only an approximation of consumer gains or losses. This is because the marginal benefit of a good depends on both the willingness and the ability of consumers to give up income to obtain more goods. Naturally, the ability to pay depends on how much income persons have. When changes in prices cause substantial changes in real income, the marginal benefit of any given quantity of a good to a consumer can change. This means the price changes can *shift* the marginal benefit curve. It can be shown that when income effects are not negligible, measuring consumer surplus as the area under a market demand curve for normal goods *underestimates* actual consumer surplus.

Using Compensated Demand Curves to Measure Consumer Surplus

Compensated demand curves Demand curves that show only substitution effects of price changes.

Compensated demand curves show only substitution effects of price changes. By removing the influence of income effects, compensated demand curves accurately measure consumer surplus when income effects are not negligible. Compensated demand curves are derived by adjusting the consumer's income to remove any variation in well-being resulting from price changes. When price falls, the increase in real income resulting from the price change is removed. When price rises, the consumer is compensated with a rebate that reflects the loss in real income associated with the price increase.

Although it is difficult to actually make such adjustments in income, it is possible to statistically estimate the income effect and on that basis to make statistical adjustments. Compensated demand curves are usually obtained through such statistical adjustments. To make the adjustments, the proportion of income spent on a good and the way consumption of that good varies with income must be approximated. The gain in income and the resulting change in the demand for X can then be estimated and actual demand adjusted accordingly.[7]

Assume that the current price of the good is P_1. Figure 5–12 shows how the compensated demand curve differs from the regular demand curve for prices above and below P_1. For such a normal good, price increases cause an income effect that reduces the quantity of the good demanded. Removing the income effect therefore increases the quantity demanded at prices above P_1. As shown, for all of these prices quantity on the compensated demand curve exceeds quantity on the regular demand curve.

[7] There is some disagreement among economists as to how much income must be adjusted to obtain the compensated demand curve. For a good discussion of this controversy, see Edward M. Gramlich, *A Guide to Benefit-Cost Analysis*, 2nd ed. (Englewood Cliffs, N.J.: Prentice Hall, 1990).

FIGURE 5–12 Compensated Demand Curve for a Normal Good

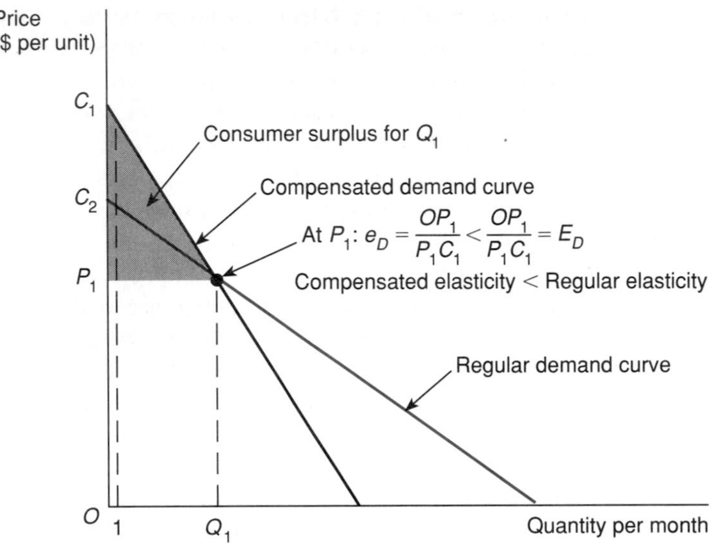

For a normal good the compensated demand curve is less elastic than the regular demand curve at all prices.

When the price of a normal good falls, the consumer experiences an income effect that serves to increase consumption of the good. Removing the income effect diminishes the consumer's response to price declines. For prices less than P_1, quantity demanded on the compensated demand curve is therefore less than quantity demanded on the regular demand curve.

For any given price of a normal good, points are less elastic on a compensated demand curve than on a regular demand curve. In Figure 5–12 this is proved using the distance formula for price elasticity of demand. This is true only for normal goods; a compensated demand curve for an inferior good is more elastic at any price than a regular demand curve. This is because the income effect for an inferior good offsets the substitution effect. When price decreases, the income effect decreases the consumption of the good whose price falls. If the influence of this effect is removed, elasticity increases because the response to a price decrease will then be greater.

Because the compensated demand curve removes the income effect, it can be used to calculate consumer surplus. It satisfies the requirement of zero income effects and enables the use of money to measure consumer surplus. Assume that the price of a good is P_1. The maximum amount the consumer would pay for the first unit would be given by the point corresponding to one unit on the compensated demand curve. Notice in Figure 5–12 that using the regular demand curve for a normal good would underestimate this maximum. This is because the regular demand curve includes the income effect of the price increase from P_1, which decreases the willingness of the consumer to pay.[8] Because the consumer can currently buy the good at a price, P_1, that is less than C_1, the maximum price he would be willing to pay for the first unit, consumer surplus is $P_1 - C_1$. If each unit of good X is represented by the smallest possible interval on the quantity axis, the consumer surplus of Q_1 units of X can be represented by the area under the compensated demand curve and above the horizontal line drawn from P_1 to the compensated demand curve. If X were cigarettes and its compensated demand curve were the one in the graph, the loss in consumer surplus from banning cigarettes would be the shaded area. Estimation of this area provides an indication of the loss in net benefits that would result from banning cigarette smoking.

Of course, the smaller the income effect for a good, the less discrepancy there is between consumer surplus measured with a regular demand curve and consumer surplus measured with a compensated demand curve. If there is reason to believe that the income effect of price changes is negligible, the regular demand curve can be used to approximate consumer surplus.

CONCEPT REVIEW

1. What is consumer surplus?
2. Why is no consumer surplus earned on the last unit of a good that each consumer purchases?
3. In what sense can taxes on the sale of goods result in an excess burden?

ESTIMATING DEMAND FUNCTIONS AND ELASTICITIES

Demand function A relationship among amounts of a good consumers will buy, its price, and all other influences on the demand for the good.

To analyze market demand fully, the influence of all determinants of the amounts consumers purchase must be taken into account. Expanding the theory of demand to do this requires the specification of a **demand function.** A demand function is a relationship among the amounts of a good consumers are willing to buy and the price of the good and all other influences on demand for the good. A demand function takes the quantity demanded of a good as a function of the price of the good. It also explicitly measures the impact on consumer purchases of income per person, the prices of related goods, and all other influences on market demand for a good.

Isolating the influence of various variables on the quantity of a good demanded is a formidable task. In actuality, it is difficult to hold "other things equal" so that the influence of one variable alone on the consumption of a good can be determined. Various techniques are used to estimate the relationships represented by a demand function. Among the common techniques are market

[8] For an in-depth analysis of the practicality of using approximations for consumer surplus, see Robert D. Willig, "Consumer's Surplus without Apology," *American Economic Review* 6, no. 4 (September 1976), pp. 589–97.

experiments, surveys of consumer intentions, and statistical methods. Techniques used to estimate demand must account for the influence of all demand determinants.

Market Experiments and Consumer Surveys

Market experiments and consumer surveys are typically used by business firms to obtain information on the responsiveness of quantities purchased to changes in price and other demand determinants. For a market experiment to produce valid results, only the price of the good must be changed. For example, if airlines attempt to determine the effect of a 10 percent reduction in airfares on the number of passengers they serve, they must be sure that only the price has changed over the period of the experiment. If the experiment lasts for six months and over this period an economic upturn increases consumer income, then the change in the number of passengers would be the combined effect of the change in price and the change in income.

The airlines would also have to be sure that consumers did not view the price reduction as temporary. If they did, there might be a surge of trips to visit long-lost relatives before the price goes back up again. In this case, price expectations, an important demand determinant, would not be held constant during the experiment. If "other things" are in fact held equal over the course of an experiment, enough data might be collected to estimate price elasticity of demand for the output of a business firm.

Other types of market experiments might be conducted to determine the influence of other demand determinants on purchases. For example, a firm might take two areas that it considers similar in every respect except income. This would allow the firm to estimate how the purchase of its product responds to variations in consumer incomes. Two areas whose consumers have similar tastes and incomes and a similar age distribution might be used to determine the influence of a product's advertising on sales. If the price of the product is the same in both areas, the experiment can isolate the influence of the advertising on sales.

Market experiments are of limited usefulness. It is very difficult to control for all of the influences on demand. Experiments of this kind also require controls over prices and other economic variables that rarely exist. The chief use of such experiments is in determining the demand for one brand of a good rather than for broad classes of goods. It is possible for an airline to see what happens if it lowers its fares, but the result observed depends on whether or not competing airlines also lower their fares.

Another common technique used by businesses is the consumer survey, or interview, which is usually conducted to uncover consumer preferences. Businesses conducting such surveys try to find out how changing the quality of their good or service might affect the quantity purchased. In this way they may uncover information on the demand for attributes of a good. Consumers might also be asked how they would react to changes in the price of a good or to changes in the prices of competing goods. Information obtained by asking existing customers questions about their income could be used to concentrate advertising campaigns in the media watched, listened to, or read by the customers most likely to buy particular goods.

A problem with the consumer survey is that there is no guarantee that the way consumers will actually behave is correlated with the way they respond to a questionnaire. There are also problems in obtaining a representative sample of consumers. If the sample is not representative of the consumers who actually buy a good, the results will be of little use.

Statistical Methods

The most sophisticated techniques for estimating demand functions involve the use of statistical methods. While elaboration of these methods is beyond the scope of this book, it is useful to discuss what they can do. The branch of economics dealing with statistical estimation of relationships among variables is called *econometrics*. Statistical methods are used to interpret observed data such as prices and quantities. These methods are used to determine whether there is in fact a cause-and-effect relationship between observed quantities, prices, and incomes. This makes it possible to test economic theories relating to both demand and supply and measure the responsiveness of one variable to a change in another variable. Statistical methods based on probability theories are used to determine whether or not what seems to be a cause-and-effect relationship is simply a chance association.

The first step required to statistically estimate a demand function is to specify the variables and the hypothesized relationships of cause and effect. For example, the researcher might specify that the quantity of some good purchased, X, depends on its own price, P; the price of a complementary good, P_C; the price of a substitute, P_S; and average consumer income, I. After this has been done, it is necessary to hypothesize the way the quantity of X purchased per person per year, Q_X, depends on its price and the other variables. The researcher may, for example, hypothesize a linear relationship. This means that the demand function may be expressed as the following linear equation:

$$Q_X = a + bP + cP_C + dP_S + eI \quad \textbf{(5–12)}$$

Demand coefficients The amounts by which quantity purchased of a good will change for each unit change in a demand determinant.

The small letters b, c, d, and e are called the **demand coefficients.** They represent the amounts by which the dependent variable Q_X will change for each unit change of an independent variable. For example, the coefficient of the variable P says that for each $1 change in the price of X, the quantity purchased will change by b units. The coefficient of the price variable therefore gives the change in quantity demanded for a $1 change in the price of the good. This is the inverse of the slope of a demand curve:

$$b = \Delta Q_X/\Delta P_X \quad \textbf{(5–13)}$$

If nothing else changes, each change in P will result in the purchase of b extra units of good X. Similarly, the coefficients of P_S, P_C, and I represent the changes in the annual amount of X that would be purchased per person for each unit change in the respective variable. The coefficient c is the change in X purchased for each $1 change in the price of the complementary good. The coefficient d is the change in the purchase of X for each $1 change in the price of the substitute good. The coefficient e gives the change in the amount of X that would be bought for each $1 change in average consumer income. The intercept of the demand function, a, represents the amount of X that would be purchased independent of any of the specified variables.[9]

When the coefficients have been estimated, hypotheses about their signs (positive or negative) can be accepted or rejected. The sign of the b coefficient is hypothesized as negative in accordance with the law of demand. The other coefficients account for the influence of "other things" on demand. Therefore, the b coefficient represents the estimated influence of price on Q_X, given the influence of other variables. Estimation of a negative b would therefore support the hypothesis of a downward-sloping demand curve.

The Identification Problem

Identification of a demand curve The variation in observed prices and quantities that can be used to trace out a demand curve from actual data.

Estimating a demand curve from market data requires that the data do in fact correspond to points on a demand curve. Suppose that both the demand and supply curves are stationary over the period for which data have been collected. Under those circumstances there would be no significant variability in price and quantity demanded. Some random shifts in price and quantity may be caused by chance over the time the data have been collected. However, there would be no reason to believe that the demand curve could be identified from the resulting scatter of points. **Identification of a demand curve** from market data requires that the variation in observed prices and quantities actually trace out a demand curve. Figure 5–13(a) illustrates stationary demand and supply curves. The observed equilibrium points are all close to the intersection of the demand curve and the supply curve.

It is easy to fall into the trap of misinterpreting market data. Suppose, for example, data have been collected on the prices of new automobiles and on the number sold. From the data it is observed that whenever the price of new automobiles rose over the period under study, the number sold increased. Can it be concluded that, in violation of the law of demand, the demand curve for automobiles is upward sloping? If there is reason to believe that for the period under study all of the variables affecting supply were fixed while consumer income was increasing, this question can be answered negatively. The increases in consumer income would shift the demand curve outward, as shown in Figure 5–13(b). Each observation collected as data would therefore represent a point on the supply curve. The equilibrium points used as data would have identified the supply curve! The demand curve, however, would not have been identified. Data generated in that way therefore cannot be used to estimate demand curves.

---

[9] The coefficients represent the first partial derivatives of the function $Q_X = f(P, P_C, P_S, I)$ with respect to each of the variables of the analysis. For example, in Equation 5–12, $b = \partial Q_X/\partial P$ and $e = \partial Q_X/\partial I$.

FIGURE 5–13 The Identification Problem

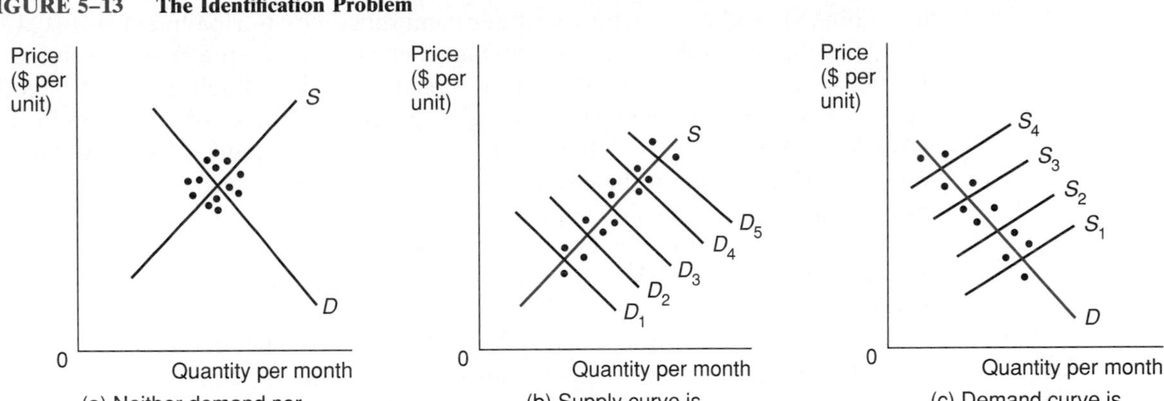

Each dot on the graphs represents an observed price and quantity sold at a given time (or location). These are equilibrium prices and quantities. Demand curves and supply curves themselves can never be directly observed. In (a) there is not enough variation in demand or supply to identify either a demand curve or a supply curve from the data. The points in (b) identify a supply curve. Only in (c) is a demand curve identified.

Market equilibrium data can identify a demand curve only when a supply variable was changing while all of the demand variables were held constant or had their effects removed by a statistical adjustment. Figure 5–13(c) shows an identified demand curve. Suppose there is reason to believe that the cost of producing automobiles increased over the period under study, thereby shifting the supply curve upward. Under these circumstances the scatter of points observed would reflect points on the demand curve. The shifting supply curve would have resulted in equilibrium prices and quantities along a given demand curve. Statisticians have developed techniques to allow identification of demand functions by including enough supply variables in their specification to allow for shifts in supply. At the same time they adjust for all influences on demand other than price. This allows statistical estimation of the coefficients of demand functions.[10]

An Estimated Demand Function for Automobiles

For example, the following statistical demand function for automobiles based on data from 1921 to 1953 was estimated by Gregory Chow:

$$Q_A = 0.3882 - 0.0235P - 0.0813S_A + 0.0100I \qquad \textbf{(5–14)}$$

where Q_A is the quantity of new automobiles purchased per year per capita, P is the dollar price of automobiles, S_A is the existing number of automobiles per

[10] For those interested in statistical estimation techniques, a good introduction is Harry H. Kelejian and Wallace E. Oates, *Introduction to Econometrics*, 2nd ed. (New York: Harper & Row, 1981).

capita in use in the previous year (an indication of available substitutes for new automobiles), and I is a measure of per capita income after payment of taxes.[11]

Quantitative methods of forecasting demand involve the use of estimated demand coefficients for variables in a demand function. Each estimated coefficient in a demand function can be used to predict the effect of a change in that variable on the quantity of the good sold. The sign in front of the coefficient indicates the direction of the effect. For example, the negative sign in front of the price variable in the equation indicates that an increase in the price of automobiles decreases the quantity demanded. The positive sign for the income coefficient indicates that an increase in income increases the quantity of automobiles purchased.

Chow used data from 1921 to 1953 to estimate automobile demand. If tastes and other demand relations have changed since then, his equation would be of little value in predicting automobile sales in 1995. If the coefficients are believed to be valid for future behavior, their estimates can be used to predict future consumption. To accomplish this, other analyses are used to predict changes in income, price, and the existing stock of old automobiles. These values are then substituted in the equation to predict the resulting change in the quantity of automobiles sold.

The coefficients of the estimated demand function can be used to compute estimated demand elasticities. For example, Chow's coefficient for his price variable is 0.0235. This estimates $\Delta Q_D/\Delta P$, changes in automobile purchases for given changes in price. Elasticity of demand is

$$P/Q_D(\Delta Q_D/\Delta P) = (P/Q_D)0.0235$$

To estimate the price elasticity of demand, select a certain P and Q_D and substitute it in the formula for elasticity. Because price elasticity of demand along a linear demand curve is different at every point, the linear specifications would give many possible elasticities. Economists using linear specifications generally calculate elasticity for the average values of price and quantity in their samples.[12] If this is done for Chow's data, a price elasticity of demand equal to about -1 is the result.[13]

Forecasting the demand for any good or service is a tricky business. It is difficult to make such predictions with 100 percent confidence. There is always the chance that an important influence on demand will change unexpectedly. For example, U.S. car manufacturers failed to predict the sharp increase in the price of oil that occurred in 1973. As a result of that increase buyers shifted to more fuel-efficient foreign cars and the demand for U.S. gas guzzlers plummeted.

---

[11] Gregory C. Chow, *Demand for Automobiles in the United States* (Amsterdam: North Holland Publishing, 1957), p. 63. The coefficients in Equation 5–14 are those estimated by Chow. The symbols for the variables, however, have been changed to conform to notations used in this book.

[12] This is not done when nonlinear specifications are used. A common nonlinear specification is based on the assumption of constant elasticity. This involves calculating the logarithms of the data and assuming a linear relationship among the logarithms of the variables.

[13] Subsequent studies of automobile demand have estimated much larger demand elasticities.

SUMMARY

1. A market demand curve shows the total quantity demanded by all consumers at any price. Market demand curves are obtained by adding up the quantities demanded by all consumers at each possible price.
2. Market demand for a product depends on all the determinants of individual demands and on population and its age distribution, income distribution among demographic groups, household size, and the number of consumers in foreign nations who are willing and able to purchase the product.
3. Price elasticity of demand measures the sensitivity of quantity of a good demanded to change in price as the percentage change in quantity demanded resulting from each 1 percent change in the price of the good.
4. Demand for a good is price elastic when the absolute value of its price elasticity of demand exceeds 1. Demand for a good is inelastic when the absolute value of its price elasticity is between zero and 1. When price elasticity of demand is exactly equal to 1, demand is of unitary elasticity.
5. The price elasticity of demand for a good depends on the availability of substitutes for the good and length of the period available for adjustment to changes in the price of the good. It can also be influenced by the portion of consumer budgets allocated to the good.
6. Estimates of the price elasticity of demand for a product can be used to forecast changes in consumer expenditures and seller revenue resulting from changes in the price of the product.
7. Price elasticity of demand varies along points of a linear demand curve.
8. Income elasticity of demand measures the percentage change in quantity purchased in response to each 1 percent change in income. Income elasticity of demand is a measure of the sensitivity of consumer purchases to changes in income. Normal goods have positive income elasticity, whereas inferior goods have negative income elasticity.
9. Cross elasticity of demand measures the sensitivity of the demand for one good to a 1 percent change in the price of another good. Positive cross elasticity of demand indicates that the two goods are substitutes; negative cross elasticity of demand indicates that the goods are complements.
10. Market demand curves provide information on the maximum price that consumers would pay for a good when a given amount of the good is available. This price can be viewed as the marginal benefit of an additional unit of the good to a consumer.
11. Consumer surplus is the difference between the market price of a good and the maximum price a consumer is willing to pay for an additional unit of the good. The total consumer surplus enjoyed by consumers is the difference between the maximum amount of money they would pay to purchase the quantity of the good sold and the amount they actually pay based on the market price. Consumer surplus is used to evaluate the gains and losses to consumers resulting from policies that affect prices.
12. Demand functions may be estimated by means of market experiments, consumer surveys, or statistical analysis of data.
13. To statistically estimate a demand function, the variables affecting the amounts purchased must be specified. Statistical methods allow the estimation of demand coefficients that measure the effect of a change in a demand determinant on the quantity of a good that buyers are willing and able to purchase. Demand coefficients can be used to estimate price, income, and cross elasticities of demand.
14. Only market equilibrium prices and quantities can be observed and used as data in statistical demand analysis. Demand curves can be identified from market data when supply curves shift and when the influences of all the demand variables on quantities purchased have been accounted for.

Important Concepts

market demand curve
price elasticity of demand
income elasticity of demand
cross elasticity of demand
consumer surplus
marginal net benefit
excess burden of a tax
compensated demand curves
demand function
demand coefficients
identification of a demand curve

Questions for Review

1. What is the difference between an individual demand curve and a market demand curve? How is the quantity demanded on a market demand curve derived for any given price?
2. Why is there reason to believe that the demand for various goods is related to the age distribution of population?
3. Explain how the average age of household heads and the average size of households in a nation can affect the demand for certain goods.
4. The price elasticity of demand for cameras is −2. What will happen to the quantity of cameras demanded if the price of cameras increases by 10 percent and nothing else changes?
5. The operator of an amusement park wants to increase monthly revenue from the sale of tickets for rides. To accomplish this goal, the operator increases the price of these tickets. Under what circumstances will the price increase actually increase revenue? Under what circumstances will the price increase *decrease* revenue?
6. Explain how the price elasticity of demand for a good is related to the slope of a demand curve. Why does a demand curve with constant slope *not* exhibit constant price elasticity?
7. If the income elasticity of demand for automobiles is 5, calculate the percentage change in automobile sales that would result from a 2 percent reduction in consumer income.
8. If the income elasticity of demand for potatoes is −0.8, what effect will a 3 percent increase in income have on potato sales? Why must the income elasticity of demand for housing be positive if a consumer spends all of his income on housing and potatoes?
9. If the cross elasticity of demand between the quantity of pork purchased and the price of beef is 0.4, what impact would a 10 percent increase in the price of beef have on the amount of pork purchased?
10. Explain why consumer surplus is always less than the marginal benefit of a unit of a good. Show how an increase in price decreases total consumer surplus. Show how a decrease in price increases total consumer surplus. Explain why consumers earn no consumer surplus on the last unit of a good purchased per month.

Problems

1. The slope of the demand curve for televisions is −0.5 at all points. If the price of televisions is currently $300 and 600 televisions are sold monthly in a small town, what is the price elasticity of demand for televisions in that town. What will happen to the revenue of the television sellers if they mark the price down by 1 percent?
2. The demand for desk lamps is linear, and the price of desk lamps is $30. The demand curve for desk lamps then shifts out parallel to itself in response to an increase in consumer income. Prove that the demand for desk lamps becomes less price elastic after the shift in the demand curve.
3. A seller wants to maximize revenue from the sale of tickets to an open-air concert. There is no limit to the number of concertgoers that can be accommodated. Assuming that the demand curve for such a concert is linear, prove that to

achieve maximum revenue, the seller must choose the price at which the price elasticity of demand equals −1.

4. Suppose the local governing authorities subsidize the cost of winter heating for low-income citizens. The subsidy pays half the price of fuel purchased by these citizens. Assume that all of them use oil heat. The subsidy reduces the price of oil from $1 to 50 cents per gallon. Consumption during a winter increases from 2 million to 3 million gallons. Calculate the gain in total consumer surplus, and prove that the dollar cost of the subsidy that winter will exceed the gains of the subsidy recipients.

5. A statistical analysis of the demand for cigarettes shows that the coefficient of the price variable is −1 million. If the price of cigarettes is $1 per pack and 4 million packs per day are sold at that price, calculate the price elasticity of demand at the current price of cigarettes. Suppose cigarette manufacturers raise the price to $1.10 per pack. Assuming that the price elasticity of demand is unchanged at the higher price, forecast what will happen to the manufacturers' revenue.

6. The diagram depicts the demand for attendance at a Broadway play. The equation of the demand curve is $P = 200 - 0.4Q_d$, where P is the ticket price in dollars and Q_d is the quantity of tickets demanded. Answer the following questions regarding this case.
   a. In the absence of any quantity constraints (that is, the seating capacity of the theater is at least 5,000), what price will the play's promoters charge to maximize total revenue from ticket sales?
   b. If the seating capacity of the theater is only 2,000 and the theater is not "overbooked," what ticket price will maximize total revenue from ticket sales? What will total revenue be at that price?
   c. If the theater capacity is greater than 2,500, will total revenue be maximized by charging the price corresponding to that capacity, or will total revenue be higher by charging a price that will not result in a sellout?
   d. Calculate the total consumer surplus corresponding to a ticket price of $80, and explain why no individual ticket purchaser will receive a consumer surplus in excess of $120 at that price.

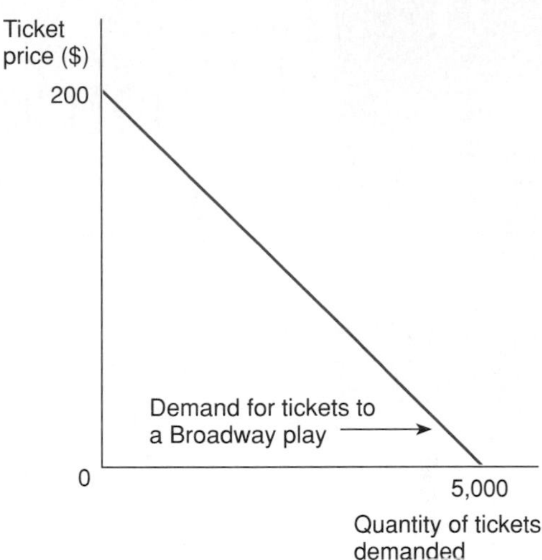

7. As chief economist for the Western Car Corporation, you are asked to predict your company's total revenue from its sale of Pronghorn cars. For each of the following changes, indicate briefly whether Western Car Corporation's total revenue from Pronghorn sales will increase, decrease, or remain the same as a result. Use the various types of demand elasticities to support your answers.
   a. A reduction in the price of the Pronghorn when the demand for Pronghorns is elastic.
   b. An increase in the price of the Pronghorn when the demand curve for Pronghorns is a rectangular hyperbola (such as that in Figure 5–4).
   c. An increase in national income.
   d. A reduction in the price of the Ford Taurus (a substitute for the Pronghorn).

6 Choices under Uncertainty

During the summer of 1991, annual interest rates on bank certificates of deposit fell from an average 8 percent earlier in the year to an average of about 6 percent. Many depositors were reluctant to buy new certificates or renew old ones because they expected interest rates to rise and thought they would be able to earn more on their savings if they waited. Instead of rising, however, interest rates fell further, and by the winter certificates of deposit were yielding only about 5 percent on average. Those who waited to buy them lost the opportunity to earn the higher rates that prevailed earlier in the year.

This example demonstrates that there is quite a bit of uncertainty about the future. When you make a purchase, you do so based on the best information you have available at the time. In many cases, however, the actual outcome of your purchase turns out to be different from the outcome you expected. For example, have you ever bought a product, such as a car or a stereo system, that did not perform the way you expected it would? Or have you ever bought some shares of stock hoping that the stock would soar in price only to find that its price plummeted instead?

The fact that actual outcomes can differ from expected outcomes is a matter that most of us consider when we make our decisions about what or how much to buy or how much to work or what occupations to enter. Our theory of choice would therefore not be complete unless we analyzed the way uncertainty affects decisions. To accomplish this, we must provide ways of measuring expected outcomes in uncertain situations. We must also provide a way of measuring risk. We can then show how attitudes toward risk influence our choices and how desires to either undertake risk or insure against it open up markets for such services as insurance. The theory we develop is particularly useful in analyzing behavior in financial markets, where traders deal with risk on a daily basis and often insure against it by diversifying the assets in their portfolios.

Probability, Expected Value, and Risk

Consumers can rarely foresee the consequences of their choices with certainty. For example, when you choose to purchase corporate stock, you do not know for sure what the future value of the stock will be or how much in dividends you will earn on the stock. Many financial assets are subject to risk because their prices and the dividends they pay are quite variable. However, some alternatives are less risky than others because the deviations of their outcomes from those expected are relatively small.

Probability

Probability
The chance that an outcome will occur.

Uncertain situation
A situation in which more than one outcome is possible and the probability of each of those outcomes is known or can be estimated.

Let's examine some of the characteristics of uncertainty. To do so, we must first define some basic concepts. **Probability** is the chance that an outcome will occur. The probability of an outcome is a number between 0 and 1. An impossible outcome has 0 probability, while a certain outcome has a probability of 1. Uncertain outcomes have probabilities of between 0 and 1. In general, an **uncertain situation** is one in which more than one outcome is possible and the probability of each of those outcomes is known or can be estimated. Assuming that the possible outcomes in the situation are mutually exclusive, so that if one occurs, the other cannot occur, the sum of the probabilities of the possible outcomes must be 1.

If we had a chance to observe a situation many times, we could measure the *objective* probability of an outcome as the number of times it would occur if the situation were repeated over and over. For example, suppose the situation is the tossing of a coin. Assume the coin is not weighted to bias the outcome for heads or tails. If you tossed the coin 1,000 times, then, on average, heads would be the outcome 500 times and tails would be the outcome 500 times. The probability that each of these outcomes would occur is equal.

The objective probability of an outcome is its frequency of occurrence, f, over a large number of times, N:

$$\text{Probability} = f/N \qquad \textbf{(6–1)}$$

For example, the probability that a head will appear on a single toss of a coin is 500/1,000 = 0.5. The probability that tails will appear on a single toss is also 0.5. If you buy a weekly ticket for lottery in which one prize is awarded for each 1,000 tickets sold each week, then your probability of winning a prize each week is 1/1,000 = 0.001.

The concept of probability has widespread application in economics and statistical analysis. For example, objective probabilities can be used to forecast the incidence of disease. The objective probability that a male of a given age will have a heart attack can be calculated by determining the entire population of males of that age and the frequency of heart attacks among those males. We might find that each year out of 10 million 45-year-old males, 10,000 have heart attacks. The probability of a heart attack for a 45-year-old male is therefore 0.001, or one out of 1,000.

Information on the probability of disease is used by hospitals to forecast the demand for medical services. Insurance companies use objective probabilities to set rates for automobile and life insurance policies.

In many cases a situation cannot easily be repeated over and over to calculate objective probabilities. For example, you might want to start up a new retail outlet in your city to sell laser discs and CD/ROM players. Because no one has ever started a store specializing in these products, you have no information on the probability that you will earn profits or incur losses. Similarly, it is difficult to set up objective probabilities about whether the stock of a particular company, say Apple Computer, will increase or decrease in value after you purchase it. In such cases, individuals formulate *subjective* estimates of probability based on intuition, experience, and current information about the company and other economic factors that influence the price of its stock. Subjective probabilities differ from objective probabilities in that they cannot be computed by repeating a situation over and over. Instead, each individual formulates his or her own estimates of probabilities of outcomes in uncertain situations and these probabilities vary among individuals. For example, you might estimate that 0.5 is the probability that the price of Apple stock will go up 50 percent this year, while your roommate, who has the same information as you have, might estimate that probability as only 0.1. Obviously, your roommate's interpretation of the information is different from yours.

Expected Value of Uncertain Situations

Payoff The value of a possible outcome in an uncertain situation measured as a sum of money.

We are primarily concerned with uncertain situations in which gains or losses can occur as a result of choices. The **payoff** of a possible outcome in an uncertain situation is the value of that outcome, measured as a sum of money, to the decision maker. If the outcome is a gain, the payoff is a sum of money received by the decision maker or an increase in the value of assets owned by the decision maker. If a loss is incurred, the payoff is negative and will require the decision maker to either make a payment or suffer a reduction in the value of assets he or she owns.

Expected value An average of the possible payoffs associated with the possible outcomes of an uncertain situation, with each outcome weighted according to its probability of occurrence.

The **expected value** of an uncertain situation is an average of the possible payoffs associated with each possible outcome. This average is obtained by multiplying each possible outcome by its probability and summing the result:

$$\text{Expected value} = \Sigma(X_i)(\text{Prob}_i) \qquad \textbf{(6–2)}$$

where X_i is the payoff to outcome i and Prob_i is the probability that X_i will occur. The sum of the probabilities for all possible outcomes must equal 1.

For example, suppose you are given the opportunity to invest in a pharmaceutical firm that is attempting to develop a new antibiotic that will succeed in treating diseases resistant to other drugs. Your payoff for each share of this firm's stock that you buy will depend on whether or not the firm develops and successfully markets the antibiotic this year. Suppose the payoff will be \$500 per share if this is done but will only be \$100 per share if it is not done. If the probability of success with the new antibiotic is 0.1, while the probability of failure is 0.9, the expected value of the gain from buying the stock this year is

$$(\$500)(0.1) + (\$100)(0.9) = \$140$$

Notice that because the probability of success is much lower than the probability of failure, the expected value of the gain from buying the stock is closer to \$100 than to \$500. This is because the concept of expected value gives a relatively lower *weight* to events of lower probability in computing the expected payoff to an uncertain situation such as buying shares of stock. Expected value is a weighted average of possible outcomes, with each outcome receiving a weight equal to its probability of occurrence.

Measuring Risk

If individuals considered only the expected value of payoffs to uncertain situations, they would always choose the outcome with the highest expected payoff. In actuality, the utility most people gain from making decisions that have an uncertain outcome depends not only on the expected value of the payoffs but also on the variability of the payoffs.

Suppose that you want to invest $10,000 so as to obtain income. You decide that you want to invest in a mutual fund specializing in either bonds or stocks. The income that you can earn each year from your investment depends on the dividends, interest, and price variability of the fund. If the price of the fund's shares goes up, you earn income in the form of a *capital gain*. Stock funds provide income in the form of dividends and capital gains. Bond funds provide interest income and a possible appreciation in share value. But there is another side of the coin for investments in mutual funds. Their prices per share can fall as well as rise! You can incur a *capital loss* if the price of the fund's shares goes down. The prices of long-term bonds can fall or rise with changes in the current market interest rates on new bonds of similar maturity. For example, a rise in the interest rates of such new bonds is likely to cause a fall in the price of a similar bond issued at a lower interest rate. This is because the existing bond has to be sold at a discount to make its effective yield equal to the yield that investors can obtain by purchasing newly issued bonds. However, the variability of bond prices is often less than that of stock prices.

Risk A situation that prevails when a person engages in an activity for which there is more than one possible outcome, with each possible outcome having a certain probability of occurrence.

Risk is a situation that prevails when a person engages in an activity for which there is more than one possible outcome, with each of the possible outcomes having a certain probability of occurrence. Risk can be measured as the variability of possible outcomes relative to the expected value of those outcomes in an uncertain situation. Let's see how we can measure the variability, and therefore the risk, of an alternative.

Table 6–1 shows how much income you can expect to earn from your $10,000 investment. Assume that if you invest the entire sum in a stock mutual fund, there is a probability of 0.6 that you will earn income of $3,000 in dividends and capital gains in one year. However, there is a probability of 0.4 that at the end of the year your stocks will be worth less than their purchase price, so that your combined

TABLE 6–1 Expected Investment Income

	Increasing Asset Prices		*Decreasing Asset Prices*	
	Income	***Probability***	***Income***	***Probability***
Stock fund	$3,000	0.6	−$1,000	0.4
Bond fund	800	0.8	400	0.2

Expected income (stock fund) = ($3,000)(0.6) + (−$1,000)0.4 = $1,400

Expected income (bond fund) = ($800)(0.8) + ($400)(0.2) = $720

MODERN MICROECONOMICS IN ACTION: INTERNATIONAL REPORT

Assessing the Risk of Foreign Investment

From a business point of view, the world has become one large global economy. Investors who seek to maximize the return on their funds look all over the world for investment opportunities. Even the small investor can engage in foreign investment by buying shares of mutual funds that specialize in foreign stocks and bonds. But foreign investment—particularly in developing countries where expected returns can be very high—can be exceedingly risky. Changes in foreign exchange rates and changes in the political conditions of foreign nations can affect the outcome of foreign investment.

The increased interest in foreign investment in recent years has given rise to a demand for information about risk in foreign nations. A market for such information has sprung up, and several firms now rate risks in foreign nations, sell that information, and provide advice to foreign investors. Two of these "risk raters" are the Economic Intelligence Unit, located in New York but a subsidiary of the Economists Group, a British firm, and International Business Communications, Ltd., a British firm, which publishes *The International Country Risk Guide*.*

The Economic Intelligence Unit rates nations as A, B, C, D, or E, with A being the least risky and E the most risky. It reports on lending risks and political or policy risks to investment, including the possibility that poor economic policies might deplete a nation's foreign exchange reserves or reduce its ability to pay back loans in other ways. *The International Country Risk (ICR) Guide* reports on such factors as government corruption and expectations for inflation, growth, and loan default.

As of August 1991 the *ICR Guide* rated 129 nations. At that time the least risky nation in which to invest was Switzerland and the most risky nations in which to invest were Iraq, Sudan, Somalia, and Liberia.

In the 1990s, many investors were considering investments in such nations as Poland, where economic reform was beginning to transform communist nations to capitalist ones. According to the risk raters, conditions were improving in Poland, but it was still risky to invest there. The Economic Intelligence Unit rated Poland as a D in 1991. However, it was safer to invest in Poland than in Czechoslovakia, whose economy was still crippled as a result of the former communist system and which still faced the risk of civil war. Because of these factors, as well as a 60 percent inflation rate, the *ICR Guide* rated Czechoslovakia as riskier than Poland. China, on the other hand, was generally agreed to be a medium-risk nation (the Economic Intelligence Unit gave it a B in 1991).

There were some relatively low-risk investment opportunities in Latin America. Chile was enjoying strong economic growth and falling inflation rates in 1991. It was also reducing its foreign debt burden. Chile therefore earned an A from the Economic Intelligence Unit, and the *ICR Guide* ranked it in the upper quarter of nations for its relatively low risk.

* See Monua Janah, "Report Card, Rating Risk in the Hot Countries," *The Wall Street Journal,* September 20, 1991, p. R4.

income from dividends and the resulting capital loss would be −$1,000. You therefore run the risk of actually losing money if you invest in the stock fund this year!

Suppose that if you invest all of your $10,000 in the bond fund, there is an 0.8 probability that you will earn interest and capital gains income of $800 in one year if bond prices rise during the year. If bond prices fall, however, your income will be only $400, and the probability of that outcome is 0.2.

Now let's calculate the expected value of your investment income for each of the two investment alternatives. As shown in Table 6–1, the expected value of the annual payoff from investing $10,000 in the stock fund is $1,400, while the expected value of the annual payoff from investing in the bond fund is only $720. If all you are concerned about is the expected value of your income, your decision would be easy—you would plunk down all of your chips on the stock fund.

However, most of us consider the riskiness of investments as well as their expected payoffs before making our choices. The next step, therefore, is to measure the risk of each investment alternative. Notice that although the stock fund has a higher expected income than the bond fund, the variation of the possible payoffs is much greater for the stock fund than for the bond fund. **Variance** is a statistical measure of the variability of payoffs in an uncertain situation that is computed by averaging the squares of the deviations of possible outcomes from the expected value of the payoffs in that situation. The squared deviations are weighted according to the probability of the outcomes. Table 6–2 shows how the variance of the payoffs for the stock fund and the bond fund is computed. Naturally, you get a very large number when you square the deviations. The variance of the payoffs for the stock fund is $3,840,000.

Variance A statistical measure of the variability of payoffs in an uncertain situation that is computed by averaging the squares of the deviations of possible outcomes from the expected value of the payoffs.

By squaring the deviations, we avoid the possibility that negative deviations can offset positive deviations, and therefore underestimate the actual variability of outcomes. However, what we are interested in is the difference between the

TABLE 6–2 Variance and Standard Deviation of Investment Income

Stock Fund

Payoff if Asset Prices Rise	***Deviation from $1,400 Expected Value***	***Deviation Squared***
$3,000	+1,600	$2,560,000

Payoff if Asset Prices Fall	***Deviation from $1,400 Expected Value***	***Deviation Squared***
−$1,000	−$2,400	$5,760,000

Variance of payoffs (stock fund) = $2,560,000(0.6) + $5,760,000(0.4) = $3,840,000
Standard deviation of payoffs (stock fund) = $\sqrt{\$3{,}840{,}000}$ = $1,959.59

Bond Fund

Payoff if Asset Prices Rise	***Deviation from $720 Expected Value***	***Deviation Squared***
$800	+$80	$6,400

Payoff if Asset Prices Fall	***Deviation from $720 Expected Value***	***Deviation Squared***
$400	−$320	$102,400

Variance of payoffs (bond fund) = $6,400(0.8) + $102,400(0.2) = $25,600
Standard deviation of payoffs (bond fund) = $\sqrt{\$25{,}600}$ = $160

Standard deviation The square root of the variance.

variance of each possible alternative among which we are choosing rather than the size of the variance. An alternative measure of risk is the **standard deviation** of payoffs, which is calculated by taking the square root of the variance. The standard deviation of payoffs from the stock fund is $1,959.59, which is a much smaller number than the variance. Standard deviation, because it is smaller and easier to handle than variance, is commonly used instead of variance to measure risk.[1]

Table 6–2 also calculates the variance and standard deviation of payoffs from the bond fund. The variance of payoffs from the bond fund is $25,600, and the standard deviation is $160. Using either variance or standard deviation of payoffs as our measure of risk, it is clear that the stock fund is a much riskier alternative than the stock fund because the variability of its payoffs is greater. If you are concerned about the riskiness of assets, you will therefore think twice about putting all of your money into the stock fund just because it has a higher expected annual payoff.

CONCEPT REVIEW

1. What is meant by the *objective probability* of an event?
2. How is the expected value of a payoff in an uncertain situation calculated?
3. How is risk measured?

UTILITY AND RISK: RISK-YIELD INDIFFERENCE CURVES

Now that we have a measure for risk, we can further analyze choices under uncertainty by considering attitudes toward risk. We can also show how the utility of income for a person can influence the choices made by that person in uncertain situations.

Risk-Yield Indifference Curves: Risk Aversion

Product attributes Characteristics of a good, service, or situation that provide utility to a person.

To examine the choices made in an uncertain situation and how attitudes toward risk affect those choices, we need to consider the way the decision maker considers the *attributes* of the situation. **Product attributes** of a good or service (such as a mutual fund or an occupation) are the characteristics that provide utility to

[1] Both the variance and standard deviation of payoffs have shortcomings as measures of risk. Both of these measures assume a symmetrical degree of risk aversion, so that deviations of outcomes *above* expected values are given the same weight as deviations *below* expected values. Of course, an investor might attach a greater weight to deviations below expected values because he does not mind doing *better* than expected.

the buyer (as in the case of a mutual fund) or seller in the case of an occupation. For example, the attributes of a car include its gas mileage, its power and acceleration, and its passenger and cargo space. The attributes of a house include its size, the number of rooms, its location, and its quality of construction. To analyze decisions regarding uncertain situations, let's assume that in considering a transaction, decision makers are interested in only two attributes: expected annual payoff, which is measured by the expected value of possible outcomes, and risk, which we will assume is measured by the standard deviation of possible outcomes.

Let's begin the analysis by assuming that as an investor you place a positive value on the annual payoff of such assets as mutual funds and a *negative* value on risk. Other things being equal, this implies that, given a choice between two mutual funds with the same expected annual payoff as measured in interest, dividends, or capital gains, you would get more utility from the one that involves less risk. A **risk averter** is a person who, other things being equal, prefers an uncertain situation with less risk to one with more risk. For a risk averter, risk, measured by either the variance or the standard deviation of payoffs, is a negatively valued attribute of an uncertain situation. For convenience, we will measure risk as the standard deviation because standard deviation is a number that is smaller and easier to handle than variance.

Risk averter A person who, other things being equal, prefers an uncertain situation with less risk to one with more risk.

Figure 6–1 plots the indifference curves between the risk and yield attributes of uncertain situations for a risk averter.[2] Notice that the indifference curves are *upward sloping* rather than downward sloping, as is usual. The upward slope indicates that risk is a negative valued attribute to the decision maker. While utility increases with increases in the expected payoff of an uncertain situation because expected payoff is a positively valued attribute, it decreases with increases in risk. To move from a position of less risk to one of more risk, the decision maker must receive a higher expected yield to avoid a reduction in utility. For the indifference map drawn in Figure 6–1, $U_3 > U_2 > U_1$.

Suppose a risk-averse investor is given a choice between two stock mutual funds with the same price per share whose annual expected payoffs and risk are represented by points S_1 and S_2, respectively on the graph. The investor will prefer the fund whose attributes correspond to S_1 to the fund whose attributes correspond to S_2 because, given the equality of the annual expected payoffs on the two funds, this fund has lower risk and therefore gives the risk averter higher utility. However, the risk-averse investor would prefer another stock fund of equal price, represented by point S_3, to either of these funds because shares of this fund would give the investor utility level U_3, which is greater than the utility level provided by either of them.

[2] In this analysis we are assuming that utility directly depends on two attributes of expected return and risk in an uncertain situation. It is also possible to *derive* an *expected utility function* from a prespecified utility function that depends only on income. The usual way of doing this is to postulate a quadratic form of the utility function that implies that $\partial U/\partial I$ is decreasing, where U is utility and I is income. It is then possible to calculate expected utility from this quadratic utility function and to show how expected utility depends on expected return and the variance of returns.

FIGURE 6–1 Risk-Yield Indifference Curves for a Risk Averter

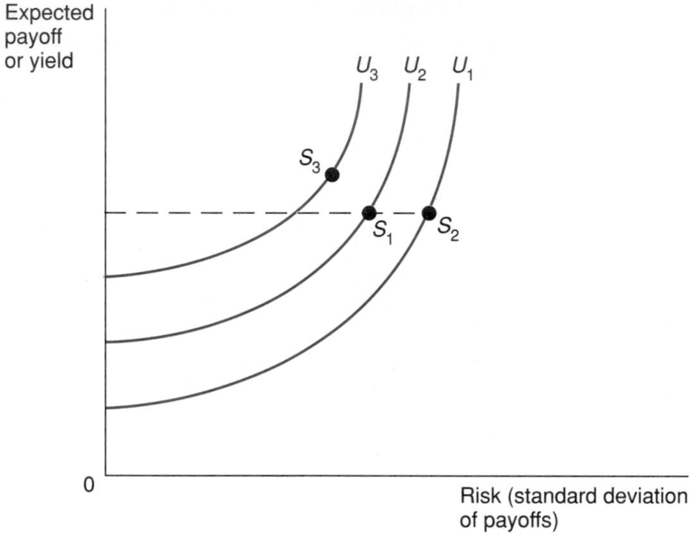

Utility increases with expected yield for a risk averter. However, additional risk, other things being equal, makes the risk averter worse off. Because risk is a negatively valued attribute, the risk-yield indifference curves are upward sloping.

Indifference Curves for Risk Lovers and Risk-Neutral Investors

Just as we differ in our preferences for goods and services, so too do we differ in our preferences for taking risk. Some people love to take risks and even thrive on doing so, and other people, although not exactly in love with risk, don't seem to mind it as risk averters do. **Risk neutrality** prevails for a decision maker if, other things being equal, additional risk in an uncertain situation neither increases nor decreases utility for that decision maker. Figure 6–2 draws the indifference curves for a risk-neutral investor. The indifference map consists of a series of horizontal indifference curves, with higher indifference curves corresponding to higher levels of utility.

Risk neutrality A situation that prevails when additional risk neither increases nor decreases utility.

A risk-neutral investor does not consider the riskiness of assets when making decisions. The only attribute of an investment situation or any other situation that can increase such an investor's level of well-being is the expected payoff of the situation. No matter what the risk level, a risk-neutral investor prefers an uncertain situation with higher expected payoff to one with lower expected payoff.

Some people, such as compulsive gamblers, enjoy taking risks. These people place a positive value on the riskiness of an uncertain situation. A **risk lover** is a person who, given the expected payoff of an uncertain situation, prefers a situation of greater risk to one of lesser risk. Assuming a diminishing marginal rate of substitution between risk and expected payoff, Figure 6–3 draws the indifference curves for a risk lover. These indifference curves have the usual downward-sloping

Risk lover A person for whom risk is a positively valued attribute of an uncertain situation.

FIGURE 6–2 Risk-Yield Indifference Curves for a Risk-Neutral Investor

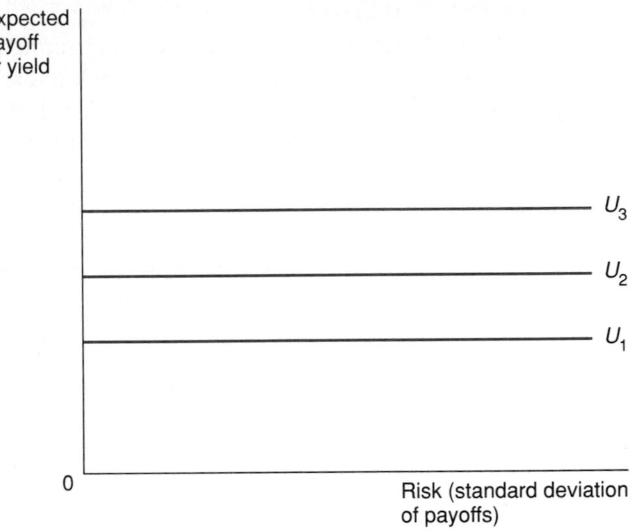

Utility increases with expected yield for a risk-neutral investor. Risk neither increases nor decreases utility for such an investor. A risk-neutral investor must maximize the expected yield or payoff in uncertain situations to maximize utility.

FIGURE 6–3 Risk-Yield Indifference Curves for a Risk Lover

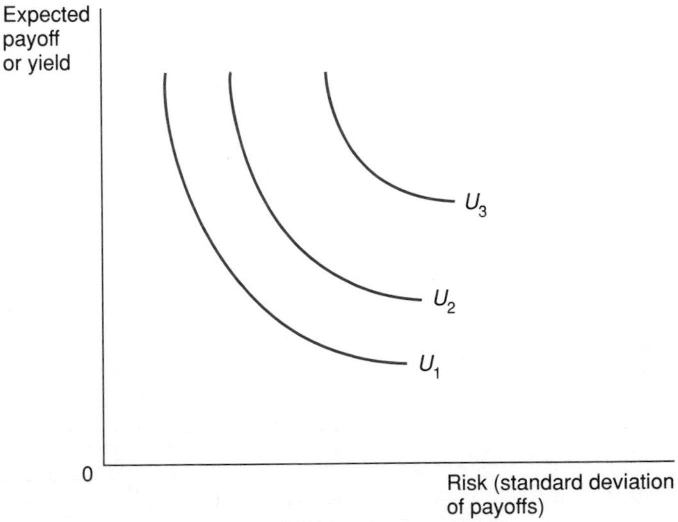

Utility increases with both expected yield and risk for a risk lover.

convex shape. For a risk lover, other things being equal, either an increase in the risk of an uncertain situation or an increase in the expected payoff of the situation increases utility.

Attitudes toward risk taking vary among investors. However, the most prevalent attitude toward risk taking is risk aversion. Most investors dislike risk and have indifference curves similar to those drawn in Figure 6–1. These investors can be induced to assume more risk only if they are compensated by a higher expected payoff for doing so. As you will soon see, this dominant attitude has important implications for behavior and pricing in financial markets, where uncertainty prevails. However, to better understand how attitudes toward risk taking are formed, we first examine the relationship between income and well-being and how that relationship influences such attitudes.

The Utility of Income and Attitudes toward Risk Taking

Most of us are better off when our annual income increases. After all, more income means that we can buy more goods and services this year or we can save to buy more in the future. Our material standard of living therefore tends to increase with increases in income. Although the total utility of income tends to increase as annual income increases, the *marginal utility* of income tends to fall for many of us. This implies that as income increases, additional dollars of income in a given year are worth less and less in terms of the utility they provide.

FIGURE 6–4 Utility and Income for a Risk Averter

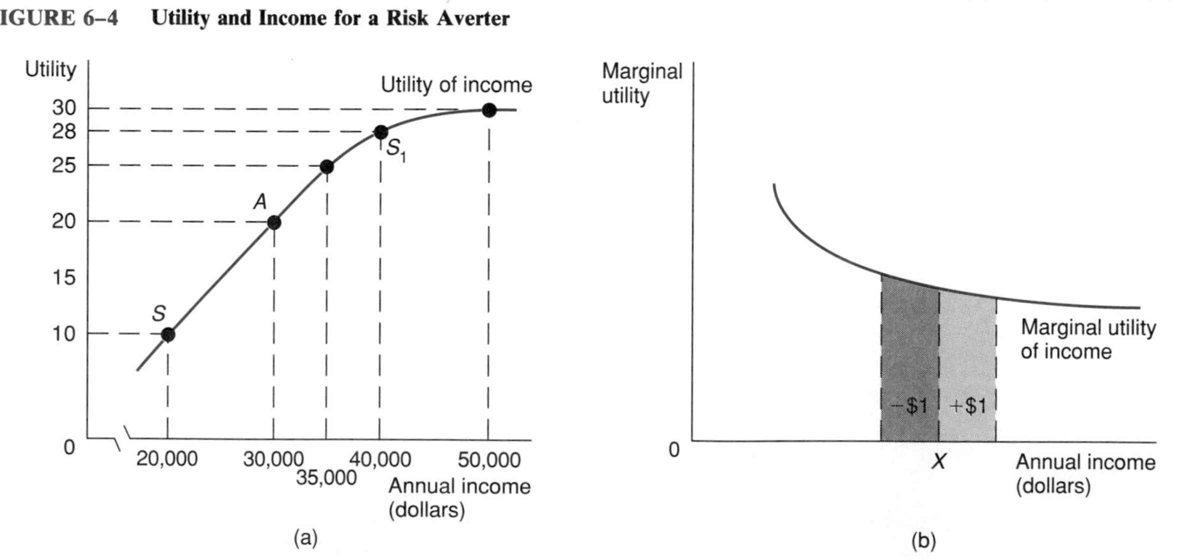

For a risk averter, the marginal utility of income declines. Confronted with a certain income of $30,000 and an uncertain situation with the same expected income, the risk averter gets higher expected utility from the certain income.

Let's examine how the way the marginal utility of income varies can affect attitudes toward risk taking. Figure 6–4(a) shows how the total utility of income for a typical investor varies. Notice that the total utility function is upward sloping but that its slope decreases as income increases. Because the slope of the total utility curve is the marginal utility of income, this curve represents the case of a person for whom that marginal utility declines. For example, suppose this person earns $30,000 a year from a job and obtains additional income from investments in stocks, bonds, and other financial assets. Suppose these investments increase the person's income from $30,000 to $35,000, which, assuming that the cardinal measurement is possible, increases the person's annual utility level from 20 units of utility to 25 units of utility. The marginal utility of this extra $5,000 in income is therefore 5 units of utility. Figure 6–4(a) shows that a further increase in annual income from $35,000 to $40,000 per year as a result of investments also increases the person's annual utility level. However, the marginal utility of this $5,000 increase is only 3 units of expected utility. Assuming that the person seeks to maximize expected utility, we need to examine how expected utility will vary with the choice to undertake or not undertake the investments.

Suppose this person is considering investments that can increase his annual income to $40,000 with an 0.5 probability but can also decrease his annual income to $20,000 with an 0.5 probability. First, let's calculate the expected value of income if the investments are made:

$$\text{Expected value of income} = 20{,}000(0.5) + 40{,}000(0.5) = \$30{,}000$$

The expected value of income is therefore the same as the certain income from his job alone that the person would enjoy if no investments were made.

Expected utility The average utility of an uncertain situation; computed by weighing the utility of the payoffs in the situation by their probabilities of occurrence.

Now let's calculate the **expected utility,** the expected utility value of income, in the uncertain situation of making investments. This is more important than the expected value of income because the person makes choices to maximize expected utility. From Figure 6–4(a), note that the expected value of an annual income of $20,000 is 10 units of utility, while the expected value of a $40,000 income is 28 units of utility. The expected utility of the certain situation of making investments is

$$\text{Expected utility} = 10(0.5) + 28(0.5) = 19$$

The expected utility enjoyed by the person if investments are not made is 20, which is the utility of getting $30,000 income this year with certainty at point *A* in Figure 6–4(a). Because the expected utility of not investing is greater than that of investing, the person whose utility function is illustrated in Figure 6–4(a) does not invest. This person can be regarded as risk averse because, confronted by the choice between a certain situation and an uncertain situation with the same expected payoff, he opts for the certain situation.

In general, risk aversion is consistent with a utility function like the one drawn in Figure 6–4, for which the marginal utility of income is declining. For such a utility function, an expected payoff of a given dollar value that is certain always provides more expected utility than an expected payoff of the same dollar value from an uncertain situation. In other words, for a given expected yield, a more risky situation provides lower expected utility than a less risky one and risk is therefore a negatively valued attribute. Remember that because the marginal utility of income declines for risk averters, the value for them (in terms of utility) of a dollar gained through a gamble in a risky situation is always less than the value of a dollar lost. Risk averters dislike variability because what they gain on the upside if they win a gamble is worth less to them than what they might lose on the downside. When confronted with the certain prospect of $\$X$ and the uncertain prospect of $\$(X - b)$ or $\$(X + b)$, each with equal probability of occurrence, the risk averter always chooses the sure $\$X$. In general, a risk averter has to be offered much better than 50–50 odds to accept a bet that involves the uncertain prospect of winning or losing a given sum of money.

However, a risk-averse individual can be induced to assume additional risk if he is compensated with a higher expected return. To see how this behavior is consistent with the utility function of Figure 6–4(a), assume that the probability is 0.5 that a \$10,000 investment in the stock market can provide the individual with a total income of \$50,000 if the stock market goes up and with a total income of \$25,000, also with a probability of 0.5, if the stock market goes down. The expected payoff of making the investment would be

$$\text{Expected income} = \$25{,}000(0.5) + \$50{,}000(0.5) = \$37{,}500$$

If the individual assumes this risk, he can increase his expected income to \$37,500 rather than the \$30,000 he can enjoy for sure without investing. Because the expected utility of the \$50,000 income is 30 units of utility, while the expected utility of the \$25,000 is 15 units, the expected utility of the uncertain situation in this case is

$$\text{Expected utility} = 15(0.5) + 30(0.5) = 22.5 \text{ units}$$

Here the expected payoff of undertaking the risk is higher than the \$30,000 received for sure. The individual will choose to make the investment because his expected utility will be higher if he does so.

We can also draw utility functions for risk neutrals and risk lovers. For a risk neutral, the marginal utility of income is constant. For a risk lover, the marginal utility of income increases as income increases. Figure 6–5(a) shows the utility function for a risk-neutral investor. That function is an upward-sloping line of constant slope. The constant slope implies constant marginal utility of income, as shown in Figure 6–5(b). For the case of risk neutrality, the utility gained when income increases by \$1 is equal to the utility lost when income declines by \$1. For a person with a utility function like the one drawn in Figure 6–5(a), risk is an attribute of an uncertain situation that is of no concern. For such a person, the expected value of $\$X$ received for sure gives the same expected utility as does the uncertain prospect of receiving $\$X + \$1$ or $\$X - \$1$, each with equal probability. This is because the gain in expected utility of adding a dollar to income equals the loss in expected utility of subtracting a dollar from income.

Figure 6–6(a) shows the utility function for a risk lover. For such a person, the marginal utility of income actually increases. Figure 6–6(b) shows the marginal utility curve for a risk lover. Such a person is eager to accept uncertain situations

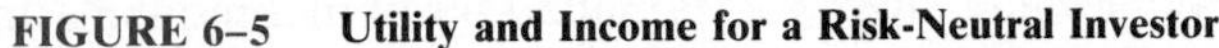

FIGURE 6–5 Utility and Income for a Risk-Neutral Investor

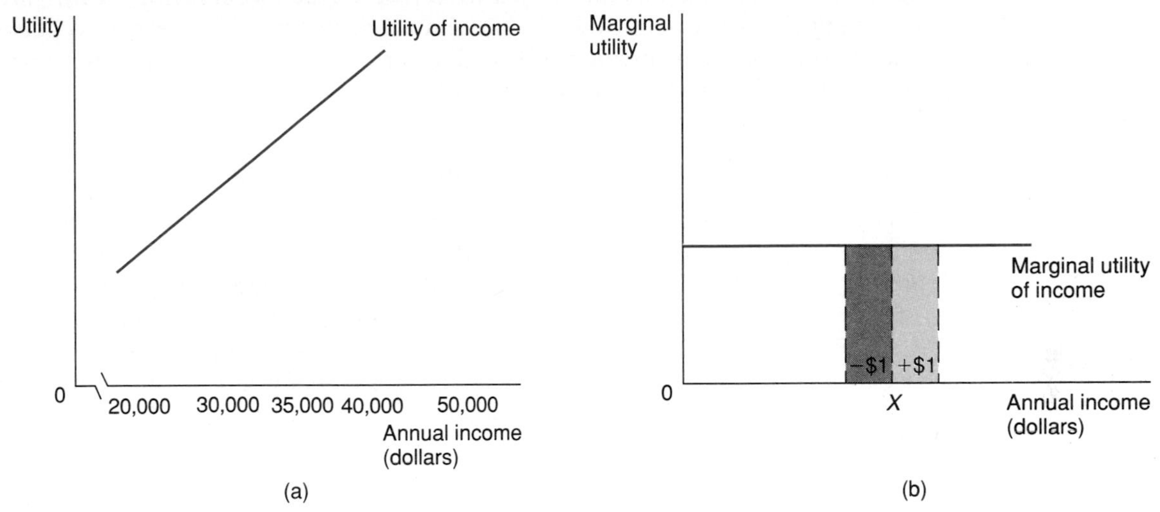

For a risk-neutral investor, the marginal utility of income is constant. For such a person, a certain income of $X provides the same expected utility as an uncertain income of the same expected value.

FIGURE 6–6 Utility and Income for a Risk Lover

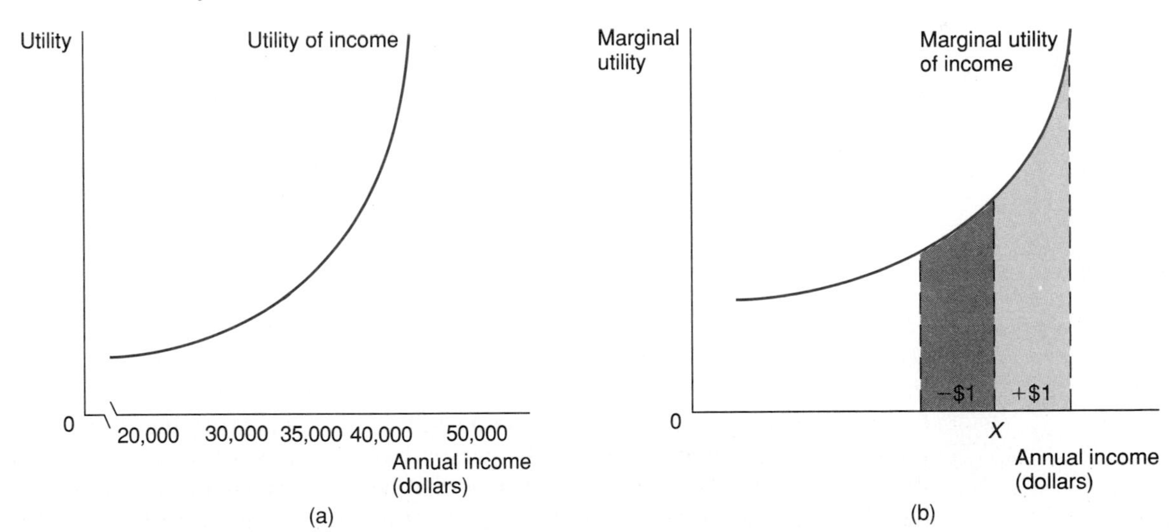

For a risk lover, the marginal utility of income increases. Such a person gets higher utility from an uncertain situation of expected value X than from a situation in which X is obtained with no uncertainty.

because he always places a greater value on an additional dollar of income than on an equal reduction in income. Faced with the prospect of receiving $\$X$ for sure or receiving either $\$(X + 1)$ or $\$ (X - 1)$ with 0.5 probability, the person will always choose the uncertain situation. For such a person, variability of income (risk) is a positively valued attribute of a situation.

More on Risk-Taking—the Friedman-Savage Hypothesis

Sometimes the same person can be viewed as behaving as a risk averter in some situations and as a risk lover in others. For example, you might be eager to insure against such risks as theft, but you might also play the state lottery, where the risk of losing is very high. In a classic analysis of this possibility Milton Friedman and L. J. Savage hypothesized that for many people the marginal utility of income declines as income increases at low levels, increases for a while after income has reached a certain level, and finally declines again after income has reached another threshold level.

Let's trace out the implications of the Friedman-Savage hypothesis for risk-taking behavior. Figure 6–7 shows how the marginal utility of income varies as income increases according to the Friedman-Savage hypothesis. The graph shows three ranges of income. In the first range, from 0 to *A*, the marginal utility of income is decreasing. In the second range, from *A* to *B*, the marginal utility of income is increasing. As income increases beyond *B*, into the third range, the marginal utility of income is again decreasing.

Suppose that a person has an annual income of $30,000 falling into the first range. This person would buy insurance because the declining marginal utility of his income implies that he is a risk averter. He would reason that the insurance premium is relatively small as compared to the losses it insures against. The dollars he gives up to pay for the insurance have relatively low utility to him, while his loss in utility from a loss of dollars of assets would be quite high even though the probability of such a loss is low as shown in the graph.

However, the same person might also gamble by purchasing a lottery ticket and thus act like a risk lover. The price of a lottery ticket is very low relative to the possible monetary payoff, though the probability of achieving that payoff (winning the lottery) is extremely low. The utility lost by buying the ticket, however, could be low relative to the expected gain in utility from accepting the gamble if the possible increase in income gets the person into the range of increasing marginal utility of income. Therefore, he reasons that the ticket is worth the price because he will gain lots of money income if he wins the lottery and the marginal utility of that income will be increasing in the range of the expected gain. However, once the person is earning annual money income of $100,000 or more, assuming that this is in the third range, beyond point *B*, the marginal utility of additional income always declines. As a result, the person's behavior will be consistently risk averse beyond point *B*.

People whose incomes are relatively low but close to the second range of Figure 6–7 are always eager to take risks to earn additional income. The entrepreneurs of a nation often have increasing marginal utility of income over the middle

FIGURE 6–7 The Friedman-Savage Hypothesis

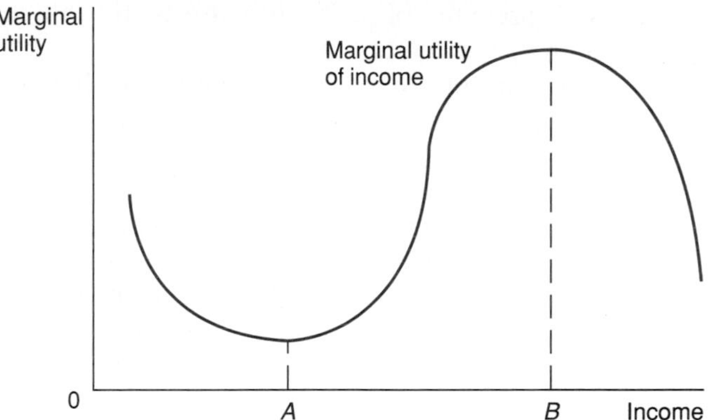

According to the Friedman-Savage hypothesis, the marginal utility of income can decline and then increase for a certain range of income before declining again. This implies that in some instances the same person would act as both a risk averter and a risk lover.

range of income. These are the innovators of society who, eager for monetary gain, take risks to increase their income. They often risk substantial portions of their current income for the possibility of future income gains even if the probability of those gains is relatively low.

Risk Premiums

Risk premium A sum of money that a risk averter would pay to avoid taking a risk.

A risk-averse person will pay to avoid taking a risk in an uncertain situation. A **risk premium** is a sum of money that a risk averter would pay to avoid taking a risk. The first step in calculating the risk premium is to find the expected level of utility that a person would derive from an uncertain situation. After this is known, the next step is to find the sum of money that gives the same level of expected utility as the uncertain situation. The risk premium is then determined by taking the difference between the expected value of the sum of money in the uncertain situation and the value of the sum of money received with certainty that would provide the same expected utility.

For example, suppose that a risk-averse person is confronted with the following uncertain situation: There is a possibility that he can have a stock of assets valued at $20,000 with a probability of 0.5 or a stock of assets valued at $40,000, also with a probability of 0.5. The expected value of this uncertain situation is therefore $30,000. Suppose that this uncertain situation gives him a level of expected utility of 19 units. If he can obtain the same level of utility from a certain situation in which a sum of money equal to $28,000 is received, the risk premium is

$$\$2,000 = \$30,000 - \$28,000$$

This person would therefore be indifferent between receiving $30,000 for sure and accepting the uncertain situation with an expected value of $30,000 along with a risk premium of $2,000 because both of these alternatives provide him with the same expected utility.

We can use our utility function to show the risk premium graphically. Figure 6–8 reproduces the utility function drawn in Figure 6–4. The uncertain prospect of either $40,000 or $20,000, each of equal probability, was shown above to provide an expected utility of 19 for the risk averter whose utility function is drawn in the graph. At point *A* the expected utility of the uncertain prospect with expected value of $30,000 is 19, which is less than the 20 units of utility that the risk averter would enjoy from $30,000 received with no uncertainty. The straight line connecting points S_1 and S_2 shows the utility that would be received from any sum expected were the investor risk neutral. Point *A* on the line represents the ex-

FIGURE 6–8 Risk Premiums

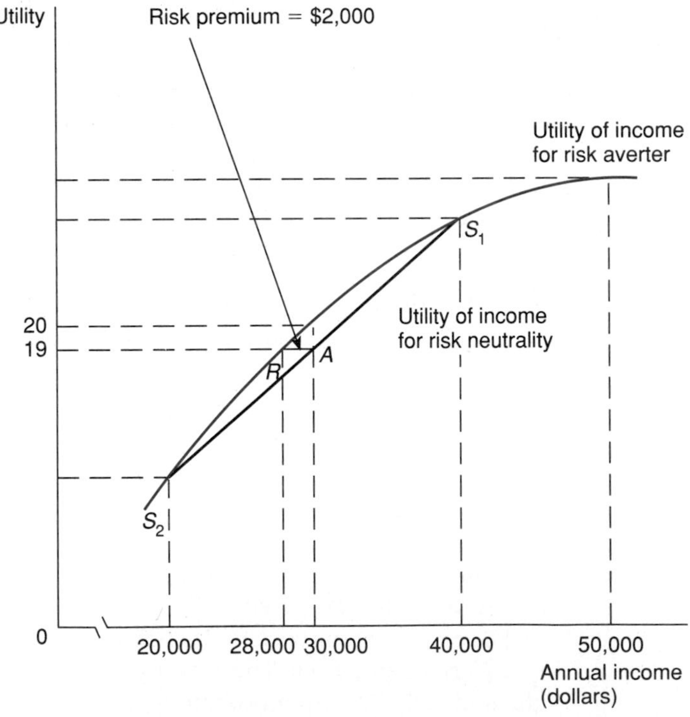

A risk averter will pay a risk premium to avoid an uncertain situation. The risk premium in the graph above is represented by the distance *RA*. It is the sum of money equal to the difference between the expected value of an uncertain situation and the expected value of a certain situation that provides the same expected utility. If the risk averter receives this sum, he will be indifferent between receiving $30,000 for sure and accepting an uncertain situation in which he could receive either $40,000 or $20,000, each with a probability of 0.5.

MODERN MICROECONOMICS IN ACTION: **GOVERNMENT AND THE ECONOMY**

Satisfying the Demand of Risk Lovers for Gambling while Raising Revenue to Finance State Government Expenditures: Government-Run Lotteries

Gambling is illegal in most states—except for government-run gambling operations. The use of lotteries is a time-honored way of raising revenue while at the same time satisfying the risk lover's demand for gambling. During and after the American Revolution, government-run lotteries raised funds for such purposes as the financing of the Continental Army and the financing of infrastructure, including bridges and schools. In the post–Civil War era, Congress enacted a series of rules that barred lottery activity in interstate commerce so there were no government-run lotteries in the United States from 1895 to 1963. In 1963, however, New Hampshire reintroduced its state lottery and as of 1989, 32 states ran lotteries and other states, hard pressed for new sources of revenue, were pressured to introduce lotteries as well.*

In most states the government-run lottery monopolizes large-scale organized gambling. The only legal competition is often the lotteries of other states. The modern lottery offers instant-win game tickets, a computerized numbers game that allows players to pick their own numbers, and lotto—a game with long odds and enormous jackpots. Lotteries are very profitable for state governments. They generate enough funds to account for more than 3 percent of state revenue on average for the states that have them.

The expected value of a lottery ticket is dismally low. The percentage of lottery revenue returned as prizes is extremely low relative to the percentage of revenue returned by commercial gambling operations. For example, horse racing and slot machine operations both return more than 80 percent of revenue collected as prizes. The payout rate for lotteries in 1989 ranged from 45 percent in West Virginia to 60 percent in Massachusetts. After deduction of operating costs, including commissions to retail sales agents, the state lotteries generated net revenue (profit) that averaged a whopping 40 percent of sales! The low odds of winning contribute to the high profits of state lotteries. Yet plenty of risk lovers rate a lottery ticket as a good buy despite the almost infinitesimally low probability of winning a large prize.

The state profit from operating lotteries can be regarded as a tax on lottery tickets, which are sold to more than 60 percent of the adults in the states that run lotteries. If the average 40 percent profit is deducted from the price of a lottery ticket and the tax collected is expressed as a percentage of expenditures net of the revenues that are returned to the state treasuries, the effective tax rate on lottery tickets is 66 percent! Thus purchasers pay high taxes on their lottery tickets in return for pretty low odds of winning! Much of the revenue generated by lotteries comes from the most active 10 percent of players, who account for about half of the receipts. The average amount spent on lottery tickets by households making $10,000 is pretty much the same as the average amount spent by households earning $60,000. Because expenditures on lottery tickets do not vary much with income, the implicit "lottery tax" is a smaller percentage of the income of upper-income groups than of the income of lower-income groups.† Apparently, the marginal utility of income is rising over the range of possible winnings for the many households with modest incomes. The biggest customers of the state lotteries are a cadre of risk lovers, many of whom have relatively low incomes.

* See Charles T. Clotfelter and Philip J. Cook, "The Economics of State Lotteries," *Journal of Economic Perspectives* 4, no. 4 (Fall 1990), pp. 105–19. The information presented here is based on research by Clotfelter and Cook.

† See ibid, p. 112.

pected value of this uncertain situation. The distance *RA* represents the risk premium of $2,000. You can think of this risk premium as the sum of money that would be necessary to pay the individual to behave as if he or she were risk neutral and therefore indifferent between certain prospects and uncertain prospects of the same expected value. The risk premium for any uncertain situation of a given expected value can be obtained by taking the horizontal distance between the risk averter's utility function and the point on the straight line corresponding to the expected value of the uncertain situation in which either S_1 or S_2 would be received. The location of the point representing the expected value of the uncertain situation would depend on the respective probabilities attached to S_1 and S_2.

The analysis of a risk premium is important to understanding the behavior of participants in markets for insurance and in financial markets in which uncertainty prevails. Let's first apply the analysis to insurance.

CONCEPT REVIEW

1. What is meant by *risk aversion*? How does the marginal utility of income vary as a risk averter's income increases?
2. How do risk lovers and risk neutrals differ from risk averters?
3. How can risk averters be induced to accept the risks of an uncertain situation over a certain situation with the same expected payoff without being made worse off?

APPLYING THE ANALYSIS: INDIFFERENCE CURVE ANALYSIS OF THE CHOICE TO INSURE AGAINST RISK

As we showed above, a risk premium represents the sum of money a person would pay to avoid taking a risk. Risk-neutral and risk-loving people do not need such premiums to induce them to accept risks because for them risk is not a negatively valued attribute of a situation. The concept of a risk premium is therefore relevant only to risk averters. Because in many situations people generally behave as if they were risk averse, risk premiums are important to understanding behavior in many markets.

Insurance markets are markets in which individuals pay to avoid risks and therefore markets in which risk premiums are relevant. The risk premium represents the maximum sum a person will pay as an insurance premium to insure against a risk. The decision to insure depends on the relationship between the insurance premium and the risk premium.

To understand the decision to insure, let's look at a very simple situation. Suppose you can purchase disability insurance through your employer. This insurance will provide you with annual income if you are unable to work as a result of illness or injury. Suppose that you estimate your chances of becoming ill or injured to an incapacitating degree as 1 in 10 for the coming year. Measure a unit of insurance on the horizontal axis of Figure 6–9 as a policy that will provide you

FIGURE 6–9 Risk Aversion and the Choice to Purchase Insurance

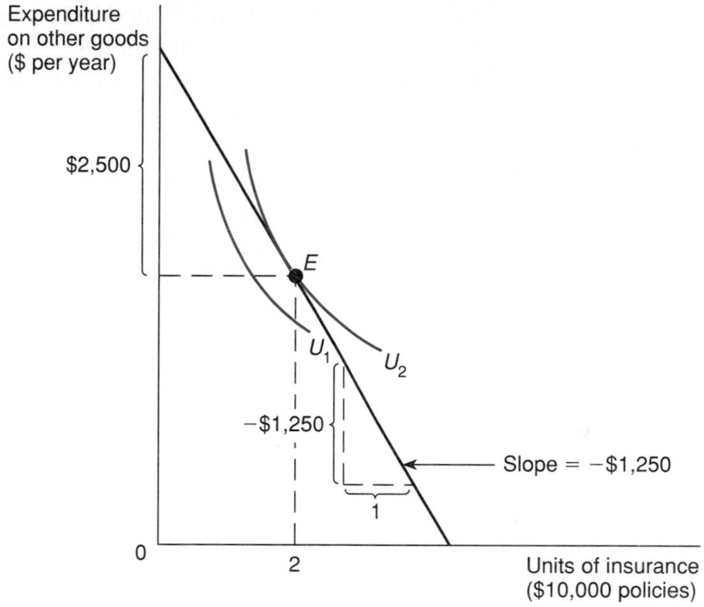

A risk averter chooses to purchase an insurance policy even when the price of the policy is higher than an actuarially fair price.

with $10,000 in annual income only if you become disabled. The expected value of the insurance is the $10,000 loss it covers multiplied by the probability that the insurance will actually be paid out to you. Because the probability of your being disabled is 1 in 10, the expected value of the loss you will avoid is $1,000. An **actuarially fair price for insurance** in an uncertain situation is one that equals the expected value of the purchase or the loss that is being insured against. In this case the actuarially fair price for the insurance policy is therefore $1,000. If the insurance company were to sell many policies providing $10,000 in coverage for that price, it would break even by paying out on average $10,000 for each $10,000 in premiums taken in. Because the insurance company has administrative, sales, and other costs, it must, of course, charge more than $1,000 per policy to break even. Suppose the price of the policy is $1,250.

Actuarially fair price for insurance A price that equals the expected value of the loss being insured against.

Figure 6–9 shows the budget line for an insurance policy whose slope is −$1,250, which represents the price of the insurance policy multiplied by −1. If a consumer is risk averse, the marginal benefit of a gamble to avoid a loss exceeds the expected value of that loss. In other words, a risk averter is willing to pay an amount greater than the expected value of a loss to avoid the risk of incurring the loss. The marginal utility of income declines for risk averters, which implies that they will pay *more than $1* to avoid a $1 expected loss. Because the marginal benefit of avoiding a gamble involving a loss exceeds the expected value of that loss, a consumer can gain by purchasing an insurance policy even though the price of the policy exceeds the expected value of the loss it covers. The consumer whose indifference curves are illustrated in Figure 6–9 is in equilibrium at point *E*. At that point he purchases two insurance policies per year, thus obtaining $20,000 of disability coverage. He gives up $2,500 of current annual income each year in exchange for avoiding the risk of losing $20,000 in income because of disability.

A risk lover, however, would not purchase any insurance at all even if it were available at an actuarially fair price. This is because for a risk lover the marginal benefit of a gamble involving a loss is always less than the expected value of that loss. Because the price of an insurance policy exceeds the expected value of the loss it covers, a risk lover would choose a corner equilibrium in Figure 6–9, at which no insurance is purchased. However, even a risk averter might choose not to purchase insurance if its price were too high. If the insurance company charges a price greater than the risk premium that the risk averter would pay to avoid a risk, it can no longer expect to sell insurance to him. For example, even if you were risk averse, you might think twice about buying a disability policy that charged you $5,000 for each $10,000 worth of income that it insured.

There are ways for persons to provide insurance for themselves. One common method of self-insurance in making investments is *diversification*. Risk averters seek to avoid reductions in the value of their investment portfolios. They can do so by purchasing a variety of assets. By diversifying their portfolios, they acquire assets whose value is likely to increase when the value of their other assets decreases. For example, if you believe that bond prices will rise whenever stock prices fall, you can diversify your portfolio by investing in both stocks and bonds. In doing so you provide yourself with insurance that the total value of your portfolio will not fall excessively when stock prices fall. Diversification is indicative of risk aversion. Let's now look at the investment choices of risk averters and show how the risk premiums demanded by risk-averse investors can affect financial markets.

Applying the Analysis: Indifference Curve Analysis of Investment Portfolio Choices

There is no way to avoid risk when dealing with financial affairs. Even if you just keep your money in a bank account (whose dollar value, unlike the prices of stocks and bonds, cannot fall), you run the risk of suffering losses in the purchasing power of that money as a result of inflation. As we pointed out in our earlier analysis of risk, the return on an asset expressed as a percentage of its purchase price can be positive or negative. The return on a financial asset, measured in real terms as the percentage increase in the value of the asset (expressed in constant dollars adjusted for changes in purchasing power resulting from inflation), depends on interest or dividends earned on the asset and on any changes in its market value that result in capital gains or capital losses.

Historically, in the United States the expected return on stocks has exceeded the expected return on corporate bonds. However, the variability of annual returns on stocks is much higher than that of annual returns on bonds, and stocks are therefore considerably riskier than bonds. Among the safest assets are Treasury bills and bank deposits, which have virtually no variability in value except that which results from changes in the inflation rate. In general, in financial markets assets with higher expected returns generally entail higher risk measured either as the variance or standard deviation of those returns. For example, over the past 60 years common stocks in the United States have averaged a real rate of return considerably higher than that of long-term corporate bonds. However, the standard deviation of stock returns has been nearly three times as high as that of bond returns. Although the expected return on stocks is higher than that on bonds, stocks are riskier than bonds, which, as you might expect, most risk averters have noticed.

The Risk-Yield Transformation Curve

Suppose that this year you have the opportunity to invest a sum of money in a bank account that will yield E_B interest and is risk free because inflation is zero. You are guaranteed a certain real annual yield on funds invested in this asset. You can also invest in stocks. The expected annual yield on stocks is E_s, with $E_s > E_B$. The risk of investing in stocks, measured by the standard deviation of doing so, is s. Because the bank account, unlike stocks, is assumed to be riskless, its standard deviation is zero.

Investment portfolio A combination of financial assets.

An **investment portfolio** is a combination of financial assets. In this simple example the portfolio consists of stocks and the risk-free asset. The *expected yield on the portfolio* depends on the proportion of funds invested in each of the two types of assets. If m is the proportion of funds invested in stocks and $(1 - m)$ is the proportion of funds invested in the risk-free asset, then the expected yield on the portfolio, E, is

$$E = mE_s + (1 - m)E_B \quad \textbf{(6–3)}$$

which is a weighted average of the expected yields on the two types of assets in the portfolio. For example, if the expected yield on stocks is 10 percent, the expected yield on the risk-free asset is 5 percent, and m is 0.4, then the expected annual yield on the portfolio is 7 percent.

The risk attributes of the portfolio are a bit more complicated to derive. However, the risk of the total portfolio depends on the riskiness of the types of assets in the portfolio and the proportion of the portfolio invested in each type of asset. In general, the greater the proportion of the portfolio invested in stocks, the greater is the risk, with the risk varying in proportion to m.

Risk-yield transformation curve A graph showing the options an investor has for trading portfolio risk for higher portfolio yield by varying the proportion of relatively risky assets in the portfolio.

$$\text{Risk} = ms \quad \textbf{(6–4)}$$

where s is the standard deviation of the return on stocks.

The problem of portfolio choice for an investor is one of choosing the combination of assets that maximizes utility. The **risk-yield transformation curve** shows the options an investor has for trading portfolio risk for higher portfolio yield in uncertain financial markets by varying the proportion of relatively risky assets in the portfolio. Figure 6–10 plots the risk-yield transformation curve for this situa-

FIGURE 6–10 Portfolio Allocation for a Risk Averter

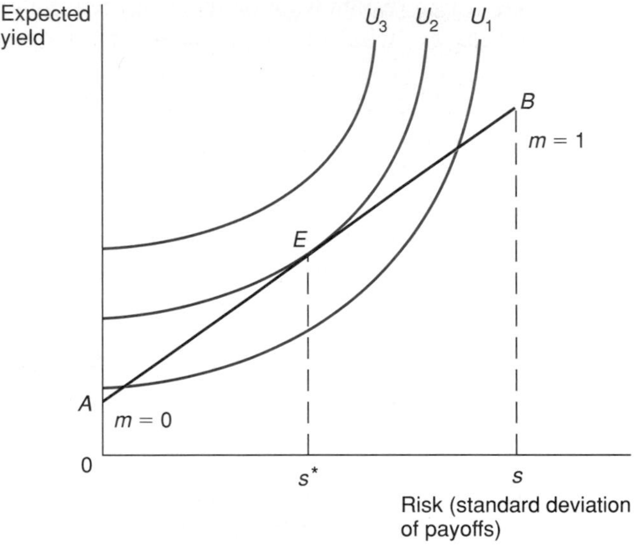

A risk averter always chooses a diversified portfolio with a mix of risky and riskless assets. Such a portfolio is shown at point *E*.

tion along with the indifference map of a typical risk-averse investor.[3] The risk-yield transformation curve is an upward-sloping line showing how the expected return on the portfolio can be increased by accepting more risk. At point *A* on the line $m = 0$. At that point the investor puts all of his funds in the risk-free asset and earns an expected return of E_B while assuming zero risk. At point *B* on the line, $m = 1$. At that point the investor puts all of his funds in stocks and earns an expected return of E_s while assuming risk equal to s.

Also shown in Figure 6–10 is the indifference map for a typical risk-averse investor. The utility-maximizing combination of the expected return and risk attributes of the portfolio corresponds to point *E*. At that point the investor has a **diversified portfolio,** which is a portfolio that consists of riskless and risky assets.

Diversified portfolio A portfolio that consists of risky and riskless assets.

[3] The equation of the risk-yield transformation curve can be derived as follows:

1. Because $E = mE_s + (1 - m)E_B$, it follows that $E = E_B + m(E_s - E_B)$.

2. Because Risk $= ms$, it follows that $m =$ Risk$/s$.

Therefore,

$$E = E_B + \text{Risk}(E_s - E_B)/s$$

which is a linear equation showing that the expected yield on the portfolio increases as risk increases, given the expected return on the risk-free asset, the expected return on stocks, and the standard deviation of the return on stocks.

FIGURE 6–11 The Degree of Risk Aversion and Portfolio Choice

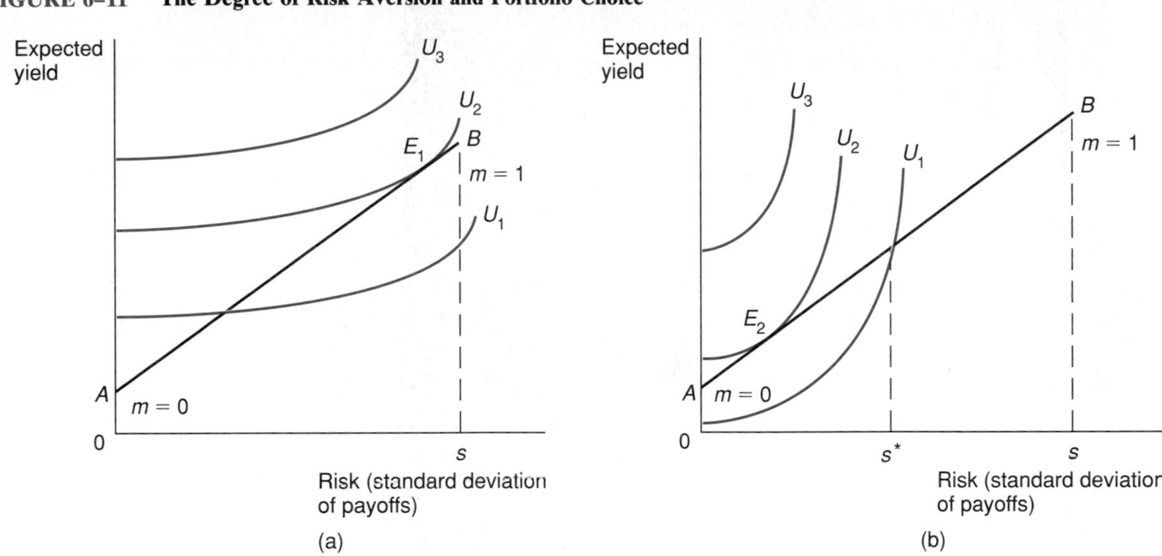

The investor in (a) is less risk averse than the investor in (b) and therefore chooses a more risky portfolio in equilibrium.

To achieve such a portfolio, the investor chooses a combination of stocks and risk-free assets so that in equilibrium $0 < m < 1$. A risk-averse investor always chooses to diversify. Depending on the degree of risk aversion, as indicated by the steepness of the indifference curves in the indifference map, the investor chooses m to maximize utility. The steeper the indifference curves, the greater is the degree of risk aversion.

Figure 6–11(a) and (b) show the different choices made by two investors who face the same risk-yield transformation curve but have different degrees of risk aversion. The first investor, Barry Bull, is far less risk averse than the second investor, Mary Bear. Barry's indifference curves are quite flat, while Mary's are very steep. As a result Barry chooses a portfolio whose value of m is close to 1 and thus is highly invested in relatively risky stocks, as shown at point E_1 in Figure 6–11(a). Mary has quite steep indifference curves in equilibrium at point E_2 in Figure 6–11(b), where her portfolio has a low risk but also has a relatively low expected return. She chooses a portfolio whose value of m is close to zero and thus contains a relatively small proportion of stocks. As you can see, investment choices are in part a matter of taste!

More on Diversification: How Careful Selection of Assets Can Reduce Risk while Not Decreasing Expected Portfolio Yields

If you carefully follow the stock market, you might observe that some stocks go up in price when others go down in price. For example, some stocks fall in price when there is a recession, while others rise in price when there is a recession.

MODERN MICROECONOMICS IN ACTION: THE BUSINESS WORLD

Stock versus Bonds: Average Yield and Risk over the Long Haul

How risky are stocks compared to bonds? How much more can you expect to earn on stocks compared to bonds if you hold them in your portfolio for a long period of time? To answer questions like these, Jack W. Wilson, professor of business at North Carolina State University, together with Charles Jones, professor of finance at NCSU, and Richard Sylla, professor of the history of financial institutions at New York University, have collected and analyzed data on U.S. stocks and other financial assets over the period 1870–1991.*

To get an idea of the expected yield on stocks, they computed the average total annual percentage rate return for stocks, estimated risk by calculating the standard deviation of returns, and then, by adjusting nominal returns for inflation, calculated real annual returns and the variability of those returns. The accompanying table shows the results of their calculations for the long haul of 121 years from 1870 to 1991 and for two subperiods, 1870–1930 and 1930–91, for common stock in the United States, assuming that dividends were reinvested monthly.

The inflation-adjusted yield on stocks has averaged 6.69 percent from 1870 to 1991 and has not increased or decreased significantly since 1930. This long-run performance of stocks suggests that an investor can expect to earn a real return of about 6.6 percent by buying stocks and holding them over a long period. The risk of holding stocks, measured by the standard deviation of inflation-adjusted returns, runs in the range of 20 and has not increased or decreased significantly since 1930.

On a year-by-year basis there has been considerable variation in stock returns. Over the period analyzed, the highest nominal (no adjustment for inflation) returns were earned in 1879, 1933, and 1954, when stocks yielded nominal returns of 57.9 percent, 55.9 percent, and 53 percent, respectively. The worst years were 1930, 1931, 1937, and 1974, when stocks yielded nominal returns of −27.3 percent, −45.7 percent, −33.2 percent, and −26.5 percent, respectively.

These data suggest that stocks are a very good investment over the long haul but if you need to get your money out of stocks soon after you put it into them, you could lose your shirt! Stocks are a great long-term investment but can be very risky short-term assets.

Now let's look at bonds. From 1870 to 1991 the nominal return on long-term government bonds in the United States averaged 4.88 percent per year. After adjusting for inflation, the real return averaged 2.83 percent per year, which was nearly 4 percent less than the average return on stocks from 1870 to 1991. Stocks therefore have a much higher expected return than government bonds. But gov-

Average Returns and Risk for U.S. Standard & Poor's 500 Common Stocks, 1870–1991

Period	*Nominal Yield* (Y) *and Risk* (s)	*Inflation-Adjusted Yield* (Y) *and Risk* (s)
1870–1991	$Y =$ 8.89%	$Y =$ 6.69%
	$s =$ 19.84	$s =$ 20.37
1870–1930	$Y =$ 7.24%	$Y =$ 6.80%
	$s =$ 18.50	$s =$ 19.21
1930–1991	$Y =$ 10.40%	$Y =$ 6.58%
	$s =$ 21.13	$s =$ 21.63

Source: Jack W. Wilson, North Carolina State University.

(*Continued*) ernment bonds are far less risky than stocks. The standard deviation of the nominal returns on government bonds from 1870 to 1991 was 6.86, less than one third of the standard deviation of the nominal returns on common stocks. The standard deviation of real returns on bonds was 8.85 over the long haul from 1870 to 1991. Government bonds are not riskless, but over the long run they are certainly less risky than common stocks.

* See Richard Sylla, Jack W. Wilson, and Charles P. Jones, "Financial Market Volatility, Panics Before 1914, and Volatility in the Long Run, 1830–1988," in *Crashes and Panics: Lessons from History*, ed. Eugene N. White (Homewood, Ill.: Dow Jones-Irwin, 1990), pp. 85–125. The analysis here is based on a more recent data set compiled by Wilson.

Cyclical stocks yield high returns when the economy is performing well and low returns when the economy is performing poorly. Countercyclical stocks do the opposite.

Suppose that the price of stock in construction firms falls during a recession, while the price of stock in videocassette rental businesses rises during a recession because more people stay home for entertainment. Suppose there is a 0.5 probability that this year we will be in a recession. If we are in a recession, you will earn a 20 percent return on your video stock, but the return on your construction will be −5 percent. If we are not in a recession, your construction stock will yield a 20 percent return and the return on your video stock will be −5 percent. Suppose you invest only in the construction firm. Your expected return will be

$$E = 20\%(0.5) + [-5\%(0.5)] = 7.5\%$$

Similarly, if you invest only in the stock of a videocassette rental business, your expected return will also be 7.5 percent. Your risk, measured by the standard deviation of the return on each of the stocks, will be $\sqrt{156.25} = 12.5$.

However, because the returns on the two stocks are perfectly negatively correlated, you can guarantee yourself 7.5 percent return *with no risk* by forming a portfolio that has one share of the construction stock for each share of the videocassette stock. To see why this is possible, note that the expected return on each of the stocks is the same and equal to 7.5 percent. The expected return on your portfolio will also be 7.5 percent if you put half of your assets in one of the stocks and half in the other stock:

$$E = (0.5)(7.5) + (0.5)(7.5) = 7.5$$

The risk on this diversified portfolio will be zero because, whether or not there is a recession, your expected return is sure to be 7.5 percent. The variance, and therefore the standard deviation, of the returns on the two stocks will be zero because of the perfectly negative correlation between those returns.

A risk-averse investor will always include in his or her portfolio combinations of stocks and other assets that achieve minimum risk for a given expected return. Naturally, it is rare to find pairs of assets whose returns are perfectly negatively correlated. However, by carefully selecting stock combinations in which a reduced return on one stock is at least partially offset by an increased return on another stock, the investor can reduce risk by *diversification*.

Diversifiable risk is risk that can be insured against by carefully considering the inverse correlation between the returns on any two assets. However, because in many cases the prices of all stocks go up or down at the same time in response to such basic changes in the economy as changes in interest or inflation rates, not all risk can be eliminated through diversification.

The Capital Asset Pricing Model

Because most investors are risk averse, they require a higher expected return on an asset to compensate them for taking additional risk. This behavior has important implications for financial markets such as the stock market. In general, if one stock is riskier than another stock, you would not expect risk-averse investors to willingly purchase the riskier stock unless it has a higher expected return than the less risky stock. However, some of the risk of buying stocks can be reduced through diversification, as we have just shown. Remember that diversification can be thought of as a form of insurance. If you know that when some stocks go up in price, others go down in price, you can consider only portfolios of stocks that have a minimum of risk for any given expected return. You can reduce the variability of the stock returns in your portfolio by carefully diversifying your assets so that you balance price increases with price declines over the business cycle. In this way you can actually minimize the risk you assume for any given expected return on the group of stocks in your overall portfolio.

Capital asset pricing model A theory of stock prices that shows how the price of any given stock depends on the various financial returns available and on the risk of buying that stock.

The **capital asset pricing model** is a theory of stock prices that shows how the price of any given stock depends on the various financial returns available and on the risk of buying that stock. According to the model, which was developed by economists William Sharpe and John Lintner, the expected return on any given stock, $E(R)$, depends on i, the current return, on a riskless security (such as short-term debt of the U.S. Treasury); $E(S)$, the expected return possible on average from a portfolio of stocks as measured by a stock index such as the Dow Jones Industrial Average; and the amount of risk that cannot be reduced through diversification that an investor undertakes when buying the stock. According to the theory, the expected return on the stock is

$$E(R) = i + [E(S) - i]\beta \qquad \textbf{(6–5)}$$

where β is a measure of the sensitivity of the return on the given stock to a change in the return on stocks in general as measured by a broad stock index.[4] For example, if each time the Dow Jones Industrial Average increases 1 percent, the

[4] This is a highly simplified treatment of a complex theory. See W. Sharpe, "Capital Asset Prices of Theory of Market Equilibrium under Conditions of Risk," *Journal of Finance,* September 1964, for Sharpe's original formulation of the theory that would help win him a Nobel prize in economics. Also see R. Westerfield, S. Ross, and J. Jaffe, *Corporate Finance,* 3rd ed. (Homewood, Ill.: Richard D. Irwin, 1993).

price of XYZ Company's stock is observed to increase 5 percent, then the value of β for XYZ Company's stock is 5. A stock whose return is generally perfectly correlated with the average price of all stocks would have a β of 1.

The higher the value of a stock's β, the greater is the variability of the stock's return and the greater is the riskiness of the stock. For example, if a stock has a β of 5, you would expect its return to increase five times as much as the average increase in the return on all stocks when the average return on all stocks is increasing. However, when the average return on all stocks is falling, you would expect the return on this stock to *fall* five times as much as the average fall in the return on all stocks.

According to Equation 6–5, given the return on the riskless asset and given the average expected return on all stocks, the expected return on any given stock tends to increase with its β. You can view the difference between the return on any given stock and the return on the riskless asset as the *risk premium* that the risk-averse investors who dominate the market demand from the given stock as compensation for taking the additional risk involved in purchasing it. Figure 6–12 draws the risk-yield transformation curve using β as a measure of risk. This line is similar to the risk-yield transformation curve we drew in Figure 6–10 when analyzing investor decisions in general. In this case, however, the curve is relevant only to a particular stock. The analysis implies that the stock's expected return increases as its variability increases relative to the variability of all stocks. The

FIGURE 6–12 Capital Asset Pricing and the Expected Yield on Stocks

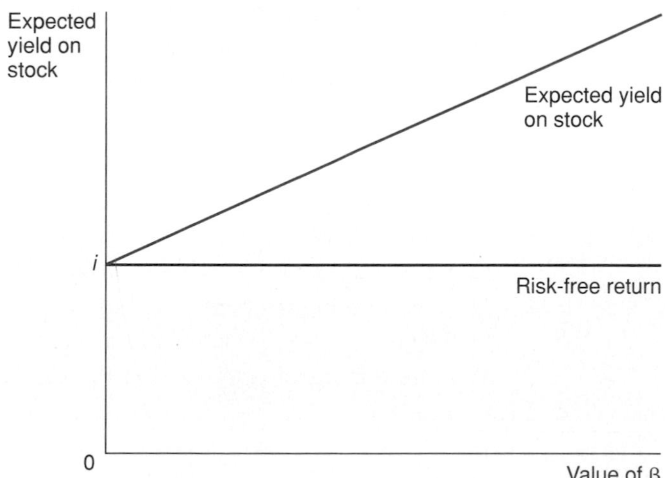

According to the capital asset pricing model, the expected yield on a stock rises above the yield on risk-free assets depending on the sensitivity of the return on the stock to changes in the average return on all stocks as measured by the β of the stock, which is an index of the stock's riskiness as compared to the average riskiness of all stocks.

TABLE 6–3 Beta Values of Selected Company Stocks, 1991

Company	*Beta Value of Stock*
Anheuser-Busch	0.3597723
Becton-Dickinson	0.7024394
Chrysler	1.490447
Dow Jones	0.6340322
Duke Power	0.1419995
Exxon	0.9131641
Intel	1.46608
PepsiCo	0.3841112
Procter & Gamble	0.1791453
Upjohn	1.493535

Source: Estimates computed by Jack Wilson, North Carolina State University.

risk premium of the stock increases as its β increases. The total expected return on a stock depends on the return possible on a risk-free investment, and the rate at which the stock's expected return increases with its β depends on the current differential of average stock yields over the yields of risk-free assets. This is because the slope of the risk-yield transformation curve in Figure 6–12 is $[E(S) - i)]$. The riskiness of stocks can easily be measured by calculating their β's. Table 6–3 shows estimated β's for various stocks as of 1991.

You can use Equation 6–5 to calculate expected yields of stocks. For example, suppose that as of January 1993 the annual return on risk-free Treasury securities is 6 percent. Suppose further that the average expected annual return on the Dow Jones Industrial Average, the S&P 500, or a similar stock index is 12 percent. You are interested in buying shares of XYZ stock, whose β is 1.5. You can expect the return on that stock to be $0.06 + (0.12 - 0.06)1.5 = 0.15$. Based on the capital asset pricing model, the expected annual return on XYZ stock is 15 percent.

CONCEPT REVIEW

1. Explain why risk averters choose to purchase insurance at premiums that exceed the actuarially fair price of the insurance.
2. How can an investor influence the expected return on an investment portfolio? What is diversifiable risk?
3. What is the significance of β in the capital asset pricing model?

Summary

1. Several outcomes are possible in an uncertain situation, and the probability of each of those outcomes is known or can be estimated.

2. Probability is the chance that an outcome will occur. Objective probability is the number of times that an outcome would occur if an uncertain situation were repeated a large number of times. Subjective probabilities are estimates based on intuition and available information that people make about the chances that an outcome will occur. Probabilities of uncertain outcome range between zero and 1. A certain outcome has a probability of 1, while an impossible outcome has a probability of zero.

3. The expected value of the payoffs in an uncertain situation is an average of the possible outcomes, with each outcome weighted according to its probability of occurrence.

4. Risk is a situation that prevails when a person engages in an activity for which there is more than one possible outcome, with each of the possible outcomes having a certain probability of occurrence. Risk is a measure of the variability of outcomes that can be approximated by using the variance or standard deviation of payoffs.

5. Attitudes toward risk can be analyzed by means of risk-yield indifference curves. For a risk averter, the expected payoff of an uncertain situation is a positively valued attribute of the situation, but risk is a negatively valued attribute. A risk averter, other things being equal, prefers an uncertain situation with less risk to one with more risk. For a risk-neutral person, other things being equal, additional risk neither increases nor decreases utility. For a risk lover, *both* risk and expected payoff are positively valued attributes of an uncertain situation.

6. Attitudes toward risk are related to the way the marginal utility of income varies as income increases. The marginal utility of income declines for risk averters. Because of the declining marginal utility of their income, risk averters prefer a certain income of a given amount to the uncertain prospect of equal increments of income above or below that amount, each having an equal probability of occurrence and each having the same expected value as the certain income. This is because for a risk averter the utility of a dollar gained is always less than the utility of a dollar lost. Risk neutrals behave as if the marginal utility of income remains constant, while risk lovers act as if the marginal utility of income increases. The marginal utility of income can decrease, then increase, and then decrease again for the same person as that person's income increases. Such as person might act as a risk averter in some situations and as a risk lover in others.

7. A risk premium is a sum of money that a risk averter would pay to avoid taking a risk. Risk premiums are the basis for the development of markets for insurance, which people buy to avoid risks. Risk averters may pay more than an actuarially fair price for insurance because of their willingness to pay risk premiums. Because risk aversion is the dominant attitude toward risk in financial markets, riskier assets typically must have higher expected payoffs to induce investors to acquire them.

8. An investment portfolio is a combination of financial assets. The expected return on a portfolio varies with its mix of risky and risk-free assets. The risk-yield transformation curve shows the opportunities an investor has to trade the risk attributes of a portfolio for higher expected payoffs by changing the composition of the assets in the portfolio. Risk averters tend to choose a diversified portfolio with a mix of risky and nonrisky assets. Some risks can be reduced to zero through diversification.

9. The β of a stock is a measure of the sensitivity of its return to a change in the return on stocks in general as measured by a broad stock index. The higher the β of a stock, the greater is its riskiness and the greater is the expected return from buying it. An increase in the β of a stock increases its expected yield because risk-averse investors demand risk premiums in exchange for acquiring riskier assets.

Important Concepts

probability
uncertain situation
payoff
expected value
risk
variance
standard deviation
product attributes
risk averter
risk neutrality
risk lover
expected utility
risk premium
actuarially fair price for insurance
investment portfolio
risk-yield transformation curve
diversified portfolio
capital asset pricing model

Questions for Review

1. What is the difference between objective probability and subjective probability? What is the probability that one dot will occur on a single throw of a single die?
2. Give an example of an uncertain situation, and show how the expected value of its payoffs can be computed.
3. The stock of the XYZ Corporation will yield a return of 10 percent this year with a projbability of 0.4 but might also yield a return of −2 percent with a probability of 0.6. What is the expected return on the stock?
4. Calculate the variance and standard deviation of the yields for the stock whose returns and their probabilities of occurrence are given in Question 3.
5. Explain why the risk-yield indifference curves for a risk-averse investor are upward sloping rather than downward sloping.
6. Tom is a risk averter. When Tom reaches age 21, his father offers him these two options:

   Option A: A gift of $10,000 in cash (with no strings attached) to be received at the end of the year.

   Option B: A gift of stock shares that have to be cashed in at the end of the year. There is a 0.5 probability that the shares will then be worth $15,000 and a 0.5 probability that they will then be worth $5,000.

   Which of the options will Tom choose? Explain your answer.
7. Show how utility and marginal utility of income will vary for a risk-neutral person. Will a risk lover be interested in purchasing an insurance policy at more than its actuarially fair price?
8. What is the Friedman-Savage hypothesis, and what does it imply about attitudes toward risk taking?
9. What is a risk premium?
10. What is the β of a stock? Why do stocks with higher β's tend to yield higher expected returns than stocks with lower β's?

Problems

1. You have the choice of two jobs when you graduate from college. The first job will pay a salary of $25,000 per year. The second is an unsalaried sales job in which you earn commission by selling machines. Based on the experience of people who have had the sales job, you know that in expansion years you can average $40,000 in commission. In recession years, however, you can average only $10,000 in commission. If the probability is 0.5 that next year will be a recession year and the probability is also 0.5 that next year will be an expansion year, calculate the expected income, variance, and standard deviation of the sales job. Assuming that you are a risk averter, which job will you take? Would your choice differ if you were risk neutral or a risk lover? Why?

2. The following table shows how the utility of income varies for John:

Income per Year (Dollars)	*Utility of Income (Utils)*
10,000	10
20,000	18
25,000	22
30,000	24
40,000	28
50,000	30

a. What is John's attitude to risk?
b. Calculate the expected income and the expected utility to John of the commission job discussed in Problem 1.
c. Suppose that John's father wants him to take the commission job. Show how the payment of a risk premium could induce John to accept the commission job over the job paying a salary of $25,000 per year.

3. The current yield on risk-free assets is 4 percent. The average expected return on stocks is 8 percent. Assuming that the capital asset pricing model holds, what is the expected return on the stocks of the companies whose β's are shown below?

Company	β
Continental Business Machines	1
Fly-by-Night Airlines	1.5
Ollies Gold Prospecting	2

Explain the meaning of the β concept.

PART III

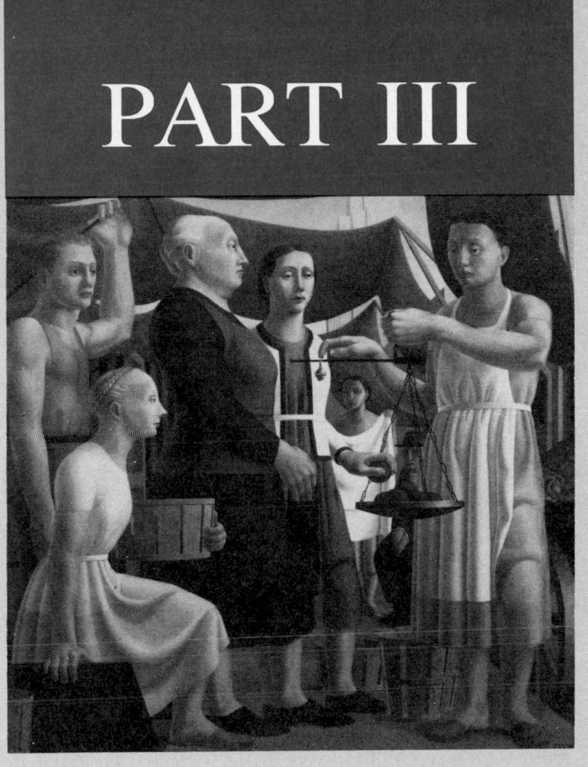

PRODUCTION, COST, AND SUPPLY IN COMPETITIVE PRODUCT MARKETS

7

The Theory of Production

Shahid Khan is the owner of a business firm in Danville, Illinois, that employs 100 workers to make bumpers for pickup trucks and sells the bumpers to automobile producers. One of his best clients in 1991 was the Toyota Motor Corporation.[1] In 1991 Toyota wanted to reduce the cost of the bumpers and dispatched a team of its manufacturing experts to Khan's Danville plant to teach his employees about the famous Toyota Production System, which is designed to minimize the cost of producing given levels of output.

Like Shahid Khan, more and more American producers have been turning to Japanese consultants for help in increasing the productivity of workers, improving product quality, and reducing production costs. For example, the Ford Motor Company's Wayne, Michigan, automobile plant is a clone of a Japanese Mazda operation and a plastics company in Kentucky is working with Toyota consultants to improve the quality of the products it supplies to Toyota, which produces its popular Camry in a Kentucky plant.[2]

The Toyota manufacturing experts who visited Khan's plant recommended that it reduce the time taken to change dies for the metal stamping presses which are used to produce a variety of bumper models. Toyota and Khan worked together to devise a method of attaching tabs to the 9-ton dies that made it easier to put them on and take them off the presses. Then the Toyota experts moved equipment around in the plant and set production goals. They sharply reduced the amount of waste metal generated in production. By the time they had finished their job of reorganizing the plant, the costs of producing a bumper had fallen and the quality of the bumpers had improved. Using what he learned from the Toyota experts, Khan planned to build a new factory off Interstate 74 in Veedersburg, Indiana, where he would employ 200 workers.

The story of Shahid Khan's "bumper works" illustrates the importance of human ingenuity in the production process. Unlike manna, economic goods and services do not fall from the heavens. They must be produced by efficiently managing the use of scarce resources. The relationship between those resources and the amounts of goods and services that they produce depends on technological knowledge. The amount of a given good or service that can be produced depends on the amount of the physical resources employed in its production and

---

[1] See Joseph P. White, "Japanese Auto Makers Help U.S. Suppliers Become More Efficient," *The Wall Street Journal,* September 9, 1991.

[2] Ibid.

on the technical "state of the art" in productive methods. Economic resources—the inputs necessary to produce outputs of goods—include labor, machines, land, and raw materials. And as you have just seen from the story of Khan's bumper works, the way the productive process is managed influences the amount of output you can get from any given combination of inputs.

Understanding the production process is a prerequisite to deriving supply curves. You can think of the supply process as involving three steps. First, managers must be aware of the possible ways of combining inputs to produce any given supply of output over a period. This is primarily a job for engineers who study the technological relationships between inputs and outputs. However, economists assume that certain "laws of production" are more or less descriptive of all productive endeavors. The most famous of these, the law of diminishing returns, will be outlined in this chapter, as will other assumptions made about the production process.

In the next step managers must choose the least costly method of producing any given output. This chapter concentrates on productive relationships, while the following chapter shows how input combinations are chosen, how costs of input combinations are measured, and how cost varies with output. Finally, the theory of supply will be fully developed in Chapters 9 and 10 by showing how information on revenue is used in conjunction with information on cost production to choose the output that maximizes profit.

The limits to the physical amount of output that can be squeezed from any combination of productive resources are the prime constraint faced by managers. Not even the best managers can accomplish the impossible. There is no way to convert lead into gold, despite centuries of trying by alchemists. Productive relationships depend on technology and on the time available. In general, production is less flexible and less responsive over shorter periods than over longer periods. Accordingly, this chapter discusses both short-run and long-run productive relationships.

PRODUCTION

Production The process of using the services of labor and equipment together with natural resources and materials to make goods and services available.

Inputs The productive services of labor, capital, and natural resources.

Production is the process of using the services of labor and equipment together with natural resources and materials to make goods and services available. The productive services of labor, capital, and natural resources are the **inputs** into the process. Goods and services are the outputs of the process. In producing automobiles, for example, the labor services used include the hours put in by machine operators, foremen, designers, managers, and all other workers, ranging from janitors to the company president. The physical capital inputs include the services of buildings, machines, and the tools used by workers. The materials used include steel, plastic, glass, tires, fuel, and other items that are needed to construct the final product—the automobile. The inputs needed to produce a rock concert include the hours put in by the performers, sound technicians, concert hall managers, and other personnel; the land on which the rock concert takes place; and such capital inputs as the concert hall, the musical instruments, the sound system, and the bus used to transport the performers.

Modern Microeconomics in Action: The Business World

Total Quality Management: The New Emphasis on Quality by U.S. Businesses and Government

Quality control was invented by American management experts. However, their techniques were most eagerly and most successfully adopted by Japanese businesses after World War II. Now quality is again a buzzword of U.S. businesses. These businesses are discovering that an emphasis on improving the quality of products and services can increase productivity and reduce costs of production.*

U.S. businesses are also discovering that the application of quality control methods to *internal* operations of the business firm can increase worker productivity. The new methods involve the joint efforts of workers and management to find better ways to carry out their functions and to produce better products. Even government is applying quality control methods to improve the services and increase the production of its employees.

Let's look at the concept of *total quality management* and how it is being used by businesses in the 1990s. Total quality management (TQM) is a set of techniques that are applied to all of a company's activities to improve the quality of its products and services. TQM seeks not only to improve the quality of products that a company offers to its customers but also to improve the quality of services that one division of a company (such as the marketing department) offers to another division (such as the product development staff). The techniques of TQM were originally developed by J. M. Juran, who called them *total quality control*. Juran applied his techniques to everyone in a firm to involve all employees at all levels in the management process. The other guru of the quality control movement has been W. Edwards Deming, who developed a technique he called *statistical quality control* to eliminate product defects by changing productive techniques rather than by improving inspection. Both Deming and Juran had a great influence on Japanese management after World War II.

TQM seeks to change both the productive and managerial processes of the firm to achieve acceptable quality levels that are agreed on by managers. The "six-sigma quality" criterion is a goal of 3.4 defects per million parts made. One of the TQM techniques is to examine a product for potential sources of defects *while it is in the design stage* and to eliminate controllable problems at that stage. For example, suppose the design of a car headlamp is such that the headlamp could be installed upside down. To prevent this from happening, the design could be changed to make it impossible for the headlamp to be installed unless it is right side up. TQM also involves working with suppliers, just as Toyota did with its U.S. bumper supplier, so that delivery will be more reliable and costs can be cut. Eastman Kodak Company was able to increase the number of patents issued to it simply by doubling the number of its patent attorneys and locating them right in its research labs. IBM involves workers in the production process at its Research Triangle Park location in North Carolina by employing agents who specialize in helping workers who feel that the company's bureaucracy is impeding improvements in the production process that can increase worker productivity. TQM techniques have also been employed by U.S. automobile manufacturers, and defects in cars have decreased considerably.

Many politicians believe that quality control can improve confidence in government. The Federal Quality Institute was established in 1988 as a resource center to promote TQM. The Internal Revenue Service developed a program that cut costs by $11 million and reduced the amount of mail that failed to get to taxpayers.

State and local governments are trying to improve quality by making their services to the public more user friendly. In many cases they find that this is best done by contracting out such services as garbage collection to private firms. Faced with the threat of replacement by employees of private firms, workers in agencies of state and local governments are often motivated to perform better.

* For an excellent discussion of quality issues in business, see *Business Week*, Special 1991 Bonus Issue: "The Quality Imperative." Many of the examples here are based on information appearing in this issue.

Technology

Technology The knowledge of how to produce goods and services.

Productive relationships are primarily technological; they are determined by engineering, physical, and human capabilities. **Technology** is the knowledge of how to produce goods and services. Over time technology improves as new scientific and other discoveries are applied to productive methods. Improved technology often results in new methods of production that allow a greater output to be made available from a given amount of resources. Improved technology also allows the development of new products.

The application of new technology alleviates the problem of scarcity by making workers, equipment, and land more productive. In recent years new technology has resulted in the development of computers that enable workers in a variety of industries to accomplish their tasks more quickly. By making workers more productive in this way, computers embodying new technology allow more output to be produced from given quantities of labor and equipment. New technology can also be embodied in workers in the form of improved education or training that represents greater technical knowledge of production.

The Production Function

Production function A relationship between inputs and the maximum attainable output under a given technology.

The relationship between any combination of input services and the maximum attainable output from that combination is described by **production function.** Production functions are defined for a given technology. An improvement in technology increases the maximum output obtainable from any combination of inputs and therefore results in a new production function. The production function can also be thought of as specifying the minimum amounts of input use necessary to produce any given amount of output under current technology.

By classifying inputs into three broad categories—labor services, capital services, and raw materials—the production function can be written as

$$Q = f(L, K, M) \tag{7–1}$$

where Q is the maximum amount of output under current technology that can be produced with any given combination of labor services, L; capital services, K; and raw materials, M.

Properties of Production Functions: The Underlying Assumptions of the Theory of Production

Economic theory assumes that when technology is given, production functions have certain properties that govern the relationship between output and input use. Although production functions differ from activity to activity, it is generally assumed that they all share the following properties:

1. *There is a limit to the extra production that can be achieved when more of one input is used while other inputs are held constant.* This implies, for example, that in a factory with a given amount of space and machines there is a limit to the extra production that can be obtained by hiring more workers.

Eventually, the extra output obtained over any period from an extra worker peters down to close to zero. A point can actually be reached at which the addition of another worker would result in a decrease rather than an increase in output! This might occur because the worker has no equipment to work with and his presence impairs the functioning of other workers.

2. *There is some complementarity among inputs, but it is possible to substitute the use of one input for the use of another input without reducing production.* Although appropriate tools are useless unless workers with appropriate skills are available to employ them, it is possible to substitute one input for another in production. For example, a given quantity and quality of furniture can be manufactured by using a highly mechanized process or by using less capital and more labor. A given amount of acreage can be farmed to produce a given yield by using many workers, hand tools, and no fertilizers or pesticides or by using few workers, complex machines, and lots of pesticides and fertilizers.

There is, however, a limit to the extent to which an increase in the use of capital can make up for a reduction in the use of labor without reducing output. Conversely, there is a limit to the extent to which the use of capital can be replaced by the use of labor. For example, in a factory you can make up for a reduction in the use of machines by hiring more workers. However, as workers are progressively substituted for machines, it requires more and more labor hours to make up for the lost machine hours.

Short run A period of production during which some inputs cannot be varied.

Long run A period of production during which all inputs can be varied.

3. *It is easier to vary the use of inputs over longer periods than over shorter periods.* The **short run** is a period of production during which some inputs cannot be varied. In the short run, for example, manufacturing firms are confined to a given factory and lack the time to expand their facilities. The **long run** is a period of production so long that producers have adequate time to vary *all* of the inputs used to produce a good. There is no limit to the extra output that can be produced when all inputs can be increased. Accordingly, producers face more constraints in making goods available in the short run than in making them available in the long run.

The period encompassed by the short run is likely to vary from activity to activity. For example, a building contractor might be able to increase all of the inputs used in producing homes in a month or two. On the other hand, an oil refinery might need years to increase the capital inputs (production facilities) required to produce more output.

Production Grids

The important aspects of production can be captured by considering only two broad classes of inputs, such as labor and capital. An advantage of using a two-input production function is that it permits graphic analysis of production. A mathematical analysis is required if more than two inputs are explicitly considered in the production function.

Table 7–1 contains hypothetical data about the relationship between the capital and labor input used to produce chairs in a furniture factory under a given technology. These data are based on the underlying relationships between inputs

TABLE 7–1 Production Grid: Chairs per Month

Labor Hours per Month	*Machine Hours per Month* 100	200	300	400
100	20	30	35	38
200	30	85	150	210
300	55	150	210	270
400	65	180	250	315
500	72	210	270	320
600	78	230	288	324
700	83	245	305	327
800	86	250	315	329

and output listed above and are assumed to be common properties of production functions. Capital input is measured by machine hours used per month; labor input is measured by labor hours used per month. Each machine hour and labor hour is of a given quality.[3]

Production grid A table that describes a production function by indicating the maximum output that can be produced with given combinations of inputs.

A **production grid** is a table that describes a production function by indicating the maximum output that can be produced with given combinations of inputs. Table 7–1 is a hypothetical production grid for a factory that produces chairs. The grid tabulates the maximum output corresponding to each combination of labor and machine hours. For example, to find the output that results from 200 labor hours and 100 machine hours, go to the row corresponding to 200 labor hours and then go across to the column corresponding to 100 machine hours. The grid indicates that the corresponding monthly output will be 30 chairs. Similarly, according to the data in the grid, monthly output would be 250 chairs if 400 labor hours and 300 machine hours were used each month.

Production Options in the Short Run: The Law of Diminishing Marginal Returns

Let's first examine production options in the short run. In the short run, some inputs are fixed and their usage cannot be varied. This limits the flexibility with which output can be varied. Assume that capital is a fixed input and labor a variable input. Suppose that a producer has a plant with equipment capable of supplying 300 machine hours of capital use each month. That capability cannot be increased or decreased in the short run. The producer must pay for the use of the equipment whether or not it is employed. You can think of the producer as owning the equipment or as having leased enough equipment to provide 300 machine hours of use per month.

[3] Clearly, if machines or labor differed in the amounts that they could produce in an hour, the hour would be a poor measure of input use. Each machine must be considered a different input, or each hour used must be adjusted according to differences in the productivity of each machine. Measuring input by hours therefore represents a considerable simplification.

Given the quantity of capital in the plant, production can be varied by adjusting the use of labor together with the available equipment according to the data in the third column of the production grid shown in Table 7–1.

In the short run, producers can be thought of as operating out of facilities of a given size. In the production facility for chairs there are a fixed number of machines, a fixed amount of equipment and space, and other fixed inputs. In a restaurant the number of tables, ovens, sinks, and stoves and the amount of space can be regarded as fixed in the short run. For a chain of department stores, the square footage and equipment of all of the stores in the chain can be regarded as fixed inputs.

In reality, some inputs are move variable in the short run than others. The proportions in which inputs are used change in the short run as output is increased. For example, although at any point in time a factory has a given number of square feet of space and a given number of machines, production can be increased in the short run by working the factory around the clock when demand for output is high. If necessary, workers can be hired to work two or three shifts each day and as much as seven days per week. In this case the proportion of labor to capital used is increased. When demand for output is low, a factory can be operated only two or three days per week or even shut down for a time by laying off workers. In this case the proportion of labor to capital used is reduced.

Total, Average, and Marginal Products of a Variable Input

Total product of a variable input The amount of output produced when a given amount of that input is used along with fixed inputs.

The **total product of a variable input** is the amount of output produced when a given amount of that input is used along with fixed inputs. The first two columns of Table 7–2 show the total product of labor (TP_L) in the chair factory in the short run based on the data from the production grid. These data correspond to the third column of the production grid shown in Table 7–1. This column shows how production varies as more labor is used together with enough capital to provide 300 machine hours per month.

TABLE 7–2 Total, Average, and Marginal Products of Labor* when K = 300 Machine Hours (Monthly)

Labor Hours	*Total Product of Labor* (TP_L)	*Average Product of Labor* $\left(AP_L = \frac{TP_L}{L}\right)$	*Marginal Product of Labor* $\left(MP_L = \frac{\Delta TP_L}{\Delta L}\right)$	*Proportion of Labor to Capital* $\left(\frac{L}{K} = \frac{\text{Labor hours}}{300}\right)$
100	35	0.35	0.35	0.3
200	150	0.75	1.15	0.6
300	210	0.70	0.60	1.0
400	250	0.63	0.40	1.3
500	270	0.54	0.20	1.7
600	288	0.48	0.18	2.0
700	305	0.44	0.17	2.3
800	315	0.39	0.10	2.7

* Total product is measured in units of chairs per month. Marginal product is measured in units of chairs per labor hour.

Average product of a variable input The total product of the variable input divided by the amount of that input used.

The **average product of a variable input** is the total product of the variable input divided by the amount of that input used. For example, the average product of labor (AP_L) is its total product divided by labor hours *(L)* used:

$$AP_L = TP_L/L \quad \textbf{(7–2)}$$

This measures the productivity of labor as output per labor hour. In this case it indicates the number of chairs produced per labor hour used. The third column of Table 7–2 calculates the average product of each 100 hours of labor used in the chair factory. For example, the average product of 100 hours of labor is 35⁄100, or 0.35 chairs per labor hour. The average product of labor increases to 0.75 chairs per labor hour when 200 labor hours are used together with the 300 machine hours. The average product of labor falls to 0.70 chairs per labor hour when 300 labor hours are used monthly. The third column of Table 7–2 shows that the average product of labor declines steadily when more than 200 labor hours per month are utilized in the short run.

Labor productivity varies considerably among factories. For example, the average product of labor in large integrated steel mills in the United States was about 0.2 tons of steel per labor hour in 1985. In the same year Japanese integrated steel mills, which employed more advanced technology and more capital than their U.S. counterparts, had an average product of labor of about 0.25 tons of steel per labor hour. On the other hand, U.S. minimills, which produced steel from scrap metal and reduced iron ore rather than crude iron ore, as is the case in the integrated mills, had an average product of labor of 0.29 tons of steel per labor hour.[4] The superior labor productivity of the U.S. minimills suggested that they were likely to be more successful than the U.S. integrated mills in competing with Japanese steel sellers.

Marginal product of a variable input The change in the total product of that input corresponding to a 1-unit change in its use.

The **marginal product of a variable input** is the change in the total product of that input corresponding to a 1-unit change in its use, other things being equal. The marginal product of labor is

$$MP_L = \Delta TP_L/\Delta L \quad \textbf{(7–3)}$$

where MP_L is the marginal product of labor and ΔTP_L is the change in the output associated with a change of ΔL units of labor used along with a fixed amount of other inputs.[5]

In Table 7–2 the marginal product at each 100-hour increment in labor used is calculated. If more data were available from the production function, the marginal product of each actual hour of labor used with the 300 hours of capital available each month could be calculated. It is assumed that the factory could not operate with zero labor, so the output of zero labor is zero. Subtracting zero from 35 gives the change in output from adding 100 hours of labor. Dividing this by 100 hours gives the marginal product of labor when 100 hours are being used. This is 0.35

[4] See Donald F. Barnett and Robert W. Crandall, *Up from the Ashes* (Washington, D.C.: Brookings Institution, 1986), table 2–1, p. 21.

[5] The marginal product of labor for very small changes in labor use is the $\partial Q/\partial L$ for the production function $Q = f(L, K)$.

chairs.[6] Adding a second 100 hours of labor to the 300 monthly machine hours results in a sharp increase in output to 150 chairs. The change in output in this case is 115 chairs. Dividing this by 100 labor hours gives 1.15 chairs. This is the marginal product of labor when 200 hours are used. Similarly, the marginal product of labor can be calculated at each 100-unit interval. This is done in the fourth column of Table 7–2. Notice how the marginal product of labor declines steadily after 200 hours are used.

The Total Product Curve

A total product curve shows how output varies as more of a variable input is used together with fixed inputs. Figure 7–1(a) shows a typical total product curve that reflects a relationship between labor use and output similar to the one shown in Table 7–2. A total product curve like the one drawn in Figure 7–1(a) shows the variation of monthly chair production when more labor hours are used together with 300 machine hours and fixed amounts of all other inputs.

Along a total product curve production can be increased by increasing the proportion of the variable input to the fixed inputs. For example, as Table 7–2 shows, the ratio of labor hours to capital hours used (L/K) increases steadily from 0.3 to 2.7 as output is increased by varying labor use and holding capital at K_1 = 300 hours per month. Notice that the total product curve indicates that a maximum amount of output can be produced when the amounts of other inputs are fixed. This maximum amount occurs at point C, where L^{**} hours per month are used together with the K_1 machine hours. If more than this amount of labor is used, the dashed portion of the total product curve shows that production would actually decrease. Points on the dashed portion of the total product curve are not included in the production function because the output corresponding to those points could be produced with the same amount of capital and less labor.

The Average Product Curve

It is possible to derive average and marginal product curves from the total product curve. The average product of labor can be gauged from the slope of a ray drawn from the origin to a point on the total product curve. At the point that the ray touches the total product curve, drop a vertical line to the horizontal axis. The length of that line represents output, Q. The distance from the point that the vertical line hits the horizontal axis to the origin represents the number of labor hours used together with the fixed inputs to produce the output Q. The slope of the ray is Q divided by L. The slope represents the average product of labor, which is Q/L at the output Q.

The maximum average product of labor is attained when the slope of a ray from the origin is just tangent to the total product curve. This occurs at point B in Figure 7–1(a), at which output is Q^* and L^* labor hours are used per month

[6] Actually, this is the average of the marginal products of each of the first 100 hours of labor. The marginal product of each hour of labor will vary. With enough data, the marginal product of each of the first 100 labor hours could be computed.

FIGURE 7–1 Total, Average, and Marginal Product of a Variable Input: The Stages of Production

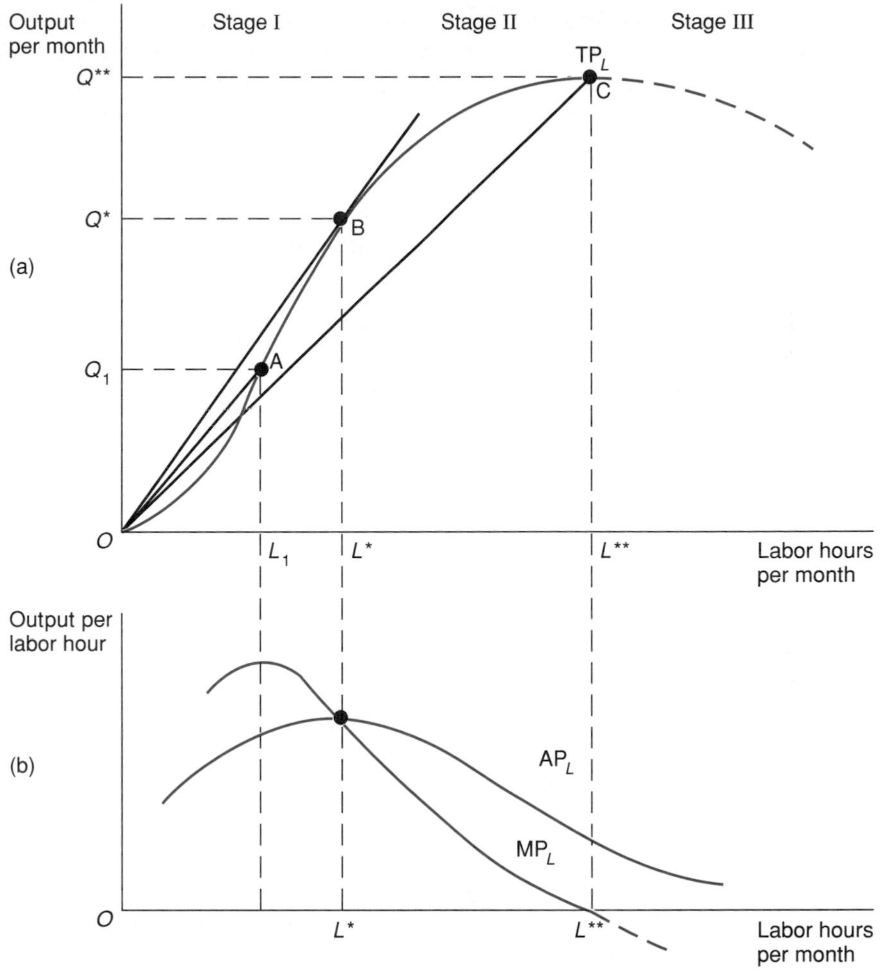

The shape of the total product curve for labor used with a fixed amount of capital reflects the law of diminishing marginal returns. The marginal product of labor increases up to point *A* and then starts declining. The average product of labor is at a maximum at point *B*, where the ray *OB* is just tangent to the total product curve. At point *C*, total product is at a maximum and marginal product of labor is equal to zero.

together with the fixed input. At that point the average product of labor is Q^*/L^*, which measures the slope of the ray *OB*. The slope of any other ray drawn in this way to the total product curve, corresponding to either less or more use than L^* labor hours per month, will be less than that of the ray drawn to point *B*. For example, the slope of the ray drawn to point *A*, corresponding to L_1 labor hours per month on the total product curve, is less than that of the ray drawn to point *B*.

At point *A* the average product of labor is therefore lower than it is at point *B*. Similarly, you can see that the average product of labor at point *C*, corresponding to L^{**} labor hours, is lower than it is at point *B* because the slope of the ray *OC* is less than the slope of the ray *OB*. By drawing rays to various points on the total product curve and noting their slopes, you can see that the average product of labor increases up to point *B*, at which L^* labor hours per month are used, and then declines as more than L^* labor hours per month are used.

The average product of labor curve is plotted directly below the total product curve in Figure 7–1(b). Points on the horizontal axis correspond to the points on the horizontal axis of the total product curve. The vertical axis measures the average product of labor in terms of output per labor hour.

The Marginal Product Curve

The slope of the total product curve at any point measures the change in output for very small changes in labor hours, $\Delta Q/\Delta L$. This slope is the marginal product of each labor hour. Point *A* is the point of inflection of the total product curve at which the concavity of the curve changes.[7] The slope of the total product curve, and therefore the marginal product of labor, increases until point *A* has been reached. Beyond this point it decreases.

Figure 7–1(b) plots the marginal product of labor on the axes that were used for its average product. Note that the marginal product of labor reaches its maximum before the average product reaches its maximum. The marginal product continues to decline until it reaches zero at L^{**} labor hours, where the slope of the total product curve is zero. If production were to continue beyond point *C*, output would actually decline. Additional labor hours beyond L^{**} would therefore have a negative marginal product.

The Relation between Average and Marginal Product

The point of maximum average product occurs where the ray *OB* from the origin is just tangent to the total product curve in Figure 7–1(a). This means that the slope of the ray is equal to the slope of the total product curve at that point. Because the slope of the ray is the average product and the slope of the total product curve is the marginal product at that point, it follows that $MP_L = AP_L$ at point *B*. The marginal product of labor therefore equals the average product of labor where the latter is at its maximum.

The average product of labor varies as more labor is used. The marginal product of labor represents the incremental output per labor hour that is added in to compute the average product of labor. If that number is above the previous average, the average must rise. For example, if the average product is 50 units per labor hour and the marginal product exceeds that, then the average product of the

---

[7] At the point of inflection, the second derivative of the production function $Q = f(L, K)$ with respect of L is zero. At this point $\partial Q/\partial L$ is at a maximum.

next labor hour must increase. This is because the last number used to calculate it exceeds the previous average. This holds for the data in Table 7–2. Notice that when the marginal product of labor exceeds the average product, the average increases. When the marginal product is below the average product, the average declines.

This is true for any relation between average and marginal numbers. If after three examinations in your economics course you have a 72 average, your marginal grade will be the grade on the next examination you take. If your marginal grade exceeds your previous average, your average must increase; if your marginal grade falls below your previous average, your average must decline.

In Figure 7–1(b) the average product of labor is at its maximum when $MP_L = AP_L$. When fewer than L^* hours of labor are used, $MP_L > AP_L$ and average product increases. When more than L^* units of labor are used, $MP_L < AP_L$ and average product decreases.

The Law of Diminishing Marginal Returns

Law of diminishing marginal returns States that as more of a variable input is used while other inputs and technology are fixed, the marginal product of the variable input will eventually decline.

The **law of diminishing marginal returns** states that as more of a variable input is used while other inputs and technology are fixed, the marginal product of the variable input will eventually decline. This law is sometimes called the *law of variable proportions* because it shows how output varies when the proportion of a variable input to fixed inputs used in production varies. It is also called the *law of diminishing returns*. According to the law, the extra production obtained from equal increments of a variable input will eventually decline as the proportion of the variable input to the fixed inputs used in production increases (assuming a given technology). The marginal product of the variable input will therefore become smaller and smaller and eventually approach zero as more and more of the variable input is employed in the short run. This means that there is a limit to the amount of output that can be obtained when only one input is variable.

Depending on the production function, the marginal product might get smaller and smaller but never reach zero. However, the marginal product might actually fall to zero and become negative if more of the variable input were used. In Figure 7–1 it is assumed that the production function is such that after L^{**} units of labor are employed per month, the marginal product of labor actually becomes negative.

The hypothesis embodied in the law of diminishing marginal returns is quite reasonable. Suppose that the law did not hold. This would mean, for example, that workers could produce an unlimited amount of food on an acre of land. If the marginal product of the workers never declined, adding more workers to that acre would always increase output at the same rate or even at an increasing rate. It would therefore be feasible to produce the entire world supply of food on 1 acre. This, of course, is unlikely.

Point of diminishing marginal returns The level of use of a variable input at which its marginal product just begins to decline.

The **point of diminishing marginal returns** is the level of use of a variable input at which its marginal product just begins to decline. In Figure 7–1(a) the point of diminishing marginal returns is point A on the total product curve. That point corresponds to the maximum marginal product of labor when L_1 labor hours per month are employed. The law of diminishing marginal returns holds that the marginal product of a variable input used together with fixed inputs must reach a point of decline in the short run in all productive endeavors.

Refer to the data on average and marginal product of labor in Table 7–2. Note that the point of diminishing marginal returns occurs at 200 labor hours when machine hours are fixed at 300. For some productive activities, diminishing returns can set in almost immediately after production begins. Where the point of diminishing returns actually occurs depends on the production function.

The Short-Run Stages of Production

Production in the short run can be divided into three stages that are shown in Figure 7–1:

Stage I: This stage begins at the start of production, where $L = 0$, and runs to the point corresponding to $L = L^*$, where the average product of labor is at a maximum.

Stage II: This stage begins at the point where the average product is at a maximum and continues to the point where the marginal product of labor becomes zero.

Stage III: In this stage the marginal product of labor actually becomes negative.

In stage I the proportion of labor to capital is too low relative to the purposes for which the productive plant was designed. Capital, the fixed input, is underutilized in this stage. A restaurant with 100 tables and only two waiters would be operating in stage I of the short-run production function. Increasing the amount of labor in stage I increases the average product of labor. For example, if the restaurant, given its 100 tables, were to double the number of its waiters, the average product of the waiters would increase. This means that twice as many waiters would be able to serve more than twice as many meals. In stage I there are increasing returns from increasing the proportion of labor, the variable input, to capital, the fixed input.

Operating in stage I involves a waste of resources in the sense that the firm incurs costs for capital equipment that it lacks the labor to utilize. The firm could produce any given output in stage I with less equipment and the same amount of labor because it does not use some of its equipment in this stage of production. However, because capital is a fixed input in the short run, the firm does not have the option of using less equipment.[8]

In stage III there is too much labor relative to capital. Now there are too many waiters relative to the number of tables, and this actually decreases the number of

[8] In Chapter 9 it will be shown that a profit-maximizing firm cannot generate enough revenue to cover its variable costs by selling output in stage I. The firm would shut down rather than operate in stage I because it loses more than its fixed costs in that range of production.

meals that can be served. The marginal product of the waiters is negative. They spill food as they distract and bump into each other. In stage III there is too much of the variable input relative to the fixed input.

Note the symmetry between stages I and III. In stage I the proportion of the variable input to the fixed input is too low, given the size of the facility. In stage III the proportion of the variable input is too high, given the size of the facility. In stage III firms pay for labor hours that result in decreases rather than increases in production. In stage I they pay for capital that is not being fully utilized because of an inadequate amount of labor.

Stage II is the only stage in which there is neither a redundancy of capital nor a redundancy of labor. It is therefore wise for firms to avoid both stages I and III and remain in stage II. By doing so, they avoid paying for underutilized capital equipment and other fixed inputs and they also avoid overutilizing labor relative to capital.

Concept Review

1. The total product of 500 labor hours used as a variable input with equipment and other fixed inputs is 50 units of output. Calculate the average product of labor.
2. Suppose that the average product of labor in a factory currently exceeds its marginal product. What will happen to output per labor hour if the factory hires more workers?
3. Explain why the average product of labor continues to increase after the point of diminishing marginal returns has been reached.

Input Substitution and Long-Run Production Options

Now let's look at the opportunities available under current technology for substituting one input for another in the production process. There are different techniques of producing a given product. For example, an automobile can be produced in a highly automated plant with many robots and very few workers or in a less capital-intensive plant that uses more workers and fewer robots.

To examine options for substituting labor for capital, let's return to the production grid of Table 7–1. Now pick out all the combinations of labor and capital that can be used to produce 210 chairs per month. For example, according to the data in Table 7–1, which are reproduced along with the graph in Figure 7–2, 200 labor hours and 400 machine hours can be used to produce 210 chairs per month. Point *A* in Figure 7–2 shows this combination of labor and capital. The same number of chairs could be produced per month if 300 labor hours and 300 machine hours were used. This is represented by point *B* in Figure 7–2. A combination of 500 labor hours and 200 machine hours per month, represented by point *D*, would also yield a monthly output of 210 chairs.

FIGURE 7–2 **An Isoquant**

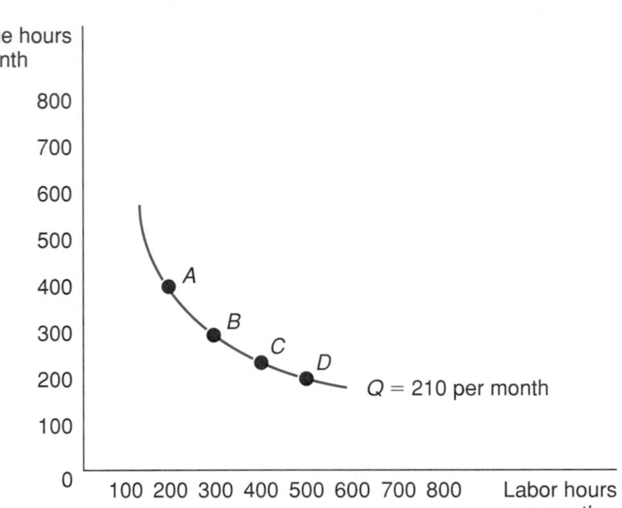

Production Grid: Chairs per Month

Labor Hours per Month	***Machine Hours per Month***			
	100	***200***	***300***	***400***
100	20	30	35	38
200	30	85	150	210
300	55	150	210	270
400	65	180	250	315
500	72	210	270	320
600	78	230	288	324
700	83	245	305	327
800	86	250	315	329

Points on the isoquant graphed here represent combinations of labor and capital that can be used to produce a monthly output of 210 chairs with a given technology and given amounts of inputs other than labor and capital.

Although not explicitly shown in the production grid, there are other combinations of labor hours and machine hours that could produce 210 chairs. One such combination is 400 labor hours and 240 machine hours per month. This is represented by point *C*.

Isoquant A curve showing all combinations of variable inputs that can be used to produce a given amount of output.

An **isoquant** is a curve showing all combinations of variable inputs that can be used to produce a given quantity of output. The isoquant for 210 chairs is illustrated in Figure 7–2. The curve is labeled $Q = 210$. Points on the curve represent all the combinations of labor and capital that can produce a maximum of 210 chairs per month, given the available technology and given the amounts of other inputs.

The isoquant illustrates that there are many ways to produce a given quantity of chairs per month. A highly mechanized operation such as the one represented by point *A* in Figure 7–2 could be used. Alternatively, the same quantity could be produced per month using few machines and lots of labor, as is the case at point *D*.

Isoquants are similar in conception to the indifference curves for consumers discussed in Chapter 3. An indifference curve gives alternative combinations of goods that provide a given level of utility and an isoquant gives alternative combinations of inputs that can be used to produce a given level of output.

Isoquant map A set of isoquants that shows the maximum output attainable from any given combination of inputs.

Isoquant Maps

An **isoquant map** is a set of isoquants that shows the maximum output attainable from any given combination of inputs. The data in the production grid allow additional isoquants to be drawn. For example, locate all the combinations of

FIGURE 7–3 An Isoquant Map

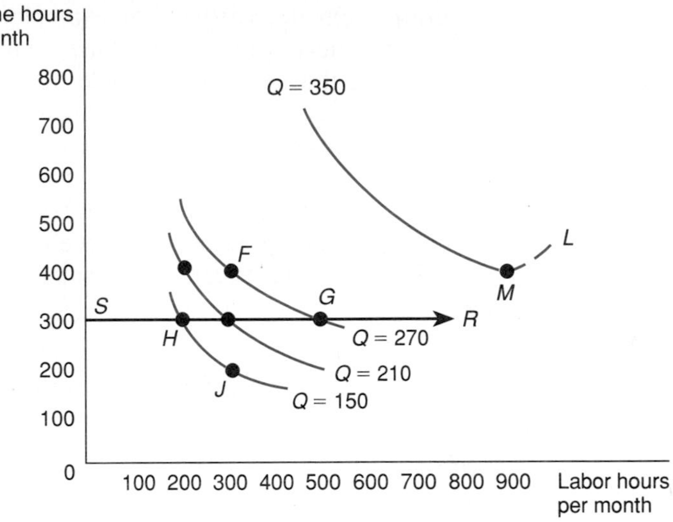

An isoquant map can be used to determine the maximum output attainable from any combination of inputs. Four isoquants have been drawn based on the data of Table 7–1. Points along the line *SR* can be used to show how production varies as variable amounts of labor hours are used together with 300 machine hours. Input combinations on an upward-sloping portion of an isoquant are not included in the production function because the same output on an upward-sloping portion such as *ML* can be produced with less input.

labor and capital in the grid that can be used to produce 270 chairs per month. The grid shows two ways of producing this output. A process using 300 labor hours and 400 machine hours is one way. This is plotted as point *F* in Figure 7–3. Another way is a process using 500 labor hours and 300 machine hours, plotted as point *G* in Figure 7–3. Tracing a smooth curve through points *F* and *G* gives the isoquant $Q = 270$. All input combinations represented by points on this isoquant can be used to produce 270 chairs per month. An isoquant for 150 chairs can be derived in the same way. Note that in the production grid a monthly combination of 200 labor hours and 300 machine hours, plotted as point *H*, can produce 150 chairs per month. The same output could be produced with 300 labor hours and 200 machine hours, represented by point *J*. The isoquant labeled $Q = 150$ is traced through these two points.

The isoquant map, like a contour map of a mountain, shows higher levels by curves. Moving away from the origin, each isoquant corresponds to a higher level of output. Isoquants other than those illustrated can be drawn through any point on the graph. The logic of the isoquant map is analogous to that of the indifference maps previously derived for consumers.

The isoquants drawn from the production grid data are *downward sloping*. This means that along a given isoquant a reduction in labor hours requires an increase in machine hours to prevent production from declining.

Positively sloped isoquants imply that an increase in the use of one input, say labor, requires an *increase* in the use of the other input, say capital, to keep production from decreasing. For example, suppose that 350 chairs per month could be produced with 400 machine hours and 850 labor hours at point M in Figure 7–3. If the same output could be produced with 900 labor hours and 450 machine hours at point L, the isoquant would be upward sloping between points M and L. However, the input combinations on ML, the dashed segment of the isoquant, would not be part of the production function because the same 350 chairs could be produced with *less* labor and *less* capital. Positively sloped portions of isoquants represent productive methods that would not be included in the production function because the same output could be produced with less input use.

Marginal Rate of Technical Substitution and the Curvature of Isoquants

Marginal rate of technical substitution of labor for capital A measure of the amount of capital that each unit of labor can replace without increasing or decreasing production.

Isoquant analysis can be used to explore the opportunities for substituting the services of one input for another. The **marginal rate of technical substitution of labor for capital** (MRTS_{LK}) is a measure of the amount of capital that each unit of labor can replace without increasing or decreasing production. It is a measure similar to the marginal rate of substitution used to analyze consumer behavior.

The isoquants that have been drawn for labor and capital in this chapter have the same convex shapes as the indifference curves that were drawn in Chapter 3 to explain consumer behavior. Figure 7–4 reproduces the isoquant map for chairs and examines the implications of its curvature for the way labor can be substituted for capital without reducing or increasing the monthly output of chairs. That output is constant at 210 chairs along the isoquant drawn.

The marginal rate of technical substitution along the isoquant at any point is the slope at that point multiplied by -1:

$$\text{MRTS}_{LK} = -\Delta K/\Delta L \qquad \textbf{(7–4)}$$

Remember that a negatively sloped isoquant implies that when machine hours in production are reduced, labor hours must be increased to keep production constant. Measuring capital input in terms of machine hours and labor input in terms of labor hours, the slope of an isoquant when multiplied by -1 at any point indicates the number of machine hours (ΔK) that each additional hour of labor use ($\Delta L = 1$) can replace without increasing or decreasing output. Alternatively, you can think of MRTS_{KL} as indicating the number of machine hours necessary to replace each labor hour withdrawn from production ($-\Delta L = 1$) without increasing or decreasing output.

The convex shape of the isoquant in Figure 7–4 implies that the marginal rate of technical substitution of labor for capital declines as labor is substituted for capital along an isoquant. This means that each labor hour can substitute for fewer and fewer machine hours as labor replaces capital and production is maintained at the same level. Conversely, you can think of diminishing marginal rates of technical substitution of labor for capital as implying that increasing numbers of machine hours are required to substitute for successive reductions of each labor hour if output is to remain constant. Moving from point D to point C on the isoquant in

FIGURE 7–4 Declining Marginal Rate of Technical Substitution of Labor for Capital

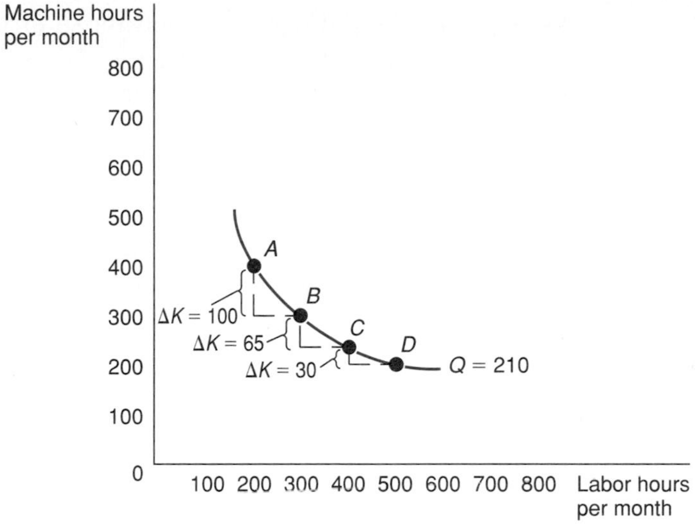

Each successive 100-hour increment in labor use replaces smaller amounts of machine use as more labor hours are used and fewer machine hours are used. Moving from point *A* to *B*, 100 labor hours replace 100 machine hours while still producing a monthly output of 210 chairs. Moving from *B* to *C*, 100 labor hours replace only 65 machine hours; moving from *C* to *D*, 100 labor hours replace only 30 machine hours.

Figure 7–4 shows that only 30 machine hours are required to make up the output lost by withdrawing 100 labor hours from production when the currently used method of production employs 200 machine hours and 500 labor hours per month. However, if the managers want to move from point *B*, at which 300 machine hours and 300 labor hours are used to produce the same monthly output, to point *A* by withdrawing 100 labor hours from use, it will take 100 machine hours to make up the output lost by doing so.

The reason for declining marginal rates of technical substitution is that inputs tend to complement each other. Complementarity between inputs is one of the underlying assumptions made by economists about production. Each input has the capability of doing something that the other either cannot do or can do only imperfectly. In most activities labor and capital are not perfect substitutes for each other. When labor hours are reduced, each additional reduction requires more machine hours to replace the lost labor time. Similarly, successive reductions in machine use require progressively more labor hours to replace the lost machine time. The curvature of the isoquants indicates the difficulty with which one input can be substituted for the other without sacrificing production. This varies from activity to activity. It may, for example, be relatively easy to substitute labor for machines in a chair factory, but it may be virtually impossible to substitute labor for capital in the production of complex chemicals (such as antifreeze).

How Variation in the Marginal Products of Inputs Affects Their Marginal Rates of Technical Substitution

The marginal rate of technical substitution of labor for capital depends on the marginal products of labor and capital. Suppose labor use is reduced by some small amount, ΔL hours, whereas capital use is increased by some amount, ΔK hours, along the isoquant in Figure 7–4. The loss in production from the decrease in labor hours is ΔL multiplied by its marginal product.[9] This loss in production would result in a movement to a lower isoquant. To remain on the same isoquant, the reduction in labor use must be offset by enough extra machine hours to get back to a point on the original isoquant. The gain in production is ΔK multiplied by its marginal product. Because the gain in production equals the loss in production, it follows that

$$-\Delta L(\text{MP}_L) = \Delta K(\text{MP}_K) \qquad \textbf{(7–5)}$$

Solving for MRTS_{KL}, the negative of the slope of the isoquant,

$$\text{MRTS}_{LK} = -\Delta K/\Delta L = \text{MP}_L/\text{MP}_K \qquad \textbf{(7–6)}$$

where MP_L is the marginal product of labor and MP_K is the marginal product of capital.[10] Assume that the marginal products of the inputs begin to decline immediately after they are employed. If this is so, Equation 7–6 can be used to show why the marginal rate of technical substitution of labor for capital declines as labor is substituted for capital. As labor use is increased, the marginal product of labor declines. This decreases the numerator of Equation 7–6. As the amount of capital used decreases when labor is substituted for it, its marginal product tends to increase. This makes the denominator larger. Both of these effects reduce the value of the ratio of the two marginal products.

Substitution of Capital for Labor in Business

Mechanization of the productive process is the hallmark of an economy's industrialization. Isoquants can be used to analyze the implications of shifts to a more mechanized productive process under a given technology. When a firm moves to a more capital-intensive productive process by substituting capital for labor, the marginal products of *both* capital and labor are affected. Assuming a given tech-

---

[9] Recall that the marginal product of labor is $\Delta Q/\Delta L$. If you multiply this by the change in labor, you will get $\Delta L[\Delta Q/\Delta L] = \Delta Q$. Similarly, a change in the amount of any input used multiplied by the marginal product of that input gives the resulting change in output.

[10] Using calculus, the same result could be obtained directly from the production function for infinitesimal changes in L and K. Suppose that the production function is $Q = f(L, K)$. To remain on a given isoquant for any substitution of labor for capital, the following condition must be satisfied:

$$dQ = (\partial Q/\partial L)dL + (\partial Q/\partial K)dK = 0$$

This implies that

$$-dK/dL = (\partial Q/\partial L)/(\partial Q/\partial K)$$

where $\partial Q/\partial L = \text{MP}_L$ and $\partial Q/\partial K = \text{MP}_K$.

nology, the use of a more capital-intensive productive process to produce a given output will result in a movement upward along any given isoquant, as shown in Figure 7–5. The isoquant in Figure 7–5 shows alternative input combinations that can be used to produce a car in a factory. Suppose that the current productive method involves the use of 1,000 labor hours and 500 machine hours per car. The labor-capital ratio is therefore currently two labor hours for each machine hour used. When the firm moves to a more capital-intensive productive process, represented by point *M*2, by installing more capital equipment, it needs less labor per car. Knowledge of the shape of the firm's isoquants for cars will tell its managers exactly how much labor reduction the new productive method calls for. At point *M*2 a car can be produced with only 500 labor hours and 1,000 machine hours. The capital-labor ratio is now only one half of a labor hour for each machine hour used per car.

Because the firm moves upward along its isoquant, the marginal rate of technical substitution of labor for capital increases as a result of mechanization of the productive process. This means that the marginal product of labor increases and the marginal product of capital declines (see Equation 7–6). The decline in the marginal product of capital reduces the potential gain from further mechanization of the productive process under current technology.

The substitution of capital for labor also *increases* the marginal product of labor. The firm is willing to pay more per hour for the reduced amount of labor now used per unit of output because the loss of an hour of labor would now result

FIGURE 7–5 Substitution of Capital for Labor

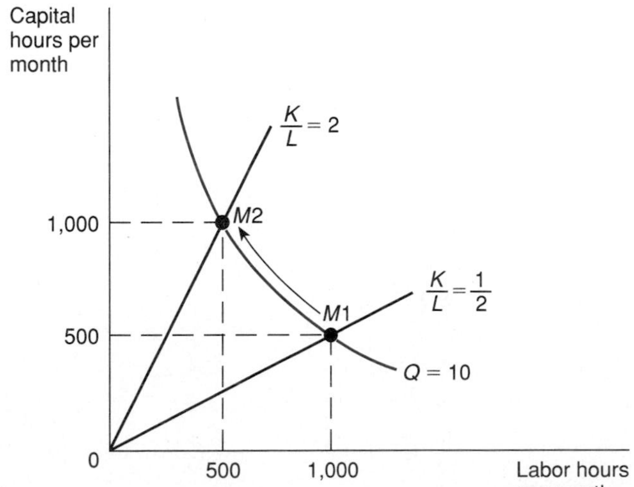

As capital is substituted for labor on the isoquant illustrated above, the capital-labor ratio increases from ½ to 2, moving from *M*1 to *M*2. The substitution results in an increase in the marginal product of labor and a decline in the marginal product of capital as the marginal rate of technical substitution of labor for capital increases.

Modern Microeconomics in Action: The Business World

An Estimated Production Function for Corn

The table below shows a production grid based on a 1977 corn fertility response study.* The data show the yield of bushels per acre on land plots that differed only in terms of the amounts of potassium (K) used per acre as fertilizer and the amounts of available nitrogen (N) per acre, other things being equal. Both inputs are measured as pounds per acre. The data show a trend similar to that of the data assumed for the chair factory example. However, as with most experimental data, there are irregularities and "gaps." Nevertheless, an underlying productive relationship between the output of corn and the use of the two inputs could be used to derive isoquants.

Two researchers in the Department of Agricultural Economics at the University of Wisconsin, Ted F. Bay and Richard A. Schoney, used computer graphics to fit the data with smooth curves.† The isoquants derived from this grid and plotted with the aid of computer graphics are shown below. Each isoquant is labeled with the number of bushels per acre.

Data Grid Yield (Bushels per Acre)

Available Potassium (K) (Lb/Acre)	***Available Nitrogen (N) (Lb/Acre)***					
	75	***131***	***187***	***243***	***299***	***355***
388	78	153		184	172	189
357		144	167	166		175
325	90	141	184	192	178	170
294	103	148	185	179	181	175
262	109	152	167	186	168	182
231	112	150	172	186	181	176
199	88	164	193	161	170	164
168	97	157	155		150	

Source: Figure and table from *American Journal of Agricultural Economics* 64, no. 2 (May 1982) pp. 289–97. Reproduced by permission.

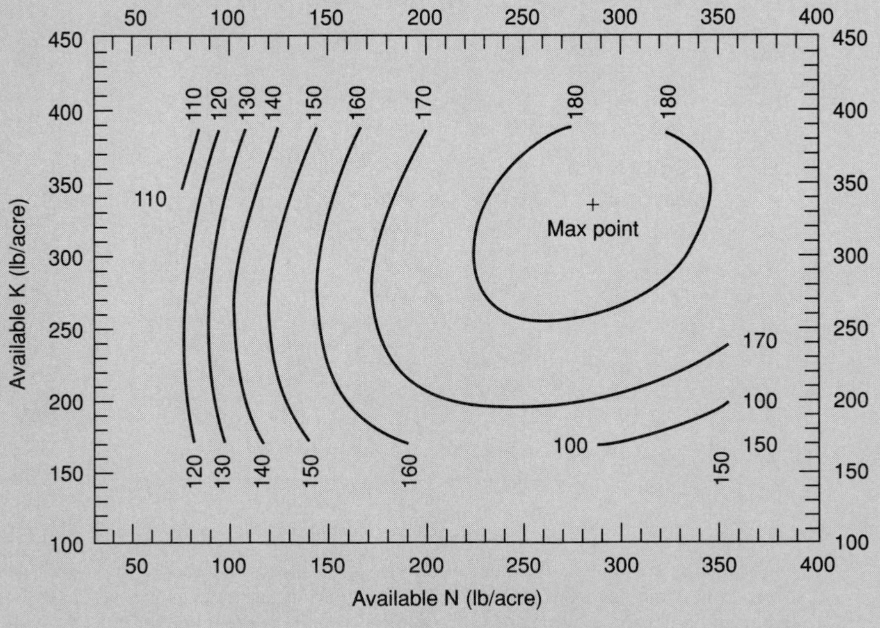

(*Continued*) Notice how the isoquants for 170 bushels per acre turn upward sloping after about 250 pounds of N are used per acre. Points on the upward-sloping portions of the isoquants are not part of the production function because the same output could be produced with less of both inputs. Each isoquant is labeled with the corresponding output per acre. The *max point* gives the combination of N and K per acre that corresponds to the maximum output of about 190 bushels per acre. If more than the amounts of N and K corresponding to the *max point* were used per acre, production per acre would decline.

* The study was conducted at the University of Wisconsin Agricultural Experiment Station at Arlington.

† Ted F. Bay and Richard A. Schoney, "Data Analysis with Computer Graphics: Production Functions," *American Journal of Agricultural Economics* 64, no. 2 (May 1982), pp. 289–97.

in the loss of more production than would have been lost previously. In this sense mechanization makes labor more valuable to firms and increases their willingness to pay more for each labor hour. This puts upward pressure on wages and thus benefits workers. When workers have more equipment to work with, their productivity tends to rise because of the complementarity between capital and labor. Even though the substitution of capital for labor reduces the firm's demand for labor per car, it increases the real value of a labor hour for the firm and therefore acts to increase the wages that the firm is willing to pay. In this way mechanization of the productive process benefits workers as well as the firm's owners.

As you will see in the next chapter, the incentive to substitute labor for capital depends on the price of labor relative to the price of capital and on the marginal product of capital relative to that of labor.

Input Substitution and the Shape of Isoquants

The way isoquants are shaped provides information about the possibility of substituting one input for the other while producing the same output. An extreme case is a fixed-proportions production function. *Fixed proportions* means that to increase output, labor and capital must always be increased in the same ratio. In the production of taxi services, for example, each hour of taxi (machine) use must be accompanied by an hour of driver (labor) use. Adding an hour of driver time without adding an hour of vehicle time will not add to output. The isoquants for a fixed-proportions production function are right angles along a ray from the origin. This is illustrated in Figure 7–6(a). Along the isoquant Q_1 the taxi trip miles per day are constant. Adding a labor hour does not increase output unless a machine hour is also added. The same holds for adding a machine (or vehicle) hour on the road. To move to a higher isoquant, each machine hour must be accompanied by a labor hour.

An isoquant with a constant marginal rate of technical substitution is illustrated in Figure 7–6(b). The slope of the isoquant drawn is -1. Along that isoquant, an hour of capital will always substitute for an hour of labor without changing output. This means the two inputs are perfect substitutes for each other. Constant marginal rates of technical substitution of one input for another imply

FIGURE 7–6 Isoquants for Fixed-Proportions and Perfect Substitution Production Functions

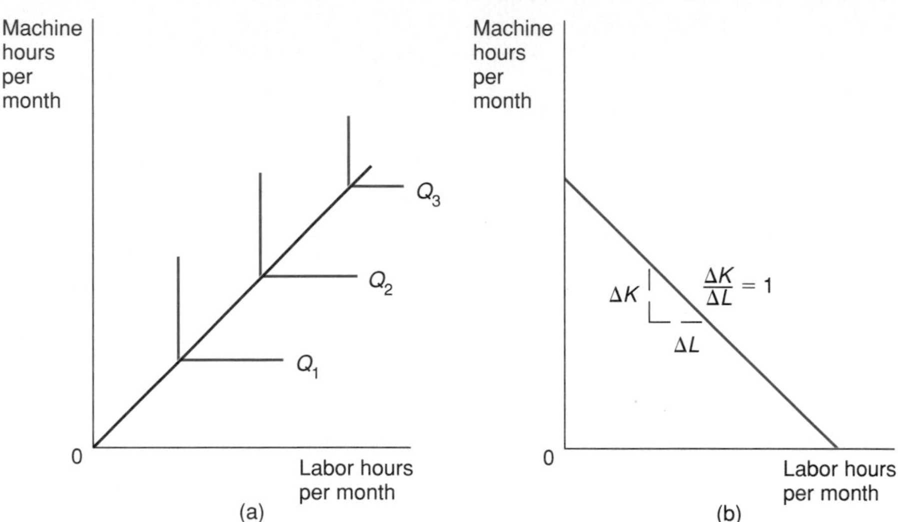

Adding machine hours without increasing labor hours by the same amount cannot increase output for the isoquants illustrated in (a). This is a fixed-proportions production function. Perfect substitution between two inputs is illustrated in (b). The marginal rate of technical substitution between labor and capital is constant. In this case one unit of capital can always replace one unit of labor without any change in production.

there is no complementarity at all between the inputs. Economists generally argue that inputs used together complement each other and that implies diminishing marginal rates of technical substitution.

The curvature of the isoquant is an indication of the ease with which one input can be substituted for another. When isoquants are close to L-shaped, so that they look almost like right angles, there is little opportunity to substitute one input for the other. On the other hand, when they look almost like downward-sloping straight lines, the opportunities for substitution are ample.

How Changes in Technology Can Affect Isoquants

As was pointed out at the beginning of this chapter, improvements in technology make inputs more productive. Improved technology causes shifts in isoquants corresponding to various output levels.

Figure 7–7 shows how the introduction of a new technology causes a single isoquant to shift inward. The isoquant labeled Q_1 shows alternative combinations of labor and capital that can be used to produce $Q_1 = 100$ units of output under the initial technology. The isoquant labeled $Q_1' = 100$ shows alternative combinations of labor and capital that can be used to produce the *same 100 units of output* under

FIGURE 7–7 Impact of Improved Technology

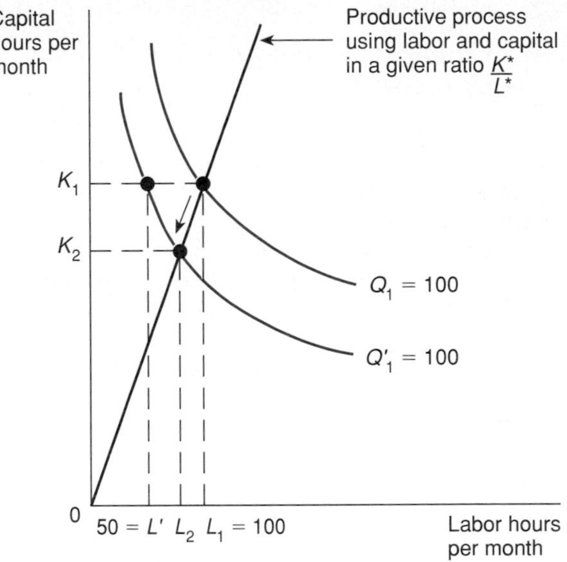

The application of improved technology causes an inward shift of any given isoquant. This means that along any ray corresponding to a given capital-labor ratio, less input will be required to produce Q_1 = 100 units of output.

an improved technology. The isoquant Q_1' lies closer to the origin than does the initial isoquant. The inward shift of the isoquant signifies that for any productive process corresponding to a given ratio of capital to labor, K^*/L^*, less of *both* labor and capital will be required to produce 100 units of output after the improvement in technology.

Improvement in technology occurs when old equipment and structures are replaced with new capital embodying more advanced technology. However, improvement in technology can also be embodied in improved managerial techniques that reflect new knowledge about the productive process and in workers who acquire new skills and new technical knowledge either through a greater amount of formal education or through on-the-job training and experience.

Improved training and knowledge on the part of workers along with improved equipment and structures have in fact reduced the physical quality of the inputs required to produce any given quantity of output over time. Advances in technology are vital to improvements in the well-being of a nation's citizens. Assume that technology improves, that there is no change in the price of labor or capital, and that firms do not change the ratio of capital to labor in production in response to the improvement in technology. Under these circumstances the 100 units of output in Figure 7–7 can now be produced with $K_2 < K_1$ units of capital and $L_2 < L_1$ units of labor.

MODERN MICROECONOMICS IN ACTION: INTERNATIONAL REPORT

Productivity Gains and International Competitiveness of U.S. Businesses

Based on 1990 output, General Motors employed 5 workers per car and Chrysler employed 4.4 workers per car in that year. During the same year the ratio of workers to cars produced was only 3.4 for Ford. Ford was the most efficient U.S. automobile producer in the early 1990s. But at that time the average Japanese automobile manufacturer, with its highly automated plants, produced cars with even less labor per unit than was used by Ford. Partly because of the smaller amount of labor required per car, Japanese cars cost $500 to $600 less per unit to produce than did similar American models.*

The high number of workers employed per car produced by General Motors in 1990 implied that the average product of the company's labor was low. When you get less from the labor you use than your competitors do and you pay about the same wages, you are going to be a high-cost producer. In today's global economy high-cost producers find it hard to compete in international markets. GM was forced to eliminate 40,000 clerical and professional jobs in the 1980s because of its declining market share. In late 1991, in an effort to make the company a leaner outfit with more productive labor, GM announced a massive downsizing that involved closing plants and laying off thousands of production workers.

Like quality, productivity has become an important buzzword for U.S. businesses of the 1990s. Fortunately, there is good news on the productivity front: American workers in the manufacturing sector have been becoming more productive, and as a result the international competitiveness of U.S. businesses has been improving.

From 1979 to 1985 the average product of U.S. workers in manufacturing, measured by output per hour, rose at an average rate of 2.8 percent per year. From 1985 to 1990, however, it rose at an average annual rate of 3.5 percent. After 1985, when the rate of productivity increase rose in the United States, it fell in 10 other major industrial nations. The improved productivity performance of the United States has been coupled with lower average annual rates of increase of labor compensation than those of competing nations. All of this has contributed to lower costs per unit of output, which has made it easier for U.S. firms to compete in international markets by charging lower prices.

In 1991, many U.S. manufacturers were selling much more in export markets than they had in the past, shipping such items as steel to Korea and transistors and other electronic components to Japan. The more efficient U.S. manufacturers were also making inroads against imports in domestic markets, selling more domestically produced machine tools, electronic items, and cars than they had sold in the past. The United States was among the lowest-cost world producers of such items as plastics and chemicals. Improvements in productivity in the U.S. steel industry, which lost international market share in the 1980s, helped make the cost of producing steel cheaper in the United States than in Japan and Germany. The total quality management program at Motorola helped raise the productivity of its workers by eliminating defects and contributed to gains in sales volume. Motorola now sells half of its output abroad.

* See Paul Ingrassia, "Auto Industry in U.S. Is Sliding Relentlessly into Japanese Hands," *The Wall Street Journal,* February 16, 1990.

Do not confuse the impact of an improvement in technology with that of a change in productive technique. A change in productive technique involves the substitution of one input for another in response to a change in economic conditions, as shown in Figure 7–5. An improvement in technology allows *any given productive technique* represented by a given ratio of capital to labor to produce *a given output* with less of *both* inputs. Of course, changes in technology and changes in productive technique through input substitution sometimes occur simultaneously.

An improvement in technology contributes to an increase in the average product of labor. For example, suppose that after adopting the new technology, the firm uses K_1 machine hours in production. Under the old technology it would have required L_1 labor hours to produce 100 units of output when K_1 machine hours were used. Under the new technology the same 100 units of output can be produced with $L' < L_1$ units of labor when K_1 machine hours are used. If $L_1 = 100$ and $L' = 50$ in Figure 7–7, then the improvement in technology increases the average product of labor from

$$100 \text{ units of output}/100 \text{ labor hours} = 1 \text{ unit of output per labor hour}$$

to

$$100 \text{ units of output}/50 \text{ labor hours} = 2 \text{ units of output per labor hour}$$

With input prices given, an improvement in technology contributes to a lowering of the costs of any given quantity of output by reducing the input use necessary to produce that output. Improvements in technology, other things being equal, therefore helps to lower the unit costs of products, which in turn results in lower prices for consumers.

Technological change also results in the availability of new products. For example, over the past 25 years improvements in technology have made possible personal computers, VCRs, compact discs, and a host of other modern miracles that would have astonished our ancestors!

Varying the Scale of Operations

Change in the scale of operations A change in the level of operation that occurs when an organization's use of all inputs is varied in the same proportion.

The long run is a period of production in which all inputs are variable. In the long run, managers can increase production by varying all inputs. They can, for example, double all of the capital, labor, and materials they use. A **change in the scale of operations** occurs when an organization's use of all inputs is varied in the *same* proportion. For example, a furniture factory would be viewed as doubling the scale of its operations if it doubled the number of machines and labor hours used and the amount of floor space and materials used.

The relationship between output and inputs used in the long run can now be examined. Assume that only two inputs are used and that the proportion of one input to the other is constant as production expands in the long run. This means that production is increased by increasing input use along a ray from the origin, as illustrated in Figure 7–8.

In the long run, no "laws" govern the relationship between inputs and outputs. Only observation and measurement can determine the variation in output as inputs are increased or decreased in the same proportion.

There are three possibilities:

1. Increasing returns to scale
2. Constant returns to scale.
3. Decreasing returns to scale.

FIGURE 7–8 **Increasing Returns to Scale**

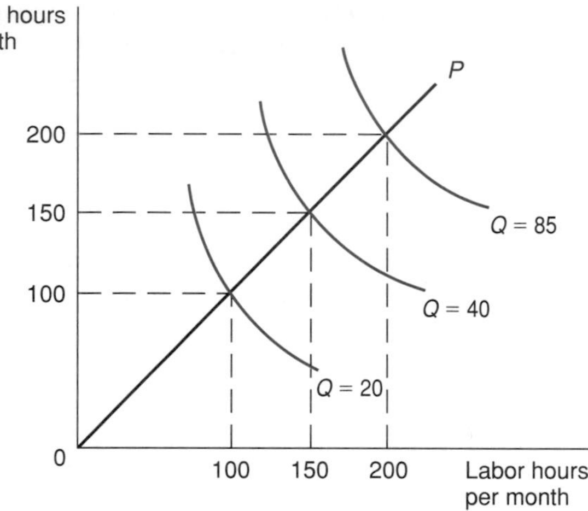

When increasing returns to scale prevail, doubling all inputs more than doubles output.

Along the ray *OP* in Figure 7–8, labor and capital are always used in a 1:1 ratio. The analysis could be carried out for any possible ratio of capital to labor. The data for the graph are from Table 7–1. Start out with 100 machine hours and 100 labor hours per month. Output from that amount of input will be 20 chairs. If both machine hours and labor hours are doubled, a monthly output of 85 chairs can be produced.[11] When output increases by a proportion that exceeds the proportion by which all inputs increase, **increasing returns to scale** prevail. Here inputs were doubled and output more than doubled. Another way to look at this is to say that when increasing returns prevail, doubling output, in this case from 20 to 40 chairs per month, requires that input use less than double. As shown in Figure 7–8, a 50 percent increase in labor and machine hours suffices to double output in this case.

Increasing returns to scale These prevail when output increases by a proportion that exceeds the proportion by which all inputs increase.

Increasing returns to scale can be the result of increases in the productivity of inputs caused by increased specialization and division of labor as the scale of operations increases. This is quite common, particularly as a firm initially expands production. With only one worker and one machine, there is little opportunity to allocate specialized tasks to labor. With two workers and two machines, one worker can specialize in machine operations and the other can specialize in hand-finishing operations. A combination of three workers and three machines offers still greater opportunities for division of labor and specialization. When workers specialize in specific tasks, their average product tends to rise.

Another cause of increasing returns to scale is that a larger scale of operations often does not require a proportionate increase in all inputs. For example, to double grazing area, a farmer does not have to double the amount of fencing. This

[11] Once again, using only two inputs is a simplification. Assume that the amount of materials is lumped together with labor and that each hour of labor always uses the same amounts of materials.

FIGURE 7–9 **Constant Returns to Scale**

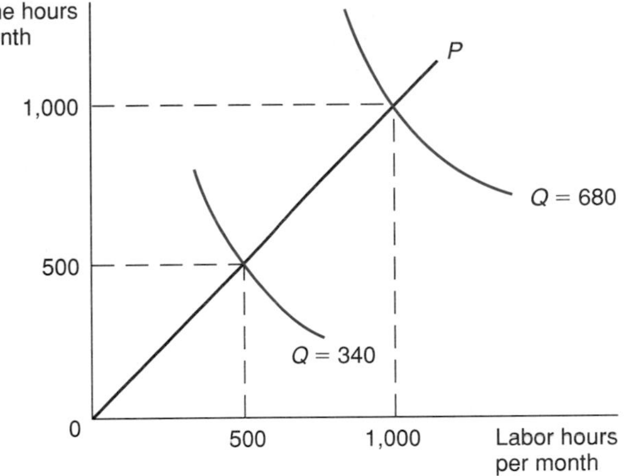

Constant returns to scale imply that doubling inputs will double output.

is a matter of simple arithmetic. When the area of a rectangle doubles, its perimeter increases by a factor of less than 2. Similarly, doubling the amount of cylindrical equipment (such as pipes and smokestacks) and spherical equipment (such as storage tanks) requires less than twice the amount of metal.

Constant returns to scale These prevail when output increases by the same proportion in which inputs increase.

Constant returns to scale prevail when output increases by the same proportion in which inputs increase. For example, a doubling of inputs would exactly double output under these circumstances. This is shown in Figure 7–9. Both labor and capital are doubled, from 500 hours to 1,000 hours per month, and output increases from 340 to 680 chairs per month.

Economies of scale Increases in input productivities that result from division of labor and savings in materials when a factory increases the scale of its operations.

Economies of scale are the increases in input productivities that result from division of labor and savings in materials when a factory increases the scale of its operations. After a while, the factory is likely to exhaust the possibilities for achieving economies of scale. As economies of scale are exhausted, a phase of constant returns to scale may set in for an operation. Identical factories at different locations could then be built to produce chairs. Each of the factories would produce the same output. It follows that doubling all inputs by building a new factory of the same size as the existing one would exactly double output.

Decreasing returns to scale These prevail when output increases by a proportion that falls short of the proportion in which inputs are increased.

A final possibility is **decreasing returns to scale.** When these prevail, output increases by a proportion that falls short of the proportion in which inputs are increased. For example, if inputs are doubled from 1,000 labor and machine hours to 2,000 labor and machine hours per month and output increases from 680 to 1,200 chairs per month, decreasing returns to scale prevail. Doubling output to 1,360 chairs per month requires more than the doubling of inputs, as shown in Figure 7–10.

Decreasing returns to scale set in when the economies of scale are more than offset by the difficulties and added input requirements of managing an organization as it becomes bigger. Difficulties in coordinating the operations of many

FIGURE 7–10 Decreasing Returns to Scale

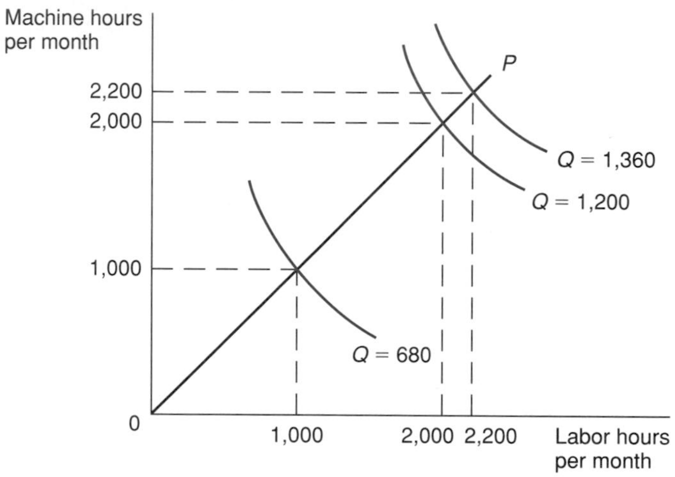

When decreasing returns to scale prevail, inputs have to more than double to double production.

factories and problems in communicating with employees could contribute to decreasing returns to scale. So too could the more than proportionate increases in managerial inputs that may be required to expand output when an organization becomes very large.

The returns to scale that are actually achievable depend on the production function. Most enterprises experience at least an initial stage of increasing returns to scale as they expand their operations. The extent to which increasing returns to scale prevail varies considerably from enterprise to enterprise. It is likely to be quite lengthy for heavy industrial enterprises such as electric power generation, automobile production, and chemical production. It can be quickly exhausted for such enterprises as home building and appliance repair. The determination of actual returns to scale requires empirical studies of particular industries.

Using Estimated Production Functions to Measure Returns to Scale

Using data on input use and output over time among firms producing a given good or service, economists have been able to estimate actual production functions. Statistical techniques are employed to analyze the data. One of the many problems involved in obtaining such estimates is measuring inputs. In reality, inputs are not homogeneous. Labor hours vary greatly in quality. Similarly, a machine hour of a complex computer cannot be added together with a machine hour of an eggbeater and give a meaningful measure of the quantity of capital input. Most of the data used to estimate production functions are based on broad aggregate measures of labor, capital, material, and land inputs. The researcher must assume that the output observed is the maximum output possible from any given input combination.

Empirical studies of production are usually based on a theoretical, or assumed, production function. Actual data are then used to test whether production in a particular industry or activity conforms to the assumed production relations. A commonly used production function is the **Cobb-Douglas production function,** which has the following form:

Cobb-Douglas production function A production function described by an equation that assumes that output varies by a constant multiplied by each input used raised to an exponential power between zero and 1.

$$Q = BL^{a1} K^{a2} M^{a3} \quad \textbf{(7–7)}$$

where Q is output, L is a measure of labor input, K is a measure of capital input, and M is a measure of the raw materials used in production. The B and the a exponents in the equation are called *coefficients of production.* The coefficients measure the percentage by which output will increase for each 1 percent increase in the use of the input, other things being equal. The data in Table 7–3 show estimated coefficients of production for selected industries. For example, the $a1$ coefficient for the food industry is 0.72. This implies that a 1 percent increase in the amount of labor used in food production will increase food output by 0.72 percent, assuming that capital and all other inputs are held fixed.

Statistical methods are used to estimate these coefficients for particular industries. Each exponent is less than 1. Convex isoquants can be derived from the function. The Cobb-Douglas production function implies declining marginal products for all inputs and also implies that good opportunities exist to substitute inputs in production without gaining or losing output.[12]

It can be shown that the production function implies constant returns to scale if the sum of the three exponents equals 1. If their sum is greater than 1, increasing returns to scale prevail. If their sum is less than 1, decreasing returns to scale prevail. To see this, assume that all inputs are increased by a factor of 2 and see what happens to output by substituting $2L$, $2K$, and $2M$ for L, K, and M in the original function:

$$\begin{aligned} Q_2 &= B(2L)^{a1}(2K)^{a2}(2M)^{a3} \\ &= B(2^{a1})L^{a1}(2^{a2})K^{a2}(2^{a3})M^{a3} \quad \textbf{(7–7)} \\ &= 2^{a1 + a2 + a3}[BL^{a1}K^{a2}M^{a3}] \end{aligned}$$

If $a1 + a2 + a3 = 1$, it follows that

$$Q_2 = 2Q_1 \quad \textbf{(7–8)}$$

Similarly, if the sum of the a exponents exceeds 1, then Q_2 will be more than twice Q_1, and vice versa because the sum is less than 1.

Estimates of Cobb-Douglas production functions are reported in Table 7–3. Most of the studies referred to in Table 7–3 used data collected from many firms in a given industry in a given year to estimate the coefficients of the production

---

[12] For an analysis of the mathematical properties of the production function, see James M. Henderson and Richard E. Quandt, *Microeconomic Theory: A Mathematical Approach,* 3rd ed. (New York: McGraw-Hill, 1980), pp. 105–14.

You can take the first derivative to Equation 7–7 with respect to each input to calculate marginal products. For example, the marginal product of labor is

$$\partial Q/\partial L = a1BL^{(a1 - 1)}K^{a2}M^{a3}$$

Because $a1 < 1$, the exponent for the L variable in the above equation will be negative. This means that as L increases, its marginal product falls.

TABLE 7–3 Estimated Exponent Coefficients for Cobb-Douglas Production Functions

Industry and Nation	*Labor (a1)*	*Capital (a2)*	*Materials (a3)*	*a1 + a2 + a3*
Foods (U.S.)*	0.72	0.35	—	1.07
Metals and machines (U.S.)*	0.71	0.26	—	0.97
Cotton (India)†	0.92	0.12	—	1.04
Jute (India)†	0.84	0.14	—	0.98
Coal (U.K.)‡	0.51	0.49	—	1.00
Crops (U.S., Montana)§	0.04	0.50	.50 ‖	1.12
Crops (U.S., Iowa)¶	0.09	0.15	.97 ‖	1.21
Livestock (U.S., Montana)¶	0.08	0.94	—	1.02

* M. Bronfenbrenner and P. A. Douglas, "Cross Section Studies in the Cobb-Douglas Function," *Journal of Political Economy* 47 (1939), pp. 761–85.

† V. N. Murti and V. K. Sastry, "Production Functions for Indian Industry," *Econometrica* 25 (1957), pp. 205–21.

‡ C. E. V. Leser, "Production Functions and British Coal Mining," *Econometrica* 23 (1955), pp. 442–46.

§ E. O. Heady and J. L. Dillon, *Agricultural Production Functions* (Ames: Iowa State University Press, 1961).

‖ Coefficient is for land input. All of these studies are reviewed in A. A. Walters, "Production and Cost Functions: An Econometric Survey," *Econometrica* 31, nos. 1–2 (January–April 1963), pp. 1–66.

¶ E. O. Heady, "Marginal Resource Productivity and Imputation of Shares for a Sample of Rented Farms," *Journal of Political Economy* 63 (1957), pp. 249–68.

function. The data fit the assumed production function well in the reported cases, implying that isoquants exhibit the diminishing marginal rates of technical substitution implied by the Cobb-Douglas function. Increasing returns to scale were found in crop production in Iowa in the early 1960s. Constant returns to scale or slightly decreasing returns to scale seem to prevail in many production functions because the sum of the exponents is close to 1.[13]

CONCEPT REVIEW

1. At current levels of use a factory manager estimates that the marginal product of labor is 5 units of output per month and that the marginal product of capital is 10 units per month. Calculate the marginal rate of technical substitution of labor for capital.
2. Why does the marginal rate of technical substitution of labor for capital decline as labor is substituted for capital?
3. If a firm expects increasing returns to scale when it expands, what will happen to output if the firm doubles all of the inputs used?

[13] These production functions, along with a discussion of some of the statistical problems of estimating their coefficients, are discussed in A. A. Walters, "Production and Cost Functions," *Econometrica* 31, nos. 1–2 (January–April 1963), pp. 1–66.

SUMMARY

1. Production transforms inputs into outputs, making the desired goods and services available.
2. A production function gives the maximum output obtainable from any given combination of inputs under current technology.
3. The short run is a period of production during which some inputs cannot be varied. Output can be increased in the short run by varying the proportions in which inputs are used. A total product curve shows how output varies when the proportion of variable inputs to fixed inputs is increased. A total product curve can be derived from an isoquant map.
4. The average product of a variable input measures output obtainable per unit of given quantities of the variable input used in combination with other fixed inputs. The average product of labor measures output per labor hour and indicates the productivity of labor. The marginal product of labor is the change in output attributed to a change in labor input.
5. The law of diminishing marginal returns describes the way output is hypothesized to vary with increased use of a variable input along with fixed inputs. According to the law, the marginal product of a variable input will eventually decline as the proportion of the variable input to the fixed input increases. The law implies that there is a limit to the amount of output that can be produced in a productive facility of given size. The law also implies that the average product of the variable input will eventually decline.
6. In the short run, three stages of production can be delineated. In the first stage the proportion of the variable input to the fixed input is too low relative to the proportions for which the plant was designed. In the third stage this proportion is too high. In the second stage the proportions are such that the average product of labor is declining but the marginal product is always positive.
7. An isoquant gives all the combinations of inputs that can produce a given output. Isoquants show that there is more than one way to produce any given output. The curvature of isoquants provides information on the ease with which one input can be substituted for another while the same output is produced.
8. A production function can be graphically depicted with an isoquant map.
9. The marginal rate of technical substitution of input X for input Y is the amount of input Y that a 1-unit increase in input X can replace without resulting in an increase or decrease in production. Because two inputs, such as labor and capital, are seldom perfect substitutes for each other, the marginal rate of technical substitution of labor for capital declines as labor is substituted for capital. Increasing numbers of machine hours are needed to replace each lost labor hour as labor hours are reduced.
10. The long run is the period of production in which all inputs are variable. The returns to expanding the scale of operations can be increasing, constant, or decreasing. The extent of increasing returns to scale depends on the opportunities for specialization of labor and economization on certain inputs as the firm expands.

IMPORTANT CONCEPTS

production
inputs
technology
production function
short run
long run
production grid
total product of a variable input
average product of a variable input
marginal product of a variable input
law of diminishing marginal returns
point of diminishing marginal returns
isoquant
isoquant map
marginal rate of technical substitution of labor for capital
change in the scale of operations
increasing returns to scale
constant returns to scale
economies of scale
decreasing returns to scale
Cobb-Douglas production function

Questions for Review

1. What relationship is defined by a production function? In what sense is waste of resources avoided by achieving technological efficiency?
2. If the average product of labor is 25 and the amount of labor employed is 100, what is the total product of labor?
3. Explain why the law of diminishing marginal returns implies that the average product of a variable input used in combination with fixed inputs will rise initially, reach a maximum, and then begin to fall.
4. A mortgage loan company can negotiate and process more loans each month by hiring additional personnel. All other inputs (vehicles, computers, office space) necessary to process loan applications are fixed. If the marginal product of a labor hour is currently 0.5 of a loan and the average product of labor is 0.7 of a loan, what will happen to the average product of labor if more personnel are hired?
5. Explain why isoquants for fixed-proportions production functions are L-shaped curves.
6. Do the positions of the average, marginal, and total product of labor curves depend on the amount of capital the firm employs? If so, how?
7. A firm has a given amount of space to produce computers. Some of the space is devoted to assembling computers, and the remaining space is devoted to building computer components. Suppose the marginal product of space used to build components exceeds the marginal product of space used to assemble computers. What can the firm do to increase its output of computers over a period?
8. Suppose that when a firm increases its use of capital from 120 to 150 and its use of labor from 500 to 625, its output increases from 200 to 220. Do constant, increasing, or decreasing returns to scale prevail in this case?
9. Show how the introduction of improved technology affects an isoquant map.
10. What factors contribute to increasing returns to scale in the long run? What factors contribute to decreasing returns to scale?

Problems

1. Suppose that the output associated with each 100 hours of machine use in the chair factory doubles. Use the data in Table 7–1 to compute a new production grid for the factory. Plot the isoquants for outputs of 420 and 540 chairs per month. Use the new data to calculate the total product of labor used in the short run in combination with 300 machine hours. Calculate the average product of labor and the marginal product of labor from the total product.
2. Show that if the marginal product of labor hours is negative and all other inputs are positive, isoquants drawn between labor and another input will be positively sloped. Show that if both labor and capital have negative marginal products, isoquants between these two inputs will be negatively sloped but nonconvex. Explain why the production function does not include either positively sloped or nonconvex portions of isoquants.
3. The production function for a small shop that frames pictures is

$$Q = 5L^{1/2}K^{1/2}$$

where Q is the number of pictures framed per day, L is labor hours, and K is machine hours.

Suppose that nine labor hours and nine machine hours are used each day. What is the maximum number of pictures that can be framed per day? Calculate the marginal product of a 10th hour of labor that day. Calculate the average product of labor when nine labor hours are used each day with nine machine hours. Suppose that the shop doubles the amounts of both labor and machine hours used per day. Calculate the increase in output. Comment on the returns to scale in this operation.
4. A firm expands in the long run by doubling both capital and labor used. Show that if constant returns to scale prevail, the average product of

both labor and capital is always the same no matter how much of them is used, provided that they are always used in the same proportion.

5.

Combination	*Output*	*Labor*	*Capital*
A	200	30	80
B	350	45	120
C	700	90	240
D	750	99	264

The above table gives labor, capital, and output isoquant data for the production of a particular good. Do the following with regard to this case:

a. Calculate the percentage changes in labor and capital use in moving from combination *A* to *B*, *B* to *C*, and *C* to *D*.

b. Identify whether increasing, decreasing, or constant returns to scale exist in moving from combination *A* to *B*, *B* to *C*, and *C* to *D*.

6. The accompanying diagram depicts the average product of labor curve for a soft-drink packaging process. Answer the following questions based on this diagram:

a. If the average product of labor is maximized at $L = 10$, does this imply that the total product of labor is maximized at $L = 10$?

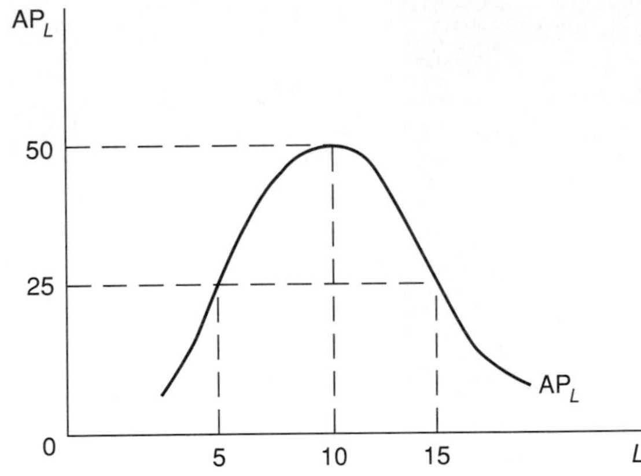

b. If $AP_L = 40$ when $L = 8$ and the marginal product of the ninth unit of labor is 60, what is the total product when $L = 9$?

c. If the marginal product is negative for the 15th unit of labor, does this imply that the average product of labor is negative when $L = 15$?

d. What is the total product when the average product of labor is 25?

e. For what level of labor use are the average and marginal product of labor the same?

8

Cost and Output

In 1990 the cost of producing a new automobile in an American-owned factory averaged $500 to $600 more than the cost of producing a similar automobile in a Japanese-owned factory.[1] In 1991 the average cost of producing a ton of steel was $535 in the United States, $614 in Japan, and $542 in Germany.[2] What accounts for these variations in unit costs of production?

In the modern global economy the international competitiveness of industries often hinges on their cost advantages. An industry that does not adopt the latest technological or managerial methods for increasing worker productivity can soon lose sales to foreign competitors. An industry whose wage increases outpace those of foreign competitors can soon find that its products are overpriced compared to the products of those competitors.

Lagging productivity gains and higher than average wage increases in the U.S. automobile industry in the 1970s and early 1980s helped cause such firms as General Motors to lose massive amounts of market share. On the other hand, gains in productivity in the U.S. steel industry helped turn a sick industry of the 1970s and early 1980s into an aggressive international competitor. As the international report in Chapter 7 showed, in recent years strong productivity gains in U.S. manufacturing have contributed to lower unit costs of production and higher exports of many U.S. industries.

The international markets of the 1990s are likely to be even more competitive than those of the past as the share of exports and imports in world output continues to grow. In 1992 economic integration in Europe reduced regulations and other government impediments that had prevented businesses there from minimizing their production costs. Many European firms will become much stronger competitors on the world market as we approach the 21st century.

Both production and cost considerations affect the decisions of business firms to supply goods and services in markets. The cost of making goods available naturally affects the profitability of doing so. A necessary prerequisite to the theory of supply is an analysis of the way cost is likely to vary with output.

The analysis of production in the previous chapter has a direct bearing on cost. The properties of the production function affect the relationship between output and cost. Now we can explore the relationship between cost and output.

---

[1] See Paul Ingrassia, "Auto Industry in U.S. Is Sliding Relentlessly into Japanese Hands," *The Wall Street Journal*, February 16, 1990.

[2] See Sylvia Nasar, "Boom in Manufactured Exports Provides Hope for U.S. Economy," *The New York Times*, April 4, 1991.

We will isolate the determinants of costs, and we will investigate the impact of changes in input prices, labor productivity, and improved technology on costs per unit of output. The way cost varies with output influences the relationship between price and the quantities supplied by business firms.

From the economist's viewpoint, cost represents the value of all forgone alternative uses of materials and input services. An appropriate starting point in the analysis of cost is a discussion of how it is measured. Once the problems of accurately measuring costs have been resolved, the relationship between cost and output can be studied. In this chapter both short-run and long-run cost curves are derived. The following two chapters draw on the analysis of cost in this chapter. Understanding how cost varies with output is the key to understanding supply by profit-maximizing firms.

Measuring Cost: Economic Cost versus Accounting Cost

Opportunity cost of using inputs The value of those inputs in their next best use.

The opportunity cost of any decision is the next best alternative that is forgone. The concept of opportunity cost, introduced in Chapter 1, is naturally relevant to measuring the cost of a business enterprise. The **opportunity cost of using inputs** is the value of those inputs in their next best use. The opportunity cost of the labor hours the owner of a business spends in running it might be the earnings the owner forgoes by not working for someone else or the value the owner places on the leisure time given up—whichever is higher.

The opportunity cost of tying up funds in a business enterprise is the highest return that could have been earned on that money had it been invested elsewhere. For example, running a furniture manufacturing business requires materials, machines, and other capital equipment. Suppose a person uses her own funds instead of borrowing to acquire these assets. The opportunity cost of funds used in this way is the return that could have been earned by investing that sum in the next best alternative. If the next best alternative is buying the stock of another firm, the dividends and other income forgone are the opportunity cost of the funds tied up in the furniture manufacturing business.

Economic cost The opportunity cost of operating a business.

Costs as measured by accountants do not include the opportunity cost of inputs supplied by a firm's owners. Accounting cost provides valuable information. Business managers are, however, aware of its shortcomings and base their decisions on opportunity cost. Those who own a business enterprise always compare the desirability of remaining in that enterprise with what they forgo by doing so. Economists therefore presume that decisions made by business firms are always based on opportunity cost. The opportunity cost of operating a business is called the **economic cost,** to distinguish it from accounting cost.

Implicit costs The value of input services that are used in production but not purchased in a market.

Calculating Economic Cost: An Example

Accounting costs diverge from economic costs because they do not include the value of the services of inputs owned by the business firm. **Implicit costs** are the value of input services that are used in production but are not purchased. Accounting costs include only explicit costs, representing payments for purchased input services. Examples of implicit costs are the opportunity costs of owner-operators' labor services and of other nonpurchased inputs, including land and capital, that owners employ in their operations. To obtain the economic costs of operating a business, a dollar value must be imputed to nonpurchased inputs so that the opportunity costs can be accurately measured by adding the implicit costs to the accounting costs.

An example will make the distinction between economic cost and accounting cost clearer. Suppose a farmer owns his own farm and devotes 40 hours a week to farming his 200 acres of land. At the end of the year his accountant provides information on the costs of operating the farm.

The information supplied by the accountant is summarized in Table 8–1. The farmer has three full-time workers to whom he has paid $40,000 in wages during the year. He has also borrowed money from the bank to finance his acquisition of capital equipment, fertilizer, and seed. He incurs total interest payments of $10,000 per year. The original cost of his capital equipment (for example, tractors, sheds, barns, pickup trucks, harvesting equipment, and plows) was $100,000. Its current market value is estimated to be $80,000.

In computing the annual cost of this equipment, the accountant spreads the original purchase price over a number of years. This accounting practice is called *depreciation*. The accountant assumes that the capital equipment will last five years before it has to be replaced. He therefore takes one fifth of its value as depreciation. This is $20,000.[3]

In measuring cost, the accountant also includes all other cash outlays, such as those for insurance, materials, gasoline, work clothing, and maintenance. These extra costs as measured by the accountant amount to $20,000. The total accounting costs are therefore $90,000, as shown in Table 8–1.

The farmer appreciates the information supplied by the accountant. He is, however, more concerned with the opportunity cost of running the farm than with the accounting cost. To find the opportunity cost of running the farm, the farmer estimates implicit costs and adds them to the explicit costs measured by the accountant. His next best alternative to running the farm is working as a farm manager for someone else. He figures that he could earn $30,000 per year managing someone else's farm. He includes this as his implicit wage. He must also impute a wage to his wife, who works 20 hours a week on the farm. His wife's next best alternative for these 20 hours per week would pay $10,000 annually. This is his wife's implicit wage.

[3] To actually reflect the rate at which equipment wears out, accounting depreciation should each year reflect the rate at which equipment wears out physically. Because it is difficult to accurately predict the rate of physical depreciation, the usual accounting procedure is to take a fixed percentage of the purchase price equipment as depreciation each year.

When the price of replacing equipment exceeds the original acquisition cost on which the depreciation calculation is based, the funds set aside for replacement on the basis of the depreciation calculation will be insufficient to replace the equipment. In periods of inflation, therefore, depreciation will understate the true cost of replacing capital.

TABLE 8–1 **Accounting Cost versus Economic Cost: An Example**

Item	*Accounting Cost*	*Economic Cost*
Wages and salaries	$40,000	$ 40,000
Interest paid	10,000	10,000
Depreciation (one fifth of the value of capital equipment)	20,000	20,000
Miscellaneous (materials, seed, fertilizer, fuel, etc.)	20,000	20,000
Implicit wage of owner	0	30,000
Implicit wage of owner's wife	0	10,000
Implicit rent	0	40,000
Implicit interest of owner's equity	0	3,000
Total	$90,000	$173,000

The farmer also forgoes the opportunity of renting the land to someone else when he farms it himself. If the annual market rent of his land is $200 per acre, then he forgoes $40,000 per year in rent payments on his 200 acres by remaining in farming. This is the opportunity cost of using the land in farming and represents the imputed rent.

Finally, the market value of the farmer's equipment is $80,000. The farmer owes the bank $50,000. If the farmer were to sell his equipment and pay off his bank loans, he would have $30,000 cash left over. By remaining in farming, he forgoes the opportunity of investing these funds elsewhere. If he could earn 10 percent on them in his next best investment, their opportunity cost is $3,000 per year. This $3,000 is included in costs as implicit interest. It must be added to the depreciation expense calculated by the accountant to get the full cost of capital.[4]

Adding all implicit costs to those figured by the accountant gives the total opportunity cost, or economic cost, of the farmer's annual operations. As shown in Table 8–1, the total economic costs for the year are $173,000, which is almost double the amount of the accounting costs.

The extent to which economic costs diverge from accounting costs varies with the amounts and kinds of inputs supplied to the firm by its owners. Typically, large corporations pay all employees wages, even if those employees are also shareholders. Thus it is rare to have implicit wages in corporations. However, corporations typically have considerable amounts of cash tied up in capital equipment and land. These costs are implicit interest and implicit rents.

[4] Alternatively, the cost of equipment could be measured as the annual rent equal to the sum of depreciation, explicit interest, and implicit interest. This rent measures the opportunity cost of choosing to use the equipment in the enterprise rather than rent it to someone else. That opportunity cost would reflect the hourly rental rate for the equipment multiplied by the number of hours' utilization over the year, assuming full-time use of the equipment.

Cost and Production

Cost function A function that describes the relationship between output and the minimum possible cost of producing that output.

The economic cost of producing a good depends on the amounts of the inputs used and on the prices of input services. When nonpurchased inputs are used by owner-operators, a price must be imputed to each unit used to measure cost accurately. A **cost function** describes the relationship between output produced and the minimum possible cost of producing that output. Technology and input prices are usually taken as given in specifying cost functions. A change in either input prices or technology will affect the minimum possible cost of producing a given amount of output.

Inefficient production implies that producers are not obtaining their output at the minimum possible cost. By changing input use, such producers could lower their cost without sacrificing output. Alternatively, it would be possible for an inefficient producer to obtain more output from a given input combination without incurring extra cost.

The cost function is related to the production function. The minimum cost at which any given output can be produced depends in part on the maximum output that can be produced with any given input combination.

Isocost Lines

Assume that labor and capital are the only two variable inputs used and that the prices of their services are P_L and P_K, respectively. The total cost, TC, of any amount of these two inputs used is

$$TC = P_L L + P_K K \tag{8–1}$$

FIGURE 8–1 Isocost Lines

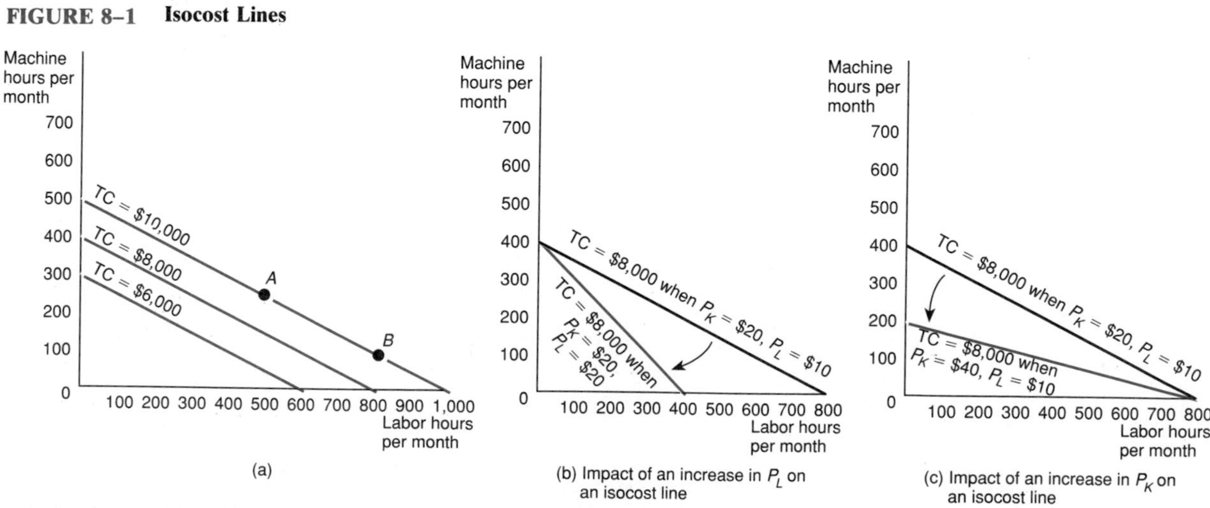

All points on an isocost line represent combinations of inputs of equal cost. A family of isocost lines is drawn in (a). As one moves farther away from the origin, more inputs are used and cost rises. The way changes in input prices affect the isocost lines is shown in (b) and (c).

where L is measured as labor hours and K is measured as machine hours. P_L is the hourly wage of labor, and P_K is the hourly rental rate for the machines.

Isocost line A line that gives all the combinations of labor and capital of equal total cost.

An **isocost line** gives all the combinations of labor and capital of equal total cost. Suppose, for example, that the price of labor services (wages) is $10 per hour, whereas the price of capital services (the machine rental rate) is $20 per hour. A monthly input combination consisting of 500 labor hours and 250 machine hours would therefore cost $10,000. This input combination lies on the same isocost line as 800 labor hours and 100 machine hours. These two input combinations are plotted as points A and B, respectively, in Figure 8–1(a). Any other monthly input combination costing $10,000 would lie on the isocost line drawn through points A and B.

Equation 8–1 defines a family of isocost lines for given prices of labor and capital. There is a different isocost line for each level of total cost. This is shown in Figure 8–1(a), where each line is labeled according to the cost of the input combinations lying on it.

When the price of labor is $10 per hour and the price of capital is $20 per hour, each machine hour given up frees $20. This can then be used to purchase two labor hours.[5] The slope of any isocost line in the family is $\Delta K/\Delta L$. The extra capital that can be purchased when an hour of labor is given up is P_L/P_K.

The ratio of the price of labor services to the price of capital services is equal to the slope of the isocost lines multiplied by -1. To see why this is so, remember that TC is constant on a given isocost line. When capital use is reduced by an amount ΔK, the effect is to reduce total cost $-P_K\Delta K$. To keep total cost constant, thereby remaining on the same isocost line outlays on extra labor hours, $P_L\Delta L$ must equal the reduction in outlays for capital. Therefore, along a given isocost line

$$P_L\Delta L = -P_K\Delta K$$

It follows that

$$-(\Delta K/\Delta L) = (P_L/P_K) \qquad \textbf{(8–2)}$$

You can also see this by solving Equation 8–1 for K:

$$K = -(P_L/P_K)L + \text{TC}/P_K \qquad \textbf{(8–3)}$$

In this case

$$\begin{aligned} P_L/P_K &= \$10/\$20 \\ &= 1/2 \end{aligned}$$

The slope of the isocost line is therefore $-1/2$.

A change in the price of either labor or capital can change the slope of a whole family of isocost lines. For example, an increase in the price of labor given the price of capital will make each of the isocost lines in the family steeper. Figure

[5] This assumes that as many or as few machine hours as desired can be rented per month. Often this is not the case. If machine time must be purchased in lumps of more than one hour, flexibility in moving from one input combination to another is limited.

8–1(b) shows how an increase in the price of labor relative to the price of capital will make any one isocost line in a family steeper. Figure 8–1(c) shows that an increase in the price of capital given the price of labor will make any one isocost line in a family flatter. When the price of capital increases relative to the price of labor, all isocost lines in a family become flatter.

The Minimum Cost Input Combination for a Given Output

Figure 8–2 reproduces one of the isoquants for the chair factory used as an example in the previous chapter. The family of isocost lines corresponding to wages of $10 per hour and an hourly machine rental rate of $20 per hour is superimposed on the same set of axes as that used for the isoquant.

What input combination will the chair producer choose to get to a point on the cost function for chairs? Remember that a cost function gives a relationship between output and the *minimum possible cost of producing that output*. The chair producer must be sure to use the input combination of labor and capital that produces each output at minimum possible cost. Suppose that the owner of the factory decides to produce 210 chairs per month. Look at the method of production used at point *M*1 on the isoquant. At that point 200 labor hours and 400 machine hours are used. Using that method, the cost of production is $10,000 per month.

FIGURE 8–2 Minimizing the Cost of Producing a Given Output

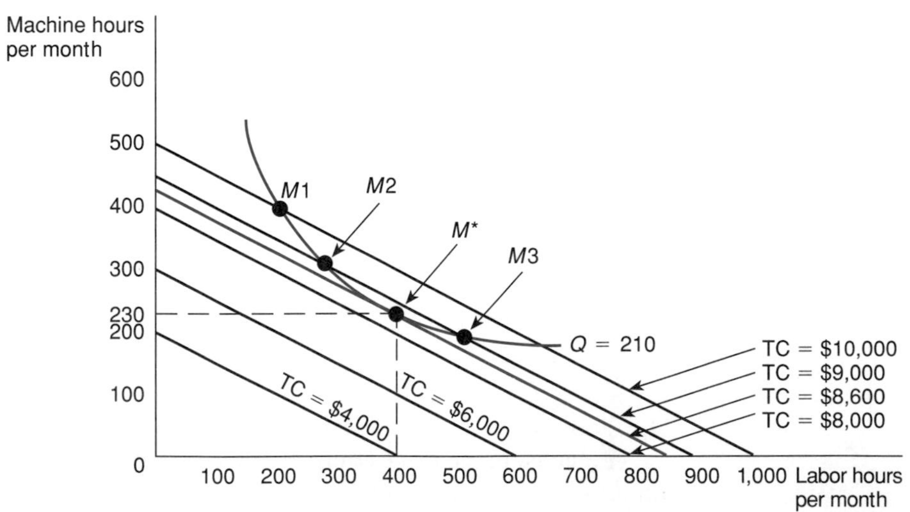

The minimum cost of producing 210 chairs per month occurs at the input combination corresponding to point *M**, where the isoquant is just tangent to an isocost line. At that point the cost of production is $8,600 per month. The cost of production for the same output is $10,000 per month at point *M*1 and $9,000 per month at points *M*2 and *M*3.

Method $M2$ uses 300 labor hours and 300 machine hours and costs $9,000 per month. Method $M3$ uses 500 labor hours and 200 machine hours and also costs $9,000 per month. The methods represented by $M2$ and $M3$ therefore lie on the same isocost line. The minimum possible cost of producing 210 chairs per month occurs at point M^*, where the isoquant is just tangent to an isocost line. At that point 400 labor hours and 230 machine hours per month are used and the cost of production is $8,600 per month. The equilibrium productive method is therefore the input combination corresponding to point M^*.

The condition for minimum cost production of a given output is that the slope of the isoquant for any two variable inputs be equal to the slope of the isocost lines for those inputs.[6] The slope of the isoquant is the marginal rate of technical substitution of labor for capital multiplied by -1. The slope of the budget line is the ratio of the price of labor to the price of capital multiplied by -1. It follows that in equilibrium

$$\text{MRTS}_{LK} = P_L/P_K \tag{8–4}$$

Because the marginal rate of technical substitution can also be written as the ratio of the marginal product of labor to the marginal product of capital (see Chapter 6 for proof),

$$\text{MP}_L/\text{MP}_K = P_L/P_K \tag{8–5}$$

Equation 8–5 defines the condition for producing any given output at the minimum possible cost. A firm must choose its input combinations for any output it chooses to satisfy that condition if it wishes to produce according to its cost function.[7]

---

[6] This condition also gives the maximum output attainable for any given fixed outlay per month. There is a certain similarity between this analysis and indifference curve analysis for consumers. However, consumers were assumed to have a fixed budget. Here the firm generates the funds to pay for inputs from the sale of output.

[7] The same result can be obtained using calculus. The firm seeks to minimize total cost subject to the constraint of its production function $Q = Q(L, K)$. With only two inputs, L and K, the total cost of any given output will be $P_L L + P_K K$. To derive the conditions for the minimum possible cost of producing any given output Q^*, form the Lagrangean expression

$$G = P_L L + P_K K + B[Q^* - Q(L, K)]$$

where B is the Lagrangean multiplier.

Differentiating the above expression with respect to L, K, and B and setting the results equal to zero to find the first-order conditions for the minimum cost allocation of inputs gives

$$\begin{aligned} \partial G/\partial L &= P_L - B(\partial Q/\partial L) = 0 \\ \partial G/\partial K &= P_K - B(\partial Q/\partial K) = 0 \\ \partial G/\partial B &= Q^* - Q(L, K) = 0 \end{aligned}$$

The second-order conditions for a minimum are satisfied if the isoquant is convex. Dividing $\partial G/\partial L$ by $\partial G/\partial K$ gives

$$\frac{P_L}{P_K} = \frac{\partial Q/\partial L}{\partial Q/\partial K}$$

But $\partial Q/\partial L$ is the marginal product of labor and $\partial Q/\partial K$ is the marginal product of capital. The last equation is therefore the same as Equation 8–5.

The Principle of Least Cost: Equimarginal Products per Dollar of Outlay on Input Services

Equation 8–5 can also be written in the following way:

$$MP_L/P_L = MP_K/P_K \tag{8–6}$$

This says that producing any given output at minimum cost requires that variable input be adjusted so that the marginal product per dollar is the same for all inputs. Alternatively, a producer meeting this condition can be viewed as maximizing the output obtainable from a given outlay.

For example, suppose that the marginal product of a machine hour in chair production is 20 chairs per month, and that the marginal product of a labor hour is 30 chairs per month. When a machine hour costs $20 and a labor hour costs $10, the marginal product of labor per dollar is three chairs per month for each $1 outlay on labor, while the marginal product of capital per dollar is only one chair for each $1 outlay on capital. If the owner of the factory were to reduce expenditure on the capital by hiring one less machine hour per month, the loss in chair output would be only 20 chairs per month. If the $20 saving were then used to hire more labor hours, the two extra labor hours employed would increase chair output by 60, assuming that the marginal product of each labor hour remained 30 chairs per month. For the same dollar outlay that month, the chair factory would then enjoy a net gain in production of 40 chairs per month! Because the gain in chair output from reallocating the dollar from the purchase of capital services to purchase of labor services outweighs the loss from doing so, monthly output increases. This means that at no increase in total cost, the firm gains more output to sell.

Whenever the marginal product per dollar of one input exceeds that of another, the firm gains salable output in this way without incurring any extra cost. You can now clearly see that by satisfying the condition for using inputs to produce any given output at minimum cost, the firm also obtains the most output for any given outlay.

As a firm reallocates input to achieve the equimarginal condition, its marginal products change. For example, as a firm uses more labor, the marginal product of labor falls. At the same time, as the firm uses less capital, the marginal product of capital rises. In this way, as the firm adjusts input use to obtain the most output from any given dollar outlay, the marginal products of inputs change until the condition in Equation 8–6 has been achieved. After that point no further net gain in salable output can be achieved by reallocating input use.

Expansion path A curve that shows how the use of variable inputs changes as output increases.

An Expansion Path

The cost function requires that input use be adjusted to satisfy the conditions in Equation 8–4 (and therefore Equations 8–5 and 8–6). An **expansion path** shows how the use of variable inputs by a producer changes as the producer expands output. Assuming that the producer minimizes the cost of producing any given

FIGURE 8–3 An Expansion Path

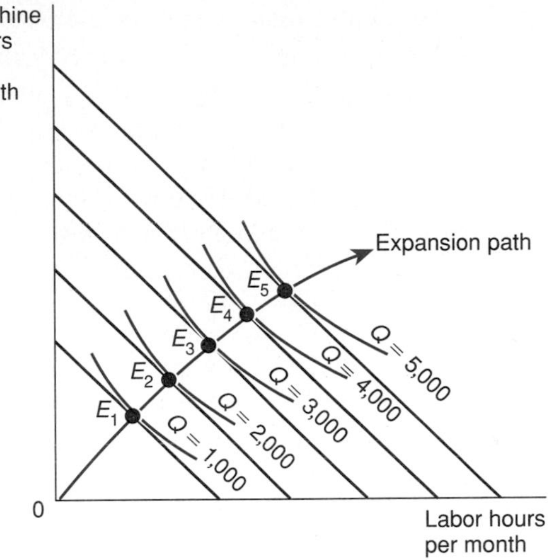

Each point of tangency gives the input combination corresponding to the minimum cost of producing the output indicated on the isoquant. Pairing the minimum cost of producing each output with the corresponding output gives points on the cost function.

TABLE 8–2 Points on a Cost Function (From a Firm's Expansion Path)

Monthly Output	*Minimum Total Cost*
1,000	$100,000
2,000	180,000
3,000	250,000
4,000	380,000
5,000	550,000

output, the expansion path can be derived by connecting the points of tangency of isoquants and isocost lines. Such an expansion path is illustrated in Figure 8–3.

Only a few isoquants have been drawn and labeled according to the amount of monthly output to which they correspond. The minimum possible cost of producing each output corresponds to the input combination given by the tangency of each isoquant and an isocost line. Table 8–2 shows the minimum total cost corresponding to each level of monthly output. It has been assumed that each successive isoquant in Figure 8–3 corresponds to an extra 1,000 units of output. The data in Table 8–2 describe the firm's cost function, assuming that labor and capital are the only inputs used.

CONCEPT REVIEW

1. Under what circumstances will the economic cost of operating a business enterprise exceed the accounting cost of doing so?
2. What information is provided by the cost function for a firm?
3. The marginal rate of technical substitution of labor for the capital used in a woodcutting operation is currently 1/4 for a firm producing 100 cords of firewood per month. If the capital equipment used rents for $50 per hour and the hourly cost of labor is $10, is the firm producing the 100 cords at the minimum possible cost?

SHORT-RUN COST

Total cost The sum of the cost of all inputs used to produce an item.

Variable cost The cost of inputs that change with output.

Fixed cost The cost of inputs that are independent of output.

In the short run, some inputs cannot be varied. During that period the firm expands output by using more variable inputs together with some fixed inputs. The **total cost** (TC) of producing a good is the sum of the cost of all inputs used in its production.

In the short run, total cost is divided into two separate components: **variable cost** (VC) and **fixed cost** (FC). Variable cost changes with output. Fixed cost is independent of output. It is the cost of inputs whose use cannot be varied in the short run. Managers often refer to their fixed costs as *overhead costs*. For example, if a producer must pay $6,000 rent per month for machines and buildings regardless of how much output is produced, the rent is a fixed cost. Similarly, insurance, depreciation on equipment, and other outlays are fixed costs in the short run.

The following identity holds:

$$TC = VC + FC \quad \textbf{(8–7)}$$

TABLE 8–3 Short-Run Cost

		Variable Cost			*Fixed Cost*	
Output (Chairs)	*Labor Hours*	*Labor Cost (P_L = $10/hr)*	*Materials Cost ($20/chair)*	*Total Variable Cost*	*Capital Cost (P_K = $20/hr)*	*Total Cost*
0	0	$ 0	$ 0	$ 0	$6,000	$ 6,000
35	100	1,000	700	1,700	6,000	7,700
150	200	2,000	3,000	5,000	6,000	11,000
210	300	3,000	4,200	7,200	6,000	13,200
250	400	4,000	5,000	9,000	6,000	15,000
270	500	5,000	5,400	10,400	6,000	16,400
288	600	6,000	5,760	11,760	6,000	17,760
305	700	7,000	6,100	13,100	6,000	19,100
315	800	8,000	6,300	14,300	6,000	20,300

Variable costs represent the cost of using variable inputs to produce any given quantity of output in the short run. The use of these variable inputs must be adjusted so that their marginal products divided by their prices are the same for each input (as indicated in Equation 8–6). Variable inputs must therefore be used in proportions that lie along an expansion path such as the one illustrated in Figure 8–3. To obtain short-run total cost, the fixed costs are simply added to the variable costs at each level of output.

A numerical example will help make this clear. Table 8–3 reproduces data from the production grid used in Chapter 7 on the output of chairs and on the labor hours required to produce those chairs. Assume that the number of machine hours used per month is fixed at 300 as a result of a contract with the firm supplying the machines. Production can be increased by using more labor hours with these 300 machine hours. Suppose that each chair requires $20 in materials. The price of labor is $10 per hour. The price of capital is $20 per hour and includes the rent of both machines and the space to house them. Assume that all of these prices accurately reflect the opportunity cost of these inputs to the owner of the chair factory.[8]

The costs of production can now be computed. The first column of Table 8–3 shows the maximum output of chairs obtainable for each 100-hour increment in the labor hours used together with 300 machine hours in the factory. The second column shows the corresponding number of labor hours used.

To obtain labor costs, simply multiply hours of labor used by the wage rate of $10 per hour. Materials costs are obtained by multiplying output by the $20 cost of materials per chair. This is the cost of the minimum amount of materials required per chair. Summing these two items gives the total variable cost of producing chairs.

Capital cost will be $6,000 per month, independent of the amount of output produced or the amount of labor used. In effect, the contract obligates the producer to pay for 300 hours of machine use and factory use at the hourly rate of $20 whether or not that amount is actually used. Total cost, shown in the last column of Table 8–3, is obtained by adding total variable cost and fixed cost.

Average Cost and Marginal Cost

Average cost The total cost per unit of output.

Average cost (AC) is total cost per unit of output. It is also called *average total cost*. Managers often refer to average cost as their *unit cost of production*. Average cost is calculated by dividing total cost of output by the number of units produced:

$$\text{AC} = \text{TC}/Q \qquad \textbf{(8–8)}$$

The average cost of producing chairs can be calculated from the data in Table 8–3 by dividing total cost at each level of output by the number of chairs produced.

[8] Cases in which this assumption is unlikely to hold are discussed in the last part of this book. For an interesting analysis of input prices and opportunity cost, see Dennis A. Johnson, "Opportunity Cost: A Pedagogical Note," *Southern Economic Journal* 50, no. 3 (January 1984), pp. 866–70.

Modern Microeconomics in Action: The Business World

Fixed Costs and Sunk Costs

You've probably heard business managers and owners talk about their "overhead." The common business term for fixed costs is *overhead costs*. Fixed, or overhead, costs are all costs that do not vary with output. Let's see how a business manager would go about measuring the fixed costs of an operation.

The following data are based on cost estimates for a fish processing plant.* The plant will dress mountain trout for shipment to urban fish markets. It will cost $67,782 to construct. The total equipment cost will be $60,337. The cost of acquiring the land for the plant will be $7,500. The plant is designed to produce 2,304 pounds of dressed trout per day.

The fixed costs include depreciation on plant and equipment, property taxes, insurance, repairs and maintenance, and forgone interest on cash invested. In addition, the plant manager's salary may be regarded as a fixed cost. Irrespective of the output level, his salary for overseeing operations or managing the plant's affairs if it is shut down must be paid.

In calculating depreciation, the plant is presumed to have a 20-year life and its equipment is presumed to have a 10-year life. A straight-line depreciation of these assets uses 1/20 of the plant cost and 1/10 of the equipment cost as a measure of annual capital cost. Forgone interest is estimated at 9 percent of one half of the total investment in land, plant, and equipment. Annual fixed, or overhead, costs are

Fixed costs =	
Depreciation	
Plant	$ 3,389
Equipment	6,034
Total	$ 9,423
Forgone interest	6,103
Property taxes	1,356
Insurance	1,239
Repairs and maintenance	1,922
Plant manager's salary	15,325
Total fixed costs	$35,368

Property taxes are estimated at 1 percent of the investment in land, plant, and equipment. Insurance is estimated at 1 percent of the investment in plant and equipment, and repairs and maintenance are estimated at 1.5 percent of the same amount.

Business managers and economists distinguish costs that can be recovered should a business be discontinued from those that cannot. *Sunk costs* are expenditures that have been made and cannot be recovered if a business is discontinued. For example, if the fish processing plant has equipment especially designed for the type of fish that it processes and is worthless in any other use, the expenditure for that equipment is a sunk cost. On the other hand, not all of the expenditure for equipment acquired for the plant is a sunk cost because some of the equipment, such as office furniture and trucks, can be sold or leased if the plant ceases to operate.

Sunk costs are not part of the opportunity cost of continuing to operate a business because they are costs that must be paid no matter what the firm does. Once incurred, a sunk cost is not part of the marginal cost of operating a business in either the short run or the long run. Because of the existence of sunk costs, we must be careful in computing fixed costs to make sure that we include only economic costs.

The existence of sunk costs implies that the fixed costs calculated by accountants can exceed the economic fixed costs as measured by economists. For example, suppose that because some of the equipment in the fish processing plant has no other use, $6,000 of the depreciation in the estimate of fixed costs is not recoverable should the plant shut down. This means that if the plant ceases to operate that depreciation, which is a measure of the annual value of the services rendered by the equipment, cannot be recovered by putting the equipment to another use or selling it to another firm. Thus, the opportunity cost of fixed inputs in the business is really only $29,368 in any given year.

It is very important to consider which costs are sunk and which are not when deciding whether to continue operating a business *once it has been*

(*Continued*) *started up*. In the case of the fish processing plant we might at first conclude that revenue of more than $35,368 over its variable costs would allow it to make a profit once it started up. Actually, however, if the plant has already been built, revenue of more than $29,368 over its variable costs would be sufficient for it to make an economic profit because $6,000 of the accounting fixed costs are sunk costs.

* J. E. Easley, *Costs and Returns of Alternative Mountain Trout Processing Facilities*, Economics Information Report no. 47, Department of Economics and Business, North Carolina State University of Raleigh, June 1976.

Average variable cost The variable cost per unit of output.

Average fixed cost The fixed cost per unit of output.

Average cost may be broken down into two components: **average variable cost** (AVC) and **average fixed cost** (AFC), where

$$\text{AVC} = \text{VC}/Q \tag{8–9}$$

and

$$\text{AFC} = \text{FC}/Q \tag{8–10}$$

Table 8–4 shows AVC, AFC, and AC for the chair factory. Variable costs are the sum of labor costs and materials costs from Table 8–3. Fixed cost is the capital cost from Table 8–3. The sum of average variable cost and average fixed cost equals average cost:

$$\text{AC} = \text{AVC} + \text{AFC} \tag{8–11}$$

The data in Table 8–4 show that both average cost and average variable cost decline at first and then begin to rise. This pattern of variation, as will be demonstrated, is rooted in the assumptions made about the way output varies with input use in the short run. Also note that because fixed cost is a constant, average fixed cost continually declines as output expands.

TABLE 8–4 Average Cost and Marginal Cost

Monthly Output	*Average Cost*	*Average Variable Cost*	*Average Fixed Cost*	ΔTC	ΔQ	*Marginal Cost*
35	$220.00	$48.57	$171.43	$1,700	35	$ 48.57
150	73.33	33.33	40.00	3,300	115	28.70
210	62.86	34.29	28.57	2,200	60	36.77
250	60.00	36.00	24.00	1,800	40	45.00
270	60.74	38.52	22.22	1,400	20	70.00
288	61.66	40.83	20.83	1,360	18	75.55
305	62.62	42.95	19.67	1,340	17	79.00
315	64.44	45.50	19.04	1,200	10	120.00

Marginal cost The change in total cost that results from a change in output; the extra cost incurred to produce another unit of output.

Marginal cost (MC) is the change in total cost associated with a change in output:

$$MC = \Delta TC/\Delta Q \tag{8–12}$$

Marginal cost represents the cost associated with producing an additional unit of output.[9]

The last column of Table 8–4 calculates marginal cost for each increment in output. When output increases from zero to 35 chairs, total cost increases from \$6,000 to \$7,700. Because ΔQ is 35, and ΔTC is \$1,700, marginal cost equals

$$\$1{,}700/35 = \$48.57$$

In Table 8–4 the change in total cost is shown for each change in output. Data are available only for 100-hour increments in labor used along with the corresponding amounts of materials and capital. The calculation estimates the marginal cost of a chair in the batch of output produced with each extra 100 hours of labor. If data on the change in total cost associated with each extra chair produced were available, marginal cost of each extra chair produced could be calculated. The change in output associated with each extra 100 hours of labor and the materials that labor uses is shown in the next-to-last column of Table 8–4. Marginal cost is calculated by dividing each change in total cost by the corresponding change in output. Marginal cost declines at first and then quickly begins to increase.

Marginal cost is independent of fixed cost because fixed cost does not change with output. Only variable costs influence marginal costs. To see this, suppose fixed cost is twice as much as the amount shown in Table 8–3. This increases total cost of output. Recalculate marginal cost based on the new \$12,000 fixed cost. You will find that marginal cost is the same as that calculated for a \$6,000 fixed cost.

Short-Run Cost Curves

Short-run costs in all enterprises are likely to follow similar patterns. This pattern of variation can be explained by the law of diminishing marginal returns (see Chapter 7). A total cost curve shows the variation in the cost of inputs used in production as output is increased. To simplify the analysis, assume that labor and capital are the only inputs used. Labor is a variable input, and the amount of capital is fixed.

Fixed cost can be measured as $P_K K$, where the amount of capital is fixed at a certain level. Think of the producer as being confined to a plant of a given size. To produce more or less, the amount of labor used in the plant can be varied. In the short run, however, it is presumed that neither the size of the plant nor the number of machines in it can be varied.

[9] Marginal cost is the first derivative of the cost function $C = f(Q)$. $MC = dC/dQ$ and measures the rate at which cost changes for small changes in output.

FIGURE 8–4 Cost and Productivity

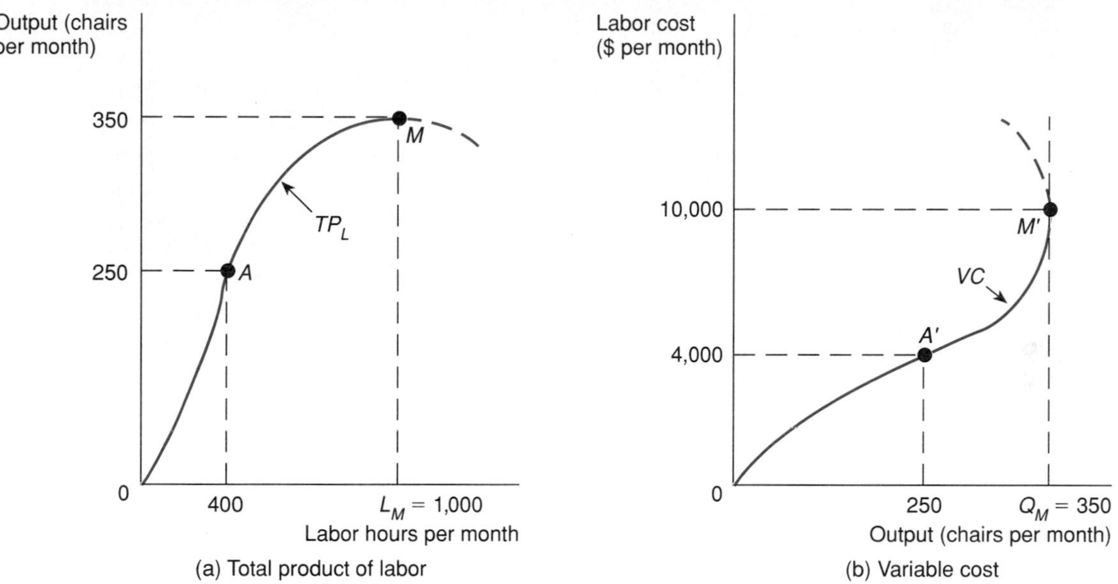

Cost is related to productivity. The short-run variable cost curve relates the value of labor used to output. The total product curve takes output as a function of the physical amount of labor used. The two curves are mirror images of each other, with the axes reversed. The variable cost curve multiplies labor by its price to obtain a dollar measure of variable cost.

Taking the price of labor as given, it is easy to show how variable costs of production are related to the total product of labor in the short run. Figure 8–4(a) depicts the total product curve for a producer. The total product curve, whose shape reflects the law of diminishing marginal returns, shows the maximum output obtainable from any amount of labor hours per month. It shows how output varies with the amount of labor used along with a given amount of capital.

The variable cost curve shows how variable costs, which in this example are measured by labor costs ($P_L L$), increase as monthly output increases. Figure 8–4(b) shows the variable cost curve for the producer. Points on this curve give the minimum labor (the variable input) cost necessary to produce the corresponding output.

Points on the variable cost curve are obtained by taking a given output level and using the total product curve to find *the minimum amount of variable labor input necessary to produce that output*. This minimum amount of labor hours per month is then multiplied by the hourly wage to obtain the variable cost of that output.

Suppose that the wage is $10 per hour. Figure 8–4(a) indicates that the minimum labor input necessary to produce 250 units of output per month is 400 labor hours, corresponding to point *A* on the total product curve. Because labor costs $10 per hour, the minimum variable cost at which it is possible to produce 250

MODERN MICROECONOMICS IN ACTION: GOVERNMENT AND THE ECONOMY

Restricting or Banning the Use of an Input

Because of the hazards of using materials that damage the environment, governments sometimes enact regulations that either restrict or ban the use of an input. For example, in the 1970s the use of many types of insecticides was restricted or banned. In the 1990s, because chlorofluorocarbons endanger the ozone layer, many governments have been taking actions to restrict or ban their use.

While the benefits of such restrictions or bans often outweigh the costs, it is important to understand the effects of the restrictions or bans on productive methods and production costs. Because restrictions or bans on input use tend to increase average costs of production, they contribute to higher product prices. In effect, by restricting or banning the use of an input, we trade off increases in the prices of goods and services for the benefits of a cleaner environment.

Let's see how restricting the use of an input affects productive methods and average costs of production. Suppose that because of the health hazards of pesticides, the amount of pesticides that can be used per acre in agriculture is limited.

Graph (a) shows an isoquant for alternative combinations of labor and pesticide per acre that can be used to produce Q_1 pounds of output. In the absence of any restriction on input use, a typical farmer would choose the input combination corresponding to point E (other things being equal). At that point the productive method uses L_E labor hours per acre and K_E pounds of pesticide per acre each session. The minimum cost per acre would be $\$TC_E$. This is the cost of the input combination at E and of any other input combination on the isocost line labeled TC_E.

Now suppose that the use of pesticides is limited to K_R pounds per acre per season. Input combinations involving more than K_R pounds of pesticide per acre will no longer be permitted. This includes all points on the dashed section of the isocost line AB, including the input combination at E. The farmer now finds that the minimum-cost method of producing Q_1 pounds of output per acre is at point R. The productive method corresponding to that point involves L_R labor hours per acre and K_R pounds of pesticide per acre each season. The cost of that productive method is $\$TC_2 > \$TC_E$. The restriction therefore increases the cost of producing a given amount of output per acre. In addition to restricting pesticide use, it increases labor (or other input) use per acre. In the long run, it is also likely to result in the substitution of land for pesticide use. With the restriction, farmers might use more acres of land to produce a given quantity of output

This conclusion must be qualified by indicating that the increase in costs results only if point E lies to the right of point R. A point such as E could lie to the left of R if the price of labor were lower relative to the price of pesticides. This would result in steeper isocost lines than those drawn on the graph. Points such as E could also lie to the left of R if the isoquants were flatter. A flatter isoquant would indicate a lower marginal product of pesticides compared with that of labor for any given amount of pesticide used than the isoquant drawn.

Assuming that point E does lie to the right of R, graph (b) shows the impact of the restriction on average cost per pound per acre. The farm's average cost curve is AC. The average cost of Q_1 pounds per acre would be TC_E/Q_1 without restriction. The restriction raises this cost to TC_2/Q_1. In general, the restriction would raise the average cost of producing any amount of output. The average cost curve would shift up to AC_R.

This example illustrates that restrictions causing less of an input to be used in production than would otherwise be the case are equivalent to cost increases. The benefits of such restrictions (in terms of reduced risk of disease and other damages) must be weighed against the increases in cost that are likely to result from them. Those increases, in turn, are likely to result in higher prices. Restricting or banning the use of pesticides is likely to increase

(*Continued*) the price of agricultural products that use pesticides as an input. Banning pesticides can be worth the costs, but it often is not obvious to citizens how such restrictions do in fact raise production costs. Economic theory clarifies this trade-off of benefits versus costs.

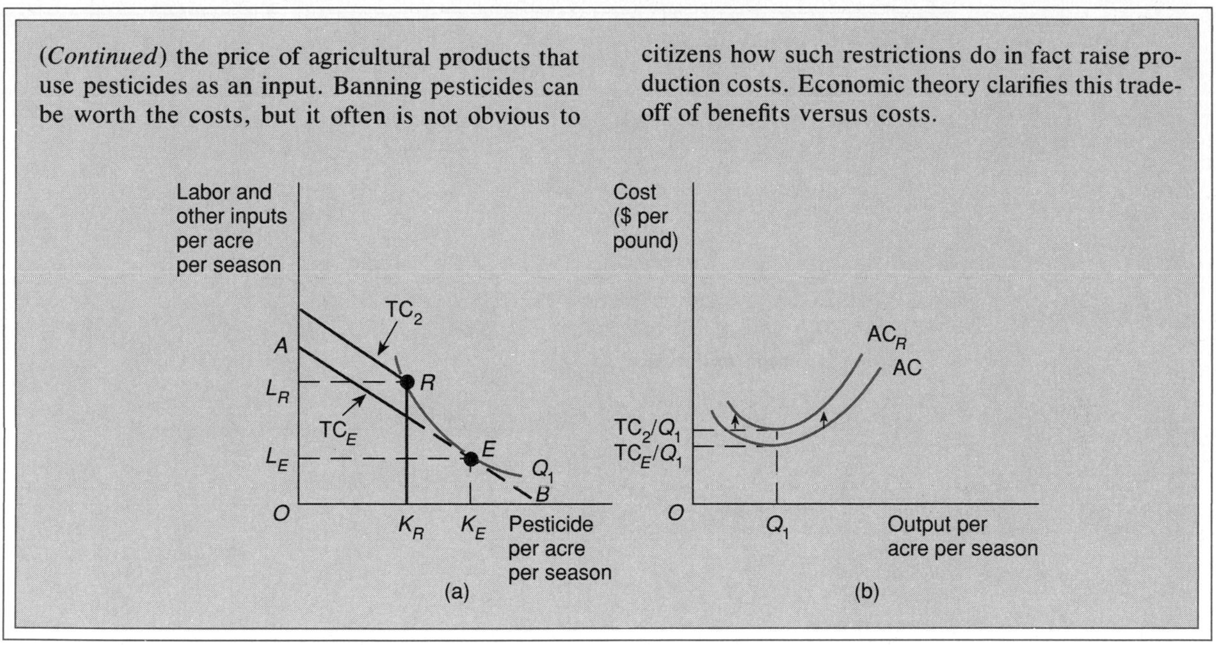

units of output per month is $4,000. In Figure 8–4(b) the variable cost of $4,000 = $P_L L$ is plotted on the vertical axis and A' is a point on the variable cost curve corresponding to 250 units of output per month. A similar exercise can be followed to obtain other points on the variable cost curve. For example, Figure 8–4(a) shows that the maximum output possible is 350 units per month given the K units of capital. To produce this output requires 1,000 labor hours, corresponding to point M on the total product curve. The corresponding point on the variable cost curve is M', which corresponds to the same 350 units of output, and a variable cost of $10,000, which equals 1,000 labor hours multiplied by the $10 wage.

The shape of the variable cost curve mirrors the shape of the total product curve. Points on the variable cost curve give the dollar value of the minimum amount of labor input necessary to produce the output per month plotted on the horizontal axis. Because the price of labor is given, the way the minimum cost of producing any given output varies with output depends entirely on the way the maximum output varies with labor use. Turn the book so that Figure 8–4(b) is on its side and hold it up to a mirror. You will see that the shape of the variable cost curve looked at in this way parallels that of the total product curve. If you need further convincing, use the data in Table 8–3 to plot total product and total cost curves on graph paper and fit a smooth curve through the points.

To obtain a total cost curve from the variable cost curve just derived, simply add fixed costs to variable costs. Fixed costs in this case are $P_K K$. For example, if fixed costs are $6,000 per month, then total cost for any given output can be calculated by adding the variable cost of that output to $6,000. In Figure 8–5(a)

FIGURE 8–5 Short-Run Cost Curves

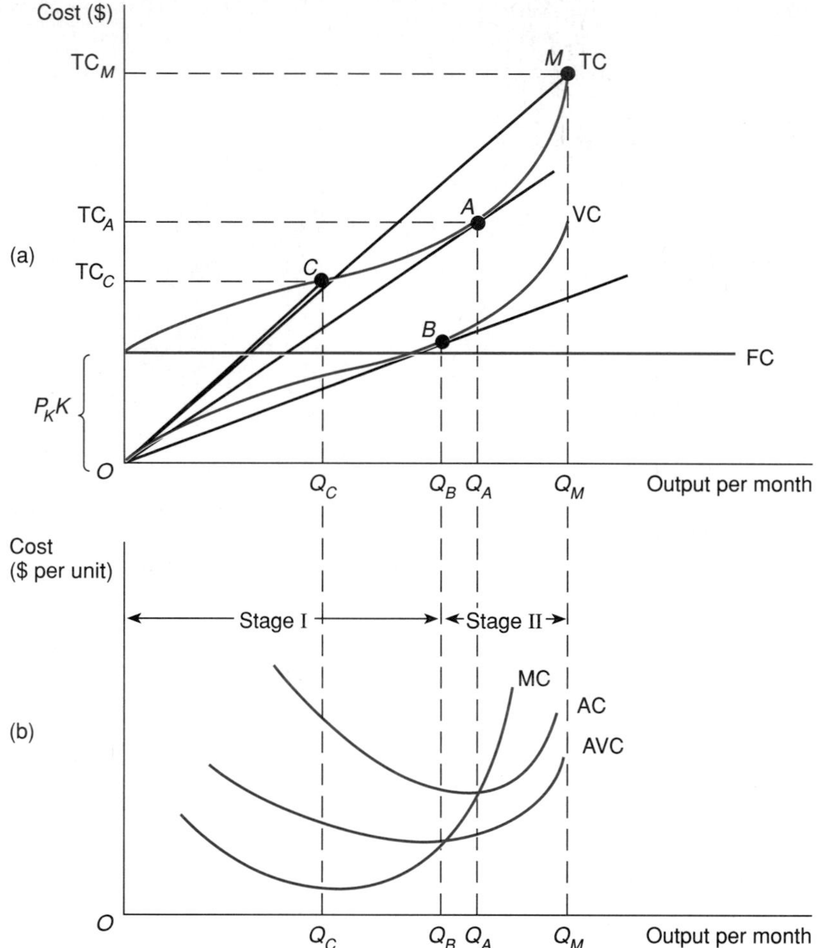

Graph (a) shows the total cost, variable cost, and fixed cost curves. Graph (b) shows the corresponding average cost, average variable cost, and marginal cost curves. Point *A* on the TC curve corresponds to the output at which AC is at a minimum. Point *B* on the VC curve corresponds to the output at which AVC is at a minimum. Point *C* on the TC curve corresponds to the output at which MC is at a minimum. Note that the MC curve intersects both the AC and AVC curves at their respective minimum points. Stage II of production runs from the point of minimum AVC to the point of maximum output.

fixed costs are represented by the horizontal line labeled FC, whose height is $P_K K$ dollars at all levels of output. Adding these fixed costs to variable costs at each output gives the total cost curve, TC, shown on the graph. Because fixed costs do not vary with output, the shape of the total cost curve reflects the shape of the variable cost curve. In this case, any variation in total cost with output is attributable to variation in labor cost alone.

Notice the broken-line portions of the variable cost and total product curves drawn in Figure 8–4. The broken-line portion of the total product curve indicates that if more labor than L_M hours per month were used in the given plant with its given number of machines, output would actually decline. This means that there is a maximum level of output that can be produced in the short run. Q_M is the maximum output that can be produced in the plant. If the managers of the plant tried to produce more than this amount by hiring more labor, output would decline. Consequently, variable costs would rise while output fell. Points along the dashed portion of the total cost curve are not part of the cost function because the outputs corresponding to those points can be produced at lower cost on the solid section of the curve.

Average Variable Cost, Average Fixed Cost, Average Cost, and Marginal Cost Curves

Average cost and its components, along with marginal cost, can be derived from the total cost curves drawn in Figure 8–5(a). The average cost of any output corresponds to the slope of a ray drawn to the point corresponding to that output on the total cost curve. For example, average cost at point *A*, which corresponds to monthly output Q_A, is TC_A/Q_A, which corresponds to the slope of the ray *OA*. The ray *OA* is just tangent to the total cost curve. The average cost of any output above or below Q_A will exceed that of Q_A. To convince yourself of this, trace rays to other points on the total cost curve corresponding to other output levels and note that their slope exceeds that of ray *OA*. For example, the average cost of the output Q_c is the slope of the ray *OC*, which is equal to TC_c/Q_c. Because the ray *OC* is steeper than the ray *OA*, the average cost when monthly output Q_c is produced exceeds the average cost when monthly output Q_A is produced. The average cost of output Q_M is also greater than the average cost of output Q_A because the ray *OM* is steeper than the ray *OA*.

The average cost of production will therefore decline at first, reach a minimum at output Q_A, and then begin to rise. Thus the average cost curve labeled AC is U-shaped, as shown in Figure 8–5(b). The units on the quantity axis are the same in Figure 8–5(a) and (b).

Average variable cost can be derived in a similar fashion. In this case the slope of a ray run from the origin just tangent to point *B* on the variable cost curve corresponds to minimum AVC. Average variable cost is also described by a U-shaped curve.

Output levels smaller than Q_B will have a larger AVC because the slope of rays drawn to the corresponding points on the variable cost curve will have a slope greater than that of the ray *OB*. Similarly, the AVC of outputs larger than Q_B will also be higher than that of output Q_B. The output corresponding to the minimum possible AVC is lower than that corresponding to the minimum AC. In Figure 8–5(b) the average variable cost curve is labeled AVC.

The vertical distance between the AC and AVC curves at any given output is the average fixed cost of that output. This follows from the fact that the sum of average variable cost and average fixed cost is average cost:

$$AC = AFC + AVC$$

Therefore,

$$\text{AFC} = \text{AC} - \text{AVC} \tag{8–13}$$

Notice how the AC and AVC curves move continually closer together as output expands in the short run. This is because average fixed cost continually declines as output is increased in the short run. This shows how overhead costs are spread over output. For example, suppose that monthly rent of $1,000 is the only fixed cost of a small shoe store. If 100 pairs of shoes are sold per month, the average fixed cost is $10. If 1,000 pairs of shoes are sold per month, the average fixed cost is only $1. You can also see how AFC declines continually with output by noting that the slope of a ray drawn to points on the FC curve in Figure 8–5(a) corresponding to higher and higher outputs declines as output goes up.

Marginal cost, $\Delta TC/\Delta Q$, is the slope of the total cost curve. Imagine running a straight edge along the total cost curve, and notice how its slope changes as output increases. Marginal cost (that is, the slope) decreases at first and reaches a minimum value at point *C*, which is the point of inflection of the total cost curve. The point of minimum marginal cost corresponds to output level Q_c. At point *M* in Figure 8–5, which corresponds to the maximum output that can be produced in the short run, marginal cost is virtually infinite. If a firm attempts to expand production beyond that point, total cost would increase, but the change in output would be zero. Marginal cost therefore approaches an infinitely large amount as Q_M is reached. The marginal cost curve is plotted in Figure 8–5(b) on the same set of axes as that used for average cost and average variable cost.

Relationship between Marginal Cost, Average Variable Cost, and Average Cost

Marginal cost equals average cost when average cost is at a minimum. This can easily be seen from Figure 8–5. Average cost is at a minimum when output is Q_A. At that output the ray *OA* from the origin is just tangent to the total cost curve. Average cost at that point equals the slope of the ray *OA*. Because the ray is tangent to the total cost curve at point *A*, the slope of the ray equals the slope of the total cost curve. The slope of the total cost curve at point *A* is the marginal cost of output Q_A. It follows that marginal cost equals average cost at that point.

Marginal cost is the cost of producing an extra unit of output after a certain number of units have already been produced. For example, in the chair factory the marginal cost of producing chairs represents the unit cost of the chairs in each extra batch produced. If this exceeds the average cost of all chairs produced previously, average cost must increase. Similarly, if the marginal cost of chairs is below the average cost, average cost must decline.

Going back to the data from Table 8–4, when the marginal cost of producing chairs is $70, notice how average cost increases from $60.74 to $61.66 as more chairs are produced. Conversely, notice how at low levels of production marginal cost is below average cost, causing average cost to decline. At an output of 150 chairs per month, average cost is $73.33 and marginal cost is only $28.70. Expansion of output to 210 chairs per month results in a decline in average cost to $62.86.

The same relationship holds between marginal cost and average variable cost. Marginal cost equals average variable cost at the latter's minimum value. When marginal cost is above average variable cost, it pulls that average up. The opposite is true when marginal cost is below average variable cost. This too can be seen from the data in Table 8–4. The minimum average variable cost occurs at a level of output between 150 and 210 chairs. Below that level MC < AVC and AVC declines. Above that level MC rises above AVC and continually pulls AVC upward.

Diminishing Returns, Costs, and the Stages of Production: More on the Relationship between Cost Functions and Production Functions

The variation in short-run costs reflects the law of diminishing marginal returns. As long as the firm can hire all the inputs it requires at constant prices, variation in short-run costs can be explained entirely by changes in the average and marginal products of its variable inputs.

If labor is the only variable input, average cost can be derived from the average product of labor. The average product of labor is output divided by labor hours used:

$$\text{AP}_L = \frac{Q}{L} \tag{8–14}$$

This is a measure of output per unit input. Average variable cost is a measure of the cost of variable input per unit of output:

$$\text{AVC} = \frac{(P_L L)}{Q} = P_L\left(\frac{L}{Q}\right) \tag{8–15}$$

But L/Q equals $1/\text{AP}_L$. Therefore,

$$\text{AVC} = P_L\left(\frac{1}{\text{AP}_L}\right) \tag{8–16}$$

Average variable cost is the inverse of the average product of labor multiplied by the price of labor when labor is the only variable input.

To obtain average cost, simply add average fixed cost to average variable cost:

$$\begin{aligned}\text{AC} &= \text{AVC} + \text{AFC}\\ &= P_L\left(\frac{1}{\text{AP}_L}\right) + \frac{(\text{P}_K K)}{Q}\end{aligned} \tag{8–17}$$

where $P_K K$ is fixed cost, assuming that capital is the only fixed input.

By means of these formulas, data on the productivity of labor can be used to calculate average variable cost and average cost, given the price of labor. Suppose it takes six hours of labor to produce 1 ton of steel and that labor is the only

MODERN MICROECONOMICS IN ACTION: INTERNATIONAL REPORT

Advanced Technology, Variable Costs, and the International Competitiveness of the U.S. Steel Industry

The U.S. steel industry was in decline throughout much of the early 1980s. From 1982 to 1986 the industry's losses totaled about $6 billion, and employment in the industry shrank from 500,000 workers in 1975 to fewer than 200,000 workers in 1987.* West European steel producers and even Japanese steel producers have also been suffering. Steel production has been growing rapidly, however, in less developed nations, where low labor costs enable producers to sell steel at lower prices than the competition.

Adjustments in the U.S. steel industry are inevitable. Even if U.S. steel mills adopt the latest technology, they are still unlikely to produce steel at lower cost than the mills in less developed nations. The new mills in such nations as Korea are also taking advantage of the cost savings possible from new technology. This coupled with their lower labor costs gives them a clear cost advantage over the U.S. mills, whose labor costs are higher. There is, however, hope for the U.S. steel industry. In fact, in recent years the average cost of producing a ton of steel in the United States has been lower than the average cost of producing comparable steel in Japan and Germany.

There are three types of steel mills: (1) integrated mills, (2) minimills, and (3) specialty-steel mills. The integrated mills are capable of producing a wide variety of steel products. Such mills currently account for about 70 percent of the nonspecialty steel produced in the United States. They produce steel directly from coal and iron ore using conventional blast furnaces. The minimills, which are much smaller than the integrated mills, reprocess scrap steel and account for about 25 percent of U.S. steel production. Finally, the specialty-steel mills are small, flexible plants that produce steel products to order from reprocessed scrap steel.

A typical U.S. integrated steel plant produces between 2 million and 5 million tons of steel products annually. Average variable costs per ton of such plants were estimated to be between $400 and $500 in the late 1980s. Their average fixed costs per ton of annual capacity are quite high in these plants because of their heavy reliance on capital equipment in blast furnace and finishing operations. Their average fixed costs in the late 1980s were estimated at about $1,600 per ton at capacity output.

Using computer-controlled, highly automated production methods, the Japanese can produce higher-quality (in terms of chemical purity) steel at lower average cost than the U.S. integrated plants. U.S. integrated mills require about six labor hours per ton of steel; Japanese producers, using more automated operations, can produce a ton of steel with less than three labor hours per ton. The Japanese also use about 80 percent less fuel per ton of steel than U.S. producers. Despite their technological advantage over U.S. steel producers, the Japanese have difficulty competing with steel producers in such nations as Korea and Taiwan, whose lower labor costs allow steel production at even lower variable costs than those of Japan. New steel producers in developing nations can build integrated mills using the latest technology, such as that employed by Japan.

U.S. minimills are better able to compete with low-cost foreign producers because their fixed costs are low relative to those of U.S. integrated mills. U.S. minimills typically produce between 300,000 and 1.2 million tons per year, and their average fixed costs per ton at capacity output are between $200 and $300. Minimills have much smaller work forces than integrated mills, and they sell their products to local buyers, thereby economizing on delivery costs. Specialty-steel mills also have lower fixed cost than integrated mills, and they can take advantage of new technologies for casting high-quality steels with special structural and mechanical properties. The table below, based on a 1987 study, compares labor input per ton of steel and average fixed cost at capacity output of a typical U.S. integrated mill and a minimill.

(*Continued*)

	Integrated Mill	*Minimill*
Labor per ton of steel	6 hours	2 to 3 hours
Capital cost per ton of steel at capacity (average fixed costs)	Up to \$1,600	\$200 to \$300

Source: Julian Szekely, "Can Advanced Technology Save the U.S. Steel Industry?" *Scientific American* 257, no. 1 (July 1987).

If labor earns a wage of \$20 per hour, the labor costs in the integrated mill would be about \$120 per ton, while labor costs in the minimill could be as low as \$40 per ton. The average cost of producing a ton of steel could be as high as \$1,720 in the integrated mill and as low as \$240 in the minimill.

In addition, to lower their average costs of production, minimills have other advantages over integrated mills. They are more flexible than integrated mills in switching to newer technologies when these become available. They are less capital intensive than integrated mills, so that it is easier to pay off and replace their equipment.

In addition to making more extensive use of minimills, U.S. steel firms have been innovating with new technology that could reduce the average cost of producing steel still further. In 1991 Inland Steel Company engaged in a joint venture with Nippon Steel Corporation, a Japanese firm, to develop a new continuous cold mill process that could substantially reduce the manufacturing time for rolled steel.† The new process weaves coils of steel in a continuous band through a plant that is the length of seven football fields. The steel can be cut to make such products as washers, dryers, and car bodies.

* Julian Szekely, "Can Advanced Technology Save the U.S. Steel Industry?" *Scientific American* 257, no. 1 (July 1987). The data here are based on figures reported by Szekely.

† See Jonathan P. Hicks, "A Faster Path of Finished Steel," *The New York Times*, April 7, 1991, p. F9.

variable input in steel production. If the price of labor (the wage rate) is \$20 per hour, then the variable cost of steel will be

$$\begin{aligned} P_L\left(\frac{L}{Q}\right) &= \$20\left(\frac{6 \text{ hours of labor}}{1 \text{ ton of steel}}\right) \\ &= \$120 \text{ per ton} \end{aligned}$$

If the fixed cost *per ton* of steel (AFC) is \$1,000 at current output, then the average cost of a ton of steel at current output will be

$$\begin{aligned} \text{AC} &= P_L\left(\frac{L}{Q}\right) + \text{AFC} \\ &= \$120 + 1{,}000 \\ &= \$1{,}120 \text{ per ton} \end{aligned}$$

The U shapes of the AC and AVC curves reflect the fact that average product of variable input first increases and then decreases in a plant. The point of minimum average variable costs corresponds to the point of maximum average product of the variable input. Figure 8–6 shows how, other things being equal, if average product of variable input is increasing, average variable cost must be decreasing, and vice versa.

It is also easy to show how marginal cost is related to the marginal product of the variable input. Assuming that labor is the only variable input, its marginal product is

$$MP_L = \frac{\Delta Q}{\Delta L} \tag{8–18}$$

Marginal cost of production is the change in labor cost, $P_L\Delta L$, which is the only variable cost in this example, divided by the change in output, ΔQ.

$$MC = \frac{(P_L\Delta L)}{\Delta Q} = P_L\left(\frac{\Delta L}{\Delta Q}\right) \tag{8–19}$$

Because $\Delta L/\Delta Q = 1/\mathrm{MP}_L$,

$$\mathrm{MC} = P_L\left(\frac{1}{\mathrm{MP}_L}\right) \tag{8–20}$$

FIGURE 8–6 The Relationship between Productivity and Cost

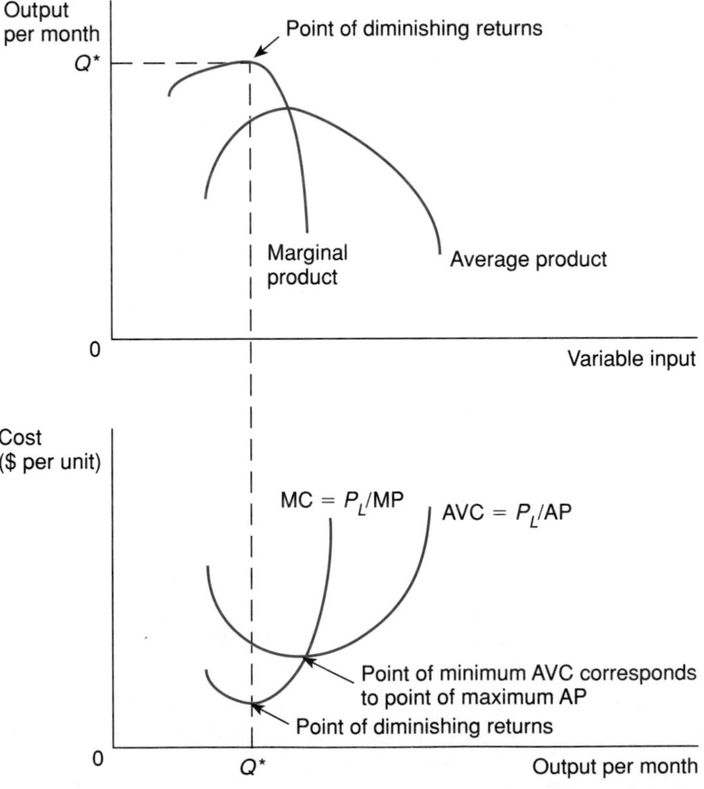

Given the prices of variable input, the patterns of variation of average variable and marginal cost in a plant depend on the way AP and MP change as more variable input is employed. As AP and MP rise, AVC and MC fall. As AP and MP fall, AVC and MC rise.

Given the price of the variable input, labor, the variation in marginal cost is entirely a result of the variation in the marginal product of labor. Recall that the point of diminishing returns occurs when the marginal product of labor begins to decline. This is precisely the point at which the marginal cost of output begins to increase. Figure 8–6 shows that at the output level Q^*, which corresponds to the point of diminishing returns, marginal cost is at a minimum.

Short-run production was divided into three stages in the previous chapter. Stage I is from zero output to the point of maximum average product of the variable input. This corresponds to the range of output from zero to the point where average variable cost is at a minimum. Stage II corresponds to the range of output for which average products of the variable inputs decline while their marginal products are positive. This is the range of output from minimum AVC to the maximum output that can be produced in the short run. In this range of production, both average cost and marginal cost increase with output. Stage III corresponds to production with a negative marginal product for the variable input. Input combinations in this stage are not included in either the production function or the cost function.

CONCEPT REVIEW

1. A firm incurs a monthly fixed cost of $10,000. If variable cost is $20,000 and the firm produces 3,000 units of output, calculate total cost, average cost, average variable cost, and average fixed cost.
2. Explain why average cost curves and marginal cost curves are U-shaped in the short run.
3. Labor is the only variable input in a computer factory. The average product of labor is currently 20 computers per worker. If workers earn a monthly wage of $3,000, calculate the current average variable cost of computers.

LONG-RUN COST

Over the long run, production managers can think about expanding or reducing the scale of operations. They can move to larger plants or smaller plants by varying the amount of fixed inputs used with variable inputs. At any given time the firm is confined to a plant of given size. Within that plant, costs will vary according to the pattern described above for the short run. At any given time short-run costs are relevant.

Long-run cost curves Curves that show the minimum cost of producing any given output when all of the inputs are variable.

Long-run cost curves show the minimum cost of producing any given output when *all* of the inputs are variable. In the long run, there are no fixed costs. All costs are variable.

The basic difference between the long run and the short run is flexibility. In the long run, producers have options that are not available in the short run. In the long run, managers can control output and costs not only by varying the intensity of operation of a given plant but also by varying the *size* and *number* of plants.

Analysis of Long-Run Costs: Variation in Plant Size

Assume that a firm manufacturing shoes can consider only five plant sizes. Assume further that each plant is sized to operate at minimum short-run AC at successive 10,000 units of monthly output. The firm's managers have the option of working in plants designed to operate at minimum short-run AC at monthly outputs of 10,000, 20,000, 30,000, 40,000, and 50,000 pairs.

Figure 8–7 shows the short-run cost curves for each of the five plants. Managers seeking to operate efficiently must determine the minimum possible level of average cost for each possible output when choosing productive methods to get the points on the long-run cost curve. They have the option of using the various plants to achieve the minimum possible cost of any given output in the long run.

Look at monthly outputs ranging from zero to 15,000 pairs of shoes in Figure 8–7. At any output below 15,000, the firm can produce at lower average cost in the first plant. For example, the average cost of a monthly output of 12,000 pairs is $20 in the first plant. For example, the average cost of a monthly output of 12,000 pairs is $20 in the first plant, whose short-run average cost curve is labeled AC_1. In the second plant, whose short-run average cost curve is labeled AC_2, it would cost $30 to produce the same output. If the managers attempted to produce this output in the second plant, much of this capital equipment would be underutilized. It is

FIGURE 8–7 A Long-Run Average Cost Curve

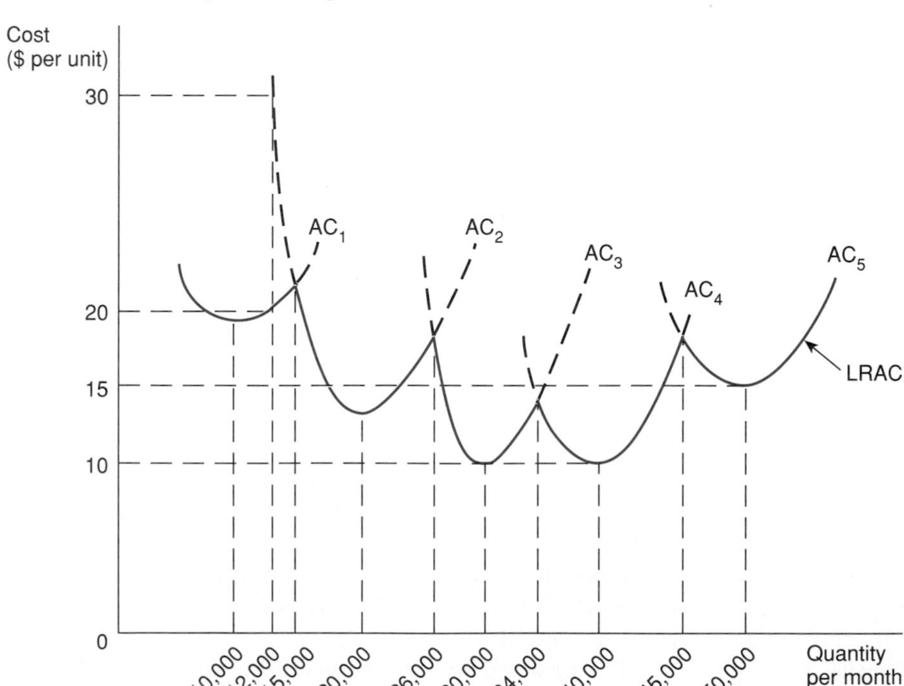

The long-run average cost curve is derived from five short-run cost curves, each corresponding to successively larger plant sizes.

cheaper to produce the 12,000 pairs in the smaller plant, even though that plant is operating above the monthly output level of 10,000 pairs at which it achieves its minimum AC.

At outputs below 15,000 pairs the relevant points on the LRAC curve are those that fall on AC_1. Beyond the point where AC_1 and AC_2 intersect on the graph, it becomes less costly to produce in the second plant. Only points on the short-run average cost curves below these points of intersection will also be points on the long-run average cost curve. This holds for all points of intersection on the curve. For example, beyond a monthly output of 26,000, where AC_2 and AC_3 intersect, it becomes less costly to produce in the third plant. The LRAC curve for all five possible plant sizes is composed of the portions of each of the five short-run cost curves corresponding to the minimum cost of producing each output. The dashed segments of each short-run average cost curve in Figure 8–7 are not included in the long-run average cost curve. It is possible to produce the output corresponding to levels of average cost on these segments at lower average cost in an alternative plant.

A smooth long-run cost curve exists when it is possible to vary plant size so that the minimum AC output for each plant is 1 unit greater than that of the previous plant. This would be the case if it were possible for the managers to expand by adding 1 square foot and the smallest fraction of a machine hour whenever they so wished. In the previous example it was presumed that additional capital had to be acquired in large "lumps" that limited the options to only five factories of widely varying capacities.

When the flexibility exists to expand to plants whose minimum AC output is 1 unit greater than that of the previous plant, the long-run average cost curve is called the *envelope* of an infinite number of short-run curves. This curve just touches each short-run cost curve but never intersects them. As the intersection points of the short-run cost curves come closer and closer together, they trace a smooth LRAC curve. Each point on the LRAC curve derived in this way corresponds to a slightly larger plant. Figure 8–8 shows some of the short-run cost curves and how the LRAC curve touches each of them. In Figure 8–8 the lowest possible average cost is $10 per unit, which is attainable in the long run when the firm produces Q^* units in the plant for which the corresponding short-run average cost curve is AC^*.

The long-run marginal cost (LRMC) curve illustrated in Figure 8–8 is derived by calculating the changes in long-run total cost for small changes in output. The long-run marginal cost curve is *not* the envelope of all the short-run marginal cost curves. Short-run marginal cost is calculated for a *given* plant. Long-run marginal cost is the rate at which cost changes with output when all costs are variable. In other words, long-run marginal cost is the incremental cost of output when the producer is free to vary the plant size. When LRMC is less than LRAC, the latter must decline. When LRMC is greater than LRAC, the latter must increase. When LRAC is constant or is at a minimum, LRMC must equal LRAC.[10]

---

[10] See James M. Henderson and Richard E. Quandt, *Microeconomic Theory: A Mathematical Approach,* 3rd ed. (New York: McGraw-Hill, 1980), pp. 88–92, for more detailed analysis of the relationship between LRAC and LRMC.

FIGURE 8–8 Long-Run Average Cost when Plant Size Is Continuously Variable

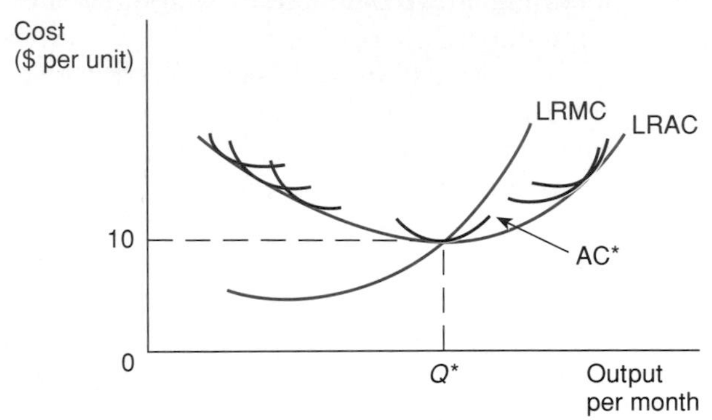

The LRAC curves above represent the envelope of an infinite number of short-run average cost curves. Each of the short-run AC curves corresponds to a plant slightly larger than the previous one. Only a few of these curves have been drawn. The output Q^* corresponds to the minimum possible LRAC of \$10.

Returns to Scale and the Shape of Long-Run Cost Curves

Just as the productive relationships between inputs and outputs influence the shape of short-run cost curves, so do such productive relationships influence the shape of long-run cost curves. To see the way productive relationships between inputs and outputs affect the shape of the long-run average cost curve, assume that a firm expands by increasing the use of all inputs in the same proportion. For example, you could think of the firm as building an identical factory at an alternative location to produce more output. If the firm initially had only one factory, it will double the scale of its operations by doubling its capital, labor, and the use of any other inputs.

The way long-run average cost varies with output when all inputs are increased in the same proportion depends on the returns to scale possible, other things being equal. If increasing returns to scale prevail, not all of the inputs used need to be doubled to double output. For example, to get a 100 percent increase in output, a 50 percent increase in labor hours and capital hours might suffice if increasing returns to scale prevail.

Figure 8–9 uses isoquant analysis to show the firm's expansion path as it increases its scale of operations. Data based on the expansion path are then used to calculate long-run average cost for various levels of output. Suppose that to increase monthly output from 1,000 units to 2,000 units, it is sufficient to increase monthly labor hours used from 500 to 750 and monthly machine hours used from 1,000 to 1,500. Because you do not have to double input use to double output in this case, increasing returns to scale prevail. Assuming no changes in hourly rates for labor or machines as the firm expands production, long-run average costs must decline when increasing returns to scale prevail. To see this, assume that the price of labor is \$10 per hour and the rental rate on capital is \$20 per hour. When

FIGURE 8–9 Returns to Scale and Long-Run Cost

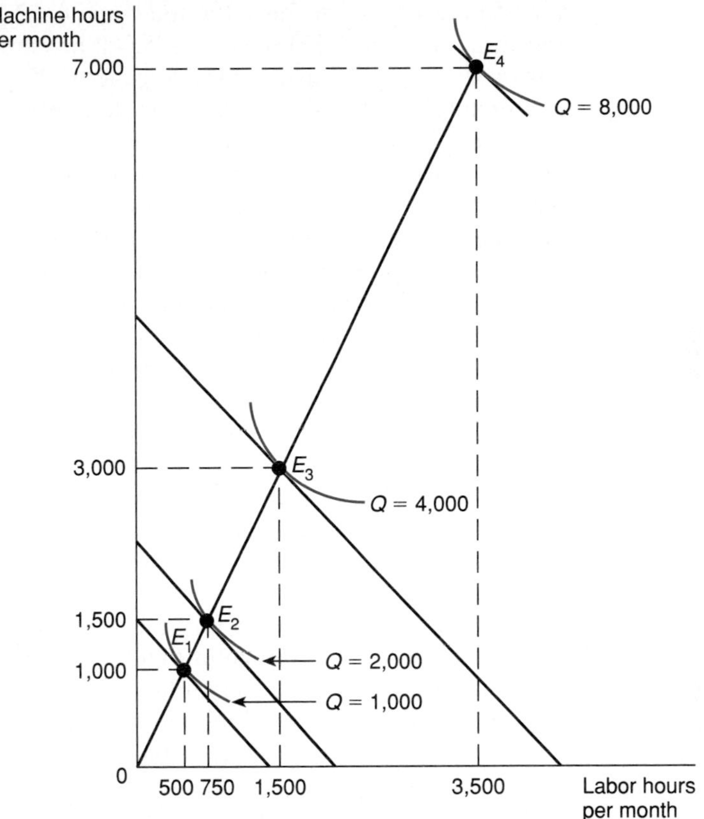

The graph shows a linear expansion path. The firm does not change the ratio of labor to capital as it expands. Between E_1 and E_2, increasing returns prevail. Between E_2 and E_3, constant returns to scale prevail. Finally, if output is increased from 4,000 to 8,000 units per month, decreasing returns to scale set in.

production is 1,000 units, total labor costs are $P_L L$, or \$5,000. Total capital costs are $P_K K$, or \$20,000. Total costs are \$25,000. Dividing these by 1,000 units of output gives an average cost of \$25 per unit. To produce 2,000 chairs requires 750 labor hours and 1,500 machine hours. Labor costs are therefore \$7,500, and capital costs are \$30,000. Dividing the total cost of \$37,500 by 2,000 units gives an average cost of \$18.75. When increasing returns to scale prevail, LRAC declines as output is increased in the long run, given input prices and technology.

It is also easy to show that constant returns to scale imply constant LRAC if input prices do not change as the firm expands. Constant returns to scale imply that input use must be doubled to double output. Suppose that this is true for output between 2,000 and 4,000 units per month. Assuming no change in input prices as production expands, long-run average costs would be constant. To increase output from 2,000 to 4,000 units per month, input use is doubled. Input cost therefore doubles. Because the total cost for 2,000 units was $37,500 per month, the total cost for 4,000 units is $75,000 per month. Dividing this by 4,000 units shows that average cost is $18.75, exactly the same as that for 2,000 units.

Finally, decreasing returns to scale imply *increasing* long-run average costs. If decreasing returns to scale prevail, input use would have to be increased in greater proportion than the desired increase in output. To double output, input use would have to more than double. Assuming that decreasing returns to scale prevail for output beyond 4,000 units per month, doubling output to 8,000 would require more than doubling input use. Machine hours would have to increase from 3,000 to 7,000 per month. Labor hours would have to increase from 1,500 to 3,500 per month. The total cost would therefore increase from $75,000 per month to $175,000 per month, assuming no changes in the prices of labor and capital. Long-run average cost at a monthly output of 8,000 chairs would therefore be $21.25, which is higher than the level that prevailed previously.

Figure 8–10 plots the long-run average cost curve for the data in the above example. A phase of increasing returns to scale up to a monthly output of 2,000 has been assumed. During this phase LRAC declines. Then, beginning at point *A*, there is a phase of constant returns to scale for monthly output from 2,000 to 4,000. During this phase, LRAC is constant. Thereafter, beginning at point *B*, there are decreasing returns to scale and LRAC rises continually.

The LRAC curve shown in Figure 8–8 assumes that the phase of increasing returns to scale is immediately followed by a phase of decreasing returns to scale and that input prices are fixed as the firm increases output. Consequently, the LRAC curve in Figure 8–8 is U-shaped.

FIGURE 8–10 Long-Run Average Cost and Returns to Scale

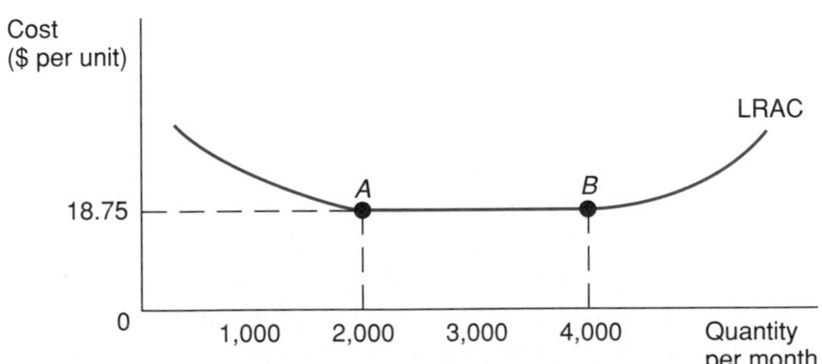

The LRAC curve is based on the expansion path of Figure 8–9. LRAC declines during the phase of increasing returns to scale. Constant returns to scale for monthly output between 2,000 and 4,000 units imply constant LRAC. Decreasing returns to scale for monthly output beyond 4,000 units result in increasing LRAC. Any output between 2,000 and 4,000 units per month can be produced at LRACmin.

EMPIRICAL STUDIES OF COST

Cost studies usually examine variation in costs associated with differences in output produced by firms of various sizes in an industry. These studies try to see how average costs of production vary with amount produced or plant size. There are a number of pitfalls in cost analysis. One pitfall is defining the output. In many cases, the output produced is easily measured and added up. For example, the output of an electric power generating company is easily measured in kilowatt-hours. But how do you measure the output of a hospital? Hospitals produce many kinds of services, some of which are more costly than others. The number of heart bypass operations cannot be added with the number of hernia operations to get a meaningful measure of output. Because heart operations are more costly than hernia operations, the number of operations performed is an imperfect measure of output. Clearly, hospitals that perform relatively more of the most costly types of surgery would show higher average costs. To take account of such differences, an adjustment has to be made for the *quality* of output. Other pitfalls of cost analysis stem from the differences between accounting cost and economic cost. If the only actual data available are accounting costs, these may have to be adjusted to include implicit costs, such as the opportunity cost of funds and forgone rents.

These problems are compounded by the usual headaches encountered in trying to fit smooth curves through actual data. The researchers must use statistical techniques to make sure that the data used actually identify a cost curve or function. They must also make sure that they control for all the determinants of cost. They must account for changes and differences in input prices among firms. They must also adjust for changes in technology.

After grappling with these difficulties, economists have managed to make sense of cost data for a variety of industries. In many cases there appears to be a lengthy stage of constant returns to scale in the long run after an initial stage of increasing returns to scale. Let's now look at the results of some of these studies.

A study of electric power generation in the United States indicated that long-run average costs decline until an output of 20 billion kilowatt-hours per year has been reached. Thereafter, the cost per kilowatt-hour is nearly constant and rises only slightly.[11] A study on sewage treatment in the United Kingdom indicates that there are significant economies of scale up to the treatment of 10 million gallons of sewage per day.[12] A study of refuse collection in cities indicates that average costs decline up to a population level of about 20,000.[13]

---

[11] Laurits R. Christensen and William H. Greene, "Economies of Scale in U.S. Electric Power Generation," *Journal of Political Economy* 84, no. 4 (August 1976), pp. 655–76.

[12] M. R. J. Knapp, "Economies of Scale in Sewage Purification and Disposal," *Journal of Industrial Economics* 27, no. 2 (December 1978), pp. 163–83.

[13] Barbara J. Stevens, "Scale, Market Structure, and the Cost of Refuse Collection," *Review of Economics and Statistics* 60, no. 3 (August 1978), pp. 438–48.

Many studies of manufacturing industries have also shown extensive stages of constant returns to scale.[14] One study of costs in British hospitals used the number of beds as an indicator of output. This study concluded that the minimum possible average cost in the long run occurred at hospitals with 310 beds. The researcher concluded that no cost savings were effected by using general ward care in larger hospitals. In fact, the researcher's analysis of cost per bed indicated that the average cost of care actually was greater in hospitals with over 1,000 beds.[15]

Economies of Scale in Powder Metallurgy Forging

New technologies are often subject to significant economies of scale. For example, a process called "powder metallurgy forging" uses powdered metal loaded into a preshaped mold instead of molten metal to forge machine parts. This process involves less waste of material and less finishing. The cast that emerges from the mold is almost finished product, so that few hand-finishing steps are required. At current prices for the powdered metal the process is still quite expensive. However, indications are that significant economies of scale exist in the production of rapidly solidified metal powders. As plant capacity increases from ½ million pounds per year to 3 million pounds per year, the average cost of these metal powders falls considerably.[16]

Economies of Scale in Banking

In the late 1980s declining profits in the U.S. banking industry and increased competition from foreign banks prompted demands that banking laws be changed to make it easier for U.S. banks to expand. One argument made in favor of such changes was that bank expansion would reduce average costs of production. It was generally believed, however, that diseconomies of scale in banking set in when the assets of banks reach $50 million to $100 million. A more recent analysis of the banking industry that concentrates on banks with assets of more than $1 billion in assets has concluded that larger banks offer services different from those of smaller banks and that this different mix of services is subject to more economies of scale.[17]

Apparently, as larger banks expand up to $3 billion in assets, greater specialization of labor and the use of computers to process both loan applications and information lead to cost saving. Above $3 billion in assets diseconomies set in

---

[14] For a good review of these studies, see A. A. Walters, "Production and Cost Functions," *Econometrica* 31, nos. 1–2 (January–April 1963), pp. 1–66.

[15] Martin Feldstein, *Economic Analysis for Health Service Efficiency* (Chicago: Markham, 1968).

[16] See Joel P. Clark and Merton C. Flemings, "Advanced Materials and the Economy," *Scientific American* 255, no. 4 (October 1986), pp. 51–57.

[17] See Athanasios G. Noulas, Subhash C. Ray, and Stephen M. Miller, "Returns to Scale and Input Substitution for Large U.S. Banks," *Journal of Money, Credit, and Banking* 22, no. 1 (February 1990), pp. 94–108.

because of difficulties in managing a large-scale organization. Thus there is some doubt as to whether the very large banks with $100 billion and more in assets that have been created in recent years can realize lower average costs than are realized by banks with between $1 billion and $3 billion in assets.

Economic Integration and Minimum Efficient Scale in Europe

As of 1992 a number of changes had occurred in Europe that could allow more industries to achieve the minimum efficient scale to lower average costs of production on their long-run average cost curves to a point like A in Figure 8–10. As of 1992, all of the differences in industrial standards and regulations among the 12 member nations of the European Community (Belgium, France, Germany, Greece, Italy, Luxembourg, The Netherlands, Denmark, Ireland, the United Kingdom, Portugal, and Spain) had been removed. Restrictions on sales among these nations were to be removed. The changes will make it easier for European-based businesses to choose the best locations for their plants, to build larger plants at a single location, and to serve the entire European Community, which comprises a market of nearly 350 million people—nearly 100 million more people than the population of the United States.

The larger scale of their operations will allow European firms to lower their average costs of production as they achieve economies of scale that were not possible until now. This means that European firms could become more formidable global competitors as they realize economies of scale that allow them to sell products at lower prices in world markets.

Changes in Input Prices and Technology

Changes in input prices and the adoption of improved technology affect a firm's cost curves. An increase in input prices shifts cost curves upward. A decrease in input prices shifts cost curves downward. This is illustrated in Figure 8–11 for the long-run average cost and marginal cost curves. The relationship between the new cost curves and the old cost curves depends on the extent of the input price changes and the opportunities that the firm has to substitute one input for another in the long run.

For example, if new minimum wage legislation increases the price of labor significantly, firms will substitute capital for labor in the long run to the maximum extent possible. This is illustrated in Figure 8–12. For example, the higher minimum wage will result in a new family of isocost lines for a restaurant operator who pays workers the minimum wage. Assume that 1,000 meals per week are served and that the initial equilibrium is at E_1, where capital and labor are used in the ratio K^*_1/L^*_1 and the minimum possible cost of serving 1,000 meals is $10,000. After the wage increase the isocost line corresponding to $10,000 lies below the isoquant corresponding to 1,000 meals per week. The cheapest method of serving 1,000 meals per week now corresponds to point E_2 on the isoquant, at which capital and labor are used in the ratio K^*_2/L^*_2, and the minimum possible total cost

FIGURE 8–11 Movements in Long-Run Costs

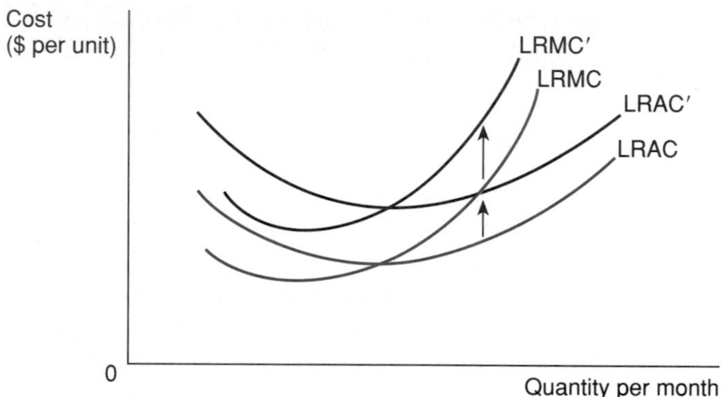

Cost curves shift upward if input prices rise, downward if input prices fall. An improvement in technology shifts the cost curves downward.

FIGURE 8–12 Changes in Input Prices and Their Impact on Long-Run Costs

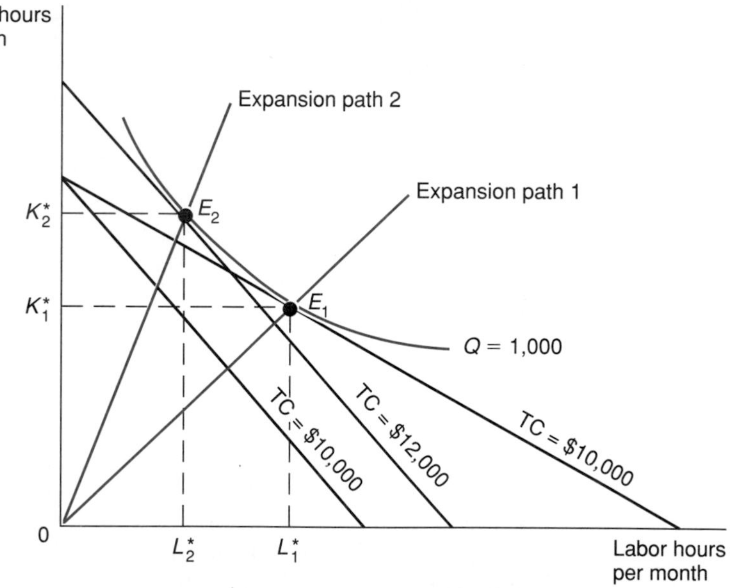

Changes in input prices induce substitution among inputs. A wage increase causes the isocost line corresponding to $10,000 to swivel downward as its intercept on the horizontal axis moves to a lower number of labor hours. After the wage increase the input combination corresponding to point E_1 is no longer the least-cost method of producing 1,000 units of output per month. The increased price of labor induces the firm to substitute capital for labor. This results in a new equilibrium at E_2 and a new long-run expansion path. After wage increase, expansion path 2 must be used to derive the long-run average cost curve. The least-cost method of producing 1,000 units of output now results in total costs of $12,000.

increases to \$12,000 per week. At that point the firm uses a method of serving meals that is more capital intensive than the method previously used because $K^*_2 > K^*_1$ and $L^*_2 < L^*_1$. In other words, the firm substitutes capital for labor as a result of the wage increase. To do so, it could use more self-service techniques, disposable plates and utensils, and anything else that might decrease reliance on labor. The total costs of producing this output rise from \$10,000 to \$12,000 per week, even after doing whatever can substitute capital for labor has been done. The higher wages increase the cost of producing any amount of output. This causes the long-run cost curve to shift upward.

An improvement in technology can also affect a firm's cost curves. Remember from the analysis in Chapter 7 that an improvement in technology implies that the firm can use less input to produce a given output. However, new technology might require that the firm use higher-priced capital and labor. Firms adopt new technology if they can reduce their costs of production for any given output by doing so. New technology therefore has the potential to shift the LRAC curve downward. In recent years, rapidly improving technology in the electronics industries has lowered the costs of producing a variety of goods, including radios, televisions, stereo equipment, calculators, computers, and automatic cameras. Technological improvements in agricultural operations, including improved farm machinery, genetic engineering advances, and improved chemical fertilizers, have sharply reduced average costs in agriculture in the past 30 years.

A technological improvement results in an entirely new isoquant map. After firms consider the price of the capital equipment or skilled labor necessary to use a new technology (such as a new computer or robot system and the programmers necessary to make the system operate) and the transaction costs of adopting it, they decide whether it can shift the LRAC curve downward. Firms will adopt a new technology only if it allows them to produce chosen outputs at lower cost than was previously possible.

New Technology and Cost: Robots

Equipment embodying more advanced technology is not always the least-cost way to produce new output. The choice to employ new technology depends on the price of the new equipment relative to the price of labor and older equipment, the expected transaction costs involved in getting the "glitches" out of the new equipment, and the gain in productivity obtained by employing the new equipment. In the mid-1980s, General Motors considered using robots to place instrument panels in cars in its new plants. However, after attempting to implement the new robot technology, GM found it cheaper to use workers to guide in the panels with the aid of special balance-weighted cranes.

The boom in the employment of robots and computerized production systems that began in the early 1980s had, in fact, slowed significantly by 1987. Many firms that employed computerized systems found that the new technology was often more costly than older technology involving less-sophisticated capital equipment and less-skilled labor. In many cases the transaction costs of the new systems were very high because it often took as long as one year to get all the glitches out of software packages designed to run automated equipment. For example, a gun manufacturer abandoned a high-technology spray-painting machine used to varnish gunstocks because it took too much time to recalibrate the machine when the type of gunstock was changed. The manufacturer returned to hand painting because it was cheaper to use this older technology for its production runs. The new machine, which cost $300,000, was put up for sale.[18]

Economic Integration in Europe, Input Prices, and LRAC

We have discussed the increased opportunities for achieving minimum efficient size of industrial plants in the European Community as its 12 member nations integrate their economies. Another aspect of European economic integration will also cause the LRAC curves in some industries to shift downward. The new laws adopted by the European Community member nations will make it easier for firms to locate their operations at locations in Europe where the inputs they use are priced as low as possible. Labor-intensive industries will find it easier to locate their operations in such nations as Greece, Portugal, and Ireland, where labor prices are relatively low. Industries that require lots of land will find it easier to select locations with low land prices or land rents.

Concept Review

1. How is a firm's long-run cost curve related to its short-run cost curves?
2. Suppose that constant returns to scale prevailed for all levels of output in the long run. What would the envelope of a firm's short-run cost curves look like?
3. Analyze the impact of an increase in the price of fuel on the productive methods and the long-run average cost curve of the trucking industry.

Summary

1. Economists measure cost as the value of inputs used in their next best alternative. This is the opportunity cost of input use.
2. The prices of purchased inputs in most cases reflect their opportunity cost. However, the opportunity cost of owner-supplied inputs must be imputed because current accounting practices do not measure them. When implicit costs exist, economic costs exceed accounting costs.
3. A cost function is a relationship between output and the minimum cost of producing that output. Firms producing at minimum cost must use variable inputs in ratios in which the marginal rate of technical substitution of one variable input for another equals the ratio of the price of that input to the other.
4. Total cost of production in the short run is the sum of variable costs and fixed costs. Variable

[18] See "Special Report: Technology in the Workplace," *The Wall Street Journal*, June 12, 1987, p. 28D.

costs change with the amount of output produced. Fixed costs remain the same, independent of the amount produced.

5. Average cost is total cost divided by output produced. Average cost is the sum of average fixed cost and average variable cost in the short run.
6. Marginal cost is the ratio of the change in cost to a change in output. It represents the cost of producing an additional unit of output.
7. Short-run cost curves reflect the law of diminishing marginal returns. Given input prices, variation in short-run costs is completely explained by variation in the average and marginal products of the variable inputs. The U-shaped short-run average cost curve reflects the fact that the average product of the variable input tends to increase at first and then to decrease as the proportion of the variable input to the fixed input increases. The point of diminishing returns is the output at which marginal cost begins to rise. This corresponds to the output at which the marginal product of the variable input begins to decline.
8. All costs are variable in the long run. In the long run, producers have the flexibility to expand or curtail output by varying all inputs. They can build more and larger factories or close factories.
9. Other influences on cost being equal, when increasing returns to scale prevail, long-run average costs decline. Long-run average costs remain constant as long as constant returns to scale prevail. Decreasing returns to scale cause long-run average costs to increase. Most types of businesses have a phase of increasing returns to scale.

Important Concepts

opportunity cost of using inputs
economic cost
implicit costs
cost function
isocost line
expansion path
total cost
variable cost
fixed cost
average cost
average variable cost
average fixed cost
marginal cost
long-run cost curves

Questions for Review

1. The current interest rate on savings accounts is 9 percent. Suppose that this is the highest rate you can expect to earn. What is the imputed annual cost of taking $4,000 out of your savings account to pay cash for a car?
2. Explain why accounting costs often differ from economic costs.
3. Suppose the marginal product of labor curve always slopes downward. Will the short-run marginal cost curve then be downward sloping, upward sloping, or U-shaped?
4. Explain why the average variable cost curve is U-shaped, whereas the average fixed cost curve always slopes downward. Also explain why changes in the price of capital affect the position of the average fixed cost curve but not the position of the short-run marginal cost curve.
5. Use an isocost-isoquant diagram to illustrate why the average cost of producing a particular level of output is generally (but not always) greater in the short run than in the long run.
6. Suppose that the marginal cost of producing shirts is $10 at a monthly output of 5,000. At that same output, average variable cost is $20. In which short-run stage of production is the firm operating?
7. Explain the difference between long-run cost curves and short-run cost curves. At any point in time a firm is operating out of a given plant, so that only short-run costs can be observed.

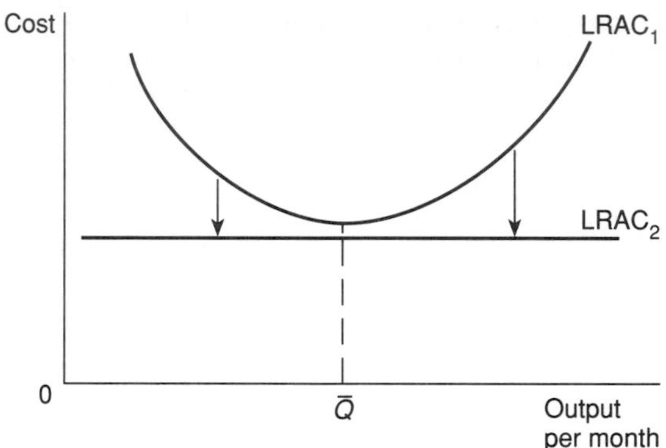

What, then, is the relevance of long-run costs from the manager's point of view?

8. Suppose that technological advance shifts the long-run average cost curve for firms in a particular industry from $LRAC_1$ to $LRAC_2$, as shown in the accompanying diagram. Suppose also that it costs a substantial amount to switch to the new technology but that this "switching cost" does not vary with the level of output. Explain why large firms producing a much greater output than $\bar{Q}$ have the most incentive to adopt the new technology. If the switching cost were paid only once rather than on a recurrent basis, might firms producing about $\bar{Q}$ units of output also choose to adopt the new technology?

9. Suppose that constant returns to scale always prevail for a firm in the long run. What does this imply about the shapes of the firm's long-run average cost and long-run marginal cost curves, assuming that input prices are independent of the firm's output in the long run?

10. Is the price of labor/price of capital ratio greater than, equal to, or less than the marginal rate of technical substitution when the total cost of producing a particular level of output is minimized in the long run? Use a diagram to explain your answer.

PROBLEMS

1. Total costs of producing radios in a certain factory are estimated at $50,000 per month when monthly output is 1,000. Fixed costs are $10,000 per month. Calculate variable cost, average cost, average variable cost, and average fixed cost.

2. Suppose that a technological innovation cuts in half the number of labor hours necessary to produce chairs. Use the data from Table 8–3 to calculate the impact on short-run cost. Assume that 300 machine hours are used each month, that the price of labor remains $10 per hour, and that the price of capital is fixed at $20 per hour. Calculate total cost, variable cost, fixed cost, average fixed cost, average variable cost, and marginal cost.

3. Suppose a lump-sum tax of $10,000 per year is levied on a producer. Show that in the short run this tax will increase average cost of production but have no effect on either average variable cost or marginal cost.

4. Suppose a firm operates a factory producing light bulbs whose output per labor hour is 50 bulbs. If labor costs $5 per hour, calculate the average variable costs of production, assuming that labor is the only variable input. If fixed costs are $5,000 per month and monthly output is 10,000 bulbs, calculate the average costs of production.

5. In the long run, the light bulb firm in Problem 4 can double output each time it doubles both labor and capital input. Assuming that the average cost of producing light bulbs that you calculated in Problem 4 is the minimum possible average cost in the factory, derive the firm's expansion path as output increases to 20,000, 30,000, 40,000, and 50,000 bulbs per month. Assume that the firm does not vary the proportions in which it uses labor and capital as it expands. Draw the long-run average cost curve and the long-run marginal cost curve. Show the impact of an increase in wages to $6 per hour on these curves.

6. Answer the following questions using the isocost-isoquant diagram.

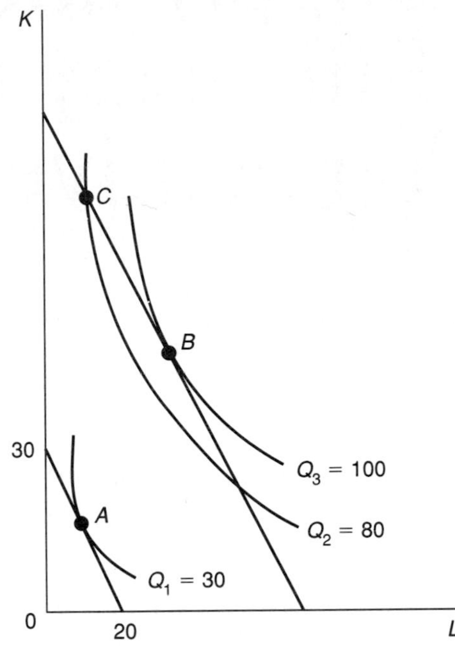

a. What is the marginal rate of technical substitution at point A?
b. If P_K = \$4 and P_L = \$6 at point B and the firm uses 50 units of capital and 30 units of labor at point B, what is the long-run average cost of producing 100 units of output?
c. Does point C represent the input combination that is used to calculate the long-run average cost of pricing 80 units of output? Why or why not?
d. Explain how input prices would have to change to make point C a cost-minimizing input combination in the long run.

7. Answer the following questions using the short-run cost diagram.

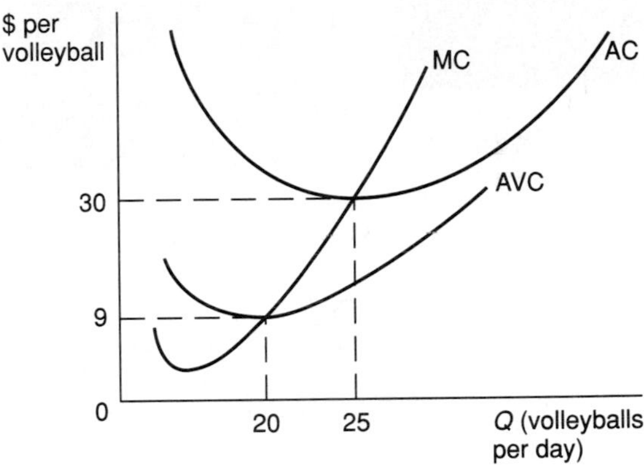

a. What is the total variable cost of producing 20 volleyballs?
b. If average fixed cost is \$12.50 at an output of 10 volleyballs, what is average variable cost at an output of 25 volleyballs?
c. Does the law of diminishing returns hold for the production function underlying these cost functions?
d. Draw in the diagram (at any output level you desire) a rectangle whose area represents total fixed cost.

9

Short-Run Supply and Allocative Efficiency in Perfectly Competitive Markets

For over 70 years the people of Russia and other republics of the former Soviet Union operated under an economic system that prohibited most private enterprise and outlawed the private pursuit of profit. In the old communist system, the government ran virtually all the productive enterprises and there was no competition among sellers. Over the long run, the system failed miserably to satisfy basic consumer demands for products. The extensive government regulation of prices and production was eventually abandoned, and as of the early 1990s the peoples of Eastern Europe and the former Soviet Union began a struggle to move toward a system of free and competitive markets to make their economies more productive and more responsive to consumer demands.

The core of the capitalistic free enterprise system that the people of former communist nations are moving toward is the pursuit of business profit and competition among sellers in free markets. Profit serves as both a signal and a reward to those who satisfy the demands for goods and services through markets. We are now ready to begin an investigation of the willingness of sellers to supply goods and services in markets. The underlying behavioral assumption of the supply model developed here is that sellers seek to maximize profits. Assuming that sellers take the price of their product as given, the model can be used to derive short-run supply curves for goods and services. The analysis explains why short-run supply curves are upward sloping. Once short-run supply curves for individual sellers have been derived, the determinants of market supply curves for a product can be delineated. The insights gleaned from an understanding of the factors affecting supply have broad applications. By means of these insights the short-run impact of various government policies and business practices on market prices and the profits of sellers can be explored.

The theory of short-run supply is an important benchmark for understanding the process by which business firms make goods and services available. Like all microeconomic models, it makes some simplifying assumptions. The most important of these is that the firm has no influence over the price of the product it sells and that only the buyers and sellers in a market are affected by the production and consumption of the product sold. Given these assumptions, we can show that the process of competition results and that the pursuit of profit serves a useful social purpose by squeezing the greatest net benefit from the resources used to satisfy consumer demands. We will derive conditions for allocative efficiency in resource use and show how such conditions can be met by a system of competitive markets.

To understand the process of supply in markets, we integrate the theories of production and cost presented in the two preceding chapters with the theory of demand and explore the relationship between market price and the quantity of goods and services supplied by sellers in the short run. Here we will show how the pursuit of profit influences the choice of how much output to supply to the market. In the following chapter, which analyzes long-run supply, we will demonstrate how over the long run the process of competition guarantees consumers the minimum prices possible and keeps profit down to levels high enough to keep firms from leaving an industry but low enough to prevent new firms from entering it.

THE BUSINESS FIRM AND PERFECT COMPETITION

Business firm An organization set up and managed for the purpose of earning profits for its owners by producing goods or services for sale in markets.

A **business firm** is an organization set up and managed for the purpose of earning profits for its owners by making one or more items available for sale in markets. As of the mid-1980s more than 17 million business firms were operating in the United States. These ranged in size from small repair shops to enormous corporations, such as General Motors.

Business firms are owned and run by people who seek to earn profit by marketing goods and services. The decisions made within firms regarding the use of inputs, the application of new technology, the choice of what to produce, and the level of production are made by its *managers*, who are either the firm's owners or agents hired by them.

The Social Functions and Internal Organization of Business Firms

A business firm is only one of various ways in which goods and services can be made available. For example, households could grow their own food, weave their own fabrics, and make their own clothes instead of purchasing their food and clothing from business firms. However, the multitude and diversity of business firms in modern nonsocialist economies testify to the fact that households gain by purchasing the items they desire from business firms instead of producing those items themselves.

One reason why firms are successful is that by specializing in production of various goods and services, they can economize on transaction costs associated with making those items available. You might be able to provide yourself with a garment by buying cotton from one neighbor, paying a second neighbor to weave the cotton into fabric, paying a third neighbor to design the garment, and paying a fourth neighbor to cut the fabric from the design and sew the garment. The time

MODERN MICROECONOMICS IN ACTION: INTERNATIONAL REPORT

The Toyota *Kyohokai:* A Unique Way of Accomplishing the Goals of Vertical Integration by Lowering the Transaction Costs of Dealing with Independent Suppliers

Vertical integration of production processes can contribute to increased business profits by reducing transaction costs. Many factory production operations involve the movement of unfinished goods through various stages until the final output is ready for shipment. Vertical integration of the stages of production within a single business firm can reduce transportation and storage costs for materials and assure a steady supply of these inputs.

The Toyota Motor Company of Japan has developed a unique way of vertically integrating the production process for the passenger automobile to lower transaction costs. It purchases raw materials such as plastics and steel from independent firms. It also purchases tires, batteries, and other car components from independent firms. It builds engines and body components and assembles and paints the final product within its own plants. However, it obtains many key components, such as piston pins, castings, and transmissions designed specifically for Toyotas, from about 230 specialized companies that have a unique relationship with it.

The 230 companies are called *Kyohokai*, which means the "Toyoto Cooperation Association." About 60 percent of Toyota's total outlay for materials and parts is accounted for by purchases from these companies. Directors of Toyota usually serve as directors of the Kyohokai companies, and Toyota usually owns a high proportion of the corporate stock of these companies. Although Toyota deals with companies other than those in the Kyohokai, its unique relationship with the Kyohokai companies allows it to coordinate planning and other activities with them so as to reduce its transaction costs. This also helps Toyota achieve reduced inventory storage costs. Toyota's detailed planning with its affiliated companies allows it to synchronize delivery of supplies so as to get car components from affiliated companies "just in time" for their assembly. The Kyohokai system has significantly reduced Toyota's costs and thus increased its profits.*

* See Toyohiro Kono, *Strategy and Structure of Japanese Enterprises* (Armonk, N.Y.: M. E. Sharpe, 1984), pp. 125–28.

and effort you would spend in obtaining the services of these specialists might be quite valuable to you. For that reason you might find it less costly to purchase clothing produced by a firm that specializes in acquiring and managing the inputs necessary to produce clothing. By specializing in the production of clothing, such a firm can produce garments and sell them profitably at a price buyers find attractive compared to the buyers' alternative of producing their own garments or managing the production process themselves.

Even business firm managers must decide which of the goods and services they use as inputs they should produce themselves and which they should purchase from other sellers. A *vertically integrated firm* would not purchase any products of other firms. For example, a vertically integrated automobile producer would make its own steel rather than purchase it from an independent steel firm. It would also acquire tires from one of its divisions rather than purchase them from another firm. A key factor in determining a firm's degree of vertical integration is the transaction costs associated with dealing with independent suppliers. To keep profit as high as possible, managers try to keep both production and transaction costs as low as possible for any given output. If an automobile producer finds that independent tire producers are unreliable suppliers and that delays in tire shipments cause lost car sales, it might choose to form (or purchase) its own tire subsidiary. By doing so, it could reduce the transaction costs of getting the tires it needs when it needs them.

There is some degree of vertical integration in all firms. However, in the effort to keep costs as low as possible, managers constantly evaluate the cost of producing goods and services used as inputs (such as accounting services) as opposed to the cost of buying those goods and services from independent sellers.[1]

Business firms provide a useful social function by acting as intermediaries between consumers of their products and owners of input services, including the workers needed to produce those products. To make a profit, business firms must be able to sell their products at prices that allow them to cover both the costs of all inputs they purchase and the opportunity cost of any owner-supplied inputs.

The Single-Product Profit-Maximizing Business Firm

To analyze the basic functions and profitability of business firms, economists make a number of simplifying assumptions about the firm's goals and operations. Two key simplifying assumptions are made in the model of the business firm developed here. First, it is assumed that the firm produces a single product, though in reality modern business firms often have a multitude of product lines.

The second simplifying assumption made by economists is that the sole goal of the firm is to maximize its profit from selling its single product over each period, though it is of course possible that firms might have other goals. They might be willing to sacrifice some profit to engage in charitable or other activities that enhance their image with the public. They might be more concerned with increasing their sales revenue or with controlling the risk of their operations than with profits. However, the behavioral assumption that firms maximize profits, although a simplification, has proved quite fruitful in enhancing our understanding of the supply process. As you will see in this chapter, a model based on the presumption that managers of a single-product firm seek to maximize profits can explain the law of supply in the short run.

Perfect competition Prevails when many competing sellers sell a standardized product in a market in which each seller has a very small share of total sales, is unconcerned about the reactions of rivals, and takes the price of the product as given; when information is freely available; and when sellers have freedom of entry into and exit out of the market.

Perfect Competition

Throughout this chapter it is assumed that many competing sellers offer their product for sale in a market with many buyers. The degree of competition among business firms and among buyers varies considerably among markets. **Perfect competition** prevails in a market in which the following conditions exist:

1. The market consists of *many competing sellers*, each selling a *standardized product* to many buyers.

[1] For analysis of the importance of transaction costs in influencing the organization of the firm, see Oliver E. Williamson, *The Economic Institutions of Capitalism* (New York: Free Press, 1985).

2. Each firm has a *very small share of the total output sold in the market*, generally less than 1 percent of total sales, over any given period.

3. No business firm in the market regards its rivals as a threat to its market share. *Firms in the market are therefore unconcerned about their competitor's production decisions.*

4. *Information is freely available* on prices, technology, and profit opportunities, and it is possible to quickly respond to changing market conditions by reallocating input use.

5. There is *freedom of entry into and exit out of the market* by sellers of the standardized good. This means that there are neither restraints to prevent a firm from choosing to sell a good in the market nor difficulties in freely choosing to cease operations as a seller.

A perfectly competitive market is one in which the conditions of perfect competition are satisfied. In a perfectly competitive market, buyers of a standardized good or service have no reason to prefer the output of one firm to that of any other firm. For example, the market for eggs is likely to be competitive. Many farmers sell eggs each day. No one farmer is likely to account for more than 1 percent of each day's output offered for sale. The first two of the aforementioned characteristics of a perfectly competitive market guarantee that no one seller in the market can influence the price of the product. Each seller's share of the total output is so small that it is impossible for any seller to shift supply enough to change price. *Accordingly, sellers in perfectly competitive markets take prices of their output as a given.*

Demand as Seen by a Competitive Firm

Competitive firm A firm that sells its output in a perfectly competitive market and thus cannot influence the price of what it sells.

A **competitive firm** is one that sells its output in a perfectly competitive market. Because competitive firms can in no way influence the market price, they can be characterized as *price takers*. The demand curve for the output of a single-product competitive firm is a horizontal line. A horizontal demand curve means that the firm can sell any amount of output without affecting the price. Each competitive firm lacks the capacity to increase or decrease the amount offered for sale sufficiently to change the market price. Do not confuse the demand curve as seen by the firm with the market demand curve. The market demand curve *is* downward sloping. It shows how the willingness of buyers to pay changes as the availability of the good changes.

Figure 9–1 shows how the market price is determined by supply and demand and how this influences the demand as seen by the firm. For example, suppose the market price of a standardized office chair produced by many independent furniture firms is $150. At this price 318,000 chairs are supplied each month. Figure 9–1(a) shows how this price is determined by the market demand for and market supply of chairs. Each firm has the capacity to produce only a small portion of the total monthly market supply. It is now easy to see why the firm's demand curve illustrated in Figure 9–1(b), is a horizontal line. Suppose 1,000 firms are producing the chair and that each firm can produce no more than 500 chairs a month. The most that any one firm can add to (or subtract from) market supply is therefore 500

FIGURE 9–1 The Demand for the Output of a Competitive Firm

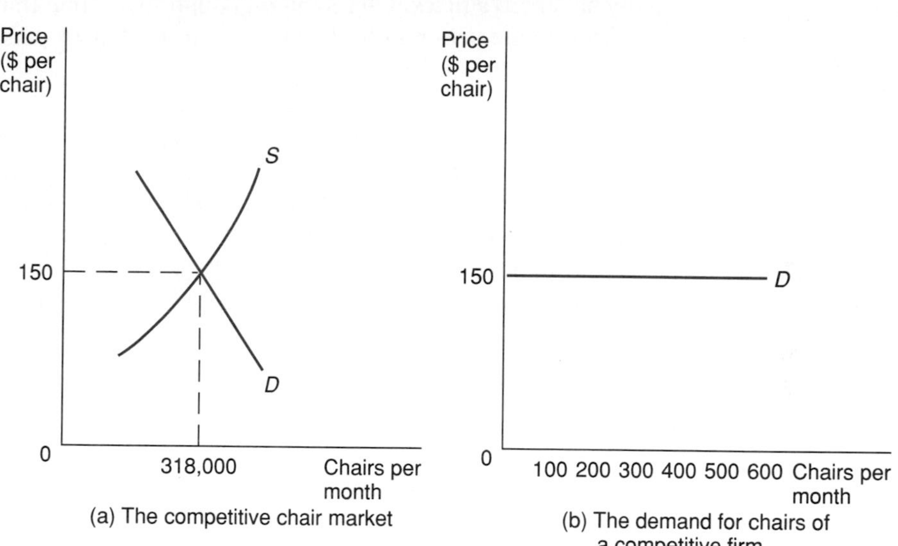

The market price of chairs is \$150. A competitive firm can sell all the chairs it wishes at that price. The demand for a competitive firm's output is infinitely elastic at the market price. The output of any one firm is a perfect substitute for that of any other firm.

units per month. Even if any one firm adds or subtracts this maximum amount, the shift in the supply curve would be so negligible as to have no effect on price. Accordingly, no one firm can influence the price by making the good produced appreciably more abundant or scarce.

The standardized product sold by any one competitive firm is a perfect substitute for that of any other competing firm. Accordingly, the demand curve viewed by the competitive firm is infinitely elastic at the market price. To verify this, note that the slope of the firm's demand curve is zero. It follows that the price elasticity of demand is minus infinity at any possible quantity along the firm's demand curve because

$$E_D = \left(\frac{P}{Q}\right)\left(\frac{\Delta Q}{\Delta P}\right)$$

The ratio $\Delta Q/\Delta P$ is the inverse of the slope of the demand curve. As the slope of a demand curve approaches zero, its inverse becomes $-1/0$, which is minus infinity. As a downward-sloping demand curve becomes flat, its price elasticity at any given quantity becomes minus infinity.

The competitive market serves as a useful abstraction. Standardized agricultural products, such as wheat, rice, corn, barley, and oats and graded meats, poultry, and dairy products, are in fact sold by a large number of firms, no one of which has a significantly large share of total supply. In other cases the products of many sellers in a market are similar enough to assume that demand as seen by any one firm, while not infinitely elastic, is at least very elastic.

CONCEPT REVIEW

1. What is the social function of a business firm?
2. What are the characteristics of a perfectly competitive market?
3. Explain why the demand curve for the product of a competitive firm is a horizontal line.

PROFIT MAXIMIZATION

The theory developed in this chapter assumes that the goal of the firm is to *maximize* profits. The firm produces a single product, the cost of which varies as more or less is produced and sold at the going market price. The managers of the firm must choose the quantity supplied so as to achieve the goal of attaining maximum profit over each sales period, such as a month.

Total Revenue, Total Cost, and Economic Profit

Profit is the difference between total revenue (TR) and total cost (TC) per sales period:

$$\text{Profit} = \text{TR} - \text{TC} \qquad \textbf{(9–1)}$$

Total revenue is the price (P) of the good sold multiplied by the amount sold (Q). The price is beyond the influence of a competitive firm. *Therefore, a competitive firm can influence its revenue only by varying the amount it offers for sale.* However, as output changes, cost changes.

Economic profits Revenue minus economic costs.

Remember that economic costs diverge from accounting costs when its firm's owners supply their own inputs rather than purchase those inputs from independent sellers (see Chapter 8). **Economic profits** are calculated by subtracting all economic costs from revenue. A firm earns economic profits when its revenue exceeds the sum of its explicit accounting costs and the implicit costs associated with the use of owner-supplied inputs. The term *profit* is used synonymously with *economic profit* in this book.

When a firm earns zero economic profit, it covers all of its economic costs. The *normal profit* is the profit that the firm's owners forgo by employing their owner-supplied inputs within their own firm. The normal profit represents the opportunity cost of the owner-supplied inputs. When owners of a firm earn zero economic profit from their operations, they cover their accounting costs and their implicit costs, thereby earning as much as they could earn in their next best alternative. A firm that earns zero economic profit is therefore regarded as earning the normal profit, which is the sum of money that covers implicit costs. Of course, the goal of the firm is to maximize economic profit, not merely to cover economic costs. When a firm cannot cover its economic costs and therefore earns less than a normal profit, its owners can earn more by using their resources in an alternative enterprise.

For example, suppose the only owner-supplied input of a corporation is capital equipment. The market value of this equipment, less any debt the firm has incurred to purchase it, is $1 million. If the corporation forgoes the opportunity to earn 10 percent per year by investing this cash elsewhere, the normal profit is $100,000 per year. An accountant would include this as part of measured profits. An economist would argue that if the firm showed annual accounting profits of only $100,000, it would merely be breaking even in the sense that revenues are exactly equal to economic costs. The $100,000 accounting profit based on accounting costs is the normal profit.

A Numerical Example: Output, Cost, Revenue, and Profit

Suppose the current market price of standardized chairs is $150. Table 9–1 provides data on output, revenues, cost, and profits for a chair producer. The production and cost data are the same as those used in Chapters 7 and 8. Additional data have been added on cost and revenues for monthly chair output between 315 and 320 chairs. These additional data allow a fine-tuned calculation of the exact monthly output level that maximizes profits.

The first column of Table 9–1 shows the monthly output of chairs ranging up to 320. The second column shows the market price of the standardized chair. The third column computes total revenue of all the monthly output levels shown. The

TABLE 9–1 Revenues, Costs, and Profits

Monthly Output (Chairs)	*Price (P = MR)*	*Total Revenue (TR)*	*Total Cost (TC)*	*Profit (TR − TC)*	*Marginal Cost* (MC)*	*Marginal Profit (MR − MC)*
0	$150	$ 0	$ 6,000	$−6,000	—	—
35	150	5,250	7,700	−2,450	$ 48.57	$101.43
150	150	22,500	11,000	11,500	28.70	121.30
210	150	31,500	13,200	18,300	36.67	113.33
250	150	37,500	15,000	22,500	45.00	105.00
270	150	40,500	16,400	24,100	70.00	80.00
288	150	43,200	17,760	25,440	75.55	74.45
305	150	45,750	19,100	26,650	78.82	71.18
315	150	47,250	20,300	26,950	120.00	30.00
316	150	47,400	20,425	26,975	125.00	25.00
317	150	47,550	20,560	26,990	135.00	15.00
318	150	47,700	20,710	26,990	150.00	0.00
319	150	47,850	20,880	26,970	170.00	−20.00
320	150	48,000	21,080	26,920	200.00	−50.00

* Marginal cost in this column represents an average of the marginal cost of output in each batch of production up to 315 chairs. Data on the marginal cost of a particular output level within each batch can exceed or fall short of the estimate of marginal cost in this column.

fourth column adds total variable costs and fixed costs to obtain total costs. Profit is shown in the fifth column. Profit is simply the difference between total revenue and total cost at each possible output level. Notice that the maximum monthly profits, $26,990, is achieved when the firm produces a monthly output of between 317 and 318 chairs. The firm can be thought of as increasing output until profits begin to decline.

Marginal Analysis of Profit Maximization

Marginal revenue The change in revenue that results from selling an additional unit of output.

The **marginal revenue** (MR) of output is the change in revenue resulting from the sale of an additional unit. Marginal revenue can be calculated for any change in output from the following formula:

$$\text{MR} = \frac{\Delta \text{TR}}{\Delta Q} \qquad \textbf{(9–2)}$$

As long as the price is unaffected by the number of units the firm sells, the marginal revenue of selling an additional chair will be its price. Each extra chair sold increases revenue by $150. The change in total revenue is always

$$\Delta \text{TR} = \Delta(PQ)$$

Because P is independent of Q for the competitive firm,

$$\Delta \text{TR} = P\Delta Q$$

Therefore,

$$\text{MR} = P(\Delta Q/\Delta Q) = P \qquad \textbf{(9–3)}$$

for a competitive firm.[2] Accordingly, the second column of Table 9–1 has been labeled P = MR.

In choosing the profit-maximizing output, managers can be thought of as comparing the marginal cost with the marginal revenue for each extra chair sold. When marginal revenue exceeds marginal cost, selling an additional chair increases profits. When marginal revenue falls short of marginal cost, sale of an additional chair decreases profits. The change in profits from selling an additional chair is the difference between the marginal revenue from that chair and its marginal cost. This is the **marginal profit.** It is calculated in the last column of Table 9–1:

Marginal profit The additional profit that results from the sale of an additional unit of output.

$$\text{Marginal profit} = \text{MR} - \text{MC} \qquad \textbf{(9–4)}$$

A firm maximizes profits by continuing to produce up to the point at which marginal revenue equals marginal cost: MR = MC. You can see this by setting marginal profit equal to zero in Equation 9–4 and solving for MR. As long as marginal profit is positive, producing more adds to profit. To exhaust all opportu-

[2] This is easy to see with calculus: TR = PQ, where P is a constant. It follows that

$$\text{MR} = d\text{TR}/dQ = P$$

nity for net gain over a period, firms must therefore increase output to the point at which MR = MC so that production continues just to the point at which it no longer adds to profit.

Because price is equal to marginal revenue for a competitive firm, maximum profits for such a firm occur when output has been adjusted to the point at which marginal cost rises to equal the market price. *The marginal condition for profit maximization by a single-product competitive firm is therefore*

$$P = \text{MC} \qquad \textbf{(9–5)}$$

The equilibrium output of a profit-maximizing competitive firm is the output for which price equals marginal cost. Any output below this level implies that the firm can increase profits by producing more. Any output above the one corresponding to P = MC implies that the firm can increase profits by producing less output.[3] You can see this by looking at the data in Table 9–1. As long as marginal cost exceeds price, marginal profit is positive and profit increases. After 318 chairs have been produced, marginal cost exceeds price and additional production results in negative marginal profit and thereby a reduction in total profit.

Graphic Analysis of Variation in Profit as Output Increases over the Short-Run Period

Figure 9–2 plots the graph of total revenue and total cost in the short run for the data in Table 9–1. The total revenue curve is a ray through the origin with slope

$$\frac{\Delta \text{TR}}{\Delta Q} = \text{MR} = \$150$$

The slope of the total revenue curve is equal to marginal revenue, which in turn is equal to the market price of the product sold by the competitive firm.

The slope of the total cost curve at any point is

$$\frac{\Delta \text{TC}}{\Delta Q} = \text{MC}$$

---

[3] This result is easily obtainable with calculus. Both total revenue and total cost are functions of quantity. This means that profit is also a function of quantity. With the symbol π representing profit:

$$\pi = f(Q) = PQ - \text{TC}$$

To maximize profits

$$d\pi/dQ = d(PQ)/dQ - d\text{TC}/dQ = 0$$

Assuming that second-order conditions for a maximum hold, it follows that maximum profits are attained at the output for which

$$d(PQ)/dQ = d\text{TC}/dQ$$

where the term on the right side of the equation is marginal revenue and the term on the left side is marginal cost. Because P is a constant under perfect competition, the equilibrium condition for maximum profit is

$$P = \text{MC}$$

FIGURE 9–2 Total Revenue, Total Costs, and Profit

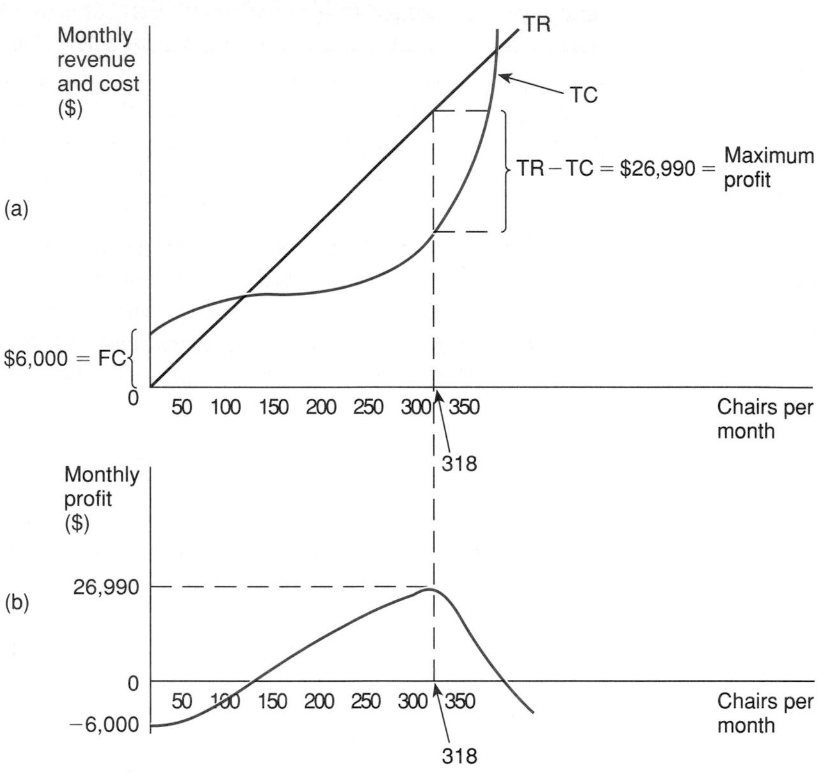

Graph (a) shows total revenue and total cost curves based on the data in Table 9–1. The difference between the two curves gives the profit per month for the indicated output. Maximum profit occurs when 318 chairs are produced each month. Graph (b) plots monthly profit. Maximum profit corresponds to the maximum distance between the TR and TC curves, which occurs when the slope of the TC curve equals the slope of the TR curve.

Note that the slope of the total cost curve decreases at first as monthly output increases but then begins to increase. This means that marginal cost declines as production begins each month and increases as monthly output grows.

The vertical distance between the total revenue and total cost curves gives profit at each level of production. This difference is plotted directly below the total revenue and total cost curves. Note that profit is negative at low levels of output. If the firm were to produce nothing during the month, its short-run losses would be equal to its fixed costs. In this case the fixed costs of $6,000 per month are the costs of capital equipment that the firm cannot avoid even if it ceases operations. As production begins, profit increases, reaching a maximum level at an output of 318 chairs per month. If the firm were to produce more than 318 chairs per month, profit would steadily decline and eventually it would become negative.

Given the price of chairs and the way total cost varies with monthly output, the firm finds that its profit varies as it varies production over the month. At low levels of output the firm is likely to incur losses because it will earn little revenue to offset its costs. As output increases from low levels, the firm's profits rise, reach a maximum at the point at which MR = MC, and then fall again as marginal costs rapidly increase above the price of the product.

At the output corresponding to maximum monthly profit, note that the slope of the total cost curve is equal to the slope of the total revenue curve. Because the slope of the total cost curve is marginal cost and the slope of the total revenue curve is marginal revenue, the point at which the slopes are equal satisfies the conditions for maximum profit.

Price, Marginal Cost, Average Cost, and the Profit-Maximizing Output

In Figure 9–3(a) the firm's demand curve is plotted on the same set of axes as its short-run marginal and average cost curves. Along the competitive firm's demand curve,

$$P = \text{MR} = \$150$$

The marginal cost curve intersects the firm's demand curve at point *B*.[4] Equilibrium output corresponding to that level of marginal cost is $Q = 318$ chairs per month. If the firm were to produce one unit more than 318 chairs per month, marginal cost would exceed marginal revenue and profit would decline.

Figure 9–3(b) shows how profit varies as the firm produces varying amounts per month when the price of chairs is $150. At the output corresponding to the point at which the marginal revenue and marginal cost curves intersect, the profit curve reaches its maximum of $26,990.

The firm's monthly profit at the equilibrium output is also represented by the area of the rectangle *ABCD* in Figure 9–3(a). The height of the rectangle is $P -$ AC. This is the profit per unit of output sold. The width of the rectangle is the quantity produced. Total profit is equal to profit per unit multiplied by the number of units sold:

$$\text{Total profit} = (P - \text{AC})Q \qquad \textbf{(9–6)}$$

According to the data in Table 9–2, at a price of $150 per chair the profit per chair is a substantial $84.87 if 318 chairs are sold. Selling 318 chairs at this price gives the firm a total profit of $26,990 per month.

Note that the maximum profit output is *not* the output for which profit per unit is highest. It would therefore be a mistake for managers of a profit-maximizing firm to use profit per unit as an indication of total profits. For the data in the table,

---

[4] For second-order conditions for a maximum to be satisfied, the marginal cost curve must rise to intersect the marginal revenue curve from below. If, instead, the marginal cost curve were falling as output rose and hit the marginal revenue curve from above, the output corresponding to the intersection would correspond to minimum profit!

FIGURE 9–3 Profit Maximization by a Competitive Firm

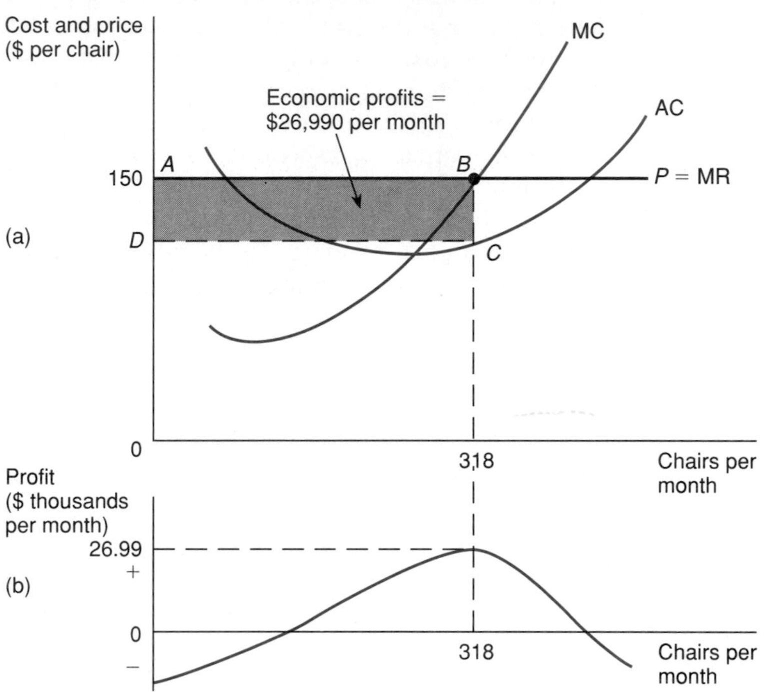

At the profit-maximizing output, $P = MC = \$150$. The firm earns economic profits equal to the shaded area *ABCD*. The profit-maximizing output is 318 chairs. Total monthly profit is $26,990 when that output is sold. Graph (b) shows how profit varies with output when the price of chairs is $150. Profit will fall if more or fewer than 318 chairs are sold per month.

TABLE 9–2 Average Cost, Price, and Profit

Output	*Average Variable Cost*	*Average Fixed Cost*	*Average Cost*	*Price*	*Profit per Unit (P − AC)*	*Total Profit (P − AC)Q*
0	—	—	—	$150	—	−$6,000
35	$48.57	$171.43	$220.00	150	−$70.00	− 2,450
150	33.33	40.00	73.33	150	76.67	11,500
210	34.29	28.57	62.86	150	87.14	18,300
250	36.00	24.00	60.00	150	90.00	22,500
270	38.52	22.22	60.74	150	89.26	24,100
288	40.83	20.83	61.66	150	88.34	25,440
305	42.95	19.67	62.62	150	87.38	26,650
315	45.50	19.04	64.44	150	85.56	26,950
316	45.65	18.99	64.64	150	85.36	26,975
317	45.94	18.92	64.86	150	85.14	26,990
318	46.26	18.87	65.13	150	84.87	26,990
319	46.58	18.81	65.45	150	84.55	26,970
320	47.13	18.75	65.88	150	84.12	26,420

the maximum profit per unit is $90. This is attained when monthly output is 250 chairs. However, at the point of actual maximum profit, profit per unit is only about $85 and output is 318 chairs per month.

Also note that given the market price, the output for which profit per unit is at a maximum corresponds to the output for which average cost of production is at a minimum. In Figure 9–3(a) this corresponds to an output of 250 chairs per month. Total profit is not necessarily maximized therefore when a manager operates a plant to minimize the average cost of production! Instead, to maximize profit, the manager must carefully gauge marginal cost and adjust output to make sure that marginal cost equals marginal revenue. Comparing *average* instead of *marginal* cost with the price does not enable a manager to choose the output that maximizes profit.

Breaking Even

When price is greater than average cost of production at the profit-maximizing output, the firm earns economic profits. Suppose, instead, the market price of the product is just equal to the average cost of production at the output corresponding to maximum profit. This possibility is illustrated in Figure 9–4(a). At a price of $60, price equals marginal cost at point *E*, which also corresponds to the point at which marginal cost equals average cost. At that price the profit-maximizing output is 250 chairs per month. Because P = AC at the output for which MR = MC, the profit per unit, P − AC, is zero; therefore, total economic profits are zero. The maximum possible economic profit at the $60 price is zero! At that price the best that the firm can do when seeking to maximize profit is to break even, which means that it just covers its economic costs.

You can see this as well by looking at Figure 9–4(b), which shows how profit varies with alternative monthly output levels. The managers of the firm can do no better than just cover their economic costs. If they choose to produce any output other than the one for which P = MC, they will incur losses. In this case, given the market price of the product, the maximum possible profit is zero. Marginal analysis still guides the managers to the maximum profit output, but in this case that profit is unfortunately zero.

The maximum possible profit a firm can earn varies with the market price of its product. Because market price is beyond the influence of any single firm, changes in overall conditions of supply and demand in the perfectly competitive market affect the market price and the opportunities to make profits by selling in the market.

Minimizing Losses when Price Is below the Minimum Possible Average Cost

When price falls below the minimum possible average cost, the firm will be unable to generate enough revenue from selling its product to cover its economic costs. Figure 9–5(a) shows the case of a firm in the unfortunate position of incurring losses at the market price of its output. At a price of $50 per unit the firm cannot avoid incurring losses because that price is below the minimum possible average

FIGURE 9–4 **A Competitive Firm Breaking Even**

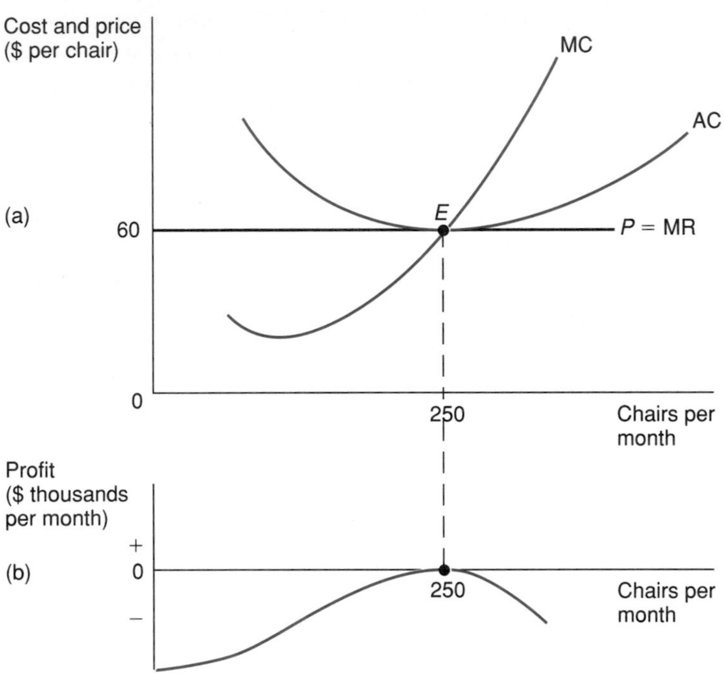

If market price were to fall to $60 per chair, the maximum possible economic profit would be zero. At the profit-maximizing output of 250 chairs per month, the firm takes in enough revenue at the $60 price to just cover its economic cost; therefore, it breaks even. Graph (b) shows that if the firm were to either increase or decrease production in relation to the current level of 250 chairs per month, it would incur losses.

cost of $60. However, by producing up to the output level at which P = MC, the firm's managers can minimize those losses. In Figure 9–5 the output corresponding to the point of minimum loss is $Q = 240$ units per month. The loss at that level of output is represented by the area *ABED*. This area represents the loss per unit of output, AC − P (which is the distance *DE* on the graph), multiplied by the output corresponding to the point at which P = MC (which corresponds to the distance *BE*).

Figure 9–5(b) also shows that if the firm chooses any output other than the one for which P = MC, it will incur still greater monthly losses. *Adjusting output to the point at which* P = *MC gives the minimum-loss output when price is below the minimum possible average cost.*

When a firm incurs losses, it has two options in the short run. It can continue to produce the output corresponding to the point at which P = MC, or it can simply shut down operations. By continuing to operate at a loss, the firm incurs both fixed costs *and* variable costs necessary to produce the loss-minimizing

FIGURE 9–5 A Competitive Firm Incurring Losses

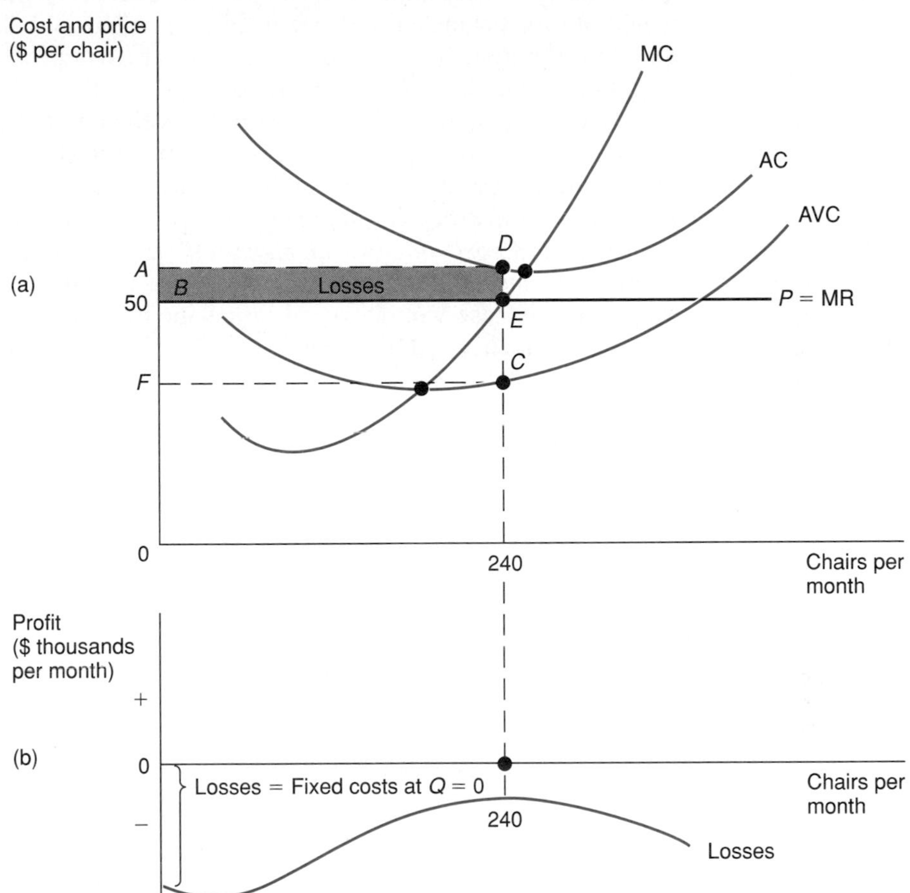

If market price were to fall to $50 per chair, the firm would incur losses equal to the area *ABED*. The loss per unit at the output where P = MC is the distance *DE*, which represents AC − P. If the firm were to cease operations, it would still incur fixed costs equal to the area *AFCD*. The firm loses less by continuing to operate in the short run.

output. It also generates some revenue by selling the output it produces. When the firm is shut down, it lays off workers and ceases to order new materials. By choosing to shut down, the managers cut variable costs to zero, but the firm still incurs losses in the short run because of its fixed costs. The firm also forgoes the opportunity to earn revenue from the sale of its product and therefore incurs losses exactly equal to its fixed costs.

It is easy to show that at a price of $50 the firm whose cost curves and demand curve are illustrated in Figure 9–5(a) will lose more by shutting down than by continuing to operate in the short run. To see this, recall that the vertical distance between the AC and AVC curves is average fixed cost (AFC). Therefore, at an output of Q = 240, fixed cost can be represented by the rectangle *AFCD*. The height of this rectangle is average fixed cost, whereas its length is the equilibrium quantity of output (Q). The area of the rectangle is average fixed cost multiplied by output sold, which equals fixed cost.

By continuing to operate, the firm loses the amount represented by the area *ABED*. Because the area *AFCD* exceeds the area *ABED*, the firm loses less by continuing to operate than by shutting down. *As long as price exceeds the minimum possible average variable cost, the loss of continuing to operate will be less than the fixed cost which is the short-run loss incurred when the plant is not in operation*. Figure 9–5(b) also shows how losses equivalent to fixed costs at zero output in this case would exceed losses incurred at an output of 240 chairs per month, at which P = MC = \$50.

The Decision to Shut Down Operations in the Short Run

Shutdown point The point reached when price falls to a level that just allows a firm to cover the minimum possible average variable cost of its output.

Under what circumstances will the firm choose to shut down in the short run when price has fallen so low that it is impossible to earn profit? When price has fallen to a level that just allows the firm to cover its minimum possible average variable cost, the firm is at the **shutdown point.** When P = AVC at the output for which P = MC, the loss per unit is equal to average fixed cost. In Figure 9–6, at a price of

FIGURE 9–6 The Shutdown Point

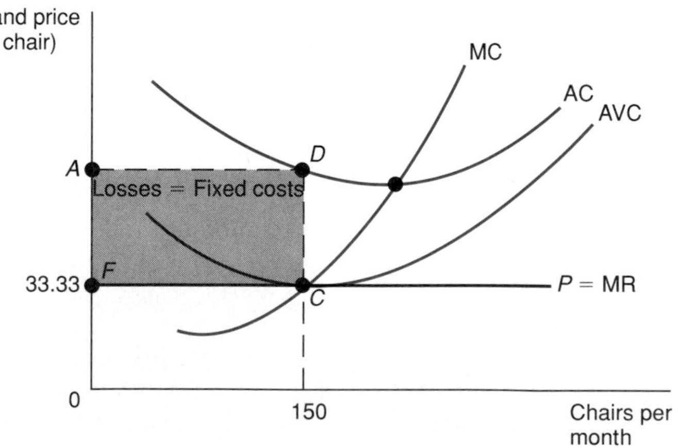

At a market price of \$33.33 per chair P = AVCmin. The firm produces 150 chairs per month. At that output (P − AC) and (AC − AVC) are both equal to the distance *DC*. The economic losses incurred by continuing to operate are equal to fixed costs. If price were to fall below \$33.33 a chair, the firm would cease operating in the short run. Therefore, the shutdown point is at *C*, where the AVC curve is at a minimum.

$33.33 per chair and an output of 150 chairs per month, the loss per chair is equal to the distance *DC*, which also represents average fixed cost. It follows that losses incurred by remaining in operation will equal fixed costs.

At any price below the minimum possible average variable cost, the loss per unit (AC − *P*) would exceed average fixed cost at the output for which *P* = MC. This is because the vertical distance between the firm's demand curve and its average cost curve would exceed the vertical distance between AC and AVC. If price were to fall below the minimum possible average variable cost, for instance, to $30 per chair, operating losses at the output for which *P* = MC would exceed fixed costs and the firm would shut down. Figure 9–7 shows that at a price of $30 per chair, which is below the minimum possible AVC, operating losses, represented by the area *ABCD*, are greater than fixed costs, represented by the area *ABFG*.

Remember that the point of minimum possible average variable cost corresponds to the point of maximum average product for the variable inputs (see Chapter 8). The output for which average variable cost of production is at a minimum corresponds to the boundary between stages I and II of production. It is now possible to show that a profit-maximizing firm will *never* operate in stage I. By using variable inputs at output levels corresponding to those in stage I, the firm will lose more by operating than by shutting down. It follows that a profit-maximizing firm avoids stage I just as surely as it avoids stage III, in which the marginal product of the variable inputs is negative.

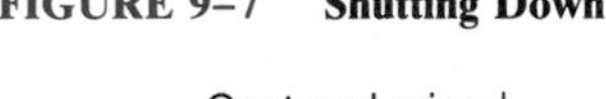

FIGURE 9–7 Shutting Down

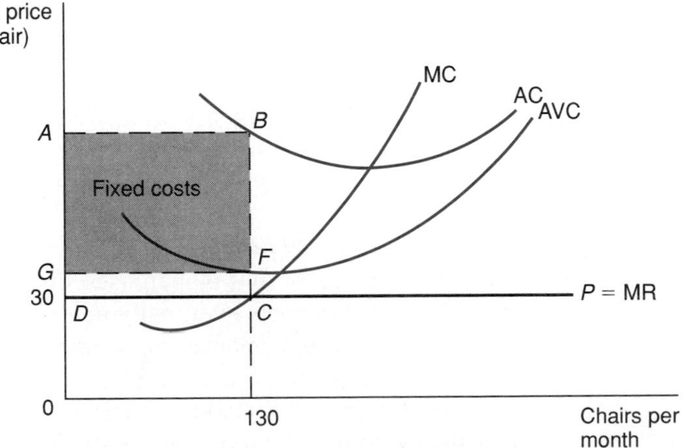

At the output corresponding to the point at which MR = MC, operating losses represented by the area *ABCD* exceed fixed costs, represented by the area *ABFG*, because *P* < AVCmin. The firm therefore immediately ceases to operate.

In summary, the firm elects to continue operating in the short run at a loss if its total revenue exceeds its variable costs. This allows the firm to generate some revenue to cover some of its fixed costs. It follows that the condition to remain in operation in the short run while incurring losses is

$$\begin{aligned} \text{TR} &> \text{VC} \\ \text{PQ} &> \text{AVC}(Q) \\ P &> \text{AVC} \end{aligned} \tag{9–7}$$

CONCEPT REVIEW

1. The price of corn is $4 per bushel. If a farmer sells corn in a perfectly competitive market, what is the marginal revenue per bushel? What must the marginal cost of corn be if the farmer maximizes profit?
2. A firm adjusts its output to the level at which MR = MC but finds that its profits are zero at this output. Draw the firm's cost curves, and show that its output is being produced at the minimum possible average cost.
3. Under what circumstances will a firm continue to operate in a market as a seller even though it cannot earn a profit by doing so?

SHORT-RUN SUPPLY

The Competitive Firm's Short-Run Supply Curve

A supply curve is a relationship between price and quantity supplied. A competitive firm always adjusts output until price is equal to marginal cost so as to maximize profits. The marginal cost curve therefore gives the relationship between price and quantity supplied by the competitive firm. However, unless the price the firm receives for its product exceeds the average variable cost of producing the output for which P = MC, the firm will cease operations. Thus, the quantity supplied by the firm at any price below minimum AVC will be zero. The competitive firm's **short-run supply curve** is therefore the portion of its marginal cost curve that lies above the minimum point of the AVC curve. This is illustrated in Figure 9–8.

Short-run supply curve The portion of a competitive firm's marginal cost curve that lies above the minimum point of its AVC curve.

Short-run supply curves slope upward because the firm's marginal costs tend to increase as its output is increased. When firms operate within a fixed plant or facility, marginal costs eventually increase. To induce a profit-maximizing firm to supply more output, market price must rise. When market price rises, marginal revenue surpasses marginal cost at current output. The firm therefore finds it profitable to increase quantity supplied at the new, higher price so as to increase marginal cost to the point at which it equals that price. After the firm has increased marginal cost to the new price by increasing quantity supplied, marginal profit again falls to zero.

Marginal costs rise, given input prices and technology, because the increased use of variable inputs along with fixed inputs in the short run results in diminishing marginal returns. The declining marginal products of variable inputs thereby con-

FIGURE 9–8 A Competitive Firm's Short-Run Supply Curve

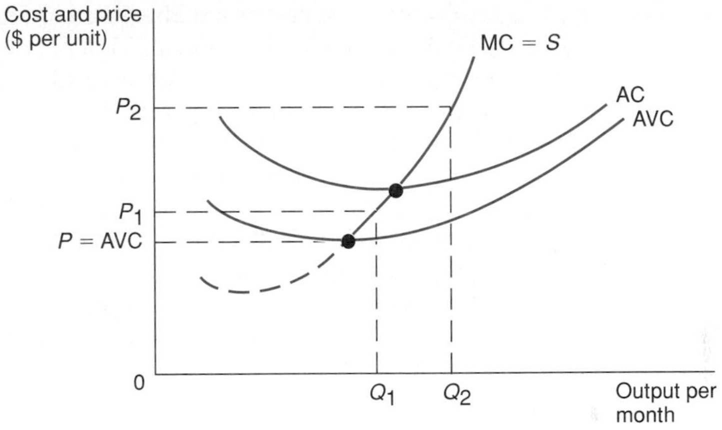

The firm's supply curve is the portion of its marginal cost curve above AVC. At any price below minimum possible AVC, the firm would cease operations and quantity supplied would be zero. To determine the quantity supplied at any price greater than minimum possible AVC, trace a horizontal line to the MC curve. Dropping a vertical line to the horizontal axis gives the quantity supplied at that price.

tribute to increasing marginal costs of production. *The law of supply is therefore rooted in the law of diminishing marginal returns!*

To determine quantity supplied by the competitive firm at any price, draw a horizontal line from that price to the marginal cost curve. At any price below minimum possible AVC, quantity supplied in the short run is zero. At a price $P_1 >$ AVC, quantity supplied is Q_1. At a higher price, P_2, quantity supplied is Q_2. This is illustrated in Figure 9–8.

Short-Run Market Supply and Its Determinants

A market supply curve gives the sum of the quantities supplied by *all firms* that offer a standardized product in the market at each possible price. Suppose that each firm supplying the standardized product to the market has exactly the same marginal cost curve.[5] Also assume that all of these firms can obtain more variable inputs that they require to produce more units without bidding up the prices of those inputs. This means that as all firms in the market acquire more inputs to increase quantity supplied, their cost curves do not shift upward as a result of higher variable input prices.[6]

[5] This, of course, is a simplification. Firms can have different marginal cost curves if they differ in size or if some firms acquire variable inputs at lower prices than those paid by their competitors.

[6] Chapter 10 will consider the consequences of rising prices for variable inputs as a result of industry expansion.

It is now easy to see how a short-run market supply curve can be derived. Suppose that each firm producing chairs has the same marginal cost curve as the typical firm whose cost curves are illustrated in Figure 9–8. The quantity supplied by the typical firm at a market price of $150 per chair is 318 chairs. If the industry comprises 1,000 identical firms, each with identical marginal cost curves, what quantity will be supplied in the market? Because each firm has the same marginal cost curve, each will supply the same output of 318 chairs per month to the market. Total quantity supplied is obtained simply by adding up the quantities supplied by each firm at that price. The quantity supplied to the market at a price of $150 will therefore be 318(1,000) = 318,000 chairs per month.

Point *A* on the market supply curve in Figure 9–9 corresponds to an output level of 318,000 chairs per month when price is $150. Because the marginal cost curves of the individual firms slope upward, you know that at any price higher than $150 each firm will supply a greater quantity, so that quantity supplied will exceed 318,000 chairs per month and that at any price lower than $150 quantity supplied will be less than 318,000 chairs per month. You also know that if the price were to fall below the minimum possible average variable cost of producing chairs, all firms in the industry would shut down. Therefore, assuming that the minimum possible AVC is $33.33 per chair, market quantity supplied will be zero at any price below this. The market supply curve therefore is not extended below a price corresponding to the minimum possible AVC. The short-run market supply, *S*, is upward sloping because the marginal cost curves of all the firms producing the standardized product slope upward. Just as diminishing marginal returns for individual firms cause their supply curves to slope upward, so do diminishing marginal returns result in an upward-sloping short-run market supply curve. You

FIGURE 9–9 Market Supply

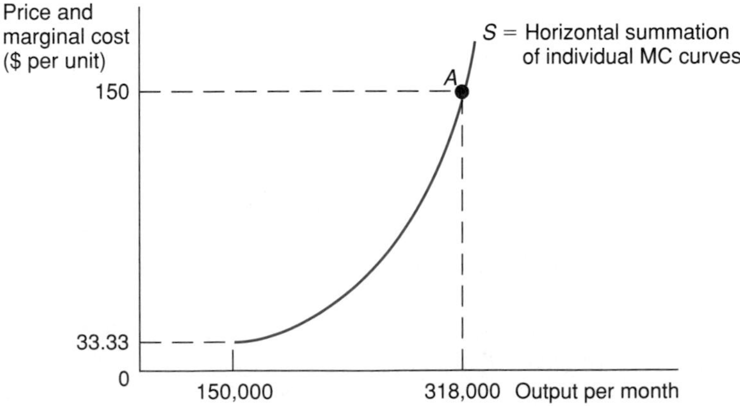

The market supply curve gives a relationship between price and the sum of the quantities supplied by all firms. At a price of P = $150 per chair, each chair producer will supply 318 chairs per month. If there are 1,000 chair producers, market quantity supplied is 318,000 chairs per month, corresponding to point *A* on the market supply curve.

can think of the market supply curve as the horizontal summation of individual marginal cost curves of firms serving the market. This means that the quantities supplied corresponding to P = MC for each firm are added at each possible price to obtain the market supply curve in Figure 9–9.

The determinants of market supply are the following:

1. The number of firms in the industry
2. The average size of firms in the industry measured by quantity of fixed inputs employed (for example, average size of factories) or productive capacity
3. The prices of variable inputs used by firms in the industry
4. The technology employed in the industry

The last three determinants affect the marginal cost curves of individual firms. For example, larger firms employ more fixed inputs, which means that their productive facilities can produce higher output. This means that larger firms achieve the minimum possible average cost and minimum possible average variable cost at a higher output level than that of smaller firms. As a result, the marginal cost curves of larger firms lie farther out from the origin. Accordingly, the larger a firm, the greater is the quantity of the good that it supplies at any given price. Therefore, the greater the average size of the firms supplying a standardized good to a market, the greater is the market quantity supplied at any given price. The higher the prices of variable inputs, the higher is the marginal cost associated with any given output. This means that an increase in the prices of variable inputs tends to shift the marginal cost curves of firms upward. As this occurs, firms will produce less output at any given price. It follows that an increase in the prices of variable inputs will decrease supply. Finally, when firms in an industry employ a new technology that reduces the marginal cost of production, the marginal cost curves of each firm will shift downward. This downward shift will increase the quantity supplied by each firm at each price. An improvement in technology that shifts marginal cost curves downward for firms in a perfectly competitive market will therefore contribute to an increase in supply.

Short-Run Price Elasticity of Supply

Price elasticity of supply A measure of the sensitivity of changes in quantity supplied to changes in price; the percentage change in quantity supplied that results from a 1 percent change in price.

Price elasticity of supply (E_S) measures the sensitivity of changes in quantity supplied to changes in price as the percentage change in quantity supplied resulting from each 1 percent change in market price. Similar in conception to price elasticity of demand, the price elasticity of supply along a supply curve can be computed from the following formula:

$$E_S = \frac{\Delta Q_S/Q_S}{\Delta P/P} = \frac{P}{Q_S}\left(\frac{\Delta Q_S}{\Delta P}\right) \quad \textbf{(9–8)}$$

Because the short-run supply curve slopes upward, the price elasticity of supply is a positive number. A 1 percent increase in the price of a good always results in some percentage increase in quantity supplied in the short run. The signs of the numerator and denominator of Equation 9–8 are therefore the same.

Modern Microeconomics in Action: The Business World

Are Markets Competitive?

As you know, the notion of a perfectly competitive market is an abstraction. In many cases, however, the conditions that exist in actual markets closely approximate those assumed for perfect competition among sellers.

Perhaps the best examples of markets in which sellers can be regarded as price takers are the markets for agricultural commodities. Agricultural commodities—wheat, corn, soybeans, tobacco, cattle, whole milk, and so on—are highly standardized products. It's rare for a buyer to see much difference between the product of one farmer and that of another. In addition, there are thousands of independent sellers of agricultural products in U.S. markets. For example, in 1987 there were nearly 1.2 million producers of cattle and calves, and slightly over 400,000 farms produced and sold soybeans. The following table shows the number of firms that sold major categories of agricultural products in 1987.

Number of Firms Producing Selected Agricultural Products, 1987

Product	*Number of Sellers*
Cattle and calves	1,176,346
Corn	788,326
Soybeans	441,899
Wheat	352,237
Dairy products	162,555
Tobacco	136,682
Peanuts	18,905
Rice	12,013

Source: U.S. Department of Commerce, Bureau of the Census, Census of Agriculture, 1987.

Two of the basic conditions necessary for firms to be price takers—standardized products and large numbers of sellers—are clearly satisfied for most agricultural products. However, doubt is often expressed about whether sellers of agricultural products actually have small market shares. After all, in recent years large corporate farms, often covering thousands of acres, have become more prevalent. The average size of U.S. farms is 456 acres. However, farms with 1,000 or more acres account for over 40 percent of all U.S. farm acreage. In recent years the top 2.6 percent of wheat producers have accounted for more than 50 percent of U.S. wheat production and the top 2 percent of broiler chicken producers have accounted for about 70 percent of market sales.* Does this mean that a few sellers could make certain agricultural products scarce enough to increase their market price?

The answer to this question is no. The reason is that the top 2 percent of producers selling an agricultural product amount to a very large number of independent firms. For example, the top 2.6 percent of grain producers that account for 50 percent of grain sales in the United States represent thousands of independent sellers! It's therefore unlikely, despite the growth of very large farms in recent years, that any one agricultural seller has a large enough market share of sales to be able to shift supply significantly. Agricultural firms thus are likely to be price takers.

Also, it's easy for firms to enter and leave agricultural markets as sellers. However, there are exceptions. Agricultural markets often have price floors and limitations on output established and enforced by government. For example, government regulations have limited the number of tobacco producers for many years.

In nonagricultural markets, product standardization is the exception rather than the rule. Producers of many consumer products differentiate their product by brand name and by quality. In some markets, such as those for new cars, one or a few sellers have large market shares and could affect price by controlling supply. Nonetheless, despite product differentiation among sellers, the products of one seller are often very good substitutes for those of others. A full-size Ford has many similarities to a full-size Chevrolet.

(*Continued*) As the following table shows for selected industries, the condition of large numbers of sellers in markets often prevails. For example, in 1987 there were over 1.9 million independent sellers of contract construction services. In many markets for nonagricultural products, therefore, the notion of firms as price takers is likely to be reasonable. Although the idea of perfect competition doesn't apply to all markets, it's an abstraction that's useful in explaining the behavior of firms in many different markets. Counting the firms in a market is, of course, not the best way to determine whether the market is competitive. However, it provides some insight into the question of whether individual sellers in the market are likely to have the power to influence the price of their product. Firms must be price takers for the theory of competitive supply to be relevant.

Number of Firms in Selected Industries in the United States, 1987

Product or Industry	*Number of Sellers*
Contract construction	1,951,509
Apparel	22,872
Millwork, plywood, and structural wood	7,930
Household furniture	5,606
Book publishers	2,856
Computer and office equipment	2,134
Knitted textiles	2,130
Iron and steel foundry products	1,231
Footwear	479
Petroleum refining	331

Source: U.S. Department of Commerce, Bureau of the Census, Census of Manufacturers, 1987, and Census of Construction Industries, 1987.

* Daniel E. Suits, "Agriculture," in *The Structure of American Industry*, 8th ed., ed. Walter Adams (New York: Macmillan, 1990).

The price elasticity of supply ranges from zero to infinity. Supply is said to be *elastic* if E_S is greater than 1; supply is said to be *inelastic* when the value of E_S is between zero and 1. Supply is said to be *unit elastic* when E_S is equal to 1. This is summarized in Table 9–3.

As with the price elasticity of demand, you must be careful not to gauge the price elasticity of supply from the slope of a supply curve. Although price elasticity of supply is related to the slope, it is not the same as the slope. A simple geometric analysis can show how the slope of a supply curve and price elasticity of supply differ. Three linear supply curves are drawn in Figure 9–10. Each has a different intercept: S_1 intercepts the vertical axis, S_2 intercepts the horizontal axis, and S_3 goes through the origin.

A supply curve with an intercept on the price axis is elastic at all possible prices. To see this, consider price P that corresponds to point A_1 on the supply curve S_1. Run a ray from the origin to point A_1. The slope of the ray to A_1 is P/Q_S.

TABLE 9–3 Price Elasticity of Supply

E_S	*Relative Responsiveness of Quantity Supplied to Price*	*Supply Response*
$0 \leq E_S < 1$	$\Delta Q_S/Q_S < \Delta P/P$	Inelastic
$E_S = 1$	$\Delta Q_S/Q_S = \Delta P/P$	Unit elastic
$1 < E_S \leq \infty$	$\Delta Q_S/Q_S > \Delta P/P$	Elastic

FIGURE 9–10 Determining Price Elasticity of Supply by the Intercept of the Supply Curve and the Axes

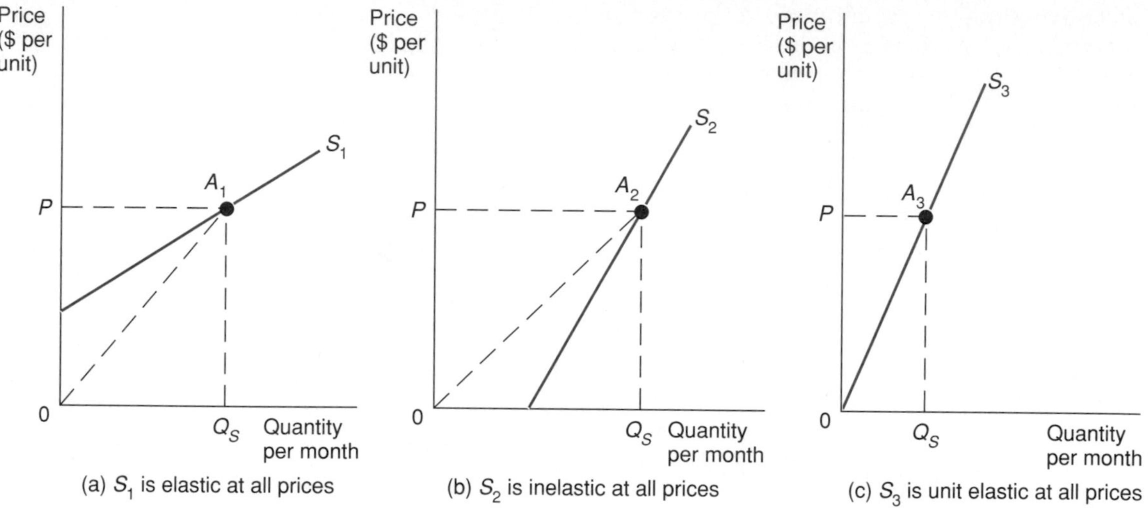

A linear supply curve that intercepts the price axis is elastic at all prices. A linear supply curve that intersects the quantity axis is inelastic at all prices. A linear supply curve that goes through the origin is unit elastic at all prices.

The price elasticity of supply may be written as

$$E_S = \frac{P}{Q_S}\left(\frac{\Delta Q}{\Delta P}\right) = \frac{P/Q_S}{\Delta P/\Delta Q} \quad \textbf{(9–9)}$$

where $\Delta P/\Delta Q$ is the slope of the supply curve. Because P/Q_S is the slope of the ray, elasticity can be determined by comparing the slope of the ray with the slope of the linear supply curve. For the supply curve S_1 shown in Figure 9–10(a), the slope of the ray exceeds the slope of the supply curve. Therefore,

$$\frac{P}{Q_S} > \frac{\Delta P}{\Delta Q} \quad \textbf{(9–10)}$$

and

$$E_S = \frac{P/Q_S}{\Delta P/\Delta Q} > 1 \text{ for all } P \quad \textbf{(9–11)}$$

Thus *for all prices* a supply curve intersecting the price axis is elastic.

Similarly, as shown in Figure 9–10(b), a supply curve whose intercept is on the quantity axis is inelastic at all points, as is shown for curve S_2. This is because P/Q_S is less than the slope of the curve for any price along such a supply curve. Finally, a supply curve going through the origin is of unitary elasticity at all prices because the ratio P/Q_S equals the slope of the supply curve at all possible prices.

The price elasticity of a nonlinear supply curve at any point can be gauged by running a line tangent to that point and observing which axis that line intercepts. For example, if the line tangent to the curve intersects the price axis, supply is

FIGURE 9–11 Short-Run Elasticity of Supply

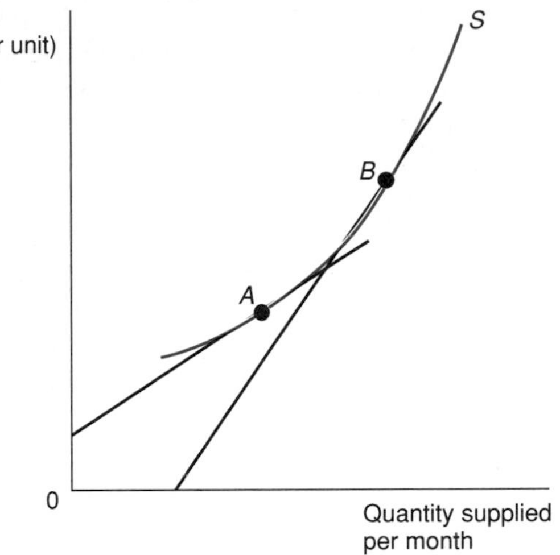

Supply tends to become more inelastic with respect to price as quantity supplied increases in the short run. At point A supply is elastic because the tangent to that point intersects the price axis. At point B supply is inelastic because the tangent to that point intersects the quantity axis.

elastic at that point. This is illustrated in Figure 9–11. The supply curve shown is elastic at point A and inelastic at point B.

Price elasticity of supply in the short run depends on how quickly marginal costs of production increase as production expands with variable inputs. With input prices held constant, short-run supply elasticity can be thought of as depending on the flexibility producers have in the short run to produce more or less with given amounts of fixed inputs. In the short run, supply tends to become more inelastic as output increases. This can be explained by the law of diminishing returns, which implies that marginal cost increases at a more rapid rate as output increases. After the point of diminishing returns, additional increases in output require progressive increases in variable inputs; this means that the marginal cost curve becomes steeper as output increases. The market supply curve also increases in slope as output increases. At the extreme, as the capacity output of firms is approached, the marginal cost curve becomes nearly infinitely sloped. This means that the price elasticity of supply approaches zero in the short run as stage III of production is approached.

It follows that the short-run elasticity of market supply for a good depends on the rate at which marginal costs increase with output. This, in turn, depends on the ease with which variable inputs can be substituted for fixed inputs. If the production function is of the fixed-proportions type between the fixed input and the variable input, it is impossible to increase supply in the short run. Firms would have to wait until additional units of the fixed input could be acquired. For example, the short-run supply of most fruits and vegetables is quite inelastic because additional land, labor, and other inputs must be put into production before their supply can increase. One estimate of the short-run elasticity of supply of spinach was 0.2.[7]

Short-run supply becomes even more inelastic when price increases in the short run if input prices increase as all firms expand production. When this is the case, the market supply curve becomes steeper at higher prices.

The period economists call the "short run" varies from industry to industry. In the long run, all inputs are variable. Firms can expand, and new firms can begin operations. Long-run supply therefore tends to be more elastic than short-run supply. There is more flexibility in the long run. However, the time necessary to add extra capacity varies from industry to industry. An airline, for example, can add extra aircraft in a relatively short time to expand capacity on a given route. However, expanding the capacity of a company generating electric power could take many years.

Applying the Theory of Short-Run Supply

A Decrease in the Price of a Variable Input

A change in input prices will affect costs of production, which will affect both the competitive firm's supply curve and the market supply. Suppose that the price of wood used in the production of chairs declines. A decrease in the price of any variable input used by firms, other things being equal, decreases variable costs. The short-run effects of a decrease in the price of this variable input on the market price of chairs, on the quantity produced, and on a typical competitive firm are illustrated in Figure 9–12.

The decrease in the price of the variable input shifts the average variable cost, average cost, and marginal cost curves downward. Figure 9–12(a) shows the impact of the decrease in the price of wood on the AC and MC curves for a typical competitive firm. The decrease in the price of the variable input shits the average and marginal cost curves downward, from MC_1 to MC_2 and from AC_1 to AC_2. If the market price were to remain at $150 a chair, its initial level, each competitive firm would increase production until MC_2 = $150. However, as all firms increase production in response to the decrease in marginal cost, the market supply increases from S_1 to S_2. Given the level of demand, this results in a decrease in the market price of chairs from $150 to $100. In equilibrium, at the new price, each firm produces to a point at which MC_2 = $100. The output corresponding to this is q_2. As all firms increase output; the market equilibrium quantity increases from Q_1 to Q_2, as shown in Figure 9–12(b). A decrease in the price of a variable input for all firms therefore results in an increase in supply. The short-run maximum possible profits of a typical chair producer change from the area *ABCD* to the area *HGEF* as the price of wood declines and as the increase in the supply of chairs lowers the price to $100.

[7] Marc Nerlove and William Addison, "Statistical Estimation of Long-Run Elasticities of Supply and Demand," *Journal of Farm Economics* 40, no. 4 (November 1958), pp. 861–80.

FIGURE 9–12 Effects of Decrease in the Price of a Variable Input

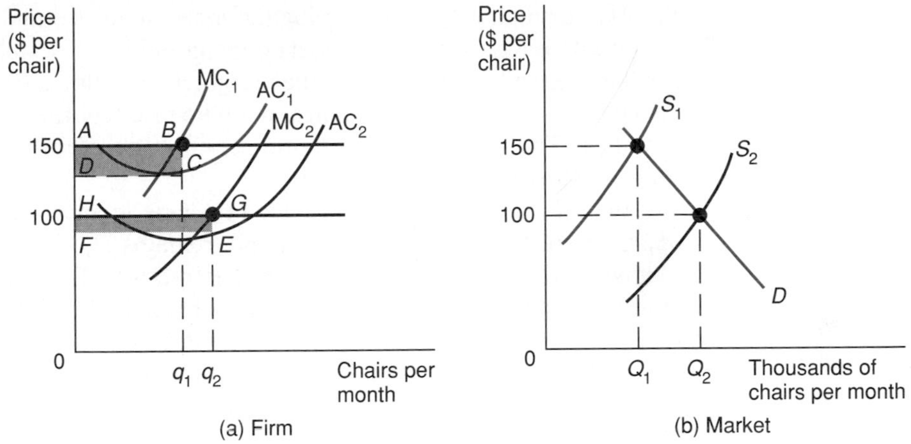

(a) Firm

(b) Market

A decrease in the price of variable input shifts both the marginal and average cost curves downward. Market supply increases, and the price of the product declines.

Suppose the decrease in the price of the variable input affected only a single firm. The market price would remain at \$150. The firm would be able to produce at the point for which MC_2 = \$150 and thereby earn more profit than it would if the market price were \$100. A change in the price of variable inputs that affects only one competitive firm will change that competitor's profit and have no effect on the market price. However, a change in input prices that affects *all* sellers of a product in a competitive market will affect market supply and therefore, other things being equal, will change the market price of output.

A Change in the Price of a Fixed Input: The Short-Run Impact of License Fees and Fixed Annual Subsidies

A change in the price of a *fixed input* affects fixed costs and average costs. However, it has *no effect* on variable costs or marginal costs. This has some interesting implications for policies that affect the prices of fixed rather than variable inputs.

Suppose the market for contractors' services in a certain state is perfectly competitive and the state government, in an effort to raise extra revenue to finance public services, then decides to triple the license fee that contractors must pay from \$1,000 to \$3,000 per year. A license fee is a fixed input in the practice of an occupation or activity. It represents an annual amount that must be paid independent of the amount of goods or services sold. In the short run, therefore, an increase in such fees is equivalent to an increase in fixed costs.

Figure 9–13(a) presumes that the price per square foot of construction is initially \$50. At that price contractors break even, thereby earning a normal profit. Before the increase in the license fee, therefore, P = AC = MC. The increase in the license fee has no effect on variable costs, however, it does increase average costs. As the average costs shift upward, the distance between the AVC curve and the AC curve increases, reflecting the increase in average fixed costs at any level of output. Because marginal costs depend only on variable costs, the increase in the license fee has no effect on the marginal cost curve. Because the marginal cost curve is unaffected by the change in the license fee, the market supply curve does not shift. The price of construction services therefore remains at $50 per square foot, as shown in Figure 9–13(b).

Each firm continues to produce the same level of output, q_1 square feet per year, where MC = $50. Market supply remains Q_1 square feet per year. Nothing changes *except* the profit earned by contractors. The typical contractor was assumed to be breaking even before the increase in AC. The increased fee therefore results in losses equal to the shaded area in Figure 9–13(a). Price is above AVC at the profit-maximum output because neither AVC nor market price is affected by the license fee increase. The short-run impact of the increased license fee is therefore confined to the profit of contractors. Neither price nor marginal costs are affected. The long-run impact is another story that is taken up in Chapter 10. However, it is clear that if losses result from the increased license fee, some contractors will cease operations in the long run as their fixed commitments expire. The long-run impact *will* therefore affect prices and quantities as firms go out of business in the state. This analysis applies to any increase in fixed costs, such as insurance payments, rents, and other items typically fixed in the short run. For example, an increase in physician's malpractice insurance premiums will not affect the physicians' short-run marginal cost but will shift their short-run average

FIGURE 9–13 A Change in the Price of a Fixed Input

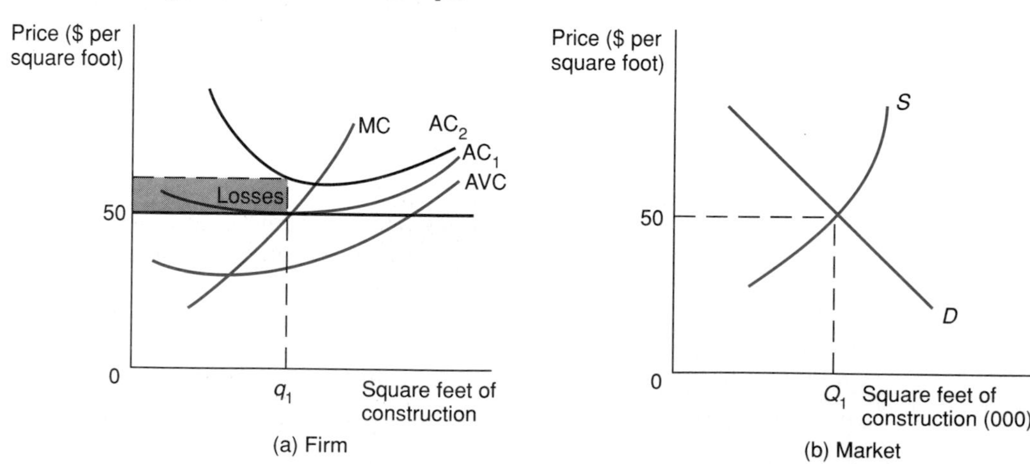

An increase in the price of a fixed input shifts the AC curve upward but has no effect on the AVC or MC curves. Because MC is not affected by the change in price, there is no change in supply and market price remains the same in the short run. If P = AC before the increase in the price of the fixed input, the firm will incur losses equal to the shaded area.

cost curves upward. An increase in insurance premiums will therefore cause the profit of firms supplying medical services to fall but will have no effect in the short run on supply or price because the MC curve will not shift.

Similarly, a *decrease* in fixed costs will not influence either price or supply in a competitive market in the short run. For example, if governing authorities *reduce* license fees for the purpose of increasing construction, there will be no effect on the amount supplied in the short run. If authorities want a rapid increase in the amount of construction services supplied, they must reduce the price of a *variable* input used by contractors.

Suppose a government offers a fixed subsidy of $10,000 a year to all farmers in an effort to get them to produce more food. This would be a windfall gain to farmers. It would decrease their average costs of operation and have no effect on their variable or marginal costs. Accordingly, their profits will increase, but there will be no increase in the quantity of food supplied in the short run. Over the long run, however, there will be an increase in supply as more persons are encouraged to enter food-related businesses.

Using Supply Curves to Calculate Producer Surplus

Producer surplus The difference between the market price of a unit of output and the minimum price required to make that extra unit available in the marketplace.

Producer surplus is the difference between the market price of a unit of output and the minimum price required to make that extra unit available in the marketplace. A firm's supply curve gives the minimum price required to make an additional unit of output available for sale. This minimum price is the marginal cost of producing that unit. The marginal cost of that unit reflects the opportunity cost of resources

FIGURE 9–14 Producer Surplus

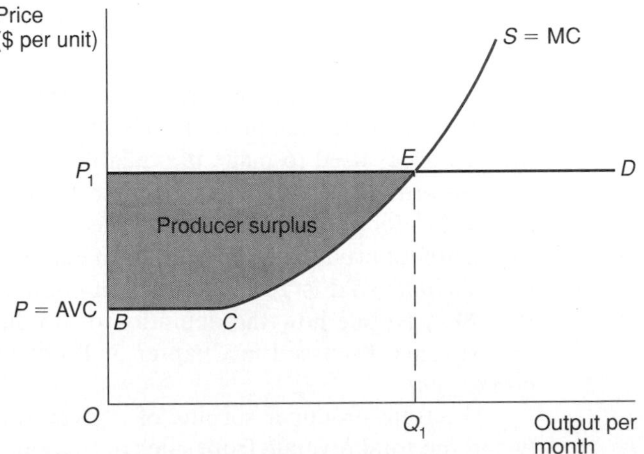

The total producer surplus of the output Q_1 is the shaded area $BCEP_1$. This area represents the difference between the seller's actual revenue and the opportunity cost of the variable inputs.

MODERN MICROECONOMICS IN ACTION: GOVERNMENT AND THE ECONOMY

How Government Policies Can Cause Losses in Producer Surplus: The Case of the Beer Industry

In 1919, the 18th Amendment to the U.S Constitution was ratified and national prohibition of alcoholic beverages became law in the United States. The amendment took the U.S. beer industry by surprise because it expected that any ban on alcoholic beverages would be limited to hard liquor. It was mistaken, and by 1920 the beer industry, which comprised a large number of firms and was highly competitive at the time, was shattered and a massive amount of producer surplus was lost in the U.S. beer industry as many brewers went out of business.

Because legal sales fell to zero, the entire producer surplus was lost. Many breweries used their plant and equipment to produce other products, such as ice cream and candy. Workers with specialized skills in brewing had to find alternative jobs, often at lower wages. Such companies as Anheuser-Busch survived the prohibition era by producing malt syrup. Although the malt syrup was marketed as a cookie ingredient, it was most commonly used to make home-brew beer!*

The beer industry of today is very different from that of the early 1900s. As of 1986 only 33 independent companies operating 67 plants produced beer in the United States. Although the industry is far less competitive today than it was early in the century, it is once again suffering from a loss in producer surplus, influenced in part by changing demographics and in part by new government policies.

In the 1980s the pool of people aged 18–34, who are major consumers of beer, shrank. Then, under federal pressure, states passed laws raising the minimum age for the purchase of alcoholic beverages to 21. Government campaigns pointing out the unfavorable health effects of alcohol abuse also reduced the demand for beer and the rate of increase in its market price. Partly as a result of such government actions, per capita beer consumption in the United States, which peaked at 24 gallons in the 1970s, stabilized in the 1980s.

* See Kenneth G. Elzinga, "The Beer Industry," in *The Structure of American Industry*, 8th ed., ed. Walter Adams (New York: Macmillan, 1990).

devoted to its production. Producer surplus can therefore be thought of as the difference between the market price of a unit of output and the opportunity cost of the resources used to make it available.

If a firm can obtain a price in excess of marginal cost by producing more, it can add to its profit. It follows that as long as $P >$ MC, a competitive firm finds expansion of production profitable. In equilibrium the producer surplus earned on the *last unit* sold is zero, because in equilibrium each firm adjusts output until $P =$ MC. Notice how the definition of producer surplus parallels that of consumer surplus discussed in Chapter 5. Producer surplus is sometimes called *economic rent*.

The total producer surplus of a given output produced is the difference between the total revenue from sales of that output and the minimum sum of money the seller would have accepted to make that amount available. This is illustrated in Figure 9–14. At a market price of P_1 a competitive firm produces output Q_1, corresponding to $P =$ MC. Total revenue is the area OP_1EQ_1. The minimum

FIGURE 9–15 The Impact of a Price Decrease on Producer Surplus

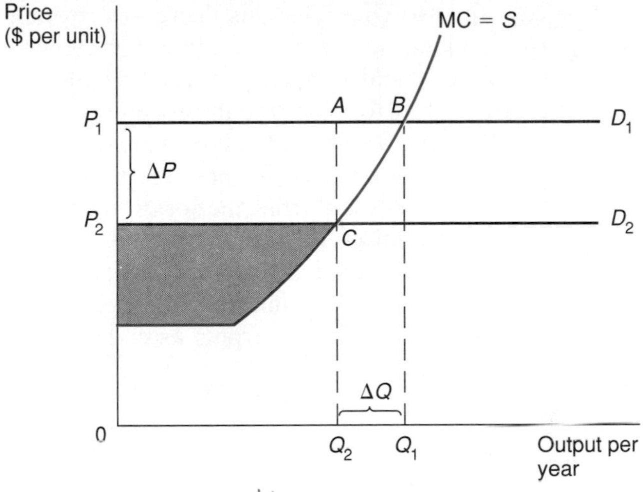

A price decrease reduces producer surplus by the shaded area. The area CBQ_1Q_2 represents the value of variable inputs transferred to alternative uses when price declines.

amount the seller will accept to make that amount available is represented by the area $OBCEQ_1$, which represents the opportunity cost of the variable inputs used to produce Q_1 units of the good. The total producer surplus of Q_1 units of output is the area $BCEP_1$. This area represents the seller's revenue in excess of the opportunity cost of the variable inputs.[8]

Price Changes and Producer Surplus

A price decrease reduces producer surplus, whereas a price increase has the opposite effect. Suppose that governments pass laws designed to discourage alcohol consumption. For example, states have recently passed laws raising the legal drinking age for alcoholic beverages from 18 to 21 and drunken driving laws that increase penalties to violators. If these laws decrease the market demand for liquor, this in turn, other things being equal, will reduce the price of liquor.

The impact of the new laws on a typical liquor producer is shown in Figure 9–15. Assuming that the market for liquor is perfectly competitive, the decline in demand reduces price from P_1 to P_2 per gallon. A typical liquor producer reacts to the price decrease by cutting back production until P_2 = MC. This results in a

[8] Note that firms with lower variable costs of production earn more total producer surplus than other firms because a firm whose variable cost is lower than that of a competitor has a marginal cost curve that lies below its competitor's for any given output. Lower cost producers also supply more goods than do higher-cost producers at any given price.

decrease in the quantity supplied by the producer from Q_1 to Q_2 per year. Producer revenue is adversely affected in two ways. First, sales decline by an amount ΔQ equal to $Q_1 - Q_2$. This decreases revenue by the area ABQ_1Q_2. In addition, the producer now receives a lower price per unit, P_2, on its remaining sales, Q_2, per year. The decline in price, ΔP, results in a loss in revenue equal to the area P_1ACP_2. The total decline in revenue is the sum of these two areas.

It would be a mistake, however, to use the decline in revenue as an indicator of the losses incurred by producers (and their distributors). The area CBQ_1Q_2 must be subtracted from the loss in revenue to obtain a measure of the loss in producer surplus. This area represents the value of variable inputs that are transferred to their next best use as a result of the decline in the price of the product. It represents the opportunity cost of input now employed in other enterprises. The total loss of producer surplus as a result of the new laws is therefore the area P_1BCP_2.

PERFECT COMPETITION AND ALLOCATIVE EFFICIENCY

Allocative efficiency A condition achieved when resources are allocated in a way that allows the maximum possible net benefit from their use.

We can now combine the concept of producer surplus with that of consumer surplus to begin evaluating equilibrium in perfectly competitive markets. First, let's set up a criterion for evaluating resource use. **Allocative efficiency** is achieved when resources are allocated in a way that allows the maximum possible net benefit from their use. When an efficient allocation of resources has been attained, it is impossible to increase the well-being of any one person without harming another person. A resource allocation satisfying this criterion is sometimes called a *Pareto optimal* after the Italian economist Vilfredo Pareto (1848–1923) developed an extensive framework for analyzing the conditions required for efficiency.

When allocative efficiency has been attained, no change in productive methods and no further exchange of goods and services among participants in an economy can result in additional net gains. It is easy to demonstrate that production in which there is waste has not achieved allocative efficiency. Suppose producers, given technology and input prices, do not manage their workers and factories well and that the transaction costs of improving management are zero. This means that with improved management, more could be produced without increasing the amount of resources used. The increased output would make at least one person better off, and at the same time no one would be made worse off because no additional resources would be required to produce that increment. This means the output of other goods enjoyed in the economy will not decline and the enjoyment from the use of those goods will not be diminished. It follows that obtaining the maximum possible output from inputs under a given technology is a necessary prerequisite for efficiency. However, there is more to efficiency than just a productive aspect, as you will now see.

Marginal Conditions for Efficiency

To see how perfectly competitive markets can achieve allocative efficiency, let's first derive the conditions under which the net gains from trading a good are at a maximum over a given period. The efficient output of a good is the output that yields a net benefit from enjoyment of the good that cannot be increased by making either more or less of the good available over a period. Let's look at the market for bread. Figure 9–16 shows how the marginal benefit and marginal cost of bread vary with the amount of bread made available each week in a market. The benefit from more bread is assumed to accrue only to the persons who obtain the bread. This means that the marginal benefit curve of bread consumers reflects all of the extra benefit associated with various quantities of bread. The marginal cost curve reflects the value of all resources used in making additional bread available after a certain amount has been produced. It is assumed that the least-cost method of production is used in making bread.

Suppose that at the current level of bread production, Q_1 per week, the marginal cost of bread is $1.50 per loaf, corresponding to point *B* on the marginal cost curve in Figure 9–16. If a buyer is willing to pay $2 for another loaf when only Q_1 loaves are available per week, corresponding to point *A* on the marginal benefit curve for bread in Figure 9–16, there is a net gain of 50 cents in producer surplus if another loaf is produced and then sold at a price of $2. If the loaf is sold for $2, the seller is made better off by 50 cents and the buyer is made no worse off because he obtains exactly $2 worth of benefit for the $2 purchase. Alternatively, if the bread is sold for $1.50, the seller is made no worse off for producing it because she

FIGURE 9–16 Consumer Surplus, Producer Surplus, and Efficiency

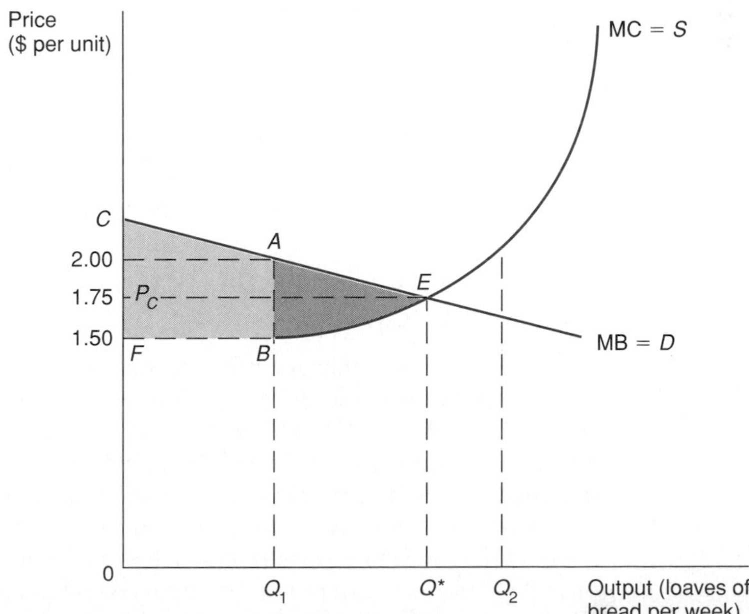

The efficient output, Q^*, maximizes the sum of producer and consumer surplus. The competitive equilibrium at point *E* is efficient because P_c = MB = MC. At Q^* the area *FCE* is the maximum possible sum of consumer and producer surplus.

exactly covers the opportunity cost associated with the additional bread. The buyer, on the other hand, receives 50 cents in consumer surplus because he obtains $2 worth of benefits for only $1.50. Any price between $1.50 and $2 for the loaf results in gains to both the buyer and the seller. The difference between the marginal benefit and the marginal cost of any given amount of bread is the *net gain* from making that additional amount available. When the marginal benefit exceeds the marginal cost, additional bread is worth more to buyers than it is to those whose resources are used to make it available.

A net gain is possible from making more bread available over any period as long as the marginal benefit (MB) of bread exceeds its marginal cost (MC). If Q_1 loaves of bread are currently being made available each week, additional net gains corresponding to the area *AEB* are possible by increasing the availability of bread until the marginal cost of bread equals its marginal benefit. At point *E* the net benefit from bread is at a maximum. The output corresponding to point *E* is Q^* loaves of bread per week. The efficient output of bread is therefore Q^* loaves per week. No additional net gains are possible from making more than Q^* units per week available because the marginal benefit of bread falls short of its marginal cost for outputs in excess of Q^*.

Efficiency is achieved when trading is undertaken just up to the point at which the marginal benefit of a good equals its marginal cost. At that point, no additional net gains from further trade are possible. Further exchange will result in losses to one of the traders as long as marginal benefits decline and marginal costs are constant or increasing. For each of the goods that can be produced in an economy, the **marginal conditions for the efficient output of a good** are

Marginal conditions for the efficient output of a good Conditions that are met when the marginal benefit of the good equals its marginal cost.

$$MB = MC \tag{9–12}$$

In Figure 9–16 Q_1 is an inefficient output because its marginal benefit exceeds its marginal cost. If production were increased from Q_1 to Q^*, additional gains equal to the shaded area *AEB* could be distributed between the traders. Similarly, Q_2 is an inefficient output because its marginal cost exceeds its marginal benefit.

The Efficient Output of a Good Maximizes the Sum of Producer and Consumer Surplus

Figure 9–16 shows that the efficient output of a good can be thought of as the number of units produced per period that maximizes the sum of producer and consumer surplus. At the efficient output, Q^*, the marginal benefit of the good just equals its marginal cost. This corresponds to the point on the graph where the marginal benefit and marginal cost curves intersect. The efficient output would be sold if the market price of the good were P_C = $1.75. At that price buyers of the good earn consumer surplus equal to the triangular area P_CCE. Similarly, at output Q^*, sellers earn producer surplus equal to the area P_CEF. The shaded areas on the graph represent the sum of producer and consumer surplus at the efficient output.

It is easy to prove that the sum of consumer and producer surplus is at a maximum at the efficient output of Q^* units per year. Suppose that one unit less than Q^* were produced per year. At that output it would be possible to increase either producer or consumer surplus. This is because the maximum price consumers would pay for the unit exceeds the minimum price sellers would accept to cover the opportunity cost of the resources required to make the unit available (MB > MC). Similarly, if one unit more than Q^* were produced per year, its marginal cost would exceed its marginal benefit. It follows that production beyond the efficient output of Q^* per year would reduce the sum of producer and consumer surplus from the maximum value possible at Q^*. The area *FCE* therefore corresponds to the maximum net benefit (sometimes called the *economic surplus*) to producers and consumers that is achieved only if the efficient output is made available over a given period.

Perfectly Competitive Markets and Efficiency

In perfectly competitive markets prices are determined impersonally by the interaction of many rival buyers and many rival sellers. Each seller adjusts production until the marginal cost of the product is equal to the market price to maximize profit. It follows that, given the price of a good, sellers will always adjust quantity supplied in a perfectly competitive market until

$$P = \text{MC}$$

This holds for all goods if each of the goods in an economy is traded in a system of perfectly competitive markets.

Buyers also take the market price as given, and each buyer purchases each good in quantities up to the point at which the marginal benefit of the good equals its price. This is because consumers who seek the greatest possible utility from their budgets react to the market price by purchasing goods up to the point at which their market price equals their marginal benefit. Therefore, given the market price of a good, buyers continue to purchase it until

$$P = \text{MB}$$

This is true in each of the markets in which buyers have no control over price. It follows that when perfect competition prevails in all markets,

$$P = \text{MB} = \text{MC}$$

In perfectly competitive markets goods are made available up to the point at which this marginal benefit equals this marginal cost. As a result efficient outputs are equilibrium outputs assuming that the marginal benefit and marginal cost curves capture all the benefits and costs associated with making the goods available.

Under perfect competition the marginal cost curve illustrated in Figure 9–16 is also the supply curve for any given period. The demand curve represents the marginal benefit of the corresponding amount of the good to consumers. The market price, P_C, corresponds to the intersection of the demand and supply curves. At that price the quantity of the good traded in the market, Q^*, is the efficient output.

A system of perfectly competitive markets would therefore receive high marks for efficiency. When trade takes place in a system of unregulated perfectly competitive markets, the maximum net benefit can be squeezed out of resources, given the willingness and ability of consumers to pay for goods under the existing distribution of income. Changes in the marginal benefit of goods result when there are changes in the willingness or ability of consumers of particular goods to pay for the items they demand. Changes in tastes or changes in the way income is distributed therefore result in shifts in the marginal benefit curves for particular items. These changes in demand change market prices and result in a new efficient resource allocation. In this sense a system of perfectly competitive markets is *responsive* to changes in the value consumers place on various goods and services. Similarly, changes in the marginal cost of making goods available shift the market supply curves. This also changes the market prices and the efficient outputs of goods. A system of perfectly competitive markets is therefore also responsive to changes in the value placed on productive resources.

SUMMARY

1. A firm is an organization that acts as an intermediary between input suppliers and buyers of the product it produces. Firms seek to make profit for their owners by managing the productive process and marketing products. Although firms can have multifaceted goals, the behavioral assumption that firms seek to maximize profits is useful in understanding the relationship between price and quantity supplied.
2. In perfectly competitive markets many firms sell a standardized product. Buyers are fully informed about the prices of the standardized product offered by these competing firms. Each firm has only a small market share of total supply and takes the price of the product as beyond its control. A competitive firm is a price taker.
3. Profits are the difference between total revenue and total cost of output sold. Because a competitive firm cannot influence price, it can vary its profit only by varying its output. Marginal revenue is the change in total revenue resulting from selling an additional unit of output. For competitive firms marginal revenue is always equal to price.
4. Economic profits are the difference between total revenue and all the opportunity costs of production. Normal profit is the opportunity cost of the owner-supplied inputs used by a firm.
5. A firm maximizes profit by adjusting output until marginal cost equals marginal revenue. At that point the marginal profit from producing another unit of output is zero. If the firm were to produce more beyond that point, profits would decrease. For a competitive firm, $P =$ MR. Maximum profits therefore occur when output is adjusted until $P =$ MC.
6. Total profit may be measured as profit per unit sold multiplied by the number of units sold. When price exceeds a firm's average cost of production at the profit-maximizing output, the firm earns economic profits. Conversely, when price is less than a firm's average cost of production, the firm suffers economic losses. The owners of the firm shut down in the short run when price falls below the minimum possible average variable cost of production.
7. A competitive firm's short-run supply curve is the portion of its marginal cost curve above average variable cost. When input prices and technology are given, the market supply curve can be derived by adding the quantities that all competitive firms supply at each price.
8. The determinants of market supply are the number of firms selling in the market, the average size of those firms as measured by their productive capability, the prices of variable inputs, and the technology employed.
9. Price elasticity of supply is the percentage change in quantity supplied resulting from each 1 percent change in market price. Because of the law of diminishing marginal returns, the short-run price elasticity of supply declines as output increases.

10. A change in the price of variable inputs shifts short-run market supply, but a change in the price of a fixed input has no effect on market supply because it does not change the marginal cost associated with each output.

11. Producer surplus is the difference between the market price and the marginal cost of producing a unit of output. The total producer surplus earned by firms measures the difference between total revenue from a given output and the opportunity cost of variable inputs used to produce that output.

12. Allocative efficiency is a criterion used to evaluate resource use. Efficiency exists when resources are used in such a way as to make it impossible to make any one person better off without harming another person.

13. Efficient output of a good is the output that maximizes the sum of consumer and producer surplus. Marginal conditions for efficiency require that MB = MC for any good. Perfectly competitive markets achieve efficiency because they result in prices that simultaneously reflect MB and MC.

Important Concepts

business firm
perfect competition
competitive firm
economic profits
marginal revenue
marginal profit
shutdown point
short-run supply curve
price elasticity of supply
producer surplus
allocative efficiency
marginal conditions for the efficient output of a good

Questions for Review

1. In a competitive market each firm selling its product is a price taker. If no firm can influence price, how does price change in response to changes in costs?

2. Marginal revenue (that is, price) may be equal to marginal cost at two different output levels for a perfectly competitive firm. Explain why the firm maximizes profit by producing the greater of these two outputs.

3. When a firm earns normal profits, its economic profits must be zero. Is this a contradiction?

4. Suppose the price of a firm's product is \$50. At the current level of output the firm estimates its marginal cost at \$30. Explain what the firm must do to maximize profits.

5. A corporation instructs its subsidiaries selling in perfectly competitive markets to maximize their profit per unit output. Each subsidiary adjusts its output to maximize the difference between market price and average costs. Explain why this policy will not necessarily maximize total profits. Explain why as a result of the policy each subsidiary will produce the output corresponding to the minimum possible average cost.

6. Explain why a firm can minimize its losses by continuing to operate in the short run when market price exceeds AVC but is less than AC.

7. "If the price of capital increases, short-run equilibrium price for a perfectly competitive industry does not change." Is this statement true or false? Explain your answer.

8. Illustrate diagrammatically why an increase in market demand will increase producer surplus for a perfectly competitive industry and for each firm in that industry.

9. Suppose you produce photocopying services and sell the services in a perfectly competitive market. The price you pay for paper increases. Explain how this will affect the price of your services, your profits, and your output if your competitors do not incur comparable increases in cost. How would your answer differ if your competitors also have increased paper cost? How will an unexpected increase in rents affect

your profits and the quantity of the services you are willing to supply in the short run?

10. Under what conditions will an economy achieve an efficient resource allocation? Suppose the marginal cost of serving a certain airline route is $2 per passenger-mile. If the marginal benefit of a passenger-mile at the current level of service is $1, is an efficient level of service being provided? What can be done to increase the net benefit of the service provided on the route?

Problems

1. Using the data in Tables 9–1 and 9–2, show how an increase in the price of chairs to $200 will affect total revenue at the various output levels. What will the monthly output of chairs be at the higher price? Calculate the firm's profit at the higher price.

2. At the end of the year an accountant tells you that your profits are $50,000. By managing your own firm, however, you forgo a salary of $30,000 that you could earn by working for someone else. You also have $100,000 of your own funds tied up in your firm. Assuming that you forgo 15 percent interest on these funds, calculate your economic profits. Will you remain in business next year?

3. Suppose you run a competitive firm that produces tomatoes. The current price of tomatoes is $1 per pound. At that price you produce 100,000 pounds per year. The average cost of production at that level of output is 50 cents per pound. Calculate the profits. Use a graph to show average cost, average variable cost, and marginal cost along with the demand for your product. Show how an increase in the price of fertilizer will affect your costs and your profit-maximizing output. Show how a lump-sum tax independent of the amount produced will affect your costs and your choice of output. What effect will a lump-sum subsidy have on the short-run supply of tomatoes?

4. Show that a firm's choice of output is independent of its fixed costs. Use the data in Table 9–1 to show the impact on output and profits of a doubling of fixed costs from $6,000 to $12,000 per month.

5. Use the data in Table 9–1 to show how the increase in fixed costs to $12,000 per month affects profit at various levels of output. Draw the total revenue and total cost curves (assuming that P = $150), and show how profit will vary with output.

6. Answer the following questions regarding a perfectly competitive firm using the short-run cost diagram.

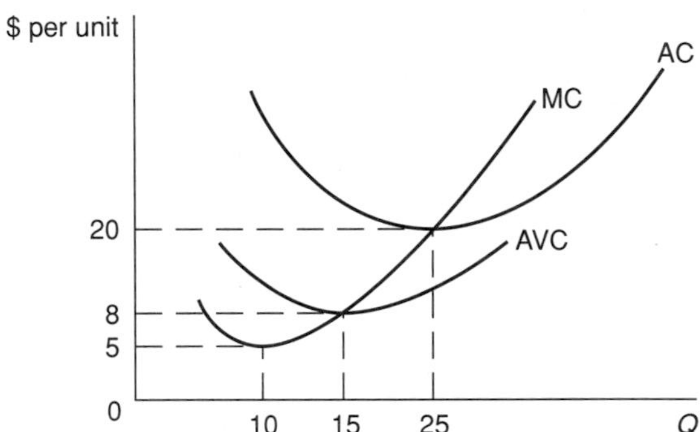

   a. Will the firm produce any output in the short run if the price of a unit is $7? Why or why not?
   b. Will the firm produce any output in the short run if the price of a unit is $10? Why or why not?
   c. If the price of a unit is $30, will the firm earn an economic profit? Draw in the diagram the rectangle whose area represents the firm's economic profit or loss at that price.
   d. Suppose the short-run equilibrium price of a unit is $25 and total fixed cost decreases for this firm and for every firm in the industry because of a decrease in the price of capital. Will the short-run equilibrium price and the short-run equilibrium industry output change as a result of this development?

7. For each of the following statements regarding perfect competition, indicate whether you believe the statement is true or false and briefly justify your answer?
   a. An increase in industry demand will increase the total producer surplus of a perfectly competitive firm.

b. A decrease in the price of labor will increase the short-run equilibrium industry output and the short-run equilibrium price.

c. The more inelastic the short-run industry supply, the greater is the price increase that a given increase in industry demand will generate.

d. The total tax revenue gained by placing a per-unit tax on a good sold in a perfectly competitive market is equal to the amount of consumer and producer surplus lost as a result of the tax.

8. Suppose buyers are willing to pay $10,000 for each additional car. Use a diagrammatic analysis of marginal benefit and marginal cost to show that efficiency has not been attained if the marginal cost of a car is currently $7,000.

9. Suppose a bus firm is forced by governing authorities to serve a route for which the maximum fare buyers will pay is less than the marginal cost per mile. Show how a reduction in the miles traveled on this route will lead to efficiency.

10

Long-Run Supply and the Effects of Government Policies in Perfectly Competitive Markets

The personal computer (PC) was introduced to Americans and the world in the early 1980s. In 1983 the market for PCs was dominated by five companies (IBM, Apple, Tandy, Hewlett-Packard, and Digital Equipment), which together accounted for 70 percent of computer sales that year. Three years later, because of ease of entry into the PC market, there were over 100 manufacturers of IBM clones that used IBM software and keyboards similar to those of the IBM PCs and that performed about as well as the more expensive IBM PCs.

The entry of new sellers into the PC market and the introduction of less costly technology for manufacturing the machines caused the supply of PCs to soar and the price of PCs to plummet throughout the 1980s. By 1993 you could easily buy a machine for $1,000 that did everything—and then some—that was done by an IBM PC system costing about $3,500 in 1983. The fierce competition in the computer industry did more than lower prices—it also caused the profits of computer manufacturers to fall. By the early 1990s, IBM's profits were down and the company was forced to reduce the size of its labor force as it adjusted to a much smaller share of the PC market than it had in the 1980s.

Economic profits are a lure that attracts investors to underwrite the expansion of enterprises. In expanding enterprises and in reallocating resources to alternative enterprises, businesses have more flexibility in the long run than they do in the short run. Another important difference between the long run and the short run is that, as with the computer industry in the 1980s, in the long run the number of firms selling a given product in a market can change. The potential for earning economic profits influences long-run supply. The long-run reaction of sellers to changes in demand and technology in free and competitive markets makes the market system responsive to change and assures consumers that they can enjoy products at minimum possible prices.

We will now supplement the short-run analysis of the previous chapter by deriving long-run supply curves. We will then explore the long-run reaction of firms to changes in economic policies and conditions. Price changes and changes in technology initiate a process of re-equilibration in markets. In the long run, firms expand their physical capacity to produce when they can increase their profits by doing so. In the long run, new firms enter competitive markets in which profit opportunities exist. Analysis of short-run supply merely scratches the surface of the theory of supply. To determine the final response of sellers to price changes, the long-run reactions of firms and investors to price changes must be considered.

The benchmark model of perfectly competitive markets explains why and how sellers respond to changes in demand and cost. Much of what was assumed in the basic supply and demand analysis of Chapter 2 can now be understood in detail. We can also use the concept of allocative efficiency that we introduced in the preceding chapter to further explore the consequences of such government policies as taxation, price controls, and entry limits in perfectly competitive markets. We will show how government intervention in markets often prevents them from achieving allocative efficiency, and we will analyze the gains and losses of economic policies.

Firms, Industries, and Perfect Competition

Industry A group of competing firms selling a certain product in a market.

An **industry** is a group of competing firms selling a certain product in a market. For example, the U.S. soybean industry comprises the half million or so U.S. farms that produce soybeans. The U.S. dairy industry comprises the nearly 200,000 U.S. dairy farmers who produce milk and milk-related products.

Throughout this chapter it is assumed that the firms in a given industry compete as sellers in perfectly competitive markets, in which freedom of enterprise is possible. In a system of perfectly competitive markets, resource owners can take advantage of profit opportunities in *all* industries in the long run. Information about input and output prices is assumed to be freely available to buyers and sellers.

Free entry A situation that exists when anyone can begin an enterprise in an industry.

Free exit A situation that exists when owners of a firm in an industry can cease operating at any time they wish.

Free entry means that anyone can begin an enterprise in an industry, with no restrictions. If a farmer believes that growing soybeans will be profitable, he can do so without any constraint. No approval from any authorities is required if free entry exists. By the same token, **free exit** means that the owners of a firm in an industry can cease operating at any time they wish. They cannot be forced to remain in an industry if they find their operations unprofitable.

Free entry and exit require that productive resources be mobile. Mobility of capital and labor allows managers and investors to take full advantage of long-run profit opportunities as they arise. As long as investors and managers remain fully informed about the prices of outputs and inputs and about technology, they can be expected to respond rapidly to changes in opportunities to earn profit. Perfect mobility means that investors are free to choose the most profitable enterprise in which to invest their funds. If investors can make more profit by employing their funds in enterprises producing microcomputers than they can elsewhere, capital and labor will flow into the microcomputer industry.

The price of the standardized product produced by firms in a perfectly competitive industry is determined by the market demand and the market supply. The competitive price is the price for which quantity demanded is equal to the quantity the industry supplies. Each firm in a perfectly competitive industry is, of course, a price taker.

LONG-RUN COMPETITIVE EQUILIBRIUM AND SUPPLY

Equilibrium of the Industry

Industry equilibrium The equilibrium that prevails when there is no tendency for firms to enter or leave an industry or to expand or reduce the scale of their operations.

Industry equilibrium prevails when there is no tendency for firms to enter or leave an industry or to expand or reduce the scale of their operations. Firms tend to expand when they can increase their profits by doing so. A firm attains maximum profits in the long run when its output and plant size have been adjusted until price (P) equals long-run marginal cost (LRMC). Just as adjusting output until P = MC gives short-run maximum profits for a competitive firm, so does adjusting output and plant size until P = LRMC give long-run maximum profits. In the long run, unlike the short run, a competitive firm can adjust output by building more and larger plants instead of just producing more within a given plant.

New firms will enter an industry if the profits in that industry exceed those that they can earn elsewhere. If existing firms in an industry are earning economic profits, those profits will lure additional firms. Positive economic profits imply that firms in the industry are earning more than a normal profit. Investors will finance new enterprises in an industry in which economic profits can be earned.

If economic profits in an industry are negative, firms in the industry cannot cover their opportunity costs. This means that they earn less than the normal profit. Because they can earn more in their next best alternative, they will leave the industry. As firms enter or leave an industry, there is a shift in the short-run market supply curve of the standardized product they produce. Consequently, given market demand for the product, price will change.

When economic profits in an industry are zero, firms have no incentive to either enter or leave the industry. Each firm just covers its economic cost and has no incentive to leave the industry. There is no tendency for new firms to enter because they will not be able to earn more in it than they can elsewhere. The number of firms in the industry will therefore be stable. It is possible to earn economic profits whenever the market price of a product exceeds the minimum possible average cost of making it available. To eliminate the incentive for new firms to enter or existing firms to expand, price must fall to the minimum possible long-run average cost (LRACmin). By the same token, when firms in a competitive industry incur losses, price must rise to LRACmin, because whenever $P <$ LRACmin, firms will leave the industry.

In summary, the conditions for industry equilibrium under perfect competition are P = LRMC and P = LRACmin. The first condition implies that no firm in the industry can earn more profit by adjusting its operations to produce more or to produce less. The second condition implies that existing firms will not leave the industry and new firms will not enter it—that no firm can expand or contract operations in the long run to make more profit and that new firms have no incentive to start operations in the industry.

Expansion of the Firm in the Long Run

A graphic analysis can help make clear the process by which a perfectly competitive industry attains an equilibrium. To do this, assume that the market price of the standard chair produced by firms in a competitive industry is $150. Based on the data in Chapter 9, the typical competitive firm in the industry can earn monthly economic profits of $26,990 at that price. In the long run, owners of such firms can think about expanding their facilities. For simplicity, assume that all firms have the same cost functions.

The incentive to expand depends of course on expected future prices. For the moment, assume that the firm's owners take the current price as the best forecast of the future price. This is illustrated in Figure 10–1. Short-run production is currently taking place in the plant, whose short-run cost curves are AC_1 and MC_1. Short-run equilibrium output is $q_1 = 318$ chairs per month. The monthly profit of $26,990 is represented by the area *APBC*. Although this profit is handsome, the firm can earn more in the long run by expanding its operations. By building a plant

FIGURE 10–1 Long-Run Profit Maximization

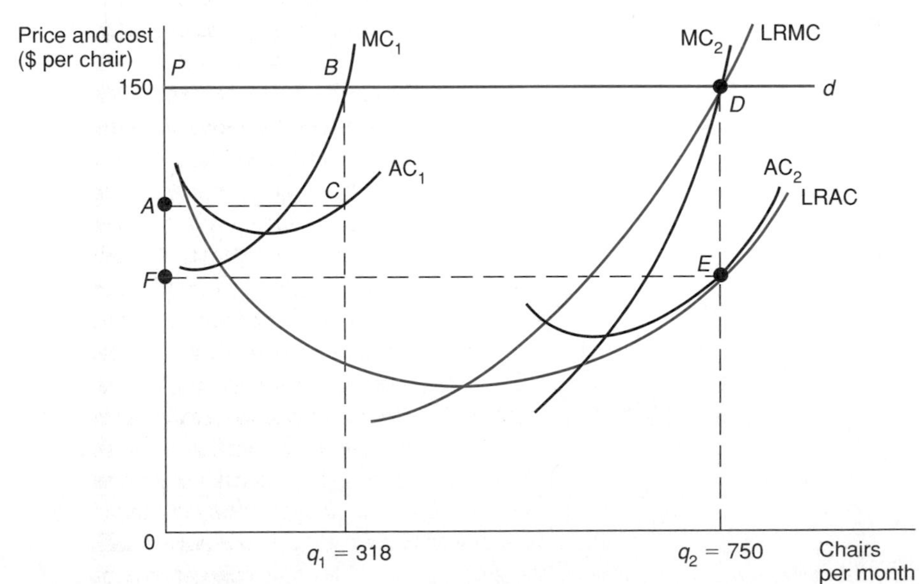

At a price of $150 per chair, the firm's short-run profits are represented by the area *APBC*. In the long run, if the price remains at $150, the firm can increase its profits by expanding until LRMC equals $150. The firm's profits would then increase to the area *PDEF*.

in which it can produce the output corresponding to the point at which P = LRMC, owners can increase its profits substantially. This is true *provided that* the price of chairs remains at $150.

In Figure 10–1 the short-run cost curves for a plant corresponding to the point at which P = LRMC are drawn along with the LRMC and LRAC curves. At a price of $150 per chair the plant (or plants because there could be more than one) for which short-run average cost and marginal cost are AC_2 and MC_2, respectively, would be constructed. That plant would be operated at the output level corresponding to $P = MC_2$. Equilibrium output would be q_2 = 750 chairs per month. Monthly profits represented by the area *PDEF* could be earned if price remained at $150 per chair. Because the area *PDEF* greatly exceeds the area *APBC,* representing current profits, the firm is tempted to expand.

Unfortunately for owners of this firm, the scenario just described will not be the final long-run outcome. New firms, attracted by economic profits, can be expected to enter the perfectly competitive industry in the long run. In addition, *all* existing firms can be expected to expand production by building more factories to make more profits. As new firms enter and as all existing firms expand, supply will increase, causing price to fall.

Long-Run Competitive Equilibrium

The impact of entry on supply, price, and profits is illustrated in Figure 10–2. After new firms enter the industry and existing firms expand, the market supply curve shifts from S_1 to S_2. Industry output increases from its initial level of Q_1 to its long-run equilibrium level of Q_2. Note that the horizontal axis of the market graph measures output in thousands of units.

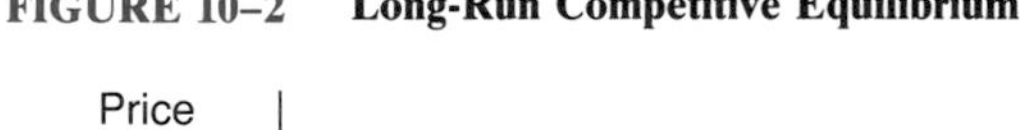

FIGURE 10–2 Long-Run Competitive Equilibrium

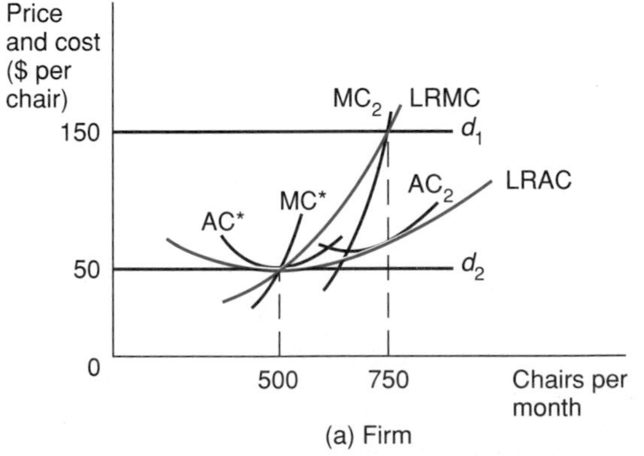

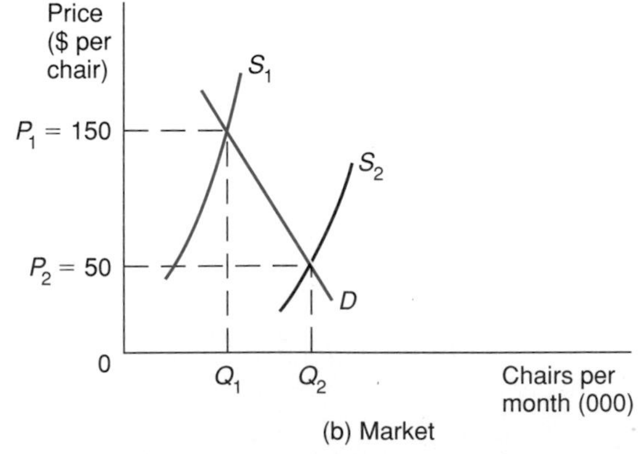

In the long run, new firms enter the chair industry. As the number of firms increases, market supply increases from S_1 to S_2 and price falls to $50 a chair. Firms continue to enter the industry until economic profits are zero. This occurs at output level Q_2. Each firm produces 500 chairs a month at the lower price and earns the normal profit because P = LRACmin at that price.

As shown in the market graph, the price of chairs falls drastically in the long run, from \$150 per unit to \$50 per unit. As this occurs, firms incur losses if they operate in the plant or plants whose short-run average cost curves are AC_2. This is true because the new market equilibrium price is below the minimum possible price attainable for that scale of operations. Maximum profits for any competitive firm in the industry are attained where P_2 = LRMC, which occurs at a monthly output of 500 chairs. At that level of operations the short-run cost curves are AC* and MC*. The monthly output of 500 chairs gives the maximum attainable long-run profits. *Maximum monthly economic profits for all of the competitive firms in the industry (assuming that they all have the same cost function) are now zero!*

Long-run competitive equilibrium The equilibrium that prevails when market output and price allow firms in an industry to earn zero economic profits.

The **long-run competitive equilibrium** is the market output and price that allow firms in an industry to earn zero economic profits. If they earned more or less, forces would be set up to either raise or lower prices until economic profits were once again zero. When economic profits are zero, firms have no incentive to enter or leave an industry because they earn a return on their owner-supplied inputs in the industry that is identical to what they can earn in their next best alternative (the normal profit).

In the long-run competitive equilibrium, prices equal not only long-run marginal costs but also long-run average costs. Finally, because demand for the product of each firm is a horizontal line, price equals LRAC at its minimum possible value (LRACmin). In Figure 10–2 the firm's demand curve, d_2, is just tangent to the minimum point of the LRAC curve. Price must also equal LRMC at that point because LRMC intersects LRAC at its minimum level. Each firm in the industry is operating in the short-run plant corresponding to AC*, the minimum possible average cost. That plant is operating at the level at which average cost is at its minimum.

Under perfect competition firms are presumed to be fully informed about the present and the future. This being the case, no competitive firm will build a plant whose short-run cost corresponds to AC_2. With perfect foresight, each competitive firm uses LRACmin as the best forecast of future prices. Accordingly, each firm can be expected to build the facilities whose short-run costs correspond to the curve AC* in the long run.

Notice the role of economic profits in ensuring the eventual establishment of the long-run competitive equilibrium. As long as the market price exceeds LRAC-min, firms can build a minimum-cost plant and earn economic profits. If economic profits fall below LRACmin, firms will be able to earn more by employing their owner-supplied inputs in another industry. Profit acts as the lure that attracts firms in competitive industries. As firms enter or leave an industry in response to opportunities to earn profit, the short-run market supply curve shifts and ensures that P = LRACmin.

Characteristics of Long-Run Competitive Equilibrium

What are the implications of the long-run competitive equilibrium for consumers? When a perfectly competitive industry is in equilibrium, the price of its product falls to the lowest possible level associated with given input prices and technology. Price is equal to the minimum possible long-run average cost of production. Each firm in the industry operates in the plant capable of producing at the lowest possible average cost in the long run. Each firm also operates that plant at the level corresponding to minimum average cost.

Firms do not keep costs as low as possible out of benevolence but out of selfish interests. Adam Smith summed this up eloquently when he argued that persons pursuing their own interests are led by an "invisible hand" to achieve an outcome that is in the common interest.[1] Competition among firms lowers price to the level of the minimum possible LRAC. Each firm seeks to maximize profit, yet in the long run no firm can earn economic profits.

Any increase or decrease in price results in forces that act to return price to the level of LRACmin. If price rises above LRACmin, economic profits prevail. In response, new firms enter the industry, existing firms expand, and supply increases until price returns to its previous equilibrium level. If price falls below LRACmin, firms exit from the industry to avoid losses. Supply then decreases until price rises to its previous equilibrium level.

The Paradox of Profits

In a perfectly competitive industry, economic profits can be enjoyed only temporarily by the owners of firms. Economic profits serve as signals. If all industries were perfectly competitive, firms would be constantly entering and leaving industries in response to their changing economic profitability. In the long run, no firm in any industry can earn more than a normal profit. In a competitive world economic profits are only temporary rewards for those who are shrewd or lucky. Economic profits are inevitably reduced to zero as they attract other producers into the industries in which they are being earned. This is the **paradox of profits:** Positive economic profits set in motion a process of resource reallocation that ultimately reduces them to zero.

Paradox of profits Positive economic profits set in motion a process of resource reallocation that ultimately reduces them to zero.

Similarly, losses are only temporary. If losses are being experienced in a perfectly competitive industry, firms will leave in the long run. As firms leave, prices rise and the losses are eventually eliminated. In the long run no firm can hope to earn more than the normal profit.

CONCEPT REVIEW

1. Under what conditions does an industry selling a product in a perfectly competitive market achieve equilibrium?
2. Why will the price of a product sold in a perfectly competitive market eventually equal the minimum possible average cost of producing it?
3. In what sense do economic profits plant the seeds of their own destruction for firms selling in a perfectly competitive market?

[1] Adam Smith, *The Wealth of Nations* (New York: Modern Library, Random House, 1937; first published in 1776), p. 423.

Long-Run Supply

Long-run supply curves for a perfectly competitive industry can be derived by tracing out the way the industry responds to changes in demand. At the outset, assume that input prices are independent of the quantity supplied by all firms in the industry, that the prices of the alternative goods that can be produced with the same inputs are constant, and that technology is a given and does not change as the industry grows. No attempt is made to explain the length of time necessary for adjustment from one equilibrium to another.

Industry Adjustment to an Increase in Demand (Constant Input Prices)

In 1990 the half million or so farmers growing soybeans in the United States had nearly 60 million acres under cultivation. The total quantity of the soybeans supplied that year, including imports, was about 2 trillion bushels. The price per bushel was nearly \$6. Assuming that the soybean industry was in equilibrium at that price, Figure 10–3 shows the long-run cost curves of the soybean producers and the equilibrium price per bushel. The equilibrium quantity supplied by the soybean industry is Q_1. The equilibrium quantity supplied by a typical soybean producer is q_1. The industry demand and supply curves are D_1 and S_1. The demand curve for a typical soybean producer is d_1, as shown in Figure 10–3(a). Because the soybean industry is assumed to be in equilibrium, P = LRACmin for the typical soybean producer.

FIGURE 10–3 Long-Run Industry Response to an Increase in Demand

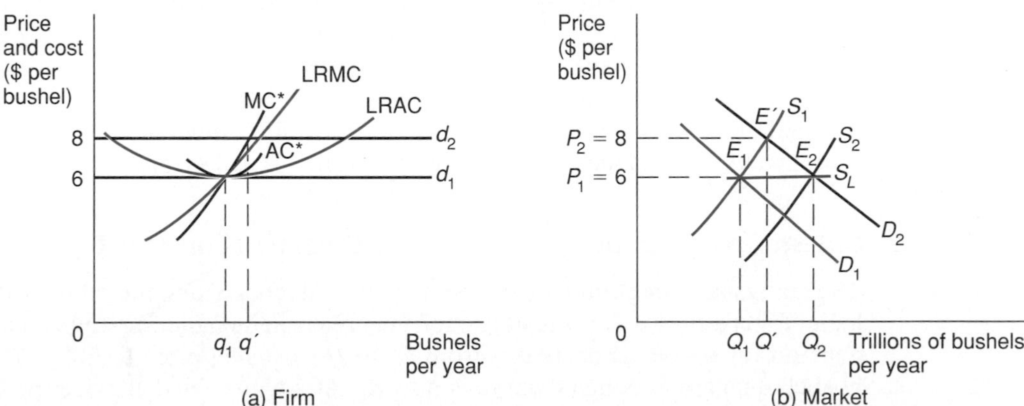

An increase in market demand for soybeans from D_1 to D_2 raises the price of soybeans from \$6 to \$8 per bushel. The typical soybean farm increases output until MC* = \$8 in the short run. This results in economic profits because P_2 exceeds the average cost of producing q'. As new firms enter the soybean industry, market supply increases from S_1 to S_2. As industry output increases, price falls to its initial level of \$6 per bushel. The long-run supply curve for the industry of constant costs is S_L which connects the points E_1 and E_2, where the industry is in equilibrium.

Suppose there is an increase in the market demand for soybeans from D_1 to D_2. In the short run, this raises the price of soybeans from P_1 = \$6 per bushel to P_2 = \$8 per bushel. A typical soybean producer's demand increases from d_1 to d_2. In the short run, at the higher price each soybean producer supplies more soybeans, so that P_2 = MC*, where MC* is the marginal cost for the farm that can achieve LRACmin. The typical soybean firm increases production from q_1 to q'. As all firms supply more soybeans at the higher price, the quantity supplied by the soybean industry increases from Q_1 to Q'. The short-run market equilibrium changes from point E_1 to point E', where the short-run industry supply curve, S_1, intersects the new demand curve, D_2.

At the higher price, firms in the soybean industry earn economic profits. These profits lure more firms to produce soybeans in the long run. In the long run, the industry supply of soybeans increases from S_1 to S_2.

The new market equilibrium therefore occurs at point E_2, where the demand curve D_2 intersects the supply curve S_2. Price returns to its initial level of \$6 per bushel. Because input prices and technology are assumed to be fixed, any other prices would diverge from LRACmin. Total market supply increases from its initial level, Q_1, equal to 2 trillion bushels, to Q_2, equal to 2.5 trillion bushels. The typical soybean firm returns to producing q_1 bushels of soybeans after the price returns to \$6 a bushel. It is once again producing soybeans at minimum possible average cost. Although each soybean firm produces the same amount as it did before the increase in demand, total industry production has increased because new firms have entered. Economic profits earned by soybean firms are once again zero.

Note that in equilibrium in the long run each firm always supplies the quantity of output corresponding to LRACmin. Market supply in equilibrium is obtained simply by adding the amounts supplied by all firms at that price. In the initial equilibrium at point E_1, each firm produces q_1 units of soybeans per year. In the final equilibrium at point E_2, each competitive firm (assuming all are the same size) once again produces q_1 units of output per year. The amount supplied to the market at this price increases despite the fact that $q_1 < q'$ because there are *more* competitive firms in the industry when the final long-run equilibrium has been attained. In the long-run equilibrium, the quantity supplied by the competitive firm always corresponds to the point at which P = LRACmin.

Industry Adjustment to a Decrease in Demand (Constant Input Prices)

The analysis of long-run industry reaction to a decrease in demand uses the same logic. Figure 10–4 traces the impact of a decrease in demand for soybeans. Market demand for soybeans decreases from D_1 to D_3, causing price to fall to P_3 = \$4 a bushel. The firm's demand curve is now d_3. At a \$4 per bushel price the firm will not be able to cover its costs. Firms will go out of business immediately if that price is below minimum possible average variable costs. If $P_2 >$ AVC, a firm will decrease production until P_2 = MC*. Output produced by a typical firm declines from q_1 to q''. As all firms respond in this way, short-run quantity supplied by the industry falls from Q_1 to Q'.

FIGURE 10–4 Long-Run Industry Response to a Decrease in Demand

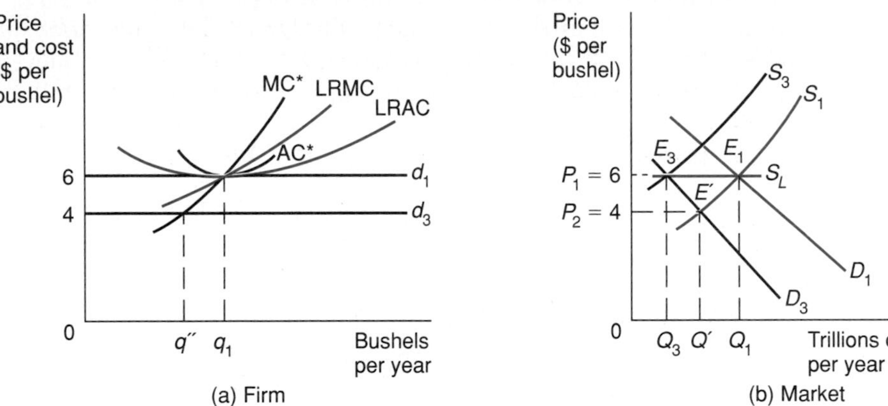

If the industry is initially in equilibrium, a decrease in demand decreases price to a level below LRACmin. Firms leave the industry in the long run to avoid losses. As a result supply decreases from S_1 to S_3. Supply continues to decrease until $P =$ LRACmin once again. For a constant-costs industry, the long-run supply curve is the horizontal line S_L.

In the long run, firms will exit from the industry. The price decline to $4 a bushel has resulted in negative economic profits. Farmers can earn more by planting alternative crops. As firms leave the industry, thereby decreasing the acreage devoted to soybean production, supply decreases from S_1 to S_3. The new long-run equilibrium is at Q_3, where 1.5 trillion bushels of soybeans are produced annually and price is again $6 per bushel. Assuming that input prices do not change as the industry contracts, price must return to its original level to eliminate losses. In the new equilibrium there are fewer soybean producers. Each remaining producer is again producing the output corresponding to LRACmin.

The Long-Run Industry Supply Curve: The Case of Constant Costs

Long-run industry supply curve A supply curve that shows the relationship between price and quantity supplied for points at which an industry is in equilibrium.

A **long-run industry supply curve** shows the relationship between price and quantity supplied *for points at which an industry is in equilibrium.* Point E_1 in Figures 10–3(b) and 10–4(b) is a point on the long-run supply curve. That is the initial equilibrium point for the soybean industry in both graphs. The curve S_1 represents the initial short-run supply curve for the industry.

After the industry expands in response to an increase in demand, a new long-run competitive equilibrium is attained at point E_2. The price and quantity corresponding to that point are another point on the long-run supply curve. The new short-run supply curve is S_2. The long-run industry supply curve, labeled S_L in Figure 10–3(b), is obtained by connecting the points E_1 and E_2. Point E' is *not* a point on the long-run supply curve because the industry is not in equilibrium at that point.

Constant-costs industry An industry for which input prices are unaffected by the quantity produced or the number of firms in the industry.

A **constant-costs industry** is one for which input prices are unaffected by the quantity produced or the number of firms in the industry. The long-run supply curve for such an industry is a horizontal line. In the long run, price must always return to the same level in such an industry to eliminate economic profits and losses. All of the points on the long-run supply curve satisfy the following condition:

$$P = \text{LRMC} = \text{LRACmin} \tag{10–1}$$

Because input prices, technology, and the prices of other outputs are independent of the quantity supplied by the industry, LRACmin is independent of the size of the industry for the case of constant costs.

Similarly, in Figure 10–4(b) point E_3 is a point on the long-run supply curve. In the long run, supply is infinitely elastic at the price of $6 per bushel as long as input prices, technology, and the prices of other goods are given.

Increasing- and Decreasing-Costs Industries and Long-Run Industry Supply Curves

Increasing-costs industry An industry for which at least some input prices increase as a direct result of the industry's expansion.

An **increasing-costs industry** is one for which the prices of at least some of the inputs used increase as a direct result of the industry's expansion. The demand for more of these inputs by the industry in the long run causes their prices to increase. An industry might buy a large share of the total supply of a particular kind of skilled labor. The increase in demand for this input results in increases in its price. For example, if the petroleum industry employs a large share of the total number of chemical engineers, the salaries that it must pay to attract them increase as the industry expands. Conversely, when the petroleum industry contracts, the salaries of chemical engineers will decline.

Suppose that as the chair industry expands, the wages of the skilled workers required to assemble chairs increase. Now consider the impact of an increase in demand for chairs assuming the industry is one of increasing costs.

The industry is initially in equilibrium at point E_1 in Figure 10–5(b). The price of chairs is $50. As demand increases a temporary short-run equilibrium is achieved at point E', where the price of chairs increases to $75. In the long run new firms enter in response to the positive economic profits that can be earned by producing chairs. However, the price of labor also increases as the industry expands. This causes an increase in average cost.

The impact of the increase in the price of labor on the LRAC curve for firms in the industry is shown in Figure 10–5(a). The increase in the price of labor input caused by the expansion of the industry causes an upward shift in the long-run average cost curve to LRAC′. As the industry achieves a new equilibrium, the market price of chairs must be higher than the initial price. This is easy to see. Suppose that price were to return to its previous level of $50 a chair. Firms would not be able to earn the normal profit at that price because the increase in labor costs has increased LRACmin from $50 to $65. The market price corresponding to LRAC′min is now $65. The new industry equilibrium is therefore at point E_2. Connecting points E_1 and E_2 gives an upward-sloping long-run supply curve, S_L. The long-run supply curve of an industry of increasing costs is therefore upward sloping.

FIGURE 10–5 An Increasing-Costs Industry

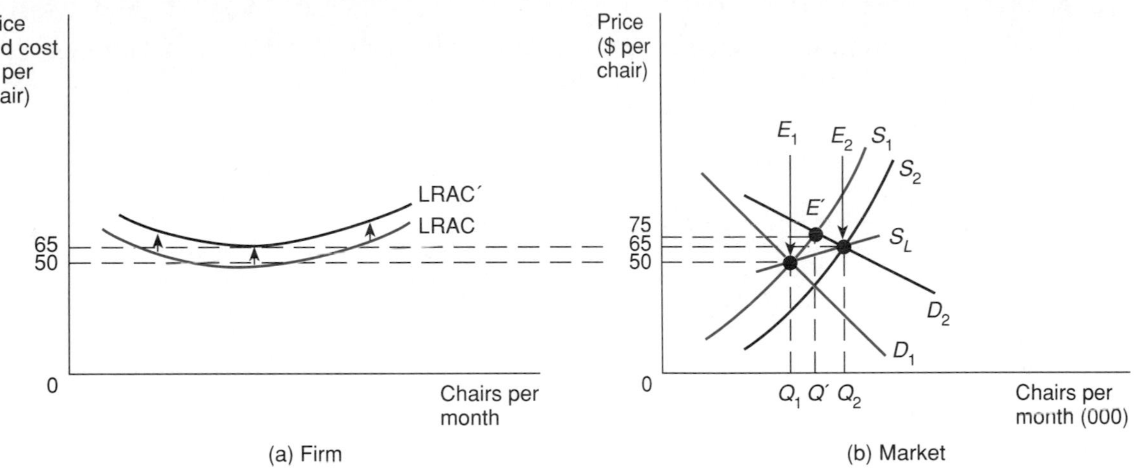

As an industry of increasing costs expands, the price of some of the inputs it uses increases. This shifts the LRAC curves upward. An initial increase in demand from D_1 to D_2 raises the price of chairs to $75. Because this price exceeds LRACmin, new firms enter and supply increases. The new equilibrium occurs at a chair price of $65. If the price of chairs were to return to its initial $50 level, firms would incur losses and leave the industry. The long-run supply curve connects points E_1 and E_2. S_L slopes upward because of the increasing costs.

Decreasing-costs industry An industry for which the prices of certain inputs used decline as a direct result of the industry's expansion.

A **decreasing-costs industry** is one for which the prices of certain inputs used decline as a direct result of the industry's expansion. Long-run average costs decline as a decreasing-costs industry expands. The long-run supply curve for such an industry is downward sloping.

The case of decreasing costs is illustrated in Figure 10–6. The initial equilibrium of the industry is at point *E*, where the price of its product is P_1. After an initial increase in demand from D_1 to D_2, a temporary short-run equilibrium is attained at E', where price increases to P'. Because this results in economic profits for firms, the industry expands. As a direct result of its expansion, the prices of some of the inputs it uses actually decline. This is a rare occurrence; however, it is possible. One economist has pointed out that expansion of the garment industry in New York City attracted firms specializing in rental of sophisticated machines for making buttonholes, fasteners, and ornaments. Individual firms in this industry were small, and no one firm could afford to purchase such machines. However, a large garment industry helped reduce the hourly rental rates for these machines by encouraging more firms to supply them.[2]

As the decreasing-costs industry adjusts, the new equilibrium price must be lower than the initial price because the firm's cost curves shift down from LRAC to LRAC′ as the industry expands. If price were to return to P_1, firms would earn

[2] See E. M. Hoover, *An Introduction to Regional Economics,* 2nd ed. (New York: Alfred A. Knopf, 1975, p. 85. Also see Robert M. Lichtenberg, *One Tenth of a Nation* (Cambridge, Mass.: Harvard University Press, 1960).

MODERN MICROECONOMICS IN ACTION: THE BUSINESS WORLD

The Impact of Advancing Technology in the Market for Computers and Other Electronic Goods

Application of improved technology in industries producing electronic goods and other "high-tech" products has resulted in rapid growth and reequilibration in these industries. The ultimate beneficiaries of the new technology have been consumers who have seen the prices of such electronic marvels as personal computers, VCRs, calculators, and quartz watches plummet in the 1980s.

The theory of long-run competitive equilibrium can easily be applied to understand the implication of improved technology in markets that are close to perfectly competitive. In the case of electronic goods, although the product is far from standardized, there is enough similarity among the goods of competing sellers and enough sellers to make the model applicable. For example, in the case of the personal computer, standardization of operating systems in the IBM PC and the IBM clones made computers of competing manufacturers very close, if not perfect, substitutes.

When new technology that reduces average costs can be employed, firms that first apply the new technology gain temporary profits. The graph shows the impact of improved technology on a typical firm in an industry. Assume that the initial price for a new computer is P_1. Using the new technology to produce the computer shifts the firm's LRAC curve down from $LRAC_1$ to $LRAC_2$. Given the price of the product, P_1, employing the new technology allows the firm to earn economic profit in the short run because $P_1 > LRAC_2min$. However, if the market is perfectly competitive, information on the new technology is freely available and existing or new competitors can employ it as well. The profits made possible by applying the new technology therefore attract new firms into the industry and result in an increase in market supply. As supply increases, the market equilibrium price falls to P_2, which is equal to $LRAC_2min$. At the new lower price the now larger industry supplies Q_2 units per year as quantity demanded increases from its initial level of Q_1.

The scenario of rapidly improving technology, ease of entry into the market, and a more or less standardized product contributed to lower prices for personal computers in the mid-1980s. In 1983 the market was dominated by five companies that accounted for 70 percent of all computer sales: IBM, Apple, Tandy, Hewlett-Packard, and Digital Equipment. By 1986 there were over 100 manufacturers of IBM clones designed to run the same software as the IBM PC. As a result of the entry of

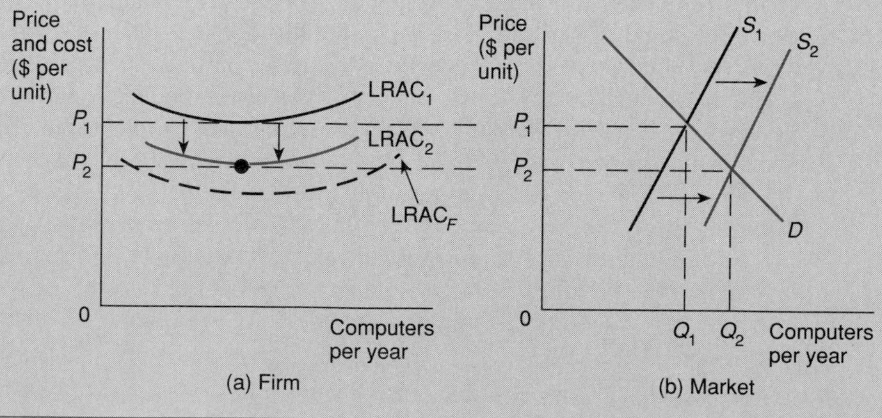

(*Continued*) many new sellers into the market—including those from Japan and South Korea—the price of personal computers plummeted in 1986. For example, an IBM PC system that cost $3,500 in 1983 could easily be purchased for about $1,500 in 1986.

After 1986 IBM's profits plummeted because of the increased competition and supply. When all nations have access to the same technology, the nation with lower labor costs can produce the same product at lower minimum possible average costs. Imported computers produced in Korea and Taiwan, where labor costs were lower, could therefore be sold in the United States at lower prices than IBM products, putting further downward pressure on prices. In the graph the dashed curve labeled $LRAC_F$ shows the long-run average cost curve for a foreign computer company employing labor priced lower than the labor employed by U.S. producers. Increased foreign competition in 1986 forced IBM to lower prices, resulting in adverse effects on its profits.

Other examples abound to show how improved technology and free entry into competitive markets result in lower prices. Such marvels of modern technology as VCRs, stereo TV monitors, and compact disc players have turned the living rooms of many Americans into substitutes for theaters and concert halls. The markets for these products have in the past been dominated by Japanese suppliers. However, South Koreans and other foreign producers have emerged as keen competitors eager to adopt new technology and supply electronic gizmos. The market for electronic goods is characterized by falling prices and improved product quality. For about $250 consumers can buy a color TV equipped with stereo sound, digital displays, and other features found only on models that cost as much as $600 or more a few years ago.

FIGURE 10–6 A Decreasing-Costs Industry

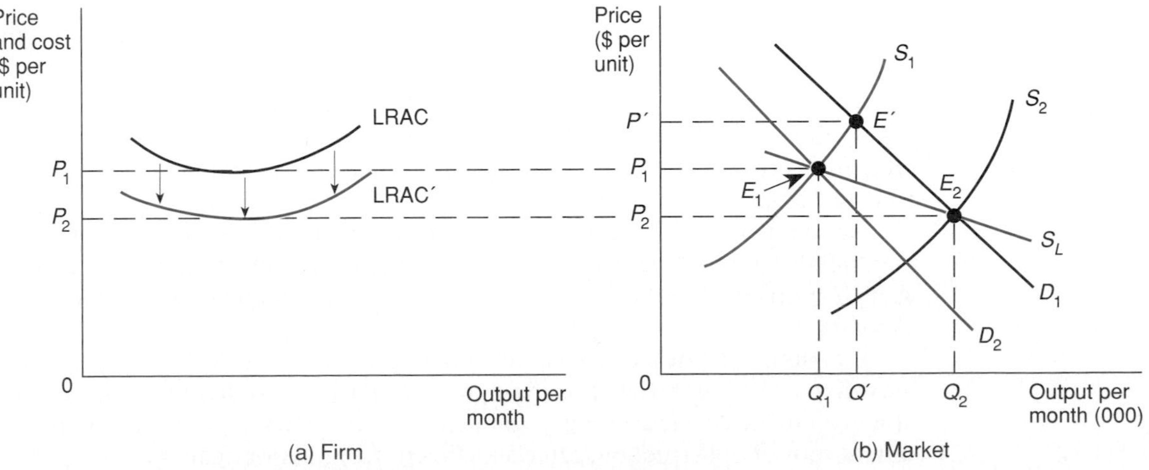

As the industry expands, the LRAC curve shifts down because the prices of some of the inputs used fall as a result. The new equilibrium is at a lower price because of the decline in LRACmin. The long-run supply curve is downward sloping.

positive economic profits and new firms would continue to enter. This would continue to occur until the price fell to LRAC′min. The new equilibrium is therefore at point E_2 for the industry, where price is P_2. Connecting the initial and final long-run equilibrium points gives a downward-sloping long-run supply curve.

In many cases an industry is incorrectly labeled as one of decreasing costs. For an industry to qualify for this label, it must be shown that price declines *as a direct result of the impact of the industry's expansion on input prices*. For this to be true, technology must be constant. This is not always the case. For example, the prices of such electronic marvels of the 1970s and 1980s as electronic calculators and the personal computer have declined since they were first introduced. Much of this decline is attributable to rapid changes in technology rather than changes in input prices resulting from the expansion of the electronics industry. The changes in technology lowered average costs of production.

Long-Run Supply versus Short-Run Supply

Short-run supply curves always slope upward for a perfectly competitive industry because the short-run supply curve reflects the upward slope of the marginal cost curves for firms in the industry. The long-run supply curve slopes upward only for increasing-costs industries. Economic profits for firms on all points along a long-run supply curve must be zero. This is not the case for points on a short-run supply curve.

Because there is more flexibility to expand in the long run, long-run supply curves can be expected to be more price elastic than corresponding short-run supply curves. For the case of constant costs, long-run price elasticity of supply is infinite. This is because the long-run supply curve for a constant-costs industry is a flat line with zero slope. For any price and quantity supplied, price elasticity on such a line is infinite because the elasticity of supply is

$$E_S = \frac{P}{Q_S}\left(\frac{\Delta Q_S}{\Delta P}\right) \qquad \textbf{(10–2)}$$

where Q_S is quantity supplied. Since $\Delta Q_S/\Delta P$ is the inverse of the slope of the supply curve, its value becomes infinite when the slope of the supply curve approaches zero. It follows that price elasticity of supply is infinite for an industry of constant costs.

For an industry of increasing costs, price elasticity of long-run supply is less than infinity but greater than zero. Long-run supply could become more inelastic at higher prices, depending on the way input prices increase when the industry expands.

Estimates of price elasticity of long-run supply suggest that constant costs prevail in many industries. For example, one study found that the long-run supply of new housing construction was infinitely elastic.[3] This implies that the price per square foot of construction, after adjustment for inflation, can be expected to be

[3] James R. Follain, Jr., "The Price Elasticity of the Long-Run Supply of New Housing Construction," *Land Economics* 55, no. 2 (May 1979), pp. 190–99.

constant in the long run. On the other hand, the long-run price elasticity of supply of many agricultural commodities has been estimated at less than 1, which suggests that agriculture is an industry of increasing costs.[4]

CONCEPT REVIEW

1. In what ways do points on a long-run industry supply curve differ from points on a short-run industry supply curve?
2. Under what circumstances is the long-run industry supply curve upward sloping?
3. Suppose that the construction industry is one of constant costs. An increase in the demand for housing construction increases the price per square foot of new construction. What will happen to the price per square foot after the industry reequilibrates?

APPLICATIONS OF THE COMPETITIVE MODEL

The Long-Run Impact of a License Fee

In the short run, the imposition of a flat-rate license fee is equivalent to an increase in fixed costs for a firm. As shown in Chapter 9, any increase in fixed costs has no impact on the output that firms produce and therefore on price in the short run. The outcome, however, is considerably different in the long run.

Suppose license fees for building contractors are tripled from \$1,000 to \$3,000 per year in a certain state. The model of competitive supply can now be used to trace the long-run implications of the increase. Of course, in the long run all costs are variable. Assume that before the introduction of the fee the industry was in equilibrium.

The increase in the license fee causes average costs to rise from LRAC to LRAC′, as shown in Figure 10–7(a). The initial price, P_1, per square foot equals LRACmin. After the increase, $P_1 <$ LRAC′min. In the long run, firms will leave the construction industry as a result of the increase. They will move to their next best alternative. For example, some firms might decide to move their operations to a state where the license fee is lower or nonexistent. As firms leave the industry, short-run supply decreases from S to S', as shown in Figure 10–7(b). Price increases until it attains the level $P_2 =$ LRAC′min. This assumes that the industry is one of constant costs. Otherwise, the curve LRAC′ would shift down as firms leave the industry, because a decrease in industry supply would decrease input prices.

It can be concluded that the long-run impact of a flat-rate annual license fee on suppliers of a particular good is a decrease in the number of suppliers. As this decrease occurs, market price increases from P_1 to P_2 and the quantity demanded

[4] Marc Nerlove and William Addison, "Statistical Estimation of Long-Run Elasticities of Supply and Demand," *Journal of Farm Economics* 40, no. 4 (November 1958), pp. 861–80.

MODERN MICROECONOMICS IN ACTION: GOVERNMENT AND THE ECONOMY

Taxi Medallions in New York City: How They Limit Entry but Keep Long-Run Economic Profits at Zero in a Competitive Industry

In the late 1930s New York City issued hack licenses to the persons who operated taxis at that time. Such licenses grant owners of vehicles the right to use them as taxis. A license of this kind is commonly referred to as a "medallion" in New York City. It is a metal plate fixed to the vehicle's hood. As of 1991 11,787 taxi medallions were available in New York City. In effect, the medallion is a government-created input required to engage in the sale of taxi services. The fixed number of medallions limits entry into the taxi industry.*

Because the supply of medallions is perfectly inelastic, their price is determined solely by the level of demand. The medallions can be sold by those who own them through brokers at a market price that varies with demand, as shown in graph (a). Given the level of demand that prevailed in 1990, the going market price for a medallion was $130,000!† When first issued in the 1930s, the medallions sold for a mere $10. Anyone wanting to enter the taxi industry in New York City in 1990 therefore first had to pay $130,000 for a medallion input plus a modest annual fee.

Fixing the supply of licenses tends to increase the price per mile of taxi service. The following analysis assumes that the price of taxi services is determined in a competitive market. Actually, in New York City changes in taxi rates require the approval of a governing authority. However, it is reasonable to assume that this authority responds to changes in demand and cost conditions in approving requests for rate changes.

Part of the opportunity cost of operating a taxi in New York City is the forgone interest on the market value of the medallion. For example, if the market price of medallions is $130,000 and the interest rate that a medallion owner can earn in the next best alternative investment is 10 percent, then each owner-operator forgoes $13,000 per vehicle per year when operating a taxi. This shifts the LRAC curve upward to $LRAC_2$, as shown in graph (b). Because the increase in costs is independent of the miles per year supplied, the medallion opportunity cost per vehicle declines as more taxi miles are supplied per vehicle.

In the absence of a fixed-supply license, the price of taxi service per mile would be P_1 and Q_1 taxi miles per year would be supplied at that price, as shown in graph (c). The medallion system reduces the market supply of taxi services to S'. The price is now $P_2 > P_1$ per mile, and the quantity demanded at that price declines in the long run from Q_1 to Q_2. The supply of output is more inelastic in the fixed-license case than would otherwise

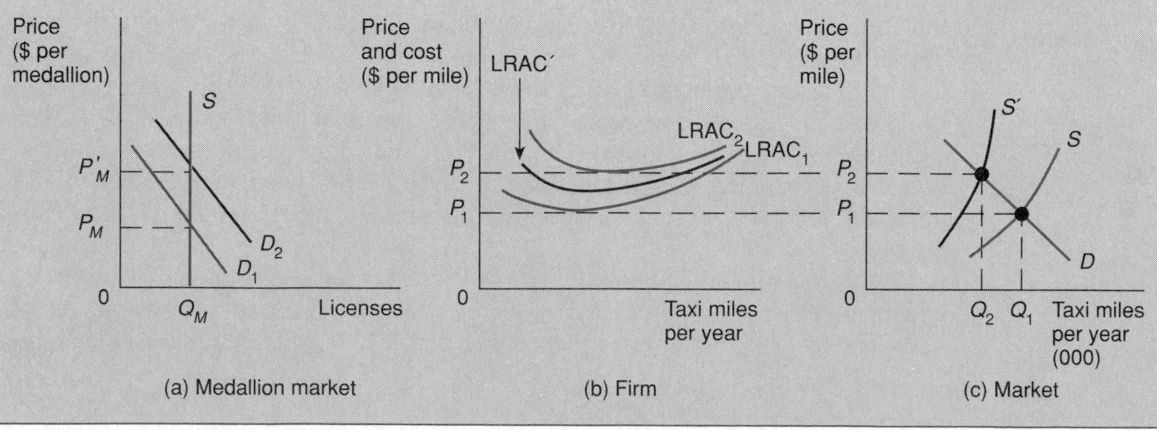

(a) Medallion market (b) Firm (c) Market

(*Continued*) be the case. Supply is not perfectly inelastic, however, because taxi owners have some flexibility in the number of hours they run their vehicles for hire on the streets.

Note that the medallion price adjusts so that no vehicle owner can earn more than normal profits. How can this result occur when the fixed-supply license system bars the entry of new vehicles? The answer lies in the fact that if the medallion price allowed economic profits, the demand for medallions would increase, as shown in graph (a). Assume that if the price of medallions were P_M, the long-run average cost curve would be LRAC′ instead of $LRAC_2$. This would allow economic profits at price P_2. This means that by purchasing a medallion, a vehicle owner could earn more than could be earned by engaging in an alternative enterprise. Demand for medallions would increase from D_1 to D_2, which would cause the price of medallions to increase from P_M to P'_M. The average cost per mile of taxi service would then increase as the opportunity cost of the medallion to owners increased. Medallion prices would continue to increase until average cost rose enough to reduce economic profits to zero. In equilibrium, $P_2 = LRAC_2min$.

A fixed-supply license limiting entry into an otherwise competitive industry therefore results in higher output prices than would otherwise prevail. However, the firms in such an industry can earn no more than the normal profit despite the effective limit to entry. The engine that exhausts profits in this case is the market price of the government-created input: the marketable license.

* For a discussion of entry restrictions in the taxi industry, see Chanock Schreiber, "The Economic Reasons for Price and Entry Regulations on Taxicabs," *Journal of Transport Economics and Policy* 9, no. 3 (September 1975), pp. 268–69.

† See *The New York Times*, October 6, 1991, p. E7. The price of medallions peaked at $140,000 in 1989. Thereafter an economic slowdown in New York City decreased the demand for taxi services and the price of medallions started to fall.

FIGURE 10–7 Long-Run Impact of a License Fee

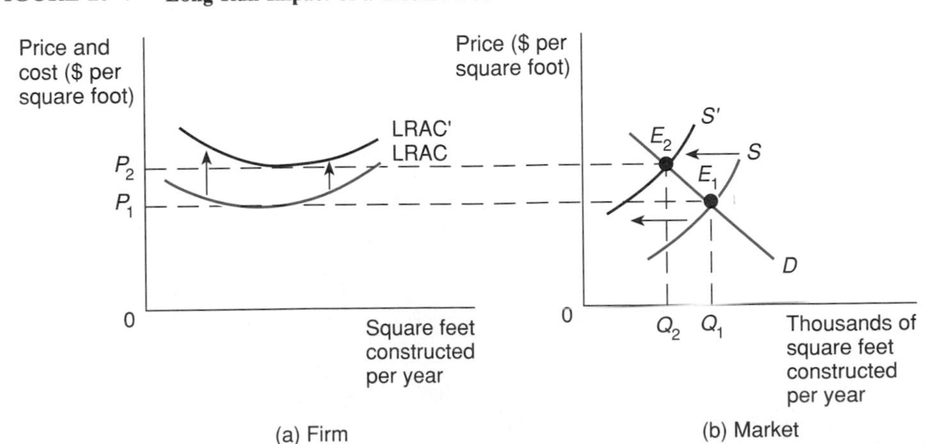

A lump-sum annual license fee shifts the average cost curve up from LRAC to LRAC′. The industry is initially in equilibrium where P_1 = LRACmin. The increase in costs causes firms to leave the industry. Supply decreases from S to S'. Price rises until a new equilibrium is attained at which P_2 = LRAC′min.

by consumers declines from Q_1 to Q_2. The extent of the price increase if the industry is one of increasing costs will be somewhat less than the extent that would prevail under constant costs.

Any change in policies or economic conditions affecting the *short-run fixed costs* of a competitive industry in equilibrium *will* reduce supply and increase price in the long run. Although the short-run impact of a change in fixed costs is nil, the long-run impact is a price increase. For example, an increase in medical malpractice insurance costs is likely in the long run to reduce the number of physician firms if the medical services industry is initially in equilibrium. Although higher malpractice insurance rates will have little effect on the price of medical services in the short run, in the long run they will decrease supply and cause price to rise.

The Long-Run Impact of Rent Controls

The impact of rent controls on market equilibrium was initially discussed in Chapter 2. Now the theory of competitive supply can be used to further explore the way rent controls affect the market for housing. In the short run, the imposition of rent controls by a local government has no effect on the supply curve of rental units. If the rent controls are established below the market equilibrium rent and the initial short-run supply curve is S_1, there will be a shortage of ΔQ units on the market in the short run. This is shown in Figure 10–8. The controlled rent, R_C, is less than the equilibrium rent, R_E, per square foot of housing. In the short run, there is little flexibility to break leases already established with tenants. As a result the short-run supply is likely to be quite inelastic. Thus, rent controls impose losses on landlords in the short run. Landlords can do little to avoid these losses until leases expire.

FIGURE 10–8 Long-Run Impact of Rent Controls

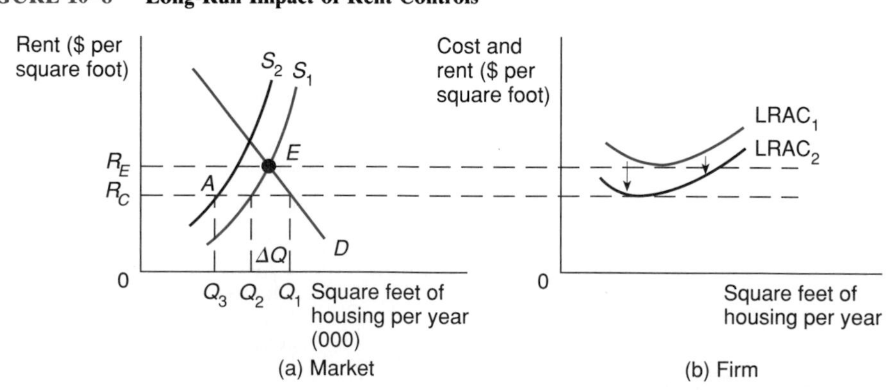

In the short run, the supply curve of housing is S_1. At the controlled rent, $R_C < R_E$, there is a shortage of Q square feet of housing per year. In the long run, firms leave the housing industry because LRAC$_1$ $> R_C$. Supply decreases to S_2, but rents cannot go up because of the controls, resulting in an increase in the housing shortage. To attain normal profits at R_C, suppliers of rental housing decrease its quality. This lower costs until LRAC$_2$ $= R_C$.

Assuming that the housing industry is initially in equilibrium at a rent of R_E per square foot, rent controls result in economic losses. Therefore, housing suppliers can be expected to convert their properties to alternative uses. They could, for example, convert rental units into condominiums and then sell the condominiums to those willing to pay the market price. They could raze rental housing units and convert the land to commercial or industrial uses. They might even choose to abandon their properties. As this occurs, the short-run supply curve shifts from S_1 to S_2. This aggravates the shortage in the long run because the quantity supplied declines to Q_3, whereas the quantity demanded remains Q_1.

If input prices do not decline as the housing industry contracts, housing suppliers will incur economic losses at a point like A. As shown in Figure 10–8(b), the minimum point of LRAC_1 is still above R_C. Landlords can eliminate the losses and thereby regain normal profits only by reducing the *quality* of the housing services they provide. They could, for example, reduce maintenance services on their apartments. New suppliers could build apartments with lower-quality materials. Such practices lower the average cost per square foot supplied per year. When landlords engage in them, the long-run average cost curve shifts down to LRAC_2, until $\text{LRAC}_2\text{min} = R_C$. Point A can be a point of long-run equilibrium for the housing industry only if suppliers find a way of reducing the average cost per square foot of housing. If they cannot, further shifts in the short-run supply curve will follow. Thus, assuming that the housing industry is one of constant costs, the long-run impact of rent controls is *both* a shortage of housing and a decrease in the quality of housing units.

Ample evidence supports the hypothesis that rent controls reduce housing quality. For example, a 1975 survey of rental housing in New York City allowed comparison of rent-controlled apartments with uncontrolled apartments of similar age. The survey revealed that rent-controlled apartments had a greater incidence of deficiencies indicative of poor housing quality. Only 13 percent of the uncontrolled apartments had a breakdown in the heating system during the year, but 34 percent of the rent-controlled apartments reported such a breakdown. Only 10 percent of the uncontrolled apartments had broken plaster or peeling paint, while 23 percent of the rent-controlled apartments suffered from such a defect. Rent-controlled apartments were twice as likely as uncontrolled apartments to have deficiencies in their plumbing systems. Rent-controlled apartments were also twice as likely as uncontrolled apartments to have holes in floors, ceilings, and walls.

In the 1970s rent controls contributed to a massive abandonment of rental housing by landlords who as a result of the controls were unable to provide adequate housing services to their tenants without incurring losses. During this period, deferral of repairs and reduced building maintenance by landlords who did not abandon rent-controlled buildings contributed to a decline in quality of housing.[5]

[5] Frank Kristof, "The Effects of Rent Control and Rent Stabilization in New York City," in *Rent Control: Myths and Reality* (Vancouver, B.C.: Fraser Institute, 1981), pp. 136–37.

Gains and Losses from Price Controls in Competitive Markets

Economic policies result in gains and losses. We can use the concepts of producer and consumer surplus developed in Chapters 5 and 9 to evaluate the gains and losses from price controls in competitive markets. Let's apply the analysis to rent controls. Figure 10–9 redraws rental housing demand and supply after the long-run effects of rent controls have worked themselves out.

The gainers from rent controls are the tenants fortunate enough to be occupying apartments that rent for amounts below the market equilibrium rents. These tenants occupy the Q_3 square feet of housing available in the long run. Their gains are equal to area A, which represents the dollar reduction in their annual rent per year that the controls make possible. However, those gains are offset by equivalent losses to landlords, whose reduction in annual income on the Q_3 square feet of housing they own is also equal to area A. In effect, rent controls and any other controls that legislate prices below equilibrium levels result in a government-mandated transfer of income from sellers to buyers. In the case of rent controls landlords finance gains in real income to tenants.

FIGURE 10–9 Gains and Losses from Rent Controls

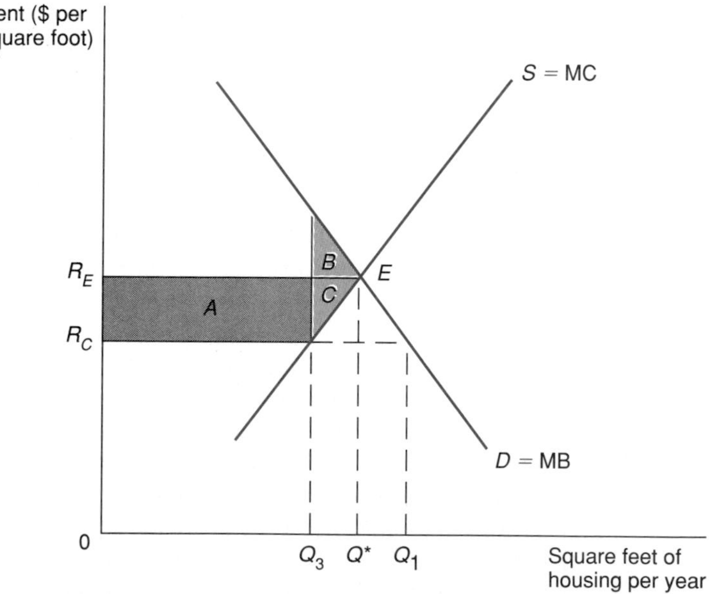

As a result of rent controls there is a gain to tenants who occupy rent-controlled units. That gain, represented by area A, is offset by an equal loss to landlords. Thus part of the effect of rent controls is a transfer of income from landlords to tenants. Rent controls also result in a deadweight loss of consumer and producer surplus, represented by the sum of areas B and C. Because of rent controls, less than the efficient amount of housing is rented and at the market output the marginal benefit of rental housing exceeds its marginal cost.

But rent controls also prevent an otherwise competitive market for rental housing from achieving efficiency. To see why this is so, remember that the demand curve indicates the marginal benefit of a product, while the supply curve indicates its marginal cost in a competitive market. The efficient amount of housing rented per year, Q^*, corresponds to point E in Figure 10–9, at which the marginal benefit of rental housing just equals its marginal cost. Because of rent controls, however, only Q_3 square feet are rented per year. At that level the marginal benefit of rental housing exceeds its marginal cost and less than the efficient amount is rented. The reduction in output below the efficient amount implies a loss in net benefits from rental housing represented by the triangular areas B and C. B is the loss in consumer surplus that results from rent controls, while C is the loss in producer surplus. The sum of the loss of producer and consumer surplus is the *deadweight loss* in net benefits that results from rent controls. Thus the net loss in benefits from resource use that results from rent controls is equal to areas B and C. Area A is merely a transfer in well-being from landlords to tenants of rent-controlled apartments. Sellers in the market as a whole lose $A + C$. Buyers in the market as a whole gain A but lose consumer surplus equal to B. The net gain from rent controls is therefore

$$\text{Gains to tenants} - \text{Losses to landlords} = (A - B) - (A + C) = -(B + C)$$

The net gain, which is negative, is the loss in producer and consumer surplus we have just identified.

Taxing the Output of a Constant-Costs Industry

Assume that the trucking industry is perfectly competitive and in equilibrium. A new tax equal to 10 cents per pound of freight shipped is imposed on trucking firms. From the truckers' point of view the tax is equivalent to a 10-cent increase in the cost of each pound shipped. Accordingly, the cost curves of all the firms in the industry will shift upward. Figure 10–10 illustrates the long-run effect of the tax on the average cost curves of truckers and on the long-run supply curve.

In the long run, firms will exit from the industry. This is because at the price of \$1, firms incur losses after the tax has been imposed and the minimum possible average cost increases from $LRAC_1min$ to $LRAC_2min$, which equals \$1.10. Firms will continue to exit until average cost of production, including the tax per pound shipped, equals price per pound. Supply therefore decreases until $P_2 = LRAC_2min$, where $LRAC_2min$ includes the tax. If the taxed industry is one of constant costs, the price per pound must rise by the amount of the tax. The long-run supply curve for an industry of constant costs is a horizontal line. Figure 10–10 shows the industry demand and supply for freight shipped by truck.

The industry is initially in equilibrium at point E_1, where the demand for trucking shipments, D, intersects long-run supply curve S_{L1}. Initially, the price of freight shipped by truck is \$1 per pound. Because the industry was assumed to be competitive and in equilibrium, it follows that LRACmin must also be \$1.

FIGURE 10–10 Taxing the Output of a Constant-Costs Industry

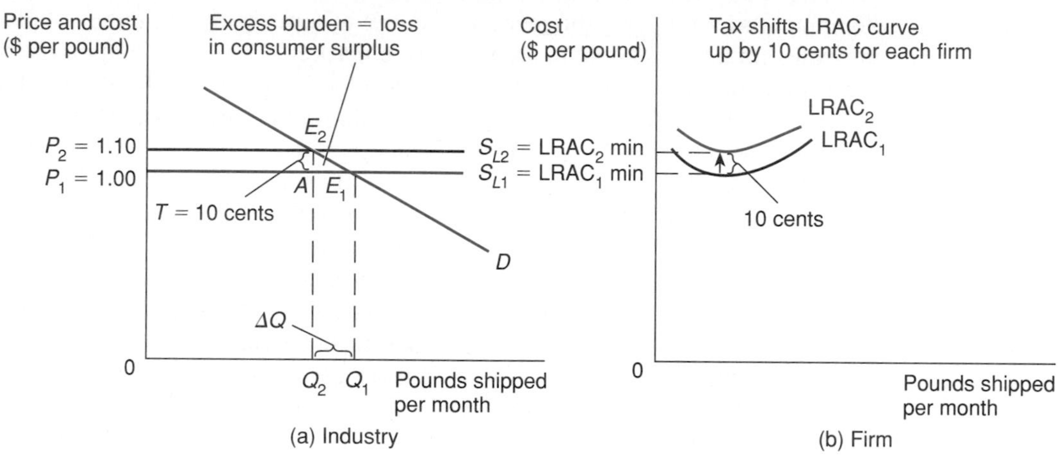

A tax on the output of a constant-costs industry results in an increase in price equal to the tax per unit. Unless the price increases $1.10 in the long run, firms will incur economic losses. The triangle AE_2E_1 is the excess burden of the tax.

The tax increases long-run average costs for trucking firms by 10 cents per pound. As a consequence the long-run supply curve shifts upward by 10 cents per pound shipped, from S_{L1} to S_{L2}. The new long-run competitive equilibrium is at point E_2, where the quantity of freight shipped declines from Q_1 to Q_2 pounds per month until the price rises to $1.10 per pound. The entire 10-cent per pound tax is completely shifted from truckers to shippers. If the price does not rise to $1.10 per pound to cover the full tax, price will fall short of LRAC. After payment of the added 10-cent per pound tax, firms *must* receive $1 per pound to cover their average cost of production exclusive of the tax. Firms will leave the industry until the long-run quantity supplied decreases enough to allow them to receive $1 per pound after payment of the 10-cent per pound tax.

Note also that the inputs used to produce ΔQ units of trucking services are transferred to other uses. The value of those inputs is represented by the area $AE_1Q_1Q_2$ in Figure 10–10. The loss in consumer benefits on these ΔQ units is the area $Q_2E_2E_1Q_1$. The difference between the loss in consumer benefits and the value of resources transferred to other use is the triangle AE_2E_1. This is the excess burden of the tax over the amount of tax revenue collected.

Taxing the Output of an Increasing-Costs Industry

When a tax is levied on an increasing-costs industry, its effects are similar to those of a tax on a constant-costs industry. However, the long-run effects of the tax cause a loss in producer and consumer surplus as resources are transferred out of the industry. In addition, because input prices decline as the size of the industry shrinks, some of the effect of the tax on prices is offset by a decrease in average costs of production as resources are transferred out of the industry. This means that the price of the taxed product does not go up by the full amount of the tax in long-run equilibrium.

Figure 10–11 shows how the long-run effects of a 10-cent tax on the trucking industry would differ if the industry were one of increasing costs. The tax shifts the supply curve upward as it increases marginal costs by 10 cents. As the supply decreases over the long run, the market equilibrium price rises, but the price increase in this case is less than 10 cents per pound. If the sellers try to keep the price at $1.10, a surplus of services will be offered in the market and price will begin to fall. As shown in Figure 10–11, the new market equilibrium price is $1.06. Sellers receive a net price of only 96 cents per pound shipped after paying the tax, which is 4 cents less than they received before the tax was levied. The tax per unit is shared by the buyers and sellers of the taxed service, with the sellers paying four cents per pound shipped and the buyers paying six cents per pound shipped.

The total tax collected, represented by area *A* in Figure 10–11, is a transfer from the service's buyers and sellers that will be used to finance government services. Area *B* is the loss in consumer surplus that results from the tax. Area *C*

FIGURE 10–11 The Effect of a Tax on an Increasing-Costs Industry

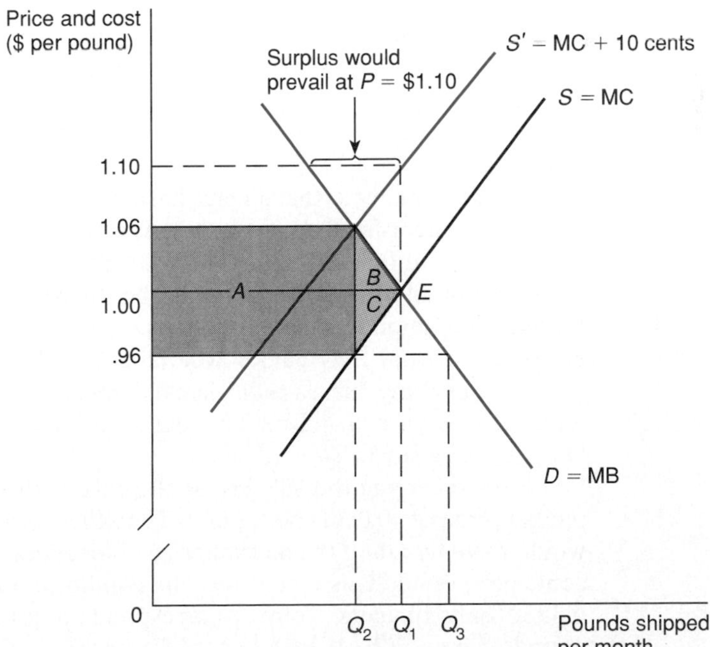

Only a portion of the tax on the output of an increasing-costs industry is shifted to buyers. The excess burden is the sum of lost producer surplus, area *C*, and lost consumer surplus, area *B*. Area *A* represents the tax revenue collected, which is a transfer from buyers and sellers of the product to the government.

is the loss in producer surplus that results for owners of the resources used to produce trucking service. The loss in producer surplus stems from the fact that input prices fall when output is reduced in an increasing-costs industry.

As Figure 10–11 shows, less than the efficient level of output is produced after the tax has been levied because at output level Q_2 the marginal benefit of trucking service is greater than its marginal cost. The excess burden of the tax is the sum of the two triangular areas B and C. The tax revenue collected must therefore be used to finance government programs whose annual benefits are equal to more than $A + B + C$ if there is to be a net gain after the tax has been paid.

Subsidizing a Competitive Industry

Suppose that the federal government subsidizes the output of insulation manufacturers. The manufacturers would receive a certain amount, for instance 10 cents, for each pound of insulation sold. This is equivalent to a 10-cent reduction in the average cost of producing insulating materials. The long-run average cost curves for the firms would shift downward.[6]

Figure 10–12 shows the long-run impact of the subsidy. Suppose that the insulation industry is one of constant costs. A subsidy of 10 cents per pound given to manufacturers will reduce the long-run average cost of producing insulation by that amount. This is shown in Figure 10–12(b). The long-run supply curve shifts downward from S_L to (S_L − 10 cents). The new long-run equilibrium occurs at point E_2, where the equilibrium price of insulation is 40 cents and the quantity sold per year is Q_2 pounds. Any price other than 40 cents per pound will result in either economic profits or economic losses. This would give rise to either entry or exit of firms.

Suppose, instead, that all purchasers of insulation, on proof of purchase, were given a payment from the government equal to 10 cents per pound. The effect of this is shown in Figure 10–12(c). The amount that consumers are willing to pay for any amount of insulation will now be 10 cents more per pound. This is true because the amount they would pay per pound after receiving the subsidy would equal the amount they paid before receiving the subsidy.

The resulting increase in demand results in a new long-run equilibrium at point E_2 in Figure 10–12(c). The market price at the new equilibrium is 50 cents. Output increases to Q_2.

After receiving the subsidy of 10 cents per pound, the buyers pay an out-of-pocket price of 40 cents per pound. They therefore buy as much insulation as they would have bought if the market price of insulation had been 40 cents instead of 50 cents per pound. This means that the equilibrium at E_2 corresponds to a net price paid of only 40 cents. Point N corresponds to a price of 40 cents and sales of Q_2 pounds per month. It makes no difference whether the cash subsidy is paid to buyers or sellers; the ultimate outcome in terms of prices paid or received and output produced is the same.

[6] The old and new LRAC curves are parallel to each other because at all outputs the subsidy reduces average costs by exactly 10 cents per pound produced.

FIGURE 10–12 Subsidizing the Output of a Constant-Costs Industry

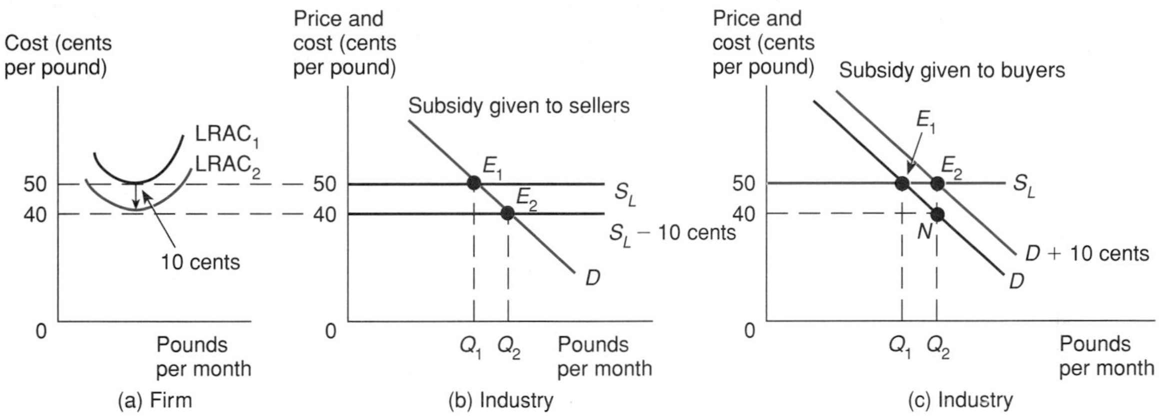

A 10-cent per pound subsidy for insulation will increase output from Q_1 to Q_2 pounds per month in the long run. The result is the same independent of whether consumers or producers receive the subsidy. In (b) the subsidy is given to sellers. In (c) the subsidy is given to buyers. The price received by sellers is the same in both cases, as is the equilibrium output.

Notice also in Figure 10–12(b) that the entire 10-cent per pound subsidy is reflected in a reduction in the price that buyers have to pay for insulation. If price does not fall by this amount, the net price received by manufacturers will be in excess of the minimum possible average costs. New firms will enter the industry until the amount of insulation supplied increases enough to reduce the price received by suppliers to 40 cents per pound.

Prices fall by the entire per unit subsidy only in the case of constant-costs industries. If the industry were one of increasing costs, price would rise to offset some of the benefit of the subsidy to consumers. For example, suppose the price of fiberglass used to produce insulation increases as the insulation industry expands. The long-run supply of insulation would be upward sloping, as shown in Figure 10–13. The effect of a 10-cent per pound subsidy received by sellers would be to shift the supply curve downward by 10 cents at all quantities of insulation. The new equilibrium occurs at point E_2, where the price has fallen to 46 cents per pound (rather than 40 cents as in the earlier example).

Minimum possible long-run average costs of production increase from 50 cents to 56 cents per pound as output expands in the long run from Q_1 to Q_2 pounds per year. This increase in average costs is attributable to the rise in the price of fiberglass. If sellers do not receive 6 cents of the 10-cent per pound subsidy, they will not supply the Q_2 pounds per year demanded by consumers. Sellers will not be able to cover their average costs of production unless they receive a total of 56 cents per pound, including the subsidy. Any market price lower than 46 cents would therefore cause firms to leave the industry. At a price of 46 cents, the 10-cent per pound subsidy allows sellers to just cover their minimum possible LRAC in equilibrium.

FIGURE 10–13 Long-Run Impact of a Subsidy: The Case of Increasing Costs

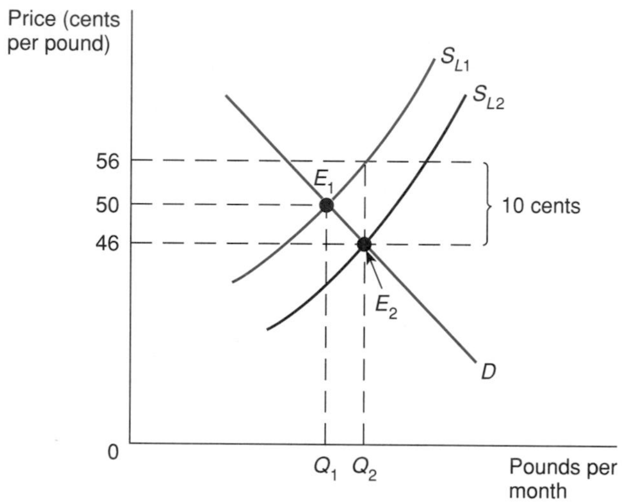

In the long run, the subsidy shifts supply downward by 10 cents per pound at each monthly output level. However, as firms in the industry increase production from Q_1 to Q_2 pounds per month, average costs of production increase. Market price falls to 46 cents per pound. After receiving the 10-cent per pound subsidy, sellers earn 56 cents per pound and just cover their opportunity costs of production.

Medical Care Subsidies

Subsidizing an increasing-costs industry therefore results in increases in the average costs of the subsidized product in the long run. This has important implications for government subsidy programs. Suppose governments provide subsidies for the consumption of particular goods by certain consumers. For example, in the United States the Medicaid and Medicare programs subsidize purchases of medical care services by the poor and elderly. These programs increase the demand for medical care by those eligible. If the medical services industry is one of increasing costs, the government subsidies will result in an increase in the price of medical services. This means that those not eligible for the programs are made worse off in two ways. First, part of the taxes they pay must go to finance the medical care of those eligible instead of other services. Second, they end up paying higher prices for their own medical care than they would pay otherwise.

Figure 10–14 shows the effect of medical care subsidies on resource use and the price of medical care. The subsidies lower the out-of-pocket price of medical care to recipients. Without any subsidies the market equilibrium would correspond to point E and the market equilibrium price would be P_E. A subsidy of G dollars per unit of service increases the supply of medical services to $S' = \text{MC} - G$, and the price to recipients of the subsidy falls to P_N, increasing the quantity of medical care services demanded from Q_1 to Q_2. To attract more resources into the medical care industry, the price per unit of service rises to P_S. Patients pay a price

FIGURE 10–14 Medical Care Subsidies, Efficiency, and the Price of Health Care

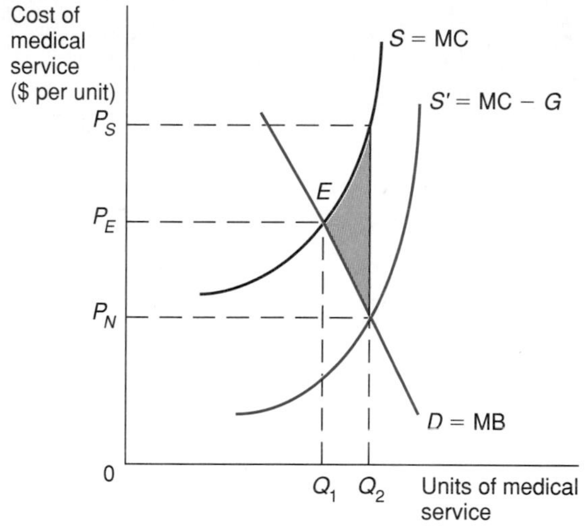

Cost of medical service ($ per unit)
P_S
P_E
P_N
0
$S = \text{MC}$
$S' = \text{MC} - G$
E
$D = \text{MB}$
Q_1 Q_2 Units of medical service

Medical care subsidies reduce the net price of medical services to patients from P_E to P_N. The subsidy of G per unit of service increases the supply of medical services to satisfy Q_2, the larger quantity demanded. If the health care industry is one of increasing costs, the price of medical services also increases. Medical care providers receive a price of P_S which is equal to $P_N + G$. The subsidy results in an overallocation of resources to medical services and a loss of net benefits from resource use equal to the shaded triangular area.

of P_N, but medical care suppliers receive P_S. The difference between the price paid by patients and the price received by suppliers is made up by G, the government subsidy payment.

The subsidy programs result in an overallocation of resources to medical care. The efficient allocation corresponds to point E, at which the marginal benefit of medical services is equal to their marginal cost. As a result of the subsidies, more than the efficient amount of resources flows into medical care over the long run, resulting in a loss of net benefits from resource use corresponding to the shaded area in Figure 10–14. Because of the subsidies, the marginal cost of medical services exceeds their marginal benefit to patients at output Q_2.

The situation depicted in Figure 10–14 explains why medical care costs have been rising so rapidly in the United States in recent years. We will discuss the market for medical care in greater detail in Chapter 17. Government subsidies that encourage the poor and elderly to consume medical care and private insurance programs that reduce the out-of-pocket costs of medical care to patients have increased the consumption and supply of medical services in the United States. In part because of these subsidies and programs, the price of medical care has increased so much that those without insurance have been priced out of the medical services market. Among the ways governments have tried to cope with this problem is to reduce the subsidies to medical care providers by limiting

MODERN MICROECONOMICS IN ACTION: INTERNATIONAL REPORT

The Globalization of Business: Input Prices and Competitive Equilibrium, or Why It's *Not* Such a Long Way to Tipperary Anymore

Remember the famous World War I song "It's a Long Way to Tipperary." Well, Tipperary is a small town about two hours' drive from Dublin, in the republic of Ireland. As of 1991 the jobless rate in the area around Tipperary was 20 percent and workers in the town were eager for even low-wage jobs. Because of improved transportation and satellite communications, it is really not a long way to Tipperary for U.S. business! Massachusetts Mutual Life Insurance Company of Springfield, Massachusetts, helped create jobs for the Irish in 1991 by satellite to McGraw-Hill's computers in Hightstown, New Jersey.*

The Cigna Corporation, a large Connecticut-based U.S. insurance firm, recently opened a claims processing office in another small Irish town, where it hired 120 Irish workers to process medical insurance claims that were flown in daily from the United States. Cigna wasn't the only U.S. firm based in the town. McGraw-Hill had offices there to maintain its circulation files, and data entered by Irish workers in those offices were linked by satellite to McGraw-Hill's computers in Hightstown, New Jersey.*

Businesses searching for ways to increase profits these days do not confine their search to the borders of their own nations. International investment and a global search for ways to keep input prices down can affect long-run competitive equilibrium. Insurance companies do not look just in the United States for plant locations that take advantage of differences in the price of labor. They look abroad too. Keeping input prices down lowers the long-run average costs of an industry and the competitive equilibrium price of its products.

Consumers of the products of perfectly competitive industries benefit through lower product prices when producers in those industries search the entire world for lower-priced inputs. Advanced communications technology and reliable intercontinental flights have made it easier for service-oriented firms such as insurance companies to locate abroad without lowering the quality of the service their clients receive. At the same time, citizens of nations with depressed economies also gain. In the case of Ireland, low taxes and high-quality but inexpensive labor have been a lure for many U.S. businesses. In Ireland a trained financial analyst will gladly work for the equivalent of $20,000 per year at the same job that pays a U.S. MBA $45,000 per year!

The search for lower input prices is a two-way street. Many German and Japanese manufacturers build plants in the United States because labor prices are lower here than in their home countries! As of 1990 Japanese businesses operated eight automobile assembly plants in the United States and their production in those plants accounted for one fifth of the cars produced in this country. Japan was even exporting some of its U.S.-built cars to Japan. Today it is hard to distinguish a U.S.-made product just by looking at the company name. For example, when you buy a Zenith TV, you might naturally assume that you are "buying American." However, Zenith makes its TVs in Mexico. On the other hand, many of the TVs of such foreign producers as Sony are made in the United States.

As business is globalized, we can expect the minimum possible average costs of production to be lower than would otherwise be possible. Lower average costs mean lower prices for you and other consumers as we move to competitive equilibrium in an increasingly competitive global economy.

* See Bernard Wysocki, Jr., "Overseas Calling: American Firms Send Office Work Abroad to Use Cheaper Labor," *The Wall Street Journal*, August 14, 1991.

payments. In the case of Medicaid patients (who are poor), whose medical bills are paid entirely by government subsidies, the payments have been reduced so much that many physicians refuse to accept such patients! These patients are therefore often served by clinics whose quality of care is well below average.

CONCEPT REVIEW

1. Explain why a license fee levied on the sellers of a product in a competitive industry will increase the price of the product in the long run.
2. Why is rent control in a perfectly competitive housing market likely to decrease the quality of housing supplied in the long run?
3. Under what circumstances will a tax on the product of firms selling in a perfectly competitive market result in an increase in the price of the product by an amount exactly equal to the tax per unit of output?

THE COMPETITIVE MODEL AS A BENCHMARK

The competitive model is an important benchmark for understanding the way markets operate. It shows how competing firms, spurred by the profit motive, respond to changing prices of inputs and outputs when they have no control over prices. The model of perfect competition is based on the simplifying assumptions of standardized products, small market shares for each firm, perfect information, and free entry and exit. When conditions in an industry fall far off these benchmark assumptions, the applicability of the competitive model must be reassessed. This will be the task of Chapters 11, 12, and 13.

Product differentiation can give rise to price variation among the products of firms selling similar but not identical goods. For example, differences in quality, appearance, and service associated with products lead to price differences. You would pay more for a Mercedes than for a Buick if you were convinced that the Mercedes would give you more value for your money. A hardware store often provides information and courteous assistance along with the products it sells. Buyers are often willing to pay more for such added service. In some cases individual firms sell a large share of the market supply of a good. Firms with large shares of the total market supply of a product are not price takers.

Imperfect buyer information can also result in price differentials among the products of firms. The benchmark assumption of perfect information may not always hold. Explicitly taking account of the costs of acquiring information can account for price differentials among standardized products. Suppose you are in the market for a stereo receiver that a dealer is selling for $200. You may be able to find the same receiver for $180 if you continue to shop. But a rational person will not shop forever. The consumer weighs the cost of additional searching for lower prices against the benefits of the money saved when such prices are found. This can explain price differentials in otherwise competitive markets. The implication of imperfect information for market equilibrium will be taken up in Chapter 17.

Summary

1. Long-run supply by firms in a perfectly competitive market is more responsive to changes in price than short-run supply. This is because firms already in the industry can expand in the long run and new entrants into the industry can begin production. The number of firms in an industry can increase or decrease in the long run.
2. An industry is in equilibrium when there is no tendency for firms to enter it, leave it, or alter their size. Firms expand production in the long run until P = LRMC.
3. In the long-run competitive equilibrium, economic profits must be zero. Profits sow the seeds of their own destruction in a competitive industry. This is the paradox of profits. Positive economic profits encourage new entrants into a perfectly competitive industry. This increases supply and decreases price until profits have been eliminated. Negative economic profits cause firms to leave an industry. Supply decreases until economic profits are again zero. In a competitive market, economic profits are signals. Once they serve their purpose of increasing or decreasing output, they return to zero.
4. A long-run industry supply curve is a relationship between price and quantity supplied at points for which the industry is in equilibrium. For all of the points on the long-run supply curve of a competitive industry, P = LRMC = LRACmin.
5. A constant-costs industry is one for which input prices are independent of the amount produced. The long-run supply curve for a constant-costs industry is a horizontal line. As long as input prices and technology are fixed, the long-run supply curve for such an industry is perfectly elastic at the one market price.
6. At least some input prices increase as a result of expansion of output in an increasing-costs industry. The long-run supply curve for such an industry is upward sloping. A decreasing-costs industry is one in which some input prices decline as a result of the industry's expansion. The long-run supply curve for such an industry is downward sloping.

Important Concepts

industry
free entry
free exit
industry equilibrium
long-run competitive equilibrium
paradox of profits
long-run industry supply curve
constant-costs industry
increasing-costs industry
decreasing-costs industry

Questions for Review

1. Explain why free entry and exit are necessary to ensure the responsiveness of firms to consumer demands.
2. When is an industry in equilibrium?
3. "An increase in market demand will increase long-run equilibrium output for a competitive industry." Is this statement true or false? Does the answer to this statement depend on whether the industry is an increasing-, decreasing-, or constant-costs industry?
4. Explain why a competitive firm that is maximizing long-run economic profits may not be in long-run equilibrium.
5. Suppose that it is possible for firms to leave—but impossible for firms to enter—a particular industry in the long run. How will the adjustment of prices in the long run in this industry be different from that of a perfectly competitive industry in which both exit and entry are free in the long run?

6. Suppose a number of plant sizes all give a firm the same profits at the long-run equilibrium price. What does this imply about the shape of the firm's long-run average cost curve?
7. In the long run, the supply of output for a perfectly competitive industry is infinitely elastic. Assuming a given technology and stable input prices, explain what would happen to consumer prices in the short run if demand for the product of this industry were to increase. What would happen to those prices in the long run?
8. Will a lump-sum annual license fee affect a producer's long-run marginal cost curve? Why? How will it affect a producer's long-run average cost curve? How will it affect (1) long-run equilibrium price, (2) long-run equilibrium industry output, (3) long-run equilibrium firm output, and (4) the number of firms in the industry in the long-run equilibrium?
9. Suppose a perfectly competitive computer industry is one of decreasing costs. Show the impact of a subsidy to computer producers on the sales and price of computers.
10. Explain how an improvement in technology will affect the number of firms and the prices in a perfectly competitive computer industry. Draw a typical firm's cost and demand curves. Also show the market demand and supply. Assume constant costs.

PROBLEMS

1. Assume that the price of computer cables is $60 for a standard 6-foot length and that the minimum possible long-run average cost of production is $40 per cable. Assume also that the computer cable industry is perfectly competitive and that firms in the industry operate in a short-run plant of capacity lower than that of the minimum-cost plant and currently earn economic profits. Assuming constant costs, draw the long-run and short-run cost curves for a typical firm in the industry. Draw the demand as seen by the firm. Finally, draw the market demand and supply. Explain how price and quantities produced will change as the industry moves toward long-run competitive equilibrium.
2. Suppose the current number of taxi licenses available for sale in a city is 4,000 and that firms in the taxi industry are currently earning normal profits. The city government creates 2,000 additional licenses and offers them for sale in the already existing market. Trace out the implications of this policy for the market price of the licenses, the market price of taxi services, the quantity of taxi miles supplied, and profits in the long run.
3. The long-run supply curve corresponds to points on both the long-run marginal cost curve and the long-run average cost curve. What would happen if in the long run $P =$ LRMC but $P >$ LRAC? What would happen if $P =$ LRMC but $P <$ LRAC?
4. The textile industry is perfectly competitive and currently in equilibrium. An increase in fuel costs occurs suddenly and unexpectedly. Use cost curves, demand curves, and supply cuves to trace out the industry's long-run and short-run reaction.
5. Show how a price floor on agricultural output above the current competitive equilibrium results in a surplus of agricultural commodities in the short run. Trace the long-run effects of the price floor. Show that entry into the industry will continue indefinitely unless the price of one or more of the inputs used increases LRAC at all levels of output. Show how the price floor results in an overallocation of resources to agricultural uses. Discuss the gains and losses that result from the price floors.
6. The diagram depicts the LRAC and LRMC curves for the typical individual corn producer. Corn is sold in a perfectly competitive market. Answer the following questions regarding this case:
   a. If the market price of corn is $4 per bushel, what is the typical corn producer's long-run profit-maximizing output and profit?
   b. Suppose that as a result of an increase in the market demand for corn, the market price of

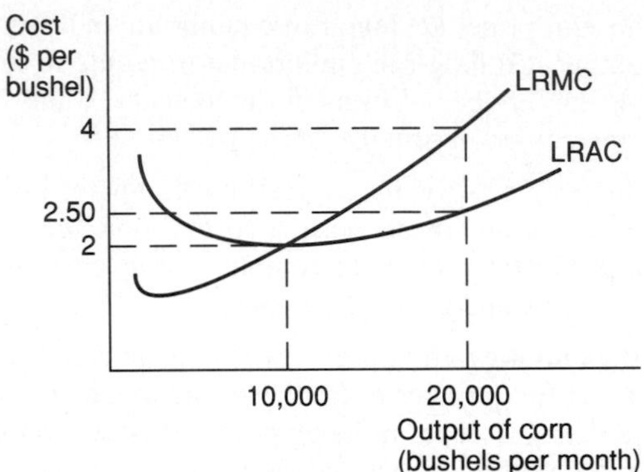

corn rises from \$2 to \$3 per bushel. Will the market supply of corn increase or decrease in response in the long run?

c. If the long-run equilibrium industry output of corn is 20 million bushels per month, how many individual corn producers will be present in the industry in long-run equilibrium?

7. Suppose the U.S. government adopts a national health insurance program, financed by tax revenue, in which the price of health care to patients is reduced to zero and the government pays all health care bills. Show how this program will affect the efficiency of resource use in each of the following cases:

a. The health care industry is one of constant costs.

b. The health care industry of one of increasing costs.

Show the gains and losses that will result from the national health insurance program. How can the government reduce the costs of the program?

PART IV

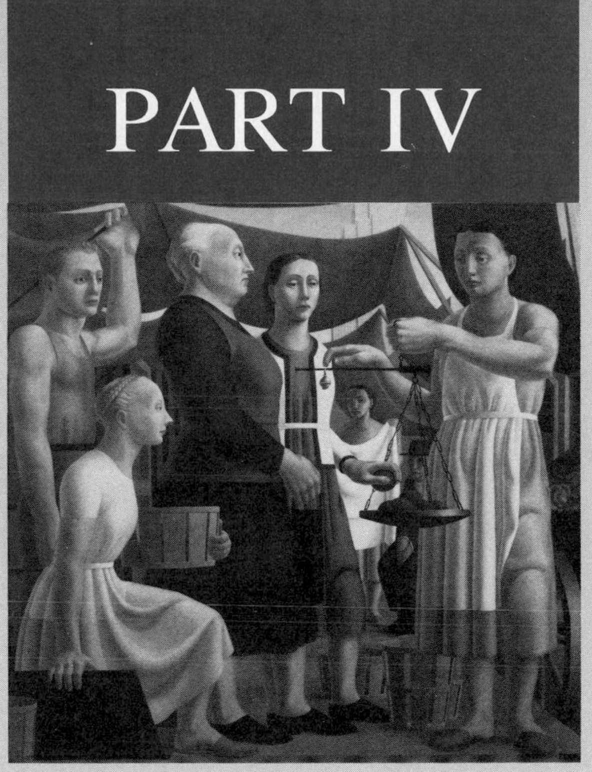

MONOPOLY AND IMPERFECTLY COMPETITIVE PRODUCT MARKETS

11 Monopoly

If you live in a city with only one cable television company, you have already experienced the consequences of dealing with a monopoly. When there is only a single seller in a market, that seller is a monopoly. A monopoly is able to control the price of the good or service it sells by making that good or service relatively scarce, and often it need not worry about the entry of competing sellers into the market it dominates. You may have dealt with a monopoly if you attend college in a small town in which textbooks and school supplies are sold by only one bookstore. If that bookstore is the sole source of supply for these items, it could set its prices at higher levels than would be the case if many competing sellers served the market. Virtually all of the people in the United States buy their electricity, local telephone service, and water from monopoly suppliers. In many cases government authorities regulate the prices these public utilities can charge.

We will now develop a model to explain prices of products sold in a market with a single profit-maximizing seller, into which the entry of additional sellers is not possible. In such a market the seller can influence the price of its product by controlling the availability of the product. In a monopoly market there is no rivalry among sellers. Consequently, the demand curve for a monopolist's product *is* the market demand curve. As you will see, a monopolist's decisions are influenced by the demand for its product, the price elasticity of that demand, and the marginal cost of producing the product.

Perfect competition is characterized by the inability of individual sellers to influence the price of the product they sell. Under perfect competition no individual firm produces a large enough share of total market supply to affect price. Monopoly, on the contrary, is characterized by the concentration of supply in the hands of a single firm's owners.

The goal of this chapter is to understand how a monopoly's influence on supply and the absence of rival sellers in the market are likely to affect the equilibrium market price. It is presumed throughout that a monopoly's owners seek to maximize profits. The monopoly price and output, once determined, can be compared with the benchmark competitive equilibrium price and quantity by analyzing the consequences of the takeover of a perfectly competitive industry by a profit-maximizing monopoly. We will also show how governments regulate the prices of monopoly public utilities like the electric company that supplies you with power for your home.

Pure Monopoly and Monopoly Power

Pure monopoly
A single seller of a product that has no close substitutes.

A **pure monopoly** is a single seller of a product that has no close substitutes. A market dominated by a monopoly contrasts sharply with a perfectly competitive market, in which many rival sellers offer a standardized good for sale. Buyers wishing to consume the product of a monopoly have only one source of supply. No rival sellers compete with a pure monopoly in its market.

The concept of pure monopoly is an abstraction. Few, if any, products have no substitutes. A local electric power company may be the sole seller of electricity in a particular area, but electricity in many of its uses does have substitutes. When the price of electricity rises, its use as a means of heating declines and natural gas or oil may be used instead.

In actuality, a national or worldwide market rarely has only one seller. De Beers Centenary, a Swiss-based South African company, accounts for about 80 percent of the annual sales of diamonds. Although De Beers cannot be regarded as a pure monopoly by the above definition, it is pretty close to one. When it offers more diamonds for sale per month, other things being equal, the price of diamonds will fall. Although De Beers is not a pure monopoly, it sells a very large share of the uncut diamonds purchased each year. It can influence diamond prices by controlling the amount it offers for sale.

Oddly enough, pure monopoly may be more common in local markets than in national markets. If there is a single physician and a single dentist in a small town, they have a local monopoly on medical and dental services. You deal with local monopolies daily because in most communities there are local public utility monopolies that provide telephone, electricity, natural gas, and transportation services. However, many local public utilities are regulated by government agencies in order to prevent them from fully exercising their power to influence prices.

Monopoly power
The ability of a firm to affect the price of its product by varying the quantity it is willing to sell.

A firm has **monopoly power** if it can affect the price of its product by varying the quantity it is willing to sell in a market. The extent to which a firm can exercise monopoly power depends on the availability of close substitutes for its product and its share of the total sales in a market. A firm need not be a *pure* monopoly to have monopoly power. The prerequisite to monopoly power is that the demand curve for a firm's output be downward sloping rather than horizontal, as is the case for a competitive firm. If a firm has a downward-sloping demand curve for its product, it can raise or lower price by varying the quantity it supplies. For example, although the Ford Motor Company does not have a pure monopoly on the sale of cars, it possesses monopoly power if it can raise the price of its cars by making fewer of them available to its dealers. It could do this if the demand curve for its cars were downward sloping. This would be the case if enough buyers of Ford cars viewed them as significantly different from the cars of competing manufacturers. Ford could also affect the price of cars if its share of the total car supply were large enough to make cars significantly scarcer or more abundant over a given period.

At the extreme the demand curve for a product sold by a *pure* monopoly *is* the downward-sloping *market* demand curve for the product. The essential difference between a monopolistic market and a competitive market is the firm's ability to

MODERN MICROECONOMICS IN ACTION: INTERNATIONAL REPORT

De Beers and Diamonds: A Global Monopoly

De Beers Centenary, an enormous diamond mining firm operating in South Africa, has a near monopoly on the sale of gem-quality diamonds. De Beers was founded in 1880 by Cecil Rhodes and two other owners of large diamond mines. Initially, most production took place on land in South Africa where the De Beers family once owned a farm. Before 1902 De Beers controlled over 99 percent of world diamond production. Currently, it mines only about 15 percent of total diamond production (measured in carats). However, it controls the sale of over 80 percent of gem-quality diamonds per year. It does so through an elaborate system of syndicates. The Central Selling Organization (CSO) of De Beers, headquartered in London, controls the marketing of the bulk of the new uncut diamonds made available in any given year.

The syndicate system was initiated in 1925 by Ernest Oppenheimer, who controlled De Beers at the time. Through the CSO the company markets not only its own production but also that of Russia and Angola and other African countries. De Beers also has other syndicates, such as the Diamond Corporation, the Diamond Trading Company, and the Diamond Trading and Purchasing Company.

It is clear that De Beers uses its monopoly position to control the price of diamonds. It can dictate the terms and prices at which it will sell. It doles out uncut diamonds to cutters at the rate it chooses. It keeps a large inventory of stones that it can use to flood the market and ruin potential competitors. For example, in 1981 sellers from the African nation of Zaire attempted to market their diamonds independently. The CSO reacted by increasing the availability of diamonds similar to those sold by Zaire. The price that the Zaire sellers could obtain for their diamonds plummeted, and they soon abandoned their plans to market their diamonds independently of the CSO.

Cutters defying De Beers' elaborate rules for buying diamonds can find themselves without a source of supply. Uncut diamonds are sold at "sights," usually held in London. De Beers usually takes orders from the cutters. At the sights the cutters are presented with a "box" of diamonds of mixed quality, usually worth at least $1 million. De Beers does not allow the buyers to pick and choose among these diamonds. The box is offered on a "take it or leave it" basis. Sightholders, as the invited buyers are called, are expected to buy whether times are good or bad. Few defy De Beers' elaborate rules and customs.*

When demand is strong, the CSO does not hesitate to raise prices. Demand increased during the first half of 1986, and De Beers responded by raising prices. The wholesale price for a 1-carat D-flawless diamond increased from $12,600 to $14,500 in March 1986.† In 1990 and 1991, when the demand for diamonds slackened because of a worldwide economic slowdown, De Beers did not raise its prices but tried to keep the price of diamonds "firm" by selling fewer diamonds. To counter the decline in demand in 1991 and 1992, De Beers stepped up its advertising by budgeting $160 million for a new campaign promoting diamonds as gifts for anniversaries and other special occasions.‡

* David E. Koskoff, *The Diamond World* (New York: Harper & Row, 1981).

† See Steve Lohr, "Why a Diamond Cartel Is Forever," *The New York Times*, September 7, 1986, p. 4F.

‡ See Neil Behrmann, "Russian Policy Won't Affect Diamond Supply, but Market Faces Crucial Christmas Sales Test," *The Wall Street Journal*, November 18, 1991.

influence the price it receives for its product. A firm with monopoly power is a *price maker* rather than a price taker.

Market structure
An indication of the number of buyers and sellers, their market shares, the degree of product standardization, and the ease of market entry and exit.

Market structure indicates the number of buyers and sellers, their shares of total output purchased or sold, the degree of product standardization, and the ease of market entry and exit. Pure monopoly and perfect competition are two extreme forms of market structure. In a pure monopoly market structure only one firm sells the entire market supply of a product; entry by other firms is not possible. Under perfect competition many firms each have small market shares and free entry is possible. In actuality, market structures lie between these extremes. The extremes, however, offer insights that enable us to understand the intermediate cases. Analysis of data pertaining to market structure is used to determine the likelihood that firms in a market can affect the price of the products they sell. This chapter concentrates on the determination of equilibrium prices and quantities under pure monopoly. Chapters 12 and 13 consider market structures in which competing firms have some degree of monopoly power.

Barriers to Entry: How Monopoly Power Is Maintained

Barrier to entry
A constraint that prevents additional sellers from entering the market of a monopoly.

Profits serve as a signal to attract new suppliers when markets are perfectly competitive. If a monopolist earns economic profits, new entrants will be tempted to compete with it by producing a similar product. The maintenance of monopoly power therefore requires conditions that prevent new sellers from competing with a monopoly. A **barrier to entry** is a constraint that prevents additional sellers from entering a market. Barriers to entry are necessary for the long-term maintenance of monopoly power. If free entry into monopoly markets were possible, the economic profits earned by monopolies would attract new sellers. Supplies would increase, as would the number of sellers. The monopolies' control over price would eventually disappear as their markets became competitive. Among the major types of barriers to entry into markets that foster and help maintain monopolies are:

1. *Government franchises.* Some barriers to entry are the result of government policies that grant single-seller status to firms. For example, local governments commonly give a single firm the right to install cable television systems. Governments typically establish monopolies that sell transportation, communication, public sanitation, electric power, natural gas, water, and sewage services. Since 1904 the funeral business in France has been controlled by General Funerals, a government-supported monopoly that sells coffins and funeral services. In many cases, the most notable being postal service, governing authorities themselves run monopolies. Many states run monopoly liquor stores and conduct lotteries that are the sole legal source of gambling.

2. *Patents and copyrights.* Patents and copyrights provide creators of new products or works of literature, art, and music with the exclusive right to sell or license the use of their creations. Patents are also granted for new productive techniques. Patents and copyrights provide monopoly positions for only a limited number of years. After they expire, these barriers to entry are removed.

Patents and copyrights are intended to encourage firms and individuals to innovate by guaranteeing them the exclusive right to market the fruits of their endeavors. However, such rights are guaranteed for only a limited period, so the monopoly they create is only temporary.

A firm that illegally enters a market as a seller by infringing on another firm's patent can be forced to cease selling by a court injunction. For example, in 1985 a federal judge ruled that the Eastman Kodak Company had infringed on seven patents granted to the Polaroid Corporation by producing and selling instant-picture cameras since 1976. When the injunction took effect, in January 1986, Kodak, which by the mid-1980s had accounted for 25 percent of annual instant-picture camera sales, had to stop producing both the cameras *and* the film it supplied for them.

3. *Ownership of the entire supply of a resource.* A monopoly can also be maintained through control of the supply of a particular input. De Beers has monopoly power in the diamond market because it controls the sale of about 80 percent of uncut gem diamonds. The Aluminum Company of America's monopoly in the U.S. aluminum market until the end of World War II was attributable in part to its control of bauxite ore, the source of aluminum, and a few excellent sources of low-cost power.

Unique ability or knowledge can also create a monopoly. Talented singers, artists, athletes—the "cream of the crop" of any profession—have monopolies on the use of their services. For example, if you were Sylvester Stallone, you could get astronomical prices for your services in each film. Stallone was paid $15 million plus a percentage of the box office receipts for his services in *Rocky IV*. He reportedly received in excess of $12 million for his services in *Over the Top*.

Firms with secret processes or technologies have monopolies if other firms cannot duplicate the techniques. For example, the Coca-Cola corporation carefully guards its formula for the syrup that goes into "Classic" Coke. The secret formula provides Coca-Cola with a monopoly on its drink. Of course, because there are many close substitute soft drinks, Coca-Cola does not have a pure monopoly.

4. *Cost advantages resulting from supplying the entire market.* Increasing returns to scale can result in lower average costs of production as a firm expands. These lower costs can contribute to the establishment of monopoly power and can also constitute an effective barrier to entry once that power has been established.

If firms can continually reduce average costs of production and increase profits by expanding to satisfy market demand, one firm will eventually emerge as the dominant supplier. Under these circumstances perfect competition would result in much higher average costs of production than would monopoly because its maintenance would require many small firms with small market shares. If perfect competition existed initially, it would end as soon as existing firms merged or as soon as one firm purchased the assets of its competitors. To achieve and take advantage of lower average costs, one firm must dominate. Once it dominates, new firms cannot enter because they would be too small initially to achieve the low average costs that the dominant firm enjoys by virtue of producing the entire market supply. The dominant firm would always be able to produce at a lower average cost than any entering firm. It could therefore temporarily lower its price and still make a profit. By temporarily lowering its price, it could put any entering firm out of business.

Figure 11–1 shows the long-run average cost curve for a single seller along with the market demand curve for its product. Notice that the average cost of production declines over the entire range of output for which the demand curve lies above the long-run AC curve. This means that at all quantities for which buyers are willing to pay a price that exceeds average cost, the single seller can always reduce average cost further by producing more. It is easy to show that under these circumstances, for any output, a single seller could supply the entire market quantity demanded at lower cost than two or more sellers. For example, a single seller could produce the output Q_1. If it offered to sell that output in the market, buyers would be willing to pay the price P_1, which would exactly equal AC_1, the average cost of that output. Total cost of production would therefore be $AC_1(Q_1)$.

Suppose, instead, two firms each produced one half of the market quantity demanded when price was set at P_1. Each of the two firms would incur average costs of production equal to $AC_2 > AC_1$, and each would offer to sell a quantity

FIGURE 11–1 The Cost Advantage of Natural Monopoly

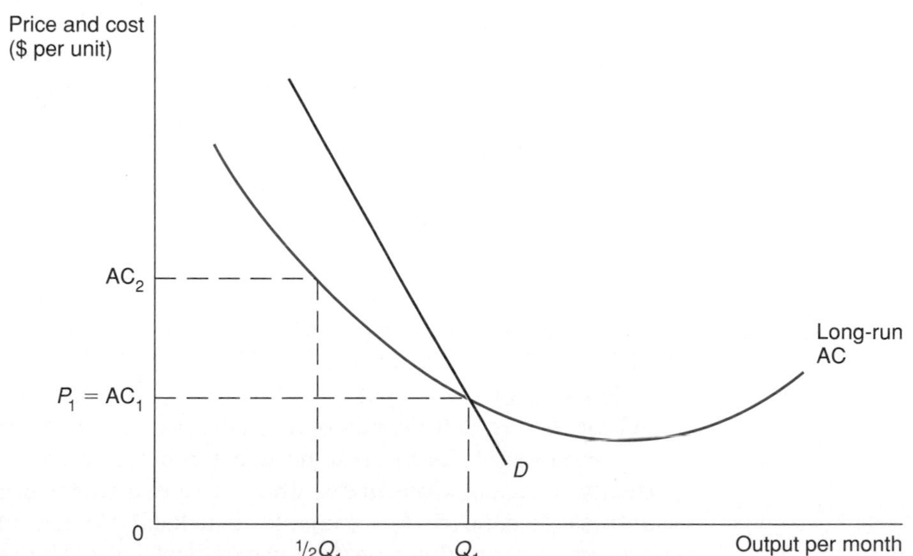

For a natural monopoly, AC declines over the entire range of output for which the demand curve lies above the long-run AC curve. The natural monopoly can produce Q_1 at lower AC than can two smaller firms, each supplying $Q_1/2$.

equal to $\frac{1}{2}Q_1$ at that price. The total costs of production for the Q_1 units of output would therefore be

$$\begin{aligned} TC_2 &= AC_2(\tfrac{1}{2}Q_1) + AC_2(\tfrac{1}{2}Q_1) \\ &= AC_2(Q_1) > AC_1(Q_1) \end{aligned} \quad \textbf{(11–1)}$$

You can see that if a price of P_1 were charged, the two smaller firms would be unable to cover their average costs of production and would therefore incur economic losses. A single large firm supplying the entire market demand can therefore produce any given output at lower total costs than can two or more smaller firms when the relationship between the demand curve and the AC curve is as shown in Figure 11–1. Such a firm could therefore put smaller firms out of business by lowering the price of its product enough to meet the entire market demand. Of course once it did so, no smaller firm could sell the product at that price and earn a profit. Having established its monopoly position in this way, the large firm would be free to cut back its output, thereby forcing the market price up. It would reduce its output in this way if it could increase its profits by doing so. If competitors attempted to enter, the large firm could again lower its prices so as to make it impossible for any competitor to earn a profit at their smaller scale of operation.

A firm that can supply the entire market demand for a product at a lower average cost than would be possible if two or more firms supplied exactly the same quantity of the product is called a **natural monopoly.** Natural monopolies can prevail for the local provision of such products as electric power, gas, and telephone services. The cost savings resulting from large-scale operation are the reason that firms are often granted monopoly franchises to serve a region. Changes in technology can change cost conditions. For example, long-distance telephone service was once considered a natural monopoly but is no longer considered so because of changes in technology. Satellite communication systems and other technological advances have made it possible for a number of firms to compete for long-distance telephone business without a larger seller having the advantage of lower average cost.

Natural monopoly A firm that can supply the entire market demand for a product at a lower average cost than would be possible if two or more firms supplied exactly the same quantity of the product.

The Demand for a Monopolist's Product

The demand for the output of a monopoly is the downward-sloping market demand for the product the monopoly sells. A common mistake made by those who criticize monopoly is to presume that the demand for a monopoly's product is perfectly inelastic. Consumers always respond to price increases by decreasing quantities demanded. For example, if a local electric monopoly raises prices, consumers will cut down on their use of electricity. They may use their air conditioners less or may be more careful about turning off lights when they leave a room. If there were only one car seller in the nation, people would buy more cars when that seller lowered prices and fewer cars when that seller raised prices.

In setting the price of a product, the managers of a monopoly consider the reactions of consumers. They know that the amount they will sell depends on the price they set. Conversely, they know that the price they can obtain for their product depends on the quantity they offer for sale over any period.

A monopolist can set the price of its product or the quantity it offers for sale over any given period. Once it sets a price, the quantity demanded is determined by the market demand curve. For example, a local telephone monopoly might decide to increase its price to increase its profits. If the price increase is approved by regulatory authorities, the monopoly will experience a decrease in the quantity of telephone service demanded. Similarly, once a monopoly chooses a quantity to make available in the market, the price buyers will pay for that amount also depends on the demand curve for the product. For example, suppose a car manufacturer that has a monopoly decides that because of higher variable costs of production it must produce and sell fewer cars each month to maximize its profits. It will therefore deliver fewer cars to its dealers. This reduction will make cars scarcer to rival buyers. Competition among these buyers for the smaller number of cars available at dealers will then put an upward pressure on price.

The output of a pure monopoly *is* the market output. The demand for a monopolist's product *is* the market demand. It is now easy to see why monopolies are not price takers. As a monopoly's output increases, price *must* fall because demand is downward sloping. Contrast a monopoly's demand with the demand faced by a competitive firm. Such a firm can sell all it likes at the market price. No matter how much it produces, it can neither increase nor decrease the market price by its own actions.

The Monopolist's Marginal Revenue

The marginal revenue of a competitive firm is the same as the price. A competitive chair company, such as the one used as an example in previous chapters, takes in an extra $150 in revenue each time it sells another chair priced at $150. A monopolist must *decrease* the price of its product to sell more. This follows from the fact that the demand curve for a monopolist's product is downward sloping. The marginal revenue of a monopolist's additional sales is less than the price.

A numerical example will make this clear. Suppose you are a popular entertainer on a par with the likes of Michael Jackson. You are the single seller of live concerts in which you are the principal performer. Your fans see no close substitute for your voice and appearance. They are crazy about you. You are, in short, a monopolist. You can set your price for a performance.

Table 11–1 provides data on the price per performance and on the number of appearances that you can sell at each price per year. At a price of $1 million per performance, only one concert hall would purchase your services. Total output of concerts per year would therefore be 1, total revenue per year would be $1 million, and marginal revenue per year would be $1 million. Marginal revenue is calculated in exactly the same way as it was for a competitive firm. It is the change in total revenue divided by the change in quantity. The third column calculates

TABLE 11–1 Demand and Marginal Revenue for a Monopoly

Performances per Year	*Price*	*Total Revenue*	*Marginal Revenue*
0	More than $1,000,000	0	—
1	$1,000,000	$1,000,000	$1,000,000
2	900,000	1,800,000	800,000
3	800,000	2,400,000	600,000
4	700,000	2,800,000	400,000
5	600,000	3,000,000	200,000
6	500,000	3,000,000	0
7	400,000	2,800,000	−200,000
8	300,000	2,400,000	−400,000

annual total revenue from the sale of performances to concert halls. Marginal revenue, shown in the fourth column, is simply the change in total revenue for each extra performance.

If you wish to give two performances per year, you must lower your price to $900,000 per concert. Total revenue will then be $1,800,000 per year, and the marginal revenue of the second concert is therefore $800,000. The marginal revenue of the second concert is $100,000 less than the price you receive for it.

Except when you give only one performance per year, marginal revenue will always be below the price charged per concert. The reason for this is that price *must* be lowered to give more than one concert a year. To sell two performances instead of one per year, you must lower your price per concert from $1 million to $900,000. This means that you forgo the opportunity of giving one concert at $1 million that year. Lowering price results in $900,000 revenue from the second concert that you would otherwise not have had the opportunity to earn. At the same time you lose the extra $100,000 that you could have earned on the first concert. The net gain in revenue from lowering price is therefore $900,000 less the $100,000 forgone on the first concert. The marginal revenue of the second concert is therefore $800,000.

Figure 11–2 plots the data of Table 11–1. At a price of $1 million, total revenue is represented by the area *OABG*, which equals $1 million. When price is reduced to $900,000, two performances are given each year. Total revenue is now the area *OCEF*, equal to $1.8 million. The marginal revenue of the second performance is the area *DEFG* minus the area *ABDC*. *DEFG* is the $900,000 gain in revenue from the second performance *ABDC* is the $100,000 in revenue lost by forgoing the opportunity to give the first performance at a price of $1 million.

Table 11–1 calculates marginal revenue for each price and quantity. After the first concert successive reductions in price increase the difference between price and marginal revenue. At a price of $500,000 per concert, marginal revenue becomes zero. At any price below $500,000, marginal revenue is negative. Giving more than six performances per year will decrease rather than increase total revenue.

FIGURE 11–2 Monopoly Demand and Marginal Revenue for Performances

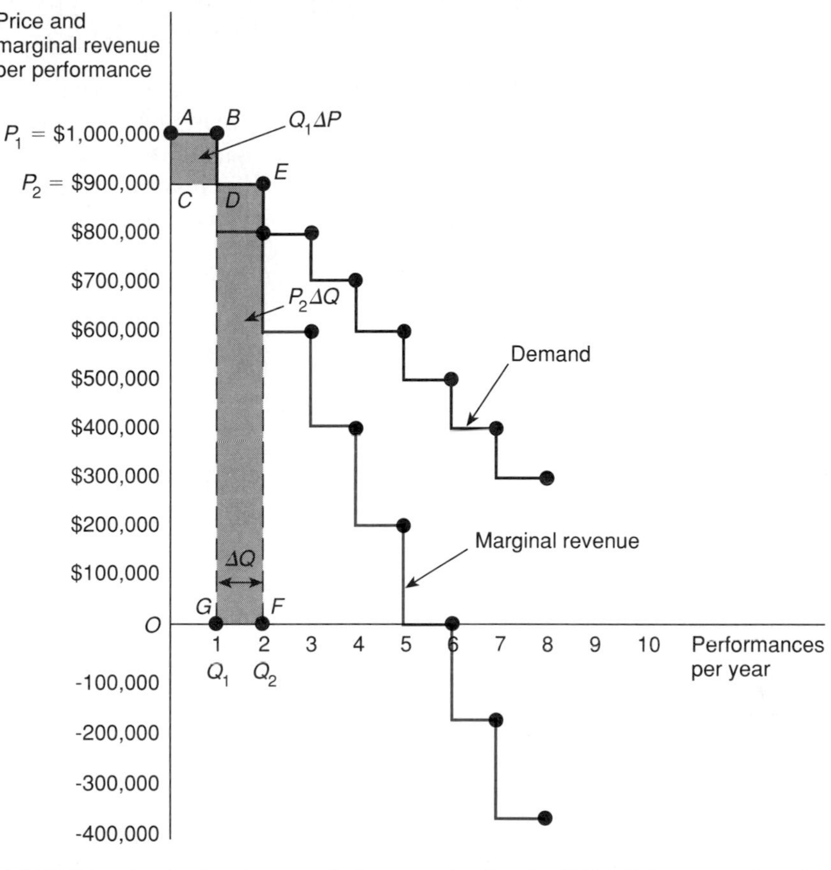

For each $100,000 reduction in price, marginal revenue declines by $200,000. For example, when price is reduced to $900,000, two performances are sold. The marginal revenue of the second performance is the area *DEFG* minus the area *ABDC*. *ABDC* is the loss in revenue on the first concert which could have been sold at a higher price, P_1. *DEFG* is the gain in revenue obtained by selling the second concert at a lower price, P_2.

Price, Marginal Revenue, and Price Elasticity of Demand

For any price decrease, an area like *ABDC* in Figure 11–2 equals $Q_1(\Delta P)$. This represents the revenue forgone on units that could have been sold at a higher price. The area *DEFG* equals $P_2(\Delta Q)$. This represents the gain in revenue obtained from additional units sold when the price falls. The change in total revenue that results from any price decline is the gain in revenue obtained by selling additional units less than the revenue forgone by giving up the opportunity to sell previous units at higher prices. For very small changes in price, the change in total revenue can therefore be written as

$$\Delta \text{TR} = P(\Delta Q) + Q(\Delta P) \quad \textbf{(11–2)}$$

where ΔP is negative and ΔQ is positive. Dividing Equation 11–2 by ΔQ gives

$$\frac{\Delta \text{TR}}{\Delta Q} = \text{MR} = P + Q\left(\frac{\Delta P}{\Delta Q}\right) \qquad \textbf{(11–3)}$$

where $\Delta P/\Delta Q$ is the slope of the demand curve. Because the monopolist's demand curve is negatively sloped, marginal revenue must be less than price.

The relationship between marginal revenue and the slope of the demand curve can easily be converted into one that relates marginal revenue to price elasticity of demand. The price elasticity of demand at a point on a demand curve is

$$E_D = (P/Q)(\Delta Q/\Delta P)$$

Therefore,

$$\Delta P/\Delta Q = P/QE_D$$

Substituting this in the equation for marginal revenue gives

$$\text{MR} = P + Q\left(\frac{P}{QE_D}\right) = P + P\left(\frac{1}{E_D}\right)$$

Therefore,

$$\text{MR} = P\left(1 + \frac{1}{E_D}\right) \qquad \textbf{(11–4)}$$

Equation 11–4 confirms the contention that for a monopolist marginal revenue is less than price. This is because E_D is negative for the monopolist's downward-sloping demand curve. Equation 11–4 shows that in general *marginal revenue of any output depends on the price of the product and the price elasticity of demand.* The equation also shows how total revenue varies with market output. Suppose that $E_D = -1$. This means demand is unit elastic. Substituting $E_D = -1$ in Equation 11–4 indicates that marginal revenue is zero. There is no change in total revenue in response to a price change when price elasticity of demand for the product is -1. Similarly, the equation shows that marginal revenue is positive when demand is elastic. This is because the value of E_D is less than -1 and greater than minus infinity when demand is elastic. Finally, marginal revenue is negative when demand is inelastic. Table 11–2 summarizes the relationship among price elasticity of demand, marginal revenue, and total revenue.

You can see that the relationship implied by Equation 11–4 is logical by analyzing the way total revenue and marginal revenue vary with quantity demanded along a linear demand curve. Figure 11–3 draws a linear demand curve and the corresponding marginal revenue curve for a monopoly. Recall that demand is price elastic when a decrease in price results in an increase in total revenue. If total revenue increases when price decreases, marginal revenue must be positive. It can therefore be concluded that whenever the marginal revenue of a price decline is positive, demand is price elastic. By the same token, if the marginal revenue of a price decline is negative, it follows that demand must be inelastic. This is because negative marginal revenue implies that the price decline results in a decrease in total revenue. Finally, when marginal revenue is zero, a change in price does not change total revenue and demand is unit elastic. This is

TABLE 11–2 Marginal Revenue, Total Revenue, and Price Elasticity of Demand for a Product

Price Elasticity of Demand	*Marginal Revenue*	*Effect of a Price Reduction on Total Revenue*
Inelastic	Negative	Total revenue declines
Unit elastic	Zero	No change in total revenue
Elastic	Positive	Total revenue increases

FIGURE 11–3 Monopoly Demand, Marginal Revenue, Total Revenue, and Elasticity

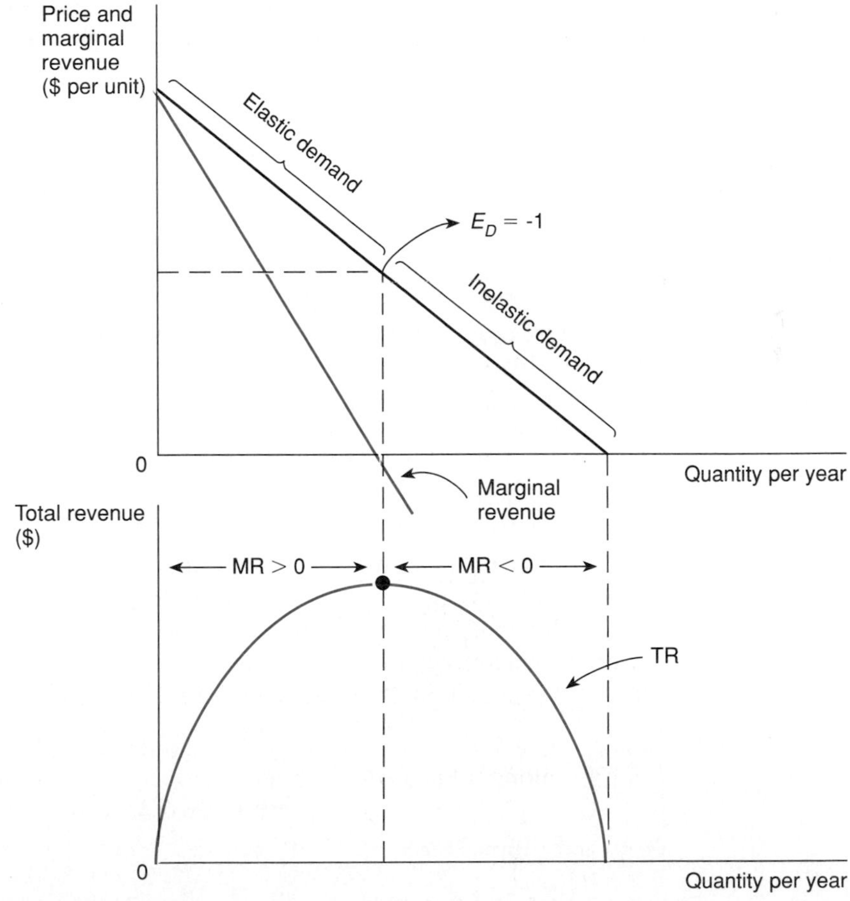

For a linear demand curve, marginal revenue declines twice as quickly as price when more is sold. When marginal revenue is positive, total revenue increases as price is reduced. When marginal revenue is negative, total revenue decreases as price is lowered. Total revenue is at a maximum when MR = 0. When MR > 0, demand is elastic. When MR < 0, demand is inelastic. Demand is of unitary elasticity when MR = 0, and total revenue is at a maximum at that point.

shown in the lower part of Figure 11–3. Maximum total revenue occurs when marginal revenue is equal to zero. At that point on the linear demand curve, the price elasticity of demand is equal to -1.

Equation 11–4 also implies that the more elastic the demand, the less difference there is between marginal revenue and price. At the extreme, if demand is infinitely elastic, the difference between price and marginal revenue becomes zero. This is because the term $1/E_D$ in Equation 11–4 approaches zero as E_D approaches minus infinity. This is in accordance with the fact that price equals marginal revenue for a competitive firm.

Notice from Table 11–1 and Figures 11–2 and 11–3 that marginal revenue declines more quickly than price as a monopolist produces more. For a linear demand curve, marginal revenue declines exactly twice as fast as price. Also notice that for each \$100,000 reduction in the price set for a performance, after the first performance, marginal revenue always declines by \$200,000. Marginal revenue becomes zero at an output level corresponding to exactly half of the amount that would be sold at a zero price.[1]

CONCEPT REVIEW

1. Under what circumstances will a firm possess monopoly power?
2. Explain why marginal revenue for any given quantity sold is less than the price at which that quantity can be sold by a monopolist.
3. If the price elasticity of demand for a monopolist's output is equal to -1 at the current level of output, can it increase its revenue by selling more or less?

PROFIT MAXIMIZATION BY MONOPOLY FIRMS

As was shown in Chapter 9, a competitive firm maximizes profit by adjusting the amount sold at the market price until marginal cost equals marginal revenue. Although a monopoly can influence the price of its product, the marginal analysis of profit maximization is the same for both the competitive and monopolistic cases. Maximization of profits implies that marginal revenue must equal marginal

[1] From Equation 11–3,

$$\text{MR} = P + Q(\Delta P/\Delta Q)$$

For a linear demand curve,

$$P = a - bQ$$

where a is the intercept of the demand curve with the price axis and b is the slope of the demand curve. When we substitute $\Delta P/\Delta Q = -b$ and $P = a - bQ$ in the equation for marginal revenue, we get

$$\text{MR} = a - 2bQ$$

The rate of change of MR with Q is twice the rate of change of price with Q.

TABLE 11–3 Costs and Determination of Profit-Maximizing Monopoly Output

Price	*Output (Performances per Year)*	*Total Cost per Year*	*Average Cost ($ per Performance)*	*Marginal Cost (MC) ($ per Performance)*	*Marginal Revenue (MR) ($ per Performance)*	*Marginal Profit (MR − MC)*	*Total Profit (TR − TC) ($ per Year)*
Over $1,000,000	0	$ 100,000	—	—	—	—	$ −100,000
$1,000,000	1	500,000	$500,000	$ 400,000	$1,000,000	$ 600,000	500,000
900,000	2	1,000,000	500,000	500,000	800,000	300,000	800,000
800,000	3	1,550,000	516,666	550,000	600,000	50,000	850,000
700,000	4	2,250,000	562,500	700,000	400,000	−300,000	550,000
600,000	5	3,150,000	630,000	900,000	200,000	−700,000	−150,000
500,000	6	4,150,000	691,666	1,000,000	0	−1,000,000	−1,150,000
400,000	7	5,550,000	792,857	1,400,000	−200,000	−1,600,000	−2,750,000
300,000	8	7,550,000	943,750	2,000,000	−400,000	−2,400,000	−5,150,000

cost at the output produced. For a monopolist, however, the marginal revenue of additional output is always less than the price at which that output is sold.[2]

Table 11–3 provides data on the costs incurred for performances. The third column of the table shows the total cost per year of all performances. The fourth column shows the average cost of each performance. Marginal cost is calculated in the fifth column as the change in total costs for each extra performance. The sixth column reproduces data on marginal revenue from Table 11–1.

Fixed costs are $100,000 per year. These include depreciation of and interest on capital equipment, such as musical instruments, sound equipment, costumes, and the vehicles used to transport you and your entourage (including bodyguards) to each performance. Even if you give no performances in a year, you still incur these costs. The last column, total profit, therefore shows that you lose $100,000 per year if you choose not to give any concerts. If you price your performances at over $1 million each, there will be no buyers. You will therefore lose an amount equal to your fixed costs.

---

[2] The price, P, that a firm with monopoly power can set is a function of Q, quantity made available for sale. Profit (π) is

$$\pi = PQ - \mathrm{TC}$$

Because $P = f(Q)$ and $\mathrm{TC} = f(Q)$,

$$d\pi/dQ = P + Q(dP/dQ) - d\mathrm{TC}/dQ$$

Assuming that second-order conditions hold, maximum profits occur where

$$[P + Q(dP/dQ)] = d\mathrm{TC}/dQ$$

The left side of the equation is marginal revenue. This expression for marginal revenue is analogous to Equation 11–3 for cases in which the changes in Q are infinitesimally small. The right side of the equation is marginal cost.

If your price is \$1 million, you will find a buyer for one performance per year. Your total costs will then be \$500,000, so you will make \$500,000 profit on that concert. The marginal cost of the first performance is \$400,000, the average variable costs of that performance. These costs include the wages you pay your assistants, accompanying musicians, and bodyguards, and the price of fuel for the vehicles that get you from location to location. The marginal revenue of the first performance is \$1 million. Marginal profit is therefore \$600,000. Recall that marginal profit is the difference between marginal revenue and marginal cost.

After your first performance, marginal revenue falls below price because you must lower your asking price to have the opportunity of giving more performances per year. The total revenue of two performances per year, from Table 11–2, is \$1.8 million. You must price your performances at \$900,000 each if you wish to sell two per year. The total cost of two concerts is \$1 million. The marginal cost of the second concert is therefore \$1 million less \$500,000, divided by 1. This gives marginal cost. Because the marginal revenue of the second performance is \$800,000, your marginal profit is positive. In this case marginal profit is \$300,000 and total profit increases from \$500,000 per year to \$800,000 per year.

As long as marginal revenue exceeds the marginal cost of a concert, total profits will increase. Total profits begin to decrease as soon as marginal costs exceed marginal revenue. You will increase your total profits if you increase your output to three concerts per year. This is because the marginal cost of the third concert is \$550,000, whereas its marginal revenue is \$600,000. Your marginal profit for the third concert is therefore \$50,000 and your total profits increase to \$850,000 per year. If you want to give three performances per year, you have to price each concert performance at \$800,000.

Would you be interested in lowering your price below \$800,000? If you were to cut your price to \$700,000, you would be able to give four performances per year. But the marginal cost of the fourth concert would be \$700,000 and its marginal revenue would be only \$400,000. Your marginal profit would therefore be −\$300,000. By cutting your price to \$700,000, you would actually reduce your total profits from \$850,000 to \$550,000 per year.

As Table 11–3 shows, at any output greater than three concerts per year, marginal cost will exceed marginal revenue. Your equilibrium price is therefore \$800,000 per performance. The equilibrium quantity that will be demanded at that price is 3. Total profits at that price are \$850,000 per year. The marginal cost of performances at that output is \$550,000. At the equilibrium output, therefore, the marginal cost is less than the price. This follows from the fact that marginal revenue is less than price under monopoly.

Monopoly Equilibrium: Graphic Analysis

Figure 11–4(a) shows the average and marginal cost curves of a monopoly firm. It also shows the demand and marginal revenue for the firm's product. The firm's output, labeled Q_M, corresponds to the point where the marginal revenue and marginal cost curves intersect. To induce buyers to purchase that output, the firm sets a price equal to P_M.

FIGURE 11–4 Monopoly Price and Output

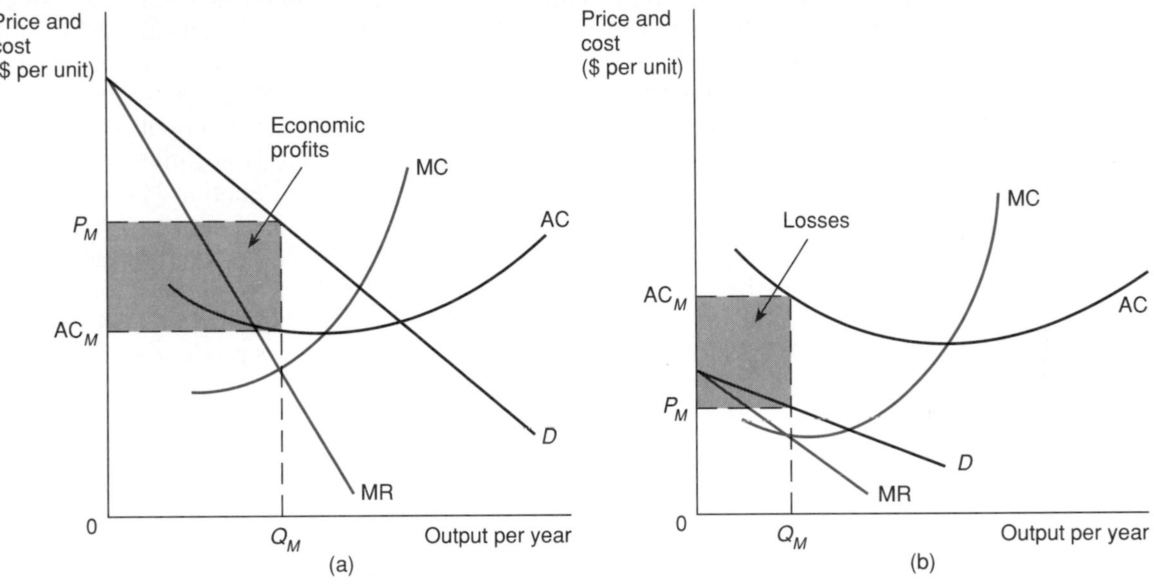

A monopoly firm maximizes profits by producing Q_M, the output corresponding to the point where MR = MC. It then sets the price, P_M, that is required to induce buyers to purchase Q_M. Having a monopoly, however, does not guarantee profits. In (a) the monopoly firm earns economic profits. In (b) demand is insufficient to allow profits at the point where MR = MC. The firm incurs economic losses because $P < \text{AC}$.

At that price and output, the monopoly firm earns a profit per unit of $(P_M - \text{AC}_M)$. Total output is Q_M. Total economic profits are therefore $(P_M - \text{AC}_M)Q_M$. For example, in equilibrium the monopoly price for performances is $800,000. The average cost of a concert is a bit less than $516,666 (the average cost shown in Table 11–3 has been rounded to the nearest dollar) when you give three performances per year. Average profit per concert is therefore $283,334. Multiplying this by 3 gives $850,000.

How much profit a monopolist actually makes depends both on costs and on the demand for its product. Should the tides of fortune change, you may find no takers for your concerts even if you offer them at a bargain price. Show business is like that; you can be here today and gone tomorrow. Having a monopoly does not guarantee that you will earn profits. Monopolists can and do go out of business when the demand for their product declines.

If the demand for and marginal revenue of a product supplied by a monopolist decline, it can be impossible for the monopolist to make a profit. If the price corresponding to the output at which MR = MC falls below average costs, a monopolist will incur losses. This is shown in Figure 11–4(b). In recent years Amtrak has had a monopoly on passenger rail service on many U.S. routes. Even with its monopoly, however, Amtrak incurred losses.

Monopoly Equilibrium and Price Elasticity of Demand

A common misconception about the behavior of monopolists is that they can earn more profit when the demand for the product they sell is inelastic. *However, a profit-maximizing monopolist will always adjust price to make sure the demand for its product is elastic rather than inelastic!* To see why this is so, consider the implications of selling in a market where the demand for a monopolist's product is inelastic. When demand is inelastic, marginal revenue is negative. This follows from the analysis presented above and summarized in Equation 11–4. Therefore, when demand is inelastic, the monopolist can increase total revenue by selling less. When it sells less, it also produces less. Total costs therefore go down. It follows that when demand is inelastic, the monopolist can increase total revenue and reduce total costs, thereby increasing profit, by selling less. A monopolist can always increase profit in this way when the demand for its product is inelastic, and it will therefore always adjust production to avoid the inelastic portions of the demand curve for its product.

You can see in still another way why the monopolist avoids selling quantities corresponding to price-inelastic points on a demand curve. Because marginal costs of a product are always positive, marginal revenue can never equal marginal cost at an output for which demand is inelastic. This is because the monopolist's marginal revenue is always negative for quantities corresponding to the inelastic portion of its demand curve. As long as marginal costs are not zero, the monopolist will find it can maximize profits by pricing its product to make sure that demand is elastic.

Monopoly Supply

A supply curve is a relationship between price and quantity supplied by a firm or an industry. Competitive firms simply react to prices. A monopoly, however, is a price maker. It can choose the price that maximizes its profits, and it lets consumers decide how much to purchase at that price. Since a monopoly does not react to price, a supply curve cannot be defined for it. A monopoly decides how much to produce on the basis of its information on the demand for its product. Given that information, it prices its product (or chooses how much of the product to make available) so that marginal revenue equals marginal cost. A supply curve for a monopoly cannot be drawn simply because the monopoly itself controls price.

Even though a monopoly has an upward-sloping marginal cost curve at any point in time, it does not necessarily increase quantity supplied when the demand for its product increases. The change in quantity supplied by a monopoly depends on the shift in the *marginal revenue* curve that results when demand increases. To see what this implies for the relationship between price and quantity supplied, suppose that the demand for the product of a monopoly increases from D_1 to D_2 in Figure 11–5. Before the increase in demand the monopoly sells the output Q_M corresponding to point E_1, at which the marginal revenue curve MR_1 intersects the monopoly's marginal cost curve. To sell this output, the monopoly chooses price P_1, which corresponds to point A on the demand curve D_1. At that price quantity demanded equals the profit-maximizing output of Q_M units per month.

FIGURE 11–5 Shifts in Demand and Monopoly Supply Decisions

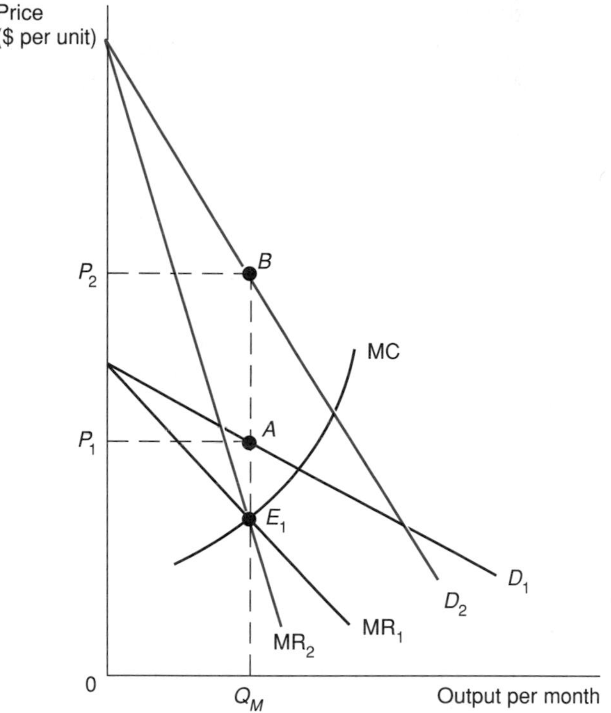

It is impossible to draw a supply curve for a monopoly. This is because a given quantity supplied by a monopoly can correspond to two or more prices. In the graph above the output, Q_M can be associated with price P_1 or P_2, depending on the level of demand and its price elasticity. If demand were to increase from D_1 to D_2, the monopoly would respond by raising price but not increasing quantity supplied.

After the increase in demand to D_2 the new marginal revenue curve is MR_2. However, MR_2 also intersects the monopoly's marginal cost curve at point E_1. The profit-maximizing output therefore remains Q_M. But, given the new demand curve, the monopoly now chooses price P_2, which corresponds to point B on the demand curve D_2, to sell Q_M. Only at price P_2, which exceeds price P_1, will the quantity demanded correspond to the profit-maximizing quantity of Q_M after the increase in demand. In this case the monopoly responds to the increase in demand by raising the price of the product but not increasing the quantity supplied!

This example points out two interesting implications of monopoly power:

1. *An increase in demand need not increase quantity supplied.* A monopoly often responds to an increase in demand merely by raising price. Its reaction depends not only on the increase in demand but also on the way the price elasticity of demand changes when demand changes. This is because a change in the price elasticity of demand associated with each price results in a new marginal revenue curve. The shift in the marginal revenue curve rather than the shift in the demand curve is the crucial determinant of the change in quantity supplied.

2. *A supply curve cannot be defined for a monopoly because two or more prices can be associated with each quantity supplied.* For example, depending on the demand and its price elasticity at each quantity, both price P_2 and price P_1 can result in a quantity supplied of Q_M in Figure 11–5. Alternatively, two or more quantities can be associated with a given price under monopoly, depending on how the price elasticity of demand changes when demand changes. Because a monopoly is a price maker rather than a price taker, a supply curve cannot be used to explain the amount of output it makes available to its market.

The lack of a supply curve also makes it difficult to predict how a monopoly will react to changes in input prices or technology that influence marginal costs of production. To forecast the impact of a shift in marginal costs, we need to know how a monopoly's marginal revenue changes and how a monopoly's output increases or decreases. This means that we need information not only on demand for the monopoly's product but also on the price elasticity of demand for that product and on how price elasticity of demand and output vary.

Monopoly Equilibrium versus Competitive Equilibrium

Using the model of perfect competition as our benchmark, we can now examine the differences between monopoly and competitive equilibrium in terms of price, output, and profits.

Assume that input prices and technology are the same no matter how many sellers are in the market. Suppose that in the long run the average cost and marginal cost of producing bread is $2 per loaf at all possible quantities. Small firms as well as large firms can produce bread at ACmin = MC = $2 in the long run. The purpose of this assumption is to assure that a single firm accommodating all of the buyers in a market has no inherent cost advantage that is unavailable to the many smaller firms that sell in a perfectly competitive market. Assuming an industry of constant costs, the long-run supply curve is therefore a horizontal line corresponding to ACmin = MC = $2 under conditions of perfect competition. This is illustrated in Figure 11–6.

The Consequences of a Monopoly Takeover of a Competitive Industry

Suppose that the market for bread is currently served by 1,000 independently owned bakeries that compete nationally for sales. Each of these bakeries sells bread in a perfectly competitive national market in which the forces of supply and demand determine prices. In Figure 11–6, given the demand for bread, the long-run competitive equilibrium corresponds to point E, at which the market demand curve intersects the horizontal long-run supply curve. The equilibrium output is

FIGURE 11–6 Monopoly versus Competitive Equilibrium

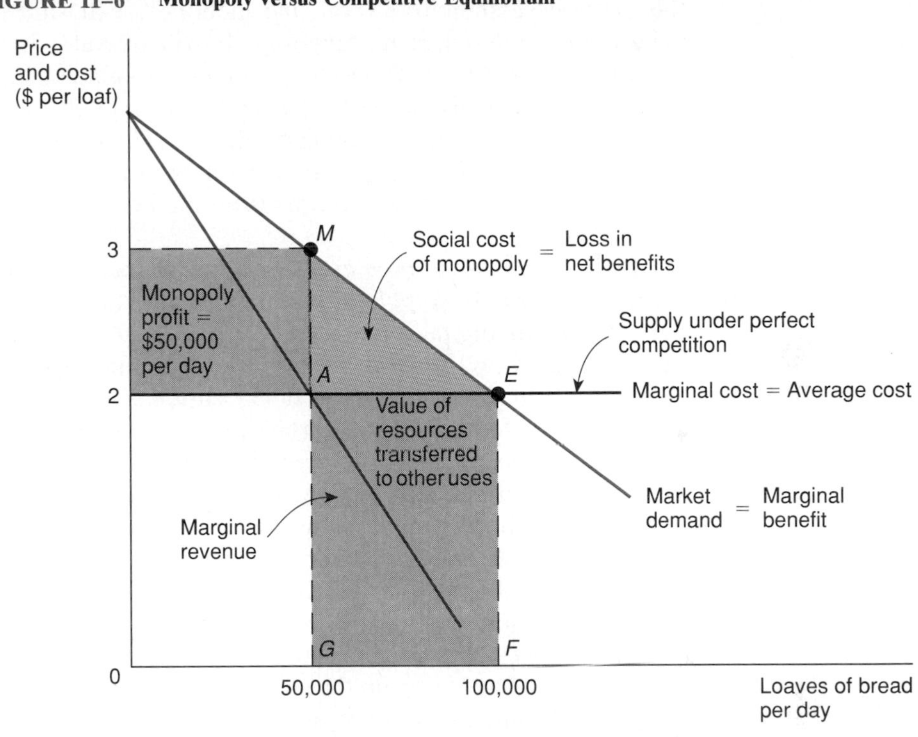

Monopolization of a perfectly competitive industry of constant costs would result in an increase in price and a decrease in quantity supplied. The social cost of monopoly is the loss in net benefits, represented by the area *AME*, resulting from the monopoly's reduction of output to maximize profit.

100,000 loaves of bread per day, and the competitive equilibrium price is $2 per loaf. At that price each bakery earns zero economic profit.

Now suppose that in a dramatic move all of the 1,000 bakeries are taken over by a single seller that now monopolizes the sale of the nation's bread. To maximize profits, the new monopoly sets price so as to sell the output at which marginal revenue equals marginal cost. The output corresponding to point *A*, at which the marginal revenue curve intersects the MC curve, is 50,000 loaves of bread per day. To sell this quantity each day, the monopoly must set a price of $3 per loaf, corresponding to point *M* on the market demand curve in Figure 11–6. The monopoly therefore immediately cuts back its daily bread output from 100,000 loaves to 50,000 loaves. Consumers of bread find it scarcer, and as a result of competition among them for the available quantity of bread, the price of bread increases to $3 per loaf.

To reduce output, the monopoly is likely to shut down some of the plants that were operated as independent bakeries prior to the takeover. This means that it will dismiss workers and sell off land and equipment. Some workers will have to search for new jobs as a result of the monopoly takeover. To cut output to half of the previous competitive level, the monopoly will shut down 500 of the 1,000 bakeries it acquired in its takeover. It will operate the remaining bakeries at output levels corresponding to the minimum possible average cost of $2 per loaf to produce a total daily output of 50,000 loaves. Given the average cost of $2 per loaf, at the $3 price the monopolist enjoys a daily profit of $1 per loaf. Total daily profit, shown as the shaded rectangular area in Figure 11–6, is therefore $50,000.

The monopoly outcome differs from the benchmark competitive equilibrium in the following respects:

1. *The monopoly price exceeds the price that prevails under perfect competition, and the monopoly output is less than the competitive equilibrium output.* The monopoly takeover therefore results in a redistribution of income from consumers of bread to the owners of the monopoly. Buyers of bread pay $1 more per loaf, and that extra dollar enriches the owners of the monopoly by allowing them to earn $50,000 profit on the 50,000 loaves sold per day.

2. *The monopoly earns economic profits by charging a price that exceeds ACmin and marginal cost.* When a pure monopoly is established, the absence of free entry into the market will prevent an increase in supplies that causes price to fall to ACmin and marginal cost. The monopoly enjoys economic profits, whereas in equilibrium competitive firms must be content with zero economic profits.

In summary, in monopoly markets prices are higher and outputs are lower than the prices and outputs that prevail in perfectly competitive markets. Other things being equal, consumers are better off when they can purchase products in perfectly competitive markets rather than monopoly markets. The higher prices paid under a monopoly enrich its owners at the expense of consumers.

The Social Cost of Monopoly

Monopolies make consumers worse off by decreasing the available amounts of goods relative to the amounts that would be available under perfect competition. The **social cost of monopoly** is a measure of the loss in net benefits resulting from the reduced availability of a good when a monopoly maximizes profit. Figure 11–6 shows how the social cost of monopoly can be measured and how the monopolist supplies *less than* the efficient amount of output when it chooses output so as to maximize profit.

Social cost of monopoly A measure of the loss in net benefits that results from a monopoly's control of output.

Assume that the demand curve for bread also reflects the marginal benefit of any given quantity of bread to consumers. In that case the area under the demand curve and above the price of the product measures the consumer surplus, or the net benefits that consumers enjoy from bread each day. The social cost of monopoly can be represented by the reduction in consumer surplus (net benefits) in Figure 11–6 that occurs when daily output is reduced from 100,000 to 50,000 loaves of bread.[3]

[3] If the supply curve were upward sloping, there would also be a loss in producer surplus stemming from the reduction in resources use that occurs when output is reduced below the competitive equilibrium level.

For example, if one more loaf of bread were made available after 50,000 per day had already been produced, the maximum price that at least one buyer would pay for that loaf would be $3. This is the marginal benefit of bread, corresponding to point *M* in Figure 11–6. The minimum price necessary to cover the opportunity cost of making that extra loaf available is only $2, which is the marginal cost of bread at point *A*. This means that the buyer can enjoy a daily marginal net benefit of $1 after compensating the seller for the $2 marginal cost of making one more loaf available daily after 50,000 have been produced. The sum of the additional net benefits possible when the daily output of bread is increased from 50,000 to 100,000 loaves is represented by the area *AME* in Figure 11–6. This area represents the gain in total consumer surplus that would be possible if the monopoly control of supply were eliminated. The area *AME* is therefore the social cost of monopoly. If barriers to entry were removed and if the market were again perfectly competitive, gains corresponding to the area *AME* would be enjoyed daily by consumers.

To maximize profit, the monopolist charges a price that exceeds the marginal cost of its product ($P >$ MC). Because consumers still purchase the good produced by the monopolist in amounts up to the point at which $P =$ MB, it must follow that $P =$ MB $>$ MC. Profit-maximizing pricing by the monopolist therefore prevents the achievement of all the net gains obtainable by trading the good.

Recall from our analysis of allocative efficiency in Chapter 9 that the *efficient output* of a good is the one for which MB = MC. Because the output supplied by the monopolist is less than the output for which MB = MC, at point *E* in Figure 11–6, *less than* the efficient output is made available to consumers. The reduction of net benefits, represented by the area *AME,* is the loss in net benefits that occurs when the monopolist produces less than the efficient output.

The area *AEFG* in Figure 11–6 represents the value of the resources that the monopolist no longer employs after the takeover. This is the total cost that would have been incurred had output not been cut to 50,000 units per day. That cost is not part of the social cost of monopoly if the owners of the resources released (such as workers and those who rent land and equipment to bakeries) can employ them in alternative enterprises after the takeover.

Attempts have been made to measure the social cost of monopoly in particular industries. For example, in the 1960s, when imported cars had only a very small share of the U.S. market, the automobile market in the United States was dominated by the General Motors Corporation, which at that time accounted for nearly 50 percent of domestic production. One study estimated that the social cost of GM's monopoly control over price at that time, represented by an area like *AME* in Figure 11–6, amounted to $1 billion per year.[4] This amount was equal to about 4 percent of GM's annual revenues. If this estimate is accurate, the social cost of GM's monopoly power in the 1960s was the equivalent of a 4 percent tax on consumers that GM added to its profits. Since the 1960s, of course, there has

---

[4] Keith C. Cowling and Dennis C. Mueller, "The Social Costs of Monopoly Power," *Economic Journal* 88 (December 1978), pp. 722–48.

been much greater competition from imports which now account for over 30 percent of U.S. automobile sales. The monopoly power exerted by GM has undoubtedly diminished since the 1960s.

Estimating the Loss in Efficiency from the Exercise of Monopoly Power

Estimating the actual social cost of monopoly is a formidable task. It requires estimating the extent to which monopoly prices in markets actually exceed marginal costs. It also requires estimating the price elasticity of demand to determine the reduction in quantity demanded that results from the monopoly price distortion over marginal cost. Gains that would not be possible if markets were competitive must be netted out of the estimate of social cost. Such gains include the lower prices that result from lower average costs and increased technological progress.

The first attempt to estimate the social cost of monopoly power in the United States was made in 1954. In a classic study Arnold Harberger estimated the value of the loss in output that resulted from monopoly power in the U.S. manufacturing sector.[5] Harberger's estimate was based on a number of simplifying assumptions. Harberger assumed that firms produced under constant costs so that their long-run average costs were constant and equal to their long-run marginal costs. He also assumed that the average price elasticity of demand for manufactured goods was unitary.

Figure 11–7 shows the model on which Harberger's estimate was based. The efficient output is Q^* and the market price that would prevail if this output were made available is P^*, corresponding to point C on the market demand curve. The actual price observed in markets would be $P^* + \Delta P$, where ΔP is the increment in price that results from monopoly power. Because pure monopoly rarely exists, this observed price is lower than the price that would prevail under pure monopoly. The social cost of monopoly power is the area of the triangle ABC.

The monopoly price distortion is ΔP. This increment in price attributable to monopoly power results in a decrease in quantity demanded equal to ΔQ. The area of the triangle ABC, representing the social cost of monopoly, is

$$W = \tfrac{1}{2}\Delta P \Delta Q \qquad \textbf{(11–5)}$$

Harberger assumed that firms that earned more than the average rate of profit of all the firms in his sample had monopoly power. He used this excess of profit over the average to compute ΔP for those firms. Then, assuming unitary elasticity of demand, he calculated the resulting decrease in quantity demanded.

The sample used by Harberger included 73 industries. Extrapolating his results to other industries, he estimated that the social cost of monopoly power in manufacturing industries was $59 million per year, or about 0.1 percent of gross national product. In 1992 dollars his estimate would amount to about $5.6 billion per year.

---

[5] Arnold C. Harberger, "Monopoly and Resource Allocation," *American Economic Review* 44 (May 1954), pp. 77–87.

FIGURE 11–7 Estimating the Social Cost of Monopoly

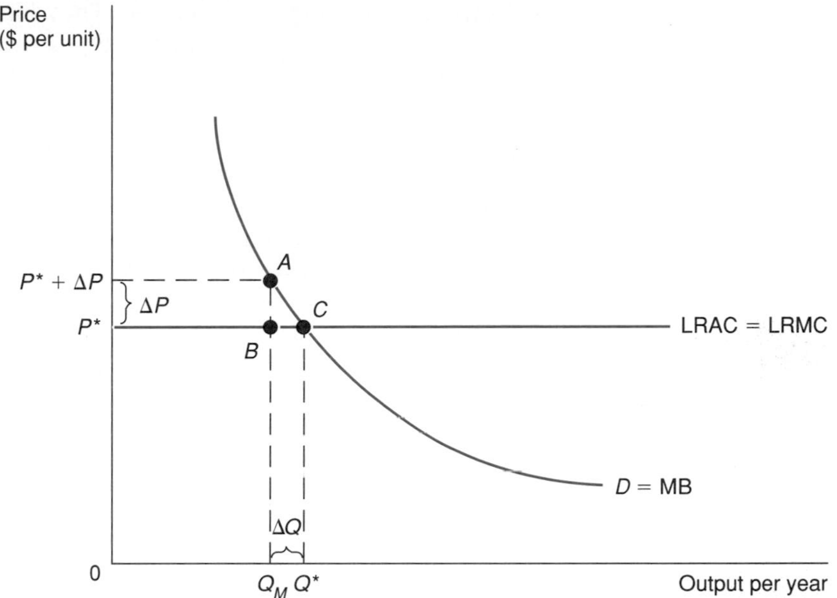

Harberger assumed constant costs and a unitary elasticity of demand. He estimated the increment in price caused by monopoly power and used that estimate, together with the presumption that $E_D = -1$, to estimate the triangular area *ABC*.

Harberger's estimate was, and still is, controversial. Critics argued that his techniques were too simple[6] and that his estimate was remarkably low. Many said that he failed to properly identify the actual exercise of monopoly power and that his estimate for the monopoly price distortion over marginal cost was too low. They argued that the average profit of all the sectors in the economy should have been used to calculate the profit and the price differential of monopoly power and that a larger price distortion would have been found if this had been done. Moreover, Harberger's estimate excluded sectors that accounted for more than three fourths of gross national product.

Harberger's assumption of unitary demand elasticity was also criticized. Unitary elasticity of demand implies that marginal revenue is zero. A firm with monopoly power would choose a price associated with zero MR only if its marginal costs were also zero. Because monopolists adjust output to make sure that demand is elastic, assuming only unitary elasticity implies an underestimate of ΔQ.

[6] See Abram Bergson, "On Monopoly Welfare Losses," *American Economic Review* 63, no. 5 (December 1973), pp. 853–70; and Richard Hartman, "On Monopoly Welfare Losses, Once Again," *Economic Inquiry* 16, no. 2 (April 1978), pp. 293–301.

In addition, Harberger's critics asserted that social costs overlooked by him are associated with the maintenance of monopoly power. Firms use resources to defend and maintain their monopoly power. They hire lawyers to defend themselves against antitrust suits. In a recent government suit against IBM, that firm spent about $100 million to defend itself against the charge that it engaged in illegal business practices to secure monopoly power. Monopolistic firms also attempt to obtain franchises from governing authorities, seek ways to prevent new domestic sellers from entering their markets, and lobby for tariffs and import quotas that restrict the entry of foreign sellers into their markets.[7]

Barriers to entry could diminish the incentive to produce output at minimum possible cost. The absence of competition could cause firms with monopoly power to be complacent about cost management.

Adjusting for these problems, more recent studies have concluded that the social cost of monopoly power in the United States is much higher than Harberger estimated. One study by Keith Cowling and Dennis C. Mueller used a sample of 734 large firms in the United States from 1963 to 1966.[8] Cowling and Mueller used a revised methodology to more accurately identify monopoly power. Their revised estimates suggest that the social cost of monopoly power in the United States, corresponding to an area like *ABC* in Figure 11–7, amounted to 4 percent of the value of the output produced by monopolistic firms. Measuring the social cost of monopoly remains a controversial undertaking. Problems involved in accurately measuring economic profits and in distinguishing them from accounting profits have not yet been solved.[9]

Are There Any Benefits from Monopolies That Can Offset the Social Cost of Monopoly?

The example used above to compare monopoly markets with perfectly competitive markets assumed that the monopoly had no cost advantage over small firms serving a market. In some cases, however, a monopoly attains its position by virtue of cost advantages that would not be possible if many smaller firms served a market. Under these circumstances benefits could be associated with monopoly power that offset the social cost of its control over price.

It is also sometimes argued that monopolies protected against competition from new entrants tend to be more innovative than sellers with many competitors. This is because monopolies know that the profits from their innovations will not be competed away in the long run. Greater innovation means more technological progress, which, in turn, leads to lower average costs.

---

[7] See Anne O. Krueger, "The Political Economy of the Rent-Seeking Society," *American Economic Review* 64, no. 3 (June 1974), pp. 291–303; and Richard A. Posner, "The Social Costs of Monopoly and Regulation," *Journal of Political Economy* 83, no. 4 (August 1975), pp. 807–27.

[8] Cowling and Mueller "Social Costs of Monopoly Power."

[9] For a lively exchange on this controversy see William F. Long and David J. Ravencraft, "The Misuse of Accounting Rates of Return: Comment," along with additional comments by Stephen Martin and Michael A. van Breda and a reply by Franklin M. Fisher, *American Economic Review* 74, no. 3 (June 1984), pp. 494–517.

Let's examine these two common arguments in favor of monopoly. First, consider the argument that economies of scale contribute to lower prices when a monopoly supplies a market. Under natural monopoly long-run average cost declines over the entire range of market demand due to economies of scale. When firms with monopoly power maximize profits, price exceeds their marginal cost and average cost. However, because both their marginal and average costs are lower than would be possible if their industry were composed of many small firms, it does not necessarily follow that consumers can gain if the industry becomes perfectly competitive. Although price would equal marginal cost under perfect competition, the marginal cost and ACmin possible under perfect competition would be much higher than the marginal cost and ACmin possible when a monopoly serves a market.

The second argument in favor of monopoly is that under monopoly technological progress is greater because monopolies have more incentive to engage in research and development and more resources to do so. Barriers to entry permit technological innovators to enjoy the fruits of their efforts for long periods. Does this imply that monopoly power increases the incentive to innovate? Are consumers better off if they are compensated by lower future prices in return for current prices that exceed marginal costs? Joseph Schumpeter forcefully argued that large monopolistic and oligopolistic firms are better suited than small competitive firms to improve technology and train workers.[10]

Schumpeter's argument is based on the belief that large firms can assemble the resources needed to conduct basic research and that such firms are able to engage in many projects at the same time, balancing the failures of many with the successes of a few. However, critics argue that large organizations stifle creativity. They point out that major technological innovations have been made on shoestring budgets in backyard garages. Innovative ideas often begin with the independent research of workers in small firms and are then sold to larger firms for the more expensive stages of later development.[11] For example, the research leading to Kodachrome color transparency film was undertaken independently by researchers who were subsidized by the Eastman Kodak Company for 10 years. Kodak acquired the rights to the invention, which it marketed as its own brand.

There is evidence both for and against Schumpeter's hypothesis that monopolies are more innovative. A study of the U.S. computer industry that did not support the hypothesis concluded that IBM was responsible for only 28 percent of 21 major computer innovations during a period in which IBM accounted for between 66 percent and 78 percent of computer sales. A study of the drug industry that supported the hypothesis found that from 1967 to 1971 the four major pharmaceutical companies accounted for nearly 50 percent of all new FDA-approved chemical drugs.[12]

---

[10] Joseph A. Schumpeter, *Capitalism, Socialism, and Democracy,* 3rd ed. (New York: Harper & Row, 1950).

[11] See John Jewkes, David Sawers, and Richard Stillerman, *The Sources of Invention,* 2nd ed. (New York: W. W. Norton, 1969).

[12] F. M. Scherer, *Industrial Market Structure and Economic Performance,* 2nd ed. (Boston: Houghton Mifflin, 1980), pp. 421–23.

MODERN MICROECONOMICS IN ACTION: THE BUSINESS WORLD

Monopoly Pricing Methods: Two-Part Tariffs

Monopolies have shown quite a bit of ingenuity in taking advantage of their power to set prices so as to maximize profits. One of their techniques requires buyers to pay a fee for the right to purchase their product and then to pay a regular price per unit of the product. For example, your cable TV company charges you a base fee for hooking into its system and then charges you extra for pay-by-view transmissions. Similarly, many local telephone companies charge a monthly base fee and then charge additional fees based on message units.

The fee for privilege of service plus prices for services consumed is called a *two-part tariff*. Theme parks such as Disney World usually employ such a pricing scheme to increase their profits. To see how the scheme works, suppose you operate a theme park and have a local monopoly. The graph shows the demand for rides at your theme park by any given tourist, along with the marginal revenue and marginal cost of the rides. If you charge a single monopoly price, your rides will be priced at $6 each and each tourist will consume four rides per visit, spending $24.

Now let's see if a bit more can be extracted from each tourist. Given the demand curve drawn, each tourist would be willing to pay more than $24 to enter your theme park and take four rides. If you know the demand curve for rides, you know that the typical tourist is enjoying a consumer surplus of $8, corresponding to the area of triangle *ABC* in the graph (area $ABC = \frac{1}{2} \times 4 \times 4$). Therefore, if you charge an entry fee of $8 in addition to $6 per ride, you can add $8 per tourist to your profit.

Given the demand curve of a typical tourist, you can add still more to your revenue from each tourist if you simply eliminate the price per ride and just charge an admission fee. For example, if the price per ride were zero, a tourist would go on 10 rides per visit and you would get revenue of $50 per tourist—0.5($10)(10)—instead of the $32 you would get from the two-part pricing scheme. But be careful. With more rides your marginal costs will increase, and thus your profit might not increase. Also, if you extract the entire consumer surplus with a single entry fee, you increase the tourists' cost per visit, so the total number of admissions will fall.

A two-part tariff is often a good way to increase profit by extracting some, but not all, of the consumer surplus from a monopolist's clients. Monopolists usually experiment with various two-part tariff pricing schemes before hitting on the one that gives them maximum profit.

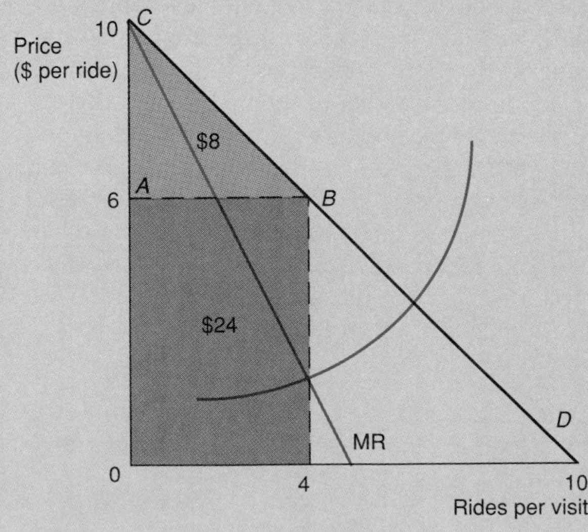

Other studies have addressed the question of whether barriers to entry encourage innovation. These studies indicate that moderate barriers to entry *encourage* innovation, that formidable barriers to entry and completely free entry *discourage* innovation, and that entering firms are often the most prolific and creative innovators.[13]

CONCEPT REVIEW

1. Explain how a monopoly sets a price for its product to maximize profit.
2. Why is it impossible to draw a supply curve for a monopoly firm?
3. Assuming that the monopoly has constant costs and no inherent cost advantages, what would be the consequences of a monopoly takeover of the soybean industry?

GOVERNMENT REGULATION OF MONOPOLY

Price Ceilings

One way to regulate monopoly power is to place a ceiling on the price a monopoly can charge. To be effective in reducing price, the ceiling must be below the price corresponding to the output at which MR = MC. Price ceilings have some very surprising effects on the way monopoly firms behave. The inevitable effect of a price ceiling in a competitive market is a shortage. This is always the case, provided that the ceiling is below the equilibrium price. Rent controls cause housing shortages. An effective ceiling on the price of gasoline results in a shortage of gasoline.

Suppose all of the fiberglass in the United States is produced by one firm. The government levies a ceiling of 25 cents a pound on the price of fiberglass. It is assumed that the monopoly firm's MC is upward sloping and that the ceiling is not lower than the firm's ACmin. If it were, the firm would cease operating in the long run.

The impact of the price ceiling is shown in Figure 11–8. The monopoly price would normally be 40 cents per pound, the price that corresponds to the quantity at which MR_1 = MC. At that price Q_1 pounds per year are sold. The price ceiling prevents the firm from charging the monopoly price. Its managers must take the ceiling price as given. The remarkable conclusion is that the monopoly now behaves as if it were a perfectly competitive firm. It can sell all it likes at 25 cents per pound up to the quantity Q_D. The demand curve under the ceiling is *ABD*. Marginal revenue, MR_2, is now equal to the price of 25 cents at all output levels up to Q_D. The monopoly produces up to the point at which MR_2 = MC. This results in an *increase* in output at the ceiling price, from Q_1 to Q_2 pounds per year.

[13] Ibid., pp. 437–38.

FIGURE 11–8 **Monopoly Reaction to a Price Ceiling**

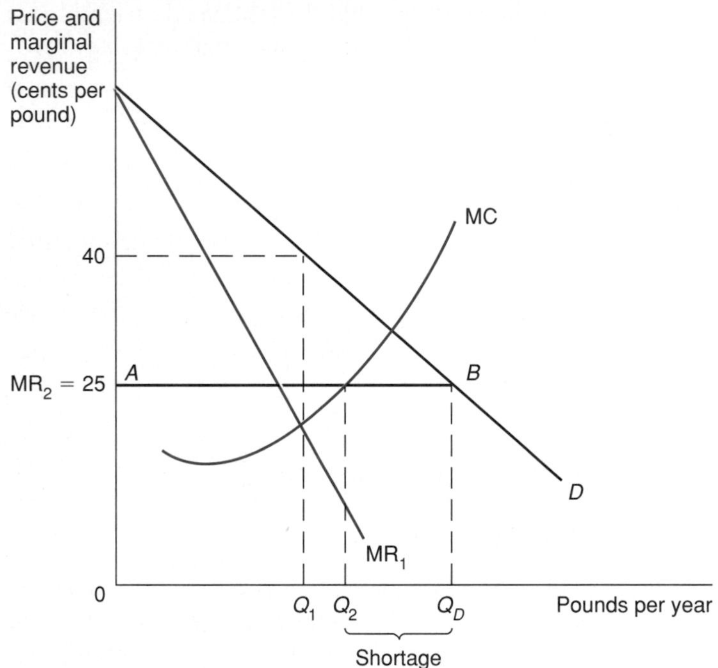

A price ceiling can cause a monopoly to increase output. The monopoly price is 40 cents per pound. Imposition of a ceiling of 25 cents per pound removes monopoly control of price. Marginal revenue is now 25 cents (the same as price) up to an output of Q_D. The monopoly equilibrium quantity increases from Q_1 to Q_2. A shortage of $(Q_D - Q_2)$ pounds per year exists at the ceiling price.

Whereas a price ceiling leads to a decrease in quantity supplied in a competitive market, it can actually *increase* quantity supplied in a monopoly market! However, a shortage still results![14] At the price ceiling of 25 cents per pound, quantity demanded, Q_D, exceeds quantity supplied, Q_2.

Regulating the Pricing of the Output of a Natural Monopoly

Recall that a natural monopoly is a firm that in the long run can satisfy market demand at any price at an average cost lower than the average cost of two or more smaller firms. The average and marginal cost curves for a natural monopoly are shown in Figure 11–9. Given the demand for its product, a profit-maximizing

[14] This conclusion holds true only if the ceiling is also below the price corresponding to the point at which the MC curve intersects the demand curve. If the ceiling is above this price but below the regular monopoly price, the reaction of the monopoly is more complicated.

FIGURE 11–9 Regulating a Natural Monopoly

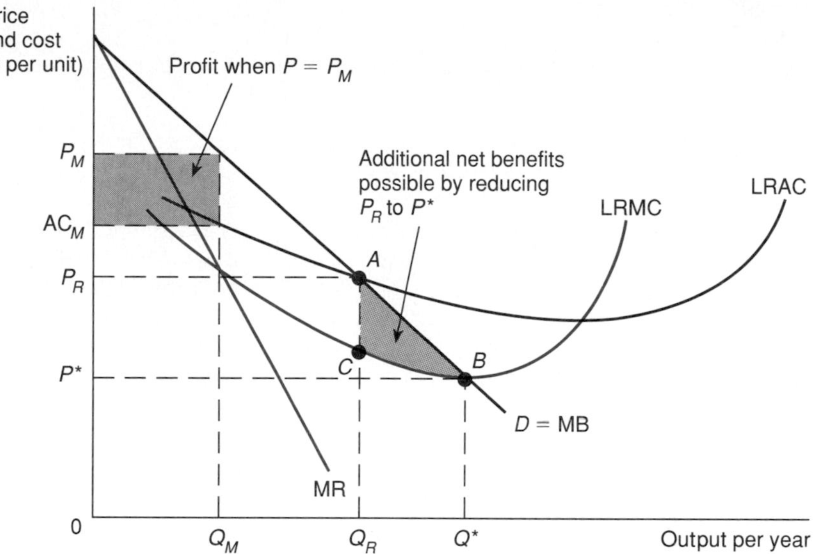

The profit-maximizing price for the monopoly is P_M. Regulators allow the monopoly to charge price P_R, which exceeds the marginal cost of Q_R, the quantity demanded at that price. The area *ABC* represents the additional net benefits that would be possible if price were reduced from P_R to P^*. However, at P^* the monopoly would incur a loss. The regulated price is the lowest price that allows the monopoly to cover its economic cost, given market demand.

monopoly produces to the point at which MR = MC over the long run. In Figure 11–9 the monopoly output, Q_M, is priced at P_M. At that price the monopoly earns economic profits because $P_M >$ AC for the output Q_M. Notice that the monopoly could lower its average costs of production further by producing beyond Q_M. Its objective, however, is to maximize profits.

Suppose that production were increased to the efficient output, Q^*, corresponding to point *B*, where the long-run marginal cost curve intersects the demand curve, which indicates the marginal benefit of each quantity. To sell Q^*, the efficient output, price would have to be set at P^*, which equals the long-run marginal cost of that output. As long as MC continually declines before it intersects the demand curve, the firm cannot cover its costs at a price that low. At Q^*, AC exceeds MC. Setting $P =$ MC to achieve the efficient output, Q^*, therefore results in losses. If a natural monopoly were forced to charge a price equal to its marginal costs, it would require a government subsidy to remain in business.

Perfect competition would require that many small firms sell the product sold by the natural monopoly. Each of these firms would produce only a fraction of the quantity demanded. The small firms would not be able to achieve average costs as low as those that the natural monopoly enjoys by virtue of its size; their average costs would be much higher than those corresponding to Q^* in Figure 11–9.

Modern Microeconomics in Action: Government and the Economy

Regulation of Electric Power Companies: Peak-Load Pricing

Electricity is a nonstorable good. Your local electric company must produce enough each day to satisfy the daily quantity demanded at the price the regulators allow it to charge. Demand for electricity fluctuates considerably between periods of peak use and off-peak use. For example, there is considerable variation in the demand for electricity over each 24-hour period. Peak use typically occurs in the late afternoon and early evening hours, whereas demand is quite slack in the late night and the early morning. There are also seasonal variations in demand. During summer heat waves, when air conditioners are running full blast, the demand for electricity soars. As the quantity of electricity demanded varies, so too does its average cost of production. Average cost of production usually increases sharply during peak demand periods because to meet the peak demand electric companies have to bring older, more costly, methods of production into use. The rate regulation commissions typically set a price for a kilowatt-hour of electricity that reflects the average cost of electricity over both the peak and off-peak periods.

The graph shows the problem faced by a typical electric company. The price set by the regulator commission is P_R, which corresponds to point A on the graph, where the demand curve D_1 for electricity intersects the average cost curve. The average quantity demanded is Q_R at the price P_R. Points on the demand curve D_1 reflect the daily marginal benefit, on average, for various quantities of electricity over a year. During periods of peak use, the demand curve shifts to D_2. Points on the demand curve D_2 reflect the marginal benefit of electricity to

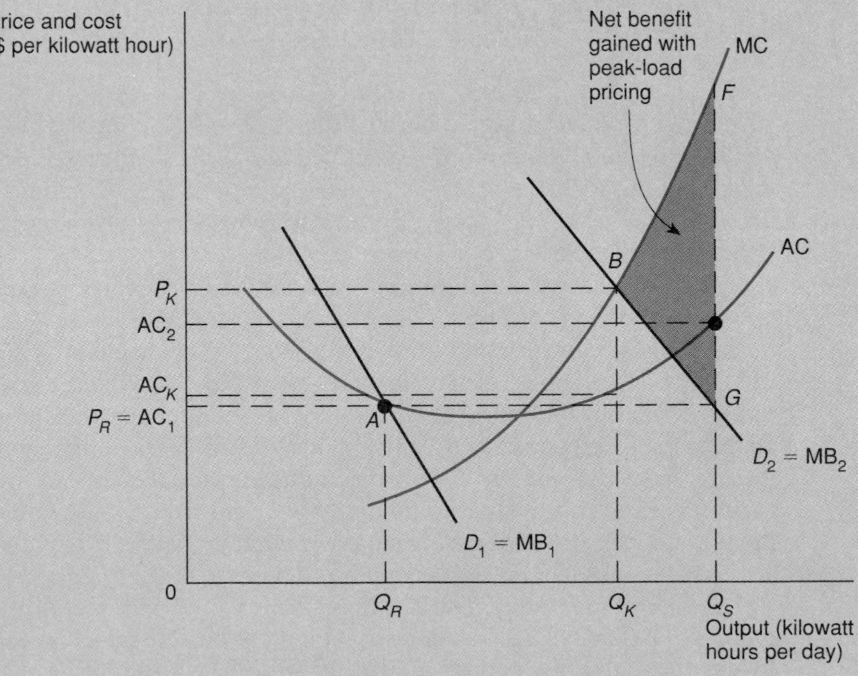

(*Continued*) consumers during such periods. At the price P_R per kilowatt-hour, the daily quantity demanded during peak periods is Q_S and the average cost of producing that quantity is AC_2. Because of the sharp increase in average cost of production above P_R during peak use, the electric company incurs losses on the electricity sold at that time.

In fact, the increase in average cost during periods of peak use is substantial. Many electric companies now operate plants generating nuclear power. Although these plants were very expensive to build, the marginal and average variable costs of operating them are quite low. On average, electricity can be generated at a cost of one cent per kilowatt-hour in a nuclear plant. In some of the older conventional plants electricity can cost over 12 cents per kilowatt-hour to generate! When demand increases beyond the capacity of nuclear plants to meet it, most electric companies have computerized controls that automatically turn on the more expensive sources of power. As demand peaks, up goes average cost and down go the electric company's profits!

The solution to this problem that many electric companies would like is *peak-load pricing*. Under this scheme the regulatory commissions would have to approve a dual pricing system under which the price of electricity would vary between periods of peak and off-peak use. For example, the peak-use rate could be set at P_K. As shown in the graph, P_K would exceed P_R and would be in effect at certain times of the day and in certain seasons. The higher peak-use rate could be set to reflect the marginal cost of electricity during peak use. This would correspond to point B, at which the demand curve D_2 intersects the marginal cost curve. The corresponding quantity demanded would be Q_K. Because P_K exceeds AC_K, the average cost of generating Q_K kilowatts, the electric company would now earn profit during periods of peak use. Naturally, the electric companies prefer profit to loss, and this is why many of them support peak-load pricing!

It would also be efficient to charge a higher price reflecting the higher marginal cost during periods of peak use. At the price P_R the quantity demanded during periods of peak use, Q_S, has a marginal cost at point F that far exceeds its marginal benefit at point G. Marginal cost exceeds marginal benefit by an amount corresponding to the distance FG on the graph when Q_S is produced. Using a peak-load price would allow increases in net benefits, represented by the area BFG in the graph, as users respond by decreasing the quantity demanded from Q_S to Q_K, at which the marginal cost equals the marginal benefit during peak use. The quantity Q_K is the efficient peak-use level of output.

Natural monopolies and government-franchised monopolies are commonly subject to the authority of government commissions. These commissions regulate the prices of the products provided by monopoly suppliers in their jurisdiction. The commissions usually consider the input prices paid by a monopoly and the interests of consumers in determining what price they allow the monopoly to charge for its product. They generally seek to allow the monopoly to at least cover its accounting costs and the opportunity costs of capital invested in it. Such commissions commonly rule on the rate requests of electric power companies, local telephone companies, franchised cable television companies, and privately operated transit services, to name a few.

Suppose that a commission approves a price allowing the owners of a natural monopoly to earn a normal profit on its operations. Figure 11–9 shows that the price allowing zero economic profits corresponds to point A, at which the demand curve intersects the average cost curve. The price approved by the commission is

P_R = AC. At that price the quantity demanded by consumers is Q_R and economic profits are zero. However, price exceeds marginal costs. Any price lower than P_R will result in economic losses for the natural monopoly. P_R is therefore the minimum price that will allow the monopoly to operate without subsidy. Because the commission allows the monopoly to sell all the output it desires at P_R, that price becomes the monopoly's marginal revenue curve up to the output Q_R. If the monopoly were to produce more than Q_R units of output, price would fall, thereby resulting in economic losses. It follows that the monopoly maximizes profits at the regulated price by producing Q_R units per month at that price, even though $P_R >$ MC at that output.

Notice that the monopoly's owners would be better off if they could charge P_M, corresponding to the output at which MR = MC. If the commission selects this price, the owners can earn maximum economic profits. Similarly, any price above P_R and below P_M will permit the owners to enjoy more than the normal profits.

At the regulated price, P_R, and the corresponding quantity, Q_R, additional net benefits from the product, represented by the area *ABC*, would be possible if price fell to the marginal cost of Q^*, the efficient output.

Criticism of Government Regulation of Pricing by Natural Monopolies

Great controversy surrounds government regulation of monopoly pricing. Part of the controversy centers on the complex question of accurately determining average costs of production. Another complex question concerns the incentives established by regulatory price rules. For example, critics of electric rate regulations argue that consumers rather than shareholders are being forced to pay for management blunders that resulted in higher average costs. The alleged management blunders include overinvestment in nuclear power plants and overexpansion of capital facilities. Critics argue that electric companies overcapitalized because they inaccurately estimated the reaction of consumers to increasing rates. Average cost includes the opportunity cost of capital. By increasing the amount of capital used, a monopoly can increase the dollar amount of normal profits. Some economists have argued that this results in production methods more capital intensive than those that would prevail in the absence of regulation. The choice of relatively inefficient capital-intensive production methods results in average costs higher than those that would otherwise prevail.[15]

The average-cost pricing rule does not provide the utilities with any incentives to minimize their cost of production. They face no competitors, and any increase in cost resulting from blunders will not affect the rate of profit they earn on their investment as long as the commission sets P = AC. In recent years opponents of average-cost pricing have attempted to shift at least part of the burden of mis-

[15] Harvey Averch and Leland L. Johnson, "The Behavior of the Firm under Regulatory Constraint," *American Economic Review* 52 (December 1962), pp. 1053–69.

management to stockholders of the electric companies. Managers of electric companies have countered such attempts by pointing out that the companies will have difficulty attracting investors if they cannot make a normal profit. Service quality would decline or electric rates would increase still more to cover interest costs if electric companies are forced to borrow because they find few buyers for their stock.

Price Discrimination

Price discrimination The selling of a good or service of given quality and average cost at different prices to different buyers.

When monopolies produce a product that buyers cannot resell, they often find it possible and in their interest to charge different prices to different buyers. The selling of a good or service of a given quality and average cost at different prices to different buyers is called **price discrimination**. The price differences in this case reflect the monopolist's ability to set different prices to different buyers rather than any differences in quality or in the costs of making the product available to these buyers.

Price discrimination is often practiced by public utilities that charge businesses higher rates than they charge household users. Many movie theaters offer discounts on admission charges to senior citizens. Similarly, drugstores sell prescription drugs and some restaurants sell meals to senior citizens at a discount. Airlines are notorious price discriminators, as may be seen from the myriad of fares available for similar seats on a given flight.

It is difficult to successfully practice price discrimination with a resellable item. If an item were resellable and the transaction costs of resale were low enough, the original purchaser who bought it at a low price would be tempted to resell it to a person who would pay a higher price. Eventually, this process would lead to the establishment of a single market price because resale would continue until those who bought the item at a low price would no longer be able to resell it at a higher price. Medical services are nonresellable. If you got a deal on your appendectomy, you could not turn around and sell it to your friend at a higher price.

Only firms with monopoly power can engage in price discrimination. A competitive firm has no control over price and therefore lacks the capacity to engage in price discrimination. To charge different buyers different prices, firms must be able to control the price of their product. Monopolies engage in price discrimination when they can increase their profits by doing so.

First-Degree Price Discrimination

Perfect, or first-degree price discrimination The price discrimination that exists when a monopoly charges each buyer a different price.

In the most extreme form of price discrimination, the monopoly charges *each* buyer a different price. This is called **perfect, or first-degree, price discrimination.** For example, suppose only one surgeon in the world is capable of performing a rare brain operation. Anyone wanting the operation must come to this surgeon. The surgeon is therefore a monopolist. Assume that this monopolist seeks to maximize profit from selling the service. Figure 11–10 illustrates the demand

FIGURE 11–10 Perfect Price Discrimination

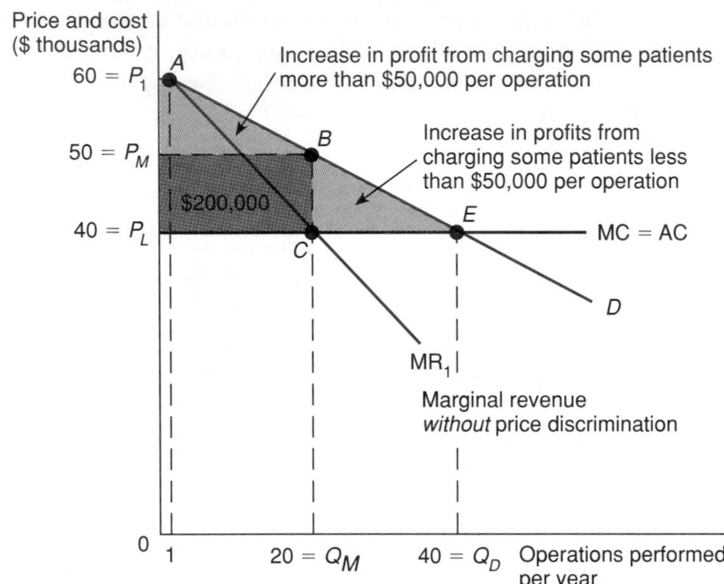

Under perfect price discrimination each buyer is charged a different price according to intensity of demand. More output is produced than under regular monopoly ($Q_D > Q_M$). The regular monopoly profits at the price P_M would be the area P_MBCP_L. The discriminating monopolist's profits exceed this level by the areas of the two triangles P_MAB and BCE.

curve for the operation, which is labeled *D*. Consumers can purchase only one of these operations in a lifetime. For simplicity, assume constant costs and the average (and therefore the marginal) cost of each operation is $40,000. If there were no price discrimination, the monopoly price of an operation would be $P_M =$ $50,000, and $Q_M = 20$ operations per year would be performed at that price. The 20 operations per year correspond to the quantity at which the curve labeled MR_1 intersects the MC curve. At that price economic profits would be $200,000 per year, represented by the area P_MBCP_L.

The surgeon clearly has the capability of engaging in price discrimination because the surgical procedure is a nonresellable personal service. It remains to be seen whether the surgeon can increase annual profits by doing so. Suppose the surgeon has each patient seeking the operation fill out a form that asks for financial information and other data that make it possible to estimate the demand curve illustrated in Figure 11–10. From this information it is clear to the surgeon that some applicants for the operation would pay more than the $40,000 marginal cost of another operation after 20 have already been performed. Remember that points on a demand curve indicate the maximum price that some consumer will offer for an item. The surgeon can see that points on the demand curve corresponding to more than 20 operations per year are above points on the marginal cost curve. The surgeon can make additional profit by charging each applicant the maximum price that the applicant is willing to pay. As long as the maximum price an applicant will pay exceeds the marginal cost of the operation, the surgeon can add to profit by serving that applicant.

In Figure 11–10 the surgeon engaging in perfect price discrimination would perform 40 operations per year and charge each applicant a different price. Only the last patient getting the operation will pay a price of $40,000, which is the marginal cost of the operation. Patients willing to pay more than the $40,000 marginal cost rather than do without the operation will be charged more. For example, the patient whose maximum price of $60,000 is represented by point *A* on the demand curve will be charged that price.

By charging patients who would have purchased their operations at the $50,000 monopoly price more than P_M, the surgeon adds to annual profit a sum represented by the triangular area P_MAB. By charging patients who would have forgone their operations at the $50,000 monopoly price *less than* P_M, the surgeon performs an additional 20 operations per year that would not otherwise have been purchased. This adds to profit a sum represented by the triangular area *BCE*. Total profit with price discrimination is now represented by the area P_LAE, which is greater than the profit that could have been earned if a single price equal to P_M had been set. It follows that the profit-maximizing surgeon engages in price discrimination because profit increases if this is done.

Under perfect price discrimination the demand curve *is* the marginal revenue curve. Equilibrium occurs at point *E*, where the maximum price paid by the last buyer equals marginal cost. Output increases from Q_M to Q_D per year under price discrimination. This is the same output that would have been supplied if the operation had been sold in a perfectly competitive market. However, only the last buyer gets the operation at the competitive benchmark price (P = MC). All other buyers pay higher prices than would have prevailed under perfect competition.

As a result of price discrimination, patients whose maximum price is on the line segment *AB* are made worse off by having to pay a higher price. Patients whose maximum price is along the line segment *BE* now choose to purchase the operation, thanks to the surgeon's willingness to charge them a price below P_M. The surgeon is better off. Profit has increased by the two triangular areas P_MAB and *BCE* as a result of price discrimination.

A perfect price discriminator captures all the consumer surplus of a good. No consumer can earn consumer surplus because the monopolist charges all consumers the maximum price that they will pay. The surplus is transferred to the monopolist as profits. The total monopoly profits, P_LP_1E, are equal to the amount of consumer surplus that would have occurred under perfect competition.

Examples of perfect price discrimination are difficult to find. However, some business practices resemble perfect price discrimination. For example, in some areas real estate agents charge a 6 percent commission on the sale of all homes. Thus the agent's fee varies according to the value of the home. A person selling a $200,000 home would pay a fee of $12,000, whereas a person selling a $30,000 home would pay a fee of only $1,800. Assuming no extra costs are involved for selling more expensive homes, this constitutes price discrimination.

Second-Degree Price Discrimination

Second-degree price discrimination The price discrimination that exists when a monopolist prices its product in blocks to extract some, but not all, of the consumer surplus.

Sometimes a monopolist does not have enough information to engage in first-degree price discrimination. When this is the case, the monopolist may engage in **second-degree price discrimination,** in which it prices its product in blocks to extract some, but not all, of the consumer surplus. This type of price discrimination takes the form of charging different prices for a product depending on *how much* of the product a consumer buys over a given period. For example, an electric power company may have a rate structure under which different rates are charged per kilowatt-hour depending on how much electricity is consumed per month. In this way the monopolist takes advantage of the fact that the marginal benefit of electricity, and therefore the willingness to pay for it, declines as more electricity is consumed.

Figure 11–11 shows how second-degree price discrimination would work in the pricing of electricity. Your price per kilowatt-hour (kwh) would depend on the amount of electricity you consumed per month. The electric company would price its output in "blocks." The first 500 kwh that you consumed per month might be priced at nine cents per kwh; the second 500, at seven cents per kwh; and the third 500, at five cents per kwh. The pricing schedule would give you a price break if you consumed more electricity per month.

FIGURE 11–11 Second-Degree Price Discrimination

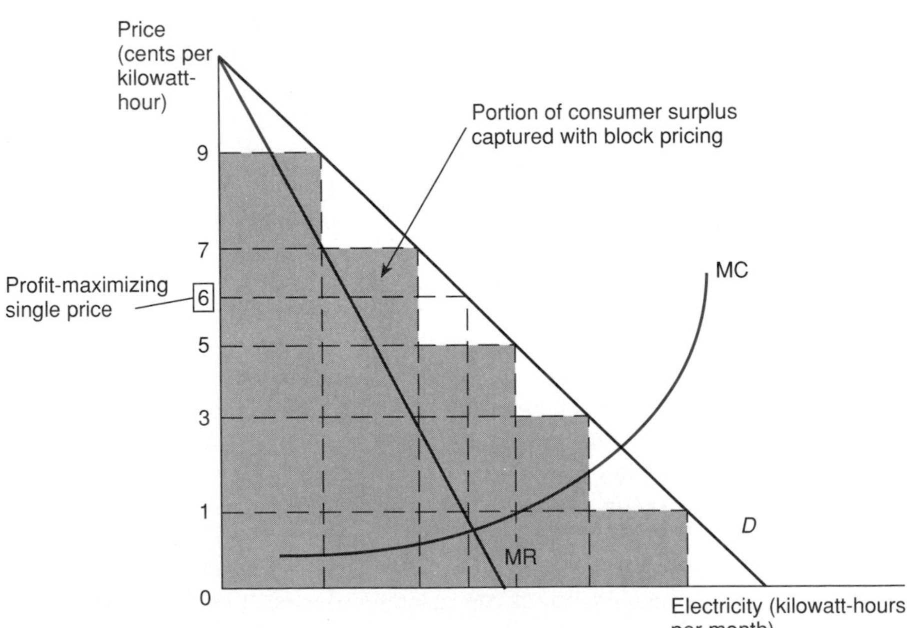

Under second-degree price discrimination the monopolist prices the product in blocks, so that the price charged depends on the amount of the product purchased over each period. Here the monopolist does not capture all of the consumer surplus but obtains more revenue than would be obtained if a single price corresponding to the output for which MR = MC were charged.

Figure 11–11 shows how this pricing schedule enables a monopoly to capture some, but not all, of the consumer surplus from its customers. If the monopoly charged a single price corresponding to the quantity at which MR = MC in the graph the price would be six cents per kwh. But because the monopoly engages in block pricing, customers who consume relatively little electricity each month pay more than six cents per kwh and very big customers, such as industrial users, pay less than six cents per kwh. As the graph shows, the monopoly earns more by engaging in second-degree price discrimination than it would earn if it charged a single price. However, because it does not price each unit at a different rate, it does not capture the entire consumer surplus. Many gas and electric companies have similar rate structures and can be regarded as engaging in second-degree price discrimination.

Price Discrimination in Segmented Markets

Segmented market A market in which two or more classes of buyers with differing responsiveness to price changes can be identified.

A **segmented market** is one in which two or more classes of buyers with differing responsiveness to price changes can be identified by certain characteristics. By charging different prices to each of these classes of buyers, the monopolist can increase its profits.

This type of price discrimination is common in airline travel. Airlines with monopoly power often perceive two classes of passengers: tourists and business travelers. Tourists have more elastic travel demands than business travelers. The business market is segmented from the tourist market by the duration of trips. Tourists on vacation tend to take trips that last one to three weeks and usually spend at least one weekend at their destination. Business travelers, on the other hand, tend to take very short or very long trips. On short trips they rarely spend a weekend at their destination. Accordingly, airlines have the opportunity to charge tourists and business travelers different prices by discriminating according to the duration of trips. The fare differential is often substantial. A business traveler sitting next to a tourist on a flight may be paying twice the tourist fare. The tourist fare is increased if the tourist ticket is used for a trip of any other duration. A tourist who extends her vacation beyond 28 days (or 45 days if that is the cutoff) and attempts to use the ticket on her return trip is in for a rude surprise when she checks in for her departure. She will have to pay the differential between the tourist rate and the business rate.

The practice of price discrimination by U.S. airlines has been on the rise since 1978, when the process of deregulating airline competition and pricing began. Since 1978 more passengers than ever have been paying discount fares with a complex of special requirements for eligibility. Travel agents now use complex computer programs to keep up with the discount fares, their advance booking requirements, and the penalties associated with violating their conditions.

Figure 11–12 shows how a monopoly airline can increase profits through price discrimination. Figure 11–12(a) shows the total demand curve for air travel on one of the airline's routes. That demand curve has a "kink" in it at the point at which tourists enter the market. At prices above the kink, only business travelers buy tickets. At prices below the kink, tourists start buying tickets. If there is no price discrimination, the airline charges the monopoly price, P_M, and sells Q_M miles of

FIGURE 11–12 Price Discrimination in Segmented Markets

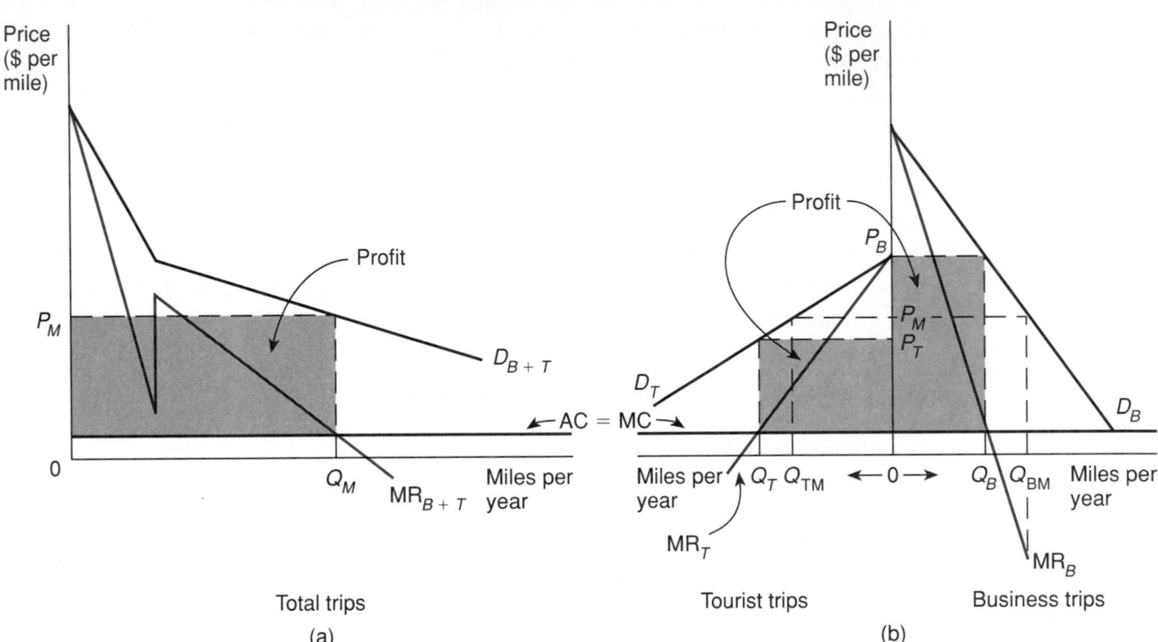

Graph (a) shows the pricing policy and profits of a nondiscriminating monopolist. In graph (b) the monopolist's market is segmented into business and tourist trips. A price-discriminating monopolist takes advantage of the segmentation by charging business travelers, whose demand is more inelastic at any price than that of tourists, a higher price than the price it charges tourists. The discriminating monopolist adjusts quantity sold in each of the market segments until $MR_T = MR_B = MC$, thereby increasing its profit above the profit that would prevail in the absence of price discrimination.

air travel per year on the route. The monopoly price is the one corresponding to the output for which MR = MC. Marginal revenue rises sharply when tourists start buying tickets. Assume that marginal costs are constant and therefore equal to average costs at all output levels.

Figure 11–12(b) shows the business and tourist segments of the market. At any price tourist demand is more elastic than business demand. Tourist demand begins at the price corresponding to the kink in the total demand curve. The curves for the two classes of consumers have been drawn back-to-back with a common price axis. Tourist miles traveled per year are measured to the left of the common origin. Business miles traveled per year are measured to the right of the origin, as is normally done.

The airline can increase its profit by price discrimination. At the single monopoly price, P_M, business travelers would consume Q_{BM} miles per year and tourists would consume Q_{TM} miles per year. Figure 11–12(b) shows that at those output levels marginal revenue is negative in the business segment and positive in the tourist segment.

Because marginal revenue in the tourist segment (MR_{TM}) exceeds that in the business market (MR_{BM}), the airline can increase its profit by selling fewer tickets to business travelers and more tickets to tourists. It accomplishes this by raising business fares and reducing tourist fares. It can continue to increase its profit until

$$MR_{TM} = MR_{BM} \tag{11–6}$$

assuming that MC is independent of the mix of sales to tourists and business travelers.

Total profit, the shaded area in both portions of Figure 11–12(b), is now the sum of the profit from tourist trips and business trips. This profit exceeds the profit that could have been earned at P_M, the single monopoly price.

Price discrimination is profitable only if price elasticity differs in the two market segments served. This can easily be proved. At any price, $MR = P(1 + 1/E_D)$. This is true for the marginal revenue of each of the segments. Marginal revenue in each of the segments must be the same for profit maximization. Therefore,

$$P_T(1 + 1/E_{DT}) = P_B(1 + 1/E_{DB}) \tag{11–7}$$

$$MR_T = MR_B$$

in equilibrium. When $E_{DB} = E_{DT}$, the price in the tourist segment must equal the price in the business segment for profit maximization:

$$P_T = P_B, \text{ if } E_{DT} = E_{DB}$$

Profit maximization results in different prices only if price elasticities of demand differ for buyers in each of the market segments. For example, if $E_{DB} < E_{DT}$ is assumed in Figure 11–12, then Equation 11–7 will be satisfied only if $P_B > P_T$. In other words, when a market is segmented, the monopolist engaging in price discrimination charges a higher price in the market segment for which demand is less elastic. One consequence of this type of price discrimination is that some market segments that would not have been served under a single-price policy are now served.

When businesses engage in price discrimination, they need information about how willingness to pay and price elasticity of demand vary across different types of consumers. In the last part of this book we will show how the costs of gathering information and the asymmetry of access to information in a market affect the incentives and mechanisms of price discrimination in the business world.

Price Discrimination in Practice

In reality firms with monopoly power use a variety of ingenious price discrimination techniques to increase their profits. Firms in the airline industry, as we just pointed out, use a variety of fares based on length of trip, day of departure, and one-way or round-trip service. Firms in other industries have also developed ways to divide buyers into groups with elastic and inelastic demands. For example, large food companies such as Nabisco and General Foods often distribute coupons through advertising that allow customers to purchase products at a discounted price. You are all familiar with these coupons, and you may have even used them to get rebates on various items or direct price reductions at the checkout counter.

Lower-income customers, who place a lower value on their time than do higher-income customers, usually clip and collect the coupons. These customers tend to have more elastic demands for many nonessential food products. By lowering the price only to customers who bother to clip and use the coupons, the food companies are able to segment their market and sell more to customers with more elastic demands.[16]

Sellers of products that can be marketed in different formats, such as books or records, can also price-discriminate. For example, book publishers can market a book in a hardback or softcover edition. Typically, they first produce a high-priced hardback edition of a new book. They assume that the persons most eager to read the book have the most inelastic demands and will pay a higher price for it. However, they also know that many additional readers whose demands are more elastic also want to buy the book. These people are willing to wait for the book. Book publishers usually issue a low-priced paperback edition after the high-priced hardback edition has fully tapped the market of eager readers with inelastic demands.

Concept Review

1. Under what circumstances can a price ceiling result in an increase in quantity supplied in a market served by a monopoly?
2. Explain why a natural monopoly would incur losses if it were required by government to charge a price equal to its marginal cost of production.
3. Under what circumstances will a monopoly engage in price discrimination?

Summary

1. A pure monopoly is a single seller of a product that has no close substitutes. Entry by new firms into a pure monopoly market must be impossible if the monopoly is to be maintained.
2. Barriers to entry include government requirements for franchises or licenses, patents and copyrights, control of particular inputs, and economies of scale.
3. A natural monopoly can produce enough to satisfy market demand in the long run under conditions of decreasing average cost. Natural monopolies are often regulated by government to limit their control of price.
4. A firm with monopoly power can influence the price of the product it sells. Such a firm is a price maker rather than a price taker.
5. The demand curve for a monopoly's output is downward sloping. The monopoly can set any price it pleases; however, its managers know that they can sell more at lower prices. Once a

[16] See Chakavarthi Narasimhan, "A Price Discrimination Theory of Coupons," *Marketing Science*, Spring 1984.

price has been set, quantity sold depends on demand. Similarly, a monopoly can choose how much to produce, and given the quantity it makes available, the price will then be determined by the demand for the product.

6. The marginal revenue of additional output sold by a monopolist falls short of its price. The relationship between price and marginal revenue depends on the price elasticity of demand for the product.
7. The monopoly firm maximizes profit by setting the price for which marginal revenue equals marginal cost. However, because $MR < P$, it follows that $MC < P$.
8. Other things being equal, prices under monopoly are higher than the prices that would prevail in a perfectly competitive market.
9. Monopoly power prevents the achievement of efficiency because it results in prices that exceed marginal costs.
10. Possible offsetting benefits of monopoly power include lower prices due to lower average and marginal costs of production and increased technological progress.
11. The social cost of monopoly is the loss in net benefits that results from monopoly power in a market.
12. The pricing policies of natural monopolies are usually regulated by government commissions. Because a natural monopoly would incur losses at a price set to equal the marginal cost of its product, these commissions usually set a price that allows the monopoly to cover its average cost of production for the level of output at which the demand curve intersects the average cost curve.
13. Price discrimination is the monopolistic practice of charging different prices for the same good. Price discrimination is possible for items that buyers cannot resell. Monopolists engage in price discrimination if they can increase their profits by doing so. They sell more by engaging in this practice than they would if they charged a single monopoly price.

Important Concepts

pure monopoly
monopoly power
market structure
barrier to entry
natural monopoly
social cost of monopoly
price discrimination
perfect, or first-degree, price discrimination
second-degree price discrimination
segmented market

Questions for Review

1. What are the characteristics that define market structure? How does the market structure corresponding to pure monopoly differ from that of perfect competition?
2. "If an industry demand curve intersects an upward-sloping portion of the LRAC curve, that industry is a natural monopoly." True or false? Explain your answer.
3. Explain why the marginal revenue curve is the same as the demand curve for a perfect price-discriminating pure monopoly.
4. Suppose a monopoly producer of steel charges a price of \$1,000 per ton. At that price marginal cost is also \$1,000. Is the monopoly maximizing profit?
5. Consider a pure monopoly that is practicing segmented market price discrimination. Suppose the quantity demanded by one buyer class exceeds the quantity demanded by another buyer class at every price level. Prove that the monopoly will sell more output to the buyer class with the greater demand.
6. Using a diagram like that in Figure 11–4(a), demonstrate that a pure monopoly will decrease its price and increase its output if the marginal cost curve shifts downward.

7. Why is it impossible to draw a supply curve for a monopoly?

8 How can a price ceiling cause a monopoly to increase the quantity supplied to a market?

9. What does the social cost of monopoly measure?

10. Explain why a natural monopoly will incur losses if it is instructed to produce at the efficient output. Show the decrease in net benefits from the product of a natural monopoly when the price is set equal to the average cost of production instead of marginal cost, given the current level of demand.

PROBLEMS

1. A monopoly cigarette producer charges a price of $1 per pack. Assuming that the monopoly is maximizing profits and the price elasticity of demand for cigarettes is −2 at that price, calculate the monopoly's marginal revenue and marginal cost. Explain why the monopoly will never sell enough cigarettes to allow demand to become inelastic.

2. Given constant returns to scale, constant costs, and a linear demand curve, prove that monopoly output will be exactly one half of the output that prevails under perfect competition.

3. Suppose a tax of $1 per pound is levied on the output of a steel producer. Assuming that the producer is a monopoly, faces a linear demand, and produces under constant costs, how much will the price of steel change?

4. Show how a price ceiling imposed on a monopoly can result in an increase in output but no shortage.

5. Suppose the price elasticity of demand for movie admission is −5 for senior citizens and −2 for persons under 65 years of age. Assume that in equilibrium a monopoly engaging in price discrimination incurs marginal costs of $3 per admission. Calculate the admission price charge to senior citizens and the admission price charged to those under age 65.

6. The short-run average cost, short-run marginal cost, demand, and marginal revenue curves of a pure monopolist are shown in the graph. Answer the following questions regarding this case.
   a. If the monopolist does not price-discriminate, what is its profit-maximizing output?

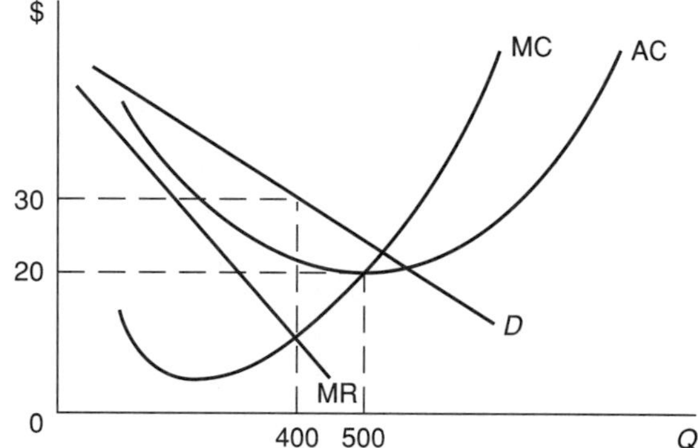

   b. Explain why the maximum profit of the pure monopolist must be less than $4,000 if it does not price-discriminate.
   c. If the monopolist practices perfect price discrimination, will its chosen output be greater than, equal to, or less than 500?

7. For each of the following statements regarding pure monopoly, indicate whether you believe the statement to be true or false and briefly justify your position:
   a. The chosen output of a natural monopoly is the output that minimizes long-run average cost.
   b. A short-run supply curve does not exist for a pure monopoly.
   c. A pure monopoly will increase its price and reduce its output in response to an upward shift of its marginal cost curve.
   d. Long-run equilibrium price will be higher and long-run equilibrium industry output will be lower if an industry is a pure monopoly rather than perfectly competitive.

12

Imperfectly Competitive Output Markets

Is a chicken a chicken, or are some chickens better than others? If you ask Frank Perdue this question, he'll be quick to tell you that there are chickens and there are *Perdue chickens*. By putting his brand name on the chickens his company sells, Frank Perdue is able to convince thousands of buyers that if they buy one of them, they will always get a Grade A well-plucked bird with less fat. Because so many people are convinced that Perdue chickens are better, they can also be sold at a price higher than that of ordinary chickens. Such a price differential would be impossible in a perfectly competitive market, in which sellers of standardized products would lose all of their sales if they priced their output even one penny higher than the price of the competition!

Let's go from the market for chickens to a very different market—the seasonal market for Passover Matzo, the unleavened bread that observant Jews eat to commemorate the exodus of their people from Egypt. Passover matzo is produced by only a handful of firms, the most famous of which is the B. Manischewitz Company of Jersey City, New Jersey. In the 1980s the price of Passover matzo was just about the same and uniformly high no matter whose brand was purchased. Then, in 1990, the Justice Department accused the executives of Manischewitz and other firms that produced Passover matzo of meeting regularly before Passover at a restaurant on Manhattan's Lower East Side in a plot to set the price of Passover matzo. The firms were subsequently found guilty of price-fixing, which is illegal in the United States. Here we have a case of a few sellers, each with a large market share, operating in collusion to keep prices high so they can make higher profits!

Imperfect competition The competition that exists when two or more sellers, each of which has some control over price, compete for sales in a market.

The two situations we have just cited are examples of **imperfect competition,** which exists when two or more sellers, each of which has some control over price, compete for sales in a market. In some cases control over price results from the fact that competing firms do not sell a standardized product. Differences in product quality or appearance, reputation for service, and other characteristics make the product of each seller in such a market unique, as is true for Perdue chickens. The uniqueness of the product gives each seller a measure of monopoly power over price.

Meals in restaurants are another good example of a differentiated product. Individual restaurants in a region differ in the type and quality of food they serve, the quality of their service, and their atmosphere. The managers of some restaurants can charge higher prices than are charged by competing restaurants without losing all of their clients. The demand curve for such a restaurant's meals is therefore downward sloping. If, instead, restaurants were standardized, the demand curve for the meals of every restaurant would be a horizontal line.

In other cases control over price stems from the large market shares of individual sellers, as was true for Passover matzos. Each of these sellers produces a large enough portion of the total market output to significantly influence supply and therefore price. For example, in the early 1980s only five U.S. firms produced lead. Because each of these firms had a fairly large share of the total market supply, each could influence the price of lead by varying the quantity it offered for sale.

In many cases control over price in a market is explainable by a combination of both product differentiation and the large market shares of individual firms. The markets for cigarettes and beer fall into this category. The four largest U.S. cigarette producers account for about 80 percent of cigarette sales. The four largest U.S. brewers account for about 75 percent of total beer sales in this country. In 1987 the five largest domestic airlines accounted for 72 percent of air passenger-miles traveled.

As we showed in the preceding chapter, the exercise of monopoly power implies losses in net benefits from resource use. However, it is not always easy to ascertain whether the firms with monopoly power actually exercise that power to jack up prices above marginal costs. In some cases the threat of competition from new entrants into the market, including suppliers of imports, restrains the exercise of monopoly power. The threat of legal action against firms that engage in unfair business practices can also restrain firms from increasing their prices above their marginal costs. Moreover, market structures in which firms are able to control prices can yield such benefits as lower production costs and product variety. Monopoly and the use of monopoly power per se is not illegal in the United States. However, firms that engage in certain business practices regarded as unfair to acquire or maintain monopoly positions are subject to prosecution. So too are firms who conspire to fix prices, as the producers of Passover matzo discovered.

In this chapter we will discuss forms of imperfect competition and techniques for diagnosing the exercise of monopoly power. In the following chapter we will examine actual business pricing and advertising strategies in imperfectly competitive markets.

MONOPOLISTIC COMPETITION

Monopolistic competition The competition that exists when many sellers compete to sell a differentiated product in a market into which the entry of new sellers is possible.

Product differentiation The sale of items that are not standardized.

Monopolistic competition exists when many sellers compete to sell a differentiated product in a market into which the entry of new sellers is possible.[1] In a monopolistically competitive market the following conditions prevail:

1. *The product of each firm selling in the market is not a perfect substitute for the product sold by competing firms.* Each seller's product has unique qualities or characteristics that make some buyers prefer it to the product of competing firms. Some buyers, for example, are willing to pay higher prices for one seller's shoes if they believe that those shoes are more comfortable. Similarly, some buyers are willing to pay premium prices for the one designer's clothing because they like the way it is cut or the quality of its detailing. **Product differentiation** means that the item sold in the market is not standardized. The differentiation can result from real differences among products or from perceived differences that result from advertising, the prestige of a brand name, or the image associated with possession or use of a product. Rolex watches, Mont Blanc pens, Mercedes Benz and BMW automobiles all have a reputation for quality and a snob appeal that give the sellers of these brands a degree of monopoly power.

2. *The market comprises a relatively large number of sellers each of which satisfies a small, but not microscopic, share of the market demand for the general type of product sold by the firm.* Under monopolistic competition market shares are generally in excess of the 1 percent or less that prevails under perfect competition. Each firm in the market typically accounts for between 1 percent and 10 percent of annual sales in the market.

3. *Sellers in the market do not consider their rival's reaction when setting the price for their products or their annual sales targets.* This characteristic results from the large number of sellers in monopolistically competitive markets. For example, if a single shoe producer cuts the price of its shoes 20 percent to sell more, its gain in sales is likely to come at the expense of many other sellers rather than just a few. Thus, no single rival is likely to suffer a significant reduction in its market share because of the price cut. Since the first firm's decision to change price does not significantly affect the opportunities of its rivals to earn a profit, its rivals have no reason to react by altering their policies. The first firm knows this and therefore does not consider any possible reactions by its rivals when it chooses its price or sales targets.

4. *Free entry and exit are possible in the market.* It is easy to enter or leave the market under monopolistic competition. Profitable conditions in a monopolistically competitive market will attract new sellers. However, entry is not quite as easy under monopolistic competition as it would be under perfect

[1] The theory of monopolistic competition was originally formulated in the 1930s. See Edward H. Chamberlin, *The Theory of Monopolistic Competition* (Cambridge, Mass.: Harvard University Press, 1933), and Joan Robinson, *The Economics of Imperfect Competition* (New York: Macmillan, 1933). The model presented here is a simplified version of Chamberlin's original formulation.

competition because new entrants with new brands or new services often find it difficult to establish their reputations. Existing firms with established reputations therefore have a competitive edge over new entrants.

Monopolistic competition is similar to monopoly in that individual firms have the power to control the price of their product. It is similar to perfect competition in that many firms sell each product and free entry and exit prevail in the market.

Defining the Industry

Product group Several closely related, but not identical, items that serve the same general purpose for consumers.

Although each seller's product is unique in a monopolistically competitive market, there is enough similarity among particular kinds of products to group the sellers of those products into industries. A **product group** comprises several closely related, but not identical, items that serve the same general purpose for consumers. The sellers in each product group can be regarded as competing firms within an industry. One example of a product group is footwear; another is women's dresses.

There are problems in defining the product groups corresponding to an industry. For example, is the footwear industry to include all types of footwear, including men's shoes, women's shoes, children's shoes, boots, athletic shoes, rubber overshoes, and so on? Clearly, arbitrary decisions are necessary to define a product group. Restaurant services could be said to constitute a product group. But are McDonald's, Burger King, and the other firms that provide fast-food services members of that product group? Perhaps not, since many buyers do not regard the meals of such firms as good substitutes for the meals of a full-service restaurant. Similarly, it might be argued that restaurants specializing in Chinese cuisine constitute a distinct product group.

When grouping firms in an industry for the purpose of defining a monopolistically competitive market, it is always necessary to make a number of arbitrary judgments.[2] However, an estimate of the cross elasticity of demand for the products of rival firms can be useful in delineating an industry. Recall that cross elasticity of demand is the percentage change in the quantity demanded of one product that results from a 1 percent change in the price of another product. In a monopolistically competitive industry the cross elasticity of demand for the product of one firm with respect to the price of the product of a rival firm should be positive and relatively large. This means that the products of competing sellers are very good substitutes for each other. If a firm within an industry raises its price above that of competing firms, it should expect to lose a significant amount of sales to competitors.

Table 12–1 shows some U.S. product groups that are likely to be monopolistically competitive. The table shows the number of firms in each product group and the percentage of the dollar value of domestic shipments in 1982 accounted for by

[2] For a technical analysis of principles for defining industries, see Kenneth D. Boyer, "Is There a Principle for Defining Industries?" *Southern Economic Journal* 50, no. 3 (January 1984), pp. 761–70.

TABLE 12–1 Shipments by the Four Largest Firms and the Eight Largest Firms in Selected Industries in Which Monopolistic Competition Prevails, 1982

Industry	*Number of Sellers*	*Annual Shipments (%)* Four Largest Firms	*Annual Shipments (%)* Eight Largest Firms
Women's and misses' dresses	5,489	6	10
Bottled and canned soft drinks	1,236	14	23
Hosiery	376	20	29
Men's and boys' shirts and nightware	535	19	29
Upholstered household furniture	1,129	17	25
Mattresses and bedsprings	786	23	31
Book publishing	2,007	17	30
Footwear (except rubber)	167	28	45
Jewelry (precious metal)	2,159	16	22

Source: U.S. Department of Commerce, Bureau of the Census, *1982 Census of Manufacturers, Concentration Ratios in Manufacturing*.

the four and eight largest domestic firms. The value of imported goods is not included in the total shipments. The total market shares of the domestic firms are therefore overstated.

In most markets that are regarded as monopolistically competitive, the four largest firms account for less than 25 percent of total domestic shipments and the eight largest firms account for less than 50 percent of total domestic shipments. For example, in 1982 there were 1,236 independent sellers of bottled and canned soft drinks. Of these sellers, the four largest accounted for 14 percent of total domestic shipments and the eight largest accounted for 23 percent.

Short-Run Equilibrium of the Firm under Monopolistic Competition

The demand curve of a monopolistically competitive firm is downward sloping. Suppose a seller in a monopolistically competitive market for soft drinks seeks to maximize profits. The seller's product is differentiated from products of competitors by its taste and by the fact that it contains more natural flavoring than in the products of competitors. The seller can raise the price of this product without reducing sales to zero because enough consumers in the market view the product as unique enough to be willing to pay a price higher than that currently charged for the products of competitive sellers. Naturally, sales of the product will decline when its price is raised, but they will not decline to zero, as would be the case if the product were a perfect substitute for the products of competing sellers. (By the same token, sales of the product will increase when its price is lowered.) The reduction in sales that results from a price increase of any product will depend on the price elasticity of demand for the product.

Demand and marginal revenue also depend on the prices set by competing soft-drink firms. If competing firms reduced their prices, this firm would sell less at any given price. The reverse would be true if competing firms raised their prices.

The following analysis concentrates on the price decision of a single firm. The prices of other firms are beyond this firm's control or influence. Remember that a monopolistically competitive firm does not consider its rivals' reactions when setting prices or sales targets.

The short-run equilibrium of the firm is illustrated in Figure 12–1. The profit-maximizing output is 2,000 liters per month. This output corresponds to the point at which MR = MC. To sell this output, the firm sets a price of $3 per liter. At that price the quantity demanded, corresponding to point *A* on the demand curve, is the profit-maximizing quantity of 2,000 liters each month.

At a price of $3 per liter the firm earns a profit per liter corresponding to the distance *AB*. Average cost of the 2,000-liter monthly output is $2. Profit per liter is therefore $1. Total monthly profit, represented by the shaded area in the graph, is $2,000. This means that firms in the industry can earn more than a normal profit. Owners of the firm therefore earn more on their owner-supplied inputs than they can in the next most profitable use of these resources.

Long-Run Equilibrium under Monopolistic Competition

In the long run, each firm producing the product in a monopolistically competitive market can expand by building new or larger facilities. New firms can enter in the long run. In the short run, the firm in the above example is able to earn economic

FIGURE 12–1 Short-Run Equilibrium of the Firm under Monopolistic Competition

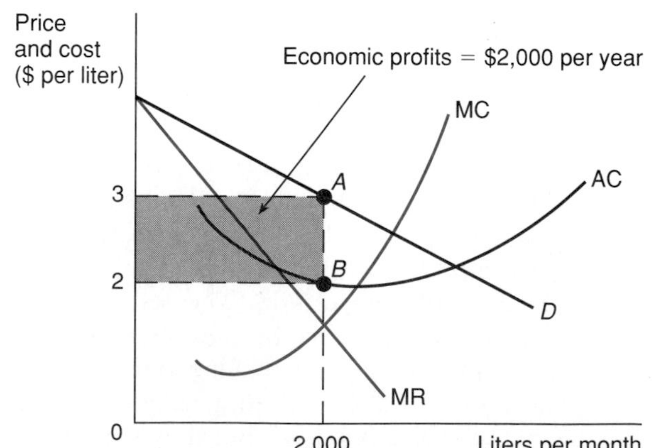

The firm produces the output corresponding to the point at which MR = MC. The profit-maximizing price is $3 per liter, which corresponds to an output of 2,000 liters per month. This allows the firm to earn economic profits equal to the shaded area. These profits will disappear in the long run because free entry exists under monopolistic competition.

profits. Those profits will attract new sellers. The firm itself will expand by estimating future marginal revenue and building the plants for which anticipated MR = LRMC. Firms that are able to produce a soft drink with the characteristics of the successful product will copy it and market it under their own brand name.

This process of innovation and imitation goes on all the time in monopolistically competitive markets. For example, Crest introduced a new tartar control toothpaste in 1985, and other companies introduced similar products soon after it became clear that Crest's new product was profitable. After Federal Express demonstrated that profit could be made by providing guaranteed overnight delivery service, other firms, such as Purolator Courier, Airborne, and UPS, entered the market with a similar service.

Soft-drink companies innovate and imitate each other on a regular basis. When one company introduces a new caffeine-free drink, you can be sure that its rivals will soon do the same if they can earn economic profits by doing so. As the number of firms producing the new drink increases and the supply of similar products becomes more abundant, the price per liter that any individual seller can charge for a given quantity declines. The firm that introduced the product will find that the demand and marginal revenue curves for the product will shift downward. This means that the price and marginal revenue the firm can expect for any given quantity that it makes available will fall in the long run because of the increased supply of the product. It is also likely that the demand for the product of any particular firm will tend to become more elastic at a given price. This is because an increase in the number of rival firms selling the product increases the substitutes available for any one firm's product. Firms continue to enter in the long run until it is no longer possible to earn economic profits from the product. This means that the price of the product produced by any monopolistically competitive firm must decline enough so that no seller in the market can earn economic profits. The long-run monopolistically competitive equilibrium is therefore similar to the long-run competitive equilibrium in that no firm earns more than normal profits.

Figure 12–2 illustrates the long-run equilibrium that can be expected for a firm under monopolistic competition. Whenever a firm earns economic profits, new firms will enter, thereby decreasing demand and marginal revenue for the firm's product. It follows that an industry cannot be in equilibrium as long as firms in the industry can charge more than the average cost of production for the profit-maximizing output. In Figure 12–2 demand for a typical firm's product has declined enough so that the price the firm must set to sell the output corresponding to the point at which MR = LRMC is equal to the average cost of that output. In long-run equilibrium the demand curve for the product of each firm in the industry is just tangent to the firm's long-run average cost curve. In Figure 12–2 the firm produces 3,000 liters per month of its product after it has expanded to take advantage of lower average costs in the long run each month. This is the output for which MR = LRMC after demand for the output has adjusted due to the entry of rival firms in the market. But the price it must set to sell that output each month is only $1.50 per liter, corresponding to point A^* on the demand curve. At that output average cost is also equal to $1.50 per liter and profit per unit is therefore zero, as is total profit. Free entry prevents firms from earning economic profits in the long run.

FIGURE 12–2 Long-Run Equilibrium of the Firm under Monopolistic Competition

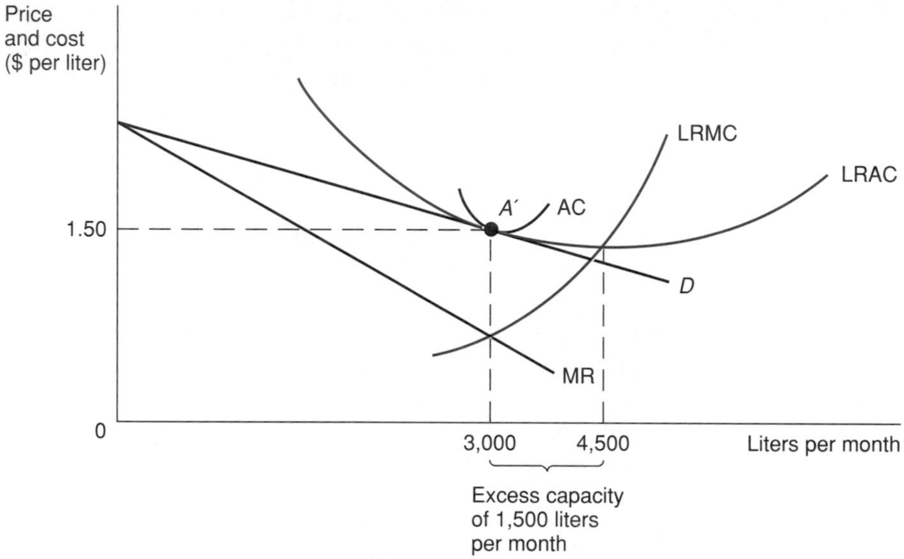

As firms enter the industry, the demand for the product of any one firm declines. In equilibrium, at the profit-maximizing output, price is equal to LRAC and economic profits are zero. The firm's capacity to produce an additional 1,500 liters per month is not utilized, and thus is excess capacity, and the price of $1.50 per liter exceeds LRACmin.

The process works in reverse as well. If the demand for the product in a monopolistically competitive market were to decline after an equilibrium had been attained, firms would exit. This is because the reduction in demand would make it impossible for firms to cover their economic costs. As shown in Figure 12–3, at the output Q_1, for which MR = LRMC after demand has decreased, a typical seller finds that P_1, the price it must set to sell that output, is less than AC_1, the average cost of producing it. Because some firms cannot cover their economic costs under these circumstances, they will leave the industry and reallocate their resources to more profitable enterprises. As this occurs, the demand and marginal revenue curves of the remaining firms shift upward. This is because the reduced availability of the product increases the maximum prices and marginal revenue that remaining firms can obtain. The exit of firms will continue until a new equilibrium has been attained at which the demand curve is again tangent to the LRAC curve and firms earn zero economic profits.

An exit process such as the one described here can also result if firms overestimate the marginal revenue obtainable from selling in the market. Overentry could make the product so abundant that firms in the market cannot cover their average costs at the output for which actual marginal revenue equals marginal cost.

FIGURE 12–3 A Monopolistically Competitive Firm Incurring Losses

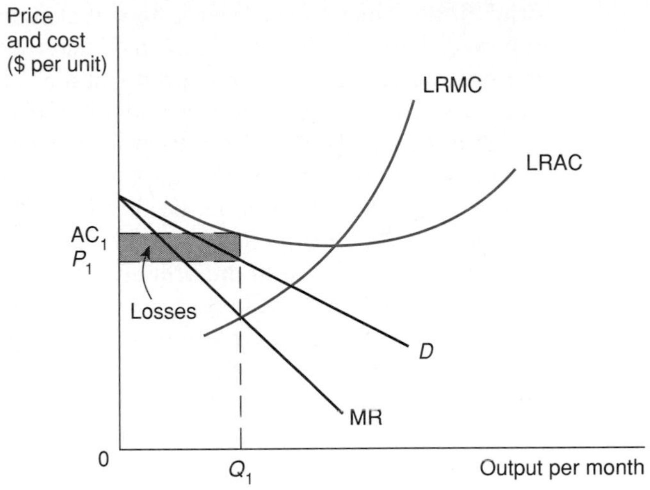

The firm whose cost and demand curves are illustrated would incur losses at the output for which LRMC = MR. The owners of this firm will reallocate their resources to alternative uses by leaving the industry.

If the demand for personal computers declines, as it did in the mid-1980s, some firms will be unable to sell the profit-maximizing quantity at a price that allows them economic profits. As a consequence firms will leave the personal computer industry and the demand for the personal computers of remaining firms will increase. This cycle of entry and exit in response to shifts in demand and profitability is a regular occurance over time in monopolistically competitive markets. A combination of a decrease in demand and overentry of new sellers contributed to such a reequilibration of the personal computer industry in the mid-1980s.

Comparison with the Benchmark Competitive Equilibrium

Consumers pay higher prices when products are differentiated than they would pay for standardized products produced by competitive firms. This conclusion holds even if the long-run average cost curve for a typical monopolistically competitive firm is exactly the same as the one that a typical firm would face under perfect competition. Price increments will prevail when costs are incurred to differentiate a product.

Under perfect competition, economic profits fall to zero for any individual firm when P = LRACmin. Under a competitive equilibrium, therefore, P = LRMC = LRACmin for each firm and consumers get the product at the lowest price possible. Prices simultaneously reflect the opportunity cost of the last unit of output produced and the average cost of producing that output.

Under monopolistic competition, economic profits decline to zero before prices reach a level that just allows firms to cover their marginal costs. The soft-drink firm in the above example finds that economic profits fall to zero in the long run before prices fall to the level that just covers its marginal cost. In Figure 12–2 the firm earns zero economic profits at a price of $1.50 per liter even though the marginal cost of its output is considerably below $1.50. At the level of output for which price equals average cost, price exceeds marginal cost. The reason for this discrepancy between average cost and marginal cost is the control of price afforded by product differentiation. Product differentiation causes demand to slope downward. This results in marginal revenue that falls short of price for any level of output. In equilibrium the firm always adjusts price until MR = MC. Because price always exceeds MR, it also exceeds MC in equilibrium.

As long as a product is differentiated among firms, it is impossible for average costs of production to reach their minimum possible level in long-run equilibrium. Elimination of economic profits requires that the demand curve be tangent to the average cost curve. This can occur only at the level of output corresponding to LRACmin if the demand curve is a horizontal line, as it is under perfect competition. Monopolistically competitive firms do not achieve all of the possible reductions in average cost in the long run. The plant size they choose in the long run is smaller than that of a competitive firm producing a standardized version of the product.

As shown in Figure 12–2, 3,000 liters of soft drinks are sold per year by the typical monopolistically competitive firm in equilibrium. However, LRACmin occurs at a monthly output of 4,500 liters. The difference between the output corresponding to LRACmin and that produced by the monopolistically competitive firm in the long run is called **excess capacity.** In Figure 12–2 there is excess capacity to produce 1,500 liters per month that the firm does not utilize in long-run equilibrium. The firm operates out of a plant whose short-run average cost curve, AC, is not the one for which LRACmin can be achieved.

Excess capacity The difference between the output corresponding to LRACmin and that produced by a monopolistically competitive firm in the long run.

The monopolistically competitive equilibrium is like the pure monopoly equilibrium in that price exceeds the marginal costs of production. Under pure monopoly, however, price can also exceed average costs in the long run because of barriers to the entry of new sellers. Under monopolistic competition entry prevents economic profits from lasting. Profits attract new firms and keep prices below the levels that would prevail if the market were supplied by a single seller. The prices for a product supplied by monopolistically competitive firms are lower than the prices that would prevail if one monopoly firm supplied it. However, those prices exceed the prices that would prevail if competitive firms supplied a standardized product.

Implications of Excess Capacity under Monopolistic Competition

Excess capacity in a monopolistically competitive industry means that the same output could be made available to consumers at lower average cost. The same output could be produced if fewer firms in the industry each produced more output at the minimum possible average cost. This means that fewer resources could produce the same output. However, an equilibrium at minimum possible average cost is possible only if the product is standardized. Standardization, a hallmark of perfect competition, implies that the demand curve for a firm is perfectly elastic, so that in long-run equilibrium each firm earns zero economic profits at the output corresponding to LRACmin. It follows that product differentiation, which implies downward-sloping demand curves for the output of individual firms, is incompatible with economizing on resource use. The real issue here is how much consumers are willing to pay for product variety. Excess capacity is a part of the cost of product differentiation under monopolistic competition.[3]

You would expect excess capacity to be more costly for consumers in markets in which a few competitors are in long-run equilibrium than in markets in which many competitors are in long-run equilibrium. The reason for this is the fewer the number of competitors, the greater is the monopoly power of each competitor. This means that the price and marginal revenue associated with any quantity for individual firms are higher in markets with a few sellers in equilibrium than in markets with many sellers in equilibrium. Thus, prices are likely to be higher in markets with fewer competitors in equilibrium. The higher the price in equilibrium, other things being equal, the greater is the excess capacity.

CONCEPT REVIEW

1. What are the distinguishing features of monopolistic competition?
2. Explain why economic profits are zero even though in long-run equilibrium prices exceed marginal cost in a monopolistically competitive market.
3. Why do firms in monopolistically competitive markets produce a level of output that falls short of the level corresponding to LRACmin? What are the consequences of excess capacity?

ADVERTISING AND PRODUCT DEVELOPMENT IN MONOPOLISTICALLY COMPETITIVE MARKETS

Costs of Nonprice Competition

In addition to incurring costs associated with excess capacity, firms in monopolistically competitive markets incur costs in seeking to convince consumers that their products differ from those of rival sellers. Monopolistically competitive markets are characterized by brand names and by continual product development and improvement. For example, many Americans use the brand name Clorox as if it were synonymous with liquid bleach. Clorox's long-standing image allows its

[3] Whether this cost is worth paying for is an interesting normative question. For an analysis of excess capacity and productive variety, see Kelvin Lancaster, "Competition and Product Variety," *Journal of Business* 53, no. 3, part 2 (July 1980), pp. S79–S105.

producer to charge significantly higher prices for this brand than are charged for rival brands. In supermarkets famous brands for a variety of products are priced higher than brands that are not as well known. Many consumers have been convinced that the quality of certain brand-name products is superior to that of competing brands and generic products.

Firms in monopolistically competitive markets are more likely to compete by improving products or developing new products than by cutting prices to increase quantity sold. A product improvement by one firm can allow it to make temporary profits until its improvement has been copied by existing rivals or new entrants. Product improvements have often been criticized as being superficial rather than substantive. Nonetheless, firms do compete in this way and many consumers do respond to changes in the quality and characteristics of products. When a firm improves a product, it usually launches an advertising campaign to inform consumers of its inspired innovation!

Selling Costs

Selling costs The costs incurred by a firm to influence the sales of its product.

The advertising and selling of products is a costly process. **Selling costs** are all the costs a firm incurs to influence the sales of its product. Advertising and other promotional expenses and salaries for sales personnel are included in selling costs. Firms incur advertising and related selling expenses in the hope of increasing revenues beyond what they would otherwise be. In recent years annual advertising expense in the United States has been in the range of $100 billion. Certain firms allocate significant portions of their annual budgets to advertising. For example, in the mid-1980s McDonald's was spending over $250 million annually on advertising.

Advertising can affect the level of demand for a firm's product and the price elasticity of that demand. It can also affect the cross elasticity of demand for a product with respect to the price of the products of competing firms. Advertising can also increase the demand for the product of *all* sellers in a product group. For example, advertising by a leading manufacturer of personal computers could increase the market demand for personal computers, including the market demand for the personal computers that its competitors sell.

There is no incentive to incur selling costs in perfectly competitive markets. In such markets the output of any one firm is a perfect substitute for that of any competing firm. In addition, perfectly competitive markets imply that buyers are fully informed. Advertising is futile in these circumstances. It can neither tell buyers something they do not already know nor differentiate the products of sellers. Firms engage in advertising and other promotional activities when these can be used to point out unique aspects of differentiated products and when information is not freely available to buyers.

When firms increase the demand for their products through advertising, their sales increase could come from a decrease in the sales of competing firms. Advertising by competing firms makes consumers aware of alternatives to their traditional sources of supply. This can increase the price elasticity of demand for the product of a given firm when all firms advertise.

Selling Cost Curves and Profit-Maximizing Advertising

There are heavy fixed costs associated with advertising and other promotional activities. A staff must be assembled to coordinate such efforts. A firm can use its own staff for that purpose or contract out this work to a specialized agency. Selling costs are discretionary. This means that they are not necessary for the production of a firm's product. When a firm advertises, it forgoes the opportunity to sell more by keeping costs and therefore prices lower. Advertising is an attempt to sell more at any given price. It is possible that a price reduction could achieve the same sales increase.

As more of a product is sold, average selling costs (selling costs per unit of output) are likely to decline at first and then to increase. Average fixed costs associated with advertising decline with an increase in sales as overhead selling costs are spread over more units. Selling costs per unit of output also decline when more advertising is undertaken if the unit price of a message declines with an increase in the number of messages. It is also possible that greater total expenditure on advertising, which means more messages to consumers, results in proportionately more incremental sales. Repeating messages in various media may increase the impact of advertising. One study of cigarette advertising found decreasing average selling costs for cigarettes up to between 20 and 30 billion cigarettes per year.[4]

An average selling costs (AC_S) curve can show how selling costs per unit vary for a given level of anticipated demand. The stronger the demand for a product, the lower are the average selling costs associated with the marketing of a given quantity of the product. Changes in the demand for a product can therefore shift the selling costs curve. For example, if that demand were stronger, meaning that buyers would purchase more of the product at any given price, the average costs of selling a given output at any price would be lower. It must also be assumed that the amount of advertising by competing firms is given. If competing firms advertise more, the average selling costs of the typical firm will increase. A change in any other influence on the demand for a firm's product will shift its average selling costs curve up or down.

The U-shaped average selling costs curve of a firm is shown in Figure 12–4. This curve gives the selling cost per unit sold, given the demand for the firm's product and the amount of advertising by rival firms. A decrease in demand shifts the average selling costs curve up, as does an increase in the advertising expenditure of competing firms. This means that the stronger the demand for a product and the lower the selling costs incurred by competing firms, the lower are the average selling costs associated with a given output of the product.

If successful, advertising increases the demand for a firm's product. Figure 12–5 shows how beginning to advertise can increase the profits of a monopolistically competitive firm. Assume that initially the monopolistically competitive market is in equilibrium with no advertising by any of the firms in the market. The

---

[4] Randall S. Brown, "Estimating Advantages to Large-Scale Advertising," *Review of Economics and Statistics* 60 (August 1978), pp. 428–37.

FIGURE 12–4 Average Selling Costs

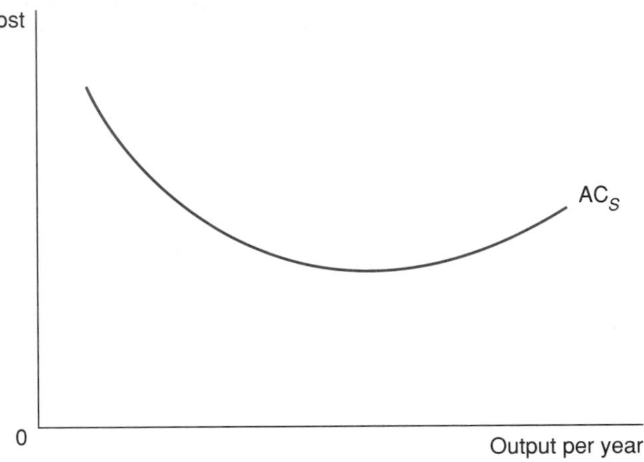

Selling costs per unit of output per year can be represented by a U-shaped curve. This curve assumes that demand for the product is fixed. The amount of advertising undertaken by this firm is independent of the amount undertaken by competing firms.

price of the product for a firm contemplating an advertising campaign is P^*, and the firm's output is Q^*. At that price $P^* = \text{AC}$, where AC is average cost of production, so the firm earns zero economic profits.

Average costs at any output after the firm has incurred advertising costs are $\text{AC} + \text{AC}_S$. Similarly, the total marginal cost of any output is now $\text{MC} + \text{MC}_S$, the sum of marginal production cost and marginal selling cost (MC_S). These cost curves have been drawn under the presumption that the firm anticipates a certain increase in demand as a result of its advertising. If the advertising is successful, the demand and marginal revenue curves for the firm's product will shift upward in response. The profit-maximizing output is now the one for which

$$\text{MR}_2 = \text{MC} + \text{MC}_S$$

In Figure 12–5 the profit-maximizing output is Q_A, assuming that demand increases after the firm's advertising campaign has been inaugurated. To sell this quantity, the firm raises its price from P^* to P_A, corresponding to point D on the demand curve D_2. The firm's advertising therefore allows it to charge a higher price for the now increased profit-maximizing output. If it were to charge the price P_A without any advertising, quantity demanded would fall to zero because P_A exceeds the maximum price that would be paid for one unit on the demand curve D_1.

The variable inputs that the firm devotes to advertising depend in part on how much demand increases after the firm's advertising campaign has begun. Total advertising costs when output is Q_A are the selling cost per unit, represented by

FIGURE 12–5 Selling Costs, Sales, and Profits

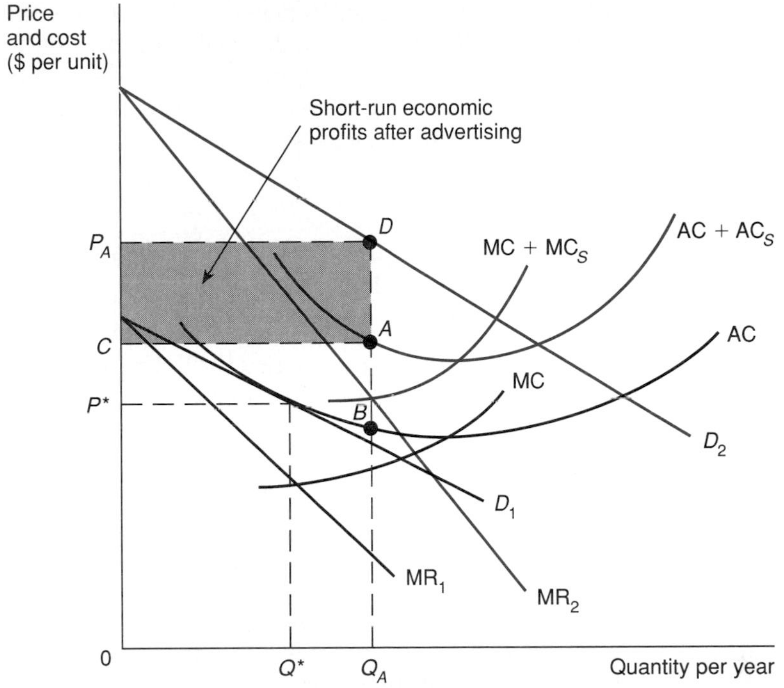

By incurring selling costs, a firm successfully shifts its demand curve from D_1 to D_2. The profit-maximizing output is the one for which MR_2 equals the marginal cost of production plus the marginal cost of selling. In the absence of any advertising the firm earns zero economic profits. The advertising campaign of the firm allows it to earn short-run economic profits.

the distance AB, multiplied by Q_A, the number of units sold per year. For the firm whose demand and cost curves have been drawn in Figure 12–5, the advertising campaign has been successful because its profits have increased from zero to the amount represented by the area P_ADAC.

After advertising has increased demand, the firm may choose to cut back on its selling costs if it thinks that the increased demand would not be lost thereby. By doing so, the firm can reduce the marginal and average costs of any given output, thus enjoying the opportunity to make still more profit. It would reduce these costs by expanding production until MR_2 falls to equal the marginal production cost.

It is difficult to precisely model a firm's behavior with regard to advertising because the decision to incur selling costs is likely to increase demand. As demand increases, the firm is tempted to increase profits further by decreasing selling costs. Decreasing selling costs may not decrease demand once consumers have been ''hooked on'' the firm's product as a result of its successful advertising.

Remember that advertising implies that a firm can increase demand and marginal revenue by incurring more selling costs. Whenever a firm incurs advertising costs, an increase in the demand for the firm's product results if the advertising is successful. If the increased demand is permanent, the advertising costs necessary to sell any given quantity decrease, and this induces the firm to cut back on advertising. The interdependence between marginal revenue and marginal cost when advertising is successful makes it impossible to predict the equilibrium level of advertising.

Long-Run Equilibrium with Advertising under Monopolistic Competition

Advertising that results in economic profits for a monopolistically competitive industry sets up a process that will eliminate those profits. Because free entry prevails under monopolistic competition, any advertising or other promotional scheme that results in economic profits can be expected to attract new sellers to the market. These sellers will produce a product similar to that of a firm earning economic profits. They will imitate the successful firm's marketing program so as to gain sales. For example, suppose that one store selling lamps places a slick advertisement in the local papers advertising an attractive stand-up lamp for $79.95. If the store makes a profit selling this lamp, other stores will carry it and will advertise it in the same way. The first store will find that it now has to advertise more often to sell the same number of lamps at the same price. As a result its selling costs curve will shift upward.

In Figure 12–5 a firm earns economic profits equal to the area P_ADAC as a result of its advertising. As new firms enter in the long run, the average selling costs curve will shift upward because of the increased advertising by competitors. This means the average selling costs associated with any given quantity of the product will be higher. When there are more rival sellers in the market, firms will have to send out more sales personnel and advertise more often to sell a given quantity of the product. In addition, as more firms enter the market of the firm that earns economic profits, the demand and marginal revenue curves for its product will shift downward. The combined effect of increased selling costs associated with any given output and decreased demand for the firm's product as new sellers enter the market will eliminate the firm's economic profits in the long run. However, insofar as advertising has increased demand for all of the sellers in the monopolistically competitive market and has encouraged entry into the market, the total quantity consumed increases.

Figure 12–6 shows the long-run equilibrium with advertising. The demand curve for each firm in equilibrium must be tangent to the AC + AC_S curve at Q_L, the profit-maximizing output. At P_L, the price necessary to sell this output, the firm earns zero economic profits. The equilibrium output Q_L is greater than Q^*, the output that would prevail in the absence of advertising. As a result of successful advertising each monopolistically competitive firm produces more than it would otherwise. This reduces the excess capacity in the industry and contributes to lower average *production* costs as firms increase plant size to achieve the

FIGURE 12–6 Long-Run Equilibrium, Profits, and Selling Costs

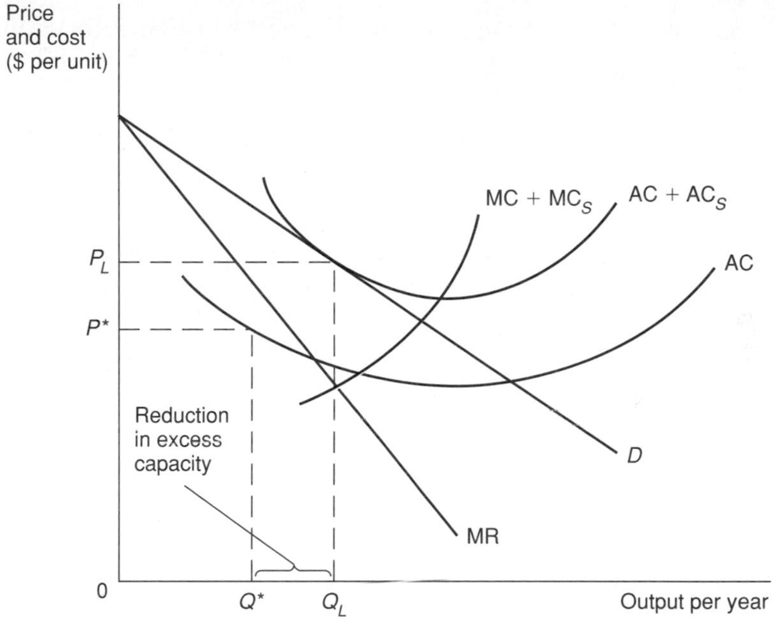

The economic profits that a firm earns by conducting a successful marketing campaign attract new firms into the industry. New firms and existing firms copy the marketing campaign, and average selling costs increase. At the same time the increased competition decreases the demand for the firm's product. Both these forces act to eliminate the profits possible from incurring selling costs in the long run. In equilibrium the profit-maximizing output is Q_L and the price set by the firm to sell that output is P_L. Because advertising has increased demand for all of the competing firms, excess capacity is lower than it would have been without advertising.

minimum possible average cost. However, consumers do not benefit because the price of the product does not fall to reflect the lower average costs of production. Instead, the average selling costs necessary to sell Q_L are reflected in P_L which is higher than P^*, the price that would have prevailed without advertising. Advertising increases demand, thus putting an upward pressure on quantity sold, but at the same time it increases average costs for the firm, thus putting an upward pressure on price.

Advertising diverts resources from the production of other goods. It is difficult to say whether consumers in the aggregate are better off as a result of advertising.[5] In a monopolistically competitive industry it is clear, however, that no firm gains from advertising in the long run. Economic profits are zero in the long-run

[5] For a discussion of the controversy, see William S. Comanor and Thomas A. Wilson, "The Effect of Advertising on Competition: A Survey," *Journal of Economic Literature* 17, no. 2 (June 1979), pp. 453–76.

Modern Microeconomics in Action: The Business World

Product Variety and Economizing on Information Costs

Many of you are suspicious of new brands or generic (unbranded) items because you don't have enough information on their quality or reliability. Supermarkets often carry generic products. Suppose these products are less expensive than the branded products. Information is rarely free. Many consumers therefore use brand names and other aspects of product differentiation as a way of assuring the reliability of the products they buy. In some cases consumers also presume that price differentials are associated with quality differentials.

Knowing that consumers are more likely to pay higher prices for products they trust, firms invest resources in advertising, showrooms, and other expenditures designed to signal the superior quality of their products. This means that product differentiation and branding can serve a useful social purpose. They act as signals of quality. Consumers are willing to pay higher prices for the benefits of such signaling. This suggests that the higher prices and excess capacity resulting from monopolistic competition reflect the value of information. The price premiums are a way of assuring product reliability. They are used by consumers to reduce the transaction costs associated with purchasing products.

Standardization of many products is impossible. Perhaps the best example is the used car. Consumers may be willing to pay more for a used car if a dealer guarantees the car for a specified period. Similarly, consumers are often willing to pay a particular seller a price premium for the assurance of reliable service.

Firms invest in advertising and other image-creating activities to signal the quality of their products. After having established their reputation in this way, they could increase their profits by lowering the quality of their products, which would lower their production costs. When consumers learn that this has been done, however, they are likely to boycott the products of such firms, which would cause those firms to lose their reputation and the value associated with the goodwill they have built up over the years. Knowledge of these consequences provides firms with incentives to perform reliably.*

Franchising chains attempt to signal quality in this way. Although the thousands of franchised fast-food restaurants are independently owned, consumers know exactly what standard of cleanliness and food quality they can expect at each of these restaurants because the franchise controls those standards. If you do not get a stomachache from eating at the local Burger King, you can be pretty sure that you will not get one if you eat at a Burger King 500 miles from home. Controlling quality assures repeat business and maintains the value of franchises. The franchisor inspects the establishments of its franchisees regularly. It is prepared to revoke franchises if quality is not upheld. If it were not prepared to do so, it would be unable to maintain the market price of its franchises. Product variety confers monopoly power on certain sellers. However, the higher prices they charge can be viewed as necessary to offset the benefits of signaling.

* See Benjamin Klein and Keith B. Leffler, "The Role of Market Forces in Assuring Contractural Performance," *Journal of Political Economy* 89, no. 4 (August 1981), pp. 615–41.

equilibrium both with and without advertising. Advertising can, however, serve a useful social purpose by providing consumers with information and reducing the transaction costs of buying.

If advertising results in brand loyalty, it gives sellers more power to raise prices without losing sales to competitors. For example, as has been noted, in supermarkets a variety of well-known brands are priced higher than competing brands that are not as well known. Many consumers believe that certain brand-name products are superior to competing brands and generic products. An example is Bayer aspirin, which sells for a significant premium over generic aspirin. Some consumers argue that Bayer's quality is superior to that of its competitors. It does, however, have the same aspirin content of lower-priced alternatives.

Some studies find a positive association between advertising and profits. This finding is interpreted to mean that advertising increases monopoly power.[6] However, others argue that advertising provides information that tends to *decrease* consumer loyalty to particular brands. This implies that advertising increases the price elasticity of demand for any individual firm's products because it makes people aware of alternatives of which they would otherwise be ignorant.[7] One study provided evidence that advertising actually decreased the price of some goods. A study of eyeglass prices concluded that they were more than twice as high in states in which the advertising of eyeglasses was not permitted than in states in which such advertising was permitted.[8]

Oligopoly

Oligopoly A market structure in which a few interdependent sellers dominate the sale of a product and into which the entry of new sellers is difficult or impossible.

Oligopoly is a market struture in which a few interdependent sellers dominate the sale of a product and into which the entry of new sellers is difficult or impossible. The product sold by oligopolistic firms can be either differentiated or standardized. The market for aluminum offers an example of an oligopoly whose product is standardized. In that market, U.S. sales are dominated by Alcoa, Reynolds, and Kaiser. Automobiles, cigarettes, and beer are examples of differentiated goods whose market structures are oligopolistic.[9]

Oligopolistic markets are typically dominated by from two to ten firms that account for half or more of the total sales of a product. The eight largest firms producing photographic equipment and supplies in the United States, for example, account for over 85 percent of the output. The market for these products is, of course, dominated by the Kodak Company. It is not, however, the single seller. The market for photographic equipment and supplies can therefore be regarded as oligopolistic.

Table 12–2 shows industries in which oligopolistic competition is likely to prevail. This table, like Table 12–1, includes only domestic shipments. Because the market share of foreign sellers is not included, the table overstates the market shares of the four largest and the eight largest firms.

---

[6] F. M. Scherer, *Industrial Market Structure and Economic Performance,* 2nd ed. (Boston: Houghton Mifflin, 1980), p. 381.

[7] Yale Brozen, "Is Advertising a Barrier to Entry?" in *Advertising and Society,* ed. Yale Brozen (New York: New York University Press, 1974), pp. 79–109.

[8] Lee Benham, "The Effect of Advertising on the Price of Eyeglasses," *Journal of Law and Economics* 15, no. 2 (October 1972), pp. 337–52.

[9] For detailed analysis of the market structure for such goods as beer, automobiles, steel, and computers, see Walter Adams, ed., *The Structure of American Industry,* 8th ed. (New York: Macmillan, 1990).

TABLE 12–2 Shipments by the Four Largest Firms and the Eight Largest Firms in Selected Oligopolistic Industries, 1982

		Annual Shipments (%)	
Industry	*Number of Sellers*	*Four Largest Firms*	*Eight Largest Firms*
Aluminum	15	64	88
Lead	5	99+	100
Steel	211	42	64
Automobiles and car bodies	28	92	97
Cereal breakfast foods	22	86	98
Flour	91	58	74
Pet food	222	52	71
Corn sugar	19	65	91
Chewing gum	9	95	99
Malt beverages (beer)	67	77	94
Roasted coffee	118	65	76
Cigars	54	60	82
Woven carpets and rugs	59	71	85
Soap and detergents	642	60	73
Tires	108	66	86
Plumbing fixtures	41	63	85

Source: U.S. Department of Commerce, Bureau of the Census, *1982 Census of Manufacturers, Concentration Ratios in Manufacturing*.

In oligopolistic markets at least some firms can influence price by virtue of their large shares of total output produced. Each of the firms in an oligopolistic market knows that when it changes price or output, the profits of all firms in the market will be affected. Each firm is aware of its interdependence with its rivals. Each is presumed to recognize that a change in its price or output will cause a reaction by competing firms. Individual sellers in oligopolistic markets *must* consider the reactions of their competitors. The response to a change in price, output, or marketing efforts that a firm expects from rival firms is a crucial determinant of its choices. The responses that individual firms expect from their rivals influence equilibrium in oligopolistic markets.

The behavior of firms in oligopolistic markets may be likened to that of armies at war. The firms are rivals; the booty is profit; and the weapons and strategies chosen include control of prices, advertising, and output. The fewness of their firms compels them to consider their opponents' reactions to their decisions.

Natural oligopoly A situation that exists when a few firms can supply the entire market output at lower long-run average costs than can many firms.

In many cases oligopolies are protected by barriers to entry similar to those discussed for monopoly firms. **Natural oligopoly** exists when the entire market output can be supplied at lower long-run average costs by a few firms than by many firms. Whether natural oligopolies exist has been a subject of controversy among economists. Industries in which natural oligopoly has been asserted to exist include petroleum refining, steel, and beer.[10]

[10] For discussions of petroleum refining and steel, see Walter S. Measday, "The Petroleum Industry," and Walter Adams and Hans Mueller, "The Steel Industry," in Adams, ed., *Structure of American Industry*. For analysis of the beer industry, see William J. Lynk, "Interpreting Rising Concentration:

In summary, an oligopolistic market has the following characteristics:

1. *Only a few firms supply the entire market.* The product these firms supply might be standardized or differentiated.
2. *At least some of the firms in the market have large market shares.* Some firms in an oligopolistic market therefore are capable of influencing the price of their product by varying its availability in the market.
3. *The firms in the market are aware of their mutual interdependence.* The firms in an oligopolistic market always consider the reactions of their rivals when choosing prices, sales targets, advertising budgets, and other business policies.

Based on the assumptions that oligopolistic firms make about the reactions of their rivals, a number of models can be developed to explain the behavior of firms in specific situations. The models presented below are designed to show you that profits tend to fall because of oligopolistic rivalry. The ruinous effects of oligopolistic rivalry on profits provide oligopolistic firms with an incentive to collude in ways that reduce competition and increase profits. In this chapter we discuss some simple models of oligopolistic rivalry and collusion. In the following chapter we examine more sophisticated models.

Conscious Rivalry: Oligopolistic Price Wars

Suppose that only a handful of firms in a local market sell a standardized product such as bricks. The pricing policy of each of these firms depends on the market demand for bricks and on how each firm thinks its rivals will react to that policy. Suppose each firm in the market seeks to maximize profit. Also suppose each firm presumes that its rivals will choose a price and stick to its decision. This implies that any given firm will presume that if it cuts its prices, its rivals will *not* cut their prices in response.

Figure 12–7 shows the market demand for bricks. For simplicity, assume that only two brick sellers are in the market and that a third brick seller will be unable to enter the market. Also assume that each of the two brick sellers in the market can produce bricks at a constant average cost of 10 cents. Currently, each of these sellers charges 20 cents per brick and both sellers are therefore earning a profit of 10 cents per brick. At 20 cents per brick quantity demanded is 100,000 bricks per month and the two sellers, the Adams Brick Company and the Baker Brick Company, each sell 50,000 bricks per month. Initially, therefore, both sellers share the market equally and earn economic profits.

Price war A bout of continual price-cutting by rival firms in an oligopolistic market.

A **price war** is a bout of continual price-cutting by rival firms in an oligopolistic market. It is one of *many* possible consequences of oligopolistic rivalry. Price wars are great for buyers but bad for the profits of sellers.

The Case of Beer," *Journal of Business* 57, no. 1 (January 1984), pp. 43–55; and Victor J. Tremblay, "Scale Economies, Technological Changes, and Firm Cost Asymmetries in the U.S. Brewing Industry," *Quarterly Review of Economics and Business* 27, no. 2 (Summer 1987), pp 71–86.

FIGURE 12–7 Impact of an Oligopolistic Price War

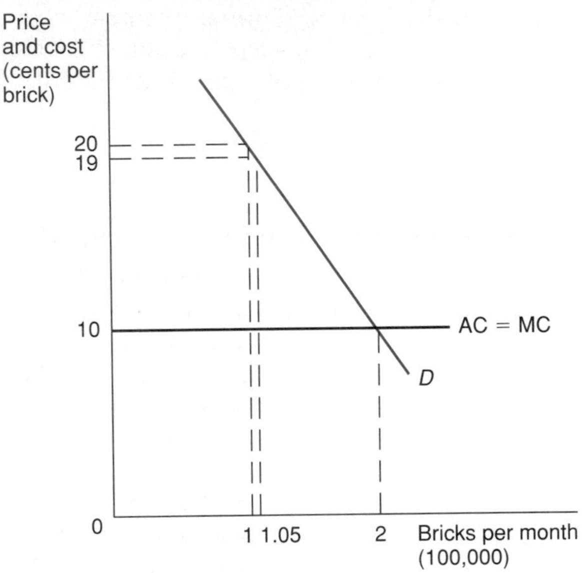

In a price war firms continually undercut each other's price until no further gain is possible from doing so. This results in an output for which $P = AC = MC$. Here the price war increases the equilibrium output from 100,000 bricks per month to 200,000 bricks per month.

It is easy to see how the two brick sellers in this example can become embroiled in a price war. Because each seller thinks the other will not react to its price cuts, there is a temptation for each of them to increase its monthly sales by cutting price. Each seller thinks that it can gain the entire market by cutting its price below that of its competitor and that it can increase its profit by doing so. For example, at the current price Baker sells 50,000 bricks per month and earns 10 cents profit per brick. It therefore earns a monthly profit of $5,000. If Baker were to lower its price per brick to 19 cents, market quantity demanded would increase to 105,000. Assuming, as Baker does, that Adams would keep its price at 20 cents, Baker could then sell 105,000 bricks per month because consumers would now buy all of this standardized product from it. Because the profit per brick would now be 9 cents Baker's profit would increase to $9,400 per month, assuming that Adams reacts as it anticipates.

Suppose that Baker yields to the temptation to cut price. Adams, enraged, reacts by setting its price a bit below Baker's price and thus gains the entire market. Adams, like Baker, assumes that its rival will not react. But Baker does react by cutting its price again.

The price war goes on until price falls to average costs. In equilibrium both firms then charge the same price: $P = AC = MC$. The total market output is the same as the output that would have been produced under perfect competition. Assuming that the other firm will always maintain its current price, a firm can always increase its profits by charging one penny less per brick than is charged by the other firm. Of course, the other firm does not maintain its current price because it realizes that it can make more profits by charging a penny less than its rival's newly announced price.

Equilibrium occurs when neither firm can benefit further from a price cut. It occurs at the level at which price is equal to average costs and economic profits are zero. Lowering price below this level will result in losses. Because each firm assumes that the other firm will not change price, there is no incentive to increase price. Doing so would result in a loss of all sales to the other firm, which is presumed to keep its price fixed at P = AC.[11] In general, equilibrium in an oligopolistic market depends on the conjectures firms make about the reactions of their rivals.

Price wars are sometimes observed in oligopolistic markets. Occasionally gas stations in a given locality engage in them. Banks serving a small market area sometimes engage in price wars by offering low-interest loans or low-cost checking accounts. Each bank attempts to make its product more attractive to consumers by charging a little less than is charged by its rival. Of course, its rival reacts by cutting the price still further.

Unfortunately for consumers, price wars are usually short-lived. Oligopolistic firms are tempted to cooperate to set prices and divide up markets so as to avoid price wars and their unfavorable effects on profits.

Collusion and Cartels

Cartel A group of firms acting together to coordinate output decisions to control price.

A **cartel** is a group of firms acting together to coordinate output decisions to control price as if they were a single monopoly. Cartels are illegal in the United States. Firms convicted of colluding to fix price and control output are subject to penalties.

There are many famous international cartels. Probably the most well known is the Organization of Petroleum Exporting Countries (OPEC). This cartel seeks to regulate its members' output of crude oil with the goal of controlling price to maximize their profits. The Central Selling Organization of the De Beers company, discussed in Chapter 11, functions as a cartel by acting as a syndicate through which major producers of uncut diamonds (of which there are only a few) can sell their products.

A cartel is a group of firms rather than a single firm. In establishing monopoly prices, it faces difficulties that do not exist for a pure monopoly. Its basic problems are coordinating decisions among its member firms and establishing a system of restrictions for those firms.

Formation of a Cartel

Suppose several producers of cement in a given region wish to form a cartel. Assume that 15 firms produce cement in the region and that the product is standardized. Buyers of cement see no differences in the output of any of the 15 firms.

[11] This is the Bertrand equilibrium, a model that was formulated by the French mathematician Joseph Bertrand.

Currently, each firm is charging a price equal to its average costs. Each firm is afraid to raise its price for fear that the other firms will not follow suit and that its economic profits will therefore become negative. Assume that for this reason output is at the competitive level and that each firm produces 1/15 of the output corresponding to Q_c in Figure 12–8(a). Point *E* corresponds to the output at which the demand curve intersects the MC curve, which is the lateral summation of the marginal cost curves of each of the producers. The MC curve would be the supply curve if the market were perfectly competitive.

Here are the four steps the cement producers must take to form a cartel:

Step 1: Make sure that a barrier to entry prevents other firms from selling cement after its price has been increased. If free entry were possible, an increase in the price of cement would attract new producers. The supply of cement would increase, and the price of cement would fall below the monopoly level that the cartel seeks to maintain.

Step 2: Organize a meeting of all cement producers to establish a target level of output. To establish this target level, estimate market demand and calculate marginal revenue at all output levels. Choose the output for which

FIGURE 12–8 Cartel Pricing and Quotas

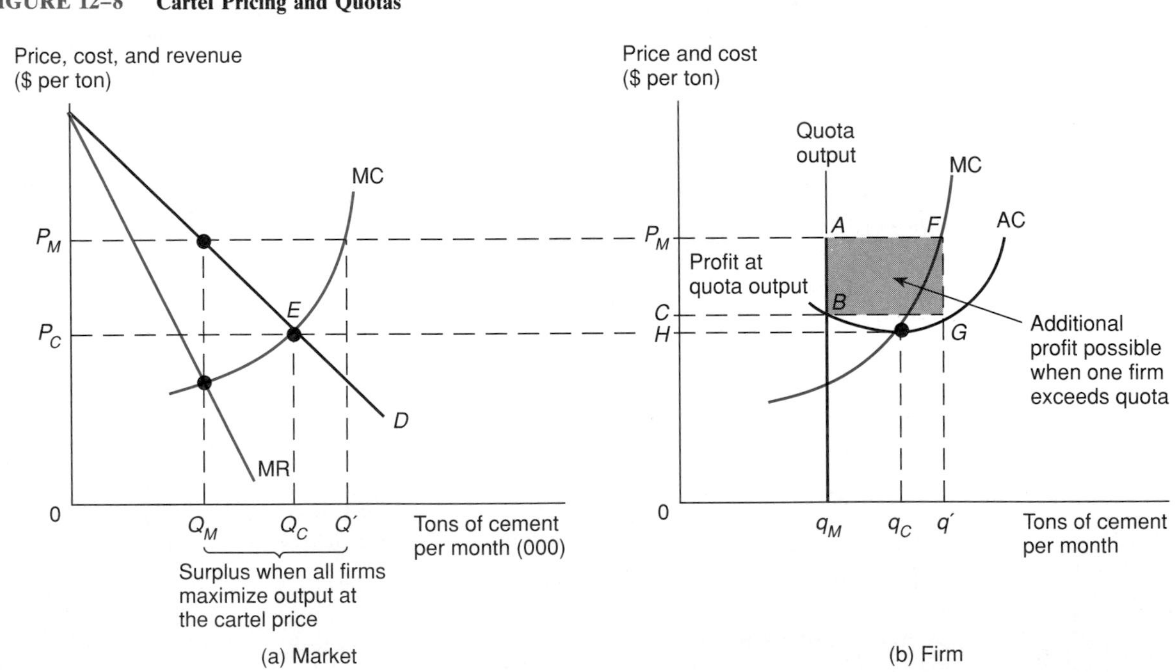

The initial equilibrium is at point *E* in graph (a) The competitive price is P_C. At that price each firm earns normal profits. At P_M, the cartel price, each firm can earn maximum profits by setting P_M = MC. If all of the firms do this, there will be a surplus of cement equal to Q_MQ' tons per month and price will fall to P_C. To maintain the cartel price, each firm must produce no more than q_M, the quota amount.

MR = MC. It is assumed that all cement producers have the same cost functions. The monopoly output will maximize the group profits of all 15 producers. This is illustrated in Figure 12–8(a). The demand curve for cement in the region is *D*. The marginal revenue corresponding to that curve is MR. The monopoly output is Q_M, which corresponds to the intersection of MR and MC. The monopoly price is P_M. The current price is P_C, and the current level of output is Q_C. The current equilibrium is the same as a competitive equilibrium.

Step 3: Set up quotas for each member of the cartel. Divide up Q_M, the total monopoly output, among the firms. For example, each firm could be instructed to deliver 1/15 of Q_M each month. If all the firms have the same cost functions, this would be equivalent to telling the firms to adjust their production until their marginal costs equal their marginal revenue. As long as the sum of the monthly output of all the firms equals Q_M, the monopoly price can be maintained.

Step 4: Establish procedures for enforcing the assigned quotas. This crucial step is difficult to enforce because the cartel price gives each firm an incentive to expand its output. If all the firms expand output, the cartel is doomed because price will then return to its competitive level. This can easily be demonstrated. Figure 12–8(b) shows the marginal and average costs of a typical cement producer. Before implementation of the cartel agreement, this firm behaves as if the demand for its output were infinitely elastic at P_C. It is afraid to raise its price for fear of losing all of its sales to its competitors. It produces output q_C. Because all of its competitors do the same, industry output is Q_C which is the output that would prevail under perfect competition.

At the newly established cartel price, the firm is allocated an output of q_M tons of cement per month, which corresponds to the point at which MR* equals each individual firm's MC. Assume that the firm's owners believe that they will not decrease market price by selling more than that amount. If they take P_M as beyond their influence, their profit-maximizing output will be q', at which P_M = MC. Assuming the market price does not fall, the firm can increase its profits from P_MABC to P_MFGC by exceeding its quota.

One firm may be able to get away with exceeding its quota without reducing market price appreciably. Suppose, however, that all cement producers exceed their quota to maximize profits at the cartel price, P_M. Industry output would increase to Q', where P_M = MC in Figure 12–8(a). There would be a surplus of cement each month because quantity demanded would fall short of quantity supplied at that price. Price will therefore fall until the surplus has been eliminated. The equilibrium price would be P_C. The cement producers would be back where they started from. They would break even at that price.

A Cement Cartel in Action

A cartel arrangement among New York City cement-pouring firms was, in fact, alleged by the U.S. Justice Department to have existed between 1981 and 1985. The cartel was administered by organized crime. The cartel increased prices by deciding which cement-pouring firm would submit a winning bid for each job. It

MODERN MICROECONOMICS IN ACTION: INTERNATIONAL REPORT

The OPEC Cartel: Can It Really Keep Oil Prices High in the 1990s?

The Organization of Petroleum Exporting Countries (OPEC) is a cartel that was formed in 1960. By 1973 it appeared to have limitless power to raise the price of crude oil in world markets. In that year members of the cartel sharply cut back shipments and the price of oil tripled. By 1979 the price of a barrel of crude oil averaged over $30. By the mid-1980s, however, there was a glut of crude oil on the market and the price of oil plummeted to less than $10 a barrel in response to the surplus. In late 1986 OPEC was struggling to raise the price of oil to $18 by instructing its members to cut back production by 7 percent. The experts of the 1970s argued that OPEC would eventually drive the price of oil up to $100 a barrel. What had happened since 1973 to diminish OPEC's ability to keep oil prices high?

First, OPEC was never able to establish a barrier to entry into the crude oil market. In response to higher prices, non-OPEC nations increased their development and production of petroleum throughout the 1970s and early 1980s. By the early 1980s, production from North Sea, Mexican, and Alaskan oil wells was putting downward pressure on crude oil prices. Second, since 1970 the demand for oil had become more elastic. Consumers had learned that there are good substitutes for petroleum products. Fuel conservation, improved insulation of homes, and more energy-efficient automobiles sharply decreased the demand for crude oil in the 1980s.

OPEC's attempt to reassert its market power in the 1980s met with some short-run success as the price of oil rose to about $22 per barrel. However, it's not clear that all of the price increase can be attributed to OPEC policies. For example, the demand for oil increased substantially in 1987 as some buyers sought to stockpile it in anticipation of future price increases resulting from the Iran-Iraq war that year. At OPEC's meeting in late 1986 there was considerable squabbling about quotas among its members, particularly between Iran and Iraq. Iraq succeeded in getting its producers exempted from quotas. The estimated daily output capacity of OPEC's member nations was nearly twice the sum of the quotas in 1987.

By 1989 OPEC had increased its target output to 20.5 million barrels of oil per day. However, cheating was rampant in 1989, and OPEC members produced an estimated 23.5 million barrels per day.* Some members, particularly Kuwait and the United Arab Emirates, seem to have been dissatisfied with their quotas. It was estimated they were producing twice the 1.1 million barrels they were supposed to ship in order to increase their individual profits. This put downward pressure on oil prices.

As OPEC's member nations disagreed on what constituted a "fair" quota for their production, OPEC began to fall apart. Pressure to increase production quotas of individual nations led to overall increases in output and put downward pressure on oil prices in early 1990. By March 1990 the average price of crude oil shipped by OPEC nations had fallen to less than $18 per barrel. There was added pressure on Kuwait and the United Arab Emirates to stop cheating on their quotas. As you know, however, the temptation to cheat on cartel agreements is often too strong to resist. It is such cheating that spells distress and eventual doom for a cartel's ability to force prices upward.

By July 1990 OPEC oil was selling for less than $14 per barrel. In August 1990 Iraq invaded Kuwait, in part to gain control of Kuwaiti oil production capacity. The resulting turmoil in the oil market in mid-1990 was enough to send the price of a barrel of crude to $40.

During the Persian Gulf War, Saudi Arabia and other OPEC nations expanded production to supply the market with oil that would normally have been supplied by Iraq and Kuwait. By the time the war ended, the price of oil had again fallen to less than $20 a barrel and total OPEC production was more than 22 million barrels per day, with Saudi Arabia supplying one third of that amount.

(*Continued*) Few astute oil market observers thought OPEC had either the ability or the desire to restrict output enough to raise the price of crude oil, and there were many who thought the price of crude oil could fall again to $15 a barrel or less! Although oil prices are volatile, the ability of OPEC to control them over the long run appears to be limited.

During 1991 the price of OPEC oil averaged about $19. In 1992 Saudi Arabia embarked on a plan to expand its production capacity 10 million barrels per day by 1994. Saudi Arabia resisted pressure from such OPEC members as Iran, Algeria, and Nigeria to scale back its production so as to raise oil prices. In the early 1990s Russia seemed likely to become a major player in the world oil market and was stepping up its efforts to develop its vast oil reserves.

* See James Tanner and Allanna Sullivan, "OPEC Is Stalled in Bid to Revise Market Shares," *The Wall Street Journal*, November 27, 1989, p. A3.

told all the other firms to submit much higher bids. Cement-pouring firms that did not abide by the cartel's rules were in for trouble. The cartel had the power to cut off the delivery of their raw materials and create labor problems that made it difficult for them to deliver cement. The cartel's bid-rigging scheme kept price up so that the monopoly output of its members could be sold. The cartel was estimated to have increased construction costs in Manhattan by as much as 20 percent during the period in which it existed.[12]

Cartels usually attempt to establish penalties for members that cheat on the cartel agreement by exceeding their quotas. The fundamental problem of cartels is that once a cartel price has been established, member firms whose profits are maximized at that price can make more by cheating. If all member firms cheat, the cartel breaks up because economic profits fall to zero.

Another problem of cartels is deciding on the monoply price and output level. This problem is particularly acute if member firms disagree on the market demand or on the price elasticity of the product or if they have different costs of production. Firms with higher average costs favor higher cartel prices. Firms are also likely to squabble about how to divide up territories. If a firm thinks its quota is too low, it has all the more reason to risk a penalty by cheating.

Price Rigidity and the Kinked Demand Curve

In the first half of the 20th century it was widely believed that prices in oligopolistic markets tended to be rigid. The model developed to explain rigid prices shows how the assumptions of individual oligopolistic firms about their rivals' reactions can lead to peculiar results. The model was believed to be applicable to the U.S. steel industry in the early 1900s and the 1920s, when, despite cost increases, the price of steel remained constant.[13]

---

[12] See Roy Rowan, "The 50 Biggest Mafia Bosses," *Fortune*, November 10, 1986, pp. 24–38.

[13] Paul Sweezy, "Demand under Conditions of Oligopoly," *Journal of Political Economy* 47 (August 1939), pp. 568–73.

Price rigidity can be explained if individual oligopolistic firms believe that any price increase will not be matched by their rivals; at the same time they believe their rivals will match their price decreases. Under these circumstances the demand curve as seen by any particular firm has a strange shape.

A price is established for the product. The model does not explain how it has been established. During the 1950s, a period of price stability, the market price for a chocolate bar was 10 cents and chocolate bars were produced by only a few firms. Assume that firms in the chocolate bar industry think that the demand for their product will be very elastic if they raise their price, because their competitors will not do likewise in response. However, they also think that if they lower their price, the demand for their product will be inelastic, because they expect their rivals to match their price cut. The sharp change in the elasticity of a firm's demand curve at the established price gives it a kinked shape.

Figure 12–9 shows this kinked demand curve along with the marginal revenue curve corresponding to it. Notice the sharp drop in marginal revenue when price falls below 10 cents, the established price. This is because of the sharp drop in revenue that occurs when a firm cuts its price while its rivals cut their prices. A

FIGURE 12–9 Oligopolistic Kinked Demand Curve

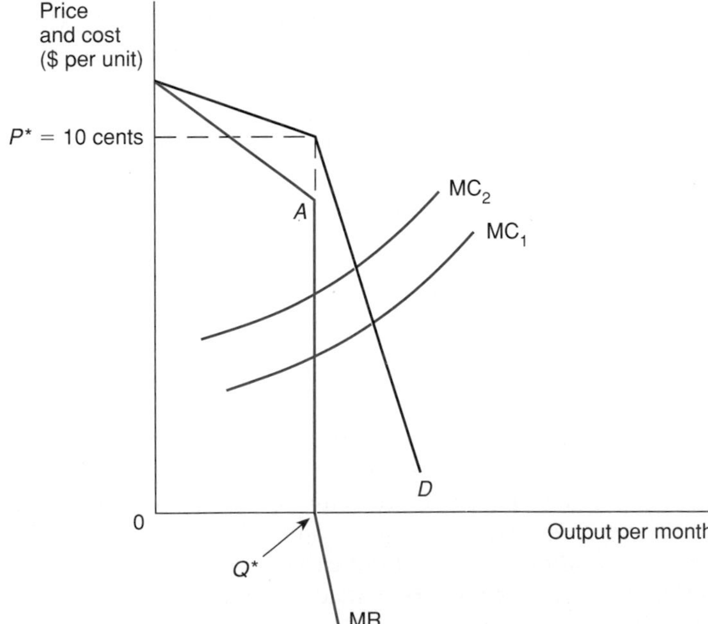

Increases in marginal cost occurring below point *A* of the marginal revenue curve will not result in a change in the price charged by the profit-maximizing firm. This explains price rigidity in the face of cost increases.

firm that cuts its price will suffer a decrease in total revenue as marginal revenue becomes negative, because demand is inelastic at prices below the established price.[14]

In Figure 12–9 maximum profits correspond to the output at which MR = MC. The marginal cost curve is MC_1. The profit-maximizing output is therefore Q^* bars per month, and P^*, the price of the product, is 10 cents.

Now suppose the price of one of the inputs necessary to produce chocolate bars increases. This shifts the marginal cost curve upward, from MC_1 to MC_2. If, after the increase, MC_2 still intersects MR in the segment below point A, the firm will change neither its output nor its price. Similarly, a decrease in marginal costs will not result in a price decrease.

The firm's price rigidity will be maintained only for cost increases that do not shift the marginal cost curve upward enough to intersect the marginal revenue curve above point A. A larger increase in marginal costs will result in a new price. There will then be a new demand curve with a new kink. The kink remains only if firms maintain the same beliefs about their rivals' price reactions after the new price has been established.

Price Leadership

Price leader A firm that sets a price to maximize its profits in a market, whose lead is followed by other firms that set the same price.

A commonly observed practice in oligopolistic markets is price leadership. One firm in an oligopolistic market, usually (but not always) the largest, acts as a **price leader.** That firm sets a price to maximize its own profits, while the other firms follow its lead. Those firms charge the same price as that set by the leader and produce the output maximizing their profits at that price. Price leadership was believed to prevail in the U.S. steel industry during the 1960s. One firm set prices, and other firms followed its lead. However, because of increased competition from foreign steel producers, steel industry observers believe that no single firm currently dominates the pricing of the U.S. steel industry.[15] Price leadership may be descriptive of pricing in banking markets. Immediately after large New York banks adjust their prime rate for loans, all other banks adjust their prime rates in the same way.

Partial monopoly A market in which one firm sets price to equate its marginal revenue and marginal cost and other firms are price takers at that price.

The dominant firm assumes that other firms in its market will not react in a way that will cause the price it sets to change. The follower firms assume that they cannot cause the dominant firm to change its price. They elect to maximize their profits at the price set by that firm. In effect, these firms become price takers at the price set by the leader. This model of price leadership is called **partial monopoly** because the leader sets a monopoly price based on its marginal revenue and marginal cost. Other firms are price takers at that price.

---

[14] The marginal revenue curve can be derived by recognizing that up to output Q^* marginal revenue corresponds to that of the elastic portion of the demand curve. When output exceeds Q^*, the marginal revenue corresponding to the inelastic portion prevails. The marginal revenue of each linear segment of the kinked demand curve always bisects a line drawn from the demand curve to the vertical axis.

[15] Adams and Mueller, "Steel Industry," in Adams, ed., *Structure of American Industry*.

FIGURE 12–10 Price Leadership

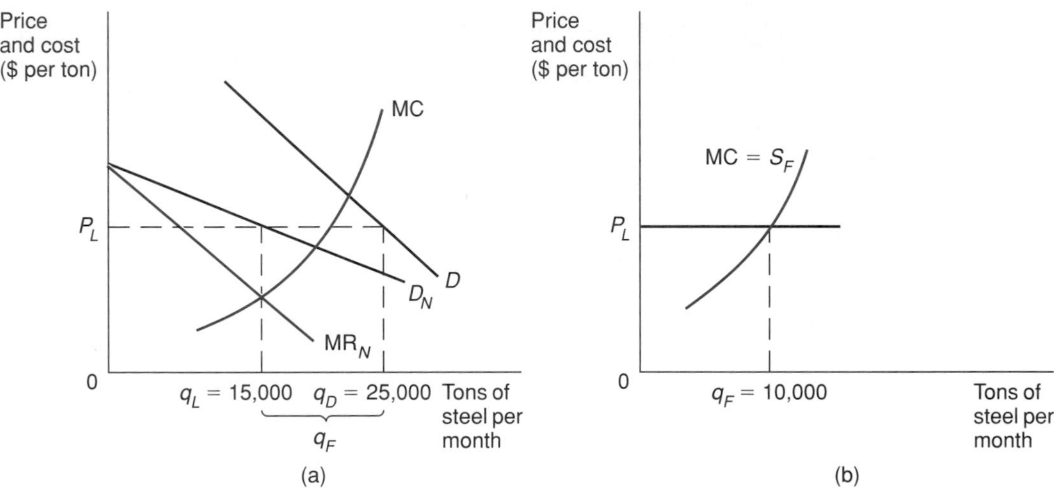

The dominant firm estimates how much other firms will sell at each possible price and subtracts this from its estimate of total market demand to obtain its net demand, D_N. It then calculates the marginal revenue for this demand, MR_N, and produces output q_L, which corresponds to the point at which $MR_N = MC$. Other firms produce where $P_L = MC$. In equilibrium $q_L + q_F = q_D$ at $P = P_L$.

Figure 12–10 shows how price is determined under partial monopoly. The dominant firm determines its demand by subtracting from market demand the amount that other firms will sell at all possible prices. The market demand curve, D, is shown in Figure 12–10(a). The supply curve of all other firms, S_F, is shown in Figure 12–10(b). The quantity supplied by the dominant firm's rivals will increase at higher prices. The dominant firm therefore makes larger deductions from market demand at higher prices.

For example, in Figure 12–10 the market quantity demanded for steel at a price of P_L per ton is 25,000 tons per month. At that price the supply curve in Figure 12–10(b) shows that the quantity supplied by other firms will be 10,000 tons per month. The remainder of the market demand for the dominant firm is therefore 15,000 tons per month. This is a point on the demand curve D_N, which gives the net sales that the dominant firm can expect to make at any price after the sales made by rival firms have been deducted.

The dominant firm maximizes its profits by choosing the price that sets MR_N, the marginal revenue of the net demand, equal to its marginal costs. Its price is therefore P_L, and it will sell q_L tons of steel at that price. Other firms take P_L as given and produce $q_F = 10{,}000$ tons per month. The dominant firm produces 15,000 tons per month, and the total quantity produced is 25,000 tons per month. At that production level price equals P_L per ton.

Price leadership can also be explained in terms of the smaller firms' fear of the dominant firm's retaliatory reactions. Such fear is particularly likely to exist if the dominant firm can produce at lower costs than the smaller firms. If this is the case, the smaller firms would hesitate to undercut the dominant firm's price. They would reason that although they would achieve temporary sales gains by doing this, they would ultimately lose a price war because the dominant firm could make economic profits at a price lower than their break-even price.

The smaller firms in an oligopolistic industry sometimes act as price followers because they believe that larger firms have superior information on market demand. They are unsure of the future demand for their output and view the price change of a larger firm as indicative of a change in that demand. This may explain price leadership in the banking industry. Smaller banks may view an increase in the prime lending rate of a large New York bank as indicative of a general excess demand for loans at the current interest rates.

Entry-Limit Pricing and Contestable Markets

Firms in an oligopolistic market may set prices so as to make it unprofitable for potential new entrants into the market to actually begin selling in the market. To accomplish this objective, firms in the market may set a price that does not maximize their current profits. They may forgo current profits to keep new firms from entering the market and putting downward pressure on future profits.

Firms either collude with one another or follow one firm's lead in setting prices to discourage entry. It is presumed that potential entrants will take the prices set by existing firms as the prices that will be maintained. To set the prices, the minimum possible long-run average cost of potential entrants into the market is estimated.

Figure 12–11(a) shows the LRAC curve of a potential entrant into an oligopolistic market. If this firm cannot expect a price of at least $P^* =$ LRACmin for its product, it will not be able to earn economic profits by entering the market. Figure 12–11(b) shows the market demand for the product. Suppose existing firms in the market organize a cartel to maximize their current profits. They would then set a price P_M corresponding to the output for which MR = MC. At that price Q_M units would be sold and existing firms would divide up the total quantity among themselves. However, because $P_M >$ LRACmin of potential entrants, the cartel is doomed to fail unless there is a barrier to entry into the market. The existing firms know that it is therefore futile to set the monopoly price. At the monopoly price more firms will enter and the quantity made available will increase. As this occurs, price will be pushed down and profits will fall.

Entry-limit price A price low enough to prevent new firms from entering a market.

What price will existing firms set? This depends on their cost curves. The **entry-limit price** is the price low enough to prevent new firms from entering the market. Suppose that the average cost curves of existing firms look exactly like those of potential entrants. In this case any price of P^* will cause entry. The existing firms will therefore have to keep price at $P^* =$ LRACmin. At that price they will sell Q_L, which is more than they would sell if price were high enough to encourage entry, but, alas, they will earn zero economic profits.

If, however, existing firms have cost advantages unavailable to potential entrants, they can earn economic profits at the price P^* in the long run while at the same time deterring new firms from entering the market. Entry-limit pricing shows

FIGURE 12–11 Entry-Limit Pricing

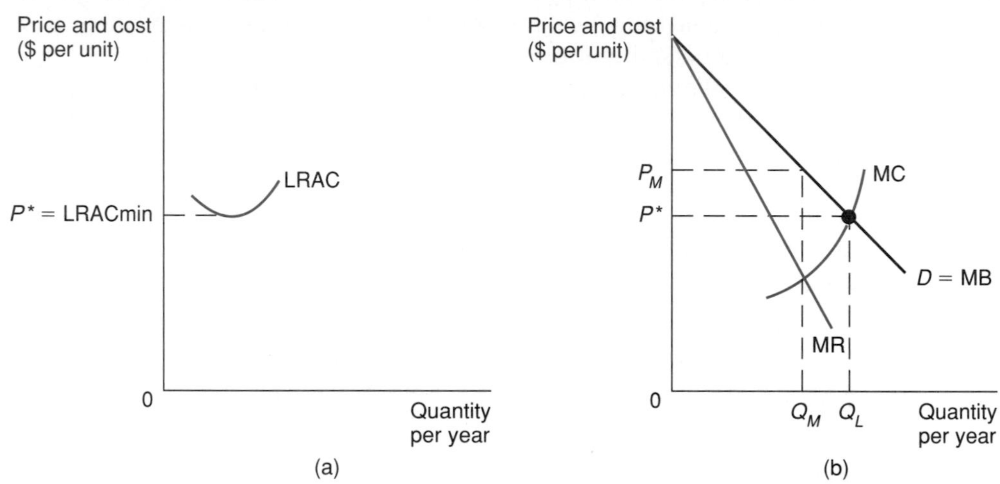

Entry-limit pricing results when existing sellers in a market set a price for the product below LRACmin of potential entrants. Graph (a) shows that LRACmin of a potential entrant is P^*. In graph (b), to prevent that firm from entering the market, existing firms set a price no higher than P^*. This price is below the profit-maximizing price of P_M.

how the fear of new entrants into a market can provide profit-maximizing sellers currently in the market with an incentive not to exercise their monopoly power.

Contestable market A market in which entry is free and exit is costless.

When firms engage in entry-limit pricing, they are usually operating in a **contestable market,** that is, a market in which entry is free and exit is costless.[16] Contestable markets need not be perfectly competitive markets in which market shares are so small that each firm must be a price taker. If entry is possible and exit is costless, an oligopolistic market in which firms are able to influence price by virtue of their high market shares can be considered contestable. Contestable markets are vulnerable to what William J. Baumol has referred to as "hit-and-run entry."[17] In hit-and-run entry an **interloper firm** quickly enters a contestable market when it can earn economic profits and leaves just as quickly before prices decline to a level that no longer permits economic profits. Assuming that the interloper firm's marginal and average costs of serving the market are the same as those of existing firms, the interloper firm can add to its profit by selling in a contestable market whenever the current price of the product is the marginal cost of making the product available. The extra profit the firm would make by entering the market is the difference between the price that can be obtained after quantity supplied increases and the marginal cost of the additional output the firm supplies.

Interloper firm A firm that quickly enters a market when it can earn economic profits and leaves quickly before prices decline to a level that no longer permits economic profits.

[16] William J. Baumol, J. C. Panzar, and R. D. Willig, *Contestable Markets and the Theory of Industry Structure* (San Diego: Harcourt Brace Jovanovich, 1982).

[17] William J. Baumol, "Contestable Markets: An Uprising in the Theory of Industry Structure," *American Economic Review* 72, no. 1 (March 1982), pp. 1–15.

An unregulated taxi market could easily be contestable. Assuming that the only input to enter the industry is an automobile, interloper entrants could make a profit whenever the price of taxi service exceeds it marginal cost. Free foreign trade can also encourage interloper firms, in this case foreign sellers, to enter domestic markets whenever prices in domestic markets exceed their marginal cost of production. Because free entry and exit prevail in a perfectly competitive market, such a market is necessarily also a perfectly contestable market.

The threat of entry by interloper firms prevents prices from deviating far from either marginal costs or average costs. When a market is contestable, it is impossible for firms already in the industry to earn economic profits for long. Such profits attract firms to the industry. The existing firms know this and therefore have an incentive to keep prices close to the average costs of production. This avoids the possibility of entry, which the existing firms know will inevitably cause prices to decline to average costs. The existing firms therefore choose to keep prices close to marginal cost to avoid a reduction in their market shares.

Firms already selling in a market must also produce any given output at minimum possible cost. If they do not do this, new firms will enter the industry and produce the same output at lower cost. This enables the new entrants to earn profits by charging a price slightly below that of existing firms. For example, suppose U.S. manufacturing firms do not employ the least-cost technology, while foreign competitors do. If this is the case, foreign competitors could enter the market of the U.S. firms and make profit by charging a price equal to or below LRACmin of those firms. To avoid this possibility, the U.S. firms have the incentive to use the best technology to achieve LRACmin and avoid encouraging foreign entrants.

The theory of contestable markets suggests that if entry and exit are free, prices equal marginal and average costs in equilibrium. If markets are, in fact, contestable, high concentration within a market does not necessarily imply that less than the efficient output will be supplied. For example, suppose that a market is served by five firms of equal size, each therefore with a market share of 20 percent. If the market is contestable, say because of the possible entry of foreign sellers, the outcome will be efficient because prices will equal marginal costs of production despite the fact that there are only a few domestic sellers.

CONCEPT REVIEW

1. What distinguishing features are common to all oligopolistic markets?
2. Under which circumstances are price wars likely to develop in oligopolistic markets?
3. Define each of the following situations: a cartel, price leadership, a contestable market. How does the behavior of sellers in these situations differ?

Diagnosing Monopoly Power

Diagnosing the symptoms of actual exercise of monopoly power in markets is not an easy matter. Do large market shares and high profits indicate the exercise of monopoly power? Do such constraints as competition from imports or the threat of legal action cause firms with monopoly power to set prices below the level that maximizes their profit?

There are a number of ways to diagnose monopoly power, none of them completely satisfactory. The economist dealing in analysis of monopoly power looks for certain symptoms. The diagnosis of monopoly power is, however, an art riddled with pitfalls.

Profits as a Symptom of Monopoly Power

Monopoly power results in prices that exceed the marginal and average costs of production. One way to measure monopoly power is to determine the extent to which market prices exceed marginal costs. The Lerner index, developed by Abba P. Lerner in the 1930s, calculates the ratio of the difference between price and marginal cost to price:

$$M = (P - \text{MC})/P \qquad \textbf{(12–1)}$$

where M is monopoly power, P is price, and MC is marginal cost of production.[18] The index takes on the value of zero under perfect competition. This is because P = MC in competitive markets. The index is positive when monopoly prevails.

It is difficult to obtain actual data on marginal cost. In long-run competitive equilibrium, however, MC = AC. When MC = AC, the index can be written as

$$M = (P - \text{AC})/P \qquad \textbf{(12–2)}$$

which is profit per unit divided by price. Multiplying Equation 12–2 by Q/Q gives

$$\begin{aligned} M &= (P - \text{AC})Q/PQ \qquad \textbf{(12–3)} \\ &= \text{Profit/Revenue} \end{aligned}$$

Using this measure, the higher the ratio of profits to sales revenue over the long run, the greater is the exercise of monopoly power. A higher profit rate as a percentage of revenue over an extended period would be taken as an indication of the exercise of monopoly power.

The Lerner index must be used with caution. One problem in using it stems from the difference between accounting profits and economic profits. Remember that accounting profits exclude implicit costs associated with owner-supplied inputs. Persistent accounting profits need *not* be indicative of monopoly power.

[18] Abba P. Lerner, "The Concept of Monopoly and the Measurement of Monopoly Power," *Review of Economic Studies* 1 (June 1934), pp. 157–75.

This is because accounting profits include normal profits. Normal profits in an industry must be deducted from accounting profits before profits can be associated with monopoly power.

Another problem in using the Lerner index is that normal profits vary from industry to industry. Normal profits are relatively high in industries with significant amounts of owner-supplied inputs. The chief input owned by large firms is capital. Firms in industries whose heavy capital requirements are supplied by shareholders require higher money profits to remain in business. The more capital invested by stockholders, the greater are normal profits.

Normal profits also vary with the riskiness of businesses. A risky business is one in which investors might earn high profits but also might encounter significant losses. The opportunity cost of investment in such a business is the next best alternative investment of equal risk. Those who invest in riskier businesses usually demand a higher return to compensate them for the risk they bear. Normal profits in riskier businesses are therefore relatively higher than normal profits in safer ventures.

Market Concentration: The Herfindahl Index

The *market share* of a firm is the percentage of annual shipments to a market accounted for by that firm. The higher the market shares of firms selling in a market, the greater is the potential of those firms to exercise monopoly power resulting in prices that exceed marginal cost. The **Herfindahl index** (H) measures market concentration by first estimating each firm's market share, S, as measured by its percentage of shipments for sale and then summing the squares of those market shares:

Herfindahl index An index that measures market concentration by estimating market shares and summing the squares of market shares of all firms in the market.

$$H = S_1^2 + S_2^2 + S_3^2 + \ldots + S_N^2 \qquad \textbf{(12–4)}$$

where S_1 is the market share of the firm accounting for the greatest number of shipments, S_2 is the market share of the second-largest shipper, and so on.

For example, for a pure monopoly the market share of the largest firm S_1 would be 100 percent and the market share of all other firms would be zero. Here the Herfindahl index would take on a value of 10,000. If a very competitive market, comprised of 100 equal-sized firms each therefore with a 1 percent market share, the Herfindahl index would take on a value of 100. H would be 1,000 for a market with 10 firms, each with a 10 percent market share. The Herfindahl index is sensitive both to the number of firms and to the individual market shares of firms. For example, a market served by 11 firms, of which the largest has a 50 percent share and each of the remaining 10 firms has a 5 percent share, would measure $H = 2{,}750$. Note that even though this market comprises 11 firms, its Herfindahl index is nearly three times as high as the index for the market with only 10 firms of equal size.

The U.S. Department of Justice uses Herfindahl indexes to assess the potential for the exercise of monopoly power in markets. It regards a market with $H =$ 1,000 or less as relatively unconcentrated and a market for which $H = 1{,}800$ or

TABLE 12–3 Herfindahl Index for 50 Largest Manufacturing Companies, Selected Industries, 1982

Industry	*Index**
Women's and misses' dresses	24
Bottled and canned soft drinks	109
Fluid milk	151
Wood office furniture	199
Men's and boy's suits and coats	201
Canned fruits and vegetables	214
Steel wire	241
Meatpacking	325
Men's footwear	378
Petroleum refining	380
Women's footwear	492
Corn sugar refining	1,416
Tires	1,591
Malt beverages	2,089
Aluminum	2,564
Turbines	2,602
Copper	2,673
Household refrigerators and freezers	2,745
Man-made fibers	2,970

* The index reported here is a Herfindahl-Hirschman index. Instead of all sellers, it includes only the 50 largest sellers.

Source: U.S. Department of Commerce, Bureau of the Census, *1982 Census of Manufacturers, Concentration Ratios in Manufacturing.*

more as highly concentrated. Table 12–3 shows the Herfindahl index for selected industries as calculated by the U.S. Department of Commerce for the largest 50 firms in each industry. The index is quite low for meat, fluid milk, and clothing. Note that for women's and misses' dresses the index is a mere 24. The index is quite high (over 2,000) for malt beverages, man-made fibers, copper, aluminum, turbines, and household refrigerators and freezers.

Keep in mind that the data used to calculate the index in Table 12–3 only include domestic shipments. For markets in which imports are a large part of sales, the Herfindahl index will overstate the degree of market concentration unless it includes the market shares of foreign sellers.

What explains high concentration in a market? Firms may have a higher share of market sales because they can make their product at a lower cost and therefore price it lower than is possible when an industry is composed of many small firms. This would hold true for natural monopoly and natural oligopoly. In such cases any discrepancy between price and marginal cost can be offset in part by lower average costs and therefore lower prices than those that would prevail under perfect competition. If a firm can produce at lower average costs than those of its competitors or if it can offer products that consumers regard as superior, it will be rewarded with high market shares. This is the outcome of competition. One expert in the field of monopoly has argued that the right question to ask is not whether a market share is high but whether a high market share would survive an attempt to earn economic profits.[19]

It follows that a highly concentrated market, say one for which the Herfindahl index is over 2,000, need not be one in which prices are higher than those that would prevail under perfect competition in the market. The persistent threat of entrants into the industry could prevent firms from exercising their monopoly power to raise prices above marginal cost. Recall the model of entry-limit pricing discussed earlier in this chapter. If existing firms believe that high prices will encourage the entry of competing firms, they may rationally forgo maximizing current profits. If the threat of entry is chronic, existing firms may prefer to keep prices close to marginal and average costs so as to maintain their large market shares rather than lose those market shares to competitors.

Mergers

Mergers are matters of concern in antitrust policy when they result in increased market shares for the merged firms. A group of firms can avoid charges of price-fixing simply by merging into one firm. Mergers that reduce competition can result in government action under the Celler-Kefauver Act. All types of U.S. mergers are scrutinized by the Justice Department and the Federal Trade Commission. Of greatest concern to policymakers are mergers of two or more competing sellers in the same market into a single firm.

In general, the Justice Department does not oppose mergers in industries in which the share of the largest firms is relatively low. Normally, a merger in a market whose Herfindahl index would be 1,000 or below after the firms combine is not opposed. The Justice Department also does not oppose the merger of firms in markets in which entry is easy. In recent years official opposition to mergers of larger corporations has been relaxed on the grounds that such mergers are necessary to reduce the costs of U.S. industries and to improve their competitive position vis-à-vis foreign sellers. In effect, this policy is based on the presumption that the contestability of the market through foreign competition is great enough to warrant reduced domestic competition. It is also based on the belief that in many cases mergers result in cost and productivity advantages that help reduce prices and make U.S. industry more competitive in world markets. The new policy was, in part, responsible for the jump in corporate acquisition of firms in the 1980s. The value of corporate acquisitions increased from about $50 billion in 1980 to nearly $200 billion in 1985.

[19] Franklin M. Fisher, "Diagnosing Monopoly," *Quarterly Review of Economics and Business* 19, no. 2 (Summer 1979), pp. 7–33.

Controlling Monopoly Power: Antitrust Policy

Antitrust statutes Statutes that seek to prevent unfair business practices that give rise to monopoly power.

Antitrust statutes seek to prevent "unfair" business practices that give rise to monopoly power. Note that monopoly power, as such, is not illegal; however, legislation outlaws certain practices that actively seek to exclude rivals from competing. The *Sherman Act of 1890* prohibits contracts, combinations, and conspiracies in restraint of trade. It also explicitly outlaws attempts to monopolize trade or commerce. However, it does not outlaw monopoly and high market shares as such. What it outlaws is the use of unfair practices to exclude rivals, not the achievement of monopoly power through superior skill or cost advantages. The Sherman Act established penalties for those convicted of violating its provisions.

The *Clayton Act,* passed in 1914, broadened the antitrust powers of the U.S. government to outlaw specific business practices and further restrain the growth of monopoly power. It also outlawed price discrimination that lessened competition. In 1914, the Federal Trade Commission was established. The commission was empowered to police markets and prevent "unfair" methods of competition. The *Celler-Kefauver Antimerger Act* was passed in 1950 to control mergers that might substantially reduce rivalry among the firms in an industry. This act specifically prohibits one corporation from acquiring the assets of another if the acquisition can be shown to create a monopoly.

Controlling Oligopolistic Price-Fixing

Any conspiracy to fix prices is illegal. Explicit price-fixing agreements among firms in an industry are subject to both civil and criminal penalties. In many cases the legal issue is whether closeness or similarity of prices among firms is evidence of intent to fix prices. An example is the 1946 case against the three major tobacco producers in the U.S. cigarette industry. American Tobacco, Reynolds, and Liggett & Myers were convicted of violating antitrust acts by virtue of their identical retail prices. In addition, these firms had pressured retailers not to lower their cigarette prices. The price of cigarettes had increased during the heart of the Great Depression of the 1930s. At that time both tobacco leaf prices and labor costs were falling. This made the price increase and the equality of prices all the more suspicious. Despite lack of evidence of any conspiracy on price among the firms, they were found guilty of price-fixing. In issuing a pronouncement on this case (which it refused to review), the Supreme Court argued that no formal agreement is necessary for proof of conspiracy. The Court concluded that conspiracy may be inferred from the acts of the accused.[20]

There is, however, often a thin line between price-fixing and price leadership. Courts in the United States have found that price leadership is, in general, not illegal. It is upheld as long as the price followers are not coerced in any way into following the leader. This principle was established in the 1920s in two key cases involving U.S. Steel and International Harvester.

[20] For an economic analysis of the case, see William H. Nicholls, "The Tobacco Case of 1946," *American Economic Review* 39, no. 3 (May 1949), pp. 284–310.

The Rule of Reason

Rule of reason A judicial rule under which acts beyond normal business practice that unduly restrain competition can be used to infer intent to monopolize.

In 1911 the Supreme Court ruled that the Standard Oil Company of New Jersey had engaged in illegal business practices with the intent and purpose of excluding other sellers from its market. This established the **rule of reason,** which holds that acts beyond normal business practice that unduly restrain competition for the purpose of excluding rivals can be used to infer intent to monopolize an industry. This rule broke up John D. Rockefeller's Standard Oil trust. It was shown that the Standard Oil Company had made use of rail rate rebates and discounts, business espionage, control of supplies to rivals, and price warfare to drive rivals out of business or to weaken them for takeover by Standard Oil.[21] The Supreme Court viewed these practices as unusual and unfair. At that time Standard Oil had a share of over 90 percent in the market for refined oil products. The rule of reason was also applied in cases that broke up the Tobacco Trust, the Powder Trust, and other trusts between 1911 and 1920.

In a case against U.S. Steel in 1920 the Supreme Court ruled that the company was not guilty of monopoly violations of the Sherman Act despite evidence of price leadership. It argued that the company did not exercise its monopoly power to exclude rivals and that its size alone was not evidence of abuse of monopoly power. This case established the legal principle that largeness, control of output, and oligopolistic price leadership are not in themselves illegal. The case also made it clear that dominant firms in an industry could expect antitrust action to be taken against them only if they used their power actively and aggressively to exclude or damage rivals.

The Relevant Market

Another significant case was decided in 1945, when a court found the Aluminum Company of America (Alcoa) guilty of monopolization and ordered it broken up. In that case the court ruled that Alcoa possessed a monopoly of primary aluminum ingots and had used its knowledge of demand to expand capacity before rivals had a chance to enter the aluminum market. The court viewed expansion of capacity as evidence of intent to monopolize the market. This decision established the precedent of inferring illegal monopolization from acts other than unreasonable business practices designed to drive competitors out of business.

The outcome of many antitrust cases depends on the resolution of disputes concerning definition of the market. The 1945 case against Alcoa hinged on the definition of the product market. Alcoa had been organized in 1888. Although some firms had attempted to enter the aluminum market before 1940, Alcoa held a dominant monopoly position in that market by virtue of its ownership or control of most of the high-grade bauxite from which aluminum was extracted. The court considered aluminum a metal with unique properties that put it in a separate product group. It was convinced that copper and steel were poor substitutes for

---

[21] For a discussion of this and related cases, see Scherer, *Industrial Market Structure and Economic Performance*, pp. 528–31.

MODERN MICROECONOMICS IN ACTION: **GOVERNMENT AND THE ECONOMY**

Antitrust Activities: On the Offensive Again in the 1990s

During the 1980s, under the Reagan administration, the Justice Department was laid back. As part of that administration's policy of encouraging mergers and growth so that U.S. firms could reap economies of scale and compete more effectively in global markets, the department did not initiate antitrust lawsuits. However, antitrust activities, particularly in high-tech, computer-related markets, have been stepped up in the 1990s.

Some antitrust lawsuits have been initiated by small new firms. These firms have argued that attempts by coalitions of companies such as IBM and Apple to establish industrywide standards for the compatibility of software and operating systems are merely a way of unfairly reducing competition. Some lawyers and economists have argued that the lawsuits could stymie joint ventures that might keep U.S. businesses on the cutting edge of technology. Others have argued that the development of standards will enhance competition in the long run by allowing smaller firms to develop machines compatible with those produced by such larger firms as IBM and Apple.*

In 1991 the Federal Trade Commission (FTC), which shares responsibility for antitrust enforcement with the Justice Department, was investigating the activities of Intel, Microsoft, and the Open Software Foundation to determine whether they were engaging in unfair business practices to limit competition. Intel, a major producer of microprocessors, was also being sued by two smaller firms, Advanced Micro Devices and Cyrix, which accused it of trying to monopolize the market for microprocessors and math processing chips. These firms claimed that Intel used its patents and copyrights to block competitors from entering its lucrative markets. Intel sued Advanced Micro for copyright infringement and claimed that Cyrix had infringed on its patents. Hewlett-Packard, which was being sued by Apple for copyright infringement, argued that Apple was trying to monopolize the market for computer screen displays.

The Open Software Foundation, which was founded by IBM, Hewlett-Packard, and Digital Equipment, develops operating systems for computers with the goal of establishing a standardized UNIX system. Software developers must submit their new operating system products to Open Software if they wish to have them incorporated into the system. The FTC is investigating the foundation's business practices to see whether they are making it difficult for smaller firms to sell their software innovations.

The effect of uniform standards in computer technology on competition in computer markets is an emerging antitrust issue of the 1990s.

* See Andrew Pollack, "Antitrust Actions on the Rise Again," *The New York Times,* November 10, 1991, p. F12.

aluminum. In defining Alcoa's market share of aluminum ingots, it did not include aluminum ingots produced from recycled scrap. Using that definition, it concluded that Alcoa's 90 percent share constituted a monopoly.

In 1956 the Supreme Court found the Du Pont company innocent of monopolizing cellophane production. Du Pont was able to convince the Court that a high cross elasticity of demand existed between cellophane and alternative packaging materials. The Supreme Court held that cellophane substituted for other wrappings to a sufficient degree to justify this broader definition of the product market.

Predatory Pricing

Predatory pricing The practice of selling a product at a price deliberately set low enough to drive rival firms out of business.

Predatory pricing is the practice of selling a product at a price deliberately set low enough to drive rival firms out of business. Often, when a firm engages in this practice, it has to sell the product below its own minimum possible average cost to achieve its objective. A firm with monopoly power can therefore suffer losses by engaging in the practice. If so, it reasons that those losses are worth the gain in future profits that it may be able to obtain by putting its rivals out of business. By demonstrating its willingness to incur losses, the firm also puts potential entrants on notice that it will lower price when they enter its market. If the market is not contestable, this implies that new entrants run the risk of incurring a loss if they enter it, because soon after entering they will have to liquidate the assets they acquire to serve the market.

Predatory pricing is regarded as an unfair practice subject to court action. For example, predatory pricing was cited by the prosecution in the Standard Oil case as one of the means used by John D. Rockefeller to drive out competition. A multiproduct firm can subsidize losses due to predatory pricing in one market if it earns profits from sales in other markets where there is less competition. In its case against IBM, the Department of Justice accused it of predatory pricing in leasing its computers.

There is a great deal of controversy as to whether firms actually engage in predatory pricing. Because many factors influence the pricing decisions of firms and data on average and marginal costs and on marginal revenue are hard to obtain, it is difficult to prove that firms have engaged in the practice.

CONCEPT REVIEW

1. What are some of the difficulties involved in diagnosing the exercise of monopoly power?
2. A market is served by two sellers, each accounting for half of the sales in the market. Calculate the Herfindahl index for this market.
3. What are some of the unfair business practices that have been outlawed by U.S. antitrust statutes?

SUMMARY

1. Markets with imperfect competition have elements of both pure monopoly and perfect competition. Firms have some control over price in such markets. They do, however, face competition from either existing or potential rivals.
2. In a monopolistically competitive market, many firms sell a differentiated product and there is free entry into the market. The demand curves for the product of any individual firm are downward sloping. Firms can control price. However, economic profits still serve the function of attracting new firms. Long-run equilibrium in monopolistically competitive markets results in elimination of economic profits. Although each firm can only break even in the long run, prices exceed marginal costs. Prices also exceed mini-

mum possible long-run average costs. Excess capacity and higher prices are social costs of product variety. When a standardized product is produced in a competitive market, prices equal MC and LRACmin.

3. Advertising and other promotional schemes are attempts by firms to increase the demand for their products. The impact of advertising on profits depends on whether competing firms also advertise. Under monopolistic competition advertising can result in only temporary increases in profits.
4. Oligopolistic markets have only a few sellers, and the entry of new sellers is difficult or impossible. The product may be standardized or differentiated among sellers. Individual firms recognize their mutual interdependence with their rivals.
5. Equilibrium in oligopoly markets depends on the conjectures that firms make about the way their rivals will react to changes in prices and quantities. Price wars in oligopolistic markets can serve to push prices down to their competitive equilibrium levels (P = LRACmin).
6. Oligopolistic firms have incentives to collude so as to avoid the unfavorable effects of price wars on profits. A cartel is a group of firms that act together to coordinate output or control price as if they were a single monopoly firm. Cartels tend to be unstable because maximization of group profits at the monopoly price is inconsistent with maximization of individual profits at that price. Firms can cheat on a cartel by selling more than their allotted quotas. If many firms do this, the cartel's monopoly price cannot be maintained.
7. Specific models of oligopoly can explain price rigidity and price leadership, as well as the incentive to forgo current profits by keeping prices low enough to deter the entry of new sellers into the market.
8. A contestable market is one in which entry and exit are free. Such markets need not be competitive. In contestable markets the threat of quick entry and exit can result in prices that equal marginal and average costs.
9. There is no generally satisfactory way of diagnosing the exercise of monopoly power. The persistence of economic profits is a symptom of monopoly power. The Herfindahl index measures market concentration by squaring each firm's market share and summing the squares. A Herfindahl index of under 1,000 usually means a market is not concentrated.

Important Concepts

imperfect competition
monopolistic competition
product differentiation
product group
excess capacity
selling costs
oligopoly
natural oligopoly
price war
cartel
price leader
partial monopoly
entry-limit price
contestable market
interloper firm
Herfindahl index
antitrust statutes
rule of reason
predatory pricing

Questions for Review

1. What factors contribute to a firm's control over price when imperfect competition exists?
2. What is a product group? Explain why arbitrary decisions must be made when defining a product group. How can the cross elasticity of demand for a product be useful in defining product groups?
3. The greater the degree of competition in a monopolistically competitive market, the flatter (more elastic) demand tends to be. How will an

increase in the amount of competition affect the degree of excess capacity of firms in the long-run equilibrium?

4. Explain why the long-run equilibrium price and output of a monopolistically competitive firm will change if other firms enter or leave the industry. Use a diagram to explain your answer.

5. How can advertising in monopolistically competitive markets reduce the costs associated with excess capacity? In what sense is the cost of excess capacity a consequence of product variety in markets?

6. How does an oligopolistic market structure differ from a monopolistically competitive one?

7. Why do oligopolistic firms have incentives to collude? What are the requirements for a successful cartel? Why are these requirements seldom met in practice?

8. If consumers benefit from lower prices, why do the courts view "predatory pricing" as harmful to consumers?

9. How is the Lerner index used to provide an indication of the exercise of monopoly power? Why is the persistence of accounting profits for a period of time in an industry not necessarily proof of the exercise of monopoly power? What does the Herfindahl index measure?

10. Have courts in the United States historically considered price leadership to be a form of price-fixing? Does price uniformity among firms in an industry necessarily imply that a price-fixing agreement is in effect?

Problems

1. Suppose that LRACmin = \$3 per gallon for ice cream. Show that if the ice cream industry is monopolistically competitive, in the long-run equilibrium the price per gallon will exceed \$3. Show how a decrease in the price of inputs used in ice cream production will affect the industry. Assume that after the decrease in costs LRAC-min = \$2.

2. The output of lumber in a certain region would be 12,000 board feet per month under perfect competition. Only two lumber producers serve the region. Assuming that AC = MC at all output levels, under what circumstances would the two sellers end up earning zero economic profits and each be selling 6,000 board feet per month?

3. The copper industry in a certain nation prices its product at \$1,000 per ton. At that price it sells 10,000 tons per year. The average cost of producing a ton of copper has been constant at \$600. Calculate the Lerner index of monopoly power, and show how it equals profit as a percentage of sales.

4. Suppose a perfectly competitive industry is organized as a cartel. Prove that maximization of group profits is inconsistent with maximization of any one firm's profits at the cartel price. Show that if all firms in the cartel maximize profits at the cartel price, the price will fall to the competitive level.

5. Show how an increase in average selling costs will affect the amount that firms spend on advertising and sales in a monopolistically competitive market.

6. Suppose that the U.S. Justice Department files a lawsuit attempting to prevent the merger of two publishers of travel books (for example, Fodor's and Frommer's Travel Guides), arguing that such a merger would violate the Celler-Kefauver Antimerger Act. How might the lawyers for the two publishers successfully defend the merger?

13

Business Strategies in Oligopolistic Markets and the Theory of Games

Suppose that you are the managing director of a large oil company and that you have to decide whether to build a new chain of gas stations to sell your brand of gas in Singapore. The price of land is very high in the urban areas of that nation, and building the new chain would require an investment of millions of dollars. Three or four other large oil companies are already in the market or are thinking about entering it, as is one of your major competitors. Your problem is to make the best guess possible about whether entering the Singapore market is going to be profitable for your company. How do you decide whether to enter the market when you know that the profit you make depends on whether your competitor decides to enter?

Because the market in question is dominated by only a few firms you have to try to guess what your competitor will do. Your profit is contingent on its output and pricing decisions because what it does will affect the demand for gasoline from your stations and therefore your profit from entering the market. If you are rational, what you will do is try to put yourself in your competitor's shoes. You will look at its options and try to guess what its profits might be under its alternatives. You will then choose a strategy based on your profit opportunities under the various scenarios that you have envisioned, given what you expect your competitor to do.

In oligopolistic markets businesses must consider the possible moves of their competitors when selecting pricing, sales, advertising, investment, and product development strategies. We are now ready to delve more deeply into the analysis of business strategies in the real world by examining how the competitive environment influences the choices made by managers. By examining the strategic choices of businesses, we will be able to get a better idea of incentives to collude or compete through various pricing and sales strategies in a variety of market situations. We will also be able to gain some insights into the factors that influence the decisions of business managers to expand their operations by building more facilities to serve an existing market or to enter a new market.

To analyze various business decisions, we will make use of standard economic analysis of demand and cost, but we will also supplement that analysis with a new and more sophisticated technique that likens the competitive environment to a match of wits similar to a game. In a game, as in an oligopolistic market, there are two or more players. Each of the players attempts to win by gaining market share or profits, but no single player can control the outcome of the game. The stakes of the game are its payoffs, which are usually measured in terms of profit, and the profit of any one participant is dependent not only on its own decisions but also on the decisions of the other players.

Theory of games A technique for analyzing the selection of strategies by persons or organizations with conflicting interests in situations whose payoffs depend on the choices made by each participant and the participant's rivals.

The **theory of games** is a technique for analyzing the selection of strategies by persons or organizations with conflicting interests in situations whose payoffs depend on the choices made by each participant and the participant's rivals. The theory of games is an ideal method for analyzing choices and options when the participants in a market are interdependent. By developing some of the simple techniques of game theory, we can show how the payoffs of choices vary with the possible choices of a rival in a gaming situation such as competition for market share. We can then show how a rational player will make choices based on assessments of the rival's actions.[1]

Duopoly: The Cournot Model and Nash Equilibrium

Duopoly A market structure in which two sellers protected from the entry of additional sellers are the sole producers of a standardized good with no close substitutes.

Let's begin our analysis of strategic behavior with a very simplified model in which there are only two sellers in a market. **Duopoly** is a market structure in which two sellers protected from the entry of additional sellers are the sole producers of a standardized good with no close substitutes. Economic models of duopoly are useful to illustrate how an individual seller's conjectures about the responses of a rival affect the equilibrium output. We have already analyzed one duopoly situation in Chapter 12, where we showed how a price war can push market prices down to the competitive level of marginal costs when sellers stubbornly believe that their rival will not match their price cuts. We can now show how other results are possible in duopoly markets under different assumptions about the conjectures that sellers might make about the business strategy of a rival.

The Cournot Model

A classic model of duopoly was formulated by the French economist Augustin Cournot in 1838. This model assumes that each of two sellers conjectures that its rival will always hold its output fixed at its current level. The model also presumes

---

[1] Game theory was originally formulated in the 1940s in a classic book by economist Oskar Morgenstern and mathematician John Von Neumann. See John Von Neumann and Oskar Morgenstern, *The Theory of Games and Economic Behavior* (New York: Science Editions, John Wiley & Sons, 1964). For applications of the theory to oligopoly, see James W. Friedman, *Game Theory with Applications to Economics* (New York: Oxford University Press, 1990). For a readable general analysis of game theory, see William Poundston, *Prisoner's Dilemma* (New York: Doubleday, 1992).

that sellers do not learn from their mistakes. These assumptions are quite different from the price war model we set up in Chapter 12, in which the sellers assumed instead that their rival would hold its prices fixed.

Let's now see how the results of the Cournot model of duopoly would differ from those of our price war model. Assume that there are only two brick producers in a region and that anyone in the region who wishes to buy bricks has to buy them from one of these producers. The bricks of each producer are standardized, and there are no quality differences. No other sellers of bricks can enter this market. Assume that both sellers can produce bricks at the same cost and that average costs are constant and therefore equal to marginal costs. Figure 13–1(a) shows the market demand for bricks, labeled D_M, along with the average and marginal costs of production. If bricks were produced in a competitive market, the output would be Q_C = 300,000 per month and the price would be P_C = AC = MC.

The two brick producers are the Adams Brick Company and the Baker Brick Company. Adams currently has the whole market to itself and presumes that the output of rival firms will always be zero. Because Adams believes that it has a monopoly, it produces the monopoly output corresponding to the point at which MR_M = MC. The resulting price is P_M. Assume a linear demand curve. This implies that marginal revenue falls twice as quickly as price as output increases. Because the marginal revenue curve bisects the line P_CE, the monopoly output is one half of the competitive output. Adams' initial profit-maximizing output is therefore 150,000 bricks per month.

Now, contrary to Adams' expectations, the Baker Brick Company enters the market. Entry of additional firms is not possible. Baker assumes that Adams will not react by changing output. It therefore begins production assuming that Adams will continue to produce 150,000 bricks each month. The demand curve it sees for its bricks is shown in Figure 13–1(b). Baker can serve all of the buyers who would buy bricks if their price fell below Adams' current price, P_M. The demand curve for Baker's output therefore begins at price P_M, at which market output is 150,000 bricks per month. This is the demand curve D_{B1}. Sales along this curve represents Baker's addition to Adams' current market output of 150,000 bricks per month.

The marginal revenue curve corresponding to this demand curve is MR_{B1}. Baker produces the output corresponding to MR_{B1} = MC. Measuring from the point at which monthly brick output is 150,000 on the quantity axis shows that this output is 75,000 bricks per month. The increase in the market supply of bricks from 150,000 to 225,000, however, decreases the price of bricks from P_M to P_1.

Table 13–1 shows the output of each firm in the first month of operation. The profit-maximizing output of each firm is always one half of the difference between Q_C and the output that it presumes the other firm produces. The competitive output is the one corresponding to P = MC, in this case 300,000 bricks per month. As Table 13–1 shows, Adams begins by producing $\frac{1}{2}Q_C$, assuming that its rival's output is zero. Baker then produces 75,000 bricks that month, which is $\frac{1}{2}(\frac{1}{2}Q_C) = \frac{1}{4}Q_C$. This is one half of the difference between the competitive output and the monopoly output initially produced by Adams.

The fall in the price of bricks caused by Baker's additional production results in a change in Adams' demand curve. Adams now assumes that Baker will continue to produce 75,000 bricks per month. It sees the demand for its bricks begin-

FIGURE 13–1 The Cournot Duopoly Model

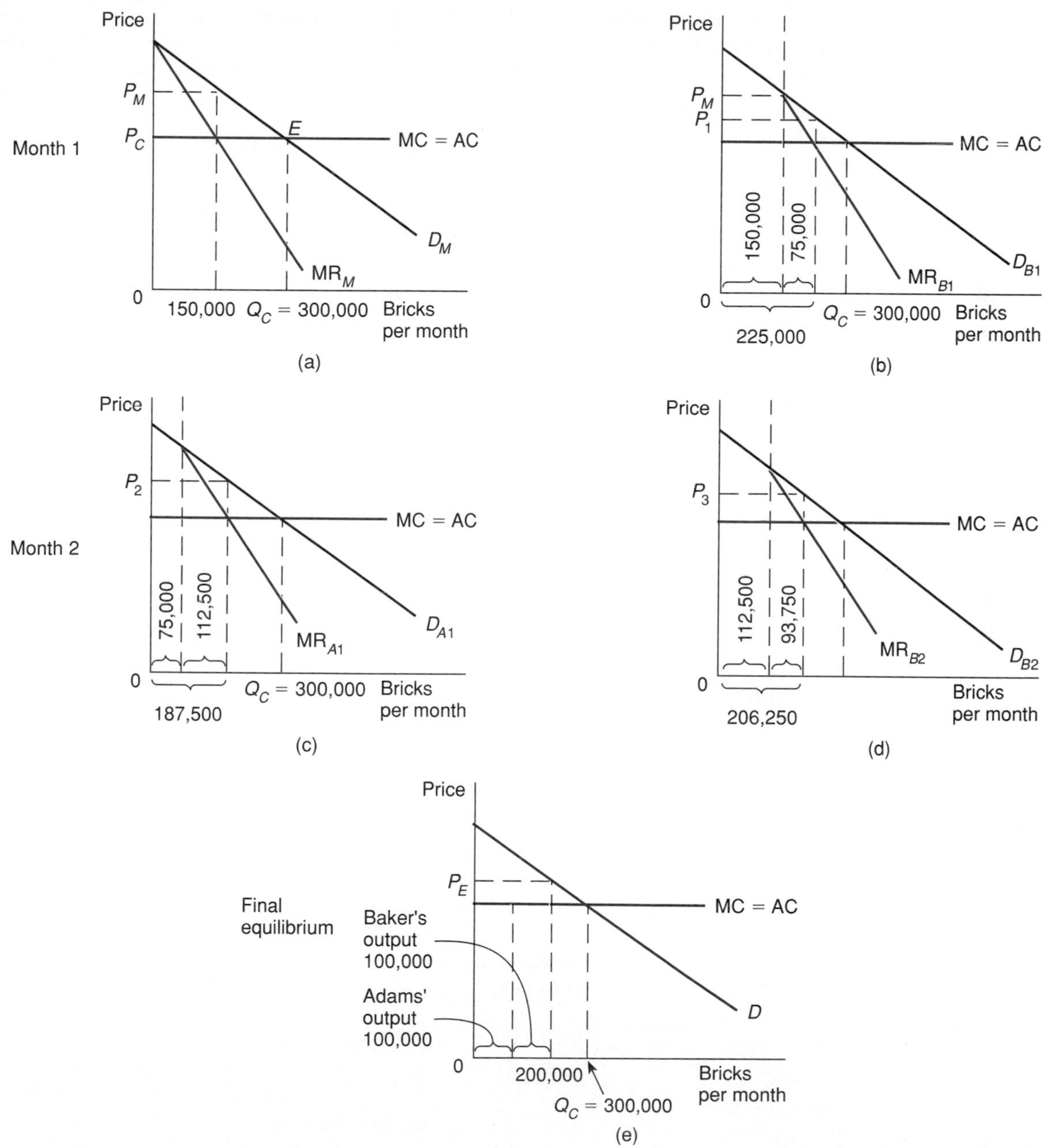

Each duopolist assumes that the other will keep producing its current output. Each month it reacts to the other's change in output. As Adams reduces production and Baker increases production, the Cournot equilibrium is approached. As shown in graph (e), each firm produces 100,000 bricks per month in equilibrium. This is equal to two thirds of the output in this market that would prevail under perfect competition.

ning at the point on the market demand curve corresponding to a monthly output of 75,000. Its demand is now D_{A1}, as shown in Figure 13–1(c). Its profit-maximizing output is now one half of the difference between the competitive output and the amount that Baker is currently producing. This occurs where $MR_{A1} = MC$. Adams assumes that Baker will continue to produce 75,000 bricks per month after it adjusts its output. The profit-maximizing output is therefore

$$\tfrac{1}{2}(300{,}000 - 75{,}000) = 112{,}500 \text{ bricks per month}$$

This can be written as

$$\tfrac{1}{2}(Q_C - \tfrac{1}{4}Q_C) = \tfrac{3}{8}Q_C \qquad \textbf{(13–1)}$$

It is shown in Table 13–1.

Now it is Baker's turn to react again. Adams has reduced its production from 150,000 to 112,500 bricks per month. This has caused the total available monthly supply of bricks to decrease from 225,000 to 187,500. As a result the price of bricks increases to P_2. Baker assumes that Adams will continue to produce this amount. It views its demand curve as beginning at the point where marked output is 112,500. This is the demand curve D_{B2}, shown in Figure 13–1(d). Maximum profit is at the point where $MR_{B2} = MC$. This equals ½ of the difference between the competitive output and the ⅜ of the competitive output currently supplied by Adams. As shown in Table 13–1, Baker now produces 5⁄16 of the competitive output (93,750 bricks per month). Total market output is now 206,250 bricks per month, and price declines to P_3.

Table 13–1 continues the calculations for months 3 and 4. Notice that each month Adams' output is declining, whereas Baker's output is increasing. Notice how the monthly output of each of the duopolists is approaching 100,000 bricks. In each month each duopolist produces half of the difference between the competitive output and the output produced by the rival firm.

Baker Brick Company increases its output by a smaller amount each month. It starts out producing ¼ of the competitive output. The next month it increases output to 5⁄16 of the competitive output. The month after that it produces 21⁄64 of

TABLE 13–1 Cournot Duopoly Equilibrium (Q_C = 300,000 Bricks per Month)

Month	*Monthly Output of Adams Brick Company*	*Monthly Output of Baker Brick Company*
1	$150{,}000 = \tfrac{1}{2}Q_C$	$75{,}000 = \tfrac{1}{2}(\tfrac{1}{2}Q_C) = \tfrac{1}{4}Q_C$
2	$112{,}500 = \tfrac{1}{2}(Q_C - \tfrac{1}{4}Q_C) = \tfrac{3}{8}Q_C$	$93{,}750 = \tfrac{1}{2}(Q_C - \tfrac{3}{8}Q_C) = \tfrac{5}{16}Q_C$
3	$103{,}125 = \tfrac{1}{2}(Q_C - \tfrac{5}{16}Q_C) = \tfrac{11}{32}Q_C$	$98{,}438 = \tfrac{1}{2}(Q_C - \tfrac{11}{32}Q_C) = \tfrac{21}{64}Q_C$
4	$100{,}781 = \tfrac{1}{2}(Q_C - \tfrac{21}{64}Q_C) = \tfrac{43}{128}Q_C$	$99{,}609 = \tfrac{1}{2}(Q_C - \tfrac{43}{128}Q_C) = \tfrac{85}{256}Q_C$

Final Equilibrium

$$Q_A = [1 - (\tfrac{1}{2} + \tfrac{1}{8} + \tfrac{1}{32} + \ldots)]Q_C = \left[1 - \frac{\tfrac{1}{2}}{1 - \tfrac{1}{4}}\right]Q_C = 100{,}000 = \tfrac{1}{3}Q_C$$

$$Q_B = (\tfrac{1}{4} + \tfrac{1}{16} + \tfrac{1}{64} + \ldots)Q_C = \frac{\tfrac{1}{4}}{1 - \tfrac{1}{4}}Q_C = 100{,}000 = \tfrac{1}{3}Q_C$$

Total output = $\tfrac{2}{3}Q_C$ = 200,000 bricks/month

the competitive output. The process goes on and on. Note that 5⁄16 can be written as 1⁄4 + 1⁄16. Similarly 21⁄64 = 1⁄4 + 1⁄16 + 1⁄64. The next term in the sum is 1⁄4 of 1⁄64. The last term in the sum is always 1⁄4 of the next to last term. Using the formula for an infinite geometric progression (see Table 13–1), the final equilibrium output of each firm approaches 1⁄3 of the competitive output. The total market output is therefore two thirds of the competitive equilibrium output, given the demand for the product. As shown in Figure 13–1(e), each firm produces 100,000 bricks per month. Total output is 200,000 bricks per month, and price is P_E. This is the Cournot duopoly equilibrium. It would prevail only if each of the rival firms stubbornly assumed that the other would never adjust its output.

Reaction Curves

Reaction curves Curves that show the profit-maximizing output produced by one firm, given the output of the rival firm.

The equilibrium for the Cournot model can be shown in another way. **Reaction curves** show the profit-maximizing output produced by one firm, given the output of the rival firm. Figure 13–2 is based on the data of Table 13–1 and plots the output of the Adams Brick Company against the corresponding output of the Baker Brick Company.

FIGURE 13–2 Reaction Curves

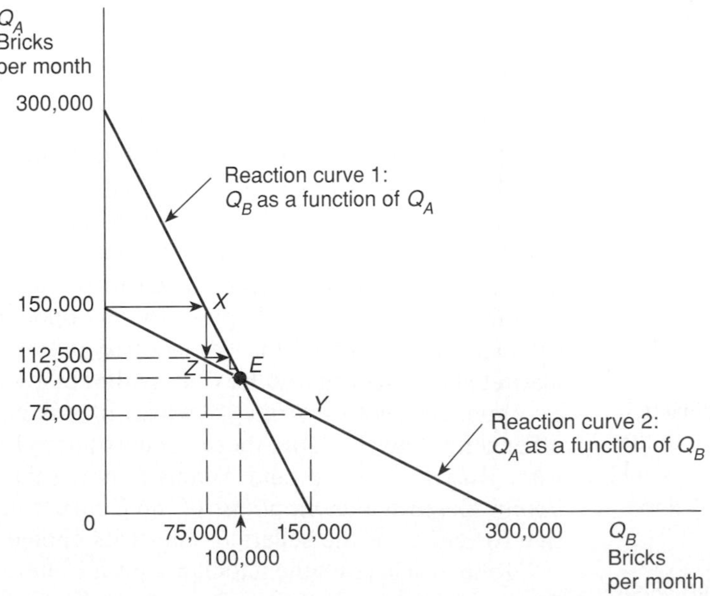

Reaction curve 1 gives Baker's profit-maximizing output per month as a function of Adams' monthly output. Reaction curve 2 gives Adams' profit-maximizing output per month as a function of Baker's monthly output. Following the arrows drawn from Q_A = 150,000 from curve to curve leads to the Cournot equilibrium at point E, where each firm produces 100,000 bricks per month.

Reaction curve 1 gives Baker's output as a function of Adams' output. It shows that if Q_A were 300,000 per month, Q_B would be zero. Similarly, reaction curve 2 gives Adams' output as a function of Baker's output. It shows that when Q_B is 300,000 per month, Q_A is zero. If either firm were to produce 300,000 bricks per month, the other firm would react by producing zero. This is because at that output price would fall to average cost. Any production in excess of 300,000 per month would not be profitable because it would cause price to fall below average cost.

If one firm produces the monopoly output, 150,000 bricks per month, the other firm responds by producing 75,000 bricks per month. At point *X*, Q_A = 150,000 and Q_B = 75,000 on reaction curve 1. Similarly, point *Y* on reaction curve 2 shows that when

$$Q_B = 150{,}000, \quad Q_A = 75{,}000$$

Reaction curves can be used to show how equilibrium is established. When Adams produces 150,000 bricks, go to reaction curve 1 to see that Baker will produce 75,000 bricks at point *X*. From point *X*, draw a line to reaction curve 2 to see how Adams then reduces output to 112,500 bricks per month. This is point *Z*. Moving from one curve to the other in this way eventually leads to point *E*. This is the Cournot equilibrium. It is attained at the output at which the two reaction curves intersect and each firm produces 100,000 bricks per month. At any other output the firms react to each other's output choice. One firm increases output, and the other decreases output until each firm produces 100,000 bricks per month and the total market output is 200,000 bricks.

Nash Equilibrium

Strategy A course of action chosen after consideration of a rival's possible courses of action in a competitive situation.

Nash equilibrium A combination of the strategies chosen by rivals in a competitive situation in which each of the rivals has no incentive to change what it is doing, given the choices of its opponents.

Let's examine the characteristics of the equilibrium in the Cournot model is greater detail. A **strategy** can be defined as a course of action chosen after consideration of a rival's possible courses of action in a competitive situation. When either of the rival sellers in a market chooses the strategy of selling one third of the competitive output level (the one corresponding to the point at which P = MC), then the maximum possible profit for its opponent will prevail if its opponent also produces one third of the competitive output level. Once that distribution of market shares has been achieved, neither of the rival sellers can increase its profit by choosing another strategy, which in this case would be the choice of some other output level. Under these circumstances Baker is doing the best it can, *given what Adams is doing*, and Adams is doing the best it can, *given what Baker is doing*. Given the assumptions of the Cournot model, there is therefore no incentive for either of the sellers to adjust its choices.

John Nash, a mathematician with an interest in economics who studied the theoretical properties of equilibrium in oligopolistic markets, developed a formal definition of the conditions of equilibrium when there is mutual interdependence among sellers. A **Nash equilibrium** is a combination of the strategies chosen by rivals in a competitive situation in which each of the rivals *has no incentive to* *change what it is doing, given the choices of its opponents.*[2] From the above analysis it is clear that the solution to the Cournot model is a Nash equilibrium.

The concept of a Nash equilibrium is extremely important in the analysis of business behavior in oligopolistic markets. When we analyzed equilibrium in perfectly competitive, pure monopoly, and monopolistically competitive markets, all we had to consider was whether firms were maximizing profits, given our information on revenue and costs. In oligopolistic markets we need more information to determine whether an equilibrium has been achieved. We need information on revenue and costs, but *we also need information on the possible strategies that rivals in the market can use.* Once we know what rivals are doing, we can use standard economic analysis to find the profit-maximizing option of any one seller. Naturally, it is more difficult to find the Nash equilibrium for an oligopolistic market, or to even be sure that one exists, than it is to find the conditions of equilibrium and the corresponding output and price in pure monopoly or perfectly competitive markets. To find a Nash equilibrium, we have to know the assumptions that a firm makes about the reactions of its rivals, and we must then search for a set of strategies, if they exist, under which each seller is doing as well as possible, given the choices of its rivals. Assuming that firms seek to maximize profit, this means that we must check all of the possible output combinations and see whether one of them corresponds to a situation in which all participants in the market are making as much profit as possible, given the choices made by all of their rivals.

The Nash equilibrium in an oligopolistic market can depend on the reaction assumptions that firms make. For example, for the Cournot duopoly model, there is a Nash equilibrium at two thirds of the competitive output levels for the entire market. In the price war duopoly model we developed in the preceding chapter, in which sellers assumed that their rival would not react to price cuts, there was a Nash equilibrium corresponding to an output level equal to the competitive output for which $P = \text{MC}$. At that output level each seller was making as much profit as possible, given what its rival was doing and assuming that its rival would not match any further price changes. At the Nash equilibrium in that model each seller earned zero economic profits!

Concept Review

1. Explain why the demand curve of any single seller in a duopoly will depend on the choices of the other seller. What are the underlying assumptions of the Cournot model of duopoly?
2. What is a reaction curve?
3. What is a Nash equilibrium? Does a Nash equilibrium exist for the Cournot model of duopoly?

[2] For a more detailed discussion of the concept of a Nash equilibrium, see David Kreps, *A Course in Microeconomic Theory* (Princeton, N.J.: Princeton University Press, 1990).

The Theory of Games

The Cournot model is highly simplified because it assumes that the sellers in the market stubbornly assume that their rival will always stick to one strategy—stonewalling on output. A similar criticism can be levied against the simplified price war model discussed in Chapter 12, in which sellers stubbornly believe that their rival will not match their price cuts or price increases. We can now begin to use the theory of games to develop more realistic models of behavior in oligopolistic markets by opening up our analysis to the possibility that sellers consider the fact that their rival can choose more than one strategy rather than only one of several possible options.

A game theoretic approach to the analysis of oligopoly involves putting each player in the market in its rival's shoes. When we apply game theory to business strategies we assume that sellers must not only consider what they can do to maximize profits, *they must also consider what their rival can do to maximize profits*. The profits of each seller are dependent not only on its own choices but also on the choices of its rival.

The Payoff Matrix

The managers of a firm are usually more sophisticated than were the owners of the two brick companies in the duopoly we discussed above. They do not stubbornly adhere to the belief that the rival firm will maintain a given price or quantity. They realize that when their firm lowers its price, the rival firm may either keep its price constant or lower it. They realize that the profits that their firm can earn depend on the rival firm's reaction.

Let's now use a game theory approach to analyze a duopoly market in which both firms have the option of starting a price war by lowering price. Assume that price is initially set at the monopoly level and each firm has the option of cutting price to gain market share. The managers of each firm calculate their profits for both the case in which the competing firm keeps its price fixed *and* the case in which it matches the price cut. Let's again examine the behavior of the Adams and Baker companies. This time, however, assume that these firms are now under new management and that they employ more sophisticated techniques in determining their prices and outputs.

The managers of each firm calculate the profits their firm can earn when it lowers price or keeps price constant. They do this for two cases. The first is the case in which the rival firm lowers price. The second is the case in which the rival firm does not lower price. The result is a **payoff matrix** that shows the gain or loss accruing to each possible strategy for each of the rival's possible reactions.

Payoff matrix A matrix that shows the gain or loss accruing to each possible strategy for each of the rival's possible reactions in a competitive situation.

Now let's use this payoff matrix to examine the options and possible profits of each seller, given the options available to its rival. Table 13–2 shows the payoff matrix. The matrix shows what will happen if either seller chooses a course of action and how the payoff to that action will vary with the choices made by the rival seller. Each box in the matrix is called a *cell*. Each cell indicates the profit that each of the sellers can expect to earn under a combination of strategies that they each choose independently. The cell in the upper left-hand corner shows the

TABLE 13–2 Payoff Matrix for a Price War

		Baker's Strategies	
		Cut Price	***Maintain Price***
Adams' Strategies	***Cut Price***	Adams' profit $45,000 Baker's profit $45,000	Adams' profit $65,000 Baker's profit $40,000
	Maintain Price	Adams' profit $40,000 Baker's profit $65,000	Adams' profit $50,000 Baker's profit $50,000

monthly profits of each of the two companies if both choose to cut price. The upper number in the cell gives Adams' monthly profit and the lower number gives Baker's monthly profit if both have cut their price from the initial monopoly price level by 1 cent per brick.

Two options are available to both companies: They can cut their price by one cent in an attempt to gain market share from their rival, or they can stand pat and maintain their price. Adams knows that if it cuts its price by one cent, it will gain sales only if Baker does not match its price cut. The first row in the payoff matrix shows the consequences of Adams' price cut. If Baker also cuts its price by one cent, Adams' profit will be $45,000 per month. If Baker maintains its price at the current level, Adams' profit will increase to $65,000 per month as a result of a sharp increase in its share of the market.

Adams' alternative strategy is to maintain its price. If it does so, it will earn a monthly profit of $40,000 if Baker responds by cutting its price. It will earn a monthly profit of $50,000 if Baker maintains its price.

The payoff matrix also shows Baker's profit for each of its possible strategies. If Adams' managers knew for sure that when Adams cut price, its rival would maintain price, they would know that the price cut would result in a profit of $65,000 per month, which is Adams' highest payoff in the matrix. However, Adams' managers know that Baker might match the price cut, in which case Adams would earn a profit of only $45,000 per month.

Dominant strategy The strategy for which a player is getting the highest possible payoff, regardless of what the rival players are doing.

Dominant Strategies and Nash Equilibriums

The managers of Adams and Baker can pursue various strategies in their attempt to maximize profits. We can search for equilibrium in a game theory model in much the same way that we do in any other model. In game theory we search for a **dominant strategy,** that is, the strategy for which a player is getting the highest possible payoff, regardless of what the rival players are doing. Let's now examine the payoff matrix in Table 13–2 to see if there is one pricing strategy that can be regarded as dominant.

Given the information in the payoff matrix, it is easy to show that cutting price is the dominant strategy for both Adams and Baker. First look at Adams' strategies. No matter what Baker does, Adams would be better off by cutting price. Look at the *upper numbers* in the first column of the payoff matrix to see why this is so. If Baker matches Adams' price cut, Adams would earn a monthly profit of $45,000. If Adams does not cut price while Baker does, its monthly profit would be $40,000. It follows that Adams would be better off by cutting price if Baker also cuts price. However, to prove that price-cutting is the dominant strategy, we also have to look at the *upper numbers* in the second column of the payoff matrix to see how Adams would do if Baker maintains price. If Baker maintains price after Adams cuts price, Adams would gain lots of market share and enjoy a profit of $65,000 per month. If, however, Adams maintains price, its profit would be only $50,000 per month. Therefore, even if Baker maintains price, Adams would make more profit if it chooses the strategy of cutting price. Based on the payoff matrix of Table 13–2 we have now proved that cutting price is Adams' dominant strategy because Adams' profit is higher when it chooses that strategy *no matter which strategy its rival chooses.*

You can also compare the *lower entries* in the rows of the matrix to prove that cutting price is Baker's dominant strategy. If Baker cuts price, it will earn $5,000 more in profit per month than it could by maintaining price when Adams maintains price. When Adams maintains price, Baker can earn $15,000 more in monthly profit by cutting price than by maintaining price. It follows that cutting price is also Baker's dominant strategy.

When both players have dominant strategies, the solution to a game theory model is a Nash equilibrium in which each of the players is getting the highest possible payoff no matter what strategy the other player chooses. Once a Nash equilibrium has been achieved, that equilibrium will be stable so that both players will have the incentive to continue choosing the same strategy and to avoid deviating from it.

A Nash Equilibrium without a Dominant Strategy for One of the Rivals

In general, we have to examine the payoff matrix in each situation to find out whether the players have a dominant strategy. In many cases the logic of the situation is such that either or both of the players does not have an obvious dominant strategy. Let's examine a situation in which one of the players does not have a dominant strategy and the other does. Suppose two car companies, Nexus and Finite, are introducing new luxury car models into an oligopolistic market. The two companies must consider whether or not to mark their entrance into the market with an aggressive television marketing campaign that could increase their market share and therefore their profit but could also decrease their profit if the expense of the campaign is greater than the extra revenue they obtain from any increase in their market share.

TABLE 13–3 Payoff Matrix for Advertising: The Case of One Rival without a Dominant Strategy

		Nexus' Strategies	
		Advertise	***Do Not Advertise***
Finite's Strategies	***Advertise***	Finite's profit $10 million Nexus' profit $ 6 million	Finite's profit $14 million Nexus' profit $ 3 million
	Do Not Advertise	Finite's profit $ 7 million Nexus' profit $ 9 million	Finite's profit $18 million Nexus' profit $ 4 million

The payoff matrix in Table 13–3 shows how the first-year annual profit of Nexus and Finite in the market would vary with advertising and not advertising. Let's examine Finite first. To do so, we look at the top number in each cell to see how Finite's profit varies under each strategy, given the choices of its rival, Nexus. If Nexus advertises, Finite's best alternative is to also advertise because its profit for the year would be $3 million higher if it advertises than if it does not advertise. If, however, Nexus does not advertise, Finite's profit for the year would be $4 million higher if *it does not advertise*. Finite's profit could be higher when it doesn't advertise, because its ad campaign is very costly and only prevents it from losing market share to Nexus if Nexus does advertise. Therefore, if Nexus does not advertise, Finite enjoys a much higher profit ($18 million for the year) than it could enjoy under any other scenario in the payoff matrix. The strategy with the highest payoff for Finite depends on which strategy Nexus chooses when it enters the market. If Nexus does not advertise, Finite is better off not to advertise and will earn $18 million in annual profit if it doesn't. If Nexus does advertise, Finite is better off to advertise and will earn $10 million in annual profit if it does.

However, based on the data in the matrix, Nexus does have a dominant strategy, which is to advertise. No matter what Finite does, Nexus has a higher profit for the year if it advertises. To see this, look at the lower numbers in each cell and compare them across rows. If Finite advertises, Nexus earns $6 million if it advertises, which is $3 million more than it would earn if it doesn't. Similarly, if Finite does not advertise, Nexus earns $9 million for the year if it advertises but only $4 million if it does not. Therefore, no matter what Finite does, Nexus is better off if it advertises. If Finite knows the payoffs to Nexus, it also knows that Nexus has a dominant strategy. Finite will therefore base its strategy on the assumption that Nexus will in fact mount a television campaign. Under these circumstances Finite's best strategy is to advertise because by doing so it can earn $10 million for the year as opposed to $7 million if it doesn't. Therefore, in this case the game has a Nash equilibrium even though one of the players lacks a dominant strategy.

More than One Nash Equilibrium

It is also possible for a game-type situation to have more than one Nash equilibrium. If so, it is possible to predict the general outcome in an oligopolistically competitive market, but it is not possible to predict the distribution of market shares among sellers. To examine the consequences of a situation in which more than one Nash equilibrium is possible, let's consider a market entry problem. Suppose that two oil companies, AxelOil and Bexico are deciding whether or not to build a new chain of gas stations in a developing African nation. Table 13–4 shows the payoff matrix for the two companies. Now suppose that AxelOil announces that it will enter the market. What will Bexico do once it learns this?

First note that, given the numbers in the cells, neither company has a dominant strategy. AxelOil's decision to enter cannot be determined unless it first knows Bexico's decision. If Bexico enters, AxelOil's best strategy is not to enter because the annual profit it would earn is $9 million if it stays out and only $6 million if it enters. However, if it knows that Bexico will not enter, then it is better off to enter because it would earn an annual profit of $9 million if it enters as opposed to only $6 million if it does not enter. Similarly, there is no dominant strategy for Bexico: If AxelOil enters, Bexico's better alternative is not to enter. Once AxelOil is in the market, Bexico's annual profit would be $6 million if it also enters but $9 million if it doesn't. On the other hand, if Bexico enters, AxelOil's

TABLE 13–4 Payoff Matrix for Market Entry: The Case of Two Nash Equilibriums

AxelOil's Strategies		*Bexico's Strategies*			
		Don't Enter		*Enter*	
Don't Enter	AxelOil's profit	$6 million	AxelOil's profit	$9 million
	Bexico's profit	$6 million	Bexico's profit	$9 million
Enter	AxelOil's profit	$9 million	AxelOil's profit	$6 million
	Bexico's profit	$9 million	Bexico's profit	$6 million

better alternative is not to enter. Apparently, the market in this nation is not big enough to handle the supplies of both companies, which, if they enter, must provide a specified minimum number of gas stations under contract with the nation's government. If both companies enter, the supply of gas would increase so much that gas prices in the nation would be pushed down, adversely affecting the profits of both companies.

Despite the fact that neither company has a dominant strategy, there can be a Nash equilibrium in this case provided that one of the companies announces its intention first. If AxelOil enters, then Bexico would be better off if it doesn't enter. This would allow it to earn an annual profit of $9 million rather than the $6 million it would earn if it enters the market once AxelOil is in it. Similarly, once AxelOil is sure that Bexico is not going to enter, it would be better off if it sticks to its decision to enter because it would then earn an annual profit of $9 million rather than the $6 million it would earn if it rescinds the decision.

Unfortunately, the Nash equilibrium we have just described is not the only possible equilibrium in this case. If, instead, Bexico announces that it will enter, AxelOil is better off it does not enter. This is because it can enjoy $9 million in annual profit by not entering as opposed to $6 million by entering. Similarly, once Bexico is sure that AxelOil will not enter, it is better off if it does not rescind its decision. These strategies also constitute a Nash equilibrium, given the numbers in the box. We can therefore predict that if the two companies act non-cooperatively, only one of them will serve the new market. However, we cannot predict which one. Note also that because annual profit is the same for both companies whether or not they serve the new market, neither has the incentive to announce first. If profit for each company were higher when it served the new market, each company would have the incentive to choose that option and it would be impossible to predict which company would announce first.

More than one Nash equilibrium is also a possibility when companies are considering the expansion of productive capacity to meet future demand. For example, suppose two companies dominate the nation's aluminum market. The demand for aluminum is expected to increase. However, because aluminum processing plants are quite large and require a minimum scale to be profitable, the strategic planners of both companies have concluded that one company would profit if it expands capacity to meet future demand but that if both companies expand capacity, the supply of aluminum would increase so much that its price would plummet and neither company would make a profit.

The payoff matrix in Table 13–5 shows how different possible scenarios would affect the annual profit of the two companies—National Aluminum Company and Federal Aluminum Company. If each company builds a plant, each would incur an annual loss of $10 million after the plants started to supply the market. If neither company builds a plant, each would earn an annual profit of $8 million. However if only one of the companies builds a plant, it would earn a profit of $15 million annually, while its competitor would earn an annual profit of $5 million. As you can see from the payoff matrix in Table 13–5, neither company has a dominant strategy. However, once either knows what its rival is going to do, the dominant strategy is clear. If Federal is convinced that National will build a

TABLE 13–5 Payoff Matrix for Building More Supply Capacity: The Advantage of Moving First

Federal's Strategies		National's Strategies: Build		National's Strategies: Don't Build	
Build	Federal's profit	−$10 million		Federal's profit	$15 million
	National's profit	−$10 million		National's profit	$5 million
Don't Build	Federal's profit	$5 million		Federal's profit	$8 million
	National's profit	$15 million		National's profit	$8 million

plant, its better alternative is not to build a plant, because it would earn $5 million in annual profit if it doesn't build one but would lose $10 million annually if it does. The same reasoning applies to Federal. If Federal knows that National will build, it is better off not to build. However, if either company is convinced that the other will build, its better alternative is to build. There are therefore two Nash equilibriums corresponding to the upper right cell and the lower left cell of the payoff matrix. We cannot predict which of the two equilibriums will emerge.

One way a firm can avoid getting into the build or do not build bind is to engage in a risky "preemptive strike" against its rival by building additional capacity before it is sure that the demand is sufficient to profitably sell the extra output. Of course, if the firm mistakenly estimates future growth in demand, it could end up with big losses. Also the firm that builds first runs the risk that its rival might not respond in a rational way or might think the market could accommodate a still larger output without causing profit to decline. If that firm also builds more capacity, profit could plummet for both firms.

Preemption can get a company into trouble with government antitrust authorities! In a famous 1945 antitrust case, the Aluminum Company of America (Alcoa) was found guilty of using unfair business practices to maintain its monopoly. The Justice Department argued that Alcoa had used its extensive knowledge of demand to expand capacity before rivals could enter the market. Here Alcoa's "preemptive strategy" was used as a way of forcing potential rivals into the dominant strategy of not building plants so they could enter the aluminum market. As a result of this case Alcoa was broken up and new aluminum firms were established.

MODERN MICROECONOMICS IN ACTION: THE BUSINESS WORLD

Business Strategies to Gain Market Share by Forcing Rivals into the Dominant Strategy of Leaving or Not Entering the Market: The Case of Retailing

In the 1970s and 1980s Sam Walton's Wal-Mart Stores developed a successful strategy for penetrating retail markets by building very large stores in urban areas with a population of less than 100,000. This strategy succeeded in forcing smaller retailers into the dominant strategy of leaving those markets. The markets were not big enough to handle more than one large retailer, so such potential entrants as Kmart were forced into the dominant strategy of staying out of them. Kmart knew that there was not enough sales volume in such markets to allow more than one large retailer to survive. Sam Walton introduced the technology of the large discount store into areas that other large retailers had shunned. In this way Wal-Mart came close to gaining a monopoly position in the discount sales market of certain areas by siphoning off sales from smaller retailers.

However, the retail market of the 1990s has been changing and Wal-Mart may have to rethink its strategy. First of all, other large retailers have realized the wisdom of Sam Walton's strategy and are now trying to be the first to enter retail markets not yet served by a large discount store. These retailers are building bigger stores than Wal-Mart built. The standard Wal-Mart store of the 1980s had an area of 76,000 square feet, but in 1990 Kmart was already operating a 148,000-square-foot Super Kmart in the town of Medina, Ohio, that sold food, apparel, and other standard discount store fare. Kmart planned to open more such superstores. Wal-Mart has responded to this challenge by upping the standard size of its stores from 76,000 square feet to 110,000 square feet.*

The heated competition for retail sales in the 1990s has come up against slowing growth in national retail sales volume. Therefore, the strategy of expansion, perhaps as a way of preempting the entry of competitors, could backfire.† Sales per store have been slowing in the 1990s. Nonetheless, the trend toward larger stores has been drawing sales away from shopping malls and department stores and could spell a change in U.S. retail sales markets as superstores drive smaller competitors into bankruptcy.

* See Isadore Barmash, "Down the Scale with the Major Store Chains," *The New York Times*, February 2, 1992, p. F5.

† Ibid.

Prisoner's Dilemma Games and the Maximum Strategy

Let's return to the payoff matrix in Table 13–2, which showed that each of the two firms in a duopoly had the dominant strategy of cutting price. The Nash equilibrium for the data in the payoff matrix corresponds to the upper left-hand cell, in which both of the participants in the market earn an annual profit of $45,000. In this game both firms would be better off if they cooperated and divided the market up. To do so, they would have to agree to maintain the current monopoly price and avoid entering into a price war that would eventually push prices down to the marginal and average costs of production, thus eliminating economic profits. If both firms maintained price, they would remain in the lower right-hand cell of the matrix, in which each would earn economic profits of $50,000. However, the dominant strategy of the two firms is to cut price so they inevitably start a price war.

Prisoner's dilemma A game-type situation in which the dominant strategy results in a Nash equilibrium in which both participants are worse off than they would have been if they had cooperated.

The type of game illustrated by the payoff in Table 13–6 is one of a general class of games called the **prisoner's dilemma,** in which the dominant strategy results in a Nash equilibrium in which both participants are worse off than they would have been if they had cooperated. The source of the prisoner's dilemma is that lack of communication between the participants and their pursuit of self-interest prevent cooperation.

The prisoner's dilemma gets its name from the well-known parable of two prisoners who are arrested after committing a crime together. They are arrested for breaking and entering, but the arresting officer suspects that they are also responsible for a string of armed robberies in the area. His job is to get them to confess to having committed the more serious crime of armed robbery. The evidence against the prisoners is spotty, so the arresting officer engages in the following ploy to extract a confession from them. Each of the prisoners is locked up and interrogated in a separate room. If neither confesses to the armed robbery, say because the evidence is inadequate, each will be convicted of breaking and entering, for which the evidence is sufficient. The sentence for breaking and entering would then be three years in jail for each prisoner. However, if one of the prisoners confesses to armed robbery, and thereby implicates the other, he would get a reduced prison term, say two years instead of the usual five years for this crime, while the other prisoner would get a longer term, say seven years instead of five, if he does not confess. If both confess, then both would get a five-year term.

If the two prisoners simply agree with each other not to confess, both would get a three-year term. But they are kept from each other while being interrogated, and each prisoner has no idea what the other will do. Unfortunately for the prisoners, but not for justice because they are really guilty, their self-interest will lead both to confess if they seek to minimize the prison term. In other words, as the payoff matrix in Table 13–6 shows, the dominant strategy for both prisoners is to confess, and that is in fact the Nash equilibrium in this case. To see this,

TABLE 13–6 Payoff Matrix for the Prisoner's Dilemma

		Killer's Strategies	
		Confess	***Don't Confess***
Bugsy's Strategies	***Confess***	Bugsy's sentence 5 years Killer's sentence 5 years	Bugsy's sentence 2 years Killer's sentence 7 years
	Don't Confess	Bugsy's sentence 7 years Killer's sentence 2 years	Bugsy's sentence 3 years Killer's sentence 3 years

remember that each prisoner wants to minimize the prison term no matter what the other prisoner does. Looking at the top numbers in the first column, you can see that for the first prisoner, call him Bugsy, the term is smaller (five years instead of seven years) if he confesses and his partner, call her Killer, also confesses. Similarly, looking at the top numbers in the second column, you can see that Bugsy is better off if he confesses even if Killer does not because in that case he would get a prison term of two years if he confesses instead of three if he does not. Confessing is therefore Bugsy's dominant strategy. If you examine the lower numbers in each row you will see that confessing is also Killer's dominant strategy. So both confess and both get a five-year term.

Notice that both prisoners would be better off if, before going into interrogation, they had been able to reach an iron-clad agreement not to confess. If each prisoner could have been sure that the other would not confess, both would have remained silent and both would have been sentenced to a three-year term instead of a five-year term. The analysis assumes that such collusion or threats—for example, Killer telling Bugsy she will do him in if he confesses—were not possible because the arresting officer's technique for extracting confessions took the two prisoners by surprise.

Maximin strategies Dominant strategies that minimize the maximum loss.

In a prisoner's dilemma situation the dominant strategies are called **maximin strategies** because they minimize the maximum loss. To demonstrate that the price war model we developed as a game theory situation earlier in the chapter is really a prisoner's dilemma game involving a maximin strategy, Table 13–7 shows the

TABLE 13–7 Payoff Matrix for a Price War: The Prisoner's Dilemma and the Maximin Strategy

		Baker's Strategies		
		Cut Price	***Maintain Price***	
Adams' Strategies	***Cut Price***	Change in Adams' profit −$5,000 Change in Baker's profit −$5,000	Change in Adams' profit $15,000 Change in Baker's profit −$10,000	Maximum losses for Adams −$5,000
	Maintain Price	Change in Adams' profit −$10,000 Change in Baker's profit $15,000	Change in Adams' profit $0 Change in Baker's profit $0	−$10,000
Maximum losses for Baker		−$5,000	−$10,000	

change in economic profits that results for each possible pair of strategies from reducing the price per brick 1 cent or from maintaining price. If the two firms in the market cooperate, they would maintain price at the initial monopoly level and split the monopoly profits. However, if the two firms choose their dominant strategy of minimizing the maximum losses, they would enter into a ruinous price war. In effect, the market participants assume that the worst possible outcome will occur for any strategy. The *worst* that can happen to Adams as a result of any strategy is shown in the table. If it cuts price, the worst possible outcome, a $5,000 decrease in profits would occur if its rival also cuts price. Similarly, if it maintains price, the worst possible outcome, a decrease in profit of $10,000 per month would occur if its rival cuts price. The strategy that results in the smallest decrease in profits is the maximin strategy. Other strategies are possible; however, the advantage of the maximin strategy is that it protects profits. In effect, it places a floor on profits. By choosing this strategy, each of the firms can be sure that its profits will not fall below a certain level.

As long as Adams does not know for sure what its rival will do, it will cut its price. If it does, the worst that can happen is that it will lose $5,000. The worst that can happen if it maintains its price is that it will lose $10,000.

Baker's management makes similar calculations. In the worst scenario it too will lose $10,000 if it maintains price and Adams cuts price and only $5,000 if it cuts price and Adams maintains price. Therefore, it also chooses the price-cutting strategy.

Each firm hopes that the other will maintain price so it can increase profits by $15,000 per month. However, if *both* firms seek to avoid the worst by pursuing the maximin strategy, each cuts price. The firms therefore start a price war. Both firms end up losing $5,000 rather than increasing profit. Each firm can increase profit only if the other firm pursues a strategy of maintaining price. When both firms employ the protective maximin strategy, neither can gain because of the resulting price war, but both choose to lower price anyway.

Both firms would be better off if both maintained price. Their rivalry and their desire to avoid the worst possible outcome assure that neither can gain from cutting price. If they realized this, they could collude and agree to maintain price. Such an agreement would neither increase nor decrease their profit. It would, however, avoid the inevitable losses that result when either firm cuts price.

Advertising under Oligopoly: Another Possible Prisoner's Dilemma Game

We briefly discussed advertising earlier in this chapter to illustrate a case in which one of two rival firms does not have a dominant strategy. We can also model advertising in oligopolistic markets as a prisoner's dilemma situation. In oligopolistic markets, individual firms consider the reactions of rival firms before engaging in advertising and other promotional expenses. An oligopolistic firm can substantially increase its market share by advertising only if rival firms do not retaliate with their own advertising.

A game theory approach to advertising is useful in understanding the problems oligopolistic firms face in choosing a marketing strategy. Assume that only two firms, Sharp and Bright, sell photographic paper in a market. Both of these firms are considering an advertising campaign to increase sales. Each realizes, however, that the gain it achieves from advertising depends on whether its rival also advertises. A payoff matrix like the one used to analyze a price war is shown in Table 13–8. If Bright advertises and Sharp does not, Bright would gain $20 million in annual profit and Sharp would lose the same amount. If, however, Sharp also advertises, both firms would lose $8 million in annual profit because both would incur selling costs, but neither would increase sales. Similarly, if Sharp advertises, it can gain only if Bright does not. Both firms would be better off if neither advertises. In that case there would be no change in their profit. This is therefore another prisoner's dilemma game.

However, if both firms seek to avoid the worst outcome by pursuing a maximin strategy, they will *both* choose to advertise. Both will go after the $20 million annual winnings, and both will come out with an $8 million annual loss. This is because each will choose the strategy with the lowest maximum loss. The last column of the table shows the maximum loss for each of Bright's strategies. If it advertises, the most it can lose is $8 million per year. If it does not advertise, the most it can lose is $20 million per year. Seeking to avoid the $20 million annual loss, it advertises. By the same reasoning, Sharp also advertises. The result is that both firms lose $8 million per year. If, instead, they had agreed not to advertise, both would have earned profit.

TABLE 13–8 Payoff Matrix for Advertising: The Case of the Prisoner's Dilemma and the Maximin Strategy

		Sharp's Strategies		
		Advertise	***Do Not Advertise***	
Bright's Strategies	***Advertise***	Change in Bright's profit −$8 million Change in Sharp's profit −$8 million	Change in Bright's profit $20 million Change in Sharp's profit −$20 million	Bright's maximum losses −$8 million
	Do Not Advertise	Change in Bright's profit −$20 million Change in Sharp's profit $20 million	Change in Bright's profit $0 Change in Sharp's profit $0	−$20 million
Sharp's maximum losses		−$8 million	−$20 million	

There is evidence that advertising in oligopolistic industries has been carried beyond the point that profit maximization would justify. The cigarette industry, which has always been characterized by heavy promotional expenses, is a good example. In the early 1970s, when cigarette advertising on television was banned, advertising outlays by firms in the industry dropped substantially. Profit in the industry, however, rose substantially. This suggests that the overall impact of advertising on profit is adverse. Advertising in oligopolistic industries apparently tends to raise costs without significantly increasing any one firm's market share. Rival firms merely cancel out the effect of each other's advertising.

The soap and detergent industry is another example of an oligopolistic industry that advertises heavily. There is evidence that this industry's advertising does little more than cancel out the effects of rival firm's promotional messages.[3] It is possible that these firms prefer nonprice competition to the alternative of a price war. They may believe that promotional efforts can provide them with temporary increases in profit if their rivals lag in reacting.

Some studies have found that advertising contributes to profits. Such studies indicate that the higher the ratio of advertising expenditures to sales in an industry, the higher are the profit rates of the industry. Insofar as higher profits indicate monopoly power, this implies that advertising leads to more monopoly control over price. It is unclear, however, whether increased advertising causes higher profits or higher profits cause increased advertising.[4]

CONCEPT REVIEW

1. What is a dominant strategy?
2. What are the consequences of a game theory situation in which more than one Nash equilibrium is possible?
3. What are the characteristics of a prisoner's dilemma game? Give two examples of situations in which each of the rivals in a market will use a maximin strategy.

APPLYING THE THEORY OF GAMES

The techniques of game theory can be applied to a variety of issues in business management. The game theory approach helps us understand why businesses choose certain courses of action and strategic plans for gaining or retaining market share. We can now apply game theoretic analysis to price-fixing, cartel quota enforcement, and strategic planning in oligopolistic markets.

---

[3] For more elaboration on these examples, see Jean Jacques Lambin, *Advertising, Competition, and Market Conduct in Oligopoly over Time* (Amsterdam: North Holland Publishing, 1976), pp. 107–13, 141–47, 167.

[4] See William S. Comanor and Thomas A. Wilson, *Advertising and Market Power* (Cambridge, Mass.: Harvard University Press, 1974); and William S. Comanor and Thomas A. Wilson, "The Effect of Advertising on Competition," *Journal of Economic Literature* 17 (June 1979), pp. 453–76.

Repeated Games and Price-Fixing

Let's return to the prisoner's dilemma game. In its original formulation the prisoner's dilemma is a *onetime* game in the sense that the players must make choices that determine a single outcome, such as a prison sentence. However, the prisoner's dilemma analysis is more complicated when it is applied to an oligopolistic market, such as one in which a firm can gain market share by cutting price. In an oligopolistic market the issue is not so much as whether the participants will have the incentive to cut price once but whether they will have the incentive to continually cut price until economic profits have been eliminated.

Repeated game A game that can be played over and over, so that the participants can develop reputations for pursuing certain strategies and can study the strategies pursued by their rival.

If the participants know that the game can be played *repeatedly,* so that they can begin another round of price-cutting once both participants have cut price, their strategies are likely to be different than they would be if price could be cut only once. A **repeated game** is one that can be played over and over, so that the participants can develop reputations for pursuing certain strategies and can study the strategies pursued by their rival. In a repeated game the participants can *learn* from their mistakes and can forecast their rival's reactions.

To understand how the outcome of a repeated game might differ from the outcome of a onetime game, imagine a duopoly market in which the initial price is set at the monopoly level so that market output is adjusted to the level at which the marginal revenue from market demand just equals the duopolists' marginal cost. Now suppose that cutting price remains the dominant strategy of the two firms in the market, Adams and Baker. However, this time suppose that each firm realizes that if either of them cuts price, so will the other, and that as a consequence profit will fall. Under these circumstances neither firm will want to cut price as long as the other firm does not cut price. However, once either firm cuts price, the other firm will respond by also cutting price.

Using the data from the payoff matrix of Table 13–2, you can see that a policy of maintaining price will guarantee each of the firms a monthly profit of $50,000, which is greater than the profit obtainable from any alternative strategy. If, however, one of the sellers begins to cut the price of bricks by one cent the scenario will be a series of games in which profits will fall by $5,000 for each round of price-cutting, as is shown in the payoff matrix of Table 13–7. Once the price war begins, it will continue until the economic profits of both firms have been eliminated.

The knowledge that one's rival is better off by not cutting price therefore leads the participants in a repeated prisoner's dilemma game to avoid choosing the maximin strategy that they would certainly choose in a onetime game. Once both firms realize that it is in their common interest to maintain price and avoid a price war, they will each choose the strategy of standing pat as long as their rival does the same.[5] Notice that this outcome is achieved without collusion between the firms. All that is necessary to convert the strategy of maintaining price into a dominant strategy is the additional reaction assumption that firms view their rival

[5] This assumes that the game is infinitely repeatable. If, instead, the game is played only a finite number of times, there is an incentive for firms to begin price-cutting in the final periods of the game so as to raise their profit at the expense of their rival. If this strategy is chosen, firms might figure out that it is best to cut price at the outset.

as unwilling to give up the luxury of maintaining the monopoly price unless it is forced to do so by the price-cutting strategy of its rival. Under these circumstances price will remain at the monopoly level. However, this equilibrium will be highly unstable because as soon as one firm gets nervous about the intentions of the other firm, it may choose to cut price first so as to gain market share.

One strategy that businesses often use to avoid a round of price-cutting in a repeated prisoners' dilemma situation is to see that their rival realizes they will match its moves in any round of the game. This strategy is sometimes called *tit for tat*—whatever you do, I will do too! By developing a reputation for using tit for tat strategies, firms can signal to their rival that its best strategy is to maintain price. One computer simulation of a repeated game in which the tit for tat strategy was employed suggests that the strategy is successful in maintaining fixed prices in a market at the monopoly level.[6] Using such a strategy of indirect signaling rather than colluding to fix prices enables firms to avoid leaving a trail of evidence that an antitrust action could use to prove that they engaged in unfair business practices to fix prices.

Enforcing Cartel Quotas

The analysis of repeated games is also applicable to cartels. As was pointed out in the previous chapter, the individual members of a cartel have an incentive to cheat because they can make more profit by exceeding the quota output at the cartel price. However, as all members cheat, market price falls from the monopoly level to the competitive level. You can now recognize the cartel situation as a classic prisoner's dilemma game in which the dominant strategy of each member is to cheat. The cheating eventually expands market supply and increases output to the competitive level, thereby driving price down to a level equal to marginal and average costs of production and eliminating profits. The Nash equilibrium for the cartel therefore appears to be a competitive-level output and price rather than a monopoly-level output and price.

However, if we view the cartel situation as a repeated game in which firms use threats of a tit for tat strategy, we have to modify our conclusion about the stability of the cartel. If the cartel organizers can convince the members that all would be better off if they maintain the cartel price and do not cheat by expanding production at that price, they can make a first step toward eliminating the incentive to cheat. But the cartel organizers must be prepared to back up their ''education'' campaign with threats of retaliation against cheaters. The threat that other price cuts will match any price cut or any expansion of output that reduces price could then be effective in removing the incentive to cheat.

An Example of Effective Cartel Enforcement

The Central Selling Organization (CSO), the marketing syndicate of the De Beers diamond mining company, which we discussed in Chapter 11, has developed a reputation for ruthless retaliation against diamond sellers who refuse to market

[6] See Robert Axelrod, *The Evolution of Cooperation* (New York: Basic Books, 1984).

their diamonds through it. For example, in 1981 sellers from the African nation of Zaire marketed their diamonds independently of the CSO in an attempt to sell more and thus increase their profits. The CSO reacted by flooding the market with the same type of diamonds that they were selling. (The CSO maintains a large stock of diamonds and is able to control diamond prices by increasing or decreasing the supply of diamonds.) The prices that the Zaire sellers could get for their diamonds plummeted as a result of the increase in supply, and they were forced to stop marketing their diamonds independently and again agree to have them sold through the CSO, which could strictly control quantities to maintain prices. The CSO's reputation for tit for tat strategic moves is a powerful deterrent to cheating on the cartel, which has been very stable since it was organized in 1925.

Even Russia and other republics of the former Soviet Union market their diamonds through the CSO and are reluctant to cheat on it. In 1992, when Russia was selling such raw materials as aluminum, gold, platinum, and uranium on world markets in a feverish attempt to earn foreign currency credits to finance imports, it remained within the CSO fold, honoring its contract to sell $5 billion in diamonds to De Beers.[7]

Competitive Strategies: Threats, Entry Deterrence, and Moving First and Sequential Games

Rivalry in oligopolistic markets is not unlike warfare, in which the combatants formulate strategic plans intended to deter the enemy from initiating offensive actions. For nearly 45 years the conflict between the East and the West involved a war of nerves in which the threat of nuclear retaliation was the strategy used to deter aggression. The logic behind this strategy was that the enemy would avoid a nuclear attack because it knew that if it did, it would sustain unacceptable damage through swift retaliation. Until the cold war was brought to an end by the political changes in the former Soviet Union in 1991 and 1992, the defense strategy of the United States was one of being poised to destroy the Soviet Union if it launched a first strike. The Soviets employed a similar strategy vis-à-vis the United States. Both superpowers knew what horrible consequences could be expected from a first strike, and both superpowers refrained from launching one. The strategy helped avoid a nuclear holocaust.

Strategic move An action that influences a rival's choice to a player's advantage.

The strategic planning of businesses in oligopolistic markets is similar to the strategic planning of a nation's military leaders. A **strategic move** is an action that influences a rival's choice to a player's advantage. A strategic move in business is designed to *signal* a rival about what to expect in reaction to its own choices.[8] An example of such a move was the CSO's flooding of the diamond market in response to the attempt of a De Beers rival to increase its market share. The reputations business firms in oligopolistic markets establish by engaging in strategic moves deter rivals from engaging in such activities as price-cutting and cheating on cartel agreements.

---

[7] See Neil Behrmann, "Russian Policy Won't Affect Diamond Supply, but Market Faces Crucial Christmas Sales Test," *The Wall Street Journal,* November 18, 1991.

[8] Two classic works in this area are Thomas C. Schelling, *The Strategy of Conflict* (New York: Oxford University Press, 1960), and Michael E. Porter, *Competitive Strategy* (New York: Free Press, 1980).

MODERN MICROECONOMICS IN ACTION: INTERNATIONAL REPORT

Strategic Trade Policy: How Government Can Reap Gains for Domestic Industry by Forcing Rival Foreign Sellers into the Dominant Strategy of Not Producing

Government policies to subsidize sellers of certain products can sometimes result in large gains in income and producer surplus to those sellers at the expense of sellers in other nations.* For example, suppose the output of a new product such as high-density television (HDTV) is subject to economies of scale, so that the average cost of production declines as more output is produced. Also suppose that the market for this product is relatively small, so that if two firms serve it, both would incur losses, but if only one firm serves it, that firm would be able to earn economic profits.

This situation amounts to a first-mover-type game with two Nash equilibriums. Suppose, for example, that Sony, a Japanese firm, is currently developing the HDTV technology. This firm therefore has a head start and is the likely first mover. Motorola, an American firm, is also able to develop the technology, but given Sony's head start and the data in the accompanying payoff matrix, Motorola's dominant strategy is not to enter the market because it knows that Sony is likely to develop the product first and therefore reap the profits. Once Sony is in, the market would not be large enough for Motorola to also earn a profit. However, the payoff matrix has two Nash equilibriums. Now let's see if there is anything that Motorola can do to obtain the first-mover advantage.

Suppose Motorola convinces the U.S. government that for various reasons it should subsidize the development of HDTV. If the subsidy is granted, then Motorola's payoff in the matrix will be different. Suppose that Motorola is granted a $20 million annual subsidy to develop the technology. As shown in the new payoff matrix, this would result in a profit of $220 million per year to Motorola if it produces the product and Sony does not, which exceeds the $200 million profit that Sony would earn if it were the sole producer. Sony knows that if it starts producing, it would lose $10 million per year if Motorola is also in the market. However, Motorola knows that with the subsidy it can earn $10 million in economic profits *even if Sony is also in the market*. Because Sony knows this too, it is then forced into the dominant strategy of leaving the market to Motorola. Here, for a $20

Payoff Matrix for Annual Profit with No Government Subsidies

		Sony's Strategies	
		Produce HDTV	***Don't Produce HDTV***
Motorola's Strategies	***Produce HDTV***	Motorola's profit −$10 million Sony's profit −$10 million	Motorola's profit $200 million Sony's profit $0
	Don't Produce HDTV	Motorola's profit $0 Sony's profit $200 million	Motorola's profit $0 Sony's profit $0

Payoff Matrix for Annual Profit with Government Subsidies

		Sony's Strategies	
		Produce HDTV	***Don't Produce HDTV***
Motorola's Strategies	***Produce HDTV***	Motorola's profit $10 million Sony's profit −$10 million	Motorola's profit $220 million Sony's profit $ 0
	Don't Produce HDTV	Motorola's profit $ 0 Sony's profit $200 million	Motorola's profit $ 0 Sony's profit $ 0

(*Continued*) million annual subsidy, the U.S. government can increase U.S. corporate profits by $220 million per year at the expense of a decrease in Japanese corporate profits. Because the corporate income tax is close to 50 percent in the United States, the additional taxes on Motorola's profits would more than finance the costs of the subsidy! The U.S. therefore appears to gain at Japan's expense.

We must, however, qualify this conclusion by pointing out that it will hold true only if the situation described can be considered a onetime game. If Japan realizes what gains a subsidy could achieve, it might use a subsidy as a competitive weapon. It might also use subsidies in other industries once it realizes how much it lost in the HDTV case. The possibility of retaliation makes it difficult to predict the overall gains that would be achieved by government intervention in international trade.

* See Paul R. Krugman, "Is Free Trade Passé?" *Journal of Economics Perspectives* 2, no. 1 (Fall 1987), pp. 131–44. The example presented here is based on a similar situation discussed in this article.

To be credible, a strategic move must be backed up by an action to convince rivals that they will be worse off if they do not behave in the way the seller initiating the move wants them to. For example, if a firm in the luxury car market raises price in the hope that its rivals will also raise price, it must convince them that it will not soon lower price if they do so. For example, if Lexus raises the price of its luxury cars, it is likely to lose market share unless it can somehow convince other sellers of luxury cars that it is in their interest to raise price also.

When one firm threatens another with a price cut or an attempt to gain market share, it must, of course, be ready for retaliation. The retaliation can be in the form of a round of price-cutting that starts a price war. One way businesses make their threats against rivals credible is to establish a *commitment* to strategic moves. A firm can signal that commitment by building a new plant, signing a long-term contract for the materials needed to produce a certain product, or other actions showing in other ways that it can increase supplies and lower prices. The commitment of De Beers' CSO is demonstrated by its willingness to hold a large stock of diamonds in inventory. Any firm thinking about the possibility of cheating on the cartel by independently marketing its own diamonds knows the De Beers organization is *willing and able* to make the strategic move of increasing the diamond supply, thereby lowering diamond prices.

By investing in such assets as productive potential to carry out strategic moves, a firm can make its threats credible to its rivals and thus effectively alter their behavior. This analysis has relevance to the question of entering markets. Recall the game that we developed earlier in this chapter in which neither of two rivals had a dominant strategy when confronted with the choice of entering a market. However, the firm that entered the market first could increase its profit and force its rival into the dominant strategy of *not entering* the market. That game had a Nash equilibrium in which one firm served the market and the other stayed out. However, the model could not be used to determine *which firm* entered the market. In effect, entering the market first was a strategic move that forced the rival firm into the dominant strategy of not entering, thereby assuring the firm that entered higher profits in the new market. The firm that entered could have established its position by making a strategic move, such as the purchase of land for gas stations. By demonstrating its commitment to enter the market in this way, it could have forced its rival into the dominant strategy of not entering. Simply announcing that you will enter a market is not sufficient to deter the entry of a rival, because the rival could make the same announcement. The first-mover advantage can be established only by convincing your rival of your credibility through a commitment of resources.

Sequential games Games in which one player acts and the other player responds to that action.

The concept of strategic moves is relevant to **sequential games,** in which one player acts and the other player responds to that action. The participants in sequential games must envisage the response of their rival to each of their actions. Chess is an example of a sequential game. The question of entering a market in which neither firm has a dominant strategy until its rival acts can be thought of as a sequential game. To obtain the rewards that accrue to the first mover in such a market, business planners must be shrewd enough to realize that once their firm enters, its rival is forced into the dominant strategy of not entering the market.

Recklessness

Another way a firm can make its strategic moves work is to establish a reputation for recklessness. For example, suppose that in competing for air travel between the Raleigh-Durham Airport and New York's LaGuardia Airport, American Airlines threatens its rival, USAir, with a fare reduction. If USAir is shrewd enough to know what American's profit would be both with the price cut and with the existing price it might reason that it should not match the price cut or, alternatively, that it should gain market share through a price cut because American will not respond with further price cuts.

For example, based on the payoff matrix shown in Table 13–9, American's dominant strategy is to maintain price. It would earn $80,000 in monthly profit by maintaining price even if USAir maintains price. It would earn only $20,000 monthly on the route if it cuts price after its rival cuts price. It would also earn

TABLE 13–9 Payoff Matrix for a Price War in which Maintaining Price Is One Rival's Dominant Strategy

		USAir's Strategies	
		Cut Price	*Maintain Price*
American's Strategies	*Cut Price*	American's profit $20,000 USAir's profit $30,000	American's profit $40,000 USAir's profit $10,000
	Maintain Price	American's profit $80,000 USAir's profit $120,000	American's profit $120,000 USAir's profit $90,000

more by maintaining price even if USAir cuts price ($120,000 per year as opposed to $40,000 per year). American's dominant strategy is therefore to maintain price. If this is the case, USAir knows that it would be irrational for American to start a price war and will therefore avoid matching any American price cut and not take seriously any threat to engage in a price war that American makes. If, however, American convinces USAir that it is willing to reduce its profits on its RDU-LaGuardia route and therefore to avoid choosing its dominant strategy, it might reduce or eliminate USAir's incentive to cut price. One way of signaling this is to demonstrate its willingness to forgo profits on other routes. If American is a very large airline that can afford to incur losses on one route because it is still making profits on other routes, its reputation for reckless strategic moves would act as a deterrent to price-cutting by rivals.

An existing firm can deter potential entrants into a market by demonstrating its willingness to lower price and thus incur reduced profits or temporary losses to prevent the entry of new firms. By establishing a reputation as a firm that will cut its profits to prevent entry, as was the case in the entry-limit pricing model we discussed in the preceding chapter, an existing firm can force potential entrants into a market into the dominant strategy of staying out of the market.

CONCEPT REVIEW

1. Why is the Nash equilibrium for a repeated prisoner's dilemma game likely to differ from the Nash equilibrium for such a game if it is played only one time?
2. How can the tit for tat strategy be effective in a noncollusive price-fixing situation?
3. What is a strategic move? Give an example of such a move and its consequence.

CONCLUSION: OLIGOPOLY AND ECONOMIC WELFARE

We have now used both standard economic analysis and the more modern game theory approach to understand business strategies in oligopolistic markets. We have seen that the outcomes in such markets can range from a competitive price equal to marginal and minimum possible average costs to a monopoly price in which the price set corresponds to the output for which the marginal revenue from market demand equals the marginal cost of production.

Although we have examined models in which firms enter into price wars or seek to deter the entry of new firms by keeping price close to their marginal and average costs of production, most of the models that we have examined suggest that prices under oligopoly will exceed marginal costs of production. The repeated game model of oligopoly suggests that firms are likely to realize, without colluding, that price wars are detrimental to their profits. The avoidance of price-cutting can therefore be the dominant strategy in an oligopolistic model.

The game theory models of cartels suggest that credible threats can give cartels more stability than might be expected in light of the simple prisoner's dilemma model. If the insights gleaned from these game theory models are correct, the implication is that in many oligopolistic industries prices are higher than they would be if the industries were competitive.

The analysis of advertising under oligopoly suggests that oligopolistic firms have incentives to advertise to increase the demand for their products. Caught in a prisoner's dilemma situation, rivals in oligopolistic markets often find advertising to be a dominant strategy. Because advertising increases both demand and the costs of making a product available, it contributes to both higher output *and* higher product prices than would prevail in competitive markets. Some of the advertising in oligopolistic markets does not provide new information to consumers but merely cancels out or counters the advertising claims of rivals. In that sense some of the advertising is wasteful.

A study of the costs of monopoly power in the United States between 1963 and 1966, based on a sample of 734 large firms, concluded that the loss in consumer surplus due to higher prices amounted to 4 percent of the value of the output of the firms in the sample. When researchers included profits and the cost of advertising as part of the costs of monopoly power, they estimated the social costs of monopoly power as 13 percent of the value of the output of the firms in the sample.[9]

However, a word of caution about analyzing oligopoly. Each oligopolistic market has its own characteristics and its own opportunities for employing various business strategies. To really know the extent to which price and output levels in oligopolistic markets actually deviate from the price and output levels of competitive or monopoly markets requires an understanding of the reaction assumptions that oligopolistic firms make about their rivals and the strategies that they

---

[9] See Keith Cowling and Dennis C. Mueller, "The Social Costs of Monopoly Power," *Economic Journal* 88 (December 1978), pp. 727–48.

MODERN MICROECONOMICS IN ACTION: **GOVERNMENT AND THE ECONOMY**

Price-Fixing: Crossing the Thin Line between Competitive Strategy and Collusion

Illegal price-fixing is often very difficult to prove. After all, sellers accused of illegal price-fixing can simply point out that in a competitive market each seller charges the same price. Therefore, when several sellers in an oligopolistic market charge identical prices for the products they sell, this in itself is not evidence of collusion. More sophisticated analysis of the strategies chosen by oligopolistic firms shows that tit for tat behavior and a reputation for recklessness can deter price-cutting in an oligopolistic market. Since these strategies do not necessarily involve illegal actions, it remains difficult to prove illegal price-fixing.

Nonetheless, firms are sometimes irresistibly impelled to engage in collusive price-fixing. Two recent cases show how the Justice Department can successfully prove price-fixing by careful investigation of business practices.

In one of these cases, the Justice Department accused the B. Manischewitz Company, a famous producer of kosher foods, of price-fixing. Manischewitz, based in Jersey City, New Jersey, denied any wrongdoing. A federal grand jury, however, indicted the company, which dominates the market for Passover matzo, on a charge of price collusion. The Justice Department claimed that Manischewitz executives met regularly with executives of two competitors at a restaurant on Manhattan's Lower East Side in a plot to fix the price of Passover matzo.

In another case, the Justice Department investigated the possibility that eight of the nation's top colleges and universities were colluding to set tuition rates. During the 1989–90 academic year the tuition fees, room, and board of the Ivy League colleges were remarkably similar. The administrators of these colleges freely admitted that they discussed tuition increases and met regularly in a "financial-aid overlap workshop" that determined how much students receiving such aid would pay. It remained for the Justice Department to determine whether such "collaboration" constitutes an illegal conspiracy to fix prices.

can employ to limit the competitive behavior of their rivals. No one theory of oligopoly is relevant to all competitive situations. We must develop our models on an ad hoc basis to see which best fits the situation we want to understand.[10]

SUMMARY

1. The theory of games is a technique for analyzing the selection of strategies by persons or organizations with conflicting interests in situations whose payoffs depend on the choices made by each participant.
2. The theory of games is useful in the analysis of duopoly, a market structure in which two sellers protected from the entry of additional sellers are the sole producers of a standardized good or service with no close substitutes.

[10] For a critical appraisal of the game theory approach, see Franklin M. Fisher, "Games Economists Play: A Noncooperative View," *Rand Journal of Economics* 20 (Spring 1989), pp. 113–24.

3. The Cournot model of duopoly assumes that each of two sellers conjectures that its rival will always hold output fixed at its current level. Each seller then chooses its own profit-maximizing output level.
4. Reaction curves for a firm in a duopoly show how the profit-maximizing output produced by that firm varies with the output produced by its rival.
5. A strategy is a course of action chosen after consideration of a rival's possible courses of action.
6. A Nash equilibrium is a combination of strategies chosen by rivals in which each of the rivals has no incentive to change what it is doing, given the choices of its opponents.
7. For the Cournot model of duopoly, a Nash equilibrium exists when each rival's level of output is one third of the competitive output level. In the Cournot model of duopoly, total market output is therefore equal to two thirds of the competitive output level. The competitive output level is the one at which marginal cost is equal to price.
8. When game theory is applied to the analysis of oligopoly, it is assumed that each competitor in a market considers what its rivals are doing to maximize profits.
9. A payoff matrix shows the gain or loss accruing to each possible strategy for each of the rival player's possible reactions in a game.
10. A dominant strategy is one in which a player in a game is getting the highest possible payoff, regardless of what the rival players are doing. When both players in a game have a dominant strategy, the solution to a game theory model is a Nash equilibrium in which each of the players is getting the highest possible payoff no matter what strategy is chosen by its rival. However, a Nash equilibrium can exist for a game in which one of the players does not have a dominant strategy and a game can have more than one Nash equilibrium.
11. In games in which one player does not have a dominant strategy, that player must know its rival's strategy before deciding what to do. For example, one firm's advertising in a market can influence the other firm's decision to advertise.
12. First-mover games are examples of games with more than one Nash equilibrium. In such games, when one player makes a move in a market, the other player is forced into the dominant strategy of not making a similar move.
13. The prisoner's dilemma is a class of games in which the dominant strategy results in a Nash equilibrium in which both participants are worse off than they would have been if they had cooperated. A price or advertising war is a possible outcome of a prisoner's dilemma situation.
14. When games are played over and over, this outcome can be different from the outcome that occurs when they are played only one time. In a repeated game the participants can develop reputations for pursuing certain strategies and can study the strategies pursued by their rival so they can learn from their mistakes. A tit for tat strategy in such a game can maintain fixed prices in a market without explicit collusion between rivals and can be useful in enforcing cartel quota agreements.
15. A strategic move influences a rival's choice to the advantage of the player that makes the move. Strategic moves signal a rival about what to expect in reaction to its choices and must be backed by commitment to be effective.
16. Although the theory of games offers important insights into business behavior in oligopolistic markets, each oligopolistic market must be analyzed according to its own characteristics to really know what strategic opportunities it makes available to firms.

Important Concepts

theory of games	strategy	dominant strategy	repeated game
duopoly	Nash equilibrium	prisoner's dilemma	strategic move
reaction curves	payoff matrix	maximin strategies	sequential games

Questions for Review

1. What assumptions underlie the Cournot model of duopoly? How is the Cournot equilibrium approached, and how does the equilibrium output in the Cournot model compare with the equilibrium output that would be produced if the market were served by a pure monopoly or by a perfectly competitive industry?
2. Why can the solution to the Cournot model be considered a Nash equilibrium?
3. How can a reaction curve for a duopolist be derived?
4. Explain how you would determine from the entries in the payoff matrix for a game whether or not a player in the game has a dominant strategy.
5. Can a Nash equilibrium exist in a duopoly even if one of the rivals *does not* have a dominant strategy? Explain your answer.
6. Under what circumstances can more than one Nash equilibrium exist in a duopoly situation? What determines which of these equilibriums actually occurs?
7. How can a seller in a regional market force its competitors into the dominant strategy of leaving or not entering the market?
8. Explain how the maximin strategy in a prisoners' dilemma game results in a Nash equilibrium in which both of the rivals are worse off than they would have been if they had cooperated.
9. How can the strategies chosen by rivals in a repeated game differ from the strategies that would be chosen if the game were played only once?
10. How can price-fixing emerge in an oligopolistic market without cooperation among the rivals?

Problems

1. The output of lumber in a certain regional market would be 12,000 board feet per month if a perfectly competitive industry served the market. Instead, the market is served by only two lumber producers and the entry of additional producers is not possible. Assuming that AC = MC for all levels of output and that the Cournot model applies, show how the Cournot equilibrium will be approached. Plot the reaction curves of each of the producers, and show how the equilibrium output compares with both the competitive output and the pure monopoly output.
2. Firm A and Firm B are the only distributors of gasoline in a small town. Firm A estimates that it can increase its profit by $2,000 per month if it cuts price by 5 percent provided that Firm B maintains price. On the other hand, if Firm B also cuts price, Firm A would find its profits fall by $1,000 per month. If Firm A maintains price, its profit would be unchanged as long as Firm B also maintains price, but if Firm A maintains price and Firm B cuts price, Firm A would find that its profits fall by $1,500 per month. Assuming that Firm B makes exactly the same calculations, set up the payoff matrix and indicate whether a Nash equilibrium exists. What is the dominant strategy for each of the two firms?
3. Only two beer distributors serve a regional market. They form a cartel under which the market is divided in half and each of its two members will sell one half of the monopoly output. Set up a matrix for the two cartel members showing how their payoffs are likely to vary with these two strategies: cheating and not cheating. Is there a Nash equilibrium?
4. The payoff matrix shows how profit can vary for two soap detergent producers that are rivals

		Tide's Strategies	
		Advertise	***Do Not Advertise***
Cheer's Strategies	***Advertise***	Cheer's profit $5 million Tide's profit $3 million	Cheer's profit $7 million Tide's profit $1.5 million
	Do Not Advertise	Cheer's profit $3.5 million Tide's profit $4.5 million	Cheer's profit $9 million Tide's profit $2 million

in an oligopolistic market. Do both producers have a dominant strategy? What is the Nash equilibrium?

5. There are economies of scale in the production of a new type of solar-powered communication satellite. The world market for this product can be served at lower average cost by one seller than by two or more sellers. Two companies are currently engaged in the development of the satellite, and their payoffs for entering or not entering the market are shown in the matrix. What can you say about the Nash equilibrium for this competitive situation?

		Seller B's Strategies	
		Don't Enter	***Enter***
Seller A's Strategies	***Don't Enter***	A's profit $6 million B's profit $6 million	A's profit $19 million B's profit $18 million
	Enter	A's profit $18 million B's profit $18 million	A's profit $12 million B's profit $12 million

6. Suppose that you produced zippers for the garment industry in New York City, that there were a small number of other zipper producers in this market, and that the prices of all these producers were exactly the same. The Justice Department accuses you of price-fixing. How can you explain to the Justice Department that the prices of different sellers can be the same without any collusion among the sellers?

PART V

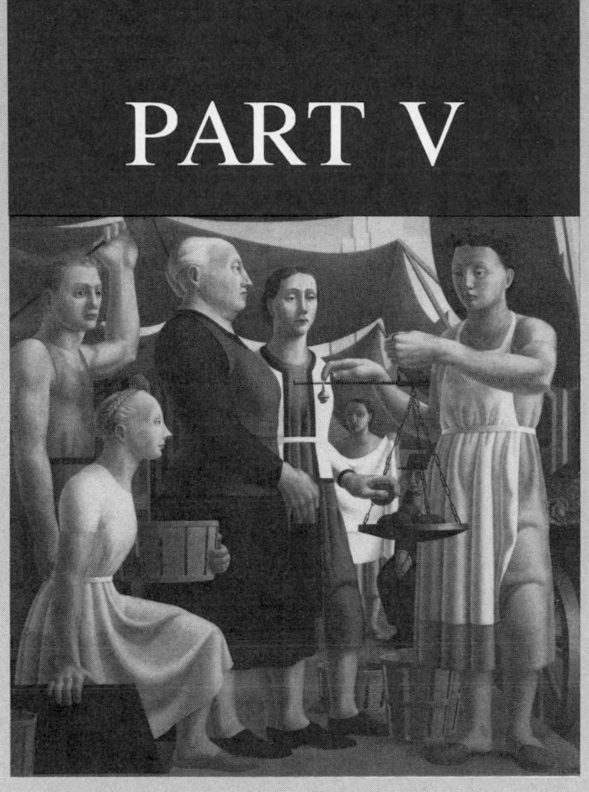

INPUT MARKETS

14

Competitive Input Markets

Hourly wages in U.S. manufacturing grew at an average annual rate of 3.5 percent during the period 1985 to 1990. Over the same period the productivity of factory workers also grew at 3.5 percent per year. In the late 1980s labor market conditions for factory workers resulted in wage increases that just compensated them for their additional productivity. This was in sharp contrast to the first half of the 1980s, from 1979 to 1985, during which hourly wages in manufacturing rose an average annual rate of 6.8 percent, while the productivity of factory workers grew by only 2.8 percent per year. Although the slower rate of wage growth in the late 1980s was bad news for workers, there was some good news as well. Reduction in wages in U.S. manufacturing industries relative to wages in comparable manufacturing industries abroad made U.S. factories more competitive in world markets. As export demand increased, so did job opportunities for U.S. factory workers. As of 1992 hourly labor costs for U.S. factory workers were lower than hourly labor costs for the factory workers in Canada, Italy, France, and Germany!

What determines the wages that workers earn in the marketplace? How do changes in input market conditions affect wages and employment opportunities? We now turn our attention to the economics of work and wages, showing how wages in labor markets are influenced by productivity, the demand for output, and the willingness of workers to trade their leisure time for income.

We will also use the techniques of analysis that we develop here to discuss capital and land markets. You will see how the supply and demand for loanable funds determine interest rates and how interest rates influence decisions to invest in the creation of new capital inputs. You will also see how interest rates affect the prices of capital assets and how the locational advantages of a site affect land rents.

Perfect Competition in Input Markets

The ability of employers of input services to influence the prices they pay for labor hours, machine hours, and other inputs they purchase depends on the extent of rivalry in the market. In a highly competitive input market the impersonal forces of supply and demand determine input prices and employers merely react to those prices. This chapter analyzes the decisions of employers of input services in competitive input markets and shows how the prices of inputs sold in such markets depend on supply and demand.

Perfectly competitive input market A market in which there is free entry and exit of sellers and buyers and in which many rival employers compete to purchase the services supplied by many sellers, each of which sells only a small share of the total supply of a standardized input and therefore cannot influence price.

A **perfectly competitive input market** is one in which the following conditions exist:

1. *Many rival employers compete to purchase input services of a given quality made available by many rival sellers.*
2. *Each employer purchases only a small share of available supplies.* This means that no employer purchases a large share of the available supply of input services and is thereby unable to shift the market demand.
3. *Each seller of input services sells only a small share of total supply and cannot appreciably affect overall market supply.* This means that no single seller can affect the price of an input by making it appreciably scarcer or more abundant.
4. *Sellers of input services are free to enter or leave each possible market and owners of inputs are able to transfer their resources from one use to another or from one location to another in response to changes in input prices.*

These characteristics imply that neither individual buyers nor individual sellers can influence the prices of input services in a perfectly competitive input market. Both employers and those who offer labor hours, machine hours, and the services of other resources for sale in competitive markets are price takers.

Derived demand Demand for inputs that is derived from the demand for products made by those inputs.

The buyers of input services are business firms and other organizations, including governments and nonprofit institutions. Their demand for input services is a **derived demand** because they purchase input services for the purpose of making products. This derived demand originates in the demand for the products made from the inputs. The numbers of labor hours, machine hours, or land acreage that business firms employ depend in part on the revenue those firms can obtain from the items they sell. For example, there would be no demand for the services of automobile workers if no one demanded cars. The demand for health care affects the demand for physicians and nurses. An insurance firm's demand for leased computer time depends on the data processing required to sell and service its insurance policies.

In a competitive input market a firm can *buy* at the market price as much of an input, such as labor, as it chooses. For example, suppose that the market supply and demand for the daily services of workers capable of doing general chores in restaurants are as illustrated in Figure 14–1(a). The current equilibrium wage of workers hired for an eight-hour workday is \$32. This wage corresponds to point E, at which the quantity of labor demanded equals the quantity supplied over a given period. The market equilibrium quantity is Q_1 worker-days of service, where a worker-day is eight hours of labor.

Because each employer in a competitive market is a price taker, it can hire all of the workers it chooses at the going market wage of \$32 per day. The supply curve of labor to each *individual* employer in the market is therefore a horizontal line that intersects the wage axis at \$32 in Figure 14–1(b). The curve showing the supply of labor to the employer reveals that the employer can purchase as many

FIGURE 14–1 Demand and Supply in a Competitive Input Market

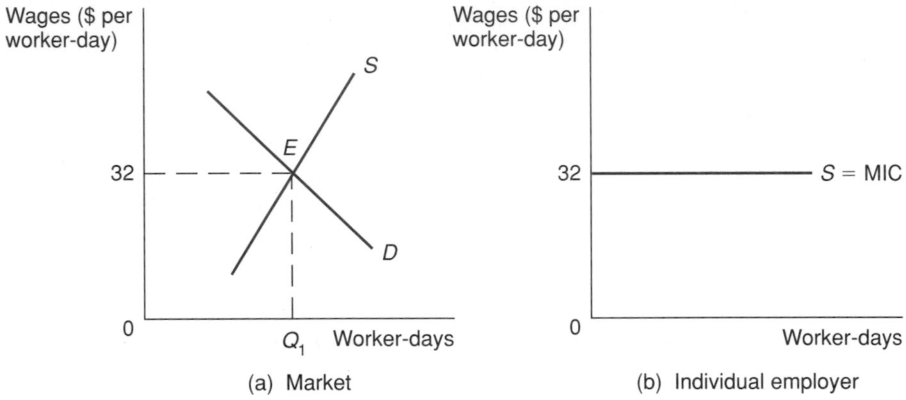

In a competitive input market the forces of supply and demand determine input price, as shown in (a). An individual employer can purchase all of the input services it wishes at the market price. In this case, as shown in (b), the individual employer can purchase all of the eight-hour worker-days at $32 without influencing the daily wage. The daily wage is the marginal input cost (MIC) of labor.

worker-days as it chooses without causing the market wage to change. Wages do change when *market* supply and demand change; however, the number of workers a particular employer hires has no effect on overall market demand.

Competitive output markets allow a firm to *sell* as much as it likes at the going market prices. If a firm operates in competitive output *and* input markets, it can buy as much input service *and* sell as much output as it chooses at the going market prices for output and input services. A firm operating in perfectly competitive output and input markets can influence neither its output prices nor its input prices.

The Marginal Revenue Product of an Input: A Measure of the Marginal Gain from Hiring an Input

Suppose a restaurant sells a pizza similar to the pizzas sold by hundreds of other restaurants in a city. The firm can sell as many pizzas as it chooses at the going market price of $5 per pizza. It has a given amount of capital equipment—ovens, chairs, tables, square footage, fountain equipment, and so on. Its managers must decide how many workers to employ per day. Although this example deals with labor, its conclusions are applicable to all inputs in the short run. Assume that the firm's managers seek to maximize profits.

Assume that all labor is of a given quality. The workers hired are unskilled and will do general chores and wait on tables. The services of unskilled workers are purchased in a competitive labor market. The firm can hire any number of

TABLE 14–1 Value of Marginal Product, Marginal Revenue Product, and Input Cost

Worker-Days (Eight Labor Hours per Day)	*Marginal Product of Labor (Pizzas per Day)*	*Price and Marginal Revenue per Unit Output*	*Value of Marginal Product of Labor and Marginal Revenue Product of Labor (VMP_L = MRP_L)*	*Marginal Labor Cost = Daily Wage ($/Eight-Hour Workday)*	*Change in Profits per Day*
0	0	$5	$ 0	$32	—
1	45	5	225	32	$193
2	30	5	150	32	118
3	20	5	100	32	68
4	7	5	35	32	3
5	3	5	15	32	−17
6	1	5	5	32	−27
7	0	5	0	32	−32
8	−5	5	−25	32	−57

labor hours per day at the going market wage of $32 per worker-day, which is the equivalent of $4 per hour for a standard eight-hour workday.

A profit-maximizing firm weighs the gain of hiring additional workers against the costs it incurs in making its hiring decisions. A marginal analysis of the hiring decisions can be used to isolate the benefits and costs of additional input service hired by a firm and to show how these influence the quantity of input service employed.

First, consider the marginal gain that the firm obtains by hiring labor. The firm hires labor for the purpose of producing and serving its product, pizza. Each extra worker hired allows the firm to produce and sell more of its product. The gain to the firm of hiring additional workers depends on the amount that each extra worker produces and on the extra revenue that can be obtained for each extra pizza sold. The extra production possible from employing another worker-day of labor after a certain number of worker-days have already been employed is the marginal product of labor.

Assume that workers are hired to work eight-hour shifts. The second column in Table 14–1 shows how the marginal product of labor varies with the number of worker-days employed. The hypothetical data in Table 14–1 assume that diminishing marginal returns in employing additional workers set in after the first worker has been hired. The marginal product of workers therefore declines as more are hired.

Marginal revenue product of an input The marginal product of an input multiplied by the marginal revenue of that output; the extra revenue possible from hiring an extra unit of an input.

The **marginal revenue product of an input** is its marginal product multiplied by the marginal revenue of that output. The marginal revenue product of labor, MRP_L, is therefore

$$MRP_L = (MP_L)(MR) \qquad \textbf{(14–1)}$$

where MR is the marginal revenue from selling output.

The marginal revenue product of an input measures the extra revenue possible from hiring each extra unit of that input. The marginal revenue product of labor measures the gain (in terms of revenue) to the firm from hiring an additional worker-day after a certain number of worker-days have already been hired over a period. This can easily be seen by noting that the marginal product of labor is the extra output associated with an extra unit of labor ($\Delta Q/\Delta L$), whereas the marginal revenue for the firm is the extra revenue that it can obtain by selling more output ($\Delta TR/\Delta Q$). The marginal revenue product of labor can therefore be written as

$$MRP_L = \left(\frac{\Delta Q}{\Delta L}\right)\left(\frac{\Delta TR}{\Delta Q}\right) = \frac{\Delta TR}{\Delta L} \qquad \textbf{(14–2)}$$

This measures the change in total revenue associated with each change in the number of labor units employed.

The marginal revenue product of labor is not associated with a *particular* worker. Rather, it shows the way the contribution of labor services to revenue varies with the number of workers hired. All workers are presumed to be equally productive. The marginal product of labor declines because of the law of diminishing marginal returns.

Value of the marginal product of an input The marginal product of an input multiplied by the price at which the additional output is sold.

The **value of the marginal product of an input** (VMP_L) is the marginal product of an input multiplied by the price at which the additional output is sold:

$$VMP_L = (MP_L)(P) \qquad \textbf{(14–3)}$$

where P is the price of the firm's product. The value of the marginal product of labor indicates the worth of the output of additional workers when that output is sold. In competitive output markets the price of a product equals its marginal revenue. It follows that as long as a firm is a price taker in its output market, the value of the marginal product of an input equals the input's marginal revenue product for any given amount used.

The third column in Table 14–1 shows that the price of pizza is constant at $5 per pie, independent of the number of worker-days hired (and therefore output sold) by the firm. Because the firm sells its output in a perfectly competitive market, the price of pizza is also the marginal revenue of pizza. The fourth column shows how the marginal revenue product of labor varies with the number of worker-days employed. The marginal revenue associated with each number of worker-days is obtained by multiplying the marginal product of that number of worker-days by the marginal revenue per unit output, which is always $5. Because the marginal revenue equals price, the data in the fourth column also indicate the value of the marginal product of labor.

For example, when the first worker is hired, the firm, other things being equal, will be able to sell 45 pizzas per day. Assuming that sales would be zero without that worker, the marginal product of labor is 45 pizzas. Multiplying this amount of output by $5 gives the marginal revenue product of labor at that point as $225 per worker-day. When the firm hires two workers, the marginal product of labor is 30 pizzas. Multiplying this by $5 gives a marginal revenue product of $150 per worker-day.

The Hiring Decision: Weighing the Marginal Gain of Additional Input Use against Its Marginal Cost

Marginal input cost The extra cost of an extra unit of input.

Marginal input cost (MIC) is the extra cost incurred to hire an extra unit of input after a certain amount has already been hired. In a perfectly competitive labor market a firm can obtain the labor services it desires at the going market wage. It follows that when a firm hires labor in a perfectly competitive labor market, the marginal input cost of each worker-day is the daily wage. For the restaurant in our example, the marginal labor cost is therefore the daily wage of $32, irrespective of how many worker-days it employs.

A profit-maximizing firm compares the extra revenue it can earn by hiring additional labor services with the extra cost it incurs by hiring those services, other things being equal. The extra revenue is the marginal revenue product of labor. In a competitive labor market the extra cost of an additional worker is the daily wage. As long as the marginal revenue product of labor exceeds it wage, additional workers will add more to revenue than to costs. Hiring those workers will therefore increase profits.

The data in Table 14–1 illustrate this. The wage is $32 for an eight-hour workday no matter how many workers are hired. When only one worker is hired, the marginal revenue product of labor is $225 per worker-day. The extra labor cost, shown in the fifth column, is $32. By hiring one worker, therefore, the firm can increase its daily profits by $193 = $225 − $32. This is shown in the last column of Table 14–1.

When two workers are employed, the marginal revenue product of labor is $150 per worker-day. Daily marginal labor cost remains at $32. Profits therefore increase by $118 per day, as shown in the last column of Table 14–1. Similarly, the

FIGURE 14–2 The Hiring Decision in a Competitive Input Market

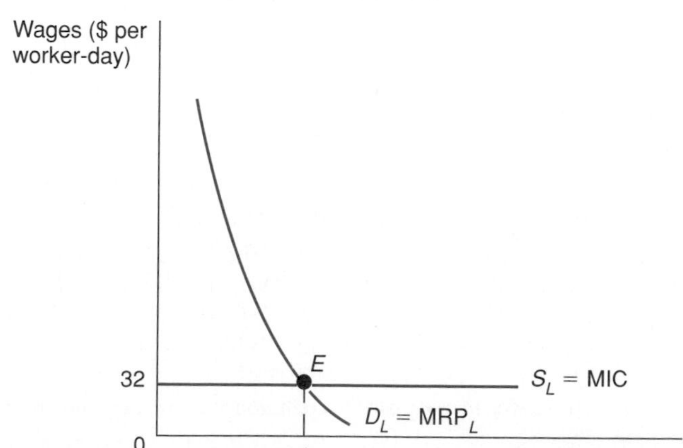

A profit-maximizing firm hires input services up to the point at which the marginal revenue product of the input equals its price. The equilibrium is at point E, where $MRP_L = w$. At the wage of $32 per day the firm hires four worker-days of labor services.

marginal revenue product of labor exceeds the wage when three workers are employed. When four workers are employed, the marginal revenue product of labor is $35 per worker-day. The extra profits from hiring this worker are $3 per day. Profits would decline if a fifth worker were employed. The marginal revenue product of labor when five workers are employed is only $15 per worker-day. Because the wage is $32 per day, profits would decline by $17 per day if a fifth worker were employed. Similarly, the marginal revenue product of labor would continue its decline if more than five workers were employed. In fact, the marginal product of labor would be zero if seven workers were employed. Given the fixed inputs in the restaurant in the short run, employing more than seven workers would decrease the number of pizzas that could be served per day.

Profits are maximized by hiring a variable input up to the point at which its marginal revenue product equals its marginal cost. This occurs when

$$MRP_L = w \qquad \textbf{(14–4)}$$

where w is the daily wage.[1]

Figure 14–2 plots the marginal revenue product of labor from the data in Table 14–1 on the same set of axes as the firm's labor supply curve. The supply of labor is perfectly elastic at the daily wage of $32, reflecting the fact that the marginal input cost is constant at $32 per worker-day. Point E, at which the MRP_L curve intersects the labor supply curve, corresponds to the number of worker-days that would result in maximum profits. The firm employs about four workers, each working an eight-hour shift, to maximize its daily profits. At that level of employment (see Table 14–1) MRP_L exceeds w by $3. If the firm could work its four employees an extra half hour or so each day, it would be able to increase its profits by about $3 by equating w and MRP_L.

A Firm's Input Demand Curve

Input demand curve A curve that shows how the quantity of input services demanded varies with the price of input services.

A firm's **input demand curve** shows how the quantity of input services demanded by the firm varies with the price of input services, given all other influences on the demand for inputs. The MRP_L curve shown in Figure 14–2 *is* the firm's input demand curve. The profit-maximizing firm buying labor services in a competitive market adjusts the quantity demanded until $MRP_L = w$ at each possible wage. To find out the number of worker-days demanded by the firm at any wage, simply locate the point corresponding to that wage on the vertical axis and find the corresponding number of worker-days on the horizontal axis associated with the

---

[1] It is easy to see that this condition maximizes profits by noting that when it holds,

$$MRP_L = MR(MP_L) = w$$

which implies that

$$w/MP_L = MR$$

If labor is the only variable input, the left side of the above equation is marginal cost (MC) (see Chapter 7). Therefore, when Equation 14–4 is satisfied, MC = MR and profit must be at its highest level.

MRP_L curve. For example, at any wage above $32 the number of worker-days employed would be less than 4 and at any wage below $32 the number of worker-days demanded would exceed 4.

There is an inverse relationship between wages and the number of workers who will be hired. This stems from the declining marginal product of labor as more labor is used in the short run. Input demand curves, like output demand curves, slope downward. The downward-sloping demand curve for an input in the short run stems from the law of diminishing marginal returns.

What Can Cause a Firm's Input Demand to Change?

Change in input demand A change in the relationship between the quantity of input demanded and the price of the input.

A **change in input demand** is a shift of an entire input demand curve that results from a change in one of the determinants of input demand other than the price of the input. In addition to the price of the input, the major determinants of input demand are as follows:

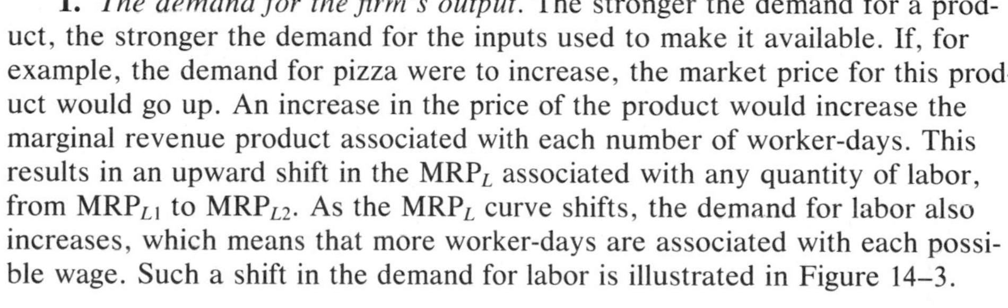

1. *The demand for the firm's output.* The stronger the demand for a product, the stronger the demand for the inputs used to make it available. If, for example, the demand for pizza were to increase, the market price for this product would go up. An increase in the price of the product would increase the marginal revenue product associated with each number of worker-days. This results in an upward shift in the MRP_L associated with any quantity of labor, from MRP_{L1} to MRP_{L2}. As the MRP_L curve shifts, the demand for labor also increases, which means that more worker-days are associated with each possible wage. Such a shift in the demand for labor is illustrated in Figure 14–3.

FIGURE 14–3 Changes in a Firm's Labor Demand

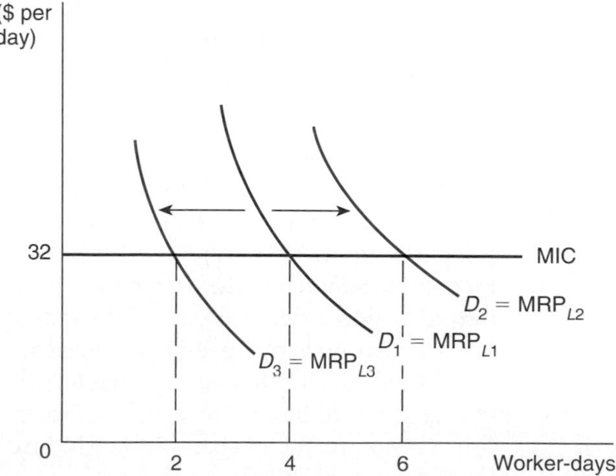

An increase in labor demand can result from an increase in the price of a firm's product or from an increase in the marginal product of labor. Either of these will increase MRP_L at any given level of labor use and shift the firm's labor demand from D_1 to D_2. Similarly, a decrease in product price or a decrease in the marginal product of labor will shift the firm's labor demand from D_1 to D_3.

After the demand for labor increases, the number of worker-days employed increases from 4 to 6 in response, assuming that the wage remains $32 per worker-day.

Similarly, a decrease in the price of the product would decrease the demand for labor, because a decrease in the price of the product would shift the marginal revenue product curve downward, from MRP_{L1} to MRP_{L3}, as shown in Figure 14–3. As a consequence the demand for labor decreases. With the decreased demand the profit-maximizing number of worker-days declines from 4 to 2.

2. *The prices and quantities of substitute and complementary inputs*. Suppose that the price of laborsaving kitchen equipment declines. This is likely to decrease the demand for labor as the firm substitutes capital for labor in response. For example, dishwashing equipment is a *substitute input for labor*. If the firm acquires more dishwashing equipment, its demand for labor declines and its demand curve shifts inwards.[2]

On the other hand, if the firm expands in the long run and acquires more tables to accommodate a stronger demand for its product, then its demand for labor will increase because it will require more workers to serve those additional tables. This will shift the demand curve for labor outward. Tables are a *complementary input for labor*.

3. *Technological change affecting the marginal product of an input*. If an improvement in technology increases the marginal product of any given number of computers employed, the marginal revenue product curve will shift upward. This means that with any given rental rate for computer hours, the quantity demanded will increase. An increase in the marginal productivity of an input at each possible level of employment therefore results in an outward shift in each firm's demand curve similar to the outward shift shown in Figure 14–3.

Industry and Market Demand for an Input

Derivation of Industry Input Demand Curves

Industry demand for an input The relationship between the amounts of input services demanded by an industry and the price of the input services.

Industry demand for an input is the sum of the amounts of input services demanded by individual firms in an industry at any price. Any one firm in the industry can hire more labor services and produce more without affecting the price of output. However, as *all* firms in the industry hire more input services, the increased supply of the industry's product causes the price of the industry's output to decrease. This causes the marginal revenue product curves of individual firms in the industry to shift downward.

Other things being equal, a decline in wages (for instance, to $3 per hour) will induce firms to hire more workers. For example, at a daily wage of $24 the pizza firm in the preceding example would hire an additional half-time worker for four

[2] This ignores the possible impact of the resulting decline in the marginal cost of output on the profit-maximizing output level. If the firm increases output as a result of the decline in the price of dishwashing equipment, some of the decline in labor employment resulting from the substitution of capital for labor will be offset by the hiring of more labor to produce more.

FIGURE 14–4 Wage Declines, Firm Demand, and Industry Demand for Labor Services

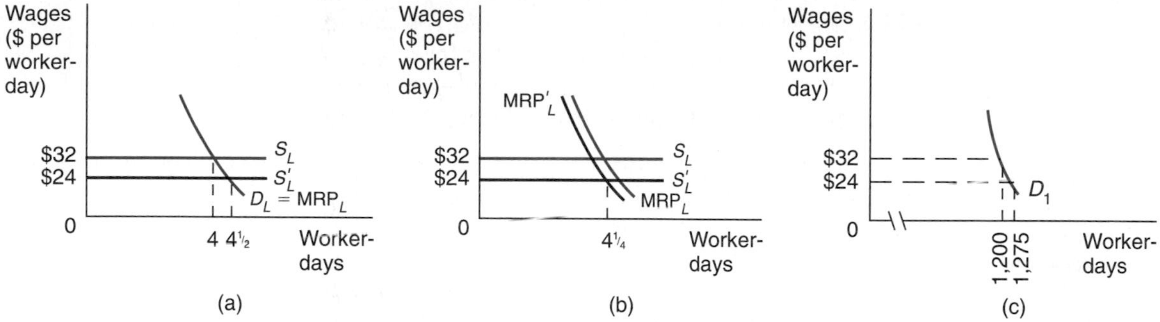

If a wage decline affects only a single firm, the firm adjusts by hiring more labor services until MRP_L equals the lower wage. This is shown in (a). When a wage decline affects all firms in an industry, increased output decreases the price of the product. This shifts the labor demand curve from MRP_L to MRP'_L and results in each firm's hiring of 4¼ instead of 4½ worker-days, as shown in (b). Graph (c) shows the industry demand for labor, which takes into account the decline in MRP_L as more workers are hired.

hours per day. The new equilibrium is shown in Figure 14–4(a). At the point at which the firm's new supply of labor intersects the demand curve for labor, 4½ worker-days are employed.

Every firm in the perfectly competitive industry hires more workers when market wages decline. As all of the pizzerias hire more workers, the production of pizza in the regional market increases. Because of the increased supply of pizzas, the equilibrium price declines from $5 to $4.50 per pizza. The decrease in the price of pizza decreases the marginal revenue product of labor at any given quantity used. This causes an inward shift in the curve representing demand for labor by any firm in the industry, as shown in Figure 14–4(b). After taking into account the decrease in the price of its output, the firm reduces by two hours the number of labor hours it uses per week. After considering the impact of the increased industry output on price and demand, the firm uses only 4¼ worker-days instead of 4½.

Suppose there are 300 identical pizzerias in the region. At a wage of $4 per hour, each pizzeria hires four workers. Total employment in the region's pizza industry is therefore 1,200 workers. Based on an eight-hour workday, the industry uses 9,600 labor hours per day.

When the wage declines to $3 per hour, total industry employment is

$$(4\tfrac{1}{4})(300) = 1{,}275 \text{ worker-days}$$
$$= 10{,}200 \text{ labor hours per day}$$

based on the full-time equivalent of eight hours per day per worker. Two points on the industry demand curve are 1,200 workers per day when the wage is $4 per hour and 1,275 workers per day when the wage is $3 per hour. This is shown in Figure 14–4(c). Connecting the two points traces out the industry labor demand curve (D_1). This curve shows the relationship between wages and employment in the industry, with the impact of the wage decline on output and product price taken into account.

Determinants of Industry Input Demand Elasticity

Wage elasticity of demand for labor The percentage change in the quantity of labor services demanded in response to each 1 percent change in wages.

The price elasticity of demand for an input is the percentage change in the quantity of the input demanded in response to each 1 percent change in its price. For example, the **wage elasticity of demand for labor** is

$$E_L = \frac{\Delta L/L}{\Delta w/w} \quad \textbf{(14–5)}$$

where L represents labor hours of work and w is the market wage.

The industry price elasticity of demand for an input is determined by several factors:

1. *The price elasticity of demand for the industry's output.* Keep in mind that the demand for an input is a derived demand. The demand for labor hours in the pizza industry therefore depends on the price elasticity of demand for pizza. The more elastic the product demand, the more elastic is the input demand. For example, suppose that wages increase. This increase in wages will increase the industry's costs of production and the price of pizza. The ultimate effect on the number of worker-days demanded by the industry depends on the responsiveness of the demand for pizza. The more elastic the demand for pizza, the more elastic is the demand for workers and the greater is the reduction in employment in the industry in response to a given increase in wages.

2. *The technical possibilities for substituting one input for another.* If wages in the pizza industry increase, the decrease in the quantity of labor demanded will depend on the ease with which capital can be substituted for labor without reducing output. If wages increase, firms can use more mechanized kitchens, disposable dishes and utensils instead of dishes and utensils that require cleaning by hand, and more prepackaged and prepared ingredients. The greater the opportunities to use machines instead of labor, the more elastic is the demand for labor.

3. *The elasticity of supply of other inputs used in the industry.* The ability to substitute one input for another can be hampered by inelastic supplies of substitute inputs. Suppose a new machine for kneading pizza dough is available. When the price of labor increases, a firm may decide to purchase one of these machines. If the supply of the machines is very inelastic, their price can rise substantially as the demand for them increases. As the price of the machine rises, fewer firms decide to use it to replace labor. The more inelastic the supply of substitute inputs, therefore, the more inelastic is the demand for the input whose price changes.

4. *Time.* The demand for an input is more elastic in the long run than in the short run. In the long run, firms have a greater opportunity to substitute one input for another.

Market Demand

Market demand for an input The relationship between the quantities of an input demanded for all uses in a market and the price of the input.

Market demand for an input is the sum of the quantities of that input demanded by *all industries* at any given price. The market demand for unskilled workers in a certain region is the sum of the demands of the region's pizza industry, other restaurant industries, and all other industries that use this type of labor. All of these industries compete for the services of workers in the same regional labor market. At any given wage the sum of the labor hours used by all of these industries must equal the quantity supplied. If one of the industries uses more workers, fewer workers will be available to work in other industries at any given wage.

Suppose unskilled workers in a region are employed in only the pizza restaurant, retailing, and construction industries. Figure 14–5 shows these industries' demand for labor. The labor demand curves are D_P, D_R, and D_C, respectively. The regional market demand (D_M) is the sum of the quantities demanded by all three industries at any wage. Note that each industry demand curve for labor includes the price effects of expansion of industry output.

The market demand for an input is obtained in the same way as the market demand for an output. At each price the quantity demanded by each industry is summed to obtain the market quantity demanded. The price elasticity of market demand is related to the price elasticity of demand for input services in each of the industries that make up the market. At any given price, market elasticity of

FIGURE 14–5 Regional Market Demand for Labor

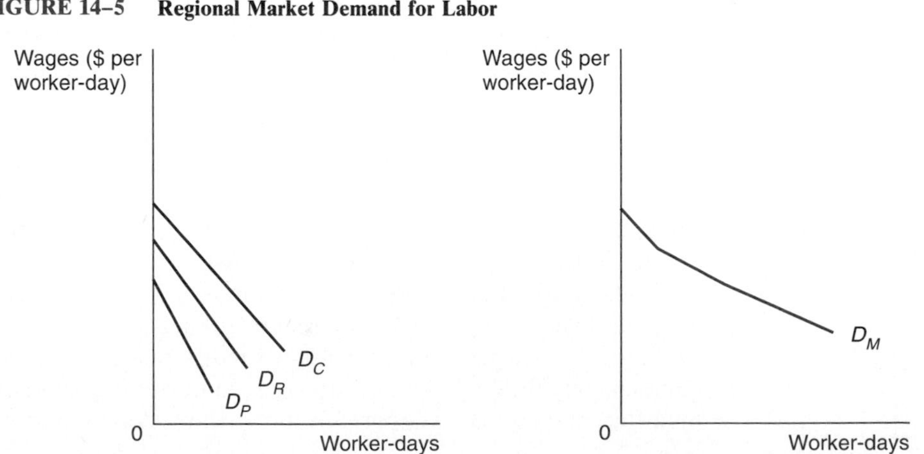

Only three industries use unskilled labor in the region. Regional labor demand is the sum of the quantities demanded by each of the three industries at all possible wages. The respective demand curves of the three industries are D_P, D_R, and D_C. The regional market demand is D_M.

demand for the input depends on the proportion of the input's services used in the various industries and on price elasticity of demand for the input in each of those industries.[3]

CONCEPT REVIEW

1. What influences the quantity of a variable input a profit-maximizing firm chooses to employ when purchasing the input in a perfectly competitive market?
2. What can increase a firm's demand for an input?
3. How is an industry's demand for an input related to the demand for the input by individual firms in the industry? How is the market demand for the input derived?

LABOR SUPPLY AND LABOR MARKETS

The Work-Leisure Choice and Labor Supply of an Individual Worker

The wage rate that persons can earn as employees is an important determinant of their decision to give up leisure time for gainful employment. Leisure is defined as any use of time other than work for pay. The person is viewed as allocating time between work for others and leisure activities. Time is a scarce resource. Work for others at the market wage yields cash income that can be spent on goods and services. Activities at home, such as preparing meals, building items, cleaning, and general household management, produce services for the person and other members of the household but do not result in cash income. These activities result in nonpurchased goods and services, but they require leisure time. They involve no transaction between a buyer and a seller. The person supplies services to himself or herself or to other members of the household without the exchange of cash.

There are 24 hours in a day, and a person must choose how to divide this time between leisure (H) and work for others at the market wage. The "price" of an hour of leisure is the cash income forgone by not using that time to work for pay. If a person earns a wage of $\$w$ per hour, then each hour retained for home use will result in the loss of $\$w$ of money income.

The amount of leisure a person chooses to take per day depends on the wage rate and on the person's preferences for leisure as opposed to money income. Figure 14–6 shows a typical person's indifference curves between money income and leisure. Both leisure and money income are regarded as economic goods. The indifference curves are therefore downward sloping and convex.

---

[3] E_{DI} is the market demand elasticity for input services with respect to price:

$$E_{DI} = \Sigma(F_i/F)E_{Di}$$

where F is the total amount of the input used at that price, F_i, is the amount used in industry i, and E_{Di} is the price elasticity of demand for the input in industry i.

FIGURE 14–6 The Work-Leisure Choice

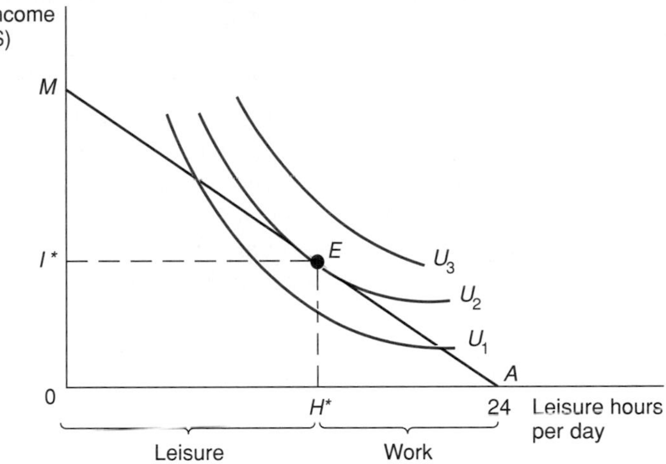

The line *MA* gives the opportunities for trading leisure for income at the market wage. The indifference curves specify the person's preferences for income and leisure. In equilibrium the person adjusts the allocation of time between work and leisure until

$$w = \text{MRS}_{HI}$$

This equilibrium occurs at point *E*, where H^* hours of leisure are consumed. The person therefore works $(24 - H^*)$ hours and earns $\$I^*$ of income.

Assume that a person has zero nonlabor income. The income-leisure budget line is *MA*. This line shows all the combinations of leisure and income that the person can enjoy when the hourly wage is $\$w$. The equation of the line is

$$I = w(24 - H) \qquad \textbf{(14–6)}$$

where I is daily income and H is hours of leisure per day. The term $(24 - H)$ represents hours of work per day. Leisure is defined as doing anything other than working for pay. For example, if the wage is \$10 per hour and a person takes 16 hours of leisure per day, and therefore works 8 hours per day, the person's income is

$$\$10(8) = \$80$$

The slope of the income-leisure budget line is $-w$. The person is a price taker in a competitive labor market. When the market wage is \$10 per hour, the person gains \$10 in income for each hour of leisure given up. The number of hours worked depends on the wage and on the preferences between income and leisure.

The person whose indifference curves are shown in Figure 14–6 is in equilibrium at point *E*, where the income-leisure budget constraint is just tangent to an indifference curve. At that point

$$\text{MRS}_{HI} = w \qquad \textbf{(14–7)}$$

where MRS_{HI} is the marginal rate of substitution of leisure for income.

In equilibrium the person whose indifference curves are shown on the graph takes H^* hours of the day as leisure and therefore works $(24 - H^*)$ hours. This person's income is therefore

$$I^* = w(24 - H^*)$$

Many workers work a standard 40-hour week. There are, however, many ways in which workers can vary the *average* number of hours worked per day or week in a given year (or over a lifetime). They can take on additional work through overtime, moonlighting on a second job, or delaying retirement. They can work at one or several part-time jobs. They can work less through longer vacations, absenteeism, early retirement, and spending more time between jobs.

Deriving a Worker's Labor Supply Curve

An increase in wages makes the income-leisure budget line steeper. This is illustrated in Figure 14–7. The wage increase swivels the budget constraint line upward from MA to $M'A$. Any given number of hours worked will result in more income because of the increase in the wage.

In Figure 14–7 the person responds to the wage increase by working more. As the wage increases, for instance, from w_1 to w_2, the person moves from an equilibrium at point E to a new equilibrium at point E'. At E' the number of hours

FIGURE 14–7 Labor Supply when the Substitution Effect Exceeds the Income Effect

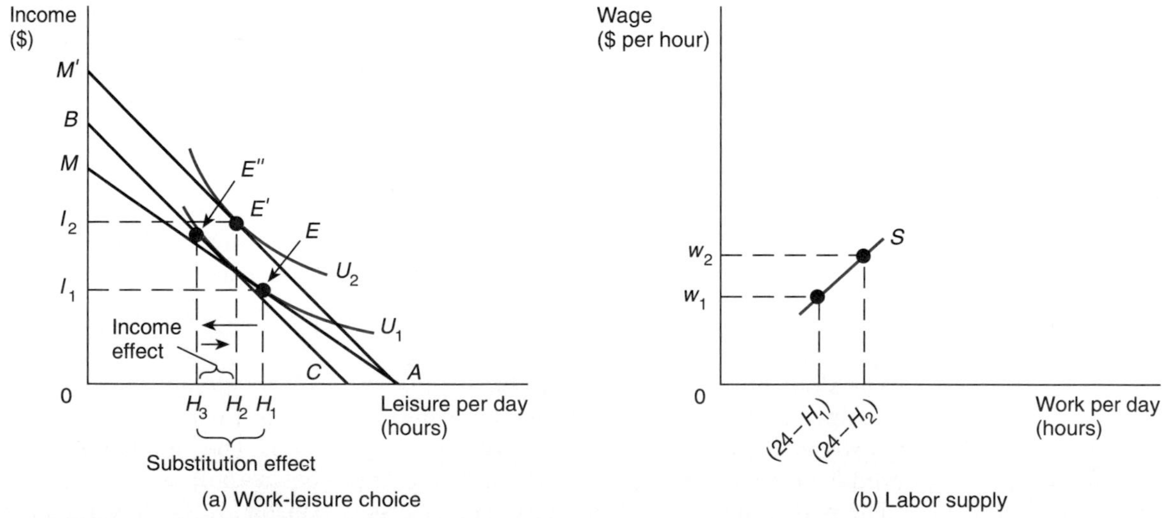

An increase in wages shifts the income line from MA to $M'A$, as shown in (a). For the person whose indifference curves are shown, equilibrium leisure decreases from H_1 to H_2. The number of hours worked increases from $(24 - H_1)$ to $(24 - H_2)$. This is consistent with an upward-sloping supply of labor hours, as shown in (b). The distance H_3H_1 is the decrease in leisure hours resulting from the substitution effect of the wage increase. The income effect increases desired leisure by H_3H_2.

retained as leisure declines to H_2 from the initial level of H_1 at point E. This implies that the person works more. At the new equilibrium, income increases to I_2 from its previous level, I_1. The increase in income is a result of the fact that the person is earning a higher wage per hour *and* is working more hours at the higher wage. Figure 14–7(b) plots the old and new wage levels and the corresponding number of hours worked per day. Connecting the two points gives an upward-sloping supply curve for labor hours for the person whose indifference curves are shown in Figure 14–7(a).

Some persons, however, will work the same number of hours per day on average or will work even *less* when wages increase. Other persons will work more when wages increase initially but will then work less when wages increase to higher levels. To fully understand individual labor supply responses, it is necessary to consider the income and substitution effects of wage changes.

Income and Substitution Effects of Wage Changes

When wages change, both income and substitution effects influence the person's choice between work and leisure. Income and substitution effects for goods and services were discussed in Chapter 4. Here the good is leisure. As wages rise, work becomes more attractive because each hour of leisure given up now results in more income. The opportunity cost (or the implicit price) of an hour of leisure is higher, which causes the person to substitute work for leisure. The substitution effect of a wage increase is therefore favorable to work. Similarly, the substitution effect of a wage decrease induces the person to substitute leisure for work and therefore to supply employers with fewer hours of work. If the substitution effect were the only impact of a change in wages, labor supply curves would always be upward sloping.

There is, however, another effect—the income effect. The income effect of a wage increase stems from the fact that it increases a person's money income for any given number of hours worked. This increase in income, even if there is no change in hours worked, induces the person to consume more of all normal goods. Leisure is for most persons a normal good. A wage increase therefore induces the person to consume more leisure hours. Consuming more leisure hours means that the person works less. The income effect of a wage increase therefore conflicts with the substitution effect.

Figure 14–7 shows how the substitution effect can be separated from the income effect of a wage increase. After wages have been increased, take away just enough of the extra earnings to make the worker as well off as before wages were increased. In Figure 14–7(a), $\$BM'$ of income are removed from the worker's earnings. The income-leisure budget line is now BC. Along that line income is reduced by $\$BM'$, but wages are at the higher level. The worker would be in equilibrium at point E″, where H_3 hours of leisure per day would be enjoyed. The distance H_3H_1 represents the substitution effect.

As long as leisure is a normal good, the income effect of a wage increase serves to decrease the number of hours worked. This can be seen by returning the income that was removed to perform this mental experiment. The return of $\$BM'$

moves the worker to point E', the actual equilibrium. This increases leisure per day by H_3H_2 hours and therefore reduces hours worked by that amount. The distance H_3H_2 is the income effect, which reduces the substitution effect's influence on the incentive to work. In Figure 14–7 the substitution effect outweighs the income effect. The overall effect of the wage increase for the worker in this case is an increase in the quantity of labor services supplied.

The reasoning is the same for a wage decrease. The substitution effect of a decline in wages decreases hours worked. The opportunity cost of an hour of leisure is less. This decreases that hour's implicit price and induces the worker to take more leisure time. At the same time, a decrease in wages reduces income for any given number of hours worked. This decrease in income leads to a reduction in the amount of leisure consumed, assuming that leisure is a normal good. The income effect of a wage decrease therefore provides an incentive to work more.

Because wages constitute the principal source of income for most persons, the income effect of a wage change can be formidable. The income effect can outweigh the substitution effect. Figure 14–8 illustrates this possibility. As wages increase from w_1 to w_2, the income line swivels upward from MA to $M'A$. The worker whose indifference curves are drawn here consumes *more* leisure. This means that the amount of work declines in response to the wage increase. Despite the decrease in hours worked, however, the worker earns higher income. Income increases from I_1 to I_2. The increase in income in this case is a result of the increase in wages only. In Figure 14–8, removing the income effect shows that the

FIGURE 14–8 Downward-Sloping Labor Supply Curve

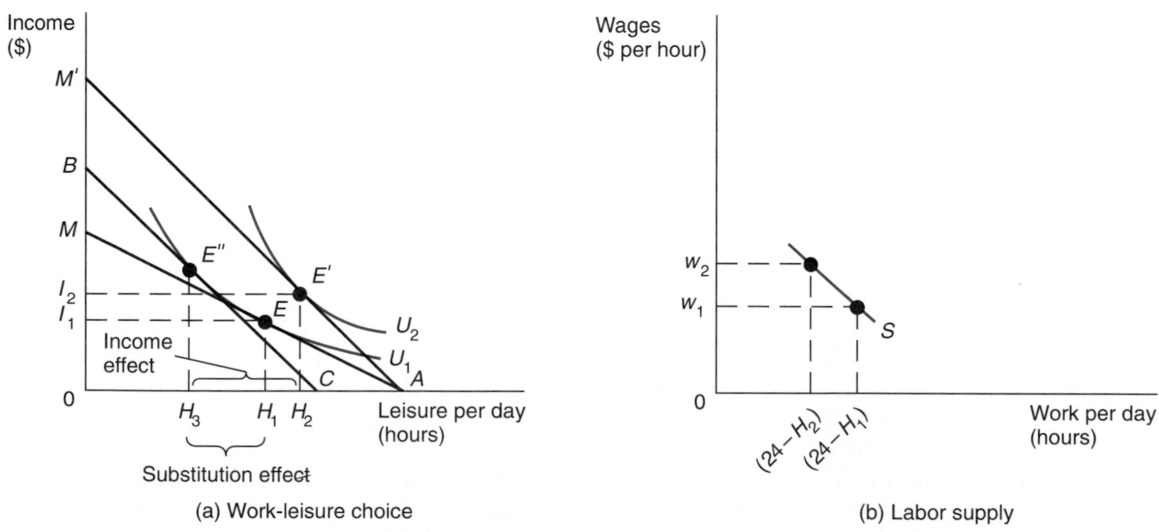

When the income effect of a wage change exceeds the substitution effect, the labor supply curve will slope downward. In the diagram, because of an increase in wages, the person consumes *more* leisure. The wage increase therefore results in a reduction in hours worked.

substitution effect still acts to increase hours worked. Taking $BM' of income away from the worker to reduce utility to its initial level, U_1, would result in an equilibrium at point E''. All points on the line BC correspond to the higher wage. The substitution effect is represented by the distance H_1H_3. After the income effect has been removed, the worker would reduce leisure per day by this amount. The worker would therefore work that much more per day. When $BM' are returned to the worker, the amount of leisure consumed increases by H_2H_3. This is the income effect. In this case $H_2H_3 > H_1H_3$. Because the income effect is greater than the substitution effect, the worker works less in response to the wage increase, as shown in Figure 14–8(b). The supply curve of labor services is negatively sloped between w_1 and w_2.

Of course, the income effect could *exactly* offset the substitution effect of a wage change. If this were the case, the worker would not alter the number of labor hours supplied in response to a change in wages. In other words, when the income effect offsets the substitution effect of a wage change, the labor supply will be perfectly inelastic.

Backward-Bending Labor Supply Curves

Backward-bending labor supply curve The labor supply curve that exists when the income effect of wage increases outweighs the substitution effect at relatively high wage levels.

A **backward-bending labor supply curve** for a person's labor services implies that the substitution effect outweighs the income effect only at relatively low wages. As wages increase, the income effect becomes stronger, and eventually it over-

FIGURE 14–9 Backward-Bending Labor Supply Curve

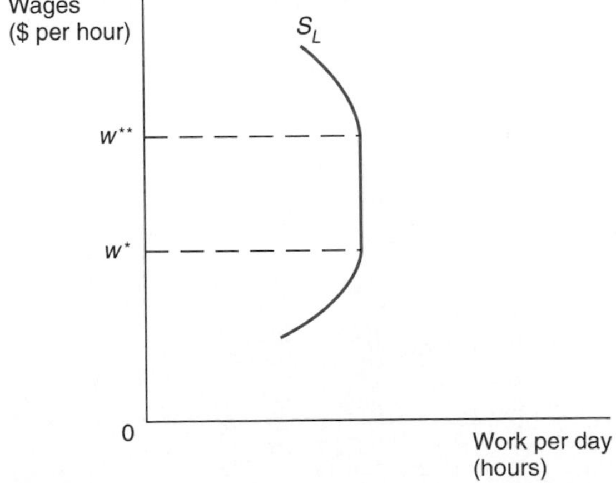

Increases in wages increase hours worked per day on the average over the year up to the hourly wage w^*. When wages are between w^* and w^{**}, the income effect exactly offsets the substitution effect and labor supply is perfectly inelastic. When hourly wages rise above w^{**}, increases in wages result in decreases in labor hours supplied because the income effect of the wage changes outweighs the substitution effect.

Modern Microeconomics in Action: Government and the Economy

Welfare and Work: How Cash Assistance to the Poor Affects Their Labor Supply Decision

Welfare programs provide eligible recipients with a cash transfer, a grant of income independent of work. The major U.S. program of cash assistance to the poor is Aid to Families with Dependent Children (AFDC). This program provides cash assistance mainly to families headed by one parent, in most cases a mother, with at least one dependent child. The program, jointly financed by state governments and the federal government, assists more than 11 million persons. Assistance under the program varies from state to state, but the average AFDC benefit is about $400 per month for a family of four. There is good reason to believe that the way the program is currently administered provides strong incentives for eligible recipients to supply less labor to the labor market.

When AFDC recipients work, their benefits are reduced by an average of 50 cents for each dollar of earnings for a period of four months. After they have worked four months, their benefits are typically reduced by $1 for each $1 of wages. However, because of various adjustments made in calculating costs associated with work, the effective reduction in benefits of AFDC recipients amounts to 70 cents for each dollar of earnings.

The daily cash transfer, T, received by an AFDC recipient with three children who receives a payment of $15 per day will vary with her earned income, I_E, according to the following formula after she has worked four months:

$$T = \$15 - 0.7I_E$$

For example, if the recipient earns $10 per day, her daily cash transfer would be

$$\$15 - 0.7(\$10) = \$8$$

Her total daily income would be the sum of her earnings and the cash transfer, which in this case would be $18.

At some point the recipient will earn enough on average each day so that the transfer will be cut off. The average daily earnings at which the cash transfer becomes zero can be obtained by setting T equal to zero:

$$T = \$15 - 0.7I_E = 0$$

which implies that when I_E = $21.43 per day on average, the recipient will no longer be eligible for a cash transfer. If the recipient earns $4 per hour at a part-time job and averages about 5.5 hours of work per day, a complete cutoff of the cash transfer will result.

Indifference curve analysis can be used to show the impact of the AFDC program on a typical recipient's choice between work and leisure. In the absence of any cash transfer, the recipient's budget line in the accompanying graph would be AM. On average, she would choose to take 18 hours of leisure per day, corresponding to point E, and to work 6 hours per day. She is eligible to receive a cash transfer, T, without working. Therefore, if she chooses to take 24 hours of leisure per day, her income would *not* be zero. The daily cash transfer under AFDC is $15, the average daily cash payment to a recipient with three children in 1990.*

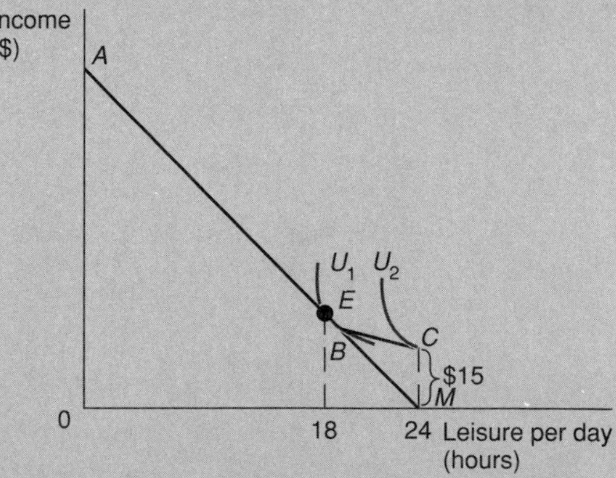

If a person is eligible for AFDC, the budget line becomes ABC, with a notch at point B that corresponds to the number of leisure hours per day

(*Continued*) at which the cash transfer is reduced to zero. The line *BC* is less steep than the line *BM* because it reflects the fact that total income will increase by only 30 cents for each dollar of earnings because the cash transfer decreases by 70 cents for each dollar of earnings when 5.5 or fewer hours per day are supplied as labor services to an employer. Assuming that the person is free to choose the number of hours of leisure she takes per day, after she becomes eligible for the program she is at a corner equilibrium at point *C* with utility level $U_2 > U_1$, at which she takes 24 hours a day in leisure and chooses not to work at all!

Numerous empirical studies and even some experiments have been conducted to determine the impact of welfare programs on labor supply. One study concluded that in the absence of AFDC transfers the women whose families received these benefits would have worked between 10 and 15 hours more per week than they actually did in the early 1980s.† However, because most AFDC recipients are unskilled and earn very low wages, this extra work would have increased their disposable income by a mere $1,500 per year—hardly enough to bring them out of poverty and certainly not enough to take the place of the AFDC transfers. Most of the experiments also suggest that AFDC transfers have an effect on work effort but that their effect on the work effort of low-income men and women with dependent children is small.‡ According to estimates based on these experiments, a 10 percent increase in the transfers would reduce hours worked less than 2 percent. These findings suggest that even if welfare benefits were reduced substantially or even if the rate at which welfare benefits are phased out with earnings were reduced, the resulting increase in work would be insufficient to bring current welfare recipients out of poverty.

* This is a meager sum. However, the recipients also receive noncash benefits such as food stamps, Medicare, and housing assistance.

† Robert A. Moffitt, "Work and the U.S. Welfare System: A Review," Department of Economics, Brown University, October 1987, mimeographed; cited in Gary Burtless, "The Economists Lament: Public Assistance in America," *Journal of Economic Perspectives* 4, no. 1 (Winter 1990), p. 73.

‡ See Burtless, "Economists Lament," p. 73.

takes the substitution effect, causing the person to work less as wages increase. Some persons prefer to work less when their hourly wage increases so as to have the time to enjoy spending their higher wages on leisure activities. As persons become more affluent, they tend to spend their higher incomes on vacations and hobby activities at home and to enjoy the luxury of relaxing. All of this requires more leisure time.

Figure 14–9 illustrates a backward-bending supply curve for a worker. When wages are below w^* per hour, increases in wages result in increases in the number of labor hours supplied. When wages are above w^* but below w^{**}, increases in wages have no effect on the number of labor hours supplied. For the range of hourly wages between w^* and w^{**}, the substitution effect is exactly offset by an equal and opposite income effect. After the wage reaches $\$w^{**}$ per hour, additional wage increases result in fewer labor hours supplied and the labor supply curve turns backward.

Competitive Labor Markets

In a competitive input market, input price and the quantity of input services sold over a given period are determined by the interaction of demand and supply. Any differences in input prices among markets, such as wage differentials for different types of labor services, can be explained in terms of differences affecting either the demand or the supply of labor services.

By making a number of simplifying assumptions, it is possible to use a model of labor market supply and demand to understand the forces influencing wages and employment in the economy. Figure 14–10 shows the demand and supply curves for factory workers in the economy. The equilibrium wage of $15 per hour measures the current average wage of factory workers in the economy. At that wage employment corresponds to Q_1 labor hours per week. Given all of the influences on the demand for factory output and the price of that output, changes in wages attributable to changes in labor market conditions can be isolated.

If the number of workers actively seeking factory jobs is increasing, as is typical, then, other things being equal, the supply of labor will increase over time. An increase in population over time tends to increase the supply of available workers. Other things being equal, this puts a downward pressure on wages. However, the depressing effect of labor supply on wages can be offset if other changes in the economy increase the demand for factory workers. If business firms make investments in new plant and equipment that increase the productivity of labor, the demand for labor shifts outward. The investments in new plant and equipment that is complementary to labor use makes workers more productive. As a result the marginal product of any given number of labor hours increases. This increases the marginal revenue product of labor and therefore increases labor

FIGURE 14–10 Population Growth, Productivity Gains, and Wages

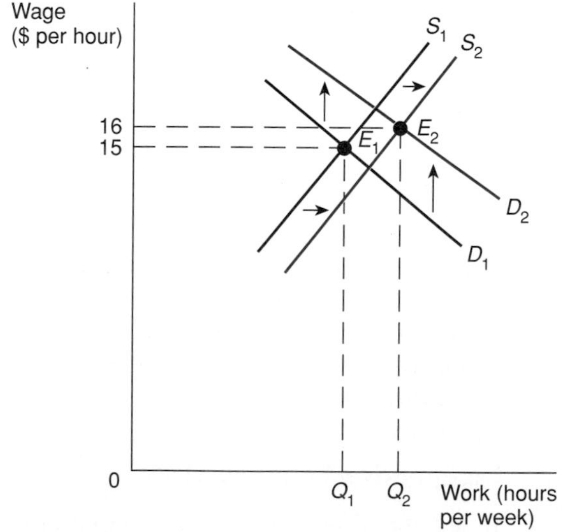

Population growth puts a downward pressure on wages by increasing labor supply. Increases in labor productivity increase labor demand, putting an upward pressure on wages.

demand.[4] If the increase in labor productivity is strong enough, the demand curve of labor shifts out sufficiently to offset the depressing effect of increased labor supply on wages, as is the case in Figure 14–10, where wages increase from $15 to $16 per hour in equilibrium.

Investments in new plant and equipment complementary to labor use can therefore benefit workers by contributing to higher wages. Other changes in the labor market that affect worker productivity can also offset supply increases. Improvements in the general productivity of workers that are associated with higher levels of education, training, and experience can also shift the demand curve for labor upward by increasing the marginal revenue product of workers.

Population growth tends to put downward pressure on wages, not only because it increases the supply of workers but also because it typically decreases the average age of workers. Population growth increases the proportion of younger workers in the labor force. Younger workers are less experienced than older workers. Since experience is an important determinant of labor productivity, a younger labor force is a less productive labor force. A decrease in the average age of workers tends to decrease the marginal revenue product of labor. This contributes to lower average wages.

In 1977, when the "baby boomers" of the late 1950s began entering the labor force, the proportion of 20-year-olds in the population was 44 percent higher than it had been in the early 1960s. This large influx of inexperienced workers into the labor force resulted in a 12–15 percent decline in the wages of new workers as compared with wages of existing workers. The increase in inexperienced workers in the labor force also sharply reduced the growth rate of real wages in the economy and contributed to an increase in the unemployment rate because younger workers are more likely than older workers to quit their jobs in search of better ones. At any point in time, therefore, more younger workers than older workers are "between jobs."

The decline in the growth rate of real wages could be reversed by the late 1990s. By that time the baby boomers will be middle-aged. They will contribute to higher average wages as the proportion of experienced workers in the labor force increases. As a result of declines in the birthrate in the 1970s, the proportion of inexperienced workers in the labor force at that time will be relatively low.

Concept Review

1. The marginal rate of substitution of leisure for income is $5 for a worker. If the worker's wage is currently $10 per hour, is the worker in equilibrium?
2. Why is there a conflict between the income and substitution effects of a wage change?
3. Explain how increases in the productivity of workers affect wage levels when population is increasing.

[4] However, the price of manufactured products will fall, offsetting some of the stimulating effect of the increased marginal product of labor on labor demand.

Modern Microeconomics in Action: International Report

Immigration and Labor Markets

According to the most recent census, the population of the United States increased by 23 million people between 1980 and 1990. Over the same period 7 million to 9 million immigrants—largely from nations in Asia, Latin America, and the Carribbean—accounted for between one third and two fifths of the growth of the U.S. population.

Immigration has always been a controversial issue in the United States. It has often been argued that immigration lowers wages and reduces employment opportunities for native-born Americans. This view is based on the faulty assumption that there are a fixed number of jobs in the economy. Fortunately, however, as the economy grows, more jobs are created. An increase in population, including an increase resulting from immigration, increases the demand for goods and services and increases job opportunities. Immigrants are not perfect substitutes for U.S. workers. They often end up taking jobs that native-born Americans shun, such as jobs in agriculture or food service.

A surprising number of economic studies have confirmed the hypothesis that immigration has no appreciable effect on the wage levels or employment of native-born Americans. The most sophisticated of these studies examine labor market outcomes in various parts of the nation where the immigrant population amounts to varying percentages of the labor force. Such studies show that a 10-percent increase in the number of immigrants as a percentage of the work force in a labor market typically results in only a 0.2 percent reduction in the wages of native workers.* They also show that increases in the proportion of immigrants in a labor market have no effect on unemployment rates and negligible effects on weeks worked per year or on labor force participation rates of natives.

Some who favor restricting immigration have argued that certain minority groups, such as blacks, are more adversely affected by immigration than other groups, through either reductions in wages or reductions in employment. However, empirical analysis shows this contention to be false.

There are, however, a number of disturbing trends. The skill levels of immigrants in the 1970s and 1980s have been markedly lower than the skill levels of pre-1970 immigrants. The immigrants of the 1970s and 1980s have been less successful than earlier immigrants in increasing their earnings over time. They have been more likely to go on welfare. They have also paid less in taxes because they have earned less. The declining skill level of recent immigrants has led to calls for changes in U.S. immigration policy in order to attract more skilled immigrants in the future. In 1990 Congress enacted a new immigration law that will make it easier for highly skilled foreign professionals to immigrate.

* See George J. Borjas, *Friends or Strangers: The Impact of Immigrants on the U.S. Economy* (New York: Basic Books, 1990), chap. 5.

Capital Markets

Capital A durable input created for the purpose of producing more goods and services.

Capital is a durable input created for the purpose of producing more goods and services. Examples of *physical* capital inputs include machines, structures, vehicles, tools, and inventories (stocks) of parts and materials. *Human* capital consists of skills, such as those of medical practitioners, created to produce various goods and services.

It takes time to create capital. For example, the construction of a new office building or the development of a new passenger aircraft can take years. During the period in which new capital is created, firms require funds to finance the costs of creating the new capital. They expend those funds today for the promise of future revenues that will be generated by the contribution of the new capital to increased production. Those who supply the funds for the creation of new capital forgo the opportunity to spend those funds on current purchases. Similarly, a person who wants to become a physician must be prepared to forgo income and incur expenses for training over the eight-year period or so that it takes to acquire the medical degree and a professional license. The essence of the decision to create new capital is a comparison of the costs involved in borrowing or sacrificing income to finance the creation of an asset that will last for a certain period and the extra revenue that asset will provide for its owner over that period.

Capital Flows and the Capital Stock

Capital includes tools, machinery, vehicles, structures, raw materials, and inventories of goods and parts in various stages of production; available skills; and expertise acquired through education and training. The *services* of capital equipment and materials are measured as flows. A flow is a measure of the value of a variable *per unit time*. When considering production decisions, the services of capital can be measured as machine hours per month or as the hourly payment for special skills, such as medical or legal professional services.

Capital itself, however, is measured as a stock. A *stock* is a measure of the value of a variable *at a given point in time*. At any point in time, a firm has a given number of machines and other types of capital. The firm's managers can vary the rate of use of those machines per month, but the actual number of machines and their value are fixed at a given point in time. Our objective in analyzing capital now is to understand the process by which the stock of capital is created and changed. To do this, we must investigate the costs involved in creating new capital and the benefits of doing so.

Interest and the Supply and Demand of Loanable Funds

Interest The price paid for the use of loanable funds.

Interest is the price paid to persons for the use of their loanable funds for a given period. Interest is usually expressed as a percentage rate per year. Suppose the interest rate is 10 percent per year. This means that suppliers of funds will be paid 10 cents for each dollar they allow others to use for a one-year period. At the end of the year, each of the dollars they lend to others will be returned along with a 10 percent premium for its use. The person who borrows funds has to pay 10 percent per year on each dollar borrowed.

The use of funds is traded in various financial markets. Those willing to lend the use of funds to others for specified periods supply funds through these markets. The equilibrium interest rate is the one for which the quantity of funds supplied by lenders equals the quantity demanded by borrowers.

In a *perfectly competitive financial market* for loanable funds, neither individual borrowers nor individual lenders can influence the interest rate. They are price takers. Each borrower demands only a small share of total funds supplied. Similarly, each lender supplies only a small share of total funds demanded.

In actuality, no one person or business firm, not even the largest of corporations, borrows a significant portion of the total funds supplied per year. Borrowers include business firms that use loanable funds to finance new capital and consumers who borrow loanable funds to finance such purchases as homes and automobiles. Governments borrow loanable funds to cover budget deficits and fund new public facilities. Those who supply funds to lenders are called savers. Savers put aside portions of their current income for use by others and are compensated with interest. Banks, life insurance companies, other specialized financial firms, and brokers act as intermediaries between savers and those who wish to borrow funds. The interest rate is determined by the supply of funds from savings and the demand for loanable funds by all borrowers.

How the Interest Rate Affects Investment Decisions

Investment The process of replenishing, or adding to, capital stock.

Physical depreciation The rate at which capital wears out or becomes obsolete.

Marginal rate of return on the investment The net increase in revenue resulting from the investment expressed as a percentage of each dollar invested.

Marginal net return on the investment The marginal rate of return less the marginal interest rate.

Investment is the process of replenishing, or adding to, capital stock. Investment represents a flow of new capital in a given year. The capital stock of a firm (and of a nation) is "used up" in production. Inventories of materials and parts are drawn down during the production process, and machines wear out or become obsolete and have to be replaced. The rate at which capital wears out is called **physical depreciation.** If in a given year new capital acquisition is less than the physical depreciation of the existing capital stock, investment will be negative in that year.

Firms make investments because new capital allows them to add to their revenues. In making an investment, a firm must decide whether the increase in revenues over time that the investment allows is worth its cost. The opportunity cost of the investment of a certain number of dollars is the interest on the sum of funds necessary to acquire the new capital.

The **marginal rate of return on the investment** (r) is the net increase in revenue resulting from the investment expressed as a percentage of each extra dollar invested. The difference between the marginal return on the investment (r) and the interest rate (i) is the **marginal net return on the investment:**

$$r - i = \text{Marginal net return on an investment} \quad \textbf{(14–8)}$$

This represents the difference between the marginal rate of return on the investment and the marginal rate of interest, which in the preceding example is 10 percent, independent of the value of the investment.

As long as r is not less than i, a firm can make additional profits by investing more. The profit-maximizing level of investment is the one for which the marginal return just equals the rate of interest. *As long as the marginal rate of return,* r, *that the firm can make on an investment is greater than the interest rate,* i, *at which funds can be borrowed (or lent), it will pay to borrow funds to finance the investment.*

Figure 14–11 plots the marginal rate of return on the investment and shows that the equilibrium quantity of investment corresponds to the point at which the marginal rate of return curve intersects the line representing the rate of interest.

FIGURE 14–11 **A Single-Period Investment**

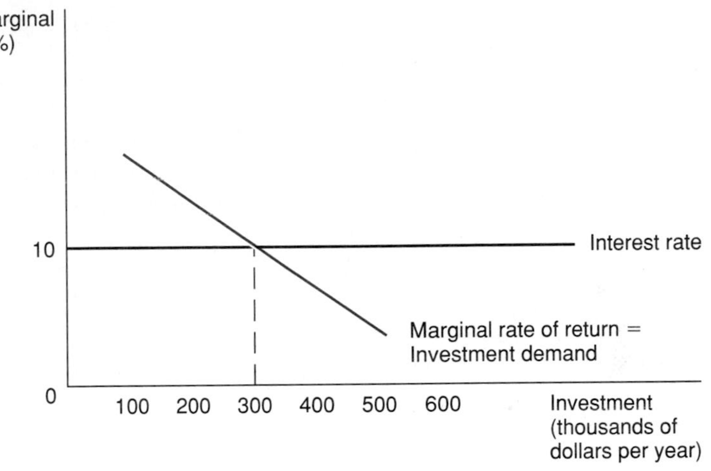

To maximize profit, the firm invests until the marginal rate of return on an investment falls to equal the interest rate.

The curve labeled ''marginal rate of return'' gives the firm's demand curve for funds. It shows the quantity of loanable funds that the firm demands for investment at each possible market interest rate. The higher the market interest rate, the smaller is the quantity of loanable funds demanded.

Multiperiod Investments

Most investments made by business firms involve multiperiod decisions. A typical addition to the capital of a firm lasts many years. Capital investments vary in their durability. The **useful life of a capital asset** is the number of years over which the newly acquired asset will contribute to a firm's revenues or reduce its costs. To calculate the return on a multiperiod investment the firm must first estimate the useful life of the new capital asset. Then it must estimate the addition to revenues that will result from the asset in each year of its use.

Useful life of a capital asset The number of years over which the newly acquired asset will contribute to a firm's revenues or reduce its costs.

Suppose a firm contemplates investing in computer software. The cost of the software is $1,000. The firm estimates that this asset will reduce costs $1,500 in its first year of use. To calculate the return on the first year of the investment, the firm must determine the annual percentage rate of return at which $1,000 will increase to $1,500 at the end of one year.

Suppose C is the marginal cost of the capital investment and R_1 is the investment's marginal contribution to either increasing revenues or decreasing costs (or a combination of the two) after one year of use. The marginal return on the investment, r, can be calculated from the following formula:

$$C(1 + r) = R_1 \tag{14–9}$$

This gives the percentage return (r) that will cause $\$C$ to grow to $\$R_1$ after one year.

The firm knows C. This is the \$1,000 cost of the software. It also knows R_1. This is the \$1,500 cost saving that will result from using the software for one year. Substituting these values for C and R_1 in Equation 14–9 allows the firm to calculate r:

$$\$1{,}000(1 + r) = \$1{,}500 \tag{14–10}$$

Internal rate of return The marginal rate of return on an investment.

In this case $r = 0.5$. The marginal rate of return on the investment, which is also commonly referred to as the investment's **internal rate of return,** is therefore 50 percent. To decide whether the investment will be profitable, the firm compares its internal rate of return with the market rate of interest. As has been shown for the single-period case, the firm can increase its profits by making the investment as long as r exceeds i. If the market rate of interest is 10 percent, the firm's net return will be 50 percent − 10 percent, which is 40 percent.

Now consider a multiperiod investment. Suppose the firm contemplates purchasing a new computer. To calculate the internal rate of return on a multiperiod investment, the firm must relate the cost of purchasing the computer to the computer's net contribution to revenues over its useful life. (The net contribution is the increase in revenues or the decrease in costs, less maintenance and depreciation costs, that results from the use of the computer.)

As a first step to understanding how this is done, calculate the internal rate of return on a two-year investment. Suppose the useful life of the computer is two years and it will cost \$10,000. It will take one year to install the computer system, so there will be no revenue or cost saving in the first year. All of the gain will be in the second year. The firm estimates that by the end of the second year the computer will result in a net increase of \$12,000 in its revenues.

If r is the internal rate of return on the investment and C is the cost of the computer, then after one year C would be worth $C(1 + r)$ and after another year it would be worth $[C(1 + r)](1 + r)$. The return after two years is therefore

$$C(1 + r)^2 = R_2 \tag{14–11}$$

The squared term takes into account the reinvestment of the principal and accumulated interest after the first year. Because $R_2 = \$12{,}000$ and $C = \$10{,}000$, the internal rate of return on the investment is

$$\$10{,}000(1 + r)^2 = \$12{,}000 \tag{14–12}$$

Solving the equation gives $r = 0.095$. Assume that the market rate of interest is still 10 percent. Since the internal rate of return is only 9.5 percent, which is less than the market rate of interest, the opportunity cost of the investment exceeds its return. More can be earned by lending the funds to another borrower at 10 percent.

Dividing the net revenue (R_1) obtained after one year from any investment by $(1 + r)$ gives (from Equation 14–9)

$$C = \frac{R_1}{(1 + r)} \tag{14–13}$$

where C is the cost of the investment. Similarly, from Equation 14–11 the following relationship holds for an investment yielding R_2 dollars after two years and nothing the first year:

$$C = \frac{R_2}{(1 + r)^2} \tag{14–14}$$

where C is the cost of the two-year investment.

In general, if C is the cost of an investment that will yield R_j dollars of net revenue in each of j years and has a useful life of N years, the following relationship holds:

$$C = \frac{R_1}{(1 + r)} + \frac{R_2}{(1 + r)^2} + \ldots + \frac{R_N}{(1 + r)^N} = \Sigma \frac{R_j}{(1 + r)^j} \tag{14–15}$$

To calculate the return on an investment, the firm will know C and estimate R_j in each year. Solving Equation 14–15 for r then gives the internal rate of return on the investment. This is the rate at which the sum C, the cost of the investment, would have to grow to generate R_j, the stream of returns. Those returns are then compared with the market rate of interest to determine whether the investment will be profitable. If $r > i$, the firm undertakes the investment.

For example, the firm might estimate the useful life of a new computer system as 10 years. If the system costs $50,000, estimate R_j for each of the 10 years and solve the equation for r. Then compare the internal rate of return with the market rate of interest.

The internal rate of return on investment tends to decline as more funds are invested in a given year. Firms undertake investments with the highest rates of return first. The downward-sloping internal rate of return curve, which resembles the curve drawn in Figure 14–11, is the firm's demand for investable funds. It represents the maximum rate of interest firms would pay to borrow loanable funds to finance a given dollar amount of investment.

Concept Review

1. What is capital, and how is the stock of capital related to investment and physical depreciation?
2. Suppose the marginal rate of return on a $5,000 investment is 10 percent. If the market rate of interest is 8 percent, would it be profitable to borrow to finance the investment? What must the firm making this investment do to maximize profit from investing?
3. The marginal return on a one-year investment is $2,000. If the investment will cost $1,800, calculate its internal rate of return.

THE SUPPLY OF SAVINGS

Time Preference

A person who saves a portion of his income forgoes the opportunity to consume something this year. The more the person saves, the more consumption he forgoes. Alternatively, a person can spend more than his income this year by borrowing. How much is saved and how much is borrowed is a matter of personal choice. That choice depends in part on preferences between consuming more this year and consuming more in the future.

Figure 14–12 shows typical indifference curves between present and future consumption of goods or services. These curves indicate preferences between consuming a given amount of current earnings immediately and postponing consumption for one year. Suppose that a person has \$20,000 in income to allocate between two periods. The more of the \$20,000 that the person spends in the current year, the less of it is available to spend next year. At point *A* all of the \$20,000 income is spent in the current year. The indifference curves show combinations of current and future expenditure of a *given amount of current income* among which the person is indifferent. Assume that there is no inflation, that goods available this year will also be available next year at the same prices. The units of measurement on both axes are dollars.

FIGURE 14–12 Time Preference

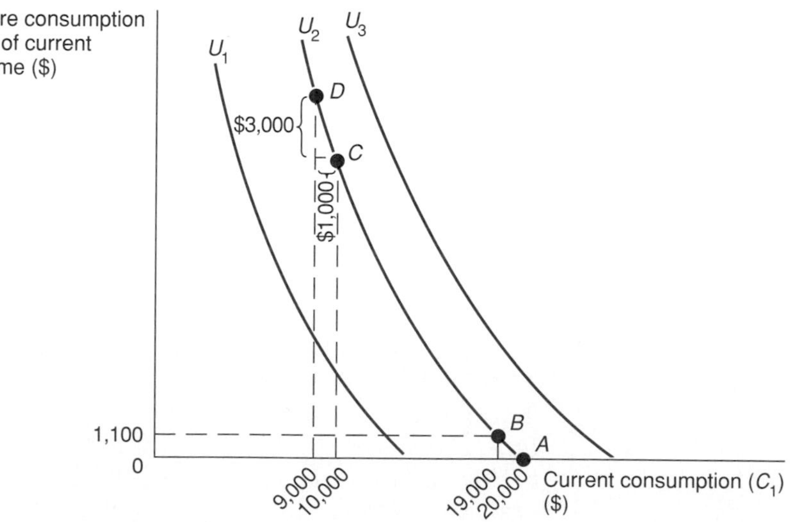

Positive time preference prevails when it takes more than a dollar of future income to compensate a person for a loss in the use of a current dollar. The MRTP is 1.1 between *A* and *B* and 3 between *C* and *D* on indifference curve U_2.

Marginal rate of time preference The value of additional future consumption required to compensate a person for giving up current consumption without making the person better or worse off.

Persons differ in their preferences for allocating earnings over present and future periods. Some are more impatient than others. Those who like instant gratification have high positive time preference and steeply sloped indifference curves. Those who are more patient and thrifty have lower positive time preference and flatter indifference curves. However, it is generally agreed that most persons have positive time preference. As will be shown, this is useful in explaining why interest rates are positive.

The **marginal rate of time preference** (MRTP) is the value of additional future consumption required to compensate a person for giving up current consumption without making the person better or worse off. The MRTP at a point on an indifference curve in Figure 14–12 is the slope of the indifference curve at that point multiplied by −1. As is the case for indifference curves in general, the MRTP declines as consumption in year 1 is substituted for consumption in year 2. This implies that as a person saves more of current income, higher returns are required in year 2 to induce her to give up each extra dollar of current consumption. For example, between points A and B on indifference curve U_2, \$1,000 of current income exchanges for \$1,100 in the second year. Therefore, between those two points

$$\text{MRTP} = \frac{\Delta C_2}{\Delta C_1} = \frac{\$1{,}100}{\$1{,}000} = 1.1 \qquad \textbf{(14–16)}$$

where ΔC_2 is the amount of consumption in the second year that it takes to induce the person to give up ΔC_1 in year 1.

The MRTP between points C and D is greater than the MRTP between points A and B. At point C the person has already saved \$10,000 out of \$20,000 income. To induce an additional \$1,000 savings would require a \$2,000 premium, so that the person would be able to consume \$3,000 after one year. Therefore, between points C and D

$$\text{MRTP} = \frac{\$3{,}000}{\$1{,}000} = 3 \qquad \textbf{(14–17)}$$

The Intertemporal Budget Constraint

Opportunities for exchanging current consumption for future consumption depend on the market rate of interest. If a person saves S dollars of current income, she will be able to consume more than S dollars in the next year. How much more depends on the market rate of interest. Suppose the interest rate is i percent per year. If the person saves S dollars, consumption in year 2 will be

$$C_2 = (1 + i)S \qquad \textbf{(14–18)}$$

S is the difference between current income and current consumption:

$$S = I - C_1 \qquad \textbf{(14–19)}$$

where I is income.

Substituting Equation 14–19 in Equation 14–18 gives

$$C_2 = (1 + i)(I - C_1) \qquad \textbf{(14–20)}$$

FIGURE 14–13 The Intertemporal Budget Constraint and Intertemporal Equilibrium

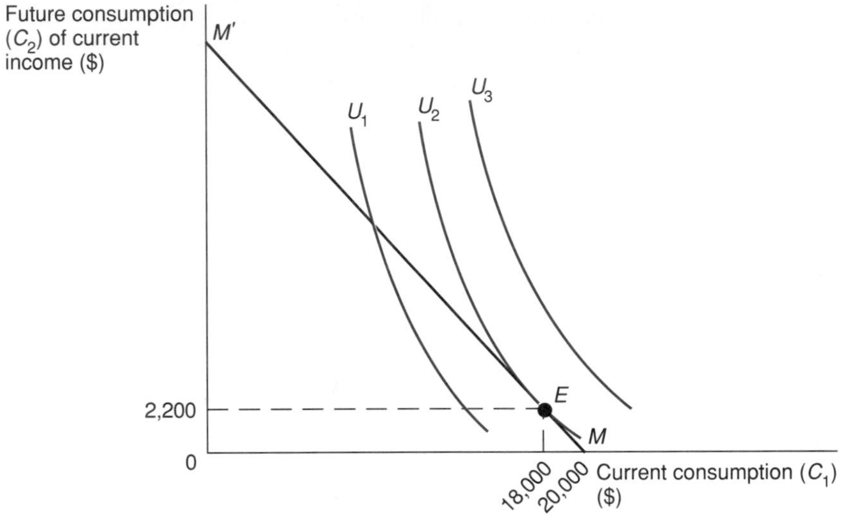

The intertemporal budget line is MM'. Along that line, $C_2 = (1 + i)(I - C_1)$. The person is in equilibrium at point E, where the intertemporal budget constraint is tangent to indifference curve U_2. At that point MRTP = $(1 + i)$ and the person saves $2,000 of current income. If $i = 0.1$, then C_2 = $2,200.

For example, if income is $20,000 and $2,000 is saved, the person will be able to consume $2,200 in year 2 in addition to income in that year when the interest rate is 10 percent. Under these circumstances, C_1 = $18,000 and C_2 = $2,200.

Figure 14–13 plots equation 14–20. This is the intertemporal budget constraint. The line MM' shows the opportunities for transforming sacrificed consumption in year 1 into consumption in year 2. The slope of the intertemporal budget constraint is $-(1 + i)$.

Intertemporal Equilibrium

In Figure 14–13 equilibrium is at point E. At that point the person consumes $18,000 of current income. The amount of saving is therefore $2,000 per year. This enables her to consume $2,200 in addition to earnings in the following year.

In equilibrium the slope of the intemporal budget line is equal to the slope of an indifference curve. The marginal rate of time preference is the slope of the indifference curve multiplied by -1. Also multiplying the slope of the budget line by -1 gives

$$\text{MRTP} = (1 + i) \qquad \textbf{(14–21)}$$

Note that the steeper the indifference curves of a person, the greater is the interest premium required to induce the person to save. It is assumed that the MRTP is greater than 1 at all points on any indifference curve. This means that a positive

FIGURE 14–14 Interest Rates and the Supply of Savings

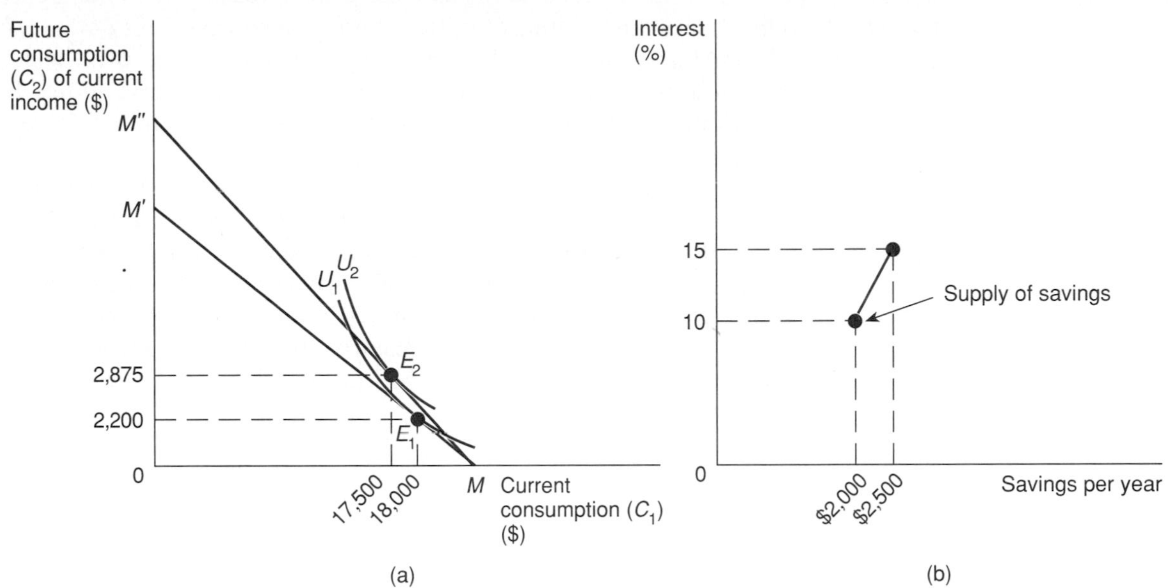

In (a), an increase in the interest rate swivels the intertemporal budget constraint up from MM′ to MM″. The new equilibrium is at point E_2. As long as the substitution effect outweighs the income effect of the increase in the interest rate, the quantity of savings supplied increases. The supply curve of savings is shown in (b).

interest rate is necessary to induce any person to save.[5] Note that the interest rate is not the sole determinant of a person's saving. Saving also depends on the person's income and preferences. A person with a very high time preference would be in equilibrium at a corner corresponding to point *M*. This person would save nothing out of current income.

Income and Substitution Effects of a Change in the Interest Rate

A change in the market rate of interest will result in both income and substitution effects. An increase in the interest rate swivels the intertemporal budget constraint upward. Assume that the interest rate increases from 10 percent to 15 percent. As shown in Figure 14–14(a), this results in a movement in the equilibrium from point E_1 to point E_2. Current consumption out of current income decreases from $18,000 to $17,500 per year. Consumption resulting from the portion of current income saved, over and above next year's income, is now

$$C_2 = (1.15)(\$2,500) = \$2,875$$

[5] The analysis can easily be adapted to allow borrowing at the market rate of interest. If a person borrows, she can consume more than her earnings in the current period. This means that saving is negative and that C_2 is also negative. If the person borrows $\$B$, $C_2 = -(1 + i)B$.

Will an increase in the interest rate induce a person to save more? This depends on the income and substitution effects of the increase. An increase in the interest rate reduces the opportunity cost of future consumption. It now costs less in terms of current dollars to obtain a dollar of future consumption. The decrease in the cost of a dollar of future consumption induces the person to substitute future for present consumption. This is the substitution effect. It results in an incentive to save more.

On the other hand, the increase in real income caused by the increase in the interest rate leads the person to consume more of all normal goods in the current period and in the future. Consumption goes up in the second period as a result of the increase in interest income received. The only way consumption can increase in the current period is for the person to save *less*. Therefore, the income effect of the increase in the interest rate provides an incentive to save less. Depending on the relative strengths of the income and substitution effects, the person saves either more or less.

A supply curve of saving can be obtained by varying the rate of interest while holding a person's current income constant. Saving is simply the difference between income and C_1, consumption in the current period. In Figure 14–14 the substitution effect of the increase in the interest rate from 10 percent to 15 percent outweighs the income effect. The amount of saving increases from $2,000 to $2,500 per year. Figure 14–14(b) shows the two corresponding points on the saving supply curve. The supply curve of saving between these two points is upward sloping.

It is possible for the income effect of an increase in interest rates to just outweigh the substitution effect. In that case a change in interest rates would have no effect on the quantity of funds saved. Of course, if the income effect outweighs the substitution effect, the supply curve of saving would be backward bending. It is also possible for the income effect to become stronger at higher levels of interest rates.

THE MARKET RATE OF INTEREST

The market rate of interest (which is an average of interest rates charged for various types of loans) depends on both the market demand for and the market supply of loanable funds. Figure 14–15(a) shows that the equilibrium interest rate is initially 10 percent at point *E*. The supply of savings depends on the time preference of savers and on the number of savers in the economy. The demand for loanable funds each year depends on the profitability of business investment and on consumer and government demands for credit. In equilibrium the quantity of funds demanded for all purposes equals the quantity supplied by all sources.

When perfect competition prevails, there is only one interest rate for all borrowers and all lenders. Both borrowers and lenders merely react to that interest rate. No person or firm can affect it in any way. The interest rate is positive because persons, on average, have a positive time preference and because the

FIGURE 14–15 The Demand for Loanable Funds, Interest Rates, and Business Investment

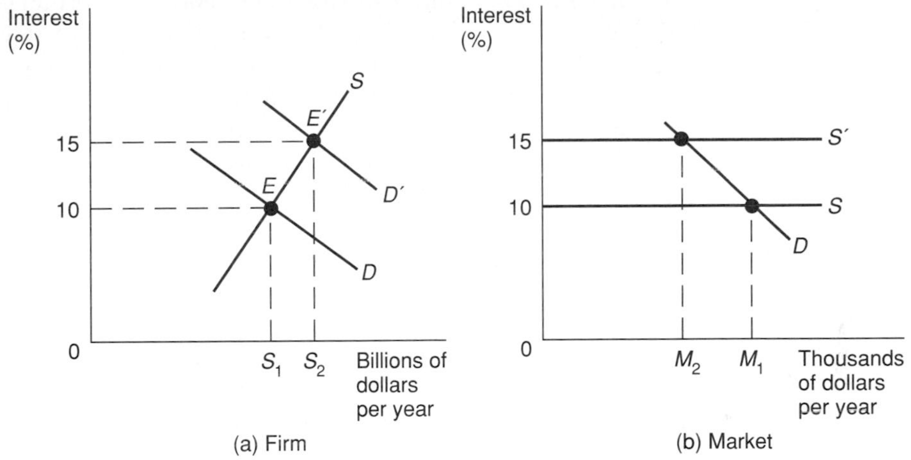

(a) Firm

(b) Market

An increase in the government's demand for funds to finance a deficit increases the market rate of interest. The quantity of savings increases from S_1 to S_2. In addition, the increase in the rate of interest decreases investment by business firms from M_1 to M_2 dollars per year.

return on business investment exceeds zero. The supply of funds for investment to any single borrower is infinitely elastic at the market rate of interest. This is shown in Figure 14–15(b).

Changes in the demand for funds or the supply of savings affect the interest rate. Changes in the interest rate in turn affect the equilibrium amount of business investment. Suppose as a result of increased government borrowing to finance a budget deficit there is an increase in the overall demand for loanable funds. Given the supply of savings, the demand for funds increases from D to D', as shown in Figure 14–15(a). Assuming that nothing else changes, the increased demand for funds increases the equilibrium interest rate from 10 percent to 15 percent as market equilibrium shifts to point E'.

Figure 14–15(b) shows the reaction of a typical firm. The higher interest rate shifts the supply of funds to the firm upward, from S to S'. At the 15 percent interest rate the amount of the firm's investment per year decreases from $\$M_1$ to $\$M_2$. The total amount of funds supplied by savers increases from $\$S_1$ to $\$S_2$. The increased saving finances a portion of the increased government borrowing. An additional portion of the increased government borrowing is financed by a reduction in the total borrowing for investment by all business firms. Each business firm reduces investment in the same way as the firm shown in Figure 14–15(b) in response to the higher interest rate. In effect, the increased government borrowing "chokes off" business investment.

An increase in the supply of savings, other things being equal, decreases the interest rate. At the lower interest rate the quantity of loanable funds demanded by *all* borrowers increases. A decrease in the market rate of interest increases the quantity of the funds per year that business firms demand for investment.

The Market Rate of Interest and the Price of Existing Capital Assets

The market rate of interest is also an important determinant of the price of ownership claims to capital assets. Changes in the market rate of interest change the prices at which ownership claims to machines, buildings, inventories, and other capital assets are traded. Be careful not to confuse the prices of ownership claims to capital with the prices of the services of capital. The services of capital inputs are flows that are priced by the hour, month, or year. The prices of ownership claims to capital assets are the prices of stocks. The price of a capital asset is related to the flow of services from that input and to the price of those services. The price of a capital asset traded in a perfectly competitive market is determined by its present and future earning potential, its useful life, and the market rate of interest.

Present value The current value of the stream of returns that can be produced from the services of a capital asset over time; the sum of money that will produce a certain stream of returns over a period when invested at a certain interest rate.

The price of a capital asset is related to the **present value** of the net revenue stream that can be produced from its services over time. That value represents the amount of loanable funds that would have to be loaned out at the current interest rate to produce the same net revenue stream over time.

Suppose a capital asset, such as 50 gallons of stored wine, is expected to sell for \$990 after one year in storage. The market rate of interest is currently 10 percent. The maximum amount an investor would pay to buy the wine is the sum of money that would grow to \$990 at the end of the year. Call this amount PV:

$$\text{PV}(1 + 0.10) = \$990 \quad \textbf{(14–22)}$$

Solving for PV gives

$$\text{PV} = \frac{\$990}{(1.10)} = \$900 \quad \textbf{(14–23)}$$

An investor who paid more than \$900 for the wine would make less than could be earned by simply lending that amount to someone else at 10 percent.

In general, the present value of \$*R* received after one year is

$$\text{PV} = \frac{R}{(1 + i)} \quad \textbf{(14–24)}$$

where *i* is the market rate of interest.

Given its return (*R*) through time, the present value of an asset declines when the market rate of interest increases. Suppose the market rate of interest increases from 10 percent to 20 percent. In that case the present value of \$990 received one year from now is

$$\text{PV} = \frac{\$990}{1.20} = \$825$$

Similarly, the present value of \$*R* received in two years can be calculated from the following formula:

$$\text{PV} = \frac{R}{(1 + i)^2} \quad \textbf{(14–25)}$$

MODERN MICROECONOMICS IN ACTION: THE BUSINESS WORLD

The Discounted Present Value of Corporate Earnings and the Volatility of Stock Prices

The willingness of investors to pay for either newly issued or existing stock in a corporation ultimately depends on their assessment of the corporation's profitability. The price of a stock represents buyers' assessment of the discounted present value of a corporation's future earnings divided by the number of its outstanding shares of stock. Variations in stock prices therefore reflect changing assessments of the corporation's current and future ability to earn profits. Changes in expectations about movements in interest rates also influence stock prices because the market rate of interest affects the discounted present value of the corporation's future stream of earnings.

One factor that investors consider in deciding whether to purchase existing or new corporate stock is the corporation's *price-earnings ratio,* which is simply the current market price of a share divided by total annual earnings per share. For example, suppose the price of a share of a certain corporation is currently $10. If the corporation's earnings per share are $1 per year, then the price-earnings ratio is 10. A price-earnings ratio of 10 corresponds roughly to an annual *current* rate of return of 10 percent in earnings per share. The higher the price-earnings ratio, the lower is the current rate of return per share. A price-earnings ratio of 20 means that earnings are currently only 5 percent of the current price per share.

By purchasing stocks with high price-earnings ratios, investors indicate that they think future profits will exceed current profits. They're willing to accept a low current return in the hope that they'll enjoy a high future return.

The return stockholders earn is in the form of either dividends or capital gains. Dividends are portions of corporate profits paid out to stockholders. A capital gain is an increase in the value of a stock over its original purchase price. If investors believe the profitability of a stock has increased, the demand for the stock will increase, and this will bid up its price. Stockholders can then sell the stock, thus converting its increased price into cash and obtaining a realized capital gain. Many stockholders who earn capital gains on their holdings don't sell their stocks because they believe their holdings will still give them good future returns compared to alternative investments. Unrealized capital gains are capital gains that are not converted into cash by selling assets.

Stock prices are volatile because assessments of the profitability of investing in stocks relative to investing in other assets are revised daily. New information causes changes in the demand for existing stocks that often spur wild gyrations in averages of stock prices and in the prices of particular stocks. Higher interest rates generally cause declines in the average price of stocks traded on stock exchanges. This is because higher interest rates make such debt instruments as bonds and mortgages more attractive alternatives and because the higher interest rate reduces the discounted present value of expected earnings per share. In addition, higher interest rates are likely to affect the future profitability of corporations. This result compounds the decrease in the demand for stocks caused by the higher yields on interest-earning debt that substitutes for stocks in investor portfolios. Similarly, lower interest rates generally cause increases in the average price of stocks traded on stock exchanges. A shrewd investor carefully follows the daily and weekly course of interest rates and makes investment decisions with interest rates in mind.

where i is the market rate of interest. PV in this case is the amount of money that must be loaned at the market rate of interest to end up with R dollars after two years. For example, when the market rate of interest is 10 percent, the present value of $10,000 revenue from an investment to be realized after two years is

$$\frac{\$10{,}000}{(1.10)^2} = \$8{,}264.46$$

Do not confuse the formula for calculating the present value of an asset with the formula for calculating the internal rate of return of an investment. The latter formula solves for r, the return on an investment, given its present cost, C, and the stream of future net returns. The present value formula uses *the market rate of interest* to discount future net revenues and to solve for their present value. In general, the present value of a capital asset that yields net revenue of R_j per year over n years is

$$PV = \Sigma \frac{R_j}{(1 + i)^j} \quad \textbf{(14–26)}$$

where $j = 1, \ldots n$.

In a perfectly competitive capital market, the price of a capital asset must equal its present value. If the market price of the asset is less than the present value of the future returns possible from owning it, persons could profit by purchasing it. This increases the demand for the asset and raises its price until its price equals its present value. For example, if the interest rate were 10 percent and the stored wine sold for less than its present value of $900, investors would compete to purchase the stored wine. This is because by investing in the wine, they could make more than the market rate of interest. At any price below $900, increased demand would increase price until it reached $900. Similarly, at a 10 percent interest rate any price above $900 means that those who hold the wine are earning less than 10 percent. They will therefore sell the wine. As the supply of stored wine offered for sale increases, its price will fall to $900.

In the long run, the price of a capital asset must equal both its present value and its average cost of production, assuming that the capital asset is sold in competitive markets. If the price of capital goods were below average costs, the producers of capital goods could not cover their opportunity costs. The supply of capital goods would decrease, and their price would rise. Similarly, if the price of capital goods were above average costs, new entrants would increase the supply of capital goods and as a result their price would fall. Finally, the price of all capital assets depends on the market rate of interest. The higher the rate of interest, the lower is the price of any capital asset.

Economic rent The difference between the payments made for input services and the minimum amount required to induce the suppliers to make those services available.

Economic Rent

Economic rent is the difference between the payments made for input services and the *minimum* amount required to induce the suppliers to make those services available. The minimum amount required for an input supplier to agree to sell any quantity of input services is the marginal cost of those services. Economic rent is a surplus over the opportunity costs of supplying an input. It is analogous to the producer surplus in output markets. For example, the economic rent a worker earns for an hour of work is the difference between the wage paid for that hour and the marginal value placed on the leisure sacrificed to work that hour. The marginal value the worker places on leisure is the marginal cost of work.

Figure 14–16 illustrates the economic rent earned in a competitive input market. At any price below P^* no one would be willing to supply the input for hire. For example, if the input is labor services, P^* might be $1. At an hourly wage below $1, the quantity of labor supplied would fall to zero. At a wage of $1 per hour, Q^* hours of work would be supplied per month. The supply curve of the input reflects the marginal cost to workers. It therefore represents the minimum price at which workers will supply additional hours.

Suppose the market equilibrium wage is $$P_1$ per hour. The economic rent earned by workers at that wage is represented by the area P_1EP^*. This area represents the difference between the total wage payments, OP_1EQ_1, made to workers and the opportunity cost to workers of supplying Q_1 hours of labor, which is represented by the area OP^*EQ_1. All workers who supply some labor services at a wage below the market wage of $4 per hour earn economic rent. The economic rent of all workers is the shaded area in Figure 14–16.

Economic rents earned by input suppliers can be removed without influencing the incentive to supply those inputs. For example, if it were possible to identify the workers who would work for less than the market wage, a tax on their rents would not change the number of hours they supply. As long as they earn enough to cover their opportunity costs, they are no better off doing anything other than

FIGURE 14–16 Economic Rent

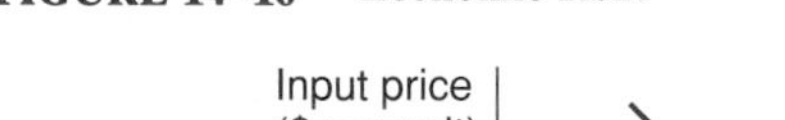

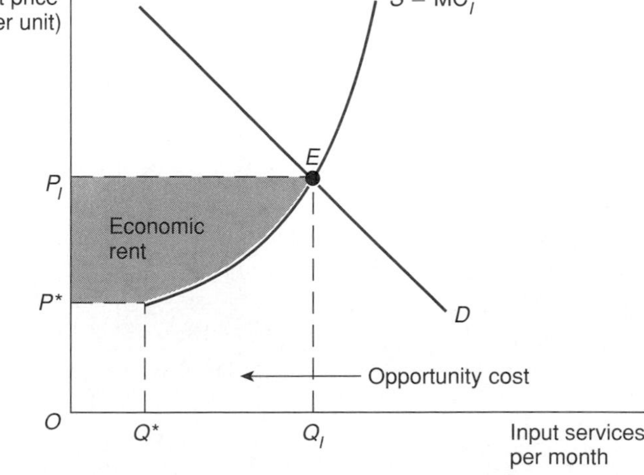

Economic rent earned from the sale of Q_1 units of input service per month is represented by the area P_1EP^*. This area represents the difference between the total payments for use of the input and the opportunity cost of the input's use to its owners.

working. On the other hand, if the wage of workers who earn zero rent is taxed, they will reduce the number of hours worked because the tax reduces their hourly wage below the opportunity cost of working.

The entire payment to an input in fixed supply is economic rent. This is illustrated in Figure 14–17(a). The supply of the input is perfectly inelastic. No matter what the price, the same amount is available for use. The supply of land in a region, for example, is perfectly inelastic. A certain number of usable acres or square miles are available for all uses. No matter what the price or monthly rent of land, no more land can be made available. Even if price drops to zero, the amount available remains the same.

Suppose there are 1,000 acres of land available for all uses at a certain location (for instance, 10 miles from the city center). The market price for the use of land is $100 per acre per month at that location. The price for the use of land per acre per month is determined by the demand for land. In a competitive land market, demand reflects the value of the marginal product of an acre. In Figure 14–17 the equilibrium price is determined by the intersection of the demand curve with the fixed supply of land. Even if the market price were zero, 1,000 acres would still be available. If the market price rises above $100, no more land can be made available at that location—the amount of land is fixed. Because the minimum price to make the land available is zero, its entire return is economic rent. In this case the total rent earned by landlords is $100,000. If the entire rental income of landlords were taxed away, the same amount of land would still be available.

However, if landowners require a certain minimum payment per acre before they will make land services available to tenants, rent will be somewhat less. This is shown in Figure 14–17(b). Suppose landlords refuse to offer the services of their land to others if rent falls below $10 per acre per month. In that case, if there are

FIGURE 14–17 Rent and the Price Elasticity of Supply of Inputs

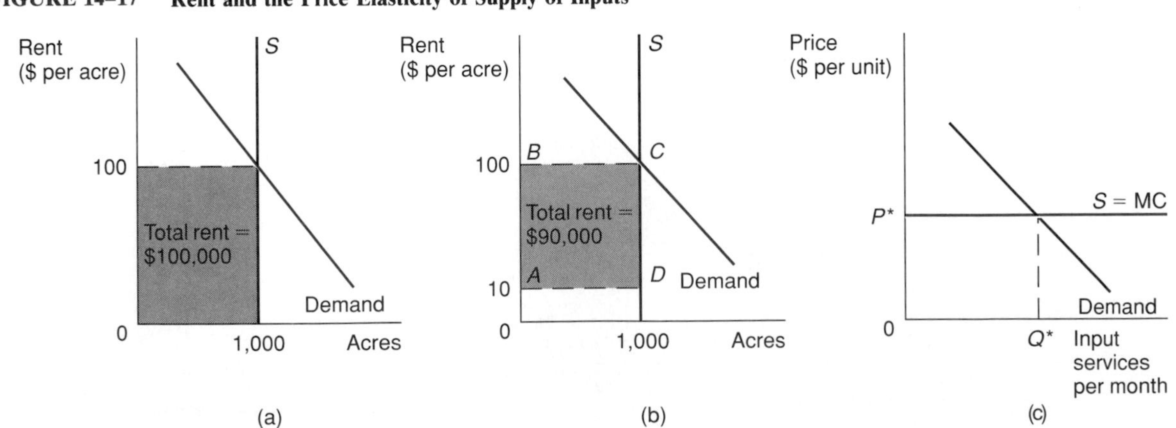

The entire payment to an input in perfectly inelastic supply, as shown in (a), is rent. If input owners require a minimum price before they will allow others to use the input, rent is somewhat less, as shown in (b). Owners of an input in perfectly elastic supply cannot earn rent because the minimum price they will take, P^*, equals the market price.

1,000 acres of land, the total rent will be $90,000 per month when the market price per acre is $100. This is represented by the area *ABCD* in Figure 14–17(b). If more than $90,000 of the rental earnings of landlords were taxed away, they would use the land themselves instead of renting it to others for cash payments.

Suppose, however, the government estimates the market rent of land and taxes it away irrespective of whether the owners or tenants use the land. The result would then be what it was in the previous case. Since landlords cannot avoid the tax or reduce the amount of the land, it is in their interest to rent the land at the market rent per acre. Otherwise, the land will not produce the income required to pay the tax.

In some cases inputs are in fixed supply for short periods. This means that those inputs can earn high rents in the short run. In the long run, supply becomes more elastic and rent earned decreases; the more elastic the supply, the less are the rents earned. Figure 14–17(c) shows the case of an input in perfectly elastic supply in the long run. If the market supply of an input looks like this, the minimum price to make the input available is the same for all suppliers. That minimum price, P^*, is the market equilibrium price. Because there is no difference between the minimum price and the market price, no economic rent is earned.

LAND MARKETS

Land is a unique input because it is immobile. The total supply of usable land at a given location is fixed. The total supply of usable land in a nation is fixed. A perfectly inelastic supply of land implies that land prices are determined by the level of demand for particular parcels. Changes in land prices or rents can be explained only with reference to changes in the level of demand. Land prices refer to the price of ownership of land parcels. Do not confuse land prices with land rents. Land rents are the prices of the services of land; land prices represent the discounted present value of future land rents. Land prices are related to land rents. The higher the rent for the services of a parcel of land, the higher is the price of the land. If R_j is the annual rent expected in year j for a given parcel of land (for example, an acre 2 miles due north from the center of a city) and i is the current market rate of interest, then the price (P_L) of the land parcel is

$$P_L = \Sigma \frac{R_j}{(1 + i)^j} \tag{14–27}$$

The useful life of a parcel of land is indefinite. The sum therefore goes from 1 to infinity. Because the factor $1/(1 + i)^j$ becomes smaller as j increases, the amount added to the sum approaches zero as j approaches infinity. The sum in Equation 14–27 therefore approaches a limit. When R_j is the same in every year, this limit is

$$P_L = \frac{R}{i} \tag{14–28}$$

where R is the annual rent and i is the market rate of interest.

Suppose a person estimates that the annual rent that can be earned on an acre of land is \$1,000. If the market rate of interest is 10 percent, then the maximum price that would be paid for the land is \$1,000/0.1, or \$10,000. In figuring the price of land, only the rent for the land is used in the calculation. The rent for structures built on the land is the return on capital. Although land lasts indefinitely, structures do not. They must be maintained and replaced.

Location, Land Use, and Land Rents

Given the rate of interest, land prices are determined by land rents. Because the supply of land at a given location is fixed, rent depends entirely on the demand for land at that location.

Those who own land must rent to the highest bidder to maximize the revenue from their land. Assume that the costs of maintaining the land are so close to zero that they may be ignored. Maximizing revenue from land is therefore equivalent to maximizing profits. Consider two parcels of land in a region. One parcel is located between Frenchman's Creek and Highway 50, two miles due north of the city. The other parcel is located between Frenchman's Creek and Highway 95, 5 miles due south of the city center. There are 50 usable acres in the first parcel and 40 usable acres in the second parcel. Assume that each parcel goes to a single use.

Figure 14–18 shows how the rent per acre is established at both of these locations. Figure 14–18(a) shows that four different types of users are interested in the land at the first location. The four demand curves show the maximum rent they would pay per acre per month. D_A is the demand for agricultural use.

FIGURE 14–18 **Land Rents**

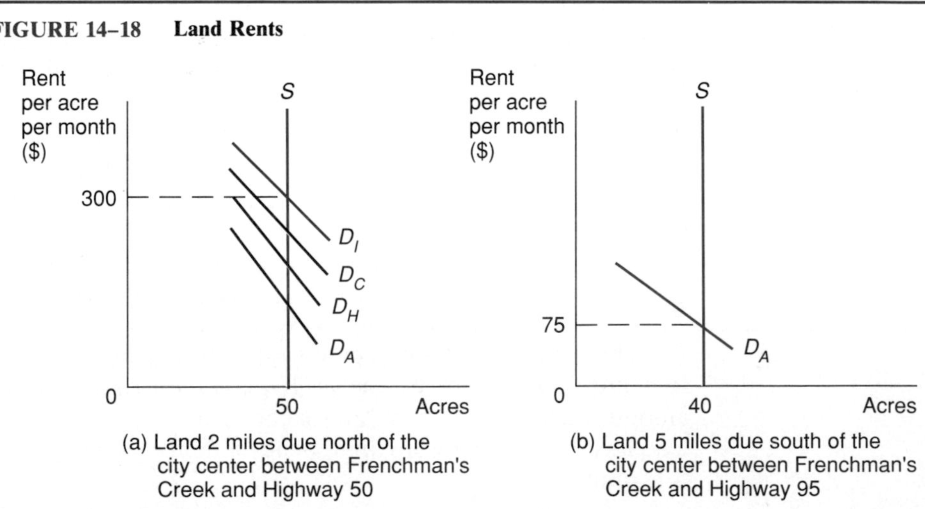

If landlords maximize profits, they rent land to the highest bidder. The supply of land at a given location is perfectly inelastic. In (a), industrial users outbid commercial, housing, and agricultural users and use all 50 acres of the land at the first location. In (b), only agricultural users bid for the land at the second location.

Farmers offer \$100 per acre for the fixed supply of 50 acres. Similarly, D_H is the demand for housing use, D_I is the demand for industrial use, and D_C is the demand for commercial use. Assume that both landlords and tenants are price takers. The highest bid for each of the 50 acres is \$300 per month. That is the amount of rent the industrial users will pay. The land at this location is therefore rented to industrial users at \$300 per acre per month.

What determines the rent that each type of user is willing to pay for the land? Except for agricultural users, no type of user is particularly concerned about land fertility. The main factor influencing the rent that the nonagricultural users are willing to pay for the land is its locational advantage. Locational advantage depends on the proximity of land to centers of work, recreation, and shopping. It also depends on neighborhood amenities such as streets, public facilities (for example, water and sewage service), and the state of repair of surrounding structures.

Rents at locations closer to centers of work and other activities rise to offset the advantages of transportation cost savings at those locations. For example, if you live far out in the suburbs and must commute 30 miles one way to work every day, you will spend a lot on gasoline or transport fares. Other things being equal, you would be willing to pay a higher monthly rent for an identical site and home only 5 miles from the city center. Competition among land users tends to bid rents up at more central sites to remove the advantage of savings in transportation costs.

Figure 14–18(b) shows that only farmers are interested in the land at the second location. The rent for the 40 acres at that location is therefore \$75 per acre per month. This is the rent corresponding to the intersection of agricultural demand and the supply at that location.

Note the implications of immobility. If land were mobile, owners of land at the location 5 miles south of the city would move their land to the location 2 miles north of the city to earn higher rents. The supply of land at various locations would adjust until rents were equal at all locations. Of course, this cannot happen. Land is fixed and cannot be moved. Differentials in land rents are the rule, not the exception, in land markets. Each site at each location has unique characteristics that affect its rent and therefore its price. Only a change in demand at that site can change the rent.

SUMMARY

1. In competitive input markets neither buyers nor sellers of input services can influence the prices of those services. The demand for input services is derived from the demand for output. Other things being equal, the greater the demand for output, the greater is input demand.
2. In a competitive input market a firm can hire all of the input services it chooses at the market price of input services. The input supply curve to a firm is perfectly elastic at the market price.
3. In a perfectly competitive input market a firm maximizes profits by hiring an input until its marginal revenue product equals its price.
4. A firm's input demand curve is its marginal revenue product curve. When a firm sells its output in competitive markets, P = MR and VMP = MRP for all inputs.
5. Market demand for an input is the sum of the amounts of that input's services demanded by

all industries at each price. Market supply of the services of an input depends on the marginal cost of making that input available for employment.

6. The work-leisure choice determined labor supply. The income-leisure budget line shows the opportunities of a worker to convert leisure into income by working for an employer. The equilibrium amount of leisure corresponds to the point at which $w = \text{MRS}_{LI}$.
7. A change in wages results in income and substitution effects. The income effect of a wage increase decreases the incentive to work. The substitution effect of a wage increase increases the incentive to work. When the substitution effect outweighs the income effect of wage increases only up to a certain level of wages, the result is a backward-bending supply curve of labor.
8. Capital includes all of the durable assets and human skills created to produce goods and services.
9. The market rate of interest depends on the demand for and supply of loanable funds. The funds for the creation of new capital are obtained from savers. The opportunity cost of funds used to create capital is the market rate of interest.
10. The prices of capital assets also depend on the market rate of interest. The price of a capital asset is the present value of the stream of returns generated by its services over time.
11. Economic rent is the difference between input payments and the minimum payments that must be made to induce the supply of inputs. Inputs earning economic rent earn more than their opportunity costs. Economic rents can be taxed away without affecting input supply.
12. Land is a unique input because it is immobile. Land prices reflect the discounted present value of future land rents. Land rents are determined by the demand for land at a particular site. The prime determinant of the demand for land is its locational advantage.

Important Concepts

perfectly competitive input market
derived demand
marginal revenue product of an input
value of the marginal product of an input
marginal input cost
input demand curve
change in input demand
industry demand for an input
wage elasticity of demand for labor
market demand for an input
backward-bending labor supply curve
capital
interest
investment
physical depreciation
marginal rate of return on the investment
marginal net return on the investment
useful life of a capital asset
internal rate of return
marginal rate of time preference
present value
economic rent

Questions for Review

1. Explain how a firm's demand for an input depends on the demand for the firm's output. What other factors influence a firm's demand for the services of a particular input in a competitive input market?
2. When will the value of the marginal product of an input equal the input's marginal revenue product for a firm?
3. How is the marginal revenue product of labor influenced by a change in the amount of capital used by a firm?
4. Using indifference curve analysis, explain how an individual's labor supply curve is obtained. Also explain why an increase in the wage rate increases the worker's maximum possible utility.

5. Under what circumstances will labor supply curves be backward bending?
6. Suppose the market rate of interest is 15 percent. What is the equilibrium return on investment for a firm that borrows loanable funds in a perfectly competitive loanable funds market?
7. What is the internal rate of return on an investment? Calculate the internal rate of return on an investment that costs $20,000 and yields $25,000 after one year. Suppose, instead, that an investment yields nothing the first year and $30,000 after two years. What is its internal rate of return?
8. Suppose your marginal rate of time preference is zero. How much interest would be necessary to induce you to save $1,000 for one year while making you just as well off as you were without saving? Suppose that your marginal rate of time preference increases and eventually exceeds 1 as you save more. Draw your indifference curves between present and future consumption.
9. What factors affect the demand for a particular parcel of land? How can real estate speculators use this knowledge to earn profits?
10. How are land prices related to land rents?

PROBLEMS

1. Suppose a new dough-kneading machine triples the marginal product of the workers in a pizza restaurant. Use the data in Table 14–1 to show how this will affect the firm's demand for labor. How many workers will the firm hire after it installs the new machine? What will happen to the firm's demand for labor after the new machine has been installed by all pizza restaurants in town? Show how a fall in the price of pizza to $2.50 per pizza will decrease the firm's demand for labor.
2. Suppose your sole source of income is wages. Draw your indifference curves between income and leisure, and show your equilibrium when the wage you can earn is $5 per hour. Suppose that an inheritance gives you a daily income of $100 without working. Show how the inheritance will affect your choice between work and leisure. Show the impact of the inheritance on your labor supply curve.
3. Use the utility maximization diagram for an individual laborer-consumer to answer the following questions:
   a. What is the hourly wage of the budget line with point A?
   b. How much labor does the individual supply when the wage is $7?
   c. Is this individual's supply of labor curve backward bending? How do you know?
   d. What is the individual's money income at point B?
   e. When the wage increases, does the individual's utility increase or decrease? Will this always be the case?

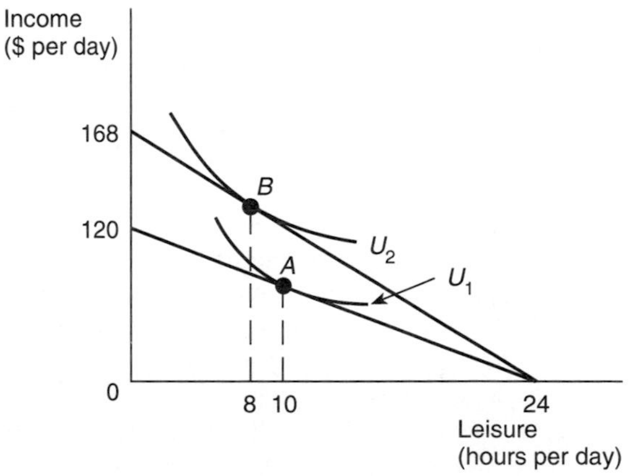

4. Suppose the interest you earn from savings is subject to a 30 percent income tax. Show how this tax will affect the equilibrium quantity of savings. Can you conclude that the quantity of savings will always decline when persons are subject to taxes on interest income?

5. Suppose the government manages to eliminate its budget deficit and to run a budget surplus that it uses to retire part of its debt. Predict the effect of these developments on interest rates and business investment.

6. Many of the modern spreadsheet programs for personal computers have routines for easily calculating internal rates of return on investments. If you have access to such a program, you can solve the following problem quickly. Suppose you are contemplating a special training program that will give you computer programming skills. The program will cost $2,000 and take one year of full-time effort. You will forgo wages of $16,500 during that time. These are your costs. You estimate that the program will increase your real income by $5,000 per year for the next 30 years. Calculate the internal rate of return on the investment. Suppose the current market rate of interest is 15 percent. Is it wise to enter the program?

7. Suppose a parcel of land is for sale at a price of $50,000. You estimate that you could rent the parcel for $4,000 per year and that it would yield this income to you and your descendants forever. Assuming that the current market rate of interest is 10 percent and that you seek to obtain the highest return possible on your $50,000, will you buy the parcel?

8. The indifference curve diagrams depict choices between current and future consumption for Sally and Theodore.
   a. What interest rate corresponds to each budget line in each diagram?
   b. Graph the supply of savings curves for each of these savers in the same diagram.
   c. Would the equilibrium interest rate tend to be higher if most people behaved like Sally or Theodore? (*Hint:* The answer depends in part on the level of the demand for loanable funds.)

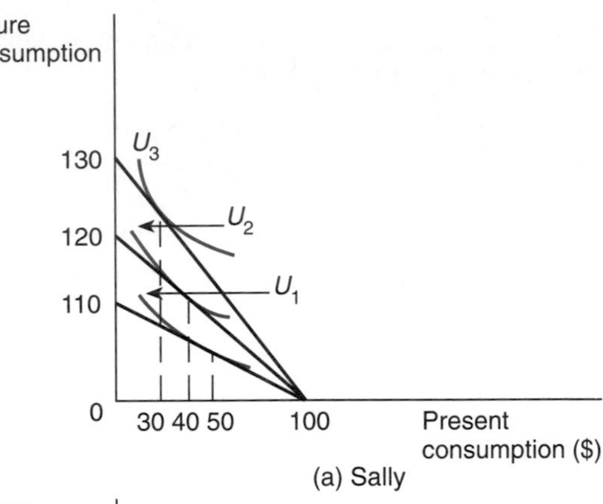

(a) Sally

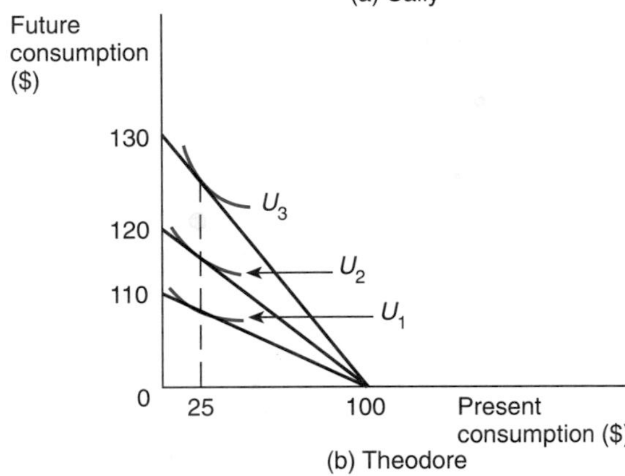

(b) Theodore

9. Suppose the equation of the demand for loanable funds curve of the XYZ Corporation is $i = 0.5 - 0.01(I)$, where i is the market interest rate and I is the amount of loanable funds (investment funding) demanded in millions of dollars. Answer the following questions regarding this case:
   a. For what interest rate will XYZ demand no loanable funds?
   b. What amount of loanable funds will XYZ demand at an interest rate of 10 percent?
   c. How many dollars of investment yield marginal rates of return (excluding interest cost) of at least 40 percent?

15

Imperfectly Competitive Input Markets

In 1992 Addamax, which makes software to enhance the security of Unix, a standard operating system for computers, cried foul. Improvements in the Unix system can be sold only to the Open Software Foundation, which then licenses the system for use by manufacturers. Open Software was founded by IBM and other major computer makers to standardize operating systems for personal computers. Addamax charged that Unix functioned as a buying cartel for its members and had used its market power to offer ridiculously low prices for software inputs into the Unix system. If the charges were true, then the market for software inputs into computer operating systems was not perfectly competitive, because one buyer was able to control the price of the inputs by limiting competition among buyers of input services.

Imperfect competition can also arise in input markets as a result of the market power exercised by sellers. Labor unions often control large blocks of labor used by industries or of labor with a certain skill. The control of labor supply gives labor unions the potential to influence wages.

We will now investigate the consequences of the exercise of control over input prices by buyers and sellers of inputs, with particular emphasis on labor markets. You will also see how employers in professional sports have operated together in the past to keep the wages of professional athletes lower than they would have been if the market were competitive. You will also see how labor unions use various methods to keep their members' wages high but how declining union membership in recent years has reduced their monopoly power.

A Monopolist's Input Demand

Let's begin by analyzing the impact of monopoly power in output markets on input demand. Monopoly power in product markets can affect the demand for input services. Firms with such power tend to produce less output than competitive firms. Because they produce less output, they demand less input services than competitive firms. The marginal revenue from additional output is less than its price for these firms. This implies that the marginal revenue product of inputs falls short of the value of their marginal product.

TABLE 15–1 Value of Marginal Product, Marginal Revenue Product, and Input Cost

Worker-Days (Eight Labor Hours per Day)	*Output*	*Marginal Product (Pizzas per Day)*	*Price, Total Revenue, and Marginal Revenue*			*Value of Marginal Product of Labor and Marginal Revenue Product of Labor*		*Marginal Labor Cost Daily Wage ($/Eight-Hour Day)*	*Change in Profits per Day*
			P	*TR*	*MR*	*VMP*$_L$	*MRP*$_L$		
0	—	0	—	—	—	—	—	$32	—
1	45	45	$4.75	$213.75	$4.75	$213.75	$213.75	32	181.75
2	75	30	4.50	337.50	4.13	135.00	123.90	32	91.90
3	95	20	4.30	408.50	3.55	86.00	71.00	32	39.00
4	102	7	4.15	423.30	2.11	29.05	14.77	32	−17.90
5	105	3	4.05	425.25	.67	12.15	2.00	32	−30.00
6	106	1	4.00	424.00	−1.25	4.00	−1.25	32	−33.75

Suppose there is only one pizzeria in a small town. This firm cannot sell all the pizzas it likes at a given price. Price will decline when more pizzas are produced. Each time another worker is hired to produce more output, the price of pizza declines. If only one worker is hired, daily output is 45 pizzas, and the price charged is $4.75 per pizza. When an additional worker is hired, output of pizzas increases to 75 per day, as shown in the second column of Table 15–1. The increase in output causes the price of a pizza to drop to $4.50. Total revenue will now be $337.50 per day. Marginal revenue can be calculated by dividing the change in revenue by the increase in output each time another worker is hired. This is done in the sixth column of Table 15–1. As a result of monopoly power marginal revenue falls below price after the first batch of pizzas has been produced by the first worker.

The seventh and eighth columns calculate the value of the marginal product of labor and its marginal revenue product as the number of workers hired increases. Because marginal revenue falls below price after the first batch of pizzas, it follows that $\text{VMP}_L > \text{MRP}_L$ beginning with the second worker. The hiring decision is based, not on VMP_L, but on the contribution of extra workers to revenue. Workers are hired up until the point at which

$$\text{MRP}_L = w \qquad \textbf{(15–1)}$$

where w is the market wage. Assume that labor is hired in a competitive input market. All the workers desired can be hired at a wage of $32 for each eight-hour worker-day. In equilibrium the monopolist will employ a bit more than three worker-days each day. The marginal revenue product of labor is $71 when three workers are hired. Hiring part-time workers increases profits until the marginal revenue product of labor is equal to the wage. If four full-time workers are hired, profits will decline because MRP_L is only $14.77 when four workers are hired.

FIGURE 15–1 Monopoly Power and the Hiring Decision

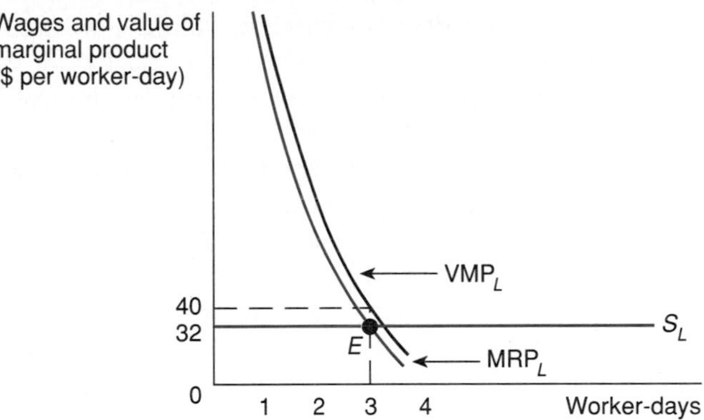

The monopoly firm can obtain all the labor it wishes at $32 per eight-hour worker-day. Equilibrium occurs at the point where the firm hires about three worker-days. VMP_L = $40 and exceeds the $32 wage because $\text{VMP}_L > \text{MRP}_L$.

Because VMP_L exceeds MRP_L, it follows from Equation 15–1 that

$$\text{VMP}_L > w \tag{15–2}$$

Workers are paid less than the value of the marginal product of labor. When pizzas are sold in competitive output markets, per the example in Chapter 14, labor is always paid a wage equal to the value of its marginal product in equilibrium.

The monopoly equilibrium is illustrated in Figure 15–1. A monopoly firm always hires less input at a given wage than a perfectly competitive firm facing the same demand for the same product. Equilibrium is at point *E* for the monopoly. This is the point at which $\text{MRP}_L = w$. At that point the value of the marginal product of labor exceeds the wage. Suppose VMP_L = $40 at that point. This is $8 above the wage. If 3.1 worker-days are employed, the difference between the value of the marginal product of labor and the wage adds 3.1($8) = $24.80 to daily profits for the monopoly. If the firm did not have monopoly power, its demand curve for labor would be VMP_L and it would hire more labor.

Monopsony

Control over the price of input services can exist on the *buyer's* side of the market if a single buyer or organization of buyers buys a significant share of the total available amount of a particular input service. For example, in some cases workers in a labor market do not have the option of offering their services to many competitive employers. At the extreme, workers in a certain region or occupation may be able to sell their services to only one employer. Suppose this employer, realizing the predicament of these workers, offers to pay them a wage *below* the marginal contribution of their labor to the firm's revenues. In a competitive labor market this firm would lose workers to rival employers, which could gain by hiring away workers who might be willing to work at those low wages. However, when a firm is the *only* employer in a market, it *can* pay wages below the marginal revenue product of labor without the fear of losing workers to a rival employer. There is therefore a tendency for wages to be lower than would otherwise be the case when only one employer purchases input services. Because wages are adversely affected by the lack of competition for labor services on the buyer's side of input markets, the lack of such competition is a matter of concern to workers.

Employers' organizations could act in consort to reduce competition for input services so that employers can pay lower wages without the fear of losing low-paid employees to rivals. For example, an organization of profit-maximizing sports teams could band together to keep the salaries of professional athletes low.

Pure monopsony A single firm that employs the entire market supply of an input that has few, if any, alternative employment opportunities.

A **pure monopsony** is a single firm that employs the entire market supply of an input that has few, if any, alternative employment opportunities. A monopsony has the power to influence the price of the input services it purchases. The supply of an input's services to a monopsony is the upward-sloping *market* supply of that input. Because the market supply of the input to the monopsony is upward sloping, the monopsony can influence the price of the input by varying the quantity of the input that it employs over a period.

Pure monopsony is as rare as pure monopoly. It could exist in a small town in which a single firm employs all workers. A mining firm that employs all workers in an isolated frontier town would be an example of such a monopsony. Although a market with only a single employer is relatively rare, it is not uncommon for a firm to employ a very large share of the total available market supply of a certain resource. For example, suppose a university employs 70 percent of the labor force of a small town. If the university increases its demand for labor, it will probably have to pay higher wages to attract workers from other towns or local workers who are currently out of the labor force. Similarly, if an aircraft producer employs 90 percent of the workers in a town, a slowdown in its business would sharply reduce wages in the town as its demand for labor declines. Such firms know that the level of their demand for labor will affect the wages they must pay to hire workers.

Oligopsony An input market structure in which a few firms purchase the entire market supply of certain inputs.

Oligopsony is an input market structure in which a few firms purchase the entire market supply of certain inputs. Professional sports leagues are a good example of oligopsony. Athletes can sell their services to a small number of firms. There are usually 20 to 30 teams in each professional sport in the United States. Most professional sports leagues have some agreed-on mechanism for reducing competition among teams. Oligopsony is similar to oligopoly in that competing firms recognize their mutual interdependence. To avoid the ruinous effects of price wars that would bid up the salaries of athletes, these teams typically seek to limit price competition. The result is an organization similar to a cartel. The firms in a league act together as if they were a single buyer. Draft rules typically limit the negotiation rights of a single player to a single team in a league. Each team has its "quota" of players, and the system prevents one team from acquiring all of the best new players.

In 1985 an arbitrator ruled that 26 major league baseball team owners acted in collusion as an oligopsony to avoid bidding up the salaries of professional players who were free agents. When firms engage in oligopsonistic collusion, the consequent reduction in rivalry serves to put downward pressure on input prices.

Marginal Input Cost for Monopsony

Monopsony power The ability of a single buyer to influence the price of some of the input services that it purchases.

Monopsony power is the ability of a single buyer to influence the price of some of the input services that it purchases. As firms with monopsony power purchase more inputs, the price they have to pay increases. Because such firms buy a significant portion of the total market supply of an input, a firm with monopsony power cannot acquire all the input services it wants at a given price. The supply of input services to a firm with monopsony power is upward sloping.

The data in Table 15–2 illustrate the effect of monopsony power on input cost. The data are for a hypothetical pure monopsony coal-mining firm in an isolated frontier region. The firm is the sole employer of workers. All of the workers are coal miners, and there are no differences in the quality of their labor services. To attract additional workers, the mining firm must increase wages. A wage increase attracts workers from other regions, induces persons not currently working to enter the labor force, and increases the number of labor hours supplied by current employees.

Columns 1 and 2 of Table 15–2 show how wages paid per day increase as additional workers are hired. When the firm employs 100 miners, it pays a daily wage of $40. It cannot, however, obtain additional workers at that wage. Currently, all who wish to work at that wage are employed by the mining firm. If it wants to attract additional labor services, it must pay higher wages.

The marginal input cost (MIC), first defined in Chapter 14, is the additional cost to the firm associated with hiring another unit of an input. In a perfectly competitive input market the marginal input cost for a firm using labor is the wage

TABLE 15–2 Input Supply, Marginal Input Cost, and Hiring by a Monopsony

Worker-Days (Eight Labor Hours per Day)	*Average Input Cost = Wages per Day*	*Labor Costs*	*Marginal Input Costs*	*Marginal Revenue Product*
100	$40	$4,000	—	—
101	41	4,141	$141	$200
102	42	4,284	143	180
103	43	4,429	145	165
104	44	4,576	147	150
105	45	4,725	149	148
106	46	4,876	151	140
107	47	5,029	153	130
108	48	5,184	155	115
109	49	5,341	157	100

because the firm can acquire as much labor service as it desires at the going market wage. However, the marginal input cost for a monopsony increases as it employs more of an input's services.

Table 15–2 shows how the marginal input cost—in this case for labor—increases as more workers are hired. If the mining firm wishes to increase its labor force to 101 workers per day, it must raise daily wages to $41. Keep in mind that all workers are paid the same hourly wage. When the firm hires more workers (each working an eight-hour day), it must pay *all workers* more, not just the last worker it hires. If it did not do so, some workers would quit and the firm would be unable to maintain a daily work force of 101 workers.

Table 15–2 shows how wages increase as the firm's management hires between 100 and 109 workers per day. Total labor costs, w_1L_1, when the firm hires each of 100 workers at a daily wage of $40 are $4,000 per day. Because the firm must increase the daily wage to $41 per day if it increases the work force to 101, total labor costs rise to $4,141 per day when it hires one more worker. The marginal input cost of labor (MIC_L) associated with the services of an extra worker is therefore

$$\$4{,}141 - \$4{,}000 = \$141$$

The marginal input cost when 101 workers are hired is the change in labor costs associated with increasing the size of the labor force to 101. The monopsonist's marginal input cost can be broken down into two separate components. The first component is the daily wage, w_2, paid to the 101st worker. The second component is the increase in the cost of employing the L_1 workers already on the staff. The wage paid to these workers must increase to maintain the labor force at the desired size. The additional cost for the L_1 worker-days already employed is

$$L_1(w_2 - w_1)$$

Marginal input cost for a monopsony The extra cost of another unit of input services that is less than the price of those services.

where w_1 is the initial wage. **Marginal input cost for a monopsony** is therefore

$$\begin{aligned} \text{MIC} &= w_2 + L_1(w_2 - w_1) \quad \textbf{(15–3)} \\ &= \$41 + \$100 \\ &= \$141 \end{aligned}$$

The marginal input cost greatly exceeds the wage paid to workers because each of the first 100 workers must be paid an extra dollar per day when the work force is increased to 101 workers. The marginal input cost is the sum of the wage of the last employee and the additional wages paid to existing employees.

As the calculations in Table 15–2 show, the marginal input cost of labor always exceeds the wage as an employer with monopsony power hires additional workers. For any given quantity of labor the marginal input cost exceeds the price of an input when a firm has monopsony power. **Average input cost** (AIC) is the total cost of hiring an input divided by the number of units used. It is easy to see that average input cost is just another name for the price of an input. For example, the average input cost of labor when L hours are used per day is

Average input cost Total input cost divided by the number of input units.

$$\frac{wL}{L} = w = \text{AIC}$$

MODERN MICROECONOMICS IN ACTION: INTERNATIONAL REPORT

The Government Budget Deficit, Credit Markets, and International Trade

The U.S. government is a big participant in credit markets. In 1991 it borrowed more than $200 billion from credit markets to cover its budget deficit. Because its borrowing is such a large share of the total borrowing each year in credit markets, the U.S. government influences total credit demand enough to bid up interest rates. High real interest rates caused by the budget deficit increase the demand for U.S. dollars by foreigners who seek to acquire those dollars to purchase U.S. government securities and other U.S. financial assets. The increased demand for the dollar caused indirectly by the budget deficit can put upward pressure on the price of the dollar in terms of foreign currencies. As the price of the dollar increases in terms of Japanese yen, German mark, and other foreign currencies, the prices of U.S. exports in foreign markets increase as well. At the same time, a high-priced dollar makes imports cheaper to Americans. The net effect of the higher price of the dollar is adverse to the balance of international trade in the United States because it discourages exports and encourages imports. A decline in net exports is a contractionary influence on the economy that hits certain industries harder than others.

There was concern in the early 1980s that high real interest rates in the United States also contributed to the higher international value of the dollar. At that time foreigners bid up the price of the dollar in terms of foreign currencies to make investments in the United States. As this occurred, the prices of U.S. exports in terms of foreign currencies soared and the balance of trade became negative. Despite a sharp reduction in the international value of the dollar in 1987, the balance of trade deficit remained negative. The federal government budget deficit can therefore indirectly prolong a balance of trade deficit if it keeps interest rates in the United States high relative to interest rates in foreign nations.

Another way the budget deficit adversely affects the balance of international trade is by contributing to an increase in disposable income in the United States. This occurs because the deficit has an expansionary effect on real GNP and because deficit financing allows lower tax rates. As the deficit increases disposable income, it increases import purchases, which tend to vary with disposable income.

To the extent that the budget deficit crowds out private investment, it can also make U.S. industries less competitive in foreign markets. Government borrowing absorbs savings that could otherwise be channeled into new investments in technology and other cost-saving advances in U.S. industries. This makes the unit costs of U.S. producers higher relative to the unit costs of foreign competitors that do make investments to keep up with advances in technology. Ultimately, this indirect effect of the budget deficit is the most harmful to the international competitiveness of U.S. industries. Private investment is the key to advances in productivity which, in turn, allow lower costs of production. When the budget deficit curbs the rate of private investment by keeping real interest rates high, it becomes harder to eliminate the trade deficit. Of course, if the deficit is used to finance government programs and investment (such as government research in new technologies) the positive impact of federal programs on productivity could offset the negative impact of reduced private investment.

In Table 15–2 the daily wage is the average input cost. When input prices increase for the firm as it hires more of an input's services, marginal input cost exceeds average input cost. This implies that AIC increases as more of the input is hired because the MIC is the last number used to compute AIC as hiring increases. For a firm hiring an input's services in a competitive input market, marginal input cost always equals average input cost because input prices are constant.

Figure 15–2 graphs the monopsony firm's MIC and AIC curves. The AIC curve is the labor supply curve S_L because it shows the wage (w) that must be paid to attract any given number of workers. The vertical difference between the two curves reflects the second term in Equation 15–3, that is, the increase in daily labor costs for the firm's existing work force when the work force is expanded by one worker-day. The marginal input cost of any given number of worker-days is obtained graphically by adding the increase in labor cost for the existing work force to the wage that must be paid in order to expand the work force by one worker-day.

Hiring Decisions in Monopsonistic Input Markets

A firm with monopsony power maximizes profits by hiring an input's services up to the point at which the marginal input cost equals the marginal revenue product of the input:

$$\text{MIC} = \text{MRP} \qquad \textbf{(15–4)}$$

FIGURE 15–2 Average Input Cost, Input Supply, and Marginal Input Cost

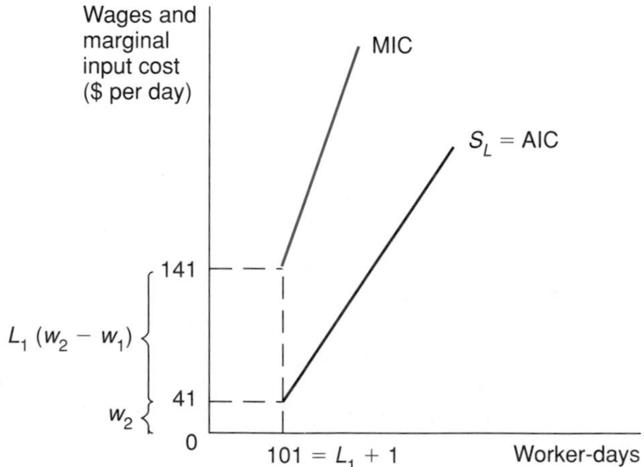

Marginal input cost (MIC) exceeds average input cost (AIC) because the firm must increase wages to hire more labor. AIC is the wage that must be paid to attract any given amount of labor. It is the labor supply curve.

The marginal revenue product measures the contribution of the extra input services to the firm's revenues. The marginal input cost is the cost of an extra unit of the input. The marginal input cost, as has been shown, exceeds the price of the input.

As long as the marginal revenue product of labor exceeds the marginal labor cost for the coal-mining firm, the firm can increase profits by hiring more workers. In Table 15–2 marginal revenue product exceeds marginal input cost as long as the firm maintains a daily work force that provides no more than 104 worker-days of labor. If the firm were to expand the daily work force to 105 worker-days, the marginal revenue product would fall to \$148, which is less than the \$149 marginal input cost associated with that work force. Maximum profits are realized when the firm hires enough workers to provide 104 worker-days of labor each day.

The profit maximizing hiring decision of the firm with monopsony power is illustrated graphically in Figure 15–3. Because the firm maximizes profits by equating MRP_L and MIC_L, it hires 104 workers per day. To obtain that many workers, it must pay wages equal to \$44 per day.

Assume that the firm sells its coal in a perfectly competitive market. There is no reason to expect that a firm possessing monopsony power in one or more of its

FIGURE 15–3 A Monopsonist's Hiring Decision

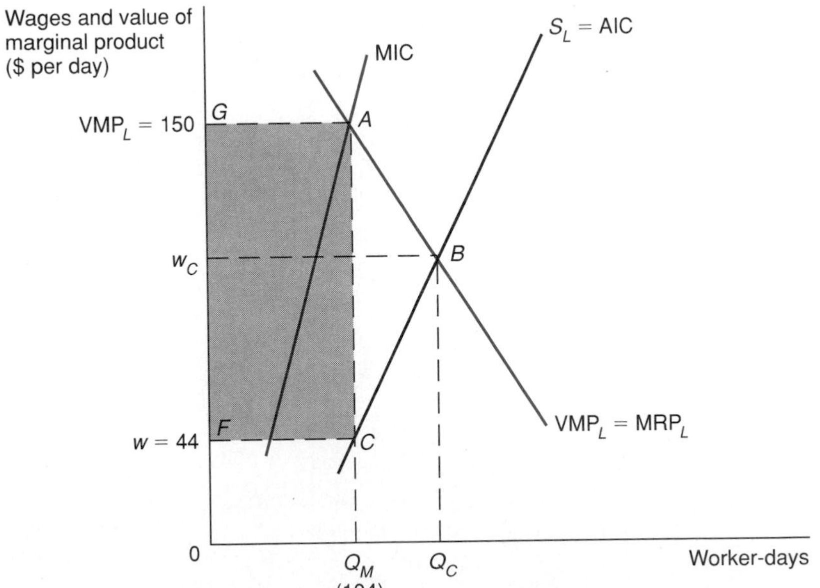

The monopsony firm hires labor services up to the point at which MRP_L = MIC. Equilibrium is at point *A*, where the firm hires 104 workers per day based on an eight-hour worker-day. Because $VMP_L > w$ at that point, the firm adds an amount equal to the area *GACF* to its profits. In the absence of monopsony power, Q_C workers would be hired daily.

MODERN MICROECONOMICS IN ACTION: GOVERNMENT AND THE ECONOMY

Taking Action against Monopsonistic Collusion in Major League Baseball

Roger Clemens and Dwight Gooden are both paid in the range of $5 million per year to play baseball. Clemens became the first major league baseball player to earn more than $5 million per year after he signed a $21.5 million contract with the Boston Red Sox. Baseball players have come a long way since 1982, when Reggie Jackson was paid a mere $975,000 salary for swinging a bat for the California Angels. The Angels posted pretty impressive results that year, and Jackson's marginal revenue product as a player was estimated to be $1.5 million in 1982. This amount was based on an estimate of how much of the revenues earned by the team was attributable to Jackson's drawing power as a player.

To estimate the marginal revenue product of a particular player, economists estimate the contribution of that player to games won and then estimate the extra revenue obtained from extra games won. Using this technique, one economist estimated that Jackson's marginal revenue product in 1982 was considerably above his salary that year.* In other words, Jackson was well worth a salary of close to $1 million in 1982 because he contributed much more than that to team revenues.

A wage below the marginal revenue product of labor suggests that the employer has monopsony power. In fact, as the text points out, major league baseball teams did have monopsony power before players were allowed to act as free agents. An analysis of career marginal revenue products and salaries by George Scully indicated that players earned salaries that were only about 15 percent of their marginal revenue products in 1977.† The graphs show how this implies a monopsony situation.

The elimination of reserve clauses allowed free agents salary increases. One estimate indicated that in the 1982 season hitters had salaries equaling 75 percent of their marginal revenue product.‡ The graphs show that the decline in the gap between marginal revenue product and wages means that the gap between wages and marginal input cost is also smaller. When monopsony power is reduced, marginal input cost for employers rises less rapidly and diverges less from the wage.

In 1987 there was further evidence suggesting that major league baseball team owners were colluding to prevent the wages of free agents from increasing. That year eight free agents seeking new contracts received *no offers* from any team but the

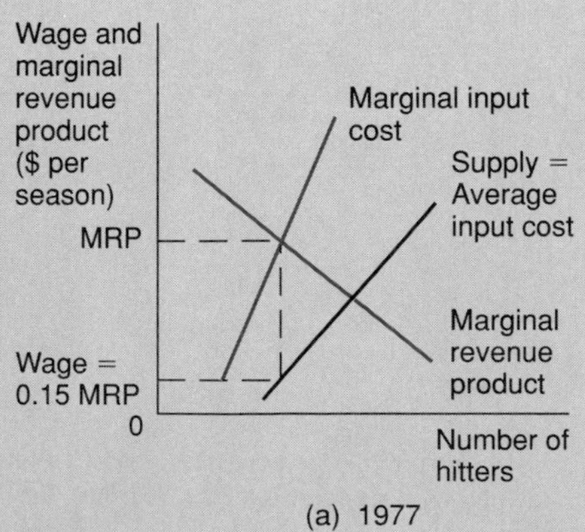

(a) 1977

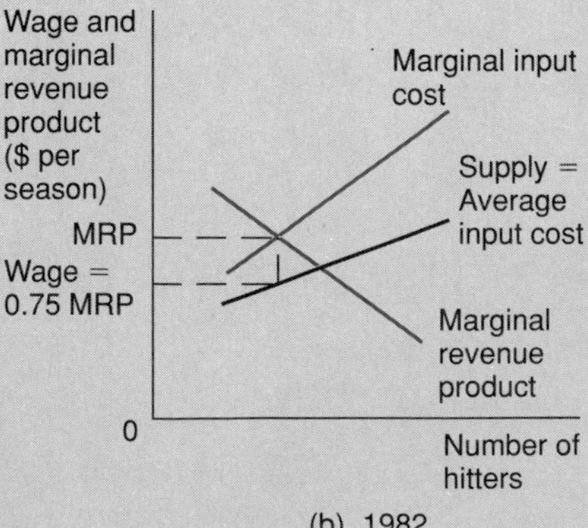

(b) 1982

(*Continued*) one for which they were currently playing. The "untouchable eight," as they were called, were Rich Gedman, Ron Guidry, Tim Raines, Doyle Alexander, Bob Horner, Andre Dawson, Lance Parrish, and Bob Boone, all of whom had just become free agents. Most of these players re-signed with their original teams that year at salaries well below the ones they were seeking. The 26 team owners claimed they weren't in collusion but that the high price of players had caused their profits to decline (as might be expected in a more competitive input market), so they chose not to bid in order to prevent further declines. A federal arbitrator disagreed with this defense.

On September 22, 1987, the arbitrator ruled that the team owners had colluded to prevent bidding for free agents. The arbitrator saw evidence of collusion in the absence of competitive offers in 1985, when only a handful of the 62 free agents in the market were signed in competitive bidding. To the players' delight, the arbitrator ruled that the team owners had entered into a scheme designed to destroy the free-agency system!

The record salaries paid to Clemens and Gooden seem to indicate that the reduced ability of team owners to exercise monopsonistic power has further increased the salaries of baseball players. Apparently, the owners of the Boston Red Sox believe that Clemens can generate more than \$21.5 million in revenue for the team through higher attendance and improved TV and radio deals!

* See Timothy Tregarthen, "Are Professional Athletes Worth the Price?" *The Margin,* November 1985, pp. 6–8. The estimates of Reggie Jackson's marginal revenue product are based on this article's quotations from the work of Howard University economist John Leonard.

† Gerald W. Scully, "Pay and Performance in Professional Sports." *American Economic Review* 64 (December 1974), pp. 915–30.

‡ See Tregarthen, *The Margin,* November 1985, pp. 6–8.

input markets will also have monopoly power. A firm that buys in an imperfectly competitive market may have to sell in a competitive output market. Because perfect competition exists in the output market, $\text{MRP}_L = \text{VMP}_L$.

In equilibrium the marginal revenue product of labor exceeds the wage paid. This follows from the fact that the marginal input cost exceeds the wage:

$$\begin{aligned} \text{VMP}_L &= \text{MRP}_L \\ &= \text{MIC} > w \end{aligned} \tag{15–5}$$

If the monopsonistic firm sells in a perfectly competitive output market, it follows that the firm also pays workers less than the value of the marginal product of labor. The difference between the VMP_L and the wage adds to the firm's profits. The shaded area in Figure 15–3 shows this addition. It is equal to

$$(\text{VMP}_L - w)Q_M \tag{15–6}$$

where Q_M is the amount of labor hired by the monopsony firm. If the market wage in equilibrium is \$44 per eight-hour worker-day and if 104 eight-hour worker-days are hired at that wage, the addition to profits is \$11,024 per day (represented by the area *GACF*) because VMP_L equals \$150 when 104 worker-days are employed. The mining firm is that much richer and the workers are that much poorer than would be the case if the workers were paid the value of the marginal product at point *A*.

Less labor is hired and lower wages are paid under monopsony than under benchmark competitive input market equilibrium. In a competitive input market, equilibrium occurs when the marginal revenue product of the input equals the price of the input. If many mining companies were competing for the services of miners in the region, equilibrium would occur at a point such as *B* in Figure 15–3. Market wages would be w_C, and Q_C worker-days would be employed. Each firm would be able to hire as many miners as it chooses at w_C. Wages for miners would be higher than monopsony wages, and *more* miners would be hired. Finally, assuming competitive output markets, each miner would be paid a wage equal to the value of the marginal product of labor. Firms could not make profits by paying miners wages below the value of their marginal product.

Monopsony Power Paired with Monopoly Power in Output Markets

When a firm has *both* monopsony power in its labor markets and monopoly power in its output market, workers are all the worse off. This case is illustrated in Figure 15–4.

The monopsony is in equilibrium at point *E*, where $\text{MRP}_L = \text{MIC}_L$. To obtain the Q_L workers per day corresponding to that point, the firm pays wages of $\$w^*$ per day. At that wage the firm adds an amount equal to the area *VRST* to its profits. This area can be broken into two components. The area *GEST* is the increments in profits resulting from the fact that $\text{MRP}_L^* > w^*$ at point *E*. The area

FIGURE 15–4 A Firm That Is Both a Monopsonist and a Monopolist

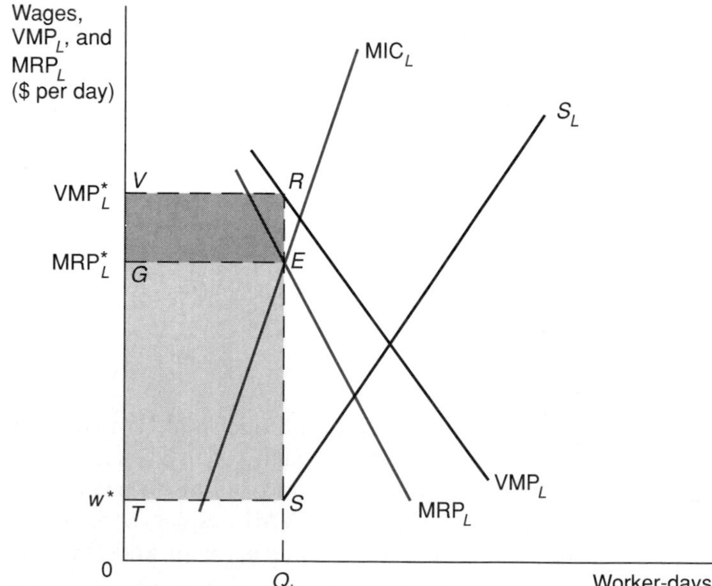

A firm with both monopsony and monopoly power hires less labor and pays lower wages than a firm with only monopsony power. Equilibrium is at point *E*, where $\text{MRP}_L = \text{MIC}$. The area *VRST* shows the additional profits of the firm with both monopsony and monopoly power.

GERV is the increment in profits resulting from the fact that $VMP_L^* > MRP_L^*$ at point *E*. The entire shaded area, *VRST*, is the addition to the firm's profit resulting from its monopsony and monopoly power.

CONCEPT REVIEW

1. How will the monopolization of an industry of constant costs affect the demand for labor in that industry?
2. Draw an input supply curve for a monopsonist, and explain why the marginal input cost of any given level of employment of the input exceeds the price necessary to attract that level of employment.
3. Prove that a monopsonist in a labor market that sells its product in a perfectly competitive output market will pay its workers a wage below the value of the marginal product of labor.

MONOPOLY POWER OF INPUT SELLERS

Suppose that a particular input were available from only a single seller. This seller would sell the entire market supply of an input whose services had few if any close substitutes. For example, if chromium were available from only one firm, then that firm would have a monopoly for that input. The analysis of monopoly power in Chapters 11 through 13 is applicable to monopoly supply of intermediate goods used as inputs. Monopoly firms charge prices that exceed marginal costs. This causes a loss in efficiency.

Except for persons with special skills or talents not possessed by anyone else, monopoly of a particular labor service is rare. However, groups of workers often form organizations designed to control the supply of labor to a market that would otherwise be competitive. We can now examine how labor unions seek to influence wages paid to union members.

Labor unions Organizations formed to represent the interests of workers in bargaining for contracts concerning wages, fringe benefits, and working conditions.

Collective bargaining Bargaining in which one negotiator acts as an agent for many independent negotiators.

Labor Unions

Labor unions are organizations formed to represent the interests of workers in bargaining for contracts concerning wages, fringe benefits, and working conditions. A labor union acts as the exclusive **collective bargaining** agent for its members. Collective bargaining substitutes one negotiator for many independent negotiators. Many industrial relations specialists argue that collective bargaining between labor and management can contribute to higher labor productivity by providing management with information on the work process and on factors influencing worker morale that would otherwise be unavailable.[1] This information

[1] See Steven G. Allen, "Unionized Construction Workers Are More Productive," *Quarterly Journal of Economics*, May 1984, pp. 251–73.

could contribute to improved managerial efficiency. Collective bargaining is viewed as more effective than individual bargaining in achieving improved pay and working conditions. Individual workers fear employer retaliation and job loss and are therefore often unwilling to individually pursue actions that would benefit all workers.

Labor unions can, however, also be viewed as organizations with potential monopoly power in the sale of labor services. A union is like a cartel of many independent sellers of a particular type of labor service. For example, a successful plumbers' union controls the entire market supply of plumbing services in a region. It has the power to influence the price of plumbing services. A successful automobile workers' union controls the supply of all workers providing services to firms producing automobiles. It has the power to control the wages of its members. Whether labor unions actually have or use monopoly power is a subject for empirical investigation. Many experts argue that the monopoly power of labor unions is minimal.[2] If unions raised wages above competitive levels for particular firms in a competitive industry, those firms would fail. Unions can succeed only by unionizing workers in an entire competitive industry or by unionizing workers in firms with monopoly power in their output markets. Under these circumstances union-negotiated wage increases in excess of productivity gains do not necessarily place firms at a competitive cost disadvantage.

A labor union faces many of the same problems that a cartel faces in establishing monopoly power. The first step for ensuring a labor union's success is to establish a barrier to entry. Like cartels, labor unions must block entry into any job or occupation for which they succeed in raising wages above the competitive level. And like cartels, labor unions suffer from potential instability. To maintain their power and the wages they set, they must prevent workers from independently negotiating with employers.

Labor unions are complex organizations. It is difficult to establish their actual goals. The analogy between labor unions and cartels is, of course, a simplification. Labor unions, unlike business firms, cannot be regarded as maximizing profits. The workers themselves are the beneficiaries of any wage increases above the competitive level that a union secures. Unions clearly seek to increase the well-being of their members. They could accomplish this by keeping their members employed or stabilizing employment. They could also pursue a variety of strategies designed to increase the labor income of their members, including strategies that seek to increase the demand for products produced with union labor. In the analysis that follows, it is presumed that labor unions seek to increase the wages earned by their members.[3] The analysis also considers the possibility that union activity affects labor productivity.

---

[2] See Richard B. Freeman and James L. Medoff, *What Do Unions Do?* (New York: Basic Books, 1984), chap. 3.

[3] For a more complete analysis of unions' objectives, see Freeman and Medoff, *What Do Unions Do?*

Union Control over Labor Supply

Unions can use their power of control over labor supply to establish wages above the competitive equilibrium wage. Assume that a union sells labor services to many independent firms, none of which has monopsony power. In the absence of union control of labor supply each firm hires as much labor as it chooses at the equilibrium wage.

Assume that the union establishes a wage for the labor services of its members above the competitive equilibrium wage. This is illustrated in Figure 15–5(a). The union wage is w_U, and the competitive equilibrium wage is w_C. The competitive wage corresponds to the intersection of the demand and supply curves of labor. Unless the union bars entry into the occupation, a surplus of labor hours will be offered each day at that wage. The daily surplus is the distance L_UL_S. For example, the union might be one of plumbers in a large city. The competitive wage might be \$10 per hour. The union's power could push that wage up to \$20 per hour. At the union wage the quantity of labor services demanded (L_U) falls to 10,000 hours per day. The quantity supplied (L_S) increases to 14,000 hours per day as plumbers from other areas search for work at the higher wage. In a competitive market the equilibrium quantity supplied would be 12,000 hours per day.

One way unions prevent the wage from falling to its equilibrium level is to negotiate a wage agreement with employers. The union agrees to supply all of the labor services employers desire up to 14,000 hours per day at the union wage. The labor supply curve now becomes w_UAS. Of course, employers hire fewer

FIGURE 15–5 Union Impact on Labor Supply and Wages

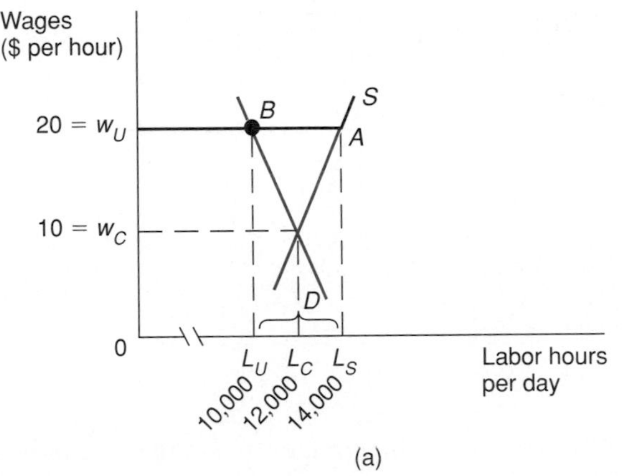

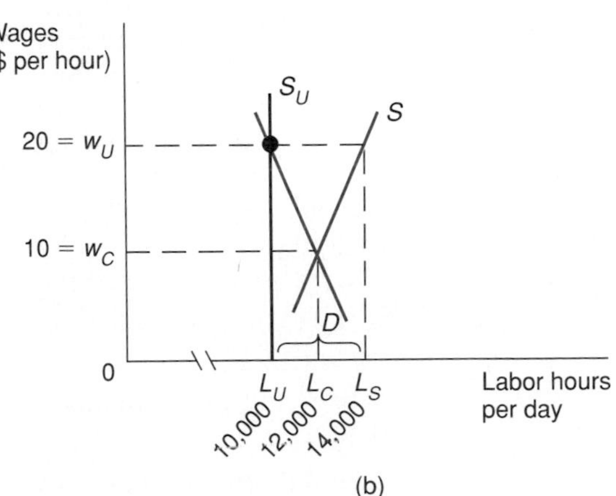

In (a) the union successfully negotiates a wage $w_U > w_C$, where w_C is the market equilibrium wage. Employers are free to hire as many workers as they wish at w_U. Adjusting employment until $w_U = \text{VMP}_L$, employers hire L_U labor hours. Because L_S hours are supplied at the union wage, there is a surplus of labor. Graph (b) illustrates a closed shop. Only union members can work, and the total supply of their labor hours is fixed at L_U. This fixed supply results in wage w_C. Because $w_U > w_C$, there is a surplus of labor and a waiting list for union membership.

MODERN MICROECONOMICS IN ACTION: THE BUSINESS WORLD

Unions in Decline

The once mighty union movement in the United States is losing strength. Between 1970 and 1989 the unionized proportion of the U.S. labor force declined from 25.4 percent to 13.5 percent. During that period unions experienced increasing difficulty in organizing workers. Import competition, high unemployment rates, deregulation in transportation industries, increased resistance to unions by employers, and other factors have all been detrimental to union strength. Whereas unions once demanded and won hefty wage increases and benefit packages, in the 1980s industrial relations between unions and manufacturing firms largely concerned wage cuts!

Particularly hard hit by the forces of change has been the steel industry. Membership in the United Steelworkers of America declined from 1.4 million dues-paying workers in 1970 to 572,000 in 1985. The demand for steel products has plummeted since the 1970s. Currently, about one quarter of the steel used in the United States is imported. New products, such as an array of high-tech plastics, substitute for steel in a variety of uses. The steelworkers spend much of their time these days negotiating contracts to maintain jobs, to minimize reductions in wages, and to prevent changes in work rules that favor employers. This is a far cry from the union's heyday, when it could threaten to strike and grind virtually all U.S. heavy manufacturing to a halt if its demands weren't met.

Although in 1985 steelworkers' wages of more than $22 per hour were still high, they had declined. Agreements worked out with LTV Steel, National Steel, and Bethlehem Steel in 1986 resulted in wage and fringe benefit reductions ranging from 99 cents to $3.15 per hour, coupled with the possibility of offsetting gains to workers in the form of profit sharing or stock ownership benefits.* In 1986 USX, formerly known as U.S. Steel, sought union concessions that would reduce worker compensation by a whopping $7 per hour, thus inducing the union to call a strike.

Despite the concessions made by unions in certain industries, up through 1984 the union wage differential in the United States had not declined substantially. Richard Edwards and Paul Swaim analyzed data on union and nonunion wages from 1979 to 1984 and observed that the wage premium enjoyed by union workers over their nonunion counterparts had not narrowed since 1979. They concluded that nongovernment unions had been content to maintain wages at the expense of losing members as nonunion labor was substituted for union counterparts.† However, Edwards and Swaim conceded that the gap in wages might be chiseled away soon if union wage concessions continued.

* See A. H. Raskin, "The Steelworkers: Limping at 50," *The New York Times*, June 15, 1986, p. F29.

† Richard Edwards and Paul Swaim, "Union-Nonunion Differentials and the Decline of Private Sector Unionism," *American Economic Review* 76, no. 2 (May 1986), pp. 97–102.

Closed shop An arrangement requiring that an employer use only union labor.

plumbers at $20 per hour than at $10 per hour, the competitive wage. Employers choose to hire 10,000 hours of plumbing service per day because that is the amount for which $w_U = \text{MRP}_L$. What happens to the surplus workers? These workers might join the union, but they will not be guaranteed work.

Another way the union can achieve its goal of higher wages is to limit the number of union members and then to negotiate a contract requiring that employers use union labor only, an arrangement called a **closed shop.** The impact of a closed shop is illustrated in Figure 15–5(b). The union neither sets nor negotiates a wage. Instead, it strictly controls union membership. This results in a perfectly inelastic supply of labor at L_U = 10,000 hours per day. The union supply curve is S_U. Given the demand for labor, this results in an equilibrium wage of w_U = \$20 an hour. At that wage there is again a surplus of labor because $w_U > w_C$. This usually means that there will be a list of plumbers waiting to join the union. Union membership acts as the control that prevents entry. The result is the same as the result of setting wages equal to \$20 per hour, as in Figure 15–5(a).

Waiting lists can be long. For example, in the mid-1970s public employee unions in New York City used their power to raise the wages of city sanitation workers. The union wages were 60 percent higher than those received for equivalent work in competing jobs elsewhere. As a result there was a waiting list of nearly 37,000 workers, although total city sanitation jobs numbered less than one third of this amount.[4]

The Impact of Unions on Wages

Empirical studies have supported the hypothesis that union workers in the United States, on average, enjoy higher wages than their nonunion counterparts of equal skill. Estimates of the positive average differential for union workers fall in the range of 10–20 percent.[5] However, these estimates neglect the fact that unions may actually depress the wages of nonunion workers. If unions are successful in increasing wages above the competitive equilibrium level, they create a surplus of workers, as was shown above. These workers seek employment in alternative nonunion jobs while hoping to obtain union jobs someday. The increase in the supply of labor hours to nonunion jobs, other things being equal, decreases wages in these jobs. Some nonunion workers, on the other hand, could benefit from union efforts to organize labor. The threat of unionization could cause many employers to pay higher wages and provide better working conditions to their nonunion employees than they would otherwise.

In the United States unions have been strongest in manufacturing, construction, mining, and transportation industries. They have been weakest in service, wholesaling, retailing, and financial industries, where they account for small percentages of the labor force. The percentage of workers belonging to unions in the southern states is also lower than the average percentage for the rest of the United States. Union power has clearly declined in recent years. In 1970 slightly over 25 percent of the labor force was unionized. However, by 1989 the number of workers belonging to unions had declined to 13.5 percent of the labor force. Union membership in such industries as steel, clothing, textiles, and oil has been declining in recent years because of a general decline in employment in the manufacturing sector of the economy.

---

[4] Ronald G. Ehrenberg and Robert S. Smith, *Modern Labor Economics: Theory and Public Policy,* 3rd ed. (Glenview, Ill.: Scott, Foresman, 1988), p. 48.

[5] C. J. Parsley, "Labor Unions and Wages: A Survey," *Journal of Economic Literature* 18, no. 1 (March 1980), pp. 1–30.

The Impact of Unionization on Labor Productivity

What do employers get in return for the higher wages paid to union workers? Higher wages cause firms to use fewer workers. The marginal revenue product of labor therefore increases as firms reduce the amount of labor input used in production. In the long run, there is a tendency to substitute capital for labor to further adjust to the higher wages. An increase in the capital-labor ratio can contribute to making union workers more productive than their nonunion counterparts.

It also appears that the working environment of union members is more structured that that of nonunion workers. Although some union work rules can decrease worker productivity, other aspects of union control can increase productivity. In firms that have entered into contracts with unions, work is generally at a faster pace and there is less employee control of overtime hours. However, unions often require minimum-size work crews and other restrictions that seek to limit the ability of employers to substitute capital for labor. Evidence also indicates that union work forces are more stable and reliable than nonunion work forces. Unions are effective in reducing worker turnover rates, which reduces training costs for employers.[6] The collective bargaining process can also contribute to increased productivity. Workers often point out improvements in the production process that mutually benefit employers and employees. Many argue that workers are more likely to do this if they possess the job security provided by unions. Whether the social gains associated with unionization of workers exceed the social costs of the monopoly power of unions remains an area of controversy.[7]

BILATERAL MONOPOLY

Bilateral monopoly A market structure in which only one buyer and one seller trade input (or output) services.

Bilateral monopoly is a market structure in which only one buyer and one seller trade input (or output) services. Both the buyer and the seller have the power to control the price of the input services. Figure 15–6 illustrates the case of bilateral monopoly. Here a monopsony is dealing with a monopoly. When a monopsony deals with a monopoly, the result can resemble a confrontation between Godzilla and King Kong! What the outcome will be for the participants is anyone's guess.

In Figure 15–6 the input supply curve is S. This shows the input price necessary to attract any quantity of the input services. Because the firm purchasing the input services is a monopsony, it will want to set a price, w_M, necessary to attract the quantity of input services corresponding to the intersection of the MIC curve with its MRP curve. This intersection occurs at point E_1. At that point the firm will want to hire L_M units of input services. It will therefore offer a price of $\$w_M$ per hour, the price necessary to attract L_M units of input services.

To maximize its profits, the monopoly seller must estimate the demand for input services. It will then seek to set a price that will induce the employer to purchase the quantity corresponding to the point at which the marginal revenue of

[6] See Ehrenberg and Smith, *Modern Labor Economics,* pp. 485–90.

[7] Freeman and Medoff provide evidence that the gains outweigh the losses. Other economists disagree with their findings.

FIGURE 15–6 Bilateral Monopoly

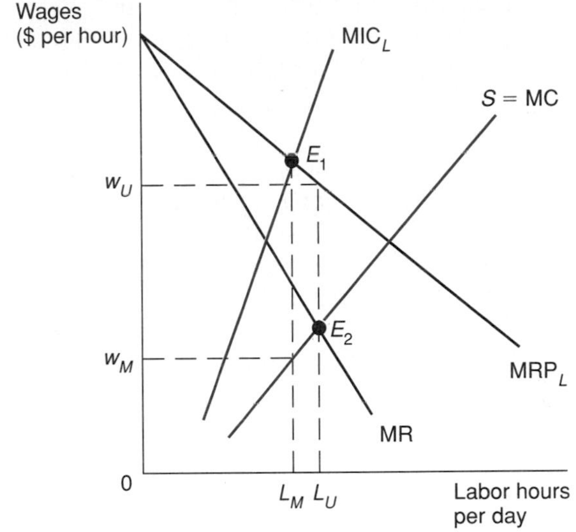

The union's optimal wage is w_U, corresponding to L_U labor hours, where the marginal revenue to the group equals the marginal cost of an hour of work to union members. The optimal wage for the monopsony is w_M, corresponding to L_M labor hours, where MIC = MRP$_L$. Bargaining between the union and the monopsony would determine actual wages, which would exceed w_M but be less than w_U.

input services sold equals the marginal cost. Assuming that the supply curve of the input services measures marginal cost, the profit-maximizing price corresponds to point E_2, where MR = MC. At that point the monopoly will want to sell L_U units of input services. To get the employer to restrict purchases to this amount, the monopoly seller will want to set a price equal to w_U.

There is no equilibrium in the market because $w_U > w_M$ and $L_M < L_U$. No trading can take place until there is agreement on price. The outcome depends on the bargaining strategies of the buyers and sellers. Eventually, the traders will agree on an input price somewhere between w_U and w_M. Each side will employ tactics to fool the other. Either side may try to hide its profit-maximizing price or threaten to cease trading. But neither side has any alternative but to trade with the other because the market has only one buyer and one seller. A game theory approach would be required to predict the final equilibrium.

Pure bilateral monopoly is rare. It is occasionally encountered when a government monopoly (such as a government tobacco or liquor monopoly) purchases goods from a single seller franchised to sell the product. The model can also be applied to the negotiations of labor unions with employers' associations. An employers' association is an organization of employers of workers that bargain as a group to set wages that will be paid by all members of the organization. For example, the Bituminous Coal Owners' Association is a national employers' association that deals principally with two major unions of employees, including the United Mine Workers. Trucking Management, Inc. is a national association of truckers that bargains with the Teamsters union. To maximize employer profits, an employers' association could attempt to set the wage at a level such as w_M, threatening that if the union did not agree to the wage, its members would cease operations and lock workers out. Although the union does not maximize profits in any meaningful sense, it will demand a wage such as w_U, which would be considerably higher than w_M, the wage offered by the employers' association. The union would threaten to strike unless its demands were met. If the difference between the wage demanded by the union and the wage offered by the employers' association is great, a long strike or lockout of workers could result. The costs of the strike or lockout to both workers and employers would eventually result in a compromise agreement.

Bilateral monopoly of this type is also quite common in professional sports in which an organization of team owners bargains with a players' union to set wages and working conditions over a contract period. For example, the National Football League Players Association (NFLPA) bargains with the Management Council of the National Football League (NFL), which represents the team owners. When the two groups cannot agree on salary and working conditions, the result is often a strike. Thus NFLPA players "walked off the job" in the fall of 1987 when the two groups could not agree on salary and other issues, particularly issues relating to free agents' rights to bargain for wage increases. The NFLPA, whose members earned an average salary of $230,000 per season, wanted to set a $90,000 minimum salary for players, with salaries escalating to $320,000 for players with 13 years of experience. These salaries correspond to a wage such as w_U in Figure 15–6. The Management Council of the NFL wanted to set a $60,000 minimum salary that would escalate to $180,000 for 13-year players and to $200,000 for 15-year players. These salaries correspond to a wage such as w_M in Figure 15–6. Other issues regarding wages were also in contention. Because a compromise agreement could not be reached at the outset, the players went out on strike in the fall of 1987.

Union Wages, Minimum Wages, and Employment in Monopsonistic Labor Markets: Some Surprising Conclusions

The impact of union-imposed wages or government-imposed minimum wages in monopsonistic labor markets differs from the impact that can be expected in competitive markets. In competitive markets any wage above the equilibrium causes a surplus of labor services. Surprisingly, this need not be the case in monopsonistic labor markets, as illustrated in Figure 15–7. Suppose all firms hiring electricians in a city have formed an employers' association. They act as a monopsony in hiring the services of electricians, who are currently not unionized. The monopsonistic cartel is in equilibrium at point E_1, where $MRP_L = MIC_L$. The curve S_L is the supply of electricians' services. The employers' association hires 10,000 labor hours of electricians' services per day and pays a wage of $8 per hour to attract that amount of labor services.

Suppose electricians now organize into a labor union. The union succeeds in negotiating a wage settlement with the employers' association that increases wage from $8 to $15 per hour. The union agrees to let the employers' association hire all

FIGURE 15–7 Union Wages and Monopsony Hiring

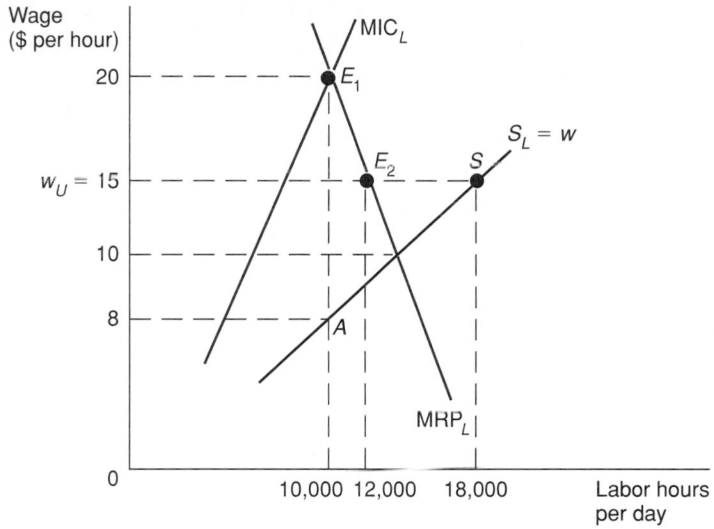

A monopsony would be in equilibrium at point E_1, where $MRP_L = MIC_L$. The wage would be \$8 per hour, and 10,000 labor hours would be hired each day. A union wage settlement results in a new MIC_L for the monopsony that is \$15 per hour up to 18,000 hours per day. In equilibrium, at the union wage the monopsony increases the amount of labor hired to 12,000 hours per day.

the workers it chooses at the union wage. Firms would normally be expected to decrease the amount of labor services hired in response to such a substantial increase in wages. In this monopsonistic market, however, firms will actually hire *more* workers as long as the union wage is less than \$20 per hour.

The wage settlement eliminates most of the monopsonistic control over wages exercised by the employers' association. Firms can now hire all of the labor hours they wish at the union wage of \$15 per hour. If firms want more than 18,000 labor hours per day, they will have to increase wages to attract more workers. The equilibrium is now at point E_2, where MRP_L equals the union wage. The union wage, which the monopsonistic firms cannot influence, is also their marginal input cost up to 18,000 hours per day. As a result of the wage settlement, the electrical contracting firms increase their employment of electricians from 10,000 to 12,000 hours per day! The electricians' union achieves the dual objective of increasing wages *and* increasing employment of electricians.

This holds only if union wages are less than \$20 per hour, the wages corresponding to point E_1, where $MRP_L = MIC_L$. If the union were to raise wages above \$20 per hour, the quantity of labor services demanded by the firms would fall below 10,000 hours per day. This is because points over \$20 on the MRP_L curve correspond to less than 10,000 hours per day. A wage settlement of over \$20 per hour would therefore reduce the daily employment of electricians.

Note also in Figure 15–7 that any wage settlement between \$8 and \$10 per hour would increase employment as the monopsony firms set MRP_L equal to these wages. However, any wage settlement below \$10 per hour, the competitive wage, would result in a shortage of electricians' services, which would increase wages to \$10 per hour.

This model is also applicable to government-imposed minimum wages. It suggests that if unskilled labor is traded in monopsonistic markets, minimum wages can *increase* rather than decrease employment. As long as the government establishes a minimum wage below the level corresponding to the point at which $MRP_L = MIC_L$ for monopsonistic employers, employers will hire more rather than fewer workers after the minimum wage has been imposed.

CONCEPT REVIEW

1. Explain how labor unions can succeed in raising wages above the levels that would prevail in a competitive labor market, and analyze the impact of their policies on employers and nonunion workers.
2. Why is it difficult to predict the effect of bargaining on input prices when bilateral monopoly prevails?
3. Under what circumstances might the imposition of a union wage exceeding the current wage increase employment in a labor market?

INPUT PRICE DIFFERENTIALS

Explaining Differences in Wages among Occupations and Jobs

The differences in wages among occupations and jobs can be explained in terms of the supply and demand for specific skills. For example, suppose only a few managers have the skills and experience necessary to be the chief executive officer (CEO) of a large corporation. The higher marginal revenue product of a CEO, combined with the scarce supply of those qualified for the post, results in very high equilibrium wages for this occupation. The equilibrium wage in Figure 15–8 is \$1 million per year on average for the 300 CEOs employed during a year.

On the other hand, the marginal revenue product of restaurant workers is much lower than that of CEOs. In addition, the supply of workers willing and able to do restaurant work is quite abundant. As shown in Figure 15–8(b), the abundant supply and relatively low marginal revenue product of such workers result in an equilibrium annual wage of only \$10,000.

Differences in skills, training, intelligence, and experience account for differences among workers that result in separate labor markets for various occupations. If you happen to be 5 feet tall, nearsighted, and lack athletic ability, you probably cannot enter the professional basketball labor market. Individual physical differences restrict the number of people who can play professional basketball. Each person has talents and skills not possessed by others. If those talents and skills are scarce and in strong demand, they can be sold at high wages. No one

FIGURE 15–8 Differences in Wages among Occupations

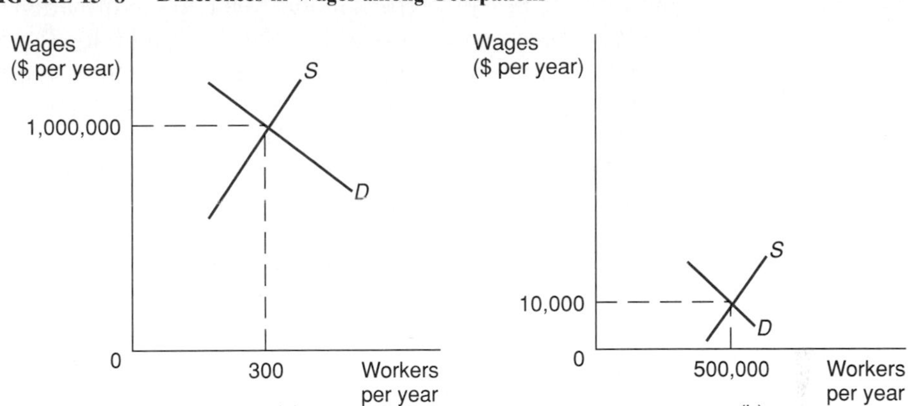

Differences in wages among occupations result from differences in the supply and demand for labor. In (a) the equilibrium wage for chief executive officers of corporations is $1 million per year, but only 300 are employed at that wage. In (b) the equilibrium wage for restaurant workers is $10,000 per year and 500,000 are employed at that wage.

would pay basketball players high wages unless there were persons willing to pay to see basketball games. Similarly, if tall and slender are among the current standards of beauty for women, and if you meet those standards and the other current standards, you may be able to make a fortune as a model. If the standards of beauty change next year, the wages you receive for your modeling services can plummet.

Another factor affecting differences in the quality of labor is the amount of training workers have. Training is costly in both time and money. In deciding to pursue training, persons weigh the opportunity cost of that time and money against the extra returns they expect to receive. Without significant positive wage differentials, many persons would be unwilling to undergo the eight years or more of postgraduate work necessary to enter certain medical specialties. Wage differentials serve to attract persons to certain occupations and to compensate them for their training costs.

This is not to say that those who spend many years studying are guaranteed high wages. Even if you spend eight years studying Slavic literature, you could have trouble finding a job if there is little demand for someone with your expertise.

How Differences in Job Quality Give Rise to Wage Differentials

Differences in the quality of the working environment can also affect wages. Workers consider factors other than money wages in their choice of jobs. Among the nonmonetary factors that affect the willingness of workers to take a particular job are working conditions.

Assume that two jobs require the same level of skill and training. Also assume that workers possess perfect mobility and full information. In a perfectly competitive labor market wages would be the same in both jobs. Suppose, however, that working conditions are not the same in the two jobs. Suppose one job involves a hazard—exposure to disease or radiation—not present in the other. If the same wages are paid in both jobs, workers are likely to prefer the safe job to the hazardous job. If workers, on average, value an unsafe working environment negatively, then equal money wages means that *real* wages are higher in the safe job. To make real wages the same in both jobs, money wages must be higher in the unsafe job. **Nonpecuniary wages** are the nonmonetary aspects of a job that must be added to money wages to obtain real wages.

Nonpecuniary wages The nonmonetary aspects of a job that must be added to money wages to obtain real wages.

Compensating wage differentials Differences in money wages needed to make the real wages of similar jobs equal when nonpecuniary wages are not equal to zero.

Nonpecuniary wages give rise to **compensating wage differentials,** which are differences in money wages needed to make the real wages of similar jobs equal when nonpecuniary wages are not equal to zero. Compensating wage differentials are positive for jobs whose nonpecuniary wages are, on average, negatively valued. This is the case for hazardous jobs. Compensating wage differentials are negative for jobs whose nonpecuniary wages are, on average, positively valued.

For example, workers who work on midsea oil-drilling rigs obtain much higher wages for their work than do workers with similar skills who work inland. The difference in the wages of the two oil-drilling jobs is the compensating wage differential for the isolation and risk of working on a floating rig. Even the military

FIGURE 15–9 Compensating Wage Differentials

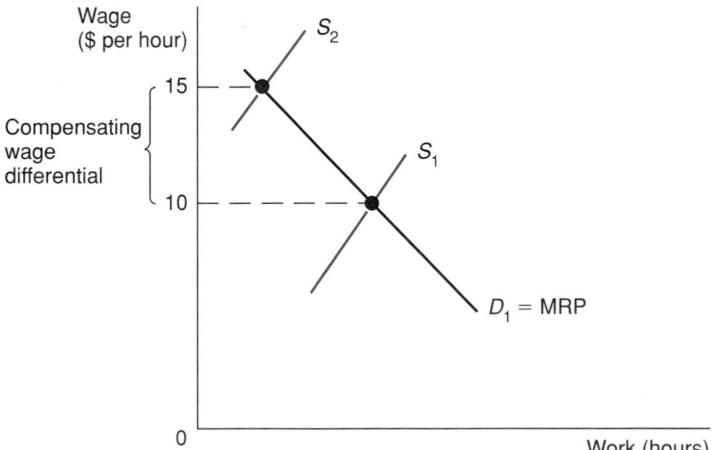

Compensating wage differentials in a given occupation can arise from differences in working conditions. Fewer workers are willing to work on offshore oil-drilling rigs. Given the demand for these workers and the supply, S_2, the equilibrium wage for offshore oil-drilling workers is \$15 per hour. The supply of workers for inland oil-drilling jobs is S_1, and those workers earn a wage of \$10 per hour. The compensating wage differential is \$5 per hour.

offers compensating wage differentials for hazardous duties. For example, those who volunteer for submarine duty in the navy are offered positive pay differentials for the hazards of undersea work.

Similarly, if labor is mobile and fully informed, employers offering work in unsanitary conditions will pay higher wages if alternative jobs exist for which working conditions are better. Here the compensating wage differential provides employers with an incentive to provide decent working conditions.

Figure 15–9 shows how the decrease in available workers for jobs of a given skill gives rise to compensating wage differentials. The supply of and demand for oil-drilling labor are S_1 and D_1 for inland jobs. The equilibrium hourly wage for such jobs is \$10. The supply curve S_2 shows the supply of labor for offshore oil-drilling jobs. The marginal revenue product for any given number of inland or offshore workers is presumed to be the same. However, because fewer workers are willing to work offshore at any given wage, the supply curve S_2 lies leftward of the supply curve S_1. The equilibrium wage for offshore workers is \$15 per hour. The \$5 difference between the wages of inland and offshore workers is the compensating wage differential for the offshore work.

Research by Thaler and Rosen has supported the hypothesis that positive wage differentials are associated with the risk of death on the job. The research indicates that, on average, in 1967 workers received \$176 extra annual wages for each 1 of 1,000 workers who died on a particular kind of job during the year. This implied that lumberjacks earned, on average, about \$450 more per year than workers of comparable skill. The annual death rate of security guards on the job was about 2.7 per 1,000 in 1967. Security guards therefore earned a compensating wage differential of \$470 per year in 1967, which after adjustment for inflation would have amounted to about \$1,400 annually in 1988.[8]

When jobs have positively valued nonpecuniary wages money wages will be lower than those in comparable jobs. If two jobs have given skill and training requirements, the one that offers such benefits as flexible working hours, opportunities for advancement, and safe and pleasant surroundings will pay lower money wages.

Nonpecuniary wages are also associated with jobs at particular locations. They can explain the regional wage differentials associated with such positively valued amenities as climate, recreational opportunities, and city size. Employers in Sunbelt areas can attract labor services at lower money wages. The lower money wages compensate for the positively valued climate of such areas. If money wages were equal in Sunbelt and other areas, workers would migrate to the Sunbelt areas until money wages fell. Studies show that wages for the same work and level of skill are higher in larger cities than in smaller cities. These results hold even after careful adjustment has been made for differences in the cost of living

---

[8] Richard Thaler and Sherwin Rosen, "The Value of Saving a Life: Evidence from the Labor Market," in *Household Production and Consumption,* ed. Nestor E. Terleckyj (New York: National Bureau of Economic Research, 1975), pp. 265–98. Also see Robert S. Smith, "Compensating Wage Differentials and Public Policy: A Review," *Industrial and Labor Relations Review* 32 (April 1979), pp. 339–52.

associated with city size.[9] The cause of the differential associated with city size has not been completely explained. A likely reason is that smaller cities offer a better quality of life. The differential may have arisen because smaller cities have less congestion, less pollution, and less exposure to crime than larger cities.

Compensating differentials are most pronounced when all persons have the same tastes. If some persons enjoy exposing themselves to hazards and other persons dislike what are commonly regarded as amenities, the differentials will be correspondingly lower.

Differences in Interest Rates

Risk and taxes can result in interest rate differentials. For example, banks typically charge their most creditworthy borrowers the lowest interest rate. This is the so-called prime rate. Other borrowers are charged higher rates. Interest rates are higher for customers who banks think have a higher risk of default. Interest rates also differ with the collateral offered to secure the loan. Collateral typically reduces the risk of default. The risk of loans is also affected by their duration. Long-term loans are generally regarded as riskier to lenders than short-term loans.

The interest rate a lender is willing to accept for a loan also depends on the tax treatment of interest on the loan. Lenders make their decisions on the basis of the net interest they receive after payment of taxes. For example, if all interest were subject to a tax of 20 percent, lenders would realize only 80 percent of gross interest earned. Suppose, however, interest earned on loans to municipal governments is tax-free. In equilibrium the gross interest charged on such loans would then be lower than the gross interest charged on other loans. Otherwise, there would be an increase in the funds available for such investments (and a decrease in the funds available for other investments) until the after-tax interest that could be earned on all loans became equal.

Discrimination in Labor Markets

Discrimination in labor markets Hiring practices that result in differing wages to equally productive workers.

Discrimination in labor markets exists when employers engage in hiring practices that result in differing wages to equally productive workers. When discrimination prevails, wages of certain groups of workers are lower than those of other equally skilled workers doing the same job. Employers are often accused of discriminating according to race, sex, age, physical handicap, religious preference, or ethnic background.

Discrimination in hiring impairs the operation of labor markets. It is an imperfection resulting in equilibrium wage differentials among demographic groups that would otherwise not be present. The differentials do not result from differences in the marginal revenue product of labor among workers. Neither do they result from differences in the marginal cost to workers of supplying labor services. Discrimination in hiring denies equality of opportunity in employment to certain workers.

[9] David N. Hyman and Robert M. Fearn, "The Influence of City Size on Labor Incomes," *Quarterly Review of Economics and Business* 18, no. 1 (Spring 1978), pp. 63–73.

In effect, it imposes a selective barrier to entry into a labor market that affects certain groups of workers. Although discrimination may be the result of the monopsony power of employers or the monopoly power of labor unions, it is generally agreed that by and large labor markets are quite competitive. The following analysis therefore discusses the impact of discrimination in labor markets that would otherwise be competitive. The analysis views discrimination as resulting from a traditional barrier to entry that either prevents certain groups from entering a market or allows them to enter the market at wages below those paid to equally productive workers who do not suffer from discrimination.

Discrimination misallocates labor resources by forcing workers who suffer from its effects to perform less productive labor services than they would perform otherwise. For example, suppose qualified women and minority group members are prevented from entering construction trades for which they are as qualified as existing workers in those trades. As a result these women and minority group members must seek alternative employment in their next best occupation. The difference between their marginal revenue product in construction work and their marginal revenue product in their next best alternative is the social cost of discrimination. In other words, discrimination results in a loss in output for the economy. As you will now see, discrimination also raises the prices of some products and lowers the prices of others.

Extreme Discrimination: Qualified Workers Are Barred from Entering the Labor Market

At the extreme, employers could refuse to hire qualified workers for reasons unrelated to the marginal revenue product or the wage at which those workers will accept employment. Discrimination could induce workers to migrate to nations or regions where they will not suffer from discriminatory practices.

Suppose that discrimination is purely the result of the prejudice of employers and that *all* employers engage in discrimination by *refusing* to hire women or members of a minority group. Figure 15–10 shows the impact of such discrimination in a labor market—for example, the construction industry. The total supply of labor and the demand for labor of given skill employed in that labor market are shown in Figure 15–10(b). If the labor market were perfectly competitive and composed of two groups of equal skill competing for available jobs, the market equilibrium wage would be w^* per hour for all workers and Q_L^* labor hours per week would be employed in the market.

Figure 15–10(a) shows that the supply of labor is composed of labor hours at various wage levels offered by two groups—men and women. The total quantity of labor supplied at any given wage in the labor market is the sum of the quantities supplied by men and women. In Figure 15–10(b) the total labor supply curve, S, is obtained by adding the quantity of labor supplied by men, Q_{LM}, to the quantity supplied by women, Q_{LW}. For example, at the equilibrium wage, w^*, Q_{LM}^* labor hours per week will be supplied by men and Q_{LW}^* labor hours per week will be supplied by women. The total quantity of labor supplied at that wage, Q_L^*, is equal to $Q_{LM}^* + Q_{LW}^*$. At that wage the marginal revenue product of *both* men and women would equal w^* in a competitive labor market.

FIGURE 15–10 Discrimination in Labor Markets

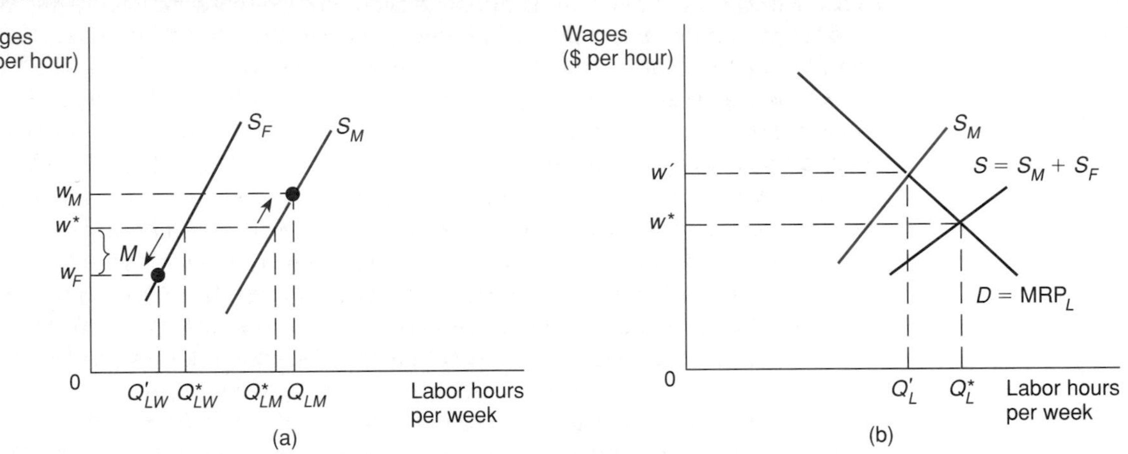

The labor supply curve S shown in (b) is the one that would prevail if both men and women could freely enter the labor market. Without any discrimination the equilibrium wage would be w^* and Q^*_L hours of labor would be hired per week. Graph (a) shows the labor supply curve of men and women. At the equilibrium wage, Q^*_{LW} hours of labor supplied by women would be used and Q^*_{LM} hours of labor supplied by men would be used. If women were excluded from the labor market by discrimination, wages paid to men would rise to w'. If, instead, women were simply paid less, labor supplied by women would decline. To maintain the labor force, wages paid to men would go up to w_M.

Now suppose that as a result of discrimination women are not hired at all in the construction industry and that the total supply of labor to this market is now composed entirely of the labor hours offered by men. The supply of labor would then be S_M in Figure 15–10(b), and equilibrium wages in the market would rise to w'. The equilibrium quantity of labor supplied would be Q'_L. Because the wages of men increase as a result of discrimination, so too does their marginal revenue product. In equilibrium the marginal revenue product of men would also increase to w' if women are prevented from competing in the labor market.

The consequences of such an extreme form of discrimination can readily be seen in Figure 15–10. Men gain as a result of the discrimination because their hourly wages increase. Women must now look for work in their next best alternative, where their marginal revenue products are presumably lower. As a result women who would otherwise work in the construction market enter other labor markets, such as the clerical and retailing markets, where wages are lower. The increase in labor supply that results from discrimination puts a further downward pressure on wages in those markets.

There are also some less obvious implications of discrimination for the economy. Because wages are now higher in construction jobs, the costs of production will also be higher. Therefore, the prices of products produced by construction firms that practice discrimination in hiring will increase. This will decrease the quantities of those products demanded and will make consumers of those products worse off. On the other hand, the flood of women into industries that do not practice discrimination will decrease labor costs in those industries and thus result in downward pressure on the prices of products that those industries produce. This is because lower wages in those industries imply lower marginal costs, which result in an increased supply of the products of those industries and a fall in their market prices.

Less Extreme Discrimination: Entry into the Market Is Permitted Only If Workers Subject to Discrimination Accept Lower Wages

Discrimination in labor markets need not be so extreme as a complete barrier to the entry of certain groups. Suppose, instead, all employers in the labor market systematically pay women lower wages than they pay men. In that case women can enter the labor market, but if they do, they will be paid wages below those paid to equally qualified male workers. For example, employers might deduct a sum of $\$M$ from the marginal revenue product of women employed in the construction industry. Assume, as before, that the equilibrium wage would otherwise be w^* and that employment at that wage would be Q_L^*. The marginal revenue product of workers in the construction industry would be MRP $= w^*$. Since employers discriminate against women, they pay them a wage of $w_F = w^* - M$. This results in a decrease, to Q'_{LW}, in the labor hours supplied by women. The amount of that decrease will depend on the elasticity of labor supply of women.

Employers cannot hire Q_L^* labor hours per week, as is required for market equilibrium in Figure 15–10(b), unless they increase the wages they pay men. Therefore, to maintain the labor force at the desired level, employees bid up the wages they pay men to w_M, and the quantity of labor supplied by men increases to Q'_{LM}. The extent of the increase varies with the elasticity of labor supply of men. Total labor supply at an *average* wage w^* is now $Q'_{LM} + Q'_{LW} = Q_L^*$. Again, wages increase for men as a result of discrimination against women, but the wage increase is less pronounced than it was when women were banned from entering the market. Some women supply less labor to the market or seek jobs in alternative markets because of the discrimination-induced wage decline.

Profit Maximization, Competition, and the Impact of These Forces on Discriminatory Wage Differentials

Discrimination is inconsistent with profit maximization by competitive firms. If some firms do not practice discrimination or if new firms can enter the input market to hire women or minority group members who are subject to discrimination, the discriminatory wage differential between men and women will eventually disappear. It is easy to see why this is so. When discrimination is practiced, women (or members of minority groups subject to it) are paid a wage that is less than their marginal revenue product. If a market in which such discrimination is practiced is perfectly competitive in all other respects, any individual firm in the market can hire all of the labor services it wishes without affecting that wage. Thus, as long as the wage paid to women is less than the marginal revenue product of their labor, a firm could gain by hiring more women and using fewer men in its labor force. A firm also gains by substituting women for men because it would be paying men whose wage $w_M > w^*$ more than their marginal revenue product. It follows that competition among employers in a competitive labor market would bid up the wages of women and bid down the wages of men until the wage differential between the two groups has been eliminated and both groups are paid w^*. A likely result of this process is that some employers would employ only women and other firms would employ only men. However, competition among employers for qualified workers would result in equal wages for the two groups.

If discrimination is practiced, employers that discriminate against workers pay for this practice with lower profits. Concern about both the unfairness and the wastefulness of discriminatory hiring practices has resulted in government action to end discrimination in U.S. labor markets.

Is Discrimination Actually Practiced?

Women earn less than men. In 1984 the hourly wages of U.S. women averaged 30 percent less than the hourly wages of U.S. men. The gap between total labor earnings of the sexes is even wider because, on average, women on full-time schedules work fewer hours per week than do men. In 1984 the median labor earnings of female workers were only about 65 percent of those earned by men. The gap between the labor earnings of men and women varies with age. The gap between the labor earnings of young women and young men is much less than the gap between middle-aged women and men. For example, the wages earned by women between the ages of 16 and 24 years were nearly 90 percent of the wages earned by men in the same age group.[10]

It is also clear that jobs in which women are concentrated pay less. In 1982 industries in which 70 percent of the employees were women had average hourly earnings of $5.71 and industries in which less than 10 percent of the employees were women had average hourly earnings of $11.56.

Studies show that wage differentials exist between men and women and between minority groups and other groups that cannot be explained by differences in the productivity of workers or differences in job conditions. As has been shown, women, on average, earn less than men in the United States. Blacks earn less than whites. One study found, however, that over 25 percent of the difference in labor earnings between U.S. men and women could be attributed to factors other than discrimination. The study also found that about 40 percent of the difference in labor earnings between blacks and whites could be attributed to factors other than discrimination.[11] The inability of economists to account for all of the wage differentials in these cases can be interpreted as suggesting (but does not prove) that some discrimination is practiced in labor markets.

Income differences among groups could reflect differences in the supply of labor by particular groups to particular occupations. They could also reflect differences in productivity among groups. A study of salary differentials between male

---

[10] Henry J. Aaron and Cameran M. Lougy, *The Comparable Worth Controversy* (Washington, D.C.: Brookings Institution, 1986), pp. 8–9.

[11] Ronald Oaxaca, "Theory and Measurement of the Economics of Discrimination," in *Equal Rights and Industrial Relations* (Madison, Wis.: Industrial Relations Research Association, 1977).

and female university professors attributed three fourths of the observed 11 percent positive differential for men to such factors as age, experience, training, rank, and academic specialty. The study did conclude, however, that the remaining fourth was the result of discrimination against women.[12]

The Issue of Comparable Worth

The Civil Rights Act of 1964 outlawed discrimination in hiring on the basis of race, color, religion, sex, or national origin. This act applies to all firms involved in interstate commerce that have at least 25 employees. Other legislation places special restrictions on the hiring practices and personnel policies of firms that have entered into contracts for services with the federal government.

Supporters of the doctrine of "comparable worth" argue that government intervention in markets is necessary to force employers to pay equal wages for equal jobs. This approach would require job evaluations to determine which jobs require similar skills and effort and the use of these evaluations to make sure that women are not paid less than men who do similar work. Under this approach the government rather than the marketplace would set wages in cases for which discrimination can be proved.

To evaluate the potential impact of government intervention to increase the wages paid to women, it is important to understand the causes of the pay gap between men and women. Unfortunately, there is no consensus among economists about the causes of that gap. One view argues that women have, on average, chosen low-paying jobs in which workers have low marginal products so as to enjoy the freedom of entering and leaving the labor force often. Women are, in fact, concentrated in jobs that require little training. Another view argues that women have been barred by traditional labor market practices from jobs for which higher wages are paid.

The fact that in the past women have tended to leave the labor force to have children has reduced their work experience relative to that of men. The lower pay gap of younger women may reflect a greater commitment to work and careers that will help eliminate the pay gap between men and women in the future. However, much of the gap has not been adequately explained and may be due to discriminatory labor market practices. This has led to the calls for government action.

What would happen if governments intervened in markets to increase the wages paid to women? One possibility is that the earnings of women as a group would actually decline. An increase in wages decreases the quantity of labor input demanded. This could result in decreased employment as the rate of hiring new workers declines. If the government wage exceeds the market equilibrium wage, a surplus of workers in the market could result. The impact of increased wages could be offset by a reduction in hours of work demanded, which would result in lower earnings.

---

[12] Nancy Gordon, Thomas E. Morton, and Ina C. Braden, "Faculty Salaries: Is There Discrimination by Sex, Race, and Discipline?" *American Economic Review* 64, no. 3 (June 1974), pp 419–27.

FIGURE 15–11 Impact of Comparable Worth Legislation

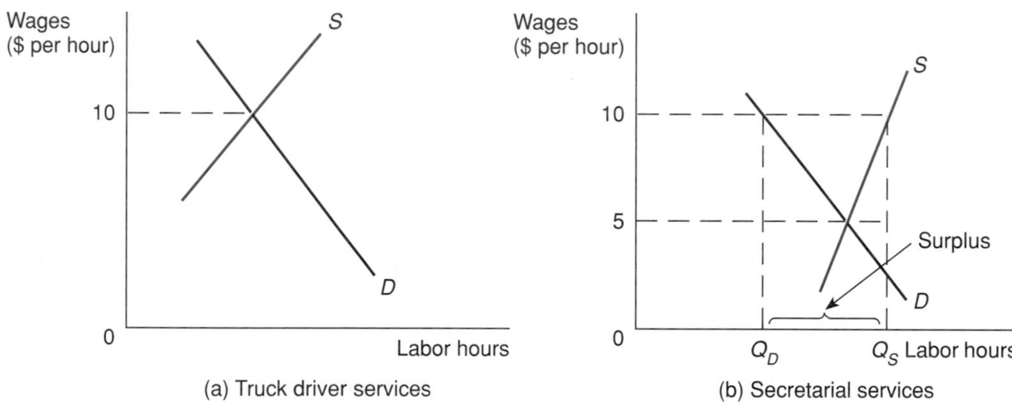

Graph (a) shows the equilibrium in the market for truck drivers, and (b) shows equilibrium in the market for secretaries. If comparable worth legislation were to require that secretaries be paid the same wage as truck drivers, there would be a surplus of secretarial labor under existing market conditions.

A basic problem in implementing a comparable worth program is the fact that the wage differential between two jobs depends not only on the marginal revenue product of labor but also on the number of workers willing to accept those jobs. For example, consider two jobs, such as a secretary and a truck driver, whose marginal revenue product curves are identical. The two jobs could be viewed as having comparable worth in the sense that the marginal revenue product of any given level of employment is the same for both. Figures 15–11(a) and 15–11(b) show that because the supply of workers willing and able to be truck drivers is less than the supply of workers willing and able to be secretaries, the wages of truck drivers exceed the wages of secretaries. Here the equilibrium wage differentials result from differences in supply rather than from discrimination. Truck drivers earn $10 per hour, and secretaries earn $5 per hour. Now suppose comparable worth legislation raises the wage of secretaries to $10 per hour. As a result the quantity of labor hours demanded in the market for secretaries will decline, whereas the quantity of labor hours supplied in that market will increase. The result will be a surplus of secretaries. Those secretaries fortunate enough to keep or find jobs at the higher wage will clearly be better off. However, because of the government-mandated wage, fewer secretaries will be employed and some secretaries who previously had jobs will be out of work!

SUMMARY

1. When a firm has monopoly power in its output market, MRP $<$ VMP for an input. The firm therefore hires less input than would otherwise be the case. Under these circumstances, for example, workers are paid wages that are less than the value of their marginal product. This allows the monopoly firm to earn more profits than are earned by a competitive firm.

2. A pure monopsony is a single buyer of input services that have few, if any, alternative employment opportunities. A monopsony can control input prices. Pure monopsony is rare. Under oligopsony a few firms have the monopsony power to influence input prices.
3. A firm with monopsony power hires input services up to the point at which the firm's marginal input cost equals the marginal revenue product of the input. Such a firm's ability to control price results in less input employment than occurs in the benchmark competitive case. When monopsony power is present, the wages paid to workers are less than the marginal revenue product of labor. The difference between wages paid and MRP_L contributes to the profits of the monopsony.
4. Labor unions can use their control over labor supply to increase the wages of workers. When wages rise above the competitive level, a worker surplus results. The surplus is rationed by the higher union wage or by closed-shop agreements that require employers to use union labor only.
5. Bilateral monopoly exists when a single seller of input services must deal with a single buyer of those services. There is no predictable equilibrium in such a market. Both buyers and sellers can control price. The profit-maximizing price for the seller is higher than the profit-maximizing price for the buyer.
6. Discrimination in labor markets is the practice of paying different wages to workers of equal productivity. Discrimination is an imperfection that prevents free entry into labor markets by all. At the extreme, certain groups are barred from entering certain labor markets. In less extreme forms of discrimination those groups are allowed to enter the labor market at wages below those of other workers.
7. Discrimination results in the payment of wage increases to groups not subject to it. It also contributes to higher prices of some goods and lower prices of others and to a distortion in resource allocation.
8. Discrimination is inconsistent with profit maximization.

Important Concepts

pure monopsony
oligopsony
monopsony power
marginal input cost for a monopsony
average input cost
labor unions
collective bargaining
closed shop
bilateral monopoly
nonpecuniary wages
compensating wage differentials
discrimination in labor markets

Questions for Review

1. Monopolists are sometimes accused of "exploiting" workers because they pay wages below the value of the marginal product of labor. Explain why monopolists do this and how such wage payments affect monopoly profits.
2. Explain why a monopsonist hirer of labor need not be a monopolist seller of output.
3. Why do monopsony firms pay workers wages that are less than the value of the marginal product of labor?
4. Explain why unionization may act to decrease the wage rates of workers in nonunionized industries. Do the relatively low wage rates of workers in service industries compared to the wage rates of workers in manufacturing industries support your explanation?
5. The postal workers' union threatens to go on strike against the U.S. Postal Service because its wage offer falls short of the union's wage demands. Can economic theory predict the wage ultimately agreed on? Explain your answer.
6. Explain why higher wage rates imposed as a result of comparable worth legislation might create unemployment.

7. Identify at least three reasons why unionization may increase labor productivity. If unionization increases labor productivity, does this imply that it reduces the average and marginal costs of production?
8. Why are some of the workers who are willing to work at the wages established by unions unlikely to find work?
9. Why is it difficult to determine how much discrimination occurs in labor markets?
10. Explain why discrimination not only decreases the wages of women and minority group members but also increases the wages of those who are not subject to discrimination.

PROBLEMS

1. A tax is levied on a monopolist's output. Assuming that labor is hired in a perfectly competitive market, show the impact of the tax on the amount of labor hired.
2. A payroll tax is levied on wages paid by a monopsony firm. Use a graphic analysis to predict the effect of the tax on the amount of labor hired.
3. Suppose a machinists' union guarantees all users of machinist labor that they can hire all they wish at the union wage of $15 per hour. This wage is above the competitive equilibrium wage. The demand for products produced by machinists increases. Show the impact of this increase on the employment of union machinists. When will firms pay *more* than the union wage?
4. A musicians' union limits its membership to 10,000 musicians. Assuming that the union establishes a closed shop, show how the union wage can exceed the competitive wage.
5. How can discrimination against minority group members in the labor market *increase* the wages of some workers? What effect is discrimination likely to have on the profits of the firms that practice it?
6. The diagram applies to a monopsonist (for example, a large factory in an isolated town) that in the absence of government or union wage restrictions will hire L^* units of labor. Answer the following questions regarding this case:

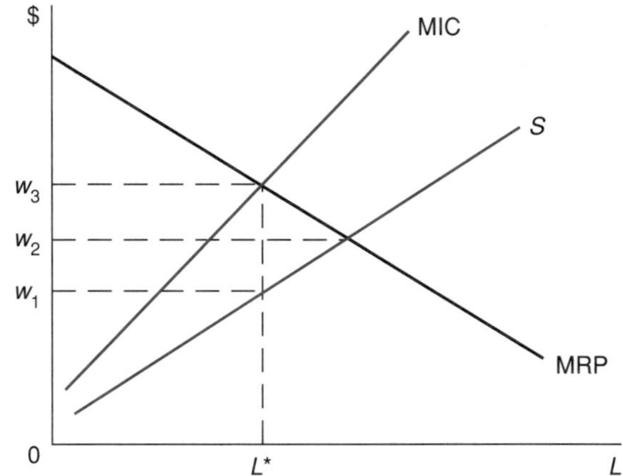

   a. In the absence of government or union wage restrictions, what wage rate will the monopsonist pay?
   b. If the government imposes a minimum wage, W_{min}, on this labor market, what level of W_{min} would create a surplus of labor?
   c. If the government imposes a minimum wage of W_3, will the monopsonist be able to earn a profit by hiring labor?
7. The National Football League Team Owners Council wants smaller team rosters than does the National Football League Players Association. Use the bilateral monopoly diagram in Figure 15–6 to explain why this should be expected.

PART VI

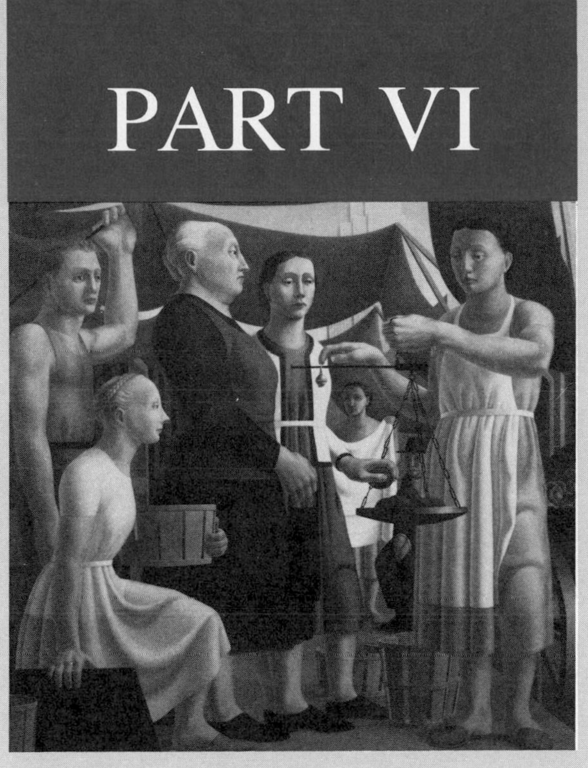

Welfare Economics, Market Failure, and the Economics of Information

16

General Equilibrium Analysis and Efficiency

The economy is like a complicated machine. If you jiggle a lever that directly affects one sector of the economy, a complex, gearlike linkage will probably cause the change in that sector to affect the operation of many other sectors of the economy. For example, an increase in the wages of skilled labor in input markets is likely to increase the average and marginal costs of producing a host of goods and services. This, in turn, is likely to increase the prices of the products produced with the now more costly labor to increase. Similarly, an increase in interest rates will increase the monthly payments on new mortgages and thus is likely to decrease the demand for new homes. As buying a new home becomes more expensive, the demand for appliances and building materials is likely to decrease, and that decrease in demand would cause changes in the prices of a wide range of products and labor services.

We will now show how interdependence among markets in the economy affects prices and quantities traded. We will also show how the concept of allocative efficiency, which we first introduced in Chapter 9, can be generalized to include all goods and services and all markets. The general equilibrium analysis we now develop will demonstrate how change in equilibrium in one market can affect equilibrium and efficiency in other markets. The interdependence of prices and quantities in all markets is an inevitable result of scarcity. By looking at that interdependence, we will be able to show how resource constraints and technology affect our ability to produce and to generate well-being. Finally, we will examine how international trade can result in mutual gains that allow nations to enjoy consumption levels surpassing the levels made possible by their domestic production.

Partial Equilibrium Analysis versus General Equilibrium Analysis

Partial equilibrium analysis Analysis of the equilibrium variables in one market.

To this point, most of the analysis of interaction between buyers and sellers in this book has focused on single markets. The analysis occasionally included explanations of the way price changes in one market affect demand or supply in other markets. A **partial equilibrium analysis** determines the equilibrium price and quantities in one market. It ignores the repercussions of a price change in that market

General equilibrium analysis Analysis of equilibrium that considers the interdependence of prices and quantities in all markets.

Feedback effects Further changes in prices and quantities in a market in response to price changes in related markets.

on equilibrium prices and quantities in other markets. A **general equilibrium analysis** traces the effects of a change in demand or supply in one market on equilibrium prices and quantities in *all* markets. General equilibrium analysis explicitly considers economic interdependence among all prices and decisions.

General equilibrium analysis can be used to consider the long-run **feedback effects** of price changes in markets. These feedback effects are further changes in prices and quantities in a market in response to price changes in related markets. Such effects can be illustrated for a hypothetical increase in the price of crude oil caused by a decrease in its supply.

Suppose a decrease in the supply of crude oil increases the price per barrel from $25 to $40. At the higher price the quantity demanded declines from 17 million to 14 million barrels per day. Figure 16–1(a) shows how the decrease in supply initially affects the oil market. A general equilibrium analysis traces the implications of the price increase in crude oil on equilibrium in other markets. Once this has been done, feedback effects in the original market can be isolated.

Crude oil is an input in the production of many goods. The increase in its price will increase the costs of producing these goods. The supply of these goods will therefore decrease, and their price will rise. For example, crude oil is an important

FIGURE 16–1 General Equilibrium Analysis of an Increase in the Price of Crude Oil

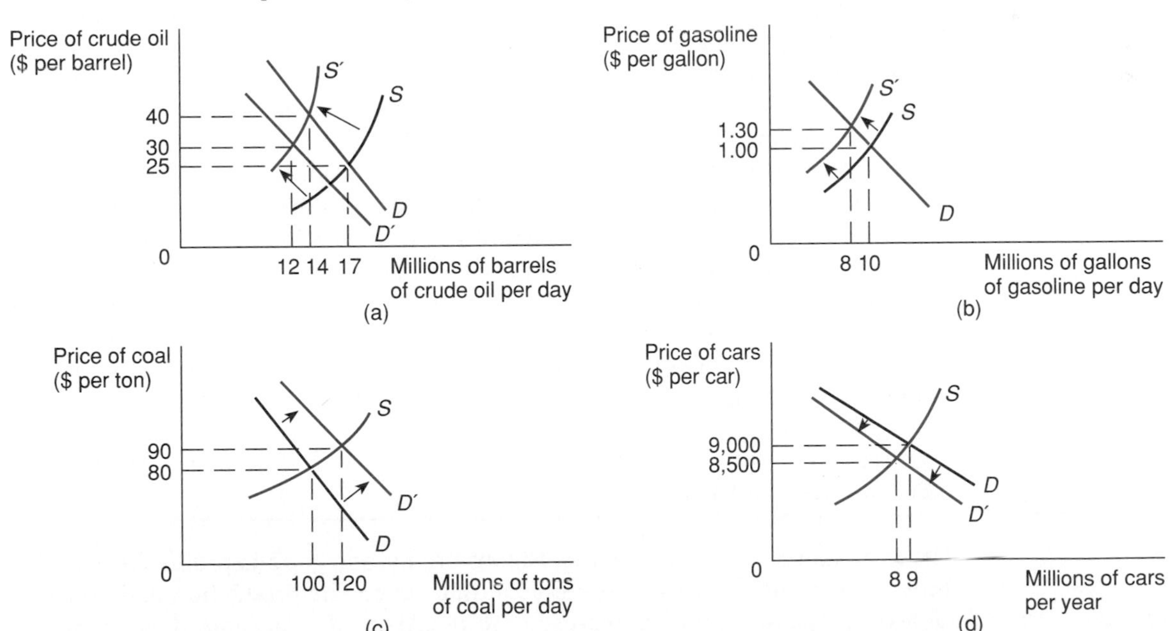

An increase in the price of crude oil increases the prices of goods for which it is an input, such as gasoline. The price of substitute inputs, such as coal, also increases. The demand for goods that are complementary to these energy sources, such as cars, declines, and their price falls. In the long run, these price effects in related markets feed back into the market for crude oil; assuming that the demand for crude oil declines, its price also declines.

input in the production of gasoline. As shown in Figure 16–1(b), the supply of gasoline will decrease and its price will increase from $1 to $1.30 per gallon. The daily quantity demanded will decline from 10 million to 8 million gallons. Similarly, the prices of all other goods produced with crude oil, such as heating oil, man-made fabrics, roofing materials, and kerosene, will also increase and the quantities of these goods sold will decline.

Figure 16–1(c) illustrates the impact of the increase in the price of crude oil on the market for its substitutes. The demand for substitute goods increases. For example, the demand for coal increases because coal is used as a substitute means of producing electrical energy. As a result of the increase in the price of crude oil, the price of coal increases from $80 to $90 per ton. The quantity supplied increases from 100 million to 120 million tons per day.

Finally, there will be a decline in the demand for goods that are complementary to goods whose prices rise as a result of the initial increase in oil prices. Figure 16–1(d) shows the impact on the market for cars. The increase in the price of gasoline causes a decrease in the demand for cars. The average price of new cars declines from $9,000 to $8,500 per unit. The quantity of new cars supplied declines from 9 million to 8 million per year.

All of these reactions to the initial increase in the price of crude oil have a feedback effect on the market for crude oil. The decreases in the quantities demanded of gasoline and other goods produced with crude oil tend to decrease the demand for crude oil. The demand for crude oil also tends to decrease because of the decrease in the demand for such goods as cars. On the other hand, the increase in the price of such substitute goods as coal tends to increase the demand for crude oil. These feedback effects may cause the demand for crude oil to either increase or decrease in the long run. In Figure 16–1 it has been assumed that the factors decreasing the demand for crude oil outweigh the factors increasing its demand in the long run. As the demand for crude oil shifts from D to D', the price of crude oil declines from $40 to $30 a barrel in the long-run equilibrium. The quantity of crude oil supplied at that price is 12 million barrels per day. A **general equilibrium** exists when prices have adjusted to a change in either demand or supply so that quantities demanded equal quantities supplied in all markets. Under these circumstances there is no tendency for further shifts in either demand or supply in any market.

General equilibrium A condition that exists when prices have adjusted to a change in either demand or supply so that quantities demanded equal quantities supplied in all markets.

General Equilibrium and Efficiency

Given resources and technology, if more of any one good is produced at a given time, less of other goods is available at that time. The production and consumption of goods and services represent an amalgam of many interdependent decisions. The outcomes of market interaction can be evaluated by comparing the resulting allocation of resources with the efficient allocation.

The essence of this interdependence can be analyzed for a simple case in which only two inputs are available to produce two goods. Assume that the two inputs are in fixed supply. At a given point in time, a fixed number of labor hours and machine hours is available to produce the two goods. This is a simplified general equilibrium analysis that can be conducted in two dimensions. The analysis can easily be generalized to many inputs and goods. However, a multidimensional analysis requires mathematical techniques to solve for the general equilibrium. A two-dimensional analysis is sufficient to understand general equilibrium without undue mathematical complexity.

The Resource Constraint

Resource constraint The total amount of input services available over a given period.

Suppose the total amount of labor services of given quality (L) available for production in a small nation is 10,000 hours per day. The only other input used in production is capital, of which 5,000 machine hours of a given quality (K) are available each day. The total amount of input services available each day is the economy's **resource constraint.** Assume that supplies of the two input services are perfectly inelastic. The limited amount of labor and capital services available each day places a constraint on the amount of goods and services that can be produced.

Assume that the only two goods produced are food (F) and clothing (C). If more input services are used to produce food each day, fewer input services are available to produce clothing. The total labor hours used each day cannot exceed 10,000. Similarly, the total number of machine hours used cannot exceed 5,000 each day. Both labor hours and machine hours are traded in perfectly competitive input markets. The only sources of personal income are earnings from the sale of labor and capital services. The competitive markets will result in prices for those services that ensure that the total quantity supplied each day equals the quantity demanded. There can be no unemployment of productive resources in competitive markets.

The resource constraint for the economy can be written in the following way:

$$L = L_F + L_C = 10{,}000 \text{ hours/day} \quad \textbf{(16–1)}$$

and

$$K = K_F + K_C = 5{,}000 \text{ hours/day} \quad \textbf{(16–2)}$$

Analysis of Production with an Edgeworth Box

The amounts of food and clothing that can be produced with the available supplies of labor and capital services depend on technology. The productive relationships in the economy are described by the production functions for food and clothing. The production function for food gives the maximum amount of food that can be produced per day with any given combination of labor hours and machine hours. Similarly, the production function for clothing gives the maximum daily output of clothing for any combination of labor and machine hours.

Edgeworth box A tool for analyzing production and the allocation of resources in an economy with fixed supplies of inputs.

An **Edgeworth box** is a convenient tool for analyzing production and the allocation of resources in an economy with fixed supplies of labor and capital.[1] An Edgeworth box is a rectangle whose sides represent the amount of input services available to produce two goods.

[1] The Edgeworth box is named after the British economist F. Y. Edgeworth, who employed a similar analysis in his well-known book *Mathematical Psychics: An Essay on the Application of Mathematics to the Moral Sciences,* published in 1891.

Each point in an Edgeworth box corresponds to an allocation of the available number of labor hours and machine hours to the production of food and clothing. This is shown in Figure 16–2. The length of the rectangle represents the 10,000 labor hours available for production per day. The width of the rectangle represents the 5,000 machine hours available per day. The number of labor hours used in food production (L_F) is measured from the origin, labeled O in the lower left corner, along the bottom of the box. The number of machine hours used in food production is measured from point O along the left-hand side of the box.

Now locate point O' at the upper right corner of the box. From that point leftward along the top of the box, measure the number of labor hours used each day in the production of clothing. The number of machine hours used each day in clothing production is measured downward along the right-hand side of the box.

Each point in the box represents an allocation of total available labor hours and machine hours to both food and clothing production. At point A within the box, for example, 7,500 labor hours and 3,000 machine hours are used each day to produce food. Whatever is not used in food production is used in clothing production. Because the total number of labor hours available each day is 10,000, the number of labor hours used in clothing production is (10,000 − 7,500) or 2,500 hours. Similarly, at point A 3,000 machine hours are used each day in food production. It follows that at that point 2,000 machine hours are used in clothing production.

FIGURE 16–2 An Edgeworth Box

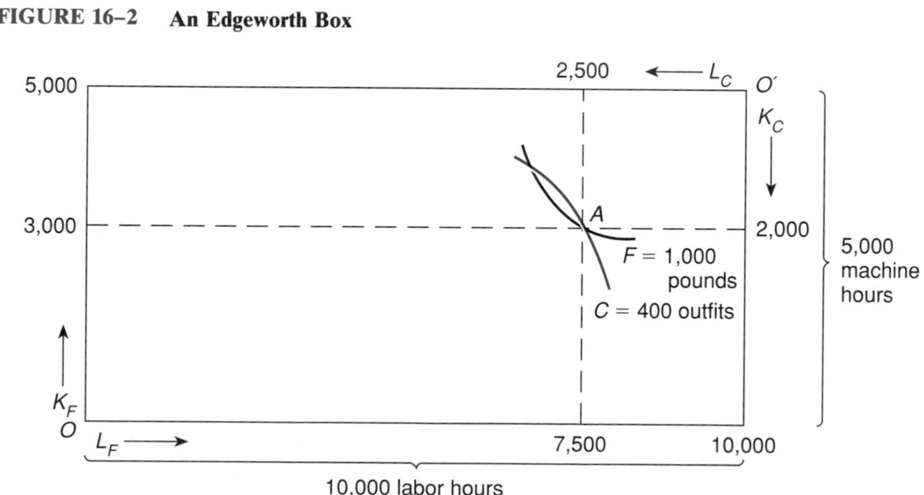

The dimensions of the Edgeworth box depend on the resource constraint. Here its length is the 10,000 labor hours available each day and its width is the 5,000 machine hours available each day. Each point in the box represents an allocation of resources for the production of food and clothing. At point A, 2,500 labor hours and 2,000 machine hours are used to produce 400 clothing outfits each day. The remaining resources, 7,500 labor hours and 3,000 machine hours, are used to produce 1,000 pounds of food each day.

The production functions for food and clothing can then be used to determine the outputs of food and clothing corresponding to the allocation of input services at point *A*. An isoquant for food and clothing can be drawn through any point in the box. Draw through point *A* the food isoquant corresponding to the output that can be produced with 7,500 labor hours and 3,000 machine hours. This isoquant indicates that these inputs correspond to daily production of 1,000 pounds of food. The isoquants corresponding to the amount of clothing that can be produced at point *A* are also drawn. That isoquant is drawn "upside down" because labor and capital in clothing production are measured from the origin *O′*. The clothing isoquant through point *A* indicates that 400 outfits of clothing are produced each day with 2,500 labor hours and 2,000 machine hours.

Each point in the Edgeworth box corresponds to an allocation of labor and machine hours to the production of the two goods. Given that allocation, the corresponding isoquants indicate the output of each of the two goods. A point in the box therefore corresponds to specific values for six variables: L_F, K_F, L_C, K_C, *F*, and *C*.

Productive Efficiency

Productive efficiency A situation that prevails when it is impossible to reallocate resources to increase the output of one good without decreasing the output of other goods.

Productive efficiency exists when it is impossible to reallocate the use of available input services to increase the output of one good without decreasing the output of any other goods. The Edgeworth box is used to isolate all of the resource allocations that attain productive efficiency. This is done in Figure 16–3.

FIGURE 16–3 **Productive Efficiency**

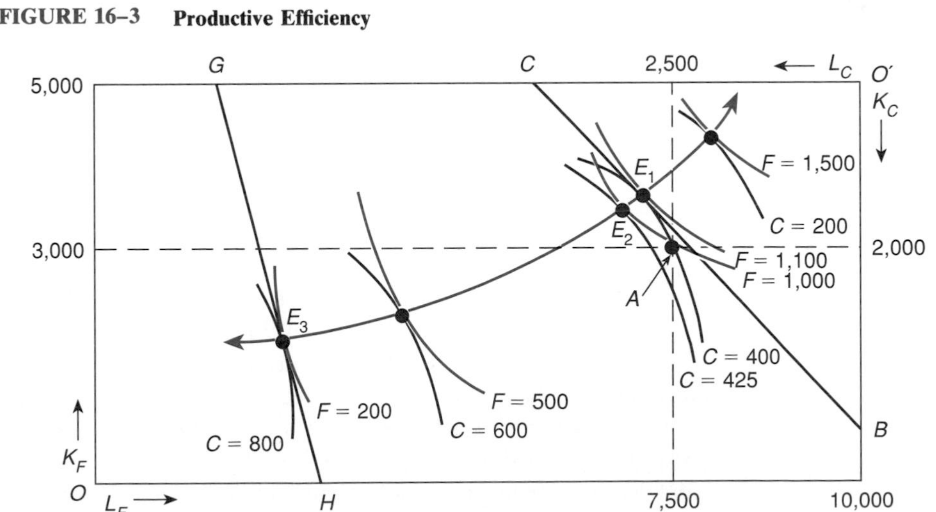

Productive efficiency exists when $MRTS^F_{LK} = MRTS^C_{LK}$. This is true for all the points of tangency between the two sets of isoquants. The line drawn through all of the tangency points is the efficiency curve for input use in the economy. For example, points E_1 and E_2 represent the efficient use of labor and capital.

It is easy to show that the daily input use at point A is inefficient. Move along the isoquant through point A, where output is 400 clothing outfits per day. That output is achieved by transferring 100 machine hours per day from food production to clothing production. At the same time, 100 labor hours per day are transferred from food production into clothing production. Clothing production remains at 400 outfits per day as a result of this reallocation of resources. However, moving from point A to point E_1, the daily production of food increases from 1,000 pounds to 1,100 pounds. Point A is inefficient because it is possible to increase the production of food at that point without decreasing the production of clothing. At point E_1 the food isoquant corresponding to 1,100 pounds per day is just tangent to the clothing isoquant for 400 outfits per day.

It is also possible to increase the production of clothing by moving away from point A without decreasing the production of food. This is accomplished by moving labor hours out of food production and replacing them with just enough machine hours to keep production constant. Staying on the isoquant corresponding to 1,000 pounds of food production, clothing production is increased from 400 to 425 outfits per day by moving from point A to point E_2. Movement beyond point E_2, which transfers more than 200 labor hours from food production, results in a decline in food production. The 200 labor hours are replaced by transferring 100 machine hours from clothing production. The two isoquants are once again tangent, at E_2.

The Edgeworth box in Figure 16–3 shows selected isoquants for food and clothing production, given the resource constraint and technology. *Only those combinations of labor hours and machine hours corresponding to tangencies between the two sets of isoquants are efficient resource allocations.* The slope of an isoquant at any point multiplied by -1 is the marginal rate of technical substitution of labor for capital. The slope of the food isoquants is $-\text{MRTS}^F_{LK}$. The slope of the clothing isoquants is $-\text{MRTS}^C_{LK}$. Efficiency requires that input services be used so that the following condition is met:

$$\text{MRTS}^F_{LK} = \text{MRTS}^C_{LK} \qquad \textbf{(16–3)}$$

Remember that the marginal rate of technical substitution of labor for capital equals the ratio of the marginal product of labor to the marginal product of capital (see Chapter 7). The efficiency condition also implies that input use must be adjusted so that MR_L/MP_K is the same in the production of all goods and services.

In Figure 16–3 a curve is drawn through all the points of tangencies satisfying Equation 16–3. This curve gives all of the efficient combinations of labor hours and machine hours. If inputs are used in any combination other than those on that curve, it will be possible to increase the production of at least one of the goods without decreasing the production of the other. Similarly, a resource allocation that leaves some inputs idle is inefficient. For example, if some labor is unemployed and the transaction cost of putting workers to work is zero, then eliminating the unemployment would make it possible to increase production of at least one good without reducing the production of another. This is because no labor hours would have to be removed from the production of any other good to put the unemployed labor to work producing food or clothing.

The Production Possibility Curve

Production possibility curve A curve showing the maximum amount of any one good that can be produced in an economy, given the output of all other goods, the resource constraint, and technology.

The **production possibility curve** shows the maximum amount of any one good that can be produced in an economy, given the output of all other goods, the resource constraint, and technology. This curve can easily be derived from the Edgeworth box. For example, one point on the production possibility curve corresponds to point E_1 in Figure 16–3. At that point the 10,000 labor hours and 5,000 machine hours available each day are being used to produce 1,100 pounds of food and 400 outfits of clothing. The production possibility curve plots clothing against food. As shown in Figure 16–4, one point on the curve, labeled E_1, is 1,100 pounds of food and 400 outfits of clothing per day. Another point corresponds to point E_2 of Figure 16–3. At that point the daily output of clothing is 425 outfits and the daily output of food is 1,000 pounds, which is shown as point E_2 in Figure 16–4. Similarly, each point of tangency between the two sets of isoquants in Figure 16–3 corresponds to a point on the production possibility curve shown in Figure 16–4. A point such as A in the Edgeworth box represents an inefficient use of input services. That point would correspond to a point within the production possibility curve. As shown in Figure 16–4, point A corresponds to 400 outfits of clothing and 1,000 pounds of food each day. By reallocating the use of input services, it is possible to move from point A to point E_1, point E_2, or any other output combination corresponding to points on the arc E_1E_2. In other words, from point A the output of food, clothing, or both can be increased without requiring any reduction in either food or clothing. Only points on the production possibility curve are efficient.

FIGURE 16–4 A Production Possibility Curve

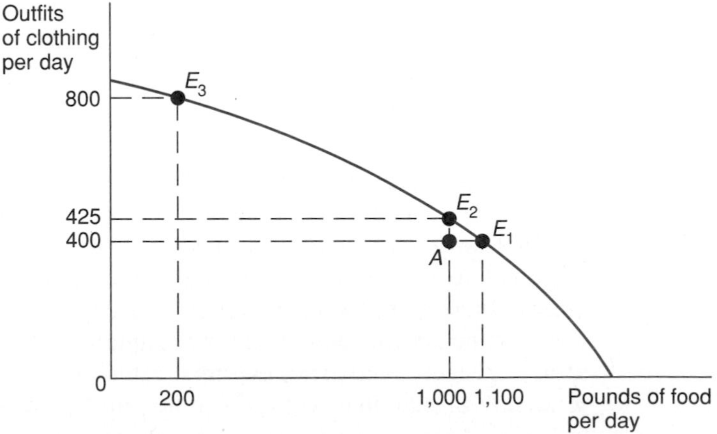

A production possibility curve can be derived from the efficiency curve in the Edgeworth box. Each point on the production possibility curve shows the maximum amount of clothing that can be produced each day, given the production of food and the available labor and machine hours each day (the resource constraint).

The Marginal Rate of Transformation

Marginal rate of transformation The amount of one good that must be sacrificed when the resources used to produce some of it are reallocated to the production of another good.

Notice the bowed shape of the production possibility curve. The slope of the curve becomes steeper as more food and less clothing are produced per day. The slope of the production possibility curve is negative, which reflects the fact that when resources are used efficiently, an increase in the production of one good can be obtained only at the expense of a decrease in the production of the other. The **marginal rate of transformation** of clothing into food reflects the amount of clothing that must be sacrificed to obtain each extra unit of food along the production possibility curve. The bowed shape of the curve implies that the marginal rate of transformation increases as more food is produced. Thus, as more resources are reallocated from clothing production to food production in the economy, *increasing amounts of clothing* are sacrificed for each extra unit of food.

The increasing marginal rate of transformation results from increasing marginal costs of production. The marginal rate of transformation of clothing into food at any point is:

$$\text{MRT}_{FC} = -\Delta C/\Delta F \tag{16–4}$$

In other words, the marginal rate of transformation is the slope of the production possibility curve multiplied by -1.

The marginal cost of an increase in food production at any point is the resulting decline in clothing production. This is the opportunity cost of the extra food production:

$$\text{MC}_F = \Delta C \tag{16–5}$$

Similarly, the marginal cost of an increase in clothing production at any point is the output of food that must be sacrificed to reallocate inputs to clothing production:

$$\text{MC}_C = \Delta F \tag{16–6}$$

Dividing Equation 16–5 by Equation 16–6 and multiplying the result by -1 gives

$$-\Delta C/\Delta F = \text{MC}_F/\text{MC}_C = \text{MRT}_{FC} \tag{16–7}$$

The bowed shape can now be explained by pointing out that as more food is produced, its marginal cost tends to increase. Similarly, a reduction in clothing production decreases the marginal cost of its production. This assumes that the marginal cost of production increases continually with the output of either of the goods. Increasing food production and decreasing clothing production increases MRT_{FC} because the denominator of Equation 16–7 decreases, whereas its numerator increases. Increasing marginal rates of transformation are explained by the tendency of marginal costs of production to increase with output.

Efficiency and General Equilibrium in Competitive Input Markets

It is easy to show that competitive input markets can result in efficient input use. Profit-maximizing firms employ input services in combinations that minimize the cost of producing any given output. Therefore, food producers react to the prices

MODERN MICROECONOMICS IN ACTION: THE BUSINESS WORLD

Are Economic Decisions within Business Firms Efficient? The Specter of X-Inefficiency

Do managers of business firms use resources *within* the firm efficiently? In evaluating the productive efficiency of markets, economists generally presume that profit-maximizing firms are compelled to achieve the maximum output from the amount of resources they utilize. When this is not the case, *X-inefficiency* is said to exist.* X-inefficiency measures the gap between potential and actual output that results from deficiencies in management skills. This type of inefficiency could stem from the difficulties that owners of business firms have in ensuring that their interests (such as profit maximization) are effectively executed by the agents who work for them. As business firms become large, these difficulties multiply.

Critics of the concept of X-inefficiency argue that X-inefficiency merely reflects output increments that cost more to achieve than they are worth.† Eliminating it would require extra management inputs. Managers weigh the costs of these inputs against the gains and rationally reject improvements that cost more than they are worth. Leibenstein, however, argues that X-efficiency is based on the skills of managers in motivating and providing incentives to workers.

X-inefficiency is a cost sometimes associated with monopoly power. Because monopoly firms have no competitors, they lack the incentive to keep costs down. One study of electricity producers found that their costs of production tended to be significantly lower, other things being equal, in cities in which two or more competing firms produced electricity.‡ This finding tended to support the Leibenstein hypothesis. Some of the cost increases attributable to monopoly may also stem from expenditures on lobbying and other activities that such firms incur to protect and maintain their monopoly power. Managers incurring these expenditures may merely be reacting to the incentives of owners to maintain long-term monopoly power and thereby maximize profits over a long period.§

* Harvey Leibenstein, "Allocative Efficiency vs. X-Efficiency," *American Economic Review* 56, no. 2 (June 1966), pp. 392–415.

† George J. Stigler, "The Xistence of X-Efficiency," *American Economic Review* 66, no. 1 (March 1976), pp. 212–16.

‡ Walter J. Primeaux, "An Assessment of X-Efficiency Gained through Competition," *Review of Economics and Statistics* 59, no. 1 (February 1977), pp. 105–8.

§ Thomas J. DiLorenzo, "Corporate Management, Property Rights, and the X-istence of the X-inefficiency," *Southern Economic Journal* 48, no. 1 (July 1981), pp. 116–23.

of labor and capital determined in competitive input markets by adjusting their use of these inputs until

$$\text{MRTS}^F_{LK} = P_L/P_K \tag{16–8}$$

Similarly, clothing producers that maximize profits also adjust input use until their marginal rate of technical substitution of labor for capital equals the ratio of the price of labor to the price of capital:

$$\text{MRTS}^C_{LK} = P_L/P_K \tag{16–9}$$

In a competitive market the price of standardized input services is the same to all users. It follows that the ratio of the price of labor services to the price of capital services must be identical for all food and clothing producers. Therefore

$$\text{MRTS}^F_{LK} = \text{MRTS}^C_{LK} \tag{16–10}$$

which is the condition for efficient input use.

A competitive input market in which input prices are the same for all users guarantees the efficient use of inputs. But which combination of outputs will be produced? This depends on the prices of labor and the prices of capital. These prices depend on the demand for food and the demand for clothing. Each point of tangency between the two sets of isoquants in the Edgeworth box corresponds to a different common value for the two marginal rates of technical substitution. Getting to each point therefore requires a certain ratio of the price of labor services to the price of capital services. The producers respond by producing the combinations of outputs corresponding to the input use implied by those marginal rates of technical substitution.

For an example, return to Figures 16–3 and 16–4. To produce the output combination implied by point E_1 (1,100 pounds of food and 400 outfits of clothing each day) requires that the ratio of the price of labor to the price of capital (P_L/P_K) be equal to the slope of the line *BC* multiplied by -1, as in Figure 16–3. If, instead, the output combination implied by point E_3 (200 pounds of food and 800 clothing outfits) were desired, the ratio of the price of labor to the price of capital would have to equal the slope of the line *GH* multiplied by -1. The line *GH* is steeper than the line *BC*. This means that the price of labor would have to rise relative to the price of capital to induce producers to decrease food production and increase clothing production. Such an increase in the relative price of labor would move the economy from point E_1 on its production possibility curve to point E_3. The next step in the analysis is to study the relationship between input prices and the demand for output.

CONCEPT REVIEW

1. What are the likely general equilibrium effects of a decrease in the price of crude oil?
2. The marginal rate of technical substitution of labor for capital in the production of steel exceeds the marginal rate of technical substitution in the production of other goods. What must be done to achieve productive efficiency?
3. Explain why the points on a production possibility curve represent output combinations that can be achieved only if productive efficiency has been attained.

EXCHANGE AND ALLOCATIVE EFFICIENCY

Allocative efficiency is achieved when a given quantity of products produced over a period is allocated among consumers in a way that makes it impossible to make any consumer better off without harming another consumer. A simple example can be used to derive the basic conditions required for the achievement of allocative efficiency.

Allocative efficiency A situation that prevails when the resources are allocated among persons so that it is impossible to make any person better off without harming another person.

Suppose two persons (and their families or tribes), *A* and *B*, consume the entire output of food and clothing in an economy. The production of food and clothing corresponds to point E_1 in Figure 16–4. An Edgeworth box showing alternative ways of allocating that amount of output between the two persons can now be drawn. This Edgeworth box is similar to the one used to analyze input use. However, the length of the rectangle now represents 1,100 pounds of food output and its width represents 400 outfits of clothing.

The Edgeworth box is drawn in Figure 16–5. Each point in the box corresponds to an allocation of the total amount of clothing and food produced between the two persons. The amount of food going to *A* (F_A) is measured from the origin *O* along the horizontal side of the box. C_A, the amount of clothing that this person receives each day, is measured along the width of the box from the origin. Similarly, the amount of food (F_B) and clothing (C_B) that *B* receives is measured from the origin *O′* in the upper right corner of the box. Each point in the box corresponds to an allocation of total output between the two persons. At point *X* in the box, *A* receives 600 pounds of food each day and *B* receives the remaining 500 pounds. Also at point *X*, *A* receives 250 outfits of clothing each day and *B* receives the remaining 150.

Is this allocation of output between the two persons efficient? To find out, plot the indifference curves between clothing and food for each of the two persons in the box. *B*'s indifference curves are upside down because they are drawn relative to the origin *O′*.

FIGURE 16–5 Exchange and Efficiency

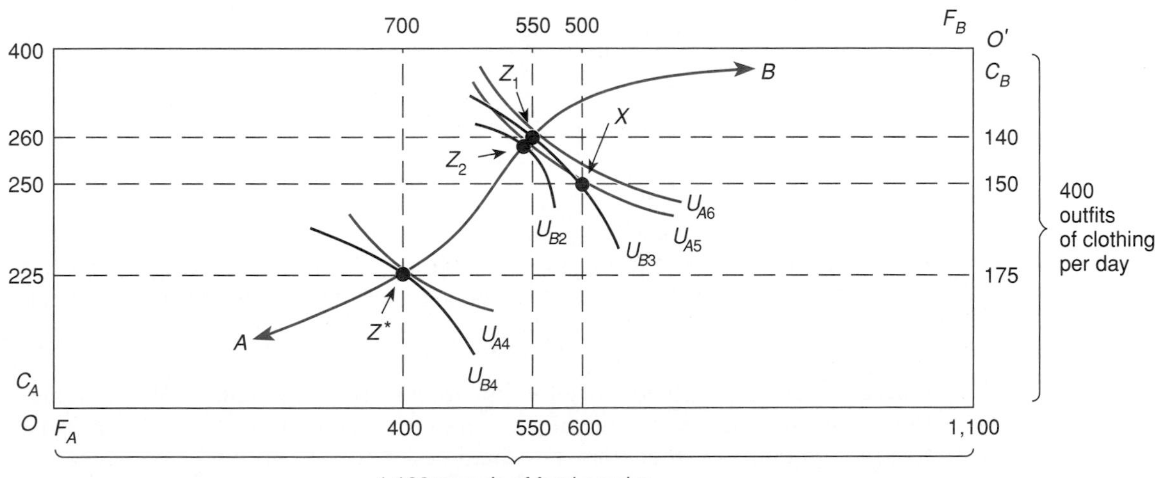

Point *X* is an inefficient allocation of 1,100 pounds of food and 400 outfits of clothing between *A* and *B*, the two persons whose indifference curves are shown. Exchange between the two persons allows movement to point Z_1, where *A* is made better off while not harming *B*. The curve *AB* shows other possible efficient allocations of the available food and clothing, including the allocations corresponding to points Z_2 and Z^*.

The allocation of products corresponding to point X is *not* efficient, because it is possible to make either A or B better off without harming the other. At point X, B enjoys utility level U_{B2}. However, if B exchanges some food each day for some of A's clothing, A becomes better off while not harming B. This exchange moves B along indifference curve U_{B2}, whereas A is made better off by moving from indifference curve U_{A5} to indifference curve U_{A6}. The exchange would continue until point Z_1 has been reached. At that point indifference curve U_{B2} is just tangent to indifference curve U_{A6}. Point Z_1 corresponds to the efficient daily allocation of 1,100 pounds of food and 400 outfits of clothing. At point Z_1 food has been allocated so that A and B each receive 550 pounds per day and clothing has been allocated so that A receives 260 outfits per day and B receives 140 outfits per day. A net gain has been achieved by moving from the resources allocation corresponding to point X to the one corresponding to point Z_1 because A has been made better off and B has been made neither better off nor worse off.

Similarly, it is possible to make B better off without harming A when the products are allocated between the two in such a way as to correspond to point X. This can be accomplished by reallocating the products between A and B so as to keep A on indifference curve U_{A5} while allowing B to move to a higher indifference curve such as U_{B3} at point Z_2. At that point indifference curve U_{B3} is tangent to indifference curve U_{A5}.

As with the allocation of inputs, there are many points of tangency, as shown in Figure 16–5. These points correspond to tangencies among indifference curves. Each point corresponds to a different distribution of well-being between A and B. For any initial allocation of available food and clothing between A and B, it will always be possible for them to trade, assuming zero transaction costs, to achieve an efficient allocation. For example, the allocation of products corresponding to point Z^* is also efficient because once that allocation has been achieved, it is not possible for either A or B to gain without the other becoming worse off. At point Z^* the indifference curve U_{A4} is tangent to the indifference curve U_{B4}. At Z^*, however, A achieves a higher level of utility and B receives a lower level than was the case at Z_1.

Therefore, an allocation of a given quantity of products between two persons is efficient if it corresponds to a tangency between the indifference curves of the two persons. Because the slopes of the indifference curves are equal, so too are the marginal rates of substitution of food for clothing at the points of tangency:

$$\text{MRS}_{FC}^{A} = \text{MRS}_{FC}^{B} \qquad \textbf{(16–11)}$$

where the superscripts identify the individual MRS of A and B. When achieved, this condition implies that the allocation of *a given quantity of products* between the two persons is such that an additional net gain through exchange of the products between the two is no longer possible. An additional net gain is possible only if either A or B (or both) can move to higher indifference curves through exchange of the products.

In Figure 16–5 the line AB connects all the possible points of tangency between the two sets of indifference curves. Changes in the allocations of the 1,100 pounds of food and the 400 outfits of clothing corresponding to points on the line would harm at least one of the two consumers. For example, moving from point A

to point B would make consumer A better off but would harm consumer B. Similarly, moving from point B to point A along the line AB would make consumer B better off but would harm consumer A. The line AB, called a **contract curve**, shows all the possible efficient allocations of two goods between two consumers. Along the contract curve, it is impossible for reallocation of the available supplies of the two goods to make either consumer better off without harming the other consumer.

Contract curve A curve showing all the possible efficient allocations of two goods between two consumers.

Efficiency in the Production and Allocation of Products

Pareto optimal resource allocation A resource allocation that achieves allocative efficiency.

When both resources and products are allocated in such a way that it is impossible to make any one person better off without harming another person, a **Pareto optimal resource allocation** has been attained. When Pareto optimality has been achieved, no additional net gain is possible from either a change in productive methods or a change in the allocation of products among consumers. *Efficiency requires that no additional net gains be possible either by reallocating the use of inputs or by allowing the exchange of available products among consumers.*

It is easy to derive the conditions under which no additional net gains are possible either through altering productive methods or through exchange of the goods and services produced. Suppose that the marginal rates of substitution of food for clothing for both A and B equal 1, so that the allocation of the *existing* quantities of food and clothing is efficient. But also suppose the marginal rate of transformation of food into clothing is 5 on the production possibility curve when the economy is producing 400 outfits and 1,100 pounds of food per day? In that case, if 1 pound of food per day were taken away from either A or B and if the resources used to produce that food were reallocated to clothing production, the daily output of clothing would increase by 5 outfits. Because $\text{MRS}_{FC} = 1$ for both A and B, it takes just one clothing outfit per day to maintain their level of well-being. Therefore, 4 clothing outfits will be left over after either A or B has been compensated for his loss of food. This extra clothing can be given to either or both of them. In any event, either or both of them are better off without harming the other.

As long as the marginal rate of transformation of clothing into food exceeds or is less than the marginal rate of substitution of food for clothing, even though the existing quantity of food is efficiently allocated, a Pareto optimal resource allocation has not been attained. All possibilities of additional gains, either through exchange among consumers or reallocation of inputs in production, must be exhausted to achieve efficiency. The efficient condition required for Pareto optimality is therefore

$$\text{MRS}^{A}_{FC} = \text{MRS}^{B}_{FC} = \text{MRT}_{FC} \tag{16–12}$$

The various resource allocations satisfying the condition for efficiency in Equation 16–12 will differ in terms of the distribution of well-being among persons and the mix of food and clothing produced to obtain that distribution. The well-being of each person depends entirely on the amount of food and clothing he or she consumes.

MODERN MICROECONOMICS IN ACTION: INTERNATIONAL REPORT

Free Trade and Efficiency: The Net Gains and Redistributive Effects of Free International Trade

Free international trade can benefit a nation's citizens by allowing a given productive capacity to make more goods and services available for consumption. It can easily be demonstrated that free trade has the potential to allow an economy to achieve points that lie *outside* the economy's production possibility curve.

The graph shows a nation's production possibility curve for annual production of clothing and food. The current market equilibrium is a resource allocation corresponding to point E_1 on the production possibility curve. At that point C_1 units of clothing and F_1 units of food are produced annually. The current equilibrium ratio of the price of food to the price of clothing is 1, which means that at current domestic output levels the economy has to sacrifice 1 unit of food to obtain an extra unit of clothing. Given the distribution of income, the efficient resource allocation (corresponding to point Z_1) results in individual A consuming C_{A1} units of clothing and F_{A1} units of food, thereby enjoying a utility level of U_A. Individual B consumes the remainder of the food and clothing output and enjoys a utility level of U_B.

Suppose that on world markets the ratio of the price of food to the price of clothing is 3. This means that through international trade this nation's citizens can obtain 3 units of clothing (instead of the 1 unit possible through reallocation of domestic resources) for each unit of food sacrificed. At that price ratio the efficient allocation of domestic inputs corresponds to point E_2, at which C_2 units of clothing and F_2 units of food are produced annually.

It can now be easily demonstrated how international trade results in net gains to citizens. From point E_2 the nation can export food in exchange for imports of clothing at the rate of 3 units of clothing

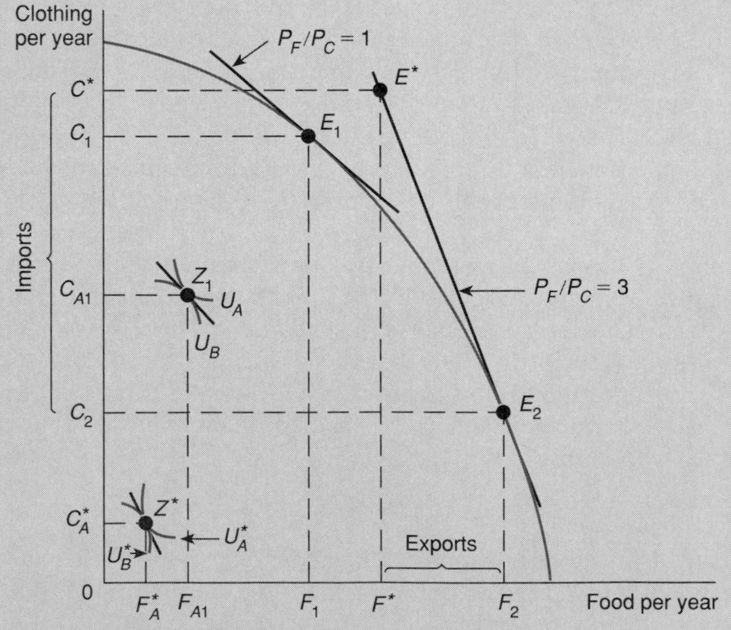

(*Continued*) for each unit of food. Depending on the demand for food and clothing in the nation, a new equilibrium is now possible that would allow the nation to enjoy more of *both* food and clothing than could have been enjoyed without international trade. Suppose that the new equilibrium occurs at point E^*, at which F^*F_2 units of food are exported annually in exchange for C^*C_2 units of clothing. *This allows the economy to enjoy a product mix that involves the consumption of both more food and more clothing than could have been consumed at point* E_1. The new equilibrium is at point E^*, at which citizens consume C^* units of food and F^* units of clothing annually. The net increase in both food and clothing will make either A or B, or both, better off.

Why is free trade often opposed despite its potential for achieving net gains in well-being? The answer to this question is that the net gains possible from free trade do not always accrue to *all* citizens. It is quite possible for free trade to make some persons worse off. To see why this is so, let us examine the process through which free trade works.

To enjoy the benefits of free trade, the nation in our example reduces its production of clothing and increases its production of food. As this occurs, workers and others who possess specialized skills or inputs used in clothing production find that the demand for their services declines as imported clothing is substituted for domestic clothing. Some of these workers must find alternative jobs in food production, often at wages lower than they enjoyed when their services were employed in clothing production. These workers and other specialized resource owners suffer a reduction in income as a result of free international trade. For example, in the graph individual A finds that because of a sharp reduction of income at the new efficient resource allocation, he can consume less of both food and clothing than before free trade began. He consumes C_A^* of clothing and F_A^* of food per year at point Z^* and has utility level $U_A^* < U_A$, the utility level that he enjoyed before the advent of free trade. Naturally, individual A will oppose free trade.

Individual B, however, gains considerably as a result of free trade. This person enjoys more clothing and more food than before trade and has utility level $U_B^* > U_B$. As a result of the increase in both clothing and food that free trade makes possible, the gainers from free trade gain enough to compensate the losers and still be better off. One way to allow the net gains from free trade to accrue to all is to find a mechanism whereby the gainers can compensate the losers. Such a compensation mechanism would eliminate much of the political opposition to free trade.*

* For a discussion of possible compensation mechanisms, see Robert Z. Lawrence and Robert E. Litan, *Saving Free Trade: A Pragmatic Approach* (Washington, D.C.: Brookings Institution, 1986).

Utility possibility curve A curve that shows how utility varies among persons for all possible efficient allocations of inputs and outputs.

Figure 16–6 shows the efficient allocation of 1,100 pounds of food and 400 clothing outfits per day between A and B. The point Z^* is the point in the Edgeworth box where the slopes of the two indifference curves are equal to each other and to the slope of the production possibility curve at point E_1. At that point, A (and his large family) consumes 400 pounds of food and 225 clothing outfits each day and B (and his horde) consumes 700 pounds of food and 175 outfits each day. It will be possible to find at least one point like Z^* for *each* Edgeworth box that can be drawn for each point on the production possibility curve. There is no unique point of efficiency.

A **utility possibility curve** shows how utility varies among persons for all possible efficient allocations of inputs and outputs. Each point on a utility possibility curve gives the maximum utility attainable by one person, given the utility level of the other person, the resource constraint, and technology. Achieving the

FIGURE 16–6 **An Efficient Allocation of Output**

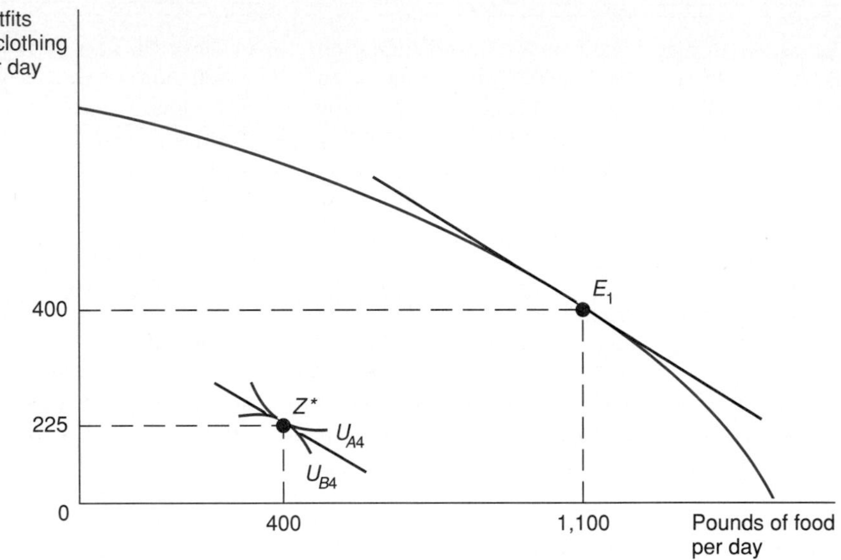

At E_1, 400 clothing outfits and 1,100 pounds of food are produced. Point Z^* gives the efficient allocation of that output between consumers A and B. At Z^*, $\text{MRS}_{FC}^{A} = \text{MRS}_{FC}^{B} = \text{MRT}_{FC}$. Consumer A receives 225 units of clothing and 400 pounds of food, and consumer B receives the remainder of the amounts produced.

FIGURE 16–7 **A Utility Possibility Curve**

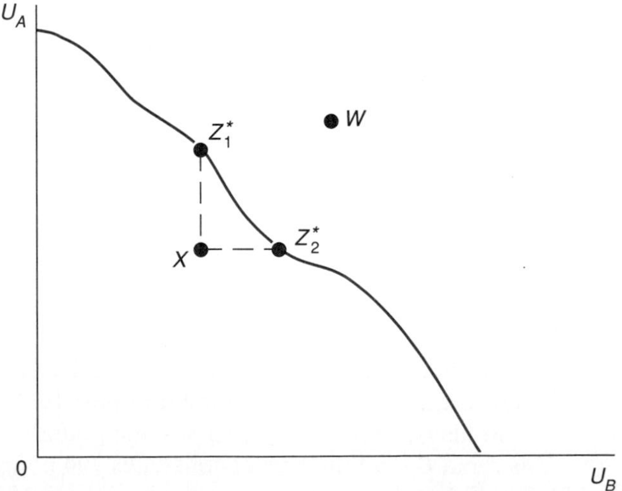

All of the points on this curve give the maximum attainable level of well-being for A given B's utility level and available resources. X is an inefficient allocation because trade between A and B or reallocation of productive resources can make either A or B better off without harming the other. A point like W is unattainable, given the available resources. A's utility and B's utility depend only on the amount of food and clothing they consume.

efficient mix of well-being among persons requires a certain allocation of output. Each point on a utility possibility curve therefore implies a certain output of goods and services. This in turn implies a certain allocation of the input services necessary to produce that output.

The utility possibility curve for the simple economy is shown in Figure 16–7. Each point on the curve is efficient. Along the curve, it is impossible to make one person better off without harming the other person. The curve is negatively sloped at all points, which reflects the fact that on the curve a gain in one person's utility can come only at the expense of another person's utility once efficiency has been attained. Points like X within the curve do not satisfy the efficiency conditions. By reallocating the use of inputs or outputs among persons, movement is possible from point X to a point on the arc $Z_1^*Z_2^*$. This makes either A or B, or both, better off without harming either A or B. A point like W is unattainable. To produce the combination of utility represented by that point, the economy would require more resources or an improvement in technology.

General Equilibrium, Perfect Competition, and the Distribution of Welfare

It has already been shown that perfectly competitive input markets can achieve productive efficiency. Perfectly competitive output markets can easily be shown to satisfy the conditions for a Pareto optimality, which is required for efficiency in general equilibrium. This is true provided that the marginal costs and marginal benefits upon which individual producers and consumers base their decisions reflect all of the costs and benefits associated with the production and exchange of goods and services.

Prices, Profit Maximization, Utility Maximization, and Efficiency

In a perfectly competitive market each food and clothing producer maximizes profits by setting price equal to marginal cost. Therefore, the outcomes of interaction between buyers and sellers of food and clothing in competitive markets are outputs that correspond to

$$P_F = \text{MC}_F$$

and

$$P_C = \text{MC}_C \qquad \textbf{(16–13)}$$

where P_F is the price per pound of food and MC_F is its marginal cost. Similarly, P_C is the price of each clothing outfit and MC_C is its marginal cost.

Dividing Equation 16–12 by Equation 16–13 gives

$$P_F/P_C = \text{MC}_F/MC_C = \text{MRT}_{FC} \qquad \textbf{(16–14)}$$

Food and clothing producers adjust outputs independently until the ratio of the price of food to that of clothing equals the marginal rate of transformation of clothing into food for the economy.

Given their incomes and tastes and the prices of food and clothing, any two consumers are assumed to maximize utility. They do so by adjusting their consumption of the two goods until the ratio of the prices of these goods equals the marginal rate of substitution of food for clothing.

$$P_F/P_C = \text{MRS}^A_{FC} = \text{MRS}^B_{FC} \tag{16–15}$$

The prices of food and clothing are the same for all consumers and producers. Combining Equations 16–14 and 16–15 gives

$$P_F/P_C = \text{MRS}^A_{FC} = \text{MRS}^B_{FC} = \text{MRT}_{FC} \tag{16–16}$$

which is the condition for achieving an efficient resource allocation that satisfies the requirements of Pareto optimality.

The general equilibrium resulting from interaction between buyers and sellers in competitive markets is therefore efficient. Achieving an efficient allocation of resources in an economy is equivalent to allowing persons to interact so as to exhaust all of the possible additional gains from trade. They do so either by reallocating resources in production or by directly exchanging goods and services with each other.

Taking an amalgam of expenditure of income on all other goods (M) as the second good and measuring expenditure in dollars gives the following efficiency condition:

$$\text{MRS}^A_{FM} = \text{MRS}^B_{FM} = \text{MRT}_{FM} = P_F \tag{16–17}$$

The first two terms of Equation 16–17 represent the willingness of either A or B to substitute dollars of expenditure on other goods for extra units of food. This measures the marginal benefit of food in dollars to each of them. The third term measures the sacrifice of dollars of expenditure on other goods that is required to pay for the input services necessary to produce an extra unit of food. This is simply the marginal cost of food measured in dollars. The last term, the price of food, measures the number of dollars that must be sacrificed to purchase an extra unit of food on the market. Equation 16–17 can now be rewritten as

$$\text{MB}^A_F = \text{MB}^B_F = \text{MC}_F = P_F \tag{16–18}$$

In general, efficiency requires that the prices of all goods and services simultaneously reflect their marginal benefit to users and their marginal cost of production. In competitive markets the prices established through the interaction of many buyers and sellers meet this condition.

The Distribution of Welfare in Competitive Markets

Which of the many possible efficient resource allocations will correspond to the general equilibrium in competitive markets? How will the distribution of welfare among persons be determined in a free market economy in which all goods are made available for sale in perfectly competitive markets?

Assume that a person's welfare depends entirely on the quantities of goods and services consumed. Their capacity to consume goods and services depends entirely on their money incomes. Under these circumstances the distribution of welfare depends entirely on the distribution of money income.[2]

In this simple economy persons obtain money income from the sale of either labor services or the services of capital inputs. A person's income therefore depends on the amount of labor services and the amount of capital services that he or she sells in each period. This depends on the amount of labor hours the person is capable of offering in each period and on the amount of capital he or she owns. It also depends on the prices of capital and labor services. Assume that all capital and labor is of a given quality so that only one price prevails for each of these input services.

Suppose that person A offers L_A hours of labor each week and that person B offers L_B hours of labor each week. In addition, A owns enough capital to offer K_A machine hours for sale each day and B offers K_B machine hours for sale each day. Given the market prices of labor and capital, the incomes of A and B, I_A and I_B, will be

$$I_A = P_L L_A + P_K K_A \quad \textbf{(16–19)}$$

and

$$I_B = P_L L_B + P_K K_B \quad \textbf{(16–20)}$$

Suppose that A works 40 hours per week and that the market wage is \$5 per hour. His weekly labor earnings are \$200. If the hourly rental rate for capital is \$20 and A rents 100 hours of capital services per week, his income from capital will be \$2,000 per week and his total income will be \$2,200 per week. Suppose B also works 40 hours per week at \$5 per hour but owns no capital. His weekly income will therefore be \$200.

Assume that the distribution of income allows A to achieve utility level U_A^* and B to achieve utility level U_B^*. To achieve his utility level, A consumes a certain amount of clothing and a certain amount of food each day. B, given his lower income, consumes a lesser amount of food and clothing to achieve his utility level. Assume that A has stronger desires for clothing than B. The price of clothing must be such that the sum of the quantities demanded by A and B equals the quantities supplied. The total amount of clothing produced will be C^*, as shown in Figure 16–8. A will consume C_A^* outfits per day, whereas B will consume the remainder. Similarly, the total amount of food produced will be F^*, of which A will consume F_A^* and B will consume the remainder. The efficient output mix is shown as E^* in Figure 16–8. Assuming competitive markets, the production of E^* and its distribution between the two consumers will be such that the common slopes of the indifference curves at point Z^* equal the slope of the production possibility curve at E^*.

---

[2] This ignores the fact that persons obtain utility from using their leisure time at home. It is easy to extend the analysis to leisure by considering leisure as a good with an implicit price rather than a market price.

FIGURE 16–8 Market Equilibrium and Efficiency

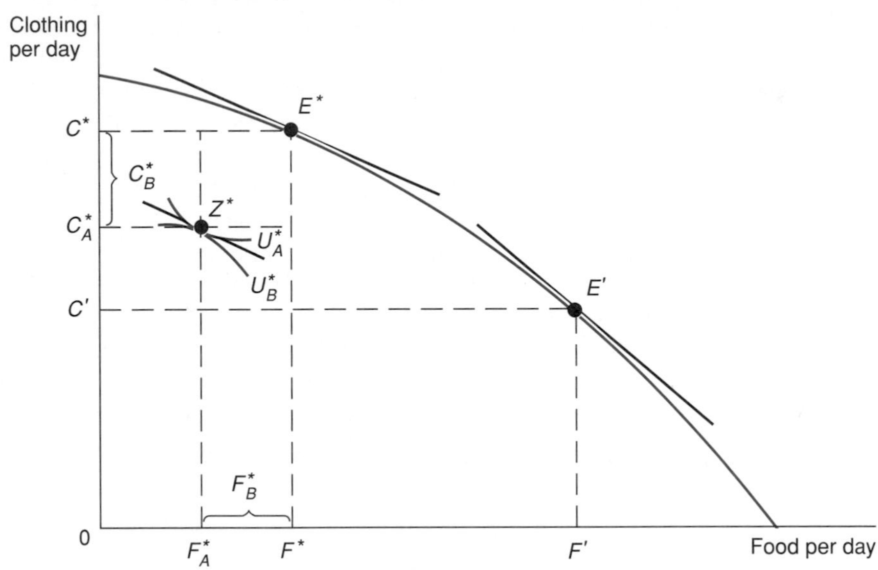

Market equilibrium results in an efficient equilibrium at point E^*, where A purchases C^*_A units of clothing and F^*_A units of food per day and B purchases the remainder of the amounts produced. A lump-sum transfer to B results in a new efficient output mix at point E'.

Changes in the Distribution of Income

Suppose governing authorities wish to change the distribution of income by taxing A and transferring the proceeds to B. To do so, they must use lump-sum taxes and transfers. Lump-sum taxes allow governments to raise revenue and transfer it among citizens without preventing the attainment of efficiency. Such taxes do not distort prices in ways that prevent persons from independently acting to set their marginal benefits equal to marginal costs. Lump-sum taxes and transfers result in income effects that cause price changes. However, their use does not result in any substitution effects. (Lump-sum taxes and transfers were discussed in detail in Chapter 5.)

An example of a lump-sum tax is one that is levied on all adults when they reach a certain age. This is sometimes called a *head tax*. All those with heads must pay the tax in a lump sum, say at age 18. They could borrow money to pay the tax out over a number of years with interest. Similarly, a lump-sum transfer would be granted to certain persons when they reach age 18. It could be paid out over a number of years. The lump sum represents the discounted present value of future annual transfers in such cases. Nothing persons do over their lifetimes can alter the amount of the initial tax or transfer.

The transfer of income from person A to person B reduces A's utility and increases B's utility. You might argue that such a transfer is desirable on grounds of equity or fairness because A has a great deal of income, whereas B is quite poor. For this reason, government policies that tax relatively well-off persons to make poor persons better off often receive enough political support to be enacted.

What are the consequences of the lump-sum taxes and transfers for the economy's product mix? This can be determined by making some assumptions about the differences in preferences between A and B and about the way their demands for products change when their incomes change. Assume that B's preference for food are stronger than A's and that when B receives the increase in income, he spends proportionately more of it on food than on clothing. Also assume that after paying the tax, A cuts down on clothing purchases to a greater degree than he cuts down on food purchases. The demand for food therefore increases and the demand for clothing decreases as a result of the redistribution of income. This moves the economy to point E' on its production possibility curve in Figure 16–8. The movement takes place because the change in the distribution of income and the consequent changes in the demand for food and clothing cause the price of food to rise relative to the price of clothing. This, in turn, could cause the prices of labor and capital services to change, which could have feedback effects on the distribution of income.

As shown in Figure 16–8, daily clothing production decreases from C^* to C' and daily food production increases from F^* to F'. The ratio of the price of food to the price of clothing increases, as shown in Figure 16–8 by lines tangent to the production possibility curve at E^* and E'. The slope of the lines tangent to the curve at each point multiplied by -1 is the ratio of the price of food to the price of clothing. As can be seen, this line is steeper at E' than at E^*. This implies that the relative price of food has risen in response to the redistribution of income. The higher relative price of food provides producers with an incentive to increase food production and decrease clothing production.

Efficiency versus Equity

The attainment of efficiency often conflicts with other social goals. For example, the efficient outcome attainable through a system of competitive markets depends on the distribution of income. Suppose that many workers earn low wages and have no capital income. Also suppose that the ownership of capital is concentrated in the hands of a few persons who enjoy high income from the sale of its services. It would seem that the use of lump-sum taxes and transfers could easily correct this problem: merely tax the rich and distribute the proceeds to the poor. Using lump-sum taxes and transfers would not prevent market interaction from attaining efficiency.

In practice, however, lump-sum taxes are difficult to administer. Incomes change over time. A lump-sum tax is a once-and-for-all levy on certain persons. When income changes, the lump-sum tax must be readjusted. If it is readjusted each year with changes in income, it becomes an income tax. When such a tax is imposed on both wages and interest, it prevents the attainment of efficiency by inducing persons to substitute leisure for work and current consumption for saving.

Given the infeasibility of using lump-sum taxes, the trade-off between efficiency and equity in income distribution becomes a political issue. For example, suppose the current allocation of resources is inefficient and a proposed new policy would achieve an efficient resource allocation. However, the efficient allocation would make the poor even worse off and the persons who gain from the efficient allocation would not share their gains with the poor. If this is the case and you are concerned about fairness to the poor, you might reasonably prefer the inefficient resource allocation to the efficient one! Similarly, workers in specific industries or in agriculture might reasonably prefer inefficient resource allocation to movements toward efficient resource allocation that would cause them to lose their jobs.

If there is no way for the gainers to compensate the losers as a result of movements from inefficient to efficient resource allocation, it is reasonable to expect some citizens to prefer the status quo to the movements toward efficiency. For example, in Figure 16–9 a movement from point X, which represents an inefficient resource allocation, to point Z^*, which represents an efficient resource allocation, will be opposed by A, who is harmed by the reallocation, but favored by B, who will gain from it.

The issue is further complicated by the fact that what is fair or equitable remains a subjective notion. What your neighbor may regard as abominably unjust

FIGURE 16–9 **Why Movements to Efficiency Are Opposed**

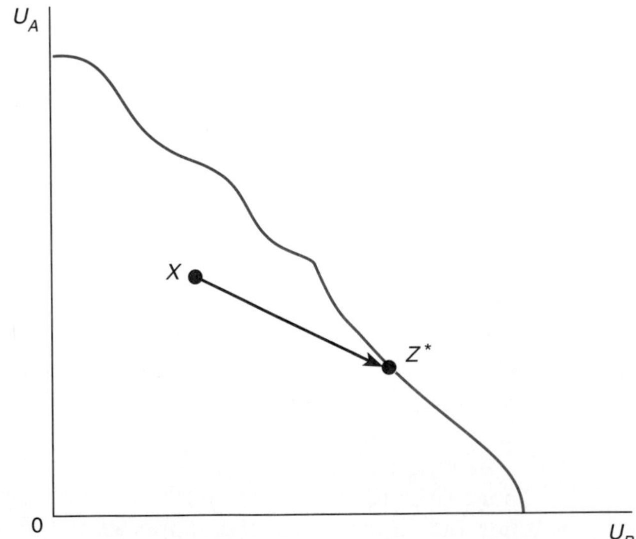

The allocation of resources corresponding to point X is inefficient. Although the allocation that would result in the achievement of point Z^* is efficient, movement from X to Z^* will be opposed by A unless B compensates A for his decline in utility.

you regard as fair. Moreover, notions of fairness are often based on selfish motives rather than altruistic considerations. Many persons benefit from the inefficient allocation of resources.[3]

When resources are allocated efficiently the size of the pie representing national economic well-being is at a maximum. But movements toward efficient resource allocations from inefficient ones must be accompanied by compensation for those who lose as a result of the change. Otherwise, those who lose will oppose the change. For example, protectionist trade policies are designed to shield national industries from "unfair" foreign competition. Free trade will make consumers better off by lowering the prices of imported goods and can benefit exporters of goods. However, workers and resource owners in industries that decline because of free trade will be made worse off by free trade. If free trade were truly efficient, the gainers would be able to compensate the losers and still have enough of their gain left over to be better off. In practice, such compensation is rarely paid, so there are gainers and losers instead of only gainers as a result of policies that lift trade barriers. Some persons can be expected to oppose movements toward efficient resource allocation because they prefer a larger slice of a smaller pie. In other words, they are better off under an inefficient resource allocation than they would be under an efficient resource allocation.

Growth in Resource Availability or Productivity

An increase in labor hours and machine hours increases the dimensions of the Edgeworth box for the allocation of input services and results in a new efficiency curve. A new production possibility curve can be derived from this new efficiency curve.

Growth in productive resources can be represented as an outward shift in the economy's production possibility curve. This is illustrated in Figure 16–10(a), which shows the shift for a production possibility curve between food and clothing. Previously unattainable combinations of food and clothing are now possible.

The increase in available input services also implies an outward shift in the utility possibility curve for the economy. More resources mean more output to be distributed among consumers. Because economic welfare depends on the goods and services available, the increase in resources allows the economy to attain combinations of well-being among persons that were previously impossible. This is shown in Figure 16–10(b), in which the utility possibility curve of two persons, *A* and *B*, are shifted outward by an increase in productive resources. The same will occur for the curves representing the mix of well-being between any two persons in the economy.

The same shifts in the two curves can result from improvements in the productivity of available resources. If more output can be obtained from a given amount of labor and capital, both the production possibility curve and the utility

---

[3] For a technical analysis of the concept of fairness, see William J. Baumol, "Applied Fairness Theory and Rationing Policy," *American Economic Review* 72, no. 4 (September 1982), pp. 639–51.

MODERN MICROECONOMICS IN ACTION: **GOVERNMENT AND THE ECONOMY**

Government Assistance to the Poor in the United States

The general equilibrium in a market economy often results in a considerable number of households with incomes so low that they live in poverty. In the United States, government provides assistance to the poor through a variety of welfare programs. To deal with the equity-efficiency trade-off, many of these programs have strict eligibility standards so only the poor who cannot work receive benefits. The eligibility standards, although subject to guidelines from the federal government, vary from state to state. The groups eligible for assistance include the disabled, the aged, and families with dependent children headed by females or disabled males. Single people who are not disabled or elderly, or who do not have dependent children, are not eligible for the major programs of government assistance even if they are poor. Similarly, able-bodied males who head a family are usually not eligible.

People become eligible for assistance if their income is below certain levels. A *means test* establishes the fact that people in the groups eligible for welfare payments have incomes and property below the minimally acceptable amounts. People who are in the eligible groups and also pass the means test are *automatically entitled to government assistance*. Therefore, government welfare programs are sometimes called *entitlement programs*.

Federal programs to assist the poor in the United States can be divided into two broad categories: programs of *cash* assistance and programs of *in-kind* assistance. The first type simply provides eligible people with financial support in the form of money income. The recipients can spend their welfare checks as they please. The second type provides those who qualify with services or assistance to purchase a certain good or service. Some in-kind assistance allows eligible people to rent government-supplied housing at a reduced price.

There are two major programs of cash assistance (or transfers) to the poor in the United States: *Aid to Families with Dependent Children* (AFDC) and *Supplemental Security Income* (SSI).

AFDC is designed mainly to aid families headed by one parent, usually a female, with dependent children. The program is jointly run and funded by the federal government and the state governments. On average the federal government bears about 54 percent of the cost of AFDC payments. Eligibility requirements and the actual amount of cash assistance under the AFDC program vary from state to state.

Under the AFDC program, there's a maximum benefit in each state for people who have no earnings. As a recipient earns income, welfare payments decline. In 1990 the maximum cash benefit for a family of four ranged from $118 per month in Alabama to $846 per month in Alaska.

You should observe that these AFDC benefits are modest compared to the poverty income level. For example, a family consisting of a mother and two dependent children receiving the maximum average benefit under AFDC would have had a cash income of $4,368 in 1990, which was less than half of the 1990 poverty income threshold of approximately $10,000 for a family of three.

Supplemental Security Income is federally funded and benefits the aged, blind, and disabled. In 1990 the maximum SSI benefit paid to a single person with zero earnings was $386 per month, while a married couple received $479 per month.

The three major government programs of in-kind assistance to the poor are

1. *Medicaid*. This program pays for medical services to eligible poor people under age 65 who pass a means test. Everyone who receives cash benefits from AFDC and SSI is automatically eligible for Medicaid. This is the most expensive government program to aid the poor in the United States.
2. *Food stamps*. This federally financed program, administered by state governments, provides the poor with stamps that can be redeemed for food and related items. The cash value of the stamps varies with the eligible recipient's earned income.
3. *Housing assistance*. A number of federally financed programs provide subsidies to help the poor pay for housing. The programs include government-provided housing at subsidized rents and payments to assist poor people who rent private housing.

FIGURE 16–10 Growth and Technological Change

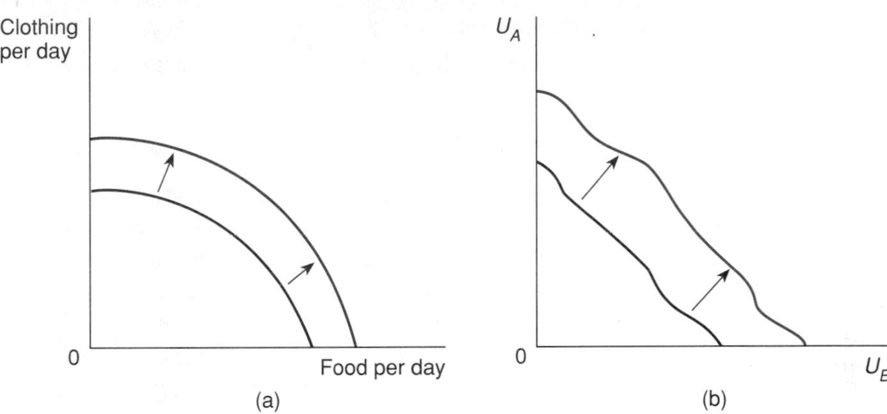

Growth in the inputs available for use or improvements in technology cause both the production possibility curve and the utility possibility curve to shift outward.

possibility curve will shift outward. For example, productivity can be increased by improvements in technology or improvements in the general level of skill and education in the work force.

When the quantity of resources is constant but their productivity increases, the Edgeworth box for input use will still have the same dimensions. There will be no change in available input services. However, the isoquants *within* the Edgeworth box would have to be relabeled and redrawn because any given combination of inputs would now produce more outputs. Productivity increases have the same impact on the production possibility curve as a growth in input services. An increase in the potential for producing goods and services means that previously unattainable combinations of well-being are now possible.

CONCEPT REVIEW

1. Explain why an economy can fail to achieve efficiency even though its managers use inputs in a way that achieves productive efficiency.
2. Use a utility possibility curve to show how net gains are possible if resource allocation is not Pareto optimal.
3. Explain why a system of perfectly competitive markets can achieve efficiency. What determines the distribution of well-being in such a system?

General Equilibrium Analysis of Market Distortions

Monopoly Power and Losses in Efficiency

In Chapter 11 we showed how exercise of monopoly power prevents prices from simultaneously reflecting the marginal benefits of production and the marginal costs of production. General equilibrium analysis can now be used to further investigate the reasons why imperfect competition causes losses in efficiency. Assume that the food industry is a monopoly. Producers in that industry maximize profits by setting their marginal revenue equal to their marginal cost. Prices exceed marginal revenue. It follows that the prices set by monopoly food producers exceed marginal costs:

$$P_F > \mathrm{MR}_F = \mathrm{MC}_F \qquad \textbf{(16–21)}$$

Assuming that perfect competition prevails in the clothing industry, the prices of clothing will equal marginal costs:

$$P_C = \mathrm{MC}_C \qquad \textbf{(16–22)}$$

Dividing Equation 16–21 by Equation 16–22 gives

$$P_F/P_C > \mathrm{MC}_F/\mathrm{MC}_C \qquad \textbf{(16–23)}$$

The ratio of prices is greater than the ratio of marginal costs because $P_F > \mathrm{MC}_F$. Therefore,

$$P_F/P_C > \mathrm{MRT}_{FC} \qquad \textbf{(16–24)}$$

Consumers, however, make their purchases on the basis of the market prices of the goods. They react to the monopoly price of food by consuming less food. For each consumer in equilibrium,

$$P_F/P_C = \mathrm{MRS}_{FC} \qquad \textbf{(16–25)}$$

It follows that for each consumer

$$\mathrm{MRS}_{FC} > \mathrm{MRT}_{FC} \qquad \textbf{(16–26)}$$

Assume that in equilibrium the ratio of the price of food to the price of clothing is 1. It follows that $\mathrm{MRS}_{FC} = 1$ for all consumers. The marginal rate of transformation of clothing into food will be less than that amount as a result of the monopoly power of the food producers. Suppose that $\mathrm{MRT}_{FC} = 1/4$. Any consumer would be just as well off as she was previously if she replaced 1 unit of clothing in her market basket with 1 unit of food each day. A marginal rate of transformation of 1/4 means that 4 units of food can be gained each day from the input services released by reducing daily clothing output by 1 unit. The unit of clothing removed from consumers can be replaced with 1 unit of food. That would maintain the consumer's well-being. However, 3 units of food would be left over. This extra food could be used to make at least one consumer better off. The monopolist's control of the price of food prevents gains like these from being realized.

If, instead, the food industry were competitive, the relative price of food would be lower. Consumers would then adjust to the lower food prices by consuming more food and less clothing. The distortion in general equilibrium caused by monopoly power causes underproduction of food *and* overproduction of clothing relative to the efficient amounts. Even if monopoly power is present only in some markets, resource allocation is distorted in *all* markets. The reason for this is that the inputs not used by the monopoly must be absorbed by other industries in the new general equilibrium. Their prices adjust to ensure that this is the case. The extra inputs in these industries result in production increases *beyond* the efficient levels. In effect, whereas the prices of the goods produced by the monopoly are too high, the prices of other goods are too low relative to the prices necessary for efficiency.

Tax-Induced Distortions

Government revenue raised by taxes other than lump-sum taxes can distort prices in ways that cause losses in efficiency. Most taxes are related to earnings from the sale of input services or the consumption of goods and services. Taxes such as the income tax or the retail sales tax affect incentives to sell input services or purchase goods and services. These taxes result in substitution effects that cause persons to alter their behavior in ways that reduce their tax burden. Such substitution effects cause losses in efficiency.

The general equilibrium-distorting effects of a tax can be easily demonstrated. Suppose that the consumption of clothing is subject to a 50 percent tax, whereas no tax is levied on the consumption of food. The tax is collected from sellers. No matter what the market price of clothing, sellers must give half of that amount to the government. On the other hand, consumers of clothing must pay the full market price.

Suppose that after the tax has been imposed, the market price of clothing is P_G per outfit. This is the gross price paid by consumers. The net price received by sellers after the imposition of the tax is P_N, where

$$P_N = P_G(1 - t) \quad \textbf{(16–27)}$$

In this case $t = 0.5$. If buyers pay \$100 for an outfit, sellers will receive only \$50 for the outfit after payment of the tax. Sellers make their production decisions on the basis of this net price. Buyers decide how much to buy on the basis of the gross price. The difference between P_G and P_N is the tax collected on each outfit sold.

The tax on clothing acts as a "wedge" between the price paid by buyers and the price received by sellers. It is this wedge that leads to a loss of efficiency in the allocation of resources. Buyers adjust their consumption of food and clothing until the ratio of the price of food to the gross price of clothing equals the marginal rate of substitution between food and clothing:

$$P_F/P_G = \text{MRS}_{FC} \quad \textbf{(16–28)}$$

Producers, however, set the ratio of the price of food to the *net* price of clothing equal to the marginal rate of transformation between food and clothing:

$$P_F/P_N = \text{MRT}_{FC} \tag{16–29}$$

Because $P_G > P_N$, it follows that

$$\text{MRS}_{FC} < \text{MRT}_{FC} \tag{16–30}$$

The tax on clothing therefore prevents an efficient resource allocation from being attained in competitive markets.

Balancing Distortions: The Theory of Second Best

Suppose that in the simple two-product economy producing food and clothing only, a monopoly that cannot be broken up is selling food. The clothing industry is, however, perfectly competitive. Is it desirable to leave this state of affairs intact, or can something be done to achieve additional net gains? By means of a general equilibrium analysis a surprising conclusion emerges about how to achieve a ''second best'' efficient allocation when a distortion preventing the attainment of efficiency in one sector of the economy cannot be removed.

The problem of inefficiency arises because the monopoly in the food industry produces *less than* the efficient output. However, this implies that the perfectly competitive clothing industry must produce *more than* the efficient output that would prevail if there were no monopoly in the food industry. This is because resources not employed by the monopoly producing food are used to produce clothing in the general equilibrium. The price of clothing is therefore lower than would otherwise be the case, since resources not used in food production are absorbed by the clothing industry and the consequent increase in the supply of clothing puts a downward pressure on its price.

This situation can be remedied by using economic policy to raise the price of clothing relative to the price of food in a way that encourages resources to flow from clothing production to food production. For example, suppose a tax were levied on the sale of clothing. As was shown previously, a tax would prevent efficiency from being attained in the clothing market. The tax would decrease the supply of clothing and raise the gross price paid by consumers. The resources released from clothing production would flow into the production of food. This would result in a general equilibrium in which food production has increased and clothing production has decreased. This second-best optimum balances the monopoly distortion with *another* distortion (in this case a tax) in another market in which efficiency would have been attained in the absence of the monopoly distortion.

General theory of second best A theory holding that it is better to depart from efficiency in one sector of the economy to balance the distortions that impair efficiency in other sectors of the economy when those distortions cannot be eliminated otherwise.

The lesson of this example is a simple one: When the efficient output cannot be attained in one sector of the economy, the resulting misallocation of resources can be corrected to some degree by pursuing policies that cause a *departure* from the efficient output in another sector. The **general theory of second best** states that it is better to depart from efficiency in one sector of an economy to balance the distortions prevailing in other sectors when those distortions cannot be eliminated otherwise.[4]

Other Distortions

Market failure Exists when exchange between buyers and sellers in an unregulated market does not result in an efficient outcome.

Other distortions that can prevent the attainment of efficient outcomes are common in systems of perfectly competitive markets. **Market failure** exists when exchange between buyers and sellers in an unregulated market does not result in an efficient outcome. A common form of market failure in perfectly competitive markets results when the marginal costs or marginal benefits upon which market participants make their choices do not reflect all of the benefits and costs that result from their trading. Under such circumstances there are discrepancies between the marginal benefits and costs on which private decisions are based and the actual marginal *social* benefits and costs. The distortions resulting from this type of market failure include environmental pollution. These distortions are so prevalent that the bulk of Chapter 18 will be devoted to an analysis of their causes and cures, especially the role of government policy in dealing with market failure.

Summary

1. General equilibrium analysis is used to determine the impact of a change in one market on prices and quantities in all markets. Partial equilibrium analysis ignores these intermarket effects. A general equilibrium exists when prices have adjusted to an initial change so that quantities demanded equal quantities supplied in all markets.
2. General equilibrium is efficient when perfect competition exists in all markets and when costs accurately reflect the value of all forgone alternatives. The amounts that can be produced are limited by an economy's resource constraint and by the state of its technology. An allocation of input services satisfies the criterion of productive efficiency when it is not possible to increase the production of any one good without reducing that of another.
3. The allocation of inputs to alternative uses can be analyzed with an Edgeworth box. The Edgeworth box is used to isolate all of the efficient input allocations.
4. Allocative efficiency is attained when a given quantity of products is allocated among consumers in such a way that no additional net gains are possible from the exchange of products among consumers.
5. A resource allocation is Pareto optimal if it is not possible to achieve additional net gains through changes in productive methods or through the exchange of products among consumers. When the conditions for Pareto optimality have been fulfilled, resources in the economy are efficiently allocated.
6. A system of perfectly competitive markets can achieve an efficient allocation of resources. The mix of output resulting from a system of such markets depends on the general equilibrium. This determines prices of outputs and inputs. Given tastes, the general equilibrium depends on the distribution of income. Lump-sum taxes and transfers can be used to change the distribution of income without impairing efficiency.

[4] See Richard G. Lipsey and Kelvin Lancaster, "The General Theory of Second Best," *Review of Economic Studies* 24 (1956), pp. 11–32.

7. The overall attainment of Pareto efficiency requires that resources be allocated so that it is no longer possible to make any one person better off without harming another person. The utility possibility curve shows all of the efficient combinations of utility between any two persons. Both the utility possibility curve and the production possibility curve are shifted outward by technological improvements and by increases in the available productive resources.

8. Using the efficiency criterion to prescribe policies often involves conflicts with other goals. In particular, movement from an inefficient to an efficient resource allocation can make some persons worse off. These persons will oppose the change unless they are compensated for their losses. The purpose of efficiency is to maximize the size of the pie measuring national welfare. In actuality, however, some persons are better off when they have a larger slice of a smaller pie.

Important Concepts

partial equilibrium analysis

general equilibrium analysis

feedback effects

general equilibrium

resource constraint

Edgeworth box

productive efficiency

production possibility curve

marginal rate of transformation

allocative efficiency

contract curve

Pareto optimal resource allocation

utility possibility curve

general theory of second best

market failure

Questions for Review

1. What are the feedback effects of price changes? How is a general equilibrium analysis useful in determining these feedback effects?

2. Explain why the avoidance of waste in production is not sufficient to achieve efficiency.

3. Goods *X* and *Y* are substitutes. Use a simplified general equilibrium analysis to show why a reduction in the supply of a resource used to produce good *X* will ultimately lead to an increase in the price of good *Y*.

4. Use an Edgeworth box for two consumers to illustrate that whenever the indifference curves of the two consumers are not tangent at the current allocation point, both consumers could gain utility through trade. Using marginal rates of substitution, explain what happens in the Edgeworth box.

5. Explain how the marginal rate of transformation changes from one point to another on a production possibility curve that is "bowed out" from the origin.

6. Explain why many resource allocations will satisfy the efficiency criterion for Pareto optimality. Use a utility possibility curve to show how these allocations will differ from one another.

7. Why does the achievement of Pareto optimality require that the marginal rate of substitution for two consumers be equal to the marginal rate of transformation? Suppose that the MRS = 6 units of clothing per unit of food and that the MRT = 4 units of clothing per unit of food. How could the production and allocation of the two goods be changed so that both consumers gain utility?

8. Show how the monopoly control of price prevents the attainment of efficiency. What are the general equilibrium effects of monopoly on resource allocation?

9. Show how taxes other than lump-sum taxes prevent an economy from achieving efficiency.

10. Using an Edgeworth box for production, explain why increases in the amounts of available resources and advances in technology shift the production possibilities curve outward.

PROBLEMS

1. Suppose the marginal rate of technical substitution of labor for capital in the production of apples is 3 and 1 in cattle production. Show that a reallocation of the inputs used to produce these two outputs is necessary for efficiency.

2. Assume the food industry is monopolized but the clothing industry is not. Also assume that these are the only two industries and it is impossible to break up the food monopoly. Show the general equilibrium implications of the food monopoly. Show how taxing the clothing industry could achieve efficiency.

3. Assume group *A* considers potatoes an inferior good but group *B* considers them a normal good. Also assume that groups *A* and *B* buy enough potatoes to influence the price of this good. Trace the impact of a redistribution of income from group *A* to group *B* on the prices and inputs of potatoes and on the efficient mix of potatoes and other goods produced.

4. Show how an increase in available labor hours per day will affect the Edgeworth production box, the production possibility curve, and the utility possibility curve. Suppose after the increase in available labor hours, the marginal rate of transformation of food into clothing exceeds the marginal rate of substitution for those two goods. Show how prices must then change to achieve efficiency.

5. Suppose the government rationing program effectively prevents any person from consuming more than 1 pound of butter per week. Suppose at the 1-pound allowance, Judy's marginal benefit of an additional pound is $5 and Joe's is $1. Assuming that the market price of butter is $1 per pound, use an Edgeworth box to show the impact of rationing on these two consumers. Show how Judy can be made better off without harming Joe if the two are allowed to exchange butter for cash between themselves.

6. The diagram shows the production possibility curve for goods *X* and *Y* in a hypothetical economy. Based on this diagram, answer the following questions:
   a. Why must the marginal rate of transformation at point *B* be greater than 4/3?

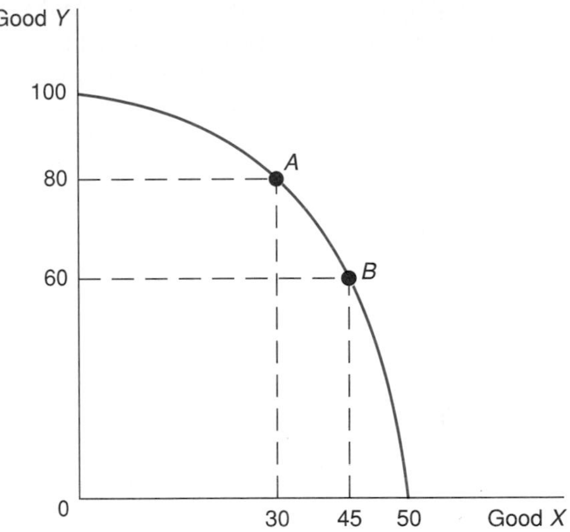

   b. Can this economy have both 80 units of good *Y* and 40 units of good *X* at the same time?
   c. Is the combination of 60 units of good *Y* and 30 units of good *X* represented by a point of tangency between isoquants in an Edgeworth production box? Why or why not?
   d. If this economy chooses point *A* and the marginal rate of transformation at point *A* is 0.8, what must the marginal rate of substitution be for the two consumers who divide the goods between themselves if the output allocation is to be efficient (that is, Pareto optimal)?

7. Suppose that this Edgeworth box applies to Jim and Mary, who have 50 units of paper and 100 units of hamburgers to divide between them,

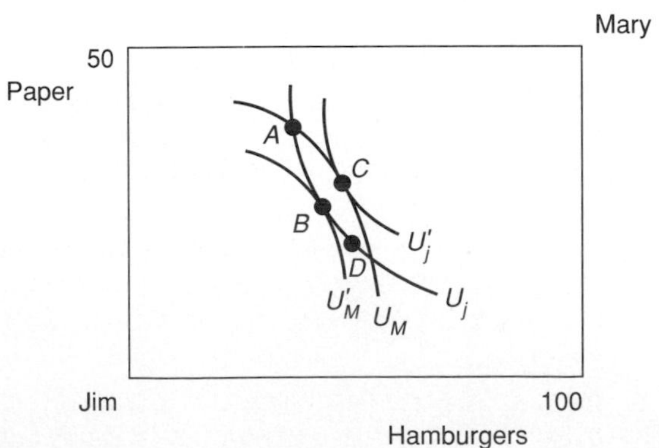

with the indifference curves for Jim and Mary as indicated. Answer the following questions regarding this case.

a. If the initial allocation is represented by point *B*, will both Jim and Mary be willing to change that allocation to the allocation represented by point *C*?

b. Will Jim be willing to move from point *B* to point *D*? Will Mary be willing to move from point *B* to point *D*?

c. Why will both Jim and Mary be willing to trade if the initial allocation is represented by point *A*? Does economic theory predict precisely what trading ratio they will establish?

17

Asymmetric Information and Market Performance

The market for health care in the United States is riddled with imperfections that impair its performance and prevent it from operating efficiently. One of its most important imperfections is the *asymmetry of information* between buyers and sellers. Patients are the buyers of medical care; physicians are the sellers. Patients usually rely on the judgments and prescriptions of their physicians because they lack enough information to do otherwise. Another imperfection that impairs the performance of U.S. health care market is the prevalence of insurance that reduces the out-of-pocket costs of health care to consumers to very low levels—often zero. Both the prevalence of insurance and the asymmetry of information between the buyers and sellers in the health care market encourage an overallocation of resources to the production of health care in the United States.

Because 87 percent of the U.S. population is covered by health insurance that pays about 80 percent of the patients' medical bills, most patients don't even think about shopping around for cheaper treatments than the ones that their physicians prescribe. For much of the U.S. population, the out-of-pocket costs for health care services are so low that there is little incentive to economize on health care. Physicians, knowing that patients pay little, if any, of the costs of treatments, feel free to prescribe expensive procedures that many patients might think twice about accepting if they had to pay the full cost and had full information on the actual benefits of the procedures.

The prevalence of health insurance and the fact that health care providers are better informed than patients on the benefits of medical procedures have contributed to soaring health care costs for Americans. In 1992 health care in the United States accounted for 14 percent of total spending for goods and services. Per capita spending on health care in the United States is twice as much as in Japan and three times as much as in the United Kingdom! Nevertheless, there is widespread dissatisfaction with the U.S. system of both health care delivery and health insurance and with the manner in which it allocates spending on health care.

We can now begin to study how the asymmetry of information affects market performance. In most of the microeconomic analysis that we have done so far, we have assumed that market participants can easily obtain information on the quality of products offered for sale, on the risks of buying and selling, and on the prices of alternatives. In reality, however, such information is often hard to come by and costly to obtain. Difficulties in obtaining information adversely affect the performance of many markets, including the markets for used products, insurance, health care services, and labor services. In some cases, difficulties in obtaining information result in allocations of resources greater than the efficient allocations that would result if full information were easily obtainable. In other cases, difficulties in obtaining information can impair market performance by not supplying enough of a product relative to the efficient amount.

Finally, imperfect information in markets encourages market participants to collect or disseminate information about what they are buying or selling. As we delve into some mysteries of the economics of information, you will see that many common business practices, including franchising, insurance examinations, guarantees, warranties, and the dissemination of information about educational or professional credentials by job applicants, can be explained as ways to cope with market inefficiencies stemming from imperfect and asymmetric information. You will also see how government policies can improve the operation of markets in which full information is unavailable to buyers or sellers and how market participants develop mechanisms for providing buyers or sellers with incentives to perform more efficiently when information on their performance is difficult to obtain.

Asymmetric Information and the Market for Used Goods

Have you ever tried to sell a used camera or a stereo system that was in really good shape? If you have, you may have been shocked by how little you could get for it as a used product. You may have then decided to give it to your kid sister or to simply trash it instead of entering the market as the seller of a perfectly good used product that could still offer many years of service to some lucky buyer.

Asymmetric information The condition that prevails in a market in which some participants (either buyers or sellers) are better informed than others.

The market for secondhand goods provides a useful starting point for examining the effects of incomplete information on market performance. **Asymmetric information** is the condition that prevails in a market in which some participants (either buyers or sellers) are better informed about product characteristics (such as the quality or prices of alternative products) than are the participants with whom they trade. For example, in the health care market the sellers (the physicians) are better informed about the services they sell than are the buyers (the patients). In the market for insurance services the buyers (the people seeking insurance coverage) are better informed about the probability that they will make a claim than are the sellers (the insurance companies).

In the market for used products the sellers are better informed than the buyers about the *quality* of the products that they are offering for sale. For example, modern cameras are loaded up with all kinds of technological innovations that can malfunction. When you buy a used camera, you can't tell whether its meter is accurate, whether its shutter speeds are correctly calibrated, or whether it has light leaks that could be expensive to fix. You also can't tell whether its various mechanisms, such as the controls that allow the lens aperture to increase or decrease, are likely to malfunction. The sellers, on the other hand, have had extensive experience with cameras and know a lot more than buyers about the quality of the cameras they are offering for sale. It is possible for buyers to check out used cameras carefully before buying them, but that might be too costly and the sellers might be unwilling to let buyers have an extensive trial period.

Perfect and Symmetric Information and Market Efficiency

Let's begin our analysis of the market for used products by assuming that information is freely available in the market (this is called *perfect information*) and that information is symmetric between buyers and sellers in that market. We will then modify the assumption of symmetric information to see how asymmetric information can affect performance in the market for used cameras.

Assume that the used cameras offered for sale can be divided into two categories: good quality and poor quality. Also assume that it is easy to distinguish good-quality used cameras from poor-quality used cameras. In that case we would expect two separate markets for used cameras to develop: one for poor-quality used cameras and one for good-quality used cameras. Assuming that both of these markets are competitive, there would be two separate equilibrium prices for these two types of cameras, with the good-quality cameras fetching a higher price than the poor-quality cameras.

The graphs in Figure 17–1 illustrate the demand and supply curves in the two markets for used cameras that would develop, given the availability of perfect and symmetric information. The demand curves reflect the marginal benefit of each

FIGURE 17–1 Markets for Used Products under Perfect and Symmetric Information

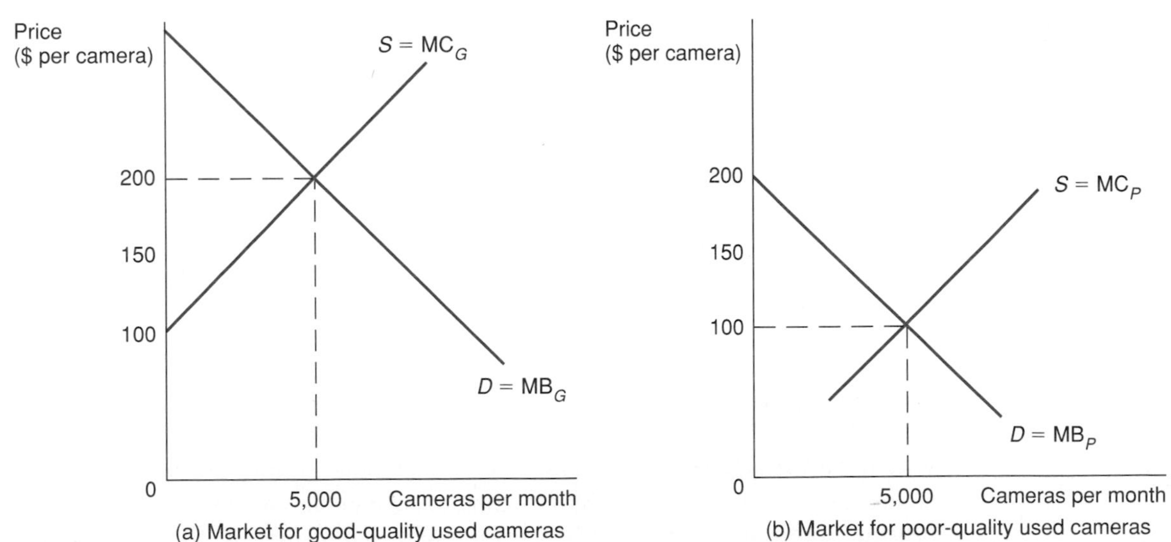

Given the availability of perfect and symmetric information, two separate markets for used cameras would develop, with a higher market equilibrium price for good-quality used cameras. The outcome is efficient because both good- and poor-quality used cameras will be sold up to the point at which their marginal benefits equal their marginal costs.

camera type to buyers. Naturally, for any given number of available cameras in each of the two markets, the marginal benefit to buyers of the good-quality cameras is higher than that of the poor-quality cameras. This is because people are willing to pay more for a good used camera that can give many years of trouble-free service than they are willing to pay for a poor used camera that can be unreliable or need repairs. The marginal benefit for used products will, of course, decline as more are made available, just as the marginal benefit of new products declines as more are made available.

The supply curves reflect the marginal cost of a given number of cameras of given quality. The marginal cost of placing a good camera on the market exceeds that of placing a poor camera on the market. After all, a good camera can still give many years of service, so the opportunity cost of parting with it is higher to those who own it. On the other hand, the opportunity cost of parting with a poor-quality camera is low because the owner knows it will not provide much additional service without expensive repairs. The supply curves of both types of cameras are upward sloping because higher prices induce more owners to place both types of cameras on the market.

Given the demand and supply curves in Figure 17–1, two separate market equilibriums are established, so that the equilibrium price of a good-quality used camera is \$200, while the equilibrium price of a poor-quality used camera is \$100. These equilibriums are efficient because at the market prices the marginal benefit of both good-quality cameras and poor-quality cameras to buyers is just equal to the marginal cost of parting with them to sellers. We can summarize the efficiency conditions for the two used camera markets as follows:

$$MB_G = MC_G \qquad \textbf{(17–1)}$$

and

$$MB_P = MC_P$$

where MB_G and MC_G are the marginal benefit and the marginal cost of the good-quality cameras, while MB_P and MC_P are the marginal benefit and the marginal cost of the poor-quality cameras.

Note that in equilibrium a total of 10,000 used cameras are sold each month—5,000 in the good-quality used camera market and 5,000 in the poor-quality used camera market.

How Asymmetric Information Can Affect Market Performance

Now let's investigate the consequences of asymmetric information for the used camera market. In reality, buyers looking for used cameras do not have sufficient information to distinguish poor-quality cameras from good-quality cameras when they enter the market through such means as responding to classified ads. Because of the asymmetry of information, buyers cannot know for sure whether they are getting a good-quality camera or a poor-quality camera when they choose to buy a used camera. This means there cannot be *two separate* markets, distin-

FIGURE 17–2 Markets for Used Goods under Asymmetric Information

(a) Good-quality cameras

(b) Poor-quality cameras

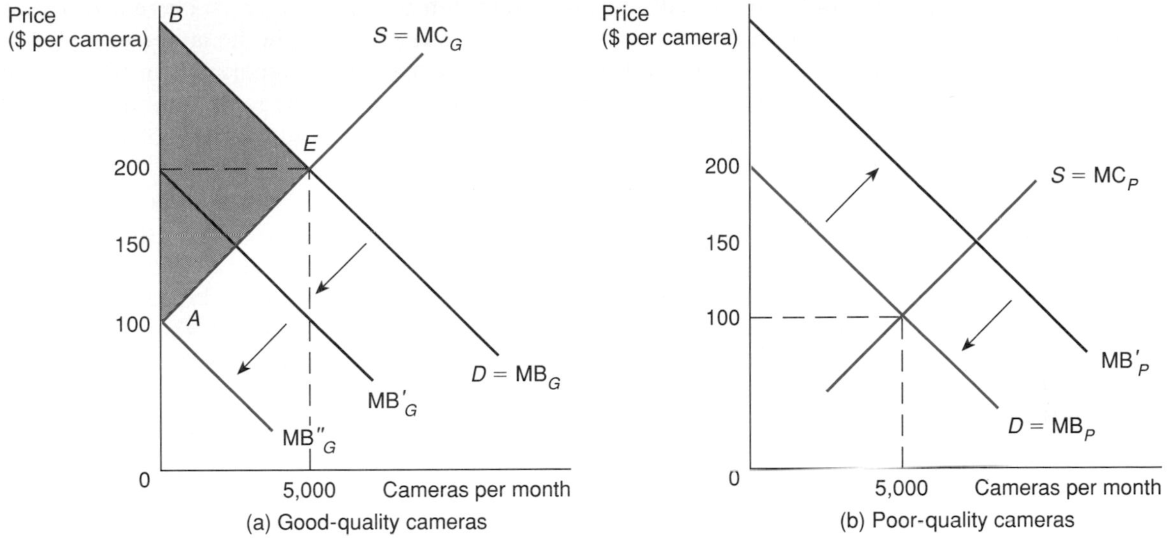

When buyers know less than sellers about product quality, poor-quality used goods drive good-quality used goods out of the market. In equilibrium 5,000 used cameras are sold each month at a price of $100, but no good-quality used cameras are sold at that price. The equilibrium is inefficient because the net benefits of area *ABE*, which would be enjoyed under perfect and symmetric information, are not achieved.

guished by quality, for used cameras. There is only one market, and sellers in that market know the quality of the products that are being offered for sale, but buyers do not.

Assume that buyers think there is a 50–50 chance that the used camera they buy will be of good or poor quality They may reason that a good-quality camera is worth $200 to them, while a poor-quality camera is worth only $100. The *expected value* of the camera they buy is therefore an average of the high price and the low price, which is $150.[1] We would therefore expect a rational buyer in the used camera market to offer only $150 for a camera that has an equal chance of being of good or poor quality. Because buyers do not know for sure whether they are getting a good- or poor-quality camera from sellers, they offer a single price for a camera, irrespective of quality.

Figure 17–2 shows the consequences for market performance of buyer behavior under asymmetric information. Buyers' lack of information on quality decreases their willingness to pay for used cameras and shifts their marginal benefit

[1] See Chapter 6 for a formal definition of the concept of expected value.

curves for both good-quality and poor-quality cameras. At first, the market appears to reach an equilibrium at a price of $150 for used cameras. However, this price is unlikely to really be an equilibrium because buyers soon realize that the emergence of a single price for cameras has changed the behavior of sellers. In Figure 17–2 the increase in the price of poor-quality cameras from $100 to $150 increases the quantity supplied by sellers. However, the reduction in the price of good-quality cameras from $200 to $150 *decreases* the quantity of good-quality cameras supplied by sellers. The mix of good-quality and poor-quality cameras changes, and buyers soon realize that the probability of getting a poor-quality used camera is now higher than 50 percent. As this realization sinks in, the willingness of buyers to pay for a used camera declines. The marginal benefit curves for both good-quality and poor-quality cameras therefore shift down. For example, if the probability of getting a poor-quality camera is now 75 percent, then the expected value of a used camera to buyers is $125 and the market price of used cameras falls accordingly.

However, the fall in the market price of used cameras results in a further reduction in the quantity of good-quality cameras supplied to the used camera market. This reduction further increases the probability that a buyer will get stuck with a poor-quality camera when making a purchase. As a consequence a further revision of the marginal benefit of buying a used camera shifts the demand curves for both good-quality and poor-quality used cameras down still more. This in turn results in a further decrease in the quantity of good-quality cameras supplied to the used camera market.

By now you can probably see where the analysis is leading. *Eventually, the demand and market price for used products decreases so much that the quantity supplied of good-quality cameras falls to zero.* When this occurs, the entire market consists of poor-quality cameras. Under the assumptions we have made, the market for used cameras is in equilibrium only when their price falls to $100 and the quantity supplied is 5,000 used cameras per month, all of poor quality. At the $100 equilibrium price the quantity of good-quality cameras supplied to the market falls to zero because those who own such cameras choose to keep them or give them to relatives or friends instead of sell them.

It is easy to demonstrate that an inefficient equilibrium emerges under asymmetric information in the market for used cameras. Under asymmetric information the equilibrium quantity of good-quality cameras is zero. However, as we demonstrated earlier, the efficient quantity of good-quality cameras that would prevail if there were perfect and symmetric information is 5,000 per month. Because of asymmetric information, the market does not achieve additional net gains from selling good-quality used cameras equal to the shaded area *ABE* in Figure 17–2(a). The market fails to sell any good-quality used cameras and therefore undersupplies a good whose marginal benefit actually exceeds its marginal cost under perfect information.

In this example, the total quantity supplied in a used product market is in effect half of the efficient amount. In equilibrium only poor-quality products are available in the used goods market and buyers in that market buy those products until their marginal benefit equals their marginal cost.

Mechanisms to Cope with Asymmetric Information: Consumer Guides, Warranties, Guarantees, and the "Lemons" Problem for Used Cars

The analysis of asymmetry of information in markets for used products suggests that there is a tendency for low-quality products to drive high-quality products off the market when sellers are better informed than buyers about product quality. However, the analysis also shows that net gains, measured by the area *ABE* in Figure 17–2(a), can be reaped by developing mechanisms that allow increased sales of higher-quality used products. It is not surprising therefore that those who wish to sell higher-quality used products seek means of signaling that quality to potential buyers.

Let's examine how net gains to buyers and sellers in highly organized markets, such as those for used cars, can result from innovations in selling. The market for used cars is like the market for other used products in that it is characterized by asymmetry of information, with sellers knowing more than buyers. However, because the average price of a used car is much higher than that of, say, a used camera, potential buyers have a much greater incentive to invest in acquiring more information about used cars than about used cameras. It might cost $50 to have a mechanic check out either a used car or a used camera, but $50 is half the price of a $100 used camera and only 1 percent of the price of a $5,000 used car. For particular years and models of used cars, potential buyers can also refer to data on frequency of repairs that are regularly published in consumer magazines. Potential buyers can obtain information on older homes, which are even more expensive than used cars, by hiring a house inspection firm to check them out. This will give potential buyers some idea of the maintenance and renovation costs they are likely to incur if they buy such a home. The greater the price of a used product, the more likely it is that the benefits of checking out the product will be greater than the costs.

Market signal A means of conveying information about a not easily seen characteristic of a product or service.

Sellers of higher-quality used products also have incentives to signal potential buyers that they handle such products. A **market signal** is a means of conveying information about a not easily seen characteristic of a product or service, such as its quality. By offering a warranty covering labor and parts for its used cars, a used car dealer signals buyers that the quality of its used cars is high, because the dealer would be unwilling to bear the cost of repairing "lemons"—products with defects that require high maintenance costs.[2] Used car dealers can charge a higher price for warrantied higher-quality cars and thus cover the costs of any warranty service they may have to provide. It would be in the best interest of used car dealers to avoid lemons if they are going to provide warranties for all of the cars they sell. In some cases a used car dealer might even identify lemons by placing an "as is" sign on certain cars and offering the cars for sale without a warranty. In this way the dealer might actually help segment the used car market into good-

[2] A classic analysis of the "lemons" problem is George Akerlof, "The Market for 'Lemons': Quality Uncertainty and the Market Mechanism," *Quarterly Journal of Economics*, August 1970, pp. 488–500.

quality and poor-quality cars, as would be required for efficiency! Some people who are good at doing their own repairs don't mind buying a lemon if they can get it at a low enough price.

Sellers of used products can establish reputations for quality that allow them to charge higher prices for the products they sell. Used car dealers, for example, could guarantee satisfaction by offering a full refund on lemons. Establishing a reputation for selling high-quality cars would enable a used-car dealer to charge higher prices and thus help overcome the problem of having poor-quality used cars push good-quality used cars out of the market. It is therefore unlikely that only poor-quality used cars will appear on the market even though the efficient mix of good-quality and poor-quality used cars may not be obtained.

From the above discussion we would expect buyers in a market with asymmetric information to expend resources on product quality information and sellers to expend resources on mechanisms that signal product quality. In making these expenditures, both buyers and sellers weigh the marginal benefit of doing so against the marginal cost and invest in information just up to the point at which the marginal benefit of doing so falls to equal the marginal cost of the information.

A Generalization: Signaling Product Quality

The analysis of asymmetric information in the markets for used products is relevant to the markets for new products. Sellers in monopolistically competitive or oligopolistic markets whose products are not standardized often have the incentive to signal product quality to consumers. Sellers regularly offer guarantees and warranties to signal the dependability of new products. (Some automobile dealers even offer free road service to buyers of new cars if the cars fail on the road.) Higher-quality brands can then be sold more easily at higher prices.

As is the case for used products, higher-quality new products are more likely to be warranted than lower-quality new products because it is more expensive for sellers to stand behind warranties for lower-quality new products. Consumers willingly pay higher prices for new products with warranties than for products with no warranties because they are convinced the quality of products with warranties is higher. Sellers of new high-quality products, like sellers of used high-quality products, have incentives to maintain their reputations for quality.

Concept Review

1. What is asymmetric information?
2. How can losses in efficiency result from asymmetry of information abut product quality in a market for used products?
3. What kinds of market signals can be used to provide information about product quality and increase the quantity of high-quality products supplied?

Asymmetric Information and the Markets for Insurance Services

A situation of asymmetric information can exist in markets in which the *sellers* are more poorly informed about the characteristics of a product than are the buyers. Insurance markets are an excellent example of markets in which buyers are better informed than sellers. In such markets sellers of insurance services offer to insure against the risk of such events as accident, illness, disability, theft, fire, and death.

When insurance companies offer their services, they base their premiums on the average probability that an event will take place. For example, suppose a 40-year-old man wants to purchase $100,000 worth of life insurance. Insurance companies estimate the probability that a man of 40 will die within the year by looking at the entire population of 40-year-old men in the nation and at the death rate for these men. If, for example, over recent years for the entire population 4 out of every 1,000 men die at the age of 40, then the probability, on average, of a man of that age dying is .004.[3] When an insurance company insures a large pool of 40-year-old men, it then figures that for each $100,000 policy it underwrites it can expect to pay out $400 in benefits during the year. Based on the probability of death for 40-year-old men, therefore, the expected payout cost of each $100,000 policy is $400. The insurance company then adds administrative costs to the expected cost of each policy, including a reasonable profit, and charges, say, $450 per year for a $100,000 life insurance policy sold to a 40-year-old man.

The problem that the insurance company now faces is that when it sells insurance policies to its clients, the actual probability that a particular client will die within the year depends on that client's health. In general, the person seeking insurance knows more about his or her health than does the seller of insurance. Remember that the insurance company bases its premiums on the average probability that a person of a given age will die. The probability of death for a particular person may, however, be higher or lower than average.

To see this, let's set up a model similar to the one we used to analyze the market for used goods. Suppose both high-risk and low-risk clients are seeking life insurance. On average, for the entire pool of 40-year-old men, the probability of dying during the year is .004. For the high-risk men in that pool, however, the probability of dying is .006 or higher on average, while for the low-risk men the probability of dying is .002 or lower. If the population of potential clients is composed of both low-risk and high-risk men, then the insurance company would be correct in assuming that the average probability of death is .004.

Ideally, if the insurance company could identify the low-risk and high-risk clients, it would know that its expected payout per $100,000 policy would be $600 for the high-risk clients but only $200 for the low-risk clients. If it added $50 of administrative cost and profit onto these payouts, given symmetry of information in the market, a $250 equilibrium premium would emerge for the low-risk clients and a $650 equilibrium premium would emerge for the high-risk clients. Assuming

[3] See Chapter 6 for a definition of the concept of probability.

that the demand and supply curves for these two separate markets reflect the marginal benefits and marginal costs of insurance, the equilibrium, as shown in Figure 17–3, would be efficient. In equilibrium 10,000 policies of $100,000 life insurance would be sold to 10,000 high-risk males at a price of $650 per year, while another 10,000 policies of $100,000 life insurance would be sold to low-risk males at a price of $250 per year.

Because of the asymmetry of information, however, the insurance company does not know whether it is selling a policy to a high-risk or low-risk male. If it reasons that the probability of any client being high risk or low risk is .5, it will charge an average of the high- and low-risk premiums, which is $450, for its $100,000 insurance policies for 40-year-old males.

But at the $450 rate, insurance is a better deal for high-risk clients than for low-risk clients. At the average rate, therefore, the insurance company will in effect supply more policies to high-risk clients than to low-risk clients. In Figure 17–3 the supply of policies to high-risk clients is S_{H2} and the quantity of policies demanded by such clients at that rate is 15,000. On the other hand, the quantity of policies demanded at that rate by low-risk clients is 5,000 per year at the $450 premium, as shown in Figure 17–3.

We now have a situation similar to the one that prevailed in the market for used products. The insurance company now finds that 75 percent of its insurance applications are coming from high-risk clients. It therefore revises its average

FIGURE 17–3 Asymmetric Information and the Market for Insurance

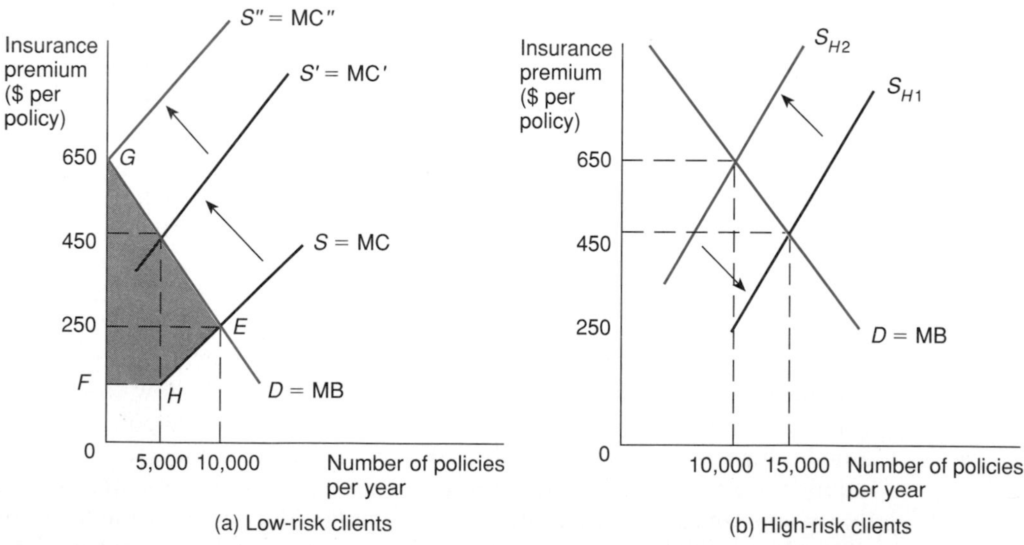

When buyers of insurance know more than the sellers about the risk of making a claim, insurance companies end up charging higher premiums to all buyers to cover their risks. The higher prices drive low-risk clients from the market with a consequent loss in net benefits corresponding to the shaded area in (a).

payouts upward and shifts the supply of insurance policies to the left. It reasons that if 75 percent of its clients are now high risk, a rate of $550 should be set for its policy. The higher rate results in a decrease in the quantity of insurance policies demanded.

You can now see where we are headed: Each time the insurance company raises its rate, it can expect a further decline in applications from low-risk clients. Eventually, the rate rises to $650 and, as shown in Figure 17–3(a), at that rate the quantity demanded by low-risk clients falls to zero. Because of the asymmetry of information, the insurance company in effect ends up serving *only* high-risk clients and low-risk clients are priced out of the market! The resulting market equilibrium is inefficient compared to the symmetric information equilibrium, in which two separate markets prevail—one for low-risk clients, the other for high-risk clients. Low-risk clients choose not to purchase life insurance even though the marginal benefit of doing so would exceed the marginal cost under full and symmetric information. In Figure 17–3(a) the loss in net benefits to low-risk clients under asymmetric information is equal to the area *FGEH*.

Adverse Selection and Mechanisms to Cope with It

Adverse selection A problem in insurance of high-risk customers dominating the demand for insurance when premiums are based on the average probability of loss.

When insurance companies set rates based on the average probability of a loss, they get an **adverse selection** of high-risk clients from the pool of potential clients because high-risk clients know that their probability of loss is higher than average. Insurance companies, realizing that they are likely to get an adverse selection of clients, then charge higher rates. As premiums rise, low-risk clients choose not to apply for insurance. The adverse selection problem occurs for all kinds of insurance, not just life insurance. People who know they are ill are more likely to seek health insurance coverage than people who are in good health. Similarly, people who live in high-crime areas are more likely to seek theft insurance than people who live in low-crime areas. This pushes up the average price of theft insurance, which causes low-risk people to go without such insurance.

However, as Figure 17–3(a) shows, net gains are possible if mechanisms are developed to distinguish high-risk clients from low-risk clients or to establish a pool of clients so large that average probabilities can be reliably used to estimate payout rates. Let's look at mechanisms of these kinds that have been developed in insurance markets. Insurance companies often insist on complete medical examinations for clients and waiting periods before health or life insurance becomes effective. Many homeowners' policies do not insure jewelry and other very valuable items that are easy candidates for theft to provide homeowners with incentives to either insure such items separately or to take precautions against theft. To protect themselves against very costly risks, insurance companies also typically place upper limits on coverage for homeowner's personal property and for health insurance claims. In the case of health or life insurance, insurance companies offer discounts to nonsmokers because the probability of early death or such catastrophic diseases as cancer and emphysema is linked to smoking. However, all of these mechanisms are unlikely to do more than partly solve the adverse selection problem.

Another mechanism that insurance companies use to cope with the adverse selection problem is to sell insurance programs to large groups, all of whose members are required to enroll in the programs. This avoids the adverse selection problem by assuring a diverse group whose average risks are more likely than the average risks of individual clients to be in the range estimated by data from the overall population pool of potential clients. For example, the risk of adverse selection is much less for a health insurer that underwrites a policy covering the 10,000 employees of a large corporation than for a health insurer that accepts applications from 10,000 *individual* clients. At the extreme, the adverse selection problems could be *completely eliminated* if *all the people of a nation* were *required* to purchase a certain type of insurance coverage. The group of insured clients would then be the same as the population pool that is used to compute the average probability of loss and payout. For example, government provision of insurance against very costly illnesses and injury could be provided at very low cost per person if everyone were required to carry the insurance and if its costs were financed by either compulsory premiums or general taxes.

Government therefore often plays a very important role in insurance markets by providing compulsory coverage for large groups in which adverse selection could be a serious problem. For example, the Medicare program of health insurance for the elderly, a system of government-provided health insurance for persons over 65, is financed mainly by taxes. Because of the adverse selection problem, private insurance companies would be unlikely to underwrite such individual health insurance for the elderly at rates based on average probability.

The Problem of Moral Hazard

Moral hazard The increased risk of payout for insurance firms that results from behavioral changes caused by insurance coverage.

Another important problem in insurance markets stems from the fact that the availability of insurance can change the behavior of the insured in ways that increase the probability of losses and therefore the probability of payouts by insurance companies. The **moral hazard** of insurance is the increased risk of payout that results from behavioral changes caused by the insurance coverage itself.[4] For example, a person who is insured against the theft of an automobile might take fewer precautions to reduce the probability of theft. Without insurance she might normally lock her car whenever it is parked; with insurance, she might often choose not to lock it. Similarly, fire insurance may reduce the incentive to take costly precautions that prevent fires, such as regular inspections of chimneys, furnaces, and electrical wiring. The moral hazard of insurance implies that the availability of insurance changes the risks of providing it! After an insurance market develops, insurance firms must reassess the probabilities of loss that were based on lack of insurance to see how those probabilities have changed once insurance has become available.

The problem of moral hazard is particularly severe in the market for health insurance. Health insurance reduces incentives to take preventive care measures, including exercise, regular checkups, and the elimination of habits that damage

[4] For a good discussion of the economics of moral hazard, see Mark V. Pauly, "The Economics of Moral Hazard: Comment," *American Economic Review*, June 1968, pp. 531–538.

health, such as smoking and drinking. Even more important, health insurance also reduces the out-of-pocket costs of visits to physicians and of medical procedures, including expensive operations. The fact that health insurance lowers what the patient pays for medical procedures increases the incentive of physicians to prescribe them. The moral hazard of health insurance combined with the asymmetry of information between health care providers and patients has led to an overproduction of health care services in the United States in recent years. Let's now examine the market for health care services and see how health insurance has affected it in the United States.

The Moral Hazard of Health Insurance and Mechanisms to Cope with It

Third-party payments Full or partial payments for market-provided services by an organization that is neither the buyer nor the seller of the services.

Deductible Minimum amount of out-of-pocket payments required by a third-party payer before it begins to pay for services.

Coinsurance The portion of the costs of services that persons covered by a third-party payment plan must incur as out-of-pocket costs.

Most expenditures on health care services in the United States are financed by **third-party payments.** The third party is neither the buyer nor the seller of the services but a health insurance provider, usually either a private company or a government program such as Medicare. When an insured person needs health care services, the insurer typically pays all but a small portion of the bill. The typical insurance plan requires patients to first incur a certain amount of health care expenditure each year, called the **deductible,** before the plan starts paying benefits. After the patient has paid the annual deductible, the plan pays most of the additional expenses incurred over each year up to a certain maximum per lifetime that varies from plan to plan.

Coinsurance, the patient's out-of-pocket costs, varies from plan to plan but is typically 20 percent of the total cost. After a patient has incurred the deductible, the insurance plan therefore pays 80 percent of the patient's covered expenses. Usually, after the patient has made a certain maximum annual out-of-pocket payment for coinsurance, the insurer pays all of the bills up to a certain annual and lifetime maximum.

The system of third-party payments increases the incentive to both consume and provide health care services. Figure 17–4 shows the demand and supply curves for health care services. If there were no health insurance and patients had to pay their own medical bills, the equilibrium price on average of health care services would be P^* and the equilibrium quantity sold per year would be Q^*. Assuming that the demand for health care services reflects the marginal benefit of such services and that the supply reflects their marginal cost, the efficient quantity of health care services would be produced, because at P^* the marginal benefit of health care equals its marginal cost.

However, health insurance reduces the price per unit of health care services below P^*. This is because after having met their deductible, patients pay only a small fraction of the actual charge for various health care services, such as surgery, hospital stays, and prescription drugs. As a result of the decline in out-of-pocket costs, say to P_H, the quantity of health care services demanded increases from Q^* to Q_H. To prevent shortages in the market, the quantity supplied must increase as the quantity demanded increases. However, to attract the additional resources required to increase the availability of health care services, the price paid to health care providers must increase. In Figure 17–4 the price to health care providers per unit of service must increase on average from P^* to P_S to induce

MODERN MICROECONOMICS IN ACTION: GOVERNMENT AND THE ECONOMY

The Moral Hazard of Deposit Insurance: Bank Failure

During the Great Depression of the early 1930s, thousands of bank failures wiped out the savings of millions of people. In 1934, to prevent future bank failures and maintain confidence in the banking system, the Federal Deposit Insurance Corporation (FDIC) was set up to guarantee bank deposits. The FDIC currently insures all deposits up to $100,000 per account from loss. The now defunct Federal Savings and Loan Insurance Corporation (FSLIC) formerly insured deposits at savings and loan associations (S&Ls) and other thrift institutions that are now insured by the FDIC.

Like any insurance system, the FDIC works if there is a small, predictable number of bank failures each year. In the 1980s, however, a dramatic rise in U.S. bank failures placed a tremendous burden on the FDIC. By 1992 the FDIC's insurance fund was exhausted by expenditures to pay off the deposit liabilities of hundreds of savings and loan associations, other thrift institutions, and banks that had failed because of poor investments and poor management. The federal government may have to budget as much as $500 billion in the 1990s to pay off the insured deposits of failed banks and S&Ls.

What caused the rash of failures, and why are billions of government dollars necessary to bail out the failed financial institutions? The answers to these questions might surprise you: The federal deposit insurance system that protects your S&L and bank deposits must itself share the blame for the failure of the S&Ls and banks in recent years! Asymmetric information and the moral hazard implicit in insurance were the culprits.

Let's look at the S&L fiasco and at the role played by deposit insurance in the incentives of managers and depositors.

To understand the causes of the savings and loan disaster, we have to go back to 1980. In that year Congress enacted the Depository Institutions Deregulation and Monetary Control Act, which allowed savings and loan associations and other thrift institutions to issue checkable deposits and to compete more aggressively for loanable funds. The increased competition caused a rise in the interest rates that thrift institutions had to pay to attract loanable funds. Since most thrift institutions had in the past specialized in low-yielding mortgage loans, they were now pressured to seek more lucrative loans to compensate for the low interest yield of their portfolios. Many thrifts made riskier loans at higher interest rates to achieve higher profits. The Garn–St Germain Act of 1982 increased their ability to do so by allowing S&Ls to expand their lending into new commercial ventures and speculative land development.

In many ways deposit insurance provided by the FDIC and FSLIC contributed to the risk-taking by owners and managers of depository institutions and precipitated many of the bank failures that occurred in the late 1980s. Many depositors believed that amounts in excess of $100,000 would be protected in the event of a bank failure. Most of the depositors who supplied their loanable funds to the thrifts were fully protected by deposit insurance and therefore cared little about their bank's financial health or about the way it was managed! When a poorly managed bank becomes insolvent, its net worth becomes negative. When this occurs, bank owners have none of their own capital at risk and therefore become more willing to take risks with funds they obtain from insured depositors. In some notorious cases, officers of thrift institutions used depositors' funds for extravagant and sometimes fraudulent personal uses that contributed to the insolvency of their institutions.

In the mid-1980s, a number of unfortunate events contributed to the failure of many S&Ls, particularly those located in such oil-producing states as Texas, Louisiana, and Oklahoma. As oil prices and land prices tumbled, risky loans based on the prospects of a prosperous oil industry turned sour. Many S&Ls discovered that their assets were not sufficient to meet their deposit liabilities. Weak institutions offered higher interest rates to attract depositors, and depositors continued to supply funds to insolvent institutions because of deposit

(*Continued*) insurance. *The system of deposit insurance that prevented bank panics also encouraged risk-taking that ultimately led to bank failures!* The losers were not the depositors or the owners—the losers were the taxpayers and the economy itself, whose operation was severely impaired.

There is no easy solution for the S&L disaster. Some experts recommend more regulation of the thrift industry to control risk-taking and bank failure; others recommend that the whole U.S. banking system be overhauled; still others recommend that deposit insurance coverage be reduced or that banks pay premiums for deposit insurance that more accurately reflect the riskiness of their portfolios. Currently, all banks, pay the same rate of insurance per $100 of deposits, no matter how risky their assets. Finally, some experts recommend that owners of thrift insurance institutions have more of their own money at stake (net worth) in these institutions.

health care providers to make Q_H units of service available per year. The system of third-party payments therefore reduces the price that patients pay for health care services and increases the price that providers receive for health care services, while at the same time increasing the amount of resources devoted to health care.

FIGURE 17–4 Third-Party Payments and the Moral Hazard of Health Insurance

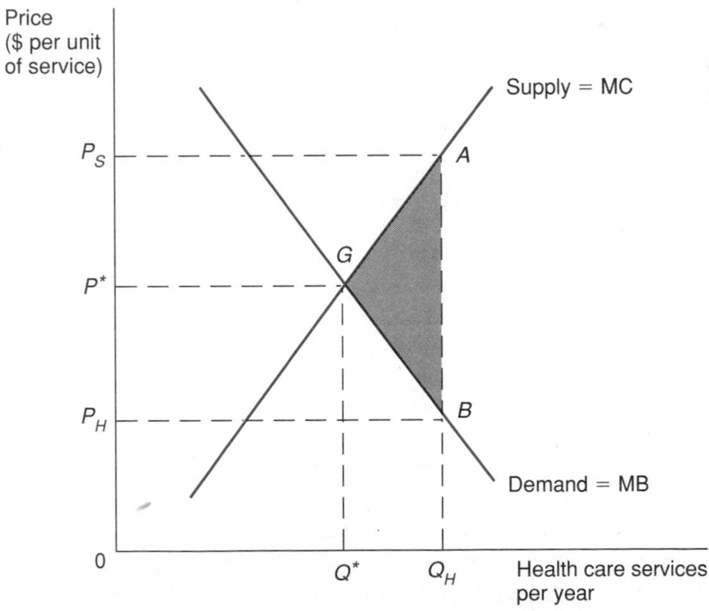

Third-party payments for health care reduce the price to patients and increase the quantity demanded. The price received by health care sellers must increase to increase quantity supplied. Expenditure on health care increases because both the price per unit paid to providers and the quantity demanded by patients increases.

Modern Microeconomics in Action: The Business World

Asymmetric Information and the Market for Health Care Services

Buying health care services is not like buying cookies or cassette tapes. The market for health care services is one in which out-of-pocket costs to consumers are reduced by third-party payments that prevent prices in the marketplace from serving their normal function of rationing quantities. The insurance-based system of health care in the United States encourages consumers to demand more and better health care services than they would otherwise. Suppliers of such services have responded to this demand by developing effective but costly new methods of treatment.

Decision making in the market for health care services is dominated by physicians who have the knowledge needed to prescribe medication and procedures and who control access to the technological marvels of modern medicine. Patients find it difficult to obtain information about alternative methods of treatment. In other words, the market for health care services is dominated by asymmetry of information between the providers and the consumers of such services.

As in any other market in which there is asymmetry of information, the resulting losses in net gains provide incentives for the development of new means of disseminating information. Recently, the Foundation for Informed Medical Decision Making, a not-for-profit foundation based in Hanover, New Hampshire, produced a series of videos designed to inform patients of options available for the treatment of four common health problems: prostate disease, low back pain, high blood pressure, and early stage breast cancer.* These interactive videos describe treatments and their risks. The video developers believe that patients will make more efficient choices if they are provided with more information on treatments. At one HMO in Denver the rate of prostate surgeries was reduced by 44 percent after patients began viewing the videos. Surgeries at another HMO were reduced by 60 percent after the HMO started using the videos.

The videos therefore have the potential for reducing the overallocation of resources to health care that results from asymmetry of information and the moral hazard of health insurance. Many insurance companies have recommended the videos as alternatives to second opinions when a physician recommends surgery.

* See Ron Winslow, "Videos, Questionnaires Aim to Expand Role of Patients in Treatment Decision," *The Wall Street Journal,* February 25, 1992.

The moral hazard of health care insurance reduces the incentive of both consumers and providers of health care services to economize on the use of such services. Patients visit physicians more often for minor ailments than they might if they had to pay the full price of the visits. Physicians and other health care practitioners, knowing that patients pay only a fraction of the price for health care services, prescribe more services than they would otherwise. Naturally, because price paid per unit of services to providers increases as a result of health care insurance, while quantities demanded and supplied also increase, total expenditures on health care increase. The bulk of the expenditures for health care services are paid directly to health care providers by private and government insurers. The amount paid by insurers is represented by the area P_HP_SAB.

More than the efficient amount of resources is allocated to health care services as a result of third-party payments and the consequent moral hazard effect. In Figure 17–4 insurance results in the demand for Q_H units of health care per year. At that level of consumption the marginal cost of health care services exceeds their marginal benefit to consumers. There is therefore an overproduction of health care services, with a consequent loss in net benefits from resource use equal to the shaded area *GAB*.

The system of health care insurance that has evolved in the United States provides the insured with financing for both routine medical problems and catastrophic illnesses. The effects of insurance in the market for health care are much more pronounced than the effects of insurance in other markets, such as insurance for automobiles, fire, and theft. People rarely crash their cars or set fire to their property just because they have automobile or fire insurance. However, in the market for health care services many people do visit physicians more often and do accept health care procedures that they might decline if they had to pay the full price of those services.

Because out-of-pocket costs for health care services are low to insured consumers they agree to procedures and prescriptions more readily than they would in the absence of insurance. Another reason for the increase in the quantity of health care services demanded is that insurance coverage reduces the incentive to take adequate precautions against incurring an insured health care expense. The magnitude of the moral hazard of health care insurance depends on the elasticity of demand for health care services. The more elastic the demand, the greater is the magnitude of the moral hazard. An additional aspect of moral hazard is the increased incentive that insurance gives providers to supply health care services or to prescribe services that increase the demand for health care.

Coping with the Moral Hazard of Health Insurance and Controlling Health Care Costs: Increasing Coinsurance and Deductibles

Concern about the moral hazard problem has resulted in the development of various schemes to make consumers more price conscious. Insurance companies often limit their payments for certain services to fixed amounts. If these amounts do not cover the full costs, the insured has to make up the difference or the provider has to absorb the difference. This technique of limiting payments provides both the consumers and providers of health care services with incentives to economize on the quantity and quality of those services. Health insurance companies sometimes pay providers only the "usual, customary, and reasonable charges" for certain medical procedures. The patient has to make up any differences between these payments and the actual charges.

The federal government has learned some lessons from private health insurance companies. Government health insurance programs have sought to reduce the moral hazard by limiting the amounts they pay physicians, hospitals, and other health care providers. The state-administered Medicaid programs, which provide health care services to the poor, place stringent limits on reimbursement rates. Unfortunately, these limits have made it more difficult for Medicaid patients to obtain health care because the providers must absorb the difference between what they receive from the government and what they charge. The reimbursement limits for Medicaid patients are lower than those on most private insurance. This has decreased the willingness of providers to offer health care services to Medicaid patients.

The most obvious way of controlling health care spending is to increase the out-of-pocket costs of health care services to the individuals who consume them. Increasing the price of health care to consumers will decrease the quantity demanded. Increased sharing of health care costs will provide consumers with incentives to economize on the use of health care services. The declining share of health care costs paid by consumers has, in fact, been a major cause of the increases in the price and volume of health care services. A classic RAND Corporation study of health care spending in the late 1970s and early 1980s found that spending per person for health care was 45 percent higher in insurance plans that required no cost sharing than in an alternative plan that required 95 percent cost sharing (meaning that health insurance paid only 5 percent of the health care bills of insurees) up to an annual maximum of $1,000.

Increased cost sharing both in private health insurance plans and in such government plans as Medicare or veterans' benefits, where the policyholders have the ability to pay (as opposed to Medicaid, where the recipients of health care services are indigent and presumably incapable of paying), have a great potential for reducing health care spending. However, for increased cost sharing to be effective, governments would have to ban the development of supplementary health insurance (such as the Medigap policies purchased by Medicare enrollees) that would turn the patient's share of costs into a third-party payment. In other words, increased cost sharing would have to be made mandatory and would have to apply to all insurance plans—public and private. This would require increased government regulation of the health insurance industry.

There are two ways of increasing consumer cost sharing. One way is to increase the deductible amounts that consumers have to incur before they became eligible for insurance payments. This would increase the price consciousness of the relatively healthy consumers who incur health care costs below the deductible. Presumably, these consumers would compare the marginal benefit of their health care services with the marginal cost and would consume health care services up to the point at which the marginal benefit falls to equal the marginal cost. A disadvantage of increasing the deductible is that this might discourage patients from seeking early tests or care that could avert high future health care costs.

The other way of increasing consumer cost sharing is to increase the coinsurance rate paid by consumers. This would decrease the quantity of health care services demanded and the quantity supplied. The effect of increasing the coinsurance rate is illustrated in Figure 17–5. Suppose the coinsurance rate is initially set at 20 percent after the deductible has been met. At that level of coinsurance third-party payers absorb 80 percent of the price of the insuree's health care services. If the coinsurance rate were increased to 40 percent, the share of the price of health care services absorbed by third parties would be reduced to 60 percent, the quantity of health care services demanded would decline from Q_1 to Q_2, and there would be a corresponding reduction in the quantity supplied. As a result of the

MODERN MICROECONOMICS IN ACTION: INTERNATIONAL REPORT

National Health Insurance in Great Britain

Many politicians have been calling for a system of national health insurance for the United States. Such a system would finance all health care through taxes and thus guarantee health care to all Americans. To see how the system works, let's examine the famous National Health Service (NHS) that was set up in Great Britain after World War II to finance and provide health care for British citizens. Under the NHS the government actually supplies the bulk of the nation's health care services. The NHS provides universal coverage for physician and hospital services, long-term care, and prescription drugs. Those services are funded almost entirely through taxes, which pay for 97 percent of NHS services. Since British citizens pay little or nothing for the health care services they consume, the moral hazard of this system would seem to be very high. However, with this danger in mind, the system has developed methods of rationing health care so as to prevent inefficient consumption of medical services.

The NHS has a virtual monopoly on the supply of hospital services in Great Britain, accounting for nearly 80 percent of the nation's hospital beds. British citizens have very little choice among health care providers. To obtain health care services, a British citizen must register with a general practice (GP) physician who is currently accepting patients. The GP controls the patient's access to the health system in much the same way as GPs control the patient's access to health care services in an HMO in the United States. GPs refer patients to specialists who can order tests and admit patients to hospitals. Once hospitalized, a patient is treated by salaried NHS specialists on the hospital staff.

GPs receive a fixed "capitation" payment from the NHS for each of their patients, irrespective of the number and kinds of services that they give the patient. This provides GPs with incentives to economize on the use of health care services. NHS specialists are salaried employees of regional health authorities. However, some physicians do receive fee-for-service payments for such services as preventive medicine and family planning services. Physicians who serve private hospitals are also paid on a fee-for-service basis.

Budgeting for capital expenditures is done by the government. Regional boards participate in decisions to acquire such new equipment as CT scanners. The budgetary limits on capital expenditures and payments to physicians often result in service shortages and long waiting lists. Typically, there is no problem in getting emergency care in Great Britain, but there are often long waits (weeks and even months) to obtain an appointment with a specialist. Doctors classify patients according to their needs for hospitalization and surgery, and the classification system determines the sequence in which patients are admitted to hospitals. As of early 1991 more than 700,000 people were on waiting lists for surgery in Great Britain. Of this number, about 200,000 had been on the lists for more than a year! It typically takes about a year to get to the top of a list for such common operations as hernia repairs, hip replacements, and cataract removals. Limitations on the amounts hospital budgets can pay surgeons have resulted in longer waiting lists.*

Frustrated by the long waits for health care services, many British citizens have undergone operations in private hospitals, where they must pay the *full cost* of the services provided. Although a heart bypass operation coupled with a valve replacement costs $26,250 at a private hospital, even patients of modest means have chosen to pay that large sum rather than risk the chance of dying while waiting to be admitted into an NHS hospital!† Britain spends about 6 percent of its GNP on health care—about half of the percentage spent in the United States. However, there are not enough health care services to go around, so those services are rationed by long waiting lists. Health care services are free to all, but not readily available.

* See Craig R. Whitney, "British Health Service, Much Beloved but Inadequate, Is Facing Changes," *The New York Times,* June 9, 1991, p. 11.

† Ibid.

FIGURE 17–5 The Effect of Increasing Coinsurance Payments

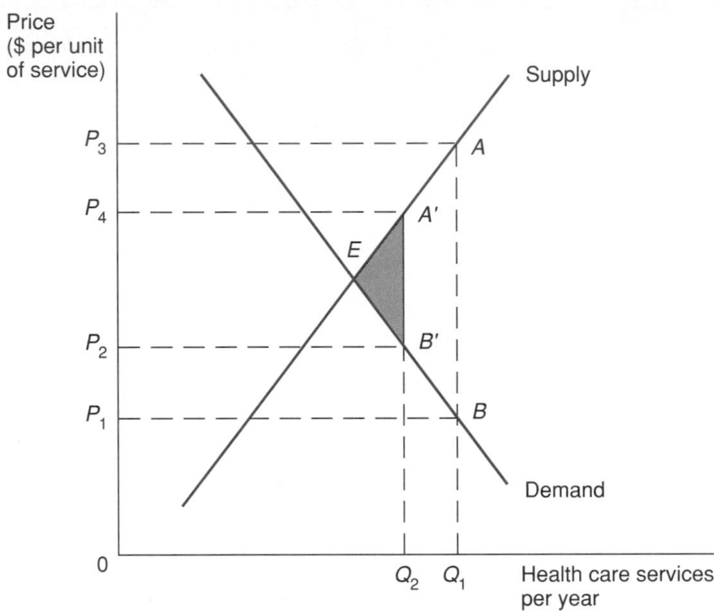

As coinsurance payments increase, the out-of-pocket costs to patients under health insurance plans increase. The resulting decrease in the quantity of health care services demanded reduces the loss in net benefits resulting from the overallocation of resources to health care services.

increased coinsurance the average market price of health care services would also decline. Both the decline in the quantity of health care services demanded and the decline in the price of those services would contribute to a decline in health care expenditures. There would also be a reduction in the overallocation of resources to health care services, and the loss in net benefits resulting from the inefficient use of those services would decline from an amount represented by the area *ABE* to an amount represented by the smaller area *A'B'E*.

Concept Review

1. Why is adverse selection a problem in insurance markets? What market mechanisms can reduce the problem of adverse selection?
2. What is the moral hazard of insurance?
3. How has the moral hazard problem contributed to soaring health care expenditures in the United States in recent years?

Asymmetric Information, Price Dispersion, and Advertising

Have you ever bought an item such as a stereo system only to find that you could have bought the same item at another store in your area for 20 percent less? Did this make you angry? If it gives you any comfort, asymmetric information may have been the culprit and it really might not have been worth your while to search for that low-priced store.

In a perfectly competitive market products are standardized. Because the product of any seller is a perfect substitute for the product of any other seller, we would naturally expect that if a seller tries to charge more than other sellers for its product, its sales will fall to zero. However, because of asymmetric information in the marketplace, it is possible for the prices of one seller to differ from the prices of other sellers even though products are standardized.

Price Dispersion in Retail Markets

Just think about your own situation when you are shopping for a product such as a TV. Suppose you want to buy a 21-inch color TV. You know that there are as many as 100 brands of such a TV on the market but that all of these brands are more or less the same. For the sake of argument, however, let's assume that you want to buy a particular Sony model and that many stores in your city sell this model. Let's also assume that all these stores have a policy of not quoting prices over the telephone, so you have to visit a store to see if it has what you want and to check its price.

When you are searching for information about prices, you are therefore going to have to use up time and some gasoline. Sellers know that their customers are not likely to be fully informed about the prices set by all competing sellers. As a result they know that if they raise the price of the TV you want above the prices set by some of their competitors, their sales of that TV will *not* fall to zero. Asymmetric information on prices can therefore cause the demand curve for a *particular seller's* products to become downward sloping, instead of being perfectly elastic at a competitive price, in an otherwise competitive market. Thus asymmetric information, with buyers being less informed than sellers about price, can bestow some monopoly power on sellers in markets that we would otherwise believe to be competitive. For this reason it is not unusual to observe **price dispersion,** a variety of prices for the same standardized product, in a market in which perfect competition appears to prevail.

Price dispersion The existence of a variety of prices for the same standardized product in a market in which perfect competition appears to prevail.

The cause of that price dispersion is the costs that buyers must incur to inform themselves about prices. To see why it is perfectly rational not to seek the lowest possible price for a product such as a TV, let's see how you might behave if you were in the market for a 21-inch Sony color TV. You might first visit the seller of this TV closest to your home and find that a local appliance store sells it for $300. You might then visit the Wal-Mart and find that it does not carry the model you want. You have therefore used some time, say one hour, and some gasoline

Search costs The costs that buyers incur to inform themselves about prices.

without getting any more information. The next day you go to Circuit City and find that it does have the model you want and that it is on sale for $279! Do you buy the TV at that point, or do you search some more for a lower price? If you are rational, what you will do is estimate the additional **search costs** you would have to incur: the time and resources you would have to use up, including the costs of telephone calls and materials that you might buy to obtain information. For example, if you consider going to Kmart to see whether it has the model you want at a lower price, you will weigh the additional search costs of going to Kmart against the expected return you might get from those costs. *You will continue to search the market for a lower price only up to the point at which the expected marginal benefit from such search falls to equal the marginal cost.*

You might estimate that a trip to Kmart will cost you two hours of time that you value at $10 per hour and $2 worth of gasoline. The marginal cost of continuing to search for a lower price would therefore be $22. If you reason that there is only a 50 percent chance that Kmart will have the TV at a price $22 lower than that of Circuit City, you will then reason that the expected return for going to Kmart will be only $11, which is half of $22. Because the marginal cost ($12) exceeds the marginal benefit ($11) of more searching, you will therefore buy the TV at Circuit City and stop searching!

On the other hand, someone who values her time more highly than you value yours might choose to buy the TV at the local appliance store even though it costs $300 there. For such a person, searching for a price lower than $300 is not worth the cost. This is why small retail stores can survive even though they charge higher prices than those charged by the large discounters. Of course, these stores may also be more friendly and offer better service than the large discounters, and this may influence the willingness of consumers to pay them higher prices.

If search costs were zero and information on prices were freely and symmetrically available to market participants, only one price would prevail in a competitive market. However, because of asymmetry of information and positive search costs, it is reasonable to expect some price dispersion even in markets that are otherwise competitive. It is also reasonable to expect less price dispersion for high-priced items than for lower-priced items. After all, certain costs of shopping around, such as the costs of travel time and telephone calls, are the same no matter what the price of the item. The marginal cost of searching for a lower price is therefore not likely to vary much from item to item. However, the marginal benefit of searching for a lower price tends to vary with the price of the item. If you are in the market for a new Mercedes with a list price of $65,000, a 1 percent price saving amounts to $650. On the other hand, a 1 percent price saving on a TV with a list price of $300 is only $3. If the probability that you will get a lower price by traveling to another seller is 50 percent, then it would be rational to make the trip to another Mercedes seller if that trip costs less than $325, but it would be rational to make the trip to another TV seller only if it costs less than $1.50! Analysis by economists does in fact support the hypothesis that price dispersion is less likely to be observed for high-priced items than for low-priced items. For example, price dispersion in a regional market for a given brand and model of a car is much less than price dispersion for a given brand and model of a household appliance such as a washing machine.[5]

Mechanisms that Reduce Price Dispersion in Product Markets

In product markets retailers often employ mechanisms that can reduce price dispersion. For example, Circuit City advertises a price "guarantee" under which customers who return with proof that a local competitor offers the same model TV at a lower price get a check for the price difference plus an additional 10 percent of that difference. Naturally, this guarantee reduces the incentive of buyers to search further and is likely to increase Circuit City's sales. Although the guarantee might be expected to reduce price dispersion, it is unlikely to reduce it to zero. Many people might buy a TV from Circuit City because of the guarantee, but not all of these buyers would search for a lower price after buying it! In addition, even the buyers who do find a lower price will weigh the extra costs of making another trip to Circuit City to collect their refund plus 10 percent against the marginal cost of doing so. If the trip requires two hours of time that you value at $10 per hour and $2 in gasoline, then you make the trip only if the refund amounts to more than $22!

Firms may also advertise or offer phone price quotes to provide buyers with better information. Insofar as advertising lowers the costs that buyers incur to collect information, it reduces search costs and price dispersion in markets. This reasoning leads to a surprising conclusion about advertising. Remember when we discussed advertising in a monopolistically competitive market we reasoned that advertising could make the demand for a seller's product more inelastic by establishing brand loyalty. In a highly competitive market, however, advertising can actually make the demand for any given seller *more elastic* by disseminating information that reduces search costs. When many sellers in a market advertise their prices, consumers become better informed about prices. This reduction in the asymmetry of information reduces the ability of any given seller in the market to raise price above the competitive level and not lose all of its sales. For example, your task of buying the Sony TV would have been a lot easier if you could have found the information you needed by looking at the ads in the local Sunday paper. If ads from your local appliance store, Wal-Mart, Kmart, and Circuit City each listed TV model numbers and prices, you could have just selected the store that offered the lowest price for the TV model you wanted and gone to that store. Easy access to telephone price quotes would have also made your job of buying the TV easier. Over the long run, advertising would therefore make the demand for any given seller more elastic and push all sellers to charge the same price.

[5] See George J. Stigler, "The Economics of Information," *Journal of Political Economy* 69 (June 1961), pp. 213–25.

In a classic study of the effect of advertising on the price of eyeglasses, one researcher concluded that allowing price quotes in eyeglass advertising contributed to lower prices. In fact, the prices of eyeglasses were much lower in states that allowed such advertising than in states that prohibited them.[6]

Tourists and Locals in Resorts

Have you ever visited a resort such as a beach during the summer or a tourist center such as Venice, Italy, and been shocked by the prices for meals in restaurants or even for such basics as toothpaste? In many cases, when you visit such an area, you plan to stay only a short period, maybe a week or two, and then return home. It is likely that the items you demand for your stay are available at much lower prices elsewhere in the area. In fact, the local residents are unlikely to be paying the exorbitant prices that you pay for toothpaste and meals because they are much better informed than you are about the alternatives in the area. However, is it really worth searching for lower prices as a tourist when you know that you are going to be in the area for only a week or two and that you are unlikely to return soon? The answer for most tourists is probably no!

Retailers in resort areas are well aware that tourists are more poorly informed about prices than are locals and that search costs are higher and have a smaller marginal return for tourists because they result in price savings over only a short period. It is therefore reasonable to expect considerably more price dispersion in a resort or tourist market than is normally observed in other retail markets.

In a resort or tourist area the high-priced outlets typically locate their operations near hotels or tourist attractions. They are therefore successful in sorting out tourists from the locals who will not pay the higher prices because they have information on the lower-priced alternatives in the area. Aside from the asymmetry of information, another reason why tourists pay higher prices is that land prices tend to be higher in the central tourist areas, which contributes to higher average costs of serving tourists at those locations. However, the high-priced outlets also provide a service to tourists by satisfying their demands at convenient locations. In many cases tourists gladly pay the higher prices rather than search for lower prices. For example, the hot dog stand at your college football stadium may charge $2 for a crummy hot dog. You could easily buy a much better hot dog for $1.25 at your local delicatessen. But would you risk missing the second half of the game by running out to the deli at halftime to satisfy your urge for a hot dog at a saving of 75 cents? Probably not. Similarly, tourists who value their time on vacations very highly are unlikely to search for lower prices if this means traveling an hour down ugly highways to visit the same kinds of suburban shopping centers they went on vacation to escape from!

The tourists-locals model of price dispersion therefore suggests that price dispersion is quite reasonable in tourist areas. It also suggests that such price dispersion may actually be efficient because it arises out of differences between

---

[6] See Lee Benham, "The Effect of Advertising on the Price of Eyeglasses," *Journal of Law and Economics* 15 (October 1972), pp. 45–74.

tourists and locals in the value and the marginal benefits of search costs. Finally, it suggests the *sorting* of high-priced and low-priced retail outlets by location. The high-priced outlets serve *only tourists* and are located near or in resort areas or near hotels. The low-priced outlets serve only locals and are located in areas away from hotels and tourist attractions.

CONCEPT REVIEW

1. What is price dispersion?
2. What are search costs, and how do they give rise to price dispersion?
3. What market mechanisms can reduce price dispersion?

ASYMMETRIC INFORMATION IN LABOR MARKETS

Asymmetry of information can adversely affect the markets for inputs. Sellers of labor services are typically much more knowledgeable about the quality of their services (their motivation, reliability, and skills) than are the employers who buy labor services in competitive labor markets. In general, employers take a gamble when they hire a new worker because they do not really know whether that worker will deliver what he or she promises. However, it is costly to hire a worker who does not perform well or who is ill suited for the job. Businesses typically invest a lot in training new workers and can significantly increase their production costs by hiring workers who perform poorly or who quit soon after having received their training.

In labor markets, as in most markets in which asymmetric information is a problem, mechanisms have been developed to reduce the costs associated with the asymmetry of information. These mechanisms include screening applicants for characteristics associated with good work performance and installing incentive-based pay plans designed to increase labor productivity. Let's now examine how employers cope with informational problems in labor markets.

Staffing, Signaling, and Screening

Staffing The process of recruiting and hiring workers to perform various tasks required to produce goods and services.

Staffing is the process of recruiting and hiring workers to perform the various tasks required to produce goods and services. This process includes advertising positions, evaluating applicants, and ranking applicants according to their qualifications. It also includes orientation and on-the-job training. Employers can add to their profits by keeping their staffing costs as low as possible.

There are various ways in which workers can *signal* their qualifications to employers. When you graduate from college, you will probably prepare a résumé that lists your educational accomplishments, experience, and skills. Employers will evaluate the signals you provide as indicators of the future productivity that they can expect from you. Employers realize that evaluation of those signals is no substitute for evaluation of your on-the-job performance. However, the signals

Labor market screening The process of limiting the applicants for a job to those who the employer believes are most likely to succeed in the organization.

you provide as an applicant offer employers a quick, cheap method of **labor market screening.** This is the process of limiting the applicants for a job to those who the employer believes are most likely to succeed in the organization. In deciding which applicants to interview, employers evaluate such signals as experience and education. For example, employers may consider only college graduates for certain positions or only persons who have taken a course in computer programming or have had actual experience in programming computers. By screening, employers seek to cut hiring costs and to select new employees from a pool of the most qualified applicants.

By far the most widespread screening device used by employers, particularly for entry-level positions, is education. As a result more and more people have attended college. The proportion of the labor force with a college education increased from 14 percent in 1970 to 27 percent in 1990. College-educated workers earn on average nearly twice as much as non-college-educated workers. The wage premium for a college education is largely due to the use of college education as a screen by employers. This has increased the incentive of high school students to go to college.

Let's now examine the role of a college education as a screening device.

Education as a Signal and a Screen

Workers with a college education may not be any smarter than workers who never attended college. Also, many jobs that require a college education—for example, many law enforcement jobs and many sales-oriented jobs—can be done by workers who never attended college. Why are employers so interested in a college degree when such a degree is not essential to the jobs they offer.

To find out why employers use a college education as a screen, let's set up a simple model of the labor market under conditions of asymmetric information with workers better informed than employers about the characteristics that affect their on-the-job performance. Suppose that workers can be divided into two categories: good quality and poor quality. Good-quality workers are well motivated, intelligent, reliable, and in general more productive than poor-quality workers. Suppose that half of the workers in the labor force are of good quality and that the other half are of poor quality.

Employers do not have perfect information on the quality of the pool of job applicants, but they do know that there is a 50 percent chance that any worker hired at random is of poor quality. Hiring workers at random would be costly because the poor-quality workers would produce less than the good-quality workers and would eventually have to be let go. Employers often invest a lot in on-the-job training, and such an investment would be wasted for the poor-quality, low-productivity workers whose period of employment is brief.

Suppose that on average good-quality workers are twice as productive as poor-quality workers. If it were possible to segment the labor market into good-quality and poor-quality workers and to pay workers of each category according to the value of their marginal product, then the wages of the good-quality workers would be twice as high as the wages of the poor-quality workers. Figure 17–6

FIGURE 17–6 The Effect of Signaling and Screening in Labor Markets

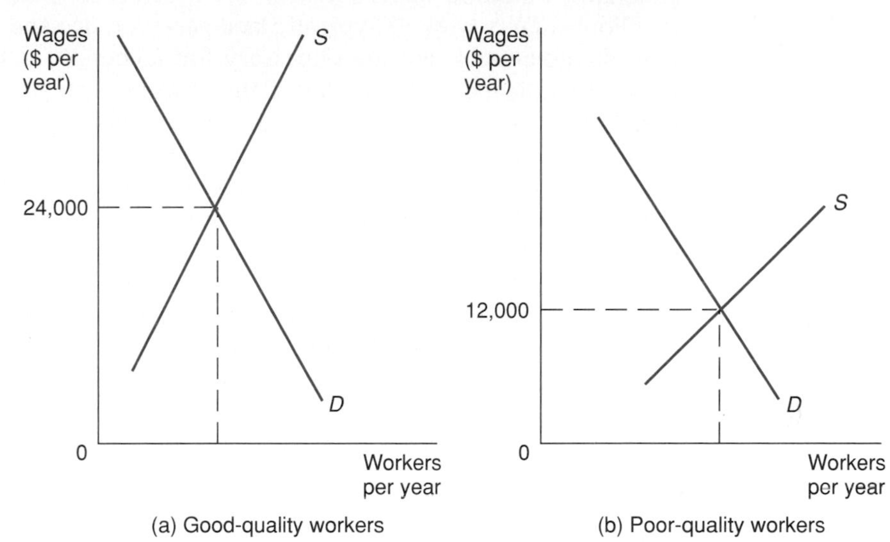

Workers signal their quality to employers through college degrees, and employers use screening to separate good-quality workers from poor-quality workers. This screening segments the labor market. College graduates are offered higher wages than are offered to workers without college degrees. In this way the labor market is segmented into two separate labor markets.

shows the wages, based on the value of the marginal product of poor- and good-quality workers, that would result when there is no asymmetry of information. The equilibrium wage is $12,000 per year for poor-quality workers and $24,000 per year for good-quality workers.

Because of the asymmetry of information, however, employers cannot identify the good-quality workers and would therefore be expected to offer all workers an initial wage of only $18,000 per year. This wage offer would alter the mix of good- and poor-quality workers in the manner now familiar to you for markets with asymmetric information. Wage offers would be revised downward as the probability of getting poor-quality workers increases. This would lead to labor market inefficiencies, which in turn would provide good-quality workers with incentives to signal their quality to employers and employers with incentives to seek means for screening to identify good-quality workers.

Education provides an ideal screen and signal in labor markets.[7] Education, as you all know, is a costly process for students. In addition to incurring costs for tuition, books, and the like, students must forgo employment opportunities and leisure time in order to do the hard work necessary to pass courses and earn the

[7] See A. Michael Spence, "Job Market Signaling," *Quarterly Journal of Economics*, August 1973, pp. 355–74.

college degree. In general, it is reasonable to assume that the costs of a college education would be higher for poor-quality workers than for good-quality workers. Poor-quality workers typically lack perseverance and motivation, two important characteristics that are necessary for success in college. Also, because of various handicaps, including lower than average intelligence and poor organizational skills, people who end up being poor-quality workers *would take longer* to complete the requirements for a college degree because they would be more likely to fail and therefore to repeat courses. Employers realize these facts and are therefore likely to screen workers according to their education even though education itself may not make workers more productive! From the employers' point of view, the value of education is that it serves as an indicator of other characteristics that are likely to be correlated with high productivity in the work force.

Thus employers use the education screen as a mechanism to segment labor markets. Applicants with a college degree are presumed to be good-quality workers and are therefore offered a wage of $24,000 per year, as shown in Figure 17–6(a). Applicants without a college degree are offered a wage of $12,000. Employers also segment workers by jobs. Workers without a college degree are placed in jobs whose marginal products are typically low, while workers with a college degree are placed in jobs whose marginal products are typically high. For example, all of the assembly line positions in a company may be offered to workers without a college degree, but all of the managerial positions may be offered to college graduates.

Once it is clear to prospective workers that employers pay college graduates more, won't they all want to go to college so they can offer this signal to the labor market and get higher wages? The answer to this question is no because of the differences in the costs of a college education among individuals. Remember, attending college is not sufficient to get the $24,000 wage, because employers offer that wage to college graduates only. Therefore, in deciding whether to attend college, high school graduates compare the marginal cost of a college education that results in a degree with the marginal benefit of the wage increment that they can expect from the degree.

Suppose that the discounted present value of the additional real wages after taxes that obtaining a college degree makes possible for a worker over a lifetime is $150,000.[8] Also suppose that good-quality workers estimate that the discounted present value of a college education, including forgone earnings and the sacrifice of leisure time required to pass courses, is $110,000. For these good-quality workers, the net gain from getting a college degree therefore has a discounted present value of $40,000. Assuming that there are no other costs or benefits from getting a college degree, these people will choose to get the degree and to offer it as a signal in labor markets.

However, as we have pointed out, getting a college degree is much more costly for poor-quality workers than for good-quality workers. Thus, poor-quality workers may find that for them the discounted present value of the costs of a

[8] See Chapter 14 for a definition of the concept of discounted present value of a stream of future earnings.

TABLE 17–1 Net Gain or Net Loss of a College Degree

Type of Worker	*Good Quality*	*Poor Quality*
Benefits	$150,000	$150,000
Costs	110,000	160,000
Net gain	40,000	−10,000

college education is $160,000. This means that getting a degree will result in a net loss with a discounted present value of $10,000. Poor-quality workers therefore do not attend college. Table 17–1 summarizes the data from this example and shows the net gain or net loss of a college degree for the two types of workers.

We can now conclude that education is remarkably efficient *both* as a screening and as a sorting device. Even if education did not increase worker productivity, the college degree would serve to screen high-productivity workers from low-productivity workers and thus improve the efficiency of labor markets. And because education does in fact impart useful skills, employers get an extra bonus when they use it as a screening device because they often obtain a skill premium from education that increases worker productivity.

An important lesson of this exercise is that a key factor influencing the demand for a college education is the wage premium that students can expect from a college degree. Since 1967 this premium has increased substantially for both men and women. In 1967 a typical woman with a college degree could expect to earn 1.8 times as much as a woman who did not attend college. By 1990 she could expect to earn 2.1 times as much. A typical man with a college degree could expect to earn 1.47 times as much as a male high school graduate in 1967 and 1.75 times as much as a male high school graduate in 1990. The increase in wage premiums for a college degree contributed to increased college enrollments in the 1980s, and perhaps to a decrease in the quality of the students who attended college, as more students for whom college work was difficult chose to attend college, lured by the incentive of higher lifetime earnings. You too are seeking to signal your worth to employers by working toward a college degree!

The Principal-Agent Problem and Shirking

Shirking Behavior by workers that prevents an employer from achieving the maximum possible marginal product from its work force over a given period.

Another informational problem that prevails in labor markets occurs *after* workers have been hired. As a practical matter, employers often lack information on the actual job performance of workers. Employers must incur costs to ascertain whether workers are actually performing assigned tasks to the best of their abilities. **Shirking** is behavior by workers that prevents an employer from achieving the maximum possible marginal product from its work force over a given period. Shirkers are of concern to employers because they increase costs above the minimum possible levels, because they cause the average product of other workers to fall, and because they make it necessary for other workers to compensate for their inadequate efforts.

Monitoring, or observing, workers to compare their performance with objective standards is a difficult and costly process. However, some monitoring is necessary when the *principals* of an organization, whose goals are affected by the performance of its workers, have goals that differ from the goals of the workers, who are their *agents*. When the goals of an organization's principals and agents differ, a **principal-agent problem** exists.

Principal-agent problem The problem that exists when the goals of an organization's principals and agents differ.

The principals of a business firm are its owners, whose goal is presumably to maximize profit from the firm's use of resources. In a corporation the principals are the stockholders. The agents are the workers, whose goal may be to minimize their workloads or to minimize their stress on the job rather than to work effectively so as to ensure profit maximization. The principal-agent problem in a business firm forces the firm's owners to incur extra costs to monitor the work force. The owners must balance these extra costs against the gains they obtain from added productivity and lower production costs when shirking is reduced. The costs of excessive monitoring and the resentment it arouses have led many firms to choose other methods of dealing with the principal-agent problem. For example, the total quality management system we discussed in Chapter 7 is really a way to help solve the principal-agent problem by improving communication between workers and employers.

Compensation Plans and Efficiency Wages

A common method of dealing with the principal-agent problem is to compensate workers so that they have a greater incentive to assist the business firm in maximizing profit. Compensation plans based on bonus payments and profit sharing are designed to make it in the interest of workers not to shirk by allowing them to earn more as the firm's profit increases. For example, a profit sharing plan reduces the differences between the goals of workers and the goals of employers by giving workers a share of profits as a supplement to wages. Managers of corporations are typically given stock options as part of their compensation. Such options allow managers to buy a corporation's stock at a set low price as of a given date. Because the price of the stock is favorably influenced by the corporation's long-term potential for earning profits, stock options give managers an incentive to increase its profitability. Managers can then buy the stock at the set price and enjoy an immediate capital gain.

Similarly, assembly line workers can be given inducements to work harder by being paid partly in the form of stock or of bonuses based on profits. Professional athletes often earn bonuses based on annual paid admissions to games. Such bonuses motivate these athletes to perform their best in order to win games and maximize attendance.

Performance-based contracts are another method of dealing with the principal-agent problem. This method often gives workers certain annual production or sales quotas that they are encouraged to meet or exceed. After achieving their quotas, they receive cash bonuses based on the additional output or sales they have generated. This method provides an incentive-based solution rather than a monitoring-based solution to the principal-agent problem.

A method that business firms often employ to ensure performance is to pay experienced workers higher wages than they can earn by working in alternative jobs or occupations for which they are qualified. For example, if the competitive market equilibrium wage of experienced assembly line workers in the personal computer industry is $10 per hour, the Dynamic Computer Company might choose to pay its experienced assembly line workers $15 per hour. This higher wage coupled with good working conditions provides Dynamic's workers with an incentive to work hard. Why? Because they know that if they were to lose their job because of poor performance, they would take a very sharp reduction in pay and perhaps suffer a deterioration in working conditions.

Efficiency wages Wages set above market equilibrium wages in order to eliminate shirking.

Efficiency wages are wages set above competitive equilibrium wages in order to eliminate shirking. Efficiency wages vary with the extent of unemployment in the economy. In general, they tend to be set at high levels when labor markets are tight because of low unemployment. When the economy is booming, competitive equilibrium wages are also high, so efficiency wages must be increased to avoid losing workers to competing firms. In recessions, however, when workers know they have few, if any, alternative employment opportunities, employers can pay lower wages and yet avoid shirking because workers fear that if they lose their job, it will be hard to find another.

The theory of efficiency wages suggests that as all firms seek to avoid shirking, market equilibrium wage rates rise above competitive equilibrium levels and unemployment increases. Then, even though all workers are earning more than the competitive equilibrium wage, they still tend to avoid shirking because they know that if they are fired, they might be unemployed for a long time before being rehired.[9]

The efficiency wage model presumes that worker productivity can be influenced by the wage employers pay. Higher wages attract better workers and reduce the incentive to shirk. Many employers realize that "you get what you pay for" and find that good pay and good working conditions contribute to higher productivity and higher profits!

Internal labor market A labor market within a firm used to fill new and upper-level positions.

A method to avoid shirking that resembles efficiency wages is the use of an **internal labor market,** a labor market within a firm, to fill new and upper-level positions. This labor market considers only the most promising employees for upper-level positions. After the productivity of lower-level screened workers has been evaluated, the best workers are promoted to those positions. This serves the dual purpose of minimizing hiring costs and providing workers with incentives not to shirk. For example, to obtain a position with a package delivery firm, a worker may first have to work in the freight terminal as a sorter. If the worker performs well in that position, the firm is likely to promote the worker to delivery driver or supervisor at significantly higher pay.

---

[9] See Janet Yellen, "Efficiency Wage Models of Unemployment," *American Economic Review* 74 (May 1984), pp. 200–205.

Concept Review

1. What is screening?
2. Why is a college education both a good signal and a good screening device?
3. What is the principal-agent problem, and what methods can be used to solve it?

Conclusion: Information and Market Performance

Through the various models of product and input markets discussed in this chapter, we have shown how asymmetry of information can impair the performance of markets. We have also shown how human ingenuity can result in net gains by developing mechanisms that generate information at relatively low cost. Information is a scarce good. Therefore, we can expect market participants to invest in mechanisms that generate information up to the point at which the marginal benefit falls to equal the marginal cost of doing so.

Summary

1. Asymmetry of information exists in a market if either buyers or sellers are better informed about product characteristics than those with whom they trade.
2. In markets for used products the sellers are typically better informed than the buyers about the quality of the products offered for sale.
3. If information were freely available, markets for used products would be segmented by quality. Asymmetry of information in those markets, however, makes such segmentation impossible. If buyers are less informed than sellers about product quality, they base their offer price on the expected value of the used product, which is derived from their assessment of the probability of getting stuck with a poor-quality product.
4. Asymmetry of information in the markets for used products results in losses of net benefits as good-quality products are driven off the markets by poor-quality products. In markets with asymmetric information, the decrease in the offer price for good-quality used products can reduce to zero the quantity supplied of such products.
5. In markets with asymmetric information sellers usually develop mechanisms to signal the characteristics of the products they offer for sale. In markets for used products guarantees, warranties, and information on product quality are used to signal the sale of high-quality used products.
6. In monopolistically competitive markets whose products are not standardized, guarantees, warranties, and franchises are often used to signal product quality.
7. Insurance markets are characterized by asymmetry of information in which sellers are more poorly informed than buyers.
8. In insurance markets the problem of adverse selection can result in losses for insurance companies if they base premiums on the average probability of a claim. Under adverse selection insurance purchasers are better informed about risks than are insurance companies. Adverse selection of clients results in increases in premiums that can drive low-risk clients out of the market as insurance becomes a bad deal for them.
9. To deal with the adverse selection problem, insurance companies gather more information about applicants for insurance or sell insurance

programs to large groups, all of whose members are required to enroll in the programs. For such groups, the probability of claims is likely to be closer to the average for the population as a whole than the probability of claims for individual applicants.

10. Because of the adverse selection problem, government can play an important role in insurance markets by requiring everybody to enroll in insurance programs and basing premiums on average probabilities of loss for the entire population.

11. The problem of moral hazard in insurance results from the fact that the risk of payout increases as the availability of insurance reduces the precautions people normally take against losses.

12. Moral hazard is a particularly severe problem for health insurance because third-party payments for health care services increase the quantity of such services demanded and reduce the incentive to take precautionary measures that can improve health. The moral hazard of health insurance reduces the incentive of both consumers and providers to economize on the use of health care services. As a result more than the efficient amount of resources is allocated to the provision of such services.

13. Most health insurance plans start paying benefits only after the patient has incurred a deductible and require coinsurance in which the patient pays part of the additional health care costs. Increasing deductibles and coinsurance can reduce the overallocation of resources to health care that results from the moral hazard problem.

14. Asymmetry of information about products can lead to price dispersion even in competitive markets with standardized products. Price dispersion exists because rational consumers search for a lower price only up to the point at which they expect marginal benefit of doing so falls to the marginal cost of searching. Price dispersion can be reduced by price guarantees or by improved information about prices through such means as telephone quotes and advertising.

15. Asymmetry of information prevails in labor markets because workers are typically better informed about their skills, motivation, and other factors affecting their productivity than are the employers who buy their services. Education is commonly used as a screen in labor markets to separate good-quality workers from poor-quality workers. Typically, only good-quality workers find that the benefits of a college degree are worth its costs, so a college degree is a reliable means of sorting good-quality workers from poor-quality workers.

16. The principal-agent problem exists when the goals of workers differ from the goals of owners of firms. Compensation plans that link the pay of workers to the profitability of firms can help deal with this problem.

17. Efficiency wages are wages set above competitive equilibrium wages in order to eliminate shirking. Efficiency wages induce workers to perform better because they know that if they lose their job, they will not find another that pays as well. Efficiency wage levels are inversely related to unemployment rates in the economy.

Important Concepts

asymmetric information
market signal
adverse selection
moral hazard
third-party payments
deductible
coinsurance
price dispersion
search costs
staffing
labor market screening
shirking
principal-agent problem
efficiency wages
internal labor market

Questions for Review

1. Under what circumstances will asymmetric information prevail in a market?
2. Explain how asymmetric information about product quality can affect the decisions of buyers and sellers in a market for secondhand furniture.
3. What is a market signal?
4. Explain how the provision of insurance services to large groups of clients can reduce the impact of the adverse selection problem on the profitability of selling insurance.
5. Explain how the system of health insurance in the United States has contributed to soaring health care expenditures?
6. What types of moral hazards might an insurance company encounter in selling comprehensive theft and damage insurance for automobiles?
7. How can we explain differences in the prices that competitors charge for a standardized product?
8. What types of signals and screens are used to deal with the problem of asymmetric information in labor markets?
9. Why is there likely to be a principal-agent problem in large corporations?
10. What are efficiency wages?

Problems

1. Suppose that automobile mechanics in your city offer a new service to purchasers of used cars. For $50 they will evaluate any used car whose purchase a person is considering and give an estimate of the car's expected repair and maintenance costs over the next two years. Use supply and demand analysis to show how this service is likely to affect the prices and the efficiency of the used car market.
2. In recent years health insurance underwriters have moved from "community rating" to "experience rating" of the risks of providing group insurance to employees of small businesses. Under experience rating they base the premiums of a group on the expected payouts *for that group*. Each year, based on experience with the group, the premiums are adjusted. Experience rating results in low premiums for healthy groups of employees but in very high premiums for groups of employees that include employees who incur high medical costs. Explain how experience rating can be viewed as a response to asymmetric information in insurance markets. How can experience rating diminish the moral hazard problem of health insurance?
3. Many health insurance companies now include heart and liver transplants among the medical procedures covered by their policies. Draw demand and supply curves for heart transplant operations and show how third-party payments for these operations affect the market and are likely to result in more than the efficient number of heart transplants per year.
4. Suppose that a law is passed requiring that all health insurance policies have a $1,000 deductible and a 50 percent coinsurance rate, which represents a considerable increase over the current levels. Under this law, however, after a patient has incurred more than $3,000 in out-of-pocket costs per year for health care services, the insurance company is required to pay all of the remaining costs. Show how the increase in the deductible and coinsurance will affect the market for health care services.
5. In recent years the wage premium of college graduates over high school graduates has increased substantially. Explain why an increase in the lifetime income gain from having a college degree is likely both to increase college enrollments and to decrease the average quality of college students.
6. The Dynamic Computer Software Company pays its employees wages and fringe benefits that average 25 percent above the market equilibrium wages paid to workers of similar skill and education in its labor market. Explain this differential in terms of the mechanisms used to reduce the costs of the principal-agent problem.

18 Externalities and Public Goods

Suppose you live near a chemical manufacturing firm that disposes of its wastes in a stream near your home. You are undoubtedly concerned that the wastes will pollute the stream, diminishing its recreational value as wildlife dies and swimming becomes risky. Worst of all, the wastes could contaminate drinking water, thereby imperiling your health. The manufacturing firm's production of chemicals for the benefit of its customers therefore affects you as well, by diminishing your benefits from the stream and increasing the risk of damage to your health. Naturally, your concern about these problems is going to lead you to demand that government do something about them.

The role of government in society is a deeply personal issue for most people. Governments have an important place in our society through activities that regulate markets and provide basic services that we rely on daily, such as police and fire protection, national defense, improvements in environmental quality, education, and roads.

We demand government services because even perfectly competitive markets often fail to allocate resources efficiently. Polluted air and water, congestion in cities, and inadequate market supplies of education, social insurance, and cultural activities are all symptoms of the failure of markets to achieve efficient output levels. When markets fail to achieve efficient output levels or when trading in markets has such unfortunate side effects as environmental damage and neglect of social problems, we often look to government for solutions. The fact is that many useful products and services cannot be provided in efficient amounts through markets.

In the preceding chapter we examined the losses in efficiency caused by asymmetry of information. We will now examine some other causes of market failure and government policies to correct it. In 1990, for example, Congress enacted legislation to provide Americans with cleaner air. The Clean Air Act of 1990 will require automakers to spend billions of dollars to reduce the pollutants emitted by cars. The act's new restrictions on the burning of high-sulfur coal by electric power plants will force these power companies to pay for the right to emit sulfur dioxides.

In 1991 governments in the United States spent nearly $2 trillion, or about one third of the GNP. In that year the federal government spent $273 billion on national defense. Because the cold war has ended, however, the benefits of defense spending are likely to decline in the future. As you will see, the efficient level of spending for public services depends on both the benefits and the costs of such services.

EXTERNALITIES

Externalities Costs or benefits of market transactions not reflected in prices.

Externalities are costs or benefits of market transactions not reflected in prices. These costs or benefits are "external" to the market prices of the goods whose production or consumption generates them. Externalities are effects on third parties not participating in market exchanges that are not reflected in the market values of the traded goods.

Negative externality A cost of resource use not reflected in the price of a product.

A **negative externality** is a cost of resource use not reflected in the price of a product. Negative externalities can result from either the production or the consumption of a good exchanged in markets. For example, a chemical manufacturing firm that disposes of wastes in a stream without paying for the damage done by those wastes is causing a negative externality from production. When a negative externality exists, the opportunity cost of using the stream as a dump is not included as part of the marginal cost of producing the firm's product. Consequently, the marginal cost of using the stream is not reflected in the price of the product.

The damages done by the wastes include the loss of the stream's recreational and commercial benefits. For example, the more wastes there are in the stream, the fewer are the stream's benefits from such alternative uses as fishing, swimming, and boating. If a way could be developed for those who bear these costs, such as fishermen and vacationers, to negotiate with either the buyers or the sellers of the chemical product for payment of damages, the price of the product would rise.

When you drive your car, you are responsible for a negative externality because you damage air quality and are not charged for that damage. Similarly, noisy neighbors are responsible for negative externalities through their consumption of housing services if they are not charged for the discomfort they cause.

Positive externality A benefit not reflected in prices.

A **positive externality** is a benefit not reflected in prices. For example, if your efforts to keep your lawn and garden attractive benefit your neighbors, you are generating a positive externality if your neighbors do not pay for the benefit they receive from those efforts. Third parties might be willing to contribute to your gardening costs. The existence of the positive externality enables them to obtain the benefit of your efforts without doing so.

Fire prevention is another activity that generates positive externalities. If you live in an apartment building or a group of attached condominiums, you benefit from your neighbors' fire prevention efforts without having to pay for them, though you might be willing to contribute to those efforts. Similarly, good sanitation services provide benefits to persons other than the buyers and sellers of the services. If your neighbor refused to hire someone to remove trash, you and other neighbors might be willing to pay at least part of the cost of its removal because you would benefit from having it removed.

Do not confuse externalities with price changes caused by changes in the relative scarcity of goods or services. A sharp increase in the demand for skiing is likely to increase the prices of items related to skiing. This means that the prices of bindings, lift fees, room rates at resorts, and other ski-related items are likely to go up. Persons who already ski are clearly made worse off when these prices rise. Is there an externality in this case? The answer is no! It is true that new skiers do not consider the fact that existing skiers are being made worse off by their sudden interest in skiing. But the increase in the price of ski-related items is merely a signal that these items are now scarcer relative to the demand for them. The price increases in response to the increased demand merely reflect the fact that the market functions well. If price did not increase, there would be a shortage of ski-related items.

By the same token, a sudden decrease in the demand for such items would not result in an external benefit as their prices fell. It would merely signal the fact that the relative scarcity of the items has declined. All of the costs and benefits are still reflected in prices. There is therefore no externality.

Negative Externalities

Let's first examine the consequences of negative externalities. Suppose that firms producing chemicals operate under conditions of perfect competition. Assume that all of the firms in the chemical industry pollute streams and lakes. Also suppose that each ton of the chemicals that these firms produce causes $10 worth of damage to parties other than the parties that produce or consume the chemicals.

Marginal external cost The extra cost imposed on third parties, for which producers are not charged, for each extra unit of output.

The **marginal external cost** (MEC) is the extra cost imposed on third parties, for which producers are not charged, resulting from each extra unit of output. In this example the marginal external cost is assumed to be $10 per ton of chemicals. The way marginal external costs vary with the output of goods depends on the particular industry involved. For example, it is quite possible for pollution to be a more costly problem at higher levels of output than at lower levels of output. In that case the marginal external cost would increase with output. Assuming a constant marginal external cost simplifies the analysis. The main points to be made from the analysis of a negative externality also hold when marginal external cost is not constant.

Marginal private cost The marginal cost of production incurred by sellers.

Marginal social cost The sum of the marginal private cost and the marginal external cost of a product.

Figure 18–1 shows the market demand and supply for chemicals. The current market equilibrium price is $100 per ton, and at that price 10,000 tons per day are sold. The demand for the chemicals reflects their marginal benefits to users. The industry supply curve of chemicals reflects the marginal costs of production incurred by individual producers. This is the **marginal private cost** (MPC) of producing chemicals. *The marginal private cost of each unit of output does not include the marginal external cost when a negative externality prevails.* Only the value of input services purchased or owned by individual firms is included in marginal private cost.

Adding the marginal external cost to the marginal private cost gives the **marginal social cost** (MSC) of producing the chemicals. This is the value of all opportunities forgone in producing each extra ton of chemicals.

FIGURE 18–1 A Negative Externality

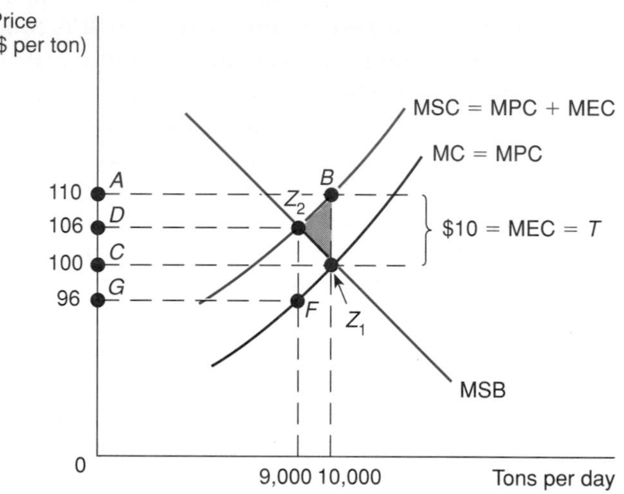

The market equilibrium occurs at Z_1, where P = MSB = MPC. The marginal social cost is MSC = MPC + MEC. The efficient output is at point Z_2, where MSC = MSB. The competitive market results in excessive production relative to the efficient amount. A corrective tax of $\$T$ = \$MEC per unit of output increases the market price to \$106 and reduces the production of chemicals to 9,000 tons per day, the efficient amount.

When a negative externality exists, marginal private cost is less than marginal social cost. Producers make their decisions about how much to produce on the basis of costs that are too low. In effect, they are not being charged for the use of all resources whose value they reduce in alternative uses. In this case the reduction in the value of water resources for recreation, fishing, drinking, and other competing uses is not included in the costs of producing the chemicals.

Figure 18–1 shows the marginal social cost of chemicals; this cost is obtained by adding the \$10 marginal external cost to the marginal private cost of each possible output. *The efficient output and price correspond to the point at which marginal social cost equals the marginal social benefit of chemicals produced.* The **marginal social benefit** (MSB) of any quantity is the extra benefit enjoyed when one more unit of a good is produced. If there are no beneficiaries of the chemical output other than consumers, the marginal social benefit is the marginal benefit obtained by buyers.

Marginal social benefit The extra benefit enjoyed when one more unit of a good or service is made available.

In Figure 18–1 the efficient output corresponds to point Z_2, at which

$$\text{MSB} = \text{MSC} \tag{18–1}$$

The efficient output is 9,000 tons per day, and the price necessary to achieve sales of that amount is \$106 per ton, corresponding to point Z_2. The market equilibrium, however, corresponds to point Z_1, at which the price of chemicals is only \$100 per ton and daily output sold is 10,000 tons. The market equilibrium corresponds to the point at which the MPC curve intersects the MSB curve. Given that each ton of chemicals results in $10 in damage to other users of the stream at the 10,000-ton market output, the total external cost is $100,000 of damage resulting from water pollution each day. That damage is represented by the area ABZ_1C in Figure 18–1. At the market output the marginal social cost of chemicals exceeds the marginal social benefit. As a result more than the efficient output is produced. The loss in efficiency is represented by the area Z_1Z_2B. This represents the net gains that would be possible if the output of chemicals were reduced to the efficient quantity of 9,000 tons per day.

If the third parties were able to charge chemical firms a price of $10 per ton of chemicals, the marginal cost of production would increase to

$$\text{MSC} = \text{MPC} + \text{MEC} = \text{MPC} + \$10 \qquad \textbf{(18–2)}$$

Firms in the chemical industry would cut back production to 9,000 tons per day. As shown in Figure 18–1, the price of a ton of chemicals would rise from $100 to $106. At the reduced output pollution damage would fall to $90,000 per day. This is the amount represented by the area DZ_2FG in Figure 18–1, which is $10 per ton multiplied by the 9,000-ton daily output.

Although pollution damage is reduced when the chemical firm is charged for that damage, it is not eliminated in this case. This is because at the $106 market price the firm finds it profitable to pay for the damage but produce less. The outcome of charges for the damage depends on other alternatives available to chemical firms. For example, if the increase in variable costs resulting from the damage charge makes it impossible for chemical firms to earn a profit, they will eventually go out of business. Chemical firms will also compare their maximum possible profit when they pay the cost of pollution damage with the profit that they could earn by changing production methods to reduce or eliminate pollution.

At the efficient output chemical firms use the stream to dispose of their wastes, but they pay the full marginal external cost of that use. At the efficient output chemical firms would pay $90,000 in damages to other users of the stream, an amount equal to the damage of $10 per ton multiplied by the efficient output.

The general condition for efficiency when a negative externality exists is

$$\text{MPC} + \text{MEC} = \text{MSC} = \text{MSB} \qquad \textbf{(18–3)}$$

Adding the value of the marginal external cost to the marginal private cost of production adjusts those costs upward to the marginal social cost. When a negative externality is present, the sale of a good in a competitive market results in too much output and a price that is too low relative to the efficient price and output.

Positive Externalities

Now let's examine a situation in which a positive externality prevails. Assume that a positive externality is associated with college education. In that case third parties other than students and colleges, the consumers and suppliers of the services associated with college education, gain when those services are exchanged. Also assume that college education is supplied by a competitive higher

FIGURE 18–2 A Positive Externality

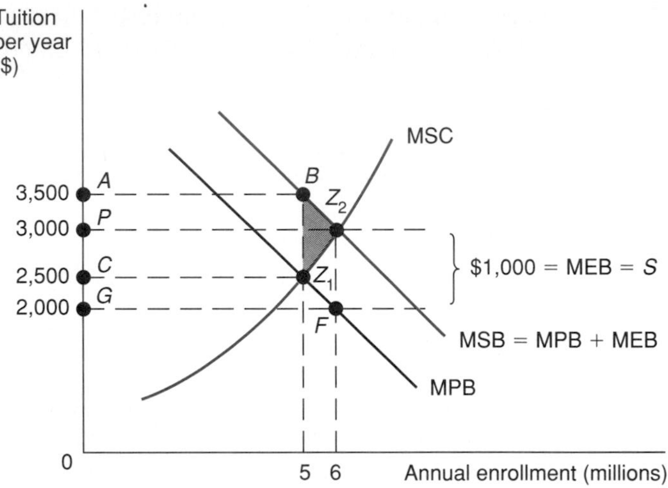

When a positive externality is present, marginal private benefit falls short of marginal social benefit. Market equilibrium at point Z_1 results in too little output relative to the efficient amount. The efficient amount is at point Z_2 where MPB + MEB = MSC. A corrective subsidy of \$$S$ = \$MEB per student increases demand for higher education to achieve the efficient enrollment.

education industry. Independent colleges and universities providing a standardized curriculum and standardized instruction compete for students. The equilibrium tuition established in the market for higher education services is $2,500 per year. At that price annual enrollment is 5 million full-time students pursuing degrees. This is illustrated in Figure 18–2. The market equilibrium corresponds to point Z_1. The supply of higher educational services reflects their marginal social cost of production.

Marginal private benefit The benefit obtained by the buyer when one more unit of an item is sold.

The **marginal private benefit** (MPB) of a good is the marginal benefit obtained by the buyer of one more unit sold. This is the benefit received by students and reflects the maximum tuition that students will pay to enroll in college for each possible level of enrollment supplied. *When a positive externality exists, the marginal private benefit of a given quantity of a good falls short of its marginal social benefit*. The value of the marginal benefits to third parties must be added to the value of marginal private benefits to obtain the marginal social benefit associated with each quantity.

Marginal external benefit The marginal benefit received by third parties other than the buyers or sellers of a good or service.

The **marginal external benefit** (MEB) of a good is the marginal benefit received by third parties other than buyers or sellers of the good. Suppose the benefits to third parties amount to $1,000 per student per year. Recipients of these external benefits believe that they benefit from living in a society in which people are better educated. They may believe that this decreases crime rates and improves the rate of technological advance. No matter what the reason, these recipients would be willing to contribute to the tuition of students who enroll in colleges and universities.

MODERN MICROECONOMICS IN ACTION: INTERNATIONAL REPORT

Global Externalities: Ozone Depletion and Global Warming

As we approach the year 2000, externalities are becoming more global in scope. Depletion of the stratospheric ozone layer is an issue of global relevance. Continued deforestation and continued use of fossil fuels may affect the global climate. Even though the effects of global environmental degradation may not be felt for many years, we need to assess current policies to make sure that future generations will not suffer from those effects.

Depletion of the ozone layer could increase exposure to solar ultraviolet radiation, thereby increasing the incidence of cancer and cataracts. It could also have unfavorable effects on crops, fish, and materials used in production. A major cause of ozone depletion is the emission of chlorofluorocarbons (CFCs) and other chemicals that are used in aerosol propellants, refrigerants, and fire extinguishers and in the production of solvents and insulation board. CFCs disperse in the atmosphere no matter where they are used and increase the chlorine and bromine concentrations that are responsible for ozone depletion. To reduce the CFC problem, *all* countries must act together. Major users of CFCs have signed international agreements to cut their production in half by 1998. It has been estimated that the cost of these agreements for the United States alone will be $2.7 billion during the 1990s.

Another global environmental issue is climate change. Many environmentalists believe that the burning of fossil fuels, certain agricultural practices, and deforestation will increase the concentration of atmospheric gases that absorb heat and allow the heat to radiate toward the earth. This "greenhouse effect," by warming the earth's climate, might have disastrous results in agricultural and coastal areas. Scientists disagree about the seriousness of this threat. However, the issue could result in international conflict if the world's advanced nations "square off" against less developed countries to reduce deforestation. Net carbon dioxide emissions depend on the extent of the world forest cover. Deforestation in Africa and Brazil could contribute to the greenhouse effect by lowering the planetary absorption of carbon dioxide. Attempts to reduce the harvesting or clearing of forests in less developed nations and low-income regions of more advanced nations can slow growth and thus impair health and living standards in areas whose people are already very poor. The nations affected by such attempts are likely to resist them unless they receive compensation from the nations that will benefit from them.

One way to avert the greenhouse effect is to discourage the use of fossil fuels by taxing them at a high rate. However, the resulting increase in energy costs could significantly slow the economic growth of advanced and developing nations alike unless low-cost nonfossil energy (such as solar power) becomes available.

The current scientific information on the greenhouse effect is inconclusive. Any benefits from action to forestall the effect will accrue in the future. Those future benefits must be discounted to obtain their current values, which can then be compared with current costs.

Adding the $1,000 marginal external benefit to the marginal private benefit received by each student gives the marginal social benefit of any given level of enrollment. In Figure 18–2 the marginal social benefit associated with any enrollment level is

$$\text{MSB} = \text{MPB} + \text{MEB} = \text{MPB} + \$1{,}000 \tag{18–4}$$

The efficient level of enrollment corresponds to point Z_2, at which

$$\text{MSB} = \text{MPB} + \text{MEB} = \text{MSC} \tag{18–5}$$

The efficient output is enrollment of 6 million full-time students. The marginal cost of producing that output is $3,000 tuition per student per year. However, to induce the annual enrollment of an additional 1 million students, tuition would have to be reduced to $2,000 per year, corresponding to point F on the MPB curve. This is because students still base their decisions on the marginal private benefit. The efficient equilibrium at point Z_2 would therefore require tuition of $2,000 per year. Third parties would have to make up the difference between the $2,000 tuition paid by students and the $3,000 marginal cost required by suppliers to accommodate 1 million more students. This difference reflects the $1,000 marginal external benefit per student.

The market equilibrium at point Z_1, however, results in positive externalities represented by the area ABZ_1C. The value of these externalities is $5 billion at the market equilibrium ($1,000 multiplied by 5 million students). Allowing third parties to contribute $1,000 per student would increase yearly enrollment to 6 million full-time students. The sum of $6 billion would be paid per year by third parties to students and colleges now participating in the exchange of higher education services. That sum is represented by the area PZ_2FG in Figure 18–2.

When a positive externality exists, market equilibrium results in the exchange of less than the efficient amount of a good or service. To achieve the efficient output, a way must be found to enable the third parties that enjoy the positive externality to contribute to its production and consumption. A portion of that contribution would be used to reduce the price paid by consumers so as to induce them to consume more. The remainder would be used to cover any increases in marginal costs necessary to induce producers to supply more.

Internalization of Externalities

Internalization of an externality The condition that results when marginal private costs or benefits associated with the market exchange of an item are adjusted to reflect actual marginal social costs or benefits of choices.

Corrective tax A levy on the output of a good or service that increases its marginal private cost to a level equal to its marginal social cost.

Internalization of an externality results when marginal private costs or benefits associated with the market exchange of a good are adjusted to reflect actual marginal social costs or benefits of choices. To internalize a negative externality, the marginal external cost must be added to the marginal private cost. Internalization of a negative externality results in an upward pressure on the price of the good that generates the externality and causes quantity demanded of the good to decline. To internalize a positive externality, the price of a good to consumers must fall so as to encourage more consumption of the good.

Corrective Taxes

A **corrective tax** is a levy on the output of a good or service that increases its marginal private cost to a level equal to its marginal social cost. A corrective tax internalizes a negative externality by raising the marginal cost of an item by an amount equal to the marginal external cost. This puts an upward pressure on the price of a good sold in a perfectly competitive market until that price rises to equal the marginal social cost of the good.

Suppose such a tax is levied on the output of chemical firms when a $10 marginal external cost is associated with each ton of output. A tax of $10 on each ton of chemicals produced increases the marginal costs of producers by $10 per ton of chemical produced. This is exactly equal to the damage associated with each ton of chemicals. The corrective tax per unit of output (T) is therefore equal to the marginal external cost:

$$T = \text{MEC} = \$10 \text{ per ton}$$

The effect of the tax can be analyzed by use of Figure 18–1. The initial market equilibrium corresponds to point Z_1. Imposition of the $10 tax shifts the marginal private cost curve upward by $10. After the tax has been imposed, the market equilibrium corresponds to point Z_2. The market price of chemicals increases from $100 to $106 per ton, causing quantity demanded to decline from 10,000 to 9,000 tons per day. After paying the tax the producers receive a net price per ton equal to $96, the marginal private cost of producing 9,000 tons per day. The tax collects $90,000 per day. This is represented by the area DZ_2FG in Figure 18–1. This revenue is sufficient to pay for the damage still being borne by alternative users of the stream. The $106 equilibrium price now reflects the $96 cost of a ton of the chemicals to sellers plus the $10 marginal external costs per ton borne by third parties. The externality has been internalized because the price of the product now equals the marginal social cost of producing it, including the marginal external cost.

The market equilibrium after the tax has been imposed is efficient because the output of 9,000 tons per day, corresponding to point Z_2, is the one for which

$$\text{MPC} + \text{MEC} = \text{MSC} = \text{MSB}$$

because T = MEC. The gain in efficiency that results from the tax is represented by the area Z_1Z_2B. This triangular area is the reduction in net social costs that results from reducing the output of chemicals to the point at which MSC = MSB.

Notice that in this case internalization of the externality does not reduce damages to zero. However, the tax does collect exactly enough revenue to compensate those who bear the damages for their costs. In effect, the tax revenue collected represents payment for the opportunity cost of using the resources that provides benefits to third parties to the market exchange of the chemicals.

Corrective Subsidies

Corrective subsidy A payment to either consumers or producers of a good whose use generates a positive externality; designed to internalize the externality.

A **corrective subsidy** is a payment to either consumers or producers of a good whose use generates a positive externality. The subsidy is designed to internalize the externality by putting downward pressure on the price of consuming the good so as to increase its market output to the efficient level. In the higher education example a $1,000 annual external benefit was associated with each full-time college student. Suppose the government announces a subsidy program under which each full-time student receives a grant of $1,000 per year for attending college. The corrective subsidy (S) equals the marginal external benefit of enrollment:

$$S = \text{MSB} = \$1{,}000$$

The $1,000 grant increases the demand for higher education by students. It is added to the marginal private benefit students receive by enrolling in college, to reflect the $1,000 positive externality. This is shown in Figure 18–2. The initial market equilibrium corresponds to point Z_1. The \$1,000 grant shifts the market demand curve upward as students add it to the marginal private benefit they receive by enrolling in college. The new market equilibrium corresponds to point Z_2. At the new equilibrium tuition rises to \$3,000 per year from its presubsidy level of \$2,500. The net tuition paid by students is \$2,000. The market equilibrium tuition falls by only \$500 of the \$1,000 grant after the increase in demand. The remaining \$500 of the grant per student accrues to colleges and universities to cover the increased marginal cost of expanding annual enrollment from 5 million to 6 million.

The corrective subsidy costs taxpayers \$6 billion per year. Ideally, the taxes collected to pay for the subsidy program would be levied on those who enjoy the positive externality. The efficient output is attained as a result of the subsidy as annual enrollment increases by 1 million. The subsidy increases enrollment until the marginal social cost of enrollment equals its marginal social benefit. The gain in net benefits from additional enrollment is the area Z_1BZ_2.

Administering Corrective Taxes and Subsidies: Problems of Measurement and Identification

A corrective tax or subsidy is easy to design in theory. In practice, however, it is often difficult to obtain the information necessary to achieve efficiency. The simple examples used up to this point assume that the marginal cost or benefit of the externality was directly correlated with output. This made it easy to levy per-unit taxes and subsidies to adjust costs or benefits to reflect the externality. In fact, the externality is often difficult to trace. In the case of chemical pollution, more than one substance may cause damage. The emission of these substances is often associated with the use of particular inputs rather than outputs. In practice, internalizing the externality requires that the charge for each type of emission be set at the marginal external cost of that emission. This requires a means of measuring such emissions and a mechanism for levying the emissions charges at rates that reflect their marginal external cost at any time.

For example, if mercury is emitted by chemical firms, a way to measure the amount that is dumped is required. Similarly, the amounts of other dumped chemical wastes must be measured. If the marginal external cost varies with output or other conditions, the charges for emissions should vary with these conditions.

There is, however, often considerable disagreement about the value of the damages. This is particularly true if human life and health are involved. The long-term effects of pollution are often uncertain, and some of those effects may be irreversible. Choosing the level of a corrective tax or emissions charge is often subject to considerable political controversy.

Finally, those who lose as a result of corrective taxes or emissions charges often oppose implementation of these means of internalizing negative externalities. For example, as a result of a charge for the emissions of chemical firms or corrective taxes on the output of such firms, the price of chemicals will rise, the output of chemicals will decline, and the profits of firms in the chemical industry will be reduced. Consumers and producers of chemicals are made worse off by the higher prices.

A properly administered corrective tax will result in gains that exceed losses. However, unless the losers are compensated for the consequences of losing their rights to pollute without charge, they will oppose the tax. Internalizing an externality always involves political considerations. In the absence of compensation for the loss of rights, it is difficult to predict whether a corrective tax will in fact be implemented.

A similar problem exists with corrective subsidies. Improving efficiency requires identification of the source of the positive externality. For example, should grants be given only to full-time students? Should students in all disciplines receive grants on an equal basis, or should a larger proportion of grants be given to students in such fields as natural science and mathematics? Is it simply going to college that benefits third parties or is it mastery of certain subjects? How is the positive externality valued? The corrective subsidy will not improve efficiency if all the benefits of a college education accrue only to students. In the absence of perfect information, it is doubtful that the most efficient distribution of a corrective subsidy can be determined.

Concept Review

1. Explain why market equilibrium under perfect competition will not result in the efficient output when a negative externality exists.
2. How does a positive externality prevent efficient market outcomes?
3. Explain how a corrective tax can internalize a negative externality.

What Causes Negative Externalities?

Property Rights Disputes

Negative externalities result from competing uses for resources in cases in which property rights to each use have not been established. In the case of a negative externality, the issue is the right of buyers and sellers to impose costs on third parties. For example, third parties are harmed by the external effects of exchanges between buyers and sellers of chemicals. Do the chemical producers have the right to dump their wastes into streams without paying for that right? The problem is that no one owns the streams. Because ownership rights to the use of streams are not clear, chemical firms can dump their wastes without payment.

Citizens who are harmed by the damaging effects of chemical wastes have a competing claim on the use of the streams for alternative purposes. Internalizing the externality involves the establishment of property rights in the use of resources. Once established, such rights can be traded for cash payments.

The relationship between externalities and property rights can be understood better by analyzing how externalities might be internalized when the transaction costs of establishing and tracing property rights are negligible. In such cases externalities might exist only temporarily as disputes concerning resource use. Provided that information is freely available, such disputes can be resolved through private negotiation.

The Coase Theorem

Coase theorem A theorem holding that when transaction costs are negligible, externalities can be internalized by governments establishing property rights to resource use and allowing free exchange of those rights.

Governments can often aid in achieving efficiency merely by assigning property rights to resource use and developing methods that allow exchange of those rights at low transaction costs. The **Coase theorem** maintains that when transaction costs are negligible, externalities can be internalized by governments establishing property rights to resource use and allowing free exchange of those rights. It makes no difference who is assigned the rights. As long as free exchange is allowed, the resulting resource allocation will be the same. Ronald H. Coase formulated this theorem and explored the relationship among property right assignments, exchange, and efficiency.[1]

For example, suppose there are only two possible uses for an isolated lake. One use is as a source of fish for a commercial fishing firm. The other use is as a convenient place to dump the wastes of a meat-packing firm. The two uses conflict. The more wastes dumped into the lake, the fewer the fish that will be available, because decomposition of the wastes uses up the lake's oxygen and decreases its capacity to support aquatic life. According to the Coase theorem, the use of the lake will be the same no matter to which user the government grants the initial right to use it. If the fishing firm is granted the right to a pollution-free lake, it can trade that right for a payment from the meat packer. The fishing firm will engage in this transaction if it can increase its profits by doing so. If the government grants the meat packer the right to dump its wastes into the lake, the fishing firm can bargain with the meat packer to reduce its dumping. The fishing firm will do so if it can increase its profit by this transaction.

Clearly, the user granted the initial right is ahead at the start. That user has the option of selling the government-granted right. Holding a valuable property right increases the holder's income whether the right is used or sold. The distribution of income between the two users is therefore affected by the initial assignment of the right to use the lake. However, as will be shown, the mix of fish and meat produced with the aid of the lake's services will be the same in both cases. The lake is an input into meat production by virtue of its function as a convenient waste disposal site. It is an input into fish production by virtue of its function as a breeding area.

A Numerical Example

A simple numerical example can be used to show the alternatives available to each user of the lake. Assume that both the fishing firm and the meat-packing firm seek to minimize profits. Both firms sell their output in competitive markets. The price of both meat and fish is $2 per pound. Each firm can sell all of the output it wishes at that price.

The two uses conflict. If the meat-packing firm uses the lake to dump wastes, the fishing firm's catch then declines. Assume that the quantity of wastes emitted is a function of the quantity of meat produced. Therefore, part of the cost of

---

[1] Ronald H. Coase, "The Problem of Social Cost," *Journal of Law and Economics* 3 (October 1960), pp. 1–44.

TABLE 18–1 An Illustration of the Coase Theorem: Meat Output, Fish Losses, and the Meat-Packer's Profits

Daily Output of Meat (Pounds)	*Daily Profits*	*Fish Losses per Day (Pounds)*	*Value of Fish Lost at $2 per Pound*	*Net Social Gain per Day Based on Full Social Cost*
0	$ 0	0	$ 0	$ 0
1,000	1,000	50	100	900
2,000	1,200	100	200	1,000
3,000	1,500	150	300	1,200
4,000	1,625	200	400	1,225
5,000	1,650	250	500	1,150
6,000	1,600	300	600	1,000
7,000	1,500	350	700	800
8,000	1,200	400	800	400

increasing the production of meat is a decrease in the lake's output of fish for any given amount of fishing. This increases the fishing firm's costs of production.

Table 18–1 shows the relationships among output of meat, fish losses, and profits of the meat packer. The first column shows the daily output of meat that the meat-packing firm can produce if it makes use of the lake. The second column shows the daily profits that it would earn if it were not liable for damages from pollution of the lake. These profits are based on the firm's private costs of production. The value of the fish lost as a result of the firm's production is not included in its costs. The third column shows the daily loss of fish output associated with various levels of meat output. It is assumed that the marginal external cost of meat production is 50 pounds of fish for each 1,000-pound increase in meat produced. Because the price of fish is $2 per pound, each 1,000 pounds of meat produced reduces the value of fish caught by $100. At the current market price of fish the marginal external cost is therefore $100 for each 1,000 pounds of meat, or 10 cents per pound of meat. The fourth column shows how the total value of fish lost varies with the output of meat. The last column shows the net daily social gain for each increment in meat output. Net social gain is equal to the profits of the meat packer less the losses of the fishing firm. In effect, the last column gives the meat packer's profits on the basis of the full social costs of its meat production, including the damage that production does to the fish catch.

The maximum profits for the meat packer would occur at a daily output of 5,000 pounds if it were not liable for damage. This is illustrated in Figure 18–3(a). The maximum profits correspond to the output at point Z_1, where P = MPC. At that output, as shown in Table 18–1, the firm earns daily profits of $1,650. However, the efficient output, based on marginal social costs, is 4,000 pounds per day. This corresponds to point Z_2, where MPC + MEC = P. In this case E is equal to $100 per 1,000 pounds of meat. The efficient output is 4,000 pounds per day. At that output the net social gain is at a maximum of $1,225 per day.[2]

[2] For an excellent geometric analysis of the Coase Theorem, see Adam Gifford, Jr., "Externalities in the Coase Theorem: A Graphical Analysis," *Quarterly Review of Economics and Business* 14, no. 4 (Winter 1974), pp. 7–21.

FIGURE 18–3 The Coase Theorem: An Example

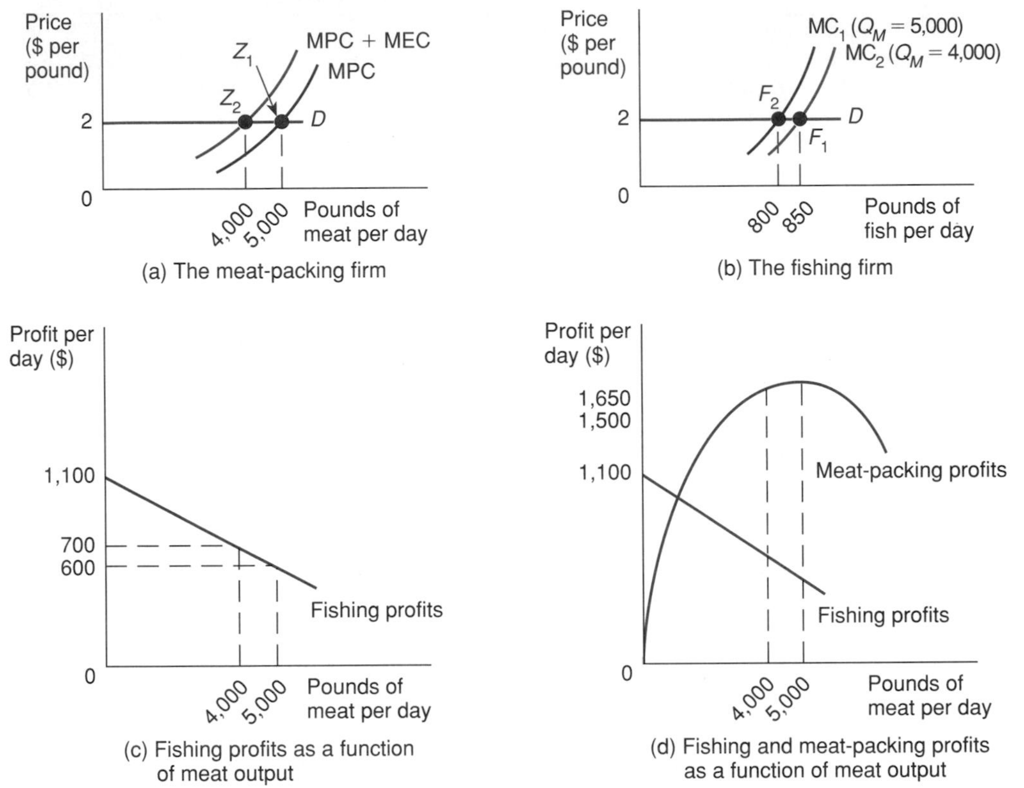

The graphs above are based on the extended numerical example in the text. They illustrate the interrelationship between costs and profits for two competing users of a lake.

Table 18–2 shows how the fish output of the lake and profits from fishing vary with the output of the meat packer. Figure 18–3(b) shows how the increase in the output of meat affects the profit-maximizing output of fish per day. This graph is based on the data of Table 18–2. The marginal cost of fish depends on the output of meat. Each increase in daily meat output increases the marginal cost of fishing. Figure 18–3(b) shows the marginal cost curve of fish output when the output of meat is 5,000 pounds and 4,000 pounds. MC_1 is the marginal cost curve of fish output when $Q_M = 5{,}000$. The profit-maximizing fish catch per day is 800 pounds. When Q_M is 4,000 pounds per day, the marginal cost curve of fish output is MC_2 and the profit-maximizing catch is 850 pounds per day. Figure 18–3(c) shows how the profits of the fishing firm vary with the output of meat. Each 1,000-pound increase in meat output reduces fishing profits by $100 per day. If the meat packer did not use the lake at all, the fishing firm could earn $1,100 per day. If the meat packer has the unrestricted right to pollute the lake with its wastes, daily meat output will be 5,000 pounds. The most the fishing firm can earn when that much meat is processed is $600 per day.

TABLE 18–2 The Coase Theorem: Meat Output, Fish Output, and Profits

Daily Output of Meat (Pounds)	*Daily Output of Fish (Pounds)*	*Daily Profits of the Fishing Firm*	*Sum of Daily Meat-Packing and Fishing Profits*
0	1,050	$1,100	$1,100
1,000	1,000	1,000	2,000
2,000	950	900	2,100
3,000	900	800	2,300
4,000	850	700	2,325
5,000	800	600	2,250
6,000	750	500	2,100
7,000	700	400	1,900
8,000	650	300	1,400

Case 1: The Emitter Has the Right to Dump Wastes

Suppose the meat packer is granted the right to dump its wastes in the lake. Clearly, this makes the fishing firm worse off. Its profits are reduced from $1,100 to $600 per day. What options are now available to the fishing firm? One option is to negotiate with the meat packer to reduce its meat output. Each 1,000-pound reduction in meat output would increase the fishing firm's daily profits by $100.

Figure 18–3(d) graphs the profits of the meat packer and the fishing firm on the same axes. Both profits are plotted against meat output. The profit-maximizing output for the meat-packing firm is 5,000 pounds of meat per day. At that meat output the daily profits of the fishing firm would be $600. For each 1,000-pound reduction in daily meat output that the fishing firm can secure, its daily profits will increase by $100 per day. The fisherman would therefore be willing to pay up to $100 per 1,000 pounds to purchase the meat packer's right to produce that last 1,000 pounds of meat.

What is the minimum payment the meat-packing firm would accept to reduce its output from 5,000 to 4,000 pounds per day? This depends on the reduction in its profits. Table 18–1 shows that its profits decline from $1,650 to $1,625 per day when output is reduced to 4,000 pounds. The change in profits is only $25 per day. When the daily output of meat declines to 4,000 pounds from 5,000 pounds, the fishing firm's daily profits increase from $600 to $700. As long as the meat-packing firm receives a payment in excess of its $25 reduction in profits, it will be better off. Because the maximum price the fishing firm will pay exceeds the minimum price the meat packer will accept to reduce output by 1,000 pounds, gains from trading the right to produce that amount exist. A bargain can be struck at some price greater than $25 but less than $100 to reduce the output of meat.

It will not, however, be mutually gainful to reduce meat output any further. A further 1,000-pound reduction in output by the meat packer will reduce its profits to $1,500 per day. Because this $125 reduction in profits exceeds the fishing firm's $100 gain in profits, no additional gains from trading are possible. At an output of 4,000 pounds of meat per day, the sum of the profits of the two goods produced with the lake's services is maximized at a total of $2,325 per day. This is shown in the last column of Table 18–2. The negotiated equilibrium results in 4,000 pounds of meat and 850 pounds of fish being produced each day on the lake. The cost of the damage borne by the fishing firm is $400. The fishing firm earns daily profits of $700, and the meat-packing firm enjoys daily profits of $1,625.

Case 2: The Emitter Does Not Have the Right to Dump Wastes

Now suppose the tables are turned and the government grants the fishing firm the right to a pollution-free lake. Would the fishing firm be willing to allow the meat packer to begin production on the lake in exchange for a cash payment? How much would the meat-packing firm be willing to offer to produce the first daily 1,000 pounds of meat on the lake? Table 18–1 shows that the firm's daily profits will increase from zero to $1,000 if it produces 1,000 pounds per day on the lake. The loss to the fishing firm is only $100 in profits per day. Because its gain exceeds its loss, the meat packer pays $100 to the fishing firm for the right to produce the first 1,000 pounds of output. The meat packer can earn profits even after deducting the cost of purchasing this right.

For each 1,000-pound increment in daily production up to 4,000 pounds, the meat-packing firm can gain from paying for the right to use the lake. What would happen if the firm increased its output to 5,000 pounds per day? Doing so would increase its profits by $25 per day but it would have to pay the fishing firm $100 per day for the right to increase its daily output that extra 1,000 pounds. If it were to make that payment, its profits would decline by $75 per day. No net gains are possible for the meat packer beyond an output of 4,000 pounds.

In equilibrium the mix of output between fish and meat produced on the lake is therefore the same, independent of which firm has the right to use the lake. In this case, as before, the meat-packing firm produces 4,000 pounds of meat and the fishing firm produces 850 pounds of fish. This maximizes the sum of the two firms' profits. However, there is now one important difference. In this case the meat packer bears the cost of the damage. Its daily profits are only $1,225 after it pays the fishing firm $400 per day for the right to use the lake. The fishing firm enjoys $700 per day from the sale of fish and an additional $400 per day from the sale of its right to use the lake. Its total daily profits are therefore $1,100, the same daily profits it would have enjoyed if there were no competing use of the lake.

This output mix is the same as the output mix that would have prevailed if a corrective tax had been levied on the damage done by the meat producer. Private negotiation results in the efficient output mix, irrespective of which firm is granted the initial right to use the lake. Note also that the efficient result is the one that maximizes the *sum* of the profits of fishing and meat-packing uses of the lake.

Additional Alternatives and Profits

The above analysis can also be used to consider other ways in which the two firms might further increase their profits. For example, the meat-packing firm, when liable for damage, has other alternatives besides making payments to the fishing firm. It could take steps to eliminate the dumping of wastes. It could choose to locate its operations elsewhere or go out of business. Finally, it could buy out the fishing firm and thereby eliminate the competing use for the lake. At each stage the firm looks at the costs of these alternatives and at the impact of those costs on its profits. It chooses the alternative that allows it to maximize its profits.

Suppose, for example, the meat-packing firm could eliminate dumping by installing a device that processes all wastes so they can be hauled away. Suppose the cost of this process per 1,000 pounds of output per day is $20. This is less than the maximum amount necessary to purchase the right to dump the wastes associated with that amount of output per day. By means of the process the meat-packing firm could make more profits by locating on the lake but not abusing the fishing firm's right to a pollution-free environment. This is shown in Table 18–3. Maximum profits would rise to $1,550 per day. Meat output would be 5,000 pounds per day, and fish output would be 1,050 pounds per day.

If the meat packer had the right to dump wastes in the lake without being liable for the damages, it would be better off not to avoid dumping because it could then make $1,650 per day. However, it would now be in the interest of the fishing firm to pay the meat packer to eliminate the dumping because the fishing firm could then increase its profits to $1,100 per day. This $400 daily increase in profits exceeds the $100 daily cost of the waste control system for the meat-packing firm.

A similar analysis could be conducted for other alternatives, such as ceasing either fishing or meat-packing operations on the lake. No matter which firm has the right to use the lake, the mix of fish and meat produced on the lake would be the same. The outcome that maximizes the sum of the profits of the two uses is the one that emerges from negotiation.

Significance of the Coase Theorem

The Coase theorem shows that externalities are disputes concerning the right to use resources. These disputes can be settled through negotiation when it is clear who has the property right to use resources and who must pay whom for their use.

TABLE 18–3 The Coase Theorem: Profits and the Cost of Eliminating the Dumping of Wastes

Daily Output of Meat	*Daily Profits*	*Daily Cost of Eliminating Dumping*	*Net Profits per Day*
0	$ 9	$ 0	$ 0
1,000	1,000	20	980
2,000	1,200	40	1,160
3,000	1,500	60	1,440
4,000	1,625	80	1,545
5,000	1,650	100	1,550
6,000	1,600	120	1,480
7,000	1,500	140	1,360

MODERN MICROECONOMICS IN ACTION: THE BUSINESS WORLD

The Evolution of Grazing Rights

The establishment of property rights depends on the costs and benefits of enforcing those rights. The grazing rights to land in the Great Plains region of the United States evolved with changes in the price of cattle and the costs of fencing.*

In the early 1800s the territories that occupied the region were characterized by vast expanses of land, little tree cover, and scarce supplies of water. The lack of trees meant a scarcity of wood, which was the cheapest and primary source of fencing material. Property rights to grazing land in the territories were not enforced or guaranteed.

Land prices in the Great Plains region rose dramatically in the 1860s and 1870s as the demand for cattle and sheep production increased. Cattle ranchers formed associations for the purpose of establishing ownership and use rights for the vast cattle ranges. This eventually led to formal leasing of unclaimed land and entry or use restrictions on public land. However, the high cost of fencing still made it difficult to enforce exclusive rights to land use.

Incursions on private land were common. Shepherds drove their sheep onto the cattle ranges, and cattle ranchers were not averse to violating the land rights of shepherds. Range wars were the prevalent way of settling disputes concerning the right to use land for competing purposes.

Finally, in the 1870s, the invention of barbed wire lowered the costs of enforcing exclusive property rights to land. Barbed wire enabled homesteaders to protect their crops from damage by cattle herds. It also enabled ranchers to control access to their own pastures. This, along with the increase in land prices, made it possible and desirable to establish exclusive property rights to the land.

* See Terry L. Anderson, and P. J. Hill, "The Evolution of Property Rights: A Study of the American West," *Journal of Law and Economics* 18 (April 1975), pp. 163–79.

In general, this is likely to be the case when the parties to the disputes are small in number and when it is easy to measure damages. Government intervention is unnecessary to resolve the disputes. Externalities in such cases are merely temporary disagreements that are settled through negotiation and payment for the exchange of initially assigned rights. Because transaction costs are likely to be negligible when only a few parties are involved, a temporary externality is called a **small-number externality.**

Small-number externality An externality in which only few parties are involved and the transaction costs of bargaining to internalize the externality are therefore likely to be low.

Government functions merely to assign the rights. Once it has assigned the rights, they can be traded for cash payments. Efficiency is guaranteed when transaction costs are negligible. However, the party initially assigned the rights is better off than it would have been had the rights been assigned to the other party.

The Coase theorem is not applicable when transaction costs are high enough to outweigh the benefits of private negotiation. For example, suppose that motorists have the right to use their vehicles near your home. If the resulting pollution harms you, with whom would you negotiate to pay for its reduction? There are so many motorists that it might be difficult to prevent them from driving in your area even if you paid them not to do so. How would you establish the value of your damages? This is a case of a **large-number externality.** Because many parties are involved in such cases, the transaction costs of bargaining to trade property rights are not negligible. Thus private negotiation will not achieve efficiency.

Large-number externality An externality in which a large number of people are involved and the transaction costs of bargaining to trade property rights are therefore very high.

Pollution Rights

The Coase theorem can be applied to pollution control policy. Assume that there is general agreement on the efficient amount of organic wastes that should be dumped into streams. Also assume that 1 million pounds of biochemical oxygen demand (BOD) units are dumped each day, whereas the efficient amount is 500,000 pounds per day. One way to achieve that efficient amount is to require each user of streams for dumping purposes to purchase "rights" to dump. One pollution right would be required for each pound of BOD, for a total of 500,000 rights, and the rights would be auctioned off in a market. Assume that the costs of enforcing the requirement of one right per pound are negligible.

Figure 18–4 shows how the price of the pollution rights would be established. The demand for the rights depends on the value of the services of streams as places to dump wastes. The supply of pollution rights is perfectly inelastic at 500,000. The equilibrium price is established at the point at which quantity demanded equals quantity supplied. Before the issuance of pollution rights, firms could dump their wastes into streams at no cost. The new equilibrium price for dumping wastes is now $5 per pound. Many firms choose not to buy the rights at that price. They reduce dumping in various ways or cease operations.

Once the pollution rights have been initially issued and sold, the government would allow them to be traded in a market. By establishing pollution rights and their price, the government facilitates trade among those who dump wastes into streams and those who have competing uses for the streams. Environmentalists

FIGURE 18–4 Pollution Rights

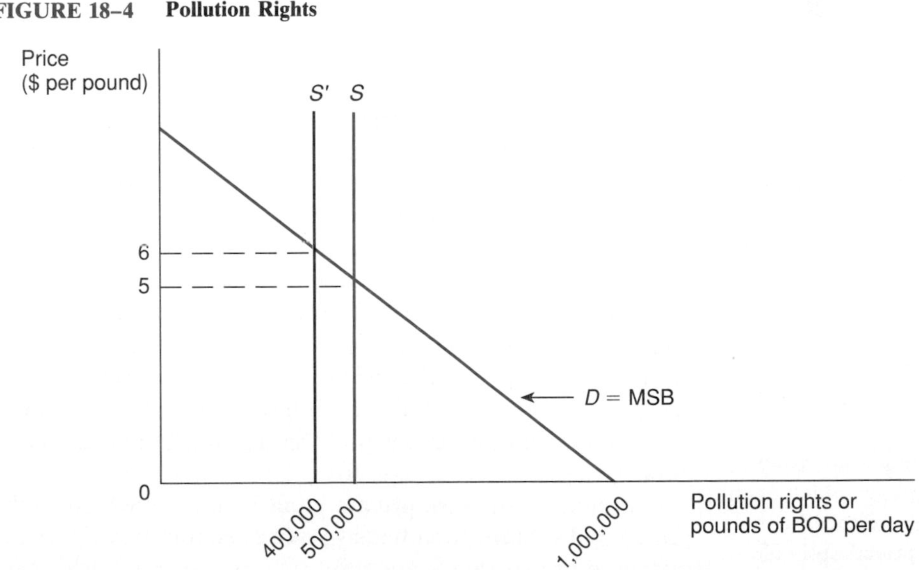

One pollution right is required for each pound of BOD dumped into streams per day. If the supply of pollution rights is fixed at 500,000 per day, the market price at auction of a pollution right would be $5. The removal of 100,000 rights per day from circulation would raise the price to $6.

could, for example, bid to purchase these rights from dumpers. By buying rights and holding them, they would decrease the amount of BOD dumping. The Sierra Club could purchase 100,000 pollution rights and remove them from the market. This would decrease the supply of pollution rights to 400,000. The price of the rights would rise accordingly to $6, and the quantity demanded would fall to 400,000. Because there would then be 100,000 fewer rights available, BOD dumping would fall by 100,000 pounds per day. If the government did not initially issue the efficient number of pollution rights, further gains from their trade would be possible. Additional transactions like the Sierra Club's purchase would help achieve efficiency.

Concept Review

1. What causes externalities to arise in market economies?
2. What is the significance of the Coase theorem?
3. How can pollution rights be used to reduce pollution?

Public Goods versus Private Goods

Markets are unlikely to provide efficient amounts of goods that all persons can consume in equal quantities, whether or not they pay for them. Such goods as national defense, pollution control, and public sanitation are not packaged in a way that enables firms to sell them by the unit, as they would sell bread and bagels. The benefits of such goods are shared by large numbers of citizens who cannot be excluded from consuming them if they refuse to pay for them. If the air is cleaned up for the benefit of only one citizen, there is no way to prevent other citizens from consuming the clean air as well.

Pure public good A good whose units of production are consumed collectively by all persons, whether or not they pay for it.

A **pure public good** is one whose units of production are consumed collectively by all persons, whether or not they pay for it. The market sale of a pure public good means that the purchaser of the good will make it available not only for his own use but for everyone else's use as well. In other words, the provision of a pure public good for a single consumer's benefit is impossible. If a person provides a pure public good for his own benefit, that person also benefits everyone else. In this sense a pure public good is one that results in positive externalities for all as soon as it is made available to one. For example, a very rich person who hires his own police force to improve public safety in a region benefits both himself and all other citizens of that region. Public safety is therefore pure public good.

Pure private good A good for which each unit produced can be priced and sold to individuals so that each unit benefits the buyer exclusively.

In contrast, a **pure private good** is one for which each unit produced can be priced and sold to individuals so that each unit benefits the buyer exclusively. The purchase of a pure private good in a market provides a benefit only to the buyer and imposes no positive or negative externalities on anyone else. Markets are ideally suited to the provision of private goods. Buyers know that when they purchase such goods, the price they pay gives them the right to the exclusive use and benefit of the goods they purchase. A loaf of bread is an example of a pure private good. When a person purchases bread, he acquires the exclusive right to its use. No one else benefits when the person eats bread purchased in a market.

National defense is an example of a pure public good. If the borders of a nation are protected from foreign attack for any one person, every other person in the nation simultaneously benefits.

Characteristics of Pure Public Goods

Pure public goods have two basic distinguishing characteristics:

Nonrival in consumption A property of a pure public good that allows a given quantity of the good to be consumed by any one person without reducing the availability of the good to other persons.

1. Pure public goods are **nonrival in consumption,** which means that consumption of a given quantity of the good by any one person does not reduce the availability of the good to others. No consumer is made worse off when an additional person consumes a given amount of a pure public good. Additional consumers can be accommodated without decreasing the benefits available to existing consumers. The marginal cost of allowing an additional consumer to enjoy the benefits of a pure public good is zero. This is because no one is made worse off when another consumer is allowed to enjoy the benefits of any given quantity of a pure public good.

On the other hand, a pure private good is rival in consumption. On any given day a certain amount of bread is produced in this country. If any one consumer obtains more of that bread, less bread is available to the remaining consumers. Buyers compete for the available amounts of bread. When a good is rival in consumption, buyers know that they must compete with others to obtain the available amounts of that good.

Nonexclusive in consumption A property of a pure public good that prevents it from being withheld from consumers who do not pay for it.

2. Pure public goods are **nonexclusive in consumption,** which means that they cannot be withheld from consumers who do not pay for them. A nonexclusive good is one whose units of production cannot be withheld from consumers who choose not to pay the price. When a good is nonexclusive, the transaction costs of excluding a person from obtaining it are extremely high. In effect, payment for the right to consume the good cannot be imposed on individual consumers. A given quantity of a pure public good can only be shared; there is no way to parcel the good out in neat little packages that can be sold over the counter. Once each "package" of the good has been produced, the benefits of that package cannot be refused to those who will not pay because it is impossible to selectively restrict the consumption of a pure public good to specific persons. For example, someone who refuses to pay for national defense services cannot be excluded from its benefits.

Efficient Output of Pure Public Goods

The *marginal social benefit* of each unit of a pure public good is the *sum* of the marginal benefits of all consumers. This is because each extra unit of the good benefits not one consumer but all consumers. For example, suppose steps are taken to improve the nation's air quality. What is the marginal social benefit of this improvement? If improving air quality is a pure public good that benefits all citizens, the benefit of the improvement is the benefit you get plus the benefit your neighbor gets and so on until the benefits to all persons are added to yours. This is true of increases in any pure public good. The marginal benefits of all consumers must be summed to obtain the marginal social benefit.

The efficient output of a pure public good corresponds to the amount for which its marginal social benefit equals its marginal social cost. The marginal social cost of producing an extra unit of a pure public good is the value of the resources necessary to produce that unit. This is no different from the marginal social cost of producing a pure private good. More national defense requires more tanks, more ships, more aircraft, more weapons, and more military personnel. Increasing national defense therefore absorbs extra resources. The efficiency conditions for a pure public good are

$$\text{MSC} = \text{MSB} = \Sigma\text{MB} \qquad \textbf{(18–6)}$$

where MSC is the marginal social cost of an extra unit of a pure public good and ΣMB is the sum of the marginal benefits received by all individual consumers of that extra unit.

Table 18–4 provides hypothetical data to show how the efficient output of a pure public good can be determined. Suppose a condominium community consists of five residents who wish to hire security guards to protect their property. The security protection is a pure public good for the five residents. Assume that the amount of security protection varies with the number of guards hired. The cost per guard is $200 per week. This is both the average and marginal cost of security protection. The five residents are Adams, Baker, Cline, Dalton, and Eames. Table 18–4 shows how the marginal benefit of each of these consumers varies with the number of security guards made available.

TABLE 18–4 Marginal Benefits of Security Guards and Cost per Guard per week

Resident	*One Guard*	*Two Guards*	*Three Guards*	*Four Guards*	*Five Guards*
Adams	$100	$ 90	$ 80	$ 70	$ 60
Baker	80	70	60	50	40
Cline	50	40	30	20	10
Dalton	40	30	20	10	0
Eames	30	20	10	0	0
ΣMB	$300	$250	$200	$140	$110

ΣMB = MC at $Q = 3$

Total cost of three guards per week = 3(200) = $600

of which

Adams pays:	80(3) =	$240 per week
Baker pays:	60(3) =	$180 per week
Cline pays:	30(3) =	$90 per week
Dalton pays:	20(3) =	$60 per week
Eames pays:	10(3) =	$30 per week

MODERN MICROECONOMICS IN ACTION: **GOVERNMENT AND THE ECONOMY**

The Clean Air Act of 1990 and the New Market for Pollution Rights

Clean air is a public good. By eliminating harmful pollutants from the atmosphere, we could improve health, preserve environmental resources, and increase recreational benefits. However, clean air is not free. We must sacrifice material goods and services to gain the benefits of clean air. Ideally, we would like to obtain those benefits at the minimum possible cost.

The Clean Air Act of 1990 requires sharp reductions in the emission of pollutants into the atmosphere. As a result of the act automakers will spend an estimated additional $7.5 billion to reduce car emissions. By 1994 new emissions-control regulations could boost the prices of new cars hundreds of dollars. The act also requires cleaner-burning gasoline, which will increase gasoline prices.

The act's restrictions on burning high-sulfur coal could cost thousands of coal-mining jobs in Appalachia and result in substantial increases in the price of electricity. Reducing sulfur dioxide emissions of power plants would reduce acid rain, but much of the costs would be borne by people in the Midwest and Southeast, where power plants in nine states emit 51 percent of the sulfur dioxide.* U.S. industry spent an estimated $33 billion on air pollution control in 1990. The provisions of the Clean Air Act of 1990 could raise those annual costs to over $50 billion.

The Clean Air Act of 1990 also introduced some innovative techniques to make sure that the emission of pollutants is reduced at the minimum possible cost. For example, it established the property rights necessary to create a new market for emission rights! The Chicago Board of Trade, the nation's largest commodity market, will be used to buy and sell rights to emit sulfur dioxide. Under the new act firms that generate electric power must reduce their emission of sulfur dioxide to 50 percent of the current levels by the year 2000. The EPA has allocated rights to dump limited amounts of sulfur dioxide to these firms. Each right entitles its owner to dump one ton of sulfur dioxide into the atmosphere per year. Firms that do not use all of their allotted emission rights can sell their remaining rights in the new market to firms that want to use more than their allotted rights allow or to any other purchasers that are willing to pay the price.

The trading of the emission rights is likely to allow electric power companies to meet the new emission reduction requirements at lower costs than would otherwise be possible. For example, suppose the market price of the right to emit a ton of sulfur dioxide is $1,000. If a power company can recycle or remove that ton of wastes from its smokestack for only $500, it can add $500 to its annual profits by selling one pollution right for $1,000 on the market. Power companies can also reduce their emission of sulfur dioxide by shifting to low-sulfur coal. The only companies that would want the emission rights would be those for which the cost of cleaning up sulfur dioxide emissions is greater than the market price of the rights. Naturally, the price of such a right may vary with the value of emitting sulfur dioxide. If new technologies for the control of such emissions are developed, the price of a right would probably fall.

The trading of emission rights encourages electric power companies to develop new technologies for reducing sulfur dioxide emissions. In this way they can add to their profits by selling their rights! This new market-based approach to emissions reduction is a great improvement over the old command-and-control approach. Under that approach all firms were required to reduce their emissions by the same percentage and the technology that they used to achieve that result was often dictated.

* See Barbara Rosewicz and Rose Gutfeld, "Clean-Air Legislation Will Cost Americans $21.5 Billion a Year," *The Wall Street Journal,* March 28, 1990; and Barbara Rosewicz, "Price Tag Is Producing Groans Already," *The Wall Street Journal,* October 29, 1990.

FIGURE 18–5 Efficient Output of a Pure Public Good

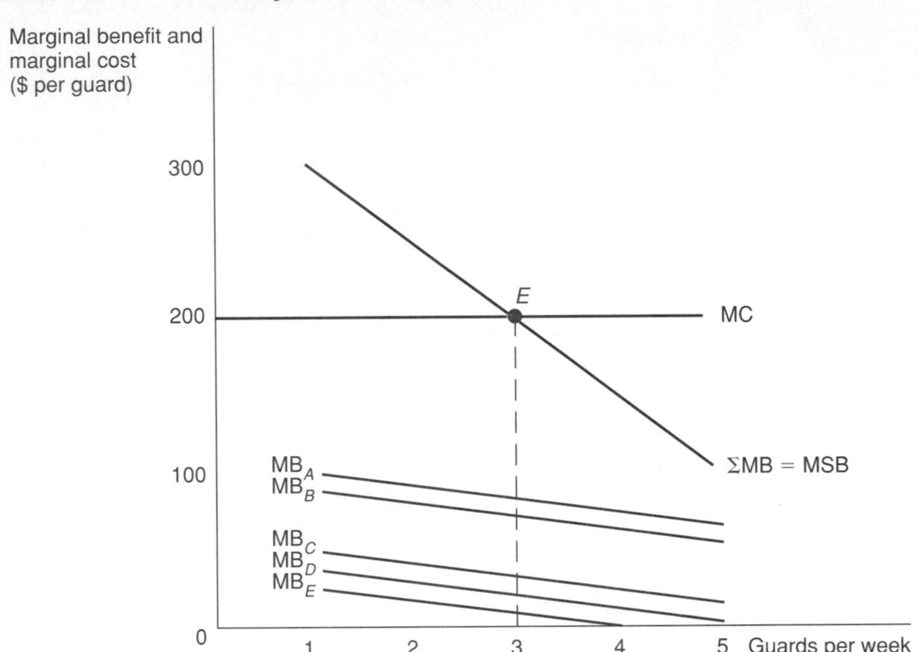

At the current price of $200 per week, no single resident will hire a security guard because all of the individual marginal benefits fall short of the price. The efficient output corresponds to point *E*, where the sum of the individual marginal benefits equals the marginal cost.

Figure 18–5 graphs each of the five individual marginal benefit curves for security protection from the data in Table 18–4. Adams' marginal benefit curve is MB_A. Similarly, the marginal benefit curve for the four other consumers is indicated by their initial. The marginal benefit declines for each consumer as more security protection is made available. For each possible quantity of the pure public good, the marginal benefits of the five consumers must be summed to obtain the marginal social benefit associated with that quantity. In Figure 18–5 the curve showing the sum of the marginal benefits is labeled ΣMB = MSB. The efficient output is three security guards. This corresponds to the point *E*, where the sum of the marginal benefits is just equal to the $200 marginal social cost of production.

Suppose that security protection were offered for sale in a market for individual consumption. How much of this pure public good would be purchased by each of the five residents if it were offered for sale at a price equal to its marginal cost? In this case the answer is zero! At a price of $200 per guard per week, not one of the five residents would choose to purchase the good. This is because the $200 weekly price per guard exceeds the highest amount any of them would be willing to pay for even one guard. The marginal social benefit of the first guard is $300.

This is the sum of the marginal benefits of the five residents. Because the marginal social benefit of the first guard exceeds its marginal social cost of production, not hiring any guards is inefficient.

An efficient arrangement for producing the pure public good requires cooperation among the consumers. An arrangement must be worked out to share the costs of production. No one consumer in this example chooses to purchase the good at a competitive price equal to marginal cost. However, all of these consumers would be made better off if they shared the cost of producing the good and worked out an arrangement for agreeing on the efficient output. At that output all five residents would share the benefits offered by security guards and would also share a weekly cost of $600 for three guards. Because security protection is presumed to be a pure public good, none are any worse off by sharing the patrol's benefits with their neighbors.

Cooperative Supply of Pure Public Goods

How do consumers provide themselves with pure public goods? One alternative is a cooperative sharing arrangement. When the size of the group enjoying the benefits of the pure public good is small enough, its positive externalities can be internalized through voluntary cooperation. Consumers must agree on the quantity of the good and on the way to divide its costs among themselves. This method of supply is often used by religious congregations and other organizations with a close-knit membership. Persons are called upon to contribute voluntarily to finance shared facilities available for the exclusive use of the group's members, such as social halls and child-care facilities. If a proposal to extend the facilities and therefore increase the output of the pure public good for members is adopted, a collection is taken. If all members are honest, they will contribute the full marginal benefit in dollars of that extension in output. Assume that full information about the tastes and economic circumstances of each member is available to all members. There is no incentive to lie about marginal benefits because each member knows what the true marginal benefit is for every other member.

If more is collected than the costs of producing the good, it can be inferred that the marginal benefit of that output exceeds its marginal cost. Additional units of the good would then be proposed for consideration. If the contributions fell short of the marginal cost of a unit, output would have to be reduced to make marginal benefit equal to marginal cost. In this way the group's members could interact to move toward a point like E in Figure 18–5.

Assume that the five members of the condominium community from the preceding example must get together to decide how many security guards to hire. Table 18–4 shows the marginal benefits that each member receives for one to five security guards hired per week. Adams, Baker, Cline, Dalton, and Eames must unanimously agree on the quantity to hire because all of them must consume the same amount. In equilibrium the contribution of each member must be adjusted so that the quantity of security guards demanded is the same for all five members. In addition, enough revenue must be raised from voluntary contributions to cover the cost of the security guards per week. The average cost and the marginal cost of guards is always $200.

The last row of Table 18–4 adds the marginal benefits of the five residents. If only one guard is hired, ΣMB will exceed the marginal cost of that guard. The marginal benefit of that first guard for the five residents is $300, whereas the marginal cost is only $200. Additional gains are possible by hiring another guard. Similarly, ΣMB for two guards is $250, which also exceeds the marginal cost of $200. Additional gains from trade are no longer possible when three guards are hired each week. At that amount, $\Sigma MB = MC = \$200$ per week. Hiring a fourth guard would reduce the sum of the marginal benefits to $140 per week. Because this is less than the marginal cost of the fourth guard, the net gain from the fourth guard would be negative.

In equilibrium each resident agrees to pay an amount for each guard equal to his or her marginal benefit corresponding to the quantity supplied. At three guards, Adams' marginal benefit is $80. His total weekly bill for the three guards will therefore be $240. Similarly, as shown in Table 18–4, the weekly share of the cost of the three guards for each of the residents is their marginal benefit multiplied by the equilibrium quantity of three guards. This raises $600 per week, which covers the total cost of the three guards, each of whom costs $200 per week.

In general, when average costs are constant

$$\Sigma MB = MC = AC \qquad \textbf{(18–7)}$$

in equilibrium. It follows that

$$\begin{aligned}(\Sigma MB)Q &= (AC)Q \\ \text{Total revenue} &= \text{Total cost}\end{aligned} \qquad \textbf{(18–8)}$$

In equilibrium all persons consume the same quantity of the pure public good. It is impossible to make any one person better off by changing either the contributions for the good or its quantity without harming another person. The output and the sharing of costs are therefore efficient.[3] Note that in equilibrium each person pays an amount per security guard that reflects the marginal benefit he or she receives.

The Free-Rider Problem

Free-rider problem The incentive of people to contribute less than their marginal benefit to the cost of financing a pure public good in the hope that others will contribute enough to make the good available.

The cooperative equilibrium for pure public goods assumes that consumers would truthfully reveal their marginal benefits. In fact, strong incentives *not* to reveal the marginal benefit of the public good are likely to prevail. Consumers receive the benefits of a pure public good whether or not they contribute to its costs. Knowledge of this fact provides persons with an incentive to contribute less than their marginal benefit. They do so in the hope that others will contribute enough to allow some of the public good to be produced. This is called the **free-rider prob-**

[3] For a more detailed analysis of the cooperative supply of pure public goods, see David N. Hyman, *Public Finance: A Contemporary Application of Theory to Policy,* 4th ed. (Fort Worth, Tex.: Dryden Press, 1993), chap. 4.

lem. Free riders understate the worth of the public good in the hope of obtaining the benefits of others' contributions and efforts at a cost below their own marginal benefit.

The effects of the free-rider problem can be illustrated with the same example. Suppose that Adams and Baker truthfully reveal their marginal benefits each time the hat is passed to collect money for the security guards. However, Cline, Dalton, and Eames try to be free riders by contributing less per guard than their marginal benefits for each quantity. Table 18–5 shows the consequences of their behavior. Suppose that Cline will contribute only $40 to the cost of the first guard, although his true marginal benefit is $50. Dalton agrees to contribute only $20 per week per guard when only one guard is hired, although her true marginal benefit is $40. Similarly, Eames understates his true marginal benefit by $20, contributing $10 when only one guard is hired.

The sum of the contributions equals $260. This exceeds the cost of the first guard. The residents presume that additional gains are possible, so they see if they can collect enough to support two guards. Comparing the data in Tables 18–4 and 18–5 shows that Cline, Dalton, and Eames once again contribute less per guard than their marginal benefits. Enough is collected to cover the cost of two guards. However, the efficient number of guards is three. As shown in Table 18–5 not enough can be collected now to achieve the efficient equilibrium. Only two guards will be hired. The total weekly cost will be $400. Table 18–5 shows how the cost of these two guards is distributed among the five residents.

At an output of only two guards, net gains based on the true marginal benefits are possible if an additional guard is hired. However, to raise enough revenue to pay for three guards, Cline and the other free riders would have to reveal their true marginal benefits. If they do, all three would be worse off than they would have

TABLE 18–5 The Free-Rider Problem

	Contribution per Guard		
Resident	*One Guard*	*Two Guards*	*Three Guards*
Adams	$100	$ 90	$ 80
Baker	80	70	80
Cline	40	25	15
Dalton	20	10	5
Eames	10	5	0
	$260	$200	$160

These amounts understate the true marginal benefits.
Equilibrium shares of the total cost of $400 per week:

Adams: $180
Baker: $140
Cline: $ 50
Dalton: $ 20
Eames: $ 10

been by continuing to enjoy their free ride. Cline would be better off by $30 if the third guard were hired. However, he would have to contribute $90 a week to support three guards (see Table 18–4). The $40 increase in his weekly cost outweighs this $30 gain. He is better off being a free rider. By ceasing to be a free rider, Dalton would gain $20 in benefits but would suffer increased costs of $40 per week. Finally, Eames would gain only $10 in benefits, but his weekly costs would rise by $20. All three are better off as free riders.

At the extreme, if all five residents tried to be free riders, the number of security guards hired could be zero. The free-rider problem prevents additional gains from trade from being achieved. It results in less than the efficient amount of a public good when costs are financed by voluntary contributions. Yet any one consumer can make himself or herself better off by becoming a free rider. Although free riding prevents efficiency, it is rational and to be expected when persons maximize the net benefits they receive from exchange.

In general, the free-rider problem is more serious in larger groups than in smaller groups. Information about consumers and their preferences is more difficult to obtain as the size of a group increases. Anonymity increases the incentive to be a free rider because, given anonymity, a person's dishonesty is less likely to be uncovered. On the other hand, in small groups in which persons are familiar with one another, as is the case for social and religious organizations, there is less incentive to attempt a free ride because moral and social pressures, coupled with the high probability of discovery, offset the gains from free riding.

Public television and radio are good examples of voluntary cooperation as a means of supporting a public good. They are also good examples of the free-rider problem in action. Public radio and television stations typically raise revenue at least once a year by inviting listeners and viewers to pledge voluntary contributions. How many of you who listen to and watch such stations contribute? If you benefit from public broadcasting and do not contribute, then you are a free rider. There are probably many free riders enjoying the benefits of public broadcasting. The voluntary contributions received undoubtedly fall far short of the true marginal social benefits of public broadcasting.

In fact, governments rarely rely on voluntary contributions as a means of financing the costs of the public goods and services they supply. Public goods and services supplied by governments are typically financed through taxation and other compulsory payments. However, what you receive in benefits may be worth less than what you pay in taxes.

Concept Review

1. How do the characteristics of pure public goods differ from those of pure private goods?
2. Under what conditions is the efficient quantity of a pure public good supplied?
3. Why is market provision of a pure public good likely to provide less than the efficient quantity?

Congestible and Excludable Public Goods

Congestible public goods Public goods that are nonrival in consumption only up to a certain level of use over a given period.

Excludable public goods Public goods that are nonrival in consumption but for which the transaction costs of excluding additional consumers are quite low.

Many goods and services have characteristics that place them somewhere between pure public goods and pure private goods. Some goods are nonrival in consumption only up to a certain level of use. These are called **congestible public goods.** After a given point an additional user decreases the benefits enjoyed by the existing users. Other goods are nonrival in consumption, but the transaction costs of excluding additional consumers are quite low. These are **excludable public goods.**

An example of a congestible public good is a road. Additional users do not reduce the availability of the road's services to others until the point of congestion. At that point an additional user slows down existing users and makes the road more hazardous. An example of an excludable public good is television broadcasting. The use of fees and charges for hookups allows exclusion from its benefits if persons refuse to pay. When exclusion is possible at low transaction costs, market supply by competing firms is a possibility.

Congestible Public Goods

The marginal cost of allowing another consumer to enjoy the benefits of a pure public good is zero. For example, suppose that one fireworks display is produced at a cost of $500. If fireworks displays are a pure public good, then this is the cost of making the good available to any one consumer. What is the marginal cost of allowing a second or third consumer to enjoy the display? The answer is zero if fireworks displays are indeed a pure public good. This follows from the fact that the pure public good is nonrival in consumption. Additional viewers do not decrease the benefits of existing viewers.

Figure 18–6(a) shows how the marginal cost of allowing additional viewers to consume a fireworks display varies with the number of viewers. The marginal cost of providing the display to one viewer is $500. However, the marginal cost of accommodating a second viewer immediately drops to zero. An unlimited number of additional consumers can enjoy a given quantity of a pure public good.

Do not confuse the cost of allowing an additional consumer to enjoy the fireworks display with the cost of producing another display. Producing another display will cost an additional $500. The cost of allowing additional consumers to enjoy any given number of displays is always zero.

Point of congestion The point at which the number of consumers of a congestible public good begins to raise the marginal cost of accommodating additional consumers above zero.

Suppose the benefits of the fireworks display *are* subject to congestion. After a certain number of people congregate to see the display, they begin to detract from the benefit that others receive. At the point of congestion, the marginal cost of accommodating an additional consumer is positive. After that point has been reached, efficiency requires a price equal to this marginal cost to be charged. If this is feasible, the price will force consumers to consider the reduction in benefits that they impose on others.

Figure 18–6(b) shows how the marginal cost of accommodating viewers varies when a fireworks display is a congestible public good. The **point of congestion** is the point at which the number of consumers just raises the marginal cost of accommodating consumers above zero. This occurs at N^* viewers in Figure 18–

FIGURE 18–6 Congestion

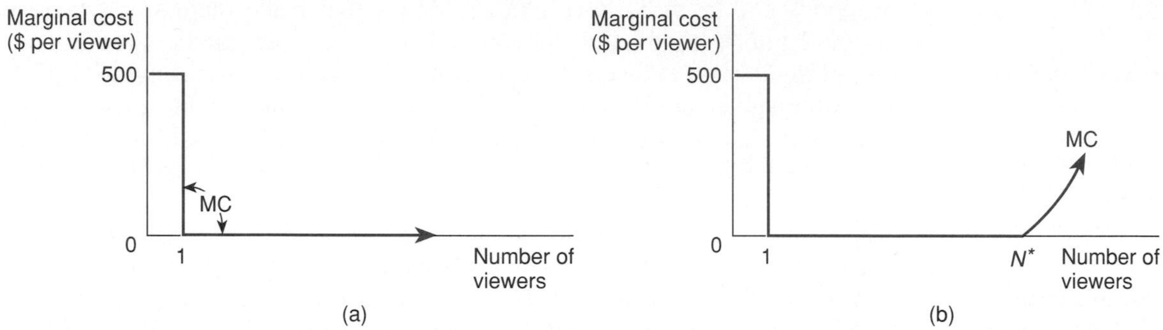

A pure public good is one that additional consumers can enjoy at zero marginal cost to existing consumers. In (a) fireworks displays have been assumed to be a pure public good. A display costing $500 can be viewed by any number of persons at zero marginal cost. In (b) congestion develops after N^* viewers have assembled. Additional viewers decrease the benefits of other viewers, resulting in a positive marginal cost after N^*.

6(b). If more than N^* persons will be viewing the fireworks display, efficiency requires that each of these persons be charged a price equal to the marginal cost that he or she imposes on others. If fewer than N^* viewers are anticipated, efficiency requires a zero price. The congestion price serves to ration the number of consumers who enjoy the pure public good after the point of congestion has been reached.

An example of a good subject to congestion is a road. For a road of a given size, there is a limit to the number of users that can be accommodated at zero marginal cost. When there are a limited number of access points on the road, the transaction costs of imposing congestion tolls are quite low.

Similarly, a bridge or tunnel has only one point of entrance and one point of exit. This makes it easy to establish tolls to ration the use of the facility. The tolls can vary with the amount of traffic. In cases in which there are predictable flows of traffic at various times of the day, the toll can vary with time of use. Thus a higher toll would be charged during rush hours. At off-hours or weekends the toll would be reduced. The toll could be set at zero when no congestion exists.

It may even be possible to ration the use of city streets in this way. The many points of access and exit on city streets have in the past made the transaction costs of imposing tolls too high. However, modern electronic technology is changing this. Cars could easily be required to have electronic tracking equipment. The streets would then be equipped with electronic sensors at various locations. A display in each car run by a small computer would alert drivers to the toll rates for various routes. Each vehicle user would then receive a monthly bill based on the toll rates for the routes and the times traveled.

Tolls on roads not only ration the use of the road's services, they also provide revenue. This revenue can be used in lieu of taxes to maintain roads and fund new and expanded facilities.

Excludable Public Goods

Excludable public goods are public goods that can be priced easily. An example of an excludable public good in an inoculation. Another example is schooling. Although it is possible to ration the use of these goods by fees and charges, the positive externalities associated with their use make this undesirable. Because inoculations benefit all by helping to eradicate disease, they are commonly made available at no charge to users and their costs are publicly financed. Similarly, public schooling is free in almost all nations. The costs of public schooling are financed mainly by taxation.

Another example of an excludable public good is knowledge. Knowledge can either be publicly distributed without charge or sold for a fee. It is clearly possible to exclude persons from the benefits of technical know-how. Yet the benefits of knowledge are nonrival. Allowing a person knowledge of how to build a certain computer does not take that knowledge away from others. Yet patents for inventions exclude persons other than inventors from the use of knowledge. This creates a valuable property for the inventors and thus is believed to encourage persons to devote their resources to the production of new knowledge.

Excludable public goods can be produced by governments or by private firms offering goods for sale in markets. Private supply implies that costs are financed through revenues from the sale of the good. Government supply can be financed through taxes, with free distribution of the goods, as in the case of public schools. Government can also charge fees for the goods they provide. Government-run hospitals and universities commonly charge fees for their services. In many cases the fees are lower than they would otherwise be because of subsidies. Of course, governments could also subsidize private firms to produce the same goods. This would have the effect of lowering prices to encourage the consumption of such goods as schooling and health services while allowing private operation.

Even goods commonly thought to be nonexcludable are often ingeniously priced by enterprising firms. The services of a lighthouse are nonrival. When the light shines to warn one ship of coastal dangers, it also shines for all other ships in the area. Surprisingly, it is possible to exclude ships from the benefits of lighthouses at a low transaction cost.

In England during the 18th and early 19th centuries, lighthouses were privately owned, profit-making operations. How did they extract payment from the shippers? Shipowners were assessed fees on the basis of the tonnage of their ships while in nearby docks. In fact, there was rarely more than one ship in the vicinity of a lighthouse at any point in time. Lighthouse owners could easily identify ships by their flags. If the ship in sight had not paid the fee for service, the benefits of light were not provided for its passage. The ships of those who refused to pay were excluded from the service.[4]

Similarly, persons often form private clubs to provide themselves with shared facilities. They set dues and other fees in ways that avoid congestion. This is a commonly used method of providing such recreational facilities as pools, golf

[4] See Ronald Coase, "The Lighthouse in Economics," *Journal of Law and Economics* 17, no. 2 (October 1974), pp. 357–76.

courses, tennis courts, and entertainment. By joining a club, members pay only a portion of the costs of its facilities and are made better off by benefiting from facilities that they do not choose to purchase for their own exclusive use.[5]

SUMMARY

1. Externalities are costs or benefits of market transactions not reflected in prices.
2. When a negative externality exists, marginal social cost exceeds marginal private cost.
3. A positive externality is a benefit not reflected in prices. When this is the case, marginal social benefit exceeds marginal private benefit.
4. An externality is internalized when prices are adjusted to reflect full marginal social costs or benefits. A corrective tax is a way of increasing prices by raising marginal private costs to marginal social costs. A corrective subsidy is a way of reducing prices by reducing marginal private benefits so that they equal marginal social benefits.
5. Corrective taxes and subsidies can be used to achieve efficiency. To administer these taxes, the source of the externality must be identified and its marginal value to third parties must be determined.
6. Negative externalities result from disputes concerning property rights to resource use. When relatively few parties are involved and transaction costs are low, these disputes can be resolved through private negotiation.
7. The Coase theorem states that when transaction costs are negligible, externalities are only temporary disputes concerning resource use that are resolved through private negotiation. It makes no difference which party is assigned the right to use a resource. As long as the right is tradable, the efficient resource allocation will always emerge through bargaining. However, the user who is granted the initial right is always better off at the outset than the user who must purchase that right when it is in its interest to do so. Governments can act to assign property rights and facilitate the trading of such rights to improve efficiency.
8. Pure public goods are nonrival in consumption and nonexclusive. Additional consumers do not reduce the availability of such goods to others. It is not feasible to exclude those who refuse to pay from the benefits of a pure public good.
9. The efficient output of a pure public good occurs at the point at which the sum of the marginal benefits of individual consumers equals the marginal cost of production.
10. In small groups a pure public good can be supplied cooperatively. Consumers must have incentives to reveal the true marginal benefits of the good. Voluntary contributions are used to finance each unit of production. In equilibrium each person contributes according to his marginal benefit. All persons consume the same quantity of the good, and the total contributions must cover the total costs of production.
11. Because of the free-rider problem, voluntary contributions are likely to be unsuccessful in large groups seeking to supply public goods. Consumers have incentives to understate their marginal benefits in the hope of obtaining benefits at costs below their actual worth. As a result, less than the efficient amount of the goods is made available.
12. Congestible public goods are public goods whose consumption is nonrival up to only a certain number of consumers. Efficiency requires that congestible public goods be priced at their marginal congestion cost when feasible.
13. Excludable public goods are public goods that are nonrival in consumption but for which the transaction cost of excluding consumers is relatively low. Such goods can be supplied by firms that operate in order to earn a profit.

[5] For a discussion of efficient dues for club members, see James M. Buchanan, "An Economic Theory of Clubs," *Economica* 32 (February 1965), pp. 1–14.

Important Concepts

externalities
negative externality
positive externality
marginal external cost
marginal private cost
marginal social cost
marginal social benefit
marginal private benefit
marginal external benefit
internalization of an externality
corrective tax
corrective subsidy
Coase theorem
small-number externality
large-number externality
pure public good
pure private good
nonrival in consumption
nonexclusive in consumption
free-rider problem
congestible public goods
excludable public goods
point of congestion

Questions for Review

1. Give some examples of negative externalities. Explain why markets tend to produce more than the efficient amounts of these goods. What is meant by internalization of a negative externality?
2. Although negative externalities (for example, pollution) are more commonly generated by production, they can also be generated by consumption. Explain how the consumption of alcohol may generate negative externalities. Also explain why the marginal social benefit curve of a good whose consumption generates negative externalities lies below the marginal private benefit curve for that good.
3. Suppose the production of electricity results in five cents of external cost per kilowatt-hour. Show how a corrective tax can internalize the external cost.
4. Why does the Coase theorem argue that government assignment of property rights is enough to internalize externalities? Does the choice of the party to which the rights are assigned make any difference? When is the theorem likely to be applicable?
5. The Coase theorem argues that individual bargaining with regard to resource rights maximizes the total income of those involved in the process. Do you agree? Explain your answer.
6. Contrast the characteristics of a pure public good with those of a pure private good. Explain why market supply of a pure public good is unlikely to be efficient.
7. Which type of public goods—congestible or excludable—is more likely to be produced by private markets? Is a national park (for example, Yellowstone) a congestible public good, an excludable public good, a pure public good, or a pure private good?
8. Explain why consumers who purchase a pure public good up to the point at which its marginal benefit equals its marginal cost of production will not consume the efficient amount.
9. Suppose police patrols are pure public goods. Is it possible for you to consume four patrols per evening, whereas your neighbor consumes eight?
10. When a pure public good is cooperatively supplied, how is the equilibrium share of the costs for each participant determined? How does the free-rider problem prevent efficiency in the cooperative provision of pure public goods?

Problems

1. A negative externality in the form of pollution damage is believed to be associated with gasoline. Suppose the damage is believed to be 5 cents per gallon. Show how a corrective tax can internalize the externality. Assume that the initial price of gasoline is $1 per gallon and that

daily consumption is 9 million gallons. Show the impact of the tax on the pollution damage and government revenues. Explain why a plan to ban the use of gasoline is likely to be inefficient.

2. The use of smoke detectors results in positive externalities. Show how a corrective subsidy will increase both the demand and the market price for these devices. Show expenditure on smoke detectors both before and after the subsidy. Show the net price and net expenditures on smoke detectors by consumers after they receive the subsidy.

3. Suppose that disputes concerning damage to wheat by cattle from adjoining ranges can always be settled through private negotiation among the parties involved. Show that the imposition of a corrective tax on cattle equal to the damage per steer will prevent the attainment of efficiency if bargaining occurs after it has been imposed.

4. Use the graphs in Figure 18–3 to show the impact of a decrease in the price of meat to $1 per pound on the equilibrium mix of meat and fish producted on the lake.

5. Suppose the price of security guards increases from $200 to $300 per week. Use the data in Table 18–4 and Figure 18–5 to show how this would affect the efficient amount of guards for members of the condominium community.

6. When you take measures to keep weeds out of your garden, you benefit you neighbors by reducing the risk that weed seeds will blow over to them. Show how each gardener in the neighborhood will produce less than the efficient amount of weed control.

7. Suppose the average cost of a pure public good increases as more of the good is produced. Show that at the efficient output of the pure public good there will be a budget surplus when the good is financed by a group's voluntary contributions. Assume that the group is small enough to permit disregarding the free-rider problem.

GLOSSARY

Actuarially fair price for insurance A price that equals the expected value of the loss being insured against.

Adverse selection A problem in insurance of high-risk customers dominating the demand for insurance when premiums are based on the average probability of loss.

Allocative efficiency A situation that prevails when the resources are allocated among persons so that it is impossible to make any person better off without harming another person.

Allocative efficiency A condition achieved when resources are allocated in a way that allows the maximum possible net benefit from their use.

Antitrust statutes Statutes that seek to prevent unfair business practices that give rise to monopoly power.

Asymmetric information The condition that prevails in a market in which some participants (either buyers or sellers) are better informed than others.

Average cost The total cost per unit of output.

Average fixed cost The fixed cost per unit of output.

Average input cost Total input cost divided by the number of input units.

Average product of a variable input The total product of the variable input divided by the amount of that input used.

Average variable cost The variable cost per unit of output.

Backward-bending labor supply curve The labor supply curve that exists when the income effect of wage increases outweighs the substitution effect at relatively high wage levels.

Barrier to entry A constraint that prevents additional sellers from entering a market.

Behavioral assumptions Assumptions about the motivations of people.

Bilateral monopoly A market structure in which only one buyer and one seller trade input (or output) services.

Budget constraint The market baskets of goods and services that a consumer can afford, given the consumer's income and the prices of the goods and services in the baskets.

Budget line A line showing all combinations of two goods that a consumer can afford if all income is spent over a period.

Business firm An organization set up and managed for the purpose of earning profits for its owners by producing goods or services for sale in markets.

Capital A durable input created for the purpose of producing more goods and services.

Capital asset pricing model A theory of stock prices that shows how the price of any given stock depends on the various financial returns available and on the risk of buying that stock.

Cardinal measurement Placing a number on alternatives so that their utility can be added.

Cartel A group of firms acting together to coordinate output decisions to control price.

Change in demand A change in the relationship between the price of an item and the quantity demanded caused by a change in something other than the price of the item.

Change in input demand A change in the relationship between the quantity of input demanded and the price of the input.

Change in quantity demanded A change in the amount of an item buyers are willing and able to buy in response to a change in its price.

Change in quantity supplied A change in the amount of an item offered for sale in response to a change in its price, other things being equal.

Change in the relative price of a good A change in the price of a good relative to the change in the average prices of all goods.

Change in the scale of operations A change in the level of operation that occurs when an organization's use of all inputs is varied in the same proportion.

Change in supply A change in the relationship between the price of a good and the quantity supplied that results from a change in something other than the price of the good.

Circular flow diagram A diagram that demonstrates how households and business firms are linked through input and output markets and how expenditure on products generates revenue that business firms use to pay for productive services.

Closed shop An arrangement requiring that an employer use only union labor.

Coase theorem A theorem holding that when transaction costs are negligible, externalities can be internalized by governments establishing property rights to resource use and allowing free exchange of those rights.

Cobb-Douglas production function A production function described by an equation that assumes that output varies by a constant multiplied by each input used raised to an exponential power between zero and one.

Coinsurance The portion of the costs of services that persons covered by a third-party payment plan must incur as out-of-pocket costs.

Collective bargaining Bargaining in which one negotiator acts as an agent for many independent negotiators.

Comparative static analysis The use of logic to trace out the effects of a change in economic conditions on equilibrium values of the variables of an economic model.

Compensated demand curves Demand curves that show only substitution effects of price changes.

Compensating wage differentials Differences in money wages needed to make the real wages of similar jobs equal when nonpecuniary wages are not equal to zero.

Competitive firm A firm that sells its output in a perfectly competitive market and thus cannot influence the price of what it sells.

Congestible public goods Public goods that are nonrival in consumption only up to a certain level of use over a given period.

Constant-costs industry An industry for which input prices are unaffected by the quantity produced or the number of firms in the industry.

Constant returns to scale These prevail when output increases by the same proportion in which inputs increase.

Consumer equilibrium A condition that is achieved when the consumer purchases the market basket that maximizes utility, subject to the budget constraint; achieved when consumption is adjusted so that $MRS_{XY} = P_X/P_y$ for any two goods.

Consumer surplus The difference between the market price of a good and the maximum price a consumer is willing to pay for an additional unit of the good.

Contestable market A market in which entry is free and exit is costless.

Contract curve A curve showing all the possible efficient allocations of two goods between two consumers.

Corner equilibrium A consumer equilibrium in which one of the goods is not purchased.

Corrective subsidy A payment to either consumers or producers of a good whose use generates a positive externality; designed to internalize the externality.

Corrective tax A levy on the output of a good or service that increases its marginal private cost to a level equal to its marginal social cost.

Cost function A function that describes the relationship between output and the minimum possible cost of producing that output.

Cross elasticity of demand The percentage change in the quantity of a good consumed in response to each 1 percent change in the price of some other good.

Decreasing-costs industry An industry for which the prices of certain inputs used decline as a direct result of the industry's expansion.

Describing returns to scale These prevail when output increases by a proportion that falls short of the proportion in which inputs are increased.

Deductible Minimum amount of out-of-pocket payments required by a third-party payer before it begins to pay for services.

Demand The relationship between the price of an item and the quantity buyers are willing and able to purchase.

Demand coefficients The amounts by which quantity purchased of a good will change for each unit change in a demand determinant.

Demand curve A graph of the relationship between price and quantity demanded.

Demand function A relationship among amounts of a good consumers will buy, its price, and all other influences on the demand for the good.

Demand schedule A table showing how the quantity demanded of an item varies with the price of the item.

Derived demand Demand for inputs that is derived from the demand for products made by those inputs.

Diminishing marginal rates of substitution of *X* for *Y* The assumption that as good *X* is substituted for good *Y* along an indifference curve, while keeping utility constant, there is a decline in the amount of good *Y* that the consumer will give up for each additional unit of good *X*.

Discrimination in labor markets Hiring practices that result in differing wages to equally productive workers.

Diversified portfolio A portfolio that consists of risky and riskless assets.

Dominant strategy The strategy for which a player is getting the highest possible payoff, regardless of what the rival players are doing.

Duopoly A market structure in which two sellers protected from the entry of additional sellers are the sole producers of a standardized good with no close substitutes.

Economic cost The opportunity cost of operating a business.

Economic model A simplified way of expressing how some sector of the economy functions; consists of assumptions that establish relationships among economic variables.

Economic profits Revenue minus economic costs.

Economic rent The difference between the payments made for input services and the minimum amount required to induce the suppliers to make those services available.

Economics The study of how scarce resources are allocated among alternative uses.

Economic variables Measurable quantities that can take on a number of possible values.

Economies of scale Increases in input productivities that result from division of labor and savings in materials when a factory increases the scale of its operations.

Edgeworth box A tool for analyzing production and the allocation of resources in an economy with fixed supplies of inputs.

Efficiency wages Wages set above market equilibrium wages in order to eliminate shirking.

Engle curve A graph showing the relationship between money income and the quantity of a good purchased.

Entry-limit price A price low enough to prevent new firms from entering a market.

Equilibrium A balance of forces that keeps economic variables from increasing or decreasing.

Equimarginal principle Equalization of the marginal utility per dollar spent on all goods so as to maximize utility given income.

Excess burden of a tax The difference between the dollar value of consumer surplus lost as a result of the tax and the tax revenue collected.

Excess capacity The difference between the output corresponding to LRACmin and that produced by a monopolistically competitive firm in the long run.

Excludable public goods Public goods that are nonrival in consumption but for which the transaction costs of excluding additional consumers are quite low.

Expansion path A curve that shows how the use of variable inputs changes as output increases.

Expected utility The average utility of an uncertain situation; computed by weighting the utility of the payoffs in the situation by their probabilities of occurrence.

Expected value An average of the possible payoffs associated with the possible outcomes of an uncertain situation, with each outcome weighted according to its probability of occurrence.

Externalities Costs or benefits of market transactions not reflected in prices.

Feedback effects Further changes in prices and quantities in a market in response to price changes in related markets.

Fixed cost The cost of inputs that are independent of output.

Free and competitive market A market in which many sellers compete for sales to many buyers who compete for available supplies and in which there are no restrictions on the participation of buyers or sellers.

Free entry A situation that exists when anyone can begin an enterprise in an industry.

Free exit A situation that exists when owners of a firm in an industry can cease operating at any time they wish.

Free-rider problem The incentive of people to contribute less than their marginal benefit to the cost of financing a pure public good in the hope that others will contribute enough to make the good available.

General equilibrium A condition that exists when prices have adjusted to a change in either demand or supply so that quantities demanded equal quantities supplied in all markets.

General equilibrium analysis Analysis of equilibrium that considers the interdependence of prices and quantities in all markets.

General theory of second best A theory holding that it is better to depart from efficiency in one sector of the economy to balance the distortions that impair efficiency in other sectors of the economy when those distortions cannot be eliminated otherwise.

Giffen good An inferior good for which the income effect exceeds the substitution effect.

Herfindahl index An index that measures market concentration by estimating market shares and summing the squares of market shares of all firms in the market.

Identification of a demand curve The variation in observed prices and quantities that can be used to trace out a demand curve from actual data.

Imperfect competition Exists when two or more sellers, each of which has some control over price, compete for sales in a market.

Implicit costs The value of input services that are used in production but not purchased in a market.

Import quotas Restrictions on the quantity of foreign goods that can be sold in a nation.

Income-consumption curve A graph connecting equilibrium points on a consumer's indifference map as income changes showing how consumption of goods varies as income changes.

Income effect The change in the consumption of a good that results from the change in real income caused by a change in the price of the good.

Income elasticity of demand The percentage change in quantity purchased of a product in response to each 1 percent change in income.

Increasing-costs industry An industry for which at least some input prices increase as a direct result of the industry's expansion.

Increasing returns to scale These prevail when output increases by a proportion that exceeds the proportion by which all inputs increase.

Indifference curve A curve connecting points on a graph that correspond to market baskets of equal utility to a consumer.

Indifference map A set of indifference curves used to describe a person's preferences.

Industry A group of competing firms selling a certain product in a market.

Industry demand for an input The relationship between the amounts of input services demanded by an industry and the price of the input services.

Industry equilibrium The equilibrium that prevails when there is no tendency for firms to enter or leave an industry or to expand or reduce the scale of their operations.

Inferior goods Goods that a consumer purchases less of as income increases.

Input demand curve A curve that shows how the quantity of input services demanded varies with the price of input services.

Inputs The productive services of labor, capital, and natural resources.

Interest The price paid for the use of loanable funds.

Interloper firm A firm that quickly enters a market when it can earn economic profits and leaves quickly before prices decline to a level that no longer permits economic profits.

Internalization of an externality The condition that results when marginal private costs or benefits associated with the market exchange of an item are adjusted to reflect actual marginal social costs or benefits of choices.

Internal labor market A labor market within a firm used to fill new and upper-level positions.

Internal rate of return The marginal rate of return on an investment.

Investment The process of replenishing, or adding to, capital stock.

Investment portfolio A combination of financial assets.

Isocost line A line that gives all the combinations of labor and capital of equal total cost.

Isoquant A curve showing all combinations of variable inputs that can be used to produce a given amount of output.

Isoquant map A set of isoquants that shows the maximum output attainable from any given combination of inputs.

Labor market screening The process of limiting the applicants for a job to those who the employer believes are most likely to succeed in the organization.

Labor unions Organizations formed to represent the interests of workers in bargaining for contracts concerning wages, fringe benefits, and working conditions.

Large-number externality An externality in which a large number of people are involved and the transaction costs of bargaining to trade property rights are therefore very high.

Laspeyres price index A measure of changes in the price level that calculates the cost of living in the current year relative to the cost of living in a base year.

Law of demand The lower the price of an item, the greater is the quantity demanded, other things being equal.

Law of diminishing marginal returns States that as more of a variable input is used while other inputs and technology are fixed, the marginal product of the variable input will eventually decline.

Law of supply The higher the price of an item, the greater is the quantity supplied.

Long run A period of production during which all inputs can be varied.

Long-run competitive equilibrium The equilibrium that prevails when market output and price allow firms in an industry to earn zero economic profits.

Long-run cost curves Curves that show the minimum cost of producing any given output when all of the inputs are variable.

Long-run industry supply curve A supply curve that shows the relationship between price and quantity supplied for points at which an industry is in equilibrium.

Lump-sum tax A tax that does not distort relative prices and therefore has only an income effect on incentives.

Marginal analysis A technique of analyzing the way persons who seek to maximize net gains make decisions.

Marginal benefit The extra benefit of one more unit of something.

Marginal benefit of a good A measure of the number of dollars of expenditure on all other goods a consumer will sacrifice to purchase a particular item.

Marginal conditions for the efficient output of a good Conditions that are met when the marginal benefit of the good equals its marginal cost.

Marginal cost The change in total cost that results from a change in output; the extra cost incurred to produce another unit of output.

Marginal cost The extra cost of one more unit of something.

Marginal external benefit The marginal benefit received by third parties other than the buyers or sellers of a good or service.

Marginal external cost The extra cost imposed on third parties, for which producers are not charged, for each extra unit of output.

Marginal input cost The extra cost of an extra unit of input.

Marginal input cost for a monopsony The extra cost of another unit of input services that is less than the price of those services.

Marginal net benefit The difference between a consumer's marginal benefit from a good and the price of that good.

Marginal net return on the investment The marginal rate of return less the marginal interest rate.

Marginal private benefit The benefit obtained by the buyer when one more unit of an item is sold.

Marginal private cost The marginal cost of production incurred by sellers.

Marginal product of a variable input The change in the total product of that input corresponding to a 1-unit change in its use.

Marginal profit The additional profit that results from the sale of an additional unit of output.

Marginal rate of return on the investment The net increase in revenue resulting from the investment expressed as a percentage of each dollar invested.

Marginal rate of substitution of *X* for *Y* The amount of good *Y* that a consumer would give up to obtain one more unit of good *X* while holding utility constant.

Marginal rate of technical substitution of labor for capital A measure of the amount of capital that each unit of labor can replace without increasing or decreasing production.

Marginal rate of time preference The value of additional future consumption required to compensate a person for giving up current consumption without making the person better or worse off.

Marginal rate of transformation The amount of one good that must be sacrificed when the resources used to produce some of it are reallocated to the production of another good.

Marginal revenue The change in revenue that results from selling an additional unit of output.

Marginal revenue product of an input The marginal product of an input multiplied by the marginal revenue of that output; the extra revenue possible from hiring an extra unit of an input.

Marginal social benefit The extra benefit enjoyed when one more unit of a good or service is made available.

Marginal social cost The sum of the marginal private cost and the marginal external cost of a product.

Marginal utility The gain in utility obtained from consuming another unit of an item.

Market An arrangement through which buyers and sellers can meet for the purpose of trading goods or services.

Market basket A combination of goods and services for consumption over a period.

Market demand curve A demand curve derived from individual demand curves for a product in a market by adding the quantities demanded by all consumers at each possible price.

Market demand for an input The relationship between the quantities of an input demanded for all uses in a market and the price of the input.

Market equilibrium A condition that exists in a market when price adjusts so that quantity demanded equals quantity supplied.

Market failure Exists when exchange between buyers and sellers in an unregulated market does not result in an efficient outcome.

Market signal A means of conveying information about a not easily seen characteristic of a product or service.

Market structure An indication of the number of buyers and sellers, their market shares, the degree of product standardization, and the ease of market entry and exit.

Maximin strategies Dominant strategies that minimize the maximum loss.

Microeconomics The study of public choices, business choices, and personal choices to understand how the economy functions.

Monopolistic competition The competition that exists when many sellers compete to sell a differentiated product in a market into which the entry of new sellers is possible.

Monopoly power The ability of a firm to affect the price of its product by varying the quantity it is willing to sell.

Monopsony power The ability of a single buyer to influence the price of some of the input services that it purchases.

Moral hazard The increased risk of payout for insurance firms that results from behavioral changes caused by insurance coverage.

Nash equilibrium A combination of the strategies chosen by rivals in a competitive situation in which each of the rivals has no incentive to change what it is doing, given the choices of its opponents.

Natural monopoly A firm that can supply the entire market demand for a product at a lower average cost than would be possible if two or more firms supplied exactly the same quantity of the product.

Natural oligopoly A situation that exists when a few firms can supply the entire market output at lower long-run average costs than can many firms.

Negative externality A cost of resource use not reflected in the price of a product.

Nonexclusive in consumption A property of a pure public good that prevents if from being withheld from consumers who do not pay for it.

Nonpecuniary wages The nonmonetary aspects of a job that must be added to money wages to obtain real wages.

Nonprice rationing The distribution of available amounts of goods and services on a basis other than willingness or ability to pay.

Nonrival in consumption A property of a pure public good that allows a given quantity of the good to be consumed by any one person without reducing the availability of the good to other persons.

Normal goods Goods that a consumer purchases more of as income increases.

Normative economic analysis Analysis of the desirability of alternative outcomes on the basis of underlying value judgments.

Oligopoly A market structure in which a few interdependent sellers dominate the sale of a product and into which the entry of new sellers is difficult or impossible.

Oligopsony An input market structure in which a few firms purchase the entire market supply of certain inputs.

Opportunity cost of a choice The next best alternative use of resources sacrificed by making a choice.

Opportunity cost of using inputs The value of those inputs in their next best use.

Ordinal measurement The ranking of alternatives as first, second, third, and so on.

Paradox of profits Positive economic profits set in motion a process of resource reallocation that ultimately reduces them to zero.

Pareto optimal resource allocation A resource allocation that achieves allocative efficiency.

Partial equilibrium analysis Analysis of the equilibrium variables in one market.

Partial monopoly A market in which one firm sets price to equate its marginal revenue and marginal cost and other firms are price takers at that price.

Payoff The value of a possible outcome in an uncertain situation measured as a sum of money.

Payoff matrix A matrix that shows the gain or loss accruing to each possible strategy for each of the rival's possible reactions in a competitive situation.

Perfect competition Prevails when many competing sellers sell a standardized product in a market in which each seller has a very small share of total sales, is unconcerned about the reactions of rivals, and takes the price of the product as given; when information is freely available; and when sellers have freedom of entry into and exit out of the market.

Perfect, or first-degree, price discrimination The price discrimination that exists when a monopoly charges each buyer a different price.

Perfectly competitive input market A market in which there is free entry and exit of sellers and buyers and in which many rival employers compete to purchase the services supplied by many sellers, each of which sells only a small share of the total supply of a standardized input and therefore cannot influence price.

Physical depreciation The rate at which capital wears out or becomes obsolete.

Point of congestion The point at which the number of consumers of a congestible public good begins to raise the marginal cost of accommodating additional consumers above zero.

Point of diminishing marginal returns The level of use of a variable input at which its marginal product just begins to decline.

Positive economic analysis Analysis of the effects of changes in economic policies or economic conditions on economic variables.

Positive externality A benefit not reflected in prices.

Predatory pricing The practice of selling a product at a price deliberately set low enough to drive rival firms out of business.

Preferences The rankings consumers give to the alternative opportunities available to them.

Present value The current value of the stream of returns that can be produced from the services of a capital asset over time; the sum of money that will produce a certain stream of returns over a period when invested at a certain interest rate.

Price ceilings Maximum prices established by law.

Price-consumption curve A graph connecting points of consumer equilibrium as prices change; shows how the consumption of a good changes as its price changes.

Price discrimination The selling of a good or service of given quality and average cost at different prices to different buyers.

Price dispersion The existence of a variety of prices for the same standardized product in a market in which perfect competition appears to prevail.

Price elasticity of demand The percentage change in quantity demanded that would result from each 1 percent change in price along a demand curve.

Price elasticity of supply A measure of the sensitivity of changes in quality supplied to changes in price; the percentage change in quantity supplied that results from a 1 percent change in price.

Price floor A minimum price established by law.

Price leader A firm that sets a price to maximize its profits in a market, whose lead is followed by other firms that set the same price.

Prices The sum of money that must be given up to obtain a unit of a good or service.

Price war A bout of continual price-cutting by rival firms in an oligopolistic market.

Principal-agent problem The problem that exists when the goals of an organization's principals and agents differ.

Prisoner's dilemma A game-type situation in which the dominant strategy results in a Nash equilibrium in which both participants are worse off than they would have been if they had cooperated.

Probability The chance that an outcome will occur.

Producer surplus The difference between the market price of a unit of output and the minimum price required to make that extra unit available in the marketplace.

Product attributes Characteristics of a good, service, or situation that provide utility to a person.

Product differentiation The sale of items that are not standardized.

Product group Several closely related, but not identical, items that serve the same general purpose for consumers.

Production The process of using the services of labor and equipment together with natural resources and materials to make goods and services available.

Production function A relationship between inputs and the maximum attainable output under a given technology.

Production grid A table that describes a production function by indicating the maximum output that can be produced with given combinations of inputs.

Production possibility curve A curve showing the maximum amount of any one good that can be produced in an economy, given the output of all other goods, the resource constraint, and technology.

Productive efficiency A situation that prevails when it is impossible to reallocate resources to increase the output of one good without decreasing the output of other goods.

Property rights Privileges to own or use scarce resources.

Pure monopoly A single seller of a product that has no close substitutes.

Pure monopsony A single firm that employs the entire market supply of an input that has few, if any, alternative employment opportunities.

Pure private good A good for which each unit produced can be priced and sold to individuals so that each unit benefits the buyer exclusively.

Pure public good A good whose units of production are consumed collectively by all persons, whether or not they pay for it.

Quantity demanded The amount of an item that would be purchased at a certain price given all of the other influences on demand.

Quantity supplied The amount of an item that would be supplied at a certain price given all of the other influences on supply.

Reaction curves Curves that show the profit-maximizing output produced by one firm, given the output of the rival firm.

Repeated game A game that can be played over and over, so that the participants can develop reputations for pursuing certain strategies and can study the strategies pursued by their rival.

Resource constraint The total amount of input services available over a given period.

Risk A situation that prevails when a person engages in an activity for which there is more than one possible outcome, with each possible outcome having a certain probability of occurrence.

Risk averter A person who, other things being equal, prefers an uncertain situation with less risk to one with more risk.

Risk lover A person for whom risk is a positively valued attribute of an uncertain situation.

Risk neutrality A situation that prevails when additional risk neither increases nor decreases utility.

Risk premium A sum of money that a risk averter would pay to avoid taking a risk.

Risk-yield transformation curve A graph showing the options an investor has for trading portfolio risk for higher portfolio yield by varying the proportion of relatively risky assets in the portfolio.

Rule of reason A judicial rule under which acts beyond normal business practice that unduly restrain competition can be used to infer intent to monopolize.

Scarcity The imbalance between desires for goods and services and the means of satisfying those desires.

Search costs The costs that buyers incur to inform themselves about prices.

Second-degree price discrimination The price discrimination that exists when a monopolist prices its product in blocks to extract some, but not all, of the consumer surplus.

Segmented market A market in which two or more classes of buyers with differing responsiveness to price changes can be identified.

Selling costs The costs incurred by a firm to influence the sales of its product.

Sequential games Games in which one player acts and the other player responds to that action.

Shirking Behavior by workers that prevents an employer from achieving the maximum possible marginal product from its work force over a given period.

Shortage The difference between quantity demanded and quantity supplied in a market when quantity demanded is greater than quantity supplied.

Short run A period of production during which some inputs cannot be varied.

Short-run supply curve The portion of a competitive firm's marginal cost curve that lies above the minimum point of its AVC curve.

Shutdown point The point reached when price falls to a level that just allows a firm to cover the minimum possible average variable cost of its output.

Small-number externality An externality in which only few parties are involved and the transaction costs of bargaining to internalize the externality are therefore likely to be low.

Social cost of monopoly A measure of the loss in net benefits that results from a monopoly's control of output.

Staffing The process of recruiting and hiring workers to perform various tasks required to produce goods and services.

Standard deviation The square root of the variance.

Strategic move An action that influences a rival's choice to a player's advantage.

Strategy A course of action chosen after consideration of a rival's possible courses of action in a competitive situation.

Substitution effect The change in the consumption of a good that results from the change in its price relative to the prices of other goods.

Supply A relationship between price and quantity supplied.

Supply curve A graph of the relationship between price and quantity supplied.

Supply schedule A table showing how the quantity supplied of an item varies with the price of that item.

Surplus The difference between quantity supplied and quantity demanded in a market when quantity supplied is greater than quantity demanded.

Tariffs Taxes levied on imported goods.

Technology The knowledge of how to produce goods and services.

Theory A framework for understanding relationships of cause and effect.

Theory of games A technique for analyzing the selection of strategies by persons or organizations with conflicting interests in situations whose payoffs depend on the choices made by each participant and the participant's rivals.

Third-party payments Full or partial payments for market-provided services by an organization that is neither the buyer nor the seller of the services.

Total cost The sum of the cost of all inputs used to produce an item.

Total product of a variable input The amount of output produced when a given amount of that input is used along with fixed inputs.

Transaction costs The value of the resources used in locating trading partners, negotiating terms of trade, drawing up contracts, and enforcing the property rights acquired in a transaction.

Transitivity A property of preferences indicating that a person who prefers alternative *A* to alternative *B* and alternative *B* to alternative *C* must also prefer *A* to *C*.

Uncertain situation A situation in which more than one outcome is possible and the probability of each of those outcomes is known or can be estimated.

Useful life of a capital asset The number of years over which the newly acquired asset will contribute to a firm's revenues or reduce its costs.

Utility The satisfaction obtained from consuming an item.

Utility function A relationship between the quantities of goods and services consumed and the utility level achieved by the consumer.

Utility possibility curve A curve that shows how utility varies among persons for all possible efficient allocations of inputs and outputs.

Value of the marginal product of an input The marginal product of an input multiplied by the price at which the additional output is sold.

Variable cost The cost of inputs that change with output.

Variance A statistical measure of the variability of payoffs in an uncertain situation that is computed by averaging the squares of the deviations of possible outcomes from the expected value of the payoffs.

Wage elasticity of demand for labor The percentage change in the quantity of labor services demanded in response to each 1 percent change in wages.

Answers to Even-Numbered Problems

Chapter 1

2. If you were to attend another concert this month you would incur a net loss of $45 − $25 = $20 because the price of the ticket exceeds your marginal benefit. If you are rational, you will not attend any more concerts this month.

Chapter 2

2. A horizontal supply curve means that a price increase is not necessary to induce firms to increase quantity supplied. If the supply of rental housing over a five-year period were a horizontal line, over that period an increase in demand would increase quantity supplied but would have no effect on the market equilibrium price.

4. At the ceiling price of $10 the quantity demanded is

   $$600 - 2(10) = 580 \text{ backpacks per month}$$

   and the quantity supplied is

   $$300 + 4(10) = 340 \text{ backpacks per month}$$

   At the ceiling price there will be a monthly shortage of 240 backpacks.

6. **a.** It will increase. Oranges and grapefruits are substitutes. A reduction in the grapefruit supply causes the price of grapefruits to rise. This causes the demand for oranges to increase, which causes both equilibrium price and quantity of oranges to increase.

   b. It will increase, because an increase in the demand for oranges increases both equilibrium price and quantity of oranges.

   c. A reduction in the grapefruit supply causes the equilibrium price of grapefruits to rise and the equilibrium quantity of grapefruits to fall. The higher grapefruit price causes the demand for oranges to rise, so both the equilibrium price and quantity of oranges will rise.

Chapter 3

2. With a $40 weekly allowance, good X (rock concerts) priced at $10, and good Y (ice cream) priced at $4 per half gallon, the budget constraint line has a slope of $-P_x/P_y = -2.5$. The intercept on the X axis is four rock concerts per week. The intercept on the Y axis is 10 half-gallon packages of ice cream per week.

   A cut in the weekly allowance shifts the budget constraint line inward parallel to itself and halves the intercept values on both X and

Y. An increase in the price of rock concerts to \$20 changes the slope of the budget line to -5, as shown in (a). It halves the X-axis intercept to two concerts but has no effect on the Y-axis intercept.

A quantity discount on ice cream results in a convex budget constraint line. When only 1 half gallon is purchased per week, the slope of the line is -2.5. When more than 1 half gallon is purchased per week, the slope is $-\$10/\$2 = -5$. It is possible for a single indifference curve with declining MRS_{XY} to be tangent to both the flat and steep portion of this budget constraint line. This means that market baskets B_1 and B_2 are the two most-preferred outcomes, as shown in (b).

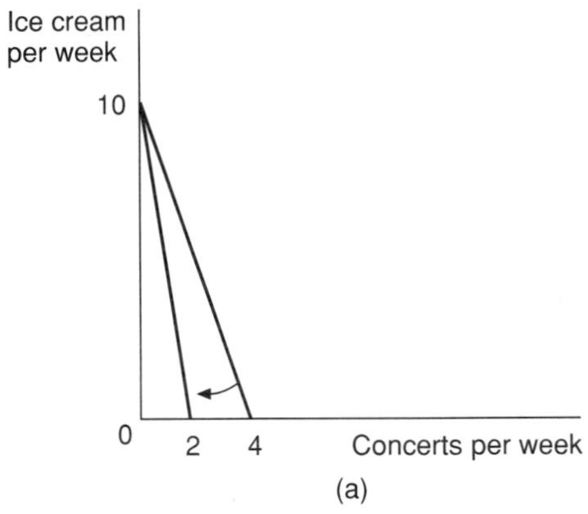

(a)

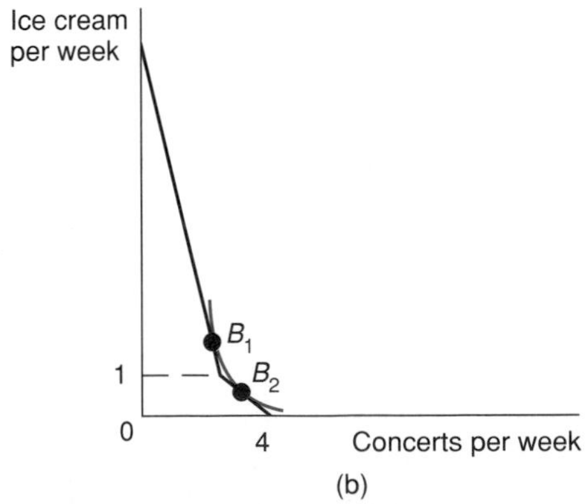

(b)

4. Because MU/P of shoes exceeds MU/P of shirts, you have not attained equilibrium. Equilibrium requires that the consumption of all goods be adjusted until their marginal utilities per dollar are equal.

Plot shoes on the X axis and shirts on the Y axis. If $MU_X/P_X > MU_X/P_Y$, it must follow that $MU_X/MU_Y > P_X/P_Y$. But the ratio of marginal utilities is MRS_{XY}. It therefore follows that the budget line intersects the indifference curve at point A because it is less steeply sloped than the indifference curve at point A. To achieve equilibrium, you must substitute shoes for shirts until you have reached point E.

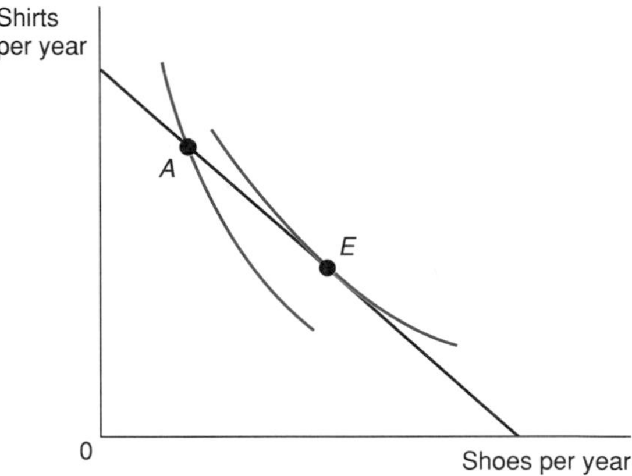

6. **a.** The horizontal intercept of the budget line is equal to income divided by the price of X, and the vertical intercept of the budget line is equal to income divided by the price of Y. So $P_X = \$30$ and $P_Y = \$15$.

   b. Since $MRS_{XY} = P_X/P_Y =$ Absolute value of the slope of the budget line at a consumer equilibrium of this sort, the MRS_{XY} at $A = 2$.

   c. Since the indifference curve is convex, the MRS_{XY} at B must be less than two, as can be verified by drawing a tangent to the indifference curve at B. So the MRS_{XY} cannot be 5 at point B.

   d. The price of good Y must increase and the price of good X must decrease to make point B a consumer equilibrium, assuming income is constant. Drawing a tangent at B shows that the budget line's vertical intercept must decrease and the horizontal intercept must increase.

CHAPTER 4

2. Note that the budget line $I_l F_l$ in Figure 4–16 in the text jumps to point B at point C. It is possible for a given convex indifference curve to touch this budget line at *both* point B and a point to the right of point B.

4. **a.** At point A income = \$400, the vertical intercept of the budget line. Since the horizontal intercept of the same budget line is 40, the price of good X must be \$10.

   b. At point A the consumer purchases 30 units of X at \$10 each, so her total spending on good X is \$300, leaving \$100 for spending on other goods. At point B, her spending on other goods is

   $$\$600 - (\$10)(45) = \$150.$$

   c. At point A income = \$400 and good X consumption = 30. At point B income = \$600 and good X consumption = 45. These are the coordinates of two points on the consumer's Engel curve for good X.

   d. Good X cannot be inferior for the consumer at an income level of \$600 because at point B her income-consumption curve slopes upward. At an income level of \$2,000 her income-consumption curve may be backward bending; without further labeling of the diagram, this cannot be definitely determined. So good X may or may not be inferior for her at an income of \$2,000.

   e. The consumer's marginal rate of substitution of spending on other goods for good X consumption is the same at all points on her income-consumption curve because the budget lines forming the indifference curve–budget line tangencies all have the same slope (that is, the price of good X is held constant).

CHAPTER 5

2. The new demand curve for desk lamps will intercept the price axis at a higher price. Using the distance formula for price elasticity of demand, the distance PC on the new curve will exceed the distance PC on the old curve, while the distance OP is the same at the price of \$30. It follows that, ignoring the minus sign, the absolute value of the price elasticity of demand will be smaller at a price of \$30 after the increase in demand. Demand at a price of \$30 is therefore less price elastic after the demand curve shifts.

4. Sellers still receive \$1 a gallon for oil. The total cost of the subsidy is \$0.5 (3 million gallons), which equals \$1.5 million. Use the formula $G = SQ_1 + \frac{1}{2}S\Delta Q$ to calculate the gain in consumer surplus. In this case

   $$SQ_1 = \$1 \text{ million}$$

   and

   $$\tfrac{1}{2}S\Delta Q = \$250{,}000$$

   The total gains to the subsidy recipients are therefore \$1.25 million, which falls short of the \$1.5 million cost of the subsidy to taxpayers.

6. **a.** To maximize total revenue when no quantity constraint exists, the promoters will charge the price corresponding to the midpoint of the demand curve, which is \$100.

   b. With a quantity constraint of 2,000 (which is less than 2,500, the quantity at which demand is unit elastic), total revenue is maximized by charging \$120, the price corresponding to a quantity demanded of 2,000. Lowering price from \$120 to \$100 would lower rather than raise revenue, given the quantity constraint. Total revenue at a price of \$120 is (\$120)(2,000) = \$240,000.

   c. Total revenue is maximized by charging \$100, as indicated in **a.** The quantity constraint in this case is not binding—that is, it does not affect the revenue-maximizing price of the promoters. So 500 of the 2,500 seats will be empty.

d. Total consumer surplus = \$180,000, which is the area under the demand curve and above the ticket price of \$80. Since the highest price anyone is willing and able to pay for a ticket is \$200, no one will receive a consumer surplus of more than \$120 from purchasing a ticket.

CHAPTER 6

2. The following table shows the marginal utility of each \$10,000 increment in income.

Income per Year (Dollars)	*Marginal Utility of Income (Utils)*
10,000	10
20,000	8
30,000	6
40,000	4
50,000	2

a. Because the marginal utility of income declines, John is a risk averter.

b. Expected income = \$40,000(0.5) + \$10,000(0.5) = \$25,000
Expected utility = 28(0.5) + 10(0.5) = 19 utils

c. In the absence of a risk premium John would choose the straight salary job because the \$25,000 income provides him with 22 utils, which exceeds the expected utility of the commission job. If John's father gives him a high enough risk premium, John could be induced to accept the commission job. The extra income would have to provide him with more than 3 utils per year.

CHAPTER 7

2. The slope of the isoquants is $-MP_K/MP_L$. If any one of the inputs has a negative marginal product, the slope will be positive. If both inputs have negative marginal products, the slope would again be positive. However, under those circumstances the production would be taking place on the nonconvex portions of the isoquants. The positively sloped and nonconvex portions of the isoquants are technologically inefficient because the marginal products of one or more inputs are negative. This means that the same output could be produced with less input use. Points on the production function only include input combinations that produce a given output with minimum input use.

4. If constant returns to scale prevail, then whenever input use doubles, so will output. If the average product of labor at initial use is Q/L, then the average product of labor after the firm doubles both labor use and capital use will be

$$2Q/2L = Q/L$$

Similarly, if the average product of capital is initially Q/K, then doubling labor and capital use will mean that the average product of capital is

$$2Q/2K = Q/K$$

Doubling input use therefore has no effect on the average product of labor or capital.

6. **a.** No. Total product keeps increasing as labor use increases as long as the marginal product of labor is positive. Since MP_L is positive (and equal to AP_L) when AP_L is maximized, we know that $L = 10$ cannot maximize total product.

b. $\text{Total product}_{L=9} = \text{Total product}_{L=8} + MP_L$ of the 9th unit of labor
$= (40)(8) + 60$
$= 320 + 60 = 380$

c. No. AP_L can never be negative, since total product can never be negative.

d. $Q = (25)(5) = 125$
$Q = (25)(15) = 375$ (Note that $AP_L = 25$ for two different Ls.)

e. $L = 10$, because $MP_L = AP_L$ when AP_L is maximized.

CHAPTER 8

2. The data in the third column of Table 8–3 will now be reduced by one half for each 100 labor hours because each output listed will now require only half as many labor hours per month. There are no changes in materials cost and capital cost. Fixed cost remains unchanged, as does average fixed cost. Variable cost will decline, as will average variable cost and marginal cost.

4. $\text{AVC} = P_L\left(\frac{1}{\text{AP}_L}\right) = \$5\left(\frac{1}{50}\right) = \$0.1$

$\text{AC} = \text{AVC} + \text{AFC} = \$0.1 + \frac{\$5,000}{10,000} = \$0.6$

6. **a.** Since, at an isoquant-isocost tangency such as point A, the $\text{MRTS}_{LK} = P_L/P_K$ = Slope of the isocost line, the MRTS_{LK} at $A = 30/20 = 1.5$.

b. Total spending on inputs at point B is \$420, so the LRAC for an output of 100 is merely \$4.20.

c. No, point C does not yield the LRAC of producing 80 units of output because it is not the cost-minimizing input combination for producing $Q = 80$ when capital use is variable. Point C would yield the SRAC of producing $Q = 80$ if the firm's capital was fixed in the short run at the level corresponding to point C.

d. The isocost line would have to "twist" as shown. Thus P_K would have to decrease and P_L would have to increase.

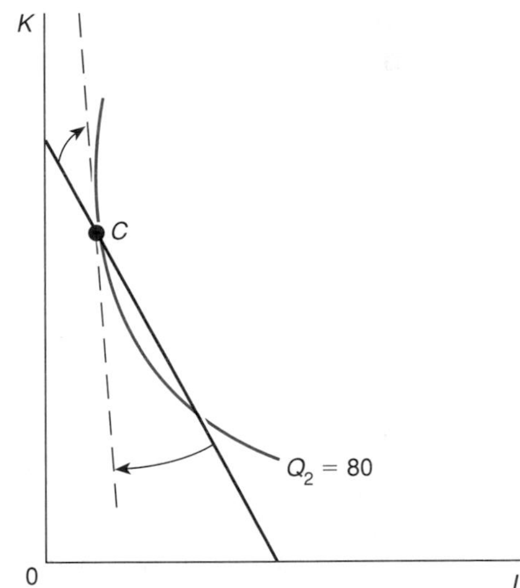

CHAPTER 9

2. Imputed economic costs are \$30,000 imputed wages and \$15,000 imputed interest. Subtracting these costs from accounting profits gives \$5,000 economic profits. Because you are more than covering your opportunity costs, you will remain in business.

4. A change in fixed costs shifts average cost but has no effect on AVC or MC. Other things being equal, a change in fixed costs has no impact on the equilibrium output because the marginal cost curve will not shift. Doubling the fixed costs in Table 9–1 confirms this.

6. **a.** No, because the minimum value of average variable cost is \$8. If the firm set MR = P = MC when price is \$7, it would lose an amount greater than its total fixed cost. Rather than do that, it will produce nothing and take a loss equal to total fixed cost. Whenever price is less than the minimum value of AVC, the firm minimizes its short-run loss by producing nothing.

b. Yes. It will set MR = MC = \$10 and produce a positive output. Since \$10 is less than the minimum value of AC of \$20, it will suffer an economic loss, but since $10 is greater than the minimum value of AVC, that loss will be less than its total fixed cost, so it will minimize its loss by producing the output level at which MC = $10.

c. Yes. Whenever price exceeds the minimum value of average total cost, the firm will earn an economic profit by choosing the output for which P = MR = MC. The area of the shaded rectangle in the diagram is the firm's maximum economic profit at a price of $30.

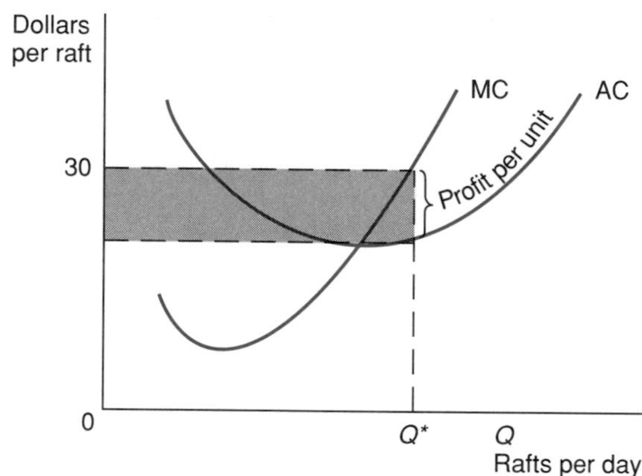

d. Short-run equilibrium industry price and output will *not* change, because the decrease in the price of capital and total fixed cost for each firm does not affect the positions of the firm's short-run marginal cost curves, which are determined only by variable costs. So the short-run industry supply curve does not shift and short-run equilibrium price and industry output remain the same.

8. Because MB > MC, less than the efficient output of cars is being produced.

Chapter 10

2. The sale of an additional 2,000 licenses will decrease the market price of these inputs. This will allow economic profits to be earned in the taxi industry. All taxi firms will experience a decrease in average costs as the opportunity cost of the licence (the forgone interest) declines. New firms will enter until the price of the licenses is at a level that allows firms in the industry to earn no more than the normal profit. In the new long-run equilibrium the price of taxi services will decline, the quantity of taxi miles supplied will increase, and economic profits will again be zero.

4. The increase in fuel costs increases variable costs and therefore shifts the LRAC curve upward. Because the industry was initially in equilibrium, the increase in fuel prices results in $P <$ LRACmin. Firms will leave the industry in the long run until supply decreases enough to increase price so as to allow the remaining firms to cover all costs (including the normal profit). In the long run, therefore, there is a decrease in the supply of textiles and an increase in their market price.

6. **a.** Q = 20,000; Profit = $30,000 per month.

b. Market supply will increase because new firms will enter the industry.

c. There will be 2,000 firms each producing 10,000 bushels per month.

Chapter 11

2. When demand is linear, marginal revenue declines twice as fast as price as more output is produced. Constant returns to scale and constant costs imply a horizontal average cost

curve where AC = MC. It follows that the marginal revenue curve will bisect the marginal cost line at the midpoint between P = MC = AC (which corresponds to the competitive output) and the vertical axis. As illustrated, this means that the monopoly output is exactly one half of the competitive output.

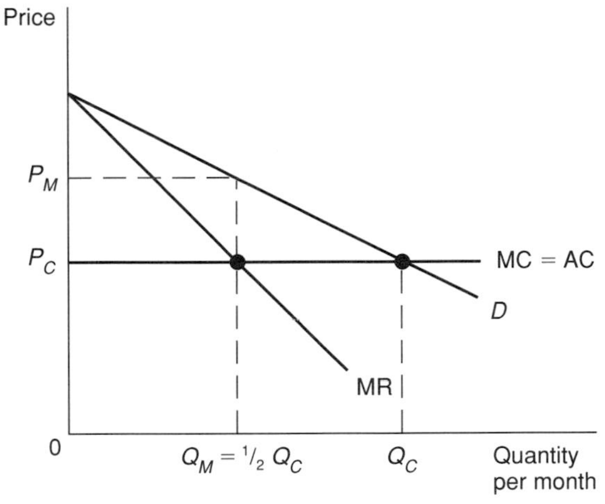

4. If the price ceiling is established at the level corresponding to the point at which the demand curve intersects LRMC, output will increase, but there will be no shortage.

6. **a.** The monopolist's profit-maximizing output with no price discrimination is 400, the output at which MR = MC.

   b. AC at an output of 400 must be greater than \$20, so the profit per unit must be less than \$10 at that output. Hence, the total profit at an output of 400 must be less than \$4,000.

   c. The monopolist's chosen output in this case will be greater than 500, which is the output at which the demand curve intersects the short-run marginal cost curve.

Chapter 12

2. In equilibrium each of the lumber producers would be selling one half of the competitive output as the end result of a price war or if the market is contestable.

4. At the established cartel price any individual firm maximizes profits by adjusting output until marginal cost equals the cartel price. If all of the firms in the industry do this, there will be a surplus at the cartel price, and price will fall to the competitive level.

6. The key factor the court would use in ruling on this case is its conception of the "relevant market" in which the two publishers compete. The Justice Department would argue for a narrow definition of the market. If the two travel book publishers both produce very practical travel guides with detailed information about hotels, restaurants, and so on, the Justice Department would argue that the relevant market is the market for detailed travel guides, so that the apparent increase in concentration (that is, reduction of competition) is made to look as large as possible. The two publishers would argue that the relevant market is much broader, including travel magazines and more general travel publications, so that the increase in concentration resulting from the merger appears to be insignificant. Which market definition the court accepts would depend on whether it believes that travel magazines and more general travel publications are close substitutes for detailed travel guides.

Chapter 13

2. Based on the payoff matrix, the dominant strategy for both A and B is to cut price, which is the Nash equilibrium corresponding to the upper left-hand cell in the matrix.

		B's Strategies	
		Cut Price	***Maintain Price***
A's Strategies	***Cut Price***	A's profit change −$1,000 B's profit change −$1,000	A's profit change $2,000 B's profit change −$1,500
	Maintain Price	A's profit change −$1,500 B's profit change $2,000	A's profit change $0 B's profit change $0

4. Only Tide has a dominant strategy, which is to advertise. Cheer does not have a dominant strategy, and whether it chooses to advertise depends on the strategy chosen by Tide. Cheer, knowing the payoffs to Tide, will assume that Tide will advertise. Cheer will therefore choose to advertise because its profits will be higher if it advertises and Tide also advertises.

6. You might argue that the situation in the market is similar to a repeated game and that there is no illegal collusion. You simply know whenever price is cut, your rivals will also cut price and you will not gain. The tit-for-tat strategy pursued by all firms in the market for price cuts does not constitute illegal collusion.

Chapter 14

2. In equilibrium MRS_{HI} = $5. A $100 per day inheritance will result in an income effect unfavorable to work. There will be no substitution effect because the wage is unaffected by the inheritance. The quantity of labor hours supplied at any wage level will be less after the inheritance. The labor supply will decrease.

4. A 30 percent tax on savings reduces the net return to savings. This will decrease the quantity of funds saved, provided that the income effect of the rate reduction does not outweigh the substitution effect.

6. The answer to this problem requires access to a microcomputer to calculate the internal rate of return on the investment. If the internal rate of return is less than 15 percent, it is unwise to enter the training program because you could earn a higher return by investing elsewhere the $18,500 that you forgo if you enter the program. Using a spreadsheet program, you will find that the internal rate of return on the investment is 27 percent. Because this exceeds the 15 percent opportunity cost, entering the training program would be a good investment.

8. **a.** With a horizontal intercept of 100 and vertical intercepts of 110, 120, and 130, the corresponding interest rates must be 10 percent, 20 percent, and 30 percent, respectively.

   b.

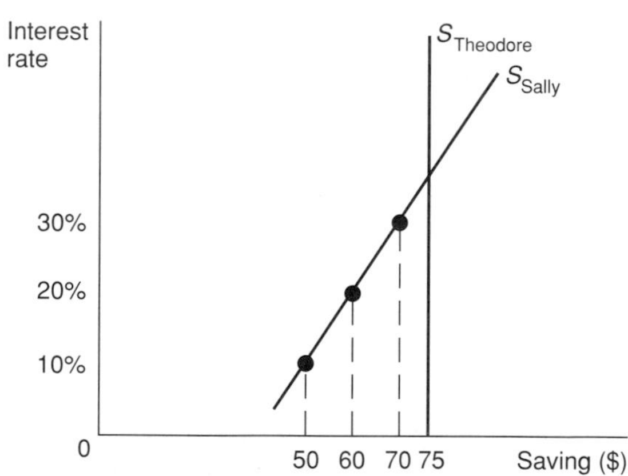

   c. This depends on the position of the market demand curve for loanable funds. The curves derived in **b** indicate that if the market demand for loanable funds is "low," the equilibrium interest rate will be higher for Sally, whereas if the market demand for loanable funds is "high," the equilibrium interest rate will be higher for Theodore.

Chapter 15

2. The payroll tax increases both the average input cost and the marginal input cost of labor. Assuming no change in the marginal revenue product of labor, this will decrease the amount of labor hired from Q_1 to Q_2, as shown. After the tax has been levied, the net wages paid to workers fall to W_N, whereas gross wages rise to $W_G > W_1$.

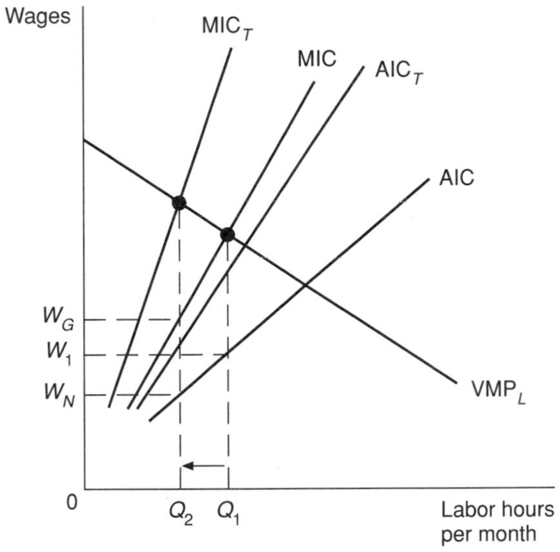

4. The supply of musicians is limited to 10,000. If this is less than the equilibrium quantity that would prevail in the absence of a closed shop, the union wage will exceed the competitive wage.

6. **a.** The monopsonist will pay a wage of W_1, the lowest wage it needs to pay to obtain L^* units of labor, as indicated by the supply of labor curve.

   b. Any minimum wage above W_2 would create a labor surplus. With a minimum wage, the left-hand portion of the MIC curve will be a horizontal line at the level of the minimum wage extending out to the MRP curve. If the minimum wage exceeds W_2, the monopsonist, by setting MIC = MRP, will demand less labor than will be supplied.

   c. Yes, the monopsonist will earn a profit by hiring labor. With a minimum wage of W_3, it will hire L^* units of labor and its total labor cost will be W_3L^*. Its total revenue from hiring labor will be the area underneath the MRP curve from $L = 0$ to $L = L^*$, which is clearly a greater area than the area of the W_3L^* rectangle.

Chapter 16

2. This is a problem of balancing distortions. The basic problem is an underallocation of resources to the monopoly industry and a consequent overallocation of resources to the competitive industry relative to the efficient allocation. A tax on the clothing industry would cause resources to flow out of that industry to the food monopoly, thereby correcting the misallocation of resources.

4. An increase in labor hours will increase the width of the Edgeworth production box and shift the production possibility curve and the utility possibility curve outward. If the marginal rate of transformation of food into clothing exceeds the marginal rate of substitution of food for clothing (given the amount of food actually produced), the consumption of food must decrease, thereby raising its MRS. To achieve this, the price of food must increase relative to the price of clothing for consumers of these two goods.

6. **a.** Because the slope of a line drawn between A and B is $-4/3$, and the slope of a tangent to the production possibility curve drawn at B—which is the marginal rate of transformation at B—must be greater than $4/3$ in absolute terms.

   b. No, because this combination lies beyond the production possibility curve.

c. No. If 60 units of Y and 30 units of X are produced, it is possible to increase the production of both goods through exchange of inputs, so the $Q = 60$ good Y isoquant and the $Q = 30$ good X isoquant cannot be tangent.

d. MRT = MRS = 0.8 when efficiency is achieved. If the MRS is not 0.8, the chosen output combination and the distribution of output could be changed in such a way that both consumers gain utility.

Chapter 17

2. Under experience rating an insurance company reduces the adverse selection problem by taking on a new group only if it has information on the past claim activity of that group. Because the group's future premiums increase with its health expenditures, the employer providing the insurance for the group has the incentive to take preventive measures that improve the group's health and to screen new workers to make sure they are healthy. Thus the incentives that result from experience rating diminish the moral hazard problem by encouraging behavior to reduce future claims.

4. The increase in the deductible and in the coinsurance rate increases out-of-pocket costs for initial medical care of less than $3,000 per year. This will reduce the quantity of health care services demanded and thus reduce the overallocation of resources to health care that results from the moral hazard problem.

6. The firm is paying efficiency wages in an attempt to reduce shirking.

Chapter 18

2. Assuming that the supply of smoke detectors is not infinitely elastic, an increase in demand will raise the market price of these devices. The corrective subsidy increases demand, and the increase in demand increases expenditures on smoke detectors. The net price paid by purchasers declines as a result of the subsidy, and their net expenditures on the devices may increase or decrease, depending on the price elasticity of demand. Figure 18–2 illustrates the impact of a corrective subsidy.

4. A decrease in the price of meat to $1 per pound will decrease the efficient output of meat to less than 4,000 pounds. The new efficient output would correspond to the point at which MPC + E = $1. This will increase the efficient output of fish (assuming that the price of fish is unchanged) because at the lower efficient output of beef, the marginal cost of producing fish will also be lower and will therefore correspond to a higher output.

6. There is a positive externality here. Because each gardener does not consider the benefit of weed reduction to neighbors, less than the efficient amount of weed control is provided

INDEX

D

I

J

K

L

Q

R

S

T

U

V

W

X

Y